CW01023218

THE ARCADES PROJECT

THE
ARCADES
PROJECT

WALTER BENJAMIN

Translated by Howard Eiland and Kevin McLaughlin

PREPARED ON THE BASIS OF THE GERMAN VOLUME EDITED BY ROLF TIEDEMANN

THE BELKNAP PRESS OF HARVARD UNIVERSITY PRESS
CAMBRIDGE, MASSACHUSETTS, AND LONDON, ENGLAND

Copyright © 1999 by the President and Fellows of Harvard College
All rights reserved
Printed in the United States of America

Second printing, 1999

This work is a translation of Walter Benjamin, *Das Passagen-Werk,* edited by Rolf Tiedemann, copyright © 1982 by Suhrkamp Verlag; volume 5 of Walter Benjamin, *Gesammelte Schriften,* prepared with the co-operation of Theodor W. Adorno and Gershom Scholem, edited by Rolf Tiedemann and Hermann Schweppenhäuser, copyright © 1972, 1974, 1977, 1982, 1985, 1989 by Suhrkamp Verlag. "Dialectics at a Standstill," by Rolf Tiedemann, was first published in English by MIT Press, copyright © 1988 by the Massachusetts Institute of Technology.

Publication of this book has been supported by a grant from the National Endowment for the Humanities, an independent federal agency.

Publication of this book has also been aided by a grant from Inter Nationes, Bonn.

Cover photo: Walter Benjamin, ca. 1932. Photographer unknown. Courtesy of the Theodor W. Adorno Archiv, Frankfurt am Main.

Frontispiece: Passage Jouffroy, 1845–1847. Photographer unknown. Courtesy Musée Carnavalet, Paris. Photo copyright © Photothèque des Musées de la Ville de Paris.

Vignettes: pages i, 1, 825, 891, 1074, Institut Français d'Architecture; page 27, Hans Meyer-Veden; page 869, Robert Doisneau.

Library of Congress Cataloging-in-Publication Data

Benjamin, Walter, 1892–1940.
    [Passagen-Werk. English]
    The arcades project / Walter Benjamin;
  translated by Howard Eiland and Kevin McLaughlin;
  prepared on the basis of the German volume edited by Rolf Tiedemann.
      p. cm.
    Includes index.
    ISBN 0-674-04326-X (alk. paper)
    I. Tiedemann, Rolf. II. Title.
  PT2603.E455 P33513   1999
  944′ .361081—dc21   99-27615

Designed by Gwen Nefsky Frankfeldt

CONTENTS

Illustrations

Translators' Foreword

The materials assembled in Volume 5 of Walter Benjamin's *Gesammelte Schriften,* under the title *Das Passagen-Werk* (first published in 1982), represent research that Benjamin carried out, over a period of thirteen years, on the subject of the Paris arcades—*les passages*—which he considered the most important architectural form of the nineteenth century, and which he linked with a number of phenomena characteristic of that century's major and minor preoccupations. A glance at the overview preceding the "Convolutes" at the center of the work reveals the range of these phenomena, which extend from the literary and philosophical to the political, economic, and technological, with all sorts of intermediate relations. Benjamin's intention from the first, it would seem, was to grasp such diverse material under the general category of *Urgeschichte,* signifying the "primal history" of the nineteenth century. This was something that could be realized only indirectly, through "cunning": it was not the great men and celebrated events of traditional historiography but rather the "refuse" and "detritus" of history, the half-concealed, variegated traces of the daily life of "the collective," that was to be the object of study, and with the aid of methods more akin—above all, in their dependence on chance—to the methods of the nineteenth-century collector of antiquities and curiosities, or indeed to the methods of the nineteenth-century ragpicker, than to those of the modern historian. Not conceptual analysis but something like dream interpretation was the model. The nineteenth century was the collective dream which we, its heirs, were obliged to reenter, as patiently and minutely as possible, in order to follow out its ramifications and, finally, awaken from it. This, at any rate, was how it looked at the outset of the project, which wore a good many faces over time.

Begun in 1927 as a planned collaboration for a newspaper article on the arcades, the project had quickly burgeoned under the influence of Surrealism, a movement toward which Benjamin always maintained a pronounced ambivalence. Before long, it was an essay he had in mind, "Pariser Passagen: Eine dialektische Feerie" (Paris Arcades: A Dialectical Fairyland), and then, a few years later, a book, *Paris, die Hauptstadt des XIX. Jahrhunderts* (Paris, the Capital of the Nineteenth Century). For some two-and-a-half years, at the end of the Twenties, having expressed his sense of alienation from contemporary German writers and his affinity with the French cultural milieu, Benjamin worked intermittently on reams of notes and sketches, producing one short essay, "Der

Saturnring oder Etwas vom Eisenbau" (The Ring of Saturn, or Some Remarks on Iron Construction), which is included here in the section "Early Drafts." A hiatus of about four years ensued, until, in 1934, Benjamin resumed work on the arcades with an eye to "new and far-reaching sociological perspectives." The scope of the undertaking, the volume of materials collected, was assuming epic proportions, and no less epic was the manifest interminability of the task, which Benjamin pursued in his usual fearless way—step by step, risking engulfment— beneath the ornamented vaulting of the reading room of the Bibliothèque Nationale in Paris. Already in a letter of 1930, he refers to *The Arcades Project* as "the theater of all my struggles and all my ideas."

In 1935, at the request of his colleagues at the Institute of Social Research in New York, Benjamin drew up an exposé, or documentary synopsis, of the main lines of *The Arcades Project;* another exposé, based largely on the first but more exclusively theoretical, was written in French, in 1939, in an attempt to interest an American sponsor. Aside from these remarkably concentrated essays, and the brief text "The Ring of Saturn," the entire *Arcades* complex (without definitive title, to be sure) remained in the form of several hundred notes and reflections of varying length, which Benjamin revised and grouped in sheafs, or "convolutes," according to a host of topics. Additionally, from the late Twenties on, it would appear, citations were incorporated into these materials—passages drawn mainly from an array of nineteenth-century sources, but also from the works of key contemporaries (Marcel Proust, Paul Valéry, Louis Aragon, André Breton, Georg Simmel, Ernst Bloch, Siegfried Kracauer, Theodor Adorno). These proliferating individual passages, extracted from their original context like collectibles, were eventually set up to communicate among themselves, often in a rather subterranean manner. The organized masses of historical objects—the particular items of Benjamin's display (drafts and excerpts)—together give rise to "a world of secret affinities," and each separate article in the collection, each entry, was to constitute a "magic encyclopedia" of the epoch from which it derived. An *image* of that epoch. In the background of this theory of the historical image, constituent of a historical "mirror world," stands the idea of the monad—an idea given its most comprehensive formulation in the pages on origin in the prologue to Benjamin's book on German tragic drama, *Ursprung des deutschen Trauerspiels* (Origin of the German Trauerspiel)—and back of this the doctrine of the reflective medium, in its significance for the object, as expounded in Benjamin's 1919 dissertation, "Der Begriff der Kunstkritik in der deutschen Romantik" (The Concept of Criticism in German Romanticism). At bottom, a canon of (nonsensuous) similitude rules the conception of the *Arcades.*

Was this conception realized? In the text we have before us, is the world of secret affinities in any sense perceptible? Can one even speak of a "world" in the case of a literary fragment? For, since the publication of the *Passagen-Werk,* it has become customary to regard the text which Benjamin himself usually called the *Passagenarbeit,* or just the *Passagen,* as at best a "torso," a monumental fragment or ruin, and at worst a mere notebook, which the author supposedly intended to mine for more extended discursive applications (such as the carefully outlined and possibly half-completed book on Baudelaire, which he worked on from 1937 to 1939). Certainly, the project as a whole is unfinished; Benjamin abandoned work on it in the spring of 1940, when he was forced to flee Paris before the advancing German army. Did he leave behind anything more than a large-scale plan or prospectus? No, it is argued, *The Arcades Project* is just that: the blueprint for an unimaginably massive and labyrinthine architecture—a dream city, in effect. This argument is predicated on the classic distinction between research and application, *Forschung* and *Darstellung* (see, for example, entry N4a,5 in the "Convolutes"), a distinction which Benjamin himself invokes at times, as in a letter to Gershom Scholem of March 3, 1934, where he wonders about ways in which his research on the arcades might be put to use, or in a letter of May 3, 1936, where he tells Scholem that not a syllable of the actual text *(eigentlichen Text)* of the *Passagenarbeit* exists yet. In another of his letters to Scholem of this period, he speaks of the future construction of a literary form for this text. Similar statements appear in letters to Adorno and others. Where *The Arcades Project* is concerned, then, we may distinguish between various stages of research, more or less advanced, but there is no question of a realized work. So runs the lament.

Nevertheless, questions remain, not least as a consequence of the radical status of "study" in Benjamin's thinking (see the Kafka essay of 1934, or Convolute m of the *Arcades*, "Idleness"). For one thing, as we have indicated, many of the passages of reflection in the "Convolutes" section represent revisions of earlier drafts, notes, or letters. Why revise for a notebook? The fact that Benjamin also transferred masses of quotations from actual notebooks to the manuscript of the convolutes, and the elaborate organization of these cited materials in that manuscript (including the use of numerous epigraphs), might likewise bespeak a compositional principle at work in the project, and not just an advanced stage of research. In fact, the montage form—with its philosophic play of distances, transitions, and intersections, its perpetually shifting contexts and ironic juxtapositions—had become a favorite device in Benjamin's later investigations; among his major works, we have examples of this in *Einbahnstrasse* (One-Way Street), *Berliner Kindheit um Neunzehnhundert* (A Berlin Childhood around 1900), "Über den Begriff der Geschichte" (On the Concept of History), and "Zentralpark" (Central Park). What is distinctive about *The Arcades Project*—in Benjamin's mind, it always dwelt apart—is the working of quotations into the framework of montage, so much so that they eventually far outnumber the commentaries. If we now were to regard this ostensible patchwork as, de facto, a determinate literary form, one that has effectively constructed itself (that is, fragmented itself), like the *Journaux intimes* of Baudelaire, then surely there would be significant repercussions for the direction and tempo of its reading, to say the least. The transcendence of the conventional book form would go together, in this case, with the blasting apart of pragmatic historicism—grounded, as this always is, on the premise of a continuous and homogeneous temporality. Citation and commentary might then be perceived as intersecting at a thousand different angles, setting up vibrations across the epochs of recent history, so as to effect "the cracking open of natural teleology." And all this would unfold through the medium of hints or "blinks"—a discontinuous presentation deliberately opposed to traditional modes of argument. At any rate, it seems undeniable that despite the informal, epistolary announcements of a "book" in the works, an *eigentlichen Buch,* the research project had become an end in itself.

Of course, many readers will concur with the German editor of the *Passagen-Werk,* Rolf Tiedemann, when he speaks, in his essay "Dialectics at a Standstill" (first published as the introduction to the German edition, and reproduced here in translation), of the "oppressive chunks of quotations" filling its pages. Part of Benjamin's purpose was to document as concretely as possible, and thus lend a "heightened graphicness" to, the scene of revolutionary change that was the nineteenth century. At issue was what he called the "commodification of things." He was interested in the unsettling effects of incipient high capitalism on the most intimate areas of life and work—especially as reflected in the work of art (its composition, its dissemination, its reception). In this "projection of the historical into the intimate," it was a matter not of demonstrating any straightforward cultural "decline," but rather of bringing to light an uncanny sense of crisis *and* of security, of crisis *in* security. Particularly from the perspective of the nineteenth-century domestic interior, which Benjamin likens to the inside of a mollusk's shell, things were coming to seem more entirely material than ever and, at the same time, more spectral and estranged. In the society at large (and in Baudelaire's writing par excellence), an unflinching realism was cultivated alongside a rhapsodic idealism. This essentially ambiguous situation—one could call it, using the term favored by a number of the writers studied in *The Arcades Project,* "phantasmagorical"—sets the tone for Benjamin's deployment of motifs, for his recurrent topographies, his mobile cast of characters, his gallery of types. For example, these nineteenth-century types (flâneur, collector, and gambler head the list) generally constitute figures in the middle—that is, figures residing within as well as outside the marketplace, between the worlds of money and magic—figures on the threshold. Here, furthermore, in the wakening to crisis (crisis masked by habitual complacency), was the link to present-day concerns. Not the least cunning aspect of this historical awakening—which is, at the same time, an awakening to myth—was the critical role assigned to humor, sometimes humor of an infernal kind. This was one way in which the documentary and the artistic, the sociological and the theological, were to meet head-on.

To speak of awakening was to speak of the "afterlife of works," something brought to pass through the medium of the "dialectical image." The latter is Benjamin's central term, in *The Arcades Project,* for the historical object of interpretation: that which, under the divinatory gaze of the collector, is taken up into the collector's own particular time and place, thereby throwing a pointed light on what has been. Welcomed into a present moment that seems to be waiting just for it—"actualized," as Benjamin likes to say—the moment from the past comes alive as never before. In this way, the "now" is itself experienced as preformed in the "then," as its distillation—thus the leading motif of "precursors" in the text. The historical object is reborn as such into a present day capable of receiving it, of suddenly "recognizing" it. This is the famous "now of recognizability" (*Jetzt der Erkennbarkeit*), which has the character of a lightning flash. In the dusty, cluttered corridors of the arcades, where street and interior are one, historical time is broken up into kaleidoscopic distractions and momentary come-ons, myriad displays of ephemera, thresholds for the passage of what Gérard de Nerval (in *Aurélia*) calls "the ghosts of material things." Here, at a distance from what is normally meant by "progress," is the *ur*-historical, collective redemption of lost time, of the times embedded in the spaces of things.

The German edition of the *Passagen-Werk* contains—besides the two exposés we have mentioned, the long series of convolutes that follow, the "Erste Notizen" (here translated as "First Sketches") and "Frühe Entwürfe" ("Early Drafts") at the end—a wealth of supplementary material relating to the genesis of *The Arcades Project*. From this textual-critical apparatus, drawn on for the Translators' Notes, we have extracted three additional sets of preliminary drafts and notations and translated them in the Addenda; we have also reproduced the introduction by the German editor, Rolf Tiedemann, as well as an account of Benjamin's last days written by Lisa Fittko and printed in the original English at the end of the German edition. Omitted from our volume are some 100 pages of excerpts from letters to and from Benjamin, documenting the growth of the project (the majority of these letters appear elsewhere in English); a partial bibliography, compiled by Tiedemann, of 850 works cited in the "Convolutes"; and, finally, precise descriptions of Benjamin's manuscripts and manuscript variants (see translators' initial note to the "Convolutes"). In an effort to respect the unique constitution of these manuscripts, we have adopted Tiedemann's practice of using angle brackets to indicate editorial insertions into the text.

A salient feature of the German edition of Benjamin's "Convolutes" ("Aufzeichnungen und Materialien") is the use of two different typefaces: a larger one for his reflections in German and a smaller one for his numerous citations in French and German. According to Tiedemann's introduction, the larger type was used for entries containing significant commentary by Benjamin. (In "First Sketches," the two different typefaces are used to demarcate canceled passages.) This typographic distinction, designed no doubt for the convenience of readers, although it is without textual basis in Benjamin's manuscript, has been maintained in the English translation. We have chosen, however, to use typefaces differing in style rather than in size, so as to avoid the hierarchical implication of the German edition (the privileging of Benjamin's reflections over his citations, and, in general, of German over French). What Benjamin seems to have conceived was a dialectical relation—a formal and thematic interfusion of citation and commentary. It is an open, societary relation, as in the protocol to the imaginary world inn (itself an unacknowledged citation from Baudelaire's *Paradis artificiels*) mentioned in the "Convolutes" at J75,2.

As for the bilingual character of the text as a whole, this has been, if not entirely eliminated in the English-language edition, then necessarily reduced to merely the citation of the original titles of Benjamin's sources. (Previously published translations of these sources have been used, and duly noted, wherever possible; where two or more published translations of a passage are available, we have tried to choose the one best suited to Benjamin's context.) In most cases we have regularized the citation of year and place of book publication, as well as volume and issue number of periodicals; bits of information, such as first names, have occasionally been supplied in angle brackets. Otherwise, Benjamin's irregular if relatively scrupulous editorial practices have been preserved.

As a further aid to readers, the English-language edition of *The Arcades Project* includes an extensive if not exhaustive "Guide to Names and Terms"; translators' notes intended to help contextualize Benjamin's citations and reflections; and cross-references serving to link particular items in the "First Sketches" and "Early Drafts" to corresponding entries in the "Convolutes."

Translation duties for this edition were divided as follows: Kevin McLaughlin translated the Exposé of 1939 and the previously untranslated French passages in Convolutes A–C, F, H, K, M (second half), O, Q–l, and p–r. Howard Eiland translated Benjamin's German throughout and was responsible for previously untranslated material in Convolutes D, E, G, I, J, L, M (first half), N, P, and m, as well as for the Translators' Foreword.

In conclusion, a word about the translation of *Konvolut*. As used for the grouping of the thirty-six alphabetized sections of the *Passagen* manuscript, this term, it would seem, derives not from Benjamin himself but from his friend Adorno (this according to a communication from Rolf Tiedemann, who studied with Adorno). It was Adorno who first sifted through the manuscript of the "Aufzeichnungen und Materialien," as Tiedemann later called it, after it had been hidden away by Georges Bataille in the Bibliothèque Nationale de France during the Second World War and then retrieved and delivered to New York at the end of 1947. In Germany, the term *Konvolut* has a common philological application: it refers to a larger or smaller assemblage—literally, a bundle—of manuscripts or printed materials that belong together. The noun "convolute" in English means "something of a convoluted form." We have chosen it as the translation of the German term over a number of other possibilities, the most prominent being "folder," "file," and "sheaf." The problem with these more common English terms is that each carries inappropriate connotations, whether of office supplies, computerese, agriculture, or archery. "Convolute" is strange, at least on first acquaintance, but so is Benjamin's project and its principle of sectioning. Aside from its desirable closeness to the German rubric, which, we have suggested, is both philologically and historically legitimated, it remains the most precise and most evocative term for designating the elaborately intertwined collections of "notes and materials" that make up the central division of this most various and colorful of Benjaminian texts.

The translators are grateful to the National Endowment for the Humanities for a two-year grant in support of the translation, and to the Dean of the Graduate School of Brown University, Peder Estrup, for a generous publication subvention. Special thanks are due Michael W. Jennings for checking the entire manuscript of the translation and making many valuable suggestions. We are further indebted to Winfried Menninghaus and Susan Bernstein for reading portions of the manuscript and offering excellent advice. Rolf Tiedemann kindly and promptly answered our inquiries concerning specific problems. The reviewers enlisted by Harvard University Press to evaluate the translation also provided much help with some of the more difficult passages. Other scholars who generously provided bibliographic information are named in the relevant Translators' Notes. Our work has greatly benefited at the end from the resourceful, vigilant editing of Maria Ascher and at every stage from the foresight and discerning judgment of Lindsay Waters.

EXPOSÉS

Paris, the Capital of the Nineteenth Century

‹Exposé of 1935›

> The waters are blue, the plants pink; the evening is sweet to
>   look on;
> One goes for a walk; the *grandes dames* go for a walk; behind
>   them stroll the *petites dames*.
>
> —Nguyen Trong Hiep, *Paris, capitale de la France: Recueil de vers*
>   (Hanoi, 1897), poem 25

I. Fourier, or the Arcades

The magic columns of these palaces
Show to the amateur on all sides,
In the objects their porticos display,
That industry is the rival of the arts.

—*Nouveaux Tableaux de Paris* (Paris, 1828), vol. 1, p. 27

Most of the Paris arcades come into being in the decade and a half after 1822. The first condition for their emergence is the boom in the textile trade. *Magasins de nouveautés,* the first establishments to keep large stocks of merchandise on the premises, make their appearance.[1] They are the forerunners of department stores. This was the period of which Balzac wrote: "The great poem of display chants its stanzas of color from the Church of the Madeleine to the Porte Saint-Denis."[2] The arcades are a center of commerce in luxury items. In fitting them out, art enters the service of the merchant. Contemporaries never tire of admiring them, and for a long time they remain a drawing point for foreigners. An *Illustrated Guide to Paris* says: "These arcades, a recent invention of industrial luxury, are glass-roofed, marble-paneled corridors extending through whole blocks of buildings, whose owners have joined together for such enterprises. Lining both sides of these corridors, which get their light from above, are the most elegant shops, so that the *passage* is a city, a world in miniature." The arcades are the scene of the first gas lighting.

The second condition for the emergence of the arcades is the beginning of iron construction. The Empire saw in this technology a contribution to the revival of architecture in the classical Greek sense. The architectural theorist Boetticher expresses the general view of the matter when he says that, "with regard to the art forms of the new system, the formal principle of the Hellenic mode" must come to prevail.[3] Empire is the style of revolutionary terrorism, for which the state is an end in itself. Just as Napoleon failed to understand the functional nature of the state as an instrument of domination by the bourgeois class, so the architects of his time failed to understand the functional nature of iron, with which the constructive principle begins its domination of architecture. These architects design supports resembling Pompeian columns, and factories that imitate residential houses, just as later the first railroad stations will be modeled on chalets. "Construction plays the role of the subconscious."[4] Nevertheless, the concept of engineer, which dates from the revolutionary wars, starts to gain ground, and the rivalry begins between builder and decorator, Ecole Polytechnique and Ecole des Beaux-Arts.

For the first time in the history of architecture, an artificial building material appears: iron. It undergoes an evolution whose tempo will accelerate in the course of the century. This development enters a decisive new phase when it becomes clear that the locomotive—on which experiments have been conducted since the end of the 1820s—is compatible only with iron tracks. The rail becomes the first prefabricated iron component, the precursor of the girder. Iron is avoided in home construction but used in arcades, exhibition halls, train stations—buildings that serve transitory purposes. At the same time, the range of architectural applications for glass expands, although the social prerequisites for its widened application as building material will come to the fore only a hundred years later. In Scheerbart's *Glasarchitektur* (1914), it still appears in the context of utopia.[5]

Each epoch dreams the one to follow.

—Michelet, "Avenir! Avenir!"[6]

Corresponding to the form of the new means of production, which in the beginning is still ruled by the form of the old (Marx), are images in the collective consciousness in which the old and the new interpenetrate. These images are wish images; in them the collective seeks both to overcome and to transfigure the immaturity of the social product and the inadequacies in the social organization of production. At the same time, what emerges in these wish images is the resolute effort to distance oneself from all that is antiquated—which includes, however, the recent past. These tendencies deflect the imagination (which is given impetus by the new) back upon the primal past. In the dream in which each epoch entertains images of its successor, the latter appears wedded to elements of primal history ‹*Urgeschichte*›—that is, to elements of a classless society. And the experiences of such a society—as stored in the unconscious of the collective—engender, through interpenetration with what is new, the utopia that has left its trace in a thousand configurations of life, from enduring edifices to passing fashions.

These relations are discernible in the utopia conceived by Fourier. Its secret cue is the advent of machines. But this fact is not directly expressed in the Fourierist literature, which takes, as its point of departure, the amorality of the business world and the false morality enlisted in its service. The phalanstery is designed to restore human beings to relationships in which morality becomes superfluous. The highly complicated organization of the phalanstery appears as machinery. The meshing of the passions, the intricate collaboration of *passions mécanistes* with the *passion cabaliste,* is a primitive contrivance formed—on analogy with the machine—from materials of psychology. This mechanism made of men produces the land of milk and honey, the primeval wish symbol that Fourier's utopia has filled with new life.

In the arcades, Fourier saw the architectural canon of the phalanstery. Their reactionary metamorphosis with him is characteristic: whereas they originally serve commercial ends, they become, for him, places of habitation. The phalanstery becomes a city of arcades. Fourier establishes, in the Empire's austere world of forms, the colorful idyll of Biedermeier. Its brilliance persists, however faded, up through Zola, who takes up Fourier's ideas in his book *Travail,* just as he bids farewell to the arcades in his *Thérèse Raquin.*—Marx came to the defense of Fourier in his critique of Carl Grün, emphasizing the former's "colossal conception of man."[7] He also directed attention to Fourier's humor. In fact, Jean Paul, in his "Levana," is as closely allied to Fourier the pedagogue as Scheerbart, in his *Glass Architecture,* is to Fourier the utopian.[8]

II. Daguerre, or the Panoramas

Sun, look out for yourself!

—A. J. Wiertz, *Oeuvres littéraires* (Paris, 1870), p. 374

Just as architecture, with the first appearance of iron construction, begins to outgrow art, so does painting, in its turn, with the first appearance of the panoramas. The high point in the diffusion of panoramas coincides with the introduction of arcades. One sought tirelessly, through technical devices, to make panoramas the scenes of a perfect imitation of nature. An attempt was made to reproduce the changing daylight in the landscape, the rising of the moon, the rush of waterfalls. ⟨Jacques-Louis⟩ David counsels his pupils to draw from nature as it is shown in panoramas. In their attempt to produce deceptively lifelike changes in represented nature, the panoramas prepare the way not only for photography but for ⟨silent⟩ film and sound film.

Contemporary with the panoramas is a panoramic literature. *Le Livre des cent-et-un* [The Book of a Hundred-and-One], *Les Français peints par eux-mêmes* [The French Painted by Themselves], *Le Diable à Paris* [The Devil in Paris], and *La Grande Ville* [The Big City] belong to this. These books prepare the belletristic collaboration for which Girardin, in the 1830s, will create a home in the feuille-ton. They consist of individual sketches, whose anecdotal form corresponds to the panoramas' plastically arranged foreground, and whose informational base corresponds to their painted background. This literature is also socially pano-ramic. For the last time, the worker appears, isolated from his class, as part of the setting in an idyll.

Announcing an upheaval in the relation of art to technology, panoramas are at the same time an expression of a new attitude toward life. The city dweller, whose political supremacy over the provinces is demonstrated many times in the course of the century, attempts to bring the countryside into town. In panoramas, the city opens out to landscape—as it will do later, in subtler fashion, for the flâneurs. Daguerre is a student of the panorama painter Prévost, whose estab-lishment is located in the Passage des Panoramas. Description of the panoramas of Prévost and Daguerre. In 1839 Daguerre's panorama burns down. In the same year, he announces the invention of the daguerreotype.

⟨François⟩ Arago presents photography in a speech to the National Assembly. He assigns it a place in the history of technology and prophesies its scientific applications. On the other side, artists begin to debate its artistic value. Photogra-phy leads to the extinction of the great profession of portrait miniaturist. This happens not just for economic reasons. The early photograph was artistically superior to the miniature portrait. The technical grounds for this advantage lie in the long exposure time, which requires of a subject the highest concentration; the social grounds for it lie in the fact that the first photographers belonged to the avant-garde, from which most of their clientele came. Nadar's superiority to his colleagues is shown by his attempt to take photographs in the Paris sewer system: for the first time, discoveries were demanded of the lens. Its importance becomes still greater as, in view of the new technological and social reality, the subjective strain in pictorial and graphic information is called into question.

The world exhibition of 1855 offers for the first time a special display called "Photography." In the same year, Wiertz publishes his great article on photogra-phy, in which he defines its task as the philosophical enlightenment of painting.[9] This "enlightenment" is understood, as his own paintings show, in a political sense. Wiertz can be characterized as the first to demand, if not actually foresee, the use of photographic montage for political agitation. With the increasing scope of communications and transport, the informational value of painting di-minishes. In reaction to photography, painting begins to stress the elements of color in the picture. By the time Impressionism yields to Cubism, painting has created for itself a broader domain into which, for the time being, photography cannot follow. For its part, photography greatly extends the sphere of commodity exchange, from mid-century onward, by flooding the market with countless im-ages of figures, landscapes, and events which had previously been available either not at all or only as pictures for individual customers. To increase turnover, it renewed its subject matter through modish variations in camera technique—innovations that will determine the subsequent history of photography.

III. Grandville, or the World Exhibitions

Yes, when all the world from Paris to China
Pays heed to your doctrine, O divine Saint-Simon,
The glorious Golden Age will be reborn.
Rivers will flow with chocolate and tea,
Sheep roasted whole will frisk on the plain,
And sautéed pike will swim in the Seine.
Fricasseed spinach will grow on the ground,
Garnished with crushed fried croutons;
The trees will bring forth apple compotes,
And farmers will harvest boots and coats.
It will snow wine, it will rain chickens,
And ducks cooked with turnips will fall from the sky.

—Langlé and Vanderburch, *Louis-Bronze et le Saint-Simonien*
    (Théâtre du Palais-Royal, February 27, 1832)[10]

World exhibitions are places of pilgrimage to the commodity fetish. "Europe is off to view the merchandise," says Taine in 1855.[11] The world exhibitions are preceded by national exhibitions of industry, the first of which takes place on the Champ de Mars in 1798. It arises from the wish "to entertain the working classes, and it becomes for them a festival of emancipation."[12] The worker occupies the foreground, as customer. The framework of the entertainment industry has not yet taken shape; the popular festival provides this. Chaptal's speech on industry opens the 1798 exhibition.—The Saint-Simonians, who envision the industrialization of the earth, take up the idea of world exhibitions. Chevalier, the first authority in the new field, is a student of Enfantin and editor of the Saint-Simonian newspaper *Le Globe*. The Saint-Simonians anticipated the development of the global economy, but not the class struggle. Next to their active participation in industrial and commercial enterprises around the middle of the century stands their helplessness on all questions concerning the proletariat.

World exhibitions glorify the exchange value of the commodity. They create a framework in which its use value recedes into the background. They open a phantasmagoria which a person enters in order to be distracted. The entertainment industry makes this easier by elevating the person to the level of the commodity. He surrenders to its manipulations while enjoying his alienation from himself and others.—The enthronement of the commodity, with its luster of distraction, is the secret theme of Grandville's art. This is consistent with the split between utopian and cynical elements in his work. Its ingenuity in representing inanimate objects corresponds to what Marx calls the "theological niceties" of the commodity.[13] They are manifest clearly in the *spécialité*—a category of goods which appears at this time in the luxuries industry. Under Grandville's pencil, the whole of nature is transformed into specialties. He presents them in the same spirit in which the advertisement (the term *réclame* also originates at this point) begins to present its articles. He ends in madness.

Fashion: "Madam Death! Madam Death!"

—Leopardi, "Dialogue between Fashion and Death"[14]

World exhibitions propagate the universe of commodities. Grandville's fantasies confer a commodity character on the universe. They modernize it. Saturn's ring becomes a cast-iron balcony on which the inhabitants of Saturn take the evening air. The literary counterpart to this graphic utopia is found in the books of the Fourierist naturalist Toussenel.—Fashion prescribes the ritual according to which the commodity fetish demands to be worshipped. Grandville extends the authority of fashion to objects of everyday use, as well as to the cosmos. In taking it to an extreme, he reveals its nature. Fashion stands in opposition to the organic. It couples the living body to the inorganic world. To the living, it defends the rights of the corpse. The fetishism that succumbs to the sex appeal of the inorganic is its vital nerve. The cult of the commodity presses such fetishism into its service.

For the Paris world exhibition of 1867, Victor Hugo issues a manifesto: "To the Peoples of Europe." Earlier, and more unequivocally, their interests had been championed by delegations of French workers, of which the first had been sent to the London world exhibition of 1851 and the second, numbering 750 delegates, to that of 1862. The latter delegation was of indirect importance for Marx's founding of the International Workingmen's Association.—The phantasmagoria of capitalist culture attains its most radiant unfolding in the world exhibition of 1867. The Second Empire is at the height of its power. Paris is acknowledged as the capital of luxury and fashion. Offenbach sets the rhythm of Parisian life. The operetta is the ironic utopia of an enduring reign of capital.

IV. Louis Philippe, or the Interior

The head . . .
On the night table, like a ranunculus,
Rests.

—Baudelaire, "Une Martyre"[15]

Under Louis Philippe, the private individual makes his entrance on the stage of history. The expansion of the democratic apparatus through a new electoral law coincides with the parliamentary corruption organized by Guizot. Under cover of this corruption, the ruling class makes history; that is, it pursues its affairs. It furthers railway construction in order to improve its stock holdings. It promotes the reign of Louis Philippe as that of the private individual managing his affairs. With the July Revolution, the bourgeoisie realized the goals of 1789 (Marx).

For the private individual, the place of dwelling is for the first time opposed to the place of work. The former constitutes itself as the interior. Its complement is the office. The private individual, who in the office has to deal with reality, needs the domestic interior to sustain him in his illusions. This necessity is all the more pressing since he has no intention of allowing his commercial considerations to impinge on social ones. In the formation of his private environment, both are kept out. From this arise the phantasmagorias of the interior—which, for the private man, represents the universe. In the interior, he brings together the far away and the long ago. His living room is a box in the theater of the world.

Excursus on Jugendstil. The shattering of the interior occurs via Jugendstil around the turn of the century. Of course, according to its own ideology, the Jugendstil movement seems to bring with it the consummation of the interior. The transfiguration of the solitary soul appears to be its goal. Individualism is its theory. With van de Velde, the house becomes an expression of the personality. Ornament is to this house what the signature is to a painting. But the real meaning of Jugendstil is not expressed in this ideology. It represents the last attempted sortie of an art besieged in its ivory tower by technology. This attempt mobilizes all the reserves of inwardness. They find their expression in the mediumistic language of the line, in the flower as symbol of a naked vegetal nature confronted by the technologically armed world. The new elements of iron construction—girder forms—preoccupy Jugendstil. In ornament, it endeavors to win back these forms for art. Concrete presents it with new possibilities for plastic creation in architecture. Around this time, the real gravitational center of living space shifts to the office. The irreal center makes its place in the home. The consequences of Jugendstil are depicted in Ibsen's *Master Builder:* the attempt by the individual, on the strength of his inwardness, to vie with technology leads to his downfall.

I believe . . . in my soul: the Thing.

—Léon Deubel, *Oeuvres* (Paris, 1929), p. 193

The interior is the asylum of art. The collector is the true resident of the interior. He makes his concern the transfiguration of things. To him falls the Sisyphean task of divesting things of their commodity character by taking possession of them. But he bestows on them only connoisseur value, rather than use value. The collector dreams his way not only into a distant or bygone world but also into a better one—one in which, to be sure, human beings are no better provided with what they need than in the everyday world, but in which things are freed from the drudgery of being useful.

The interior is not just the universe but also the étui of the private individual. To dwell means to leave traces. In the interior, these are accentuated. Coverlets and antimacassars, cases and containers are devised in abundance; in these, the traces of the most ordinary objects of use are imprinted. In just the same way, the traces of the inhabitant are imprinted in the interior. Enter the detective story, which pursues these traces. Poe, in his "Philosophy of Furniture" as well as in his detective fiction, shows himself to be the first physiognomist of the domestic interior. The criminals in early detective novels are neither gentlemen nor apaches, but private citizens of the middle class.

V. Baudelaire, or the Streets of Paris

Everything becomes an allegory for me.

—Baudelaire, "Le Cygne"[16]

Baudelaire's genius, which is nourished on melancholy, is an allegorical genius. For the first time, with Baudelaire, Paris becomes the subject of lyric poetry. This poetry is no hymn to the homeland; rather, the gaze of the allegorist, as it falls on the city, is the gaze of the alienated man. It is the gaze of the flâneur, whose way of life still conceals behind a mitigating nimbus the coming desolation of the big-city dweller. The flâneur still stands on the threshold—of the metropolis as of the middle class. Neither has him in its power yet. In neither is he at home. He seeks refuge in the crowd. Early contributions to a physiognomics of the crowd are found in Engels and Poe. The crowd is the veil through which the familiar city beckons to the flâneur as phantasmagoria—now a landscape, now a room. Both become elements of the department store, which makes use of flânerie itself to sell goods. The department store is the last promenade for the flâneur.

In the flâneur, the intelligentsia sets foot in the marketplace—ostensibly to look around, but in truth to find a buyer. In this intermediate stage, in which it still has patrons but is already beginning to familiarize itself with the market, it appears as the *bohème*. To the uncertainty of its economic position corresponds the uncertainty of its political function. The latter is manifest most clearly in the professional conspirators, who all belong to the *bohème*. Their initial field of activity is the army; later it becomes the petty bourgeoisie, occasionally the proletariat. Nevertheless, this group views the true leaders of the proletariat as its adversary. The *Communist Manifesto* brings their political existence to an end. Baudelaire's poetry draws its strength from the rebellious pathos of this class. He sides with the asocial. He realizes his only sexual communion with a whore.

Easy the way that leads into Avernus.

—Virgil, *The Aeneid*[17]

It is the unique provision of Baudelaire's poetry that the image of the woman and the image of death intermingle in a third: that of Paris. The Paris of his poems is a sunken city, and more submarine than subterranean. The chthonic elements of the city—its topographic formations, the old abandoned bed of the Seine—have evidently found in him a mold. Decisive for Baudelaire in the "death-fraught idyll" of the city, however, is a social, a modern substrate. The modern is a principal accent of his poetry. As spleen, it fractures the ideal ("Spleen et idéal"). But precisely the modern, *la modernité,* is always citing primal history. Here, this occurs through the ambiguity peculiar to the social relations and products of this epoch. Ambiguity is the manifest imaging of dialectic, the law of dialectics at a standstill. This standstill is utopia and the dialectical image, therefore, dream image. Such an image is afforded by the commodity per se: as fetish. Such an image is presented by the arcades, which arc house no less than street. Such an image is the prostitute—seller and sold in one.

I travel in order to get to know my geography.

—Note of a madman, in Marcel Réja, *L'Art chez les fous* (Paris, 1907), p. 131

The last poem of *Les Fleurs du mal:* "Le Voyage." "Death, old admiral, up anchor now." The last journey of the flâneur: death. Its destination: the new. "Deep in the Unknown to find the *new!*"[18] Newness is a quality independent of the use value of the commodity. It is the origin of the illusory appearance that belongs inalienably to images produced by the collective unconscious. It is the quintessence of that false consciousness whose indefatigable agent is fashion. This semblance of the new is reflected, like one mirror in another, in the semblance of the ever recurrent. The product of this reflection is the phantasmagoria of "cultural history," in which the bourgeoisie enjoys its false consciousness to the full. The art that begins to doubt its task and ceases to be "inseparable from ‹ . . . › utility" (Baudelaire)[19] must make novelty into its highest value. The *arbiter novarum rerum* for such an art becomes the snob. He is to art what the dandy is to fashion.—Just as in the seventeenth century it is allegory that becomes the canon of dialectical images, in the nineteenth century it is novelty. Newspapers flourish, along with *magasins de nouveautés*. The press organizes the market in spiritual values, in which at first there is a boom. Nonconformists rebel against consigning art to the marketplace. They rally round the banner of *l'art pour l'art*. From this watchword derives the conception of the "total work of art"—the *Gesamtkunstwerk*—which would seal art off from the developments of technology. The solemn rite with which it is celebrated is the pendant to the distraction that transfigures the commodity. Both abstract from the social existence of human beings. Baudelaire succumbs to the rage for Wagner.

VI. Haussmann, or the Barricades

I venerate the Beautiful, the Good, and all things great;
Beautiful nature, on which great art rests—
How it enchants the ear and charms the eye!
I love spring in blossom: women and roses.

—Baron Haussmann, *Confession d'un lion devenu vieux*[20]

The flowery realm of decorations,
The charm of landscape, of architecture,
And all the effect of scenery rest
Solely on the law of perspective.

—Franz Böhle, *Theater-Catechismus* (Munich), p. 74

Haussmann's ideal in city planning consisted of long perspectives down broad straight thoroughfares. Such an ideal corresponds to the tendency—common in the nineteenth century—to ennoble technological necessities through artistic ends. The institutions of the bourgeoisie's worldly and spiritual dominance were to find their apotheosis within the framework of the boulevards. Before their completion, boulevards were draped across with canvas and unveiled like monuments.—Haussmann's activity is linked to Napoleonic imperialism. Louis Napoleon promotes investment capital, and Paris experiences a rash of speculation. Trading on the stock exchange displaces the forms of gambling handed down from feudal society. The phantasmagorias of space to which the flâneur devotes himself find a counterpart in the phantasmagorias of time to which the gambler is addicted. Gambling converts time into a narcotic. ‹Paul› Lafargue explains gambling as an imitation in miniature of the mysteries of economic fluctuation.[21] The expropriations carried out under Haussmann call forth a wave of fraudulent speculation. The rulings of the Court of Cassation, which are inspired by the bourgeois and Orleanist opposition, increase the financial risks of Haussmannization.

Haussmann tries to shore up his dictatorship by placing Paris under an emergency regime. In 1864, in a speech before the National Assembly, he vents his hatred of the rootless urban population, which keeps increasing as a result of his projects. Rising rents drive the proletariat into the suburbs. The *quartiers* of Paris in this way lose their distinctive physiognomy. The "red belt" forms. Haussmann gave himself the title of "demolition artist," *artiste démolisseur*. He viewed his work as a calling, and emphasizes this in his memoirs. Meanwhile he estranges the Parisians from their city. They no longer feel at home there, and start to become conscious of the inhuman character of the metropolis. Maxime Du Camp's monumental work *Paris* owes its inception to this consciousness.[22] The *Jérémiades d'un Haussmannisé* give it the form of a biblical lament.[23]

The true goal of Haussmann's projects was to secure the city against civil war. He wanted to make the erection of barricades in Paris impossible for all time. With the same end in mind, Louis Philippe had already introduced wooden paving. Nonetheless, barricades played a role in the February Revolution. Engels studies the tactics of barricade fighting.[24] Haussmann seeks to neutralize these tactics on two fronts. Widening the streets is designed to make the erection of barricades impossible, and new streets are to furnish the shortest route between the barracks and the workers' districts. Contemporaries christen the operation "strategic embellishment."

Reveal to these depraved,
O Republic, by foiling their plots,
Your great Medusa face
Ringed by red lightning.

—Workers' song from about 1850, in Adolf Stahr, *Zwei Monate in Paris* (Oldenburg, 1851), vol. 2, p. 199[25]

The barricade is resurrected during the Commune. It is stronger and better secured than ever. It stretches across the great boulevards, often reaching a height of two stories, and shields the trenches behind it. Just as the *Communist Manifesto* ends the age of professional conspirators, so the Commune puts an end to the phantasmagoria holding sway over the early years of the proletariat. It dispels the illusion that the task of the proletarian revolution is to complete the work of 1789 hand in hand with the bourgeoisie. This illusion dominates the period 1831–1871, from the Lyons uprising to the Commune. The bourgeoisie never shared in this error. Its battle against the social rights of the proletariat dates back to the great Revolution, and converges with the philanthropic movement that gives it cover and that is in its heyday under Napoleon III. Under his reign, this movement's monumental work appears: Le Play's *Ouvriers européens* [European Workers].[26] Side by side with the concealed position of philanthropy, the bourgeoisie has always maintained openly the position of class warfare.[27] As early as 1831, in the *Journal des débats,* it acknowledges that "every manufacturer lives in his factory like a plantation owner among his slaves." If it is the misfortune of the workers' rebellions of old that no theory of revolution directs their course, it is also this absence of theory that, from another perspective, makes possible their spontaneous energy and the enthusiasm with which they set about establishing a new society. This enthusiasm, which reaches its peak in the Commune, wins over to the working class at times the best elements of the bourgeoisie, but leads it in the end to succumb to their worst elements. Rimbaud and Courbet declare their support for the Commune. The burning of Paris is the worthy conclusion to Haussmann's work of destruction.

My good father had been in Paris.

—Karl Gutzkow, *Briefe aus Paris* (Leipzig, 1842), vol. 1, p. 58

Balzac was the first to speak of the ruins of the bourgeoisie.[28] But it was Surrealism that first opened our eyes to them. The development of the forces of production shattered the wish symbols of the previous century, even before the monuments representing them had collapsed. In the nineteenth century this development worked to emancipate the forms of construction from art, just as in the sixteenth century the sciences freed themselves from philosophy. A start is made with architecture as engineered construction. Then comes the reproduction of nature as photography. The creation of fantasy prepares to become practical as commercial art. Literature submits to montage in the feuilleton. All these products are on the point of entering the market as commodities. But they linger on the threshold. From this epoch derive the arcades and *intérieurs,* the exhibition halls and panoramas. They are residues of a dream world. The realization of dream elements, in the course of waking up, is the paradigm of dialectical thinking. Thus, dialectical thinking is the organ of historical awakening. Every epoch, in fact, not only dreams the one to follow but, in dreaming, precipitates its awakening. It bears its end within itself and unfolds it—as Hegel already noticed—by cunning. With the destabilizing of the market economy, we begin to recognize the monuments of the bourgeoisie as ruins even before they have crumbled.

Paris, Capital of the Nineteenth Century

Exposé ⟨of 1939⟩

Introduction

History is like Janus; it has two faces. Whether it looks at the past or at the present, it sees the same things.

—Maxime Du Camp, *Paris,* vol. 6, p. 315

The subject of this book is an illusion expressed by Schopenhauer in the following formula: to seize the essence of history, it suffices to compare Herodotus and the morning newspaper.[1] What is expressed here is a feeling of vertigo characteristic of the nineteenth century's conception of history. It corresponds to a viewpoint according to which the course of the world is an endless series of facts congealed in the form of things. The characteristic residue of this conception is what has been called the "History of Civilization," which makes an inventory, point by point, of humanity's life forms and creations. The riches thus amassed in the aerarium of civilization henceforth appear as though identified for all time. This conception of history minimizes the fact that such riches owe not only their existence but also their transmission to a constant effort of society—an effort, moreover, by which these riches are strangely altered. Our investigation proposes to show how, as a consequence of this reifying representation of civilization, the new forms of behavior and the new economically and technologically based creations that we owe to the nineteenth century enter the universe of a phantasmagoria. These creations undergo this "illumination" not only in a theoretical manner, by an ideological transposition, but also in the immediacy of their perceptible presence. They are manifest as phantasmagorias. Thus appear the arcades—first entry in the field of iron construction; thus appear the world exhibitions, whose link to the entertainment industry is significant. Also included in this order of phenomena is the experience of the flâneur, who abandons himself to the phantasmagorias of the marketplace. Corresponding to these phantasmagorias of the market, where people appear only as types, are the phantasmagorias of the interior, which are constituted by man's imperious need to leave the imprint of his private individual existence on the rooms he inhabits. As for the phantasmagoria of civilization itself, it found its champion in Haussmann and its manifest expression in his transformations of Paris.—Nevertheless, the pomp and the splendor with which commodity-producing society surrounds itself, as well as its illusory sense of security, are not immune to dangers; the collapse of the Second Empire and the Commune of Paris remind it of that. In the same period, the most dreaded adversary of this society, Blanqui, revealed to it, in his last piece of writing, the terrifying features of this phantasmagoria. Humanity figures there as damned. Everything new it could hope for turns out to be a reality that has always been present; and this newness will be as little capable of furnishing it with a liberating solution as a new fashion is capable of rejuvenating society. Blanqui's cosmic speculation conveys this lesson: that humanity will be prey to a mythic anguish so long as phantasmagoria occupies a place in it.

A. Fourier, or the Arcades

I

The magic columns of these *palais*
Show to enthusiasts from all parts,
With the objects their porticos display,
That industry is the rival of the arts.

—*Nouveaux Tableaux de Paris* (Paris, 1828), p. 27

Most of the Paris arcades are built in the fifteen years following 1822. The first condition for their development is the boom in the textile trade. *Magasins de nouveautés,* the first establishments to keep large stocks of merchandise on the premises, make their appearance. They are the forerunners of department stores. This is the period of which Balzac writes: "The great poem of display chants its stanzas of color from the Church of the Madeleine to the Porte Saint-Denis." The arcades are centers of commerce in luxury items. In fitting them out, art enters the service of the merchant. Contemporaries never tire of admiring them. For a long time they remain an attraction for tourists. An *Illustrated Guide to Paris* says: "These arcades, a recent invention of industrial luxury, are glass-roofed, marble-paneled corridors extending through whole blocks of buildings, whose owners have joined together for such enterprises. Lining both sides of the arcade, which gets its light from above, are the most elegant shops, so that the *passage* is a city, a world in miniature." The arcades are the scene of the first attempts at gas lighting.

The second condition for the emergence of the arcades is the beginning of iron construction. Under the Empire, this technology was seen as a contribution to the revival of architecture in the classical Greek sense. The architectural theorist Boetticher expresses the general view of the matter when he says that, "with regard to the art forms of the new system, the Hellenic mode" must come to prevail. The Empire style is the style of revolutionary terrorism, for which the state is an end in itself. Just as Napoleon failed to understand the functional nature of the state as an instrument of domination by the bourgeoisie, so the architects of his time failed to understand the functional nature of iron, with which the constructive principle begins its domination of architecture. These architects design supports resembling Pompeian columns, and factories that imitate residential houses, just as later the first railroad stations will assume the look of chalets. Construction plays the role of the subconscious. Nevertheless, the concept of engineer, which dates from the revolutionary wars, starts to gain ground, and the rivalry begins between builder and decorator, Ecole Polytechnique and Ecole des Beaux-Arts.—For the first time since the Romans, a new artificial building material appears: iron. It will undergo an evolution whose pace will accelerate in the course of the century. This development enters a decisive new phase when it becomes clear that the locomotive—object of the most diverse experiments since the years 1828–1829—usefully functions only on iron rails. The rail becomes the first prefabricated iron component, the precursor of the girder. Iron is avoided in home construction but used in arcades, exhibition halls, train stations—buildings that serve transitory purposes.

II

It is easy to understand that every mass-type "interest" which
asserts itself historically goes far beyond its real limits in the
"idea" or "imagination," when it first comes on the scene.

—Marx and Engels, *Die heilige Familie*[2]

The secret cue for the Fourierist utopia is the advent of machines. The phalanstery is designed to restore human beings to a system of relationships in which morality becomes superfluous. Nero, in such a context, would become a more useful member of society than Fénelon. Fourier does not dream of relying on virtue for this; rather, he relies on an efficient functioning of society, whose motive forces are the passions. In the gearing of the passions, in the complex meshing of the *passions mécanistes* with the *passion cabaliste,* Fourier imagines the collective psychology as a clockwork mechanism. Fourierist harmony is the necessary product of this combinatory play.

Fourier introduces into the Empire's world of austere forms an idyll colored by the style of the 1830s. He devises a system in which the products of his colorful vision and of his idiosyncratic treatment of numbers blend together. Fourier's "harmonies" are in no way akin to a mystique of numbers taken from any other tradition. They are in fact direct outcomes of his own pronouncements—lucubrations of his organizational imagination, which was very highly developed. Thus, he foresaw how significant meetings would become to the citizen. For the phalanstery's inhabitants, the day is organized not around the home but in large halls similar to those of the Stock Exchange, where meetings are arranged by brokers.

In the arcades, Fourier recognized the architectural canon of the phalanstery. This is what distinguishes the "empire" character of his utopia, which Fourier himself naively acknowledges: "The societarian state will be all the more brilliant at its inception for having been so long deferred. Greece in the age of Solon and

Pericles could already have undertaken it."[3] The arcades, which originally were designed to serve commercial ends, become dwelling places in Fourier. The phalanstery is a city composed of arcades. In this *ville en passages,* the engineer's construction takes on a phantasmagorical character. The "city of arcades" is a dream that will charm the fancy of Parisians well into the second half of the century. As late as 1869, Fourier's "street-galleries" provide the blueprint for Moilin's *Paris en l'an 2000.*[4] Here the city assumes a structure that makes it—with its shops and apartments—the ideal backdrop for the flâneur.

Marx took a stand against Carl Grün in order to defend Fourier and to accentuate his "colossal conception of man."[5] He considered Fourier the only man besides Hegel to have revealed the essential mediocrity of the petty bourgeois. The systematic overcoming of this type in Hegel corresponds to its humorous annihilation in Fourier. One of the most remarkable features of the Fourierist utopia is that it never advocated the exploitation of nature by man, an idea that became widespread in the following period. Instead, in Fourier, technology appears as the spark that ignites the powder of nature. Perhaps this is the key to his strange representation of the phalanstery as propagating itself "by explosion." The later conception of man's exploitation of nature reflects the actual exploitation of man by the owners of the means of production. If the integration of the technological into social life failed, the fault lies in this exploitation.

B. Grandville, or the World Exhibitions

I

Yes, when all the world from Paris to China
Pays heed to your doctrine, O divine Saint-Simon,
The glorious Golden Age will be reborn.
Rivers will flow with chocolate and tea,
Sheep roasted whole will frisk on the plain,
And sautéed pike will swim in the Seine.
Fricasseed spinach will grow on the ground,
Garnished with crushed fried croutons;
The trees will bring forth apple compotes,
And farmers will harvest boots and coats.
It will snow wine, it will rain chickens,
And ducks cooked with turnips will fall from the sky.

—Langlé and Vanderburch, *Louis-Bronze et le Saint-Simonien*
 (Théâtre du Palais-Royal, February 27, 1832)

World exhibitions are places of pilgrimage to the commodity fetish. "Europe is off to view the merchandise," says Taine in 1855.[6] The world exhibitions were preceded by national exhibitions of industry, the first of which took place on the Champ de Mars in 1798. It arose from the wish "to entertain the working classes, and it becomes for them a festival of emancipation."[7] The workers would constitute their first clientele. The framework of the entertainment industry has not yet taken shape; the popular festival provides this. Chaptal's celebrated speech on industry opens the 1798 exhibition.—The Saint-Simonians, who envision the industrialization of the earth, take up the idea of world exhibitions. Chevalier, the first authority in this new field, is a student of Enfantin and editor of the Saint-Simonian newspaper *Le Globe*. The Saint-Simonians anticipated the development of the global economy, but not the class struggle. Thus, we see that despite their participation in industrial and commercial enterprises around the middle of the century, they were helpless on all questions concerning the proletariat.

World exhibitions glorify the exchange value of the commodity. They create a framework in which its use value becomes secondary. They are a school in which the masses, forcibly excluded from consumption, are imbued with the exchange value of commodities to the point of identifying with it: "Do not touch the items on display." World exhibitions thus provide access to a phantasmagoria which a person enters in order to be distracted. Within these *divertissements,* to which the individual abandons himself in the framework of the entertainment industry, he remains always an element of a compact mass. This mass delights in amusement parks—with their roller coasters, their "twisters," their "caterpillars"—in an attitude that is pure reaction. It is thus led to that state of subjection which propaganda, industrial as well as political, relies on.—The enthronement of the commodity, with its glitter of distractions, is the secret theme of Grandville's art. Whence the split between its utopian and cynical elements in his work. The subtle artifices with which it represents inanimate objects correspond to what Marx calls the "theological niceties" of the commodity.[8] The concrete expression of this is clearly found in the *spécialité*—a category of goods which appears at this time in the luxuries industry. World exhibitions construct a universe of *spécialités*. The fantasies of Grandville achieve the same thing. They modernize the universe. In his work, the ring of Saturn becomes a cast-iron balcony on which the inhabitants of Saturn take the evening air. By the same token, at world exhibitions, a balcony of cast-iron would represent the ring of Saturn, and people who venture out on it would find themselves carried away in a phantasmagoria where they seem to have been transformed into inhabitants of Saturn. The literary counterpart to this graphic utopia is the work of the Fourierist savant Toussenel. Toussenel was the natural-sciences editor for a popular newspaper. His zoology classifies the animal world according to the rule of fashion. He considers woman the intermediary between man and the animals. She is in a sense the decorator of the animal world, which, in exchange, places at her feet its plumage and its furs. "The lion likes nothing better than having its nails trimmed, provided it is a pretty girl that wields the scissors."[9]

II

Fashion: "Madam Death! Madam Death!"

—Leopardi, "Dialogue between Fashion and Death"[10]

Fashion prescribes the ritual according to which the commodity fetish demands to be worshipped. Grandville extends the authority of fashion to objects of everyday use, as well as to the cosmos. In taking it to an extreme, he reveals its nature. It couples the living body to the inorganic world. To the living, it defends the rights of the corpse. The fetishism which thus succumbs to the sex appeal of the inorganic is its vital nerve. The fantasies of Grandville correspond to the spirit of fashion that Apollinaire later described with this image: "Any material from nature's domain can now be introduced into the composition of women's clothes. I saw a charming dress made of corks. . . . Steel, wool, sandstone, and files have suddenly entered the vestmentary arts. . . . They're doing shoes in Venetian glass and hats in Baccarat crystal."[11]

C. Louis Philippe, or the Interior

I

I believe . . . in my soul: the Thing.

—Léon Deubel, *Oeuvres* (Paris, 1929), p. 193

Under the reign of Louis Philippe, the private individual makes his entry into history. For the private individual, places of dwelling are for the first time opposed to places of work. The former come to constitute the interior. Its complement is the office. (For its part, the office is distinguished clearly from the shop counter, which, with its globes, wall maps, and railings, looks like a relic of the baroque forms that preceded the rooms in today's residences.) The private individual, who in the office has to deal with realities, needs the domestic interior to sustain him in his illusions. This necessity is all the more pressing since he has no intention of grafting onto his business interests a clear perception of his social function. In the arrangement of his private surroundings, he suppresses both of these concerns. From this derive the phantasmagorias of the interior—which, for the private individual, represents the universe. In the interior, he brings together remote locales and memories of the past. His living room is a box in the theater of the world.

The interior is the asylum where art takes refuge. The collector proves to be the true resident of the interior. He makes his concern the idealization of objects. To him falls the Sisyphean task of divesting things of their commodity character by taking possession of them. But he can bestow on them only connoisseur value, rather than use value. The collector delights in evoking a world that is not just distant and long gone but also better—a world in which, to be sure, human beings are no better provided with what they need than in the real world, but in which things are freed from the drudgery of being useful.

II

The head . . .
On the night table, like a ranunculus,
Rests.

—Baudelaire, "Une Martyre"[12]

The interior is not just the universe of the private individual; it is also his étui. Ever since the time of Louis Philippe, the bourgeois has shown a tendency to compensate for the absence of any trace of private life in the big city. He tries to do this within the four walls of his apartment. It is as if he had made it a point of honor not to allow the traces of his everyday objects and accessories to get lost. Indefatigably, he takes the impression of a host of objects; for his slippers and his watches, his blankets and his umbrellas, he devises coverlets and cases. He has a marked preference for velour and plush, which preserve the imprint of all contact. In the style characteristic of the Second Empire, the apartment becomes a sort of cockpit. The traces of its inhabitant are molded into the interior. Here is the origin of the detective story, which inquires into these traces and follows these tracks. Poe—with his "Philosophy of Furniture" and with his "new detectives"— becomes the first physiognomist of the domestic interior. The criminals in early detective fiction are neither gentlemen nor apaches, but simple private citizens of the middle class ("The Black Cat," "The Tell-Tale Heart," "William Wilson").

III

This seeking for *my* home . . . was *my* affliction. . . . Where is—
my home? I ask and seek and have sought for it; I have not found it.

—Nietzsche, *Also sprach Zarathustra*[13]

The liquidation of the interior took place during the last years of the nineteenth century, in the work of Jugendstil, but it had been coming for a long time. The art of the interior was an art of genre. Jugendstil sounds the death knell of the genre. It rises up against the infatuation of genre in the name of a *mal du siècle,* of a perpetually open-armed aspiration. Jugendstil for the first time takes into consideration certain tectonic forms. It also strives to disengage them from their functional relations and to present them as natural constants; it strives, in short, to stylize them. The new elements of iron construction—especially the girder— command the attention of this "modern style." In the domain of ornamentation, it endeavors to integrate these forms into art. Concrete puts at its disposal new potentialities for architecture. With van de Velde, the house becomes the plastic expression of the personality. Ornament is to this house what the signature is to a painting. It exults in speaking a linear, mediumistic language in which the flower, symbol of vegetal life, insinuates itself into the very lines of construction. (The curved line of Jugendstil appears at the same time as the title *Les Fleurs du mal.* A sort of garland marks the passage from the "Flowers of Evil" to the "souls of flowers" in Odilon Redon and on to Swann's *faire catleya.*)[14]—Henceforth, as Fourier had foreseen, the true framework for the life of the private citizen must be sought increasingly in offices and commercial centers. The fictional framework for the individual's life is constituted in the private home. It is thus that *The Master Builder* takes the measure of Jugendstil. The attempt by the individual to vie with technology by relying on his inner flights leads to his downfall: the architect Solness kills himself by plunging from his tower.[15]

D. Baudelaire, or the Streets of Paris

I

Everything for me becomes allegory.

—Baudelaire, "Le Cygne"[16]

Baudelaire's genius, which feeds on melancholy, is an allegorical genius. With Baudelaire, Paris becomes for the first time the subject of lyric poetry. This poetry of place is the opposite of all poetry of the soil. The gaze which the allegorical genius turns on the city betrays, instead, a profound alienation. It is the gaze of the flâneur, whose way of life conceals behind a beneficent mirage the anxiety of the future inhabitants of our metropolises. The flâneur seeks refuge in the crowd. The crowd is the veil through which the familiar city is transformed for the flâneur into phantasmagoria. This phantasmagoria, in which the city appears now as a landscape, now as a room, seems later to have inspired the décor of department stores, which thus put flânerie to work for profit. In any case, department stores are the last precincts of flânerie.

In the person of the flâneur, the intelligentsia becomes acquainted with the marketplace. It surrenders itself to the market, thinking merely to look around; but in fact it is already seeking a buyer. In this intermediate stage, in which it still has patrons but is starting to bend to the demands of the market (in the guise of the feuilleton), it constitutes the *bohème*. The uncertainty of its economic position corresponds to the ambiguity of its political function. The latter is manifest especially clearly in the figures of the professional conspirators, who are recruited from the *bohème*. Blanqui is the most remarkable representative of this class. No one else in the nineteenth century had a revolutionary authority comparable to his. The image of Blanqui passes like a flash of lightning through Baudelaire's "Litanies de Satan." Nevertheless, Baudelaire's rebellion is always that of the asocial man: it is at an impasse. The only sexual communion of his life was with a prostitute.

II

They were the same, had risen from the same hell,
These centenarian twins.

—Baudelaire, "Les Sept Vieillards"[17]

The flâneur plays the role of scout in the marketplace. As such, he is also the explorer of the crowd. Within the man who abandons himself to it, the crowd inspires a sort of drunkenness, one accompanied by very specific illusions: the man flatters himself that, on seeing a passerby swept along by the crowd, he has accurately classified him, seen straight through to the innermost recesses of his soul—all on the basis of his external appearance. Physiologies of the time abound in evidence of this singular conception. Balzac's work provides excellent examples. The typical characters seen in passersby make such an impression on the senses that one cannot be surprised at the resultant curiosity to go beyond them and capture the special singularity of each person. But the nightmare that corresponds to the illusory perspicacity of the aforementioned physiognomist consists in seeing those distinctive traits—traits peculiar to the person—revealed to be nothing more than the elements of a new type; so that in the final analysis a person of the greatest individuality would turn out to be the exemplar of a type. This points to an agonizing phantasmagoria at the heart of flânerie. Baudelaire develops it with great vigor in "Les Sept Vieillards," a poem that deals with the seven-fold apparition of a repulsive-looking old man. This individual, presented as always the same in his multiplicity, testifies to the anguish of the city dweller who is unable to break the magic circle of the type even though he cultivates the most eccentric peculiarities. Baudelaire describes this procession as "infernal" in appearance. But the newness for which he was on the lookout all his life consists in nothing other than this phantasmagoria of what is "always the same." (The evidence one could cite to show that this poem transcribes the reveries of a hashish eater in no way weakens this interpretation.)

III

Deep in the Unknown to find the *new!*

—Baudelaire, "Le Voyage"[18]

The key to the allegorical form in Baudelaire is bound up with the specific signification which the commodity acquires by virtue of its price. The singular debasement of things through their signification, something characteristic of seventeenth-century allegory, corresponds to the singular debasement of things through their price as commodities. This degradation, to which things are subject because they can be taxed as commodities, is counterbalanced in Baudelaire by the inestimable value of novelty. *La nouveauté* represents that absolute which is no longer accessible to any interpretation or comparison. It becomes the ultimate entrenchment of art. The final poem of *Les Fleurs du mal:* "Le Voyage." "Death, old admiral, up anchor now."[19] The final voyage of the flâneur: death. Its destination: the new. Newness is a quality independent of the use value of the commodity. It is the source of that illusion of which fashion is the tireless purveyor. The fact that art's last line of resistance should coincide with the commodity's most advanced line of attack—this had to remain hidden from Baudelaire.

"Spleen et idéal"—in the title of this first cycle of poems in *Les Fleurs du mal,* the oldest loanword in the French language was joined to the most recent one.[20] For Baudelaire, there is no contradiction between the two concepts. He recognizes in spleen the latest transfiguration of the ideal; the ideal seems to him the first expression of spleen. With this title, in which the supremely new is presented to the reader as something "supremely old," Baudelaire has given the liveliest form to his concept of the modern. The linchpin of his entire theory of art is "modern beauty," and for him the proof of modernity seems to be this: it is marked with the fatality of being one day antiquity, and it reveals this to whoever witnesses its birth. Here we meet the quintessence of the unforeseen, which for Baudelaire is an inalienable quality of the beautiful. The face of modernity itself blasts us with its immemorial gaze. Such was the gaze of Medusa for the Greeks.

E. Haussmann, or the Barricades

I

I venerate the Beautiful, the Good, and all things great;
Beautiful nature, on which great art rests—
How it enchants the ear and charms the eye!
I love spring in blossom: women and roses.

—Baron Haussmann, *Confession d'un lion devenu vieux*[21]

Haussmann's activity is incorporated into Napoleonic imperialism, which favors investment capital. In Paris, speculation is at its height. Haussmann's expropriations give rise to speculation that borders on fraud. The rulings of the Court of Cassation, which are inspired by the bourgeois and Orleanist opposition, increase the financial risks of Haussmannization. Haussmann tries to shore up his dictatorship by placing Paris under an emergency regime. In 1864, in a speech before the National Assembly, he vents his hatred of the rootless urban population. This population grows ever larger as a result of his projects. Rising rents drive the proletariat into the suburbs. The *quartiers* of Paris in this way lose their distinctive physiognomy. The "red belt" forms. Haussmann gave himself the title of "demolition artist." He believed he had a vocation for his work, and emphasizes this in his memoirs. The central marketplace passes for Haussmann's most successful construction—and this is an interesting symptom. It has been said of the Ile de la Cité, the cradle of the city, that in the wake of Haussmann only one church, one public building, and one barracks remained. Hugo and Mérimée suggest how much the transformations made by Haussmann appear to Parisians as a monument of Napoleonic despotism. The inhabitants of the city no longer feel at home there; they start to become conscious of the inhuman character of the metropolis. Maxime Du Camp's monumental work *Paris* owes its existence to this dawning awareness. The etchings of Meryon (around 1850) constitute the death mask of old Paris.

The true goal of Haussmann's projects was to secure the city against civil war. He wanted to make the erection of barricades in the streets of Paris impossible for all time. With the same end in mind, Louis Philippe had already introduced wooden paving. Nevertheless, barricades had played a considerable role in the February Revolution. Engels studied the tactics of barricade fighting. Haussmann seeks to forestall such combat in two ways. Widening the streets will make the erection of barricades impossible, and new streets will connect the barracks in straight lines with the workers' districts. Contemporaries christened the operation "strategic embellishment."

II

The flowery realm of decorations,
The charm of landscape, of architecture,
And all the effect of scenery rest
Solely on the law of perspective.

—Franz Böhle, *Theater-Catechismus* (Munich), p. 74

Haussmann's ideal in city planning consisted of long straight streets opening onto broad perspectives. This ideal corresponds to the tendency—common in the nineteenth century—to ennoble technological necessities through spurious artistic ends. The temples of the bourgeoisie's spiritual and secular power were to find their apotheosis within the framework of these long streets. The perspectives, prior to their inauguration, were screened with canvas draperies and unveiled like monuments; the view would then disclose a church, a train station, an equestrian statue, or some other symbol of civilization. With the Haussmannization of Paris, the phantasmagoria was rendered in stone. Though intended to endure in quasi-perpetuity, it also reveals its brittleness. The Avenue de l'Opéra —which, according to a malicious saying of the day, affords a perspective on the porter's lodge at the Louvre—shows how unrestrained the prefect's megalomania was.

III

Reveal to these depraved,
O Republic, by foiling their plots,
Your great Medusa face
Ringed by red lightning.

—Pierre Dupont, *Chant des ouvriers*

The barricade is resurrected during the Commune. It is stronger and better designed than ever. It stretches across the great boulevards, often reaching a height of two stories, and shields the trenches behind it. Just as the *Communist Manifesto* ends the age of professional conspirators, so the Commune puts an end to the phantasmagoria that dominates the earliest aspirations of the proletariat. It dispels the illusion that the task of the proletarian revolution is to complete the work of '89 in close collaboration with the bourgeoisie. This illusion had marked the period 1831–1871, from the Lyons riots to the Commune. The bourgeoisie never shared in this error. Its battle against the social rights of the proletariat dates back to the great Revolution, and converges with the philanthropic movement that gives it cover and that was in its heyday under Napoleon III. Under his reign, this movement's monumental work appeared: Le Play's *Ouvriers européens* [European Workers].

Side by side with the overt position of philanthropy, the bourgeoisie has always maintained the covert position of class struggle.[22] As early as 1831, in the *Journal des débats,* it acknowledged that "every manufacturer lives in his factory like a plantation owner among his slaves." If it was fatal for the workers' rebellions of old that no theory of revolution had directed their course, it was this absence of theory that, from another perspective, made possible their spontaneous energy and the enthusiasm with which they set about establishing a new society. This enthusiasm, which reaches its peak in the Commune, at times won over to the workers' cause the best elements of the bourgeoisie, but in the end led the workers to succumb to its worst elements. Rimbaud and Courbet took sides with the Commune. The burning of Paris is the worthy conclusion to Baron Haussmann's work of destruction.

Conclusion

Men of the nineteenth century, the hour of our apparitions is
fixed forever, and always brings us back the very same ones.

—Auguste Blanqui, *L'Eternité par les astres* (Paris, 1872), pp. 74–75

During the Commune, Blanqui was held prisoner in the fortress of Taureau. It was there that he wrote his *L'Eternité par les astres* [Eternity via the Stars]. This book completes the century's constellation of phantasmagorias with one last, cosmic phantasmagoria which implicitly comprehends the severest critique of all the others. The ingenuous reflections of an autodidact, which form the principal portion of this work, open the way to merciless speculations that give the lie to the author's revolutionary élan. The conception of the universe which Blanqui develops in this book, taking his basic premises from the mechanistic natural sciences, proves to be a vision of hell. It is, moreover, the complement of that society which Blanqui, near the end of his life, was forced to admit had defeated him. The irony of this scheme—an irony which doubtless escaped the author himself—is that the terrible indictment he pronounces against society takes the form of an unqualified submission to its results. Blanqui's book presents the idea of eternal return ten years before *Zarathustra*—in a manner scarcely less moving than that of Nietzsche, and with an extreme hallucinatory power.

This power is anything but triumphant; it leaves, on the contrary, a feeling of oppression. Blanqui here strives to trace an image of progress that (immemorial antiquity parading as up-to-date novelty) turns out to be the phantasmagoria of history itself. Here is the essential passage:

> The entire universe is composed of astral systems. To create them, nature has only a hundred *simple bodies* at its disposal. Despite the great advantage it derives from these resources, and the innumerable combinations that these resources afford its fecundity, the result is necessarily a *finite* number, like that of the elements themselves; and in order to fill its expanse, nature must repeat to infinity each of its *original* combinations or *types*. So each heavenly body, whatever it might be, exists in infinite number in time and space, not only in *one* of its aspects but as it is at each second of its existence, from birth to death. . . . The earth is one of these heavenly bodies. Every human being is thus eternal at every second of his or her existence. What I write at this moment in a cell of the Fort du Taureau I have written and shall

write throughout all eternity—at a table, with a pen, clothed as I am now, in circumstances like these. And thus it is for everyone. . . . The number of our doubles is infinite in time and space. One cannot in good conscience demand anything more. These doubles exist in flesh and bone—indeed, in trousers and jacket, in crinoline and chignon. They are by no means phantoms; they are the present eternalized. Here, nonetheless, lies a great drawback: there is no progress. . . . What we call "progress" is confined to each particular world, and vanishes with it. Always and everywhere in the terrestrial arena, the same drama, the same setting, on the same narrow stage—a noisy humanity infatuated with its own grandeur, believing itself to be the universe and living in its prison as though in some immense realm, only to founder at an early date along with its globe, which has borne with deepest disdain the burden of human arrogance. The same monotony, the same immobility, on other heavenly bodies. The universe repeats itself endlessly and paws the ground in place. In infinity, eternity performs—imperturbably—the same routines.[23]

This resignation without hope is the last word of the great revolutionary. The century was incapable of responding to the new technological possibilities with a new social order. That is why the last word was left to the errant negotiators between old and new who are at the heart of these phantasmagorias. The world dominated by its phantasmagorias—this, to make use of Baudelaire's term, is "modernity." Blanqui's vision has the entire universe entering the modernity of which Baudelaire's seven old men are the heralds. In the end, Blanqui views novelty as an attribute of all that is under sentence of damnation. Likewise in *Ciel et enfer* [Heaven and Hell], a vaudeville piece that slightly predates the book: in this piece the torments of hell figure as the latest novelty of all time, as "pains eternal and always new." The people of the nineteenth century, whom Blanqui addresses as if they were apparitions, are natives of this region.

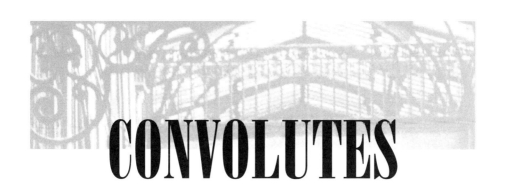

CONVOLUTES

Overview

[Arcades, *Magasins de Nouveautés*, Sales Clerks]

> The magic columns of these palaces
> Show to the amateur on all sides,
> In the objects their porticos display,
> That industry is the rival of the arts.
>
> —"Chanson nouvelle," cited in *Nouveaux Tableaux de Paris, ou Observations sur les moeurs et usages des Parisiens au commencement du XIXe siècle* (Paris, 1828), vol. 1, p. 27

> For sale the bodies, the voices, the tremendous unquestionable wealth, what will never be sold.
>
> —Rimbaud[1]

"In speaking of the inner boulevards," says the *Illustrated Guide to Paris,* a complete picture of the city on the Seine and its environs from the year 1852, "we have made mention again and again of the arcades which open onto them. These arcades, a recent invention of industrial luxury, are glass-roofed, marble-paneled corridors extending through whole blocks of buildings, whose owners have joined together for such enterprises. Lining both sides of these corridors, which get their light from above, are the most elegant shops, so that the arcade is a city, a world in miniature ▢ Flâneur ▢, in which customers will find everything they need. During sudden rainshowers, the arcades are a place of refuge for the unprepared, to whom they offer a secure, if restricted, promenade—one from which the merchants also benefit." ▢ Weather ▢

This passage is the locus classicus for the presentation of the arcades; for not only do the divagations on the flâneur and the weather develop out of it, but, also, what there is to be said about the construction of the arcades, in an economic and architectural vein, would have a place here. [A1,1]

Names of *magasins de nouveautés*: La Fille d'Honneur, La Vestale, Le Page Inconstant, Le Masque de Fer ‹The Iron Mask›, Le Petit Chaperon Rouge ‹Little Red Riding Hood›, Petite Nanette, La Chaumière allemande ‹The German Cottage›, Au Mamelouk, Le Coin de la Rue ‹On the Streetcorner›—names that mostly come from successful vaudevilles. ▢ Mythology ▢ A glover: Au Ci-Devant Jeune Homme. A confectioner: Aux Armes de Werther.

"The name of the jeweler stands over the shop door in large *inlaid letters*—inlaid with fine imitation gems." Eduard Kroloff, *Schilderungen aus Paris* (Hamburg, 1839), vol. 2, p. 73. "In the Galerie Véro-Dodat, there is a grocery store; above its door, one reads the inscription: 'Gastronomie Cosmopolite.' The individual characters of the sign are formed, in comic fashion, from snipes, pheasants, hares, antlers, lobsters, fish, bird kidneys, and so forth." Kroloff, *Schilderungen aus Paris*, vol. 2, p. 75. □ Grandville □   [A1,2]

As business increased, the proprietor would purchase stock for a week and, to make room for the goods being stored, would withdraw to the entresol. In this way, the *boutique* became a *magasin*.   [A1,3]

It was the time in which Balzac could write: "The great poem of display chants its stanzas of color from the Church of the Madeleine to the Porte Saint-Denis." *Le Diable à Paris* (Paris, 1846), vol. 2, p. 91 (Balzac, "Les Boulevards de Paris").
                                          [A1,4]

"The day the word *specialty* was discovered by Her Majesty Industry, queen of France and of neighboring regions: on that day, it is said, Mercury, *special* god of merchants and of several other social *specialties*, knocked three times with his caduceus on the front of the Stock Exchange and swore by the beard of Proserpine that the word was fine with him." □ Mythology □ The word is used initially, however, only for luxury items. *La Grande Ville: Nouveau Tableau de Paris* (Paris, 1844), vol. 2, p. 57 (Marc Fournier, "Les Spécialités parisiennes").   [A1,5]

"The narrow streets surrounding the Opéra and the hazards to which pedestrians were exposed on emerging from this theater, which is always besieged by carriages, gave a group of speculators in 1821 the idea of using some of the structures separating the new theater from the boulevard. / This enterprise, a source of riches for its originators, was at the same time of great benefit to the public. / By way of a small, narrow covered arcade built of wood, one had, in fact, direct access, with all the security of the Opéra's vestibule, to these galleries, and from there to the boulevard. . . . Above the entablature of Doric pilasters dividing the shops rise two floors of apartments, and above the apartments—running the length of the galleries—reigns an enormous glass-paned roof." J. A. Dulaure, *Histoire physique, civile et morale de Paris depuis 1821 jusqu'à nos jours* (Paris, 1835), vol. 2, pp. 28–29.   [A1,6]

Until 1870, the carriage ruled the streets. On the narrow sidewalks the pedestrian was extremely cramped, and so strolling took place principally in the arcades, which offered protection from bad weather and from the traffic. "Our larger streets and our wider sidewalks are suited to the sweet flânerie that for our fathers was impossible except in the arcades." □ Flâneur □ Edmond Beaurepaire, *Paris d'hier et d'aujourd'hui: La Chronique des rues* (Paris, 1900), p. 67.   [A1a,1]

Names of arcades: Passage des Panoramas, Passage Véro-Dodat, Passage du Désir (leading in earlier days to a house of ill repute), Passage Colbert, Passage Vivienne, Passage du Pont-Neuf, Passage du Caire, Passage de la Réunion, Passage de l'Opéra, Passage de la Trinité, Passage du Cheval-Blanc, Passage Pressière ‹Bessières?›, Passage du Bois de Boulogne, Passage Grosse-Tête. (The Passage des Panoramas was known at first as the Passage Mirès.) [A1a,2]

The Passage Véro-Dodat (built between the Rue de Bouloy and the Rue Grenelle-Saint-Honoré) "owes its name to two rich pork butchers, Messieurs Véro and Dodat, who in 1823 undertook its construction together with that of the adjacent buildings—an immense development. This led someone at the time to describe this arcade as a 'lovely work of art framed by two neighborhoods.'" J. A. Dulaure, *Histoire physique, civile et morale de Paris depuis 1821 jusqu'à nos jours* (Paris, 1835), vol. 2, p. 34. [A1a,3]

The Passage Véro-Dodat had marble flooring. The actress Rachel lived there for a while. [A1a,4]

No. 26, Galerie Colbert: "There, in the guise of a female glover, shone a beauty that was approachable but that, in the matter of youth, attached importance only to its own; she required her favorites to supply her with the finery from which she hoped to make a fortune. . . . This young and beautiful woman under glass was called 'the Absolute'; but philosophy would have wasted its time pursuing her. Her maid was the one who sold the gloves; she wanted it that way." ☐ Dolls ☐ Prostitutes ☐ ‹Charles› Lefeuve, *Les Anciennes Maisons de Paris*, vol. 4 ‹Paris, 1875›, p. 70. [A1a,5]

Cour du Commerce: "Here (using sheep) the first experiments were conducted with the guillotine; its inventor lived at that time on the Cour du Commerce and the Rue de l'Ancienne-Comédie." Lefeuve, *Les Anciennes Maisons de Paris*, vol. 4, p. 148. [A1a,6]

"The Passage du Caire,[2] where the main business is lithographic printing, must have decked itself out in lights when Napoleon III abolished the stamp duty on commercial circulars; this emancipation made the arcade rich, and it showed its appreciation with expenditures for beautification. Up to that point, when it rained, umbrellas had been needed in its galleries, which in several places lacked glass covering." Lefeuve, *Les Anciennes Maisons de Paris*, vol. 2, p. 233. ☐ Dream Houses ☐ Weather ☐ (Egyptian ornamentation). [A1a,7]

Impasse Maubert, formerly d'Amboise. Around 1756, at Nos. 4–6, a poisoner resided with her two assistants. All three were found dead one morning—killed through inhalation of toxic fumes. [A1a,8]

Shops in the Passage Véro-Dodat. Courtesy of the Musée Carnavalet, Paris. Photo copyright © Photothèque des Musées de la Ville de Paris. See A1a,4.

Years of reckless financial speculation under Louis XVIII. With the dramatic signage of the *magasins de nouveautés,* art enters the service of the businessman.
[A1a,9]

"After the Passage de Panoramas, which went back to the year 1800 and which had an established reputation in society, there was, by way of example, the gallery that was opened in 1826 by the butchers Véro and Dodat and that was pictured in the 1832 lithograph by Arnout. After 1800 we must go all the way to 1822 to meet with a new arcade: it is between this date and 1834 that the majority of these singular passageways are constructed. The most important of them are grouped in

Glass roof and iron girders, Passage Vivienne. Photographer unknown. Collection of Johann Friedrich Geist; courtesy Prestel Verlag, Munich. See A1a,2.

The Passage des Panoramas. Watercolor by an unknown artist, ca. 1810. Courtesy of
Agence Giraudon. See A2,1.

an area bounded by the Rue Croix-des-Petits-Champs to the south, the Rue de la Grange-Batelière to the north, the Boulevard de Sébastopol to the east, and the Rue Ventadour to the west." Marcel Poëte, *Une vie de cité* (Paris, 1925), pp. 373–374. [A1a,10]

Shops in the Passage des Panoramas: Restaurant Véron, reading room, music shop, Marquis, wine merchants, hosier, haberdashers, tailors, bootmakers, hosiers, bookshops, caricaturist, Théâtre des Variétés. Compared with this, the Passage Vivienne was the "solid" arcade. There, one found no luxury shops. ☐ Dream Houses: arcade as nave with side chapels. ☐ [A2,1]

People associated the "genius of the Jacobins with the genius of the industrials," but they also attributed to Louis Philippe the saying: "God be praised, and my shops too." The arcades as temples of commodity capital. [A2,2]

The newest Paris arcade, on the Champs-Elysées, built by an American pearl king; no longer in business. ☐ Decline ☐ [A2,3]

"Toward the end of the ancien régime, there were attempts to establish bazaar-like shops and fixed-price stores in Paris. Some large *magasins de nouveautés*—such as Le Diable Boiteux, Les Deux Magots, Le Petit Matelot, Pygmalion—were founded during the Restoration and during the reign of Louis Philippe; but these were businesses of an inferior sort compared to today's establishments. The era of the department stores dates, in fact, only from the Second Empire. They have undergone a great deal of development since 1870, and they continue to develop." E‹mile› Levasseur, *Histoire du commerce de la France,* vol. 2 (Paris, 1912), p. 449. [A2,4]

Arcades as origin of department stores? Which of the *magasins* named above were located in arcades? [A2,5]

The regime of specialties furnishes also—this said in passing—the historical-materialist key to the flourishing (if not the inception) of genre painting in the Forties of the previous century. With the growing interest of the bourgeoisie in matters of art, this type of painting diversified; but in conformity with the meager artistic appreciation initially displayed by this class, it did so in terms of the content, in terms of the objects represented. There appeared historical scenes, animal studies, scenes of childhood, scenes from the life of monks, the life of the family, the life of the village—all as sharply defined genres. ☐ Photography ☐ [A2,6]

The influence of commercial affairs on Lautréamont and Rimbaud should be looked into! [A2,7]

"Another characteristic deriving chiefly from the Directory [presumably until around 1830??] would be the lightness of fabrics; on even the coldest days, one was seen only rarely in furs or warm overcoats. At the risk of losing their skin, women clothed themselves as though the harshness of winter no longer existed, as though nature had suddenly been transformed into an eternal paradise." ‹John› Grand-Carteret, *Les Elégances de la toilette* (Paris), p. xxxiv. [A2,8]

In other respects as well, the theater in those days provided the vocabulary for articles of fashion. Hats à la Tarare, à la Théodore, à la Figaro, à la Grande-Prêtresse, à la Iphigénie, à la Calprenade, à la Victoire. The same *niaiserie* that seeks in ballet the origin of the real betrays itself when—around 1830—a newspaper takes the name *Le Sylphe*. ▯ Fashion ▯ [A2,9]

Alexandre Dumas at a dinner party given by Princess Mathilde. The verse is aimed at Napoleon III.

> In their imperial splendor,
> The uncle and nephew are equal:
> The uncle seized the capitals,
> The nephew seizes our capital.

Icy silence followed. Reported in *Mémoires du comte Horace de Viel-Castel sur le règne de Napoléon III*, vol. 2 (Paris, 1883), p. 185. [A2,10]

"The *coulisse*[3] guaranteed the ongoing life of the Stock Exchange. Here there was never closing time; there was almost never night. When the Café Tortoni finally closed its doors, the column of stock jobbers would head across the adjacent boulevards and meander up and down there, collecting in front of the Passage de l'Opéra." Julius Rodenberg, *Paris bei Sonnenschein und Lampenlicht* (Leipzig, 1867), p. 97. [A2,11]

Speculation in railroad stocks under Louis Philippe. [A2,12]

"Of the same extraction, furthermore [that is, from the house of Rothschild], is the amazingly eloquent Mirès, who needs only to speak in order to convince his creditors that losses are profits—but whose name, after the scandalous trial against him, was nonetheless obliterated from the Passage Mirès, which thereupon became the Passage des Princes (with the famous dining rooms of Peters restaurant)." Rodenberg, *Paris bei Sonnenschein und Lampenlicht* (Leipzig, 1867), p. 98. [A2a,1]

Cry of the vendors of stock-exchange lists on the street: In the event of a rise in prices, "Rise in the stock market!" In the event of a fall, "Variations in the stock market!" The term "fall" was forbidden by the police. [A2,a,2]

In its importance for the affairs of the *coulisse,* the Passage de l'Opéra is comparable to the Kranzlerecke. Speculator's argot "in the period preceding the outbreak of the German war [of 1866]: the 3-percent interest was called *Alphonsine;* the land credit, *le gros Ernest;* the Italian revenue, *le pauvre Victor;* the credit for movables, *le petit Jules.*" In Rodenberg ⟨Leipzig, 1867⟩, p. 100. [A2a,3]

Range of a stockbroker's fee: between 2,000,000 ⟨*sic*⟩ and 1,400,000 francs.
  [A2a,4]

"The arcades, nearly all of which date from the Restoration." Théodore Muret, *L'Histoire par le théâtre* (Paris, 1865), vol. 2, p. 300. [A2a,5]

Some details concerning *Avant, pendant, et après* ⟨Before, During, and After⟩, by Scribe and Rougemont. Premier on June 28, 1828. The first part of the trilogy represents the society of the ancien régime, the second part depicts the Reign of Terror, and the third takes place in the society of the Restoration period. The main character, the General, has in peacetime become an industrialist and indeed a great manufacturer. "Here manufacturing replaces, at the highest level, the field worked by the soldier-laborer. The praises of industry, no less than the praises of *warriors* and *laureates*, were sung by Restoration vaudeville. The bourgeois class, with its various levels, was placed opposite the class of nobles: the fortune acquired by work was opposed to ancient heraldry, to the turrets of the old manor house. This Third Estate, having become the dominant power, received in turn its flatterers." Théodore Muret, *L'Histoire par le théâtre,* vol. 2, p. 306. [A2a,6]

The Galeries de Bois, "which disappeared in 1828–1829 to make room for the Galerie d'Orléans, were made up of a triple line of shops that could hardly be called luxurious. There were two parallel lanes covered by canvas and planks, with a few glass panes to let the daylight in. Here one walked quite simply on the packed earth, which downpours sometimes transformed into mud. Yet people came from all over to crowd into this place, which was nothing short of magnificent, and stroll between the rows of shops that would seem like mere booths compared to those that have come after them. These shops were occupied chiefly by two industries, each having its own appeal. There were, first, a great many milliners, who worked on large stools facing outward, without even a window to separate them; and their spirited expressions were, for many strollers, no small part of the place's attraction. And then the Galeries de Bois were the center of the new book trade." Théodore Muret, *L'Histoire par le théâtre,* vol. 2, pp. 225–226.
  [A2a,7]

Julius Rodenberg on the small reading room in the Passage de l'Opéra: "What a cheerful air this small, half-darkened room has in my memory, with its high bookshelves, its green tables, its red-haired *garçon* (a great lover of books, who was always reading novels instead of bringing them to others), its German newspapers, which every morning gladdened the heart of the German abroad (all except the Cologne paper, which on average made an appearance only once in ten days). But when there is any news in Paris, it is here that one can receive it. Softly whispered (for the redhead keeps a sharp lookout to make sure that neither he nor other readers will be disturbed by this), it passes from lips to ear, passes almost imperceptibly from pen to paper, and finally from writing desk to nearby letterbox. The good *dame du bureau* has a friendly smile for all, and papers and envelopes for correspondents. The early mail is dispatched, Cologne and Augsburg have their news; and now—it is noontime!—to the tavern." Rodenberg, *Paris bei Sonnenschein und Lampenlicht* (Leipzig, 1867), pp. 6–7. [A2a,8]

"The Passage du Caire is highly reminiscent, on a smaller scale, of the Passage du Saumon, which in the past existed on the Rue Montmartre, on the site of the present-day Rue Bachaumont." Paul Léautaud, "Vieux Paris," *Mercure de France* (October 15, 1927), p. 503. [A3,1]

"Shops on the old model, devoted to trades found nowhere else, surmounted by a small, old-fashioned mezzanine with windows that each bear a number, on an escutcheon, corresponding to a particular shop. From time to time, a doorway giving onto a corridor; at the end of the corridor, a small stairway leading to these mezzanines. Near the knob of one of these doors, this handwritten sign:

> The worker next door
> would be obliged if,
> in closing the door,
> you refrained from slamming it.

[A3,2]

Another sign is cited in the same place (Léautaud, "Vieux Paris," *Mercure de France* [1927], pp. 502–503):

> ANGELA
>
> 2nd floor, to the right

[A3,3]

Old name for department stores: *docks à bon marché*—that is, "discount docks." ⟨Sigfried⟩ Giedion, *Bauen in Frankreich* ⟨Leipzig and Berlin, 1928⟩, p. 31. [A3,4]

Evolution of the department store from the shop that was housed in arcades. Principle of the department store: "The floors form a single space. They can be taken in, so to speak, 'at a glance.'" Giedion, *Bauen in Frankreich,* p. 34. [A3,5]

Giedion shows (in *Bauen in Frankreich,* p. 35) how the axiom, "Welcome the crowd and keep it seduced" (*Science et l'industrie,* 143 [1925], p. 6), leads to corrupt architectural practices in the construction of the department store Au Printemps (1881–1889). Function of commodity capital! [A3,6]

"Even women, who were forbidden to enter the Stock Exchange, assembled at the door in order to glean some indications of market prices and to relay their orders to brokers through the iron grating." *La Transformation de Paris sous le Second Empire* (authors Poëte, Clouzot, Henriot) ‹Paris, 1910›, on the occasion of the exhibition of the library and the historical works of the city of Paris, p. 66.
[A3,7]

"We have no specialty"—this is what the well-known dealer in secondhand goods, Frémin, "the man with the head of gray," had written on the signboard advertising his wares in the Place des Abbesses. Here, in antique bric-à-brac, reemerges the old physiognomy of trade that, in the first decades of the previous century, began to be supplanted by the rule of the *spécialité*. This "superior scrap-yard" was called *Au Philosophe* by its proprietor. What a demonstration and demolition of stoicism! On his placard were the words: "Maidens, do not dally under the leaves!" And: "Purchase nothing by moonlight."
[A3,8]

Evidently people smoked in the arcades at a time when it was not yet customary to smoke in the street. "I must say a word here about life in the arcades, favored haunt of strollers and smokers, theater of operations for every kind of small business. In each arcade there is at least one cleaning establishment. In a salon that is as elegantly furnished as its intended use permits, gentlemen sit upon high stools and comfortably peruse a newspaper while someone busily brushes the dirt off their clothing and boots." Ferdinand von Gall, *Paris und seine Salons*, vol. 2 ‹Oldenburg, 1845›, pp. 22–23.
[A3,9]

A first winter garden—a glassed-in space with flower beds, espaliers, and fountains, in part underground—on the spot where, in the garden of the Palais-Royal in 1864 (and today as well?), the reservoir was located. Laid out in 1788.   [A3,10]

"It is at the end of the Restoration that we see the first *magasins de nouveautés*: Les Vêpres Siciliennes, Le Solitaire, La Fille Mal Gardée, Le Soldat Laboureur, Les Deux Magots, Le Petit Saint-Thomas, Le Gagne-Denier ‹Penny Winnings›." ‹Lucien› Dubech and ‹Pierre› d'Espezel, *Histoire de Paris* (Paris, 1926), p. 360.
[A3,11]

"In 1820 . . . the Passage Viollet and the Passage des Deux Pavillons were opened. These arcades were among the novelties of their day. The result of private initiative, they were covered galleries housing shops that fashion made prosperous. The most famous was the Passage des Panoramas, which flourished from 1823 to 1831. 'On Sundays,' observed Musset, one went en masse 'to the Panoramas or else to the boulevards.' It was also private initiative that created, somewhat haphazardly, the housing developments known as *cités*, the short streets or dead ends built at shared expense by a syndicate of property owners." Lucien Dubech and Pierre d'Espezel, *Histoire de Paris* (Paris, 1926), pp. 355–356.   [A3a,1]

In 1825, opening of the "Passages Dauphine, Saucède, Choiseul" and of the Cité Bergère. "In 1827 . . . the Passages Colbert, Crussol, de l'Industrie. . . . 1828 saw the opening . . . of the Passages Brady and des Gravilliers and the beginnings of the Galerie d'Orléans at the Palais-Royal, which replaced the wooden galleries that had burned down that year." Dubech and d'Espezel, *Histoire de Paris*, pp. 357–358.   [A3a,2]

"The ancestor of the department stores, La Ville de Paris, appeared at 174 Rue Montmartre in 1843." Dubech and d'Espezel, *Histoire de Paris*, p. 389.   [A3a,3]

"Rainshowers annoy me, so I gave one the slip in an arcade. There are a great many of these glass-covered walkways, which often cross through the blocks of buildings and make several branchings, thus affording welcome shortcuts. Here and there they are constructed with great elegance, and in bad weather or after dark, when they are lit up bright as day, they offer promenades—and very popular they are—past rows of glittering shops." Eduard Devrient, *Briefe aus Paris* (Berlin, 1840), p. 34.   [A3a,4]

Rue-galerie.—"The *street-gallery* . . . is the most important feature of a Phalanstery and . . . cannot be conceived of in civilization. . . . Street-galleries . . . are heated in winter and ventilated in summer. . . . The street-gallery, or *continuous peristyle*, extends along the second story. . . . Those who have seen the gallery of the Louvre may take it as a model for the street-gallery in Harmony." E. Silberling, *Dictionnaire de sociologie phalanstérienne* (Paris, 1911), p. 386; citing ⟨Charles⟩ Fourier, *Théorie de l'unité universelle* (1822), p. 462, and *Le Nouveau Monde industriel et sociétaire* (1829), pp. 69, 125, 272. In addition: *Galerie.*— "All portions of the central edifice can be traversed by means of a wide gallery which runs along the second floor. . . . Thus, everything is linked by a series of passageways which are sheltered, elegant, and comfortable in winter thanks to the help of heaters and ventilators." E. Silberling, *Dictionnaire*, pp. 197–198; citing Fourier, *Théorie mixte, ou spéculative, et synthèse routinière de l'association*, p. 14.[4]   [A3a,5]

The Passage du Caire adjoining the former Cour des Miracles. Built in 1799 on the site of the old garden of the Convent of the Daughters of God.   [A3a,6]

Trade and traffic are the two components of the street. Now, in the arcades the second of these has effectively died out: the traffic there is rudimentary. The arcade is a street of lascivious commerce only; it is wholly adapted to arousing desires. Because in this street the juices slow to a standstill, the commodity proliferates along the margins and enters into fantastic combinations, like the tissue in tumors.—The flâneur sabotages the traffic. Moreover, he is no buyer. He is merchandise.   [A3a,7]

For the first time in history, with the establishment of department stores, consumers begin to consider themselves a mass. (Earlier it was only scarcity which taught them that.) Hence, the circus-like and theatrical element of commerce is quite extraordinarily heightened. [A4,1]

With the appearance of mass-produced articles, the concept of specialty arises. Its relation to the concept of originality remains to be explored. [A4,2]

"I grant that business at the Palais-Royal has had its day; but I believe that this should be attributed not to the absence of streetwalkers but to the erection of new arcades, and to the enlargement and refurbishing of several others. I will mention the Passages de l'Opéra, du Grand-Cerf, du Saumon, de Véro-Dodat, Delorme, de Choiseul, and des Panoramas." F. F. A. Béraud, *Les Filles publiques de Paris et la police qui les régit* (Paris and Leipzig, 1839), vol. 1, p. 205. [A4,3]

"I do not know if business at the Palais-Royal has really suffered from the absence of *femmes de débauche*; but what is certain is that public decency there has improved enormously. . . . It seems to me, furthermore, that respectable women now willingly do their shopping in the shops of the galleries . . . ; this has to be an advantage for the merchants. For when the Palais-Royal was invaded by a swarm of practically nude prostitutes, the gaze of the crowd was turned toward them, and the people who enjoyed this spectacle were never the ones who patronized the local businesses. Some were already ruined by their disorderly life, while others, yielding to the allure of libertinism, had no thought then of purchasing any goods, even necessities. I believe I can affirm . . . that, during those times of inordinate tolerance, several shops at the Palais-Royal were closed, and in others buyers were rare. Thus, business did not at all prosper there, and it would be more accurate to say that the stagnation of business at that time was owing rather to the free circulation of the *filles publiques* than to their absence, which today has brought back into the galleries and the garden of this palace numerous strollers, who are far more favorable to business than prostitutes and libertines." F. F. A. Béraud, *Les Filles publiques de Paris* (Paris and Leipzig, 1839), vol. 1, pp. 207–209. [A4,4]

> The cafés are filled
> With gourmets, with smokers;
> The theaters are packed
> With cheerful spectators.
> The arcades are swarming
> With gawkers, with enthusiasts,
> And pickpockets wriggle
> Behind the flâneurs.

Ennery and Lemoine, *Paris la nuit*, cited in H. Gourdon de Genouillac, *Les Refrains de la rue de 1830 à 1870* (Paris, 1879), pp. 46–47.—To be compared with Baudelaire's "Crépuscule du soir." [A4a,1]

"And those who cannot pay for . . . a shelter? They sleep wherever they find a place, in passages, arcades, in corners where the police and the owners leave them undisturbed." Friedrich Engels, *Die Lage der arbeitenden Klasse in England,* 2nd ed. (Leipzig, 1848), p. 46 ("Die grossen Städte").[5] [A4a,2]

"In all the shops, like a uniform, the oak counter is adorned with counterfeit coins, in every kind of metal and in every format, mercilessly nailed in place like birds of prey on a door—unimpeachable evidence of the proprietor's scrupulous honesty." Nadar, *Quand j'étais photographe* (Paris ‹1900›), p. 294 ("1830 et environs"). [A4a,3]

Fourier on the street-galleries: "To spend a winter's day in a Phalanstery, to visit all parts of it without exposure to the elements, to go to the theater and the opera in light clothes and colored shoes without worrying about the mud and the cold, would be a charm so novel that it alone would suffice to make our cities and castles seem detestable. If the Phalanstery were put to civilized uses, the mere convenience of its sheltered, heated, and ventilated passageways would make it enormously valuable.[6] Its property value . . . would be double that of another building its size." E. Poisson, *Fourier* [Anthology] (Paris, 1932), p. 144. [A4a,4]

"The street-galleries are a mode of internal communication which would alone be sufficient to inspire disdain for the palaces and great cities of civilization. . . . The king of France is one of the leading monarchs of civilization; he does not even have a porch in his Tuileries palace. The king, the queen, the royal family, when they get into or out of their carriages, are forced to get as wet as any petty bourgeois who summons a cab before his shop. Doubtless the king will have on hand, in the event of rain, a good many footmen and courtiers to hold an umbrella for him . . . ; but he will still be lacking a porch or a roof that would shelter his party. . . . Let us describe the street-galleries which are one of the most charming and precious features of a Palace of Harmony. . . . The Phalanx has no outside streets or open roadways exposed to the elements. All portions of the central edifice can be traversed by means of a wide gallery which runs along the second floor of the whole building. At each extremity of this spacious corridor there are elevated passages, supported by columns, and also attractive underground passages which connect all the parts of the Phalanx and the adjoining buildings. Thus, everything is linked by a series of passageways which are sheltered, elegant, and comfortable in winter thanks to the help of heaters and ventilators. . . . The street-gallery, or *continuous peristyle,* extends along the second story. It could not be placed on the ground floor, since the lower part of the building will be traversed by carriage entrances. . . . The street-galleries of a Phalanx wind along just one side of the central edifice and stretch to the end of each of its wings. All of these wings contain a double row of rooms. Thus, one row of rooms looks out upon the fields and gardens, and the other looks out upon the street-gallery. The street-gallery, then, will be three stories high with windows on one side. . . . The kitchens and some of the public halls will be located on the ground floor. There will also be trap doors in the floors of the dining rooms on the second story. Thus, the tables may be set in the kitchens below and simply raised through the trap doors when it is time to eat. These trap doors will be particularly useful during festivities, such as the visits of traveling caravans and legions, when there will be too many people to eat in the ordinary dining rooms. Then double rows of tables will be set in the street-galleries, and the food will be passed up from the kitchen. / The principal public halls should not be situated on the ground floor. There are two reasons for this. The first is that the patriarchs and children, who have difficulty climbing stairs, should be lodged in the lower parts of the building. The second is that the children should be kept in isolation from the nonindustrial activities of the adults." Poisson, *Fourier* [Anthology] (Paris, 1932), pp. 139–144.[7]   [A5]

> Yes, *parbleu!* You know the power of Tibet.
> Implacable enemy of proud innocence,
> Hardly does it appear than it carries away
> The bookkeeper's wife and the burgher's daughter,
> The stern prude and the frigid coquette:
> It signals the victory of lovers;
> For fashion tolerates no resistance,
> And not to have it puts one to shame.
> Its fabric, braving the current bon mot,
> Softens in its folds the arrows of ridicule;
> Seeing it, you think of a magical talisman:
> It braces the spirits and subjugates the heart;
> For it to appear is already a triumph, its coming a conquest;
> It reigns as conqueror, as sovereign, as master;
> And treating its quiver as a burden quite useless,
> Love has fashioned its bandeau of cashmere.

Edouard [d'Anglemont], *Le Cachemire,* one-act comedy in verse, performed for the first time in Paris at the Théâtre Royal de l'Odéon, on December 16, 1826 (Paris, 1827), p. 30.   [A5a,1]

Delvau on Chodruc-Duclos: "Under the reign of Louis Philippe, who owed him nothing, he . . . did what he had done under the reign of Charles X, who in fact owed him something. . . . His bones took more time to rot than his name took to erase itself from the memory of men." Alfred Delvau, *Les Lions du jour* (Paris, 1867), pp. 28–29.   [A5a,2]

"It was not until after the expedition to Egypt,[8] when people in France gave thought to expanding the use of precious cashmere fabric, that a woman, Greek by birth, introduced it to Paris. M. Ternaux . . . conceived the admirable project of raising Hindustani goats in France. Since then, . . . there have been plenty of workers to train and trades to establish, in order for us to compete successfully against products renowned through so many centuries! Our manufacturers are beginning to triumph . . . over women's prejudice against French shawls. . . . We have managed to make women forget for a moment the ridiculous fabric-designs of the Hindus by happily reproducing the vividness and brilliant harmony of the flowers found in our own gardens. There is a book in which all these interesting subjects are discussed both knowledgeably and elegantly. *L'Histoire des schalls*, by M. Rey, though written for the shawl manufacturers of Paris, is guaranteed to captivate women. . . . This book, together with its author's magnificent manufactured goods, will undoubtedly help to dissipate French people's infatuation with the work of foreigners. M. Rey, manufacturer of shawls made of wool, cashmere, etc. . . . has brought out several cashmeres ranging in price from 170 to 500 francs. We owe to him, among other improvements, . . . the graceful imitation of native-grown flowers in place of the bizarre palms of the Orient. Our praise would not be equal to the benefits he has bestowed, . . . nor could it render the high honor that this litterateur-manufacturer deserves for his long research and his talents. We must be content merely to name him." Chenoue and H. D., *Notice sur l'exposition des produits de l'industrie et des arts qui a lieu à Douai en 1827* (Douai, 1827), pp. 24–25. [A6,1]

After 1850: "It is during these years that the department stores are created: Au Bon Marché, Le Louvre, La Belle Jardinière. Total sales for Au Bon Marché in 1852 were only 450,000 francs; by 1869 they had risen to 21 million." Gisela Freund, *La Photographie du point de vue sociologique* (manuscript, pp. 85–86); citing Lavisse, *Histoire de France*. [A6,2]

"The printers . . . were able to appropriate, at the end of the eighteenth century, a vast area: . . . the Passage du Caire and its environs. . . . But with the extension of the boundaries of Paris, printers . . . were dispersed to all parts of the city. . . . Alas! A glut of printers! Today workers corrupted by the spirit of speculation ought to remember that . . . between the Rue Saint-Denis and the Cour des Miracles there still exists a long, smoke-filled gallery where their true household gods lie forgotten." Edouard Foucaud, *Paris inventeur* (Paris, 1844), p. 154. [A6,3]

Description of the Passage du Saumon, "which, by way of three stone steps, opened onto the Rue Montorgueil. It was a narrow corridor decorated with pilasters supporting a ridged glass roof, which was littered with garbage thrown from neighboring houses. At the entrance, the signboard—a tin salmon indicating the main characteristic of the place: the air was filled with the smell of fish . . . and also the smell of garlic. It was here, above all, that those arriving in Paris from the south of France would arrange to meet. . . . Through the doors of the shops, one spied dusky alcoves where sometimes a piece of mahogany furniture, the classic furniture of the period, would manage to catch a ray of light. Further on, a small bar hazy with the smoke of tobacco pipes; a shop selling products from the colonies and emitting a curious fragrance of exotic plants, spices, and fruits; a ballroom open for dancing on Sundays and workday evenings; finally the reading room of

A branch of La Belle Jardinière in Marseilles. From *Le Monde illustré,* March 28, 1863. See A6,2.

Sieur Ceccherini, who offered to patrons his newspapers and his books." J. Lucas-Dubreton, *L'Affaire Alibaud, ou Louis-Philippe traqué* (1836; rpt. Paris, 1927), pp. 114–115.   [A6a,1]

On the occasion of disturbances associated with the burial of General Lamarque on June 5, 1832, the Passage du Saumon was the scene of a battle waged on barricades, in which 200 workers confronted the troops.   [A6a,2]

"*Martin:* Business, you see, sir, . . . is the ruler of the world!—*Desgenais:* I am of your opinion, Monsieur Martin, but the ruler alone is not enough; there must be subjects. And that is where painting, sculpture, music come in. . . .—*Martin:* A little of that is necessary, surely, . . . and . . . I myself have encouraged the arts. Why, in my last establishment, the Café de France, I had many paintings on allegorical subjects. . . . What is more, I engaged musicians for the evenings. . . . Finally, if I may invite you to accompany me . . . , you will see under my peristyle two very large, scantily attired statues, each with a light fixture on its head.—*Desgenais:* A light fixture?—*Martin:* That is my idea of sculpture: it must serve some purpose. . . . All those statues with an arm or a leg in the air—what are they good

for, since they've had no pipe installed to carry gas? . . . What are they good for?"
Théodore Barrière, *Les Parisiens*, produced at the Théâtre du Vaudeville on December 28, 1854 (Paris, 1855), p. 26. [The play is set in 1839.]   [A6a3]

There was a Passage du Désir. ‹See A1a,2.›   [A6a,4]

Chodruc-Duclos—a supernumerary at the Palais-Royal. He was a royalist, an opponent of the Vendée, and had grounds for complaining of ingratitude under Charles X. He protested by appearing publicly in rags and letting his beard grow.   [A6a,5]

Apropos of an engraving that pictures a shopfront in the Passage Véro-Dodat: "One cannot praise this arrangement too highly—the purity of its lines; the picturesque and brilliant effect produced by the gaslight globes, which are placed between the capitals of the two double columns bordering each shop; and finally the shop partitions, which are set off by reflecting plate glass." Cabinet des Estampes ‹in the Bibliothèque Nationale, Paris›.   [A7,1]

At No. 32 Passage Brady there was a dry-cleaning establishment, Maison Donnier. It was ‹famous› for its "giant workrooms" and its "numerous personnel." A contemporary engraving shows the two-story building crowned by small mansards; female workers in great numbers are visible through the windows; from the ceilings hangs the linen.   [A7,2]

Engraving from the Empire: *The Dance of the Shawl among the Three Sultanas*. Cabinet des Estampes.   [A7,3]

Sketch and floor plan of the arcade at 36 Rue Hauteville, in black, blue, and pink, from the year 1856, on stamped paper. A hotel attached to the arcade is likewise represented. In boldface: "Property for lease." Cabinet des Estampes.   [A7,4]

The first department stores appear to be modeled on oriental bazaars. From engravings one sees that, at least around 1880, it was the fashion to cover with tapestries the balustrades of the staircases leading to the atrium. For example, in the store called City of Saint-Denis. Cabinet des Estampes.   [A7,5]

"The Passage de l'Opéra, with its two galleries, the Galerie de l'Horloge and the Galerie du Baromètre. . . . The opening of the Opéra on the Rue Le Peletier, in 1821, brought this arcade into vogue, and in 1825 the duchesse de Berry came in person to inaugurate a 'Europama' in the Galerie du Baromètre. . . . The grisettes of the Restoration danced in the Idalia Hall, built in the basement. Later, a café called the Divan de l'Opéra was established in the arcade. . . . Also to be found in the Passage de l'Opéra was the arms manufacturer Caron, the music publisher

The Passage de l'Opéra, 1822-1823. Courtesy of the Musée Carnavalet, Paris. Photo copyright © Photothèque des Musées de la Ville de Paris. See A7,6.

Street scene in front of the Passage des Panoramas. Lithograph by Opitz, 1814. Courtesy of the Bibliothèque Nationale de France. See A7,7.

Marguerie, the pastry chef Rollet, and finally the perfume shop of the Opéra. . . . In addition, . . . there was Lemonnier, *artiste en cheveux*—which is to say, manufacturer of handkerchiefs, reliquaries, and funeral items made of hair." Paul d'Ariste, *La Vie et le monde du boulevard, 1830–1879* (Paris ⟨1930⟩), pp. 14–16.

[A7,6]

"The Passage des Panoramas, so named in memory of the two panoramas that stood on either side of its entranceway and that disappeared in 1831." Paul d'Ariste, *La Vie et le monde du boulevard* (Paris), p. 14.   [A7,7]

The beautiful apotheosis of the "marvel of the Indian shawl," in the section on Indian art in Michelet's *Bible de l'humanité* (Paris, 1864).   [A7a,1]

> And Jehuda ben Halevy,
> In her view, would have been honored
> Quite enough by being kept in
> Any pretty box of cardboard
>
> With some very swanky Chinese
> Arabesques to decorate it,
> Like a bonbon box from Marquis
> In the Passage Panorama.

Heinrich Heine, *Hebräische Melodien*, "Jehuda ben Halevy," part 4, in *Romanzero*, book 3 (cited in a letter from Wiesengrund).[9]   [A7a,2]

Signboards. After the rebus style came a vogue for literary and military allusions. "If an eruption of the hilltop of Montmartre happened to swallow up Paris, as Vesuvius swallowed up Pompeii, one would be able to reconstruct from our signboards, after fifteen hundred years, the history of our military triumphs and of our literature." Victor Fournel, *Ce qu'on voit dans les rues de Paris* (Paris, 1858), p. 286 ("Enseignes et affiches").   [A7a,3]

Chaptal, in his speech on protecting brand names in industry: "Let us not assume that the consumer will be adept, when making a purchase, at distinguishing the degrees of quality of a material. No, gentlemen, the consumer cannot appreciate these degrees; he judges only according to his senses. Do the eye or the touch suffice to enable one to pronounce on the fastness of colors, or to determine with precision the degree of fineness of a material, the nature and quality of its manufacture?" ‹Jean-Antoine-Claude› Chaptal, *Rapport au nom d'une commission spéciale chargée de l'examen du projet de loi relatif aux altérations et suppositions de noms sur les produits fabriqués* [Chambre des Pairs de France, session of July 17, 1824], p. 5.—The importance of good professional standing is magnified in proportion as consumer know-how becomes more specialized.   [A7a,4]

"What shall I say now of that *coulisse* which, not content with harboring a two-hour illegal session at the Stock Exchange, spawned once again not long ago, in the open air, two demonstrations per day on the Boulevard des Italiens, across from the Passage de l'Opéra, where five or six hundred market speculators, forming a compact mass, followed clumsily in the wake of some forty unlicensed brokers, all the while speaking in low voices like conspirators, while police officers prodded them from behind to get them to move on, as one prods fat, tired sheep being led to the slaughterhouse." M. J. Ducos (de Gondrin), *Comment on se ruine à la Bourse* (Paris, 1858), p. 19. [A7a,5]

It was at 271 Rue Saint-Martin, in the Passage du Cheval Rouge, that Lacenaire committed his murders. [A7a,6]

A sign: "L'épé-scié" ⟨The Sawed-Off Epé[e]⟩.[10] [A7a,7]

From a prospectus: "To the inhabitants of the Rues Beauregard, Bourbon-Villeneuve, du Caire, and de la Cour des Miracles. . . . A plan for two covered arcades running from the Place du Caire to the Rue Beauregard, ending directly in front of the Rue Sainte-Barbe, and linking the Rue Bourbon-Villeneuve with the Rue Hauteville. . . . Gentlemen, for some time now we have been concerned about the future of this neighborhood, and it pains us to see that properties so close to the boulevard carry a value so far below what they ought to have. This state of affairs would change if lines of communication were opened. Since it is impossible to construct new streets in this area, due to the great unevenness of the ground, and since the only workable plan is the one we have the honor of submitting to you here, we hope, Gentlemen, that in your capacity as owners . . . you will in turn honor us with your cooperation and affiliation. . . . Every partner will be required to pay an installment of 5 francs on each 250-franc share in the future company. As soon as a capital sum of 3,000 francs is realized, this provisional subscription will become final—said sum being judged at present sufficient. . . . Paris, this 20th of October, 1847." Printed prospectus inviting subscriptions. [A8,1]

"In the Passage Choiseul, M. Comte, 'Physician to the King,' presents his celebrated troupe of child actors *extraordinaires* in the interval between two magic shows in which he himself performs." J.-L. Croze, "Quelques spectacles de Paris pendant l'été de 1835" (*Le Temps*, August 22, 1935). [A8,2]

"At this turning point in history, the Parisian shopkeeper makes two discoveries that revolutionize the world of *la nouveauté*: the display of goods and the male employee. The display, which leads him to deck out his shop from floor to ceiling and to sacrifice three hundred yards of material to garland his façade like a flagship; and the male employee, who replaces the seduction of man by woman—something conceived by the shopkeepers of the ancien régime—with the seduction of woman by man, which is psychologically more astute. Together with these comes the fixed price, the known and nonnegotiable cost." H. Clouzot and R.-H. Valensi, *Le Paris de "La Comédie humaine": Balzac et ses fournisseurs* (Paris, 1926), pp. 31–32 ("Magasins de nouveautés"). [A8,3]

When a *magasin de nouveautés* rented the space formerly occupied by Hetzel, the editor of *La Comédie humaine*, Balzac wrote: "*The Human Comedy* has yielded to the comedy of cashmeres." (Clouzot and Valensi, *Le Paris de "La Comédie humaine,"* p. 37.) [A8,4]

Passage du Commerce-Saint-André: a reading room. [A8a,1]

"Once the socialist government had become the legitimate owner of all the houses of Paris, it handed them over to the architects with the order . . . to establish *street-galleries.* . . . The architects accomplished the mission entrusted to them as well as could be expected. On the second story of every house, they took all the rooms that faced the street and demolished the intervening partitions; they then opened up large bays in the dividing walls, thereby obtaining street-galleries that had the height and width of an ordinary room and that occupied the entire length of a block of buildings. In the newer *quartiers,* where neighboring houses have their floors at approximately the same height, the galleries could be joined together on a fairly even level. . . . But on older streets . . . the floors had to be carefully raised or lowered, and often the builders had to resign themselves to giving the floor a rather steep slant, or breaking it up with stairs. When all the blocks of houses were thus traversed by galleries occupying . . . their second story, it remained only to connect these isolated sections to one another in order to constitute a network . . . embracing the whole city. This was easily done by erecting covered walkways across every street. . . . Walkways of the same sort, but much longer, were likewise put up over the various boulevards, over the squares, and over the bridges that cross the Seine, so that in the end . . . a person could stroll through the entire city without ever being exposed to the elements. . . . As soon as the Parisians had got a taste of the new galleries, they lost all desire to set foot in the streets of old—which, they often said, were fit only for dogs." Tony Moilin, *Paris en l'an 2000* (Paris, 1869), pp. 9–11. [A8a,2]

"The second floor contains the street-galleries. . . . Along the length of the great avenues, . . . they form street-salons. . . . The other, much less spacious galleries are decorated more modestly. They have been reserved for retail businesses that here display their merchandise in such a way that passersby circulate no longer in front of the shops but in their interior." Tony Moilin, *Paris en l'an 2000* (Paris, 1869), pp. 15–16 ("Maisons-modèles"). [A8a,3]

Sales clerks: "There are at least 20,000 in Paris. . . . A great number of sales clerks have been educated in the classics . . . ; one even finds among them painters and architects unaffiliated with any workshop, who use a great deal of their knowledge . . . of these two branches of art in constructing displays, in determining the design of new items, in directing the creation of fashions." Pierre Larousse, *Grand Dictionnaire universel du XIXᵉ siècle*, vol. 3 (Paris, 1867), p. 150 (article on "Calicot"). [A9,1]

"Why did the author of *Etudes de moeurs*[11] ⟨Studies of Manners⟩ choose to present, in a work of fiction, lifelike portraits of the notables of his day? Doubtless for his own amusement first of all. . . . This explains the descriptions. For the direct citations, another reason must be found—and we see none better than his unmistakable aim of providing publicity. Balzac is one of the first to have divined the power of the advertisement and, above all, the disguised advertisement. In those days, . . . the newspapers were unaware of such power. . . . At the very most, around midnight, as workers were finishing up the layout, advertising writers might slip in at the bottom of a column some lines on Pâte de Regnault or Brazilian Blend. The newspaper advertisement as such was unknown. More unknown still was a process as ingenious as citation in a novel. . . . The tradesmen named by Balzac . . . are clearly his own. . . . No one understood better than the author of *César Birotteau* the unlimited potential of publicity. . . . To confirm this, one need only look at the epithets . . . he attaches to his manufacturers and their products. Shamelessly he dubs them: the *renowned* Victorine; Plaisir, an *illustrious* hairdresser; Staub, the *most celebrated* tailor of his age; Gay, a *famous* haberdasher . . . on the Rue de la Michodière (even giving the address!); . . . 'the cuisine of the Rocher de Cancale, . . . the premier restaurant in Paris . . . , which is to say, in the *entire world*.'" H. Clouzot and R.-H. Valensi, *Le Paris de "La Comédie humaine": Balzac et ses fournisseurs* (Paris, 1926), pp. 7–9 and 177–179.   [A9,2]

The Passage Véro-Dodat connects the Rue Croix-des-Petits-Champs with the Rue Jean-Jacques-Rousseau. In the latter, around 1840, Cabet held his meetings in his rooms. We get an idea of the tone of these gatherings from Martin Nadaud's *Mémoires de Léonard, ancien garçon maçon:* "He was still holding in his hand the towel and razor he had just been using. He seemed filled with joy at seeing us respectably attired, with a serious air: 'Ah, Messieurs,' he said (he did not say 'Citizens'), 'if your adversaries could only see you now! You would disarm their criticisms. Your dress and your bearing are those of well-bred men.'" Cited in Charles Benoist, "L'Homme de 1848," part 2, *Revue des deux mondes* (February 1, 1914), pp. 641–642.—It was characteristic of Cabet to believe that workers need not busy themselves with writing.   [A9,3]

Street-salons: "The largest and most favorably situated among these [street-galleries] were tastefully decorated and sumptuously furnished. The walls and ceilings were covered with . . . rare marble, gilding, . . . mirrors, and paintings. The windows were adorned with splendid hangings and with curtains embroidered in marvelous patterns. Chairs, fauteuils, sofas . . . offered comfortable seating to tired strollers. Finally, there were artistically designed objects, antique cabinets, . . . glass cases full of curiosities, . . . porcelain vases containing fresh flowers, aquariums full of live fish, and aviaries inhabited by rare birds. These completed the decoration of the street-galleries, which lit up the evening with . . . gilt candelabras and crystal lamps. The government had wanted the streets belonging to the people of Paris to surpass in magnificence the drawing rooms of the most powerful sovereigns. . . . First thing in the morning, the street-galleries are turned over to attendants who air them out, sweep them carefully, brush, dust, and polish the furniture, and everywhere impose the most scrupulous cleanliness. Then, depending on the season, the windows are either opened or closed, and either a fire is lit or the blinds are lowered. . . . Between nine and ten o'clock this cleaning is all completed, and passersby, until then few and far between, begin to appear in greater numbers. Entrance to the galleries is strictly forbidden to anyone who is dirty or to carriers of heavy loads; smoking and spitting are likewise prohibited here." Tony Moilin, *Paris en l'an 2000* (Paris, 1869), pp. 26–29 ("Aspect des rues-galeries").   [A9a,1]

The *magasins de nouveautés* owe their existence to the freedom of trade established by Napoleon I. "Of those establishments, famous in 1817, which gave themselves names like La Fille Mal Gardée, Le Diable Boiteux, Le Masque de Fer, or Les Deux Magots, not one remains. Many of those which replaced them under Louis Philippe also foundered later on—like La Belle Fermière and La Chaussée d'Antin. Or else they were sold at little profit—like Le Coin de Rue and Le Pauvre Diable." G. d'Avenel, "Le Mécanisme de la vie moderne," part 1: "Les Grands Magasins," *Revue des deux mondes* (July 15, 1894), p. 334.   [A9a,2]

The office of Philipon's weekly *La Caricature* was in the Passage Véro-Dodat.   [A9a,3]

Passage du Caire. Erected after Napoleon's return from Egypt. Contains some evocations of Egypt in the reliefs—sphinx-like heads over the entrance, among other things. "The arcades are sad, gloomy, and always intersecting in a manner disagreeable to the eye. . . . They seem . . . destined to house lithographers' studios and binders' shops, as the adjoining street is destined for the manufacture of straw hats; pedestrians generally avoid them." Elie Berthet, "Rue et Passage du Caire," *Paris chez soi* (Paris ‹1854›), p. 362.   [A10,1]

"In 1798 and 1799, the Egyptian campaign lent frightful importance to the fashion for shawls. Some generals in the expeditionary army, taking advantage of the proximity of India, sent home shawls . . . of cashmere to their wives and lady friends. . . . From then on, the disease that might be called cashmere fever took on significant proportions. It began to spread during the Consulate, grew greater under the Empire, became gigantic during the Restoration, reached colossal size under the July Monarchy, and has finally assumed Sphinx-like dimensions since the February Revolution of 1848." *Paris chez soi* (Paris), p. 139 (A. Durand, "Châles—Cachemires indiens et français"). Contains an interview with M. Martin, 39 Rue Richelieu, proprietor of a store called The Indians; reports that shawls which earlier were priced between 1,500 and 2,000 francs can now be bought for 800 to 1,000 francs.   [A10,2]

From Brazier, Gabriel, and Dumersan, *Les Passages et les rues*, vaudeville in one act, presented for the first time, in Paris, at the Théâtre des Variétés on March 7, 1827 (Paris, 1827).—Beginning of a song by the shareholder Dulingot:

> For the arcades, I form
> Continual refrains of thanks:

In the Passage Delorme
I've put a hundred thousand francs. (Pp. 5–6)

"I hear they want to roof all the streets of Paris with glass. That will make for lovely hothouses; we will live in them like melons" (p. 19).   [A10,3]

From Girard, *Des Tombeaux, ou De l'Influence des institutions funèbres sur les moeurs* (Paris, 1801): "The new Passage du Caire, near the Rue Saint-Denis, . . . is paved in part with funerary stones, on which the Gothic inscriptions and the emblems have not yet been effaced." The author wishes to draw attention here to the decline of piety. Cited in Edouard Fournier, *Chroniques et légendes des rues de Paris* (Paris, 1864), p. 154.   [A10,4]

Brazier, Gabriel, and Dumersan, *Les Passages et les rues, ou La Guerre déclarée*, vaudeville in one act, performed for the first time, in Paris, at the Théâtre des Variétés on March 7, 1827 (Paris, 1827).—The party of arcades-adversaries is composed of M. Duperron, umbrella merchant; Mme. Duhelder, wife of a carriage provider; M. Mouffetard, hatter; M. Blancmanteau, merchant and manufacturer of clogs; and Mme. Dubac, rentier—each one coming from a different part of town. M. Dulingot, who has bought stock in the arcades, has championed their cause. His lawyer is M. Pour; that of his opponents, M. Contre. In the second to last (fourteenth) scene, M. Contre appears at the head of a column of streets, which are decked with banners proclaiming their names. Among them are the Rue aux Ours, Rue Bergère, Rue du Croissant, Rue du Puits-qui-Parle, Rue du Grand-Hurleur. Likewise in the next scene—a procession of arcades with their banners: Passage du Saumon, Passage de l'Ancre, Passage du Grand-Cerf, Passage du Pont-Neuf, Passage de l'Opéra, Passage du Panorama ‹*sic*›. In the following scene, the last (sixteenth), Lutèce[12] emerges from the bowels of the earth, at first in the guise of an old woman. In her presence, M. Contre takes up the defense of the streets against the arcades. "One hundred forty-four arcades open their mouths wide to devour our customers, to siphon off the ever-rising flow of our crowds, both active and idle. And you want us streets of Paris to ignore this clear infringement of our ancient rights! No, we demand . . . the interdiction of our one hundred forty-four opponents and, in addition, fifteen million, five hundred thousand francs in damages and interest" (p. 29). The argument by M. Pour in favor of the arcades takes the form of verse. An extract:

> We whom they would banish—we are more than useful.
> Have we not, by virtue of our cheerful aspect,
> Encouraged all of Paris in the fashion
> Of bazaars, those marts so famous in the East?
> . . . . .
> And what are these walls the crowd admires?
> These ornaments, these columns above all?
> You'd think you were in Athens; and this temple
> Is erected to commerce by good taste. (Pp. 29–30)

Lutèce arbitrates the differences: "'The affair is settled. Genies of light, hearken to my voice.' (At this moment the whole gallery is suddenly illuminated by gas-light.)" (p. 31). A ballet of streets and arcades concludes the vaudeville.   [A10a,1]

"I do not at all hesitate to write—as monstrous as this may seem to serious writers on art—that it was the sales clerk who launched lithography. . . . Condemned to imitations of Raphael, to Briseises by Regnault, it would perhaps have died; the sales clerk saved it." Henri Bouchot, *La Lithographie* (Paris ‹1895›), pp. 50–51.
[A11,1]

> In the Passage Vivienne
> She told me: "I'm from Vienna."
> And she added:
> "I live with my uncle,
> The brother of Papa!
> I take care of his furuncle—
> It has its charms, this fate."
> I promised to meet the damsel again
> In the Passage Bonne-Nouvelle;
> But in the Passage Brady
> I waited in vain.
> . . . . .
> And there you have it: arcade amours!

Narcisse Lebeau, cited by Léon-Paul Fargue, "Cafés de Paris," part 2 [in *Vu*, 9, no. 416 (March 4, 1936)].   [A11,2]

"There seems no reason, in particular, at the first and most literal glance, why the story should be called after the Old Curiosity Shop. Only two of the characters have anything to do with such a shop, and they leave it for ever in the first few pages. . . . But when we feel the situation with more fidelity we realize that this title is something in the nature of a key to the whole Dickens romance. His tales always started from some splendid hint in the streets. And shops, perhaps the most poetical of all things, often set his fancy galloping. Every shop, in fact, was to him the door of romance. Among all the huge serial schemes . . . it is a matter of wonder that he never started an endless periodical called the *The Street*, and divided it into shops. He could have written an exquisite romance called *The Baker's Shop*; another called *The Chemist's Shop*; another called *The Oil Shop*, to keep company with *The Old Curiosity Shop*." G. K. Chesterton, *Dickens*, trans. Laurent and Martin-Dupont (Paris, 1927), pp. 82–83.[13]   [A11,3]

"One may wonder to what extent Fourier himself believed in his fantasies. In his manuscripts he sometimes complains of critics who take literally what is meant as figurative, and who insist moreover on speaking of his 'studied whims.' There may have been at least a modicum of deliberate charlatanism at work in all this—an attempt to launch his system by means of the tactics of commercial advertising, which had begun to develop." F. Armand and R. Maublanc, *Fourier* (Paris, 1937), vol. 1, p. 158. ⬜ Exhibitions ⬜ [A11a,1]

Proudhon's confession near the end of his life (in his book *De la justice*[14]—compare with Fourier's vision of the phalanstery): "It has been necessary for me to become civilized. But need I approve? The little bit of civilizing I've received disgusts me. . . . I hate houses of more than one story, houses in which, by contrast with the social hierarchy, the meek are raised on high while the great are settled near the ground." Cited in Armand Cuvillier, *Marx et Proudhon: A la lumière du Marxisme*, vol. 2, part 1 (Paris, 1937), p. 211. [A11a,2]

Blanqui: "'I wore,' he says, 'the first tricolored cockade of 1830, made by Madame Bodin in the Passage du Commerce.'" Gustave Geffroy, *L'Enfermé* (Paris, 1897), p. 240. [A11a,3]

Baudelaire can still write of "a book as dazzling as an Indian handkerchief or shawl." Baudelaire, *L'Art romantique* (Paris), p. 192 ("Pierre Dupont").[15]
[A11a,4]

The Crauzat Collection possesses a beautiful reproduction of the Passage des Panoramas from 1808. Also found there: a prospectus for a bootblacking shop, in which it is a question mainly of Puss in Boots. [A11a,5]

Baudelaire to his mother on December 25, 1861, concerning an attempt to pawn a shawl: "I was told that, with the approach of New Year's Day, there was a glut of cashmeres in the stores, and that they were trying to discourage the public from bringing any more in." Charles Baudelaire, *Lettres à sa mère* (Paris, 1932), p. 198. [A11a,6]

"Our epoch will be the link between the age of isolated forces rich in original creativeness and that of the uniform but leveling force which gives monotony to its products, casting them in masses, and following out one unifying idea—the ultimate expression of social communities." H. de Balzac, *L'Illustre Gaudissart*, ed. Calmann-Lévy (Paris, 1837), p. 1.[16] [A11a,7]

Sales at Au Bon Marché, in the years 1852 to 1863, rose from 450,000 to 7 million francs. The rise in profits could have been considerably less. "High turnover and small profits" was at that time a new principle, one that accorded with the two dominant forces in operation: the multitude of purchasers and the mass of goods. In 1852, Boucicaut allied himself with Vidau, the proprietor of Au Bon Marché, the *magasin de nouveautés*. "The originality consisted in selling guaranteed merchandise at discount prices. Items, first of all, were marked with fixed prices, another bold innovation which did away with bargaining and with 'process sales'—that is to say, with gauging the price of an article to the physiognomy of the buyer; then the 'return' was instituted, allowing the customer to

Au Bon Marché department store in Paris. Woodcut, ca. 1880. See A12,1.

cancel his purchase at will; and, finally, employees were paid almost entirely by commission on sales. These were the constitutive elements of the new organization." George d'Avenel, "Le Mécanisme de la vie moderne: Les Grands Magasins," *Revue des deux mondes,* 124 (Paris, 1894), pp. 335–336. [A12,1]

The gain in time realized for the retail business by the abolition of bargaining may have played a role initially in the calculations of department stores. [A12,2]

A chapter, "Shawls, Cashmeres," in Börne's *Industrie-Ausstellung im Louvre* ‹Exhibition of Industry in the Louvre›. Ludwig Börne, *Gesammelte Schriften* (Hamburg and Frankfurt am Main, 1862), vol. 3, p. 260. [A12,3]

The physiognomy of the arcade emerges with Baudelaire in a sentence at the beginning of "Le Joueur généreux": "It seemed to me odd that I could have passed this enchanting haunt so often without suspecting that here was the entrance." ‹Baudelaire, *Oeuvres*, ed. Y.-G. Le Dantec (Paris, 1931),› vol. 1, p. 456.[17] [A12,4]

Specifics of the department store: the customers perceive themselves as a mass; they are confronted with an assortment of goods; they take in all the floors at a glance; they pay fixed prices; they can make exchanges. [A12,5]

"In those parts of the city where the theaters and public walks . . . are located, where therefore the majority of foreigners live and wander, there is hardly a building without a shop. It takes only a minute, only a step, for the forces of attraction to gather; a minute later, a step further on, and the passerby is standing before a different shop. . . . One's attention is spirited away as though by violence, and one has no choice but to stand there and remain looking up until it returns. The name of the shopkeeper, the name of his merchandise, inscribed a dozen times on placards that hang on the doors and above the windows, beckon from all sides; the exterior of the archway resembles the exercise book of a schoolboy who writes the few words of a paradigm over and over. Fabrics are not laid out in samples but are hung before door and window in completely unrolled bolts. Often they are attached high up on the third story and reach down in sundry folds all the way to the pavement. The shoemaker has painted different-colored shoes, ranged in rows like battalions, across the entire façade of his building. The sign for the locksmiths is a six-foot-high gold-plated key; the giant gates of heaven could require no larger. On the hosiers' shops are painted white stockings four yards high, and they will startle you in the dark when they loom like ghosts. . . . But foot and eye are arrested in a nobler and more charming fashion by the paintings displayed before many storefronts. . . . These paintings are, not infrequently, true works of art, and if they were to hang in the Louvre, they would inspire in connoisseurs at least pleasure if not admiration. . . . The shop of a wigmaker is adorned with a picture that, to be sure, is poorly executed but distinguished by an amusing conception. Crown Prince Absalom hangs by his hair from a tree and is pierced by the lance of an enemy. Underneath runs the verse: 'Here you see Absalom in his hopes quite debunked, / Had he worn a peruke, he'd not be defunct.' Another . . . picture, representing a village maiden as she kneels to receive a garland of roses—token of her virtue—from the hands of a chevalier, ornaments the door of a milliner's shop." Ludwig Börne, *Schilderungen aus Paris (1822 und 1823)*, ch. 6 ("Die Läden" ‹Shops›), in *Gesammelte Schriften* (Hamburg and Frankfurt am Main, 1862), vol. 3, pp. 46–49. [A12a]

On Baudelaire's "religious intoxication of great cities":[18] the department stores are temples consecrated to this intoxication. [A13]

B

[Fashion]

Fashion: Madam Death! Madam Death!
—Giacomo Leopardi, "Dialogue between Fashion and Death"[1]

Nothing dies; all is transformed.
—Honoré de Balzac, *Pensées, sujets, fragments* (Paris, 1910), p. 46

And boredom is the grating before which the courtesan teases death.
☐ Ennui ☐   [B1,1]

Similarity of the arcades to the indoor arenas in which one learned to ride a bicycle. In these halls the figure of the woman assumed its most seductive aspect: as cyclist. That is how she appears on contemporary posters. Chéret the painter of this feminine pulchritude. The costume of the cyclist, as an early and unconscious prefiguration of sportswear, corresponds to the dream prototypes that, a little before or a little later, are at work in the factory or the automobile. Just as the first factory buildings cling to the traditional form of the residential dwelling, and just as the first automobile chassis imitate carriages, so in the clothing of the cyclist the sporting expression still wrestles with the inherited pattern of elegance, and the fruit of this struggle is the grim sadistic touch which made this ideal image of elegance so incomparably provocative to the male world in those days.
☐ Dream Houses ☐   [B1,2]

"In these years [around 1880], not only does the Renaissance fashion begin to do mischief, but on the other side a new interest in sports—above all, in equestrian sports—arises among women, and together these two tendencies exert an influence on fashion from quite different directions. The attempt to reconcile these sentiments dividing the female soul yields results that, in the years 1882–1885, are original if not always beautiful. To improve matters, dress designers simplify and take in the waist as much as possible, while allowing the skirt an amplitude all the more rococo." *70 Jahre deutsche Mode* (1925), pp. 84–87.   [B1,3]

Here fashion has opened the business of dialectical exchange between woman and ware—between carnal pleasure and the corpse. The clerk, death, tall and loutish, measures the century by the yard, serves as mannequin himself to save costs, and manages single-handedly the liquidation that in French is called *révolution*. For fashion was never anything other than the parody of the motley cadaver, provocation of death through the woman, and bitter colloquy with decay whispered between shrill bursts of mechanical laughter. That is fashion. And that is why she changes so quickly; she titillates death and is already something different, something new, as he casts about to crush her. For a hundred years she holds her own against him. Now, finally, she is on the point of quitting the field. But he erects on the banks of a new Lethe, which rolls its asphalt stream through arcades, the armature of the whores as a battle memorial. □ Revolution □ Love □

[B1,4]

Squares, o square in Paris, infinite showplace,
where the modiste Madame Lamort
winds and binds the restless ways of the world,
those endless ribbons, to ever-new
creations of bow, frill, flower, cockade, and fruit—

R. M. Rilke, *Duineser Elegien* (Leipzig, 1923), p. 23.[2]   [B1,5]

"Nothing has a place of its own, save fashion appoints that place." *L'Esprit d'Alphonse Karr: ‹Pensées extraites de ses oeuvres complètes›* (Paris, 1877), p. 129. "If a woman of taste, while undressing at night, should find herself constituted in reality as she has pretended to be during the day, I like to think she'd be discovered next morning drowned in her own tears." Alphonse Karr, cited in F. Th. Vischer, *Mode und Zynismus* (Stuttgart, 1879), pp. 106–107.   [B1,6]

With Karr, there appears a rationalist theory of fashion that is closely related to the rationalist theory of the origin of religions. The motive for instituting long skirts, for example, he conceives to be the interest certain women would have had in concealing an unlovely ‹foot›. Or he denounces, as the origin of certain types of hats and certain hairstyles, the wish to compensate for thin hair.   [B1,7]

Who still knows, nowadays, where it was that in the last decade of the previous century women would offer to men their most seductive aspect, the most intimate promise of their figure? In the asphalted indoor arenas where people learned to ride bicycles. The woman as cyclist competes with the cabaret singer for the place of honor on posters, and gives to fashion its most daring line.

[B1,8]

For the philosopher, the most interesting thing about fashion is its extraordinary anticipations. It is well known that art will often—for example, in pictures—precede the perceptible reality by years. It was possible to see streets or rooms that shone in all sorts of fiery colors long before technology, by means of illuminated signs and other arrangements, actually set them under such a light. Moreover, the sensitivity of the individual artist to what is coming certainly far exceeds that of the *grande dame*. Yet fashion is in much steadier, much more precise contact with the coming thing, thanks to the incomparable nose which the feminine collective has for what lies waiting in the future. Each season brings, in its newest creations, various secret signals of things to come. Whoever understands how to read these semaphores would know in advance not only about new currents in the arts but also about new legal codes, wars, and revolutions.[3]—Here, surely, lies the greatest charm of fashion, but also the difficulty of making the charming fruitful. [B1a,1]

"Whether you translate Russian fairy tales, Swedish family sagas, or English picaresque novels—you will always come back in the end, when it is a question of setting the tone for the masses, to France, not because it is always the truth but because it will always be the fashion." ‹Karl› Gutzkow, *Briefe aus Paris,* vol. 2 ‹Leipzig, 1842›, pp. 227–228. Each time, what sets the tone is without doubt the newest, but only where it emerges in the medium of the oldest, the longest past, the most ingrained. This spectacle, the unique self-construction of the newest in the medium of what has been, makes for the true dialectical theater of fashion. Only as such, as the grandiose representation of this dialectic, can one appreciate the singular books of Grandville, which created a sensation toward the middle of the century. When Grandville presents a new fan as the "fan of Iris" and his drawing suggests a rainbow, or when the Milky Way appears as an avenue illuminated at night by gaslamps, or when "the moon (a self-portrait)" reposes on fashionable velvet cushions instead of on clouds[4]—at such moments we first come to see that it is precisely in this century, the most parched and imagination-starved, that the collective dream energy of a society has taken refuge with redoubled vehemence in the mute impenetrable nebula of fashion, where the understanding cannot follow. Fashion is the predecessor—no, the eternal deputy—of Surrealism. [B1a,2]

A pair of lascivious engravings by Charles Vernier entitled *A Wedding on Wheels*— showing the departure and the return. The bicycle offered unsuspected possibilities for the depiction of the raised skirt. [B1a,3]

A definitive perspective on fashion follows solely from the consideration that to each generation the one immediately preceding it seems the most radical anti-aphrodisiac imaginable. In this judgment it is not so far wrong as might be supposed. Every fashion is to some extent a bitter satire on love; all sexual perversities are suggested in every fashion by the most ruthless means; every fashion is filled with secret resistances to love. It is worthwhile reflecting on the following observation by Grand-Carteret, superficial though it is: "It is in scenes from the amorous life that one may in fact perceive the full ridiculousness of certain fashions. Aren't men and women grotesque in these gestures and attitudes—in the tufted forelock (already extravagant in itself), in the top hat and the nipped-waisted frockcoat, in the shawl, in the *grandes pamélas,* in the dainty fabric boots?" Thus, the confrontation with the fashions of previous generations is a

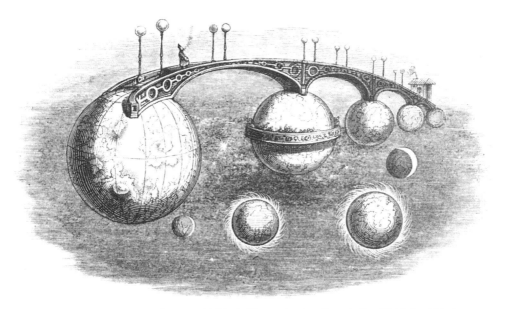

Le Pont des planètes (Interplanetary Bridge). Engraving by Grandville, 1844. See B1a,2.

matter of far greater importance than we ordinarily suppose. And one of the most significant aspects of historical costuming is that—above all, in the theater—it undertakes such a confrontation. Beyond the theater, the question of costume reaches deep into the life of art and poetry, where fashion is at once preserved and overcome.   [B1a,4]

A kindred problem arose with the advent of new velocities, which gave life an altered rhythm. This latter, too, was first tried out, as it were, in a spirit of play. The loop-the-loop came on the scene, and Parisians seized on this entertainment with a frenzy. A chronicler notes around 1810 that a lady squandered 75 francs in one evening at the Parc de Montsouris, where at that time you could ride those looping cars. The new tempo of life is often announced in the most unforeseen ways. For example, in posters. "These images of a day or an hour, bleached by the elements, charcoaled by urchins, scorched by the sun—although others are sometimes collected even before they have dried—symbolize to a higher degree even than the newspapers the sudden, shock-filled, multiform life that carries us away." Maurice Talmeyr, *La Cité du sang* (Paris, 1901), p. 269. In the early days of the poster, there was as yet no law to regulate the posting of bills or to provide protection for posters and indeed *from* posters; so one could wake up some morning to find one's window placarded. From time immemorial this enigmatic need for sensation has found satisfaction in fashion. But in its ground it will be reached at last only by theological inquiry, for such inquiry bespeaks a deep affective attitude toward historical process on the part of the human being. It is tempting to connect this need for sensation to one of the seven deadly sins, and it is not surprising that a chronicler adds apocalyptic prophecies to this connection and foretells a time when people will have been blinded by the effects of too much electric light and maddened by the tempo of news reporting. From Jacques Fabien, *Paris en songe* (Paris, 1863). [B2,1]

"On October 4, 1856, the Gymnasium Theater presented a play entitled *Les Toilettes Tapageuses* ⟨The Flashy Dressers⟩. It was the heyday of the crinoline, and puffed-out women were in fashion. The actress playing the leading role, having grasped the satirical intentions of the author, wore a dress whose skirt, exaggerated by design, had a fullness that was comical and almost ridiculous. The day after opening night, she was asked by more than twenty fine ladies to lend her dress as a model, and eight days later the crinoline had doubled in size." Maxime Du Camp, *Paris*, vol. 6 ⟨Paris, 1875⟩, p. 192. [B2,2]

"Fashion is the *recherche*—the always vain, often ridiculous, sometimes dangerous quest—for a superior ideal beauty." Du Camp, *Paris*, vol. 6, p. 294. [B2,3]

The epigraph from Balzac is well suited to unfolding the temporality of hell: to showing how this time does not recognize death, and how fashion mocks death; how the acceleration of traffic and the tempo of news reporting (which conditions the quick succession of newspaper editions) aim at eliminating all discontinuities and sudden ends; and how death as caesura belongs together with all the straight lines of divine temporality.—Were there fashions in antiquity? Or did the "authority of the frame"[5] preclude them? [B2,4]

"She was everybody's contemporary." ⟨Marcel⟩ Jouhandeau, *Prudence Hautechaume* (Paris, 1927), p. 129. To be *contemporaine de tout le monde*—that is the keenest and most secret satisfaction that fashion can offer a woman. [B2,5]

An emblem of the power of fashion over the city of Paris: "I have purchased a map of Paris printed on a pocket handkerchief." Gutzkow, *Briefe aus Paris,* vol. 1 ⟨Leipzig, 1842⟩, p. 82. [B2a,1]

Apropos of the medical discussion concerning the crinoline: Some people thought to justify its use, together with that of the petticoat, by noting "the agreeable and salutary coolness which the limbs enjoyed underneath. . . . Among doctors, [however,] it is acknowledged that this celebrated coolness has already led to chills, and these have occasioned the unfortunately premature end of a situation which it was the original purpose of the crinoline to conceal." F. Th. Vischer, *Kritische Gänge,* new series, no. 3 (Stuttgart, 1861), p. 100: "Vernünftige Gedanken über die jetzige Mode" ⟨Reasonable Opinions on Current Fashions⟩. [B2a,2]

It was "madness for the French fashions of the Revolution and the First Empire to mimic Greek proportions with clothing cut and sewn in the modern manner." Vischer, "Vernünftige Gedanken über die jetzige Mode," p. 99. [B2a,3]

Des dames d'un demi-monde, mais n'ayant pas de demi-jupes .

Fashionable courtesans wearing crinolines. Lithograph by Honoré Daumier, 1855. The caption reads: "Ladies of the demi-monde, but having no demi-skirts." See B2,2.

A knit scarf—a brightly striped muffler—worn also, in muted colors, by men.
[B2a,4]

F. Th. Vischer on the men's fashion of wide sleeves that fall below the wrist: "What we have here are no longer arms but the rudiments of wings, stumps of penguin wings, fish fins. The movement of these shapeless appendages resembles the gesticulations—the sliding, jerking, paddling—of a fool or simpleton." Vischer, "Vernünftige Gedanken über die jetzige Mode," p. 111. [B2a,5]

Important political critique of fashion from the standpoint of the bourgeois: "When the author of these reasonable opinions first saw, boarding a train, a young man wearing the newest style of shirt collar, he honestly thought that he was looking at a priest; for this white band encircles the neck at the same height as the well-known collar of the Catholic cleric, and moreover the long smock was black. On recognizing a layman in the very latest fashion, he immediately understood all that this shirt collar signifies: 'O, for us everything, everything is one—concordats included! And why not? Should we clamor for enlightenment like noble youths? Is not hierarchy more distinguished than the leveling effected by a shallow spiritual liberation, which in the end always aims at disturbing the pleasure of refined people?'—It may be added that this collar, in tracing a neat little line around the neck, gives its wearer the agreeable air of someone freshly beheaded, which accords so well with the character of the blasé." To this is joined the violent reaction against purple. Vischer, "Vernünftige Gedanken über die jetzige Mode," p. 112. [B2a,6]

On the reaction of 1850–1860: "To show one's colors is considered ridiculous; to be strict is looked on as childish. In such a situation, how could dress not become equally colorless, flabby, and, at the same time, narrow?" Vischer, p. 117. He thus brings the crinoline into relation with that fortified "imperialism which spreads out and puffs up exactly like its image here, and which, as the last and strongest expression of the reflux of all the tendencies of the year 1848, settles its dominion like a hoop skirt over all aspects, good and bad, justified and unjustified, of the revolution" (p. 119). [B2a,7]

"At bottom, these things are simultaneously free and unfree. It is a twilight zone where necessity and humor interpenetrate. . . . The more fantastic a form, the more intensely the clear and ironic consciousness works by the side of the servile will. And this consciousness guarantees that the folly will not last; the more consciousness grows, the nearer comes the time when it acts, when it turns to deed, when it throws off the fetters." Vischer, pp. 122–123. [B2a,8]

One of the most important texts for elucidating the eccentric, revolutionary, and surrealist possibilities of fashion—a text, above all, which establishes thereby the connection of Surrealism to Grandville and others—is the section on fashion in Apollinaire's *Poète assassiné* (Paris, 1927), pp. 74ff.[6] [B2a,9]

How fashion takes its cue from everything: Programs for evening clothes appeared, as if for the newest symphonic music. In 1901, in Paris, Victor Prouvé exhibited a formal gown with the title, "Riverbank in Spring." [B2a,10]

Hallmark of the period's fashions: to intimate a body that never knows full nakedness. [B3,1]

"Around 1890 people discover that silk is no longer the most elegant material for street clothes; henceforth it is allotted the previously unknown function of lining. From 1870 to 1890, clothing is extraordinarily expensive, and changes in fashion are accordingly limited in many cases to prudent alterations by which new apparel can be derived from remodeling the old." *70 Jahre deutsche Mode* (1925), p. 71. [B3,2]

"1873 . . . , when the giant skirts that stretched over cushions attached to the derrière, with their gathered draperies, their pleated frills, their embroidery, and their ribbons, seem to have issued less from the workshop of a tailor than from that of an upholsterer." J. W. Samson, *Die Frauenmode der Gegenwart* (Berlin and Cologne, 1927), pp. 8–9.   [B3,3]

No immortalizing so unsettling as that of the ephemera and the fashionable forms preserved for us in the wax museum. And whoever has once seen her must, like André Breton, lose his heart to the female figure in the Musée Grévin who adjusts her garter in the corner of a loge. ⟨Breton,⟩ *Nadja* ⟨Paris, 1928⟩, p. 199.[7]   [B3,4]

"The flower trimmings of large white lilies or water lilies with stems of rush, which look so charming in any coiffure, unintentionally remind one of delicate, gently floating sylphids and naiades. Just so, the fiery brunette cannot adorn herself more delightfully than with fruit braided in graceful little branches—cherries, red currants, even bunches of grapes mingled with ivy and flowering grasses—or than with long vivid red velvet fuchsias, whose leaves, red-veined and as though tinged with dew, form a crown; also at her disposal is the very lovely *cactus speciosus*, with its long white filaments. In general, the flowers chosen for decorating the hair are quite large; we saw one such headdress of very picturesque and beautiful white roses entwined with large pansies and ivy branches, or rather boughs. The arrangement of the gnarled and tendriled branches was so felicitous that it seemed nature itself had lent a hand—long branches bearing buds and long stems swayed at the sides with the slightest motion." *Der Bazar,* third year (Berlin, 1857), p. 11 (Veronika von G., "Die Mode").   [B3,5]

The impression of the old-fashioned can arise only where, in a certain way, reference is made to the most topical. If the beginnings of modern architecture to some extent lie in the arcades, their antiquated effect on the present generation has exactly the same significance as the antiquated effect of a father on his son.
                                                                                                [B3,6]

In my formulation: "The eternal is in any case far more the ruffle on a dress than some idea."[8] ▢ Dialectical Image ▢   [B3,7]

In fetishism, sex does away with the boundaries separating the organic world from the inorganic. Clothing and jewelry are its allies. It is as much at home with what is dead as it is with living flesh. The latter, moreover, shows it the way to establish itself in the former. Hair is a frontier region lying between the two kingdoms of *sexus*. Something different is disclosed in the drunkenness of passion: the landscapes of the body. These are already no longer animated, yet are still accessible to the eye, which, of course, depends increasingly on touch and smell to be its guides through these realms of death. Not seldom in the dream, however, there are swelling breasts that, like the earth, are all appareled in woods and rocks, and gazes have sent their life to the bottom of glassy lakes that slumber in the valleys. These landscapes are traversed by paths which lead sexuality into the world of the inorganic. Fashion itself is only another medium enticing it still more deeply into the universe of matter. [B3,8]

"'This year,' said Tristouse, 'fashions are bizarre and common, simple and full of fantasy. Any material from nature's domain can now be introduced into the composition of women's clothes. I saw a charming dress made of corks. . . . A major designer is thinking about launching tailor-made outfits made of old bookbindings done in calf. . . . Fish bones are being worn a lot on hats. One often sees delicious young girls dressed like pilgrims of Saint James of Compostella; their outfits, as is fitting, are studded with coquilles Saint-Jacques. Steel, wool, sandstone, and files have suddenly entered the vestmentary arts. . . . Feathers now decorate not only hats but shoes and gloves; and next year they'll be on umbrellas. They're doing shoes in Venetian glass and hats in Baccarat crystal. . . . I forgot to tell you that last Wednesday I saw on the boulevards on old dowager dressed in mirrors stuck to fabric. The effect was sumptuous in the sunlight. You'd have thought it was a gold mine out for a walk. Later it started raining and the lady looked like a silver mine. . . . Fashion is becoming practical and no longer looks down on anything. It ennobles everything. It does for materials what the Romantics did for words.'" Guillaume Apollinaire, *Le Poète assassiné*, new edition (Paris, 1927), pp. 75–77.[9] [B3a,1]

A caricaturist—circa 1867—represents the frame of a hoop skirt as a cage in which a girl imprisons hens and a parrot. See Louis Sonolet, *La Vie parisienne sous le Second Empire* (Paris, 1929), p. 245. [B3a,2]

"It was bathing in the sea . . . that struck the first blow against the solemn and cumbersome crinoline." Louis Sonolet, *La Vie parisienne sous le Second Empire* (Paris, 1929), p. 247. [B3a,3]

"Fashion consists only in extremes. Inasmuch as it seeks the extremes by nature, there remains for it nothing more, when it has abandoned some particular form, than to give itself to the opposite form." *70 Jahre deutsche Mode* (1925), p. 51. Its uttermost extremes: frivolity and death. [B3a,4]

"We took the crinoline to be the symbol of the Second Empire in France—of its overblown lies, its hollow and purse-proud impudence. It toppled . . . , but . . . just before the fall of the Empire, the Parisian world had time to indulge another side of its temperament in women's fashions, and the Republic did not disdain to follow its lead." F. Th. Vischer, *Mode und Cynismus* (Stuttgart, 1879), p. 6. The new fashion to which Vischer alludes is explained: "The dress is cut diagonally across the body and stretched over . . . the belly" (p. 6). A little later he speaks of the women thus attired as "naked in their clothes" (p. 8). [B3a,5]

Friedell explains, with regard to women, "that the history of their dress shows surprisingly few variations. It is not much more than a regular rotation of a few quickly altering, but also quickly reinstated, nuances: the length of the train, the height of the coiffure, the shortness of the sleeves, the fullness of the skirt, the placement of the neckline and of the waist. Even radical revolutions like the boyish haircuts fashionable today are only the 'eternal return of the same.'" Egon Friedell, *Kulturgeschichte der Neuzeit*, vol. 3 (Munich, 1931), p. 88. Women's fashions are thus distinguished, according to the author, from the more diverse and more categorical fashions for men. [B4,1]

"Of all the promises made by ⟨Etienne⟩ Cabet's novel *Voyage en Icarie* ⟨Voyage to Icaria⟩, at least one has been realized. Cabet had in fact tried to prove in the novel, which contains his system, that the communist state of the future could admit no product of the imagination and could suffer no change in its institutions. He had therefore banned from Icaria all fashion—particularly the capricious priestesses of fashion, the modistes—as well as goldsmiths and all other professions that serve luxury, and had demanded that dress, utensils, and the like should never be altered." Sigmund Engländer, *Geschichte der französischen Arbeiter-Associationen* (Hamburg, 1864), vol. 2, pp. 165–166. [B4,2]

In 1828 the first performance of *La Muette de Portici* took place.[10] It is an undulating musical extravaganza, an opera made of draperies, which rise and subside over the words. It must have had its success at a time when drapery was beginning its triumphal procession (at first, in fashion, as Turkish shawls). This revolt, whose premier task is to protect the king from its own effect, appears as a prelude to that of 1830—to a revolution that was indeed no more than drapery covering a slight reshuffle in the ruling circles. [B4,3]

Does fashion die (as in Russia, for example) because it can no longer keep up the tempo—at least in certain fields? [B4,4]

Grandville's works are true cosmogonies of fashion. Part of his oeuvre could be entitled "The Struggle of Fashion with Nature." Comparison between Hogarth and Grandville. Grandville and Lautréamont.—What is the significance of the hypertrophy of captions in Grandville? [B4,5]

"Fashion . . . is a witness, but a witness to the history of the great world only, for in every country . . . the poor people have fashions as little as they have a history, and their ideas, their tastes, even their lives barely change. Without doubt, . . . public life is beginning to penetrate the poorer households, but it will take time." Eugène Montrue, *Le XIXᵉ siècle vécu par deux français* (Paris), p. 241. [B4,6]

The following remark makes it possible to recognize how fashion functions as camouflage for quite specific interests of the ruling class. "Rulers have a great aversion to violent changes. They want everything to stay the same—if possible, for a thousand years. If possible, the moon should stand still and the sun move no farther in its course. Then no one would get hungry any more and want dinner. And when the rulers have fired their shot, the adversary should no longer be permitted to fire; their own shot should be the last." Bertolt Brecht, "Fünf Schwierigkeiten beim Schreiben der Wahrheit," *Unsere Zeit,* 8, nos. 2–3 (Paris, Basel, Prague, April 1935), p. 32.   [B4a,1]

MacOrlan, who emphasizes the analogies to Surrealism in Grandville's work, draws attention in this connection to the work of Walt Disney, on which he comments: "It is not in the least morbid. In this it diverges from the humor of Grandville, which always bore within itself the seeds of death." ⟨Pierre⟩ MacOrlan, "Grandville le précurseur," *Arts et métiers graphiques,* 44 (December 15, 1934), ⟨p. 24⟩.   [B4a,2]

"The presentation of a large couture collection lasts two to three hours. Each time in accord with the tempo to which the models are accustomed. At the close, a veiled bride traditionally appears." Helen Grund, *Vom Wesen der Mode* (Munich: Privately printed, 1935), p. 19. In this practice, fashion makes reference to propriety while serving notice that it does not stand still before it.   [B4a,3]

A contemporary fashion and its significance. In the spring of 1935, something new appeared in women's fashions: medium-sized embossed metal plaquettes, which were worn on jumpers or overcoats and which displayed the initial letters of the bearer's first name. Fashion thus profited from the vogue for badges which had arisen among men in the wake of the patriotic leagues. On the other hand, the progressive restrictions on the private sphere are here given expression. The name—and, to be sure, the first name—of persons unknown is published on a lapel. That it becomes easier thereby to make the acquaintance of a stranger is of secondary importance.   [B4a,4]

"The creators of fashions . . . like to frequent society and extract from its grand doings an impression of the whole; they take part in its artistic life, are present at premieres and exhibitions, and read the books that make a sensation. In other words, they are inspired by the . . . ferment . . . which the busy present day can offer. But since no present moment is ever fully cut off from the past, the latter also will offer attractions to the creator, . . . though only that which harmonizes with the reigning tone can be used. The toque tipped forward over the forehead, a style we owe to the Manet exhibition, demonstrates quite simply our new readiness to confront the end of the previous century." Helen Grund, *Vom Wesen der Mode,* p. 13.   [B4a,5]

On the publicity war between the fashion house and the fashion columnists: "The fashion writer's task is made easier by the fact that our wishes coincide. Yet it is made more difficult by the fact that no newspaper or magazine may regard as new what another has already published. From this dilemma, we and the fashion writer are saved only by the photographers and designers, who manage through the pose and lighting to bring out different aspects of a single piece of clothing. The most important magazines . . . have their own photo studios, which are equipped with all the latest technical and artistic refinements, and which employ highly talented specialized photographers. . . . But the publication of these documents is not permitted until the customer has made her choice, and that means usually four to six weeks after the initial showing. The reason for this measure?—The woman who appears in society wearing these new clothes will herself not be denied the effect of surprise." Helen Grund, *Vom Wesen der Mode*, pp. 21–22.   [B5,1]

According to the summary of the first six issues, the magazine published by Stéphane Mallarmé, *La Dernière Mode* (Paris, 1874), contains "a delightful sportive sketch, the result of a conversation with the marvelous naturalist Toussenel." Reproduction of this summary in *Minotaure*, 2, no. 6 (Winter 1935) ‹p. 27›.
      [B5,2]

A biological theory of fashion that takes its cue from the evolution of the zebra to the horse, as described in the abridged Brehm (p. 771):[11] "This evolution spanned millions of years. . . . The tendency in horses is toward the creation of a first-class runner and courser. . . . The most ancient of the existing animal types have conspicuously striped coats. Now, it is very remarkable that the external stripes of the zebra display a certain correspondence to the arrangement of the ribs and the vertebra inside. One can also determine very clearly the arrangement of these parts from the unique striping on the upper foreleg and upper hind leg. What do these stripes signify? A protective function can be ruled out. . . . The stripes have been . . . preserved despite their 'purposelessness and even unsuitableness,' and therefore they must . . . have a particular significance. Isn't it likely that we are dealing here with outward stimuli for internal responses, such as would be especially active during the mating season? What can this theory contribute to our theme? Something of fundamental importance, I believe.—Ever since humanity passed from nakedness to clothing, 'senseless and nonsensical' fashion has played the role of wise nature. . . . And insofar as fashion in its mutations . . . prescribes a constant revision of all elements of the figure, . . . it ordains for the woman a continual preoccupation with her beauty." Helen Grund, *Vom Wesen der Mode*, pp. 7–8.   [B5,3]

At the Paris world exhibition of 1900 there was a Palais du Costume, in which wax dolls arranged before a painted backdrop displayed the costumes of various peoples and the fashions of various ages.   [B5a,1]

"But as for us, we see . . . around us . . . the effects of confusion and waste inflicted by the disordered movement of the world today. Art knows no compromise with hurry. Our ideals are good for ten years! The ancient and excellent reliance on the judgment of posterity has been stupidly replaced by the ridiculous superstition of *novelty*, which assigns the most illusory ends to our enterprises, condemning them to the creation of what is most perishable, of what must be perishable by its nature: the sensation of newness. . . . Now, everything to be seen here has been enjoyed, has charmed and delighted through the centuries, and the whole glory of it calmly tells us: 'I AM NOTHING NEW. Time may well spoil the material in which I exist; but for so long as it does not destroy me, I cannot be destroyed by the indifference or contempt of any man worthy of the name." Paul Valéry, "Préambule" (preface to the catalogue of the exhibition "Italian Art from Cimabue to Tiepolo," at the Petit Palais, 1935), pp. iv, vii.[12]   [B5a,2]

"The ascendancy of the bourgeoisie works a change in women's wear. Clothing and hairstyles take on added dimensions . . . ; shoulders are enlarged by leg-of-mutton sleeves, and . . . it was not long before the old hoop-petticoats came back into favor and full skirts were the thing. Women, thus accoutered, appeared destined for a sedentary life—family life—since their manner of dress had about it nothing that could ever suggest or seem to further the idea of movement. It was just the opposite with the advent of the Second Empire: family ties grew slack, and an ever-increasing luxury corrupted morals to such an extent that it became difficult to distinguish an honest woman from a courtesan on the basis of clothing alone. Feminine attire had thus been transformed from head to toe. . . . Hoop skirts went the way of the accentuated rear. Everything that could keep women from remaining seated was encouraged; anything that could have impeded their walking was avoided. They wore their hair and their clothes as though they were to be viewed in profile. For the profile is the silhouette of someone . . . who passes, who is about to vanish from our sight. Dress became an image of the rapid movement that carries away the world." Charles Blanc, "Considérations sur le vêtement des femmes" (Institut de France, October 25, 1872), pp. 12–13.   [B5a,3]

"In order to grasp the essence of contemporary fashion, one need not recur to motives of an individual nature, such as . . . the desire for change, the sense of beauty, the passion for dressing up, the drive to conform. Doubtless such motives have, at various times, . . . played a part . . . in the creation of clothes. . . . Nevertheless, fashion, as we understand it today, has no individual motives but only a social motive, and it is an accurate perception of this social motive that determines the full appreciation of fashion's essence. This motive is the effort to distinguish the higher classes of society from the lower, or more especially from the middle classes. . . . Fashion is the barrier—continually raised anew because continually torn down—by which the fashionable world seeks to segregate itself from the middle region of society; it is the mad pursuit of that class vanity through which a single phenomenon endlessly repeats itself: the endeavor of one group to establish a lead, however minimal, over its pursuers, and the endeavor of the other group to make up the distance by immediately adopting the newest fashions of the leaders. The characteristic features of contemporary fashion are thus explained: above all, its origins in the upper circles and its imitation in the middle strata of society. Fashion moves from top to bottom, not vice versa. . . . An attempt by the middle classes to introduce a new fashion would . . . never succeed, though nothing would suit the upper classes better than to see the former with their own set of fashions. ([Note:] Which does not deter them from looking for new designs in the sewer of the Parisian demi-monde and bringing out fashions that clearly bear the mark of their unseemly origins, as Fr. Vischer . . . has pointed out in his . . . widely censured but, to my mind, . . . highly meritorious essay on fashion.) Hence the unceasing variation of fashion. No sooner have the middle classes adopted a newly introduced fashion than it . . . loses its value for the upper classes. . . . Thus, novelty is the indispensable condition for all fashion. . . . The duration of a fashion is inversely proportional to the swiftness of its diffusion; the ephemerality of fashions has increased in our day as the means for their diffusion have expanded via our perfected communications techniques. . . . The social motive referred to above explains, finally, the third characteristic feature of contemporary fashion: its . . . tyranny. Fashion comprises the outward criterion for judging whether or not one 'belongs in polite society.' Whoever does not repudiate it altogether must go along, even where he . . . firmly refuses some new development. . . . With this, a judgment is passed on fashion. . . . If the classes that are weak and foolish enough to imitate it were to gain a sense of their own proper worth, . . . it would be all up with fashion, and beauty could once again assume the position it has had with all those peoples who . . . did not feel the need to accentuate class differences through clothing or, where this occurred, were sensible enough to respect them." Rudolph von Jhering, *Der Zweck im Recht*, vol. 2 (Leipzig, 1883), pp. 234–238.[13]

[B6; B6a,1]

On the epoch of Napoleon III: "Making money becomes the object of an almost sensual fervor, and love becomes a financial concern. In the age of French Romanticism, the erotic ideal was the working girl who gives herself; now it is the tart who sells herself. . . . A hoydenish nuance came into fashion: ladies wore collars and cravats, overcoats, dresses cut like tailcoats, . . . jackets à la Zouave, dolmans, walking sticks, monocles. Loud, harshly contrasting colors are preferred—for the coiffure as well: fiery red hair is very popular. . . . The paragon of fashion is the *grande dame* who plays the cocotte." Egon Friedell, *Kulturgeschichte der Neuzeit*, vol. 3 (Munich, 1931), p. 203. The "plebeian character" of this fashion represents, for the author, an "invasion . . . from below" by the nouveaux riches.

[B6a,2]

"Cotton fabrics replace brocades and satins, . . . and before long, thanks to . . . the revolutionary spirit, the dress of the lower classes becomes more seemly and agreeable to the eye." Edouard Foucaud, *Paris inventeur: Physiologie de l'industrie française* (Paris, 1844), p. 64 (referring to the Revolution of 1789). [B6a,3]

An assemblage which, on closer inspection, proves to be composed entirely of pieces of clothing together with assorted dolls' heads. Caption: "Dolls on chairs, mannequins with false necks, false hair, false attractions—voilà Longchamp!" Cabinet des Estampes. [B6a,4]

"If, in 1829, we were to enter the shops of Delisle, we would find a multitude of diverse fabrics: Japanese, Alhambresque, coarse oriental, stocoline, meotide, silenian, zinzoline, Chinese Bagazinkoff. . . . With the Revolution of 1830, . . . the court of fashion had crossed the Seine and the Chaussée d'Antin had replaced the aristocratic faubourg." Paul d'Ariste, *La Vie et le monde du boulevard, 1830–1870* ‹Paris, 1930›, p. 227.   [B6a,5]

"The well-to-do bourgeois, as a friend of order, pays his suppliers at least once a year; but the man of fashion, the so-called lion, pays his tailor every ten years, if he pays him at all." *Acht Tage in Paris* (Paris, July 1855), p. 125.   [B7,1]

"It is I who invented *tics*. At present, the lorgnon has replaced them. . . . The tic involves closing the eye with a certain movement of the mouth and a certain movement of the coat. . . . The face of an elegant man should always have . . . something irritated and convulsive about it. One can attribute these facial agitations either to a natural satanism, to the fever of the passions, or finally to anything one likes." *Paris-Viveur,* by the authors of the memoirs of Bilboquet [Taxile Delord] (Paris, 1854), pp. 25–26.   [B7,2]

"The vogue for buying one's wardrobe in London took hold only among men; the fashion among women, even foreigners, has always been to be outfitted in Paris." Charles Seignobos, *Histoire sincère de la nation française* (Paris, 1932), p. 402.
                                                                                     [B7,3]

Marcelin, the founder of *La Vie Parisienne,* has set forth "the four ages of the crinoline."   [B7,4]

The crinoline is "the unmistakable symbol of reaction on the part of an imperialism that spreads out and puffs up . . . , and that . . . settles its dominion like a hoop skirt over all aspects, good and bad, justified and unjustified, of the revolution. . . . It seemed a caprice of the moment, and it has established itself as the emblem of a period, like the Second of December."[14] F. Th. Vischer, cited in Eduard Fuchs, *Die Karikatur der europäischen Völker* (Munich ‹1921›), vol. 2, p. 156.   [B7,5]

In the early 1840s, there is a nucleus of modistes on the Rue Vivienne.   [B7,6]

Simmel calls attention to the fact that "the inventions of fashion at the present time are increasingly incorporated into the objective situation of labor in the economy. . . . Nowhere does an article first appear and then become a fashion; rather, articles are introduced for the express purpose of becoming fashions." The contrast put forward in the last sentence may be correlated, to a certain extent, with that between the feudal and bourgeois eras. Georg Simmel, *Philosophische Kultur* (Leipzig, 1911), p. 34 ("Die Mode").[15]   [B7,7]

Simmel explains "why women in general are the staunchest adherents of fashion. . . . Specifically: from the weakness of the social position to which women have been condemned for the greater part of history derives their intimate relation with all that is 'etiquette.'" Georg Simmel, *Philosophische Kultur* (Leipzig, 1911), p. 47 ("Die Mode").[16]　　　　　　　　　　　　　　　　　　　　　　　　[B7,8]

The following analysis of fashion incidentally throws a light on the significance of the trips that were fashionable among the bourgeoisie during the second half of the century. "The accent of attractions builds from their substantial center to their inception and their end. This begins with the most trifling symptoms, such as the . . . switch from a cigar to a cigarette; it is fully manifest in the passion for traveling, which, with its strong accentuations of departure and arrival, sets the life of the year vibrating as fully as possible in several short periods. The . . . tempo of modern life bespeaks not only the yearning for quick changes in the qualitative content of life, but also the force of the formal attraction of the boundary—of inception and end." Georg Simmel, *Philosophische Kultur* (Leipzig, 1911), p. 41 ("Die Mode").[17]　　　　　　　　　　　　　　　　　　[B7a,1]

Simmel asserts that "fashions differ for different classes—the fashions of the upper stratum of society are never identical with those of the lower; in fact, they are abandoned by the former as soon as the latter prepares to appropriate them." Georg Simmel, *Philosophische Kultur* (Leipzig, 1911), p. 32 ("Die Mode").[18]

　　　　　　　　　　　　　　　　　　　　　　　　　　　　　　　[B7a,2]

The quick changing of fashion means "that fashions can no longer be so expensive . . . as they were in earlier times. . . . A peculiar circle . . . arises here: the more an article becomes subject to rapid changes of fashion, the greater the demand for *cheap* products of its kind; and the cheaper they become, the more they invite consumers and constrain producers to a quick change of fashion." Georg Simmel, *Philosophische Kultur* (Leipzig, 1911), pp. 58–59 ("Die Mode").[19]　　　　　[B7a,3]

Fuchs on Jhering's analysis of fashion: "It must . . . be reiterated that the concern for segregating the classes is only one cause of the frequent variation in fashions, and that a second cause—the private-capitalist mode of production, which in the interests of its profit margin must continually multiply the possibilities of turnover—is of equal importance. This cause has escaped Jhering entirely, as has a third: the function of erotic stimulation in fashion, which operates most effectively when the erotic attractions of the man or the woman appear in ever new settings. . . . Friedrich Vischer, who wrote about fashion . . . twenty years before Jhering, did not yet recognize, in the genesis of fashion, the tendencies at work to keep the classes divided; . . . on the other hand, he was fully aware of the erotic problems of dress." Eduard Fuchs, *Illustrierte Sittengeschichte vom Mittelalter bis zur Gegenwart: Das bürgerliche Zeitalter*, enlarged edition (Munich ⟨1926?⟩), pp. 53–54.　　　　　　　　　　　　　　　　　　　　　　　　　　[B7a,4]

Eduard Fuchs (*Illustrierte Sittengeschichte vom Mittelalter bis zur Gegenwart: Das bürgerliche Zeitalter*, enlarged ed., pp. 56–57) cites—without references—a

remark by F. Th. Vischer, according to which the gray of men's clothing symbolizes the "utterly blasé" character of the masculine world, its dullness and inertia.
[B8,1]

"One of the surest and most deplorable symptoms of that weakness and frivolity of
character which marked the Romantic age was the childish and fatal notion of
rejecting the deepest understanding of technical procedures, . . . the consciously
sustained and *orderly* carrying through of a work . . . —all for the sake of the
spontaneous impulses of the individual sensibility. The idea of creating works of
lasting value lost force and gave way, in most minds, to the desire to astonish; art
was condemned to a whole series of breaks with the past. There arose an automatic
audacity, which became as obligatory as tradition had been. Finally, that switching—at high frequency—of the tastes of a given public, which is called Fashion,
replaced with its essential changeableness the old habit of slowly forming styles,
schools, and reputations. To say that Fashion took over the destinies of the fine
arts is as much as to say that commercial interests were creeping in." Paul Valéry,
Pièces sur l'art (Paris), pp. 187–188 ("Autour de Corot").[20]   [B8,2]

"The great and fundamental revolution has been in cotton prints. It has required
the combined efforts of science and art to force rebellious and ungrateful cotton
fabrics to undergo every day so many brilliant transformations and to spread
them everywhere within the reach of the poor. Every woman used to wear a blue or
black dress that she kept for ten years without washing, for fear it might tear to
pieces. But now her husband, a poor worker, covers her with a robe of flowers for
the price of a day's labor. All the women of the people who display an iris of a
thousand colors on our promenades were formerly in mourning." J. Michelet, *Le
Peuple* (Paris, 1846), pp. 80–81.[21]   [B8,3]

"It is no longer art, as in earlier times, but the clothing business that furnishes the
prototype of the modern man and woman. . . . Mannequins become the model for
imitation, and the soul becomes the image of the body." Henri Pollès, "L'Art du
commerce," *Vendredi*, ‹12› (February 1937). Compare tics and English fashions
for men.   [B8,4]

"One can estimate that, in Harmony, the changes in fashion . . . and the imperfec-
tions in manufacturing would occasion an annual loss of 500 francs per person,
since even the poorest of Harmonians has a wardrobe of clothes for every season. . . . As far as clothing and furniture are concerned, . . . Harmony . . . aims
for infinite variety with the least possible consumption. . . . The excellence of the
products of societary industry . . . entail perfection for each and every manufactured object, so that furniture and clothing . . . become eternal." ‹Fourier,› cited
in Armand and Maublanc, *Fourier* (Paris, 1937), vol. 2, pp. 196, 198.   [B8a,1]

"This taste for modernity is developed to such an extent that Baudelaire, like
Balzac, extends it to the most trifling details of fashion and dress. Both writers

study these things in themselves and turn them into moral and philosophical questions, for these things represent immediate reality in its keenest, most aggressive, and perhaps most irritating guise, but also as it is most generally experienced." [Note:] "Besides, for Baudelaire, these matters link up with his important theory of dandyism, where it is a question, precisely, of morality and modernity." Roger Caillois, "Paris, mythe moderne," *Nouvelle Revue française*, 25, no. 284 (May 1, 1937), p. 692. [B8a,2]

"Sensational event! The *belles dames*, one fine day, decide to puff up the derrière. Quick, by the thousands, *hoop* factories! . . . But what is a simple *refinement* on illustrious coccyxes? A trumpery, no more. . . . 'Away with the rump! Long live crinolines!' And suddenly the civilized world turns to the production of ambulatory bells. Why has the fair sex forgotten the delights of hand bells? . . . It is not enough to keep one's place; you must make some noise down there. . . . The *quartier* Bréda and the Faubourg Saint-Germain are rivals in piety, no less than in plasters and chignons. They might as well take the church as their model! At vespers, the organ and the clergy take turns intoning a verse from the Psalms. The fine ladies with their little bells could follow this example, words and tintinnabulation by turns spurring on the conversation." A. Blanqui, *Critique sociale* (Paris, 1885), vol. 1, pp. 83–84 ("Le Luxe").—"Le Luxe" is a polemic against the luxury-goods industry. [B8a,3]

Each generation experiences the fashions of the one immediately preceding it as the most radical antiaphrodisiac imaginable. In this judgment it is not so far off the mark as might be supposed. Every fashion is to some extent a bitter satire on love; in every fashion, perversities are suggested by the most ruthless means. Every fashion stands in opposition to the organic. Every fashion couples the living body to the inorganic world. To the living, fashion defends the rights of the corpse. The fetishism that succumbs to the sex appeal of the inorganic is its vital nerve. [B9,1]

Where they impinge on the present moment, birth and death—the former through natural circumstances, the latter through social ones—considerably restrict the field of play for fashion. This state of affairs is properly elucidated through two parallel circumstances. The first concerns birth, and shows the natural engendering of life "overcome" ⟨*aufgehoben*⟩ by novelty in the realm of fashion. The second circumstance concerns death: it appears in fashion as no less "overcome," and precisely through the sex appeal of the inorganic, which is something generated by fashion. [B9,2]

The detailing of feminine beauties so dear to the poetry of the Baroque, a process in which each single part is exalted through a trope, secretly links up with the image of the corpse. This parceling out of feminine beauty into its noteworthy constituents resembles a dissection, and the popular comparisons of bodily parts to alabaster, snow, precious stones, or other (mostly inorganic) formations makes the same point. (Such dismemberment occurs also in Baudelaire: "Le Beau Navire.")   [B9,3]

Lipps on the somber cast of men's clothing: He thinks that "our general aversion to bright colors, especially in clothing for men, evinces very clearly an oft-noted peculiarity of our character. Gray is all theory; green—and not only green but also red, yellow, blue—is the golden tree of life.[22] In our predilection for the various shades of gray . . . running to black, we find an unmistakable social reflection of our tendency to privilege the theory of the formation of intellect above all else. Even the beautiful we can no longer just enjoy; rather, . . . we must first subject it to criticism, with the consequence that . . . our spiritual life becomes ever more cool and colorless." Theodor Lipps, "Über die Symbolik unserer Kleidung," *Nord und Süd*, 33 (Breslau and Berlin, 1885), p. 352.   [B9,4]

Fashions are a collective medicament for the ravages of oblivion. The more short-lived a period, the more susceptible it is to fashion. Compare K2a,3.   [B9a,1]

Focillon on the phantasmagoria of fashion: "Most often . . . it creates hybrids; it imposes on the human being the profile of an animal. . . . Fashion thus invents an artificial humanity which is not the passive decoration of a formal environment, but that very environment itself. Such a humanity—by turns heraldic, theatrical, fantastical, architectural—takes, as its ruling principle, the poetics of ornament, and what it calls 'line' . . . is perhaps but a subtle compromise between a certain physiological canon . . . and imaginative design." Henri Focillon, *Vie des formes* (Paris, 1934), p. 41.[23]   [B9a,2]

There is hardly another article of dress that can give expression to such divergent erotic tendencies, and that has so much latitude to disguise them, as a woman's hat. Whereas the meaning of male headgear in its sphere (the political) is strictly tied to a few rigid patterns, the shades of erotic meaning in a woman's hat are virtually incalculable. It is not so much the various possibilities of symbolic reference to the sexual organs that is chiefly of interest here. More surprising is what a hat can say about the rest of the outfit. H‹elen› Grund has made the ingenious suggestion that the bonnet, which is contemporaneous with the crino-line, actually provides men with directions for managing the latter. The wide brim of the bonnet is turned up—thereby demonstrating how the crinoline must be turned up in order to make sexual access to the woman easier for the man.
                                                                                      [B10,1]

For the females of the species *homo sapiens*—at the earliest conceivable period of its existence—the horizontal positioning of the body must have had the greatest advantages. It made pregnancy easier for them, as can be deduced from the back-bracing girdles and trusses to which pregnant women today have recourse. Proceeding from this consideration, one may perhaps venture to ask: Mightn't walking erect, in general, have appeared earlier in men than in women? In that case, the woman would have been the four-footed companion of the man, as the dog or cat is today. And it seems only a step from this conception to the idea that the frontal encounter of the two partners in coitus would have been originally a kind of perversion; and perhaps it was by way of this deviance that the woman would have begun to walk upright. (See note in the essay "Eduard Fuchs: Der Sammler und der Historiker.")[24]   [B10,2]

"It would . . . be interesting to trace the effects exerted by this disposition to upright posture on the structure and function of the rest of the body. There is no doubt that all the particulars of an organic entity are held together in intimate cohesion, but with the present state of our scientific knowledge we must maintain that the extraordinary influences ascribed herewith to standing upright cannot in fact be proved. . . . No significant repercussion can be demonstrated for the structure and function of the inner organs, and Herder's hypotheses—according to which all forces would react differently in the upright posture, and the blood stimulate the nerves differently—forfeit all credibility as soon as they are referred to differences manifestly important for behavior." Hermann Lotze, *Mikrokosmos* (Leipzig, 1858), vol. 2, p. 90.[25]   [B10a,1]

A passage from a cosmetics prospectus, characteristic of the fashions of the Second Empire. The manufacturer recommends "a cosmetic . . . by means of which ladies, if they so desire, can give their complexion the gloss of rose taffeta." Cited in Ludwig Börne, *Gesammelte Schriften* (Hamburg and Frankfurt am Main, 1862), vol. 3, p. 282 ("Die Industrie-Ausstellung im Louvre").   [B10a,2]

C

[Ancient Paris, Catacombs, Demolitions, Decline of Paris]

> Easy the way that leads into Avernus.
> —Virgil[1]

> Even the automobiles have an air of antiquity here.
> —Guillaume Apollinaire[2]

How gratings—as allegories—have their place in hell. In the Passage Vivienne, sculptures over the main entrance representing allegories of commerce.   [C1,1]

Surrealism was born in an arcade. And under the protection of what muses!
[C1,2]

The father of Surrealism was Dada; its mother was an arcade. Dada, when the two first met, was already old. At the end of 1919, Aragon and Breton, out of antipathy to Montparnasse and Montmartre, transferred the site of their meetings with friends to a café in the Passage de l'Opéra. Construction of the Boulevard Haussmann brought about the demise of the Passage de l'Opéra. Louis Aragon devoted 135 pages to this arcade; in the sum of these three digits hides the number nine—the number of muses who bestowed their gifts on the newborn Surrealism. They are named Luna, Countess Geschwitz, Kate Greenaway, Mors, Cléo de Mérode, Dulcinea, Libido, Baby Cadum, and Friederike Kempner. (Instead of Countess Geschwitz: Tipse?)[3]   [C1,3]

Cashier as Danae.   [C1,4]

Pausanias produced his topography of Greece around A.D. 200, at a time when the cult sites and many other monuments had begun to fall into ruin.   [C1,5]

Few things in the history of humanity are as well known to us as the history of Paris. Tens of thousands of volumes are dedicated solely to the investigation of this tiny spot on the earth's surface. Authentic guides to the antiquities of the old Roman city—Lutetia Parisorum—appear as early as the sixteenth century. The catalogue of the imperial library, printed during the reign of Napoleon III, contains nearly a hundred pages under the rubric "Paris," and this collection is far from complete. Many of the main thoroughfares have their own special literature, and we possess written accounts of thousands of the most inconspicuous houses. In a beautiful turn of phrase, Hugo von Hofmannsthal called ‹this city› "a landscape built of pure life." And at work in the attraction it exercises on people is the kind of beauty that is proper to great landscapes—more precisely, to volcanic landscapes. Paris is a counterpart in the social order to what Vesuvius is in the geographic order: a menacing, hazardous massif, an ever-active hotbed of revolution. But just as the slopes of Vesuvius, thanks to the layers of lava that cover them, have been transformed into paradisal orchards, so the lava of revolutions provides uniquely fertile ground for the blossoming of art, festivity, fashion. ⬜ Fashion ⬜ [C1,6]

Balzac has secured the mythic constitution of his world through precise topographic contours. Paris is the breeding ground of his mythology—Paris with its two or three great bankers (Nucingen, du Tillet), Paris with its great physician Horace Bianchon, with its entrepreneur César Birotteau, with its four or five great cocottes, with its usurer Gobseck, with its sundry advocates and soldiers. But above all—and we see this again and again—it is from the same streets and corners, the same little rooms and recesses, that the figures of this world step into the light. What else can this mean but that topography is the ground plan of this mythic space of tradition ‹ *Traditionsraum*›, as it is of every such space, and that it can become indeed its key—just as it was the key to Greece for Pausanias, and just as the history and situation of the Paris arcades are to become the key for the underworld of *this* century, into which Paris has sunk. [C1,7]

To construct the city topographically—tenfold and a hundredfold—from out of its arcades and its gateways, its cemeteries and bordellos, its railroad stations and its . . . , just as formerly it was defined by its churches and its markets. And the more secret, more deeply embedded figures of the city: murders and rebellions, the bloody knots in the network of the streets, lairs of love, and conflagrations. ⬜ Flâneur ⬜ [C1,8]

Couldn't an exciting film be made from the map of Paris? From the unfolding of its various aspects in temporal succession? From the compression of a centuries-long movement of streets, boulevards, arcades, and squares into the space of half an hour? And does the flâneur do anything different? ⬜ Flâneur ⬜ [C1,9]

"Two steps from the Palais-Royal, between the Cour des Fontaines and the Rue Neuve-des-Bons-Enfants, there is a dark and tortuous little arcade adorned by a public scribe and a greengrocer. It could resemble the cave of Cacus or of Tro-

phonius, but it could never resemble an arcade—even with good will and gas
lighting." ⟨Alfred⟩ Delvau, *Les Dessous de Paris* (Paris, 1860), pp. 105–106.
[C1a,1]

One knew of places in ancient Greece where the way led down into the underworld. Our waking existence likewise is a land which, at certain hidden points,
leads down into the underworld—a land full of inconspicuous places from which
dreams arise. All day long, suspecting nothing, we pass them by, but no sooner
has sleep come than we are eagerly groping our way back to lose ourselves in the
dark corridors. By day, the labyrinth of urban dwellings resembles consciousness; the arcades (which are galleries leading into the city's past) issue unremarked onto the streets. At night, however, under the tenebrous mass of the
houses, their denser darkness protrudes like a threat, and the nocturnal pedestrian hurries past—unless, that is, we have emboldened him to turn into the
narrow lane.

But another system of galleries runs underground through Paris: the Métro,
where at dusk glowing red lights point the way into the underworld of names.
Combat, Elysée, Georges V, Etienne Marcel, Solférino, Invalides, Vaugirard—
they have all thrown off the humiliating fetters of street or square, and here in the
lightning-scored, whistle-resounding darkness are transformed into misshapen
sewer gods, catacomb fairies. This labyrinth harbors in its interior not one but a
dozen blind raging bulls, into whose jaws not one Theban virgin once a year but
thousands of anemic young dressmakers and drowsy clerks every morning must
hurl themselves. ▯ Street Names ▯ Here, underground, nothing more of the colli-
sion, the intersection, of names—that which aboveground forms the linguistic
network of the city. Here each name dwells alone; hell is its demesne. Amer,
Picon, Dubonnet are guardians of the threshold.   [C1a,2]

"Doesn't every *quartier* have its true apogee some time before it is fully built up?
At that point its planet describes a curve as it draws near businesses, first the large
and then the small. So long as the street is still somewhat new, it belongs to the
common people; it gets clear of them only when it is smiled on by fashion. Without
naming prices, the interested parties dispute among themselves for the rights to
the small houses and the apartments, but only so long as the beautiful women, the
ones with the radiant elegance that adorns not only the salon but the whole house
and even the street, continue to hold their receptions. And should the lady become
a pedestrian, she will want some shops, and often the street must pay not a little for
acceding too quickly to this wish. Courtyards are made smaller, and many are
entirely done away with; the houses draw closer together. In the end, there comes
a New Year's Day when it is considered bad form to have such an address on one's
visiting card. By then the majority of tenants are businesses only, and the gateways
of the neighborhood no longer have much to lose if now and again they furnish
asylum for one of the small tradespeople whose miserable stalls have replaced the
shops." ⟨Charles⟩ Lefeuve, *Les Anciennes Maisons de Paris sous Napoléon III*
(Paris and Brussels, 1873), vol. 1, p. 482.[4] ▯ Fashion ▯   [C1a,3]

It is a sad testimony to the underdeveloped *amour-propre* of most of the great European cities that so very few of them—at any rate, none of the German cities—have anything like the handy, minutely detailed, and durable map that exists for Paris. I refer to the excellent publication by Taride, with its twenty-two maps of all the Parisian *arrondissements* and the parks of Boulogne and Vincennes. Whoever has stood on a streetcorner of a strange city in bad weather and had to deal with one of those large paper maps—which at every gust swell up like a sail, rip at the edges, and soon are no more than a little heap of dirty colored scraps with which one torments oneself as with the pieces of a puzzle—learns from the study of the *Plan Taride* what a city map can be. People whose imagination does not wake at the perusal of such a text, people who would not rather dream of their Paris experiences over a map than over photos or travel notes, are beyond help.   [C1a,4]

Paris is built over a system of caverns from which the din of Métro and railroad mounts to the surface, and in which every passing omnibus or truck sets up a prolonged echo. And this great technological system of tunnels and thorough-fares interconnects with the ancient vaults, the limestone quarries, the grottoes and catacombs which, since the early Middle Ages, have time and again been reentered and traversed. Even today, for the price of two francs, one can buy a ticket of admission to this most nocturnal Paris, so much less expensive and less hazardous than the Paris of the upper world. The Middle Ages saw it differently. Sources tell us that there were clever persons who now and again, after exacting a considerable sum and a vow of silence, undertook to guide their fellow citizens underground and show them the Devil in his infernal majesty. A financial venture far less risky for the swindled than for the swindlers: Must not the church have considered a spurious manifestation of the Devil as tantamount to blasphemy? In other ways, too, this subterranean city had its uses, for those who knew their way around it. Its streets cut through the great customs barrier with which the Farmers General had secured their right to receive duties on imports, and in the sixteenth and eighteenth centuries smuggling operations went on for the most part below ground. We know also that in times of public commotion mysterious rumors traveled very quickly via the catacombs, to say nothing of the prophetic spirits and fortunetellers duly qualified to pronounce upon them. On the day after Louis XVI fled Paris, the revolutionary government issued bills ordering a thorough search of these passages. And a few years later a rumor suddenly spread through the population that certain areas of town were about to cave in.   [C2,1]

To reconstruct the city also from its *fontaines* ‹springs, wells›. "Some streets have preserved these in name, although the most celebrated among them, the Puits d'Amour ‹Well of Love›, which was located not far from the marketplace on the Rue de la Truanderie, has been dried, filled up, and smoothed over without a trace remaining. Hence, there is hardly anything left of the echoing wells which provided a name for the Rue du Puits-qui-Parle, or of the wells which the tanner

Adam-l'Hermite had dug in the *quartier* Saint-Victor. We have known the Rues de Puits-Mauconseil, du Puits-de-Fer, du Puits-du-Chapitre, du Puits-Certain, du Bon-Puits, and finally the Rue du Puits, which, after being the Rue du Bout-du-Monde, became the Impasse Saint-Claude-Montmartre. The marketplace wells, the bucket-drawn wells, the water carriers are all giving way to the public wells, and our children, who will easily draw water even on the top floors of the tallest buildings in Paris, will be amazed that we have preserved for so long these primitive means of supplying one of humankind's most imperious needs." Maxime du Camp, *Paris: Ses organes, ses fonctions et sa vie* (Paris, 1875), vol. 5, p. 263.

[C2,2]

A different topography, not architectonic but anthropocentric in conception, could show us all at once, and in its true light, the most muted *quartier:* the isolated fourteenth *arrondissement.* That, at any rate, is how Jules Janin already saw it a hundred years ago. If you were born into that neighborhood, you could lead the most animated and audacious life without ever having to leave it. For in it are found, one after another, all the buildings of public misery, of proletarian indigence, in unbroken succession: the birthing clinic, the orphanage, the hospital (the famous Santé), and finally the great Paris jail with its scaffold. At night, one sees on the narrow unobtrusive benches—not, of course, the comfortable ones found in the squares—men stretched out asleep as if in the waiting room of a way station in the course of this terrible journey.

[C2,3]

There are architectonic emblems of commerce: steps lead to the apothecary, whereas the cigar shop has taken possession of the corner. The business world knows to make use of the threshold. In front of the arcade, the skating rink, the swimming pool, the railroad platform, stands the tutelary of the threshold: a hen that automatically lays tin eggs containing bonbons. Next to the hen, an automated fortuneteller—an apparatus for stamping our names automatically on a tin band, which fixes our fate to our collar.

[C2,4]

In old Paris, there were executions (for example, by hanging) in the open street.

[C2,5]

Rodenberg speaks of the "stygian existence" of certain worthless securities—such as shares in the Mirès fund—which are sold by the "small-time crooks" of the Stock Exchange in the hope of a "future resurrection brought to pass by the day's market quotations." Julius Rodenberg, *Paris bei Sonnenschein und Lampenlicht* (Berlin, 1867), pp. 102–103.

[C2a,1]

Conservative tendency of Parisian life: as late as 1867, an entrepreneur conceived the plan of having five hundred sedan chairs circulate throughout the city.

[C2a,2]

Concerning the mythological topography of Paris: the character given it by its gates. Important is their duality: border gates and triumphal arches. Mystery of

the boundary stone which, although located in the heart of the city, once marked the point at which it ended.—On the other hand, the Arc de Triomphe, which today has become a traffic island. Out of the field of experience proper to the threshold evolved the gateway that transforms whoever passes under its arch. The Roman victory arch makes the returning general a conquering hero. (Absurdity of the relief on the inner wall of the arch? A classicist misunderstanding?)
[C2a,3]

The gallery that leads to the Mothers[5] is made of wood. Likewise, in the large-scale renovations of the urban scene, wood plays a constant though ever-shifting role: amid the modern traffic, it fashions, in the wooden palings and in the wooden planking over open substructions, the image of its rustic prehistory.
▢ Iron ▢
[C2a,4]

"It is the obscurely rising dream of northerly streets in a big city—not only Paris, perhaps, but also Berlin and the largely unknown London—obscurely rising, in a rainless twilight that is nonetheless damp. The streets grow narrow and the houses right and left draw closer together; ultimately it becomes an arcade with grimy shop windows, a gallery of glass. To the right and left: Are those dirty bistros, with waitresses lurking in black-and-white silk blouses? It stinks of cheap wine. Or is it the garish vestibule of a bordello? As I advance a little further, however, I see on both sides small summer-green doors and the rustic window shutters they call *volets*. Sitting there, little old ladies are spinning, and through the windows by the somewhat rigid flowering plant, as though in a country garden, I see a fair-skinned young lady in a gracious apartment, and she sings: 'Someone is spinning silk. . . .'" Franz Hessel, manuscript. Compare Strindberg, "The Pilot's Trials."[6]
[C2a,5]

At the entrance, a mailbox: last opportunity to make some sign to the world one is leaving.
[C2a,6]

Underground sightseeing in the sewers. Preferred route: Châtelet–Madeleine.
[C2a,7]

"The ruins of the Church and of the aristocracy, of feudalism, of the Middle Ages, are sublime—they fill the wide-eyed victors of today with admiration. But the ruins of the bourgeoisie will be an ignoble detritus of pasteboard, plaster, and coloring." ‹Honoré de Balzac and other authors,› *Le Diable à Paris* (Paris, 1845), vol. 2, p. 18 (Balzac, "Ce qui disparait de Paris"). ▢ Collector ▢
[C2a,8]

. . . All this, in our eyes, is what the arcades are. And they were nothing of all this. "It is only today, when the pickaxe menaces them, that they have at last become the true sanctuaries of a cult of the ephemeral, the ghostly landscape of damnable pleasures and professions. Places that yesterday were incomprehensible, and that tomorrow will never know." Louis Aragon, *Le Paysan de Paris* (Paris, 1926), p. 19.[7] ▢ Collector ▢
[C2a,9]

Sudden past of a city: windows lit up in expectation of Christmas shine as though their lights have been burning since 1880.   [C2a,10]

The dream—it is the earth in which the find is made that testifies to the primal history of the nineteenth century. ▯ Dream ▯   [C2a,11]

Reasons for the decline of the arcades: widened sidewalks, electric light, ban on prostitution, culture of the open air.   [C2a,12]

The rebirth of the archaic drama of the Greeks in the booths of the trade fair. The prefect of police allows only dialogue on this stage. "This third character is mute, by order of Monsieur the Prefect of Police, who permits only dialogue in theaters designated as nonresident." Gérard de Nerval, *Le Cabaret de la Mère Saguet* (Paris ‹1927›), pp. 259–260 ("Le Boulevard du Temple autrefois et aujourd'hui").   [C3,1]

At the entrance to the arcade, a mailbox: a last opportunity to make some sign to the world one is leaving.   [C3,2]

The city is only apparently homogeneous. Even its name takes on a different sound from one district to the next. Nowhere, unless perhaps in dreams, can the phenomenon of the boundary be experienced in a more originary way than in cities. To know them means to understand those lines that, running alongside railroad crossings and across privately owned lots, within the park and along the riverbank, function as limits; it means to know these confines, together with the enclaves of the various districts. As threshold, the boundary stretches across streets; a new precinct begins like a step into the void—as though one had unexpectedly cleared a low step on a flight of stairs.   [C3,3]

At the entrance to the arcade, to the skating rink, to the pub, to the tennis court: *penates*. The hen that lays the golden praline-eggs, the machine that stamps our names on nameplates and the other machine that weighs us (the modern *gnōthi seauton*),[8] slot machines, the mechanical fortuneteller—these guard the threshold. They are generally found, it is worth noting, neither on the inside nor truly in the open. They protect and mark the transitions; and when one seeks out a little greenery on a Sunday afternoon, one is turning to these mysterious *penates* as well. ▯ Dream House ▯ Love ▯   [C3,4]

The despotic terror of the hand bell, the terror that reigns throughout the apartment, derives its force no less from the magic of the threshold. Some things shrill as they are about to cross a threshold. But it is strange how the ringing becomes melancholy, like a knell, when it heralds departure—as in the Kaiserpanorama, when it starts up with the slight tremor of the receding image and announces another to come. ▯ Dream House ▯ Love ▯   [C3,5]

These gateways—the entrances to the arcades—are thresholds. No stone step serves to mark them. But this marking is accomplished by the expectant posture of the handful of people. Tightly measured paces reflect the fact, altogether unknowingly, that a decision lies ahead. ☐ Dream House ☐ Love ☐ [C3,6]

Other courts of miracles besides the one in the Passage du Caire that is celebrated in *Notre-Dame de Paris* ⟨The Hunchback of Notre Dame.⟩ "In the old Paris neighborhood of the Marais, on the Rue des Tournelles, are the Passage and the Cour des Miracles. There were other *cours des miracles* on the Rue Saint-Denis, the Rue du Bac, the Rue de Neuilly, the Rue des Coquilles, the Rue de la Jussienne, the Rue Saint-Nicaise, and the promontory of Saint-Roch." ⟨Emile de⟩ Labédollière, *Histoire ⟨des environs⟩ du nouveau Paris* (Paris ⟨1861?⟩), p. 31. [The biblical passages after which these courts were named: Isaiah 26.4–5 and 27.] [C3,7]

In reference to Haussmann's successes with the water supply and the drainage of Paris: "The poets would say that Haussmann was inspired more by the divinities below than by the gods above." Lucien Dubech and Pierre d'Espezel, *Histoire de Paris* (Paris, 1926), p. 418. [C3,8]

Métro. "A great many of the stations have been given absurd names. The worst seems to belong to the one at the corner of the Rue Bréguet and the Rue Saint-Sabin, which ultimately joined together, in the abbreviation 'Bréguet-Sabin,' the name of a watchmaker and the name of a saint." Dubech and d'Espezel, *Histoire de Paris*, p. 463. [C3,9]

Wood an archaic element in street construction: wooden barricades. [C3,10]

June Insurrection. "Most of the prisoners were transferred via the quarries and subterranean passages which are located under the forts of Paris, and which are so extensive that half the population of the city could be contained there. The cold in these underground corridors is so intense that many had to run continually or move their arms about to keep from freezing, and no one dared to lie down on the cold stones. . . . The prisoners gave all the passages names of Paris streets, and whenever they met one another, they exchanged addresses." Engländer, ⟨*Geschichte der französischen Arbeiter-Associationen* (Hamburg, 1864)⟩, vol. 2, pp. 314–315. [C3a,1]

"The Paris stone quarries are all interconnected. . . . In several places pillars have been set up so that the roof does not cave in. In other places the walls have been reinforced. These walls form long passages under the earth, like narrow streets. On several of them, at the end, numbers have been inscribed to prevent wrong turns, but without a guide one is not . . . likely to venture into these exhausted seams of limestone . . . if one does not wish . . . to risk starvation."—"The legend according to which one can see the stars by day from the tunnels of the Paris quarries" originated in an old mine shaft "that was covered over on the surface by a stone slab in which there is a small hole some six millimeters in diameter. Through this hole, the daylight shines into the gloom below like a pale star." J. F. Benzenberg, *Briefe geschrieben auf einer Reise nach Paris* (Dortmund, 1805), vol. 1, pp. 207–208. [C3a,2]

"A thing which smoked and clacked on the Seine, making the noise of a swimming dog, went and came beneath the windows of the Tuileries, from the Pont Royal to the Pont Louis XV; it was a piece of mechanism of no great value, a sort of toy, the daydream of a visionary, a Utopia—a steamboat. The Parisians looked upon the useless thing with indifference." Victor Hugo, *Les Misérables*, part 1,[9] cited in Nadar, *Quand j'étais photographe* (Paris ‹1900›), p. 280. [C3a,3]

"As if an enchanter or a stage manager, at the first peal of the whistle from the first locomotive, gave a signal to all things to awake and take flight." Nadar, *Quand j'étais photographe* (Paris), p. 281. [C3a,4]

Characteristic is the birth of one of the great documentary works on Paris—namely, Maxime Du Camp's *Paris: Ses organes, ses fonctions et sa vie dans la seconde moitié du XIXe siècle,* in six volumes (Paris, 1893–1896). About this book, the catalogue of a secondhand bookshop says: "It is of great interest for its documentation, which is as exact as it is minute. Du Camp, in fact, has not been averse to trying his hand at all sorts of jobs—performing the role of omnibus conductor, street sweeper, and sewerman—in order to gather materials for his book. His tenacity has won him the nickname 'Prefect of the Seine *in partibus,*' and it was not irrelevant to his elevation to the office of senator." Paul Bourget describes the genesis of the book in his "Discours académique du 13 juin 1895: Succession à Maxime Du Camp" (*Anthologie de l'Académie Française* [Paris, 1921], vol. 2, pp. 191–193). In 1862, recounts Bourget, after experiencing problems with his vision, Du Camp went to see the optician Secrétan, who prescribed a pair of spectacles for farsightedness. Here is Du Camp: "Age has gotten to me. I have not given it a friendly welcome. But I have submitted. I have ordered a lorgnon and a pair of spectacles." Now Bourget: "The optician did not have the prescribed glasses on hand. He needed a half hour to prepare them. M. Maxime Du Camp went out to pass this half hour strolling about the neighborhood. He found himself on the Pont Neuf. . . . It was, for the writer, one of those moments when a man who is about to leave youth behind thinks of life with a resigned gravity that leads him to find in all things the image of his own melancholy. The minor physiological decline which his visit to the optician had just confirmed put him in mind of what is so quickly forgotten: that law of inevitable destruction which governs everything human. . . . Suddenly he began—he, the voyager to the Orient, the sojourner through mute and weary wastes where the sand consists of dust of the dead—to envision a day when this town, too, whose enormous breath now filled his senses, would itself be dead, as so many capitals of so many empires were dead. The idea came to him that it would be extraordinarily inter-esting for us to have an exact and complete picture of an Athens at the time of

Pericles, of a Carthage at the time of Barca, of an Alexandria at the time of the Ptolemies, of a Rome at the time of the Caesars. . . . By one of those keen intuitions with which a magnificent subject for a work flashes before the mind, he clearly perceived the possibility of writing about Paris this book which the historians of antiquity had failed to write about their towns. He regarded anew the spectacle of the bridge, the Seine, and the quay. . . . The work of his mature years had announced itself." It is highly characteristic that the modern administrative-technical work on Paris should be inspired by classical history. Compare further, concerning the decline of Paris, Léon Daudet's chapter on Sacré Coeur in his *Paris vécu* ‹Experiences of Paris›.[10]   [C4]

The following remarkable sentence from the bravura piece "Paris souterrain," in Nadar's *Quand j'étais photographe:* "In his history of sewers, written with the genial pen of the poet and philosopher, Hugo mentions at one point (after a description that he has made more stirring than a drama) that, in China, not a single peasant returns home, after selling his vegetables in the city, without bearing the heavy load of an enormous bucket filled with precious fertilizer" (p. 124).
                                                                    [C4a,1]

Apropos of the gates of Paris: "Until the moment you saw the toll collector appear between two columns, you could imagine yourself before the gates of Rome or of Athens." *Biographie universelle ancienne et moderne*, new edition published under the direction of M. Michaud, vol. 14 (Paris, 1856), p. 321 (article by P. F. L. Fontaine).   [C4a,2]

"In a book by Théophile Gautier, *Caprices et zigzags*, I find a curious page. 'A great danger threatens us,' it says. 'The modern Babylon will not be smashed like the tower of Lylak; it will not be lost in a sea of asphalt like Pentapolis, or buried under the sand like Thebes. It will simply be depopulated and ravaged by the rats of Montfaucon.' Extraordinary vision of a vague but prophetic dreamer! And it has in essence proven true. . . . The rats of Montfaucon . . . have not endangered Paris; Haussmann's arts of embellishment have driven them off. . . . But from the heights of Montfaucon the proletariat have descended, and with gunpowder and petroleum they have begun the destruction of Paris which Gautier foresaw." Max Nordau, *Aus dem wahren Milliardenlande: Pariser Studien und Bilder* (Leipzig, 1878), vol. 1, pp. 75–76 ("Belleville").   [C4a,3]

In 1899, during work on the Métro, foundations of a tower of the Bastille were discovered on the Rue Saint-Antoine. Cabinet des Estampes.   [C4a,4]

Halls of wine: "The warehouse, which consists partly of vaults for the spirits and partly of wine cellars dug out of stone, forms . . ., as it were, a city in which the streets bear the names of the most important wine regions of France." *Acht Tage in Paris* (Paris, July 1855), pp. 37–38.   [C4a,5]

"The cellars of the Café Anglais . . . extend quite a distance under the boulevards, forming the most complicated defiles. The management took the trouble to divide them into streets. . . . You have the Rue du Bourgogne, the Rue du Bordeaux, the Rue du Beaune, the Rue de l'Ermitage, the Rue du Chambertin, the crossroads of . . . Tonneaux. You come to a cool grotto . . . filled with shellfish . . . ; it is the grotto for the wines of Champagne. . . . The great lords of bygone days conceived the idea of dining in their stables. . . . But if you want to dine in a really eccentric fashion: *vivent les caves!*" Taxile Delord, *Paris-viveur* (Paris, 1854), pp. 79–81, 83–84.   [C4a,6]

"Rest assured that when Hugo saw a beggar on the road, . . . he saw him for what he is, for what he really is in reality: the ancient mendicant, the ancient supplicant, . . . on the ancient road. When he looked at a marble slab on one of our mantlepieces, or a cemented brick in one of our modern chimneys, he saw it for what it is: the stone of the hearth. The ancient hearthstone. When he looked at a door to the street, and at a doorstep, which is usually of cut stone, he distinguished clearly on this stone the ancient line, the sacred threshold, for it is one and the same line." Charles Péguy, *Oeuvres complètes, 1873–1914: Oeuvres de prose* (Paris, 1916), pp. 388–389 ("Victor-Marie, Comte Hugo").   [C5,1]

"The wine shops of the Faubourg Antoine resemble those taverns on Mount Aventine, above the Sibyl's cave, which communicated with the deep and sacred afflatus; taverns whose tables were almost tripods, and where men drank what Ennius calls 'the sibylline wine.'" Victor Hugo, *Oeuvres complètes*, novels, vol. 8 (Paris, 1881), pp. 55–56 (*Les Misérables*, part 4).[11]   [C5,2]

"Those who have traveled in Sicily will remember the celebrated convent where, as a result of the earth's capacity for drying and preserving bodies, the monks at a certain time of year can deck out in their ancient regalia all the grandees to whom they have accorded the hospitality of the grave: ministers, popes, cardinals, warriors, and kings. Placing them in two rows within their spacious catacombs, they allow the public to pass between these rows of skeletons. . . . Well, this Sicilian convent gives us an image of our society. Under the pompous garb that adorns our art and literature, no heart beats—there are only dead men, who gaze at you with staring eyes, lusterless and cold, when you ask the century where the inspiration is, where the arts, where the literature." ⟨Alfred⟩ Nettement, *Les Ruines morales et intellectuelles* (Paris, October 1836), p. 32. This may be compared with Hugo's "A l'Arc de Triomphe" of 1837.   [C5,3]

The last two chapters of Léo Claretie's *Paris depuis ses origines jusqu'en l'an 3000* (Paris, 1886) are entitled "The Ruins of Paris" and "The Year 3000." The first contains a paraphrase of Victor Hugo's verses on the Arc de Triomphe. The second reproduces a lecture on the antiquities of Paris that are preserved in the famous "Académie de Floksima . . . located in La Cénépire. This is a new continent . . .

discovered between Cape Horn and the southern territories in the year 2500"
(p. 347).   [C5,4]

"There was, at the Châtelet de Paris, a broad long cellar. This cellar was eight feet
deep below the level of the Seine. It had neither windows nor ventilators . . . ; men
could enter, but air could not. The cellar had for a ceiling a stone arch, and for a
floor, ten inches of mud. . . . Eight feet above the floor, a long massive beam
crossed this vault from side to side; from this beam there hung, at intervals, chains
. . . and at the end of these chains there were iron collars. Men condemned to the
galleys were put into this cellar until the day of their departure for Toulon. They
were pushed under this timber, where each had his iron swinging in the darkness,
waiting for him. . . . In order to eat, they had to draw their bread, which was
thrown into the mire, up their leg with their heel, within reach of their hand. . . .
In this hell-sepulcher, what did they do? What can be done in a sepulcher: they
agonized. And what can be done in a hell: they sang. . . . In this cellar, almost all
the argot songs were born. It is from the dungeon of the Grand Châtelet de Paris
that the melancholy galley refrain of Montgomery comes: 'Timaloumisaine, timou-
lamison.' Most of these songs are dreary; some are cheerful." Victor Hugo,
Oeuvres complètes novels, vol. 8 (Paris, 1881), pp. 297–298 *(Les Misérables)*.[12]
▯ Subterranean Paris ▯   [C5a,1]

On the theory of thresholds: "'Between those who go on foot in Paris and those
who go by carriage, the only difference is the running board,' as a peripatetic
philosopher has said. Ah, the running board! . . . It is the point of departure from
one country to another, from misery to luxury, from thoughtlessness to thoughtful-
ness. It is the hyphen between him who is nothing and him who is all. The question
is: where to put one's foot." Théophile Gautier, *Etudes philosophiques: Paris et les
Parisiens au XIXe siècle* (Paris, 1856), p. 26.   [C5a,2]

Slight foreshadowing of the Métro in this description of model houses of the future:
"The basements, very spacious and well lit, are all connected, forming long galleries which follow the course of the streets. Here an underground railroad has been
built—not for human travelers, to be sure, but exclusively for cumbersome merchandise, for wine, wood, coal, and so forth, which it delivers to the interior of the
home. . . . These underground trains acquire a steadily growing importance."
Tony Moilin, *Paris en l'an 2000* (Paris, 1869), pp. 14–15 ("Maisons-modèles").
                                                                                             [C5a,3]

Fragments from Victor Hugo's ode "A l'Arc de Triomphe":

                                        II
        . . . . .
        Always Paris cries and mutters.
        Who can tell—unfathomable question—
        What would be lost from the universal clamor
        On the day that Paris fell silent!

III

Silent it will be nonetheless!—After so many dawns,
So many months and years, so many played-out centuries,
When this bank, where the stream breaks against the echoing bridges,
Is returned to the modest and murmuring reeds;

When the Seine shall flee the obstructing stones,
Consuming some old dome collapsed into its depths,
Heedful of the gentle breeze that carries to the clouds
The rustling of the leaves and the song of birds;

When it shall flow, at night, pale in the darkness,
Happy, in the drowsing of its long-troubled course,
To listen at last to the countless voices
Passing indistinctly beneath the starry sky;

When this city, mad and churlish *ouvrière*,
That hastens the fate reserved for its walls,
And, turning to dust under the blows of its hammer,
Converts bronze to coins and marble to flagstones;

When the roofs, the bells, the tortuous hives,
Porches, pediments, arches full of pride
That make up this city, many-voiced and tumultuous,
Stifling, inextricable, and teeming to the eye,

When from the wide plain all these things have passed,
And nothing remains of pyramid and pantheon
But two granite towers built by Charlemagne
And a bronze column raised by Napoleon,

You, then, will complete the sublime triangle!
. . . . .

IV

Thus, arch, you will loom eternal and intact
When all that the Seine now mirrors in its surface
   Will have vanished forever,
When of that city—the equal, yes, of Rome—
Nothing will be left except an angel, an eagle, a man
   Surmounting three summits!

V

No, time takes nothing away from things.
More than one portico wrongly vaunted
In its protracted metamorphoses
Comes to beauty in the end.
On the monuments we revere
Time casts a somber spell,
Stretching from façade to apse.
Never, though it cracks and rusts,

Is the robe which time peels from them
Worth the one it puts back on.

It is time who chisels a groove
In an indigent arch-stone;
Who rubs his knowing thumb
On the corner of a barren marble slab;
It is he who, in correcting the work,
Introduces a living snake
Midst the knots of a granite hydra.
I think I see a Gothic roof start laughing
When, from its ancient frieze,
Time removes a stone and puts in a nest.

. . . . .

VIII

. . . . .

No, everything will be dead. Nothing left in this campagna
But a vanished population, still around,
But the dull eye of man and the living eye of God,
But an arch, and a column, and there, in the middle
Of this silvered-over river, still afoam,
A church half-stranded in the mist.

                                        February 2, 1837.

Victor Hugo, *Oeuvres complètes*, Poetry, vol. 3 (Paris, 1880), pp. 233–245.
                                                          [C6; C6a,1]

Demolition sites: sources for teaching the theory of construction. "Never have circumstances been more favorable for this genre of study than the epoch we live in today. During the past twelve years, a multitude of buildings—among them, churches and cloisters—have been demolished down to the first layers of their foundations; they have all provided . . . useful instruction." Charles-François Viel, *De l'Impuissance des mathématiques pour assurer la solidité des bâtimens* (Paris, 1805), pp. 43–44.   [C6a,2]

Demolition sites: "The high walls, with their bister-colored lines around the chimney flues, reveal, like the cross-section of an architectural plan, the mystery of intimate distributions. . . . A curious spectacle, these open houses, with their floorboards suspended over the abyss, their colorful flowered wallpaper still showing the shape of the rooms, their staircases leading nowhere now, their cellars open to the sky, their bizarre collapsed interiors and battered ruins. It all resembles, though without the gloomy tone, those uninhabitable structures which Piranesi outlined with such feverish intensity in his etchings." Théophile Gautier, *Mosaïque de ruines: Paris et les Parisiens au XIXe siècle*, by Alexandre Dumas, Théophile Gautier, Arsène Houssaye, Paul de Musset, Louis Enault, and Du Fayl (Paris, 1856), pp. 38–39.   [C7,1]

Conclusion of ⟨Louis⟩ Lurine's article "Les Boulevards": "The boulevards will die of an aneurism: the explosion of gas." *Paris chez soi* (Paris ⟨1854⟩), p. 62 (anthology issued by Paul Boizard). [C7,2]

Baudelaire to Poulet-Malassis on January 8, 1860, concerning Meryon: "In one of his large plates, he substituted for a little balloon a cloud of predatory birds, and when I pointed out to him that it was implausible that so many eagles could be found in a Parisian sky, he answered that it was not without a basis in fact, since 'those men' (the emperor's government) had often released eagles to study the presages according to the rites, and that this had been reported in the newspapers—even in *Le Moniteur*."[13] Cited in Gustave Geffroy, *Charles Meryon* (Paris, 1926), pp. 126–127. [C7,3]

On the triumphal arch: "The triumph was an institution of the Roman state and was conditioned on the possession of the field-commander's right—the right of the military *imperium*—which, however, was extinguished on the day of the triumph. . . . Of the various provisions attaching to the right of triumph, the most important was that the territorial bounds of the city . . . were not to be crossed prematurely. Otherwise the commander would forfeit the rights of the auspices of war—which held only for operations conducted outside the city—and with them the claim to triumph. . . . Every defilement, all guilt for the murderous battle (and perhaps originally this included the danger posed by the spirits of the slain), is removed from the commander and the army; it remains . . . outside the sacred gateway. . . . Such a conception makes it clear . . . that the *porta triumphalis* was nothing less than a monument for the glorification of victory." Ferdinand Noack, *Triumph und Triumphbogen*, Warburg Library Lectures, vol. 5 (Leipzig, 1928), pp. 150–151, 154. [C7,4]

"Edgar Poe created a character who wanders the streets of capital cities; he called him the Man of the Crowd. The restlessly inquiring engraver is the Man of Stones. . . . Here we have . . . an . . . artist who did not study and draw, like Piranesi, the remnants of a bygone existence, yet whose work gives one the sensation of persistent nostalgia. . . . This is Charles Meryon. His work as an engraver represents one of the profoundest poems ever written about a city, and what is truly original in all these striking pictures is that they seem to be the image, despite being drawn directly from life, of things that are finished, that are dead or about to die. . . . This impression exists independently of the most scrupulous and realistic reproduction of subjects chosen by the artist. There was something of the visionary in Meryon, and he undoubtedly divined that these rigid and unyielding forms were ephemeral, that these singular beauties were going the way of all flesh. He listened to the language spoken by streets and alleys that, since the earliest days of the city, were being continually torn up and redone; and that is why his evocative poetry makes contact with the Middle Ages through the nineteenth-century city, why it radiates eternal melancholy through the vision of immediate appearances. "*Old* Paris is gone (no human heart / changes half so fast as a city's face)."[14] These two lines by Baudelaire could serve as an epigraph to Meryon's entire oeuvre." Gustave Geffroy, *Charles Meryon* (Paris, 1926), pp. 1–3.   [C7a,1]

"There is no need to imagine that the ancient *porta triumphalis* was already an arched gateway. On the contrary, since it served an entirely symbolic act, it would originally have been erected by the simplest of means—namely, two posts and a straight lintel." Ferdinand Noack, *Triumph und Triumphbogen*, Warburg Library Lectures, vol. 5 (Leipzig, 1928), p. 168.   [C7a,2]

The march through the triumphal arch as *rite de passage:* "The march of the troops through the narrow gateway has been compared to a 'rigorous passage through a narrow opening,' something to which the significance of a rebirth attaches." Ferdinand Noack, *Triumph und Triumphbogen*, Warburg Library Lectures, vol. 5 (Leipzig, 1928), p. 153.   [C7a,3]

The fantasies of the decline of Paris are a symptom of the fact that technology was not accepted. These visions bespeak the gloomy awareness that along with the great cities have evolved the means to raze them to the ground.

[C7a,4]

Noack mentions "that Scipio's arch stood not above but opposite the road that leads up to the Capitol (adversus viam, qua in Capitolium ascenditur). . . . We are thus given insight into the purely monumental character of these structures, which are without any practical meaning." On the other hand, the cultic significance of these structures emerges as clearly in their relation to special occasions as in their isolation: "And there, where many . . . later arches stand—at the beginning and end of the street, in the vicinity of bridges, at the entrance to the forum, at the city limit—there was operative for the . . . Romans a conception of the sacred as boundary or threshold." Ferdinand Noack, *Triumph und Triumphbogen*, Warburg Library Lectures, vol. 5 (Leipzig, 1928), pp. 162, 169.

[C8,1]

Apropos of the bicycle: "Actually one should not deceive oneself about the real purpose of the fashionable new mount, which a poet the other day referred to as the horse of the Apocalypse." *L'Illustration*, June 12, 1869, cited in *Vendredi*, October 9, 1936 (Louis Chéronnet, "Le Coin des vieux").   [C8,2]

Concerning the fire that destroyed the hippodrome: "The gossips of the district see in this disaster a visitation of the wrath of heaven on the guilty spectacle of the velocipedes." *Le Gaulois*, October 2 (3?), 1869, cited in *Vendredi*, October 9, 1936 (Louis Chéronnet, "Le Coin des vieux"). The hippodrome was the site of ladies' bicycle races.   [C8,3]

To elucidate *Les Mystères de Paris* and similar works, Caillois refers to the *roman noir*, in particular *The Mysteries of Udolpho*, on account of the "preponderance of vaults and underground passages." Roger Caillois, "Paris, mythe moderne," *Nouvelle Revue française*, 25, no. 284 (May 1, 1937), p. 686.

[C8,4]

"The whole of the *rive gauche*, all the way from the Tour de Nesle to the Tombe Issoire . . . , is nothing but a hatchway leading from the surface to the depths. And if the modern demolitions reveal the mysteries of the upper world of Paris, perhaps one day the inhabitants of the Left Bank will awaken startled to discover the mysteries below." Alexandre Dumas, *Les Mohicans de Paris*, vol. 3 (Paris, 1863).

[C8,5]

"This intelligence of Blanqui's, . . . this tactic of silence, this politics of the catacombs, must have made Barbès hesitate occasionally, as though confronted with . . . an unexpected stairway that suddenly gapes and plunges to the cellar in an unfamiliar house." Gustave Geffroy, *L'Enfermé* (Paris, 1926), vol. 1, p. 72.

[C8,6]

‹Régis› Messac (‹in *Le "Detective Novel" et l'influence de la pensée scientifique* [Paris, 1929],› p. 419) quotes from Vidocq's *Mémoires* (chapter 45): "Paris is a spot on the globe, but this spot is a sewer and the emptying point of all sewers."

[C8a,1]

Le Panorama (a literary and critical revue appearing five times weekly), in volume 1, number 3 (its last number), February 25, 1840, under the title "Difficult Questions": "Will the universe end tomorrow? Or must it—enduring for all eternity—see the end of our planet? Or will this planet, which has the honor of bearing us, outlast all the other worlds?" Very characteristic that one could write this way in a literary revue. (In the first number, "To Our Readers," it is acknowledged, furthermore, that *Le Panorama* was founded to make money.) The founder was the vaudevillian Hippolyte Lucas. [C8a,2]

> Saint who each night led back
> The entire flock to the fold, diligent shepherdess,
> When the world and Paris come to the end of their term,
> May you, with a firm step and a light hand,
> Through the last yard and the last portal,
> Lead back, through the vault and the folding door,
> The entire flock to the right hand of the Father.

Charles Péguy, *La Tapisserie de Sainte-Geneviève*, cited in Marcel Raymond, *De Baudelaire au Surréalisme* (Paris, 1933), p. 219.[15] [C8a,3]

Distrust of cloisters and clergy during the Commune: "Even more than with the incident of the Rue Picpus, everything possible was done to excite the popular imagination, thanks to the vaults of Saint-Laurent. To the voice of the press was added publicizing through images. Etienne Carjat photographed the skeletons, 'with the aid of electric light.' . . . After Picpus, after Saint-Laurent, at an interval of some days, the Convent of the Assumption and the Church of Notre-Dame-des-Victoires. A wave of madness overtook the capital. Everywhere people thought they were finding buried vaults and skeletons." Georges Laronze, *Histoire de la Commune de 1871* (Paris, 1928), p. 370.   [C8a,4]

1871: "The popular imagination could give itself free reign, and it took every opportunity to do so. There wasn't one civil-service official who did not seek to expose the method of treachery then in fashion: the subterranean method. In the prison of Saint-Lazare, they searched for the underground passage which was said to lead from the chapel to Argenteuil—that is, to cross two branches of the Seine and some ten kilometers as the crow flies. At Saint-Sulpice, the passage supposedly abutted the château of Versailles." Georges Laronze, *Histoire de la Commune de 1871* (Paris, 1928), p. 399.   [C8a,5]

"As a matter of fact, men had indeed replaced the prehistoric water. Many centuries after it had withdrawn, they had begun a similar overflowing. They had spread themselves in the same hollows, pushed out in the same directions. It was down there—toward Saint-Merri, the Temple, the Hôtel de Ville, toward Les Halles, the Cemetery of the Innocents, and the Opéra, in the places where water had found the greatest difficulty escaping, places which had kept oozing with infiltrations, with subterranean streams—that men, too, had most completely saturated the soil. The most densely populated and busiest *quartiers* still lay over what had once been marsh." Jules Romains, *Les Hommes de bonne volonté*, book 1, *Le 6 octobre* (Paris ‹1932›), p. 191.[16]   [C9,1]

Baudelaire and the cemeteries: "Behind the high walls of the houses, toward Montmartre, toward Ménilmontant, toward Montparnasse, he imagines at dusk the cemeteries of Paris, these three other cities within the larger one—cities smaller in appearance than the city of the living, which seems to contain them, but in reality how much more populous, with their closely packed little compartments arranged in tiers under the ground. And in the same places where the crowd circulates today—the Square des Innocents, for example—he evokes the ancient ossuaries, now leveled or entirely gone, swallowed up in the sea of time with all their dead, like ships that have sunk with all their crew aboard." François Porché, *La Vie douloureuse de Charles Baudelaire*, in series entitled *Le Roman des Grandes Existences*, no. 6 (Paris ‹1926›), pp. 186–187.   [C9,2]

Parallel passage to the ode on the Arc de Triomphe. Humanity is apostrophized:

> As for your cities, Babels of monuments
> Where all events clamor at once,
> How substantial are they? Arches, towers, pyramids—
> I would not be surprised if, in its humid incandescence,
> The dawn one morning suddenly dissolved them,

Along with the dewdrops on sage and thyme.
And all your noble dwellings, many-tiered,
End up as heaps of stone and grass
Where, in the sunlight, the subtle serpent hisses.

Victor Hugo, *La Fin de Satan: Dieu* (Paris, 1911), pp. 475–476 ("Dieu–L'Ange").
[C9,3]

Léon Daudet on the view of Paris from Sacré Coeur. "From high up you can see this population of palaces, monuments, houses, and hovels, which seem to have gathered in expectation of some cataclysm, or of several cataclysms—meteorological, perhaps, or social. . . . As a lover of hilltop sanctuaries, which never fail to stimulate my mind and nerves with their bracing harsh wind, I have spent hours on Fourvières looking at Lyons, on Notre-Dame de la Garde looking at Marseilles, on Sacré Coeur looking at Paris. . . . And, yes, at a certain moment I heard in myself something like a tocsin, a strange admonition, and I saw these three magnificent cities . . . threatened with collapse, with devastation by fire and flood, with carnage, with rapid erosion, like forests leveled en bloc. At other times, I saw them preyed upon by an obscure, subterranean evil, which undermined the monuments and neighborhoods, causing entire sections of the proudest homes to crumble. . . . From the standpoint of these promontories, what appears most clearly is the menace. The agglomeration is menacing; the enormous labor is menacing. For man has need of labor, that is clear, but he has other needs as well. . . . He needs to isolate himself and to form groups, to cry out and to revolt, to regain calm and to submit. . . . Finally, the need for suicide is in him; and in the society he forms, it is stronger than the instinct for self-preservation. Hence, as one looks out over Paris, Lyons, or Marseilles, from the heights of Sacré Coeur, the Fourvières, or Notre-Dame de la Garde, what astounds one is that Paris, Lyons, and Marseilles have endured." Léon Daudet, *Paris vécu*, vol. 1, *Rive droite* (Paris ‹1930›), pp. 220–221.
[C9a,1]

"In a long series of classical writers from Polybius onward, we read of old, renowned cities in which the streets have become lines of empty, crumbling shells, where the cattle browse in forum and gymnasium, and the amphitheater is a sown field, dotted with emergent statues and herms. Rome had in the fifth century of our era the population of a village, but its imperial palaces were still habitable." Oswald Spengler, *Le Déclin de l'Occident* ‹trans. M. Tazerout›, vol. 2, pt. 1 (Paris, 1933), p. 151.[17]
[C9a,2]

[Boredom, Eternal Return]

> Must the sun therefore murder all dreams,
> the pale children of my pleasure grounds?
> The days have grown so still and glowering.
> Satisfaction lures me with nebulous visions,
> while dread makes away with my salvation—
> as though I were about to judge my God.
>
> —Jakob van Hoddis[1]

> Boredom waits for death.
>
> —Johann Peter Hebel[2]

> Waiting is life.
>
> —Victor Hugo[3]

Child with its mother in the panorama. The panorama is presenting the Battle of Sedan. The child finds it all very lovely: "Only, it's too bad the sky is so dreary."—"That's what the weather is like in war," answers the mother. ☐ Dioramas ☐

Thus, the panoramas too are in fundamental complicity with this world of mist, this cloud-world: the light of their images breaks as through curtains of rain.
[D1,1]

"This Paris [of Baudelaire's] is very different from the Paris of Verlaine, which itself has already faded. The one is somber and rainy, like a Paris on which the image of Lyons has been superimposed; the other is whitish and dusty, like a pastel by Raphael. One is suffocating, whereas the other is airy, with new buildings scattered in a wasteland, and, not far away, a gate leading to withered arbors." François Porché, *La Vie douloureuse de Charles Baudelaire* (Paris, 1926), p. 119.
[D1,2]

The mere narcotizing effect which cosmic forces have on a shallow and brittle personality is attested in the relation of such a person to one of the highest and most genial manifestations of these forces: the weather. Nothing is more characteristic than that precisely this most intimate and mysterious affair, the working of the weather on humans, should have become the theme of their emptiest chatter. Nothing bores the ordinary man more than the cosmos. Hence, for him, the deepest connection between weather and boredom. How fine the ironic overcoming of this attitude in the story of the splenetic Englishman who wakes up one morning and shoots himself because it is raining. Or Goethe: how he managed to illuminate the weather in his meteorological studies, so that one is tempted to say he undertook this work solely in order to be able to integrate even the weather into his waking, creative life. [D1,3]

Baudelaire as the poet of *Spleen de Paris:* "One of the central motifs of this poetry is, in effect, boredom in the fog, ennui and indiscriminate haze (fog of the cities). In a word, it is spleen." François Porché, *La Vie douloureuse de Charles Baudelaire* (Paris, 1926), p. 184. [D1,4]

In 1903, in Paris, Emile Tardieu brought out a book entitled *L'Ennui,* in which all human activity is shown to be a vain attempt to escape from boredom, but in which, at the same time, everything that was, is, and will be appears as the inexhaustible nourishment of that feeling. To hear this, you might suppose the work to be a mighty monument of literature—a monument *aere perennius* in honor of the *taedium vitae* of the Romans.[4] But it is only the self-satisfied shabby scholarship of a new Homais, who reduces all greatness, the heroism of heroes and the asceticism of saints, to documents of his own spiritually barren, petty-bourgeois discontent. [D1,5]

"When the French went into Italy to maintain the rights of the throne of France over the duchy of Milan and the kingdom of Naples, they returned home quite amazed at the precautions which Italian genius had taken against the excessive heat; and, in admiration of the arcaded galleries, they strove to imitate them. The rainy climate of Paris, with its celebrated mud and mire, suggested the pillars, which were a marvel in the old days. Here, much later on, was the impetus for the Place Royale. A strange thing! It was in keeping with the same motifs that, under Napoleon, the Rue de Rivoli, the Rue de Castiglione, and the famous Rue des Colonnes were constructed." The turban came out of Egypt in this manner as well. *Le Diable à Paris* (Paris, 1845), vol. 2, pp. 11–12 (Balzac, "Ce qui disparaît de Paris").
   How many years separated the war mentioned above from the Napoleonic expedition to Italy? And where is the Rue des Colonnes located?[5] [D1,6]

"Rainshowers have given birth to ‹many› adventures."[6] Diminishing magical power of the rain. Mackintosh. [D1,7]

As dust, rain takes its revenge on the arcades.—Under Louis Philippe, dust settled even on the revolutions. When the young duc d'Orléans "married the princess of Mecklenburg, a great celebration was held at that famous ballroom where the first symptoms of the Revolution ‹of 1830› had broken out. When they came to prepare the room for the festivities of the young couple, the people in charge found it as the Revolution had left it. On the ground could be seen traces of the military banquet—candle ends, broken glasses, champagne corks, trampled cockades of the Gardes du Corps, and ceremonial ribbons of officers from the Flanders regiment." Karl Gutzkow, *Briefe aus Paris* (Leipzig, 1842), vol. 2, p. 87. A historical scene becomes a component of the panopticon. ☐ Diorama ☐ Dust and Stifled Perspective ☐ [D1a,1]

"He explains that the Rue Grange-Batelière is particularly dusty, that one gets terribly grubby in the Rue Réaumur." Louis Aragon, *Le Paysan de Paris* (Paris, 1926), p. 88.[7] [D1a,2]

Plush as dust collector. Mystery of dustmotes playing in the sunlight. Dust and the "best room." "Shortly after 1840, fully padded furniture appears in France, and with it the upholstered style becomes dominant." Max von Boehn, *Die Mode im XIX. Jahrhundert,* vol. 2 (Munich, 1907), p. 131. Other arrangements to stir up dust: the trains of dresses. "The true and proper train has recently come back into vogue, but in order to avoid the nuisance of having it sweep the streets, the wearer is now provided with a small hook and a string so that she can raise and carry the train whenever she goes anywhere." Friedrich Theodor Vischer, *Mode und Zynismus* (Stuttgart, 1879), p. 12. ☐ Dust and Stifled Perspective ☐ [D1a,3]

The Galerie du Thermomètre and the Galerie du Baromètre, in the Passage de l'Opéra. [D1a,4]

A feuilletonist of the 1840s, writing on the subject of the Parisian weather, has determined that Corneille spoke only once (in *Le Cid*) of the stars, and that Racine spoke only once of the sun. He maintains, further, that stars and flowers were first discovered for literature by Chateaubriand in America and thence transplanted to Paris. See Victor Méry, "Le Climat de Paris," in *Le Diable à Paris* ‹vol. 1 (Paris, 1845), p. 245›. [D1a,5]

Concerning some lascivious pictures: "It is no longer the fan that's the thing, but the umbrella—invention worthy of the epoch of the king's national guard. The umbrella encouraging amorous fantasies! The umbrella furnishing discreet cover. The canopy, the roof, over Robinson's island." John Grand-Carteret, *Le Décolleté et le retroussé* (Paris ‹1910›), vol. 2, p. 56. [D1a,6]

"Only here," Chirico once said, "is it possible to paint. The streets have such gradations of gray. . . ." [D1a,7]

The Parisian atmosphere reminds Carus[8] of the way the Neapolitan coastline looks when the sirocco blows. [D1a,8]

Only someone who has grown up in the big city can appreciate its rainy weather, which altogether slyly sets one dreaming back to early childhood. Rain makes everything more hidden, makes days not only gray but uniform. From morning until evening, one can do the same thing—play chess, read, engage in argument—whereas sunshine, by contrast, shades the hours and discountenances the dreamer. The latter, therefore, must get around the days of sun with subterfuges—above all, must rise quite early, like the great idlers, the waterfront loafers and the vagabonds: the dreamer must be up before the sun itself. In the "Ode to Blessed Morning," which some years past he sent to Emmy Hennings, Ferdinand Hardekopf, the only authentic decadent that Germany has produced, confides to the dreamer the best precautions to be taken for sunny days.[9]

[D1a,9]

"To give to this dust a semblance of consistency, as by soaking it in blood." Louis Veuillot, *Les Odeurs de Paris* (Paris, 1914), p. 12.   [D1a,10]

Other European cities admit colonnades into their urban perspective, Berlin setting the style with its city gates. Particularly characteristic is the Halle Gate—unforgettable for me on a blue picture postcard representing Belle-Alliance Platz by night. The card was transparent, and when you held it up to the light, all its windows were illuminated with the very same glow that came from the full moon up in the sky.   [D2,1]

"The buildings constructed for the new Paris revive all the styles. The ensemble is not lacking in a certain unity, however, because all the styles belong to the category of the tedious—in fact, the most tedious of the tedious, which is the emphatic and the aligned. *Line up! Eyes front!* It seems that the Amphion of this city is a corporal. . . . / He moves great quantities of things—showy, stately, colossal—and all of them are tedious. He moves other things, extremely ugly; they too are tedious. / These great streets, these great quays, these great houses, these great sewers, their physiognomy poorly copied or poorly dreamed—all have an indefinable something indicative of unexpected and irregular fortune. They exude tedium." Veuillot, *Les Odeurs de Paris* ⟨Paris, 1914⟩, p. 9. ☐ Haussmann ☐   [D2,2]

Pelletan describes a visit with a king of the Stock Exchange, a multimillionaire: "As I entered the courtyard of the house, a squad of grooms in red vests were occupied in rubbing down a half dozen English horses. I ascended a marble staircase hung with a giant gilded chandelier, and encountered in the vestibule a majordomo with white cravat and plump calves. He led me into a large glass-roofed gallery whose walls were decorated entirely with camellias and hothouse plants. Something like suppressed boredom lay in the air; at the very first step, you breathed a vapor as of opium. I then passed between two rows of perches on which parakeets from various countries were roosting. They were red, blue, green, gray, yellow, and white; but all seemed to suffer from homesickness. At the extreme end of the gallery stood a small table opposite a Renaissance-style fireplace, for at this hour the master of the house took his breakfast. . . . After I had waited a quarter of an hour, he deigned to appear. . . . He yawned, looked sleepy, and seemed continually on the point of nodding off; he walked like a somnambulist. His fatigue had infected the walls of his mansion. The parakeets stood out like his separate thoughts, each one materialized and attached to a pole. . . . " ☐ Interior ☐ ‹Julius› Rodenberg, *Paris bei Sonnenschein und Lampenlicht* (Leipzig, 1867), pp. 104–105. [D2,3]

Fêtes françaises, ou Paris en miniature ‹French Festivities, or Paris in Miniature›: produced by Rougemont and Gentil at the Théâtre des Variétés. The plot has to do with the marriage of Napoleon I to Marie-Louise, and the conversation, at this point, concerns the planned festivities. "Nevertheless," says one of the characters, "the weather is rather uncertain."—Reply: "My friend, you may rest assured that this day is the choice of our sovereign." He then strikes up a song that begins:

> At his piercing glance, doubt not—
> The future is revealed;
> And when good weather is required,
> We look to his star.

Cited in Théodore Muret, *L'Histoire par le théâtre, 1789–1851* (Paris, 1865), vol. 1, p. 262. [D2,4]

"This dull, glib sadness called ennui." Louis Veuillot, *Les Odeurs de Paris* (Paris, 1914), p. 177. [D2,5]

"Along with every outfit go a few accessories which show it off to best effect—that is to say, which cost lots of money because they are so quickly ruined, in particular by every downpour." This apropos of the top hat. ☐ Fashion ☐ F. Th. Vischer, *Vernünftige Gedanken über die jetzige Mode* ‹in *Kritische Gänge*, new series, no. 3 (Stuttgart, 1861)›, p. 124. [D2,6]

We are bored when we don't know what we are waiting for. That we do know, or think we know, is nearly always the expression of our superficiality or inattention. Boredom is the threshold to great deeds.—Now, it would be important to know: What is the dialectical antithesis to boredom? [D2,7]

The quite humorous book by Emile Tardieu, *L'Ennui* (Paris, 1903), whose main thesis is that life is purposeless and groundless and that all striving after happiness and equanimity is futile, names the weather as one among many factors supposedly causing boredom.—This work can be considered a sort of breviary for the twentieth century. [D2,8]

Boredom is a warm gray fabric lined on the inside with the most lustrous and colorful of silks. In this fabric we wrap ourselves when we dream. We are at home then in the arabesques of its lining. But the sleeper looks bored and gray within his sheath. And when he later wakes and wants to tell of what he dreamed, he communicates by and large only this boredom. For who would be able at one stroke to turn the lining of time to the outside? Yet to narrate dreams signifies nothing else. And in no other way can one deal with the arcades—structures in which we relive, as in a dream, the life of our parents and grandparents, as the embryo in the womb relives the life of animals. Existence in these spaces flows then without accent, like the events in dreams. Flânerie is the rhythmics of this slumber. In 1839, a rage for tortoises overcame Paris. One can well imagine the elegant set mimicking the pace of this creature more easily in the arcades than on the boulevards. ▢ Flâneur ▢   [D2a,1]

Boredom is always the external surface of unconscious events. For this reason, it has appeared to the great dandies as a mark of distinction. Ornament and boredom.   [D2a,2]

On the double meaning of the term *temps*[10] in French.   [D2a,3]

Factory labor as economic infrastructure of the ideological boredom of the upper classes. "The miserable routine of endless drudgery and toil in which the same mechanical process is repeated over and over again is like the labor of Sisyphus. The burden of labor, like the rock, always keeps falling back on the worn-out laborer." Friedrich Engels, *Die Lage der arbeitenden Klasse in England* ‹2nd ed. (Leipzig, 1848)›, p. 217; cited in Marx, *Kapital* (Hamburg, 1922), vol. 1, p. 388.[11]   [D2a,4]

The feeling of an "incurable imperfection in the very essence of the present" (see *Les Plaisirs et les jours,* cited in Gide's homage)[12] was perhaps, for Proust, the main motive for getting to know fashionable society in its innermost recesses, and it is an underlying motive perhaps for the social gatherings of all human beings.   [D2a,5]

On the salons: "All faces evinced the unmistakable traces of boredom, and conversations were in general scarce, quiet, and serious. Most of these people viewed dancing as drudgery, to which you had to submit because it was supposed to be good form to dance." Further on, the proposition that "no other city in Europe, perhaps, displays such a dearth of satisfied, cheerful, lively faces at its soirées as Paris does in its salons. . . . Moreover, in no other society so much as in this one, and by reason of fashion no less than real conviction, is the unbearable boredom so roundly lamented." "A natural consequence of this is that social affairs are marked by silence and reserve, of a sort that at larger gatherings in other cities would most certainly be the exception." Ferdinand von Gall, *Paris und seine Salons*, vol. 1 (Oldenburg, 1844), pp. 151–153, 158.   [D2a,6]

The following lines provide an occasion for meditating on timepieces in apartments: " A certain blitheness, a casual and even careless regard for the hurrying time, an indifferent expenditure of the all too quickly passing hours—these are qualities that favor the superficial salon life." Ferdinand von Gall, *Paris und seine Salons,* vol. 2 (Oldenburg, 1845), p. 171. [D2a,7]

Boredom of the ceremonial scenes depicted in historical paintings, and the *dolce far niente* of battle scenes with all that dwells in the smoke of gunpowder. From the *images d'Epinal* to Manet's *Execution of Emperor Maximilian,* it is always the same—and always a new—fata morgana, always the smoke in which Mogreby ⟨?⟩ or the genie from the bottle suddenly emerges before the dreaming, absent-minded art lover. ☐ Dream House, Museums ☐[13] [D2a,8]

Chess players at the Café de la Régence: "It was there that clever players could be seen playing with their backs to the chessboard. It was enough for them to hear the name of the piece moved by their opponent at each turn to be assured of winning." *Histoire des cafés de Paris* (Paris, 1857), p. 87. [D2a,9]

"In sum, classic urban art, after presenting its masterpieces, fell into decrepitude at the time of the *philosophes* and the constructors of systems. The end of the eighteenth century saw the birth of innumerable projects; the Commission of Artists brought them into accord with a body of doctrine, and the Empire adapted them without creative originality. The flexible and animated classical style was succeeded by the systematic and rigid pseudoclassical style. . . . The Arc de Triomphe echoes the gate of Louis XIV; the Vendôme column is copied from Rome; the Church of the Madeleine, the Stock Exchange, the Palais-Bourbon are so many Greco-Roman temples." Lucien Dubech and Pierre d'Espezel, *Histoire de Paris* (Paris, 1926), p. 345. ☐ Interior ☐ [D3,1]

"The First Empire copied the triumphal arches and monuments of the two classical centuries. Then there was an attempt to revive and reinvent more remote models: the Second Empire imitated the Renaissance, the Gothic, the Pompeian. After this came an epoch of vulgarity without style." Dubech and d'Espezel, *Histoire de Paris* (Paris, 1926), p. 464. ☐ Interior ☐ [D3,2]

Announcement for a book by Benjamin Gastineau, *La Vie en chemin de fer* ⟨Life on the Railroad⟩: "*La Vie en chemin de fer* is an entrancing prose poem. It is an epic of modern life, always fiery and turbulent, a panorama of gaiety and tears passing before us like the dust of the rails before the windows of the coach." By Benjamin Gastineau, *Paris en rose* (Paris, 1866), p. 4. [D3,3]

Rather than pass the time, one must invite it in. To pass the time (to kill time, expel it): the gambler. Time spills from his every pore.—To store time as a battery stores energy: the flâneur. Finally, the third type: he who waits. He takes in the time and renders it up in altered form—that of expectation.[14] [D3,4]

"This recently deposited limestone—the bed on which Paris rests—readily crumbles into a dust which, like all limestone dust, is very painful to the eyes and lungs.

A little rain does nothing at all to help, since it is immediately absorbed and the surface left dry once again." "Here is the source of the unprepossessing bleached gray of the houses, which are all built from the brittle limestone mined near Paris; here, too, the origin of the dun-colored slate roofs that blacken with soot over the years, as well as the high, wide chimneys which deface even the public buildings, . . . and which in some districts of the old city stand so close together that they almost block the view entirely." J. F. Benzenberg, *Briefe geschrieben auf einer Reise nach Paris* (Dortmund, 1805), vol. 1, pp. 112, 111.   [D3,5]

"Engels told me that it was in Paris in 1848, at the Café de la Régence (one of the earliest centers of the Revolution of 1789), that Marx first laid out for him the economic determinism of his materialist theory of history." Paul Lafargue, "Persönliche Erinnerungen an Friedrich Engels," *Die neue Zeit*, 23, no. 2 (Stuttgart, 1905), p. 558.   [D3,6]

Boredom—as index to participation in the sleep of the collective. Is this the reason it seems distinguished, so that the dandy makes a show of it?   [D3,7]

In 1757 there were only three cafés in Paris.   [D3a,1]

Maxims of Empire painting: "The new artists accept only 'the heroic style, the sublime,' and the sublime is attained only with 'the nude and drapery.' . . . Painters are supposed to find their inspiration in Plutarch or Homer, Livy or Virgil, and, in keeping with David's recommendation to Gros, are supposed to choose . . . 'subjects known to everyone.' . . . Subjects taken from contemporary life were, because of the clothing styles, unworthy of 'great art.'" A. Malet and P. Grillet, *XIXᵉ siècle* (Paris, 1919), p. 158. ☐ Fashion ☐   [D3a,2]

"Happy the man who is an observer! Boredom, for him, is a word devoid of sense." Victor Fournel, *Ce qu'on voit dans les rues de Paris* (Paris, 1858), p. 271.   [D3a,3]

Boredom began to be experienced in epidemic proportions during the 1840s. Lamartine is said to be the first to have given expression to the malady. It plays a role in a little story about the famous comic Deburau. A distinguished Paris neurologist was consulted one day by a patient whom he had not seen before. The patient complained of the typical illness of the times—weariness with life, deep depressions, boredom. "There's nothing wrong with you," said the doctor after a thorough examination. "Just try to relax—find something to entertain you. Go see Deburau some evening, and life will look different to you." "Ah, dear sir," answered the patient, "I *am* Deburau."   [D3a,4]

Return from the *Courses de la Marche:* "The dust exceeded all expectations. The elegant folk back from the races are virtually encrusted; they remind you of Pom-

peii. They have had to be exhumed with the help of a brush, if not a pickaxe."
H. de Pène, *Paris intime* (Paris, 1859), p. 320. [D3a,5]

"The introduction of the Macadam system for paving the boulevards gave rise to
numerous caricatures. Cham shows the Parisians blinded by dust, and he proposes to erect . . . a statue with the inscription: 'In recognition of Macadam, from
the grateful oculists and opticians.' Others represent pedestrians mounted on
stilts traversing marshes and bogs." *Paris sous la République de 1848: Exposition
de la Bibliothèque et des Travaux historiques de la Ville de Paris* (1909) [Poëte,
Beaurepaire, Clouzot, Henriot], p. 25. [D3a,6]

"Only England could have produced dandyism. France is as incapable of it as its
neighbor is incapable of anything like our . . . lions, who are as eager to please as
the dandies are disdainful of pleasing. . . . D'Orsay . . . was naturally and passionately pleasing to everyone, even to men, whereas the dandies pleased only in
displeasing. . . . Between the lion and the dandy lies an abyss. But how much
wider the abyss between the dandy and the fop!" Larousse, ‹*Grand Dictionnaire
universelle*› *du dix-neuvième siècle*‹, vol. 6 (Paris, 1870), p. 63 (article on the
dandy)›. [D4,1]

In the second-to-last chapter of his book *Paris: From Its Origins to the Year 3000*
(Paris, 1886), Léo Claretie speaks of a crystal canopy that would slide over the city
in case of rain. "In 1987" is the title of this chapter. [D4,2]

With reference to Chodruc-Duclos: "We are haunted by what was perhaps the
remains of some rugged old citizen of Herculaneum who, having escaped from
his underground bed, returned to walk again among us, riddled by the thousand
furies of the volcano, living in the midst of death." *Mémoires de Chodruc-Duclos,*
ed. J. Arago and Edouard Gouin (Paris, 1843), vol. 1, p. 6 (preface). The first
flâneur among the *déclassés*. [D4,3]

The world in which one is bored—"So what if one is bored! What influence can it
possibly have?" "What influence! . . . What influence, boredom, with us? But an
enormous influence, . . . a decisive influence! For ennui, you see, the Frenchman
has a horror verging on veneration. Ennui, in his eyes, is a terrible god with a
devoted cult following. It is only in the grip of boredom that the Frenchman can be
serious." Edouard Pailleron, *Le Monde où l'on s'ennuie* (1881), Act 1, scene 2; in
Pailleron, *Théâtre complet*, vol. 3 (Paris ‹1911›), p. 279. [D4,4]

Michelet "offers a description, full of intelligence and compassion, of the condition
of the first specialized factory workers around 1840. There were 'true hells of
boredom' in the spinning and weaving mills: '*Ever, ever, ever,* is the unvarying
word thundering in your ears from the automatic equipment which shakes even
the floor. One can never get used to it.' Often the remarks of Michelet (for example, on reverie and the rhythms of different occupations) anticipate, on an intui-

tive level, the experimental analyses of modern psychologists." Georges Friedmann, *La Crise du progrès* (Paris ⟨1936⟩), p. 244; quotation from Michelet, *Le
Peuple* (Paris, 1846), p. 83.[15]   [D4,5]

Faire droguer, in the sense of *faire attendre*, "to keep waiting," belongs to the
argot of the armies of the Revolution and of the Empire. According to ⟨Ferdinand⟩
Brunot, *Histoire de la langue française*, vol. 9, *La Révolution et l'Empire* (Paris,
1937) ⟨p. 997⟩.   [D4,6]

Parisian Life: "The contemporary scene is preserved, like a specimen under glass,
in a letter of recommendation to Metella given by Baron Stanislas de Frascata to
his friend Baron Gondremarck. The writer, tied to the 'cold country' in which he
lives, sighs for the champagne suppers, Metella's sky-blue boudoir, the songs, the
glamor of Paris, the gay and glittering city, throbbing with warmth and life, in
which differences of station are abolished. Metella reads the letter to the strains of
Offenbach's music, which surrounds it with a yearning melancholy, as though
Paris were paradise lost, and at the same time with a halo of bliss as though it were
the paradise to come; and, as the action continues, one is given the impression that
the picture given in the letter is beginning to come to life." S. Kracauer, *Jacques
Offenbach und das Paris seiner Zeit* (Amsterdam, 1937), pp. 348–349.[16]
                                                                                   [D4a,1]

"Romanticism ends in a theory of boredom, the characteristically modern sentiment; that is, it ends in a theory of power, or at least of energy. . . . Romanticism,
in effect, marks the recognition by the individual of a bundle of instincts which
society has a strong interest in repressing; but, for the most part, it manifests the
abdication of the struggle. . . . The Romantic writer . . . turns toward . . . a poetry
of refuge and escape. The effort of Balzac and of Baudelaire is exactly the reverse
of this and tends to integrate into life the postulates which the Romantics were
resigned to working with only on the level of art. . . . Their effort is thus linked to
the myth according to which imagination plays an ever-increasing role in life."
Roger Caillois, "Paris, mythe moderne," *Nouvelle Revue française*, 25, no. 284
(May 1, 1937), pp. 695, 697.   [D4a,2]

1839: "France is bored" (Lamartine).   [D4a,3]

Baudelaire in his essay on Guys: "Dandyism is a mysterious institution, no less
peculiar than the duel. It is of great antiquity, Caesar, Catiline, and Alcibiades
providing us with dazzling examples; and very widespread, Chateaubriand having
found it in the forests and by the lakes of the New World." Baudelaire, *L'Art
romantique* (Paris), p. 91.[17]   [D4a,4]

The Guys chapter in *L'Art romantique*, on dandies: "They are all representatives
. . . of that compelling need, alas only too rare today, for combating and destroying
triviality. . . . Dandyism is the last spark of heroism amid decadence; and the type
of dandy discovered by our traveler in North America does nothing to invalidate

this idea; for how can we be sure that those tribes which we call 'savage' may not in fact be the *disjecta membra* of great extinct civilizations? . . . It is hardly necessary to say that when Monsieur G. sketches one of his dandies on paper, he never fails to give him his historical personality—his legendary personality, I would venture to say, if we were not speaking of the present time and of things generally considered frivolous." Baudelaire, *L'Art romantique*, vol. 3, ed. Hachette (Paris), pp. 94–95.[18]   [D5,1]

Baudelaire describes the impression that the consummate dandy must convey: "A rich man, perhaps, but more likely an out-of-work Hercules!" Baudelaire, *L'Art romantique* (Paris), p. 96.[19]   [D5,2]

In the essay on Guys, the crowd appears as the supreme remedy for boredom: "'Any man,' he said one day, in the course of one of those conversations which he illumines with burning glance and evocative gesture, 'any man . . . who can yet be *bored in the heart of the multitude* is a blockhead! A blockhead! And I despise him!" Baudelaire, *L'Art romantique*, p. 65.[20]   [D5,3]

Among all the subjects first marked out for lyric expression by Baudelaire, *one* can be put at the forefront: bad weather.   [D5,4]

As attributed to a certain "Carlin," the well-known anecdote about Deburau (the actor afflicted with boredom) forms the pièce de résistance of the versified *Eloge de l'ennui* ‹Encomium to Boredom›, by Charles Boissière, of the Philotechnical Society (Paris, 1860).—"Carlin" is the name of a breed of dogs; it comes from the first name of an Italian actor who played Harlequin.   [D5,5]

"Monotony feeds on the new." Jean Vaudal, *Le Tableau noir;* cited in E. Jaloux, "L'Esprit des livres," *Nouvelles littéraires*, November 20, 1937.   [D5,6]

Counterpart to Blanqui's view of the world: the universe is a site of lingering catastrophes.   [D5,7]

On *L'Eternité par les astres:* Blanqui, who, on the threshold of the grave, recognizes the Fort du Taureau as his last place of captivity, writes this book in order to open new doors in his dungeon.   [D5a,1]

On *L'Eternité par les astres:* Blanqui yields to bourgeois society. But he's brought to his knees with such force that the throne begins to totter.   [D5a,2]

On *L'Eternité par les astres:* The people of the nineteenth century see the stars against a sky which is spread out in this text.   [D5a,3]

It may be that the figure of Blanqui surfaces in the "Litanies of Satan": "You who give the outlaw that serene and haughty look" (‹Baudelaire, *Oeuvres,*› ed. Le

Dantec, ‹vol. 1 [Paris, 1931],› p. 138).[21] In point of fact, Baudelaire did a drawing from memory that shows the head of Blanqui. [D5a,4]

To grasp the significance of *nouveauté,* it is necessary to go back to novelty in everyday life. Why does everyone share the newest thing with someone else? Presumably, in order to triumph over the dead. This only where there is nothing really new. [D5a,5]

Blanqui's last work, written during his last imprisonment, has remained entirely unnoticed up to now, so far as I can see. It is a cosmological speculation. Granted it appears, in its opening pages, tasteless and banal. But the awkward deliberations of the autodidact are merely the prelude to a speculation that only this revolutionary could develop. We may call it theological, insofar as hell is a subject of theology. In fact, the cosmic vision of the world which Blanqui lays out, taking his data from the mechanistic natural science of bourgeois society, is an infernal vision. At the same time, it is a complement of the society to which Blanqui, in his old age, was forced to concede victory. What is so unsettling is that the presentation is entirely lacking in irony. It is an unconditional surrender, but it is simultaneously the most terrible indictment of a society that projects this image of the cosmos—understood as an image of itself—across the heavens. With its trenchant style, this work displays the most remarkable similarities both to Baudelaire and to Nietzsche. (Letter of January 6, 1938, to Horkheimer.)[22] [D5a,6]

From Blanqui's *L'Eternité par les astres:* "What man does not find himself sometimes faced with two opposing courses? The one he declines would make for a far different life, while leaving him his particular individuality. One leads to misery, shame, servitude; the other, to glory and liberty. Here, a lovely woman and happiness; there, fury and desolation. I am speaking now for both sexes. Take your chances or your choice—it makes no difference, for you will not escape your destiny. But destiny finds no footing in infinity, which knows no alternative and makes room for everything. There exists a world where a man follows the road that, in the other world, his double did not take. His existence divides in two, a globe for each; it bifurcates a second time, a third time, thousands of times. He thus possesses fully formed doubles with innumerable variants, which, in multiplying, always represent him as a person but capture only fragments of his destiny. All that one might have been in this world, one is in another. Along with one's entire existence from birth to death, experienced in a multitude of places, one also lives, in yet other places, ten thousand different versions of it." Cited in Gustave Geffroy, *L'Enfermé* (Paris, 1897), p. 399. [D6,1]

From the conclusion of *L'Eternité par les astres:* "What I write at this moment in a cell of the Fort du Taureau I have written and shall write throughout all eternity—at a table, with a pen, clothed as I am now, in circumstances like these." Cited in Gustave Geffroy, *L'Enfermé* (Paris, 1897), p. 401. Right after this, Geffroy writes: "He thus inscribes his fate, at each instant of its duration, across the numberless stars. His prison cell is multiplied to infinity. Throughout the entire universe, he is the same confined man that he is on this earth, with his rebellious strength and his freedom of thought." [D6,2]

From the conclusion of *L'Eternité par les astres:* "At the present time, the entire life of our planet, from birth to death, with all its crimes and miseries, is being lived partly here and partly there, day by day, on myriad kindred planets. What we call 'progress' is confined to each particular world, and vanishes with it. Always and everywhere in the terrestrial arena, the same drama, the same setting, on the same narrow stage—a noisy humanity infatuated with its own grandeur, believing itself to be the universe and living in its prison as though in some immense realm, only to founder at an early date along with its globe, which has borne with deepest disdain, the burden of human arrogance. The same monotony, the same immobility, on other heavenly bodies. The universe repeats itself endlessly and paws the ground in place." Cited in Gustave Geffroy, *L'Enfermé* (Paris, 1897), p. 402. [D6a,1]

Blanqui expressly emphasizes the scientific character of his theses, which would have nothing to do with Fourierist frivolities. "One must concede that each particular combination of materials and people 'is bound to be repeated thousands of times in order to satisfy the demands of infinity.'" Cited in Geffroy, *L'Enfermé* (Paris, 1897), p. 400. [D6a,2]

Blanqui's misanthropy: "The variations begin with those living creatures that have a will of their own, or something like caprices. As soon as human beings enter the scene, imagination enters with them. It is not as though they have much effect on the planet. . . . Their turbulent activity never seriously disturbs the natural progression of physical phenomena, though it disrupts humanity. It is therefore advisable to anticipate this subversive influence, which . . . tears apart nations and brings down empires. Certainly these brutalities run their course without even scratching the terrestrial surface. The disappearance of the disruptors would leave no trace of their self-styled sovereign presence, and would suffice to return nature to its virtually unmolested virginity." Blanqui, *L'Eternité ⟨par les astres* (Paris, 1872)⟩>, pp. 63–64. [D6a,3]

Final chapter (8, "Résumé") of Blanqui's *L'Eternité par les astres:* "The entire universe is composed of astral systems. To create them, nature has only a hundred *simple bodies* at its disposal. Despite the great advantage it derives from these resources, and the innumerable combinations that these resources afford its fecundity, the result is necessarily a *finite* number, like that of the elements themselves; and in order to fill its expanse, nature must repeat to infinity each of its *original* combinations or *types.* / So each heavenly body, whatever it might be, exists in infinite number in time and space, not only in *one* of its aspects but as it is at each second of its existence, from birth to death. All the beings distributed across its surface, whether large or small, living or inanimate, share the privilege of this perpetuity. / The earth is one of these heavenly bodies. Every human being is thus eternal at every second of his or her existence. What I write at this moment in a cell of the Fort du Taureau I have written and shall write throughout all eternity—at a table, with a pen, clothed as I am now, in circumstances like these. And thus it is for everyone. / All worlds are engulfed, one after another, in the revivifying flames, to be reborn from them and consumed by them once more—monotonous flow of an hourglass that eternally empties and turns itself over. The new is always old, and the old always new. / Yet won't those who are interested in extraterrestrial life smile at a mathematical deduction which accords them not only immortality but eternity? The number of our doubles is infinite in time and space. One cannot in good conscience demand anything more. These doubles exist in flesh and bone—indeed, in trousers and jacket, in crinoline and chignon. They are by no means phantoms; they are the present eternalized. / Here, nonetheless, lies a great drawback: there is no progress, alas, but merely vulgar revisions and reprints. Such are the exemplars, the ostensible 'original editions,' of all the worlds past and all the worlds to come. Only the chapter on bifurcations is still open to hope. Let us not forget: *all that one might have been in this world, one is in another.* / In this world, progress is for our descendants alone. They will have more of a chance than we did. All the beautiful things ever seen on our world have, of course, already been seen—are being seen at this instant and will always be seen—by our descendants, and by their doubles who have preceded and will follow them. Scions of a finer humanity, they have already mocked and reviled our existence on dead worlds, while overtaking and succeeding us. They continue to scorn us on the living worlds from which we have disappeared, and their contempt for us will have no end on the worlds to come. / They and we, and all the inhabitants of our planet, are reborn prisoners of the moment and of the place to which destiny has assigned us in the series of Earth's avatars. Our continued life depends on that of the planet. We are merely phenomena that are ancillary to its resurrections. Men of the nineteenth century, the hour of our apparitions is fixed forever, and always brings us back the very same ones, or at most with a prospect of felicitous variants. There is nothing here that will much gratify the yearning for improvement. What to do? I have sought not at all my pleasure, but only the truth. Here there is neither revelation nor prophecy, but rather a simple deduction on the basis of spectral analysis and Laplacian cosmogony. These two discoveries make us eternal. Is it a windfall? Let us profit from it. Is it a mystification? Let us resign ourselves to it. / . . . / At bottom, this eternity of the human being among the stars is a melancholy thing, and this sequestering of kindred worlds by the inexorable barrier of space is even more sad. So many identical populations pass away without suspecting one another's existence! But no—this has finally been discovered, in the nineteenth century. Yet who is inclined to believe it? / Until now, the past has, for us, meant barbarism, whereas the future has signified progress, science, happiness, illusion! This past, on all our counterpart worlds, has seen the most brilliant civilizations disappear without leaving a trace, and they will continue to disappear without leaving a trace. The future will witness yet again, on billions of worlds, the ignorance, folly, and cruelty of our bygone eras! / At the present time, the entire life of our planet, from birth to death, with all its crimes and miseries, is being lived partly here and partly there, day by day, on myriad kindred planets. What we call 'progress' is confined to each particular world, and vanishes with it. Always and everywhere in the terrestrial arena, the same drama, the same setting, on the same narrow stage—a noisy humanity infatuated with its own grandeur, believing itself to be the universe and living in its prison as though in some immense realm, only to founder at an early date along with its globe, which has borne with deepest disdain the burden of human arrogance. The same monotony, the same immobility, on other heavenly bodies. The universe repeats itself endlessly and paws the ground in place. In infinity, eternity performs—imperturbably—the same routines." Auguste Blanqui, *L'Eternité par les astres: Hypothèse astronomique* (Paris, 1872), pp. 73–76. The elided paragraph dwells on the "consolation" afforded by the idea that the doubles of loved ones departed from Earth are at this very hour keeping our own doubles company on another planet.   [D7; D7a]

"Let us think this thought in its most terrible form: existence as it is, without meaning or aim, yet recurring inevitably without any finale into nothingness: *the eternal return* [p. 45]. . . . We deny end goals: if existence had one, it would have to have been reached." Friedrich Nietzsche, *Gesammelte Werke* (Munich ‹1926›), vol. 18 (*The Will to Power*, book 1), p. 46.[23]   [D8,1]

"The doctrine of eternal recurrence would have *scholarly* presuppositions." Nietzsche, *Gesammelte Werke* (Munich), vol. 18 (*The Will to Power*, book 1), p. 49.[24]   [D8,2]

"The old habit, however, of associating a goal with every event . . . is so powerful that it requires an effort for a thinker not to fall into thinking of the very aimlessness of the world as intended. This notion—that the world intentionally *avoids* a goal . . .—must occur to all those who would like to force on the world the capacity for *eternal novelty* [p. 369]. . . . The world, as force, may not be thought of as unlimited, for it *cannot* be so thought of. . . . Thus—the world also lacks the capacity for eternal novelty." Nietzsche, *Gesammelte Werke*, vol. 19 (*The Will to Power*, book 4), p. 370.[25]   [D8,3]

"The world . . . lives on itself: its excrements are its nourishment." Nietzsche, *Gesammelte Werke*, vol. 19 (*The Will to Power*, book 4), p. 371.[26]   [D8,4]

The world "without goal, unless the joy of the circle is itself a goal; without will, unless a ring feels good will toward itself." Nietzsche, *Gesammelte Werke*, vol. 19 (*The Will to Power*, book 4), p. 374.[27]   [D8,5]

On eternal recurrence: "The great thought as a Medusa head: all features of the world become motionless, a frozen death throe." Friedrich Nietzsche, *Gesammelte Werke* (Munich ‹1925›), vol. 14 (*Unpublished Papers, 1882–1888*), p. 188.

[D8,6]

"We have created the weightiest thought—now *let us create the being* for whom it is light and pleasing!" Nietzsche, *Gesammelte Werke* (Munich), vol. 14 *(Unpublished Papers, 1882–1888)*, p. 179. [D8,7]

Analogy between Engels and Blanqui: each turned to the natural sciences late in life. [D8,8]

"If the world may be thought of as a certain definite quantity of force and as a certain definite number of centers of force—and every other representation remains . . . *useless*—it follows that, in the great dice game of existence, it must pass through a calculable number of combinations. In infinite time, every possible combination would at some time or another be realized; more: it would be realized an infinite number of times. And since between every combination and its next recurrence all other possible combinations would have to take place, . . . a circular movement of absolutely identical series is thus demonstrated. . . . This conception is not simply a mechanistic conception; for if it were that, it would not condition an infinite recurrence of identical cases but a final state. *Because* the world has not reached this, mechanistic theory must be considered an imperfect and merely provisional hypothesis." Nietzsche, *Gesammelte Werke* (Munich ⟨1926⟩), vol. 19 (*The Will to Power*, book 4), p. 373.[28] [D8a,1]

In the idea of eternal recurrence, the historicism of the nineteenth century capsizes. As a result, every tradition, even the most recent, becomes the legacy of something that has already run its course in the immemorial night of the ages. Tradition henceforth assumes the character of a phantasmagoria in which primal history enters the scene in ultramodern get-up. [D8a,2]

Nietzsche's remark that the doctrine of eternal recurrence does not embrace mechanism seems to turn the phenomenon of the *perpetuum mobile* (for the world would be nothing else, according to his teachings) into an argument against the mechanistic conception of the world. [D8a,3]

On the problem of modernity and antiquity. "The existence that has lost its stability and its direction, and the world that has lost its coherence and its significance, come together in the will of 'the eternal recurrence of the same' as the attempt to repeat—on the peak of modernity, in a symbol—the life which the Greeks lived within the living cosmos of the visible world." Karl Löwith, *Nietzsches Philosophie der ewigen Wiederkunft des Gleichen* (Berlin, 1935), p. 83. [D8a,4]

L'Eternité par les astres was written four, at most five, years after Baudelaire's death (contemporaneously with the Paris Commune?).—This text shows what the stars are doing in that world from which Baudelaire, with good reason, excluded them. [D9,1]

The idea of eternal recurrence conjures the phantasmagoria of happiness from the misery of the Founders Years.[29] This doctrine is an attempt to reconcile the

mutually contradictory tendencies of desire: that of repetition and that of eternity. Such heroism has its counterpart in the heroism of Baudelaire, who conjures the phantasmagoria of modernity from the misery of the Second Empire.
[D9,2]

The notion of eternal return appeared at a time when the bourgeoisie no longer dared count on the impending development of the system of production which they had set going. The thought of Zarathustra and of eternal recurrence belongs together with the embroidered motto seen on pillows: "Only a quarter hour."
[D9,3]

Critique of the doctrine of eternal recurrence: "As natural scientist . . ., Nietzsche is a philosophizing dilettante, and as founder of a religion he is a 'hybrid of sickness and will to power'" [preface to *Ecce Homo*] (p. 83).[30] "The entire doctrine thus seems to be nothing other than an experiment of the human will and an attempt to eternalize all our doings and failings, an atheistic surrogate for religion. With this accords the homiletic style and the composition of *Zarathustra*, which down to its tiniest details often imitates the New Testament" (pp. 86–87). Karl Löwith, *Nietzsches Philosophie der ewigen Wiederkunft des Gleichen* (Berlin, 1935).
[D9,4]

There is a handwritten draft in which Caesar instead of Zarathustra is the bearer of Nietzsche's tidings (Löwith, p. 73). That is of no little moment. It underscores the fact that Nietzsche had an inkling of his doctrine's complicity with imperialism.
[D9,5]

Löwith calls Nietzsche's "new divination . . . the synthesis of divination from the stars with divination from nothingness, which is the last verity in the desert of the freedom of individual capacity" (p. 81).
[D9,6]

From "Les Etoiles" ‹The Stars›, by Lamartine:

> Thus these globes of gold, these islands of light,
> Sought instinctively by the dreaming eye,
> Flash up by the thousands from fugitive shadow,
> Like glittering dust on the tracks of night;
> And the breath of the evening that flies in its wake
> Sends them swirling through the radiance of space.
>
> All that we seek—love, truth,
> These fruits of the sky, fallen on earth's palate,
> Throughout your brilliant climes we long to see—
> Nourish forever the children of life;
> And one day man perhaps, his destiny fulfilled,
> Will recover in you all the things he has lost.

‹Alphonse de› Lamartine, *Oeuvres complètes*, vol. 1 (Paris, 1850), pp. 221, 224 (*Méditations*). This meditation closes with a reverie in which Lamartine is pleased to imagine himself transformed into a star among stars.
[D9a,1]

From "L'Infini dans les cieux" ‹Infinity in the Skies›, by Lamartine:

> Man, nonetheless, that indiscoverable insect,
> Crawling about the hollows of an obscure orb,
> Takes the measure of these fiery planets,
> Assigns them their place in the heavens,
> Thinking, with hands that cannot manage the compass,
> To sift suns like grains of sand.
>
> And Saturn bedimmed by its distant ring!

Lamartine, *Oeuvres complètes* (Paris, 1850), pp. 81–82, 82 (*Harmonies poétiques et religieuses*). [D9a,2]

Dislocation of hell: "And, finally, what is the place of punishments? All regions of the universe in a condition analogous to that of the earth, and still worse." Jean Reynaud, *Terre et ciel* (Paris, 1854), p. 377. This uncommonly fatuous book presents its theological syncretism, its *philosophie religieuse,* as the new theology. The eternity of hell's torments is a heresy: "The ancient trilogy of Earth, Sky, and Underworld finds itself reduced, in the end, to the druidical duality of Earth and Sky" (p. xiii). [D9a,3]

Waiting is, in a sense, the lined interior of boredom. (Hebel: boredom waits for death.) [D9a,4]

"I always arrived first. It was my lot to wait for her." J.-J. Rousseau, *Les Confessions*, ed. Hilsum (Paris ‹1931›), vol. 3, p. 115.[31] [D9a,5]

First intimation of the doctrine of eternal recurrence at the end of the fourth book of *Die fröhliche Wissenschaft:* "How, if some day or night a demon were to sneak after you into your loneliest loneliness and say to you: 'This life as you now live it and have lived it, you will have to live once more and innumerable times more; and there will be nothing new in it, but every pain and every joy and every thought and sigh and everything immeasurably small or great in your life must return to you— all in the same succession and sequence—even this spider and this moonlight between the trees, and even this moment and I myself. The eternal hourglass of existence is turned over and over, and you with it, a dust grain of dust.' Would you not . . . curse the demon who spoke thus? Or did you once experience a tremendous moment when you would have answered him: 'You are a god and never have I heard anything more godly!'"[32] Cited in Löwith, *Nietzsches Philosophie der ewigen Wiederkunft ‹des Gleichen* (Berlin, 1935)›, p. 57–58. [D10,1]

Blanqui's theory as a *répétition du mythe*—a fundamental example of the primal history of the nineteenth century. In every century, humanity has to be held back a grade in school. See the basic formulation of the problem of primal history, of *Urgeschichte,* in N3a,2; also N4,1. [D10,2]

"Eternal return" is the *fundamental* form of the *urgeschichtlichen,* mythic conscious-ness. (Mythic because it does not reflect.) [D10,3]

L'Eternité par les astres should be compared with the spirit of '48, as it animates Reynaud's *Terre et ciel.* With regard to this, Cassou: "On discovering his earthly destiny, man feels a sort of vertigo and cannot at first reconcile himself to this destiny alone. He must link it up to the greatest possible immensity of time and space. Only in the context of its most sweeping breadth will he intoxicate himself with being, with movement, with progress. Only then can he in all confidence and in all dignity pronounce the sublime words of Jean Reynaud: 'I have long made a practice of the universe.'" "We find nothing in the universe that cannot serve to elevate us, and we are genuinely elevated only in taking advantage of what the universe offers. The stars themselves, in their sublime hierarchy, are but a series of steps by which we mount progressively toward infinity." ‹Jean› Cassou, *Quar-ante-huit* ‹Paris, 1939›, pp. 49, 48. [D10,4]

Life within the magic circle of eternal return makes for an existence that never emerges from the auratic. [D10a,1]

As life becomes more subject to administrative norms, people must learn to wait more. Games of chance possess the great charm of freeing people from having to wait. [D10a,2]

The boulevardier (feuilletonist) has to wait, whereupon he really waits. Hugo's "Waiting is life" applies first of all to him. [D10a,3]

The essence of the mythical event is return. Inscribed as a hidden figure in such events is the futility that furrows the brow of some of the heroic personages of the underworld (Tantalus, Sisyphus, the Danaides). Thinking once again the thought of eternal recurrence in the nineteenth century makes Nietzsche the figure in whom a mythic fatality is realized anew. (The hell of eternal damnation has perhaps impugned the ancient idea of eternal recurrence at its most formida-ble point, substituting an eternity of torments for the eternity of a cycle.) [D10a,4]

The belief in progress—in an infinite perfectibility understood as an infinite ethical task—and the representation of eternal return are complementary. They are the indissoluble antinomies in the face of which the dialectical conception of historical time must be developed. In this conception, the idea of eternal return appears precisely as that "shallow rationalism" which the belief in progress is accused of being, while faith in progress seems no less to belong to the mythic mode of thought than does the idea of eternal return. [D10a,5]

E

[Haussmannization, Barricade Fighting]

> The flowery realm of decorations,
> The charm of landscape, of architecture,
> And all the effect of scenery rest
> Solely on the law of perspective.
>
> —Franz Böhle, *Theater-Catechismus, oder humoristische Erklärung ver-*
> *schiedener vorzüglich im Bühnenleben üblicher Fremdwörter* (Munich),
> p. 74

> I venerate the Beautiful, the Good, and all things great;
> Beautiful nature, on which great art rests—
> How it enchants the ear and charms the eye!
> I love spring in blossom: women and roses.
>
> —*Confession d'un lion devenu vieux* (Baron Haussmann, 1888)

> The breathless capitals
> Opened themselves to the cannon.
>
> —Pierre Dupont, *Le Chant des étudiants* (Paris, 1849)

The characteristic and, properly speaking, sole decoration of the Biedermeier room "was afforded by the curtains, which—extremely refined and compounded preferably from several fabrics of different colors—were furnished by the upholsterer. For nearly a whole century afterward, interior decoration amounts, in theory, to providing instructions to upholsterers for the tasteful arrangement of draperies." Max von Boehn, *Die Mode im XIX. Jahrhundert,* vol. 2 (Munich, 1907), p. 130. This is something like the interior's perspective on the window.
[E1,1]

Perspectival character of the crinoline, with its manifold flounces. At least five to six petticoats were worn underneath. [E1,2]

Peep-show rhetoric, perspectival figures of speech: "Incidentally, the figure of greatest effect, employed by all French orators from their podiums and tribunes, sounds pretty much like this: 'There was in the Middle Ages a book which concen-

trated the spirit of the times as a mirror concentrates the rays of the sun, a book which towered up in majestic glory to the heavens like a primeval forest, a book in which . . . a book for which . . . finally, a book which . . . by which and through which [the most long-winded specifications follow] . . . a book . . . a book . . . this book was the *Divine Comedy.*' Loud applause." Karl Gutzkow, *Briefe aus Paris* (Leipzig, 1842), vol. 2, pp. 151–152.   [E1,3]

Strategic basis for the perspectival articulation of the city. A contemporary seeking to justify the construction of large thoroughfares under Napoleon III speaks of them as "unfavorable 'to the habitual tactic of local insurrection.'" Marcel Poëte, *Une vie de cité* (Paris, 1925), p. 469. "Open up this area of continual disturbances." Baron Haussmann, in a memorandum calling for the extension of the Boulevard de Strasbourg to Châtelet. Emile de Labédollière, *Le Nouveau Paris,* p. 52. But even earlier than this: "They are paving Paris with wood in order to deprive the Revolution of building materials. Out of wooden blocks there will be no more barricades constructed." Gutzkow, *Briefe aus Paris,* vol. 1, pp. 60–61. What this means can be gathered from the fact that in 1830 there were 6,000 barricades.   [E1,4]

"In Paris . . . they are fleeing the arcades, so long in fashion, as one flees stale air. The arcades are dying. From time to time, one of them is closed, like the sad Passage Delorme, where, in the wilderness of the gallery, female figures of a tawdry antiquity used to dance along the shopfronts, as in the scenes from Pompeii interpreted by Guerinon Hersent. The arcade that for the Parisian was a sort of salon-walk, where you strolled and smoked and chatted, is now nothing more than a species of refuge which you think of when it rains. Some of the arcades maintain a certain attraction on account of this or that famed establishment still to be found there. But it is the tenant's renown that prolongs the excitement, or rather the death agony, of the place. The arcades have one great defect for modern Parisians: you could say that, just like certain paintings done from stifled perspectives, they're in need of air." Jules Claretie, *La Vie à Paris, 1895* (Paris, 1896), pp. 47ff.   [E1,5]

The radical transformation of Paris was carried out under Napoleon III mainly along the axis running through the Place de la Concorde and the Hôtel de Ville. It may be that the Franco-Prussian War of 1870 was a blessing for the architectural image of Paris, seeing that Napoleon III had intended to alter whole districts of the city. Stahr thus writes, in 1857, that one had to make haste now to see the old Paris, for "the new ruler, it seems, has a mind to leave but little of it standing." ⟨Adolf Stahr, *Nach fünf Jahren,* vol. 1 (Oldenburg, 1857), p. 36.⟩   [E1,6]

The stifled perspective is plush for the eyes. Plush is the material of the age of Louis Philippe. ▢ Dust and Rain ▢   [E1,7]

Regarding "stifled perspectives": "'You can come to the *panorama* to do drawings from nature,' David told his students." Emile de Labédollière, *Le Nouveau Paris* (Paris), p. 31.   [E1,8]

Among the most impressive testimonies to the age's unquenchable thirst for perspectives is the perspective painted on the stage of the opera in the Musée Grévin. (This arrangement should be described.)   [E1,9]

"Having, as they do, the appearance of walling-in a massive eternity, Hauss-mann's urban works are a wholly appropriate representation of the absolute gov-erning principles of the Empire: repression of every individual formation, every organic self-development, 'fundamental hatred of all individuality.'" J. J. Honeg-ger, *Grundsteine einer allgemeinen Kulturgeschichte der neuesten Zeit*, vol. 5 (Leipzig, 1874), p. 326. But Louis Philippe was already known as the *Roi-Maçon* ‹Mason King›.   [E1a,1]

On the transformation of the city under Napoleon III: "The subsoil has been profoundly disturbed by the installation of gas mains and the construction of sewers. . . . Never before in Paris have so many building supplies been moved about, so many houses and apartment buildings constructed, so many monuments restored or erected, so many façades dressed with cut stone. . . . It was necessary to act quickly and to take advantage of properties acquired at a very high cost: a double stimulus. In Paris, shallow basements have taken the place of deep cellars, which required excavations a full story deep. The use of concrete and cement, which was first made possible by the discoveries of Vicat, has contributed both to the reasonable cost and to the boldness of these substructions." E. Levasseur, *Histoire des classes ouvrières et de l'industrie en France de 1789 à 1870*, vol. 2 (Paris, 1904), pp. 528–529. ☐ Arcades ☐   [E1a,2]

"Paris, as we find it in the period following the Revolution of 1848, was about to become uninhabitable. Its population had been greatly enlarged and unsettled by the incessant activity of the railroad (whose rails extended further each day and linked up with those of neighboring countries), and now this population was suffo-cating in the narrow, tangled, putrid alleyways in which it was forcibly confined." ‹Maxime› Du Camp, *Paris*, vol. 6 ‹Paris, 1875›, p. 253.   [E1a,3]

Expropriations under Haussmann. "Certain barristers made a specialty of this kind of case. . . . They defended real estate expropriations, industrial expropria-tions, tenant expropriations, sentimental expropriations; they spoke of a roof for fathers and a cradle for infants. . . . 'How did you make your fortune?' a parvenu was asked: 'I've been expropriated,' came the response. . . . A new industry was created, which, on the pretext of taking in hand the interests of the expropriated, did not shrink from the basest fraud. . . . It sought out small manufacturers and equipped them with detailed account books, false inventories, and fake merchan-

dise that often was nothing more than logs wrapped in paper. It would even procure groups of customers to fill the shop on the day the jury made their prescribed
visit. It fabricated leases—exaggerated, extended, antedated—on sheets of old
paper bearing official stamps, which it had managed to procure. It would have
stores newly repainted and staffed with improvised clerks, whom it paid three
francs a day. It was a sort of midnight gang that rifled the till of the city government." Du Camp, *Paris*, vol. 6, pp. 255–256. [E1a,4]

Engels' critique of barricade tactics: "The most that the insurrection can actually
implement in the way of tactical practice is the correct construction and defense of
a single barricade." But "even in the classic period of street fighting, . . . the
barricade produced more of a moral than a material effect. It was a means of
shaking the steadfastness of the military. If it held on until this was attained, then
victory was won; if not, there was defeat." Friedrich Engels, Introduction to Karl
Marx, *Die Klassenkämpfe in Frankreich, 1848–1850* (Berlin, 1895), pp. 13, 14.[1]
[E1a,5]

No less retrograde than the tactic of civil war was the ideology of class struggle.
Marx on the February Revolution: "In the ideas of the proletarians, . . . who
confused the finance aristocracy with the bourgeoisie in general; in the imagination of good old republicans, who denied the very existence of classes or, at most,
admitted them as a result of the constitutional monarchy; in the hypocritical
phrases of the segments of the bourgeoisie up till now excluded from power—in
all these, the *rule of the bourgeoisie* was abolished with the introduction of the
republic. All the royalists were transformed into republicans, and all the million-
aires of Paris into workers. The phrase which corresponded to this imagined
liquidation of class relations was *fraternité*." Karl Marx, *Die Klassenkämpfe in
Frankreich* (Berlin, 1895), p. 29.[2] [E1a,6]

In a manifesto in which he proclaims the right to work, Lamartine speaks of
the "advent of the industrial Christ." *Journal des économistes*, 10 (1845), p. 212.[3]
▯ Industry ▯ [E1a,7]

"The reconstruction of the city . . . , by obliging the workers to find lodgings in
outlying *arrondissements*, has dissolved the bonds of neighborhood that previously united them with the bourgeoisie." Levasseur, *Histoire des classes ouvrières et de l'industrie en France*, vol. 2 ⟨Paris, 1904⟩, p. 775. [E2,1]

"Paris is musty and close." Louis Veuillot, *Les Odeurs de Paris* (Paris, 1914),
p. 14. [E2,2]

Parks, squares, and public gardens first installed under Napoleon III. Between
forty and fifty were created. [E2,3]

Construction in the Faubourg Saint-Antoine: Boulevard Prince Eugène, Boulevard Mazas, and Boulevard Richard Lenoir, as strategic axes.   [E2,4]

The heightened expression of the dull perspective is what you get in panoramas.
It signifies nothing to their detriment but only illuminates their style when Max
Brod writes: "Interiors of churches, or of palaces or art galleries, do not make for
beautiful panorama images. They come across as flat, dead, obstructed." ‹Max
Brod,› *Über die Schönheit hässlicher Bilder* (Leipzig, 1913), p. 63. An accurate
description, except that it is precisely in this way that the panoramas serve the
epoch's will to expression. ☐ Dioramas ☐   [E2,5]

On June 9, 1810, at the Théâtre de la Rue de Chartres, a play by Barré, Radet,
and Desfontaines is given its first performance. Entitled *Monsieur Durelief, ou Les
Embellissements de Paris*, it presents a series of rapid scenes as in a review, showing the changes wrought in Parisian life by Napoleon I. "An architect who is the
bearer of one of those significant names formerly in use on the stage, M. Durelief,
has fabricated a miniature Paris, which he intends to exhibit. Having labored
thirty years on this project, he thinks he has finished it at last; but suddenly a
'creative spirit' appears, and proceeds to prune and sharpen the work, creating
the need for incessant corrections and additions:

> This vast and wealthy capital,
> Adorned with his fine monuments,
> I keep as a cardboard model in my room,
> And I follow the embellishments.
> But always I find myself in arrears—
> By my word, it's getting desperate:
> Even in miniature, one cannot do
> What that man does full-scale."

The play ends with an apotheosis of Marie-Louise, whose portrait the goddess of
the city of Paris holds, as her loveliest ornament, high above the heads of the
audience. Cited in Théodore Muret, *L'Histoire par le théâtre, 1789–1851* (Paris,
1865), vol. 1, pp. 253–254.   [E2,6]

Use of omnibuses to build barricades. The horses were unharnessed, the passengers were put off, the vehicle was turned over, and the flag was fastened to an axle.
                                                                        [E2,7]

On the expropriations: "Before the war, there was talk of demolishing the Passage
du Caire in order to put a circus on the site. Today there's a shortage of funds, and
the proprietors (all forty-four of them) are hard to please. Let's hope there's a
shortage of funds for a long time to come and the proprietors become still harder to
please. The hideous gap of the Boulevard Haussmann at the corner of the Rue
Drouot, with all the charming houses it has brought down, should content us for
the moment." Paul Léautaud, "Vieux Paris," *Mercure de France* (October 15,
1927), p. 503.   [E2,8]

Haussmann and the Chamber of Deputies: "One day, in an excess of terror, they accused him of having created a *desert* in the very center of Paris! That desert was the Boulevard Sébastopol." Le Corbusier, *Urbanisme* (Paris ‹1925›), p. 149.[4]

[E2,9]

Very important: "Haussmann's Equipment"—illustrations in Le Corbusier, *Urbanisme*, p. 150.[5] Various shovels, picks, wheelbarrows, and so on.

[E2,10]

Jules Ferry, *Comptes fantastiques d'Haussmann* ‹Paris, 1868›. Pamphlet directed against Haussmann's autocratic management of finances.

[E2,11]

"The avenues [Haussmann] cut were entirely arbitrary: they were not based on strict deductions of the science of town planning. The measures he took were of a financial and military character." Le Corbusier, *Urbanisme* (Paris), p. 250.[6]

[E2a,1]

". . . the impossibility of obtaining permission to photograph an adorable wax-work figure in the Musée Grévin, on the left, between the hall of modern political celebrities and the hall at the rear of which, behind a curtain, is shown 'an evening at the theater': it is a woman fastening her garter in the shadows, and is the only statue I know of with eyes—the eyes of provocation." André Breton, *Nadja* (Paris, 1928), pp. 199–200.[7] Very striking fusion of the motif of fashion with that of perspective. ☐ Fashion ☐

[E2a,2]

To the characterization of this suffocating world of plush belongs the description of the role of flowers in interiors. After the fall of Napoleon Bonaparte, an attempt was made at first to return to rococo. But this was hardly feasible. The European situation after the Restoration was the following: "Typically, Corinthian columns are used almost everywhere. . . . This pomp has something oppressive about it, just as the restless bustle accompanying the city's transformation robs natives and foreigners alike of both breathing space and space for reflection. . . . Every stone bears the mark of despotic power, and all the ostentation makes the atmosphere, in the literal sense of the words, heavy and close. . . . One grows dizzy with this novel display; one chokes and anxiously gasps for breath. The feverish haste with which the work of several centuries is accomplished in a decade weighs on the senses." *Die Grenzboten,* Journal of politics and literature (‹Leipzig,› 1861), semester 2, vol. 3, pp. 143–144 ("Die Pariser Kunstausstellung von 1861 und die bildende Kunst des 19[ten] Jahrhunderts in Frankreich"). The author probably Julius Meyer. These remarks are aimed at Haussmann. ☐ Plush ☐

[E2a,3]

Remarkable propensity for structures that convey and connect—as, of course, the arcades do. And this connecting or mediating function has a literal and spatial as well as a figurative and stylistic bearing. One thinks, above all, of the way the Louvre links up with the Tuileries. "The imperial government has built practically no new independent buildings, aside from barracks. But, then, it has been all the more zealous in completing the barely begun and half-finished works of previous centuries. . . . At first sight, it seems strange that the government has made it its business to preserve existing monuments. . . . The government, however, does not aim to pass over the people like a storm; it wants to engrave itself lastingly in their existence. . . . Let the old houses collapse, so long as the old monuments remain." *Die Grenzboten* (1861), semester 2, vol. 3, pp. 139–141 ("Die Pariser Kunstausstellung von 1861"). ☐ Dream House ☐   [E2a,4]

Connection of the railroads to Haussmann's projects. From a memorandum by Haussmann: "The railway stations are today the principal entryways into Paris. To put them in communication with the city center by means of large arteries is a necessity of the first order." E. de Labédollière, *Histoire du nouveau Paris*, p. 32. This applies in particular to the so-called Boulevard du Centre: the extension of the Boulevard de Strasbourg to Châtelet by what is today the Boulevard Sébastopol.   [E2a,5]

Opening of the Boulevard Sébastopol like the unveiling of a monument. "At 2:30 in the afternoon, at the moment the [imperial] procession was approaching from the Boulevard Saint-Denis, an immense scrim, which had masked the entrance to the Boulevard de Sébastopol from this side, was drawn like a curtain. This drapery had been hung between two Moorish columns, on the pedestals of which were figures representing the arts, the sciences, industry, and commerce." Labédollière, *Histoire du nouveau Paris*, p. 32.   [E2a,6]

Haussmann's predilection for perspectives, for long open vistas, represents an attempt to dictate art forms to technology (the technology of city planning). This always results in kitsch.   [E2a,7]

Haussmann on himself: "Born in Paris, in the old Faubourg du Roule, which is joined now to the Faubourg Saint-Honoré at the point where the Boulevard Haussmann ends and the Avenue de Friedland begins; student at the Collège Henri IV and the old Lycée Napoléon, which is situated on the Montagne Sainte-Geneviève, where I later studied at the law school and, at odd moments, at the Sorbonne and the Collège de France. I took walks, moreover, through all parts of the city, and I was often absorbed, during my youth, in protracted contemplation of a map of this many-sided Paris, a map which revealed to me weaknesses in the network of public streets. / Despite my long residence in the provinces (no less than twenty-two years!), I have managed to retain my memories and impressions of former times, so that, when I was suddenly called upon, some days ago, to direct the transformation of the Capital of the Empire (over which the Tuileries and City Hall are currently at loggerheads), I felt myself, in fact, better prepared than one might have supposed to fulfill this complex mission, and ready, in any case, to enter boldly into the heart of the problems to be resolved." *Mémoires du Baron Haussmann*, vol. 2 (Paris, 1890), pp. 34–35. Demonstrates very well how it is often distance alone that, intervening between plan and work, enables the plan to be realized.   [E3,1]

How Baron Haussmann advanced upon the dream city that Paris still was in 1860. From an article of 1882: "There were hills in Paris, even on the Boulevards. . . . We lacked water, markets, light in those remote times—scarcely thirty years ago. Some gas jets had begun to appear—that is all. We lacked Churches, too. A number of the more ancient ones, including the most beautiful, were serving as stores, barracks, or offices. The others were wholly concealed by a growth of tumbledown hovels. Still, the Railroads existed; each day in Paris they discharged torrents of travelers who could neither lodge in our houses nor roam through our tortuous streets. / . . . He [Haussmann] demolished some *quartiers*—one might say, entire towns. There were cries that he would bring on the plague; he tolerated such outcries and gave us instead—through his well-considered architectural breakthroughs—air, health, and life. Sometimes it was a Street that he created, sometimes an Avenue or Boulevard; sometimes it was a Square, a Public Garden, a Promenade. He established Hospitals, Schools, Campuses. He gave us a whole river. He dug magnificent sewers." *Mémoires du Baron Haussmann*, vol. 2 (Paris, 1890), pp. x, xi. Extracts from an article by Jules Simon in *Le Gaulois*, May 1882. The numerous capital letters appear to be a characteristic orthographic intervention by Haussmann.   [E3,2]

From a conversation, later on, between Napoleon III and Haussmann. Napoleon: "How right you are to maintain that the People of France, who are generally thought so fickle, are at bottom the most routine people in the world!" "Yes, Sire, though I would add: with regard to things! . . . I myself am charged with the double offense of having unduly disturbed the Population of Paris by *bouleversant*, by 'boulevardizing,' almost all the *quartiers* of the city, and of having allowed it to keep the same profile in the same setting for too long." *Mémoires du Baron Haussmann*, vol. 2 (Paris, 1890), pp. 18–19. ⟨Compare E9,1.⟩   [E3,3]

From a discussion between Napoleon III and Haussmann on the latter's assuming his duties in Paris. Haussmann: "I would add that, although the population of Paris as a whole was sympathetic to the plans for the transformation—or, as it was called then, the 'embellishment'—of the Capital of the Empire, the greater part of the bourgeoisie and almost all the aristocracy were hostile." Why though? *Mémoires du Baron Haussmann*, vol. 2 (Paris, 1890), p. 52.   [E3,4]

"I left Munich on the sixth of February, spent ten days in archives in northern Italy, and arrived in Rome under a pouring rain. I found the Haussmannization of the city well advanced." *Briefe von Ferdinand Gregorovius an den Staatssekretär Hermann von Thile*, ed. Hermann von Petersdorff (Berlin, 1894), p. 110.
                                                                          [E3,5]

Nickname for Haussmann: "Pasha Osman." He himself makes the comment, with reference to his providing the city with spring water: "I must build myself an

aqueduct." Another bon mot: "My titles? . . . I have been named artist-demoli-
tionist." [E3,6]

"In 1864, defending the arbitrary character of the city's government, [Hauss-
mann] adopted a tone of rare boldness. 'For its inhabitants, Paris is either a great
marketplace of consumption, a giant stockyard of labor, an arena of ambitions, or
simply a rendezvous of pleasures. It is not their home. . . .' Then the statement
that polemicists will attach to his reputation like a stone: 'If there are a great many
who come to find an honorable situation in the city, . . . there are also others,
veritable nomads in the midst of Parisian society, who are absolutely destitute of
municipal sentiment.' And, recalling that everything—railroads, administrative
networks, branches of national activity—eventually leads to Paris, he concluded:
'It is thus not surprising that in France, country of aggregation and of order, the
capital almost always has been placed, with regard to its communal organization,
under an emergency regime.'" Georges Laronze, *Le Baron Haussmann* (Paris,
1932), pp. 172–173. Speech of November 28, 1864. [E3a,1]

Political cartoons represented "Paris as bounded by the wharves of the English
Channel and those of the south of France, by the highways of the Rhine valley and
of Spain; or, according to Cham, as the city which gets for Christmas the houses in
the suburbs! . . . One caricature shows the Rue de Rivoli stretching to the horizon." Georges Laronze, *Le Baron Haussmann* (Paris, 1932), pp. 148–149.
[E3a,2]

"New arteries . . . would link the center of Paris with the railroad stations, reducing congestion in the latter. Others would take part in the battle against poverty
and revolution; they would be strategic routes, breaking through the sources of
contagion and the centers of unrest, and permitting, with the influx of better air,
the arrival of an armed force, hence connecting, like the Rue de Turbigo, the
government with the barracks, and, like the Boulevard du Prince-Eugène, the
barracks with the suburbs." Georges Laronze, *Le Baron Haussmann*, pp. 137–
138. [E3a,3]

"An independent deputy, the comte de Durfort-Civrac, . . . objected that these
new boulevards, which were supposed to aid in repressing disturbances, would
also make them more likely because, in order to construct them, it was necessary
to assemble a mass of workers." Georges Laronze, *Le Baron Haussmann*, p. 133.
[E3a,4]

Haussmann celebrates the birthday—or name day (April 5)?—of Napoleon III.
"Running the length of the Champs-Elysées, from the Place de la Concorde to the
Etoile, there was a scalloped border of 124 sculpted arcades reposing on a double
row of columns. 'It is a reminiscence,' *Le Constitutionnel* sought to explain, 'of
Cordova and the Alhambra.' . . . The visual effect was thus very striking, with the
swirling branches of the fifty-six great streetlights along the avenue, the reflections

from the surfaces below, and the flickering of flames from the five hundred thousand jets of gas." Georges Laronze, *Le Baron Haussmann*, p. 119. ☐ Flâneur ☐
[E3a,5]

On Haussmann: "Paris now ceased forever to be a conglomeration of small towns, each with its distinctive physiognomy and way of life—where one was born and where one died, where one never dreamed of leaving home, and where nature and history had collaborated to realize variety in unity. The centralization, the megalomania, created an artificial city, in which the Parisian (and this is the crucial point) no longer feels at home; and so, as soon as he can, he leaves. And thus a new need arises: the craving for holidays in the country. On the other hand, in the city deserted by its inhabitants, the foreigner arrives on a specified date—the start of 'the season.' The Parisian, in his own town, which has become a cosmopolitan crossroads, now seems like one deracinated." Lucien Dubech and Pierre d'Espezel, ⟨*Histoire de Paris* (Paris, 1926),⟩ pp. 427–428.
[E3a,6]

"Most of the time, it was necessary to resort to a jury of expropriations. Its members, cavilers from birth, adversaries on principle, showed themselves generous with funds which, as they supposed, cost them nothing and from which each was hoping one day to benefit. In a single session where the city might offer a million and a half, the jury would demand from it nearly three million. The beautiful field of speculation! Who wouldn't want to do his part? There were barristers specializing in the matter; there were agencies guaranteeing (in return for a commission) a serious profit; there were operations for simulating a lease or a commercial transaction, and for doctoring account books." Georges Laronze, *Le Baron Haussmann* (Paris, 1932), pp. 190–191.
[E4,1]

From the *Lamentations* raised against Haussmann: "You will live to see the city grown desolate and bleak. / Your glory will be great in the eyes of future archaeologists, but your last days will be sad and bitter. / . . . / And the heart of the city will slowly freeze. / . . . / Lizards, stray dogs, and rats will rule over this magnificence. The injuries inflicted by time will accumulate on the gold of the balconies, and on the painted murals. / . . . . / And loneliness, the tedious goddess of deserts, will come and settle upon this new empire you will have made for her by so formidable a labor." *Paris désert: Lamentations d'un Jérémie haussmannisé* ⟨(Paris, 1868), pp. 7–8⟩.
[E4,2]

"The problem of the embellishment—or, more precisely, of the regeneration—of Paris arose about 1852. Until then, it had been possible to leave this great city in its state of dilapidation, but now it became necessary to deal with the matter. This was because, by a fortuitous coincidence, France and the countries around it were completing the construction of those long lines of railroad tracks which crisscross Europe." *Paris nouveau jugé par un flâneur* (Paris, 1868), p. 8.
[E4,3]

"I read, in a book which enjoyed great success last year, that the streets of Paris had been enlarged to permit ideas to circulate and, above all, regiments to pass.

This malicious statement (which comes in the wake of others) is the equivalent of saying that Paris has been strategically embellished. Well, so be it. . . . I do not hesitate to proclaim that strategic embellishments are the most admirable of embellishments." *Paris nouveau jugé par un flâneur* (Paris, 1868), pp. 21–22.
[E4,4]

"They say that the city of Paris has condemned itself to forced labor, in the sense that, if it ever ceased its various construction projects and forced its numerous workers to return to their respective provinces, from that day forward its toll revenues would diminish considerably." *Paris nouveau jugé par un flâneur* (Paris, 1868), p. 23.
[E4,5]

Proposal to link the right to vote for the Paris municipal council to proof of at least fifteen months' residence in the city. Part of the reasoning: "If you examine the matter closely, you will soon realize that it is precisely during the agitated, adventurous, and turbulent period of his existence . . . that a man resides in Paris." *Paris nouveau jugé par un flâneur*, p. 33.
[E4,6]

"It is understood that the follies of the city promote reason of state." Jules Ferry, *Comptes fantastiques d'Haussmann* (Paris, 1868), p. 6.
[E4,7]

"The concessions, worth hundreds of millions, are apportioned sub rosa. The principle of public adjudication is set aside, as is that of cooperation." Ferry, *Comptes fantastiques*, p. 11.
[E4a,1]

Ferry analyzes (pp. 21–23 of his *Comptes fantastiques*) the judgments rendered in cases of expropriation—judgments which, in the course of Haussmann's projects, took on a tendency unfavorable to the city. Following a decree of December 27, 1858—which Ferry regards as merely the normalization of an ancient right, but which Haussmann regards as the establishment of a new right—the city was denied the possibility of expropriating in their entirety properties which lay in the way of the new arteries. The expropriation was limited to those portions immediately required for the construction of the streets. In this way, the city lost out on the profits it had hoped to make from the sale of remaining plots of land, whose value was driven up by the construction.
[E4a,2]

From Haussmann's memorandum of December 11, 1867: "There is a deep-rooted and long-standing conviction that the last two methods of acquisition did not by any means automatically terminate the tenants' occupancy. But the Court of Appeals has ruled, in various decisions spanning the period 1861–1865, that, vis-à-vis the city, the judgment requiring the consent of the seller, taken together with the private contract, has the effect *ipso jure* of dissolving the lease of the tenants. As a consequence, many of the tenants doing business in houses acquired for the city by mutual agreement . . . have acted to annul their leases before the date of expropriation and have demanded to be immediately evicted and compensated. . . . The city . . . has had to pay enormous, unforeseen indemnities." Cited in Ferry, *Comptes fantastiques*, p. 24.   [E4a,3]

"Louis-Napoléon Bonaparte felt his vocation to be the securing of the 'bourgeois order.' . . . Industry and trade, the affairs of the bourgeoisie, were to prosper. An immense number of concessions were given out to the railroads; public subventions were granted; credit was organized. The wealth and luxury of the bourgeois world increased. The 1850s saw the . . . beginnings of the Parisian department stores: Au Bon Marché, Au Louvre, La Belle Jardinière. The turnover at Au Bon Marché—which, in 1852, was only 450,000 francs—rose, by 1869, to 21 million." Gisela Freund, "Entwicklung der Photographie in Frankreich" [manuscript].[8]
                                                                              [E4a,4]

Around 1830: "The Rue Saint-Denis and Rue Saint-Martin are the principal arteries in this *quartier*, a godsend for rioters. The war for the streets was deplorably easy there. The rebels had only to rip up the pavement and then pile up various objects: furniture from neighboring houses, crates from the grocer's, and, if need be, a passing omnibus, which they would stop, gallantly helping the ladies to disembark. In order to gain these Thermopylaes, it was thus necessary to demolish the houses. The line infantry would advance into the open, heavily armed and well equipped. A handful of insurgents behind a barricade could hold an entire regiment at bay." Dubech and d'Espezel, *Histoire de Paris* (Paris, 1926), pp. 365–366.
                                                                              [E4a,5]

Under Louis Philippe: "In the interior of the city, the governing idea seems to have been to rearrange the strategic lines that played so important a role in the historic days of July: the line of the quays, the line of the boulevards. . . . Finally, at the center, the Rue de Rambuteau, grandsire of the Haussmannized thoroughfares: it presented, at Les Halles, in the Marais, a breadth that seemed considerable then—thirteen meters." Dubech and d'Espezel, *Histoire de Paris* (Paris, 1926), pp. 382–383.   [E5,1]

Saint-Simonians: "During the cholera epidemic of 1832, they called for the demolition of crowded, closely built neighborhoods, which was excellent. But they demanded that Louis Philippe and Lafayette set the pace with shovel and pickaxe; the workers were supposed to work under the direction of uniformed Polytechnicians, and to the sound of military music; the most beautiful women in Paris were to come and offer their encouragement." Dubech and d'Espezel, *Histoire de Paris*, pp. 392–393. ▯ Industrial Development ▯ Secret Societies ▯   [E5,2]

"All efforts notwithstanding, the newly constructed buildings did not suffice to accommodate the expropriated. The result was a grave crisis in rents: they doubled. In 1851, the population was 1,053,000; after the annexation in 1866, it increased to more than 1,825,000. At the end of the Second Empire, Paris had 60,000 houses and 612,000 apartments, of which 481,000 were rented for less than

500 francs. Buildings grew taller, but ceilings became lower. The government had to pass a law requiring a minimum ceiling height of 2 meters 60 centimeters." Dubech and d'Espezel, pp. 420–421.   [E5,3]

"Scandalous fortunes were amassed by those in the prefect's inner circle. A legend attributes to Madame Haussmann a naive remark in a salon: 'It is curious that every time we buy a house, a boulevard passes through it.'" Dubech and d'Espezel, p. 423.   [E5,4]

"At the end of his wide avenues, Haussmann constructs—for the sake of perspective—various monuments: a Tribunal of Commerce at the end of the Boulevard Sébastopol, and bastard churches in all styles, such as Saint-Augustin (where Baltard copies Byzantine structures), a new Saint-Ambroise, and Saint-François-Xavier. At the end of the Chaussée d'Antin, the Church of La Trinité imitates the Renaissance style. Sainte-Clotilde imitates the Gothic style, while Saint-Jean de Belleville, Saint-Marcel, Saint-Bernard, and Saint-Eugène are all products of iron construction and the hideous embrasures of false Gothic. . . . Though Haussmann had some good ideas, he realized them badly. He depended heavily on perspectives, for example, and took care to put monuments at the end of his rectilinear streets. The idea was excellent, but what awkwardness in the execution! The Boulevard de Strasbourg frames the enormous flight of steps at the Tribunal of Commerce, and the Avenue de l'Opéra provides a vista of the porter's lodge at the Louvre." Dubech and d'Espezel, pp. 416, 425.   [E5,5]

"Above all, the Paris of the Second Empire is cruelly lacking in beauty. Not one of these great straight avenues has the charm of the magnificent curve of the Rue Saint-Antoine, and no house of this period affords anything like the tender delights of an eighteenth-century façade, with its rigorous and graceful orders. Finally, this illogical city is structurally weak. Already the architects are saying that the Opéra is cracked, that La Trinité is crumbling, and that Saint-Augustin is brittle." Dubech and d'Espezel, p. 427.   [E5,6]

"In Haussmann's time, there was a need for new roads, but not necessarily for the new roads he built. . . . The most striking feature of his projects is their scorn for historical experience. . . . Haussmann lays out an artificial city, like something in Canada or the Far West. . . . His thoroughfares rarely possess any utility and never any beauty. Most are astonishing architectural intrusions that begin just about anywhere and end up nowhere, while destroying everything in their path; to curve them would have been enough to preserve precious old buildings. . . . We must not accuse him of too much Haussmannization, but of too little. In spite of the megalomania of his theories, his vision was, in practice, not large enough. Nowhere did he anticipate the future. His vistas lack amplitude; his streets are too narrow. His conception is grandiose but not grand; neither is it just or provident." Dubech and d'Espezel, pp. 424–426.   [E5a,1]

"If we had to define, in a word, the new spirit that was coming to preside over the transformation of Paris, we would have to call it megalomania. The emperor and his prefect aim to make Paris the capital not only of France but of the world. . . . Cosmopolitan Paris will be the result." Dubech and d'Espezel, p. 404.   [E5a,2]

"Three facts will dominate the project to transform Paris: a strategic fact that demands, at the city's center, the break-up of the ancient capital and a new arrangement of the hub of Paris; a natural fact, the push westward; and a fact entailed by the systematic megalomania of the idea of annexing the suburbs." Dubech and d'Espezel, p. 406.   [E5a,3]

Jules Ferry, opponent of Haussmann, at the news of the surrender at Sedan: "The armies of the emperor are defeated!" Cited in Dubech and d'Espezel, p. 430.
     [E5a,4]

"Until Haussmann, Paris had been a city of moderate dimensions, where it was logical to let experience rule; it developed according to pressures dictated by nature, according to laws inscribed in the facts of history and in the face of the landscape. Brusquely, Haussmann accelerates and crowns the work of revolutionary and imperial centralization. . . . An artificial and inordinate creation, emerged like Minerva from the head of Jupiter, born amid the abuse of the spirit of authority, this work had need of the spirit of authority in order to develop according to its own logic. No sooner was it born, than it was cut off at the source. . . . Here was the paradoxical spectacle of a construction artificial in principle but abandoned in fact only to rules imposed by nature." Dubech and d'Espezel, pp. 443–444.   [E5a,5]

"Haussmann cut immense gaps right through Paris, and carried out the most startling operations. It seemed as if Paris would never endure his surgical experiments. And yet, today, does it not *exist* merely as a consequence of his daring and courage? His equipment was meager; the shovel, the pick, the wagon, the trowel, the wheelbarrow—the simple tools of every race . . . before the mechanical age. His achievement was truly admirable." Le Corbusier, *Urbanisme* (Paris ‹1925›), p. 149.[9]   [E5a,6]

The mighty seek to secure their position with blood (police), with cunning (fashion), with magic (pomp).   [E5a,7]

The widening of the streets, it was said, was necessitated by the crinoline. [E5a,8]

Manner of life among the masons, who often came from Marche or Limousin. (The description dates from 1851—before the great influx of this social stratum in the wake of Haussmann's works.) "The masons, whose way of life is more distinct than that of other emigrants, belong ordinarily to families of small farmer-householders established in the rural townships and provided with individual pasturage, allow-

Tools used by Haussmann's workers. Artist unknown. See E5a,6.

ing for the maintenance of at least one dairy cow per family. . . . During his so-journ in Paris, the mason lives with all the economy that is consistent with an unmarried situation; his provisions . . . come to approximately thirty-eight francs a month; his lodgings . . . cost only eight francs a month. Workers of the same profession ordinarily share a room, where they sleep two by two. This chamber is barely heated; it is lit by means of a tallow candle, which the lodgers take turns in buying. . . . Having reached the age of forty-five, the mason . . . henceforth re-mains on his property to cultivate it himself. . . . This way of life forms a marked contrast to that of the sedentary population; nevertheless, after some years, it tends visibly to alter. . . . Thus, during his stay in Paris, the young mason shows himself more willing than before to contract illegitimate unions, to spend money on clothing, and to frequent various gathering places and places of pleasure. As he becomes less capable of elevating himself to the condition of proprietor, he finds himself more susceptible to feelings of jealousy toward the upper classes of society. This depravity, to which he succumbs far from the influence of his family, . . . and in which the love of gain develops without the counterweight of religious sentiment, leads sometimes to the sort of coarseness found . . . among the sedentary workers of Paris." F. Le Play, *Les Ouvriers européens* (Paris, 1855), p. 277.   [E6,1]

On the politics of finance under Napoleon III: "The financial policy of the Empire has been consistently guided by two main concerns: to compensate for the insufficiency of normal revenues and to multiply the construction projects that keep capital moving and provide jobs. The trick was to borrow without opening the ledger and to undertake a great number of works without immediately overloading the budget. . . . Thus, in the space of seventeen years, the imperial government has had to procure for itself, in addition to the natural products of taxation, a sum of four billion three hundred twenty-two million francs. With the gathering of this enormous subsidy, whether by direct loans (on which it was necessary to pay interest) or by putting to work available capital (on which revenues were lost), there has resulted from these extra-budgetary operations an increase of debts and liabilities for the state." André Cochut, *Opérations et tendances financières du Second Empire* (Paris, 1868), pp. 13, 20–21.   [E6,2]

Already at the time of the June Insurrection, "they broke through walls so as to be able to pass from one house to another." Sigmund Engländer, *Geschichte der französischen Arbeiter-Associationen* (Hamburg, 1864), vol. 2, p. 287.   [E6,3]

"In 1852, . . . being a Bonapartist opened up all the pleasures in the world. It was these people who, humanly speaking, were the most avid for life; therefore, they conquered. Zola was agitated and amazed at this thought; suddenly, here was the formula for those men who, each in his own way and from his own vantage point, had founded an empire. Speculation (chief of the vital functions of this empire), unbridled self-enrichment, pleasure seeking—all three were glorified theatrically in exhibitions and festivals, which by degrees took on the aspect of a Babylon. And along with these brilliant masses taking part in the apotheosis, close behind them, . . . the obscure masses who were awaking and moving to the forefront." Heinrich Mann, *Geist und Tat* (Berlin, 1931), p. 167 ("Zola").   [E6a,1]

Around 1837, Dupin, in the Galerie Colbert, issued a series of colored lithographs (signed Pruché <?>, 1837) representing the theatergoing public in various postures. A few plates in the series: *Spectators in High Spirits, Spectators Applauding, Spectators Intriguing, Spectators Accompanying the Orchestra, Attentive Spectators, Weeping Spectators*.   [E6a,2]

Beginnings of city planning in Boissel's *Discours contre les servitudes publiques* <Discourse against Public Easements> of 1786: "Since the natural community of goods has been broken up and distributed, every individual property owner has built as he pleases. In the past, the social order would not have suffered from this trend, but now that urban construction proceeds at the entire discretion, and to the entire advantage, of the owners, there is no longer any consideration at all for the security, health, or comfort of society. This is particularly the case in Paris, where churches and palaces, boulevards and walkways are built in abundance, while housing for the great majority of inhabitants is relegated to the shadows. Boissel describes in graphic detail the filth and perils that threaten the poor pedestrian on the streets of Paris. . . . To this miserable arrangement of streets he now turns his attention, and he effectively solves the problem by proposing to transform the ground floors of houses into airy arcades, which would offer protection from the vehicles and the weather. He thus anticipates Bellamy's idea of 'one umbrella over all heads.'"[10] C. Hugo, "Der Sozialismus in Frankreich während der grossen Revolution," part 1, "François Boissel," *Die neue Zeit*, 11, no. 1 (Stuttgart, 1893), p. 813. [E6a,3]

On Napoleon III around 1851: "He is a socialist with Proudhon, a reformer with Girardin, a reactionary with Thiers, a moderate republican with the supporters of the republic, and an enemy of democracy and revolution with the legitimists. He promises everything and subscribes to everything." Friedrich Szarvady, *Paris*, vol. 1 [the only volume to appear] (Berlin, 1852), p. 401. [E6a,4]

"Louis Napoleon, . . . this representative of the lumpenproletariat and of every type of fraud and knavery, slowly draws . . . all power to himself. . . . With glad élan, Daumier reemerges. He creates the brilliant figure of Ratapoil, an audacious pimp and charlatan. And this ragged marauder, with his murderous cudgel forever concealed behind his back, becomes for Daumier the embodiment of the downfallen Bonapartist idea." Fritz Th. Schulte, "Honoré Daumier," *Die neue Zeit*, 32, no. 1 (Stuttgart ‹1913–1914›), p. 835. [E7,1]

With reference to the transformation of the city: "Nothing less than a compass is required, if you are to find your way." Jacques Fabien, *Paris en songe* (Paris, 1863), p. 7. [E7,2]

The following remark, by way of contrast, throws an interesting light on Paris: "Where money, industry, and riches are present, there are façades; the houses have assumed faces that serve to indicate the differences in class. In London, more than elsewhere, the distances are pitilessly marked. . . . A proliferation of ledges, bow windows, cornices, columns—so many columns! The column is nobility." Fernand Léger, "Londres," *Lu*, 5, no. 23 (June 7, 1935), p. 18. [E7,3]

> The distant native of the age-old Marais
> Rarely sets foot in the Quartier d'Antin,
> And from Ménilmontant, calm lookout point,
> He surveys Paris as from a height;
> His thrift and frugality won't let him budge
> From this spot where the gods have dropped him.

[Léon Gozlan,] *Le Triomphe des omnibus: Poème héroï-comique* (Paris, 1828), p. 7. [E7,4]

"Hundreds of thousands of families, who work in the center of the capital, sleep in the outskirts. This movement resembles the tide: in the morning the workers stream into Paris, and in the evening the same wave of people flows out. It is a melancholy image. . . . I would add . . . that it is the first time that humanity has assisted in a spectacle so dispiriting for the people." A. Granveau, *L'Ouvrier devant la société* (Paris, 1868), p. 63 ("Les Logements à Paris"). [E7,5]

July 27, 1830: "Outside the school, men in shirtsleeves were already rolling casks; others brought in paving stones and sand by wheelbarrow; a barricade was begun." G. Pinet, *Histoire de l'Ecole polytechnique* (Paris, 1887), p. 142. [E7a,1]

1833: "The plan to surround Paris with a belt of fortifications . . . aroused passionate interest at this time. It was argued that detached forts would be useless for the defense of the interior, and threatening only to the population. The opposition was universal. . . . Steps were taken to organize a large popular demonstration on July 27. Informed of these preparations . . . , the government abandoned the project. . . . Nevertheless, . . . on the day of the review, numerous cries of 'Down with the forts!' echoed in advance of the procession: '*A bas les forts détachés! A bas les bastilles!*'" G. Pinet, *Histoire de l'Ecole polytechnique* (Paris, 1887), pp. 214–215. The government ministers took their revenge with the affair of the "Gunpowder Conspiracy."[11] [E7a,2]

Engravings from 1830 show how the insurgents threw all sorts of furniture down on the troops from out of the windows. This was a feature especially of the battles on the Rue Saint-Antoine. Cabinet des Estampes. [E7a,3]

Rattier invokes a dream Paris, which he calls "the false Paris"—as distinguished from the real one: "the purer Paris, . . . the truer Paris, . . . the Paris that doesn't exist" (p. 99): "It is grand, at this moment in time, to set well-guarded Babylon walzing in the arms of Memphis, and to set London dancing in the embrace of Peking. . . . One of these fine mornings, France will have a rude awakening when it realizes it is confined within the walls of Lutetia, of which she forms but a crossroads. . . . The next day, Italy, Spain, Denmark, and Russia will be incorporated by decree into the Parisian municipality; three days later, the city gates will be pushed back to Novaya Zemlya and to the Land of the Papuans. Paris will be the world, and the universe will be Paris. The savannahs and the pampas and the Black Forest will compose the public gardens of this greater Lutetia; the Alps, the Pyrenees, the Andes, the Himalayas will be the Aventine and the scenic hills of this incomparable city—knolls of pleasure, study, or solitude. But all this is still nothing: Paris will mount to the skies and scale the firmament of firmaments; it will annex, as suburbs, the planets and the stars." Paul-Ernest de Rattier, *Paris n'existe pas* (Paris, 1857), pp. 47–49. These early fantasies should be compared with the satires on Haussmann published ten years later.   [E7a,4]

Already Rattier assigns to his false Paris "a unique and simple system of traffic control that links geometrically, and in parallel lines, all the avenues of this false Paris to a single center, the Tuileries—this being an admirable method of defense and of maintaining order." Paul-Ernest de Rattier, *Paris n'existe pas* (Paris, 1857), p. 55.   [E8,1]

"The false Paris has the good taste to recognize that nothing is more useless or more immoral than a riot. Though it may gain the upper hand for a few minutes, it is quelled for several centuries. Instead of occupying itself with politics, . . . it is peaceably absorbed in questions of economy. . . . A prince who is against fraud . . . knows . . . very well . . . that gold, a great deal of gold, is required . . . on our planet to build a stepladder to the sky." Paul-Ernest de Rattier, *Paris n'existe pas* (Paris, 1857), pp. 62, 66–67.   [E8,2]

July Revolution: "Fewer were felled . . . by bullets than by other projectiles. The large squares of granite with which Paris is paved were dragged up to the top floors of the houses and dropped on the heads of the soldiers." Friedrich von Raumer, *Briefe aus Paris und Frankreich im Jahre 1830* (Leipzig ‹1831›), vol. 2, p. 145.
                                                                                   [E8,3]

Report of a third party, in Raumer's book: "I saw a group of Swiss, who had been kneeling and begging for their lives, killed amid jeering, and I saw the stripped bodies of the gravely wounded thrown contemptuously onto the barricades to make them higher." Friedrich von Raumer, *Briefe aus Paris und Frankreich in Jahre 1830* (Leipzig, 1831), vol. 2, p. 256.   [E8,4]

Descriptions of barricades of 1830: Ch. Motte, *Révolutions de Paris, 1830: Plan figuratif des barricades ainsi que des positions et mouvements des citoyens armés et des troupes* (published by the author ‹Paris, 1830›).   [E8,5]

Caption for a plate in *Les Ruines de Paris: 100 photographies*, by A. Liébert (Paris, 1871), vol. 1: "Barricade of the Federates, Constructed by Gaillard Senior."   [E8,6]

"When the emperor . . . enters his capital, the fifty horses of his carriage are at a gallop; between the Gateway of Paris and his Louvre, he pauses under two thousand triumphal arches and passes before fifty colossi erected in his image. . . . And this idolizing of the sovereign by his subjects causes some dismay among the latter-day pious, to whom it occurs that their idols were never recipients of such homage." Arsène Houssaye, "Le Paris futur"; in ‹Dumas, Gautier, Houssaye, and others,› *Paris et les Parisiens au XIXe siècle* (Paris, 1856), p. 460.   [E8,7]

High daily allowances for the deputies under Napoleon III.   [E8,8]

"The 4,054 barricades of the 'Three Glorious Days' were made from . . .
8,125,000 paving stones." *Le Romantisme* [Exhibition catalogue (at the Bibliothèque Nationale), January 22–March 10, 1930; explanatory note to no. 635,
A. de Grandsagne and M. Plant, *Révolution de 1830, plan des combats de Paris*].
                                                                                               [E8,9]

"When, last year, thousands of workers marched through the streets of the capital
in a menacing calm; when, at a time of peace and commercial prosperity, they
interrupted the course of their work . . . , the government's first responsibility was
to take forceful measures against a disturbance that was all the more dangerous
for not knowing itself as such." L. de Carné, "Publications démocratiques et
communistes," *Revue des deux mondes*, 27 (Paris, 1841), p. 746.   [E8a,1]

"What fate does the present movement of society have in store for architecture?
Let us look around us. . . . Ever more monuments, ever more palaces. On all sides
rise up great stone blocks, and everything tends toward the solid, the heavy, the
vulgar; the genius of art is imprisoned by such an imperative, in which the imagination no longer has any room to play, can no longer be great, but rather is
exhausted in representing . . . the tiered orders on façades and in decorating
friezes and the borders of window frames. In the interior, one finds still more of
the court, more of the peristyle, . . . with the little rooms more and more confined,
the studies and boudoirs exiled to the niches under the spiral staircase, . . . where
they constitute pigeonholes for people; it is the cellular system applied to the
family group. The problem becomes how, in a given space, to make use of the least
amount of materials and to pack in the greatest number of people (while isolating
them all from one another). . . . This tendency—indeed, this fait accompli—is the
result of progressive subdividing. . . . In a word, *each for himself and each by
himself* has increasingly become the guiding principle of society, while the public
wealth . . . is scattered and squandered. Such are the causes, at this moment in
France, for the demise of monumentally scaled residential architecture. For private habitations, as they become narrower, are able to sustain but a narrow art.
The artist, lacking space, is reduced to making statuettes and easel paintings. . . .
In the presently emerging conditions of society, art is driven into an impasse where
it suffocates for lack of air. It is already suffering the effects of this new norm of
limited artistic facility, which certain souls, supposedly advanced, seem to regard
as the goal of their philanthropy. . . . In architecture, we do not make art for art's
sake; we do not raise monuments for the sole purpose of occupying the imagination
of architects and furnishing work for painters and sculptors. What is necessary,
then, is to apply the monumental mode of construction . . . to all the elements of
human dwelling. We must make it possible not only for a few privileged individuals
but for all people to live in palaces. And if one is to occupy a palace, one should
properly live there together with others, in bonds of association. . . . Where art is
concerned, therefore, it is only the association of all elements of the community

that can launch the immense development we are outlining." D. Laverdant, *De la mission de l'art et du rôle des artistes: Salon de 1845* (Paris, 1845), from the offices of *La Phalange*, pp. 13–15.   [E8a,2]

"For some time now, . . . there have been efforts to discover where this word *boulevard* could have come from. As for me, I am finally satisfied as to the etymology: it is merely a variant of the word *bouleversement* ‹commotion, upheaval›." Edouard Fournier, *Chroniques et légendes des rues de Paris* (Paris, 1864), p. 16.   [E9,1]

"Monsieur Picard, attorney for the city of Paris, . . . has energetically defended the interests of the city. What he has been presented with in the way of antedated leases at the moment of expropriations, what he has had to contend with in order to nullify fantastic titles and reduce the claims of the expropriated is almost beyond belief. A collier for the city one day placed before him a lease, antedated some years, on paper bearing official stamps. The simple man believed himself already in possession of a weighty sum for his shanty. But he did not know that this paper bore, in its watermark, the date of its manufacture. The attorney raised it to the light; it had been made three years after the date stamped." Auguste Lepage, *Les Cafés politiques et littéraires de Paris* (Paris ‹1874›), p. 89.   [E9,2]

Observations on the physiology of the uprising, in Niépovié's book: "Nothing has changed on the surface, but there is something unusual in the air. The cabriolets, omnibuses, and hackney coaches seem to have quickened their pace, and the drivers keep turning their heads as though someone were after them. There are more groups standing around than is usual. . . . People look at one another with anxious interrogation in their eyes. Perhaps this urchin or this worker hastening by will know something; and he is stopped and questioned. What's going on? ask the passersby. And the urchin or the worker responds, with a smile of utter indifference, 'They are gathering at the Place de la Bastille,' or 'They are gathering near the Temple' (or somewhere else), and then hurries off to wherever they are gathering. . . . On the sites themselves, the scene is pretty much as he said: the population has massed to such an extent that you can hardly get through. The pavement is strewn with sheets of paper. What is it? A proclamation of *Le Moniteur républicain,* which dates from the Year 50 of the one and indivisible French republic. People have gathered, you are told, to discuss the proclamation. The shops have not yet been closed; shots have not yet been fired. . . . Now then, behold the saviors. . . . All of a sudden, the holy battalion has halted before a house, and, just as quickly, the third-story windows are thrown open and packets of cartridges rain down. . . . The distribution is accomplished in the twinkling of an eye and, with that, the battalion is dispatched on the run—a portion to one side, a portion to the other. . . . Vehicles are no longer passing on the streets; there is less noise. And that's why one can hear, if I do not deceive myself . . . Listen, they're beating the drum. It is the call to arms. The authorities are roused."

Gaëtan Niépovié, *Etudes physiologiques sur les grandes métropoles de l'Europe occidentale: Paris* (Paris, 1840), pp. 201–204, 206. [E9,3]

A barricade: "At the entrance to a narrow street, an omnibus lies with its four wheels in the air. A pile of crates, which had served perhaps to hold oranges, rises to the right and to the left, and behind them, between the rims of the wheels and the openings, small fires are blazing, continually emitting small blue clouds of smoke." Gaëtan Niépovié, *Etudes physiologiques sur les grandes métropoles de l'Europe occidentale: Paris* (Paris, 1840), p. 207. [E9a,1]

1868: death of Meryon. [E9a,2]

"It has been said that Charlet and Raffet by themselves prepared the way for the Second Empire in France." Henri Bouchot, *La Lithographie* (Paris ‹1895›), pp. 8–9. [E9a,3]

From Arago's letter on the encirclement of Paris (Associations Nationales en Faveur de la Presse Patriote) [extract from *Le National* of July 21, 1833]: "All the projected forts, with regard to distance, would give access to the most populous districts of the capital" (p. 5). "Two of the forts, those of Italie and Passy, would be enough to set fire to all sections of Paris on the Left Bank of the Seine; . . . two others, Fort Philippe and Fort Saint-Chaumont, could cover the rest of the city with their circle of fire" (p. 8). [E9a,4]

In *Le Figaro* of April 27, ‹1936,› Gaëtan Sanvoisin cites this remark by Maxime Du Camp: "If there were only Parisians in Paris, there would be no revolutionaries." Compare with similar statements by Haussmann. [E9a,5]

"A one-act play by Engels, written in haste and performed in September 1847 at the German Alliance for Workers in Brussels, already represented a battle on the barricades in a German petty state—a battle which ended with the abdication of the prince and the proclamation of a republic." Gustav Mayer, *Friedrich Engels*, vol. 1, *Friedrich Engels in seiner Frühzeit*, 2nd ed. (Berlin ‹1933›), p. 269.[12]
[E9a,6]

During the suppression of the June Insurrection, artillery came to be used for the first time in street fighting. [E9a,7]

Haussmann's attitude toward the Parisian population recalls that of Guizot toward the proletariat. Guizot characterized the proletariat as the "external population." (See Georgi Plekhanov, "Über die Anfänge der Lehre vom Klassenkampf," *Die neue Zeit,* 21, no. 1 (Stuttgart, 1903), p. 285. [E9a,8]

The building of barricades appears in Fourier as an example of "nonsalaried but impassioned work." [E9a,9]

The practice of bamboozling the municipal expropriations committee became an industry under Haussmann. "Small traders and shopkeepers . . . would be supplied with false books and inventories, and, when necessary, their premises would (it turned out) be newly redecorated and refurnished; while during the visit of the committee to the premises, a constant stream of unexpected customers would pour in." S. Kracauer, *Jacques Offenbach und das Paris seiner Zeit* (Amsterdam, 1937), p. 254.[13]   [E10,1]

City planning in Fourier: "Each avenue, each street, should open onto some particular prospect, whether the countryside or a public monument. The custom of civilized nations—where streets come to an end with a wall, as in fortresses, or with a heap of earth, as in the newer sections of Marseilles—should be avoided. Every house that faces the street should be obliged to have ornamentation of the first class, in the gardens as well as on the buildings." Charles Fourier, *Cités ouvrières: Des modifications à introduire dans l'architecture des villes* ‹extracts from *La Phalange*› (Paris, 1849), p. 27.   [E10,2]

In connection with Haussmann: "The mythic structure develops rapidly: opposing the vast city is the legendary hero destined to conquer it. In fact, there are hardly any works of the period that do not contain some invocation inspired by the capital, and the celebrated cry of Rastignac[14] is of unusual simplicity. . . . The heroes of Ponson du Terrail are more lyrical in their inevitable apostrophe to the 'modern Babylon' (this is always the name used for Paris). See, for example, that . . . of the . . . false Sir Williams in the novel *Le Club des Valets de coeur:* 'O Paris, Paris! You are the true Babylon, the true arena of intellectual battle, the true temple where evil has its cult and its priesthood; and I am sure that the breath of the archangel of shadows passes over you eternally, like the winds over the infinity of the seas. O motionless tempest, ocean of stone, I want to be that dark eagle which, amid your angry waves, disdains the lightning and sleeps cheerfully on the thunderstorm, his great wing extended. I want to be the genius of evil, the vulture of the seas, of this most perfidious and tempestuous sea on which the human passions toss and unfurl.'" Roger Caillois, "Paris, mythe moderne," *Nouvelle Revue française*, 25, no. 284 (May 1, 1937), p. 686.   [E10,3]

Blanquist revolt of May 12, 1839: "He had waited a week to profit from the installation of new troops unfamiliar with the maze of Paris streets. The thousand men on whom he counted for the engagement were supposed to assemble between the Rue Saint-Denis and the Rue Saint-Martin. . . . Under a magnificent sun . . . toward three in the afternoon, in the midst of a burgeoning Sunday crowd, the revolutionary band all at once musters and appears. Immediately a vacuum, a silence, sets in around them." Gustave Geffroy, *L'Enfermé* (Paris, 1926), vol. 1, pp. 81–82.   [E10a,1]

In 1830, rope was used, among other things, to barricade the streets.   [E10a,2]

Rastignac's famous challenge (cited in Messac ‹Le "Detective Novel" et l'influence de la pensée scientifique [Paris, 1929]›, pp. 419–420): "Eugène, now alone, walked a few steps to the topmost part of the graveyard. He saw Paris, spread windingly along the two banks of the Seine. Lights were beginning to twinkle. His gaze fixed itself almost avidly on the space between the column in the Place Vendôme and the cupola of Les Invalides. There lived the world into which he had wished to penetrate. He fastened on the murmurous hive a look that seemed already to be sucking the honey from it, and uttered these words: 'Now I'm ready for you!'"[15]   [E10a,3]

To the theses of Haussmann corresponds the tabulation of Du Camp, according to which the population of Paris during the Commune was 75.5 percent foreigners and provincials.   [E10a,4]

For the Blanquist putsch of August 14, 1870, 300 revolvers and 400 heavy daggers were made available. It is characteristic of the street fighting in this period that the workers preferred daggers to revolvers.   [E10a,5]

Kaufmann places at the head of his chapter entitled "Architectural Autonomy" an epigraph from Le Contrat social: "a form . . . in which each is united with all, yet obeys only himself and remains as free as before.—Such is the fundamental problem that the social contract solves" (p. 42).[16] In this chapter (p. 43): "[Ledoux] justifies the separation of the buildings in the second project for Chaux with the words: 'Return to principle. . . . Consult nature; man is everywhere isolated' (Architecture, p. 70). The feudal principle of prerevolutionary society . . . can have no further validity now. . . . The autonomously grounded form of every object makes all striving after theatrical effect appear senseless. . . . At a stroke, it would seem, . . . the Baroque art of the prospect disappears from sight." E. Kaufmann, Von Ledoux bis Le Corbusier (Vienna and Leipzig, 1933), p. 43.   [E10a,6]

"The renunciation of the picturesque has its architectural equivalent in the refusal of all prospect-art. A highly significant symptom is the sudden diffusion of the silhouette. . . . Steel engraving and wood engraving supplant the mezzotint, which had flourished in the Baroque age. . . . To anticipate our conclusions, . . . let it be said that the autonomous principle retains its efficacy . . . in the first decades after the architecture of the Revolution, becoming ever weaker with the passage of time until, in the later decades of the nineteenth century, it is virtually unrecognizable." Emil Kaufmann, Von Ledoux bis Le Corbusier (Vienna and Leipzig, 1933), pp. 47, 50.   [E11,1]

Napoléon Gaillard: builder of the mighty barricade that, in 1871, stood at the entrance of the Rue Royale and the Rue de Rivoli.   [E11,2]

"At the corner of the Rue de la Chaussée-d'Antin and the Rue Basse-du-Rampart, there sits a house that is remarkable for the caryatids on the façade facing the Rue

Basse-du-Rampart. Because this latter street must disappear, the magnificent house with the caryatids, built only twenty years ago, is going to be demolished. The jury for expropriations grants the three million francs demanded by the owner and approved by the city. Three million! What a useful and productive expenditure!" Auguste Blanqui, *Critique sociale*, vol. 2, *Fragments et notes* (Paris, 1885), p. 341. [E11,3]

"Against Paris. Obdurate scheme to clear out the city, to disperse its population of workers. Hypocritically—on a humanitarian pretext—they propose to redistribute throughout the 38,000 townships of France the 75,000 workers affected by unemployment. 1849." Blanqui, *Critique sociale*, vol. 2, *Fragments et notes* (Paris, 1885), p. 313. [E11,4]

"A Monsieur d'Havrincourt recently expounded on the strategic theory of civil war. The troops must never be allowed to spend much time in the main areas of disturbance. They are corrupted by contact with the rebels and refuse to fire freely when repression becomes necessary. . . . The best system: construct citadels dominating the suspect towns and ready at any moment to crush them. Soldiers must be kept garrisoned, away from the popular contagion." Auguste Blanqui, *Critique sociale*, vol. 2 (Paris, 1885), pp. 232–233 ("Saint-Etienne, 1850").
[E11,5]

"The Haussmanization of Paris and the provinces is one of the great plagues of the Second Empire. No one will ever know how many thousands of unfortunates have lost their lives as a consequence of deprivations occasioned by these senseless constructions. The devouring of so many millions is one the principal causes of the present distress. . . . 'When building goes well, everything goes well,' runs a popular adage, which has attained the status of economic axiom. By this standard, a hundred pyramids of Cheops, rising together into the clouds, would attest to overflowing prosperity. Singular calculus. Yes, in a well-ordered state, where thrift did not strangle exchange, construction would be the true measure of public fortune. For then it would reveal a growth in population and an excess of labor that . . . would lay a foundation for the future. In any other circumstances, the trowel merely betrays the murderous fantasies of absolutism, which, when its fury for war momentarily slackens, is seized by the fury for building. . . . All mercenary tongues have been loosed in a chorus of celebration for the great works that are renewing the face of Paris. Nothing so sad, so lacking in social spontaneity, as this vast shifting of stones by the hand of despotism. There is no more dismal symptom of decadence. In proportion as Rome collapsed in agony, its monuments grew more numerous and more colossal. It was building its own sepulcher and making ready to die gloriously. But as for the modern world—it has no wish to die, and human stupidity is nearing its end. People are weary of grandiose homicidal acts. The projects that have so disrupted the capital, conditioned as they are on repression and vanity, have failed the future no less than the present." A. Blanqui,

Critique sociale, vol. 1, *Capital et travail* (Paris, 1885), pp. 109–111 (conclusion of "Le Luxe"). The foreword to *Capital et travail* is dated May 26, 1869.

[E11a,1]

"The illusions about the fantastic structures are dispelled. Nowhere are there materials other than the hundred *simple bodies*. . . . It is with this meager assortment that the universe is necessarily made and remade, without respite. M. Haussmann had just as much to rebuild Paris with; he had precisely these materials. It is not variety that stands out in his constructions. Nature, which also demolishes in order to reconstruct, does a little better with the things it creates. It knows how to make such good use of its meager resources that one hesitates to say there is a limit to the originality of its works." A. Blanqui, *L'Eternité par les astres: Hypothèse astronomique* (Paris, 1872), p. 53.

[E11a,2]

Die neue Weltbühne, 34, no. 5 (February 3, 1938), in an essay by H. Budzislawski, "Croesus Builds" (pp. 129–130), quotes Engels' "Zur Wohnungsfrage" ‹On the Housing Question› of 1872: "In reality the bourgeoisie has only one method of settling the housing question after *its* fashion—that is to say, of settling it in such a way that the solution continually poses the question anew. This method is called 'Haussmann.' By the term 'Haussmann,' I do not mean merely the specifically Bonapartist manner of the Parisian Haussmann—cutting long, straight, broad streets right through closely built working-class neighborhoods and lining them on both sides with big luxurious buildings, the intention having been, apart from the strategic aim of making barricade fighting more difficult, to develop a specifically Bonapartist building-trades proletariat dependent on the government, and to turn the city into a luxury city pure and simple. By 'Haussmann' I mean the practice, which has now become general, of making breaches in the working-class neighborhoods of our big cities, particularly in those which are centrally situated. . . . The result is everywhere the same: the most scandalous alleys . . . disappear to the accompaniment of lavish self-glorification by the bourgeoisie . . . , but—they reappear at once somewhere else, often in the immediate neighborhood." [17]—With this goes the prize question: Why was the mortality rate in London so much higher in the new working-class districts (around 1890?) than in the slums?—Because people went hungry so that they could afford the high rents. And Peladan's observation: the nineteenth century forced everyone to secure lodgings for himself, even at the cost of food and clothing.

[E12,1]

Is it true, as Paul Westheim maintains in his article "Die neue Siegesallee" (*Die neue Weltbühne,* 34, no. 8, p. 240), that Haussmann spared Parisians the misery of large blocks of flats?

[E12,2]

Haussmann who, faced with the city plan of Paris, takes up Rastignac's cry of "A nous deux maintenant!"

[E12,3]

"The new boulevards have introduced light and air into unwholesome districts, but have done so by wiping out, along their way, almost all the courtyards and gardens—which moreover have been ruled out by the progressive rise in real estate prices." Victor Fournel, *Paris nouveau et Paris futur* (Paris, 1868), p. 224 ("Conclusion").   [E12,4]

The old Paris bewails the monotony of the new streets; whereupon the new Paris responds:

> Why all these reproaches? . . .
> Thanks to the straight line, the ease of travel it affords,
> One avoids the shock of many a vehicle,
> And, if one's eyes are good, one likewise avoids
> The fools, the borrowers, the bailiffs, the bores;
> Last but not least, down the whole length of the avenue,
> Each passerby now avoids the others, or nods from afar.

M. Barthélemy, *Le Vieux Paris et le nouveau* (Paris, 1861), pp. 5–6.   [E12a,1]

The old Paris: "The rent devours all, and they go without meat." M. Barthélemy, *Le Vieux Paris et le nouveau* (Paris, 1861), p. 8.   [E12a,2]

Victor Fournel, in his *Paris nouveau et Paris futur* (Paris, 1868), particularly in the section "Un chapitre des ruines de Paris moderne," gives an idea of the scale on which Haussmann engineered destruction in Paris. "Modern Paris is a parvenu that goes back no further in time than its own beginnings, and that razes the old palaces and old churches to build in their place beautiful white houses with stucco ornaments and pasteboard statues. In the previous century, to write the annals of the monuments of Paris was to write the annals of Paris itself, from its origins up through each of its epochs; soon, however, it will be . . . merely to write the annals of the last twenty years of our own existence" (pp. 293–294).   [E12a,3]

Fournel, in his eminent demonstration of Haussmann's misdeeds: "From the Faubourg Saint-Germain to the Faubourg Saint-Honoré, from the Latin Quarter to the environs of the Palais-Royal, from the Faubourg Saint-Denis to the Chaussée d'Antin, from the Boulevard des Italiens to the Boulevard du Temple, it seemed, in each case, that you were passing from one continent to another. It all made for so many distinct small cities within the capital city—a city of study, a city of commerce, a city of luxury, a city of refuge, a city of movement and of popular pleasures—all of them nonetheless linked to one another by a host of gradations and transitions. And this is what is being obliterated . . . by the construction everywhere of the same geometrical and rectilinear street, with its unvarying mile-long perspective and its continuous rows of houses that are always the same house." Victor Fournel, *Paris nouveau et Paris futur*, pp. 220–221 ("Conclusion").   [E12a,4]

"They . . . transplant the Boulevard des Italiens in its entirety to the Montagne Sainte-Geneviève—with about as much utility and profit as a hothouse flower in the forest—and they create Rues de Rivoli in the ancient city center, which has no need of them. Eventually this cradle of the capital, having been demolished, will comprise at most a barracks, a church, a hospital, and a palace." Victor Fournel, *Paris nouveau et Paris futur* (Paris, 1868), p. 223. The last thought echoes a stanza from Hugo's "A l'Arc de Triomphe." [E13,1]

Haussmann's work is accomplished today, as the Spanish war makes clear, by quite other means. [E13,2]

Temporary tenants under Haussmann: "The industrial nomads among the new ground-floor Parisians fall into three principal categories: commercial photographers; dealers in bric-à-brac who run bazaars and cheap shops; and exhibitors of curiosities, particularly of female giants. Up to now, these interesting personages have numbered among those who have profited the most from the transformation of Paris." Victor Fournel, *Paris nouveau et Paris futur* (Paris, 1868), pp. 129–130 ("Promenade pittoresque à travers le nouveau Paris"). [E13,3]

"The covered market of Les Halles, by universal consent, constitutes the most irreproachable construction of the past dozen years. . . . It manifests one of those logical harmonies which satisfy the mind by the obviousness of its signification." Victor Fournel, *Paris nouveau et Paris futur*, p. 213. [E13,4]

Already Tissot invites speculation: "The city of Paris is supposed to make a series of loans totaling hundreds of millions of francs and, at the same time, purchase the better part of a *quartier* in order to rebuild it in a manner conforming to the requirements of taste, hygiene, and ease of communication. Here is matter for speculation." Amédée de Tissot, *Paris et Londres comparés* (Paris, 1830), pp. 46–47. [E13,5]

In *Le Passé, le présent, l'avenir de la Republique* (Paris, 1850), p. 31 (cited in ⟨Jean⟩ Cassou, *Quarante-huit* ⟨Paris, 1939⟩, pp. 174–175), Lamartine already speaks of the "nomadic, indecisive, and dissolute city dwellers who are corrupted by their idleness in public places and who go whichever way the wind of factionalism blows, heeding the voice of him who shouts the loudest." [E13a,1]

Stahl on the Parisian tenement houses: "It was already [in the Middle Ages] an overpopulated metropolis that was squeezed within the tight belt of a walled fortification. For the mass of people, there were neither single-family houses nor separately owned houses nor even modest cottages. Buildings of many stories were erected on the narrowest of lots, generally allowing only two, often only one, front window (though elsewhere three-window houses were the rule). These buildings usually remained wholly unadorned, and when they did not simply come to a stop at the top, there was at most a single gable affixed there. . . . On the roofs, the situation was strange enough, with unassuming superstructures and mansardes nestled next to the chimney flues, which were placed extremely close to one another." Stahl sees, in the freedom of the roofing structures—a freedom to which modern architects in Paris likewise adhere—"a fantastic and thoroughly Gothic element." Fritz Stahl, *Paris* (Berlin ‹1929›), pp. 79–80.   [E13a,2]

"Everywhere . . . the peculiar chimneys serve only to heighten the disorder of these forms [the mansardes]. This is . . . a trait common to all Parisian houses. Even the oldest of them have that high wall from which the tops of the chimney flues extend. . . . We are far removed here from the Roman style, which has been taken to be the foundation of Parisian architecture. We are in fact nearer its opposite, the Gothic, to which the chimneys clearly allude. . . . If we want to call this more loosely a "northern style," then we can see that a second . . . northern element is present to mitigate the Roman character of the streets. This is none other than the modern boulevards and avenues . . . , which are planted, for the most part, with trees; . . . and rows of trees, of course, are a feature of the northern city." Fritz Stahl, *Paris* (Berlin), pp. 21–22.   [E13a,3]

In Paris, the modern house has "developed gradually out of the preexisting one. This could happen because the preexisting one was already a large townhouse of the type created here . . . in the seventeenth century on the Place Vendôme, where today the residential palaces of former times have come to harbor business establishments of every kind—without having suffered the least alteration to their façades." Fritz Stahl, *Paris* (Berlin), p. 18.   [E14]

A plea for Haussmann: "It is well known that . . . the nineteenth century entirely lost, together with other fundamental concepts of art, the concept of the city as . . . a unified whole. Henceforth there was no longer any city planning. New buildings were introduced into the old network of streets without a plan, and they were expanded without a plan. . . . What can properly be called the architectural history of a city . . . was in this way everywhere terminated. Paris is the only exception, and as such it was greeted with incomprehension and disapproval" (pp. 13–14). "Three generations failed to understood what city planning is. We know what it is, but in our case this knowledge generally brings only regret for missed opportunities. . . . These considerations make it possible to appreciate the only city planner of genius in the modern world—a man, moreover, who indirectly created all the American metropolises" (pp. 168–169). "It is solely in this perspective, then, that Haussmann's great thoroughfares take on their real meaning. With them, the new city . . . intervenes in the old and, in a certain sense, draws on the old, without otherwise violating its character. Thus, these thoroughfares may be said to have, along with their utility, an aesthetic effect, such that the old city and the new are not left standing opposite each other, as is the case everywhere else, but are drawn together into one. The moment you come out of some ancient lane onto one of Haussmann's avenues, you're in contact with this newer Paris—the

Paris of the past three centuries. For Haussmann took over not only the form of the avenue and boulevard but also the form of the house from the imperial capital laid out by Louis XIV. That is why his streets can perform the function of making the city into a conspicuous unity. No, he has not destroyed Paris; rather, he has brought it to completion. . . . This must be acknowledged even when you realize how much beauty was sacrificed. . . . Haussmann was assuredly a fanatic—but his work could be accomplished only by a fanatic." Fritz Stahl, *Paris: Eine Stadt als Kunstwerk* (Berlin), pp. 173–174. [E14a]

[Iron Construction]

Each epoch dreams the one to follow.
—Michelet, "Avenir! Avenir!" (*Europe*, 73, p. 6)

Dialectical deduction of iron construction: it is contrasted both with Greek construction in stone (raftered ceiling) and with medieval construction in stone (vaulted ceiling). "Another art, in which another static principle establishes a tone even more magnificent than that of the other two, will struggle from the womb of time to be born. . . . A new and unprecedented ceiling system, one that will naturally bring in its wake a whole new realm of art forms, can . . . make its appearance only after some particular material—formerly neglected, if not unknown, as a basic principle in that application—begins to be accepted. Such a material is . . . iron, which our century has already started to employ in this sense. In proportion as its static properties are tested and made known, iron is destined to serve, in the architecture of the future, as the basis for the system of ceiling construction; and with respect to statics, it is destined to advance this system as far beyond the Hellenic and the medieval as the system of the arch advanced the Middle Ages beyond the monolithic stone-lintel system of antiquity. . . . If the static principle of force is thus borrowed from vaulted constructions and put to work for an entirely new and unprecedented system, then, with regard to the art forms of the new system, the formal principle of the Hellenic mode must find acceptance." *Zum hundertjährigen Geburtstag Karl Boettichers* (Berlin, 1906), pp. 42, 44–46. (The principle of Hellenic architecture and Germanic architecture as carried over into the architecture of our time.)   [F1,1]

Glass before its time, premature iron. In the arcades, both the most brittle and the strongest materials suffered breakage; in a certain sense, they were deflowered. Around the middle of the past century, it was not yet known how to build with glass and iron. Hence, the light that fell from above, through the panes between the iron supports, was dirty and sad.   [F1,2]

"The mid-1830s see the appearance of the first iron furniture, in the form of bedsteads, chairs, small tables, *jardinières*; and it is highly characteristic of the epoch that this furniture was preferred because it could be made to imitate perfectly any type of wood. Shortly after 1840, fully padded furniture appears in France, and with it the upholstered style becomes dominant." Max von Boehn, *Die Mode im XIX. Jahrhundert,* vol. 2 (Munich, 1907), p. 131.   [F1,3]

The two great advances in technology—gas[1] and cast iron—go together. "Aside from the great quantity of lights maintained by the merchants, these galleries are illuminated in the evening by thirty-four jets of hydrogen gas mounted on cast-iron volutes on the pilasters." The quote is probably referring to the Galerie de l'Opéra. J. A. Dulaure, *Histoire de Paris . . . depuis 1821 jusqu'à nos jours,* vol. 2 ‹(Paris, 1835), p. 29›.   [F1,4]

"The stagecoach gallops up to the quay, by the Seine. A bolt of lightning flashes over the Pont d'Austerlitz. The pencil comes to rest." Karl Gutzkow, *Briefe aus Paris,* vol. 2 ‹Leipzig, 1842›, p. 234. The Austerlitz Bridge was one of the first iron structures in Paris. With the lightning flash above, it becomes an emblem of the dawning technological age. Close by, the stagecoach with its team of black horses, whose hoofs strike romantic sparks. And the pencil of the German author who sketches them: a splendid vignette in the style of Grandville.
                    [F1,5]

"In reality, we know of no beautiful theaters, no beautiful railroad stations, no beautiful exhibition halls, no beautiful casinos—that is to say, no beautiful houses of industry or of frivolity." Maurice Talmeyr, *La Cité du sang* (Paris, 1908), p. 277.   [F1,6]

Magic of cast iron: "Hahblle[2] was able then to convince himself that the ring around this planet was nothing other than a circular balcony on which the inhabitants of Saturn strolled in the evening to get a breath of fresh air." Grandville, *Un autre monde* (Paris ‹1844›), p. 139. ▢ Hashish ▢   [F1,7]

In mentioning factories built in the style of residential houses, and other things of this kind, we must take into account the following parallel from the history of architecture: "I said earlier that in the period of 'sensibility,' temples were erected to friendship and tenderness; as taste subsequently turned to the classical style, a host of temples or temple-like buildings immediately sprang up in gardens, in parks, on hills. And these were dedicated not only to the Graces or to Apollo and the Muses; farm buildings, too, including barns and stables, were built in the style of temples." Jacob Falke, *Geschichte des modernen Geschmacks* (Leipzig, 1866), pp. 373–374. There are thus masks of architecture, and in such masquerade the architecture of Berlin around 1800 appears on Sundays, like a ghost at a costume ball.   [F1a,1]

"Every tradesman imitates the materials and methods of others, and thinks he has accomplished a miracle of taste when he brings out porcelain cups resembling the work of a cooper, glasses resembling porcelains, gold jewelry like leather

thongs, iron tables with the look of rattan, and so on. Into this arena rushes the confectioner as well—quite forgetting his proper domain, and the touchstone of his taste—aspiring to be a sculptor and architect." Jacob Falke, *Geschichte des modernen Geschmacks,* p. 380. This perplexity derived in part from the superabundance of technical processes and new materials that had suddenly become available. The effort to assimilate them more thoroughly led to mistakes and failures. On the other hand, these vain attempts are the most authentic proof that technological production, at the beginning, was in the grip of dreams. (Not architecture alone but all technology is, at certain stages, evidence of a collective dream.)
[F1a,2]

"With iron construction—a secondary genre, it is true—a new art was born. The east-side railroad station designed by Duquesnay, the Gare de l'Est, was in this regard worthy of architects' attention. The use of iron greatly increased in that period, thanks to the new combinations to which it lent itself. Two quite different but equally remarkable works in this genre deserve to be mentioned first: the Bibliothèque Sainte-Geneviève and the cental marketplace, Les Halles. The latter is . . . a veritable archetype: reproduced several times in Paris and other cities, it proceeded, as the Gothic cathedral had done, to appear all over France. . . . Notable improvements can be observed in the details. The monumental lead-work has become rich and elegant; the railings, candelabras, and mosaic flooring all testify to an often successful quest for beauty. Technological advances have made it possible to sheathe cast iron with copper, a process which must not be abused. Advances in luxury have led, even more successfully, to the replacement of cast iron by bronze, something which has turned the streetlamps in certain public places into *objets d'art.*" ☐ Gas ☐ Note to this passage: "In 1848, 5,763 tons of iron entered Paris; in 1854, 11,771; in 1862, 41,666; in 1867, 61,572." E. Levasseur, *Histoire des classes ouvrières et de l'industrie en France de 1789 à 1870,* vol. 2 (Paris, 1904), pp. 531–532. [F1a,3]

"Henri Labrouste, an artist whose talents are sober and severe, successfully inaugurated the ornamental use of iron in the construction of the Bibliothèque Sainte-Geneviève and the Bibliothèque Nationale." Levasseur, *Histoire des classes ouvrières,* p. 197. [F1a,4]

First construction of Les Halles in 1851, long after the project had been approved by Napoleon in 1811. It met with general disfavor. This stone structure was known as *le fort de la Halle.* "It was an unfortunate attempt which will not be repeated. . . . A mode of construction better suited to the end proposed will now be sought. The glassed sections of the Gare de l'Ouest and the memory of the Crystal Palace, which had housed the world exhibition at London in 1851, were no doubt responsible for the idea of using glass and cast iron almost exclusively. Today we can see the justification for turning to such lightweight materials, which, better than any others, fulfilled the conditions laid down for these establishments. Work on Les

Halles has not let up since 1851, yet they are still not finished." Maxime Du Camp, *Paris* (Paris, 1875), vol. 2, pp. 121–122. [F1a,5]

Plan for a train station intended to replace the Gare Saint-Lazare. Corner of Place de la Madeleine and Rue Tronchet. "According to the report, the rails—supported by 'elegant cast-iron arches rising twenty feet above the ground, and having a length of 615 meters'—would have crossed the Rue Saint-Lazare, the Rue Saint-Nicolas, the Rue des Mathurins, and the Rue Castellane, each of which would have had its own station." ☐ Flâneur. Railroad station near <?> the streets ☐ ". . . Merely by looking at them, we can see how little these plans actually anticipated the future of the railroads. Although described as 'monumental,' the façade of this train station (which, fortunately, was never built) is of unusually small dimensions; it would not even serve to accommodate one of those shops that nowadays extend along the corners of certain intersections. It is a sort of Italianate building, three stories high, with each story having eight windows; the main entrance is marked by a stairway of twenty-four steps leading to a semicircular porch wide enough for five or six persons to pass through side by side." Du Camp, *Paris*, vol. 1, pp. 238–239. [F2,1]

The Gare de l'Ouest (today?) presents "the double aspect of a factory in operation and a ministry." Du Camp, *Paris*, vol. 1, p. 241. "With your back to the three tunnels that pass under the Boulevard des Batignolles, you can take in the whole of the train station. You see that it almost has the shape of an immense mandolin: the rails would form the strings, and the signal posts, placed at every crossing of the tracks, would form the pegs." Du Camp, *Paris*, vol. 1, p. 250. [F2,2]

"Charon . . . ruined by the installation of a wire footbridge over the Styx." Grandville, *Un autre monde* (Paris, 1844), p. 138. [F2,3]

The first act of Offenbach's *Vie parisienne* takes place in a railroad station. "The industrial movement seems to run in the blood of this generation—to such an extent that, for example, Flachat has built his house on a plot of land where, on either side, trains are always whistling by." Sigfried Giedion, *Bauen in Frankreich* (Leipzig and Berlin ‹1928›), p. 13. Eugène Flachat (1802–1873), builder of railroads, designer. [F2,4]

On the Galerie d'Orléans in the Palais-Royal (1829–1831): "Even Fontaine, one of the originators of the Empire style, is converted in later years to the new material. In 1835–1836, moreover, he replaced the wooden flooring of the Galerie des Batailles in Versailles with an iron assembly.—These galleries, like those in the Palais-Royal, were subsequently perfected in Italy. For us, they are a point of departure for new architectural problems: train stations, and the like." Sigfried Giedion, *Bauen in Frankreich*, p. 21. [F2,5]

"The complicated construction (out of iron and copper) of the Corn Exchange in 1811 was the work of the architect Bellangé and the engineer Brunet. It is the first time, to our knowledge, that architect and engineer are no longer united in one person. . . . Hittorff, the builder of the Gare du Nord, got his insight into iron construction from Bellangé.—Naturally, it is a matter more of an application of iron than a construction in iron. Techniques of wood construction were simply transposed to iron." Sigfried Giedion, *Bauen in Frankreich*, p. 20. [F2,6]

Apropos of Veugny's covered market built in 1824 near the Madeleine: "The slenderness of the delicate cast-iron columns brings to mind Pompeian wall paintings. 'The construction, in iron and cast iron, of the new market near the Madeleine is one of the most graceful achievements in this genre. One cannot imagine anything more elegant or in better taste. . . .' Eck, *Traité*." Sigfried Giedion, *Bauen in Frankreich*, p. 21. [F2,7]

"The most important step toward industrialization: mechanical prefabrication of specific forms (sections) out of wrought iron or steel. The fields interpenetrate: . . . in 1832, railroad workers began not with building components but with rails. Here is the point of departure for sectional iron, which is the basis of iron construction. [Note to this passage: The new methods of construction penetrate slowly into industry. Double-T iron was used in flooring for the first time in Paris in 1845, when the masons were out on strike and the price of wood had risen due to increased construction and larger spans.]" Giedion, *Bauen in Frankreich*, p. 26. [F2,8]

The first structures made of iron served transitory purposes: covered markets, railroad stations, exhibitions. Iron is thus immediately allied with functional moments in the life of the economy. What was once functional and transitory, however, begins today, at an altered tempo, to seem formal and stable. [F2,9]

"Les Halles consist of two groups of pavilions joined to each other by covered lanes. It is a somewhat timid iron structure that avoids the generous spans of Horeau and Flachat and obviously keeps to the model of the greenhouse." Giedion, *Bauen in Frankreich*, p. 28. [F2a,1]

On the Gare du Nord: "Here they have entirely avoided that abundance of space which is found in waiting rooms, entryways, and restaurants around 1880, and which led to the problem of the railroad station as exaggerated baroque palace." Giedion, *Bauen in Frankreich*, p. 31. [F2a,2]

"Wherever the nineteenth century feels itself to be unobserved, it grows bold." Giedion, *Bauen in Frankreich,* p. 33. In fact, this sentence holds good in the general form that it has here: the anonymous art of the illustrations in family magazines and children's books, for example, is proof of the point. [F2a,3]

Railroad stations ‹*Bahnhöfe*› used to be known as *Eisenbahnhöfe*.[3]   [F2a,4]

There is talk of renewing art by beginning with forms. But are not forms the true mystery of nature, which reserves to itself the right to remunerate—precisely through them—the accurate, the objective, the logical solution to a problem posed in purely objective terms? When the wheel was invented, enabling continuous forward motion over the ground, wouldn't someone there have been able to say, with a certain justification, "And now, into the bargain, it's round—it's in the *form of a wheel?*" Are not all great conquests in the field of forms ultimately a matter of technical discoveries? Only now are we beginning to guess what forms—and they will be determinative for our epoch—lie hidden in machines. "To what extent the old forms of the instruments of production influenced their new forms from the outset is shown, . . . perhaps more strikingly than in any other way, by the attempts, before the invention of the present locomotive, to construct a locomotive that actually had two feet, which, after the fashion of a horse, it raised alternately from the ground. It is only after considerable development of the science of mechanics, and accumulated practical experience, that the form of a machine becomes settled entirely in accordance with mechanical principles, and emancipated from the traditional form of the tool that gave rise to it." (In this sense, for example, the supports and the load, in architecture, are also "forms.") Passage is from Marx, *Kapital,* vol. 1 (Hamburg, 1922), p. 347n.[4]   [F2a,5]

Through the Ecole des Beaux-Arts, architecture is linked with the plastic arts. "That was a disaster for architecture. In the Baroque age, this unity had been perfect and self-evident. In the course of the nineteenth century, however, it became untenable." Sigfried Giedion, *Bauen in Frankreich* ‹Leipzig and Berlin, 1928›, p. 16. This not only provides a very important perspective on the Baroque; it also indicates that architecture was historically the earliest field to outgrow the concept of art, or, better, that it tolerated least well being contemplated as "art"—a category which the nineteenth century, to a previously unimagined extent but with hardly more justification at bottom, imposed on the creations of intellectual productivity.   [F3,1]

The dusty fata morgana of the winter garden, the dreary perspective of the train station, with the small altar of happiness at the intersection of the tracks—it all molders under spurious constructions, glass before its time, premature iron. For in the first third of the previous century, no one as yet understood how to build with glass and iron. That problem, however, has long since been solved by hangars and silos. Now, it is the same with the human material on the inside of the arcades as with the materials of their construction. Pimps are the iron bearings of this street, and its glass breakables are the whores.   [F3,2]

"The new 'architecture' ‹*Bauen*› has its origin in the moment of industry's formation, around 1830—the moment of mutation from the craftsmanly to the industrial production process." Giedion, **Bauen in Frankreich**, p. 2.   [F3,3]

"Railroad tracks," with the peculiar and unmistakable dream world that attaches to them, are a very impressive example of just how great the natural symbolic power of technological innovation can be. In this regard, it is illuminating to learn of the bitter polemic waged against iron rails in the 1830s. In *A Treatise in Elementary Locomotion,* for example, A. Gordon argued that the steam carriage (as it was called then) should run on lanes of granite. It was deemed impossible to produce enough iron for even the very small number of railway lines being planned at that time. [F3,4]

It must be kept in mind that the magnificent urban views opened up by new constructions in iron—Giedion, in his *Bauen in Frankreich* (illustrations 61–63), gives excellent examples with the Pont Transbordeur in Marseilles—for a long time were evident only to workers and engineers. ▯ Marxism ▯ For in those days who besides the engineer and the proletarian had climbed the steps that alone made it possible to recognize what was new and decisive about these structures: the feeling of space? [F3,5]

In 1791, the term *ingénieur* began to be used in France for those officers skilled in the arts of fortification and siege. "At the same time, and in the same country, the opposition between 'construction' and 'architecture' began to make itself felt; and before long it figured in personal attacks. This antithesis had been entirely unknown in the past. . . . But in the innumerable aesthetic treatises which after the storms of the Revolution guided French art back into regular channels, . . . the *constructeurs* stood opposed to the *décorateurs,* and with this the further question arose: Did not the *ingénieurs,* as the allies of the former, necessarily occupy with them, socially speaking, a distinct camp?" A. G. Meyer, *Eisenbauten* (Esslingen, 1907), p. 3. [F3,6]

"The technique of stone architecture is stereotomy; that of wood is tectonics. What does iron construction have in common with the one or the other?" Alfred Gotthold Meyer, *Eisenbauten* (Esslingen, 1907), p. 5. "In stone we feel the natural spirit of the mass. Iron is, for us, only artificially compressed durability and tenacity" (p. 9). "Iron has a tensile strength forty times greater than that of stone and ten times greater than that of wood, although its net weight is only four times that of stone and only eight times that of wood. In comparison with a stone mass of the same dimensions, therefore, an iron body possesses, with only four times the weight, a load limit forty times higher" (p. 11). [F3,7]

"This material, in its first hundred years, has already undergone essential transformations—cast iron, wrought iron, ingot iron—so that today the engineer has at his disposal a building material completely different from that of some fifty years ago. . . . In the perspective of historical reflection, these are 'ferments' of a disquieting instability. No other building material offers anything remotely similar. We stand here at the beginning of a development that is sure to proceed at a furious pace. . . . The . . . conditions of the material . . . are volatilized in 'limitless possibilities.'" A. G. Meyer, *Eisenbauten*, p. 11. Iron as revolutionary building material! [F3a,1]

Meanwhile, how it looked in the vulgar consciousness is indicated by the crass yet typical utterance of a contemporary journalist, according to whom posterity will one day have to confess, "In the nineteenth century, ancient Greek architecture once again blossomed in its classical purity." *Europa,* 2 (Stuttgart and Leipzig, 1837), p. 207. [F3a,2]

Railroad stations as "abodes of art." "If Wiertz had had at his disposal . . . the public monuments of modern civilization—railway stations, legislative chambers, university lecture halls, marketplaces, town halls— . . . who can say what bright and dramatic new worlds he would have traced upon his canvas!" A. J. Wiertz, *Oeuvres littéraires* (Paris, 1870), pp. 525–526. [F3a,3]

The technical absolutism that is fundamental to iron construction—and fundamental merely on account of the material itself—becomes apparent to anyone who recognizes the extent to which it contrasts with traditional conceptions of the value and utility of building materials. "Iron inspired a certain distrust just because it was not immmediately furnished by nature, but instead had to be artificially prepared as a building material. This distrust is only a specific application of that general sentiment of the Renaissance to which Leon Battista Alberti (*De re aedificatoria* [Paris, 1512], fol. xliv) gives expression at one point with the words: 'Nam est quidem cujusquis corporis pars indissolubilior, quae a natura concreta et counita est, quam quae hominum manu et arte conjuncta atque, compacta est' ‹For there is, in each thing, a part that is the work and the assemblage of nature, and that is more indissoluble than that which is produced and assembled by the hand of man with his art›." A. G. Meyer, *Eisenbauten* (Esslingen, 1907), p. 14. [F3a,4]

It is worth considering—and it appears that the answer to this question would be in the negative—whether, at an earlier period, technical necessities in architecture (but also in the other arts) determined the forms, the style, as thoroughly as they do today, when such technological derivation seems actually to become the signature of everything now produced. With iron as a material, this is already clearly the case, and perhaps for the first time. Indeed, the "basic forms in which iron appears as a building material are . . . already themselves, as distinct syntheses, partly new. And their distinctiveness, in large measure, is the product and expression of the natural properties of the building material, since such properties have been technically and scientifically developed and exploited precisely for *these* forms. The systematic industrial process which converts raw material into immediately available building material begins, with iron, at a much earlier stage than with previously existing building materials. Between matter and material, in this case, there is a relationship quite different from that between stone and ashlar, clay and tile, timber and beam: with iron, building material and structural form are, as it were, more homogeneous." A. G. Meyer, *Eisenbauten* (Esslingen, 1907), p. 23. [F3a,5]

1840–1844: "The construction of fortifications, inspired by Thiers. . . . Thiers, who thought that railroads would never work, had gates constructed in Paris at the very moment when railroad stations were needed." Dubech and d'Espezel, *Histoire de Paris* (Paris, 1926), p. 386. [F3a,6]

"From the fifteenth century onward, this nearly colorless glass, in the form of window panes, rules over the house as well. The whole development of interior space obeys the command: 'More light!'[5]—In seventeenth-century Holland, this development leads to window openings that, even in houses of the middle class, ordinarily take up almost half the wall. . . . / The abundance of light occasioned by this practice must have . . . soon become disagreeable. Within the room, curtains offered a relief that was quickly to become, through the overzealous art of the upholsterer, a disaster. . . . / The development of space by means of glass and iron had come to a standstill. / Suddenly, however, it gained new strength from a perfectly inconspicuous source. / Once again, this source was a 'house,' one designed to 'shelter the needy,' but it was a house neither for mortals nor for divinities, neither for hearth fires nor for inanimate goods; it was, rather, a house for plants. / The origin of all present-day architecture in iron and glass is the greenhouse." A. G. Meyer, *Eisenbauten,* p. 55. □ Light in the Arcades □ Mirrors □ The arcade is the hallmark of the world Proust depicts. Curious that, like this world, it should be bound in its origin to the existence of plants. [F4,1]

On the Crystal Palace of 1851: "Of all the great things about this work, the greatest, in every sense of the word, is the vaulted central hall. . . . Now, here too, at first, it was not a space-articulating architect who did the talking but a—gardener. . . . This is literally true: the main reason for the elevation of the central hall was the presence, in this section of Hyde Park, of magnificent elm trees, which neither the Londoners nor Paxton himself wished to see felled. Incorporating them into his giant glass house, as he had done earlier with the exotic plants at Chatsworth, Paxton almost unconsciously—but nonetheless fundamentally—enhanced the architectural value of his construction." A. G. Meyer, *Eisenbauten* (Esslingen, 1907), p. 62. [F4,2]

In opposition to the engineers and builders, ‹Charles-François› Viel, as architect, publishes his extremely violent, comprehensive polemic against static calculation, under the title *De l'Impuissance des mathématiques pour assurer la solidité des bâtiments* ‹On the Uselessness of Mathematics for Assuring the Stability of Buildings› (Paris, 1805). [F4,3]

The following holds good for the arcades, particularly as iron structures: "Their most essential component . . . is the roof. Even the etymology of the word 'hall'[6] points to this. It is a covered, not an enclosed space; the side walls are, so to

Interior of the Crystal Palace, London, from a photograph by William Henry Fox Talbot. See F4,2.

speak, 'concealed.'" This last point pertains in a special sense to the arcades, whose walls have only secondarily the function of partitioning the hall; primarily, they serve as walls or façades for the commercial spaces within them. The passage is from A. G. Meyer, *Eisenbauten,* p. 69.   [F4,4]

The arcade as iron construction stands on the verge of horizontal extension. That is a decisive condition for its "old-fashioned" appearance. It displays, in this regard, a hybrid character, analogous in certain respects to that of the Baroque church—"the vaulted 'hall' that comprehends the chapels only as an extension of its own proper space, which is wider than ever before. Nevertheless, an attraction 'from on high' is also at work in this Baroque hall—an upward-tending ecstasy, such as jubilates from the frescoes on the ceiling. So long as ecclesiastical spaces aim to be more than spaces for gathering, so long as they strive to safeguard the idea of the eternal, they will be satisfied with nothing less than an overarching unity, in which the vertical tendency outweighs the horizontal." A. G. Meyer, *Eisenbauten,* p. 74. On the other hand, it may be said that something sacral, a vestige of the nave, still attaches to this row of commodities that is the arcade. From a functional point of view, the arcade already occupies the field of horizontal amplitude; architecturally, however, it still stands within the conceptual field of the old "hall."   [F4,5]

The Galerie des Machines, built in 1889,[7] was torn down in 1910 "out of artistic sadism."   [F4,6]

Historical extension of the horizontal: "From the palaces of the Italian High Renaissance, the châteaux of the French kings take the 'gallery,' which—as in the case of the 'Gallery of Apollo' at the Louvre and the 'Gallery of Mirrors' at Versailles— becomes the emblem of majesty itself. . . . / Its new triumphal advance in the nineteenth century begins under the sign of the purely utilitarian structure, with those halls known as warehouses and markets, workshops and factories; the problem of railroad stations and, above all, of exhibitions leads it back to art. And everywhere the demand for continuous horizontal extension is so great that the stone arch and the wooden ceiling can have only very limited applications. . . . In Gothic structures, the walls turn into the ceiling, whereas in iron halls of the type . . . represented by the Gallery of Machines in Paris, the ceiling slides over the walls without interruption." A. G. Meyer, *Eisenbauten,* pp. 74–75.   [F4a,1]

Never before was the criterion of the "minimal" so important. And that includes the minimal element of quantity: the "little," the "few." These are dimensions that were well established in technological and architectural constructions long before literature made bold to adapt them. Fundamentally, it is a question of the earliest manifestation of the principle of montage. On building the Eiffel Tower: "Thus, the plastic shaping power abdicates here in favor of a colossal span of spiritual energy, which channels the inorganic material energy into the smallest, most efficient forms and conjoins these forms in the most effective manner. . . . Each of the twelve thousand metal fittings, each of the two and a half million rivets, is machined to the millimeter. . . . On this work site, one hears no chisel-blow liberating form from stone; here thought reigns over muscle power, which it transmits via cranes and secure scaffolding." A. G. Meyer, *Eisenbauten*, p. 93. ☐ Precursors ☐ [F4a,2]

"Haussmann was incapable of having what could be called a policy on railroad stations. . . . Despite a directive from the emperor, who justly baptized *les gares* 'the new gateways of Paris,' the continued development of the railroads surprised everyone, surpassing all expectations. . . . The habit of a certain empiricism was not easily overcome." Dubech and d'Espezel, *Histoire de Paris* (Paris, 1926), p. 419. [F4a,3]

Eiffel Tower. "Greeted at first by a storm of protest, it has remained quite ugly, though it proved useful for research on wireless telegraphy. . . . It has been said that this world exhibition marked the triumph of iron construction. It would be truer to say that it marked its bankruptcy." Dubech and d'Espezel, *Histoire de Paris*, pp. 461–462. [F4a,4]

"Around 1878, it was thought that salvation lay in iron construction. Its 'yearning for verticality' (as Salomon Reinach put it), the predominance of empty spaces over filled spaces, and the lightness of its visible frame raised hopes that a style was emerging in which the essence of the Gothic genius would be revived and rejuvenated by a new spirit and new materials. But when engineers erected the Galerie des Machines and the Eiffel Tower in 1889, people despaired of the art of iron. Perhaps too soon." Dubech and d'Espezel, *Histoire de Paris*, p. 464. [F4a,5]

Béranger: "His sole reproach to the regime of Louis Philippe was that it put the republic to grow in a hothouse." Franz Diederich, "Victor Hugo," *Die neue Zeit*, 20, no. 1 (Stuttgart, 1901), p. 648. [F4a,6]

"The path that leads from the Empire form of the first locomotive to the finished objective and functional form of today marks an evolution." Joseph Aug. Lux, "Maschinenästhetik," *Die neue Zeit*, 27, no. 2 (Stuttgart, 1909), p. 439. [F4a,7]

"Those endowed with an especially fine artistic conscience have hurled down, from the altar of art, curse after curse on the building engineers. It suffices to mention Ruskin." A. G. Meyer, *Eisenbauten* (Esslingen, 1907), p. 3. [F5,1]

Concerning the artistic idea of Empire. On Daumier: "He displayed the greatest enthusiasm for muscular excitations. Tirelessly his pencil exalts the tension and movement of muscles. . . . But the public of which he dreamed was proportioned differently from this ignoble . . . society of shopkeepers. He yearned for a social milieu that would have provided, like that of ancient Greece, a base from which people could raise themselves, as from a pedestal, in vigorous beauty. . . . A grotesque distortion must . . . result when the bourgeoisie is viewed from the angle of such ideals. Daumier's caricatures were thus the almost involuntary consequence of a lofty ambition that failed in its aim of attunement with the middle-class public. . . . In 1835, an attempt on the life of the king[8] presented an . . . opportunity to curtail . . . the boldness of the press, which had been publicly blamed for the deed. Political caricature became impossible. . . . Hence, the drawings of lawyers done in this period are . . . by far the most passionate and animated. The courtroom is the only place where pitched battles can still be waged in all their fury, and lawyers are the only people in whom an emphatically muscular rhetoric and a professionally dramatic pose have made for an elaborate physiognomy of the body." Fritz Th. Schulte, "Honoré Daumier," *Die neue Zeit*, 32, no. 1 (Stuttgart ‹1913›), pp. 833–835. [F5,2]

The miscarriage of Baltard's design for Les Halles, built in 1853, is due to the same unfortunate combination of masonry and ironwork as in the original project for the London exhibition hall of 1851, the work of the Frenchman Horeau. Parisians referred to Baltard's structure, which was subsequently torn down, as *le fort de la Halle*. [F5,3]

On the Crystal Palace, with the elms in its midst: "Under these glass arches, thanks to awnings, ventilators, and gushing fountains, visitors revel in a delicious coolness. In the words of one observer: 'You might think you were under the billows of some fabulous river, in the crystal palace of a fairy or naiad.'" A. Démy, *Essai historique ‹sur les expositions universelles de Paris* (Paris, 1907)›, p. 40. [F5,4]

"After the closing of the London Exhibition in 1851, people in England wondered what was to become of the Crystal Palace. Although a clause inserted in the deed of concession for the grounds required . . . the demolition . . . of the building, public opinion was unanimous in asking for the abrogation of this clause. . . . The newspapers were full of proposals of all kinds, many of which were distinctly eccentric. A doctor wanted to turn the place into a hospital; another suggested a bathing establishment. . . . One person had the idea of making it a gigantic library. An Englishman with a violent passion for flowers insisted on seeing the whole palace become a garden." The Crystal Palace was acquired by Francis Fuller and transferred to Sydenham. A. S. de Doncourt, *Les Expositions universelles* (Lille and Paris ‹1889›), p. 77. Compare F6a,1. The Bourse could *represent* anything; the Crystal Palace could be *used* for anything. [F5a,1]

"Furniture making in tubular iron . . . rivals furniture making in wood, and even surpasses it. Furniture of such iron, with baked-on color, . . . enameled with flowers or with patterns imitating those of inlaid wood, is elegant and nicely turned, like the tops of Boucher's gates." Edouard Foucaud, *Paris inventeur: Physiologie de l'industrie française* (Paris, 1844), pp. 92–93. [F5a,2]

The square opposite the Gare du Nord was known in 1860 as the Place de Roubaix. [F5a,3]

In engravings of the period, horses are prancing across railroad station esplanades, and stagecoaches roll by in clouds of dust. [F5a,4]

Caption for a woodcut representing a catafalque in the Gare du Nord: "Last respects paid to Meyerbeer in Paris at the *gare de chemin de fer du Nord*." [F5a,5]

Factories with galleries inside and winding iron staircases. Early prospectuses and illustrations show production rooms and display rooms, which are often under the same roof, fondly represented in cross-section like doll houses. Thus a prospectus of 1865 for the footwear company Pinet. Not infrequently one sees ateliers, like those of photographers, with sliding shades in front of the skylight. Cabinet des Estampes. [F5a,6]

The Eiffel Tower: "It is characteristic of this most famous construction of the epoch that, for all its gigantic stature, . . . it nevertheless feels like a knickknack, which . . . speaks for the fact that the second-rate artistic sensibility of the era could think, in general, only within the framework of genre and the technique of filigree." Egon Friedell, *Kulturgeschichte der Neuzeit*, vol. 3 (Munich, 1931), p. 363. [F5a,7]

"Michel Chevalier sets down his dreams of the new temple in a poem:

> I would have you see my temple, the Lord God said.
> . . . . .
> The columns of the temple
> Were strong beams;
> Of hollow cast-iron columns
> Was the organ of this new temple.
>
> . . . . .
> The framework was of iron, of molded steel,
> Of copper and of bronze.
> The architect had placed it upon the columns
> Like a stringed instrument upon a woodwind.
>
> . . . . .
> From the temple came, moreover, at each moment of the day,
> The sounds of a new harmony.
> The slender spire rose up like a lightning rod;
> It reached to the clouds,

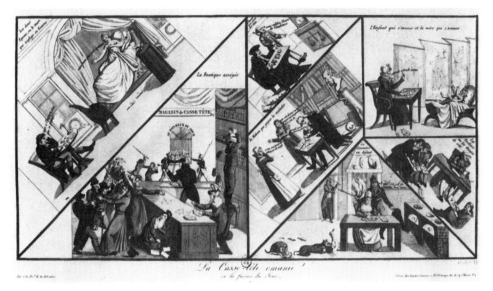

La Casse-tête-omanie, ou La Fureur du jour (Picture Puzzle Mania, or They're All the Rage These Days). See F6,2.

To seek there electric force;
Storms have charged it with vitality and tension.

. . . . .

At the top of the minarets
The telegraph was waving its arms,
Bringing from all parts
Good news to the people."

Henry-René D'Allemagne, *Les Saint-Simoniens, 1827–1837* (Paris, 1930), p. 308.
[F6,1]

The "Chinese puzzle," which comes into fashion during the Empire, reveals the century's awakening sense for construction. The problems that appear, in the puzzles of the period, as hatched portions of a landscape, a building, or a figure are a first presentiment of the cubist principle in the plastic arts. (To verify: whether, in an allegorical representation in the Cabinet des Estampes, the brain-teaser undoes the kaleidoscope or vice versa.)   [F6,2]

"Paris à vol d'oiseau" ‹A Bird's-Eye View of Paris›—*Notre-Dame de Paris,* vol. 1, book 3—concludes its overview of the architectural history of the city with an ironic characterization of the present day, which culminates in a description of the architectural insignificance of the Stock Exchange. The importance of the chapter is underlined by a note added to the definitive edition of 1832, which says: "The author . . . enlarges, in one of these chapters, upon the current decadence of architecture and the now (in his view) almost inevitable demise of this king of the arts—a view which is, unhappily, deeply rooted in him and deeply pondered." Victor Hugo, *Oeuvres complètes,* novels, vol. 3 (Paris, 1880), p. 5.[9]   [F6,3]

Before the decision to build the Palais de l'Industrie[10] was made, a plan had existed to roof over a section of the Champs-Elysées—along with its trees—in the manner of the Crystal Palace.   [F6,4]

Victor Hugo, in *Notre-Dame de Paris*, on the Bourse: "If it be the rule that the architecture of a building should be adapted to its function, . . . we can hardly wonder enough at a monument which might equally well be a king's palace, a house of commons, a town hall, a college, a riding school, an academy, a warehouse, a law court, a museum, a barracks, a sepulcher, a temple, or a theater. For the present, it is a stock exchange. . . . It is a stock exchange in France just as it would have been a temple in Greece. . . . We have the colonnade encircling the monument, beneath which, on days of high religious solemnity, the theory of stockbrokers and jobbers can be majestically expounded. These, for sure, are very stately monuments. If we add to them many fine streets, as amusing and diverse as the Rue de Rivoli, then I do not despair but that one day a balloon's-eye view of Paris will offer us that wealth of lines, . . . that diversity of aspect, that somehow . . . unexpected beauty, which characterizes a checkerboard." Victor Hugo, *Oeuvres complètes*, novels, vol. 3 (Paris, 1880), pp. 206–207 (*Notre-Dame de Paris*).[11]

[F6a,1]

The Paris Stock Exchange, mid-nineteenth century. Courtesy of the Paris Stock Exchange. See F6a,1.

The Palais de l'Industrie at the world exhibition of 1855. See F6a,2.

Palais de l'Industrie: "One is struck by the elegance and lightness of the iron framework; yet the engineer, . . . Monsieur Barrault, has shown more skill than taste. As for the domed glass roof, . . . it is awkwardly placed, and the idea evoked . . . is . . . that of a large cloche: industry in a hothouse. . . . On each side of the entrance have been placed two superb locomotives with their tenders." This last arrangement presumably occasioned by the distribution of prizes which closed the exhibition on November 15, 1855. Louis Enault, "Le Palais de l'Industrie," in *Paris et les Parisiens au XIXe siècle* (Paris, 1856), pp. 313, 315. [F6a,2]

From Charles-François Viel, *De l'Impuissance des mathématiques pour assurer la solidité des bâtiments* (Paris, 1805): Viel distinguishes *ordonnance* ‹planning, layout› from *construction* and faults the younger architects above all for insufficient knowledge of the former. Ultimately responsible is "the new direction that public instruction in this art has taken, in the wake of our political tempests" (p. 9). "As for the geometers who practice architecture, their buildings—as regards invention and construction—prove the nullity of mathematics where *ordonnance* and structural stability are concerned" (p. 10). "The mathematicians . . . claim to have . . . reconciled boldness with stability. It is only under the aegis of algebra that these two words can meet" (p. 25; it remains to be determined whether this last sentence is meant ironically, or whether it distinguishes between algebra and mathematics). The author criticizes the Pont du Louvre and the Pont de la Cité (both bridges from 1803) in accordance with the principles of Leon Battista Alberti.   [F6a,3]

According to Viel, the first bridges to be built on a constructive basis would have been undertaken around 1730.   [F7,1]

In 1855, the Hôtel du Louvre was constructed at a rapid tempo, so as to be in place for the opening of the world exhibition. "For the first time, the entrepreneurs used electric light on the site, in order to double the day's labor; some unexpected delays occurred; the city was just coming out of the famous carpenters' strike, which put an end to wood-frame structures in Paris. Consequently, the Hôtel du Louvre possesses the rare distinction of having wedded, in its design, the wood paneling of old houses to the iron flooring of modern buildings." Vte G. d'Avenel, "Le Mécanisme de la vie moderne," part 1, "Les Grands Magasins," *Revue des deux mondes* (July 15, 1894), p. 340.   [F7,2]

"In the beginning, railroad cars look like stagecoaches, autobuses like omnibuses, electric lights like gas chandeliers, and the last like petroleum lamps." Léon Pierre-Quint, "Signification du cinéma," *L'Art cinématographique*, 2 (Paris, 1927), p. 7.   [F7,3]

Apropos of the Empire style of Schinkel: "The building that brings out the location, the substructure that embodies the true seat of invention, . . . these things resemble—a vehicle. They convey architectural ideals, which only in this sort of way can still be 'practiced.'" Carl Linfert, "Vom Ursprung grosser Baugedanken," *Frankfurter Zeitung*, January 9, 1936.   [F7,4]

On the world exhibition of 1889: "We can say of this festivity that it has been celebrated, above all, to the glory of iron. . . . Having undertaken to give readers of *Le Correspondant* a rough idea of industry in connection with the Exposition du Champ de Mars, we have chosen for our theme 'Metal Structures and Railroads.'" Albert de Lapparent, *Le Siècle du fer* (Paris, 1890), pp. vii–viii.   [F7,5]

On the Crystal Palace: "The architect, Paxton, and the contractors, Messrs. Fox and Henderson, had systematically resolved not to use parts with large dimensions. The heaviest were hollow cast-iron girders, eight meters long, none of which weighed more than a ton. . . . Their chief merit was that they were economical. . . . Moreover, the execution of the plan was remarkably rapid, since all the parts were of a sort that the factories could undertake to deliver quickly." Albert de Lapparent, *Le Siècle du fer* (Paris, 1890), p. 59.   [F7,6]

Lapparent divides iron structures into two classes: iron structures with stone facings and true iron structures. He places the following example among the first sort. "Labrouste . . . , in 1868, . . . gave to the public the reading room of the Bibliothèque Nationale. . . . It is difficult to imagine anything more satisfying or more harmonious than this great chamber of 1,156 square meters, with its nine fretted cupolas, incorporating arches of iron lattice and resting on sixteen light cast-iron columns, twelve of which are set against the walls, while four, completely free-standing, rise from the floor on pedestals of the same metal." Albert de Lapparent, *Le Siècle du fer* (Paris, 1890), pp. 56–57. [F7a,1]

The engineer Alexis Barrault, who with Viel built the Palace of Industry in 1855, was a brother of Emile Barrault. [F7a,2]

In 1779, the first cast-iron bridge (that of Coalbrookdale). In 1788, its builder[12] was awarded the Gold Medal of the English Society of Arts. "Since it was in 1790, furthermore, that the architect Louis completed the wrought-iron framework for the Théâtre Français in Paris, we may say that the centenary of metal construction coincides almost exactly with that of the French Revolution." A. de Lapparent, *Le Siècle du fer* (Paris, 1890), pp. 11–12. [F7a,3]

Paris, in 1822: a "woodwork strike." [F7a,4]

On the subject of the Chinese puzzle, a lithograph: *The Triumph of the Kaleidoscope, or the Demise of the Chinese Game.* A reclining Chinese man with a brainteaser spread out on the ground before him. On his shoulder, a female figure has planted her foot. In one hand, she carries a kaleidoscope; in the other, a paper or a scroll with kaleidoscope patterns. Cabinet des Estampes (dated 1818). [F7a,5]

"The head turns and the heart tightens when, for the first time, we visit those fairy halls where polished iron and dazzling copper seem to move and think by themselves, while pale and feeble man is only the humble servant of those steel giants." J. Michelet, *Le Peuple* (Paris, 1846), p. 82. The author in no way fears that mechanical production will gain the upper hand over human beings. The individualism of the consumer seems to him to speak against this: each "man now . . . wants to be himself. Consequently, he will often care less for products fabricated *by classes*, without any individuality that speaks to his own" (ibid., p. 78).[13] [F7a,6]

"Viollet-le-Duc (1814–1879) shows that the architects of the Middle Ages were also engineers and resourceful inventors." Amédée Ozenfant, "La Peinture murale," *Encyclopédie française*, vol. 16, *Arts et littératures dans la société contemporaine*, part 1, p. 70, column 3. [F8,1]

Protest against the Eiffel Tower: "We come, as writers, painters, sculptors, architects, . . . in the name of French art and French history, both of which are threatened, . . . to protest against the construction, in the very heart of our capital, of the useless and monstrous Eiffel Tower. . . . Its barbarous mass overwhelms Notre-Dame, the Sainte-Chapelle, the Tower of Saint-Jacques. All our monuments

Le Triomphe du kaléidoscope, ou Le Tombeau du jeu chinois (The
Triumph of the Kaleidoscope, or The Demise of the Chinese
Game), 1818. Courtesy of the Bibliothèque Nationale, Paris.
See F7a,5.

are debased, our architecture diminished." Cited in Louis Chéronnet, "Les Trois
Grand-mères de l'exposition," *Vendredi*, April 30, 1937.   [F8,2]

Supposedly there were trees within Musard's "Harmony Hall," on the Boulevard
Montmartre.   [F8,3]

"It was in 1783, in the construction of the Théâtre Français, that iron was employed for the first time on a large scale, by the architect Louis. Never perhaps,
has a work so audacious been attempted. When, in 1900, the theater was rebuilt in
the aftermath of a fire, it was with a weight of iron one hundred times greater than
that which the architect Louis had used for the same trusswork. Construction in
iron has provided a succession of buildings, of which the great reading room of the
Bibliothèque Nationale by Labrouste was the first, and one of the most successful. . . . But iron requires costly maintenance. . . . The world exhibition of 1889

marked the triumph of exposed ironwork . . . ; at the exhibition of 1900, nearly all the iron frames were covered with plasterwork." *L'Encyclopédie française*, vol. 16, 16–68, pp. 6–7 (Auguste Perret, "Les Besoins collectifs et l'architecture").

[F8,4]

The "triumph of exposed ironwork" in the age of the genre: "It may be . . . the . . . enthusiasm for machine technology and the faith in the superior durability of its materials that explains why the attribute 'iron' is used . . . whenever . . . power and necessity are supposed to be manifest. Iron are the laws of nature, and iron is the 'stride of the worker battalion'; the . . . union of the German empire is supposedly made of iron, and so is . . . the chancellor himself." Dolf Sternberger, *Panorama* (Hamburg, 1938), p. 31. [F8,5]

The iron balcony. "In its most rigorous form, the house has a uniform façade. . . . Articulation results only from doors and windows. In France, the window is, without exception, even in the poorest house, a *porte-fenêtre*, a 'French window' opening to the floor. . . . This makes a railing necessary; in the poorer houses it is a plain iron bar, but in the wealthier houses it is of wrought iron. . . . At a certain stage, the railing becomes an ornament. . . . It further contributes to the articulation of the façade by . . . accenting the lower line of the window. And it fulfills both functions without breaking the plane of the façade. For the great architectural mass of the modern house, with its insistent lateral extension, this articulation could not possibly suffice. The architects' building-sense demanded that the ever stronger horizontal tendency of the house . . . be given expression. . . . And they discovered the means for this in the traditional iron grille. Across the entire length of the building front, on one or two stories, they set a balcony provided with an iron grating of this type, which, being black, stands out very distinctly and makes a vigorous impression. These balconies, . . . up to the most recent period of building, were kept very narrow; and if through them the severity of the surface is overcome, what can be called the relief of the façade remains nonetheless quite flat, overcoming the effect of the wall as little as does the sculpted ornamentation, likewise kept flat. In the case of adjoining houses, these balcony railings fuse with one another and consolidate the impression of a walled street; and this effect is heightened by the fact that, wherever the upper stories are used for commercial purposes, the proprietors put up . . . not signboards but matched gilded letters in roman style, which, when well spaced across the ironwork, appear purely decorative." Fritz Stahl, *Paris* (Berlin ‹1929›), pp. 18–19. [F8a]

G

[Exhibitions, Advertising, Grandville]

Yes, when all the world from Paris to China
Pays heed to your doctrine, O divine Saint-Simon,
The glorious Golden Age will be reborn.
Rivers will flow with chocolate and tea,
Sheep roasted whole will frisk on the plain,
And sautéed pike will swim in the Seine.
Fricasseed spinach will grow on the ground,
Garnished with crushed fried croutons;
The trees will bring forth apple compotes,
And farmers will harvest boots and coats.
It will snow wine, it will rain chickens,
And ducks cooked with turnips will fall from the sky.

—Ferdinand Langlé and Emile Vanderburch, *Louis-Bronze et le Saint-Simonien: Parodie de Louis XI* (Théâtre du Palais-Royal, February 27, 1832), cited in Théodore Muret, *L'Histoire par le théâtre, 1789–1851* (Paris, 1865), vol. 3, p. 191

Music such as one gets to hear on the pianofortes of Saturn's ring.

—Hector Berlioz, *A travers chants,* authorized German edition prepared by Richard Pohl (Leipzig, 1864), p. 104 ("Beethoven im Ring des Saturn")

From a European perspective, things looked this way: In all areas of production, from the Middle Ages until the beginning of the nineteenth century, the development of technology proceeded at a much slower rate than the development of art. Art could take its time in variously assimilating the technological modes of operation. But the transformation of things that set in around 1800 dictated the tempo to art, and the more breathtaking this tempo became, the more readily the dominion of fashion overspread all fields. Finally, we arrive at the present state of things: the possibility now arises that art will no longer find time to adapt somehow to technological processes. The advertisement is the ruse by which the dream forces itself on industry. [G1,1]

Within the frames of the pictures that hung on dining room walls, the advent of whiskey advertisements, of Van Houten cocoa, of Amieux canned food is heralded. Naturally, one can say that the bourgeois comfort of the dining room has survived longest in small cafés and other such places; but perhaps one can also say that the space of the café, within which every square meter and every hour are paid for more punctually than in apartment houses, evolved out of the latter. The apartment from which a café was made is a picture puzzle ‹*Vexierbild*› with the caption: Where is the capital hiding? [G1,2]

Grandville's works are the sibylline books of *publicité*. Everything that, with him, has its preliminary form as joke, or satire, attains its true unfolding as advertisement. [G1,3]

Handbill of a Parisian textiles dealer from the 1830s: "Ladies and Gentlemen: / I ask you to cast an indulgent eye on the following observations; my desire to contribute to your eternal salvation impels me to address you. Allow me to direct your attention to the study of the Holy Scriptures, as well as to the extremely moderate prices which I have been the first to introduce into the field of hosiery, cotton goods, and related products. No. 13, Rue Pavé-Saint-Sauveur." Eduard Kroloff, *Schilderungen aus Paris* (Hamburg, 1839), vol. 2, pp. 50–51. [G1,4]

Superposition and advertising: "In the Palais-Royal, not long ago, between the columns on the upper story, I happened to see a life-sized oil painting representing, in very lively colors, a French general in full-dress uniform. I take out my spectacles to examine more closely the historical subject of the picture, and my general is sitting in an armchair holding out a bare foot: the podiatrist, kneeling before him, excises the corns." J. F. Reichardt, *Vertraute Briefe aus Paris* (Hamburg, 1805), vol. 1, p. 178. [G1,5]

In 1861, the first lithographic poster suddenly appeared on walls here and there around London. It showed the back of a woman in white who was thickly wrapped in a shawl and who, in all haste, had just reached the top of a flight of stairs, where, her head half turned and a finger upon her lips, she is ever so slightly opening a heavy door, through which one glimpses the starry sky. In this way Wilkie Collins advertised his latest book, one of the greatest detective novels ever written: *The Woman in White*. See Talmeyr, *La Cité du sang* (Paris, 1901), pp. 263–264. [G1,6]

It is significant that Jugendstil failed in interior design, and soon afterward in architecture too, whereas in the street, with the poster, it often found very successful solutions. This is fully confirmed in Behne's discerning critique: "By no means was Jugendstil ridiculous in its original intentions. It was looking for renewal because it clearly recognized the peculiar contradictions arising between imitation Renaissance art and new methods of production determined by the machine. But it gradually became ridiculous because it believed that it could resolve the enormous objective tensions formally, on paper, in the studio." ☐ Interior ☐ Adolf Behne, *Neues Wohnen—Neues Bauen* (Leipzig, 1927), p. 15. Of course, in the end, the law according to which an action brings about an opposite reaction holds true for Jugendstil. The genuine liberation from an epoch, that is, has the structure of awakening in this respect as well: it is entirely ruled by cunning. Only with cunning, not without it, can we work free of the realm of dream. But there is also a false liberation; its sign is violence. From the beginning, it condemned Jugendstil to failure. ☐ Dream Structure ☐   [G1,7]

Innermost, decisive significance of the advertisement: "Good posters exist . . . only in the domain of trifles, of industry, or of revolution." Maurice Talmeyr, *La Cité du sang* (Paris, 1901), p. 277. The same thought with which the bourgeois here detects the tendency of advertising in its early period: "In short, the moral of the poster has nothing to do with its art, and its art nothing to do with the moral, and this defines the character of the poster" (ibid., p. 275).   [G1,8]

Just as certain modes of presentation—genre scenes and the like—begin, in the course of the nineteenth century, to "cross over" into advertising, so also into the realm of the obscene. The Nazarene style and the Makart style have their black and their colored lithographic cousins in the field of obscene graphics. I saw a plate that, at first glance, could have passed as something like Siegfried's bath in dragon blood: green sylvan solitude, crimson mantle of the hero, naked flesh, a sheet of water—it was the most complicated embrace of three human bodies, and it looked like the frontispiece of an inexpensive book for young people. This is the language of color characteristic of the posters that flourished in the arcades. When we hear that portraits of famous cancan dancers like Rigolette and Frichette would have hung there, we have to imagine them colored like this. Falser colors are possible in the arcades; that combs are red and green surprises no one. Snow White's stepmother had such things, and when the comb did not do its work, the beautiful apple was there to help out—half red, half poison-green, like cheap combs. Everywhere gloves play a starring role, colored ones, but above all the long black variety on which so many, following Yvette Guilbert, have placed their hopes for happiness, and which will bring some, let us hope, to Margo Lion. And laid out on a side table in a tavern, stockings make for an ethereal meat counter.   [G1a,1]

The writings of the Surrealists treat words like trade names, and their texts are, at bottom, a form of prospectus for enterprises not yet off the ground. Nesting today in trade names are figments such as those earlier thought to be hidden in the cache of "poetic" vocables.   [G1a,2]

In 1867, a wallpaper dealer put up his posters on the columns of bridges. [G1a,3]

Many years ago, on the streetcar, I saw a poster that, if things had their due in this world, would have found its admirers, historians, exegetes, and copyists just as surely as any great poem or painting. And, in fact, it was both at the same time.

As is sometimes the case with very deep, unexpected impressions, however, the shock was too violent: the impression, if I may say so, struck with such force that it broke through the bottom of my consciousness and for years lay irrecoverable somewhere in the darkness. I knew only that it had to do with "Bullrich Salt" and that the original warehouse for this seasoning was a small cellar on Flottwell Street, where for years I had circumvented the temptation to get out at this point and inquire about the poster. There I traveled on a colorless Sunday afternoon in that northern Moabit, a part of town that had already once appeared to me as though built by ghostly hands for just this time of day. That was when, four years ago, I had come to Lützow Street to pay customs duty, according to the weight of its enameled blocks of houses, on a china porcelain city which I had had sent from Rome. There were omens then along the way to signal the approach of a momentous afternoon. And, in fact, it ended with the story of the discovery of an arcade, a story that is too *berlinisch* to be told just now in this Parisian space of remembrance. Prior to this incident, however, I stood with my two beautiful companions in front of a miserable café, whose window display was enlivened by an arrangement of signboards. On one of these was the legend "Bullrich Salt." It contained nothing else besides the words; but around these written characters there was suddenly and effortlessly configured that desert landscape of the poster. I had it once more. Here is what it looked like. In the foreground, a horse-drawn wagon was advancing across the desert. It was loaded with sacks bearing the words "Bullrich Salt." One of these sacks had a hole, from which salt had already trickled a good distance on the ground. In the background of the desert landscape, two posts held a large sign with the words "Is the Best." But what about the trace of salt down the desert trail? It formed letters, and these letters formed a word, the word "Bullrich Salt." Was not the preestablished harmony of a Leibniz mere child's play compared to this tightly orchestrated predestination in the desert? And didn't that poster furnish an image for things that no one in this mortal life has yet experienced? An image of the everyday in Utopia? [G1a,4]

"The store known as La Chaussée d'Antin had recently announced its new inventory of yard goods. Over two million meters of barege, over five million of grenadine and poplin, and over three million of other fabrics—altogether about eleven million meters of textiles. *Le Tintamarre* now remarked, after recommending La Chaussée d'Antin to its female readers as the 'foremost house of fashion in the world,' and also the 'most dependable': 'The entire French railway system comprises barely ten thousand kilometers of tracks—that is, only ten million meters. This *one* store, therefore, with its stock of textiles, could virtually stretch a tent over all the railroad tracks of France, "which, especially in the heat of summer, would be very pleasant."' Three or four other establishments of this kind publish similar figures, so that, with all these materials combined, one could place not only Paris . . . but the whole *département* of the Seine under a massive canopy, 'which likewise would be welcome in rainy weather.' But we cannot help asking: How are stores supposed to find room to stock this gigantic quantity of goods? The answer is very simple and, what is more, very logical: each firm is always larger than the others.

"You hear it said: 'La Ville de Paris, the largest store in the capital,' 'Les Villes de France, the largest store in the Empire,' 'La Chaussée d'Antin, the largest store in Europe,' 'Le Coin de Rue, the largest store in the world.'—'In the world': that is to say, on the entire earth there is none larger; you'd think that would be the limit. But no: Les Magasins du Louvre have not been named, and they bear the title 'The largest stores in the universe.' The universe! Including Sirius apparently, and maybe even the 'disappearing twin stars' of which Alexander von Humboldt speaks in his *Kosmos*."[1]

Here we see the connection between capitalism's evolving commercial advertising and the work of Grandville.

‹Adolf Ebeling,› *Lebende Bilder aus dem modernen Paris,* 4 vols. (Cologne, 1863–1866), vol. 2, pp. 292–294. [G2,1]

"Now then, you princes and sovereign states, resolve to pool your riches, your resources, your energies in order to ignite, as we do our gas jets, long-extinct volcanoes [whose craters, though filled with snow, are spewing torrents of inflammable hydrogen]; high cylindrical towers would be necessary to conduct the hot springs of Europe into the air, from which—so long as care is taken to avoid any premature contact with cooling waters—they will tumble down in cascades [and thereby warm the atmosphere]. Artificial concave mirrors, arranged in a semicircle on mountaintops to reflect the rays of the sun, would suitably augment the tendency of these springs to heat the air." F. v. Brandenburg, *Victoria! Eine neue Welt! Freudevoller Ausruf in Bezug darauf, daß auf unserm Planeten, besonders auf der von uns bewohnten nördlichen Halbkugel eine totale Temperatur-Veränderung hinsichtlich der Vermehrung der atmosphärischen Wärme eingetreten ist,*[2] 2nd expanded ed. (Berlin, 1835) ‹pp. 4–5›. ▯ Gas ▯

This fanatasy of an insane mind effectively constitutes, under the influence of the new invention, an advertisement for gas lighting—an advertisement in the comic-cosmic style of Grandville. In general, the close connection between advertising and the cosmic awaits analysis. [G2,2]

Exhibitions. "All regions and indeed, retrospectively, all times. From farming and mining, from industry and from the machines that were displayed in operation, to raw materials and processed materials, to art and the applied arts. In all these we see a peculiar demand for premature synthesis, of a kind that is characteristic of the nineteenth century in other areas as well: think of the total work of art. Apart from indubitably utilitarian motives, the century wanted to generate a vision of the human cosmos, as launched in a new movement." Sigfried Giedion, *Bauen in Frankreich* ‹Leipzig and Berlin, 1928›, p. 37. But these "premature syntheses" also bespeak a persistent endeavor to close up the space of existence and of development. To prevent the "airing-out of the classes." [G2,3]

Apropos of the exhibition of 1867, organized according to statistical principles: "**To take a turn about this place, circular like the equator, is literally to travel**

around the world, for all nations have come here; enemies are coexisting in peace. Just as, at the origin of things, the divine spirit was hovering over the orb of the waters, so now it hovers over this orb of iron." *L'Exposition universelle de 1867 illustrée: Publication internationale autorisée par la commission impériale*, vol. 2, p. 322 (cited in Giedion, ‹*Bauen in Frankreich*,› p. 41).   [G2,4]

In connection with the exhibition of 1867. On Offenbach. "For the past ten years, this verve of the comic author and this joyous inspiration of the composer have been vying with each other for fantastic and serendipitous effects; but only in 1867, the year of the Universal Exposition, did they attain the height of hilarity, the ultimate expression of their exuberance.[3] The success of this theater company, already so great, became delirious—something of which our petty victories of today can furnish no idea. Paris, that summer, suffered sunstroke." From the speech before the Académie Française by Henri Lavedan, December 31, 1899 (on the election of Meilhac).   [G2a,1]

Advertising is emancipated in Jugendstil. Jugendstil posters are "large, always figurative, refined in their colors but not gaudy; they show balls, night clubs, movie theaters. They are made for a frothy life—a life with which the sensual curves of Jugendstil are well matched." *Frankfurter Zeitung,* signed F. L. On an exhibition of posters in Mannheim in 1927. ☐ Dream Consciousness ☐   [G2a,2]

The first London exhibition brings together industries from around the world. Following this, the South Kensington museum is founded. Second world exhibition in 1862, likewise in London. With the Munich exhibition of 1875, the German Renaissance style comes into fashion.   [G2a,3]

Wiertz on the occasion of a world exhibition: "What strikes one at first is not at all the things people are making today but the things they will be making in the future. / The human spirit begins to accustom itself to the power of matter." A. J. Wiertz, *Oeuvres littéraires* (Paris, 1870), p. 374.   [G2a,4]

Talmeyr calls the poster "the art of Gomorrah." *La Cité du sang* (Paris, 1901), p. 286. ☐ Jugendstil ☐   [G2a,5]

Industrial exhibitions as secret blueprint for museums. Art: industrial products projected into the past.   [G2a,6]

Joseph Nash painted a series of watercolors for the king of England showing the Crystal Palace, the edifice built expressly for London's industrial exhibition in 1851. The first world exhibition and the first monumental structure in glass and iron! From these watercolors, one sees with amazement how the exhibitors took pains to decorate the colossal interior in an oriental-fairy-tale style, and how—alongside the assortment of goods that filled the arcaded walks—bronze monu-

ments, marble statues, and bubbling fountains populated the giant halls. ☐ Iron
☐ Interior ☐   [G2a,7]

The design for the Crystal Palace is by Joseph Paxton, chief gardener to the duke
of Devonshire, for whom he had built a conservatory (greenhouse) of glass and
iron at Chatsworth House. His design provided for fireproofing, plenty of light,
and the possibility of speedy and inexpensive assembly, and it prevailed over
those of the London Building Committee, whose competition was held in vain.[4]
                                                                                [G2a,8]

"Yes, long live the beer of Vienna! Is it native to this land that produces it? In
truth, I do not know. But of one thing, there can be no doubt: it is a refined and
comforting brew. It is not like the beer of Strasbourg . . . or Bavaria. . . . It is
divine beer, . . . clear as the thought of a poet, light as a swallow in flight, robust
and alcohol-charged as the pen of a German philosopher. It is digested like the
purest water, and it refreshes like ambrosia." Advertisement for Fanta Beer of
Vienna. No. 4, Rue Halévy, near the Nouvel Opéra, New Year's 1866. *Almanach
indicateur parisien* (Paris, 1866), p. 13.   [G2a,9]

"Another new word: *la réclame* (advertisement). Will it make a fortune?" Nadar,
Quand j'étais photographe (Paris ⟨1900⟩), p. 309.   [G2a,10]

Between the February Revolution and the June Insurrection: "All the walls were
covered with revolutionary posters which, some years later, Alfred Delvau reprinted in two thick volumes under the title *Les Murailles révolutionnaires*, so
that today we can still get some idea of this remarkable poster literature. There
was scarcely a palace or a church on which these notices could not be seen. Never
before was such a multitude of placards on view in any city. Even the government
made use of this medium to publish its decrees and proclamations, while thousands of other people resorted to *affiches* in order to air their views publicly on all
possible questions. As the time for the opening of the National Assembly drew
near, the language of the posters grew wilder and more passionate. . . . The number of public criers increased every day; thousands and thousands of Parisians,
who had nothing else to do, became news vendors." Sigmund Engländer,
Geschichte der französischen Arbeiter-Associationen (Hamburg, 1864), vol. 2,
pp. 279–280.   [G3,1]

"A short merry piece that is customarily presented here before the performance of
a new play: *Harlequin afficheur* ⟨Harlequin the Bill-Sticker⟩. In one quite funny
and charming scene, a poster for the comedy is stuck on Columbine's house." J. F.
Reichardt, *Vertraute Briefe aus Paris* (Hamburg, 1805), vol. 1, p. 457.   [G3,2]

"These days, a good many houses in Paris appear to be decorated in the style of
Harlequin's costume; I mean a patchwork of large green, yellow, [a word illegible]
and pink pieces of paper. The bill-stickers wrangle over the walls and come to

blows over a streetcorner. The best of it is that all these posters cover one another up at least ten times a day." Eduard Kroloff, *Schilderungen aus Paris* (Hamburg, 1839), vol. 2, p. 57. [G3,3]

"Paul Siraudin, born in 1814, has been active in the theater since 1835; he has supplemented this activity with practical efforts in the field of confectionery. The results of these efforts beckon no less temptingly from the large display window in the Rue de la Paix than the sugar almonds, bonbons, honey cakes, and sweet crackers offered to the public in the form of one-act dramatic sketches at the Palais-Royal." Rudolf Gottschall, "Das Theater und Drama des Second Empire," in *Unsere Zeit: Deutsche Revue—Monatsschrift zum Conversationslexicon* (Leipzig, 1867), p. 933. [G3,4]

From Coppée's speech to the Académie Française ("Response to Hérédia," May 30, 1895), it can be inferred that a strange sort of written image could formerly be seen in Paris: "Calligraphic masterpieces which, in the old days, were exhibited on every streetcorner, and in which we could admire the portrait of Béranger or 'The Taking of the Bastille' in the form of paraphs" ‹p. 46›. [G3,5]

Le Charivari of 1836 has an illustration showing a poster that covers half a housefront. The windows are left uncovered, except for one, it seems. Out of that a man is leaning while cutting away the obstructing piece of paper.

[G3,6]

"Essence d'Amazilly, fragrance and antiseptic; hygienic toiletries from Duprat and Company." "If we have named our essence after the daughter of a cacique, it is only to indicate that the vegetal ingredients to which this distillation owes its surprising effectiveness come from the same torrid climate as she does. The term 'antiseptic' belongs to the lexicon of science, and we use it only to point out that, apart from the incomparable benefits our product offers to ladies, it possesses hygienic virtues calculated to win the confidence of all those willing to be convinced of its salutary action. For if our lotion, unlike the waters of the Fountain of Youth, has no power to wash away the accumulated years, at least it does have, in addition to other merits, the inestimable advantage (we believe) of restoring to the full extent of its former radiance the lost majesty of that consummate entity, that masterpiece of Creation which, with the elegance, purity, and grace of its forms, makes up the lovelier half of humanity. Without the providential supervention of our discovery, this most brilliant and delicate ornament—resembling, in the tender charms of its mysterious structure, a fragile blossom that wilts at the first hard rain—would enjoy, at best, but a fugitive splendor, after the fading of which it must needs languish under the ruinous cloud of illness, the fatiguing demands of nursing, or the no less injurious embrace of the pitiless corset. Developed, above all, in the interests of ladies, our Essence d'Amazilly answers to the most exacting and most intimate requirements of their toilette. It unites, thanks to a happy infusion, all that is necessary to revive, foster, and enhance natural attractions, without the slightest detriment." ⟨Cited in⟩ Charles Simond, *Paris de 1800 à 1900* (Paris, 1900), vol. 2, p. 510 ("Une Réclame de parfumeur en 1857").[5]   [G3a,1]

"Gravely, the sandwich-man bears his double burden, light as it is. A young lady whose rotundity is only temporary smiles at the walking poster, yet wishes to read it even as she smiles. The happy author of her abdominal salience likewise bears a burden of his own." ⟨The husband has his wife on his right arm and a large box under his left. Along with four other people, they are clustered around a sandwich-man seen from the back.⟩ Text accompanying a lithograph entitled "L'Homme-affiche sur la Place des Victoires," from *Nouveaux Tableaux de Paris*, text to plate 63 [the lithographs are by Marlet]. This book is a sort of Hogarth *ad usum Delphini*.   [G3a,2]

Beginning of Alfred Delvau's preface to *Les Murailles révolutionnaires:* "These revolutionary placards—at the bottom of which we set our obscure name—form an immense and unique composition, one without precedent, we believe, in the history of books. They are a collective work. The author is Monsieur Everyone— Mein Herr Omnes, as Luther says." *Les Murailles révolutionnaires de 1848*, 16th ed. (Paris ⟨1852⟩), vol. 1, p. 1.   [G3a,3]

"When, in 1798, under the Directory, the idea of public exhibitions was inaugurated on the Champ de Mars, there were 110 exhibitors, of whom twenty-five were awarded medals." *Palais de l'Industrie* (distributed by H. Plon).   [G4,1]

"Beginning in 1801, the products of newly emerging industries were exhibited in the courtyard of the Louvre." Lucien Dubech and Pierre d'Espezel, *Histoire de Paris* (Paris, 1926), p. 335.   [G4,2]

"Every five years—in 1834, 1839, and 1844—the products of industry are exhibited in Marigny Square." Dubech and d'Espezel, *Histoire de Paris*, p. 389.
          [G4,3]

"The first exhibition dates back to 1798; set up on the Champ de Mars, it was . . . an exhibition of the products of French industry and was conceived by François de Neufchâteau. There were three national exhibitions under the Empire (in 1801, 1802, and 1806), the first two in the courtyard of the Louvre, the third at the Invalides. There were three during the Restoration (in 1819, 1823, and 1827), all at the Louvre; three during the July Monarchy (in 1834, 1839, and 1844), on the Place de la Concorde and the Champs-Elysées; and one under the Second Republic, in 1849. Then, following the example of England, which had organized an international exhibition in 1851, Imperial France held world exhibitions on the Champ de Mars in 1855 and 1867. The first saw the birth of the Palais de l'Industrie, demolished during the Republic; the second was a delirious festival marking the high point of the Second Empire. In 1878, a new exhibition was organized to attest to rebirth after defeat; it was held on the Champ de Mars in a temporary palace erected by Formigé. It is characteristic of these enormous fairs to be ephemeral, yet each of them has left its trace in Paris. The exhibition of 1878 was responsible for the Trocadéro, that eccentric palace clapped down on the top of Chaillot by Davioud and Bourdais, and also for the footbridge at Passy, built to replace the Pont d'Iéna, which was no longer usable. The exhibition of 1889 left behind the Galerie des Machines, which was eventually torn down, although the Eiffel Tower still stands." Dubech and d'Espezel, *Histoire de Paris* (Paris, 1926), p. 461.   [G4,4]

"'Europe is off to view the merchandise,' said Renan—contemptuously—of the 1855 exhibition." Paul Morand, *1900* (Paris, 1931), p. 71.   [G4,5]

"'This year has been lost for propaganda,' says a socialist orator at the congress of 1900." Paul Morand, *1900* (Paris, 1931), p. 129.   [G4,6]

"In 1798, a universal exposition of industry was announced; it was to take place . . . on the Champ de Mars. The Directory had charged the minister of the interior, François de Neufchâteau, with organizing a national festival to commemorate the founding of the Republic. The minister had conferred with several people, who proposed holding contests and games, like greasy-pole climbing. One person suggested that a great market be set up after the fashion of country fairs, but on a larger scale. Finally, it was proposed that an exhibition of paintings be included. These last two suggestions gave François de Neufchâteau the idea of presenting an exhibition of industry in celebration of the national festival. Thus, the first industrial exposition is born from the wish to amuse the working classes, and it becomes for them a festival of emancipation. . . . The increasingly popular character of industry starts to become evident. . . . Silk fabrics are replaced by woolens, and satin and lace by materials more in keeping with the domestic requirements of the Third Estate: woolen bonnets and corduroys. . . . Chaptal, the spokesman for this exhibition, calls the industrial state by its name for the first time." Sigmund Engländer, *Geschichte der französischen Arbeiter-Associationen* (Hamburg, 1864), vol. 1, pp. 51–53.   [G4,7]

"In celebrating the centenary of the great Revolution, the French bourgeoisie has, as it were, intentionally set out to demonstrate to the proletariat *ad oculos* the economic possibility and necessity of a social uprising. The world exhibition has given the proletariat an excellent idea of the unprecedented level of development which the means of production have reached in all civilized lands—a development far exceeding the boldest utopian fantasies of the century preceding this one. . . . The exhibition has further demonstrated that modern development of the forces of production must of necessity lead to industrial crises that, given the anarchy currently reigning in production, will only grow more acute with the passage of time, and hence more destructive to the course of the world economy." G. Plekhanov, "Wie die Bourgeoisie ihrer Revolution gedenkt," *Die neue Zeit*, 9, no. 1 (Stuttgart, 1891), p. 138.   [G4a,1]

"Despite all the posturing with which Teutonic arrogance tries to represent the capital of the Reich as the brightest beacon of civilization, Berlin has not yet been able to mount a world exhibition. . . . To try to excuse this deplorable fact by claiming that world exhibitions have had their day and now are nothing but gaudy and grandiose vanity fairs, and so forth, is a crass evasion. We have no wish to deny the drawbacks of world exhibitions . . . ; nevertheless, in every case they remain incomparably more powerful levers of human culture than the countless barracks and churches with which Berlin has been inundated at such great cost. The recurrent initiatives to establish a world exhibition have foundered, first of all, on the lack of energy . . . afflicting the bourgeoisie, and, second, on the poorly disguised resentment with which an absolutist-feudal militarism looks on anything that could threaten its—alas!—still germinating roots." ⟨Anonymous,⟩ "Klassenkämpfe," *Die neue Zeit*, 12, no. 2 (Stuttgart, 1894), p. 257.   [G4a,2]

On the occasion of the world exhibition of 1867, Victor Hugo issued a manifesto to the peoples of Europe.   [G4a,3]

Chevalier was a disciple of Enfantin. Editor of *Le Globe*.   [G4a,4]

Apropos of Roland de la Platière's *Encyclopédie méthodique:* "Turning to *les manufactures,* . . . Roland writes: 'Industry is born of need. . . .' It might appear from this that the term is being used in the classical sense of *industria*. What follows provides clarification: 'But this fecund and perverse riverhead, of irregular and retrogressive disposition, eventually came down from the uplands to flood the fields, and soon nothing could satisfy the need which overspread the land.' . . . What is significant is his ready employment of the word *industrie*, more than thirty years before the work of Chaptal." Henri Hauser, *Les Débuts du capitalisme* (Paris, 1931), pp. 315–316.   [G4a,5]

"With price tag affixed, the commodity comes on the market. Its material quality and individuality are merely an incentive for buying and selling; for the social measure of its value, such quality is of no importance whatsoever. The commodity has become an abstraction. Once escaped from the hand of the producer and divested of its real particularity, it ceases to be a product and to be ruled over by human beings. It has acquired a 'ghostly objectivity' and leads a life of its own. 'A commodity appears, at first sight, to be a trivial and easily understood thing. Our analysis shows that, in reality, it is a vexed and complicated thing, abounding in metaphysical subtleties and theological niceties.' Cut off from the will of man, it aligns itself in a mysterious hierarchy, develops or declines exchangeability, and, in accordance with its own peculiar laws, performs as an actor on a phantom stage. In the language of the commodities exchange, cotton 'soars,' copper 'slumps,' corn 'is active,' coal 'is sluggish,' wheat 'is on the road to recovery,' and petroleum 'displays a healthy trend.' Things have gained autonomy, and they take on human features. . . . The commodity has been transformed into an idol that, although the product of human hands, disposes over the human. Marx speaks of the fetish character of the commodity. 'This fetish character of the commodity world has its origin in the peculiar social character of the labor that produces commodities. . . . It is only the particular social relation between people that here assumes, in the eyes of these people, the phantasmagorical form of a relation between things.'"[6] Otto Rühle, *Karl Marx* (Hellerau ‹1928›), pp. 384–385.   [G5,1]

"According to official estimates, a total of about 750 workers, chosen by their comrades or else named by the entrepreneurs themselves, visited London's world exhibition in 1862. . . . The official character of this delegation, and the manner in which it was constituted, naturally inspired little confidence in the revolutionary and republican émigrés from France. This circumstance perhaps explains why the idea of an organized reception for this deputation originated with the editors of an organ dedicated to the cooperative movement. . . . At the urging of the editorial staff of *The Working Man*, a committee was formed to prepare a welcome for the French workers. . . . Those named to participate included . . . J. Morton Peto, . . . and *Joseph Paxton*. . . . The interests of industry were put foremost, . . . and the need for an agreement between workers and entrepreneurs, as the *sole* means of bettering the difficult condition of the workers, was strongly underlined. . . . We cannot . . . regard this gathering as the birthplace . . . of the International Workingmen's Association. That is a legend. . . . The truth is simply that this visit acquired, through its indirect consequences, momentous importance as a key step on the way to an understanding between English and French workers." D. Rjazanov, "Zur Geschichte der ersten Internationale," in *Marx-Engels Archiv*, vol. 1 ‹Frankfurt am Main, 1928›, pp. 157, 159–160.   [G5,2]

"Already, for the first world exhibition in 1851, some of the workers proposed by the entrepreneurs were sent to London at the state's expense. There was also, however, an independent delegation dispatched to London on the initiative of Blanqui (the economist) and Emile de Girardin. . . . This delegation submitted a general report in which, to be sure, we find no trace of the attempt to establish a permanent liaison with English workers, but in which the need for peaceful relations between England and France is stressed. . . . In 1855, the second world exhibition took place, this time in Paris. Delegations of workers from the capital, as well as from the provinces, were now totally barred. It was feared that they would give workers an opportunity for organizing." D. Rjazanov, "Zur Geschichte der ersten Internationale," in *Marx-Engels Archiv*, ed. Rjazanov, vol. 1 (Frankfurt am Main), pp. 150–151.   [G5a,1]

The subtleties of Grandville aptly express what Marx calls the "theological niceties"[7] of the commodity.   [G5a,2]

"The sense of taste is a carriage with four wheels, which are: (1) Gastronomy; (2) Cuisine; (3) Company; (4) Culture." From ‹Fourier's› *Nouveau Monde industriel et sociétaire* (1829), cited in E. Poisson, *Fourier* (Paris, 1932), p. 130.   [G5a,3]

Connection of the first world exhibition in London in 1851 with the idea of free trade. [G5a,4]

"The world exhibitions have lost much of their original character. The enthusiasm that, in 1851, was felt in the most disparate circles has subsided, and in its place has come a kind of cool calculation. In 1851, we were living in the era of free trade. . . . For some decades now, we have witnessed the spread of protectionism. . . . Participation in the exhibition becomes . . . a sort of representation . . . ; and whereas in 1850 the ruling tenet was that the government need not concern itself in this affair, the situation today is so far advanced that the government of each country can be considered a veritable entrepreneur." Julius Lessing, *Das halbe Jahrhundert der Weltausstellungen* (Berlin, 1900), pp. 29–30. [G5a,5]

In London, in 1851, "appeared . . . the first cast-steel cannon by Krupp. Soon thereafter, the Prussian minister of war placed an order for more than 200 exemplars of this model." Julius Lessing, *Das halbe Jahrhundert der Weltausstellungen* (Berlin, 1900), p. 11. [G5a,6]

"From the same sphere of thought that engendered the great idea of free trade arose . . . the notion that no one would come away empty-handed—rather, the contrary—from an exhibition at which he had staked his best so as to be able to take home the best that other people had to offer. . . . This bold conception, in which the idea for the exhibition originated, was put into action. Within eight months, everything was finished. 'An absolute wonder that has become a part of history.' At the foundation of the entire undertaking, remarkably enough, rests the principle that such a work must be backed not by the state but by the free activity of its citizens. . . . Originally, two private contractors, the Munday brothers, offered to build, at their own risk, a palace costing a million marks. But grander proportions were resolved on, and the necessary funds for guaranteeing the enterprise, totaling many millions, were subscribed in short order. The great new thought found a great new form. The engineer Paxton built the Crystal Palace. In every land rang out the news of something fabulous and unprecedented: a palace of glass and iron was going to be built, one that would cover eighteen acres. Not long before this, Paxton had constructed a vaulted roof of glass and iron for one of the greenhouses at Kew, in which luxuriant palms were growing, and this achievement gave him the courage to take on the new task. Chosen as a site for the exhibition was the finest park in London, Hyde Park, which offered in the middle a wide open meadow, traversed along its shorter axis by an avenue of splendid elms. But anxious onlookers soon raised a cry of alarm lest these trees be sacrificed for the sake of a whim. 'Then I shall roof over the trees,' was Paxton's answer, and he proceeded to design the transept, which, with its semicylindrical vault elevated 112 feet above the ground, . . . accommodated the whole row of elms. It is in the highest degree remarkable and significant that this Great Exhibition of London— born of modern conceptions of steam power, electricity, and photography, and modern conceptions of free trade—should at the same time have afforded the decisive impetus, within this period as a whole, for the revolution in artistic forms. To build a palace out of glass and iron seemed to the world, in those days, a fantastic inspiration for a temporary piece of architecture. We see now that it was the first great advance on the road to a wholly new world of forms. . . . The constructive style, as opposed to the historical style, has become the watchword of the modern movement. When did this idea make its triumphal entry into the world? In the year 1851, with the Crystal Palace in London. At first, people thought it impossible that a palace of colossal proportions could be built from glass and iron. In the publications of the day, we find the idea of assembling iron components, so familiar to us now, represented as something extraordinary. England can boast of having accomplished this quite novel task in the space of eight months, using its existing factories, without any additional capacity. One points out triumphantly that . . . in the sixteenth century a small glazed window was still a luxury item, whereas today a building covering eighteen acres can be constructed entirely out of glass. To a man like Lothar Bucher, the meaning of this new structure was clear: it was the undisguised architectural expression of the transverse strength of slender iron components. But the fantastic charm which the edifice exerted on all souls went well beyond such a characterization, however crucial for the program of the future; and in this regard, the preservation of the magnificent row of trees for the central transept was of capital importance. Into this space were transported all the horticultural glories which the rich conservatories of England had been able to cultivate. Lightly plumed palms from the tropics mingled with the leafy crowns of the five-hundred-year-old elms; and within this enchanted forest the decorators arranged masterpieces of plastic art, statuary, large bronzes, and specimens of other artworks. At the center stood an imposing crystal fountain. To the right and to the left ran galleries in which visitors passed from one national exhibit to the other. Overall, it seemed a wonderland, appealing more to the imagination than to the intellect. 'It is with sober economy of phrase that I term the prospect incomparably fairy-like. This space is a summer night's dream in the midnight sun' (Lothar Bucher). Such sentiments were registered throughout the world. I myself recall, from my childhood, how the news of the Crystal Palace reached us in Germany, and how pictures of it were hung in the middle-class parlors of distant provincial towns. It seemed then that the world we knew from old fairy tales—of the princess in the glass coffin, of queens and elves dwelling in crystal houses—had come to life . . ., and these impressions have persisted through the decades. The great transept of the palace and part of the pavilions were transferred to Sydenham, where the building stands today;[8] there I saw it in 1862, with feelings of awe and the sheerest delight. It has taken four decades, numerous fires, and many depredations to ruin this magic, although even today it is still not completely vanished." Julius Lessing, *Das halbe Jahrhundert der Weltausstellungen* (Berlin, 1900), pp. 6–10.   [G6; G6a,1]

Organizing the New York exhibition of 1853 fell to Phineas Barnum.   [G6a,2]

"Le Play has calculated that the number of years required to prepare a world exhibition equals the number of months it runs. . . . There is obviously a shocking

Exterior of the Crystal Palace, London. See G6; G6a,1.

disproportion here between the period of gestation and the duration of the enterprise." Maurice Pécard, *Les Expositions internationales au point de vue économique et social, particulièrement en France* (Paris, 1901), p. 23.   [G6a,3]

A bookseller's poster appears in *Les Murailles revolutionnaires de 1848* with the
following explanatory remark: "We offer this *affiche,* as later we shall offer others
unrelated to the elections or to the political events of the day. We offer it because it
tells why and how certain manufacturers profit from certain occasions." From the
poster: "Read this important notice against Swindlers. Monsieur Alexandre
Pierre, wishing to stop the daily abuses created by the general ignorance of the
Argot and Jargon of swindlers and dangerous men, has made good use of the
unhappy time he was forced to spend with them as a victim of the fallen Government; now restored to liberty by our noble Republic, he has just published the
fruit of those sad studies he was able to make in prison. He is not afraid to descend

into the midst of these horrible places, and even into the Lions' Den, if by these means . . . he can shed light on the principal words of their conversations, and thus make it possible to avoid the misfortunes and abuses that result from not knowing these words, which until now were intelligible only to swindlers. . . . On sale from public vendors and from the Author." *Les Murailles révolutionnaires de 1848* (Paris ‹1852›), vol. 1, p. 320. [G7,1]

If the commodity was a fetish, then Grandville was the tribal sorcerer. [G7,2]

Second Empire: "The government's candidates . . . were able to print their proclamations on white paper, a color reserved exclusively for official publications." A. Malet and P. Grillet, *XIXe siècle* (Paris, 1919), p. 271. [G7,3]

In Jugendstil we see, for the first time, the integration of the human body into advertising. ⌑Jugendstil⌑ [G7,4]

Worker delegations at the world exhibition of 1867. At the top of the agenda is the demand for the abrogation of Article 1781 of the Civil Code, which reads: "The employer's word shall be taken as true in his statement of wages apportioned, of salary paid for the year ended, and of accounts given for the current year" (p. 140).—"The delegations of workers at the exhibitions of London and Paris in 1862 and in 1867 gave a direction to the social movement of the Second Empire, and even, we may say, to that of the second half of the nineteenth century. . . . Their reports were compared to the records of the Estates General; the former were the signal for a social evolution, just as the latter, in 1789, had been the cause of a political and economic revolution" (p. 207).—[This comparison comes from Michel Chevalier.] Demand for a ten-hour workday (p. 121).—"Four hundred thousand free tickets were distributed to the workers of Paris and various *départements*. A barracks with more than 30,000 beds was put at the disposal of the visiting workers" (p. 84). Henry Fougère, *Les Délégations ouvrières aux expositions universelles* (Montluçon, 1905). [G7,5]

Gatherings of worker delegations of 1867 at the "training ground of the Passage Raoul." Fougère, p. 85. [G7a,1]

"The exhibition had long since closed, but the delegates continued their discussions, and the parliament of workers kept holding sessions in the Passage Raoul." Henry Fougère, *Les Délégations ouvrières aux expositions universelles sous le second empire* (Montluçon, 1905), pp. 86–87. Altogether, the sessions lasted from July 21, 1867, until July 14, 1869. [G7a,2]

International Association of Workers. "'The Association . . . dates from 1862, from the time of the world exhibition in London. It was there that English and French workers first met, to hold discussions and seek mutual enlightenment.' Statement made by M. Tolain on March 6, 1868, . . . during the first suit brought by the government against the International Association of Workers." Henry Fougère, *Les Délégations ouvrières aux expositions universelles sous le second empire* (Montluçon, 1905), p. 75. The first great meeting in London drafted a declaration of sympathy for the liberation of the Poles.   [G7a,3]

In the three or four reports by the worker delegations who took part in the world exhibition of 1867, there are demands for the abolition of standing armies and for general disarmament. Delegations of porcelain painters, piano repairmen, shoemakers, and mechanics. See Fougère, pp. 163–164.   [G7a,4]

1867. "Whoever visited the Champ de Mars for the first time got a singular impression. Arriving by the central avenue, he saw at first . . . only iron and smoke. . . . This initial impression exerted such an influence on the visitor that, ignoring the tempting diversions offered by the arcade, he would hasten toward the movement and noise that attracted him. At every point . . . where the machines were momentarily still, he could hear the strains of steam-powered organs and the symphonies of brass instruments." A. S. de Doncourt, *Les Expositions universelles* (Lille and Paris ‹1889›), pp. 111–112.   [G7a,5]

Theatrical works pertaining to the world exhibition of 1855: *Paris trop petit*, August 4, 1855, Théâtre du Luxembourg; Paul Meurice, *Paris*, July 21, Porte-Saint-Martin; Théodore Barrière and Paul de Kock, *L'Histoire de Paris* and *Les Grands Siècles*, September 29; *Les Modes de l'exposition*; *Dzim boom boom: Revue de l'exhibition*; Sébastien Rhéal, *La Vision de Faustus, ou L'Exposition universelle de 1855*. In Adolphe Démy, *Essai historique sur les expositions universelles de Paris* (Paris, 1907), p. 90.   [G7a,6]

London's world exhibition of 1862: "No trace remained of the edifying impression made by the exhibition of 1851. . . . Nevertheless, this exhibition had some noteworthy results. . . . The greatest surprise . . . came from China. Up to this time, Europe had seen nothing of Chinese art except . . . the ordinary porcelains sold on the market. But now the Anglo-Chinese war had taken place . . . , and the Summer Palace had been burned to the ground, supposedly as punishment.[9] In truth, however, the English had succeeded even more than their allies, the French, in carrying away a large portion of the treasures amassed in that palace, and these treasures were subsequently put on exhibit in London in 1862. For the sake of discretion, it was women rather than men . . . who acted as exhibitors." Julius Lessing, *Das halbe Jahrhundert der Weltausstellungen* (Berlin, 1900), p. 16.
                    [G8,1]

Lessing (*Das halbe Jahrhundert der Weltausstellungen* [Berlin, 1900], p. 4) points up the difference between the world exhibitions and the fairs. For the latter, the merchants brought their whole stock of goods along with them. The world exhibitions presuppose a considerable development of commercial as well as industrial credit—that is to say, credit on the part of the customers, as well as on the part of the firms taking their orders. [G8,2]

"You deliberately had to close your eyes in order not to realize that the fair on the Champ de Mars in 1798, that the superb porticoes of the courtyard of the Louvre and the courtyard of the Invalides constructed in the following years, and, finally, that the memorable royal ordinance of January 13, 1819,[10] have powerfully contributed to the glorious development of French industry. . . . It was reserved for the king of France to transform the magnificent galleries of his palace into an immense bazaar, in order that his people might contemplate . . . these unbloodied trophies raised up by the genius of the arts and the genius of peace." ⟨Joseph-Charles⟩ Chenou and H.D., *Notice sur l'exposition des produits de l'industrie et des arts qui a eu lieu à Douai en 1827* (Douai, 1827), p. 5. [G8,3]

Three different delegations of workers were sent to London in 1851; none of them accomplished anything significant. Two were official: one represented the National Assembly, and one the municipality of Paris. The private delegation was put together with the support of the press, in particular of Emile de Girardin. The workers themselves played no part in assembling these delegations. [G8,4]

The dimensions of the Crystal Palace, according to A. S. Doncourt, *Les Expositions universelles* (Lille and Paris ⟨1889⟩), p. 12. The long sides measured 560 meters. [G8,5]

On the workers' delegations to the Great Exhibition in London in 1862: "Electoral offices were being rapidly organized when, on the eve of elections, an incident . . . arose to impede the operations. The Paris police . . . took umbrage at this unprecedented development, and the Workers Commission was ordered to cease its activities. Convinced that this measure . . . could only be the result of a misunderstanding, members of the Commission took their appeal directly to His Majesty. . . . The emperor . . . was, in fact, willing to authorize the Commisssion to pursue its task. The elections . . . resulted in the selection of two hundred delegates. . . . A period of ten days had been granted to each group to accomplish its mission. Each delegate received, on his departure, the sum of 115 francs, a second-class round-trip train ticket, lodging, and a meal, as well as a pass to the exhibition. . . . This great popular movement took place without the slightest incident that . . . could have been termed regrettable." *Rapports des délégués des ouvriers parisiens à l'exposition de Londres en 1862, publiés par la Commission ouvrière* (Paris, 1862–1864) [1 vol.!], pp. iii–iv. (The document contains fifty-three reports by delegations from the different trades.) [G8a,1]

Paris, 1855. "Four locomotives were guarding the hall of machines, like those great bulls of Ninevah, or like the sphinxes to be seen at the entrance to Egyptian temples. This hall was a land of iron and fire and water; the ears were deafened, the eyes dazzled. . . . All was in motion. One saw wool combed, cloth twisted, yarn clipped, grain threshed, coal extracted, chocolate refined, and on and on. All exhibitors without exception were allowed motility and steam, contrary to what went on in London in 1851, when only the English exhibitors had had the benefit of fire and water." A. S. Doncourt, *Les Expositions universelles* (Lille and Paris ‹1889›), p. 53. [G8a,2]

In 1867, the "oriental quarter" was the center of attraction. [G8a,3]

Fifteen million visitors to the exhibition of 1867. [G8a,4]

In 1855, for the first time, merchandise could be marked with a price. [G8a,5]

"Le Play had . . . understood how necessary it would become to find what we call, in modern parlance, 'a draw'—some star attraction. He likewise foresaw that this necessity would lead to mismanagement of the exhibitions, and this is the issue . . . to which M. Claudio-Janet addressed himself in 1889: 'The economist M. Frédéric Passy, a worthy man, has for many years now, in his speeches to Parliament and to the Académie, been denouncing the abuses of the street fairs. Everything he says about the gingerbread fair . . . can also be said (allowing for differences in magnitude) of the great centennial celebration.'" A note at this point: "The centennial celebration, in fact, was so successful that the Eiffel Tower, which cost 6 million francs, had already earned, by the fifth of November, 6,459,581 francs." Maurice Pécard, *Les Expositions internationales au point de vue économique et sociale, particulièrement en France* (Paris, 1901), p. 29. [G9,1]

The exhibition palace of 1867 on the Champ de Mars—compared by some to Rome's Colosseum: "The arrangement conceived by Le Play, the head of the exhibition committee, was a most felicitous one. The objects on exhibit were distributed, according to their materials, in eight concentric galleries; twelve avenues . . . branched out from the center, and the principal nations occupied the sectors cut by those radii. In this way, . . . by strolling around the galleries, one could . . . survey the state of one particular industry in all the different countries, whereas, by strolling up the avenues that crossed them, one could survey the state of the different branches of industry in each particular country." Adolphe Démy, *Essai historique sur les expositions universelles de Paris* (Paris, 1907), p. 129.—Cited here is Théophile Gautier's article about the palace in *Le Moniteur* of September 17, 1867: "We have before us, it seems, a monument created on another planet, on Jupiter or Saturn, according to a taste we do not recognize and with a coloration to which our eyes are not accustomed." Just before this: "The great azure gulf, with its blood-colored rim, produces a vertiginous effect and unsettles our ideas of architecture.'" [G9,2]

Resistance to the world exhibition of 1851: "The king of Prussia forbade the royal prince and princess . . . from traveling to London. . . . The diplomatic corps refused to address any word of congratulations to the queen. 'At this moment,' wrote . . . Prince Albert to his mother on April 15, 1851, . . . 'the opponents of the Exhibition are hard at work. . . . The foreigners, they cry, will start a radical revolution here; they will kill Victoria and myself and proclaim a red republic. Moreover, the plague will surely result from the influx of such multitudes and will devour those who have not been driven away by the high prices on everything.'" Adolphe Démy, *Essai historique sur les expositions universelles* (Paris, 1907), p. 38. [G9,3]

François de Neufchâteau on the exhibition of 1798 (in Démy, *Essai historique sur les expositions universelles*). "'The French,' he declared, . . . 'have amazed Europe by the swiftness of their military successes; they should launch a career in commerce and the arts with just the same fervor'" (p. 14). "This initial exposition . . . is really an initial campaign, a campaign disastrous for English industry" (p. 18).—Martial character of the opening procession: "(1) a contingent of trumpeters; (2) a detachment of cavalry; (3) the first two squads of mace bearers; (4) the drums; (5) a military marching band; (6) a squad of infantry; (7) the heralds; (8) the festival marshal; (9) the artists registered in the exhibition; (10) the jury" (p. 15).—Neufchâteau awards the gold medal to the most heroic assault on English industry. [G9a,1]

The second exhibition, in Year IX,[11] was supposed to bring together, in the courtyard of the Louvre, works of industry and of the plastic arts. But the artists refused to exhibit their work alongside that of manufacturers (Démy, p. 19). [G9a,2]

Exhibition of 1819. "The king, on the occasion of the exhibition, conferred the title of baron on Ternaux and Oberkampf. . . . The granting of aristocratic titles to industrialists had provoked some criticisms. In 1823, no new titles were conferred." Démy, *Essai historique*, p. 24. [G9a,3]

Exhibition of 1844. Madame de Girardin's comments on the event, ‹in› Vicomte de Launay, *Lettres parisiennes*, vol. 4, p. 66 (cited in Démy, *Essai historique*, p. 27): "'It is a pleasure,' she remarked, 'strangely akin to a nightmare.' And she went on to enumerate the singularities, of which there was no lack: the flayed horse, the colossal beetle, the moving jaw, the chronometric Turk who marked the hours by the number of his somersaults, and—last but not least—M. and Mme. Pipelet, the concierges in *Les Mystères de Paris*,[12] as angels." [G9a,4]

World exhibition of 1851: 14,837 exhibitors; that of 1855: 80,000. [G9a,5]

In 1867, the Egyptian exhibit was housed in a building whose design was based on an Egyptian temple. [G9a,6]

In his novel *The Fortress*, Walpole describes the precautions that were taken in a lodging-house specially designed to welcome visitors to the world exhibition of

1851. These precautions included continuous police surveillance of the dormitories, the presence of a chaplain, and a regular morning visit by a doctor.   [G10,1]

Walpole describes the Crystal Palace, with the glass fountain at its center and the old elms—the latter "looking almost like the lions of the forest caught in a net of glass" (p. 307). He describes the booths decorated with expensive carpets, and above all the machines. "There were in the machine-room the 'self-acting mules,' the Jacquard lace machines, the envelope machines, the power looms, the model locomotives, centrifugal pumps, the vertical steam-engines, all of these working like mad, while the thousands nearby, in their high hats and bonnets, sat patiently waiting, passive, unwitting that the Age of Man on this Planet was doomed." Hugh Walpole, *The Fortress* (Hamburg, Paris, and Bologna ‹1933›), p. 306.[13]   [G10,2]

Delvau speaks of "men who, each evening, have their eyes glued to the display window of La Belle Jardinère to watch the day's receipts being counted." Alfred Delvau, *Les Heures parisiennes* (Paris, 1866), p. 144 ("Huit heures du soir").
[G10,3]

In a speech to the Senate, on January 31, 1868, Michel Chevalier makes an effort to save the previous year's Palace of Industry from destruction. Of the various possibilities he lays out for salvaging the building, the most noteworthy is that of using the interior—which, with its circular form, is ideally suited to such a purpose—for practicing troop maneuvers. He also proposes developing the structure into a permanent merchandise mart for imports. The intention of the opposing party seems to have been to keep the Champ de Mars free of all construction—this for military reasons. See Michel Chevalier, *Discours sur une pétition réclamant contre la destruction du palais de l'Exposition universelle de 1867* (Paris, 1868).
[G10,4]

"The world exhibitions . . . cannot fail to provoke the most exact comparisons between the prices and the qualities of the same article as produced in different countries. How the school of absolute freedom of trade rejoices then! The world exhibitions contribute . . . to the reduction, if not the abolition, of custom duties." Achille de Colusont ‹?›, *Histoire des expositions des produits de l'industrie française* (Paris, 1855), p. 544.   [G10a,1]

> Every industry, in exhibiting its trophies
> In this bazaar of universal progress,
> Seems to have borrowed a fairy's magic wand
> To bless the Crystal Palace.
> . . . . .
> Rich men, scholars, artists, proletarians—
> Each one labors for the common good;
> And, joining together like noble brothers,
> All have at heart the happiness of each.

Clairville and Jules Cordier, *Le Palais de Cristal, ou Les Parisiens à Londres* [Théâtre de la Porte-Saint-Martin, May 26, 1851] (Paris, 1851), p. 6.   [G10a,2]

The last two tableaux from Clairville's *Palais de Cristal* take place in front of and inside the Crystal Palace. The stage directions for the ‹next to› last tableau: "The main gallery of the Crystal Palace. To the left, downstage, a bed, at the head of which is a large dial. At center stage, a small table holding small sacks and pots of earth. To the right, an electrical machine. Toward the rear, an exhibition of various products (based on the descriptive engraving done in London)" (p. 30).
[G10a,3]

Advertisement for Marquis Chocolates, from 1846: "Chocolate from La Maison Marquis, 44 Rue Vivienne, at the Passage des Panoramas.—The time has come when chocolate praline, and all the other varieties of *chocolat de fantaisie*, will be available . . . from the House of Marquis in the most varied and graceful of forms. . . . We are privileged to be able to announce to our readers that, once again, an assortment of pleasing verses, judiciously selected from among the year's purest, most gracious, and most elevated publications, will accompany the exquisite confections of Marquis. Confident in the favorable advantage that is ours alone, we rejoice to bring together that puissant name with so much lovely verse." Cabinet des Estampes.   [G10a,4]

Palace of Industry, 1855: "Six pavilions border the building on four sides, and 306 arcades run through the lower story. An enormous glass roof provides light to the interior. As materials, only stone, iron, and zinc have been used; building costs amounted to 11 million francs. . . . Of particular interest are two large paintings on glass at the eastern and western ends of the main gallery. . . . The figures represented on these appear to be life-size, yet are no less than six meters high." *Acht Tage in Paris* (Paris, July 1855), pp. 9–10. The paintings on glass show figures representing industrial France and Justice.   [G11,1]

"I have . . . written, together with my collaborators on *L'Atelier*, that the moment for economic revolution has come . . . , although we had all agreed some time previously that the workers of Europe had achieved solidarity and that it was necessary now to move on, before anything else, to the idea of a political federation of peoples." A. Corbon, *Le Secret du peuple de Paris* (Paris, 1863), p. 196. Also p. 242: "In sum, the political attitude of the working class of Paris consists almost entirely in the passionate desire to serve the movement of federation of nationalities."   [G11,2]

Nina Lassave, Fieschi's beloved, was employed, after his execution on February 19, 1836, as a cashier at the Café de la Renaissance on the Place de la Bourse.
[G11,3]

Animal symbolism in Toussenel: the mole. "The mole is . . . not the emblem of a single character. It is the emblem of a whole social period: the period of industry's infancy, the Cyclopean period. . . . It is the . . . allegorical expression of the absolute predominance of brute force over intellectual force. . . . Many estimable analogists find a marked resemblance between moles, which upturn the soil and pierce passages of subterranean communication, . . . and the monopolizers of railroads and stage routes. . . . The extreme nervous sensibility of the mole, which fears the light . . . , admirably characterizes the obstinate obscurantism of those monopolizers of banking and of transportation, who also fear the light." A. Toussenel, *L'Esprit des bêtes: Zoologie passionnelle—Mammifères de France* (Paris, 1884), pp. 469, 473–474.[14]   [G11,4]

Animal symbolism in Toussenel: the marmot. "The marmot . . . loses its hair at its work—in allusion to the painful labor of the chimney sweep, who rubs and spoils his clothes in his occupation." A. Toussenel, *L'Esprit des bêtes* (Paris, 1884), p. 334.[15]   [G11,5]

Plant symbolism in Toussenel: the vine. "The vine loves to gossip . . . ; it mounts familiarly to the shoulder of plum tree, olive, or elm, and is intimate with all the trees." A. Toussenel, *L'Esprit des bêtes* (Paris, 1884), p. 107.   [G11,6]

Toussenel expounds the theory of the circle and of the parabola with reference to the different childhood games of the two sexes. This recalls the anthropomorphisms of Grandville. "The figures preferred by childhood are invariably round—the ball, the hoop, the marble; also the fruits which it prefers: the cherry, the gooseberry, the apple, the jam tart. . . . The analogist, who has observed these games with continued attention, has not failed to remark a characteristic difference in the choice of amusements, and the favorite exercises, of the children of the two sexes. . . . What then has our observer remarked in the character of the games of feminine infancy? He has remarked in the character of these games a decided proclivity toward the ellipse. / I observe among the favorite games of feminine infancy the shuttlecock and the jump rope. . . . Both the rope and the cord describe parabolic or elliptical curves. Why so? Why, at such an early age, this preference of the minor sex for the elliptical curve, this manifest contempt for marbles, ball, and top? Because the ellipse is the curve of love, as the circle is that of friendship. The ellipse is the figure in which God . . . has profiled the form of His favorite creatures—woman, swan, Arabian horse, dove; the ellipse is the essentially attractive form. . . . Astronomers were generally ignorant as to why the planets describe ellipses and not circumferences around their pivot of attraction; they now know as much about this mystery as I do." A. Toussenel, *L'Esprit des bêtes,* pp. 89–91.[16]   [G11a,1]

Toussenel posits a symbolism of curves, according to which the circle represents friendship; the ellipse, love; the parabola, the sense of family; the hyperbola, ambition. In the paragraph concerning the hyperbola, there is a passage closely related to Grandville: "The hyperbola is the curve of ambition. . . . Admire the determined persistence of the ardent asymptote pursuing the hyperbola in headlong eagerness: it approaches, always approaches, its goal . . . but never attains it." A. Toussenel, *L'Esprit des bêtes* (Paris, 1884), p. 92.[17]   [G11a,2]

Animal symbolism in Toussenel: the hedgehog. "Gluttonous and repulsive, it is also the portrait of the scurvy slave of the pen, trafficking with all subjects, selling postmaster's appointments and theater passes, . . . and drawing . . . from his sorry Christian conscience pledges and apologies at fixed prices. . . . It is said that the hedgehog is the only quadruped of France on which the venom of the viper has no effect. I should have guessed this exception merely from analogy. . . . For explain . . . how calumny (the viper) can sting the literary blackguard." A. Toussenel, *L'Esprit des bêtes* (Paris, 1884), pp. 476, 478.[18]   [G11a,3]

"Lightning is the kiss of clouds, stormy but faithful. Two lovers who adore each other, and who will tell it in spite of all obstacles, are two clouds animated with opposite electricities, and swelled with tragedy." A. Toussenel, *L'Esprit des bêtes: Zoologie passionnelle—Mammifères de France*, 4th ed. (Paris, 1884), pp. 100–101.[19]   [G12,1]

The first edition of Toussenel's *L'Esprit des bêtes* appeared in 1847.   [G12,2]

"I have vainly questioned the archives of antiquity to find traces of the setter dog. I have appealed to the memory of the most lucid somnambulists to ascertain the epoch when this race appeared. All the information I could procure . . . leads to this conclusion: the setter dog is a creation of modern times." A. Toussenel, *L'Esprit des bêtes* (Paris, 1884), p. 159.[20]   [G12,3]

"A beautiful young woman is a true voltaic cell, . . . in which the captive fluid is retained by the form of surfaces and the isolating virtue of the hair; so that when this fluid would escape from its sweet prison, it must make incredible efforts, which produce in turn, by influence on bodies differently animated, fearful ravages of attraction. . . . The history of the human race swarms with examples of intelligent and learned men, intrepid heroes, . . . transfixed merely by a woman's eye. . . . The holy King David proved that he perfectly understood the condensing properties of polished elliptical surfaces when he took unto himself the young Abigail." A. Toussenel, *L'Esprit des bêtes* (Paris, 1884), pp. 101–103.[21]   [G12,4]

Toussenel explains the rotation of the earth as the resultant of a centrifugal force and a force of attraction. Further on: "The star . . . begins to waltz its frenetic waltz. . . . Everything rustles, stirs, warms up, shines on the surface of the globe, which only the evening before was entombed in the frigid silence of night. Marvelous spectacle for the well-placed observer—change of scene wonderful to behold. For the revolution took place between two suns and, that very evening, an amethyst star made its first appearance in our skies" (p. 45). And, alluding to the volcanism of earlier epochs of the earth: "We know the effects which the first waltz usually has on delicate constitutions. . . . The Earth, too, was rudely awakened by its first ordeal." A. Toussenel, *L'Esprit des bêtes: Zoologie passionnelle* (Paris, 1884), pp. 44–45.   [G12,5]

Principle of Toussenel's zoology: "The rank of the species is in direct proportion to its resemblance to the human being." A. Toussenel, *L'Esprit des bêtes* (Paris, 1884), p. i. Compare the epigraph to the work: "'The best thing about man is his dog.'—Charlet."   [G12a,1]

The aeronaut Poitevin, sustained by great publicity, undertook an "ascent to Uranus" accompanied in the gondola of his balloon by young women dressed as mythological figures. *Paris sous la République de 1848: Exposition de la Bibliothèque et des travaux historiques de la Ville de Paris* (1909), p. 34.   [G12a,2]

We can speak of a fetishistic autonomy not only with regard to the commodity but also—as the following passage from Marx indicates—with regard to the means of production: "If we consider the process of production from the point of view of the simple labor process, the laborer stands, in relation to the means of production, . . . as the mere means . . . of his own intelligent productive activity. . . . But it is different as soon as we deal with the process of production from the point of view of the process of surplus-value creation. The means of production are at once changed into means for the absorption of the labor of others. It is now no longer the laborer that employs the means of production, but the means of production that employ the laborer. Instead of being consumed by him as material elements of his productive activity, they consume him as the ferment necessary to their own life process. . . . Furnaces and workshops that stand idle by night, and absorb no living labor, are a 'mere loss' to the capitalist. Hence, furnaces and workshops constitute lawful claims upon the night labor of the workpeople."[22] This observation can be applied to the analysis of Grandville. To what extent is the hired laborer the "soul" of Grandville's fetishistically animated objects?   [G12a,3]

"Night distributes the stellar essence to the sleeping plants. Every bird which flies has the thread of the infinite in its claw." Victor Hugo, *Oeuvres complètes* (Paris, 1881), novels, vol. 8, p. 114 (*Les Misérables*, book 4).[23]   [G12a,4]

Drumont calls Toussenel "one of the greatest prose writers of the century." Edouard Drumont, *Les Héros et les pitres* (Paris ‹1900›), p. 270 ("Toussenel").
                                                                [G12a,5]

Technique of exhibition: "A fundamental rule, quickly learned through observation, is that no object should be placed directly on the floor, on a level with the walkways. Pianos, furniture, physical apparatus, and machines are better displayed on a pedestal or raised platform. The best exhibits make use of two quite distinct systems: displays under glass and open displays. To be sure, some products, by their very nature or because of their value, have to be protected from contact with the air or the hand; others benefit from being left uncovered." *Exposition universelle de 1867, à Paris: Album des installations les plus remarquables de l'Exposition de 1862, à Londres, publié par la commission impériale pour servir de renseignement aux exposants des diverses nations* (Paris, 1866) ‹p. 5›. Album of plates in large folio, with very interesting illustrations, some in color, showing—in cross-section or longitudinal section, as the case may be—the pavilions of the world exhibition of 1862. Bibliothèque Nationale, V.644.   [G13,1]

Paris in the year 2855: "Our many visitors from Saturn and Mars have entirely forgotten, since arriving here, the horizons of their mother planet! Paris is henceforward the capital of creation! . . . Where are you, Champs-Elysées, favored theme of newswriters in 1855? . . . Buzzing along this thoroughfare that is paved with hollow iron and roofed with crystal are the bees and hornets of finance! The capitalists of Ursa Major are conferring with the stockbrokers of Mercury! And coming on the market this very day are shares in the debris of Venus half consumed by its own flames!" Arsène Houssaye, "Le Paris futur," in *Paris et les Parisiens au XIXe siècle* (Paris, 1856), pp. 458–459.   [G13,2]

At the time of the establishment, in London, of the General Council of the Workers International,[24] the following remark circulated: "The child born in the workshops of Paris was nursed in London." See Charles Benoist, "Le 'Mythe' de la classe ouvrière," *Revue des deux mondes* (March 1, 1914), p. 104.   [G13,3]

"Seeing that the gala ball is the sole occasion on which men contain themselves, let us get used to modeling all our institutions on gatherings such as these, where the woman is queen." A. Toussenel, *Le Monde des oiseaux*, vol. 1 (Paris, 1853), p. 134. And: "Many men are courteous and gallant at a ball, doubting not that gallantry is a commandment of God" (ibid., p. 98).   [G13,4]

On Gabriel Engelmann: "When he published his *Essais lithographiques* in 1816, great care was taken to reproduce this medallion as the frontispiece to his book, with the inscription: 'Awarded to M. G. Engelmann of Mulhouse (Upper Rhine). Large-scale execution, and refinement, of the art of lithography. Encouragement. 1816.'" Henri Bouchot, *La Lithographie* (Paris ‹1895›), p. ‹38›.   [G13,5]

On the London world exhibition: "In making the rounds of this enormous exhibition, the observer soon realizes that, to avoid confusion, . . . it has been necessary to cluster the different nationalities in a certain number of groups, and that the only useful way of establishing these industrial groupings was to do so on the basis of—oddly enough—religious beliefs. Each of the great religious divisions of humanity corresponds, in effect, . . . to a particular mode of existence and of industrial activity." Michel Chevalier, *Du Progrès* (Paris, 1852), p. 13.   [G13a,1]

From the first chapter of *Capital:* "A commodity appears, at first sight, a very trivial thing and easily understood. Its analysis shows that in reality it is a very queer thing, abounding in metaphysical subtleties and theological niceties. So far as it is a value in use, there is nothing mysterious about it. . . . The form of wood is altered by making a table out of it; nevertheless, this table remains wood, an ordinary material thing. As soon as it steps forth as commodity, however, it is transformed into a material immaterial thing. It not only stands with its feet on the ground, but, in the face of all other commodities, it stands on its head, and out of its wooden brain it evolves notions more whimsically than if it had suddenly begun to dance."[25] Cited in Franz Mehring, "Karl Marx und das Gleichnis," in *Karl Marx als Denker, Mensch, und Revolutionär,* ed. Rjazanov (Vienna and Berlin ‹1928›), p. 57 (first published in *Die neue Zeit,* March 13, 1908).   [G13a,2]

Renan compares the world exhibitions to the great Greek festivals, the Olympian games, and the Panathenaea. But in contrast to these, the world exhibitions lack poetry. "Twice, Europe has gone off to view the merchandise and to compare products and materials; and on returning from this new kind of pilgrimage, no one has complained of missing anything." Some pages later: "Our century tends toward neither the good nor the bad; it tends toward the mediocre. What succeeds in every endeavor nowadays is mediocrity." Ernest Renan, *Essais de morale et de critique* (Paris, 1859), pp. 356–357, 373 ("La Poésie de l'Exposition").   [G13a,3]

Hashish vision in the casino at Aix-la-Chapelle. "The gaming table at Aix-la-Chapelle is nothing short of an international congress, where the coins of all kingdoms and all countries are welcome. . . . A storm of Leopolds, Friedrich Wilhelms, Queen Victorias, and Napoleons rain down . . . on the table. Looking over this shining alluvium, I thought I could see . . . the effigies of the sovereigns . . . irrevocably fade from their respective écus, guineas, or ducats, to make room for other visages entirely unknown to me. A great many of these faces . . . wore grimaces . . . of vexation, of greed, or of fury. There were happy ones too, but only a few. . . . Soon this phenomenon . . . grew dim and passed away, and another sort of vision, no less extraordinary, now loomed before me. . . . The bourgeois effigies which had supplanted the monarchs began themselves to move about within the metallic disks. . . that confined them. Before long, they had separated from the disks. They appeared in full relief; then their heads burgeoned out into rounded forms. They had taken on . . . not only faces but living flesh. They had all sprung Lilliputian bodies. Everything assumed a shape . . . somehow or other; and creatures exactly like us, except for their size, . . . began to enliven the gaming table, from which all currency had vanished. I heard the ring of coins struck by the steel of the croupier's rake, but this was all that remained of the old resonance . . . of louis and écus, which had become men. These poor myrmidons were now taking to their heels, frantic at the approach of the murderous rake of the croupier; but escape was impossible. . . . Then . . . the dwarfish stakes, obliged to admit defeat, were ruthlessly captured by the fatal rake, which gathered them into the croupier's clutching hand. The croupier—how horrible!—took up each small body daintily between his fingers and devoured it with gusto. In less than half an hour, I saw some half-dozen of these imprudent Lilliputians hurled into the abyss of this terrible tomb. . . . But what appalled me the most was that, on raising my eyes (altogether by chance) to the gallery surrounding this valley of death, I noticed not just an extraordinary likeness but a complete identity between the several kingpins playing the life-sized game and the miniature humans struggling there on the table. . . . What's more, these kingpins . . . appeared to me . . . to collapse in desperation precisely as their childlike facsimiles were overtaken by the formidable rake. They seemed to share . . . all the sensations of their little doubles; and never, for as long as I live, will I forget the look and the gesture—full of hatred and despair—which one of those gamblers directed toward the bank at the very moment that his tiny simulacrum, coralled by the rake, went to satisfy the ravenous appetite of the croupier." Félix Mornand, *La Vie des eaux* (Paris, 1862), pp. 219–221 ("Aix-la-Chapelle"). [G14]

It would be useful to compare the way Grandville portrays machines to the way Chevalier, in 1852, still speaks of the railroad. He calculates that two locomotives, having a total of 400 horsepower, would correspond to 800 actual horses. How would it be possible to harness them up? How supply the fodder? And, in a note, he adds: "It must also be kept in mind that horses of flesh and blood have to rest after a brief journey; so that to furnish the same service as a locomotive, one must have on hand a very large number of animals." Michel Chevalier, *Chemins de fer: Extrait du dictionnaire de l'économie politique* (Paris, 1852), p. 10. [G14a,1]

The principles informing the exhibition of objects in the Galerie des Machines of 1867 were derived from Le Play. [G14a,2]

A divinatory representation of architectural aspects of the later world exhibitions is found in Gogol's essay "On Present-Day Architecture," which appeared in the mid-Thirties in his collection *Arabesques*. "Away with this academicism which commands that buildings be built all one size and in one style! A city should consist of many different styles of building, if we wish it to be pleasing to the eye. Let as many contrasting styles combine there as possible! Let the solemn Gothic and the richly embellished Byzantine arise in the same street, alongside colossal Egyptian halls and elegantly proportioned Greek structures! Let us see there the slightly concave milk-white cupola, the soaring church steeple, the oriental miter, the Italianate flat roof, the steep and heavily ornamented Flemish roof, the quadrilateral pyramid, the cylindrical column, the faceted obelisk!"[26] Nikolai Gogol, "Sur l'Architecture du temps présent," cited in Wladimir Weidlé, *Les Abeilles d'Aristée* (Paris ‹1936›), pp. 162–163 ("L'Agonie de l'art"). [G14a,3]

Fourier refers to the folk wisdom that for some time has defined "Civilization" as *le monde à rebours* ‹the world contrariwise›. [G14a,4]

Fourier cannot resist describing a banquet held on the banks of the Euphrates to honor the victors in both a competition among zealous dam workers (600,000) and a contest of pastry cooks. The 600,000 athletes of industry are furnished with 300,000 bottles of champagne, whose corks, at a signal from the "command tower," are all popped simultaneously. To echo throughout the "mountains of the Euphrates." Cited in ‹Armand and› Maubl‹anc, *Fourier* (Paris, 1937)›, vol. 2, pp. 178–179. [G14a,5]

"Poor stars! Their role of resplendence is really a role of sacrifice. Creators and servants of the productive power of the planets, they possess none of their own and must resign themselves to the thankless and monotonous career of providing torchlight. They have luster without enjoyment; behind them shelter, invisible, the living creatures. These slave-queens are nevertheless of the same stuff as their happy subjects. . . . Dazzling flames today, they will one day be dark and cold, and only as planets can they be reborn to life after the shock that has volatilized the retinue and its queen into a nebula." A. Blanqui, *L'Eternité par les astres* (Paris, 1872), pp. 69–70. Compare Goethe: "Euch bedaur' ich, unglückselge Sterne" ‹I pity you, unhappy stars›.[27] [G15,1]

"The sacristy, the stock exchange, and the barracks—those three musty lairs that together vomit night, misery, and death upon the nations. October 1869." Auguste Blanqui, *Critique sociale* (Paris, 1885), vol. 2, p. 351 ("Fragments et notes").
[G15,2]

"A rich death is a closed abyss." From the fifties. Auguste Blanqui, *Critique sociale* (Paris, 1885), vol. 2, p. 315 ("Fragments et notes"). [G15,3]

An *image d'Epinal* by Sellerie shows the world exhibition of 1855. [G15,4]

Elements of intoxication at work in the detective novel, whose mechanism is described by Caillois (in terms that recall the world of the hashish eater): "The characters of the childish imagination and a prevailing artificiality hold sway over this strangely vivid world. Nothing happens here that is not long premeditated; nothing corresponds to appearances. Rather, each thing has been prepared for use at the right moment by the omnipotent hero who wields power over it. We recognize in all this the Paris of the serial installments of *Fantômas*." Roger Caillois, "Paris, mythe moderne," *Nouvelle Revue française*, 25, no. 284 (May 1, 1937), p. 688. [G15,5]

"Every day I see passing beneath my window a certain number of Kalmucks, Osages, Indians, Chinamen, and ancient Greeks, all more or less Parisianized." Charles Baudelaire, *Oeuvres*, ‹ed. and annotated by Y.-G. Le Dantec (Paris, 1932),› vol. 2, p. 99 ("Salon de 1846," section 7, "De l'Idéal et du modèle").[28]
[G15,6]

Advertising under the Empire, according to Ferdinand Brunot, *Histoire de la langue française des origines à 1900*, vol. 9, *La Révolution et l'Empire*, part 9,

"Les Evénements, les institutions et la langue" (Paris, 1937): "We shall freely imagine that a man of genius conceived the idea of enshrining, within the banality of the vernacular, certain vocables calculated to seduce readers and buyers, and that he chose Greek not only because it furnishes inexhaustible resources to work with but also because, less widely known than Latin, it has the advantage of being . . . incomprehensible to a generation less versed in the study of ancient Greece. . . . Only, we know neither who this man was, nor what his nationality might be, nor even whether he existed or not. Let us suppose that . . . Greek words gained currency little by little until, one day, . . . the idea . . . was born . . . that, by their own intrinsic virtue, they could serve for advertising. . . . I myself would like to think that . . . several generations and several nations went into the making of that verbal billboard, the Greek monster that entices by surprise. I believe it was during the epoch I'm speaking of that the movement began to take shape. . . . The age of 'comagenic' hair oil had arrived." Pp. 1229–1230 ("Les Causes du triomphe du grec"). [G15a,1]

"What would a modern Winckelmann say . . . were he confronted by a product from China—something strange, bizarre, contorted in form, intense in color, and sometimes so delicate as to be almost evanescent? It is, nevertheless, an example of universal beauty. But in order to understand it, the critic, the spectator, must effect within himself a mysterious transformation; and by means of a phenomenon of the will acting on the imagination, he must learn by himself to participate in the milieu which has given birth to this strange flowering." Further along, on the same page, appear "those mysterious flowers whose deep color enslaves the eye and tantalizes it with its shape." Charles Baudelaire, *Oeuvres*, ‹ed. Le Dantec (Paris, 1932),› vol. 2, pp. 144–145 ("Exposition universelle, 1855").[29] [G15a,2]

"In French poetry before Baudelaire, as in the poetry of Europe generally, the style and accents of the Orient were never more than a faintly puerile and factitious game. With *Les Fleurs du mal*, the strange color is not produced without a keen sense of escape. Baudelaire . . . invites himself to absence. . . . In making a journey, he gives us the feel of . . . unexplored nature, where the traveler parts company with himself. . . . Doubtless, he leaves the mind and spirit unchanged; but he presents a new vision of his soul. It is tropical, African, black, enslaved. Here is the true country, an actual Africa, an authentic Indies." André Suarès, Preface to Charles Baudelaire, *Les Fleurs du mal* (Paris, 1933), pp. xxv–xxvii. [G16,1]

Prostitution of space in hashish, where it serves for all that has been.[30] [G16,2]

Grandville's masking of nature with the fashions of midcentury—nature understood as the cosmos, as well as the world of animals and plants—lets history, in the guise of fashion, be derived from the eternal cycle of nature. When Grandville presents a new fan as the "fan of Iris," when the Milky Way appears as an "avenue" illuminated at night by gas lamps, when "the moon (a self-portrait)" reposes on fashionable velvet cushions instead of on clouds, then history is being secularized and drawn into a natural context as relentlessly as it was three hundred years earlier with allegory.   [G16,3]

The planetary fashions of Grandville are so many parodies, drawn by nature, of human history. Grandville's harlequinades turn into Blanqui's plaintive ballads.
[G16,4]

"The exhibitions are the only properly modern festivals." Hermann Lotze, *Mikrokosmos*, vol. 3 (Leipzig, 1864), p. ?   [G16,5]

The world exhibitions were training schools in which the masses, barred from consuming, learned empathy with exchange value. "Look at everything; touch nothing."   [G16,6]

The entertainment industry refines and multiplies the varieties of reactive behavior among the masses. In this way, it makes them ripe for the workings of advertising. The link between this industry and the world exhibitions is thus well established.   [G16,7]

Proposal for urban planning in Paris: "It would be advisable to vary the forms of the houses and, as for the districts, to employ different architectural orders, even those in no way classical—such as the Gothic, Turkish, Chinese, Egyptian, Burmese, and so forth." Amédée de Tissot, *Paris et Londres comparés* (Paris, 1830), p. 150.—The architecture of future exhibitions!   [G16a,1]

"As long as this unspeakable construction [the Palace of Industry] survives, . . . I shall take satisfaction in renouncing the title 'man of letters'. . . . Art and industry! Yes, it was in fact for them alone that, in 1855, this impossible tangle of galleries was reserved, this jumble where the poor writers have not even been granted six square feet—the space of a grave! Glory to thee, O Stationer. . . . Mount to the Capitol, O Publisher . . . ! Triumph, you artists and industrials, you who have had the honors and the profit of a world exhibition, whereas poor literature . . ." (pp. v–vi). "A world exhibition for the man of letters, a Crystal Palace for the author-modiste!" Whisperings of a scurrilous demon whom Babou, according to his "Lettre à Charles Asselineau," is supposed to have encountered one day along the Champs-Elysées. Hippolyte Babou, *Les Payens innocents* (Paris, 1858), p. xiv.   [G16a,2]

Exhibitions. "Such transitory installations, as a rule, have had no influence on the configuration of cities. . . . It is otherwise . . . in Paris. Precisely in the fact that here giant exhibitions could be set up in the middle of town, and that nearly always they would leave behind a monument well suited to the city's general aspect—precisely in this, one can recognize the blessing of a great original layout and of a continuing tradition of urban planning. Paris could . . . organize even the most immense exhibition so as to be . . . accessible from the Place de la Concorde. Along the quays leading west from this square, for a distance of kilometers, the curbs have been set back from the river in such a way that very wide lanes are opened, which, abundantly planted with rows of trees, make for the loveliest possible exhibition routes." Fritz Stahl, *Paris* (Berlin ‹1929›), p. 62.   [G16a,3]

[The Collector]

> All these old things have a moral value.
> —Charles Baudelaire[1]

> I believe . . . in my soul: the Thing.
> —Léon Deubel, *Oeuvres* (Paris, 1929), p. 193

Here was the last refuge of those infant prodigies that saw the light of day at the time of the world exhibitions: the briefcase with interior lighting, the meter-long pocket knife, or the patented umbrella handle with built-in watch and revolver. And near the degenerate giant creatures, aborted and broken-down matter. We followed the narrow dark corridor to where—between a discount bookstore, in which dusty tied-up bundles tell of all sorts of failure, and a shop selling only buttons (mother-of-pearl and the kind that in Paris are called *de fantaisie*)—there stood a sort of salon. On the pale-colored wallpaper full of figures and busts shone a gas lamp. By its light, an old woman sat reading. They say she has been there alone for years, and collects sets of teeth "in gold, in wax, and broken." Since that day, moreover, we know where Doctor Miracle got the wax out of which he fashioned Olympia.[2] □ Dolls □ [H1,1]

"The crowd throngs to the Passage Vivienne, where people never feel conspicuous, and deserts the Passage Colbert, where they feel perhaps too conspicuous. At a certain point, an attempt was made to entice the crowd back by filling the rotunda each evening with harmonious music, which emanated invisibly from the windows of a mezzanine. But the crowd came to put its nose in at the door and did not enter, suspecting in this novelty a conspiracy against its customs and routine pleasures." *Le Livre des cent-et-un,* vol. 10 (Paris, 1833), p. 58. Fifteen years ago, a similar attempt was made—likewise in vain—to boost the ‹Berlin› department store W. Wertheim. Concerts were given in the great arcade that ran through it. [H1,2]

Never trust what writers say about their own writings. When Zola undertook to defend his *Thérèse Raquin* against hostile critics, he explained that his book was a scientific study of the temperaments. His task had been to show, in an example, exactly how the sanguine and the nervous temperaments act on one another—to the detriment of each. But this explanation could satisfy no one. Nor does it explain the admixture of colportage, the bloodthirstiness, the cinematic goriness of the action. Which—by no accident—takes place in an arcade.[3] If this book really expounds something scientifically, then it's the death of the Paris arcades, the decay of a type of architecture. The book's atmosphere is saturated with the poisons of this process: its people drop like flies.   [H1,3]

In 1893, the cocottes were driven from the arcades.   [H1,4]

Music seems to have settled into these spaces only with their decline, only as the orchestras themselves began to seem old-fashioned in comparison to the new mechanical music. So that, in fact, these orchestras would just as soon have taken refuge there. (The "theatrophone" in the arcades was, in certain respects, the forerunner of the gramophone.) Nevertheless, there was music that conformed to the spirit of the arcades—a panoramic music, such as can be heard today only in old-fashioned genteel concerts like those of the casino orchestra in Monte Carlo: the panoramic compositions of ‹Félicien› David, for example—*Le Désert, Christoph Colomb, Herculanum*. When, in the 1860s (?), an Arab political delegation came to Paris, the city was very proud to be able to mount a performance of *Le Désert* for them in the great Théâtre de l'Opéra (?).   [H1,5]

"Cineoramas. The Grand Globe Céleste: a gigantic sphere forty-six meters in diameter, where you can hear the music of Saint-Saëns." Jules Claretie, *La Vie à Paris 1900* (Paris, 1901), p. 61. ☐ Diorama ☐   [H1,6]

Often these inner spaces harbor antiquated trades, and even those that are thoroughly up to date will acquire in them something obsolete. They are the site of information bureaus and detective agencies, which there, in the gloomy light of the upper galleries, follow the trail of the past. In hairdressers' windows, you can see the last women with long hair. They have richly undulating masses of hair, which are "permanent waves," petrified coiffures. They ought to dedicate small votive plaques to those who made a special world of these buildings—to Baudelaire and Odilon Redon, whose very name sounds like an all too well-turned ringlet. Instead, they have been betrayed and sold, and the head of Salome made into an ornament—if that which dreams of the console there below is not the embalmed head of Anna Czyllak.[4] And while these things are petrified, the masonry of the walls above has become brittle. Brittle, too, are ☐ Mirrors ☐ ‹See R1,3.›   [H1a,1]

What is decisive in collecting is that the object is detached from all its original functions in order to enter into the closest conceivable relation to things of the same kind. This relation is the diametric opposite of any utility, and falls into the peculiar category of completeness. What is this "completeness"? It is a grand attempt to overcome the wholly irrational character of the object's mere presence at hand through its integration into a new, expressly devised historical system: the collection. And for the true collector, every single thing in this system becomes an encyclopedia of all knowledge of the epoch, the landscape, the industry, and the owner from which it comes. It is the deepest enchantment of the collector to enclose the particular item within a magic circle, where, as a last shudder runs through it (the shudder of being acquired), it turns to stone. Everything remembered, everything thought, everything conscious becomes socle, frame, pedestal, seal of his possession. It must not be assumed that the collector, in particular, would find anything strange in the *topos hyperouranios*—that place beyond the heavens which, for Plato,[5] shelters the unchangeable archetypes of things. He loses himself, assuredly. But he has the strength to pull himself up again by nothing more than a straw; and from out of the sea of fog that envelops his senses rises the newly acquired piece, like an island.—Collecting is a form of practical memory, and of all the profane manifestations of "nearness" it is the most binding. Thus, in a certain sense, the smallest act of political reflection makes for an epoch in the antiques business. We construct here an alarm clock that rouses the kitsch of the previous century to "assembly." [H1a,2]

Extinct nature: the shell shop in the arcades. In "The Pilot's Trials," Strindberg tells of "an arcade with brightly lit shops." "Then he went on into the arcade. . . . There was every possible kind of shop, but not a soul to be seen, either behind or before the counters. After a while he stopped in front of a big window in which there was a whole display of shells. As the door was open, he went in. From floor to ceiling there were rows of shells of every kind, collected from all the seas of the world. No one was in, but there was a ring of tobacco smoke in the air. . . . So he began his walk again, following the blue and white carpet. The passage wasn't straight but winding, so that you could never see the end of it; and there were always fresh shops there, but no people; and the shopkeepers were not to be seen." The unfathomability of the moribund arcades is a characteristic motif. Strindberg, *Märchen* (Munich and Berlin, 1917), pp. 52–53, 59.[6] [H1a,3]

One must make one's way through *Les Fleurs du mal* with a sense for how things are raised to allegory. The use of uppercase lettering should be followed carefully. [H1a,4]

At the conclusion of *Matière et mémoire,* Bergson develops the idea that perception is a function of time. If, let us say, we were to live vis-à-vis some things more calmly and vis-à-vis others more rapidly, according to a different rhythm, there would be nothing "subsistent" for us, but instead everything would happen right before our eyes; everything would strike us. But this is the way things are for the great collector. They strike him. How he himself pursues and encounters them, what changes in the ensemble of items are effected by a newly supervening item—all this shows him his affairs in constant flux. Here, the Paris arcades are examined as though they were properties in the hand of a collector. (At bottom, we may say, the collector lives a piece of dream life. For in the dream, too, the rhythm of perception and experience is altered in such a way that everything—even the seemingly most neutral—comes to strike us; everything concerns us. In order to understand the arcades from the ground up, we sink them into the deepest stratum of the dream; we speak of them as though they had struck us.)

[H1a,5]

"Your understanding of allegory assumes proportions hitherto unknown to you; I will note, in passing, that allegory—long an object of our scorn because of maladroit painters, but in reality a most *spiritual* art form, one of the earliest and most natural forms of poetry—resumes its legitimate dominion in a mind illuminated by intoxication." Charles Baudelaire, *Les Paradis artificiels* (Paris, 1917), p. 73.[7] (On the basis of what follows, it cannot be doubted that Baudelaire indeed had allegory and not symbol in mind. The passage is taken from the chapter on hashish.) The collector as allegorist. ⬜ Hashish ⬜

[H2,1]

"The publication ‹in 1864› of *L'Histoire de la société française pendant la Révolution et sous le Directoire* opens the era of the curio—and the word 'curio' should not be taken as pejorative. In those days, the historical curio was called a 'relic.'" Remy de Gourmont, *Le Deuxième Livre des masques* (Paris, 1924), p. 259. This passage concerns a work by Edmond and Jules de Goncourt.

[H2,2]

The true method of making things present is to represent them in our space (not to represent ourselves in their space). (The collector does just this, and so does the anecdote.) Thus represented, the things allow no mediating construction from out of "large contexts." The same method applies, in essence, to the consideration of great things from the past—the cathedral of Chartres, the temple of Paestum—when, that is, a favorable prospect presents itself: the method of receiving the things into our space. We don't displace our being into theirs; they step into our life.

[H2,3]

Fundamentally a very odd fact—that collector's items as such were produced industrially. Since when? It would be necessary to investigate the various fashions that governed collecting in the nineteenth century. Characteristic of the Biedermeier period (is this also the case in France?) is the mania for cups and saucers. "Parents, children, friends, relatives, superiors, and subordinates make their feelings known through cups and saucers. The cup is the preferred gift, the most popular kind of knickknack for a room. Just as Friedrich Wilhelm III filled his study with pyramids of porcelain cups, the ordinary citizen collected, in the cups and saucers of his sideboard, the memory of the most important events, the most precious hours, of his life." Max von Boehn, *Die Mode im XIX. Jahrhundert,* vol. 2 (Munich, 1907), p. 136.

[H2,4]

Possession and having are allied with the tactile, and stand in a certain opposition to the optical. Collectors are beings with tactile instincts. Moreover, with the recent turn away from naturalism, the primacy of the optical that was determinate for the previous century has come to an end. ☐ Flâneur ☐ The flâneur optical, the collector tactile.[8]   [H2,5]

Broken-down matter: the elevation of the commodity to the status of allegory. Allegory and the fetish character of the commodity.   [H2,6]

One may start from the fact that the true collector detaches the object from its functional relations. But that is hardly an exhaustive description of this remarkable mode of behavior. For isn't this the foundation (to speak with Kant and Schopenhauer) of that "disinterested" contemplation by virtue of which the collector attains to an unequaled view of the object—a view which takes in more, and other, than that of the profane owner and which we would do best to compare to the gaze of the great physiognomist? But how his eye comes to rest on the object is a matter elucidated much more sharply through another consideration. It must be kept in mind that, for the collector, the world is present, and indeed ordered, in each of his objects. Ordered, however, according to a surprising and, for the profane understanding, incomprehensible connection. This connection stands to the customary ordering and schematization of things something as their arrangement in the dictionary stands to a natural arrangement. We need only recall what importance a particular collector attaches not only to his object but also to its entire past, whether this concerns the origin and objective characteristics of the thing or the details of its ostensibly external history: previous owners, price of purchase, current value, and so on. All of these—the "objective" data together with the other—come together, for the true collector, in every single one of his possessions, to form a whole magic encyclopedia, a world order, whose outline is the *fate* of his object. Here, therefore, within this circumscribed field, we can understand how great physiognomists (and collectors are physiognomists of the world of things) become interpreters of fate. It suffices to observe just one collector as he handles the items in his showcase. No sooner does he hold them in his hand than he appears inspired by them and seems to look through them into their distance, like an augur. (It would be interesting to study the bibliophile as the only type of collector who has not completely withdrawn his treasures from their functional context.)   [H2,7; H2a,1]

The great collector Pachinger, Wolfskehl's friend, has put together a collection that, in its array of proscribed and damaged objects, rivals the Figdor collection in Vienna. He hardly knows any more how things stand in the world; explains to his visitors—alongside the most antique implements—the use of pocket handkerchiefs, hand mirrors, and the like. It is related of him that, one day, as he was crossing the Stachus, he stooped to pick something up. Before him lay an object he had been pursuing for weeks: a misprinted streetcar ticket that had been in circulation for only a few hours.   [H2a,2]

An apology for the collector ought not to overlook this invective: "Avarice and old age, remarks Gui Patin, are always in collusion. With individuals as with societies, the need to accumulate is one of the signs of approaching death. This is confirmed in the acute stages of preparalysis. There is also the mania for collection, known in neurology as 'collectionism.' / From the collection of hairpins to the cardboard box bearing the inscription: 'Small bits of string are useless.'" *Les Sept Péchés capitaux* (Paris, 1929), pp. 26–27 (Paul Morand, "L'Avarice"). But compare collecting done by children! [H2a,3]

"I am not sure I should have been so thoroughly possessed by this one subject, but for the heaps of fantastic things I had seen huddled together in the curiosity-dealer's warehouse. These, crowding on my mind, in connection with the child, and gathering round her, as it were, brought her condition palpably before me. I had her image, without any effort of imagination, surrounded and beset by everything that was foreign to its nature, and farthest removed from the sympathies of her sex and age. If these helps to my fancy had all been wanting, and I had been forced to imagine her in a common chamber, with nothing unusual or uncouth in its appearance, it is very probable that I should have been less impressed with her strange and solitary state. As it was, she seemed to exist in a kind of allegory." Charles Dickens, *Der Raritätenladen* (Leipzig, ed. Insel), pp. 18–19.⁹ [H2a,4]

Wiesengrund, in an unpublished essay on *The Old Curiosity Shop*, by Dickens: "Nell's death is decided in the sentence that reads: 'There were some trifles there—poor useless things—that she would have liked to take away; but that was impossible.'. . . Yet Dickens recognized that the possibility of transition and dialectical rescue was inherent in this world of things, this lost, rejected world; and he expressed it, better than Romantic nature-worship was ever able to do, in the powerful allegory of money with which the depiction of the industrial city ends: '. . . two old, battered, smoke-encrusted penny pieces. Who knows but they shone as brightly in the eyes of angels, as golden gifts that have been chronicled on tombs?'"¹⁰ [H2a,5]

"Most enthusiasts let themselves be guided by chance in forming their collection, like bibliophiles in their browsing. . . . M. Thiers has proceeded otherwise: before assembling his collection, he formed it as a whole in his head; he laid out his plan in advance, and he has spent thirty years executing it. . . . M. Thiers possesses what he wanted to possess. . . . And what was the point? To arrange around himself a miniature of the universe—that is, to gather, within an environment of eighty square meters, Rome and Florence, Pompeii and Venice, Dresden and the Hague, the Vatican and the Escorial, the British Museum and the Hermitage, the Alhambra and the Summer Palace. . . . And M. Thiers has been able to realize this vast project with only modest expenditures made each year over a thirty-year period. . . . Seeking, in particular, to adorn the walls of his residence with the most precious souvenirs of his voyages, M. Thiers had reduced copies made of the most famous paintings. . . . And so, on entering his home, you find yourself immediately surrounded by masterpieces created in Italy during the age of Leo X. The wall facing the windows is occupied by *The Last Judgment*, hung between *The Dispute of the Holy Sacrament* and *The School of Athens.* Titian's *Assumption* adorns the mantelpiece, between *The Communion of Saint Jerome* and *The Transfiguration. The Madonna of Saint Sixtus* makes a pair with *Saint Cécila,* and on the pilaster are framed the Sibyls of Raphael, between the *Sposalizio* and the picture representing Gregory IX delivering the decretals to a delegate of the Consistory. . . . These copies all being reduced in accordance with the same scale, or nearly so, . . . the eye discovers in them, with pleasure, the relative proportions of the originals. They are painted in watercolor." Charles Blanc, *Le Cabinet de M. Thiers* (Paris, 1871), pp. 16–18. [H3,1]

"Casimir Périer said one day, while viewing the art collection of an illustrious enthusiast . . . : 'All these paintings are very pretty—but they're dormant capital.'. . . Today, . . . one could say to Casimir Périer . . . that . . . paintings . . ., when they are indeed authentic, that drawings, when recognizably by the hand of a master, . . . sleep a sleep that is restorative and profitable. . . . The . . . sale of the curiosities and paintings of Monsieur R. . . . has proven in round figures that works of genius possess a value just as solid as the Orléans ‹Railroad Co.› and a little more secure than bonded warehouses." Charles Blanc, *Le Trésor de la curiosité*, vol. 2 (Paris, 1858), p. 578. [H3,2]

The *positive* countertype to the collector—which also, insofar as it entails the liberation of things from the drudgery of being useful, represents the consummation of the collector—can be deduced from these words of Marx: "Private property has made us so stupid and inert that an object is *ours* only when we have it, when it exists as capital for us, or when . . . we *use* it." Karl Marx, *Der historische Materialismus,* in *Die Frühschriften,* ed. Landshut and Mayer (Leipzig ‹1932›), vol. 1, p. 299 ("Nationalökonomie und Philosophie").[11] [H3a,1]

"*All* the physical and intellectual senses have been replaced by the simple alienation of *all* these senses, the sense of *having.* . . . (On the category of *having,* see Hess in *Twenty-One Sheets*)." Karl Marx, *Der historische Materialismus* (Leipzig), vol. 1, p. 300 ("Nationalökonomie und Philosophie").[12] [H3a,2]

"I can, in practice, relate myself humanly to an object only if the object relates itself humanly to man." Karl Marx, *Der historische Materialismus* (Leipzig), vol. 1, p. 300 ("Nationalökonomie und Philosophie").[13] [H3a,3]

The collections of Alexandre du Sommerard in the holdings of the Musée Cluny. [H3a,4]

The quodlibet has something of the genius of both collector and flâneur. [H3a,5]

The collector actualizes latent archaic representations of property. These representations may in fact be connected with taboo, as the following remark indicates: "It . . . is . . . certain that taboo is the primitive form of property. At first emotively and 'sincerely,' then as a routine legal process, declaring something taboo would have constituted a title. To appropriate to oneself an object is to render it sacred and redoubtable to others; it is to make it 'participate' in oneself." N. Guterman and H. Lefebvre, *La Conscience mystifiée* (Paris, 1936), p. 228.

[H3a,6]

Passages by Marx from "Nationalökonomie und Philosophie": "Private property has made us so stupid and inert that an object is ours only when we *have* it." "All the physical and intellectual senses . . . have been replaced by the simple alienation of all these senses, the sense of having."[14] Cited in Hugo Fischer, *Karl Marx und sein Verhältnis zu Staat und Wirtschaft* (Jena, 1932), p. 64.

[H3a,7]

The ancestors of Balthazar Claës were collectors.

[H3a,8]

Models for Cousin Pons: Sommerard, Sauvageot, Jacaze.

[H3a,9]

The physiological side of collecting is important. In the analysis of this behavior, it should not be overlooked that, with the nest-building of birds, collecting acquires a clear biological function. There is apparently an indication to this effect in Vasari's treatise on architecture. Pavlov, too, is supposed to have occupied himself with collecting.

[H4,1]

Vasari is supposed to have maintained (in his treatise on architecture?) that the term "grotesque" comes from the grottoes in which collectors hoard their treasures.

[H4,2]

Collecting is a primal phenomenon of study: the student collects knowledge.

[H4,3]

In elucidating the relation of medieval man to his affairs, Huizinga occasionally adduces the literary genre of the "testament": "This literary form can be . . . appreciated only by someone who remembers that the people of the Middle Ages were, in fact, accustomed to dispose of even the meanest [!] of their possessions through a separate and detailed testament. A poor woman bequeathed her Sunday dress and cap to her parish, her bed to her godchild, a fur to her nurse, her everyday dress to a beggar woman, and four pounds *tournois* (a sum which constituted her entire fortune), together with an additional dress and cap, to the Franciscan friars (Champion, *Villon,* vol. 2, p. 182). Shouldn't we recognize here, too, a quite trivial manifestation of the same cast of mind that sets up every case of virtue as an eternal example and sees in every customary practice a divinely willed ordinance?" J. Huizinga, *Herbst des Mittelalters* (Munich, 1928), p. 346.[15] What strikes one most about this noteworthy passage is that such a relation to movables would perhaps no longer be possible in an age of standardized mass production. It would follow quite naturally from this to ask whether or not the forms of argumentation to which the author alludes, and indeed certain forms of Scholastic thought in general (appeal to hereditary authoritary), belong together with the forms of production. The collector develops a similar relationship with his objects, which are enriched through his knowledge of their origin and their duration in history—a relationship that now seems archaic.   [H4,4]

Perhaps the most deeply hidden motive of the person who collects can be described this way: he takes up the struggle against dispersion. Right from the start, the great collector is struck by the confusion, by the scatter, in which the things of the world are found. It is the same spectacle that so preoccupied the men of the Baroque; in particular, the world image of the allegorist cannot be explained apart from the passionate, distraught concern with this spectacle. The allegorist is, as it were, the polar opposite of the collector. He has given up the attempt to elucidate things through research into their properties and relations. He dislodges things from their context and, from the outset, relies on his profundity to illuminate their meaning. The collector, by contrast, brings together what belongs together; by keeping in mind their affinities and their succession in time, he can eventually furnish information about his objects. Nevertheless—and this is more important than all the differences that may exist between them—in every collector hides an allegorist, and in every allegorist a collector. As far as the collector is concerned, his collection is never complete; for let him discover just a single piece missing, and everything he's collected remains a patchwork, which is what things are for allegory from the beginning. On the other hand, the allegorist—for whom objects represent only keywords in a secret dictionary, which will make known their meanings to the initiated—precisely the allegorist can never have enough of things. With him, one thing is so little capable of taking the place of another that no possible reflection suffices to foresee what meaning his profundity might lay claim to for each one of them.[16]   [H4a,1]

Animals (birds, ants), children, and old men as collectors.   [H4a,2]

A sort of productive disorder is the canon of the *mémoire involontaire,* as it is the canon of the collector. "And I had already lived long enough so that, for more than one of the human beings with whom I had come in contact, I found in antipodal regions of my past memories another being to complete the picture. . . . In much the same way, when an art lover is shown a panel of an altar screen, he remembers in what church, museum, and private collection the other panels are dispersed (likewise, he finally succeeds, by following the catalogues of art sales or frequenting antique shops, in finding the mate to the object he possesses and thereby completing the pair, and so can reconstruct in his mind the predella and the entire altar)." Marcel Proust, *Le Temps retrouvé* (Paris), vol. 2, p. 158.[17] The *mémoire volontaire,* on the other hand, is a registry providing the object with a classificatory number behind which it disappears. "So now we've been there." ("I've had an experience.") How the scatter of allegorical properties (the patchwork) relates to this creative disorder is a question calling for further study.   [H5,1]

I

[The Interior, The Trace]

"In 1830, Romanticism was gaining the upper hand in literature. It now invaded architecture and placarded house façades with a fantastic gothicism, one all too often made of pasteboard. It imposed itself on furniture making. 'All of a sudden,' says a reporter on the exhibition of 1834, 'there is boundless enthusiasm for strangely shaped furniture. From old châteaux, from furniture warehouses and junk shops, it has been dragged out to embellish the salons, which in every other respect are modern. . . .' Feeling inspired, furniture manufacturers have been prodigal with their 'ogives and machicolations.' You see beds and armoires bristling with battlements, like thirteenth-century citadels." E. Levasseur, ‹*Histoire des classes ouvrières et de l'industrie en France, de 1789 à 1870* (Paris, 1904),› vol. 2, pp. 206–207. [I1,1]

Apropos of a medieval armoire, this interesting remark from Behne: "Movables ‹furniture› quite clearly developed out of immovables ‹real estate›." The armoire is compared to a "medieval fortress. Just as, in the latter, a tiny dwelling space is surrounded in ever-widening rings by walls, ramparts, and moats, forming a gigantic outwork, so the contents of the drawers and shelves in the armoire are overwhelmed by a mighty outwork." Adolf Behne, *Neues Wohnen—Neues Bauen* (Leipzig, 1927), pp. 59, 61–62. [I1,2]

The importance of movable property, as compared with immovable property. Here our task is slightly easier. Easier to blaze a way into the heart of things abolished or superseded, in order to decipher the contours of the banal as picture puzzle—in order to start a concealed William Tell from out of wooded entrails, or in order to be able to answer the question, "Where is the bride in this picture?" Picture puzzles, as schemata of dreamwork, were long ago discovered by psychoanalysis. We, however, with a similar conviction, are less on the trail of the psyche than on the track of things. We seek the totemic tree of objects within the thicket of primal history. The very last—the topmost—face on the totem pole is that of kitsch. [I1,3]

The confrontation with furniture in Poe. Struggle to awake from the collective dream. [I1,4]

How the interior defended itself against gaslight: "Almost all new houses have gas today; it burns in the inner courtyards and on the stairs, though it does not yet have free admission to the apartments. It has been allowed into the antechamber and sometimes even into the dining room, but it is not welcome in the drawing room. Why not? It fades the wallpaper. That is the only reason I have run across, and it carries no weight at all." Du Camp, *Paris,* vol. 5, p. 309.

[I1,5]

Hessel speaks of the "dreamy epoch of bad taste." Yes, this epoch was wholly adapted to the dream, was furnished in dreams. The alternation in styles—Gothic, Persian, Renaissance, and so on—signified: that over the interior of the middle-class dining room spreads a banquet room of Cesare Borgia's, or that out of the boudoir of the mistress a Gothic chapel arises, or that the master's study, in its iridescence, is transformed into the chamber of a Persian prince. The photomontage that fixes such images for us corresponds to the most primitive perceptual tendency of these generations. Only gradually have the images among which they lived detached themselves and settled on signs, labels, posters, as the figures of advertising.

[I1,6]

A series of lithographs from 18‹—› showed women reclining voluptuously on ottomans in a draperied, crepuscular boudoir, and these prints bore inscriptions: *On the Banks of the Tagus, On the Banks of the Neva, On the Banks of the Seine,* and so forth. The Guadalquivir, the Rhone, the Rhine, the Aar, the Tamis—all had their turn. That a national costume might have distinguished these female figures one from another may be safely doubted. It was up to the *légende,* the caption inscribed beneath them, to conjure a fantasy landscape over the represented interiors.

[I1,7]

To render the image of those salons where the gaze was enveloped in billowing curtains and swollen cushions, where, before the eyes of the guests, full-length mirrors disclosed church doors and settees were gondolas upon which gaslight from a vitreous globe shone down like the moon.

[I1,8]

"We have witnessed the unprecedented—marriages between styles that one would have believed eternally incompatible: hats of the First Empire or the Restoration worn with Louis XV jackets, Directory-style gowns paired with high-heeled ankle boots—and, still better, low-waisted coats worn over high-waisted dresses." John Grand-Carteret, *Les Elégances de la toilette* (Paris), p. xvi.

[I1a,1]

Names of different types of traveling car from the early years of the railroad: berlin (closed and open), diligence, furnished coach, unfurnished coach. ▢ Iron Construction ▢

[I1a,2]

"This year, too, spring arrived earlier and more beautiful than ever, so that, to tell the truth, we could not rightly remember the existence of winter in these parts, nor whether the fireplace was there for any purpose other than supporting on its mantel the timepieces and candelabra that are known to ornament every room here; for the true Parisian would rather eat one course less per day than forgo his 'mantelpiece arrangement.'" *Lebende Bilder aus dem modernen Paris*, 4 vols. (Cologne, 1863–1866), vol. 2, p. 369 ("Ein kaiserliches Familienbild"). [I1a,3]

Threshold magic. At the entrance to the skating rink, to the pub, to the tennis court, to resort locations: *penates*. The hen that lays the golden praline-eggs, the machine that stamps our names on nameplates, slot machines, fortunetelling devices, and above all weighing devices (the Delphic *gnōthi seauton*[1] of our day)—these guard the threshold. Oddly, such machines don't flourish in the city, but rather are a component of excursion sites, of beer gardens in the suburbs. And when, in search of a little greenery, one heads for these places on a Sunday afternoon, one is turning as well to the mysterious thresholds. Of course, this same magic prevails more covertly in the interior of the bourgeois dwelling. Chairs beside an entrance, photographs flanking a doorway, are fallen household deities, and the violence they must appease grips our hearts even today at each ringing of the doorbell. Try, though, to withstand the violence. Alone in an apartment, try not to bend to the insistent ringing. You will find it as difficult as an exorcism. Like all magic substance, this too is once again reduced at some point to sex—in pornography. Around 1830, Paris amused itself with obscene lithos that featured sliding doors and windows. These were the *Images dites à portes et à fenêtres*, by Numa Bassajet. [I1a,4]

Concerning the dreamy and, if possible, oriental interior: "Everyone here dreams of instant fortune; everyone aims to have, at one stroke, what in peaceful and industrious times would cost a lifetime of effort. The creations of the poets are full of sudden metamorphoses in domestic existence; they all rave about marquises and princesses, about the prodigies of the *Thousand and One Nights*. It is an opium trance that has overspread the whole population, and industry is more to blame for this than poetry. Industry was responsible for the swindle in the Stock Exchange, the exploitation of all things made to serve artificial needs, and the . . . dividends." Gutzkow, *Briefe aus Paris* ⟨Leipzig, 1842⟩, vol. 1, p. 93. [I1a,5]

While art seeks out the intimate view, . . . industry marches to the fore." Octave Mirbeau, in *Le Figaro* (1889). (See *Encyclopédie d'architecture* [1889] p. 92.) [I1a,6]

On the exhibition of 1867. "These high galleries, kilometers in length, were of an undeniable grandeur. The noise of machinery filled them. And it should not be forgotten that, when this exhibition held its famous galas, guests still drove up to the festivities in a coach-and-eight. As was usual with rooms at this period, attempts were made—through furniture-like installations—to prettify these twenty-five-meter-high galleries and to relieve the austerity of their design. One stood in fear of one's own magnitude." Sigfried Giedion, *Bauen in Frankreich* ⟨Leipzig and Berlin, 1928⟩, p. 43. [I1a,7]

Under the bourgeoisie, cities as well as pieces of furniture retain the character of fortifications. "Till now, it was the *fortified city* which constantly paralyzed town planning." Le Corbusier, *Urbanisme* (Paris ‹1925›), p. 249.[2]   [I1a,8]

The ancient correspondence between house and cabinet acquires a new variant through the insertion of glass roundels in cabinet doors. Since when? Were these also found in France?   [I1a,9]

The bourgeois pasha in the imagination of contemporaries: Eugène Sue. He had a castle in Sologne. There, it was said, he kept a harem filled with women of color. After his death, the legend arose that he had been poisoned by the Jesuits.[3]   [I2,1]

Gutzkow reports that the exhibition salons were full of oriental scenes calculated to arouse enthusiasm for Algiers.   [I2,2]

On the ideal of "distinction." "Everything tends toward the flourish, toward the curve, toward intricate convolution. What the reader does not perhaps gather at first sight, however, is that this manner of laying and arranging things also incorporates a setting apart—one that leads us back to the knight. / The carpet in the foreground lies at an angle, diagonally. The chairs are likewise arranged at an angle, diagonally. Now, this could be a coincidence. But if we were to meet with this propensity to situate objects at an angle and diagonally in all the dwellings of all classes and social strata—as, in fact, we do—then it can be no coincidence. . . . In the first place, arranging at an angle enforces a distinction—and this, once more, in a quite literal sense. By the obliquity of its position, the object sets itself off from the ensemble, as the carpet does here. . . . But the deeper explanation for all this is, again, the unconscious retention of a posture of struggle and defense. / In order to defend a piece of ground, I place myself expressly on the diagonal, because then I have a free view on two sides. It is for this reason that the bastions of a fortification are constructed to form salient angles. . . . And doesn't the carpet, in this position, recall such a bastion? . . . / Just as the knight, suspecting an attack, positions himself crosswise to guard both left and right, so the peace-loving burgher, several centuries later, orders his art objects in such a way that each one, if only by standing out from all the rest, has a wall and moat surrounding it. He is thus truly a *Spiessbürger,* a militant philistine." Adolf Behne, *Neues Wohnen—Neues Bauen* (Leipzig, 1927), pp. 45–48. In elucidating this point, the author remarks half-seriously: "The gentlemen who could afford a villa wanted to mark their higher standing. What easier way than by borrowing feudal forms, knightly forms?" (ibid., p. 42). More universal is Lukács' remark that, from the perspective of the philosophy of history, it is characteristic of the middle classes that their new opponent, the proletariat, should have entered the arena at a moment when the old adversary, feudalism, was not yet vanquished. And they will never quite have done with feudalism.   [I2,3]

Maurice Barrès has characterized Proust as "a Persian poet in a concierge's box." Could the first person to grapple with the enigma of the nineteenth-century interior be anything else? (The citation is in Jacques-Emile Blanche, *Mes Modèles* [Paris, 1929] ?)[4] [I2,4]

Announcement published in the newspapers: "Notice.—Monsieur Wiertz offers to paint a picture free of charge for any lovers of painting who, possessing an original Rubens or Raphael, would like to place his work as a pendant beside the work of either of these masters." A. J. Wiertz, *Oeuvres littéraires* (Paris, 1870), p. 335. [I2,5]

Nineteenth-century domestic interior. The space disguises itself—puts on, like an alluring creature, the costumes of moods. The self-satisfied burgher should know something of the feeling that the next room might have witnessed the coronation of Charlemagne as well as the assassination of Henri IV, the signing of the Treaty of Verdun as well as the wedding of Otto and Theophano. In the end, things are merely mannequins, and even the great moments of world history are only costumes beneath which they exchange glances of complicity with nothingness, with the petty and the banal. Such nihilism is the innermost core of bourgeois coziness—a mood that in hashish intoxication concentrates to satanic contentment, satanic knowing, satanic calm, indicating precisely to what extent the nineteenth-century interior is itself a stimulus to intoxication and dream. This mood involves, furthermore, an aversion to the open air, the (so to speak) Uranian atmosphere, which throws a new light on the extravagant interior design of the period. To live in these interiors was to have woven a dense fabric about oneself, to have secluded oneself within a spider's web, in whose toils world events hang loosely suspended like so many insect bodies sucked dry. From this cavern, one does not like to stir.[5] [I2,6]

During my second experiment with hashish. Staircase in Charlotte Joël's studio. I said: "A structure habitable only by wax figures. I could do so much with it plastically; Piscator and company can just go pack. Would be possible for me to change the lighting scheme with tiny levers. I can transform the Goethe house into the Covent Garden opera; can read from it the whole of world history. I see, in this space, why I collect colportage images. Can see everything in this room— the sons of Charles III and what you will."[6] [I2a,1]

"The serrated collars and puffed sleeves . . . which were mistakenly thought to be the garb of medieval ladies." Jacob Falke, *Geschichte des modernen Geschmacks* (Leipzig, 1866), p. 347. [I2a,2]

"Since the glittering arcades have been cut through the streets, the Palais-Royal has effectively lost out. Some would say: since the times have grown more virtuous. What were once small *cabinets particuliers* of ill repute have now become smoking

rooms in coffeehouses. Each coffeehouse has a smoking room known as the *divan*." Gutzkow, *Briefe aus Paris* (Leipzig, 1842), vol. 1, p. 226. ▯ Arcades ▯
[I2a,3]

"The great Berlin industrial exhibition is full of imposing Renaissance rooms; even the ashtrays are in antique style, the curtains have to be secured with halberds, and the bull's-eye rules in window and cabinet." *70 Jahre deutsche Mode* (1925), p. 72.
[I2a,4]

An observation from the year 1837. "In those days, the classical style reigned, just as the rococo does today. With a stroke of its magic wand, fashion . . . transformed the salon into an atrium, armchairs into curule seats, dresses with trains into tunics, drinking glasses into goblets, shoes into buskins, and guitars into lyres." Sophie Gay, *Der Salon der Fräulein Contet* (in *Europa: Chronik der gebildeten Welt,* ed. August Lewald, vol. 1 [Leipzig and Stuttgart, 1837], p. 358). Hence the following: "What is the height of embarrassment?" "When you bring a harp to a party and no one asks you to play it." This piece of drollery, which also illuminates a certain type of interior, probably dates from the First Empire.
[I2a,5]

"As to Baudelaire's 'stage properties'—which were no doubt modeled on the fashion in interior decoration of his day—they might provide a useful lesson for those elegant ladies of the past twenty years, who used to pride themselves that not a single 'false note' was to be found in their town houses. They would do well to consider, when they contemplate the alleged purity of style which they have achieved with such infinite trouble, that a man may be the greatest and most artistic of writers, yet describe nothing but beds with 'adjustable curtains' . . . , halls like conservatories . . . , beds filled with subtle scents, sofas deep as tombs, whatnots loaded with flowers, lamps burning so briefly . . . that the only light comes from the coal fire." Marcel Proust, *Chroniques* (Paris ‹1927›), pp. 224–225[7] (the titles of works cited are omitted). These remarks are important because they make it possible to apply to the interior an antinomy formulated with regard to museums and town planning—namely, to confront the new style with the mystical-nihilistic expressive power of the traditional, the "antiquated." Which of these two alternatives Proust would have chosen is revealed not only by this passage, it may be added, but by the whole of his work (compare *renfermé*—"closed-up," "musty").
[I2a,6]

Desideratum: the derivation of genre painting. What function did it serve in the rooms that had need of it? It was the last stage—harbinger of the fact that soon these spaces would no longer, in general, welcome pictures. "Genre painting. . . . Conceived in this way, art could not fail to resort to the specialties so suited to the marketplace: each artist wants to have his own specialty, from the pastiche of the Middle Ages to microscopic painting, from the routines of the bivouac to Paris fashions, from horses to dogs. Public taste in this regard does not discriminate. . . . The same picture can be copied twenty times without exhausting demand and, as the vogue prescribes, each well-kept drawing room wants to have one of these fashionable *furnishings*." Wiertz, *Oeuvres littéraires* ‹Paris, 1870›, pp. 527–528.   [I2a,7]

Against the armature of glass and iron, upholstery offers resistance with its textiles.   [I3,1]

One need only study with due exactitude the physiognomy of the homes of great collectors. Then one would have the key to the nineteenth-century interior. Just as in the former case the objects gradually take possession of the residence, so in the latter it is a piece of furniture that would retrieve and assemble the stylistic traces of the centuries. ▯ World of Things ▯   [I3,2]

Why does the glance into an unknown window always find a family at a meal, or else a solitary man, seated at a table under a hanging lamp, occupied with some obscure niggling thing? Such a glance is the germ cell of Kafka's work.   [I3,3]

The masquerade of styles, as it unfolds across the nineteenth century, results from the fact that relations of dominance become obscured. The holders of power in the bourgeoisie no longer necessarily exercise this power in the places where they live (as rentiers), and no longer in direct unmediated forms. The style of their residences is their false immediacy. Economic alibi in space. Interior alibi in time.   [I3,4]

"The art would be to be able to feel homesick, even though one is at home. Expertness in the use of illusion is required for this." Kierkegaard, *Sämtliche Werke* ‹properly: *Gesammelte Werke*›, vol. 4 ‹Jena, 1914›, p. 12 ‹*Stages on Life's Way*›.[8] This is the formula for the interior.   [I3,5]

"Inwardness is the historical prison of primordial human nature." Wiesengrund-Adorno, *Kierkegaard* (Tübingen, 1933), p. 68.[9]   [I3,6]

Second Empire. "It is this epoch that sees the birth of the logical specialization by genus and species that still prevails in most homes, and that reserves oak and solid walnut for the dining room and study, gilded wood and lacquers for the drawing room, marquetry and veneering for the bedroom." Louis Sonolet, *La Vie parisienne sous le Second Empire* (Paris, 1929), p. 251.   [I3,7]

"What dominated this conception of furnishing, in a manner so pronounced as to epitomize the whole, was the taste for draped fabrics, ample hangings, and the art of harmonizing them all in a visual ensemble." Louis Sonolet, *La Vie parisienne sous le Second Empire* (Paris, 1929), p. 253.   [I3,8]

"The drawing rooms of the Second Empire contained . . . a piece of furniture quite recently invented and today completely extinct: it was the *fumeuse*. You sat on it astride, while leaning back on upholstered arm-rests and enjoying a cigar." Louis Sonolet, *La Vie parisienne sous le Second Empire* (Paris, 1929), p. 253. [I3,9]

On the "filigree of chimneys" as "fata morgana" of the interior: "Whoever raises his eyes to the housetops, with their iron railings tracing the upper edge of the long gray boulevard blocks, discovers the variety and inexhaustibility of the concept 'chimney.' In all degrees of height, breadth, and length, the smokestacks rise from their base in the common stone flues; they range from simple clay pipes, oftentimes half-broken and stooped with age, and those tin pipes with flat plates or pointed caps, . . . to revolving chimney cowls artfully perforated like visors or open on one side, with bizarre soot-blackened metal flaps. . . . It is the . . . tender irony of the one single form by which Paris . . . has been able to preserve the magic of intimacy. . . . So it is as if the urbane coexistence . . . that is characteristic of this city were to be met with again up there on the rooftops." Joachim von Helmersen, "Pariser Kamine," *Frankfurter Zeitung*, February 10, 1933. [I3,10]

Wiesengrund cites and comments on a passage from the *Diary of a Seducer*—a passage that he considers the key to Kierkegaard's "entire oeuvre": "Environment and setting still have a great influence upon one; there is something about them which stamps itself firmly and deeply in the memory, or rather upon the whole soul, and which is therefore never forgotten. However old I may become, it will always be impossible for me to think of Cordelia amid surroundings different from this little room. When I come to visit her, the maid admits me to the hall; Cordelia herself comes in from her room, and, just as I open the door to enter the living room, she opens her door, so that our eyes meet exactly in the doorway. The living room is small, comfortable, little more than a cabinet. Although I have now seen it from many different viewpoints, the one dearest to me is the view from the sofa. She sits there by my side; in front of us stands a round tea table, over which is draped a rich tablecloth. On the table stands a lamp shaped like a flower, which shoots up vigorously to bear its crown, over which a delicately cut paper shade hangs down so lightly that it is never still. The lamp's form reminds one of oriental lands; the shade's movement, of mild oriental breezes. The floor is concealed by a carpet woven from a certain kind of osier, which immediately betrays its foreign origin. For the moment, I let the lamp become the keynote of my landscape. I am sitting there with her outstretched on the floor, under the lamp's flowering. At other times I let the osier rug evoke thoughts of a ship, of an officer's cabin—we sail out into the middle of the great ocean. When we sit at a distance from the window, we gaze directly into heaven's vast horizon. . . . Cordelia's environment must have no foreground, but only the infinite boldness of far horizons" (*Gesammelte Schriften* ⟨properly: *Werke* (Jena, 1911)⟩, vol. 1, pp. 348–349 [*Either/Or*]). Wiesengrund remarks: "Just as external history is 'reflected' in internal history, semblance ⟨*Schein*⟩ is in the *intérieur* space. Kierkegaard no more discerned the element of semblance in all merely reflected and reflecting intrasubjective reality than he sees through the semblance of the spatial in the image of the interior. But here he is exposed by the material. . . . The contents of the interior are mere decoration, alienated from the purposes they represent, deprived of their own use value, engendered solely by the isolated dwelling-space. . . . The self is overwhelmed in its own domain by commodities and their historical essence. Their semblance-character is historically-economically produced by the alienation of thing from use value. But in the interior, things do not remain alien. . . . Foreignness transforms itself from alienated things into expression; mute things speak as 'symbols.' The ordering of things in the dwelling-space is called 'arrangement.' Historically illusory ‹*Geschichtlich scheinhafte*› objects are arranged in it as the semblance of unchangeable nature. In the interior, archaic images unfold: the image of the flower as that of organic life; the image of the orient as specifically the homeland of yearning; the image of the sea as that of eternity itself. For the semblance to which the historical hour condemns things is eternal." Theodor Wiesengrund-Adorno, *Kierkegaard* (Tübingen, 1933), pp. 46–48.[10]   [I3 a]

The bourgeois who came into ascendancy with Louis Philippe sets store by the transformation of nature into the interior. In 1839, a ball is held at the British embassy. Two hundred rose bushes are ordered. "The garden," so runs an eye-witness account, "was covered by an awning and had the feel of a drawing room. But what a drawing room! The fragrant, well-stocked flower beds had turned into enormous *jardinières,* the graveled walks had disappeared under sumptuous carpets, and in place of the cast-iron benches we found sofas covered in damask and silk; a round table held books and albums. From a distance, the strains of an orchestra drifted into this colossal boudoir."   [I4,1]

Fashion journals of the period contained instructions for preserving bouquets.
          [I4,2]

"Like an odalisque upon a shimmering bronze divan, the proud city lies amid warm, vine-clad hills in the serpentine valley of the Seine." Friedrich Engels, "Von Paris nach Bern," *Die neue Zeit*, 17, no. 1 (Stuttgart, 1899), p. 10.   [I4,3]

The difficulty in reflecting on dwelling: on the one hand, there is something age-old—perhaps eternal—to be recognized here, the image of that abode of the human being in the maternal womb; on the other hand, this motif of primal history notwithstanding, we must understand dwelling in its most extreme form as a condition of nineteenth-century existence. The original form of all dwelling is existence not in the house but in the shell. The shell bears the impression of its occupant. In the most extreme instance, the dwelling becomes a shell. The nineteenth century, like no other century, was addicted to dwelling. It conceived the residence as a receptacle for the person, and it encased him with all his appurtenances so deeply in the dwelling's interior that one might be reminded of the inside of a compass case, where the instrument with all its accessories lies embedded in deep, usually violet folds of velvet. What didn't the nineteenth century invent some sort of casing for! Pocket watches, slippers, egg cups, thermometers, playing cards—and, in lieu of cases, there were jackets, carpets, wrappers, and covers. The twentieth century, with its porosity and transparency, its tendency toward the well-lit and airy, has put an end to dwelling in the old sense. Set off against the doll house in the residence of the master builder Solness are the "homes for human beings."[11] Jugendstil unsettled the world of the shell in a radical way. Today this world has disappeared entirely, and dwelling has diminished: for the living, through hotel rooms; for the dead, through crematoriums.

[I4,4]

"To dwell" as a transitive verb—as in the notion of "indwelt spaces";[12] herewith an indication of the frenetic topicality concealed in habitual behavior. It has to do with fashioning a shell for ourselves.

[I4,5]

"From under all the coral branches and bushes, they swam into view; from under every table, every chair; from out of the drawers of the old-fashioned cabinets and wardrobes that stood within this strange clubroom—in short, from every hand's-breadth of hiding which the spot provided to the smallest of fish, they suddenly came to life and showed themselves." Friedrich Gerstäcker, *Die versunkene Stadt* (Berlin: Neufeld and Henius, 1921), p. 46.

[I4a,1]

From a review of Eugène Sue's *Juif errant* ‹Wandering Jew›, criticized for various reasons, including the denigration of the Jesuits and the unmanageable abundance of characters who do nothing but appear and disappear: "A novel is not a place one passes through; it is a place one inhabits." Paulin Limayrac, "Du Roman actuel et de nos romanciers," *Revue des deux mondes*, 11, no. 3 (Paris, 1845), p. 951.

[I4a,2]

On literary Empire. Népomucène Lemercier brings onto the stage, under allegorical names, the Monarchy, the Church, the Aristocracy, the Demagogues, the Empire, the Police, Literature, and the Coalition of European powers. His artistic means: "the fantastic applied emblematically." His maxim: "Allusions are my weapons; allegory, my buckler." Népomucène Lemercier, *Suite de la Panhypocrisiade, ou Le Spectacle infernal du dix-neuvième siècle* (Paris, 1832), pp. ix, vii.

[I4a,3]

From the "Exposé préliminaire" to Lemercier's *Lampélie et Daguerre*: "A short preamble is necessary to introduce my audience to the compositional strategy of this poem, whose subject is praise for the discovery made by the illustrious artist M. Daguerre; this is a discovery of equal interest to the Academy of Science and the Academy of Fine Arts, for it concerns the study of drawing as much as the study of physics. . . . On the occasion of such an homage, I would like to see a new invention in poetry applied to this extraordinary discovery. We know that ancient mythology . . . explained natural phenomena by symbolic beings, active representations of the particular principles embodied in things. . . . Modern imitations have, up to now, borrowed only the forms of classical poetry; I am endeavoring to appropriate for us the principle and the substance. The tendency of the versifiers of our century is to reduce the art of the muses to practical and trivial realities, easily comprehensible by the average person. This is not progress but decadence. The original enthusiasm of the ancients, by contrast, tended to elevate the human intelligence by initiating it into those secrets of nature revealed by the elegantly ideal fables. . . . It is not without encouragement that I lay bare for you the foundations of my theory, which I have applied . . . to Newtonian philosophy in my *Atlantiade*. The learned geometer Lagrange has been so generous as to voice approval of my attempt to create for our modern muses that great rarity: a theosophy . . . conforming to acquired knowledge." Népomucène Lemercier, *Sur la Découverte de l'ingénieux peintre du diorama: Séance publique annuelle des cinq académies de jeudi 2 mai 1839* (Paris, 1839), pp. 21–23.   [I4a,4]

On the illusionistic painting of the Juste Milieu:[13] "The painter must . . . be a good dramatist, a good costumer, and a skillful director. . . . The public . . . is much more interested in the subject than in the artistic qualities. 'Isn't the most difficult thing the blending of colors?—No, responds a connoisseur, it's getting the fish's scales right. Such was the idea of aesthetic creation among professors, lawyers, doctors; everywhere one admired the miracle of trompe-l'oeil. Any minimally successful imitation would garner praise.'" Gisela Freund, "La Photographie du point de vue sociologique" (Manuscript, p. 102). The quotation is from Jules Breton, *Nos peintres du siècle*, p. 41.   [I5,1]

Plush—the material in which traces are left especially easily.   [I5,2]

Furthering the fashion in knickknacks are the advances in metallurgy, which has its origins in the First Empire. "During this period, groups of cupids and bacchantes appeared for the first time. . . . Today, art owns a shop and displays the marvels of its creations on shelves of gold or crystal, whereas in those days masterpieces of statuary, reduced in precise proportion, were sold at a discount. The *Three Graces* of Canova found a place in the boudoir, while the *Bacchantes* and the *Faun* of Pradier had the honors of the bridal chamber." Edouard Foucaud, *Paris inventeur: Physiologie de l'industrie française* (Paris, 1844), pp. 196–197.   [I5,3]

"The science of the poster . . . has attained that rare degree of perfection at which skill turns into art. And here I am not speaking of those extraordinary placards . . . on which experts in calligraphy . . . undertake to represent Napoleon on horseback by an ingenious combination of lines in which the course of his history is simultaneously narrated and depicted. No, I shall confine myself to ordinary posters. Just see how far these have been able to push the eloquence of typography, the seductions of the vignette, the fascinations of color, by using the most varied and brilliant of hues to lend perfidious support to the ruses of the publishers!" Victor Fournel, *Ce qu'on voit dans les rues de Paris* (Paris, 1858), pp. 293–294 ("Enseignes et affiches"). [I5,4]

Interior of Alphonse Karr's apartment: "He lives like no one else. These days he's on the sixth or seventh floor above the Rue Vivienne. The Rue Vivienne for an artist! His apartment is hung in black; he has windowpanes of violet or white frosted glass. He has neither tables nor chairs (at most, a single chair for exceptional visitors), and he sleeps on a divan—fully dressed, I'm told. He lives like a Turk, on cushions, and writes sitting on the floor. . . . His walls are decorated with various old things . . . ; Chinese vases, death-heads, fencer's foils, and tobacco pipes ornament every corner. For a servant, he has a mulatto whom he outfits in scarlet from head to toe." Jules Lecomte, *Les Lettres de Van Engelgom*, ed. Almeras (Paris, 1925), pp. 63–64. [I5,5]

From Daumier's *Croquis pris au Salon* ‹Sketches Made at the Salon›. A solitary art-lover indicating a picture on which two miserable poplars are represented in a flat landscape: "What society could be as degenerate and corrupt as ours? . . . Everyone looks at pictures of more or less monstrous scenes, but no one stops before an image of beautiful and pure nature." [I5a,1]

On the occasion of a murder case in London which turned on the discovery of a sack containing the victim's body parts, together with remnants of clothing; from the latter, the police were able to draw certain conclusions. "'So many things in a minuet!' a celebrated dancer used to say. So many things in an overcoat!—when circumstances and men make it speak. You will say it's a bit much to expect a person, each time he acquires a topcoat, to consider that one day it may serve him as a winding sheet. I admit that my suppositions are not exactly rose-colored. But, I repeat, . . . the week's events have been doleful." H. de Pène, *Paris intime* (Paris, 1859), p. 236. [I5a,2]

Furniture at the time of the Restoration: "sofas, divans, ottomans, love seats, recliners, settees." Jacques Robiquet, *L'Art et le goût sous la Restauration* (Paris, 1928), p. 202. [I5a,3]

"We have already said . . . that humanity is regressing to the state of cave dweller, and so on—but that it is regressing in an estranged, malignant form. The savage in his cave . . . feels . . . at home there. . . . But the basement apartment of the poor man is a hostile dwelling, 'an alien, restraining power, which gives itself up to him only insofar as he gives up to it his blood and sweat.' Such a dwelling can never feel like home, a place where he might at last exclaim, 'Here I am at home!' Instead, the poor man finds himself in someone else's home, . . . someone who daily lies in wait for him and throws him out if he does not pay his rent. He is also aware of the contrast in quality between his dwelling and a human dwelling—a residence in that other world, the heaven of wealth." Karl Marx, *Der historische Materialismus*, ed. Landshut and Mayer (Leipzig ‹1932›), vol. 1, p. 325 ("Nationalökonomie und Philosophie").[14]   [I5a,4]

Valéry on Poe. He underlines the American writer's incomparable insight into the conditions and effects of literary work in general: "What distinguishes a truly general phenomenon is its fertility. . . . It is therefore not surprising that Poe, possessing so effective and sure a method, became the inventor of several different literary forms—that he provided the first . . . examples of the scientific tale, the modern cosmogonic poem, the detective novel, the literature of morbid psychological states." Valéry, "Introduction" to Baudelaire, *Les Fleurs du mal* ‹Paris, 1926›, p. xx.[15]   [I5a,5]

In the following description of a Parisian salon, Gautier gives drastic expression to the integration of the individual into the interior: "The eye, entranced, is led to the groups of ladies who, fluttering their fans, listen to the talkers half-reclining. Their eyes are sparkling like diamonds; their shoulders glisten like satin; and their lips open up like flowers." (Artificial things come forth!) *Paris et les Parisiens aux XIXe siècle* (Paris, 1856), p. iv (Théophile Gautier, "Introduction").   [I6,1]

Balzac's interior decorating in the rather ill-fated property Les Jardies:[16] "This house . . . was one of the romances on which M. de Balzac worked hardest during his life, but he was never able to finish it. . . . 'On these patient walls,' as M. Gozlan has said, 'there were charcoal inscriptions to this effect: "Here a facing in Parian marble"; "Here a cedar stylobate"; "Here a ceiling painted by Eugène Delacroix"; "Here a fireplace in cipolin marble."'" Alfred Nettement, *Histoire de la littérature française sous le gouvernement de juillet* (Paris, 1859), vol. 2, pp. 266–267.   [I6,2]

Development of "The Interior" chapter: entry of the prop into film.   [I6,3]

E. R. Curtius cites the following passage from Balzac's *Petits Bourgeois:* "The hideous unbridled speculation that lowers, year by year, the height of the ceilings, that fits a whole apartment into the space formerly occupied by a drawing room and declares war on the garden, will not fail to have an influence on Parisian morals. Soon it will become necessary to live more outside the house than within it." Ernst Robert Curtius, *Balzac* (Bonn, 1923), p. 28. Increasing importance of the streets, for various reasons.   [I6,4]

Perhaps there is a connection between the shrinking of residential space and the elaborate furnishing of the interior. Regarding the first, Balzac makes some telling observations: "Small pictures alone are in demand because large ones can no longer be hung. Soon it will be a formidable problem to house one's library. . . . One can no longer find space for provisions of any sort. Hence, one buys things that are not calculated to wear well. 'The shirts and the books won't last, so there

you are. The durability of products is disappearing on all sides.'" Ernst Robert
Curtius, *Balzac* (Bonn, 1923), pp. 28–29.   [I6,5]

"Sunsets cast their glowing colors on the walls of dining room and drawing room,
filtering softly through lovely hangings or intricate high windows with mullioned
panes. All the furniture is immense, fantastic, strange, armed with locks and
secrets like all civilized souls. Mirrors, metals, fabrics, pottery, and works of the
goldsmith's art play a mute mysterious symphony for the eye." Charles Baudelaire, *Le Spleen de Paris*, ed. R. Simon (Paris), p. 27 ("L'Invitation au voyage").[17]
                                                                                [I6a,1]

Etymology of the word "comfort." "In English, it used to mean *consolation* ('Com-
forter' is the epithet applied to the Holy Spirit). Then the sense became, instead,
well-being. Today, in all languages of the world, the word designates nothing more
than rational convenience." Wladimir Weidlé, *Les Abeilles d'Aristée* (Paris
‹1936›), p. 175 ("L'Agonie de l'art").   [I6a,2]

"The artist-midinettes . . . no longer occupy rooms; rather, they live in studios.
(More and more, you hear every place of habitation called a 'studio,' as if people
were more and more becoming artists or students.)" Henri Pollès, "L'Art du commerce," *Vendredi*, February 12, 1937.   [I6a,3]

Multiplication of traces through the modern administrative apparatus. Balzac
draws attention to this: "Do your utmost, hapless Frenchwomen, to remain
unknown, to weave the very least little romance in the midst of a civilization
which takes note, on public squares, of the hour when every hackney cab comes
and goes; which counts every letter and stamps them twice, at the exact time they
are posted and at the time they are delivered; which numbers the houses . . . ;
which ere long will have every acre of land, down to the smallest holdings . . . ,
laid down on the broad sheets of a survey—a giant's task, by command of a
giant." Balzac, *Modeste Mignon*,[18] cited in Régis Messac, *Le "Detective Novel" ‹et
l'influence de la pensée scientifique›* (Paris, 1929), p. 461.   [I6a,4]

"Victor Hugo works standing up, and, since he cannot find a suitable antique to
serve as his desk, he writes on a stack of stools and large books which is covered
with a carpet. It is on the Bible, it is on the Nuremberg Chronicles, that the poet
leans and spreads his paper." Louis Ulbach, *Les Contemporains* (Paris, 1833),
cited in Raymond Escholier, *Victor Hugo raconté par ceux qui l'ont vu* (Paris,
1931), p. 352.   [I7,1]

The Louis Philippe style: "The belly overspreads everything, even the timepieces."   [I7,2]

There is an apocalyptic interior—a complement, as it were, of the bourgeois
interior at midcentury. It is to be found with Victor Hugo. He writes of spiritual-

istic manifestations: "I have been checked for a moment in my miserable human *amour-propre* by actual revelation, coming to throw around my little miner's lamp a streak of lightning and of meteor." In *Les Contemplations,* he writes:

> We listen for any sounds in these dismal empty spaces;
> Wandering through the shadows, we listen to the breath
>   That makes the darkness shudder;
> And now and then, lost in unfathomable nights,
> We see lit up by mighty lights
>   The window of eternity.

(Cited in Claudius Grillet, *Victor Hugo spirite* ‹Lyons and Paris, 1929›, pp. 52, 22.)   [I7,3]

Lodgings around 1860: "The apartment . . . was situated on the Rue d'Anjou. It was decorated . . . with carpets, door curtains, fringed valances, double draperies, so that you would think the Stone Age had been succeeded by an Age of Hangings." Louise Weiss, *Souvenirs d'une enfance républicaine* (Paris ‹1937›), p. 212.   [I7,4]

The relation of the Jugendstil interior to its predecessors comes down to the fact that the bourgeois conceals his alibi in history with a still more remote alibi in natural history (specifically in the realm of plants).   [I7,5]

The étuis, dust covers, sheaths with which the bourgeois household of the preceding century encased its utensils were so many measures taken to capture and preserve traces.   [I7,6]

On the history of the domestic interior. The residential character of the rooms in the early factories, though disconcerting and inexpedient, adds this homely touch: that within these spaces one can imagine the factory owner as a quaint figurine in a landscape of machines, dreaming not only of his own but of their future greatness. With the dissociation of the proprietor from the workplace, this characteristic of factory buildings disappears. Capital alienates the employer, too, from his means of production, and the dream of their future greatness is finished. This alienation process culminates in the emergence of the private home.
                                                                                                         [I7a,1]

"During the first decades of the nineteenth century, furniture and the objects that surrounded us for use and pleasure were relatively simple and durable, and accorded with the needs of both the lower and the upper strata. This resulted in people's attachment, as they grew up, to the objects of their surroundings. . . . The differentiation of objects has broken down this situation in three different ways. . . . First, the sheer quantity of very specifically formed objects make a close . . . relationship to each of them more difficult. . . . This is expressed . . . in the housewife's complaint that the care of the household becomes ceremonial fetishism. . . . This concurrent differentiation has the same effect as consecutive differentiation. Changes in fashion disrupt that . . . process of . . . assimilation between subject and object. . . . [In the third place, there is] the multitude of styles that confronts us when we view the objects that surround us." Georg Simmel, *Philosophie des Geldes* (Leipzig, 1900), pp. 491–494.[19]　　　　　　　　　　[I7a,2]

On the theory of the trace. To "the Harbor-Master, . . . [as] a sort of . . . deputy-Neptune for the circumambient seas, . . . I was, in common with the other seamen of the port, merely a subject for official writing, filling up of forms with all the artificial superiority of a man of pen and ink to the men who grapple with realities outside the consecrated walls of official buildings. What ghosts we must have been to him! Mere symbols to juggle with in books and heavy registers, without brains and muscles and perplexities; something hardly useful and decidedly inferior." Joseph Conrad, *Die Schattenlinie* (Berlin ‹1926›), p. 51.[20] (Compare with the Rousseau passage ‹cited below›.)　　　　　　　　　　[I7a,3]

On the theory of the trace. Practice is eliminated from the productive process by machinery. In the process of administration, something analogous occurs with heightened organization. Knowledge of human nature, such as the senior employee could acquire through practice, ceases to be decisive. This can be seen when one compares Conrad's observations in "The Shadow-Line" with a passage from *Les Confessions*.　　　　　　　　　　[I8,1]

On the theory of the trace: administration in the eighteenth century. As secretary to the French embassy in Venice, Rousseau had abolished the tax on passports for the French. "As soon as the news got around that I had reformed the passport tax, my only applicants were crowds of pretended Frenchmen who claimed in abominable accents to be either from Provence, Picardy, or Burgundy. As I have a fairly good ear, I was not easily fooled, and I doubt whether a single Italian cheated me out of my *sequin,* or a single Frenchmen paid it." Jean-Jacques Rousseau, *Les Confessions,* ed. Hilsum (Paris ‹1931›), vol. 2, p. 137.[21]　　　　[I8,2]

Baudelaire, in the introduction to his translation of Poe's "Philosophy of Furniture," which originally appeared in October 1852 in *Le Magasin des familles:* "Who among us, in his idle hours, has not taken a delicious pleasure in constructing for himself a model apartment, a dream house, a house of dreams?" Charles Baudelaire, *Oeuvres complètes*, ed. Crépet, *Histoires grotesques et sérieuses par Poe* (Paris, 1937), p. 304.　　　　　　　　　　[I8,3]

J

[Baudelaire]

> For it pleases me, all for your sake, to row
> My own oars here on my own sea,
> And to soar heavenward by a strange avenue,
> Singing you the unsung praises of Death.
>
> —Pierre Ronsard, "Hymne de la Mort," *A Louys des Masures*[1]

"Baudelaire's problem . . . must have . . . posed itself in these terms: 'How to be a great poet, but neither a Lamartine nor a Hugo nor a Musset.' I do not say that these words were consciously formulated, but they must have been latent in Baudelaire's mind; they even constituted what was the essential Baudelaire. They were his *raison d'état*. . . . Baudelaire considered Victor Hugo; and it is not impossible to imagine what he thought of him. . . . Everything that might scandalize, and thereby instruct and guide a pitiless young observer in the way of his own future art, . . . Baudelaire must have recorded in his mind, distinguishing the admiration forced upon him by Hugo's wonderful gifts from the impurities, the imprudences, . . . that is to say, the chances for life and fame that so great an artist left behind him to be gleaned." Paul Valéry, Introduction (Charles Baudelaire, *Les Fleurs du mal*, with an introduction by Paul Valéry [Paris ‹1926›], pp. x, xii, xiv).[2] Problem of the *poncif*.[3]   [J1,1]

"For a few years before the Revolution of 1848, everyone is hesitating between a pure art and a social art, and it is only well after 1852 that *l'art pour l'art* gains the upper hand." C. L. de Liefde, *Le Saint-Simonisme dans la poésie française entre 1825 et 1865* ‹Haarlem, 1927›, p. 180.   [J1,2]

Leconte de Lisle, in the preface to his *Poèmes et poésies* of 1855: "The hymns and odes inspired by steam power and electric telegraphy leave me cold." Cited in C. L. de Liefde, *Le Saint-Simonisme dans la poésie française entre 1825 et 1865*, p. 179.   [J1,3]

Baudelaire's "Les Bonnes Soeurs" ‹The Kind Sisters› may be compared with the Saint-Simonian poem "La Rue" ‹The Street›, by Savinien Lapointe, shoemaker.

Charles Baudelaire, 1855. Photo by Nadar. Musée d'Orsay, Paris; photo copyright
© RMN.

The latter is concerned *only* with prostitution and, at the end, evokes memories of
the youth of the fallen young women:

> Oh! Do not seek to know all that debauchery does
> To wither the flowers and mow them down;
> In its working, it is premature as death
> And will make you old despite your eighteen years.
>
> . . . .

. . . .
Have pity on them! Pity!
When on the corner you should knock against them,
Their angelic faces bathed in the glow of good recalled.

Olinde Rodrigues, *Poésies sociales des ouvriers* (Paris, 1841), pp. 201, 203.
[J1,4]

Dates. Baudelaire's first letter to Wagner: February 17, 1860. Wagner's concerts in Paris: February 1 and 8, 1860. Paris premiere of *Tannhäuser:* March 13, 1861. When was Baudelaire's article in *La Revue européenne?*[4]   [J1,5]

Baudelaire planned "an enormous work on the *peintres des moeurs* ⟨painters of manners⟩." Crépet, in this connection, cites his statement: "Images—my great, my primitive passion."[5] Jacques Crépet, "Miettes baudelairiennes," *Mercure de France*, 46th year, vol. 262, no. 894, pp. 531–532.   [J1,6]

"Baudelaire . . . can still write, in 1852, in the preface to Dupont's *Chansons:* 'Art was thereafter inseparable from morality and utility.' And he speaks there of the 'puerile Utopia of the school of *art for art's sake.*'[6] . . . Nevertheless, he changes his mind soon after 1852. This conception of social art may perhaps be explained by his youthful relations. Dupont was his friend at the moment when Baudelaire, 'almost fanatically republican under the monarchy,' was meditating a realistic and communicatory poetry." C. L. de Liefde, *Le Saint-Simonisme dans la poésie française entre 1825 et 1865* ⟨Haarlem, 1927⟩, p. 115.   [J1a,1]

Baudelaire soon forgot the February Revolution.[7] Telling evidence of this fact has been published by Jacques Crépet, in "Miettes baudelairiennes" ⟨Baudelairean Morsels⟩ (*Mercure de France*, vol. 262, no. 894, p. 525), in the form of a review of the *Histoire de Neuilly et de ses châteaux*, by the abbé Bellanger, a review which Baudelaire probably composed at the request of his friend the lawyer Ancelle, and which at the time presumably appeared in the press. There Baudelaire speaks of the history of the place "from Roman times to the terrible days of February, when the château was the theater and spoil of the most ignoble passions, of orgy and destruction."   [J1a,2]

Nadar describes the outfit worn by Baudelaire, who is encountered in the vicinity of his residence ⟨of 1843–1845⟩, the Hôtel Pimodan. "Black trousers drawn well above his polished boots; a blue workman's blouse, stiff in its new folds; his black hair, naturally curly, worn long—his only coiffure; bright linen, strictly without starch; a faint moustache under his nose and a bit of beard on his chin; rose-colored gloves, quite new. . . . Thus arrayed and hatless, Baudelaire walked about his *quartier* of the city at an uneven pace, both nervous and languid, like a cat, choosing each stone of the pavement as if he had to avoid crushing an egg." Cited in Firmin Maillard, *La Cité des intellectuels* (Paris ⟨1905⟩), p. 362.   [J1a,3]

Baudelaire—after his enforced sea voyage[8]—was a well-traveled man.   [J1a,4]

Baudelaire to Poulet-Malassis, on January 8, 1860, after a visit from Meryon: "After he left me, I wondered how it was that I, who have always had the mind and the nerves to go mad, have never actually gone mad. In all seriousness, I gave heaven a Pharisee's thanks for this."[9] Cited in Gustave Geffroy, *Charles Meryon* (Paris, 1926), p. 128.   [J1a,5]

From the ⟨eighth⟩ section of Baudelaire's "Salon de 1859." There one finds, apropos of Meryon, this phrase: "the profound and complex charm of a capital city which has grown old and worn in the glories and tribulations of life." A little further on: "I have rarely seen the natural solemnity of an immense city more poetically reproduced. Those majestic accumulations of stone; those spires 'whose fingers point to heaven'; those obelisks of industry, spewing forth their conglomerations of smoke against the firmament; those prodigies of scaffolding 'round buildings under repair, applying their openwork architecture, so paradoxically beautiful, upon architecture's solid body; that tumultuous sky, charged with anger and spite; those limitless perspectives, only increased by the thought of all the drama they contain;—he forgot not one of the complex elements which go to make up the painful and glorious décor of civilization. . . . But a cruel demon has touched M. Meryon's brain. . . . And from that moment we have never ceased waiting anxiously for some consoling news of this singular naval officer who in one short day turned into a mighty artist, and who bade farewell to the ocean's solemn adventures in order to paint the gloomy majesty of this most disquieting of capitals."[10] Cited in Gustave Geffroy, *Charles Meryon* (Paris, 1926), pp. 125–126.
[J2,1]

The editor Delâtre conceived a plan to publish an album of Meryon's etchings with text by Baudelaire. The plan fell through; but it had already been ruined for Baudelaire when Meryon demanded, instead of a text suited to the poet, a pedantic explication of the pictured monuments. Baudelaire complains of the matter in his letter of February 16, 1860, to Poulet-Malassis.   [J2,2]

Meryon placed these lines under his etching *Le Pont-Neuf*:

> Here lies the exact likeness
> Of the late Pont-Neuf,
> All newly refurbished
> Per recent ordinance.
> O learned doctors,
> Skillful surgeons,
> Why not do for us
> What's been done for this stone bridge?

According to Geffroy—who evidently takes them from another version of the etching—the last two lines are: "Will tell why renovations / Have been forced on this stone bridge." Gustave Geffroy, *Charles Meryon* (Paris, 1926), p. 59.   [J2,3]

The Pont-Neuf. Etching by Charles Meryon, 1853-1854. See J2,3.

Bizarre features on plates by Meryon. "The Rue des Chantres": squarely in the foreground, affixed at eye-level on the wall of what would seem to be a nearly windowless house, is a poster bearing the words "Sea Baths." ‹See Geffroy, *Charles Meryon*, p. 144.›—"The Collège Henry IV," about which Geffroy writes: "All around the school, the gardens, and neighboring houses, the space is empty, and suddenly Meryon begins to fill it with a landscape of mountain and sea, replacing the ocean of Paris. The sails and masts of a ship appear, some flocks of sea birds are taking wing, and this phantasmagoria gathers around the most rigorous design, the tall buildings of the school regularly pierced by windows, the courtyard planted with trees, . . . and the surrounding houses, with their dark rooftops, crowded chimneys, and blank façades" (Geffroy, *Charles Meryon*, p. 151).—"The Admiralty": in the clouds a troop of horses, chariots, and dolphins advances upon the ministry; ships and sea serpents are not lacking, and several human-shaped creatures are to be seen in the multitude. "This will be . . . the last view of Paris engraved by Meryon. He bids adieu to the city where he suffered that onslaught of dreams at the house, stern as a fortress, in which he did service as a young ensign, in the springtime of his life, when he was just setting out for the distant isles" (Geffroy, *Charles Meryon*, p. 161). ▯ Flâneur ▯ [J2a,1]

"Meryon's execution is incomparable, Béraldi says. The most striking thing is the beauty and dignity of his firm, decisive line. Those fine straight edges are said to be executed thus: the plate is set upright on an easel, the etching needle is held at arm's length (like a rapier), and the hand moves slowly from top to bottom." R. Castinelli, "Charles Meryon," Introduction to Charles Meryon, *Eaux-fortes sur Paris*, p. iii. [J2a,2]

Meryon produced his twenty-two etchings of Paris between 1852 and 1854. [J2a,3]

When did the "Paris article" ‹*article de Paris*› first appear? [J2a,4]

What Baudelaire says about a drawing by Daumier on the subject of cholera could also apply to certain engravings by Meryon: "True to its ironic custom in times of great calamity and political upheaval, the sky of Paris is superb; it is quite white and incandescent with heat." Charles Baudelaire, *Les Dessins de Daumier* (Paris ‹1924›), p. 13. ‹See J52a,4.› ☐ Dust, Boredom ☐ [J2a,5]

"The splenetic cupola of the sky"—a phrase from Charles Baudelaire, *Le Spleen de Paris*, ed. Simon (Paris), p. 8 ("Chacun sa chimère").[11] [J2a,6]

"The philosophical and literary Catholicism . . . of Baudelaire had need of an intermediate position . . . where it could take up its abode between God and the Devil. The title *Les Limbes* ‹Limbo› marked this geographic determination of Baudelaire's poems, making it possible to understand better the order Baudelaire wanted to establish among them, which is the order of a journey—more exactly, a fourth journey after Dante's three journeys in *Inferno*, *Purgatorio*, and *Paradiso*. The poet of Florence lived on in the poet of Paris." Albert Thibaudet, *Histoire de la littérature française de 1789 à nos jours* (Paris ‹1936›), p. 325.[12] [J3,1]

On the allegorical element. "Dickens . . . mentions, among the coffee shops into which he crept in those wretched days, one in St. Martin's Lane, 'of which I only recollect that it stood near the church, and that in the door there was an oval glass plate with COFFEE ROOM painted on it, addressed towards the street. If I ever find myself in a very different kind of coffee room now, but where there is such an inscription on glass, and read it backwards on the wrong side, MOOR EEFFOC (as I often used to do then in a dismal reverie), a shock goes through my blood.' That wild word, 'Moor Eeffoc,' is the motto of all effective realism." G. K. Chesterton, *Dickens* (series entitled *Vie des hommes illustres*, no. 9), trans. from the English by Laurent and Martin-Dupont (Paris, 1927), p. 32.[13] [J3,2]

Dickens and stenography: "He describes how, after he had learnt the whole exact alphabet, 'there then appeared a procession of new horrors, called arbitrary characters—the most despotic characters I have ever known; who insisted, for instance, that a thing like the beginning of a cobweb meant "expectation," and that a pen-and-ink skyrocket stood for "disadvantageous."' He concludes, 'It was almost heartbreaking.' But it is significant that somebody else, a colleague of his, concluded, 'There never *was* such a shorthand writer.'" G. K. Chesterton, *Dickens* (series entitled *Vie des hommes illustres*, no. 9), trans. Laurent and Martin-Dupont (Paris, 1927), pp. 40–41.[14]   [J3,3]

Valéry (Introduction to *Les Fleurs du mal* [Paris, 1926], p. xxv) speaks of a combination of "eternity and intimacy" in Baudelaire.[15]   [J3,4]

From the article by Barbey d'Aurevilly in *Articles justicatifs pour Charles Baudelaire, auteur des Fleurs du mal* (Paris, 1857), a booklet of thirty-three pages, with other contributions by Dulamon, Asselineau, and Thierry, which was printed at Baudelaire's expense for the trial:[16] "The poet, terrifying and terrified, wanted us to inhale the abomination of that dread basket that he carries, pale canephore, on his head bristling with horror. . . . His talent . . . is itself a flower of evil cultivated in the hothouses of Decadence. . . . There is something of Dante in the author of *Les Fleurs du mal*, but it is the Dante of an epoch in decline, an atheist and modernist Dante, a Dante come after Voltaire." Cited in W. T. Bandy, *Baudelaire Judged by His Contemporaries* (New York ⟨1933⟩), pp. 167–168 ⟨collection of texts in French⟩.   [J3a,1]

Gautier's note on Baudelaire in *Les Poètes français: Recueil des chefs-d'oeuvre de la poésie française*, ed. Eugène Crépet (Paris, 1862), vol. 4, *Les Contemporains:* "We never read *Les Fleurs du mal* . . . without thinking involuntarily of that tale by Hawthorne ⟨entitled "Rappaccini's Daughter"⟩. . . . His muse resembles the doctor's daughter whom no poison can harm, but whose pallid and anemic complexion betrays the influence of the milieu she inhabits." Cited in W. T. Bandy, *Baudelaire Judged by His Contemporaries* (New York), p. 174. ⟨See J29a,3⟩.   [J3a,2]

Main themes of Poe's aesthetic, according to Valéry: philosophy of composition, theory of the artificial, theory of modernity, theory of the strange and exceptional.   [J3a,3]

"Thus, Baudelaire's problem might have—indeed, must have—posed itself in these terms: 'How to be a great poet, but neither a Lamartine nor a Hugo nor a Musset.' I do not say that these words were consciously formulated, but they must have been latent in Baudelaire's mind; they even constituted what was the essential Baudelaire. They were his *raison d'état*. In the domain of creation, which is also the domain of pride, the need to come out and be distinct is part of life itself." Paul Valéry, Introduction to Baudelaire, *Les Fleurs du mal* (Paris, 1928), p. x.[17]   [J3a,4]

Régis Messac (⟨*Le "Detective Novel" et l'influence de la pensée scientifique* [Paris, 1929],⟩ p. 421) points to the influence of the "Two Crépuscules" ⟨"Le Crépuscule du matin" and "Le Crépuscule du soir," in *Les Fleurs du mal*⟩, first published February 1, 1852, in *La Semaine théâtrale*, on certain passages in Ponson du Terrail's *Drames de Paris*, which began to appear, in installments, in 1857.   [J3a,5]

The title originally planned for *Spleen de Paris* was *Le Promeneur solitaire*. For *Le Fleurs du mal* it was *Les Limbes* ‹Limbo›. [J4,1]

From "Conseils aux jeunes littérateurs": "If one is willing to live in stubborn contemplation of tomorrow's work, daily perseverance will serve inspiration." Charles Baudelaire, *L'Art romantique*, ed. Hachette, vol. 3 (Paris), p. 286.[18] [J4,2]

Baudelaire confesses to having had, "in childhood, the good fortune—or the misfortune—of reading only books for adults." Charles Baudelaire, *L'Art romantique* (Paris), p. 298 ("Drames et romans honnêtes").[19] [J4,3]

On Heine: "‹his› works are corrupted by materialistic sentimentality." Baudelaire, *L'Art romantique*, p. 303 ("L'Ecole païenne").[20] [J4,4]

A motif that wandered from *Spleen de Paris* to "L'Ecole païenne": "Why don't the poor wear gloves when they beg? They would make a fortune." Baudelaire, *L'Art romantique* (Paris), p. 309.[21] [J4,5]

"The time is not far off when it will be understood that every literature that refuses to walk hand in hand with science and philosophy is a homicidal and suicidal literature." Baudelaire, *L'Art romantique* (Paris), p. 309 (concluding sentence of "L'Ecole païenne").[22] [J4,6]

Baudelaire on the child raised in the company of the Pagan School: "His soul, constantly excited and unappeased, goes about the world, the busy, toiling world; it goes, I say, like a prostitute, crying: *Plastique! Plastique!* The plastic—that frightful word gives me goose flesh." Baudelaire, *L'Art romantique* (Paris), p. 307.[23] Compare J22a,2. [J4,7]

A passage from the portrait of Victor Hugo in which Baudelaire, like an engraver who sketches his own image in a remarque, has portrayed himself in a subordinate clause: "If he paints the sea, no *seascape* will equal his. The ships which furrow its surface or which cut through its foam will have, more than those of any other painter, the appearance of fierce combatants, the character of will and of animality which mysteriously emerges from a geometric and mechanical apparatus of wood, iron, ropes, and canvas; a monstrous animal created by man to which the wind and the waves add the beauty of movement." Baudelaire, *L'Art romantique* (Paris), p. 321 ("Victor Hugo").[24] [J4,8]

A phrase apropos of Auguste Barbier: "the natural indolence of those who depend on inspiration." Baudelaire, *L'Art romantique* (Paris), p. 335.[25] [J4a,1]

Baudelaire describes the poetry of the lyric poet—in the essay on Banville—in a way that, point for point, brings into view the exact opposite of his own poetry: "The word 'apotheosis' is one of those that unfailingly appear under the pen of the poet when he has to describe . . . a mingling of glory and light. And if the lyric poet has occasion to speak of himself, he will not depict himself bent over a table, . . . wrestling with intractable phrases, . . . any more than he will show himself in a poor, wretched, or disorderly room; nor, if he wishes to appear dead, will he show himself rotting beneath a linen shroud in a wooden casket. That would be lying." Baudelaire, *L'Art romantique* (Paris), pp. 370–371.[26]   [J4a,2]

In his essay on Banville, Baudelaire mentions mythology together with allegory, and then continues: "Mythology is a dictionary of living hieroglyphics." Baudelaire, *L'Art romantique* (Paris), p. 370.[27]   [J4a,3]

Conjunction of the modern and the demonic: "Modern poetry is related at one and the same time to painting, music, sculpture, decorative art, satiric philosophy, and the analytic spirit. . . . Some could perhaps see in this symptoms of depravity of taste. But that is a question which I do not wish to discuss here." Nevertheless, a page later, after a reference to Beethoven, Maturin, Byron, and Poe, one reads: "I mean that modern art has an essentially demoniacal tendency. And it seems that this satanic side of man . . . increases every day, as if the devil, like one who fattens geese, enjoyed enlarging it by artificial means, patiently force-feeding the human race in his poultry yard in order to prepare himself a more succulent dish." Baudelaire, *L'Art romantique* (Paris), pp. 373–374.[28] The concept of the demonic comes into play where the concept of modernity converges with Catholicism.   [J4a,4]

Regarding Leconte de Lisle: "My natural predilection for Rome prevents me from feeling all the enjoyment that I should in the reading of his Greek poems." Baudelaire, *L'Art romantique* (Paris), pp. 389–390.[29] Chthonic view of the world. Catholicism.   [J4a,5]

It is very important that the modern, with Baudelaire, appear not only as the signature of an epoch but as an energy by which this epoch immediately transforms and appropriates antiquity. Among all the relations into which modernity enters, its relation to antiquity is critical. Thus, Baudelaire sees confirmed in Hugo "the fatality which led him . . . partially to transform ancient ode and ancient tragedy into the poems and dramas that we know." Baudelaire, *L'Art romantique* (Paris), p. 401 *("Les Misérables")*.[30] This is also, for Baudelaire, the function of Wagner.   [J5,1]

The gesture with which the angel chastises the miscreant: "Is it not useful for the poet, the philosopher, to take egoistic Happiness by the hair from time to time and say to it, while rubbing its nose in blood and dung: 'See your handiwork and swallow it'?" Charles Baudelaire, *L'Art romantique* (Paris), p. 406 *("Les Misérables")*.[31]   [J5,2]

"The Church, . . . that Pharmacy where no one has the right to slumber!" Baudelaire, *L'Art romantique* (Paris), p. 420 *("Madame Bovary")*.[32]   [J5,3]

"Madame Bovary, in what is most forceful, most ambitious, and also most contemplative in her nature, has remained a man. Just as Pallas Athena sprang fully armed from the head of Zeus, so this strange androgynous creature has kept all the attraction of a virile soul in a charming feminine body." Further along, on Flaubert: "All *intellectual* women will be grateful to him for having raised the female to so high a level . . . and for having made her share in that combination of calculation and reverie which constitutes the perfect being." Baudelaire, *L'Art romantique*, pp. 415, 419.[33]   [J5,4]

"Hysteria! Why couldn't this physiological mystery be made the sum and substance of a literary work—this mystery which the Académie de Médecine has not yet solved and which, manifesting itself in women by the sensation of a lump in the throat that seems to rise . . . , shows itself in excitable men by every kind of impotence as well as by a tendency toward every kind of excess." Baudelaire, *L'Art romantique* (Paris), p. 418 *("Madame Bovary")*.[34]   [J5,5]

From "Pierre Dupont": "Whatever the party to which one belongs, . . . it is impossible not to be moved by the sight of that sickly throng breathing the dust of the workshops, . . . sleeping among vermin . . .—that sighing and languishing throng . . . which looks long and sadly at the sunshine and shadows of the great parks." Baudelaire, *L'Art romantique* (Paris), pp. 198–199.[35]   [J5a,1]

From "Pierre Dupont": "By excluding morality, and often even passion, the puerile Utopia of the school of *art for art's sake* was inevitably sterile. . . . When there appeared a poet, awkward at times, but almost always great, who proclaimed in impassioned language the sacredness of the Revolution of 1830 and sang of the destitution of England and Ireland, despite his defective rhymes, despite his pleonasms, . . . the question was settled, and art was thereafter inseparable from morality and utility." Baudelaire, *L'Art romantique* (Paris), p. 193.[36] The passage refers to Barbier.   [J5a,2]

"The optimism of Dupont, his unlimited trust in the natural goodness of man, his fanatical love of nature constitute the greatest share of his talent." Baudelaire, *L'Art romantique* (Paris), p. 201.[37]   [J5a,3]

"I was not at all surprised to find . . . in *Tannhäuser, Lohengrin,* and *The Flying Dutchman,* an excellent method of construction, a spirit of order and division that recalls the architecture of ancient tragedies." Baudelaire, *L'Art romantique* (Paris), p. 225 ("Richard Wagner et *Tannhäuser*").[38]   [J5a,4]

"If, in his choice of subjects and in his dramatic method, Wagner resembles antiquity, by the passionate energy of his expression he is today the truest representative of modern nature." Baudelaire, *L'Art romantique* (Paris), p. 250.[39]

[J5a,5]

Baudelaire in "L'Art philosophique," an essay concerned mainly with Alfred Re-thel: "Here everything—place, decor, furnishings, accessories (see Hogarth, for example)—everything is allegory, allusion, hieroglyph, rebus." Baudelaire, *L'Art romantique*, p. 131.[40] There follows a reference to Michelet's interpretation of Dürer's *Melancholia I*.   [J5a,6]

Variant of the passage on Meryon cited by Geffroy, in "Peintres et aqua-fortistes" (1862): "Just the other day a young American artist, M. Whistler, was showing . . . a set of etchings . . . representing the banks of the Thames; wonderful tangles of rigging, yardarms and rope; farragos of fog, furnaces, and corkscrews of smoke; the profound and intricate poetry of a vast capital. . . . M. Meryon, the true type of the consummate etcher, could not neglect the call. . . . In the pungency, finesse, and sureness of his drawing, M. Meryon recalls all that was best in the old etchers. We have rarely seen the natural solemnity of a great capital more poetically de-picted. Those majestic accumulations of stone; those 'spires whose fingers point to heaven'; those obelisks of industry, spewing forth their conglomerations of smoke against the firmament; those prodigies of scaffolding 'round buildings under re-pair, applying their openwork architecture, of such paradoxical and arachnean beauty, upon architecture's solid body; that foggy sky, charged with anger and spite; those limitless perspectives, only increased by the thought of the dramas they contain—he forgot not one of the complex elements which go to make up the painful and glorious décor of civilization." Baudelaire, *L'Art romantique* (Paris), pp. 119–121.[41]   [J6,1]

On Guys: "The festivals of the Bairam, . . . in the midst of which, like a pale sun, can be discerned the endless ennui of the late sultan." Baudelaire, *L'Art roman-tique* (Paris), p. 83.[42]   [J6,2]

On Guys: "Wherever those deep, impetuous desires, war, love, and gaming, are in full flood, like Orinocos of the human heart . . . , our observer is always punctu-ally on the spot." Baudelaire, *L'Art romantique* (Paris), p. 87.[43]   [J6,3]

Baudelaire as antipode of Rousseau, in the maxim from his essay on Guys: "For no sooner do we take leave of the domain of needs and necessities to enter that of pleasures and luxury than we see that nature can counsel nothing but crime. It is this infallible Mother Nature who has created parricide and cannibalism." Baude-laire, *L'Art romantique* (Paris), p. 100.[44]   [J6,4]

"Very difficult to note down in shorthand"—this, from the essay on Guys, is Baudelaire's appreciation, obviously very modern, of the movement of carriages. Baudelaire, *L'Art romantique* (Paris), p. 113.[45]   [J6,5]

Closing sentences of the Guys essay: "He has gone everywhere in quest of the ephemeral, the fleeting forms of beauty in the life of our day, the characteristic traits of what, with the reader's permission, we have called 'modernity.' Often bizarre, violent, excessive, but always full of poetry, he has succeeded, in his drawings, in distilling the bitter or heady flavor of the wine of Life." Baudelaire, *L'Art romantique* (Paris), p. 114.[46]   [J6a,1]

The figure of the "modern" and that of "allegory" must be brought into relation with each other: "Woe unto him who seeks in antiquity anything other than pure art, logic, and general method! By plunging too deeply into the past, . . . he renounces the . . . privileges provided by circumstances; for almost all our origi nality comes from the stamp that *time* imprints upon our feelings ‹*sensations*›." Baudelaire, *L'Art romantique* (Paris), p. 72 ("Le Peintre de la vie moderne").[47] But the privilege of which Baudelaire speaks also comes into force, in a mediated way, vis-à-vis antiquity: the stamp of time that imprints itself on antiquity presses out of it the allegorical configuration.   [J6a,2]

Concerning "Spleen et idéal," these reflections from the Guys essay: "Modernity is the transitory, the fugitive, the contingent; it is one half of art, the other half being the eternal and immutable. . . . If any particular modernity is to be worthy of becoming antiquity, one must extract from it the mysterious beauty that human life involuntarily gives it. It is to this task that Monsieur G. particularly addresses himself." Baudelaire, *L'Art romantique* (Paris), p. 70. In another place (p. 74), he speaks of "this *legendary* translation of external life."[48]   [J6a,3]

Motifs of the poems in the theoretical prose. "Le Coucher du soleil romantique" ‹Romantic Sunset›: "Dandyism is a sunset; like the declining daystar, it is glori- ous, without heat and full of melancholy. But alas, the rising tide of democracy . . . is daily overwhelming these last representatives of human pride" (*L'Art roman- tique*, p. 95).—"Le Soleil" ‹The Sun›: "At a time when others are asleep, Monsieur G. is bending over his table, darting onto a sheet of paper the same glance that a moment ago he was directing toward external things, skirmishing with his pencil, his pen, his brush, splashing his glass of water up to the ceiling, wiping his pen on his shirt, in a ferment of violent activity, as though afraid that the images might escape him, cantankerous though alone, elbowing himself on" (*L'Art romantique*, p. 67).[49]   [J6a,4]

Nouveauté: "The child sees everything in a state of newness; he is always *drunk*. Nothing more resembles what we call inspiration than the delight with which a child absorbs form and color. . . . It is by this deep and joyful curiosity that we may explain the fixed and animally ecstatic gaze of a child confronted with something new." Baudelaire, *L'Art romantique* (Paris), p. 62 ("Le Peintre de la vie moderne"). Perhaps this explains the dark saying in "L'Oeuvre et la vie d'Eugène Delacroix": "For it is true to say that, generally speaking, the child, in relation to the man, is much closer to original sin" (*L'Art romantique*, p. 41).[50]   [J7,1]

The sun: "the boisterous sun beating a tattoo upon his windowpane" (*L'Art ro- mantique*, p. 65); "the landscapes of the great city . . . buffeted by the sun" (*L'Art romantique*, pp. 65–66).[51]   [J7,2]

In "L'Oeuvre et la vie d'Eugène Delacroix": "The whole visible universe is but a storehouse of images and signs." Baudelaire, *L'Art romantique*, p. 13.[52]   [J7,3]

From the Guys essay: "Beauty is made up of an eternal, invariable element . . . and of a relative, circumstantial element, which will be . . . the age—its fashions, its morals, its emotions. Without this second element, which might be described as the amusing, enticing, appetizing icing on the divine cake, the first element would be beyond our powers of digestion." Baudelaire, *L'Art romantique*, pp. 54–55.[53]
[J7,4]

On *nouveauté:* "Night! you'd please me more without these stars / which speak a language I know all too well." *Fleurs ‹du mal›*, ed. Payot, p. 139 ("Obsession").[54]
[J7,5]

The subsequent appearance of the flower in Jugendstil is not without significance for the title *Les Fleurs du mal*. This work spans the arch that reaches from the *taedium vitae* of the Romans to Jugendstil.   [J7,6]

It would be important to determine Poe's relation to Latinity. Baudelaire's interest in the technique of composition could have led him—in the end—as surely to Latin culture as his interest in the artificial led him to Anglo-Saxon culture. Working through Poe, this latter area of culture also conditions—at the outset— Baudelaire's theory of composition. Hence, it becomes more urgent to ask whether this doctrine does not, in the end, bear a Latin stamp.   [J7,7]

The Lesbians—a painting by Courbet.   [J7,8]

Nature, according to Baudelaire, knows this one luxury: crime. Thus the significance of the artificial. Perhaps we may draw on this thought for the interpretation of the idea that children stand nearest to original sin. Is it because, exuberant by nature, they cannot get out of harm's way? At bottom, Baudelaire is thinking of parricide. (Compare *L'Art romantique* [Paris], p. 100.)[55]   [J7a,1]

The key to the emancipation from antiquity—which (see in the Guys essay, *L'Art romantique,* p. 72)[56] can furnish only the canon of composition—is for Baudelaire allegorese.   [J7a,2]

Baudelaire's manner of reciting. He gathered his friends—Antonio Watripon, Gabriel Dantrague, Malassis, Delvau—"in a modest café on the Rue Dauphine. . . . The poet began by ordering punch; then, when he saw us all disposed toward benevolence . . . , he would recite to us in a voice at once mincing, soft, fluty, oily, and yet mordant, some enormity or other—"Le Vin de l'assassin" ‹The Murderer's Wine› or "Une Charogne" ‹Carrion›. The contrast between the violence of the images and the perfect placidity, the suave and emphatic accentuation, of the delivery was truly striking." Jules Levallois, *Milieu de siècle: Mémoires d'un critique* (Paris ‹1895›), pp. 93–94.   [J7a,3]

"The famous phrase, 'I who am the son of a priest'; the glee he was said to feel in eating nuts, when he would imagine he was munching the brains of small children; the story of the glazier who, at his request, climbed six flights of stairs under a heavy load of windowpanes in oppressive summer heat, only to be told he was not needed—all just so many insanities, and probably falsehoods, which he delighted in amassing." Jules Levallois, *Milieu de siècle: Mémoires d'un critique* (Paris), pp. 94–95.   [J7a,4]

A remarkable pronouncement by Baudelaire on Gautier (cited in Jules Levallois, *Milieu de siècle: Mémoires d'un critique* [Paris], p. 97). It is recorded by Charles de Lovenjoul, "Un Dernier Chapitre de l'histoire des oeuvres de Balzac," in *L'Echo des théâtres* of August 25, 1846, as follows: "Fat, lazy, sluggish, he has no ideas, and can only string words together as the Osage strings beads for a necklace." ‹See J36a,1.›   [J7a,5]

Highly significant letter from Baudelaire to Toussenel: "Monday, January 21, 1856. My dear Toussenel, I really want to thank you for your gift. I didn't know the value of your book—I admit it simply and baldly. . . . For a long time I've been rejecting almost all books with a feeling of disgust. It's been a long time, too, since I've read anything so *absolutely instructive and amusing*. The chapter on the falcon and the birds that hunt on man's behalf is a masterpiece in itself. / There are expressions in your book that recall those of the great masters and which are cries of truth—expressions whose tone is irresistibly philosophical, such as, 'Every animal is a sphinx,' and, with regard to analogy, 'What repose the mind finds in gentle quietude, sheltered by so fertile and so simple a doctrine, for which none of God's works is a mystery!' . . . What is beyond doubt is that you are a poet. I've been saying for a very long time that the poet is *supremely* intelligent . . . and that *imagination* is the most *scientific* of faculties, for it alone can understand the *universal analogy*, or what a mystic religion calls *correspondence*. But when I try to publish such statements, I'm told I'm mad. . . . What is absolutely certain is that I have a philosophical cast of mind that allows me to see clearly what is true, even in zoology, although I'm neither a huntsman nor a naturalist. . . . One idea has been uppermost in my thoughts since I started reading your book—and this is that you're a true intelligence which has wandered into a sect. All things considered, what do you owe to *Fourier?* Nothing, or very little. Without Fourier you would still be what you are. *Rational men* didn't await Fourier's arrival on earth to realize that nature is a *language*, an allegory, a mold, an *embossing*, if you like. . . . Your book arouses in me a great many dormant thoughts—and where *original sin* is concerned, as well as . . . *form molded on an idea*, I've often thought that noxious, disgusting animals were, perhaps, merely the coming to life in bodily form of man's *evil thoughts*. . . . Thus, the whole of *nature* participates in original sin. / Don't hold my boldness and straightforwardness against me, but believe

Théophile Gautier, 1854-1855. Photo by Nadar. Musée d'Orsay,
Paris; photo copyright © RMN. See J7a,5.

that I am your devoted . . . Ch. Baudelaire."[57] Henri Cordier, *Notules sur Baudelaire* (Paris, 1900), pp. 5–7. The middle section of the letter polemicizes against
Toussenel's faith in progress and his denunciation of de Maistre.   [J8]

"Origin of the name Baudelaire. Here is what M. Georges Barral has written on
this subject in the *La Revue des curiosités révolutionnaires:* Baudelaire explained
the etymology of his name, which, he said, came not from *bel* or *beau* but from
band or *bald*. 'My name is something terrible,' he declared. 'As a matter of fact,
the *badelaire* was a saber with a short, broad blade and a convex cutting edge,
hooked at the tip. . . . It was introduced into France after the Crusades and used
in Paris until around 1560 for executing criminals. Some years ago, in 1861, during excavations carried out near the Pont-au-Change, they recovered the *badelaire* used by the executioner at the Grand Châtelet in the twelfth century. It was
deposited in the Musée de Cluny. Go and have a look. It is frightening to see. I
shudder to think how the profile of my face approximates the profile of this *bade-*

laire.'—'But your name is *Baudelaire*,' I replied, 'not *Badelaire*.'—'Badelaire, Baudelaire by corruption. It's the same thing.'—'Not at all,' I say. 'Your name comes from *baud* (merry), *baudiment* (merrily), *s'ébaudir* (to make merry). You are kind and cheerful.'—'No, no, I am wicked and sad.'" Louis Thomas, *Curiosités sur Baudelaire* (Paris, 1912), pp. 23–24.   [J8a,1]

Jules Janin published an article in 1865, in *L'Indépendance belge*, reproaching Heine for his melancholy; Baudelaire drafted a letter in response. "Baudelaire maintains that melancholy is the source of all sincere poetry." Louis Thomas, *Curiosités sur Baudelaire* (Paris, 1912), p. 17.   [J8a,2]

On a visit to an Academician,[58] Baudelaire refers to *Les Fleurs du bien* that appeared in 1858 and claims the name of the author—Henry (probably Henri) Bordeaux—as his own pseudonym. See L. Thomas, *Curiosités sur Baudelaire* (Paris, 1912), p. 43.   [J8a,3]

"On the Ile Saint-Louis, Baudelaire felt at home everywhere; he was as perfectly at his ease in the street or on the quays as he would have been in his own room. To go out into the island was in no way to quit his domain. Thus, one met him in slippers, bareheaded, and dressed in the tunic that served as his work clothes." Louis Thomas, *Curiosités sur Baudelaire* (Paris, 1912), p. 27.   [J8a,4]

"'When I'm *utterly alone*,' he wrote in 1864, 'I'll seek out a religion (Tibetan or Japanese), for I despise the Koran too much, and on my deathbed I'll forswear that last religion to show beyond doubt my disgust with universal stupidity.'"[59] Louis Thomas, *Curiosités sur Baudelaire* (Paris, 1912), pp. 57–58.   [J8a,5]

Baudelaire's production is masterly and assured from the beginning.   [J9,1]

Dates. *Fleurs du mal*: 1857, 1861, 1866. Poe: 1809–1849. Baudelaire's discovery of Poe: around the end of 1846.   [J9,2]

Remy de Gourmont has drawn a parallel between Athalie's dream and "Les Métamorphoses du vampire"; Fontainas has endeavored to do likewise with Hugo's "Fantômes" (in *Les Orientales*) and "Les Petites Vieilles." Hugo: "How many maidens fair, alas! I've seen fade and die. . . . One form, above all . . ."[60]   [J9,3]

Laforgue on Baudelaire: "After all the liberties of Romanticism, he was the first to discover these rough comparisons which suddenly, in the midst of a harmonious period, cause him to put his foot in his plate; obvious, exaggerated comparisons which seem at times downright American; disconcerting purplish flash and dazzle: 'Night was thickening . . . like a partition!' (Other examples abound.) ‹Her walk is like› a serpent at the end of a stick; her hair is an ocean; her head sways with the gentleness of a young elephant; her body leans like a frail vessel plunging its yardarms into the water; her saliva mounts to her mouth like a wave swollen by the melting of rumbling glaciers; her neck is a tower of ivory; her teeth are sheep perched on the hills above Hebron.—This is Americanism superimposed on the metaphorical language of the 'Song of Songs.'" Jules Laforgue, *Mélanges posthumes* (Paris, 1903), pp. 113–114 ("Notes sur Baudelaire").[61] Compare J86a,2.

[J9,4]

"In the fogs along the Seine, the storm of his youth and the marine suns of his memories have loosened the strings of an incurably plaintive and shrill Byzantine viol." Jules Laforgue, *Mélanges posthumes* (Paris, 1903), p. 114 ("Notes sur Baudelaire").[62]

[J9,5]

When the first edition of *Les Fleurs du mal* appeared, Baudelaire was thirty-six years old.

[J9,6]

Le Vavasseur describes him around 1844: "Byron attired like Beau Brummell."

[J9,7]

The *Petits Poèmes en prose* were first collected posthumously.

[J9,8]

"He was the first to break with the public." Laforgue, *Mélanges posthumes* (Paris, 1903), p. 115.[63]

[J9,9]

"Baudelaire the cat, Hindu, Yankee, episcopal, alchemist.—Cat: his way of saying 'my dear' in that solemn piece that opens with 'Behave, my Sorrow!'—Yankee: the use of 'very' before an adjective; his curt descriptions of landscape, and the line 'Mount, my spirit, wander at your ease,' which the initiated recite in metallic tones; his hatred of eloquence and of poetic confidences; 'Vaporous pleasure will drift out of sight / As . . .' what then? Hugo, Gautier, and others before him would have made a French, oratorical comparison; he makes a Yankee one and, without settled prejudice, remains in the air: 'As a sylphid pirouettes into the wings' (you can see the iron wires and stage machinery).—Hindu: his poetry is closer to the Indian than that of Leconte de Lisle with all his erudition and dazzling intricacy: 'of sobbing fountains and of birds that sing / endless obbligatos to my trysts.' Neither a great heart nor a great intellect, but what plaintive nerves! What open senses! What a magical voice!" Jules Laforgue, *Mélanges posthumes* (Paris, 1903), pp. 118–119 ("Notes sur Baudelaire").[64]

[J9a,1]

One of the few clearly articulated passages of the *Argument du livre sur la Belgique*—in chapter 27, "Promenade à Malines": "Profane airs, adapted to peals of bells. Through the crossing and recrossing melodies, I seemed to hear notes from "La Marseillaise." The hymn of the rabble, as broadcast from the belfries, had lost a little of its harshness. Chopped into small pieces by the hammers, this was not the usual gloomy howling; rather, it had taken on, to my ears, a childish grace. It was as though the Revolution had learned to stutter in the language of heaven." Baudelaire, *Oeuvres,* vol. 2, ed. Y‹ves›-G‹érard› Le Dantec ‹Paris, 1931–1932›, p. 725. [J9a,2]

From the "Note détachée" in the book on Belgium: "I am no dupe, and I have never been a dupe! I say, 'Long live the Revolution!' as I would say, 'Long live Destruction! Long live Expiation! Long live Punishment! Long live Death!'" Baudelaire, *Oeuvres,* vol. 2, ed. Y.-G. Le Dantec, pp. 727–728.[65] [J9a,3]

Argument du livre sur la Belgique, chapter 25, "Architecture—Churches—Religions." "Brussels. Churches: Sainte-Gudule. Magnificent stained-glass windows. Beautiful intense colors, like those with which a profound soul invests all the objects of life." Baudelaire, *Oeuvres,* vol. 2, ed. Y.-G. Le Dantec, p. 722.—"Mort des amants"—Jugendstil—Hashish. [J9a,4]

"I asked myself whether Baudelaire . . . had not sought, through histrionics and psychic transfer, to revive the adventures of the prince of Denmark. . . . There would have been nothing surprising in his having performed for himself the drama of Elsinore." Léon Daudet, *Flambeaux* (Paris ‹1929›), p. 210 ("Baudelaire"). [J10,1]

"The inner life . . . of Charles Baudelaire . . . seems to have passed . . . in constant fluctuation between euphoria and aura. Hence the double character of his poems, which, on the one hand, represent a luminous beatitude and, on the other, a state of . . . *taedium vitae.*" Léon Daudet, *Flambeaux* (Paris), p. 212 ("Baudelaire"). [J10,2]

Jeanne Duval, Madame Sabatier, Marie Daubrun. [J10,3]

"Baudelaire was out of place in the stupid nineteenth century. He belongs to the Renaissance. . . . This can be felt even in the beginnings of his poems, which recall those of Ronsard." Léon Daudet, *Flambeaux* (Paris), p. 216 ("Baudelaire: Le Malaise et 'l'aura'"). [J10,4]

Léon Daudet voices a very unfavorable judgment on Sainte-Beuve's *Baudelaire.* [J10,5]

Among those who have pictured the city of Paris, Balzac is, so to speak, the primitive; his human figures are larger than the streets they move in. Baudelaire is the first to have conjured up the sea of houses, with its multistory waves. Perhaps in a context with Haussmann. [J10,6]

"The baudelaire . . . is a kind of cutlass. . . . Broad and short and double-edged, . . . the baudelaire ensures a deadly thrust, for the hand that holds it is near the point." Victor-Emile Michelet, *Figures d'évocateurs* (Paris, 1913), p. 18 ("Baudelaire, ou Le Divinateur douloureux"). [J10,7]

"The dandy, Baudelaire has said, 'should aspire to be sublime, continually. He should live and sleep in front of a mirror.'"[66] Louis Thomas, *Curiosités sur Baudelaire* (Paris, 1912), pp. 33–34.   [J10,8]

Two stanzas by Baudelaire, found on the page of an album:

> Noble strong-armed woman, who sleep and dream
> throughout long days with no thought of good or evil,
> who wear robes proudly slung in Grecian style;
> you whom for many years (which seem slow to me now)
> my lips, well versed in luscious kisses,
> cherished with all the devotion of a monk;
>
> priestess of debauch, my sister in lust,
> who disdained to carry and nourish
> a male child in your hallowed urn,
> but fear and flee the appalling stigmata
> which virtue carved with its degrading blade
> in pregnant matrons' flanks.[67]

Louis Thomas, *Curiosités sur Baudelaire* (Paris, 1912), p. 37.   [J10,9]

"He was the *first* to write about himself in a moderate confessional manner, and to leave off the inspired tone. / He was the first to speak of Paris from the point of view of one of her daily damned (the lighted gas jets flickering with the wind of Prostitution, the restaurants and their air vents, the hospitals, the gambling, the logs resounding as they are sawn and then dropped on the paved courtyards, and the chimney corner, and the cats, beds, stockings, drunkards, and modern perfumes)—all in a noble, remote, and superior fashion. . . . The first also who accuses himself rather than appearing triumphant, who shows his wounds, his laziness, his bored uselessness at the heart of this dedicated, workaday century. / The first to bring to our literature the boredom implicit in sensuality, together with its strange décor: the sad alcove, . . . and to take pleasure in doing so. . . . The Painted Mask of Woman and its heavenly extension in sunset . . . Spleen and illness (not the poetic aspects of consumption but rather neurosis) without ever once using the word." Laforgue, *Mélanges posthumes* (Paris, 1903), pp. 111–112.[68]   [J10a,1]

"From the mysterious darkness in which they had germinated, sent out secret roots, and reared their fecund stalks, *Les Fleurs du mal* have gone on to blossom magnificently, opening up their somber jagged corollas veined with the colors of life and, under an endless sky of glory and scandal, scattering their heady perfumes of love, of sorrow, and of death." Henri de Regnier, ‹"Baudelaire et *Les Fleurs du mal*," introductory essay› in Charles Baudelaire, *"Les Fleurs du mal" et autres poèmes* (Paris ‹1930›), p. 18.   [J10a,2]

"He is always polite to what is ugly." Jules Laforgue, *Mélanges posthumes* (Paris, 1903), p. 114.[69]
[J10a,3]

Roger Allard—in *Baudelaire et "l'Esprit nouveau"* (Paris, 1918), p. 8—compares Baudelaire's poems to Madame Sabatier with Ronsard's poems to Hélène.
[J10a,4]

"Two writers profoundly influenced Baudelaire, or rather two books. . . . One is the delicious *Diable amoureux*, by Cazotte; the other, Diderot's *La Religieuse*. To the first, many of the poems owe their restless frenzy . . . ; with Diderot, Baudelaire gathers the somber violets of Lesbos." At this point, in a note, a citation from Apollinaire's commentary to his edition of Baudelaire's *Oeuvres poétiques:* "One would probably not go wrong in taking Cazotte as the hyphen that had the honor of uniting, in . . . Baudelaire, the spirit of the Revolution's writers with that of Edgar Poe." Roger Allard, *Baudelaire et "l'Esprit nouveau"* (Paris, 1918), pp. 9–10. ‹See J20a,2.›
[J10a,5]

"The flavor of late autumn . . . which Baudelaire savored . . . in the literary decomposition of low Latin." Roger Allard, *Baudelaire et "l'Esprit nouveau"* (Paris, 1918), p. 14.
[J11,1]

"Baudelaire . . . is the most musical of French poets, along with Racine and Verlaine. But whereas Racine plays only the violin, Baudelaire plays the whole orchestra." André Suarès, Preface to Charles Baudelaire, *Les Fleurs du mal* (Paris, 1933), pp. xxxiv–xxxv.
[J11,2]

"If Baudelaire is supremely contained, as no one since Dante has been, it is because he always concentrates on the inner life, as Dante focused on dogma." André Suarès, Preface to Baudelaire, *Les Fleurs du mal* (Paris, 1933), p. xxxviii.
[J11,3]

Les Fleurs du mal is the *Inferno* of the nineteenth century. But Baudelaire's despair carries him infinitely beyond the wrath of Dante." André Suarès, Preface to Baudelaire, *Les Fleurs du mal* (Paris, 1933), p. xiii.
[J11,4]

"There is no artist in verse superior to Baudelaire." André Suarès, Preface to Baudelaire, *Les Fleurs du mal* (Paris, 1933), p. xxiii.
[J11,5]

Apollinaire: "Baudelaire is the scion of Laclos and Edgar Poe." Cited in Roger Allard, *Baudelaire et "l'Esprit nouveau"* (Paris, 1918), p. 8.
[J11,6]

The "Choix de maximes consolantes sur l'amour" ‹Selected Consolatory Maxims on Love› contains an excursus on ugliness (first published March 3, 1846, in *Le Corsaire-Satan*). The beloved has contracted smallpox and suffered scars, which from then on are the lover's delight: "You run a grave risk, if your pockmarked mistress betrays you, of being able to console yourself only with pockmarked women. For certain spirits, more precious and more jaded, delight in ugliness proceeds from an obscurer sentiment still—the thirst for the unknown and the taste for the horrible. It is this sentiment . . . which drives certain poets into the dissecting room or the clinic, and women to public executions. I am sincerely sorry for the man who cannot understand this—he is a harp who lacks a bass string!" Baudelaire, *Oeuvres*, vol. 2, ed. Y.-G. Le Dantec, p. 621.[70]   [J11,7]

The idea of "correspondences" surfaces already in the "Salon de 1846," where a passage of *Kreisleriana* is cited. (See the note by Le Dantec, *Oeuvres*, vol. 1, p. 585.)[71]   [J11,8]

In considering the aggressive Catholicism displayed in Baudelaire's later work, one must bear in mind that his writing had met with scant success during his lifetime. This could have led Baudelaire, in rather unusual fashion, to align himself or rather to identify himself with the completed works. His particular sensuality found its theoretical equivalents only in the process of poetic composition; these equivalents, however, the poet appropriated to himself as such, unconditionally and without any sort of revision. They bear the trace of this origin precisely in their aggressiveness.   [J11a,1]

"He has on a blood-red cravat and rose gloves. Yes, it is 1840. . . . Some years, even green gloves were worn. Color disappeared from outfits only reluctantly. For Baudelaire was not alone in sporting that purple or brick-colored cravat. Not alone in wearing pink gloves. His trademark is in the combination of the two effects with the black outfit." Eugène Marsan, *Les Cannes de M. Paul Bourget et le bon choix de Philinte* (Paris, 1923), pp. 236–237.   [J11a,2]

"His utterances, Gautier thought, were full of 'capital letters and italics.' He appeared . . . surprised at what he himself said, as if he heard in his own voice the words of a stranger. But it must be admitted that his women and his sky, his perfumes, his nostalgia, his Christianity and his demon, his oceans and his tropics, made for a subject matter of stunning novelty. . . . I do not even criticize his jerky gait, . . . which made people compare him to a spider. It was the beginning of that angular gesticulation which, little by little, would displace the rounded graces of the old world. Here, too, he is a precursor." Eugène Marsan, *Les Cannes de M. Paul Bourget et le bon choix de Philinte* (Paris, 1923), pp. 239–240.   [J11a,3]

"His gestures were noble, slow, kept in close to the body. His politeness seemed affected because it was a legacy of the eighteenth century, Baudelaire being the son of an old man who had known the salons." Eugène Marsan, *Les Cannes de M. Paul Bourget et le bon choix de Philinte* (Paris, 1923), p. 239.   [J11a,4]

There are two different versions of Baudelaire's debut in Brussels.[72] Georges Rency, who reproduces both, prefers the one by the chronicler Tardieu. "In a horrible funk," writes the latter, "Baudelaire read and stammered and trembled, his teeth chattering, his nose buried in his manuscript. It was a disaster." Camille Lemonnier, on the other hand, came away with the "impression of a magnificent talker." Georges Rency, *Physionomies littéraires* (Brussels, 1907), pp. 267, 268 ("Charles Baudelaire"). [J12,1]

"He . . . never made a serious effort to understand what was external to him." Georges Rency, *Physionomies littéraires* (Brussels, 1907), p. 274 ("Charles Baudelaire"). [J12,2]

"Baudelaire is as incapable of love as of labor. He loves as he writes, by fits and starts, and then relapses into the dissolute egoism of a flâneur. Never does he show the slightest curiosity about human affairs or the slightest consciousness of human evolution. . . . His art could therefore be said . . . to sin by reason of its narrowness and singularity; these, indeed, are defects which put off sane and upright minds such as love clear works of universal import." Georges Rency, *Physionomies littéraires* (Brussels, 1907), p. 288 ("Charles Baudelaire"). [J12,3]

"Like many another author of his day, he was not a writer but a stylist. His images are almost always inappropriate. He will say of a look that it is 'gimlet-sharp.' . . . He will call repentance 'the last hostelry.' . . . Baudelaire is a still worse writer in prose than in verse. . . . He does not even know grammar. 'No French writer,' he says, 'ardent for the glory of the nation, can, without pride and without regrets, divert his gaze. . .' The solecism here is not only flagrant; it is foolish." Edmond Scherer, *Etudes sur la littérature contemporaine*, vol. 4 (Paris, 1886), pp. 288–289 ("Baudelaire"). [J12,4]

"Baudelaire is a sign not of decadence in letters but of the general lowering of intelligence." Edmond Scherer, *Etudes sur la littérature contemporaine*, vol. 4 (Paris, 1886), p. 291 ("Charles Baudelaire"). [J12,5]

Brunetière recognizes, with Gautier, that Baudelaire has opened new territory for poetry. Among the criticisms registered against him by the literary historian is this: "Moreover, he was a poet who lacked more than one element of his art—notably (according to people who knew him) the gift of thinking directly in verse." F‹erdinand› Brunetière, *L'Evolution de la poésie lyrique en France au XIXe siècle*, vol. 2 (Paris, 1894), p. 232 ("Le Symbolisme"). [J12,6]

Brunetière (*L'Evolution de la poésie lyrique en France au XIXe siècle*, vol. 2 [Paris, 1894]) distinguishes Baudelaire on one side from the school of Ruskin, and on the other from the Russian novelists. In both these movements he sees currents which, with good reason, resist the *décadence* proclaimed by Baudelaire, opposing to everything hypercultivated the primitive simplicity and innocence of natural man. A synthesis of these antithetical tendencies would be represented by Wagner.—Brunetière arrived at this relatively positive estimation of Baudelaire only belatedly (1892). [J12a,1]

On Baudelaire in relation to Hugo and Gautier: "He treats the great masters he learned from as he treats women: he adores and vilifies them." U.-V. Chatelain, *Baudelaire, l'homme et le poète* (Paris), p. 21. [J12a,2]

Baudelaire on Hugo: "Not only does he express precisely and translate literally what is clearly and distinctly visible, but he expresses with indispensable obscurity what is obscure and vaguely revealed." Citing this sentence in *Baudelaire, l'homme et le poète* (Paris), p. 22, Chatelain rightly says that Baudelaire is perhaps the only man of his time to have understood the "secret Mallarméism" of Hugo. [J12a,3]

"Barely sixty people followed the hearse in the sweltering heat; Banville and Asselineau, under a gathering storm, made beautiful speeches that nobody could hear. With the exception of Veuillot in *L'Univers*, the press was cruel. Everything bore down on his remains. A gale dispersed his friends; his enemies . . . called him 'mad.'" U.-V. Chatelain, *Baudelaire, l'homme et le poète* (Paris), p. 16. [J12a,4]

For the experience of the *correspondances*, Baudelaire refers occasionally to Swedenborg, and also to hashish. [J12a,5]

Baudelaire at a concert: "Two piercing black eyes, gleaming with a peculiar vividness, alone animated the figure that seemed frozen in its shell." Lorédan Larchey, *Fragments de souvenirs* (Paris, 1901), p. 6 ("Le Boa de Baudelaire—L'Impeccable Banville"). [J12a,6]

Larchey is an eyewitness to Baudelaire's first visit to an Academician—a call paid to Jules Sandeau. Larchey finds himself in the entrance hall soon after Baudelaire. "When I arrived, . . . at the appointed hour, a bizarre spectacle informed me I had been preceded. All around the hat-pegs of the antechamber was coiled a long scarlet boa, one of those boas in chenille of which young working-class women are particularly fond." L. L‹archey, *Fragments de souvenirs*›, p. 7. [J12a,7]

Tableau of decadence: "Behold our great cities under the fog of tobacco smoke that envelops them, thoroughly sodden by alcohol, infused with morphine: it is there that humanity comes unhinged. Rest assured that this source breeds more epileptics, idiots, and assassins than poets." Maurice Barrès, *La Folie de Charles Baudelaire* (Paris ‹1926›), pp. 104–105. [J13,1]

"In conclusion, I would like to imagine that a government such as we conceive after the model of Hobbes would strive to arrest, by some vigorous therapeutic method, the spread of these doctrines, which are as productive of malingerers and troublemakers as they are useless for forming citizens. . . . But I think that the wise despot, after careful reflection, would refrain from intervening, faithful to the tradition of an agreeable philosophy: *Après nous le déluge*." Maurice Barrès, *La Folie de Charles Baudelaire* (Paris), pp. 103–104. [J13,2]

"Baudelaire was perhaps only a hard-working soul who felt and understood what was new through Poe, and who disciplined himself in the course of his life to become specialized." Maurice Barrès, *La Folie de Charles Baudelaire* (Paris), p. 98. [J13,3]

"Let us perhaps guard against taking these poets too quickly for Christians. The liturgical language, the angels, the Satans . . . are merely a *mise en scène* for the artist who judges that the picturesque is well worth a Mass."[73] Maurice Barrès, *La Folie de Charles Baudelaire* (Paris), pp. 44–45. [J13,4]

"His best pages are overwhelming. He rendered superb prose into difficult verse." Maurice Barrès, *La Folie de Charles Baudelaire* (Paris), p. 54. [J13,5]

"Scattered across the sky like luminous seeds of gold and silver, radiating out from the deep darkness of night, the stars represent [for Baudelaire] the ardor and energy of the human imagination." Elisabeth Schinzel, *Natur und Natursymbolik bei Poe, Baudelaire und den französischen Symbolisten* (Düren [Rhineland], 1931), p. 32. [J13,6]

"His voice . . . muffled like the nighttime rumble of vehicles, filtering into plushly upholstered bedrooms." Maurice Barrès, *La Folie de Charles Baudelaire* (Paris), p. 20. [J13,7]

"It might seem, at first, that Baudelaire's oeuvre was relatively infertile. Some wits compared it to a narrow basin dug with effort in a gloomy spot shrouded in haze. . . . The influence of Baudelaire was revealed in *Le Parnasse contemporain* . . . of 1865. . . . Three figures emerge: . . . Stéphane Mallarmé, Paul Verlaine, and Maurice Rollinat." Maurice Barrès, *La Folie de Charles Baudelaire* (Paris), pp. 61, 63, 65. [J13,8]

"And the place occupied by racial epithets among the rabble at that time!" Maurice Barrès, *La Folie de Charles Baudelaire* (Paris), p. 40. [J13a,1]

Flaubert to Baudelaire: "You praise the flesh without loving it, in a melancholy, detached way that I find sympathetic. Ah! how well you understand the boredom of existence!"[74] Cited in Maurice Barrès, *La Folie de Charles Baudelaire* (Paris), p. 31. [J13a,2]

Baudelaire's predilection for Juvenal may well have to do with the latter's being one of the first urban poets. Compare this observation by Thibaudet: "In surveying the great epochs of urban life, we see that the more the city provides poets and other people with their intellectual and moral life, the more forcefully poetry is pushed outside the city. When, . . . in the Greek world, that life was fostered within the great cosmopolitan centers of Alexandria and Syracuse, these cities gave birth to pastoral poetry. When the Rome of Augustus came to occupy a similar position of centrality, the same poetry of shepherds, . . . of pristine nature, appeared with the *Bucolics* and the *Georgics* of Virgil. And in eighteenth-century France, at the most brilliant moment . . . of Parisian existence, the pastoral re-appears as part of a return to antiquity. . . . The only poet in whom one might find a foretaste of Baudelairean urbanism (and of other things Baudelairean as well) would be perhaps, at certain moments, Saint-Amant." Albert Thibaudet, *Intérieurs* (Paris ‹1924›), pp. 7–9. [J13a,3]

"In passing from all these Romantic poets to Baudelaire, we pass from a landscape of nature to a landscape of stone and flesh. . . . A religious awe of nature, which, for these . . . Romantics, was part of their familiarity with nature, has become with Baudelaire a hatred of nature." [?] [J13a,4]

Baudelaire on Musset: "Except at the age of one's first Communion—in other words, at the age when everything having to do with prostitutes and silk stockings produces a religious effect—I have never been able to endure that paragon of lady-killers, his spoiled-child's impudence, invoking heaven and hell in tales of dinner-table conversations, his muddy torrent of mistakes in grammar and pros-ody, and finally his utter incapacity to understand the process by which a reverie becomes a work of art."[75] Thibaudet, who quotes this remark in *Intérieurs* (p. 15), juxtaposes it with one by Brunetière on Baudelaire: "He's just a Satan with a furnished apartment, a Beelzebub of the dinner table" (p. 16). [J13a,5]

"A sonnet like 'A Une Passante' ‹To a Woman Passing By›, a stanza like the last stanza of that sonnet[76] . . . could blossom only in the milieu of a great capital, where human beings live together as strangers to one another and yet as travelers on the same journey. Among all the capitals, Paris alone produces such beings as a natural fruit." Albert Thibaudet, *Intérieurs* (Paris), pp. 22 ("Baudelaire").
[J14,1]

"He carried about him as sorrowful trophy . . . a burden of memories, so that he seemed to live in a continual paramnesia. . . . The poet carries within himself a living *durée* ‹perduration› which odors call forth . . . and with which they min-gle. . . . This city is a *durée*, an inveterate life-form, a memory. . . . If he loved in . . . a Jeanne Duval some immemorial stretch of night . . . , this will be only a symbol . . . of that true *durée* . . . that is consubstantial with the life and being of Paris, the *durée* of those very old, rumpled creatures who (it seemed to him) ought to form, like the capital itself, massive blocks and unending embankments of memories." (Reference is to "Les Petites Vieilles.") Albert Thibaudet, *Intérieurs* (Paris), pp. 24–27 ("Baudelaire"). [J14,2]

Thibaudet juxtaposes Baudelaire's "Une Charogne" ‹Carrion› with Gautier's "La Comédie de la mort" ‹The Comedy of Death› and Hugo's "L'Epopée du ver" ‹The Epic of the Worm› ‹*Intérieurs*, p. 46›.   [J14,3]

Thibaudet adverts very aptly to the connection between confession and mystification in Baudelaire. Through the latter, Baudelaire's pride compensates itself for the former. "Ever since Rousseau's *Confessions,* it seems that all our literature of the personal has taken its departure from the broken-down furniture of religion, from a debunked confessional." Thibaudet, *Intérieurs* (Paris), p. 47 ("Baudelaire"). Mystification a figure of original sin.   [J14,4]

Thibaudet (*Intérieurs*, p. 34) cites a remark from 1887, in which Brunetière calls Baudelaire "a species of oriental idol, monstrous and misshapen, whose natural deformity is heightened by strange colors."   [J14,5]

In 1859 Mistral's *Mireille* appeared. Baudelaire was incensed at the book's success.   [J14,6]

Baudelaire to Vigny: "The only praise I ask for this book is that readers recognize it's not a mere album, but has a beginning and an end."[77] Cited in Thibaudet, *Intérieurs* (Paris), p. 5.   [J14,7]

Thibaudet concludes his essay on Baudelaire with the allegory of the sick muse, who, on Rastignac Hill on the Right Bank of the Seine, forms a pendant to the Montagne Sainte-Geneviève on the Left Bank (pp. 60–61).   [J14,8]

Baudelaire: "of all our great poets, the one who writes worst—if Alfred de Vigny be excepted." Thibaudet, *Intérieurs* (Paris), p. 58 ("Baudelaire").   [J14,9]

Poulet-Malassis had his "shop" in the Passage des Princes, called in those days the Passage Mirès.   [J14a,1]

"Violet boa on which curled his long graying locks, carefully maintained, which gave him a somewhat clerical appearance." ‹Jules Husson› Champfleury, *Souvenirs et portraits de jeunesse* (Paris, 1872), p. 144 ("Rencontre de Baudelaire").   [J14a,2]

"He worked, not always consciously, at that misunderstanding which isolated him in his own time; he worked at it all the more as this misunderstanding was already taking shape in himself. His private notes, published posthumously, are painfully revealing in this respect. . . . As soon as this artist of incomparable subtlety speaks of himself, he is astonishingly awkward. Irreparably he lacks pride—to the point where he reckons incessantly with fools, either to astound them, to shock them, or after all to inform them that he absolutely does not reckon with fools." André

Gide, Preface to Charles Baudelaire, *Les Fleurs du mal*, ed. Edouard Pelletan (Paris, 1917), pp. xiii-xiv.[78]   [J14a,3]

"'This book has not been written for my wives, my daughters, or my sisters,' he says, speaking of *Les Fleurs du mal*. Why warn us? Why this sentence? Oh, simply for the pleasure of affronting bourgeois morals, with the words 'my wives' slipped in, as if carelessly. He values them, however, since we find in his private journal: 'This cannot shock my wives, my daughters, or my sisters.'" André Gide, Preface to Charles Baudelaire, *Les Fleurs du mal*, ed. Edouard Pelletan (Paris, 1917), p. xiv.[79]   [J14a,4]

"Without doubt, Baudelaire is the artist about whom the most nonsense has been written." André Gide, Preface to Ch‹arles› B‹audelaire›, *Les Fleurs du mal*, ed. Edouard Pelletan (Paris, 1917), p. xii.[80]   [J14a,5]

"*Les Fleurs du mal* is dedicated to what Gautier claimed to be: magician of French letters, pure artist, impeccable writer—and this was a way of saying: Do not be deceived; what I venerate is the art and not the thought; my poems will have merit not because of their movement, passion, or thought, but because of their form." André Gide, Preface to Ch. B., *Les Fleurs du mal*, ed. Edouard Pelletan (Paris, 1917), pp. xi–xii.[81]   [J14a,6]

"Now he quietly converses with each one of us." André Gide, Preface to Ch. B., *Les Fleurs du mal*, ed. E. Pelletan (Paris, 1917), p. xv.[82]   [J14a,7]

Lemaître in his article "Baudelaire," published originally in the "Feuilleton Dramatique" section of *Le Journal des débats*, and written on the occasion of Crépet's edition of the *Oeuvres posthumes et Correspondances inédites*: "Worst of all, I sense that the unhappy man is perfectly incapable of developing these sibylline notes. The *pensées* of Baudelaire are most often only a sort of painful and pretentious stammering. . . . One cannot imagine a less philosophical mind." Jules Lemaître, *Les Contemporains*, 4th series (Paris, 1895), p. 21 ("Baudelaire"). Brooding! ‹See J55a,1›.   [J15,1]

After Calcutta. "On his return, he enters into possession of his patrimony, seventy thousand francs. Within two years, he has spent half of it. . . . For the next twenty years, he lives on the income provided by the remaining thirty-five thousand francs. . . . Now, during these twenty years, he runs up no more than ten thousand francs in new debts. Under these conditions, as you can imagine, he couldn't have indulged very often in Neronian orgies!" Jules Lemaître, *Les Contemporains*, 4th series (Paris, 1895), p. 27.   [J15,2]

Bourget draws a comparison between Leonardo and Baudelaire: "We are drawn irresistibly to prolonged meditation on the enigma of this painter, of this poet. On

being studiously contemplated, the enigma surrenders its secret." Paul Bourget, *Essais de psychologie contemporaine*, vol. 1 (Paris, 1901), p. 4 ("Baudelaire").
[J15,3]

"He excels at beginning a poem with words of unforgettable solemnity, at once tragic and rueful: 'What does it matter to me that you are wise? / Be lovely—and be sad! . . .' Elsewhere: "Sudden as a knife you thrust / into my sorry heart. . . .' And elsewhere: "Pensive as cattle resting on the beach, / they are staring out to sea. . . .'" Paul Bourget, *Essais de psychologie contemporaine*, vol. 1 (Paris, 1901), pp. 3–4.[83]
[J15,4]

Bourget sees in Benjamin Constant, Amiel, and Baudelaire three kindred spirits, intellects stamped by the *esprit d'analyse*, types determined by *décadence*. The detailed appendix to "Baudelaire" is concerned with Constant's *Adolphe*. Together with the spirit of analysis, Bourget considers ennui an element of decadence. The third and last chapter of his essay on Baudelaire, "Théorie de la decadence," develops this idea with reference to the late Roman Empire.   [J15,5]

1849 or 1850: Baudelaire draws from memory the head of Blanqui. See Philippe Soupault, *Baudelaire* (Paris ‹1931›), illustration on p. 15.
[J15,6]

"It is all a harmony of artifices, of deliberate contradictions. Let us try to note some of these. Realism and idealism are mingled. Along with description that takes extravagant pleasure in the most dismal details of physical reality there is, at the same time, refined expression of ideas and beliefs that exceed the immediate impression made on us by bodies—There is a union of the most profound sensuality with Christian asceticism. 'A horror of life, and an ecstatic joy in life,' writes Baudelaire somewhere.[84] . . . There is also, speaking of love, the combination of adoration and contempt for woman. . . . Woman is seen as a slave, as an animal, . . . yet to her the same homage, the same prayers are addressed as to the immaculate Virgin. Or rather, she is seen as the universal trap . . . and worshipped for her deadly power. And that is not all: even as one seeks to render the most ardent passion, one also labors to find for it . . . the most unexpected form . . .— that is, what bespeaks the greatest sang-froid and even absence of passion. . . . One believes, or one pretends to believe, in the devil; he is envisaged by turns, or simultaneously, as the Father of Evil and as the great Loser and great Victim; and one delights in proclaiming one's impiety in the language of . . . the faithful. 'Progress' is cursed; the industrial civilization of the century is execrated, . . . and, at the same time, the poet revels in the special color and brilliancy this civilization has brought to human life. . . . Such, I believe, is the basic intent of Baudelairism: always to unite two opposed orders of feeling . . . and, at bottom, two divergent conceptions of the world and of life—the Christian and the other, or, if you like, the past and the present. It is a masterpiece of the Will (like Baudelaire, I capitalize), the last word in inventiveness in the realm of feeling." Jules Lemaître, *Les Contemporains*, 4th series (Paris, 1895), pp. 28–31 ("Baudelaire").   [J15a,1]

Lemaître observes that Baudelaire really did create a *poncif*, a cliché, as he set out to do.   [J15a,2]

"The bloody apparatus of destruction"—where is this phrase in Baudelaire? In "La Destruction."[85]   [J15a,3]

"You could put him down as the perfect embodiment of the 'Parisian pessimist,' two words which earlier would have jarred on being coupled." Paul Bourget, *Essais de psychologie contemporaine*, vol. 1 (Paris, 1901), p. 14.   [J15a,4]

Baudelaire had briefly considered reproducing, as the frontispiece to the second edition of *Les Fleurs*, a dance of death by H. Langlois.   [J15a,5]

"Three different men inhabit this man at one and the same time. . . . These three men are all quite modern, and more modern still is their synthesis. The crisis of religious faith, the city life of Paris, and the scientific spirit of the age . . . are so thoroughly allied here as to appear inseparable. . . . Faith has died out, whereas mysticism, though intellectually discredited, still permeates the sensibility. . . . We could note . . . the use of liturgical terminology to celebrate sensual pleasure . . . or that curious work of 'prose' in decadent Latin style which he entitled 'Franciscae meae laudes.' . . . On the other hand, his libertine tastes came from Paris. Everywhere in his . . . poems is a backdrop of Parisian vice, as well as a backdrop of Catholic ritual. He has obviously penetrated—and with hair-raising experiences, we may be sure—the most wretched strata of this unchaste city. He has eaten at common dinner tables beside painted women whose mouths drip blood through masks of ceruse. He has slept in brothels, and has known the rancor of broad daylight illuminating, along with the faded curtains, the still more faded face of the woman-for-hire. He has sought out . . . the unthinking spasm that . . . cures the *mal de penser*. And, at the same time, he has stopped and chatted at every street-corner in town. . . . He has led the life of the literary man, . . . and he has . . . whetted the blade of his spirit where that of others would have been dulled." Paul Bourget, *Essais de psychologie contemporaine*, vol. 1 (Paris, 1901), pp. 7–9 ("Baudelaire").   [J16,1]

Rivière provides a sequence of felicitous glosses on Baudelaire's poetic procedure: "Strange procession of words! Sometimes like a weariness of the voice, . . . an utterance full of frailty: 'I dream of new flowers, but who can tell / if this sordid swamp of mine affords / the mystic nourishment on which they thrive [qui *ferait* leur vigueur].' Or: 'a favoring Goddess makes the desert bloom [Cybèle, qui les aime, *augmente* ses verdures]. . . .' Like those who feel themselves completely in command of what they want to say, he seeks at first the most remote of terms; he then invites their approach, conciliates them, and infuses them with a quality you would not have thought could be theirs. . . . Such poetry cannot be the product of inspiration. . . . And just as the unfolding thought . . . slowly breaks free of the obscurity in which it began, so the poetic trajectory retains a certain slowness from its long virtuality: 'How sweet the greenish light of your elongated eyes.' . . . Every one of Baudelaire's poems is a movement. . . . Each constitutes some particular phrase, question, reminder, invocation, or dedication, which has a specific direction." Jacques Rivière, *Etudes* (Paris), pp. 14–18.[86]   [J16,2]

Frontispiece (by Rops) to the collection of Baudelaire's poems entitled *Les Epaves* ‹Wreckage›. It presents a multifaceted allegory.—Plan to use an etching by Bracquemond as the frontispiece to the ‹second edition of› *Les Fleurs du mal.* Baudelaire describes it: "A skeleton turning into a tree, with legs and ribs forming the trunk, the arms stretched out to make a cross and bursting into leaves and buds, sheltering several rows of poisonous plants in little pots, lined up as if in a gardener's hothouse."[87]   [J16,3]

Curious notion of Soupault's: "Almost all of the poems are more or less directly inspired by a print or a painting. . . . Can it be said that he sacrificed to fashion? He dreaded being alone. . . . His weakness obliged him to look for things to lean on." Philippe Soupault, *Baudelaire* (Paris ‹1931›), p. 64.   [J16a,1]

"In the years of his maturity and resignation, he never spoke a word of regret or complaint about his childhood." Arthur Holitscher, "Charles Baudelaire," *Die Literatur*, vol. 12, pp. 14–15.   [J16a,2]

"These images . . . do not aim to caress our imagination; they are distant and studied, the way a voice sounds when it emphasizes something. . . . Like a word spoken in our ear when we least expected it, the poet is suddenly hard by: 'You remember? You remember what I'm saying? Where did we see that together, we who don't even know each other?" Jacques Rivière, *Etudes* (Paris), pp. 18–19.   [J16a,3]

"Baudelaire understood the clairvoyance of the heart that does not acknowledge all it experiences. . . . It is a hesitation, a holding back, a modest gaze." Jacques Rivière, *Etudes* (Paris), p. 21.   [J16a,4]

"Lines of verse so perfect, so measured, that at first one hesitates to grant them all their meaning. A hope stirs for a minute—doubt as to their profundity. But one need only wait." Jacques Rivière, *Etudes* (Paris), p. 22.   [J16a,5]

On Baudelaire's "Crépuscule du matin" ‹Twilight of Daybreak›: "Each line of "Crépuscule du matin"—without stridency, with devotion—evokes a misfortune." Jacques Rivière, *Etudes* (Paris), p. 29.   [J16a,6]

"The devotion of a heart moved to ecstasy by weakness. . . . Though he speaks of the most horrible things, the fierceness of his respect lends him a subtle decency." Jacques Rivière, *Etudes* (Paris), pp. 27–28.   [J16a,7]

According to Champfleury, Baudelaire would have bought up all the unsold items from the Salon of 1845. [J16a,8]

"Baudelaire knew the art of transforming his features as well as any escaped convict." ⟨Jules⟩ Champfleury, *Souvenirs et portraits de jeunesse* (Paris, 1872), p. 135 ("Rencontre de Baudelaire").—Courbet complained of the trouble he had completing the portrait of Baudelaire; the subject looked different from one day to the next. [J16a,9]

Baudelaire's liking for porter. [J16a,10]

"Baudelaire's favorite flowers were neither daisy, carnation, nor rose; he would break into raptures at the sight of those thick-leaved plants that look like vipers about to fall on their prey, or spiny hedgehogs. Tormented forms, bold forms— such was this poet's ideal." Champfleury, *Souvenirs et portraits de jeunesse* (Paris, 1872), p. 143. [J16a,11]

Gide, in his preface to *Les Fleurs du mal,* lays emphasis on the "centrifugal and disintegrating" force which Baudelaire, like Dostoevsky, recognized in himself and which he felt to be in opposition to his productive concentration (p. xvii).[88] [J17,1]

"This taste for Boileau and Racine was not an affectation in Baudelaire. . . . There is something more in *Les Fleurs du mal* than the 'thrill of the new'; there is a return to traditional French verse. . . . Even in his nervous malaise, Baudelaire retains a certain sanity." Remy de Gourmont, *Promenades littéraires,* 2nd series (Paris, 1906), pp. 85–86 ("Baudelaire et le songe d'Athalie"). [J17,2]

Poe (as cited in Remy de Gourmont, *Promenades littéraires* [Paris, 1904], p. 371: "Marginalia sur Edgar Poe et sur Baudelaire"): "The assurance of the wrong or error of any action is often the one unconquerable *force* which impels us, and alone impels us, to its prosecution."[89] [J17,3]

Construction of "L'Echec de Baudelaire" ⟨Baudelaire's defeat⟩, by René Laforgue. As a child, Baudelaire is supposed to have witnessed the coitus of his nurse or his mother with her (first or second?) husband; he would find himself in the position of third person in a love relationship and would settle down in that position; he would become a voyeur and frequent bordellos mainly as a voyeur; owing to this same fixation on the visual, he would become a critic and experience a need for objectivity, "so that nothing is 'lost to view.'" He would belong to a clearly defined category of patients: "For them, to see means to soar above everything, like eagles, in complete security, and to realize a sort of omnipotence by identification at once with the man and with the woman. . . . These are the people who then develop that fatal taste for the absolute . . . , and who, taking refuge in the domain of pure imagination, lose the use of their hearts" (*L'Echec de Baudelaire* [Paris, 1931], pp. 201, 204).[90]   [J17,4]

"Baudelaire loved Aupick without being aware of it, and . . . his reason for continually provoking his stepfather was in order to be loved by him. . . . If Jeanne Duval played a part in the poet's emotional life analogous to that played by Aupick, we can understand why Baudelaire was . . . sexually possessed by her. And so . . . this union stood, rather, for a homosexual union, in which Baudelaire chiefly played the passive role—that of the woman." René Laforgue, *L'Echec de Baudelaire* (Paris, 1931), pp. 175, 177.[91]   [J17,5]

His friends sometimes called Baudelaire "Monseigneur Brummell."   [J17,6]

On the compulsion to lie, as seen in Baudelaire: "The direct and spontaneous expression of a truth becomes, for these subtle and tormented consciences, the equivalent of success . . . in incest; success, that is to say, in a sphere in which it can be realized simply by 'good sense.' . . . For in those cases where normal sexuality is repressed, *good sense* is fated to lack an object." René Laforgue, *L'Echec de Baudelaire* (Paris, 1931), p. 87.[92]   [J17,7]

Anatole France—*La Vie littéraire*, vol. 3 (Paris, 1891)—on Baudelaire: "His legend, created by his friends and admirers, abounds in marks of bad taste" (p. 20). "The most wretched woman encountered at night in the shadows of a disreputable alley takes on, in his mind, a tragic grandeur: seven demons are in them [!] and the whole mystical sky looks down on this sinner whose soul is in peril. He tells himself that the vilest kisses resound through all eternity, and he brings to bear on this momentary encounter eighteen centuries of devilishness" (p. 22). "He is attracted to women only to the point necessary for irrevocable loss of his soul. He is never a lover, and he would not even be a debauchee if debauchery were not superlatively impious. . . . He would have nothing to do with women if he were not hoping that, through them, he could offend God and make the angels weep" (p. 22).
                                                                          [J17a,1]

"At bottom, he had but half a faith. Only his spirit was completely Christian. His heart and intellect remained empty. There is a story that one day a naval officer, one of his friends, showed him a manitou that he had brought back from Africa, a monstrous little head carved from a piece of wood by a poor black man.—'It is awfully ugly,' says the officer, and he threw it away disdainfully.—'Take care,' Baudelaire said in an anxious tone, 'lest it prove the true god!' They were the most profound words he ever uttered. He believed in unknown gods—not least for the pleasure of blaspheming." Anatole France, *La Vie littéraire*, vol. 3 (Paris, 1891), p. 23 ("Charles Baudelaire").   [J17a,2]

Letter to Poulet-Malassis of February 18, 1860.   [J17a,3]

"The hypothesis of Baudelaire's P.G. ⟨*paralyse générale*⟩ has persisted for half a century and still reigns in certain quarters. Nevertheless, it is based on a gross and demonstrable error and is without any foundation in fact. . . . Baudelaire did not die from P.G. but from softening of the brain, the consequence of a stroke . . . and of a hardening of the cerebral arteries." Louis-Antoine-Justine Caubert, *La Névrose de Baudelaire* (Bordeaux, 1930), pp. 42–43. The argument against general paralysis is made, likewise in a treatise, by Raymond Trial, *La Maladie de Baudelaire* (Paris, 1926), p. 69. But he sees the brain disorder as a consequence of syphilis, whereas Caubert believes that syphilis has not been conclusively established in Baudelaire's case (see p. 46); he cites Remond and Voivenel, *Le Génie littéraire* (Paris, 1912), p. 41: "Baudelaire was . . . the victim of sclerosis of the cerebral arteries."   [J17a,4]

In his essay "Le Sadisme chez Baudelaire," published in *La Chronique médicale* of November 15, 1902, Cabanès defends the thesis that Baudelaire was a "sadistic madman" (p. 727).   [J18,1]

Du Camp on Baudelaire's voyage "to the Indies": "He arranged supplies of livestock for the English army . . . , and rode about on elephants while composing verse." Du Camp adds in a note: "I have been told that this anecdote is spurious; I have it from Baudelaire himself, and I have no reason to doubt its veracity, though it may perhaps be faulted for a surplus of imagination." Maxime Du Camp, *Souvenirs littéraires*, vol. 2 (Paris, 1906), p. 60.   [J18,2]

Indicative of the reputation that preceded Baudelaire before he had published anything of importance is this remark by Gautier: "I fear that with Baudelaire it will be as it once was with Petrus Borel. In our younger days, we used to say: Hugo has only to sit and wait; as soon as Petrus publishes something, he will disappear. . . . Today, the name of Baudelaire is brandished before us; we are told that when he publishes his poems, Musset, Laprade, and I will dissolve into thin air. I don't believe it for a moment. Baudelaire will burn out just as Petrus did." Cited in Maxime Du Camp, *Souvenirs littéraires*, vol. 2 (Paris, 1906), pp. 61–62.
                                                                 [J18,3]

"As a writer, Baudelaire had one great defect, of which he had no inkling: he was ignorant. What he knew, he knew well; but he knew very little. History, physiology, archaeology, philosophy all eluded him. . . . The external world scarcely interested him; he saw it perhaps, but assuredly he never studied it." Maxime Du Camp, *Souvenirs littéraires*, vol. 2 (Paris, 1906), p. 65.   [J18,4]

From the evaluations of Baudelaire by his teachers at the Lycée Louis-le-Grand: "Ready mind. A few lapses in taste" (in Rhetoric). "Conduct sometimes rather unruly. This student, as he himself admits, seems convinced that history is perfectly useless" (in History).—Letter of August 11, 1839, to his stepfather, after earning his baccalaureate: "I did rather poorly in my examinations, except for

Latin and Greek—in which I did very well. And this is what saved me."[93] Charles Baudelaire, *Vers latins*, ed. Jules Mouquet (Paris, 1933), pp. 17, 18, 26.   [J18,5]

According to ⟨Joséphin⟩ Péladan, "Théorie plastique de l'androgyne" (*Mercure de France*, 21 [1910], p. 650), the androgyne appears in Rossetti and Burne-Jones.   [J18,6]

Ernest Seillière, *Baudelaire* (Paris, 1931), p. 262, on "the death of artists": "Re-reading his work, I tell myself that, were he making his debut as a writer now, not only would he not be singled out for distinction, but he would be judged maladroit."   [J18,7]

Seillière refers to the story "La Fanfarlo" as a document whose importance for Baudelaire's biography has not been sufficiently recognized ⟨*Baudelaire*, p. 72⟩.   [J18,8]

"Baudelaire will keep to the end this intermittent awkwardness which was so foreign to the dazzling technique of a Hugo." Ernest Seillière, *Baudelaire*, p. 72.   [J18a,1]

Key passages on the unsuitability of passion in art: the second preface to Poe, the study of Gautier.[94]   [J18a,2]

The first lecture in Brussels was concerned with Gautier. Camille Lemonnier compares it to a Mass celebrated in honor of the master. Baudelaire is said to have displayed, on this occasion, "the grave beauty of a cardinal of letters officiating at the altar of the Ideal." Cited in Seillière, *Baudelaire* (Paris, 1931), p. 123.   [J18a,3]

"In the drawing room on the Place Royale, Baudelaire had himself introduced as a fervent disciple but . . . Hugo, ordinarily so skillful in sending away his visitors happy, did not understand the *artificialiste* character and the exclusively Parisian predilections of the young man. . . . Their relations nonetheless remained cordial, Hugo having evidently not read the 'Salon de 1846'; and, in his 'Réflexions sur quelques-uns de mes contemporains' ⟨Reflections on Some of My Contemporaries⟩, Baudelaire showed himself very admiring, even rather perceptive, if without great profundity." Ernest Seillière, *Baudelaire* (Paris, 1931), p. 129.   [J18a,4]

Baudelaire, reports Seillière (p. 129), is supposed to have enjoyed strolling often along the Canal de l'Ourcq.   [J18a,5]

About the Dufays—Baudelaire's forebears on his mother's side—nothing is known.   [J18a,6]

"In 1876, in an article entitled 'Chez feu mon maître' ⟨At the Home of My Late Mentor⟩, Cladel would evoke . . . the macabre trait in the physiognomy of the poet.

Never, according to this witness, . . . was he more forbidding than when he wanted to appear jovial; his voice took on a disquieting edge, while his *vis comica* made one shudder. On the pretext of exorcizing the evil spirits of his auditors, and with bursts of laughter piercing as sobs, he told them outrageous tales of trysts beyond the grave which froze the blood in their veins." Ernest Seillière, *Baudelaire* (Paris, 1931), p. 150.   [J18a,7]

Where in Ovid is the passage in which it is said that the human face was made to mirror the stars?[95]   [J18a,8]

Seillière notes that the poems attributed apocryphally to Baudelaire were all necrophilic in character (p. 152).   [J18a,9]

"Finally, as we know, the passional anomaly has a place in the art of Baudelaire, at least under one of its aspects, that of Lesbos; the other has not yet been made admissible by the progress of moral naturism." Ernest Seillière, *Baudelaire* (Paris, 1931), p. 154.   [J18a,10]

The sonnet "Quant à moi, si j'avais un beau parc planté d'ifs" ‹As for me, if only I had a fine park, planted with yews›,[96] which Baudelaire apparently addressed to a young lady of Lyons some time around 1839–1840, is reminiscent, in its closing line—"And you know that too, my beauty, whose eyes are too shrewd"—of the last line of "A Une Passante."   [J19,1]

The piece "Vocations," in *Spleen de Paris,* is of great interest—particularly the account of the third child, who "lowered his voice: 'It certainly gives you a funny feeling not to be sleeping alone, and to be in bed with your nurse, and in the dark. . . . If you ever get the chance, try to do the same—you'll see!' / While he was talking, the eyes of the young author of this revelation had widened with a sort of stupefaction at what he was still feeling, and the light of the setting sun playing in his untidy red curls seemed to be lighting up a sulfurous aureole of passion." [97] The passage is as notable for Baudelaire's conception of the sinful as for the aura of public *confessio.*   [J19,2]

Baudelaire to his mother on January 11, 1858 (cited in Charles Baudelaire, *Vers latins*, ed. Mouquet [Paris, 1933], p. 130): "You haven't noticed that in *Les Fleurs du mal* there are two poems concerning you, or at least alluding to intimate details of our former life, going back to that time of your widowhood which left me with such strange and sad memories—one: 'Je n'ai pas oublié, voisine de la ville' (Neuilly), and the other, which follows it: 'La servante au grand coeur dont vous étiez jalouse' (Mariette)? I left these poems without titles and without any further clarification, because I have a horror of prostituting intimate family matters. . . ."[98]   [J19,3]

Leconte de Lisle's opinion that Baudelaire must have composed his poems by versifying a prose draft is taken up by Pierre Louÿs, *Oeuvres complètes*, vol. 12 (Paris, 1930), p. liii ("Suite à poétique"). Jules Mouquet comments on this view in Charles Baudelaire, *Vers latins*, introduction and notes by Jules Mouquet (Paris, 1933), p. 131: "Leconte de Lisle and Pierre Louÿs, carried away by their antipathy to the *Christian* poet of *Les Fleurs du mal*, deny that he had any poetic gift!—Now, according to the testimony of friends of his youth, Baudelaire had started out by writing thousands of lines of fluent verse 'on any and every subject,' which he could hardly have done without 'thinking in verse.' He deliberately reined in this facility when . . . , at about the age of twenty-two, he began to write the poems which he entitled first *Les Lesbiennes*, then *Les Limbes*. . . . The *Petits Poèmes en prose* . . . , in which the poet returns to themes he had already treated in verse, were composed at least ten years after *Les Fleurs du mal*. That Baudelaire had difficulty fashioning verse is a legend which he himself perhaps . . . helped spread." [J19,4]

According to Raymond Trial, in *La Maladie de Baudelaire* (Paris, 1926), p. 20, recent research has shown that hereditary syphilis and acquired syphilis are not mutually exclusive. Thus, in Baudelaire's case, acquired syphilis would have joined with the hereditary strain transmitted by the father and manifest through hemiplegia in both sons and in his wife. [J19a,1]

Baudelaire, 1846: "If ever your flâneur's curiosity has landed you in a street brawl, perhaps you will have felt the same delight as I have often felt to see a protector of the public's slumbers—a policeman or a municipal guard (the real army)—thumping a republican. And if so, like me, you will have said in your heart: 'Thump on, thump a little harder. . . . The man whom thou thumpest is an enemy of roses and of perfumes, and a maniac for *utensils*. He is the enemy of Watteau, the enemy of Raphael."[99] Cited in R. Trial, *La Maladie de Baudelaire* (Paris, 1926), p. 51. [J19a,2]

"Speak neither of opium nor of Jeanne Duval if you would criticize *Les Fleurs du mal*." Gilbert Maire, "La Personnalité de Baudelaire," *Mercure de France*, 21 (January 16, 1910), p. 244. [J19a,3]

"To conceive Baudelaire without recourse to his biography—this is the fundamental object and final goal of our undertaking." Gilbert Maire, "La Personnalité de Baudelaire," *Mercure de France*, 21 (January 16, 1910), p. 244. [J19a,4]

"Jacques Crépet would like us to look on Baudelaire in such a way that the sincerity of his life would assure us of the value of his work, and that, sympathizing with the man, we would learn to love both life and work." Gilbert Maire, "La Personnalité de Baudelaire," *Mercure de France*, 21 (February 1, 1910), p. 414. [J19a,5]

Maire writes (p. 417) that the "incomparable sensibility" of Barrès was schooled on Baudelaire. [J19a,6]

To Ancelle, 1865: "One can both possess a *unique genius* and be a *fool*. Victor Hugo has given us ample proof of that. . . . The Ocean itself tired of his company."[100] [J19a,7]

Poe: "'I would not be able to love,' he will say quite clearly, 'did not death mix its breath with that of Beauty!'"[101] Cited in Ernest Seillière, *Baudelaire* (Paris, 1931), p. 229. The author refers to the time when, after the death of Mrs. Jane Stanard, the fifteen-year-old Poe would spend long nights in the graveyard, often in the rain, at the site of her grave. [J19a,8]

Baudelaire to his mother, concerning *Les Fleurs du mal:* "This book . . . possesses . . . a beauty that is sinister and cold: it was created with fury and patience."[102] [J19a,9]

Letter from Ange Pechméja to Baudelaire, February 1866. The writer expresses his admiration, in particular, for the sensuous interfusion in the poet's language. See Ernest Seillière, *Baudelaire* (Paris, 1933), pp. 254–255. [J19a,10]

Baudelaire ascribes to Hugo an "interrogative" poetic character. [J20,1]

There is probably a connection between Baudelaire's weakness of will and the abundance of power with which certain drugs under certain conditions endow the will. "Architecte de mes féeries / Je faisais, à ma volonté, / Sous un tunnel de pierreries / Passer un océan dompté."[103] [J20,2]

Baudelaire's inner experiences: "Commentators have somewhat falsified the situation . . . in insisting overmuch on the *theory* of universal analogy, as formulated in the sonnet 'Correspondances,' while ignoring the reverie to which Baudelaire was inclined. . . . There were moments of depersonalization in his existence, moments of self-forgetting and of communication with 'revealed paradises.' . . . At the end of his life . . ., he abjured the dream, . . . blaming his moral shipwreck on his 'penchant for reverie.'" Albert Béguin, *L'Ame romantique et le rêve* (Marseilles, 1937), vol. 2, pp. 401, 405. [J20,3]

In his book *Le Parnasse*, Thérive points to the decisive influence of painting and the graphic arts on a great many of Baudelaire's poems. He sees in this a characteristic feature of the Parnassian school. Moreover, he sees Baudelaire's poetry as an interpenetration of Parnassian and Symbolist tendencies. [J20,4]

"A propensity to imagine even nature through the vision that others have had of it. 'La Géante' comes out of Michelangelo; 'Rêve parisien,' out of Simone Martini; 'A

Une Madone' is a Baroque statue in a Spanish chapel." André Thérive, *Le Parnasse* (Paris, 1929), p. 101.   [J20,5]

Thérive finds in Baudelaire "certain gaucheries, which, today, one can't help thinking might be traits of the sublime." André Thérive, *Le Parnasse* (Paris, 1929), p. 99.   [J20,6]

In an article entitled "Une Anecdote controuvée sur Baudelaire" ⟨A Fabricated Anecdote about Baudelaire⟩, in the Fortnightly Review section of the *Mercure de France* (May 15, 1921), Baudelaire's alleged sojourn and activity with a conservative newspaper in Châteauroux is disputed by Ernest Gaubert, who examined all the periodicals from the town, and who traces the anecdote back to A. Ponroy (a friend of Baudelaire's who had family in Châteauroux), from whom Crépet got it. *Mercure de France*, 148, pp. 281–282.   [J20,7]

Daudet, in an inspired phrase, speaks of Baudelaire's "trap-door disposition—which is also that of Prince Hamlet." Léon Daudet, *Les Pèlerins d'Emmaüs* (*Courrier des Pays-Bas,* 4) (Paris ⟨1928⟩), p. 101 ("Baudelaire: Le Malaise et l'aura'").
[J20,8]

"Theme . . . of . . . the affirmation of a mysterious presence at the back of things, as in the depths of the soul—the presence of Eternity. Hence the obsession with timepieces, and the need to break out of the confines of one's own life through the immense prolongation of ancestral memory and of former lives." Albert Béguin, *L'Ame romantique et le rêve* (Marseilles, 1937), vol. 2, p. 403.   [J20a,1]

Roger Allard in a polemic against the introduction to *L'Oeuvre poétique de Charles Baudelaire*, edited by Guillaume Apollinaire (Paris: Bibliothèque des Curieux). In this introduction, Apollinaire advances the thesis that Baudelaire, while inaugurating the modern spirit, played little part in its development; his influence is nearly spent. Baudelaire is said to be a cross between Laclos and Poe. Allard replies: "In our view, two writers profoundly influenced Baudelaire, or rather two books. . . . One is . . . *Le Diable amoureux* ⟨The Devil in Love⟩, by Cazotte; the other, Diderot's *La Religieuse* ⟨The Nun⟩. Two notes at this point: "(1) M. Apollinaire could not do otherwise than name the author of *Le Diable amoureux* in a note concerning the last line of the sonnet 'Le Possédé': 'One would probably not go wrong in taking Cazotte as the hyphen that had the honor of uniting, in Baudelaire's mind, the spirit of the Revolution's writers with that of Edgar Poe.' (2) The poem accompanying a letter from Baudelaire to Sainte-Beuve can be found in the edition furnished by M. Apollinaire: '. . . with eyes darker and more blue than the Nun whose / sad and obscene story is known to all. . . .'[104] A few lines later, we come upon the first draft of a stanza of 'Lesbos.'" Roger Allard, *Baudelaire et "l'Esprit nouveau"* (Paris, 1918), p. 10.   [J20a,2]

Léon Daudet, in "Baudelaire: Le Malaise et l'aura,'" asks whether Baudelaire did not in some degree play Hamlet opposite Aupick and his mother.   [J20a,3]

Vigny wrote "Le Mont des oliviers" partly in order to refute de Maistre, by whom he was deeply influenced.   [J20a,4]

Jules Romains (*Les Hommes de bonne volonté*, book 2, *Crime de Quinette* ‹Paris, 1932›, p. 171) compares the flâneur to Baudelaire's "rugged swimmer reveling in the waves."[105]   [J20a,5]

Compare "the secret harvest of the heart" ("Le Soleil") with "Nothing ever grows, / once the heart is harvested" ("Semper eadem").[106] These formulations have a bearing on Baudelaire's heightened artistic consciousness: the blossom makes the dilettante; the fruit, the master.   [J20a,6]

The essay on Dupont was commissioned by Dupont's publisher.   [J21,1]

Poem to Sarah, around 1839. It contains this stanza:

> Though to get some shoes she sold her soul,
> The good Lord would laugh if with this wretch
> I struck a haughty pose like some Tartuffe,
> I who sell my thought and would be an author.[107]   [J21,2]

"Le Mauvais Vitrier"—to be compared with Lafcadio's *acte gratuit* ‹gratuitous act›.[108]   [J21,3]

> "When, your heart on fire with valor and with hope,
> you whipped the moneylenders out of that place—
> you were master then! But now, has not remorse
> pierced your side even deeper than the spear?[109]

That is, remorse at having let pass so fine an opportunity for proclaiming the dictatorship of the proletariat!" Thus inanely comments Seillière (‹*Baudelaire* [Paris, 1933],› p. 193) on "Le Reniement de Saint Pierre."   [J21,4]

Apropos these lines from "Lesbos"—"Of Sappho who died on the day of her blasphemy, / . . . insulting the rite and the designated worship"[110]—Seillière (p. 216) remarks: "It is not hard to see that the 'god,' the object of this 'august' religion, whose practice consists in blaspheming and in insulting traditional rites, is none other than Satan." Isn't the blasphemy, in this case, the love for a young man?   [J21,5]

From the obituary notice, "Charles Baudelaire," by Jules Vallès, which appeared September 7, 1867, in *La Rue:* "Will he have ten years of immortality?" (p. 190). "These are, moreover, bad times for the biblicists of the sacristy or of the cabaret!

Ours is an age of gaiety and distrust, one that never long suspends the recital of nightmares or the spectacle of ecstasies. It has now become clear that no one else had enough foresight to undertake such a campaign at the period when Baudelaire began his" (pp. 190–191). "Why didn't he become a professor of rhetoric or a dealer in scapulars, this didactician who imitated the blasted and downtrodden, this classicist who wanted to shock Prudhomme, but who, as Dusolier has said, was only a hysterical Boileau who went to play Dante among the cafés" (p. 192). Notwithstanding the resounding error in its appreciation of the importance of Baudelaire's work, the obituary contains some perceptive passages, particularly those concerned with the habitus of Baudelaire: "He had in him something of the priest, the old lady, and the ham actor. Above all, the ham actor" (p. 189). The piece is reprinted in André Billy, *Les Ecrivains de combat* (Paris, 1931); originally appeared in *La Situation*.   [J21,6]

Key passages on the stars in Baudelaire (ed. Le Dantec): "Night! you'd please me more without these stars / which speak a language I know all too well— / I long for darkness, silence, *nothing there* . . ." ("Obsession," ‹vol. 1,› p. 88).—Ending of "Les Promesses d'un visage" (‹vol. 1,› p. 170): the "enormous head of hair— / . . . which in darkness rivals you, O Night, / deep and spreading starless Night!"—"Yet neither sun nor moon appeared, / and no horizon paled" ("Rêve parisien," ‹vol. 1,› p. 116).—"What if the waves and winds are black as ink" ("Le Voyage," ‹vol. 1,› p. 149).—Compare, however, "Les Yeux de Berthe," the only weighty exception (‹vol. 1,› p. 169), and, in another perspective, the constellation of the stars with the aether, as it appears in "Delphine et Hippolyte" (‹vol. 1,› p. 160) and in "Le Voyage" (‹vol. 1,› p. 146 ‹sec. 3›). On the other hand, highly characteristic that "Le Crépuscule du soir" makes no mention of stars.[111] [J21a,1]

"Le Mort joyeux" could represent a reply to Poe's fantasies of decomposition: "and let me know if one last twinge is left. . . ."[112]   [J21a,2]

A sardonic accent marks the spot where it is said of the stars: "decent planets, at a time like this, / renounce their vigilance—" ("Sépulture").[113]   [J21a,3]

Baudelaire introduces into the lyric the figure of sexual perversion that seeks its objects on the street. What is most characteristic, however, is that he does this with the phrase "trembling like a fool" in one of his most perfect love poems, "A Une Passante."[114]   [J21a,4]

Figure of the big city whose inhabitants are frightened of cathedrals: "Vast woods, you terrify me like cathedrals" ("Obsession").[115]   [J21a,5]

"Le Voyage" (sec. 7): "Come and revel in the sweet delight / of days where it is always afternoon!"[116] Is it too bold to see in the emphasis on this time of day something peculiar to the big city?   [J21a,6]

The hidden figure that is the key to "Le Balcon": the night which holds the lovers in its embrace as, after day's departure, they dream of the dawn, is starless—"The night solidified into a wall."[117]   [J21a,7]

To the glance that encounters the "Passante" contrast George's poem "Von einer Begegnung" ⟨Encounter⟩:

> My glances drew me from the path I seek
>
> . . . . .
>
> And crazed with magic, mad to clasp, they trailed
> The slender bow sweet limbs in walking curved,
> And wet with longing then, they fell and failed
> Before into your own they boldly swerved.

Stefan George, *Hymnen; Pilgerfahrten; Algabal* (Berlin, 1922), pp. 22–23.[118]

[J22,1]

"'The unexampled ogle of a whore / glinting toward you like a silver ray / the wavering moon releases on the lake':[119] so begins the last poem. And into this extraordinary stare, which brings uncontrollable tears to the eyes of him who meets it without defenses, Berg looked long and avidly. For him, however, as for Baudelaire, the mercenary eye became a legacy of the prehistoric world. The arc-light moon of the big city shines for him like something out of the age of hetaerism. He needs only to have it reflected, as on a lake, and the banal reveals itself as the distant past; the nineteenth-century commodity betrays its mythic taboo. It was in such a spirit that Berg composed *Lulu*." Wiesengrund-Adorno, "Konzertarie 'Der Wein,'" in Willi Reich, *Alban Berg*, with Berg's own writings and with contributions by Theodor Wiesengrund-Adorno and Ernst Krenek (Vienna, Leipzig, Zurich ⟨1937⟩), p. 106.   [J22,2]

What's with the dilation of the sky in Meryon's engraving?   [J22,3]

"Le Crépuscule du matin" occupies a crucial position in *Les Fleurs du mal*. The morning wind disperses the clouds of myth. Human beings and their affairs are exposed to view. The prerevolutionary dawn glimmers in this poem. (In fact, it was probably composed after 1850.)   [J22,4]

The antithesis between allegory and myth has to be clearly developed. It was owing to the genius of allegory that Baudelaire did not succumb to the abyss of myth that gaped beneath his feet at every step.   [J22,5]

"'The depths being the multitudes,' Victor Hugo's solitude becomes a solitude overrun, a swarming solitude." Gabriel Bounoure, "Abîmes de Victor Hugo," *Mesures*, (July 15, 1936), p. 39. The author underscores the element of passivity in Hugo's experience of the crowd.   [J22,6]

"Nachtgedanken" ‹Night Thoughts›, by Goethe: "I pity you, unhappy stars, / who are so beautiful and shine so splendidly, / gladly guiding the struggling sailor with your light, / and yet have no reward from gods or men: / for you do not love, you have never known love! / Ceaselessly by everlasting hours / your dance is led across the wide heavens. / How vast a journey you have made already / since I, reposing in my sweetheart's arms, / forgot my thoughts of you and of the midnight!"[120]   [J22a,1]

The following argument—which dates from a period in which the decline of sculpture had become apparent, evidently prior to the decline of painting—is very instructive. Baudelaire makes exactly the same point about sculpture from the perspective of painting as is made today about painting from the perspective of film. "A picture, however, is only what it wants to be; there is no other way of looking at it than on its own terms. Painting has but one point of view; it is exclusive and absolute, and therefore the painter's expression is much more forceful." Baudelaire, *Oeuvres,* vol. 2, p. 128 ("Salon de 1846"). Just before this (pp. 127–128): "The spectator who moves around the figure can choose a hundred different points of view, except the right one."[121] ‹Compare› J4,7.   [J22a,2]

On Victor Hugo, around 1840: "At that same period, he began to realize that if man is the solitary animal, the solitary man is a man of the crowds [p. 39]. . . . It was Victor Hugo who gave Baudelaire that sense of the irradiant life of the crowd, and who taught him that 'multitude and solitude [are] equal and interchangeable terms for the poet who is active and productive. . . .'[122] Nevertheless, what a difference between the solitude which the great artist of spleen chose for himself in Brussels in order 'to gain an inalienable individual tranquillity' and the solitude of the magus of Jersey, haunted at that same moment by shadowy apparitions! . . . Hugo's solitude is not an envelope, a *Noli me tangere,* a concentration of the individual in his difference. It is, rather, a participation in the cosmic mystery, an entry into the realm of primitive forces" (pp. 40–41). Gabriel Bounoure, "Abîmes de Victor Hugo," *Mesures* (July 15, 1936), pp. 39–41.   [J22a,3]

From *Le Collier des jours* ‹The Necklace of Days›, vol. 1, cited by Remy de Gourmont in *Judith Gautier* (Paris, 1904), p. 15: "A ring of the bell interrupted us and then, without a sound, a very singular person entered the room and made a slight bow of the head. I had the impression of a priest without his cassock. 'Ah, here's Baldelarius!' cried my father, extending his hand to the newcomer." Baudelaire offers a gloomy jest on the subject of Judith's nickname, "Ouragan" ‹Hurricane›.   [J23,1]

"At the café called the Divan Le Peletier, Théodore de Banville would see Baudelaire sitting fiercely, 'like an angry Goethe' (as he says in a poem), next to 'the gentle Asselineau.'" Léon Daudet, *Le Stupide XIXᵉ Siècle* (Paris, 1922), pp. 139–140.   [J23,2]

Apropos of "The greathearted servant . . ." and the end of "Le Voyage" ("O Death, old captain . . ."), L. Daudet speaks of a Ronsardian flight (in *Le Stupide XIXᵉ Siècle*, p. 140). [J23,3]

"My father had caught a glimpse of Baudelaire, and he told me about his impression: a bizarre and atrabilious prince among boors." Léon Daudet, *Le Stupide XIXᵉ Siècle* (Paris, 1922), p. 141. [J23,4]

Baudelaire calls Hugo a "genius without borders."[123] [J23,5]

It is presumably no accident that, in searching for a poem by Hugo to provide with a pendant, Baudelaire fastened on one of the most banal of the banal—"Les Fantômes." In this sequence of six poems, the first begins: "How many maidens fair, alas! I've seen / Fade and die." The third: "One form above all,—'twas a Spanish maid." And further on: "What caused her death? Balls, dances—dazzling balls; / They filled her soul with ecstasy and joy." This is followed by the story of how she caught cold one morning, and eventually sank into the grave. The sixth poem resembles the close of a popular ballad: "O maidens, whom such festive *fêtes* decay! / Ponder the story of this Spanish maid."[124] [J23,6]

With Baudelaire's "La Voix" ‹The Voice› compare Victor Hugo's "Ce qu'on entend sur la montagne" ‹What Is Heard on the Mountain›. The poet gives ear to the world storm:

> Soon with that voice confusedly combined,
> Two other voices, vague and veiled, I find.
> . . . . .
> And seemed each voice, though mixed, distinct to be,
> As two cross-currents 'neath a stream you see.
>
> One from the seas—triumphant, blissful song!
> Voice of the waves, which talked themselves among;
> The other, which from the earth to heaven ran,
> Was full of sorrow—the complaint of man.

The poem takes, as its object, the dissonance of the second voice, which is set off against the harmony of the first. Ending:

> Why God . . .
> Joins in the fatal hymn since earth began,
> The song of Nature, and the cries of man?[125] [J23,7]

Isolated observations from Barbey d'Aurevilly's "M. Charles Baudelaire": "I sometimes imagine . . . that, if Timon of Athens had had the genius of Archilochus, he would have been able to write in this manner on human nature and to insult it while rendering it!" (p. 381). "Conceive, if you will, a language more plastic than poetic, a language hewn and shaped like bronze and stone, in which each phrase has its volutes and fluting" (p. 378). "This profound dreamer . . . asked himself

... what would become of poetry in passing through a head organized, for example, like that of Caligula or Heliogabalus" (p. 376).—"Thus, like the old Goethe who transformed himself into a seller of Turkish pastilles in his *Divan* . . . , the author of *Les Fleurs du mal* turned villainous, blasphemous, impious for the sake of his thought" (pp. 375–376). ⟨Jules⟩ Barbey d'Aurevilly, *XIX Siècle: Les Oeuvres et les hommes*, vol. 3, *Les Poètes* (Paris, 1862).   [J23a,1]

"A critic (M. Thierry, in *Le Moniteur*) made the point recently in a very fine appreciation: to discover the parentage of this implacable poetry . . . one must go back to Dante . . . !" (p. 379). This analogy Barbey makes emphatically his own: "Dante's muse looked dreamily on the Inferno; that of *Les Fleurs du mal* breathes it in through inflamed nostrils, as a horse inhales shrapnel" (p. 380). Barbey d'Aurevilly, *XIXe Siècle: Les Oeuvres et les hommes*, vol. 3, *Les Poètes* (Paris, 1862).   [J23a,2]

Barbey d'Aurevilly on Dupont: "Cain triumphs over the gentle Abel in this man's talent and thinking—the Cain who is coarse, ravenous, envious, and fierce, and who has gone to the cities to consume the dregs of accumulated resentments and share in the false ideas that triumph there!" Barbey d'Aurevilly, *Le XIXe Siècle: Les Oeuvres et les hommes*, vol. 3, *Les Poètes* (Paris, 1862), p. 242 ("M. Pierre Dupont").   [J23a,3]

A manuscript of Goethe's "Nachtgedanken" bears the notation, "Modeled on the Greek."   [J23a,4]

At the age of eleven, Baudelaire experienced first hand the workers' rebellion of 1832 in Lyons. It appears that no trace remained in him of any impressions that event might have left.   [J23a,5]

"One of the arguments he makes to his guardian, Ancelle, is rather curious. It seems to him that 'the new Napoleonic regime, after illustrations depicting the battlefield, ought to seek illustrations depicting the arts and letters.'" Alphonse Séché, *La Vie des Fleurs du mal* (Paris, 1928), p. 172.   [J23a,6]

The sense of "the abyssal" is to be defined as "meaning." Such a sense is always allegorical.   [J24,1]

With Blanqui, the cosmos has become an abyss. Baudelaire's abyss is starless; it should not be defined as cosmic space. But even less is it the exotic space of theology. It is a secularized space: the abyss of knowledge and of meanings. What constitutes its historical index? In Blanqui, the abyss has the historical index of mechanistic natural science. In Baudelaire, doesn't it have the social index of *nouveauté?* Is not the arbitrariness of allegory a twin to that of fashion?
                          [J24,2]

Explore the question whether a connection exists between the works of the allegorical imagination and the *correspondances*. In any case, these are two wholly distinct sources for Baudelaire's production. That the first of them has a very considerable share in the specific qualities of his poetry cannot be doubted. The nexus of meanings might be akin to that of the fibers of spun yarn. If we can distinguish between spinning and weaving activity in poets, then the allegorical imagination must be classed with the former.—On the other hand, it is not impossible that the correspondences play at least some role here, insofar as a word, in its way, calls forth an image; thus, the image could determine the meaning of the word, or else the word that of the image. [J24,3]

Disappearance of allegory in Victor Hugo. [J24,4]

Do flowers lack souls? Is this an implication of the title *Les Fleurs du mal?* In other words, are flowers a symbol of the whore? Or is this title meant to recall flowers to their true place? Pertinent here is the letter accompanying the two *crépuscule* ‹twilight› poems which Baudelaire sent to Fernand Desnoyers for his *Fontaine-bleau: Paysages, légendes, souvenirs, fantaisies* (1855). ‹See below, 24a,1.› [J24,5]

Utter detachment of Poe from great poetry. For one Fouqué, he would give fifty Molières. The *Iliad* and Sophocles leave him cold. This perspective would accord perfectly with the theory of *l'art pour l'art*. What was Baudelaire's attitude?
[J24,6]

With the mailing of the "Crépuscules" to Fernand Desnoyers for his *Fontaine-bleau* (Paris, 1855): "My dear Desnoyers: You ask me for some verses for your little anthology, verses about *Nature*, I believe; about forests, great oak trees, verdure, insects—and perhaps even the sun? But you know perfectly well that I can't become sentimental about vegetation and that my soul rebels against this strange new religion. . . . I shall never believe that *the souls of the gods live in plants*. . . . I have always thought, even, that there was something irritating and impudent about *Nature* in its fresh and rampant state."[126] Cited in A. Séché, *La Vie des Fleurs du mal* ‹Amiens, 1928›, pp. 109–110. [J24a,1]

"Les Aveugles" ‹Blind Men›: Crépet gives as source for this poem of Baudelaire's a passage from "Des Vetters Eckfenster" ‹My Cousin's Corner Window›—a passage about the way blind people hold their heads. Hoffmann considers the heavenward gaze to be edifying. ‹See T4a,2.› [J24a,2]

Louis Goudall criticized Baudelaire on November 4, 1855, on the basis of poems published in *La Revue des deux mondes*. "Poetry that is . . . nauseating, glacial, straight from the charnel house and the slaughterhouse." Cited in François Por-ché, *La Vie douloureuse de Charles Baudelaire* (series entitled *Le Roman des grandes existences*, vol. 6) (Paris ‹1926›), p. 202. [J24a,3]

The reviews by ‹Barbey› d'Aurevilly and Asselineau were turned down by *Le Pays* and *La Revue française*, respectively.   [J24a,4]

The famous statement by Valéry on Baudelaire ‹see J1,1› goes back, in essence, to the suggestions Sainte-Beuve sent to Baudelaire for his courtroom defense. "In the field of poetry, everything was taken. Lamartine had taken the skies. Victor Hugo, the earth—and more than the earth. Laprade, the forests. Musset, the dazzling life of passion and orgy. Others, the hearth, rural life, and so on. Théophile Gautier, Spain and its vibrant colors. What then remained? What Baudelaire has taken. It was as though he had no choice in the matter. . . ." Cited in Porché, *La Vie douloureuse de Charles Baudelaire* ‹Paris, 1926›, p. 205.   [J24a,5]

Very plausible indication in Porché to the effect that Baudelaire did not produce the many decisive variants to his poems while seated at his desk. (See Porché, p. 109.)   [J24a,6]

"Finding the poet one evening at a public ball, Charles Monselet accosted him: 'What are you doing here?'—'My dear fellow,' replied Baudelaire, 'I'm watching the death's heads pass!'" Alphonse Séché, *La Vie des Fleurs du mal* (‹Amiens,› 1928), p. 32.   [J25,1]

"His earnings have been reckoned: the total for his entire life does not exceed sixteen thousand francs. Catulle Mendès calculated that the author . . . would have received about one franc seventy centimes per day as payment for his literary labors." Alphonse Séché, *La Vie des Fleurs du mal* (‹Amiens,› 1928), p. 34.
                                                                                  [J25,2]

According to Séché, Baudelaire's aversion to a sky that was "much too blue"—or rather, much too bright—would have come from his stay on the island of Mauritius. (See Séché, p. 42.)   [J25,3]

Séché speaks of a pronounced similarity between Baudelaire's letters to Mlle. Daubrun and his letters to Mme. Sabatier. (See p. 53.)   [J25,4]

According to Séché (p. 65), Champfleury would have taken part with Baudelaire in the founding of *Le Salut public*.   [J25,5]

Prarond on the period around 1845: "We understood little of the use of tables for working, thinking, composing. . . . For my part, I saw him composing verses on the run while he was out in the streets; I never saw him seated before a ream of paper." Cited in Séché, *La Vie des Fleurs du mal* (1928), p. 84.   [J25,6]

The way Baudelaire presented himself during his Brussels lecture on Gautier, as described by Camille Lemonnier in *La Vie belge:* "Baudelaire made one think of a man of the church, with those beautiful gestures of the pulpit. His soft linen cuffs fluttered like the sleeves of a clerical frock. He developed his subject with an almost evangelical unctuousness, proclaiming his veneration for a literary master in the liturgical tones of a bishop announcing a mandate. To himself, no doubt, he was celebrating a Mass full of glorious images; he had the grave beauty of a cardinal of letters officiating at the altar of the Ideal. His smooth, pale visage was shaded in the halftone of the lamplight. I watched his eyes move like black suns. His mouth had a life of its own within the life and expressions of his face; it was thin and quivering with a delicate vibrancy under the drawn bow of his words. And from its haughty height the head commanded the attention of the intimidated audience." Cited in Séché, *La Vie des Fleurs du mal* (1928), p. 68.   [J25,7]

Baudelaire transferred his application for the playwright Scribe's seat in the Académie Française to that of the Catholic priest Lacordaire.   [J25a,1]

Gautier: "Baudelaire loves ample polysyllabic words, and with three or four of these words he sometimes fashions lines of verse that seem immense, lines that resonate in such a way as to lengthen the meter." Cited in A. Séché, *La Vie des Fleurs du mal* (‹Amiens,› 1928), p. 195.   [J25a,2]

Gautier: "To the extent that it was possible, he banished eloquence in poetry." Cited in A. Séché, *La Vie des Fleurs du mal* (1928), p. 197.   [J25a,3]

E. Faguet in an article in *La Revue:* "Since 1857, the neurasthenia among us has scarcely abated; one could even say that it has been on the rise. Hence, 'there is no cause for wonder,' as Ronsard once said, that Baudelaire still has his followers. . . ." Cited in Alphonse Séché, *La Vie des Fleurs du mal* (1928), p. 207.
          [J25a,4]

Le Figaro publishes (date?) an article by Gustave Bourdin that was written at the instigation of Interior Minister Billaut. The latter had shortly before, as judge or public prosecutor, suffered a setback with the acquittal of Flaubert in the trial against *Madame Bovary*. A few days later came Thierry's article in *Le Moniteur.* "Why did Sainte-Beuve . . . leave it to Thierry to tell readers of *Le Moniteur* about *Les Fleurs du mal?* Sainte-Beuve doubtless refused to write about Baudelaire's book because he deemed it more prudent to efface the ill effect his article on *Madame Bovary* had had in the inner circles of the government." Alphonse Séché, *La Vie des Fleurs du mal* (1928), pp. 156–157.[127]   [J25a,5]

The denunciation in Bourdin's article is treacherously disguised as praise for precisely those poems singled out in the indictment. After a disgusted enumeration of Baudelaire's topics, he writes: "And in the middle of it all, four poems—'Le Reniement de Saint Pierre,' then 'Lesbos,' and two entitled 'Femmes damnées'— four masterpieces of passion, of art, and of poetry. It is understandable that a poet of twenty might be led by his imagination to treat these subjects, but nothing excuses a man over thirty who foists such monstrosities on the public by means of a book." Cited in Alphonse Séché, *La Vie des Fleurs du mal* (1928), p. 158.

[J25a,6]

From Edouard Thierry's review of *Les Fleurs du mal* in *Le Moniteur* (July 14, 1857?): "The Florentine of old would surely recognize, in this French poet of today, the characteristic ardor, the terrifying utterance, the ruthless imagery, and the sonority of his brazen lines. . . . I leave his book and his talent under Dante's stern warning."[128] Cited in Alphonse Séché, *Le Vie des Fleurs du mal* (1928), pp. 160–161.

[J26,1]

Baudelaire's great dissatisfaction with the frontispiece designed by Bracquemond according to specifications provided by the poet, who had conceived this idea while perusing Hyacinthe Langlois' *Histoire des danses macabres*. Baudelaire's instructions: "A skeleton turning into a tree, with legs and ribs forming the trunk, the arms stretched out to make a cross and bursting into leaves and buds, sheltering several rows of poisonous plants in little pots, lined up as if in a gardener's hothouse." ‹See J16,3.› Bracquemond evidently runs into difficulties, and moreover misses the poet's intention when he masks the skeleton's pelvis with flowers and fails to give its arms the form of branches. From what Baudelaire has said, the artist simply does not know what a *squelette arborescent* is supposed to be, and he can't conceive how vices are supposed to be represented as flowers. (Cited in Alphonse Séché, *La Vie des Fleurs du mal* [‹Amiens,› 1928], pp. 136–137, as drawn from letters.) In the end, a portrait of the poet by Bracquemond was substituted for this planned image. Something similar resurfaced around 1862, as Poulet-Malassis was planning a luxury edition of *Les Fleurs du mal*. He commissioned Bracquemond to do the graphic design, which apparently consisted of decorative borders and vignettes; emblematic devices played a major role on these. (See Séché, p. 138.)—The subject that Bracquemond had failed to render was taken up by Rops in the frontispiece to *Les Epaves* (1866).

[J26,2]

List of reviewers for *Les Fleurs du mal*, with the newspapers Baudelaire had in mind for them: Buloz, Lacaussade, Gustave Rouland (*La Revue européenne*); Gozlan (*Le Monde illustré*); Sainte-Beuve (*Le Moniteur*); Deschanel (*Le Journal des débats*); Aurevilly (*Le Pays*); Janin (*Le Nord*); Armand Fraisse (*Le Salut public de Lyons*); Guttinguer (*La Gazette de France*). (According to Séché, p. 140.)

[J26,3]

The publication rights for Baudelaire's entire oeuvre were auctioned after his death to Michel Lévy for 1,750 francs.

[J26,4]

The "Tableaux Parisiens" appear only with the second edition of *Le Fleurs du mal*.

[J26,5]

The definitive title for the book was proposed by Hippolyte Babou in the Café Lamblin. [J26a,1]

"L'Amour et le crâne" ‹Eros and the Skull›. "This poem of Baudelaire's was inspired by two works of the engraver Henri Goltzius." Alphonse Séché, *La Vie des Fleurs du mal* (‹Amiens,› 1928), p. 111. [J26a,2]

"A Une Passante." "M. Crépet mentions as possible source a passage from 'Dina, la belle Juive,' in Petrus Borel's *Champavert* . . . : 'For me, the thought that this lightning flash that dazzled us will never be seen again . . . ; that two existences made . . . for happiness together, in this life and in eternity, are forever sundered . . .—for me, this thought is profoundly saddening.'" Cited in A. Séché, *La Vie des Fleurs du mal*, p. 108. [J26a,3]

"Rêve parisien." Like the speaker in the poem, Constantin Guys also rose at noon; hence, according to Baudelaire (letter of March 13, 1860, to Poulet-Malassis), the dedication.[129] [J26a,4]

Baudelaire (where?)[130] points to the third book of the *Aeneid* as source for "Le Cygne." (See Séché, p. 104.) [J26a,5]

To the right of the barricade; to the left of the barricade. It is very significant that, for large portions of the middle classes, there was only a shade of difference between these two positions. This changes only with Louis Napoleon. For Baudelaire it was possible (no easy trick!) to be friends with Pierre Dupont and to participate in the June Insurrection on the side of the proletariat, while avoiding any sort of run-in when he encountered his friends from the Ecole Normande, Chennevières and Le Vavasseur, in the company of a national guardsman.—It may be recalled, in this context, that the appointment of General Aupick as ambassador to Constantinople in 1848 goes back to Lamartine, who at that time was minister of foreign affairs. [J26a,6]

Work on *Les Fleurs du mal* up through the first edition: fifteen years. [J26a,7]

Proposal of a Brussels pharmacist to Poulet-Malassis: in exchange for a commitment to buy 200 copies, he would be allowed to advertise to readers, in the back pages of *Les Paradis artificiels*, a hashish extract prepared by his firm. Baudelaire's veto won out with difficulty. [J26a,8]

From ‹Barbey› d'Aurevilly's letter to Baudelaire of February 4, 1859: "Villain of genius! In poetry, I knew you to be a sacred viper spewing your venom in the faces of the *g*—*s* and the *g*—*s*. But now the viper has sprouted wings and is soaring through the clouds to shoot its poison into the very eyes of the Sun!" Cited in Ernest Seillière, *Baudelaire* (Paris, 1931). p. 157. [J27,1]

In Honfleur, he had hung two paintings over his bed. One of them, painted by his father as pendant to the other, showed an amorous scene; the other, dating from an earlier time, a Temptation of Saint Anthony. In the center of the first picture, a bacchante. [J27,2]

"Sand is inferior to Sade!"[131] [J27,3]

"We ensure that our confessions are well rewarded"[132]—this should be compared with the practice of his letters. [J27,4]

Seillière (p. 234) cites ‹Barbey› d'Aurevilly: "Poe's hidden objective was to confound the imagination of his times. . . . Hoffmann did not have this terrible power." Such *puissance terrible* was surely Baudelaire's as well. [J27,5]

On Delacroix (according to Seillière, p. 114): "Delacroix is the artist best equipped to portray modern woman in her heroic manifestations, whether these be understood in the divine or the infernal sense. . . . It seems that such color thinks for itself, independently of the objects it clothes. The effect of the whole is almost musical."[133] [J27,6]

Fourier is said to have presented his "minute discoveries" too "pompously."[134]
[J27,7]

Seillière represents as his particular object of study what in general determines the standard for the literature on Baudelaire: "It is, in effect, the theoretical conclusions imposed on Charles Baudelaire by his life experiences that I am particularly concerned with in these pages." Ernest Seillière, *Baudelaire* (Paris, 1931), p. 1. [J27,8]

Eccentric behavior in 1848: "'They've just arrested de Flotte,' he said. 'Is it because his hands smelled of gunpowder? Smell mine!'" Seillière, *Baudelaire* (Paris, 1931), p. 51. [J27,9]

Seillière (p. 59) rightly contrasts Baudelaire's postulate, according to which the advent of Napoleon III is to be interpreted in de Maistre's sense as "providential," with his comment: "My rage at the coup d'état. How many bullets I braved! Another Bonaparte! What a disgrace!" Both in "Mon Coeur mis à nu."[135]
[J27a,1]

The book by Seillière is thoroughly imbued with the position of its author, who is president of the Académie des Sciences Morales et Politiques. A typical premise: "The social question is a question of morality" (p. 66). Individual sentences by Baudelaire are invariably accompanied by the author's marginal glosses.
[J27a,2]

Bourdin: son-in-law of Villemessant. *Le Figaro* in 1863 publishes a violent attack by Pontmartin on Baudelaire. In 1864, he halts publication of the *Petits Poèmes en prose* after two installments. Villemessant: "Your poems bore everybody." See François Porché, *La Vie douloureuse de Charles Baudelaire* (series entitled *Le Roman des grandes existences*, vol. 6) (Paris ‹1926›), p. 261.   [J27a,3]

On Lamartine: "A bit of a strumpet, a bit of a whore." Cited in François Porché, *La Vie douloureuse de Charles Baudelaire* (series entitled *Le Roman des grandes existences*, vol. 6) (Paris), p. 248.   [J27a,4]

Relation to Victor Hugo: "He had solicited from him a preface to the study on Gautier, and, with the aim of forcing Victor Hugo's hand, had even dedicated some poems to him." François Porché, *La Vie douloureuse de Charles Baudelaire* (series entitled *Le Roman des grandes existences*, vol. 6) (Paris), p. 251.   [J27a,5]

Title of the first publication of pieces from *Les Paradis artificiels* in *La Revue contemporaine*, 1858: "De l'Idéal artificiel" ‹On the Artificial Ideal›.   [J27a,6]

Sainte-Beuve's article in *Le Constitutionnel* of January 20, 1862.[136] Subsequently, as early as February 9—as Baudelaire is toying with the idea of declaring his candidacy for Lacordaire's seat instead of for Scribe's, which was his original plan—the admonition: "Leave the Académie as it is, more surprised than shocked." Baudelaire withdraws his application. See Porché, *La Vie douloureuse de Charles Baudelaire* (Paris), p. 247.   [J27a,7]

"Note that this innovator has not a single new idea. After Vigny, one must wait until Sully-Prudhomme to find new ideas in a French poet. Baudelaire never entertains anything but the most threadbare platitudes. He is the poet of aridity and banality. "Bénédiction": the artist here below is a martyr. "L'Albatros": the artist flounders in reality. "Les Phares": artists are the beacons of humanity. . . . Brunetière is surely right: there is nothing more in "Une Charogne" than the words of Ecclesiasticus, 'With all flesh, both man and beast, . . . are death and bloodshed.'"[137] Emile Faguet, "Baudelaire," *La Revue*, 87 (1910), p. 619.
[J28,1]

"He has almost no imagination. His inspiration is amazingly meager." E. Faguet, "Baudelaire," *La Revue*, 87 (1910), p. 616.   [J28,2]

Faguet draws a comparison between Senancour and Baudelaire—what's more, in favor of the former.   [J28,3]

J.-J. Weiss (*Revue contemporaine*, January 1858): "This line of verse . . . resembles one of those spinning tops that would hum in the gutter." Cited in Camille Vergniol, "Cinquante ans après Baudelaire," *Revue de Paris*, 24th year (1917), p. 687.   [J28,4]

Pontmartin in his critique of the portrait of Baudelaire by Nargeot: "This engraving shows us a face that is haggard, sinister, ravaged, and malign; it is the face of a hero of the Court of Assizes, or of a pensioner from Bicêtre." Compare B2a,6 (Vischer: the "freshly beheaded" look). [J28,5]

Adverse criticism from Brunetière in 1887 and 1889. In 1892 and 1893 come the corrections. The sequence: *Questions de critique* (June 1887); *Essai sur la littérature contemporaine* (1889); *Nouveaux Essais sur la littérature contemporaine* (1892); *Evolution de la poésie lyrique en France* (1893).[138] [J28,6]

Physiognomy of Baudelaire in his last years: "He has an aridity in all his features, which contrasts sharply with the intensity of his look. Above all, he has that set to his lips which indicates a mouth long accustomed to chewing only ashes." François Porché, *La Vie douloureuse de Charles Baudelaire* (series entitled *Le Roman des grandes existences*, vol. 6) (Paris ‹1926›), p. 291. [J28,7]

1861. Suicidal impulses. Arsène Houssaye of *La Revue contemporain* learns that some of the *Petits Poèmes en prose* appearing in his journal have already appeared in the *La Revue fantaisiste*. Publication is suspended.—*La Revue des deux mondes* rejects the essay on Guys.—*Le Figaro* brings it out with an "editorial note" by Bourdin. [J28,8]

First lectures in Belgium: Delacroix, Gautier. [J28a,1]

The Ministry of the Interior refuses to issue its stamp to *Les Paradis artificiels*. (See Porché, p. 226.) What does that signify? [J28a,2]

Porché (p. 233) points out that Baudelaire throughout his life retained the mindset of a young man of good family.—Very instructive in this regard: "In every change there is something at once vile and agreeable, some element of disloyalty and restlessness. This sufficiently explains the French Revolution."[139] The sentiment recalls Proust—who was also a *fils de famille*. The historical projected into the intimate. [J28a,3]

Meeting between Baudelaire and Proudhon in 1848 at the offices of Proudhon's daily newspaper, *Le Représentant du peuple*. A chance encounter, it ends with their having dinner together on the Rue Neuve-Vivienne. [J28a,4]

The hypothesis that Baudelaire, in 1848, helped to found the conservative newspaper *Le Représentant de l'Indre* (later edited by Ponroy) comes from René Johannet. The newspaper supported the candidacy of Cavaignac. Baudelaire's collaboration at that moment, assuming it took place at all, may have involved a mystification. Without his knowledge, his trip to Châteauroux was subsidized, through Ancelle, by Aupick. [J28a,5]

According to Le Dantec, the second tercet of "Sed Non Satiata" is in some degree linked to "Les Lesbiennes." [J28a,6]

By 1843, according to Prarond, a great many poems from *Le Fleurs du mal* were already written. [J28a,7]

In 1845, "The Gold-Bug" is translated by Alphonse Borghers as "Le Scarabée d'or," in *La Revue britannique.* The next year, *La Quotidienne* publishes an adaptation, signed by initials only, of "The Murders in the Rue Morgue," wherein Poe's name goes unmentioned. Decisive for Baudelaire, according to Asselineau, was the translation of "The Black Cat" by Isabelle Meunier, in *La Démocratie pacifique* (1847). Characteristically enough, the first of Baudelaire's translations from Poe, to judge by the date of publication ⟨July 15, 1848⟩, was of "Mesmeric Revelation." [J28a,8]

1855: Baudelaire writes a letter to George Sand, interceding on behalf of Marie Daubrun. [J28a,9]

"Always very polite, very haughty, and very unctuous at the same time, there was about him something reminiscent of the monk, of the soldier, and of the cosmopolitan." Judith Cladel, *Bonshommes* (Paris, 1879), cited in E. and J. Crépet, *Charles Baudelaire* (Paris, 1906), p. 237. [J29,1]

In his "Notes et documents pour mon avocat," Baudelaire refers to the letters on art and morality which Balzac addressed to Hippolyte Castille in the newspaper *La Semaine.*[140] [J29,2]

Lyons is noted for its thick fog. [J29,3]

In 1845, apparent suicide attempt: knife wound in the chest. [J29,4]

"It is partly a life of leisure that has enabled me to grow.—To my great detriment—for leisure without fortune breeds debts. . . . But also to my great profit, as regards sensibility and meditation. . . . Other men of letters are, for the most part, base ignorant drudges."[141] Cited in Porché, ⟨*La Vie douloureuse de Charles Baudelaire* (Paris, 1926),⟩ p. 116. [J29,5]

Louis Goudall's article in *Le Figaro* of November 4, 1855, which took aim at the publication of poems in *La Revue des deux mondes,* caused Michel Lévy to give up the rights to *Les Fleurs du mal* to Poulet-Malassis. [J29,6]

1848: *Le Salut public,* with Champfleury and Toubin. First issue, February 27, written and edited in less than two hours. In that issue, presumably by the hand of Baudelaire: "A few misguided brethren have smashed some mechanical presses. . . . All machinery is sacred, like a work of art" (cited in Porché, p. 129).—Compare "the bloody apparatus of Destruction."[142]   [J29,7]

1849: *Le Représentant de l'Indre*. Baudelaire's participation not established with certainty. If the article "Actuellement" ‹At the Present Time› is written by him, then a certain mystification at the expense of the conservative principals at the newspaper is not out of the question.   [J29,8]

1851: with Dupont and La Chambaudie, *La République du peuple*, democratic almanac; "Editor, Baudelaire." Only "L'Ame du vin" ‹The Soul of the Wine› is published there with his signature.   [J29,9]

1852: with Champfleury and Monselet, *La Semaine théâtrale*.   [J29,10]

Addresses:	February 1854	Hôtel de York, Rue Sainte-Anne
	May	Hôtel du Maroc, Rue de Seine
	1858	Hôtel Voltaire, Quai Voltaire
	December 1858	22 Rue Beautreillis
	Summer 1859	Hôtel de Dieppe, Rue d'Amsterdam

[J29,11]

At the age of twenty-seven, Baudelaire was gray at the temples.   [J29,12]

From Charles Asselineau, *Baudelaire: Recueil d'Anecdotes* (in Crépet, *Charles Baudelaire* [Paris, 1908], ‹pp. 279ff.› published *in extenso*): the story of Asselineau's handkerchief.[143] Baudelaire's obstinacy. Provocative effects of his "diplomacy." His mania for shocking people.   [J29a,1]

From Gautier's obituary for Baudelaire, *Le Moniteur*, September 9, 1867: "Born in India, and possessing a thorough knowledge of the English language, he made his debut with his translations of Edgar Poe." Théophile Gautier, *Portraits contemporains* (Paris, 1874), p. 159.   [J29a,2]

A good half of Gautier's obituary notice is occupied with Poe. The part devoted to *Les Fleurs du mal* depends on metaphors which Gautier extracts from a story by Hawthorne: "We never read *Les Fleurs du mal*, by Baudelaire, without thinking involuntarily of that tale by Hawthorne ‹entitled "Rappaccini's Daughter"›; it has those somber and metallic colors, those verdigris blossoms and heady perfumes. His muse resembles the doctor's daughter whom no poison can harm, but whose pallid and anemic complexion betrays the influence of the milieu she inhabits." Théophile Gautier, *Portraits contemporains* (Paris, 1874), p. 163. ‹See J3a,2.›

[J29a,3]

Gautier's characterization of Baudelaire, in his *Histoire du Romantisme,* is not much more than a succession of questionable metaphors. "This poet's talent for concentration has caused him to reduce each piece to a single drop of essence enclosed in a crystal flagon cut with many facets," and so on (p. 350). Banality pervades the entire analysis. "Although he loves Paris as Balzac loved it; although, in his search for rhymes, he wanders through its most sinister and mysterious lanes at the hour when the reflections of the lights change the pools of rainwater into pools of blood, and when the moon moves along the broken outline of the dark roofs like an old yellow ivory skull; although he stops at times by the smoke-dimmed windows of taverns, listening to the croaking song of the drunkard and the strident laugh of the prostitute, . . . yet very often a suddenly recurring thought takes him back to India." Théophile Gautier, *Histoire du Romantisme* (Paris, 1874), p. 379 ("Le Progrès de la poésie française depuis 1830").[144] Compare Rollinat! [J29a,4]

Interior of the Hôtel Pimodan: no sideboard, no dining room table, frosted glass panes. At that point, Baudelaire had a servant. [J29a,5]

1851: new poems in *Le Messager de l'Assemblée*. The Saint-Simonian *Revue politique* turns down his manuscripts. Porché remarks that it looks very much as though Baudelaire was not really able to choose where to publish. [J30,1]

The fortune Baudelaire inherited in 1842 totaled 75,000 francs (in 1926, equivalent to 450,000 francs). To his colleagues—Banville—he passed for "very rich." He soon afterward discreetly left home. [J30,2]

As Porché nicely puts it (‹*La Vie douloureuse de Charles Baudelaire* [Paris, 1926],› p. 98), Ancelle was the embodiment of the "legal world." [J30,3]

Journey to Bordeaux in 1841 by stagecoach, one of the last.—A very severe storm Baudelaire went through on board the ship commanded by Captain Saliz, the *Paquebot des Mers du Sud,* appears to have left little trace in his work. [J30,4]

Baudelaire's mother was twenty-six and his father sixty when they married in 1819. [J30,5]

In the Hôtel Pimodan, Baudelaire wrote with a red goose quill. [J30,6]

"Mesmeric Revelation," certainly not one of Poe's more distinguished works, is the only story to be translated by Baudelaire during the American author's lifetime. 1852: Poe biography in *La Revue de Paris*. 1854: beginning of the translation work. [J30,7]

It should be remembered that Jeanne Duval was Baudelaire's first love. [J30,8]

Meetings with his mother in the Louvre during the years of dissension with Aupick. [J30,9]

The banquets organized by Philoxène Boyer. Baudelaire gives readings of "Une Charogne," "Le Vin de l'assassin," "Delphine et Hippolyte" (Porché, ‹*La Vie douloureuse de Charles Baudelaire* [Paris, 1926],› p. 158). [J30,10]

Porché (p. 98) draws attention to the fact that, with Saliz, Ancelle, and Aupick, Baudelaire had relations of a typical sort. [J30,11]

Sexual preoccupations, as revealed by the titles of projected novels: "Les Enseignements d'un monstre" ‹Education of a Monster›, "Une Infâme adorée" ‹Beloved Slattern›, "La Maîtresse de l'idiot" ‹The Idiot's Mistress›, "Les Tribades" ‹The Dykes›, "L'Entreteneur" ‹The Keeper›. [J30,12]

Consider that Baudelaire not infrequently, it appears, loved to humble himself in long conversations with Ancelle. In this, too, he is a *fils de famille*. More along these lines in his farewell letter: "I shall probably have to live a very hard life, but I shall be better off that way."[145] [J30,13]

Cladel mentions a "noble and transcendent dissertation" by Baudelaire on the physiognomy of language, having to do with the colors of words, their peculiarities as sources of light, and finally their moral characteristics. [J30a,1]

Indicative of a perhaps not uncommon tone in the exchanges between the two writers is Champfleury's letter of March 6, 1863. Baudelaire, in a letter now lost, had declined Champfleury's proposal to meet a female admirer of the *Le Fleurs du mal* and the writings of Poe, making a point of his dignity. Champfleury responds: "As for my compromised dignity, I refuse to hear of it. Stop frequenting places of far worse repute. Try to imitate my life of hard work; be as independent as I am; never have to depend on others—and then you can talk about dignity. / The word, in fact, means nothing to me, and I put it down to your peculiar ways, which are both affected and natural" (cited in E. and J. Crépet, ‹*Charles Baudelaire* [Paris, 1906],› appendix, p. 341). Baudelaire (*Lettres,* pp. 349ff.) writes back on the same day.[146] [J30a,2]

Hugo to Baudelaire, August 30, 1857. He acknowledges receipt of *Les Fleurs du mal.* "Art is like the heavens; it is the infinite field. You have just proved that. Your *Fleurs du mal* are as radiant and dazzling as the stars." Cited in Crépet, p. 113. Compare the great letter of October 6, 1859, containing the formula and credo of progress. [J30a,3]

Paul de Molènes to Baudelaire, May 14, 1860. "You have this gift for the new, something that has always seemed to me precious—indeed, almost sacred." Cited in Crépet, p. 413. [J30a,4]

Ange Pechméja, Bucharest, February 11–23, 1866. In this long letter full of great admiration, an exact outlook on *la poésie pure:* "I would say something more: I am convinced that, if the syllables that go to form verses of this kind were to be translated by the geometric forms and subtle colors which belong to them by analogy, they would possess the agreeable texture and beautiful tints of a Persian carpet or Indian shawl. / My idea will strike you as ridiculous; but I have often felt like drawing and coloring your verse." Cited in Crépet, p. 415.   [J30a,5]

Vigny to Baudelaire, January 27, 1862: "How . . . unjust you are, it seems to me, toward this lovely bouquet, so variously scented with odors of spring, for having given it a title it does not deserve, and how much I deplore that poisonous air which you sometimes pipe in from the murky bourne of Hamlet's graveyard." Cited in Crépet, p. 441.   [J30a,6]

From the letter that Baudelaire sent to Empress Eugénie, November 6, 1857: "But the fine, increased by costs that are unintelligible to me, exceeds the resources of the proverbial poverty of poets, and . . . , convinced that the heart of the Empress is open to pity for all tribulations, spiritual as well as material, I have conceived the idea, after a period of indecision and timidity that lasted ten days, of appealing to the gracious goodness of your Majesty and of entreating your intercession with the minister of justice."[147] H. Patry, "L'Epilogue du procès des *Fleurs du mal:* Une Lettre inédite de Baudelaire à l'Impératrice," *Revue d'histoire littéraire de la France,* 29th year (1922), p. 71.   [J31,1]

From Schaunard, *Souvenirs* (Paris, 1887): "'I detest the countryside,' says Baudelaire in explanation of his hasty departure from Honfleur, 'particularly in good weather. The persistent sunshine oppresses me. . . . Ah! speak to me of those everchanging Parisian skies that laugh or cry according to the wind, and that never, in their variable heat and humidity, have any effect on the stupid crops. . . . I am perhaps affronting your convictions as a landscape painter, but I must tell you further that an open body of water is a monstrous thing to me; I want it incarcerated, contained within the geometric walls of a quay. My favorite walking place is the embankment along the Canal de l'Ourcq'" (cited in Crépet, p. 160).   [J31,2]

Crépet juxtaposes Schaunard's report with the letter to Desnoyers, and then remarks in closing: "What can we conclude from all this? Perhaps simply that Baudelaire belonged to that family of unfortunates who desire only what they do not have and love only the place where they are not" (Crépet, p. 161).   [J31,3]

Baudelaire's *sincérité* was formerly much discussed. Traces of this debate are still to be found in Crépet (see p. 172).   [J31,4]

"The laughter of children is like the blossoming of a flower. . . . It is a plant-like joy. And so, in general, it is more like a smile—something analogous to the wagging of a dog's tail, or the purring of a cat. And if there still remains some distinction between the laughter of children and such expressions of animal contentment, . . . this is because their laughter is not entirely free of ambition, as is only proper to little scraps of men—that is, to budding Satans." "De l'Essence du rire," *Oeuvres*, ed. Le Dantec, vol. 2, p. 174.[148]   [J31,5]

Christ knew anger, and also tears; he did not laugh. Virginie would not laugh at the sight of a caricature. The sage does not laugh, nor does innocence. "The comic element is a damnable thing, and one of diabolical origin." "De l'Essence du rire," *Oeuvres*, ed. Le Dantec, vol. 2, p. 168.[149]   [J31a,1]

Baudelaire distinguishes the "significative comic" from the "absolute comic." The latter alone is a proper object of reflection: the grotesque.[150]   [J31a,2]

Allegorical interpretation of modern clothing for men, in the "Salon de 1846": "As for the garb, the outer husk, of the modern hero, . . . is it not the necessary garb of our suffering age, which wears the symbol of perpetual mourning even on its thin black shoulders? Notice how the black suit and the frock coat possess not only their political beauty, which is an expression of universal equality, but also their poetic beauty, which is an expression of the public soul—an endless procession of hired mourners, political mourners, amorous mourners, bourgeois mourners. We are all of us celebrating some funeral." *Oeuvres*, ed. Le Dantec, vol. 2, p. 134.[151]
[J31a,3]

The incomparable force of Poe's description of the crowd. One thinks of early lithographs by Senefelder, like "Der Spielclub" ⟨The Players' Club⟩, "Die Menge nach Einbruch der Dunkelheit" ⟨The Crowd after Nightfall⟩: "The rays of the gas lamps, feeble at first in their struggle with the dying day, had now at length gained ascendancy, and threw over everything a fitful and garish luster. All was dark yet splendid—as that ebony to which has been likened the style of Tertullian."[152] Edgar Poe, *Nouvelles Histoires extraordinaires*, trans. Charles Baudelaire (Paris ⟨1886⟩), p. 94. ▢ Flâneur ▢   [J31a,4]

"Imagination is not fantasy. . . . Imagination is an almost divine faculty which perceives . . . the intimate and secret relations of things, the correspondences and the analogies." ⟨Baudelaire,⟩ "Notes nouvelles sur Edgar Poe," *Nouvelles Histoires extraordinaires*, pp. 13–14.[153]   [J31a,5]

Purely emblematic book illustration—ornamented with devices—which Bracquemond had designed for the planned de luxe edition of *Les Fleurs du mal* around 1862. The only copy of the plate was sold by Champfleury, and later acquired by Avery (New York).   **[J31a,6]**

Concerning the conception of the crowd in Victor Hugo, two very characteristic passages from "La Pente de la rêverie" ⟨The Propensity for Reverie⟩:

> Crowd without name! Chaos!—Voices, eyes, footsteps.
> Those never seen, those never known.
> All the living!—cities buzzing in the ear
> More than any beehive or American woods.

The following passage shows the crowd depicted by Hugo as though with the burin of an engraver:

> The night with its crowd, in this hideous dream,
> Came on—growing denser and darker together—
> And, in these regions which no gaze can fathom,
> The increase of men meant the deepening of shadow.
> All became vague and uncertain; only a breath
> That from moment to moment would pass,
> As though to grant me a view of the great anthill,
> Opened in the far-reaching shadow some valleys of light,
> As the wind that blows over the tossing waves
> Whitens the foam, or furrows the wheat in the fields.

Victor Hugo, *Oeuvres complètes, Poésie,* vol. 2 (*Les Orientales, Feuilles d'automne*) (Paris, 1880), pp. 363, 365–366.   [J32,1]

Jules Troubat—Sainte-Beuve's secretary—to Poulet-Malassis, April 10, 1866: "See, then, how poets always end! Though the social machine revolves, and regulates itself for the bourgeoisie, for professional men, for workers, . . . no benevolent statute is being established to guarantee those unruly natures impatient of all restraint the possibility, at least, of dying in a bed of their own.—'But the brandy?' someone will ask. What of it? You too drink, Mister Bourgeois, Mister Grocer; you have as many vices as—and even more than—the poet. . . . Balzac burns himself out with coffee; Musset besots himself with absinthe and still produces his most beautiful stanzas; Murger dies alone in a nursing home, like Baudelaire at this very moment. And not one of these writers is a socialist!" (Cited in Crépet, ‹*Baudelaire* [Paris, 1906],› pp. 196–197.) The literary market.   [J32,2]

In a draft of the letter to Jules Janin (1865), Baudelaire plays Juvenal, Lucan, and Petronius off against Horace.   [J32,3]

Letter to Jules Janin: "melancholy, always inseparable from the feeling for beauty." *Oeuvres*, ed. Le Dantec, vol. 2, p. 610.   [J32,4]

"Every epic intention . . . is the result of an imperfect sense of art." ‹Baudelaire,› "Notes nouvelles sur Edgar Poe" (*Nouvelles Histoires extraordinaires* [Paris, 1886], p. 18).[154] This is, in embryo, the whole theory of "pure poetry." (Immobilization!)
                                                                            [J32,5]

According to Crépet (‹*Baudelaire* [Paris, 1906],› p. 155), most of the drawings left by Baudelaire portray "macabre scenes."   [J32a,1]

"Among all the books in the world today, the Bible being the sole exception, *Les Fleurs du mal* is the most widely published and the most often translated into other languages." André Suarès, *Trois Grands Vivants* (Paris ‹1938›), p. 269 ("Baudelaire et *Les Fleurs du mal*").   [J32a,2]

"The life of Baudelaire is a desert for anecdotes." André Suarès, *Trois Grands Vivants* (Paris), p. 270 ("Baudelaire et *Les Fleurs du mal*"). [J32a,3]

"Baudelaire does not describe." André Suarès, *Trois Grands Vivants* (Paris), p. 294 ("Baudelaire et *Les Fleurs du mal*"). [J32a,4]

In the "Salon de 1859," vehement invective against *l'amour*—apropos of a critique of the Neo-Greek school: "Yet aren't we quite weary of seeing paint and marble squandered on behalf of this elderly scamp . . . ? . . . His hair is thickly curled like a coachman's wig; his fat wobbling cheeks press against his nostrils and his eyes; it is doubtless the elegiac sighs of the universe which distend his flesh, or perhaps I should say his *meat*, for it is stuffed, tubulous, and blown out like a bag of lard hanging on a butcher's hook; on his mountainous back is attached a pair of butterfly wings." Ch. B., *Oeuvres*, ed. Le Dantec (Paris), vol. 2, p. 243.[155]

[J32a,5]

"There is a worthy publication in which every contributor knows all and has a word to say about all, a journal in which every member of the staff . . . can instruct us, by turns, in politics, religion, economics, the fine arts, philosophy, and literature. In this vast monument of fatuity, which leans toward the future like the Tower of Pisa, and in which nothing less than the happiness of humankind is being worked out . . ." Ch. B., *Oeuvres*, ed. Le Dantec (Paris), vol. 2, p. 258 ("Salon de 1859"). (*Le Globe?*)[156] [J32a,6]

In defense of Ricard: "Imitation is the intoxication of supple and brilliant minds, and often even a proof their superiority." Ch. B., *Oeuvres*, ed. Le Dantec, vol. 2, p. 263 ("Salon de 1859"). *Pro domo!*[157] [J32a,7]

"That touch of slyness which is always mingled with innocence." Ch. B., *Oeuvres*, ed. Le Dantec, vol. 2, p. 264 ("Salon de 1859"). On Ricard.[158] [J32a,8]

Vigny in "Le Mont des oliviers" ‹Mount of Olives›, against de Maistre:

> He has been on this earth for many long ages,
> Born from harsh masters and false-speaking sages,
> Who still vex the spirit of each living nation
> With spurious conceptions of my true redemption.[159] [J33,1]

"Perhaps only Leopardi, Edgar Poe, and Dostoevsky experienced such a dearth of happiness, such a power of desolation. Round about him, this century, which in other respects seems so flourishing and multifarious, takes on the terrrible aspect of a desert." Edmond Jaloux, "Le Centenaire de Baudelaire," *La Revue hebdomadaire*, 30th year, no. 27 (July 2, 1921), p. 77. [J33,2]

"All by himself, Baudelaire made poetry a method of analysis, a form of introspection. In this, he is very much the contemporary of Flaubert or of Claude Bernard." Edmond Jaloux, "Le Centenaire de Baudelaire," *La Revue hebdo-madaire*, 30th year, no. 27 (July 2, 1921), p. 69. [J33,3]

List of Baudelaire's topics, in Jaloux: "nervous irritability of the individual devoted to solitude . . . ; abhorrence of the human condition and the need to confer dignity upon it through religion or *through art* . . . ; love of debauchery in order to forget or punish oneself . . . ; passion for travel, for the unknown, for the new; . . . predilection for whatever gives rise to thoughts of death (twilight, autumn, dismal scenes) . . . ; adoration of the artificial; complacency in spleen." Edmond Jaloux, "Le Centenaire de Baudelaire," *La Revue hebdomadaire,* 30th year, no. 27 (July 2, 1921), p. 69. Here we see how an exclusive regard for psychological considerations blocks insight into Baudelaire's genuine originality. [J33,4]

Influence of *Les Fleurs du mal,* around 1885, on Rops, Moreau, Rodin. [J33,5]

Influence of "Les Correspondances" on Mallarmé. [J33,6]

Baudelaire's influence on Realism, then on Symbolism. Moréas, in the Symbolist manifesto of September 18, 1886 (*Le Figaro*): "Baudelaire must be considered the true precursor of the present movement in poetry." [J33,7]

Claudel: "Baudelaire has celebrated the only passion which the nineteenth century could feel with sincerity: Remorse." Cited in *Le Cinquantenaire de Charles Baudelaire* (Paris, 1917), p. 43. ‹Compare J53,1.› [J33,8]

"A Dantesque nightmare." Leconte de Lisle, cited in *Le Cinquantenaire de Charles Baudelaire* (Paris, 1917), p. 17. [J33a,1]

Edouard Thierry compares *Les Fleurs de mal* to the ode written by Mirabeau during his imprisonment at Vincennes. Cited in *Le Cinquantenaire de Charles Baudelaire* (Paris, 1917), p. 19. [J33a,2]

Verlaine (where?): "The profound originality of Baudelaire is . . . to have represented, in a powerful and essential way, modern man. . . . By this, I mean only modern man in the physical sense . . . , modern man with his senses stirred up and vibrating, his spirit painfully subtle, his brains saturated with tobacco, and his blood on fire with alcohol. . . . Charles Baudelaire . . . may be said to personify the ideal type, the Hero if you will, of this individuality in sensitivity. Nowhere else, not even in Heinrich Heine, will you find it accentuated so strongly." Cited in *Le Cinquantenaire de Charles Baudelaire* (Paris, 1917), p. 18. [J33a,3]

Lesbian motifs in Balzac (*La Fille aux yeux d'or*); Gautier (*Mademoiselle de Maupin*); Delatouche (*Fragoletta*). [J33a,4]

Poems for Marie Daubrun: "Chant d'automne," "Sonnet d'automne." [J33a,5]

Meryon and Baudelaire were born in the same year; Meryon died a year after Baudelaire. [J33a,6]

In the years 1842–1845, according to Prarond, Baudelaire was fascinated with a portrait of a woman by Greco in the Louvre. Cited in Crépet, ‹*Charles Baudelaire* [Paris, 1906],› p. 70. [J33a,7]

Project dated May 1846: "Les Amours et la mort de Lucain" ‹The Loves and the Death of Lucan›. [J33a,8]

"He was twenty-two years old, and he found himself immediately provided with employment at the town hall of the seventh *arrondissement*—'in the Registry of Deaths,' he kept repeating with an air of satisfaction." Maurice Rollinat, *Fin d'oeuvre*; cited in Gustave Geffroy, *Maurice Rollinat, 1846–1903* (Paris, 1919), p. 5. [J33a,9]

Barbey d'Aurevilly has placed Rollinat between Poe and Baudelaire; and he calls Rollinat "a poet of the tribe of Dante." Cited in Geffroy, *Maurice Rollinat*, p. 8. [J33a,10]

Composition of Baudelairean poems by Rollinat. [J33a,11]

"La Voix" ‹The Voice›: "in the pit's deepest dark, I distinctly see strange worlds."[160] [J33a,12]

According to Charles Toubin, Baudelaire in 1847 had two domiciles, on the Rue de Seine and the Rue de Babylone. On days when the rent was due, he often spent the night with friends in a third. See Crépet, ‹*Charles Baudelaire*, (Paris, 1906),› p. 48. [J34,1]

Crépet (p. 47) counts fourteen addresses for Baudelaire between 1842 and 1858, not including Honfleur and some temporary lodgings. He lived in the Quartier du Temple, the Ile Saint-Louis, the Quartier Saint-Germain, the Quartier Mont-martre, the Quartier de la République. [J34,2]

"You are passing through a great city that has grown old in civilization—one of those cities which harbor the most important archives of universal life—and your eyes are drawn upward, *sursum, ad sidera;* for in the public squares, at the corners of the crossways, stand motionless figures, larger than those who pass at their feet, repeating to you the solemn legends of Glory, War, Science, and Martyr-dom, in a mute language. Some are pointing to the sky, whither they ceaselessly aspired; others indicate the earth from which they sprang. They brandish, or they contemplate, what was the passion of their life and what has become its emblem: a tool, a sword, a book, a torch, *vitai lampada!* Be you the most heedless of men, the most unhappy or the vilest, a beggar or a banker, the stone phantom takes possession of you for a few minutes and commands you, in the name of the past, to think of things which are not of the earth. / Such is the divine role of sculpture." Ch. B., *Oeuvres,* ed. Le Dantec, vol, 2, pp. 274–275 ("Salon de 1859").[161] Baudelaire speaks here of sculpture as though it were present only in the big city. It is a sculpture that stands in the way of the passerby. This depiction contains something in the highest degree prophetic, though sculpture plays only the smallest part in that which would fulfill the prophecy. Sculpture is found ‹?› only in the city.   [J34,3]

Baudelaire speaks of his partiality for "the landscape of romance," more and more avoided by painters. From his description, it becomes evident that he is thinking of structures essentially Baroque: "But surely our landscape painters are far too herbivorous in their diet? They never willingly take their nourishment from ruins. . . . I feel a longing for . . . crenellated abbeys, reflected in gloomy pools; for gigantic bridges, towering Ninevite constructions, haunts of dizziness—for everything, in short, which would have to be invented if it did not already exist!" Ch. B., *Oeuvres,* ed. Le Dantec, vol. 2, p. 272 ("Salon de 1859").[162]
                                                                                                                                    [J34,4]

"Imagination . . . decomposes all creation; and with the raw materials accumulated and disposed in accordance with rules whose origins one cannot find except in the furthest depths of the soul, it creates a new world—it produces the sensation of newness." Ch. B., *Oeuvres*, vol. 2, p. 226 ("Salon de 1859").[163]   [J34a,1]

On the ignorance of painters, with particular reference to Troyon: "He paints on and on; he stops up his soul and continues to paint, until at last he becomes like the artist of the moment. . . . The imitator of the imitator finds his own imitators, and in this way each pursues his dream of greatness, stopping up his soul more and more thoroughly, and above all *reading nothing*, not even *The Perfect Cook*, which at any rate would have been able to open up for him a career of greater glory, if less profit." Ch. B., *Oeuvres*, vol. 2, p. 219 ("Salon de 1859").[164]
                                                                                                                                    [J34a,2]

"The pleasure of being in a crowd is a mysterious expression of sensual joy in the multiplication of number. . . . Number is in *all*. . . . Ecstasy is a number. . . . Religious intoxication of great cities." Ch. B., *Oeuvres,* vol. 2, pp. 626–627 ("Fusées").[165] Extract the root of the human being!   [J34a,3]

"The arabesque is the most spiritualistic of designs." Ch. B., *Oeuvres*, vol. 2, p. 629 ("Fusées").[166]   [J34a,4]

"For my part, I say: the sole and supreme pleasure of love lies in the absolute knowledge of doing *evil*. And man and woman know, from birth, that in evil is to be found all voluptuousness." Ch. B., *Oeuvres*, vol. 2, p. 628 ("Fusées").[167]
                                                                                                                                    [J34a,5]

"Voltaire jests about our immortal soul, which has dwelt for nine months amid excrement and urine. . . . He might, at least, have traced, in this localization, a malicious gibe or satire directed by Providence against love, and, in the way humans procreate, a sign of original sin. After all, we can make love only with the organs of excretion." Ch. Baudelaire, *Oeuvres,* vol. 2, p. 651 ("Mon Coeur mis à nu").[168] At this point, Lawrence's defense of Lady Chatterley should be mentioned. [J34a,6]

Beginnings, with Baudelaire, of a devious rationalization of the charms exerted on him by prostitution: "Love may arise from a generous sentiment—namely, the liking for prostitution; but it soon becomes corrupted by the liking for ownership" ("Fusées"), "The human heart's ineradicable love of prostitution—source of man's horror of solitude. . . . The man of genius wants to be *one*—that is, solitary. / The glorious thing . . . is to remain *one* by practicing your prostitution in your own company" ("Mon Coeur mis à nu"). Vol. 2, pp. 626, 661.[169] [J34a,7]

In 1835 Cazotte's *Le Diable amoureux* is published, with a preface by Gérard de Nerval. Baudelaire's line in "Le Possédé"—"Mon cher Belzébuth, je t'adore"—is an explicit citation of Cazotte. "Baudelaire's verse has a demoniacal sound much stranger than the diabolism of the age of Louis Philippe." Claudius Grillet, *Le Diable dans la littérature au XIXe siècle* (Lyons and Paris, 1935), pp. 95–96. [J35,1]

Letter to his mother on December 26, 1853: "Besides, I am so accustomed to physical discomforts; I know so well how to put two shirts under a torn coat and trousers so threadbare that the wind cuts through them; I know so well how to put straw or even paper soles in worn-out shoes that I hardly feel anything except moral suffering. Nevertheless, I must confess that I have reached the point of being afraid to make brusque movements or to walk very much, for fear of tearing my clothes even more." Ch. B., *Dernières Lettres inédites à sa mère,* introduction and notes by Jacques Crépet (Paris, 1926), pp. 44–45.[170] [J35,2]

The Goncourts report in their journal on June 6, 1883, the visit of a young man from whom they learn that the budding scholars at the high school are divided into two camps. The future students of the Ecole Normale have taken About and Sarcey as their models; the others, Edmond de Goncourt and Baudelaire. *Journal des Goncourts,* vol. 6 (Paris, 1892), p. 264. [J35,3]

To his mother on March 4, 1860, concerning etchings by Meryon: "The hideous and colossal figure in the frontispiece is one of the figures decorating the exterior of Notre Dame. In the background is Paris, viewed from a height. How the devil this man manages to work so calmly over an abyss, I do not know." Ch. B., *Dernières Lettres à sa mère,* introduction and notes by Jacques Crépet (Paris, 1926), pp. 132–133. [J35,4]

In the *Dernières Lettres* (p. 145), this phrase for Jeanne: "that aged beauty who has now become an invalid."[171] He wants to leave her an annuity after his death.

[J35,5]

Decisive for the confrontation between Baudelaire and Hugo is a passage from Hugo's letter of November 17, 1859, to Villemain: "Sometimes I spend the whole night meditating on my fate, before the great deep, and . . . all I can do is exclaim: Stars! Stars! Stars!" Cited in Claudius Grillet, *Victor Hugo spirite* (Lyons and Paris, 1929), p. 100.[172]

[J35,6]

The multitudes in Hugo: "The prophet seeks out solitude. . . . He goes into the desert to think. Of what? Of the multitudes." Hugo, *William Shakespeare*, ⟨part 2, book⟩ 6.

[J35,7]

Allegory in the spiritualist protocols from Jersey: "Even pure abstractions frequented Marine-Terrace: Idea, Death, the Drama, the Novel, Poetry, Criticism, Humbug. They . . . preferred to make their appearance during the day, while the dead came at night." Claudius Grillet, *Victor Hugo spirite* (Lyons and Paris, 1929), p. 27.

[J35a,1]

The "multitudes" in Hugo figure as the "depths of the shadow" in *Les Châtiments* ("La Caravane," part 4), *Oeuvres complètes*, vol. 4, *Poésie* (Paris, 1882), p. 397: "The day when our plunderers, our tyrants beyond number, / Will know that someone stirs in the depths of the shadow."

[J35a,2]

On *Les Fleurs du mal*: "Nowhere does he make a direct allusion to hashish or to opium visions. In this we must admire the superior taste of the poet, completely taken up as he is with the philosophic construction of his poem." Georges Rodenbach, *L'Elite* (Paris, 1899), pp. 18–19.

[J35a,3]

Rodenbach (p. 19) emphasizes, like Béguin, the *experience* of the *correspondances* in Baudelaire.

[J35a,4]

Baudelaire to ⟨Barbey⟩ d'Aurevilly: "Should you take Communion with hands on hips?" Cited in Georges Rodenbach, *L'Elite* (Paris, 1899), p. 6.

[J35a,5]

Three generations (according to Georges Rodenbach, *L'Elite* [Paris, 1899], pp. 6–7) revolve about the "splendid restoration of Notre Dame." The first, forming as it were an outer circle, is represented by Victor Hugo. The second, represented by ⟨Barbey⟩ d'Aurevilly, Baudelaire, and Hello, forms an inner circle of devotion. The third is made up of the group of satanists: Huysmans, Guaita, Péladan.

[J35a,6]

"However beautiful a house may be, it is first of all—before we consider its beauty—so many feet high and so many feet wide. Likewise, literature, which is the most priceless material, is first of all the filling up of so many columns, and a literary architect whose name in itself is not a guarantee of profit has to sell at all kinds of prices." Ch. B., *Oeuvres*, vol. 2, p. 385 ("Conseils aux jeunes littérateurs").[173]   [J35a,7]

Note from "Fusées": "The portrait of *Serenus* by Seneca. That of *Stagirus* by Saint John Chrysostom. *Acedia*, the malady of monks. *Taedium vitae . . .*" Charles Baudelaire, *Oeuvres*, vol. 2, p. 632.[174]   [J35a,8]

Charles-Henry Hirsch describes Baudelaire, in comparison to Hugo, as "more capable of adapting to widely varying temperaments, thanks to the keenness of his ideas, sensations, and words. . . . The lessons of Baudelaire endure by virtue of . . . the strict form which keeps them before our eyes." Cited in *Le Cinquantenaire de Charles Baudelaire* (Paris, 1917), p. 41.   [J36,1]

A remark by Nadar in his memoirs: Around 1911, the director of an agency for newspaper clippings told him that Baudelaire's name used to show up in the newspapers as often as the names of Hugo, Musset, and Napoleon. See *Le Cinquantenaire de Charles Baudelaire* (Paris, 1917), p. 43.   [J36,2]

Passage from *Le Salut publique* attributed by Crépet to Baudelaire: "Citizens should not give heed . . . to such as these—to Barthélemy, Jean Journet, and others who extol the republic in execrable verse. The emperor Nero had the laudable habit of rounding up all the bad poets in an amphitheater and flogging them cruelly." Cited in Crépet, ‹*Charles Baudelaire* (Paris, 1906),› p. 81.   [J36,3]

Passage from *Le Salut publique* attributed by Crépet to Baudelaire: "Intellects have grown. No more tragedies, no more Roman history. Are we not greater today than Brutus?" Cited in Crépet, p. 81.   [J36,4]

Crépet (p. 82) quotes the *Notes de M. Champfleury:* "De Flotte perhaps belongs with Wronski, Blanqui, Swedenborg, and others, in that somewhat bizarre pantheon which lately elevated Baudelaire, following upon the reading of his texts, the events of the day, and the notoriety attained overnight by certain figures."   [J36,5]

"The work of Edgar Poe—with the exception of few beautiful poems—is the body of an art from which Baudelaire has blasted the soul." André Suarès, *Sur la Vie* (Paris, 1925), vol. 2, p. 99 ("Idées sur Edgar Poe").   [J36,6]

Baudelaire's theory of imagination, as well as his doctrine of the short poem and the short story, are influenced by Poe. The theory of *l'art pour l'art,* in Baudelaire's formulation, seems to be a plagiarism.   [J36,7]

In his commemorative address, Banville draws attention to Baudelaire's classical technique.   [J36,8]

"Comment on paie ses dettes quand on a du génie" ‹How a Genius Pays His Debts› appeared in 1846 and contains, under the appellative "the second friend," the following portrait of Gautier: "The second friend was, and still is, fat, lazy, and sluggish; what is more, he has no ideas and can only string words together as the Osage strings beads for a necklace." Ch. B., *Oeuvres*, vol. 2, p. 393.[175]   [J36a,1]

Hugo: "As for me, I am conscious of the starry gulf in my soul." "Ave, dea—moriturus te salutat: A Judith Gautier," Victor Hugo, *Oeuvres choisies: Poésies et drames en vers* (Paris ‹1912›), p. 404.   [J36a,2]

In his famous description of the lecture Baudelaire gave on Gautier in Brussels, Camille Lemonnier represents in a fascinating way the mounting perplexity into which the lecturer's positive glorification of Gautier plunged the audience. They had got the impression, as the talk went on, that Baudelaire was going to turn with some inimitable sarcasm from all he had said, as from a kind of decoy, in order to develop a different conception of poetry. And this expectation paralyzed the listeners.   [J36a,3]

Baudelaire—Camille Pelletan's favorite poet. So says Robert de Bonnières, *Mémoires d'aujourd'hui*, vol. 3 (Paris, 1888), p. 239.   [J36a,4]

Robert de Bonnières, *Mémoires d'aujourd'hui*, vol. 3 (Paris, 1888), publishes, on pp. 287–288, an exasperated letter sent to Taine by the director of *La Revue libérale* on January 19, 1864, in which he complains of the intransigence displayed by Baudelaire in the course of negotiations over cuts in the piece "Les Vocations" (*Spleen de Paris*).   [J36a,5]

A passage from Rodenbach that exemplifies something typical in the description of the city—namely, the forced metaphor: "In these cities saddened by a choir of weathercocks, / Birds of iron dreaming [!] of flight to the skies." Cited in G. Tourquet-Milnes, *The Influence of Baudelaire in France and England* (London, 1913), p. 191.—Parisian modernity!   [J36a,6]

In the "Salon de 1846" one sees how precise Baudelaire's concept of a politics of art already was at that time: section 12 ("De l'Eclectisme et du doute") and section 14 ("De Quelques Douteurs") show that Baudelaire was conscious early on of the need to bring artistic production into line with certain fixed points. In section 17 ("Des Ecoles et des ouvriers"), Baudelaire speaks of atomization as a symptom of weakness. He lauds the schools of old: "*Then* you had schools of painting; *now* you have emancipated journeymen . . .—a school, . . . that is, the impossibility of doubt." Ch. B., *Oeuvres,* vol. 2, p. 131.[176] Compare *le poncif!*
                                                                                    [J36a,7]

On a sheet with the sketch of a female figure and two portraits of a male head, an inscription[177] dating back to the nineteenth century: "Portrait of Blanqui (Auguste), a good likeness drawn from memory by Baudelaire in 1850, perhaps 1849?" Reproduction in Féli Gautier, *Charles Baudelaire* (Brussels, 1904), p. lii.
[J37,1]

"He would *churn* his brains in order to produce astonishment." This comment by Leconte de Lisle occurs in the untitled article by Jules Claretie that appears in *Le Tombeau* and that reprints substantial portions of Claretie's obituary notice. *Le Tombeau de Charles Baudelaire* (Paris, 1896), p. 91. Effect of the endings of poems!
[J37,2]

"O Poet, you who turned the work of Dante upside down, / Exalting Satan to the heights and descending to God." Closing lines of Verhaeren's "A Charles Baude-laire," in *Le Tombeau de Charles Baudelaire* (Paris, 1896), p. 84.   [J37,3]

In *Le Tombeau de Charles Baudelaire* (Paris, 1896), there is a text by Alexandre Ourousof, "L'Architecture secrète des *Fleurs du mal.*" It represents an oft-repeated attempt to establish distinct cycles in the book, and consists essentially in the selection of the poems inspired by Jeanne Duval. It makes reference to the article published by ⟨Barbey⟩ d'Aurevilly in *Le Pays* on July 24, 1857, in which it was maintained for the first time that there is a "secret architecture" in the book.
[J37,4]

"The echoes of the unconscious are so strong in him—literary creation being, with him, so close to physical effort—the currents of passion are so strong, so drawn out, so slow and painful, that all his psychic being resides there with his physical being." Gustave Kahn, preface to Charles Baudelaire, *"Mon Coeur mis à nu" et "Fusées"* (Paris, 1909), p. 5.   [J37,5]

"If Poe had been a real influence on him, we would find some trace of this in Baudelaire's way of imagining . . . scenes of action. In fact, the greater his immer-sion in the work of the American writer, the more he avoids fantasies of action. . . . His projected works, his titles for novels . . . all had to do with various . . . psychic crises. Not one suggests an adventure of any kind." Gustave Kahn, preface to Charles Baudelaire, *"Mon Coeur mis à nu" et "Fusées"* (Paris, 1909), pp. 12–13.
[J37,6]

Kahn discerns in Baudelaire a "refusal to take the opportunity offered by the nature of the lyric pretext." Gustave Kahn, preface to Ch. B., *"Mon Coeur mis à nu" et "Fusées"* (Paris, 1909), p. 15.   [J37,7]

Of the *Fleurs du mal* illustrated by Rodin for Paul Gallimard, Mauclair writes: "You feel that Rodin has handled the book, taken it up and put it down a hundred times, that he has read it while out on walks, and at the end of a long evening has suddenly reopened it under the lamplight and, haunted by a verse, picked up his pen. One can tell where he paused, what page he creased [!], how unsparing he must have been of the volume; for he had not been given some de luxe copy needing to be protected from damage. It was very much, as he himself liked to describe it, 'his' pocket Baudelaire." Charles Baudelaire, *Vingt-Sept Poèmes des Fleurs du mal, illustrés par Rodin* (Paris, 1918), p. 7 (preface by Camille Mauclair).

[J37a,1]

The penultimate paragraph in "Chacun sa chimère" ‹To Every Man His Chimera› is distinctly reminiscent of Blanqui: "And the procession passed by me and disappeared in the haze at the horizon, just where the rounded surface of the planet prevents the human gaze from following." Ch. B., *Oeuvres,* vol. 1, p. 412.[178]

[J37a,2]

On the painter Jules Noël: "He is doubtless one of those who impose a daily amount of progress upon themselves." "Salon de 1846," *Oeuvres*, vol. 2, p. 126.[179]

[J37a,3]

In the comment on *Les Fleurs du mal* that Sainte-Beuve sends to Baudelaire in a letter of ‹June› 20, 1857, he finds this to say about the style of the book: "a curious poetic gift and an almost *precious* lack of constraint in expression." Immediately following: "with your *pearling* of the detail, with your *Petrarchism* of the horrible." Cited in Etienne Charavay, *A. de Vigny et Charles Baudelaire, candidats à l'Académie française* (Paris, 1879), p. 134.

[J37a,4]

"It seems to me that in many things you do not take yourself seriously enough." Vigny to Baudelaire on January 27, 1862, apropos of Baudelaire's candidacy for the Académie. Cited in Etienne Charavay, *A. de Vigny et Charles Baudelaire, candidats à l'Académie française* (Paris, 1879), pp. 100–101.

[J37a,5]

Jules Mouquet, in ‹the introduction to› his edition of Ch‹arles› B‹audelaire›, *Vers retrouvés: Manoël* (Paris, 1929), looks into the relation between Baudelaire and the poems published by ‹G.› Le Vavasseur, E. Prarond, and A. Argonne in *Vers* (Paris, 1843). There turn out to be a number of filiations. Apart from actual contributions by Baudelaire that appear in the second section under the name of Prarond, there are important correspondences, in particular that of "Le Rêve d'un curieux"[180] to "Le Rêve," by Argonne (pseudonym of Auguste Dozon).

[J37a,6]

Among the twenty-three poems of *Les Fleurs du mal* known to have been composed by the summer of 1843: "Allégorie," "Je n'ai pas oublié," "La Servante au grand coeur," "Le Crépuscule du matin."

[J38,1]

"Baudelaire feels a certain reserve about showing his work to the public; he publishes his poems under successive pseudonyms: Prarond, Privat d'Anglemont,

Pierre de Fayis. 'La Fanfarlo' appears . . . on January 1, 1847, signed by Charles Dufays." Ch. B., *Vers retrouvés*, ed. Jules Mouquet (Paris, 1929), p. 47.   [J38,2]

The following sonnet from the body of work by Prarond is attributed by Mouquet to Baudelaire:

> Born in the mud to a nameless jade,
> The child grew up speaking argot;
> By the age of ten, he had graduated from the sewers;
> Grown, he would sell his sister—is a jack-of-all-trades.
>
> His back has the curve of an old flying buttress;
> He can sniff out the way to every cheap bordello;
> His look is a mixture of arrogance and cunning;
> He's the one to serve as watchdog for rioters.
>
> Wax-coated string keeps his thin soles in place;
> On his uncovered pallet a dirty wench laughs
> To think of her husband deceived by unchaste Paris.
>
> Plebeian orator of the stockroom,
> He talks politics with the corner grocer.
> Here is what's called an *enfant de Paris*.

Charles Baudelaire, *Vers retrouvés*, ed. Jules Mouquet (Paris, 1929), pp. 103–104.   [J38,3]

Freund contends "that the musicality of the poem does not present itself as a specific . . . technical quality but is rather the authentic ethos of the poet. . . . Musicality is the form taken by *l'art pour l'art* in poetry." Cajetan Freund, *Der Vers Baudelaires* (Munich, 1927), p. 46.   [J38,4]

On the publication of poems under the title *Les Limbes* ‹Limbo› in *Le Messager de l'Assemblée*, April 9, 1851: "A small booklet entitled *La Presse de 1848* contains the following: 'Today we see announced in *L'Echo des marchands de vin* a collection of poems called *Les Limbes*. These are *without doubt* socialist poems and, consequently, bad poems. Yet another fellow has become a disciple of Proudhon through either *too much* or *too little* ignorance.'" A. de la Finelière and Georges Descaux, *Charles Baudelaire* (series entitled *Essais de bibliographie contemporaine*, vol. 1) (Paris, 1868), p. 12.   [J38,5]

Modernity—anticlassical and classical. Anticlassical: as antithesis to the classical period. Classical: as heroic fulfillment of the epoch that puts its stamp on its expression.   [J38a,1]

There is evidently a connection between Baudelaire's unfavorable reception in Belgium, his reputation as a police spy there, and the letter to *Le Figaro* concerning the banquet for Victor Hugo.[181]   [J38a,2]

Note the rigor and elegance of the title *Curiosités esthétiques*.[182]   [J38a,3]

The teachings of Fourier: "Although, in nature, there are certain plants which are more or less holy, certain . . . animals more or less sacred; and although . . . we may rightly conclude that certain nations . . . have been prepared . . . by Providence for a determined goal . . .—nevertheless all I wish to do here is assert their *equal* utility in the eyes of Him who is undefinable." Ch. B., *Oeuvres*, vol. 2, p. 143 ("Exposition Universelle, 1855").[183]   [J38a,4]

"One of those *narrow-minded modern professors* of aesthetics (as they are called by Heinrich Heine), . . . whose stiffened fingers, paralyzed by the pen, can no longer run with agility over the immense keyboard of *correspondences!*" Ch. B., *Oeuvres*, vol. 2, p. 145 ("Exposition Universelle, 1855").[184]   [J38a,5]

"In the manifold productions of art, there is something always new which will forever escape the rules and analyses of the school!" Ch. B., *Oeuvres*, vol. 2, p. 146 ("Exposition Universelle, 1855").[185] Analogy to fashion.   [J38a,6]

To the notion of progress in the history of art, Baudelaire opposes a monadological conception. "Transferred into the sphere of the imagination . . . , the idea of progress looms up with gigantic absurdity. . . . In the poetic and artistic order, inventors rarely have predecessors. Every flowering is spontaneous, individual. Was Signorelli really the begetter of Michelangelo? Did Perugino contain Raphael? The artist depends on himself alone. He can promise nothing to future centuries except his own works." Ch. B., *Oeuvres,* vol. 2, p. 149 ("Exposition Universelle, 1855").[186]   [J38a,7]

Toward a critique of the concept of progress in general: "For this is how disciples of the philosophers of steam and sulfur matches understand it: progress appears to them only in the form of an indefinite series. Where is that guarantee?" Ch. B., *Oeuvres*, vol. 2, p. 149 ("Exposition Universelle, 1855").[187]   [J38a,8]

"The story is told of Balzac . . . that one day he found himself in front of a . . . melancholy winter scene, heavy with hoarfrost and thinly sprinkled with cottages and wretched-looking peasants; and that, after gazing at a little house from which a thin wisp of smoke was rising, he cried, 'How beautiful it is! But what are they doing in that cottage? What are their thoughts? What are their sorrows? Has it been a good harvest? *No doubt they have bills to pay?*' Laugh if you will at M. de Balzac. I do not know the name of the painter whose honor it was to set the great novelist's soul a-quiver with anxiety and conjecture; but I think that in this way . . . he has given us an excellent lesson in criticism. You will often find me appraising a picture exclusively for the sum of ideas or of dreams that it suggests to my mind." Ch. B., *Oeuvres*, vol. 2, p. 147 ("Exposition Universelle, 1855").[188]

[J39,1]

Conclusion of the "Salon de 1845": "The painter, the true painter for whom we are looking, will be he who can snatch its epic quality from the life of today and can make us see and understand, with brush or with pencil, how great and poetic we are in our cravats and our patent-leather boots. Next year let us hope that the true seekers may grant us the extraordinary delight of celebrating the advent of the *new!*" Ch. B., *Oeuvres*, vol. 2, pp. 54–55.[189]   [J39,2]

"As for the garb, the outer husk, of the modern hero . . . , has not this much-maligned garb its own native beauty and charm? Is it not the necessary garb of our suffering age, which wears the symbol of perpetual mourning even on its thin black shoulders? Notice how the black suit and the frock coat possess not only their political beauty, which is an expression of universal equality, but also their poetic beauty, which is an expression of the public soul—an endless procession of hired mourners, political mourners, amorous mourners, bourgeois mourners. We are all of us celebrating some funeral. / A uniform livery of mourning bears witness to equality. . . . Don't these puckered creases, playing like serpents around the mortified flesh, have their own mysterious grace? / . . . For the heroes of the *Iliad* cannot compare with you, O Vautrin, O Rastignac, O Birotteau—nor with you, O Fontanarès, who dared not publicly recount your sorrows wearing the funereal and rumpled frock coat of today; nor with you, O Honoré de Balzac, you the most heroic, the most amazing, the most romantic and the most poetic of all the characters that you have drawn from your fertile bosom!" Ch. B., *Oeuvres*, vol. 2, pp. 134, 136 ("Salon de 1846: De l'Héroïsme de la vie moderne").[190] The last sentence concludes the section.   [J39,3]

"For when I hear men like Raphael and Veronese being lauded to the skies, with the manifest intention of diminishing the merit of those who came after them, . . . I ask myself if a merit which is *at least* the equal of theirs (I will even admit for a moment, and out of pure compliance, that it may be inferior) is not infinitely more *meritorious,* since it has triumphantly evolved in an atmosphere and a territory which are hostile to it." Ch. B., *Oeuvres,* vol. 2, p. 239 ("Salon de 1859").[191] Lukács says that to make a decent table today, a man needs all the genius once required of Michelangelo to complete the dome of St. Peter's.
                    [J39a,1]

Baudelaire's attitude toward progress was not always the same. Certain declarations in the "Salon de 1846" contrast clearly with remarks made later. In that essay we find, among other things: "There are as many kinds of beauty as there are habitual ways of seeking happiness. This is clearly explained by the philosophy of progress. . . . Romanticism will not consist in a perfect execution, but in a conception analogous to the ethical disposition of the age" (p. 66). In the same text: "Delacroix is the latest expression of progress in art" (p. 85). Ch. B., *Oeuvres,* vol. 2.[192]   [J39a,2]

The importance of theory for artistic creation was not something about which Baudelaire was clear, initially. In the "Salon de 1845," discussing the painter Haussoullier, he asks: "Is M. Haussoullier perhaps one of those who know too much about their art? That is a truly dangerous scourge." Ch. B., *Oeuvres,* vol. 2, p. 23.[193]   [J39a,3]

A critique of the idea of progress, such as may become necessary in connection with a presentation of Baudelaire, must take great care to differentiate itself from the latter's own critique of progress. This applies still more unconditionally to Baudelaire's critique of the nineteenth century and to that entailed by his biography. It is a mark of the warped and crassly ignorant portrait of Baudelaire drawn by Peter Klassen that the poet should appear against the background of a century painted in the colors of Gehenna. The only thing in this century really worthy of praise, in the author's view, is a certain clerical practice—namely, that moment "when, in token of the reestablished kingdom of the grace of God, the Holy of Holies was carried through the streets of Paris in an entourage of shining armaments. This will have been an experience decisive, because fundamental, for his entire existence." So begins this presentation of the poet framed in the depraved categories of the George circle. Peter Klassen, *Baudelaire* (Weimar ‹1931›), p. 9.
                                                                                               [J39a,4]

Gauloiserie in Baudelaire: "To organize a grand conspiracy for the extermination of the Jewish race. / The Jews who are *librarians* and bear witness to the *Redemption*." Ch. B., *Oeuvres,* vol. 2, p. 666 ("Mon Coeur mis à nu").[194] Céline has continued along these lines. (Cheerful assassins!)   [J40,1]

"More military metaphors: 'The poets of combat.' 'The vanguard of literature.' This weakness for military metaphors is a sign of natures that are not themselves militant, but are made for discipline—that is to say, for conformity. Natures congenitally domestic, Belgian natures that can think only in unison." Ch. B., *Oeuvres*, vol. 2, p. 654 ("Mon Coeur mis à nu").[195]   [J40,2]

"If a poet demanded from the state the right to keep a few bourgeois in his stable, people would be very surprised; whereas if a bourgeois demanded a roast poet, people would find this quite natural." Ch. B., *Oeuvres*, vol. 2, p. 635 ("Fusées").[196]   [J40,3]

"This book is not made for my wives, my daughters, or my sisters.—I have little to do with such things." Ch. B., *Oeuvres*, vol. 2, p. 635 ("Fusées").[197]   [J40,4]

Baudelaire's estrangement from the age: "Tell me in what salon, in what tavern, in what social or intimate gathering you have heard a single witty remark uttered by a spoiled child [compare p. 217: "The artist is today . . . but a *spoiled child*"] a profound remark, to make one ponder or dream . . . ? If such a remark has been thrown out, it may indeed have been not by a politician or a philosopher, but by someone of an outlandish profession, like a hunter, a sailor, or a taxidermist. But by an artist . . . , never." Ch. B., *Oeuvres,* vol. 2, p. 217 ("Salon de 1859"). This is a sort of evocation of the "amazing travelers."[198]   [J40,5]

Gauloiserie in Baudelaire: "In its most widely accepted sense, the word 'Frenchman' means *vaudevilliste.* . . . Everything that towers or plunges, above or below him, causes him prudently to take to his heels. The sublime always affects him like a riot, and he opens his Molière only in fear and trembling—and because someone has persuaded him that Molière is an amusing author." Ch. B., *Oeuvres,* vol. 2, p. 111 ("Salon de 1846: De M. Horace Vernet").[199]   [J40,6]

Baudelaire knows, in the "Salon de 1846," "the fatal law of propensities." Ch. B., *Oeuvres,* vol. 2, p. 114.[200]   [J40,7]

Re the title *Les Limbes* ‹Limbo›, compare the passage from the "Salon de 1846" on Delacroix's painting *Women of Algiers:* "This little poem of an interior . . . seems somehow to exhale the heady scent of a house of ill repute, which quickly enough guides our thoughts toward the *fathomless* limbo of sadness." Ch. B., *Oeuvres,* vol. 2, p. 85.[201]   [J40,8]

Apropos a depiction of Samson by Decamps, in the "Salon de 1845": "Samson, that ancient cousin of Hercules and Baron von Münchhausen." Ch. B., *Oeuvres,* vol. 2, p. 24.[202]   [J40a,1]

"Thus, France was diverted from its natural course, as Baudelaire has shown, to become a vehicle of the despiritualization—the 'bestialization'—of folk and state." Peter Klassen, *Baudelaire* (Weimar ‹1931›), p. 33.   [J40a,2]

Closing line of *La Légende des siècles*, part 3, section 38 ("Un Homme aux yeux profonds passait"): "O scholar of abyssal things alone!" Victor Hugo, *Oeuvres complètes, Poésie,* vol. 9 (Paris, 1883), p. 229.   [J40a,3]

"The boulder with the pensive profile." Victor Hugo, *Oeuvres complètes, Poésie,* vol. 9 (Paris, 1883), p. 191 (*Le Groupe des idylles,* no. 12, "Dante").   [J40a,4]

> Crouching on the summit, the grim sphinx Nature dreams,
> Petrifying with its abyss-gaze
>   The magus used to wondrous flights,
> The studious group of pale Zoroastrians,
> Sun-gazers and scanners of the stars,
>   The dazzled, the astounded.
>
> . . . . .
> The night revolves in riot 'round the sphinx.
> If we could once lift up its monstrous paw,
>   So fascinating to the mind of yesteryear
> (Newton just as much as ancient Hermes),

> Underneath that dark and fatal claw
> We'd find this one word: Love.

"Man deceives himself! He sees how dark all is for him." Victor Hugo, *La Légende des siècles*, part 3 ("Ténèbres"), in *Oeuvres complètes, Poésie*, vol. 9 (Paris, 1883), pp. 164–165. Ending of the poem. [J40a,5]

Ending of "La nuit! La nuit! La nuit!" ⟨Night! Night! Night!⟩:

> O sepulchers! I hear the fearful organ of the shadow,
> Formed from all the cries of somber nature
>   And the crash of rocky reefs;
> Death plays the clavier resounding through the branches,
> And the keys, now black, now white, are all
>   Your tombstones and your biers.

Victor Hugo, *La Légende des siècles*, part 3 ("Ténèbres"), in *Oeuvres complètes, Poésie*, vol. 9 (Paris, 1883), p. 161. [J40a,6]

In *La Légende des siècles* ⟨The Legend of the Ages⟩, part 3, poems like "Les Chutes: Fleuves et poètes" ⟨The Falls: Rivers and Poets⟩ and "Désintéressement" ⟨Disinterestedness⟩—the one devoted to the torrents of the Rhine, the other to Mont Blanc—provide an especially vigorous idea of the perception of nature in the nineteenth century. In these poems we find the allegorical mode of vision uniquely interfused with the spirit of the vignette. [J40a,7]

From Théodore de Banville, *Mes Souvenirs* (Paris, 1882), ch. 7 ("Charles Baudelaire"). Their first meeting: "Night had come—luminous soft enchantress. We had left the Luxembourg and were walking along the outer boulevards, through streets whose movement and mysterious tumult the poet of *Les Fleurs du mal* had always so attentively cherished. Privat d'Anglemont walked a little apart from us, in silence" (p. 77). [J41,1]

From Théodore de Banville, *Mes Souvenirs* (Paris, 1882): "I no longer recall which African country it was in which he was put up by a family to whom his parents had sent him. At any rate, he quickly became bored with the conventional manners of his hosts, and took off by himself for a mountain to live with a tall young woman of color who understood no French, and who cooked him strangely spiced ragouts in a burnished copper cauldron, around which some naked little black children were dancing and howling. Oh, but those ragouts! How well he conjured them up, and how one would have loved to try them!" (p. 79). [J41,2]

"In his lodgings at the Hôtel Pimodan, when I went there for the first time to visit him, there were no dictionaries, no separate study—not even *a table with writing materials*; nor was there a sideboard or a separate dining room, or anything else resembling the décor of a bourgeois apartment." Théodore de Banville, *Mes Souvenirs* (Paris, 1882), pp. 81–82. [J41,3]

On Joseph de Maistre: "To the pretensions and the insolence of metaphysics, he responded with the historical." J. Barbey d'Aurevilly, *Joseph de Maistre, Blanc de Saint-Bonnet, Lacordaire, Gratry, Caro* (Paris, 1910), p. 9. [J41,4]

"Some, like Baudelaire, . . . identified the demon, staggered but reoriented themselves, and once more honored God. It would nonetheless be unjust to expect from these precursors a surrender of the human faculties as complete as that required, for example, in the sort of mysterious dawn it seems we have begun to live at present." Stanislas Fumet, *Notre Baudelaire* [series entitled *Le Roseau d'or*, vol. 8] (Paris, 1926), p. iii. [J41,5]

"This great poetic success thus represents—if we add to these 1,500 copies the print-run of 1,000, plus the overruns from the first edition—a sum total of 2,790 copies maximum in circulation. What other poet of our day, except Victor Hugo, could boast of such a demand for his work?" A. de la Finelière and Georges Descaux, *Charles Baudelaire* [series entitled *Essais de bibliographie contemporaine*, vol. 1] (Paris, 1868). Note on the second edition of *Les Fleurs du mal*. [J41,6]

Poe: "Cyrano de Bergerac become a pupil of the astronomer Arago"—*Journal des Goncourt*, July 16, 1856.[203]—"If Edgar Poe dethroned Walter Scott and Mérimée, if realism and bohemianism triumphed all down the line, if certain poems about which I have nothing to say (for fairness bids me be silent) were taken seriously by . . . honest and well-intentioned men, then this would no longer be decadence but an orgy." Pontmartin, *Le Spectateur*, September 19, 1857; cited in Léon Lemonnier, *Edgar Poe et la critique française de 1845 à 1875* (Paris, 1928), pp. 187, 214. [J41a,1]

On allegory: "Limp arms, like weapons dropped by one who flees."[204] [J41a,2]

Swinburne appropriates for himself the thesis that art has nothing to do with morality. [J41a,3]

"*Les Fleurs du mal* are a cathedral." Ernest Raynaud, *Ch. Baudelaire* (Paris, 1922), p. 305 (citing Gonzague de Reynold, *Charles Baudelaire*). [J41a,4]

"Baudelaire frets and torments himself in producing the least word. . . . For him, art 'is a duel in which the artist shrieks with terror before being overcome.'"[205] Ernest Raynaud, *Ch. Baudelaire* (Paris, 1922), pp. 317–318. [J41a,5]

Raynaud recognizes the incompatibility of Baudelaire and Gautier. He devotes a long chapter to this (pp. 310–345). [J41a,6]

"Baudelaire submitted to the requirements of . . . buccaneer editors who exploited the vanity of socialites, amateurs, and novices, and accepted manuscripts only if one took out a subscription." Ernest Raynaud, *Ch. Baudelaire* (Paris, 1922), p. 319. Baudelaire's own conduct is the complement of this state of affairs. He would offer the same manuscript to several different journals and authorize reprints without acknowledging them as such. [J41a,7]

Baudelaire's essay of 1859 on Gautier: "Gautier . . . could not have misinterpreted the piece. This is made clear by the fact that, in writing the preface to the 1863 edition of *Les Fleurs du mal*, he wittily repaid Baudelaire for his essay." Ernest Raynaud, *Ch. Baudelaire* (Paris, 1922), p. 323. [J41a,8]

"In other respects, what witnesses most tellingly to the evil spell of those times is the story of Balzac, . . . who . . . all his life fairly cudgeled his brains to master a style, without ever attaining one. . . . [Note:] The discordancy of those times is underscored by the fact that the prisons of La Roquette and Mazas were built with the same gusto with which Liberty Trees were planted everywhere. Bonapartist propaganada was harshly suppressed, but the ashes of Napoleon were brought home. . . . The center of Paris was cleared and its streets were opened up, but the city was strangled with a belt of fortifications." Ernest Raynaud, *Ch. Baudelaire* (Paris, 1922), pp. 287–288. [J41a,9]

After referring to the marriage of ancient Olympus with the wood sprites and fairies of Banville: "For his part, little wishing to join the ever-swelling procession of imitators on the high road of Romanticism, Charles Baudelaire looked about him for a path to originality. . . . Where to cast his lot? Great was his indecision. . . . Then he noticed that Christ, Jehovah, Mary, Mary Magdalene, the angels, and 'their phalanxes' all occupied a place in this poetry, but that Satan never appeared in it. An error in logic; he resolved to correct this. . . . Victor Hugo had made *la diablerie* a fantastic setting for some ancient legends. Baudelaire, in contrast, *actually* incarcerated modern man—the man of the nineteenth century—in the prison of hell." Alcide Dusolier, *Nos Gens de lettres* (Paris, 1864), pp. 105–106 ("M. Charles Baudelaire").

[J42,1]

"He certainly would have made an excellent reporter for the witchcraft trials." Alcide Dusolier, *Nos Gens de lettres* (Paris, 1864), p. 109 ("M. Ch. B."). Baudelaire must have enjoyed reading that. [J42,2]

With Dusolier, considerable insight into details, but total absence of any perspective on the whole: "Obscene mysticism, or, if you prefer, mystical obscenity— here, I have said and I repeat, is the double character of *Les Fleurs du mal*." Alcide Dusolier, *Nos Gens de lettres* (Paris, 1864), p. 112. [J42,3]

"We would reserve nothing, not even praise. I attest then to the presence, in M. Baudelaire's poetic gallery, of certain *tableaux parisiens* (I would have preferred *eaux-fortes* ‹etchings› as a more accurate and more characteristic term) possessing great vigor and marvelous precision." Alcide Dusolier, *Nos Gens de lettres* (Paris, 1864), pp. 112–113 ("Meryon").   [J42,4]

There is a reference in Dusolier, apropos of "Femmes damnées," to *La Religieuse* ‹The Nun›—but Diderot is not mentioned.   [J42,5]

A further judgment from Dusolier (p. 114); "But can one say, 'Here is a poet'? Yes, if a rhetor were an orator." The legend about the relation between verse and prose in Baudelaire goes back to Dusolier. Shock!   [J42,6]

Closing words: "If I had to sum up in a phrase what Baudelaire is by nature and what he would like to persuade us that he is, I would say without any hesitation: he is a hysterical Boileau. / May 6, 1863." Alcide Dusolier, *Nos Gens de lettres* (Paris, 1864), p. 119.   [J42,7]

Baudelaire's horoscope, prepared for Raynaud by Paul Flambart: "The psychological enigma of Baudelaire is seen almost entirely in this alliance of two things ordinarily the least suited to being linked together: a wonderfully fluent poetic gift and a crushing pessimism." Ernest Raynaud, *Ch. Baudelaire* (Paris, 1922), p. 54. The Baudelairean psychological antinomy in its tritest formulation.
                                                                              [J42,8]

"Is this to say that we must necessarily assimilate Baudelaire to Dante, as M. de Reynold, following the lead of Ernest Raynaud, has done? If it is a question of poetic genius, surely admiration . . . can go no further. If it is a question of philosophical tendency, I would merely remark that Dante . . . , well in advance of his time, introduces into his work ideas that are already quite modern, as Lamennais has nicely demonstrated, whereas Baudelaire . . . gives full expression to the spirit of the Middle Ages and is, accordingly, behind the times. Thus, if the truth be told, far from continuing Dante, he differs from him altogether." Paul Souday, "Gonzague de Reynold's *Charles Baudelaire*" (*Les Temps*, April 21, 1921, "Les Livres").   [J42a,1]

"New editions of *Les Fleurs du mal* have been announced or are starting to appear. Up to now there have been only two on the market, one for six francs, the other for three francs fifty. And now one at twenty sous." Paul Souday, "Le Cinquantenaire de Baudelaire" (*Le Temps*, June 4, 1917).[206]   [J42a,2]

According to Souday—in a review of Baudelaire's letters (*Le Temps*, August 17, 1917)—Baudelaire earned a total of 15,000 francs in twenty-five years.   [J42a,3]

"These sturdy ships, with their air of idleness and nostalgia."[207]   [J42a,4]

Thesis of Paul Desjardins: "Baudelaire is lacking in verve—that is to say, he has no ideas but only sensations." Paul Desjardins, "Charles Baudelaire," *Revue bleue* (Paris, 1887), p. 22.   [J42a,5]

"Baudelaire does not give us a lifelike representation of objects; he is more concerned to steep the image in memory than to embellish or portray it." Paul Desjardins, "Charles Baudelaire," *Revue bleue* (Paris, 1887), p. 23.   [J42a,6]

Souday tries to dismiss the Christian velleities of Baudelaire with a reference to Pascal.   [J42a,7]

Kafka says: dependency keeps you young.   [J42a,8]

"This sensation is then renewed ad infinitum through astonishment. . . . All of a sudden, Baudelaire draws back from what is most familiar to him and eyes it in horror. . . . He *draws back from himself*; he looks upon himself as something quite new and prodigiously interesting, although a little unclean: 'Lord give me strength and courage to behold / My body and my heart without disgust!'"[208] Paul Desjardins, "Charles Baudelaire," *Revue bleue* (Paris, 1887), p. 18.   [J42a,9]

Baudelaire's fatalism: "At the time of the coup d'état in December, he felt a sense of outrage. 'What a disgrace!' he cried at first; then he came to see things 'from a providential perspective' and resigned himself like a monk." Desjardins, "Charles Baudelaire," *Revue bleue* (1887), p. 19.   [J42a,10]

Baudelaire—according to Desjardins—unites the sensibility of the Marquis de Sade with the doctrines of Jansenius.   [J43,1]

"True civilization . . . has nothing to do with . . . table-turning"[209]—an allusion to Hugo.   [J43,2]

"Que diras-tu ce soir . . ." ‹What Will You Say Tonight . . .› invoked as the poem of a "man in whom a decided aptitude for the most arduous speculations did not exclude a poetry that was solid, warm, colorful, essentially original and humane." Charles Barbara, *L'Assassinat du Pont-Rouge* (Paris, 1859), p. 79 (the sonnet, pp. 82–83).   [J43,3]

Barrès: "In him the simplest word betrays the effort by which he attained so high a level." Cited in Gide, "Baudelaire et M. Faguet," *Nouvelle Revue française* (November 1, 1910), p. 513.[210]   [J43,4]

"A phrase of Brunetière's is even more to our purpose: '. . . He lacks animation and imagination.' . . . Agreed that he lacks animation and imagination. . . . The question arises (since, after all, we do have *Les Fleurs du mal*) whether it is indeed essentially the imagination which makes the poet; or, since MM. Faguet and Brunetière certainly are in favor of giving the name of poetry to a kind of versified oratory, whether we would not do well to hail Baudelaire as something other and more than a poet: the first artist in poetry." André Gide, "Baudelaire et M. Faguet," *Nouvelle Revue française*, 2 (November 1, 1910), pp. 513–514. Gide quotes, in connection with this, Baudelaire's formula, "The imagination, that queen of the faculties," and concedes that the poet was unaware of the true state of affairs (p. 517).[211]   [J43,5]

"The seeming inappropriateness of terms, which will irritate some critics so much, that skillful impreciseness of which Racine already made such masterly use, . . . that air-space, that interval, between image and idea, between the word and the thing, is just where there is room for the poetic emotion to come and dwell." A. Gide, "Baudelaire et M. Faguet," *Nouvelle Revue française*, 2 (November 1, 1910), p. 512.[212]   [J43,6]

"Enduring fame is promised only to those writers who can offer to successive generations a nourishment constantly renewed; for every generation arrives on the scene with its own particular hunger." A. Gide, "Baudelaire et M. Faguet," *Nouvelle Revue française*, 2 (November 1, 1910), p. 503.[213]   [J43,7]

Faguet complains of the lack of movement in Baudelaire, and Gide, making reference to Baudelaire's "I hate all movement" and to the iterative poems, remarks: "As if the greatest novelty of his art had not been to *immobilize* his poems, to develop them in depth!" Gide, "Baudelaire et M. Faguet," *Nouvelle Revue française*, 2 (November 1, 1910), pp. 507, 508.[214]   [J43,8]

Of the line, "Limp arms . . . ," Proust says, in the preface to ⟨Paul Morand,⟩ *Tendres Stocks* ⟨Paris, 1921⟩, p. 15, that it sounds like something from Racine's *Britannicus*.[215]—The heraldic character of the image!   [J43a,1]

Very astute judgment by Proust on Sainte-Beuve's behavior toward Baudelaire, in the preface to *Tendres Stocks*.[216]   [J43a,2]

Of those "tunes . . . granting a kind of glory to the crowd," Proust remarks (⟨"A Propos de Baudelaire," *Nouvelle Revue française* [June 1, 1921],⟩ p. 646): "It would seem impossible to better that."[217]   [J43a,3]

"I have not had time to speak here of the part played in Baudelaire's work by ancient cities, or of the scarlet note they strike, here and there, in the fabric of his poetry." Marcel Proust, "A Propos de Baudelaire," *Nouvelle Revue française* (June 1, 1921), p. 656.[218]   [J43a,4]

Proust thinks that the concluding lines of both ⟨Racine's⟩ *Andromache* and ⟨Baudelaire's⟩ "Le Voyage" fall flat. He is offended by the extreme simplicity of these endings.[219]   [J43a,5]

"A capital is not wholly necessary to man." Senancour, *Obermann*, ed. Fasquelle (Paris ⟨1901⟩), p. 248.[220]   [J43a,6]

"He was the first . . . to show the woman in her *bedroom*, in the midst not only of her jewels and perfumes, but of her makeup, her *linens*, her dresses, trying to decide if she prefers a *scalloped hem or a straight hem*. He compares her . . . to animals—to the *elephant*, the *monkey*, and the *snake*." John Charpentier, "La Poésie britannique et Baudelaire," *Mercure de France*, 147 (May 1, 1921), p. 673.
[J43a,7]

On allegory: "His greatest glory, wrote Théophile Gautier [in the preface to the 1863 edition of *Les Fleurs du mal*], 'will be to have introduced into the realm of stylistic possibilities whole classes of objects, sensations, and effects left unnamed by Adam, the great nomenclator.' He *names* . . . the hopes and regrets, the curiosities and fears, that seethe in the darkness of the inner world." John Charpentier, "La Poésie britannique et Baudelaire," *Mercure de France*, 147 (May 1, 1921), p. 674.
[J43a,8]

"L'Invitation au voyage," translated into Russian by Merezhkovski, became a gypsy romance entitled "Holubka moïa."
[J43a,9]

In connection with "L'Irrémédiable," Crépet (*Les Fleurs du mal*, ed. Jacques Crépet [Paris, 1931], p. 449) cites the following passage from *Les Soirées de Saint-Pétersbourg:* "That river which one crosses but once; that pitcher of the Danaides, *always* full and *always* empty; that liver of Tityus, *always* regenerated under the beak of the vulture that *always* devours it anew, . . .—these are so many speaking hieroglyphs, about which it is impossible to be mistaken."[221]
[J43a,10]

Letter to Calonne, director of *La Revue contemporaine*, on February 11, 1859: "The dance of death is not a person but an allegory. It seems to me that it should not be capitalized. An extremely well-known allegory." *Les Fleurs du mal*, ed. Crépet (Paris, 1931), p. 459.[222]
[J44,1]

Regarding "L'Amour du mensonge" ‹Love of Deceit›. From a letter to Alphonse de Calonne: "The word 'royal' will help the reader understand the metaphor, which transforms memory into a crown of towers, like those that weigh down the brows of the goddesses of *maturity*, of *fertility*, of *wisdom*." *Fleurs du mal*, ed. Jacques Crépet (Paris, 1931), p. 461.[223]
[J44,2]

Planned cycle of poems "Onéirocritie" ‹Dream Interpretation›: "Symptoms of ruin. Vast Pelasgic buildings, one on top of the other. Apartments, rooms, temples, galleries, stairways, caeca, belvederes, lanterns, fountains, statues.—Fissures and cracks. Dampness resulting from a reservoir situated near the sky.—How to warn people and nations? Let us whisper warnings into the ears of the most intelligent. / High up, a column cracks and its two ends shift. Nothing has collapsed as yet. I can no longer find the way out. I go down, then climb back up. A tower.—Labyrinth. I never succeeded in leaving. I live forever in a building on the point of collapsing, a building undermined by a secret malady.—I reckon up in my mind, to amuse myself, whether such a prodigious mass of stones, marble blocks, statues, and walls, which are all about to collide with one another, will be greatly sullied by that multitude of brains, human flesh, and shattered bones.—I see such terrible things in my dreams that sometimes I wish I could sleep no more, if only I could be sure of not becoming too weary." Nadar, *Charles Baudelaire intime* (Paris, 1911), pp. 136–137 [⟨Baudelaire, *Oeuvres,*⟩ ed. Le Dantec, vol. 2, p. 696].[224]   [J44,3]

Proust on "Le Balcon": "Many of the lines in Baudelaire's 'Le Balcon' convey a similar impression of mystery" (p. 644). This in contrast to Hugo: "Victor Hugo always does wonderfully what he has to do. . . . But the fabricating—even when it is a fabricating of the impalpable—is always visible." Marcel Proust, "A Propos de Baudelaire," *Nouvelle Revue française*, 16 (Paris, 1921), pp. 643–644.[225]
                                                                                          [J44,4]

On the iterative poems: "The world of Baudelaire is a strange sectioning of time in which only the red-letter days can appear. This explains such frequent expressions as 'If some evening,' and so on." M. Proust, "A Propos de Baudelaire," *Nouvelle Revue française*, 16 (June 1, 1921), p. 652.[226]   [J44,5]

Meryon's letter of March 31, 1860, to Nadar: he does not wish to be photographed by him.   [J44,6]

"As to Baudelaire's 'stage properties'—. . . they might provide a useful lesson for those elegant ladies of the past twenty years, who . . . would do well to consider, when they contemplate the alleged purity of style which they have achieved with such infinite trouble, that a man may be the greatest and most artistic of writers, yet describe nothing but beds with 'adjustable curtains' ('Pièces condamnées'), halls like conservatories ('Une Martyre'), beds filled with subtle scents, sofas deep as tombs, whatnots loaded with flowers, lamps burning so briefly ('Pièces condamnées') that the only light comes from the coal fire. Baudelaire's world is a place to which, at rare moments, a perfumed breeze from the outer air brings refreshment and a sense of magic, . . . thanks to those porticoes . . . 'open onto unknown skies' ('La Mort'), or 'which the suns of the sea tinged with a thousand fires' ('La Vie antérieure')." M. Proust, "A Propos de Baudelaire," *Nouvelle Revue française*, 16 (June 1, 1921), p. 652.[227]   [J44a,1]

On the "Pièces condamnées": "They take their place once more among the grandest poems in the book, like those crystal-clear waves that heave majestically after a night of storm, and, by interposing their crests between the spectator and the immense sweep of the ocean, give a sense of space and distance to the view." Proust, "A Propos de Baudelaire," *Nouvelle Revue française*, 16 (June 1, 1921), p. 655.[228]   [J44a,2]

"How did he come to be so interested in lesbians . . . ? When Vigny, raging against women, thought to find the explanation of the mystery of their sex in the fact that women give suck . . . , in their psychology ('Always the companion whose heart is untrue'), it is easy to see why, in his frustrated and jealous passion, he could write: 'Woman will have Gomorrah, and Man will have Sodom.' But he does, at least, see the two sexes at odds, facing each other as enemies across a great gulf. . . . But this did not hold true of Baudelaire. . . . This 'connection' between Sodom and Gomorrah is what, in the final section of my novel, . . . I have shown in the person of a brutish creature, Charles Morel (it is usually to brutish creatures that this part is allotted). But it would seem that Baudelaire cast himself for it, and looked on the role as a privilege. It would be intensely interesting to know why he chose to assume it, and how well he acquitted himself. What is comprehensible in a Charles Morel becomes profoundly mysterious in the author of *Les Fleurs du mal*." Marcel Proust, "A Propos de Baudelaire," *Nouvelle Revue française*, 16 (June 1, 1921), pp. 655–656.[229]   [J44a,3]

Louis Ménard—who, under the pseudonym Louis de Senneville, had published *Prométhée délivré* ⟨Prometheus Unbound⟩—in *La Revue philosophique et religieuse* of September 1857 (cited in *Les Fleurs du mal*, ed. Crépet [Paris, 1930], pp. 362–363): "Though he talks incessantly of the vermin and scorpions in his soul and takes himself for the avatar of all vices, it is easy to see that his principal defect is an overly libertine imagination—a defect all too common among those erudite persons who have passed their youth in seclusion. . . . Let him enter into the community of human life, and he will be able to find a characteristically elevated form for vibrant, wholesome creations. He will be a paterfamilias and will publish books of the sort that could be read to his children. Until then, he will remain a schoolboy of 1828, suffering from what Geoffroy Saint-Hilaire calls arrested development."   [J45,1]

From the summation delivered by M. Pinard: "I portray evil with its intoxications, you say, but also with its miseries and shames. So be it. But what of all those many readers for whom you write (for you publish thousands of copies of your book, and at a low price) those numerous readers of every class, age, and condition? Will they take the antidote of which you speak with such complacency?" Cited in *Les Fleurs du mal*, ed. Crépet (Paris, 1930), p. 334.   [J45,2]

An article by Louis Goudall in *Le Figaro* of November 4, 1855, opens the way for criticisms of "university pedants." Goudall writes, after the publication of poems in *La Revue des deux mondes:* "After the fading of his surprise celebrity, Baudelaire will be associated exclusively with the withered fruits of contemporary poetry." Cited in *Les Fleurs du mal,* ed. Crépet (Paris, 1930), p. 306.   [J45,3]

In 1850, Asselineau saw Baudelaire with a copy of the poems inscribed by a calligrapher and bound in two gilded quarto volumes.   [J45,4]

Crépet (*Fleurs du mal*, ed. Crépet, p. 300) says that, around 1846, many of Baudelaire's friends knew his poems by heart. Only three of the poems had been published at that point.   [J45,5]

May 1852: "*Les Limbes* ‹Limbo›: intimate poems of Georges Durant, collected and published by his friend Th. Véron." [J45,6]

Announcing *Les Limbes* in the second issue of *L'Echo des marchands de vin*: "*Les Limbes:* poems by Charles Baudelaire. The book will be published on February 24, 1849, in Paris and Leipzig." [J45,7]

Leconte de Lisle in *La Revue européenne* of December 1, 1861. Among other things, he speaks of "that strange mania for dressing up the discoveries of modern industry in bad verse." He refers to Baudelaire's oeuvre as "stamped with the vigorous seal of long meditation." The *Inferno* plays a big part in his review. Cited in *Les Fleurs du mal*, ed. Crépet, pp. 385, 386. [J45a,1]

Swinburne's article in *The Spectator* of September 6, 1862. The author was twenty-five years old at the time. [J45a,2]

Paris, for Gonzague de Reynold, as "antechamber to the Baudelairean Hell." Turn to the second chapter, "La Vision de Paris," in part 2 (entitled "L'Art et l'oeuvre") of his book *Charles Baudelaire* (Paris and Geneva, 1920), and you find nothing but a longwinded, subaltern paraphrase of certain poems. [J45a,3]

Villon and Baudelaire: "In the one, we find the mystical and macabre Christianity of an age in the process of losing its faith; in the other, the more or less secularized Christianity of an age seeking to recover its faith." Gonzague de Reynold, *Charles Baudelaire* (Paris and Geneva, 1920), p. 220. [J45a,4]

Reynold draws a schematic parallel between the fifteenth and the nineteenth centuries as periods of *décadence*, in which an extreme realism prevails alongside an extreme idealism, together with unrest, pessimism, and egoism. [J45a,5]

Imitatio Christi, book 1, paragraph 20, "De amore solitudinus et silentii": "Quid potes alibi videre, quod hic non vides? Ecce caelum et terra et omnia elementa: nam ex istis omnia sunt facta."[230] [J45a,6]

Mallarmé, in the opening piece of *Divagations*, "Formerly, in the margins of a BAUDELAIRE": "This torrent of tears illuminated by the bengal light of the artificer Satan, who comes from behind." Stéphane Mallarmé, *Divagations* (Paris, 1897), p. 60. [J45a,7]

December 4, 1847: "After New Year's Day, I am starting a new kind of writing, . . . the Novel. It is not necessary for me to point out to you the gravity, the beauty, and the infinite possibilities of that art." Ch‹arles› B‹audelaire›, *Lettres à sa mère* (Paris, 1932), p. 26.[231] [J45a,8]

December 8, 1848: "Another reason I would be happy if you were able to comply with my request is that I very much fear a revolutionary uprising, and nothing is more deplorable than to be utterly without money at such a time." Ch. B., *Lettres à sa mère* (Paris, 1932), p. 33.[232]   [J45a,9]

"From the end of the Second Empire down to our own day, the evolution in philosophy and the blooming of *Les Fleurs du mal* have been concomitant. This explains the peculiar destiny of a work whose fundamental parts, though still enveloped in shadow, are becoming clearer with every passing day." Alfred Capus, *Le Gaulois*, 1921 (cited in *Les Fleurs du mal*, ed. Crépet [Paris, 1931], p. 50).
[J46,1]

On March 27, 1852, he mentions to his mother some "sickly articles, hastily written." ‹Charles Baudelaire,› *Lettres à sa mère* (Paris, 1932), p. 39.[233]   [J46,2]

March 27, 1852: "To beget children is the only thing which gives moral intelligence to the female. As for young women without status and without children, they show nothing but coquetry, implacability, and elegant debauchery." *Lettres à sa mère* (Paris, 1932), p. 43.[234]   [J46,3]

In a letter to his mother, Baudelaire refers to the reading room, in addition to the café, as a refuge in which to work.   [J46,4]

December 4, 1854: "Should I resign myself to going to bed and staying there for lack of clothes?" *Lettres à sa mère* (Paris, 1932), p. 74.[235] (On p. 101, he asks for the loan of some handkerchiefs.)   [J46,5]

December 20, 1855, after toying with the idea of petitioning for a subvention: "Never will my name appear on filthy government paper." *Lettres à sa mère*, p. 83.[236]   [J46,6]

Problematic passage from a letter of July 9, 1857, concerning *Les Fleurs du mal*: "Moreover, alarmed myself by the horror I was going to inspire, I cut out a third of it at the proof stage." *Lettres à sa mère*, p. 110.[237]   [J46,7]

Spleen de Paris appears for a time, in 1857 (see p. 111, letter of July 9, 1857), to have had the title *Poèmes nocturnes*.   [J46,8]

Planned essay (*Lettres à sa mère*, p. 139) on Machiavelli and Condorcet.   [J46,9]

May 6, 1861: "'And what about God!' you will say. I wish with all my heart (with what sincerity I alone can know) to believe that an exterior invisible being is concerned with my fate. But what can I do to make myself believe it?" *Lettres à sa mère*, p. 173.[238]   [J46,10]

May 6, 1861: "I am forty years old and I cannot think of school without pain, any more than I can think of the fear which my stepfather inspired in me." *Lettres à sa mère*, p. 176.[239]   [J46a,1]

July 10, 1861, on the planned de luxe edition: "Where is the mama who will give *Les Fleurs du mal* as a present to her children? And where is the papa?" *Lettres à sa mère*, p. 186.   [J46a,2]

His eyes strained with working in the Louvre: "Two bloodshot goggle-eyes." *Lettres à sa mère*, p. 191.   [J46a,3]

On *Les Misérables*—August 11, 1862: "The book is disgusting and clumsy. On this score, I've shown that I possess the art of lying." *Lettres à sa mère*, p. 212.[240]
[J46a,4]

June 3, 1863. He speaks of Paris, "where I have been bored for months, as no one was ever bored before." *Lettres à sa mère*, p. 218.[241]   [J46a,5]

Conclusion of "Crépuscule du soir": the muse herself, who turns away from the poet to whisper words of inspiration to the air.   [J46a,6]

Baudelaire planned a "refutation of the preface to the life of Caesar by Napoleon III."   [J46a,7]

In a letter of May 4, 1865, Baudelaire mentions to his mother an "immensely long" article appearing in *La Revue germanique. Lettres à sa mère*, p. 260.[242]   [J46a,8]

March 5, 1866: "I like nothing so much as to be alone. But that is impossible; and it seems that *the Baudelaire school* exists." *Lettres à sa mère*, p. 301.[243]   [J46a,9]

December 23, 1865: "If I can ever regain the freshness and energy I've sometimes enjoyed, I'll assuage my wrath in horrible books. I'd like to set the entire human race against me. That offers a pleasure that could console me for everything." *Lettres à sa mère*, p. 278.[244]   [J46a,10]

"As a man advances through life . . . , what the world has agreed to call 'beauty' loses much of its importance. . . . Henceforth beauty will be no more than *the promise of happiness*. . . . Beauty will be the form which promises the most kindness, the most loyalty to an oath, the most honesty in fulfilling a pledge, the most subtlety in understanding relationships" (p. 424). And a little further on, with reference to "L'Ecole païenne," to which these lines written in an album constitute a note: "How could I possibly succeed in convincing a young scatterbrain that no sensual desire is mingled with the irresistible sympathy I feel for old women—for those creatures who have suffered greatly through their lovers, their husbands, their children, and also through their own mistakes?" Ch. B., *Oeuvres complètes*, ed. Le Dantec, vol. 2, pp. 424–425.[245]   [J47,1]

"For some time, . . . it [has seemed] to me that I am having a bad dream, that I am hurtling through space and that a multitude of wooden, golden, and silver idols are falling with me, tumbling after me, bumping into me, and breaking my head and back." Ch. B., *Oeuvres complètes*, vol. 2, pp. 420–421 ("L'Ecole païenne").[246] Compare the anecdote about Baudelaire and the Mexican idol ‹J17a,2?›.   [J47,2]

Toward the end of the Second Empire, as the regime relaxes its pressure, the theory of *l'art pour l'art* suffers a loss in prestige.   [J47,3]

From the argument of the Guys essay, it would appear that Baudelaire's fascination with this artist was connected above all with his handling of backgrounds, which differs little from the handling of backgrounds in the theater. But because these pictures, unlike scenery on a stage, are to be viewed from close up, the magic of distance is canceled for the viewer without his having to renounce the judgment of distance. In the essay on Guys, Baudelaire has characterized the gaze which here *and in other places* he himself turns toward the distance. Baudelaire dwells on the expression of the oriental courtesan: "She directs her gaze at the horizon, like a beast of prey; the same wildness, the same indolent distraction, and also at times the same fixity of attention." Ch. B., *Oeuvres*, vol. 2, p. 359.[247]   [J47,4]

In his poem L'Héautontimorouménos" ‹The Self-Tormentor›, Baudelaire himself speaks of his shrill voice.   [J47,5]

A decisive value is to be accorded Baudelaire's efforts to capture the gaze in which the magic of distance is extinguished. (Compare "L'Amour du mensonge.") Relevant here: my definition of the aura as the aura of distance opened up with the look that awakens in an object perceived.[248]   [J47,6]

The gaze in which the magic of distance is extinguished: "Let your eyes plunge into the fixed stare / of satyresses or water sprites" ("L'Avertisseur" ‹The Lookout›).[249]   [J47a,1]

Among the prose poems planned but left unwritten is "La Fin du monde." Its basic theme is perhaps best indicated in the following passage from "Fusées," no. 22: "The world is about to come to an end. The only reason it should continue is that it exists. What a weak argument, compared with all the arguments to the contrary, and especially the following: 'What, in future, is the world to do in the sight of heaven?' For, supposing it continued to have material existence, would this existence be worthy of the name, or of the Encyclopedia of History? . . . For my part, I who sometimes feel myself cast in the ridiculous role of prophet, I know that I shall never receive so much as a doctor's charity. Lost in this base world, jostled by the mob, I am like a weary man who sees behind him, in the depths of the years, only disillusionment and bitterness, and in front of him only a tempest that brings nothing new. . . . I seem to have wandered off. . . . Nevertheless, I shall let these pages stand—because I wish to set an exact date to my anger." Ch. B., *Oeuvres*,

The piece that begins, "The world is coming to an end" ("Fusées," no. 22), contains, interwoven with the apocalyptic reverie, a frightfully bitter critique of Second Empire society. (It reminds one here and there, perhaps, of Nietzsche's delineation of "the last man.") This critique displays, in part, prophetic features. Of the coming society, it is said that "nothing in the sanguinary, blasphemous, or unnatural dreams of the utopians can be compared to what will actually happen. . . . Rulers will be compelled, in order to maintain their position and create a semblance of order, to resort to methods that would appall present-day mankind, hardened as it is. . . . Justice—if, in this fortunate epoch, any justice can still exist—will forbid the existence of citizens who are unable to make a fortune. . . . Those times are perhaps quite close at hand. Who knows whether they are not here already—whether it is not simply the coarsening of our natures that keeps us from noticing what sort of atmosphere we already breathe?" Ch. B., *Oeuvres,* vol. 2, pp. 640–641.[251] [J47a,3]

"The gist of it all, in the eyes of history and of the French people, is that Napoleon III's great claim to renown will have been that he showed how anybody at all, if only he gets hold of the telegraph and the printing presses, can govern a great nation. Anyone who believes that such things can be done without the people's permission is an imbecile." Ch. B., *Oeuvres,* vol. 2, p. 655 ("Mon Coeur mis à nu," no. 44).[252] [J48,1]

"A sense of solitude, since my childhood. Despite my family, and especially amid companions—a sense of an eternally lonely destiny." Ch. B., *Oeuvres,* vol. 2, p. 645 ("Mon Coeur mis à nu").[253] [J48,2]

"Truth, for all its multiplicity, is not two-faced." Ch. B., *Oeuvres,* vol. 2, p. 63 ("Salon de 1846: Aux Bourgeois").[254] [J48,3]

"Allegory is one of the noblest genres of art." Ch. B., *Oeuvres,* vol. 2, p. 30 ("Salon de 1845").[255] [J48,4]

"The will must have become a highly developed and productive faculty to be able to give its stamp . . . to works . . . of the second rank. . . . The spectator enjoys the effort, and his eye drinks in the sweat." Ch. B., *Oeuvres,* vol. 2, ⟨p. 26⟩ ("Salon de 1845"). [J48,5]

"The idea of progress. This dim beacon, an invention of contemporary philosophism, licensed without the sanction of Nature or God—this modern lantern casts dark shadows over every object of knowledge. Liberty vanishes; punishment disappears." Ch. B., *Oeuvres,* vol. 2, p. 148 ("Exposition Universelle, 1855").[256] [J48,6]

"Stupidity is often the ornament of beauty. It is what gives to the eyes that gloomy limpidity of blackish pools and that oily calm of tropical seas." Ch. B., *Oeuvres*, vol. 2, p. 622 ("Choix de maximes consolantes sur l'amour").[257]   [J48,7]

"A last, general rule: in love, beware of the *moon* and the *stars;* beware of the Venus de Milo." Ch. B., *Oeuvres*, vol. 2, p. 624 ("Choix de maximes consolantes sur l'amour").[258]   [J48,8]

Baudelaire was always after the gist. His epoch forbade him to formulate it in such a way that its social bearing would become immediately intelligible. Where he sought in fact to make it comprehensible—in the essays on Dupont, as in the theoretical musings in a Christian vein—he instead lost sight of it. Nevertheless, the formulation he attains at one point in this context—"How much can you get for a lyre, at the pawnshop?"—gives apt expression to his insistence on an art that can prove itself before society. The sentence from Ch. B., *Oeuvres,* vol. 2, p. 422 ("L'Ecole païenne").[259]   [J48,9]

With regard to allegory: "What do you expect from heaven or from the stupidity of the public? Enough money to raise altars to Priapus and Bacchus in your attics? ... I understand the rage of iconoclasts and of Muslims against images. I admit all the remorse of Saint Augustine for the too great pleasure of the eyes." Ch. B., *Oeuvres*, vol. 2, pp. 422, 423 ("L'Ecole païenne").[260]   [J48a,1]

It belongs to the physiognomic profile of Baudelaire that he fosters the gestures of the poet at the expense of the professional insignia of the writer. In this, he is like the prostitute who cultivates her physiognomy as sexual object or as "beloved" in order to conceal her professional dealings.   [J48a,2]

If the poems of *Les Epaves,* in Proust's great image,[261] are the foamy wave crests in the ocean of Baudelairean poetry, then the poems of "Tableaux parisiens" are its safe harbor. In particular, these poems contain hardly any echo of the revolutionary storms that were breaking over Paris. In this respect they resemble the poetry of Heym, composed forty years later, in which the corresponding state of affairs has now risen to consciousness while the "Marseillaise" has been interred. The last two tercets of the sonnet "Berlin III," which describes the sunset in Berlin in winter, read as follows:

> A paupers' graveyard upheaves black, stone after stone;
> The dead look out on the red sunset
> From their hole. It tastes like strong wine.
>
> They sit knitting all along the wall,
> Sooty caps on their naked temples,
> To the old attack song, the "Marseillaise."

Georg Heym, *Dichtungen* (Munich, 1922), p. 11.   [J48a,3]

A decisive line for the comparison with Blanqui: "When earth becomes a trickling dungeon" ("Spleen IV").[262]   [J48a,4]

The idea of the immobilization of nature appears, perhaps as refuge for the prescient imagination immediately before the war, in poems by Georg Heym, whose images the spleen of Baudelaire could not yet have touched: "But the seas congeal. On the waves / The ships hang rotting, morose." Georg Heym, *Dichtungen* (Munich, 1922), p. 73 (collection entitled *Umbra vitae*).   [J48a,5]

It would be a big mistake to see in the theoretical positions on art taken by Baudelaire after 1852—positions which differ so markedly from those of the period around 1848—the fruits of a development. (There are not many artists whose work attests so little to a development as that of Baudelaire.) These positions represent theoretical extremes, of which the dialectical mediation is given by Baudelaire's whole oeuvre, without being entirely present to his conscious reflection. The mediation resides in the destructive and purificatory character of the work. This art is useful insofar as it destroys. Its destructive fury is directed not least at the fetishistic conception of art. Thus it serves "pure" art, in the sense of a purified art.   [J49,1]

The first poems of *Les Fleurs du mal* are all devoted to the figure of the poet. From them it emerges, precisely insofar as the poet makes appeal to a station and a task, that society no longer has such things to confer.   [J49,2]

An examination of those places where the "I" appears in the poems of Baudelaire might result in a possible classificatory grouping. In the first five poems of *Les Fleurs du mal,* it surfaces but a single time. And further on, it is not unusual to find poems in which the "I" does not occur. More essential—and, at the same time, more deliberate—is the way in other poems, like "Réversibilité" or "Harmonie du soir," it is kept in the background.   [J49,3]

"La Belle Dorothée"—she must buy back her eleven-year-old sister.[263]   [J49,4]

"I assure you that the seconds are now strongly accented, and rush out of the clock crying, 'I am Life, unbearable and implacable Life!'" Ch. B., *Oeuvres*, vol. 1, p. 411 ("La Chambre double").[264]   [J49,5]

From "Quelques mots d'introduction" to the "Salon de 1845": "And at the very outset, with reference to that impertinent designation, 'the bourgeois,' we beg to state that we in no way share the prejudices of our great confrères in the world of art, who for some years now have been striving their utmost to cast anathema upon that inoffensive being. . . . And, finally, the ranks of the artists themselves contain so many bourgeois that it is better, on the whole, to suppress a word which does not define any particular vice of caste." *Oeuvres*, vol. 2, pp. 15–16.[265] The same tendency in the preface, "Aux Bourgeois," of the "Salon de 1846."   [J49,6]

The figure of the lesbian woman belongs among Baudelaire's heroic exemplars. [He himself gives expression to this in the language of his satanism. It would be no less comprehensible in an unmetaphysical critical language.] The nineteenth century began openly and without reserve to include the woman in the process of commodity production. The theoreticians were united in their opinion that her specific femininity was thereby endangered; masculine traits must necessarily manifest themselves in women after a while. Baudelaire affirms these traits. At the same time, however, he seeks to free them from the domination of the economy. Hence the purely sexual accent which he comes to give this developmental tendency in woman. The paradigm of the lesbian woman bespeaks the ambivalent position of "modernity" vis-à-vis technological development. (What he could not forgive in George Sand, presumably, was her having profaned, through her humanitarian convictions, this image whose traits she bore. Baudelaire says that she was worse than Sade.)[266]   [J49a,1]

The concept of exclusive rights was not so widely accepted in Baudelaire's day as it is today. Baudelaire often republished his poems two or three times without having anyone take offense. He ran into difficulties with this only toward the end of his life, with the *Petits Poèmes en prose*.   [J49a,2]

From his seventeenth year, Baudelaire led the life of a ‹littérateur?›. One cannot say that he ever thought of himself as an "intellectual" or engaged himself on behalf of "the life of the mind." The registered trademark for artistic production had not yet been invented. (In this situation, moreover, his imperious need to distinguish himself and withdraw worked to his advantage.) He refused to go along with the defamation of the bourgeois, under the banner of which there was mobilized a solidarity of artists and men of letters that he considered suspect. Thus, in the "Musée classique du Bazar Bonne-Nouvelle" ‹Classical Museum of the Good-News Bazaar› (*Oeuvres,* vol. 2, p. 61), he writes: "The bourgeois, who has few scientific notions, goes where the loud voice of the bourgeois artist directs him.—If this voice were suppressed, the grocer would carry E. Delacroix around in triumph. The grocer is a great thing, a divine being whom it is necessary to respect, *homo bonae voluntatis!*"[267] In more detail a year earlier, in the preface to the "Salon de 1845."   [J49a,3]

Baudelaire's eccentric individuality was a mask under which he tried to conceal—out of shame, you could say—the supra-individual necessity of his way of life and, to a certain extent, his life history.   [J50,1]

To interrupt the course of the world—that was Baudelaire's deepest intention. The intention of Joshua. [Not so much the prophetic one: for he gave no thought to any sort of reform.] From this intention sprang his violence, his impatience, and his anger; from it, too, sprang the ever-renewed attempts to cut the world to the heart [or sing it to sleep]. In this intention he provided death with an accompaniment: his encouragement of its work.   [J50,2]

Apropos of "Harmonie du soir" and other iterative poems: Baudelaire notes in Poe "repetitions of the same line or of several lines, insistent reiterations of phrases which simulate the obesssions of melancholy or of a fixed idea." "Notes nouvelles sur Edgar Poe," in *Nouvelles Histoires extraordinaires* (Paris ⟨1886⟩), p. 22.[268] Immobilization!   [J50,3]

"Lord give me strength and courage to behold / my body and my heart without disgust!" With this, juxtapose: "The dandy should aspire to be sublime, continually. He should live and sleep in front of a mirror." *Oeuvres*, vol. 2, p. 643 ("Mon Coeur mis à nu," no. 5). The lines of verse are from "Un Voyage à Cythère."[269]
[J50,4]

The close of "La Destruction" (published in 1855 under the title "La Volupté"!) presents the image of petrified unrest. ("Was like a Medusa-shield, / image of petrified unrest"—Gottfried Keller, "Verlorenes Recht, verlorenes Glück.")
[J50,5]

On "Le Voyage," opening stanza: the dream of distance belongs to childhood. The traveler has seen the far distant, but has lost the belief in distance.   [J50,6]

Baudelaire—the melancholic, whose star pointed him into the distance. He didn't follow it, though. Images of distance appear [in his poems] only as islands looming out of the sea of long ago, or the sea of Paris fog. These islands are seldom lacking in the Negress. And her violated body is the figure in which the distance lays itself at the feet of what Baudelaire found near: the Paris of the Second Empire.   [J50,7]

The eye growing dim at the moment of death is the *Ur*-phenomenon of expiring appearance ⟨*Schein*⟩.   [J50,8]

"Les Petites Vieilles" ⟨The Little Old Women⟩: "Their eyes . . . glint like holes where water sleeps at night."[270]   [J50,9]

Baudelaire's violent temper belongs together with his destructive animus. We get nearer the matter when we recognize here, too, in these bursts of anger, a "strange sectioning of time."[271]   [J50a,1]

Baudelaire, in his best passages, is occasionally coarse—never sonorous. His mode of expression at these points deviates as little from his experience as the gestures of a perfect prelate deviate from his person.   [J50a,2]

Although the general contours were by then already lost to view, the concept of allegory in the first third of the nineteenth century did not have the disconcerting quality that attaches to it today. In his review of *Les Poésies de Joseph Delorme,* in *Le Globe* of April 11, 1829, Charles Magnin brings together Victor Hugo and

Sainte-Beuve with the words: "They both proceed almost continually by figures, allegories, symbols." ‹Cited in Charles Augustin Sainte-Beuve,› *Vie, poésies et pensées de Joseph Delorme* (Paris, 1863), vol. 1, p. 295. [J50a,3]

A comparison between Baudelaire and Sainte-Beuve can unfold only within the narrow confines of subject matter and poetic workmanship. For Sainte-Beuve was a genial and indeed cozy sort of author. Charles Magnin justly writes in *Le Globe* of April 11, 1829: "His spirit might cloud over for a while, but no sooner does it compose itself than a fund of natural benevolence rises to the surface." (Here, it is not the benevolence but the surface that is decisive.) "Without doubt, this is the source of that sympathy and indulgence which he inspires in us." ‹Cited in› *Vie, poésies et pensées de Joseph Delorme* (Paris, 1863), vol. 1, p. 294. [J50a,4]

Miserable sonnet by Sainte-Beuve (*Les Consolations* [Paris, 1863], pp. 262–263): "I love Paris and its beautiful sunsets of autumn," with the closing lines: "And I depart, in my thoughts mingling / Paris with an Ithaca of beautiful sunsets." [J50a,5]

Charles Magnin in his review of *Les Poésies de Joseph Delorme*, in *Le Globe*, April 11, 1829: "Doubtless the alexandrine with a variable caesura calls for a stricter rhyme." ‹Cited in› *Vie, poésies et pensées de Joseph Delorme* (Paris, 1863), vol. 1, p. 298. [J50a,6]

Conception of the poet, according to Joseph Delorme: "The idea of consorting with elect beings who sing of their sorrows here below, the idea of groaning in harmony to their lead, came to him like a smile amid his sufferings and lightened them a little." *Vie, poésies et pensées de Joseph Delorme* (Paris, 1863), vol. 1, p. 16. The book has an epigraph from *Obermann;* this fact sets a limit to the influence which *Obermann* could have exercised on Baudelaire. [J51,1]

Sainte-Beuve, notes Charles Magnin, half approving and half deploring, "delights in a certain crudity of expression, and abandons himself . . . to a sort of linguistic shamelessness. . . . The harshest word, however shocking, is almost always the word he prefers." *Le Globe,* April 11, 1829, cited in *Vie, poésies et pensées de Joseph Delorme* (Paris, 1863), vol. 1, p. 296. Close on this (p. 297), Magnin reproaches the poet for having presented the girl in the poem "Ma Muse" as a consumptive: "We would not mind if the poet showed us his muse poor, grieving, or ill-clad. But consumptive!" The consumptive Negress in Baudelaire. We get some idea of Sainte-Beuve's innovations from lines like "nearby, the opening of a ravine: / A girl washes threadbare linen there day after day" ("Ma Muse," in vol. 1, p. 93), or, from a suicide fantasy, "Some local fellows, / . . . / Mixing jeers with their stupid stories, / Will chat idly over my blackened remains / Before packing them off to the graveyard in a wheelbarrow" ("Le Creux de la vallée," in vol. 1, p. 114). [J51,2]

Sainte-Beuve's characterization of his own poetry: "I have endeavored . . . to be original in my fashion, which is humble and bourgeois, . . . calling by their name the things of private life, but preferring the thatched cottage to the boudoir." *Vie, poésies et pensées de Joseph Delorme* (Paris, 1863), vol. 1, p. 170 ("Pensées," no. 19). [J51,3]

With Sainte-Beuve, a standard of sensibility: "Ever since our poets, . . . instead of saying 'a romantic grove,' a 'melancholy lake,' . . . started saying 'a green grove' and 'a blue lake,' alarm has been spreading among the disciples of Madame de Staël and the Genevan school; and already complaints can be heard about the invasion of a new materialism. . . . Above all, there is a dread of monotony, and it seems far too easy and far too simple to say that the leaves are green and the waves blue. On this point, perhaps, the adversaries of the picturesque deceive themselves. The leaves, in fact, are not always green; the waves not always blue. Or rather, we find in nature . . . neither green, nor blue, nor red, properly speaking; the natural colors of things are colors without names. . . . The picturesque is not a box of paints that can be emptied." ⟨Sainte-Beuve, *Vie, poésies et pensées de Joseph Delorme* (Paris, 1863),⟩ pp. 166–167 ("Pensées," no. 16). [J51,4]

"The alexandrine . . . resembles somewhat a pair of tongs, gleaming and golden, if straight and rigid; it is not for rummaging about in nooks and crannies.—Our modern verse is to a degree partitioned and *articulated* in the manner of insects, but, like them, it has wings." *Vie, poésies et pensées de Joseph Delorme* (Paris, 1863), vol. 1, p. 161 ("Pensées," no. 9). [J51a,1]

The sixth of Joseph Delorme's *pensées* assembles a number of examples and prefigurations of the modern alexandrine, from Rotrou, Chénier, Lamartine, Hugo, and Vigny. It notes that they are all informed by "the full, the large, the copious." Typical is this verse by Rotrou: "I myself have seen them—[the Christians] looking so serene— / *Driving their hymns to the skies in bulls of bronze*" (p. 154). [J51a,2]

"The poetry of André Chénier . . . is, as it were, the landscape for which Lamartine has done the sky." *Delorme*, vol. 1, pp. 159–160 ("Pensées," no. 8). [J51a,3]

In the preface of February 1829, Sainte-Beuve provides the poetry of Joseph Delorme with a more or less exact social index. He lays weight on the fact that Delorme comes from a good family, and even more on his poverty and the humiliations to which it has exposed him. [J51a,4]

What I propose is to show how Baudelaire lies embedded in the nineteenth century. The imprint he has left behind there must stand out clear and intact, like that of a stone which, having lain in the ground for decades, is one day rolled from its place. [J51a,5]

The unique importance of Baudelaire resides in his being the first and the most unflinching to have taken the measure of the self-estranged human being, in the double sense of acknowledging this being and fortifying it with armor against the reified world.[272]   [J51a,6]

Nothing comes closer to the task of the ancient hero in Baudelaire's sense—and in his century—than to give a form to modernity.   [J51a,7]

In the "Salon de 1846" (*Oeuvres,* vol. 2, p. 134), Baudelaire has described his social class through the clothes they wear. From this description it emerges that heroism is a quality of the one who describes, and not at all a quality of his subject. The "heroism of modern life" is a subterfuge or, if you prefer, a euphemism. The idea of death, from which Baudelaire never broke loose, is the hollow matrix readied for a knowledge that was not his. Baudelaire's concept of heroic modernity, it would seem, was first of all this: a monstrous provocation. Analogy with Daumier.   [J52,1]

Baudelaire's truest posture is ultimately not that of Hercules at rest but that of the mime who has taken off his makeup. This *gestus* is found again in the "ebbings" of his prosodic construction—something that, for several commentators, is the most precious element of his *ars poetica.*   [J52,2]

January 15, 1866, on *Le Spleen de Paris:* "Finally, I am hopeful that one of these days I'll be able to show a new Joseph Delorme linking his rhapsodic meditation to every chance event in his flânerie." Ch‹arles› B‹audelaire›, *Lettres* (Paris, 1915), p. 493.[273]   [J52,3]

January 15, 1866, to Sainte-Beuve: "In certain places in *Joseph Delorme* I find a few too many lutes, lyres, harps, and Jehovahs. This clashes with the Parisian poems. Moreover, you'd come with the aim of destroying all that." Ch. B., *Lettres* (Paris, 1915), p. 495.[274]   [J52,4]

An image that Baudelaire summons to explain his theory of the short poem, particularly the sonnet, in a letter to Armand Fraisse of February 19, 1860, serves better than any other description to suggest the way the sky looks in Meryon: "Have you ever noticed that a section of the sky seen through a vent or between two chimneys or two rocks, or through an arcade, gives a more profound idea of the infinite than a great panorama seen from a mountaintop?" Ch. B., *Lettres* (Paris, 1915), pp. 238–239.[275]   [J52,5]

Apropos of Pinelli, in "Quelques caricaturistes étrangers": "I wish that someone would invent a neologism, that someone would manufacture a word destined to destroy once and for all this species of *poncif*—the *poncif* in conduct and behavior, which creeps into the life of artists as into their works." Ch. B., *Oeuvres*, vol. 2, p. 211.[276] [J52,6]

Baudelaire's use of the concept "allegory" is not always entirely sure: "the . . . allegory of the spider weaving her web between the arm and the line of a fisherman, whose impatience never causes him to stir." Ch. B., *Oeuvres,* vol. 2, p. 204 ("Quelques caricaturistes étrangers").[277] [J52a,1]

Against the proposition "The genius makes his way." Ch. B., *Oeuvres*, vol. 2, p. 203 ("Quelques caricaturistes étrangers"). [J52a,2]

About Gavarni: "Like all men of letters—being a man of letters himself—he is slightly tainted with corruption." Ch. B., *Oeuvres*, vol. 2, p. 199 ("Quelques caricaturistes français").[278] [J52a,3]

In "Quelques caricaturistes français," on a drawing by Daumier dealing with cholera: "True to its ironic custom in times of great calamity and political upheaval, the sky of Paris is superb; it is quite white and incandescent with heat. . . . The square is deserted and like an oven—more desolate, even, than a populous square after a riot." Ch. B., *Oeuvres*, vol. 2, p. 193.[279] [J52a,4]

In *Le Globe* of March 15, 1830, Duvergier de Hauranne writes of *Les Consolations:* "It is not at all certain that the Posillipo has not inspired M. Sainte-Beuve as much as his Boulevard d'Enfer" (‹cited in Sainte-Beuve, *Les Consolations* [Paris, 1863],› p. 114). [J52a,5]

Critique of *Joseph Delorme* and *Les Consolations* by Farcy, a July insurgent who fell in battle shortly after composing these lines: "Libertinism is poetic when it is a transport of impassioned principle in us, when it is audacious philosophy, but not when it is merely a furtive aberration, a shameful confession. This state of mind . . . ill accords . . . with the poet, who should always go along unaffected, with head held high, and who requires enthusiasm, or the bitter depths of passion." From the manuscript published by C. A. Sainte-Beuve in *Les Consolations: Pensées d'août* (Paris, 1863), p. 125. [J52a,6]

From the critique of Sainte-Beuve by Farcy: "If the crowd is intolerable to him, the vastness of space oppresses him even more, a situation that is less poetic. He has not shown the pride or the range to take command of all this nature, to listen to it, understand it, and render its grand spectacles." "He was right," comments Sainte-Beuve (p. 126). C. A. Sainte-Beuve, *Les Consolations: Pensées d'août* [*Poésies de Sainte-Beuve*, part 2] (Paris, 1863), p. 125. [J52a,7]

Baudelaire's oeuvre has perhaps gained importance—moral as well as literary— through the fact that he left no novel. [J52a,8]

The mental capacities that matter in Baudelaire are "souvenirs" of the human being, somewhat the way medieval allegories are souvenirs of the gods. "Baudelaire," Claudel once wrote, "takes as his subject the only inner experience left to people of the nineteenth century—namely, remorse." Now, this very likely paints too rosy a picture: remorse was no less past its time than other inner experiences formerly canonized. Remorse in Baudelaire is merely a souvenir, like repentance, virtue, hope, and even anguish, which was overtaken the moment it relinquished its place to *morne incuriosité* ‹glum indifference›." [280]   [J53,1]

As Baudelaire, after 1850, took up the doctrine of *l'art pour l'art,* he explicitly carried through a renunciation which he had undertaken in sovereign spirit at the very instant he made allegory into the armature of his poetry: he gave up using art as category of the totality of existence.   [J53,2]

The brooder, whose startled gaze falls on the fragment in his hand, becomes an allegorist.   [J53,3]

If we call to mind just how much Baudelaire as a poet had to respect his own precepts, his own insights, his own taboos, and how strictly circumscribed, on the other hand, the tasks of his poetic labor were, then we may come to see in him a heroic trait. There is no other book of poems in which the poet as such presents himself with so little vanity and so much force. This fact provides a basis for the frequent comparison with Dante.   [J53,4]

What proved so fascinating to Baudelaire in late Latin literature, particularly in Lucan, may have been the use this literature made of the names of gods—a practice in which it prepared the way for allegory. Usener discusses this.[281]
          [J53,5]

Scenes of horror in Lucan: the Thessalian witch Erichtho, and the profanation of the dead (‹*Bellum civile,*› book 5, lines 507–569); the desecration of the head of Pompey (book 8, lines 663–691); Medusa (book 9, lines 624–653).   [J53,6]

"Le Coucher du soleil romantique"[282]—landscape as allegory.   [J53,7]

Antiquity and Christianity together determine the historical armature of the allegorical mode of perception; they provide the lasting rudiments of the first allegorical experience—that of the High Middle Ages. "The allegorical outlook has its origin in the conflict between the guilt-laden *physis,* held up as an example by Christianity, and a purer *natura deorum* [nature of the gods], embodied in the Pantheon. With the revival of paganism in the Renaissance, and of Christianity in the Counter-Reformation, allegory, the form of their conflict, also had to be renewed" (‹Walter Benjamin,› *Ursprung des deutschen Trauerspiels* [Berlin, 1928], p. 226).[283] In Baudelaire's case, the matter is clarified if we reverse the formula. The allegorical experience was primary for him; one can say that he appropriated from the antique world, as from the Christian, no more than he needed to set going in his poetry that primordial experience—which had a substrate entirely sui generis. [J53a,1]

The passion for ships and for self-propelled toys is, with Baudelaire, perhaps only another expression of the discredit into which, in his view, the world of the organic has fallen. A sadistic inspiration is palpable here. [J53a,2]

"All the miscreants of melodrama—accursed, damned, and fatally marked with a grin which runs from ear to ear—are in the pure orthodoxy of laughter. . . . Laughter is satanic; it is thus profoundly human." Ch. B., *Oeuvres*, vol. 2, p. 171 ("De l'Essence du rire").[284] [J53a,3]

It is a shock that brings someone engrossed in reverie up from the depths. Medieval legends invoke the state of shock peculiar to the researcher whose longing for more-than-human wisdom has led him to magic; the experience of shock is cited here as the "derisive laughter of hell." "Here . . . the muteness of matter is overcome. In laughter, above all, matter takes on an abundance of spirit, in highly eccentric disguise. Indeed, it becomes so spiritual that it far outstrips language. Aiming still higher, it ends in shrill laughter" (*Ursprung des deutschen Trauerspiels,* p. 227).[285] Not only was such strident laughter characteristic of Baudelaire; it reechoed in his ear and gave him much to think about. [J53a,4]

Laughter is shattered articulation. [J54,1]

On the flight of images and the theory of surprise, which Baudelaire shared with Poe: "Allegories become dated because it is part of their nature to shock."[286] The succession of allegorical publications in the Baroque represents a sort of flight of images. [J54,2]

On petrified unrest and the flight of images: "The same tendency is characteristic of Baroque lyric. The poems have 'no forward movement, but they swell up from within.' If it is to hold its own against the tendency toward absorption, the allegorical must constantly unfold in new and surprising ways." *Ursprung,* p. 182 (citing Fritz Strich).[287] [J54,3]

Once the scheme of allegory has been metaphysically determined according to its threefold illusionary nature, as "illusion of freedom—in the exploration of what is forbidden; . . . illusion of independence—in the secession from the community of the pious; . . . illusion of infinity—in the empty abyss of evil" (*Ursprung,* p. 230),[288] then nothing is easier than to assimilate whole groups of Baudelairean poems to this design. The first part can be represented by the cycle "Fleurs du mal"; the second part, by the cycle "Révolte"; while the third could be elaborated without difficulty from "Spleen et idéal." [J54,4]

The image of petrified unrest, in the Baroque, is "the bleak confusion of Golgotha, which can be recognized as the schema underlying the allegorical figures in hundreds of the engravings and descriptions of the period" (*Ursprung*, p. 232).[289]   [J54,5]

The extent of Baudelaire's impatience can be gauged from these lines in "Sonnet d'automne": "My heart, on which everything jars / except the candor of the primitive animal."[290]   [J54,6]

Experiences emptied out and deprived of their substance: "Last . . . we / [of the] Muse's priesthood . . . / have drunk without thirst and eaten without hunger!" ("L'Examen de minuit").[291]   [J54,7]

Art appears truly bare and austere in the light of an allegorical consideration:

> And on that last and terrible day,
> . . . . .
> To escape the vengeance from above,
> He must show barns whose uttermost
> Recesses swell with ripened grain,
> And blooms whose shapes and hues will gain
> The suffrage of the Heavenly Host.[292]

"La Rançon." Compare "Le Squelette laboureur."   [J54,8]

Concerning the "strange sectioning of time," the final stanza of "L'Avertisseur":

> Despite what he may hope or plan,
> There is no moment left when man
> Is not subject to the constant
> Warnings of this odious Serpent.[293]

To be compared with "L'Horloge" and "Rêve parisien."   [J54a,1]

About laughter: "Beguiled by ghostly laughter in the air / his reason falters, grasps at phantom straws." ("Sur *Le Tasse en prison* d'Eugène Delacroix.")

> His mirth is the reverse of Melmoth's sneer
> Or the snickering of Mephistopheles,
> licked by the lurid light of a Fury's torch
> that burns them to a crisp but leaves us cold.

"Vers pour le portrait de M. Honoré Daumier."[294]   [J54a,2]

The derisive laughter from the clouds in "La Béatrice."

> For I—am I not a dissonance
> in the divine accord,

> because of the greedy Irony
> which infiltrates my soul?

"L'Héautontimorouménos."[295] [J54a,3]

"La Beauté"[296]—entails petrifaction, but not the unrest on which the gaze of the allegorist falls. [J54a,4]

On the fetish:

> Precious minerals form her polished eyes,
> and in her strange symbolic nature where
> angel and sphinx unite, where diamond,
>
> gold, and steel dissolve into one light,
> shines forever, useless as a star,
> the sterile woman's icy majesty.

"Avec ses vêtements . . ."[297] [J54a,5]

"For hours? Forever! Into that splendid mane / let me braid rubies, ropes of pearls to bind / you indissolubly to my desire." ("La Chevelure.")[298] [J54a,6]

When he went to meet the consumptive Negress who lived in the city, Baudelaire saw a much truer aspect of the French colonial empire than did Dumas when he took a boat to Tunis on commission from Salvandy. [J54a,7]

Society of the Second Empire:

> Victims in tears, the hangman glorified;
> the banquet seasoned and festooned with blood:
> the poison of power clogs the despot's veins,
> and the people kiss the knout that scourges them.

"Le Voyage."[299] [J55,1]

The clouds: "Le Voyage," section 4, stanza 3. [J55,2]

Autumnal motif: "L'Ennemi," "L'Imprévu," "Semper Eadem." [J55,3]

Satan in "Les Litanies de Satan": "great king of subterranean things"—"You whose bright eye knows the deep arsenals / Where the buried race of metals slumbers."[300] [J55,4]

Granier de Cassagnac's theory of the subhuman, with regard to "Abel et Caïn." [J55,5]

On the Christian determination of allegory: it has no place in the cycle "Révolte." [J55,6]

On allegory: "L'Amour et le crâne: Vieux Cul-de-lampe," "Allégorie," "Une Gra-
vure fantastique." [J55,7]

> . . . The sky was suave, the sea serene; for me
> from now on everything was bloody and black
> —the worse for me—and as if in a shroud
> my heart lay buried in this allegory.

"Un Voyage à Cythère."[301] [J55,8]

"Steeling my nerves to play a hero's part" ("Les Sept Vieillards").[302] [J55,9]

"Les Sept Vieillards" on the subject of eternal sameness. Chorus girls.
[J55,10]

List of allegories: Art, Love, *Pleasure, Repentance, Ennui*, Destruction, the Now,
Time, Death, *Fear, Sorrow*, Evil, Truth, *Hope*, Vengeance, Hate, Respect, Jealousy, Thoughts. [J55,11]

"L'Irrémédiable"—catalogue of emblems. [J55,12]

The allegories stand for that which the commodity makes of the experiences
people have in this century. [J55,13]

The wish to sleep. "I hate all passion, and wit grates on me" ("Sonnet
d'automne").[303] [J55,14]

"A sinuous fleece . . . / . . . which in darkness rivals you, O Night, / deep and
spreading starless Night!" ("Les Promesses d'un visage").[304] [J55,15]

"The dizzying stairs that swallow up his soul" ("Sur *Le Tasse en prison* d'Eugène
Delacroix").[305] [J55,16]

The affinity Baudelaire felt for late Latin literature is probably connected with his
passion for the allegorical art that had its first flowering in the High Middle Ages.
[J55,17]

To attempt to judge Baudelaire's intellectual powers on the basis of his philosophical digressions, as Jules Lemaître has done,[306] is ill-advised. Baudelaire was a
bad philosopher, a better theorist in matters of art; but only as a brooder was he
incomparable. He has the stereotypy in motif characteristic of the brooder, the
imperturbability in warding off disturbance, the readiness each time to put the
image at the beck and call of the thought. The brooder is at home among
allegories. [J55a,1]

The attraction which a few basic situations continually exerted on Baudelaire
belongs to the complex of symptoms associated with melancholy. He appears to

have been under the compulsion of returning at least once to each of his main motifs. [J55a,2]

Baudelaire's allegory bears traces of the violence that was necessary to demolish the harmonious façade of the world that surrounded him. [J55a,3]

In Blanqui's view of the world, petrified unrest becomes the status of the cosmos itself. The course of the world appears, accordingly, as one great allegory. [J55a,4]

Petrified unrest is, moreover, the formula for Baudelaire's life history, which knows no development. [J55a,5]

The state of tension subsisting between the most cultivated sensibility and the most intense contemplation is a mark of the Baudelairean. It is reflected theoretically in the doctrine of correspondences and in the predilection for allegory. Baudelaire never attempted to establish any sort of relations between these. Nevertheless, such relations exist. [J55a,6]

Misery and terror—which, in Baudelaire, have their armature in allegorical perception—have become, in Rollinat, the object of a genre. (This genre had its "artistic headquarters" at Le Chat Noir café. Its model, if you will, may be found in a poem like "Le Vin de l'assassin." Rollinat was one of the house poets at Le Chat Noir.) [J55a,7]

"De l'Essence du rire" contains the theory of satanic laughter. In this essay, Baudelaire goes so far as to adjudge even smiling as fundamentally satanic. Contemporaries testified to something frightful in his own manner of laughing. [J55a,8]

That which the allegorical intention has fixed upon is sundered from the customary contexts of life: it is at once shattered and preserved. Allegory holds fast to the ruins. Baudelaire's destructive impulse is nowhere concerned with the abolition of what falls to it. (But compare "Révolte," J55,‹6›.) [J56,1]

Baroque allegory sees the corpse only from the outside; Baudelaire evokes it from within. [J56,2]

Baudelaire's invectives against mythology recall those of the medieval clerics. He especially detests chubby-cheeked Cupid. His aversion to this figure has the same roots as his hatred for Béranger. [J56,3]

Baudelaire regards art's workshop in itself [as a site of confusion,] as the "apparatus of destruction" which the allegories so often represent. In the notes he left for a preface to a projected third edition of *Les Fleurs du mal,* he writes: "Do we show the public . . . the mechanism behind our effects? . . . Do we display all the rags, the paint, the pulleys, the chains, the alterations, the scribbled-over proof sheets— in short, all the horrors that make up the sanctuary of art?" Ch. B., *Oeuvres,* vol. 1, p. 582.[307]   [J56,4]

Baudelaire as mime: "Being as chaste as paper, as sober as water, as devout as a woman at Holy Communion, as harmless as a sacrificial lamb, I would not be displeased to be taken for a lecher, a drunkard, an infidel, a murderer." Ch. B., *Oeuvres*, vol. 1, p. 582 (Studies for a preface to *Les Fleurs du mal*).[308]   [J56,5]

Solely for the publication of *Les Fleurs du mal* and *Petits Poèmes en prose*, Baudelaire sent notices to more than twenty-five periodicals, not counting the newspapers.   [J56,6]

Baroque detailing of the female body: "Le Beau Navire" ⟨The Fine Ship⟩. To the contrary: "Tout entière" ⟨Altogether⟩.   [J56,7]

Allegory:

> That it's foolish to build anything on human hearts—
> For everything cracks, yes, even love and beauty,
> Till Oblivion flings them into its hod
> And gives them over to Eternity!

in his "Confession."[309]   [J56,8]

Fetish: "who now, from Pit to Empyrean scorned / by all but me . . . / . . . / my jet-eyed statue, angel with brazen brows!" ("Je te donne ces vers.")[310]   [J56,9]

"Michelangelo / No man's land where every Hercules / becomes a Christ." ("Les Phares.")[311]   [J56a,1]

"An echo repeated by a thousand labyrinths." ("Les Phares.")[312]   [J56a,2]

"La Muse vénal" shows to what degree Baudelaire occasionally saw the publication of poems as a form of prostitution.   [J56a,3]

"Your Christian bloodstream coursing strong / and steadfast as the copious Classical vein." ("La Muse malade.")[313]   [J56a,4]

In Baudelaire's case, the really decisive indication of class betrayal is not the integrity which forbade his applying for a government grant but the incompatibility he felt with the ethos of journalism.   [J56a,5]

Allegory views existence, as it does art, under the sign of fragmentation and ruin. *L'art pour l'art* erects the kingdom of art outside profane existence. Common to both is the renunciation of the idea of harmonious totality in which—according to the doctrine of German Idealism no less than that of French eclecticism—art and profane existence are merged. [J56a,6]

The portrayal of the crowd in Poe shows that the description of confusion is not the same as a confused description. [J56a,7]

Flowers adorn the individual stations of this Calvary [of male sexuality]. They are flowers of evil. [J56a,8]

Les Fleurs du mal is the last book of poems to have had a European-wide reverberation. Before that: Ossian, and Heine's *Buch der Lieder* ‹Book of Songs›.
[J56a,9]

The dialectic of commodity production in advanced capitalism: the novelty of products—as a stimulus to demand—is accorded an unprecedented importance. At the same time, "the eternal return of the same" is manifest in mass production.
[J56a,10]

In Blanqui's cosmology, everything hinges on the stars, which Baudelaire banishes from his world. [J56a,11]

The renunciation of the magic of distance is a decisive moment in the lyric poetry of Baudelaire. It has found its sovereign formulation in the first stanza of "Le Voyage." [J56a,12]

It belongs to the Via Dolorosa of male sexuality that Baudelaire perceived pregnancy, in some degree, as unfair competition. On the other hand, solidarity between impotence and sterility. [J57,1]

The passage in which Baudelaire speaks of his fascination with painted theatrical backdrops—Where? Q4a,4. [J57,2]

Baudelaire's destructive impulse is nowhere concerned with the abolition of what falls to it. This is reflected in his allegory and is the condition of its regressive tendency. On the other hand, allegory has to do, precisely in its destructive furor, with dispelling the illusion that proceeds from all "given order," whether of art or of life: the illusion of totality or of organic wholeness which transfigures that order and makes it seem endurable. And this is the progressive tendency of allegory. [J57,3]

Whenever humanity—aspiring after a purer, more innocent, more spiritual existence than it has been granted—looked around for a token and pledge of this existence in nature, it generally found it in the plant or animal kingdom. Not so Baudelaire. His dream of such an existence disdains community with any terrestrial nature and holds to the clouds. Many of his poems contain cloud motifs [not to mention the transfiguration of Paris in "Paysage" ‹Landscape›]. What is most appalling is the defilement of the clouds ("La Béatrice"). [J57,4]

From the perspective of spleen, the buried man is the "transcendental subject of history."[314] [J57,5]

Baudelaire's financial misery is a moment of his personal Golgotha. It has furnished, together with his erotic misery, the defining features of the image of the poet handed down by tradition. The Passion of Baudelaire: understood as a redemption. [J57,6]

Let us emphasize the solitude of Baudelaire as a counterpart to that of Blanqui. The latter, too, had a "destiny eternally solitary" ("Mon Coeur mis à nu," no. 12).[315] [J57,7]

On the image of the crowd in Poe: How well can the image of the big city turn out when the register of its physical dangers—to say nothing of the danger to which it itself is exposed—is as incomplete as it is at the time of Poe or Baudelaire? In the crowd, we see a presentiment of these dangers. [J57,8]

Baudelaire's readers are men. It is men who have made him famous; it is them he has redeemed.[316] [J57,9]

Baudelaire would never have written poems, if he had had merely the motives for doing so that poets usually have. [J57a,1]

On impotence. Baudelaire is a "maniac, in revolt against his own impotence." Incapable of satisfying the sexual needs of a woman, he made a virtue of necessity in sabotaging the spiritual needs of his contemporaries. He himself did not fail to notice the connection, and his consciousness of this connection is seen most clearly in his style of humor. It is the cheerless humor of the rebel, not for a moment to be confused with the geniality of scoundrels, which at that time was already on the rise. This type of reaction is something very French; its name, *la rogne,* is not easily rendered into other languages.[317] [J57a,2]

It is in its transitoriness that modernity shows itself to be ultimately and most intimately akin to antiquity. The uninterrupted resonance which *Les Fleurs du mal* has found up through the present day is linked to a certain aspect of the urban scene, one that came to light only with the city's entry into poetry. It is the aspect least of all expected. What makes itself felt through the evocation of Paris in Baudelaire's verse is the infirmity and decrepitude of a great city. Nowhere, perhaps, has this been given more perfect expression than in the poem "Crépuscule du matin," which is the awakening sob of the sleeper, reproduced in the materials of urban life. This aspect, however, is more or less common to the whole cycle of "Tableaux parisiens;" it is present in the transparence of the city, as conjured by "Le Soleil," no less than in the allegorical evocation of the Louvre in "Le Cygne." [J57a,3]

On the physiognomy of Baudelaire as that of the mime: Courbet reports that he looked different every day. [J57a,4]

With the inhabitants of Romance-language nations, a refinement of the sensorium does not diminish the power of sensuous apprehension. With the Germans, on the other hand, the refinement, the advancing cultivation of sensuous enjoyment is generally purchased with a decline in the art of apprehension; here, the capacity for pleasure loses in concentration what it gains in delicacy. (Compare the "reek of wine-casks"[318] in "Le Vin des chiffonniers.") [J57a,5]

The eminent aptitude for pleasure on the part of a Baudelaire has nothing at all to do with any sort of coziness. The fundamental incompatibility of sensuous pleasure with what is called *Gemütlichkeit* is the mark of an authentic culture of the senses. Baudelaire's snobbism is the eccentric repudiation of complacency, and his satanism is the readiness to subvert this habit of mind wherever and whenever it should arise. [J58,1]

The streets of Paris, in Meryon's rendering, are chasms, high above which float the clouds. [J58,2]

Baudelaire wanted to make room for his poems, and to this end he had to push aside others. He managed to devalue certain poetic liberties of the Romantics through his classical deployment of rhyme, as he devalued the traditional alexandrine through his introduction of certain ebbings and points of rupture. In short, his poems contained special provisions for the elimination of competitors. [J58,3]

Baudelaire was perhaps the first to have had the idea of a market-oriented originality, which just for that reason was more original in its day than any other. The *création* of his *poncif*[319] led him to adopt methods that were the stock in trade of the competition. His defamatory remarks about Musset or Béranger have just as much to do with this as his imitations of Victor Hugo. [J58,4]

The relation of the crowd to the individual comes, practically of itself, to unfold as a metaphor in which the differing inspirations of these two poets—Hugo and Baudelaire—can be grasped. Words, like images, present themselves to Hugo as a surging, relentless mass. With Baudelaire, in contrast, they take the side of the solitary who, to be sure, fades into the multitude, but not before appearing with singular physiognomy to one who allows her gaze to linger. [J58,5]

What good is talk of progress to a world sinking into rigor mortis? Baudelaire found the experience of such a world set down with incomparable power in the work of Poe, who thus became irreplaceable for him. Poe described the world in which Baudelaire's whole poetic enterprise had its prerogative.   [J58,6]

The idea of Baudelaire's aesthetic Passion has given to many parties in the critical literature on Baudelaire the character of an *image d'Epinal*. These colored prints, as is well known, often showed scenes from the lives of saints.   [J58a,1]

There are weighty historical circumstances making the Golgotha-way of impotence trod by Baudelaire into one marked out in advance by his society. Only this would explain how it was that he drew, as traveling expenses along the way, a precious old coin from among the accumulated treasures of this society. It was the coin of allegory, with the scythe-wielding skeleton on one side, and, on the obverse, the figure of Melancholy plunged in meditation.   [J58a,2]

That the stars do not appear in Baudelaire is the surest indicator of that tendency of his poetry to dissolve illusory appearances.[320]   [J58a,3]

The key to Baudelaire's relationship with Gautier is to be sought in the more or less clear awareness of the younger man [?] that even in art his destructive impulse encounters no inviolable limit. In fact, such a limit cannot withstand the allegorical intention. Moreover, Baudelaire could hardly have written his essay on Dupont if the critique of the concept of art entailed by the latter's established practice had not corresponded to his own radical critique. In referring to Gautier, Baudelaire successfully undertook to cover up these tendencies.   [J58a,4]

In the flâneur, one might say, is reborn the sort of idler that Socrates picked out from the Athenian marketplace to be his interlocutor. Only, there is no longer a Socrates. And the slave labor that guaranteed him his leisure has likewise ceased to exist.   [J58a,5]

Streets of ill repute. Considering the importance of forbidden forms of sexuality in Baudelaire's life and work, it is remarkable that the bordello plays no role in either his private documents or his work. There is no counterpart, within this sphere, to a poem such as "Le Jeu." The brothel is named but once: in "Les Deux Bonnes Soeurs."   [J58a,6]

For the flâneur, the "crowd" is a veil hiding the "masses."[321]   [J59,2]

That Hugo's poetry takes up the motif of table-turning is perhaps less noteworthy than the fact that it was regularly composed in the presence of such phenomena. For Hugo in exile, the unfathomable, insistent swarm of the spirit world takes the place of the public.   [J59,3]

The primary interest of allegory is not linguistic but optical. "Images—my great, my primitive passion."[322]   [J59,4]

The elaborate theorems with which the principle of "art for art's sake" was enunciated by its original proponents, as by subsequent literary history, ultimately come down to a specific thesis: that sensibility is the true subject of poetry. Sensibility is, by its nature, involved in suffering. If it experiences its highest concretization, its richest determination, in the sphere of the erotic, then it must find its absolute consummation, which coincides with its transfiguration, in the Passion. It will define the idea of an "aesthetic Passion." The concept of the aesthetic appears here with precisely the signification that Kierkegaard gives it in his erotology. [J59,5]

The poetics of *l'art pour l'art* blends seamlessly into the aesthetic Passion of *Les Fleurs du mal*. [J59,6]

The "loss of a halo"[323] concerns the poet first of all. He is obliged to exhibit himself in his own person *on the market*. Baudelaire played this role to the hilt. His famous mythomania was a publicity stunt. [J59,7]

The new dreariness and desolation of Paris, as it is described by Veuillot, comes on the scene, together with the dreariness of men's attire, as an essential moment in the image of modernity. [J59,8]

Mystification, with Baudelaire, is an apotropaic magic, similar to the lie among prostitutes. [J59,9]

The commodity form emerges in Baudelaire as the social content of the allegorical form of perception. Form and content are united in the prostitute, as in their synthesis. [J59,10]

Baudelaire perceived the significance of the mass-produced article as clearly as did Balzac. In this, his "Americanism," of which Laforgue speaks, has its firmest foundation. He wanted to create a *poncif*, a cliché. Lemaître assures him that he succeeded. [J59a,1]

Apropos of Valéry's reflections on the situation of Baudelaire. It is important that Baudelaire met with competitive relations in the production of poetry. Of course, rivalry between poets is as old as the hills. But in the period around 1830, these rivalries began to be decided on the open market. It was victory in that field—and not the patronage of the gentry, princes, or the clergy—that was to be won. This condition weighed more heavily on the lyric than on other forms of poetry. The disorganization of styles and of poetic schools is the complement of that market, which reveals itself to the poet as the "public." Baudelaire was not based in any style, and he had no school. It was a real discovery for him that he was competing against individuals. [J59a,2]

Les Fleurs du mal may be considered an arsenal. Baudelaire wrote certain of his poems in order to destroy others written before him.   [J59a,3]

No one ever felt less at home in Paris than Baudelaire. *Every* intimacy with things is alien to the allegorical intention. To touch on things means, for it, to violate them. To recognize things means, for it, to see through them. Wherever the allegorical intention prevails, no habits of any kind can be formed. Hardly has a thing been taken up than allegory has dispensed with the situation. Thing and situation become obsolete for allegory more quickly than a new pattern for the milliner. But to become obsolete means: to grow strange. Spleen lays down centuries between the present moment and the one just lived. It is spleen that tirelessly generates "antiquity." And in fact, with Baudelaire, modernity is nothing other than the "newest antiquity." Modernity, for Baudelaire, is not solely and not primarily the object of his sensibility; it is the object of a conquest. Modernity has, for its armature, the allegorical mode of vision.   [J59a,4]

The correspondence between antiquity and modernity is the sole constructive conception of history in Baudelaire. With its rigid armature, it excludes every dialectical conception.   [J59a,5]

On the phrase, "I have little to do with such things,"[324] in the draft of a preface to *Les Fleurs du mal*. Baudelaire, who never founded a family, has given the word "familiar" in his poetry an inflection filled with meaning and with promise such as it never before possessed. It is like a slow, heavily laden haywagon in which the poet carts to the barn everything which throughout his life he had to renounce. Compare "Correspondances," "Bohémiens en voyage," "Obsession."   [J60,1]

The passage "where everything, even horror, turns to magic"[325] could hardly be better exemplified than by Poe's description of the crowd.   [J60,2]

Concerning the opening line from "La Servante au grand coeur": on the words "of whom you were so *jealous*"[326] falls an accent that one would not necessarily expect. The voice, as it were, draws back from "jealous." Therein lies the frailty of this already long-past situation.   [J60,3]

On "Spleen I": through the word "mortality," the city with its offices and its statistical registers lies embedded in spleen, as in a picture puzzle ‹*Vexierbild*›.
                                          [J60,4]

The whore is the most precious booty in the triumph of allegory—the life which signifies death. This quality is the only thing about her that cannot be bought, and for Baudelaire it is the only thing that matters.   [J60,5]

Around the middle of the century, the conditions of artistic production underwent a change. This change consisted in the fact that for the first time the form of the commodity imposed itself decisively on the work of art, and the form of the masses on its public. Particularly vulnerable to these developments, as can be seen now unmistakably in our century, was the lyric. It is the unique distinction of *Les Fleurs du mal* that Baudelaire responded to precisely these altered conditions with a book of poems. It is the best example of heroic conduct to be found in his life.   [J60,6]

The heroic bearing of Baudelaire is akin to that of Nietzsche. Though Baudelaire likes to appeal to Catholicism, his historical experience is nonetheless that which Nietzsche fixed in the phrase "God is dead." In Nietzsche's case, this experience is projected cosmologically in the thesis that nothing new occurs any more. In Nietzsche, the accent lies on eternal recurrence, which the human being has to face with heroic composure. For Baudelaire, it is more a matter of "the new," which must be wrested heroically from what is always again the same.   [J60,7]

The historical experiences which Baudelaire was one of the first to undergo (it is no accident that he belongs to the generation of Marx, whose principal work appeared in the year of his death) have become, in our day, only more widespread and persistent. The traits displayed by capital in June 1848 have, since then, been engraved still more sharply in the ruling classes. And the particular difficulties involved in mastering the poetry of Baudelaire are the obverse of the ease with which one can give oneself up to it. In a word, there is nothing yet obsolete about this poetry. This fact has determined the character of most of the books concerned with Baudelaire: they are feuilletons on an expanded scale.
      [J60a,1]

Particularly toward the end of his life, and in view of the limited success of his work, Baudelaire more and more threw himself into the bargain. He flung himself after his work, and thus, to the end, confirmed in his own person what he had said about the unavoidable necessity of prostitution for the poet.   [J60a,2]

One encounters an abundance of stereotypes in Baudelaire, as in the Baroque poets.   [J60a,3]

For the decline of the aura, one thing within the realm of mass production is of overriding importance: the massive reproduction of the image.   [J60a,4]

Impotence is the key figure of Baudelaire's solitude.[327] An abyss divides him from his fellow men. It is *this* abyss of which his poetry speaks.   [J60a,5]

We may assume that the crowd as it appears in Poe, with its abrupt and intermittent movements, is described quite realistically. In itself, the description has a higher truth. These are less the movements of people going about their business than the movements of the machines they operate. With uncanny foresight, Poe seems to have modeled the gestures and reactions of the crowd on the rhythm of these machines. The flâneur, at any rate, has no part in such behavior. Instead, he forms an obstacle in its path. His nonchalance would therefore be nothing other than an unconscious protest against the tempo of the production process. (Compare D2a,1.)   [J60a,6]

Fog appears as a consolation of the solitary man. It fills the abyss surrounding him.   [J60a,7]

Baudelaire's candidacy for the Académie was a sociological experiment.   [J61,1]

Series of types—from the national guardsman Mayeux, through Gavroche, to the ragpicker, to Vireloque, to Ratapoil.[328]   [J61,2]

Baudelaire's allegorical mode of vision was not understood by any of his contemporaries and was thus, in the end, completely overlooked.   [J61,3]

Surprising proclamations and mystery-mongering, sudden attacks and impenetrable irony, belong to the *raison d'état* of the Second Empire and were characteristic of Napoleon III. They are no less characteristic of the theoretical writings of Baudelaire.   [J61,4]

The cosmic shudder in Victor Hugo has little in common with the naked terror that seized Baudelaire in his spleen. Hugo felt perfectly at home in the world of the spirits. It is the complement of his domestic existence, which was itself not without horror.   [J61,5]

The veiled import of the first section of "Chant d'automne": the season is named only in the tiny phrase "autumn is here!"[329] and the following line says that, for the poet, it has no other meaning than as a foreboding of death. To him, it has brought no harvest.   [J61,6]

In the guise of a beggar, Baudelaire continually put the model of bourgeois society to the test. His willfully induced, if not deliberately maintained, dependence on his mother not only has a psychoanalytically identifiable cause; it also has a social cause.   [J61,7]

The labyrinth is the right path for him who always arrives early enough at his destination. For the flâneur, this destination is the marketplace.   [J61,8]

The path of one who shrinks from arriving at his goal will easily take the form of a labyrinth. [For the flâneur, this goal is the marketplace.] The same holds for the social class that does not want to know where it is heading. Moreover, nothing prevents it from reveling in this roundabout way and hence substituting the shudder of pleasure for the shudder of death. This was the case for the society of the Second Empire.   [J61,9]

What concerned Baudelaire was not manifest and short-term demand, but latent and long-term demand. *Les Fleurs du mal* demonstrates not only that he correctly assessed such a demand but, in addition, that this sureness in evaluation is inseparable from his significance as a poet. [J61,10]

One of the most powerful attractions of prostitution appears only with the rise of the metropolis—namely, its operation in the mass and through the masses. It was the existence of the masses that first enabled prostitution to overspread large areas of the city, whereas earlier it had been confined, if not to houses, at least to the streets. The masses first made it possible for the sexual object to be reflected simultaneously in a hundred different forms of allurement—forms which the object itself produced. Beyond this, salability itself can become a sexual stimulus; and this attraction increases wherever an abundant supply of women underscores their character as commodity. With the exhibition of girls[330] in rigidly uniform dress at a later period, the music hall review explicitly introduced the mass-produced article into the libidinal life of the big-city dweller. [J61a,1]

As a matter of fact, if the rule of the bourgeoisie were one day to be stabilized (which never before has happened, and never can), then the vicissitudes of history would in actuality have no more claim on the attention of thinkers than a child's kaleidoscope, which with every turn of the hand dissolves the established order into a new array. As a matter of fact, the concepts of the ruling class have in every age been the mirrors that enabled an image of "order" to prevail. [J61a,2]

In *L'Eternité par les astres,* Blanqui displayed no antipathy to the belief in progress; between the lines, however, he heaped scorn on the idea. One should not necessarily conclude from this that he was untrue to his political credo. The activity of a professional revolutionary such as Blanqui does not presuppose any faith in progress; it presupposes only the determination to do away with present injustice. The irreplaceable political value of class hatred consists precisely in its affording the revolutionary class a healthy indifference toward speculations concerning progress. Indeed, it is just as worthy of humane ends to rise up out of indignation at prevailing injustice as to seek through revolution to better the existence of future generations. It is just as worthy of the human being; it is also more like the human being. Hand in hand with such indignation goes the firm resolve to snatch humanity at the last moment from the catastrophe looming at every turn. That was the case with Blanqui. He always refused to develop plans for what comes "later." [J61a,3]

Baudelaire was obliged to lay claim to the dignity of the poet in a society that had no more dignity of any kind to confer. Hence the *bouffonnerie* of his public appearances. [J62,1]

The figure of Baudelaire has passed into his fame. For the petty-bourgeois mass of readers, his story is an *image d'Epinal,* an illustrated "life history of a libertine."

This image has contributed greatly to Baudelaire's reputation—little though its purveyors may have numbered among his friends. Over this image another imposes itself, one that has had a less widespread but more lasting effect: it shows Baudelaire as exemplar of an aesthetic Passion.   [J62,2]

The aesthete in Kierkegaard is predestined to the Passion. See "The Unhappiest Man" in *Either/Or*.   [J62,3]

The grave as the secret chamber in which Eros and Sexus settle their ancient quarrel.   [J62,4]

The stars in Baudelaire present the rebus image ‹*Vexierbild*› of the commodity. They are "the eternal return of the same" in great masses.   [J62,5]

Baudelaire did not have the humanitarian idealism of a Victor Hugo or a Lamartine. The emotional buoyancy of a Musset was not at his disposal. He did not, like Gautier, take pleasure in his times, nor could he deceive himself about them like Leconte de Lisle. It was not given him to find a refuge in devotions, like Verlaine, nor to heighten the youthful vigor of his lyric élan through the betrayal of his adulthood, like Rimbaud. As rich as Baudelaire is in knowledge of his craft, he is relatively unprovided with stratagems to face the times. And even the grand tragic part he had composed for the arena of his day—the role of the "modern"—could be filled in the end only by himself. All this Baudelaire no doubt recognized. The eccentricities in which he took such pleasure were those of the mime who has to perform before a public incapable of following the action on the stage—a mime, furthermore, who knows this about his audience and, in his performance, allows that knowledge its rightful due.   [J62,6]

In the psychic economy, the mass-produced article appears as obsessional idea. [It answers to no natural need.] The neurotic is compelled to channel it violently among the ideas within the natural circulation process.   [J62a,1]

The idea of eternal recurrence transforms the historical event itself into a mass-produced article. But this conception also displays, in another respect—on its obverse side, one could say—a trace of the economic circumstances to which it owes its sudden topicality. This was manifest at the moment the security of the conditions of life was considerably diminished through an accelerated succession of crises. The idea of *eternal* recurrence derived its luster from the fact that it was no longer possible, in all circumstances, to expect a recurrence of conditions across any interval of time shorter than that provided by eternity. The quotidian constellations very gradually began to be less quotidian. Very gradually their recurrence became a little less frequent, and there could arise, in consequence, the obscure presentiment that henceforth one must rest content with cosmic constellations. Habit, in short, made ready to surrender some of its prerogatives. Nietzsche says, "I love short-lived habits,"[331] and Baudelaire already, throughout his life, was incapable of developing regular habits. Habits are the armature of long experience ‹*Erfahrung*›, whereas they are decomposed by individual experiences ‹*Erlebnisse*›. [J62a,2]

A paragraph of the "Diapsalmata ad se ipsum" deals with boredom. It closes with the sentence: "My soul is like the Dead Sea, over which no bird can fly; when it has flown midway, then it sinks down to death and destruction." Sören Kierkegaard, *Entweder-Oder* (Jena, 1911), vol. 1, p. 33. Compare "I am a graveyard that the moon abhors" ("Spleen II").[332] [J62a,3]

Melancholy, pride, and images. "Carking care is my feudal castle. It is built like an eagle's nest upon the peak of a mountain lost in the clouds. No one can take it by storm. From this abode I dart down into the world of reality to seize my prey; but I do not remain down there, I bear my quarry aloft to my stronghold. What I capture are images." Sören Kierkegaard, *Entweder-Oder* (Jena, 1911), vol. 1, p. 38 ("Diapsalmata ad se ipsum").[333] [J62a,4]

On the use of the term "aesthetic" in Kierkegaard. In choosing a governess, one takes into account "also her aesthetic qualifications for amusing the children." Sören Kierkegaard, *Entweder-Oder* (Jena, 1911), vol. 1, p. 255 ("The Rotation Method").[334] [J63,1]

Blanqui's journey: "One tires of living in the country, and moves to the city; one tires of one's native land, and travels abroad; one is *europamüde* ‹tired of Europe›, and goes to America; and so on. Finally one indulges in a sentimental hope of endless journeyings from star to star." Sören Kierkegaard, *Entweder-Oder* (Jena, 1911), vol. 1, p. 260 ("The Rotation Method").[335] [J63,2]

Boredom: "it causes a dizziness like that produced by looking down into a yawning chasm, and this dizziness is infinite." Kierkegaard, *Entweder-Oder*, vol. 1, p. 260 ("The Rotation Method").[336] [J63,3]

On the Passion of the aesthetic man in Kierkegaard and its foundation in memory: "Memory is emphatically the real element of the unhappy man. . . . If I imagine a man who himself had had no childhood, . . . but who now . . . discovered all the beauty that there is in childhood, and who would now remember his own childhood, constantly staring back into that emptiness of the past, then I would have an excellent illustration of the truly unhappy man." Sören Kierkegaard, *Entweder-Oder* (Jena, 1911), vol. 1 pp. 203–204 ("The Unhappiest Man").[337] [J63,4]

Baudelaire's desire to write a book in which he would spew his disgust with humanity into its face recalls the passage in which Kierkegaard confesses to using the either-or as "an interjection" which he would "shout at mankind, just as boys shout 'Yah! Yah!' after a Jew." Kierkegaard, *Entweder-Oder* (Jena, 1913), vol. 2,

p. 133 ("Equilibrium between the Aesthetical and the Ethical in the Composition of Personality").[338]   [J63,5]

On the "sectioning of time." "This . . . is the most adequate expression for the aesthetic existence: it is in the moment. Hence the prodigious oscillations to which the man who lives aesthetically is exposed." Kierkegaard, *Entweder-Oder*, vol. 2, p. 196 ("Equilibrium between the Aesthetical and the Ethical in the Composition of Personality").[339]   [J63,6]

On impotence. Around the middle of the century, the bourgeois class ceases to be occupied with the future of the productive forces it has unleashed. (Now appear those counterparts to the great utopias of a More or Campanella, who had welcomed the accession of this class and affirmed the identity of its interests with the demands of freedom and justice—now appear, that is to say, the utopias of a Bellamy or a Moilin, which are mainly concerned with touching up the notion of economic consumption and its incentives.) In order to concern itself further with the future of the productive forces which it had set going, the bourgeoisie would first of all have had to renounce the idea of private income. That the habit of "coziness" so typical of bourgeois comfort around midcentury goes together with this lassitude of the bourgeois imagination, that it is one with the luxury of "never having to think about how the forces of production must develop in their hands"—these things admit of very little doubt. The dream of having children is merely a beggarly stimulus when it is not imbued with the dream of a new nature of things in which these children might one day live, or for which they can struggle. Even the dream of a "better humanity" in which our children would "have a better life" is only a sentimental fantasy reminiscent of Spitzweg when it is not, at bottom, the dream of a better nature in which they would live. (Herein lies the inextinguishable claim of the Fourierist utopia, a claim which Marx had recognized [and which Russia had begun to act on].) The latter dream is the living source of the biological energy of humanity, whereas the former is only the muddy pond from which the stork draws children. Baudelaire's desperate thesis concerning children as the creatures closest to original sin is not a bad complement to this image.   [J63a,1]

Re the dances of death: "Modern artists are far too neglectful of those magnificent allegories of the Middle Ages." Ch. B., *Oeuvres*, vol. 2, p. 257 ("Salon de 1859").[340]   [J63a,2]

It is impotence that makes for the bitter cup of male sexuality. From this impotence springs Baudelaire's attachment to the seraphic image of woman, as well as his fetishism. It follows that Keller's "sin of the poet"—namely, "to invent sweet images of women, / such as bitter earth never harbors"[341]—is certainly not his. Keller's women have the sweetness of chimeras. Baudelaire, in his female figures, remains precise, and therefore French, because with him the fetishistic and the seraphic elements do not coincide, as they always do in Keller.   [J64,1]

"Of course, Marx and Engels ironized an absolute idealist faith in progress. (Engels commends Fourier for having introduced the future disappearance of humanity into his reflections on history, as Kant introduced the future disappearance of the solar system.) In this connection, Engels also makes fun of 'the talk about illimitable human perfectibility.'"[342] Letter of ⟨Hermann⟩ Duncker to Grete Steffin, July 18, 1938.   [J64,2]

The mythic concept of the task of the poet ought to be defined through the profane concept of the instrument.—The great poet never confronts his work simply as the producer; he is also, at the same time, its consumer. Naturally, in contrast to the public, he consumes it not as entertainment but as tool. This instrumental character represents a use value that does not readily enter into the exchange value.   [J64,3]

On Baudelaire's "Crépuscule du soir": the big city knows no true evening twilight. In any case, the artificial lighting does away with all transition to night. The same state of affairs is responsible for the fact that the stars disappear from the sky over the metropolis. Who ever notices when they come out? Kant's transcription of the sublime through "the starry heavens above me and the moral law within me"[343] could never have been conceived in these terms by an inhabitant of the big city.   [J64,4]

Baudelaire's spleen is the suffering entailed by the decline of the aura. "Adorable Spring has lost its perfume."[344]   [J64,5]

Mass production is the principal economic cause—and class warfare the principal social cause—of the decline of the aura.   [J64a,1]

De Maistre on the "savage"—a reflection directed against Rousseau: "One need only glance at the savage to see the curse written . . . on the external form of his body. . . . A formidable hand weighing on these doomed races wipes out in them the two distinctive characteristics of our grandeur: foresight and perfectibility. The savage cuts the tree down to gather the fruit; he unyokes the ox that the missionary has just entrusted to him, and cooks it with wood from the plow." Joseph de Maistre, *Les Soirées de Saint-Pétersbourg*, ed. Hattier (Paris ⟨1922⟩), p. 23 (second dialogue).[345]   [J64a,2]

The Knight in the third dialogue: "I would very much like, though it cost me dearly, to discover a truth capable of shocking the whole human race. I would state it plainly to everyone's face." Joseph de Maistre, *Les Soirées de Saint-Pétersbourg*, ed. Hattier, p. 29.   [J64a,3]

"Beware, above all, one very common prejudice . . .—namely, the belief that the great reputation of a book presupposes an extensive and reasoned knowledge of that book. Such is not the case, I assure you. The great majority are capable of judging solely by the lights of a rather small number of men who first deliver an opinion. They pass on, and this opinion survives them. The new books arriving on the scene leave no time for reading any others; and soon these others are judged only according to a vague reputation." Joseph de Maistre, *Les Soirées de Saint-Pétersbourg*, ed. Hattier (Paris), p. 44 (sixth dialogue). [J64a,4]

"The whole earth, continually steeped in blood, is nothing but an immense altar on which every living thing must be sacrificed without end, without restraint, without respite, until the consummation of the world, the extinction of evil, the death of death." De Maistre, *Soirées*, ed. Hattier, p. 61 (seventh dialogue: "La Guerre").[346] [J64a,5]

The characters in *Les Soirées de Saint-Pétersbourg:* the Knight has felt the influence of Voltaire, and the Senator is a mystic, while the Count expounds the doctrine of the author himself. [J64a,6]

"But do you realize, gentlemen, the source of this flood of insolent doctrines which unceremoniously judge God and call him to account for his orders? They come to us from that great phalanx we call *savants* ‹intellectuals› and whom we have not been able in this age to keep in their place, which is a secondary one. At other times, there were very few *savants*, and a very small minority of this very small minority were ungodly; today one sees nothing but *savants*. It is a profession, a crowd, a nation, and among them the already unfortunate exception has become the rule. On every side they have usurped a limitless influence; yet if there is one thing certain in this world, it is, to my mind, that it is not for science to guide men. Nothing necessary for this is entrusted to science. One would have to be out of one's mind to believe that God has charged the academies with teaching us what he is and what we owe to him. It rests with the prelates, the nobles, the great officers of state to be the repositories and guardians of the saving truths, to teach nations what is bad and what good, what true and what false, in the moral and spiritual order. Others have no right to reason on this kind of matter. They have the natural sciences to amuse them. What are they complaining about?" De Maistre, *Les Soirées de Saint-Pétersbourg*, ed. Hattier (Paris), p. 72 (eighth dialogue).[347] [J65,1]

On judicial procedures: "Under the rule of Muslim law, authority punishes, even with death, the man it thinks deserves it, at the very moment and place it seizes him; this brusque enforcement of the law, which has not lacked blind admirers, is nevertheless one of the many proofs of the brutalization and divine censure of these peoples. Among us, things are quite different. The culprit must be arrested; he must be charged; he must defend himself; he must above all settle his conscience and his worldly affairs; practical arrangements for his punishment must be made. Finally, to take everything into account, a certain time must be left to take him to the appointed place of punishment. The scaffold is an *altar*; it cannot therefore be either set up in a certain place or moved, except by authority. These delays, praiseworthy in their very excessiveness, yet still not lacking their blind detractors, are no less a proof of our superiority." De Maistre, *Les Soirées de Saint-Pétersbourg*, ed. Hattier (Paris), p. 78 (tenth dialogue).[348]   [J65,2]

God appears in de Maistre as *mysterium tremendum*.[349]   [J65,3]

In the seventh dialogue ("La Guerre"), a series of sentences beginning with the formula "War is divine." Among these, one of the most extravagant: "War is divine in the protection granted to the great leaders, even the most daring, who are rarely struck down in battle." *Soirées de Saint-Pétersbourg*, pp. 61–62.[350]
[J65a,1]

There is, in Baudelaire a latent tension between the destructive and the idyllic aspects of death—between its bloody and its palliative nature.   [J65a,2]

Jugendstil phraseology should still be considered progressive in Baudelaire.
[J65a,3]

"Destruction's bloody retinue"[351] is the court of allegory.   [J65a,4]

The historicism of the nineteenth century is the background against which Baudelaire's "pursuit of modernity" stands out. (Villemain, Cousin.)   [J65a,5]

So long as there is semblance in history, it will find in nature its ultimate refuge. The commodity, which is the last burning-glass of historical semblance ‹*Schein*›, celebrates its triumph in the fact that nature itself takes on a commodity character. It is this commodity appearance ‹*Warenschein*› of nature that is embodied in the whore. "Money feeds sensuality," it is said, and this formula in itself affords only the barest outline of a state of affairs that reaches well beyond prostitution. Under the dominion of the commodity fetish, the sex appeal of the woman is more or less tinged with the appeal of the commodity. It is no accident that the relations of the pimp to his girlfriend, whom he sells as an "article" on the market, have so inflamed the sexual fantasies of the bourgeoisie. The modern advertisement shows, from another angle, to what extent the attractions of the woman and those of the commodity can be merged. The sexuality that in former times—on a social level—was stimulated through imagining the future of the productive forces is mobilized now through imagining the power of capital.
[J65a,6]

The circumstance of the new is perhaps nowhere better illuminated than in the figure of the flâneur. His thirst for the new is quenched by the crowd, which appears self-impelled and endowed with a soul of its own. In fact, this collective is nothing but appearance. This "crowd," in which the flâneur takes delight, is just the empty mold with which, seventy years later, the *Volksgemeinschaft* ‹People's Community›[352] was cast. The flâneur who so prides himself on his alertness, on his nonconformity, was in this respect also ahead of his contemporaries: he was the first to fall victim to an ignis fatuus which since that time has blinded many millions. [J66,1]

Baudelaire idealizes the experience of the commodity, in that he ascribes to it, as canon, the experience of allegory. [J66,2]

If it is imagination that presents correspondences to the memory, it is thinking that consecrates allegory to it. Memory brings about the convergence of imagination and thinking. [J66,3]

With the new manufacturing processes that lead to imitations, semblance is consolidated in the commodity. [J66,4]

Between the theory of natural correspondences and the repudiation of nature exists a contradiction. It is resolved insofar as within the memory impressions become detached from individual experiences, so that the long experience stored up in those impressions is released and can be fed into the allegorical *fundus*. ‹See J62a,2.› [J66,5]

‹Stefan› George translated "Spleen et Idéal" by "Trübsinn und Vergeistigung" ‹Melancholy and Spiritualization›, thus hitting upon the essential meaning of the ideal in Baudelaire. [J66,6]

With Meryon, the majesty and decrepitude of Paris come into their own. [J66,7]

In the form taken by prostitution in the big cities, the woman appears not only as commodity but, in a precise sense, as mass-produced article. This is indicated by the masking of individual expression in favor of a professional appearance, such as makeup provides. The point is made still more emphatically, later on, by the uniformed girls of the music-hall review. [J66,8]

Baudelaire's opposition to progress was the indispensable condition for his success at capturing Paris in his poetry. Compared with this poetry, all later big-city lyric must be accounted feeble. What it lacks is precisely that reserve toward its subject matter which Baudelaire owed to his frenetic hatred of progress. [J66a,1]

In Baudelaire, Paris as an emblem of antiquity contrasts with its masses as an emblem of modernity. [J66a,2]

On *Le Spleen de Paris:* news items are the leaven that allows the urban masses to rise in Baudelaire's imagination. [J66a,3]

Spleen is the feeling that corresponds to catastrophe in permanence. [J66a,4]

It is a very specific experience that the proletariat has in the big city—one in many respects similar to that which the immigrant has there. [J66a,5]

To the flâneur, his city is—even if, like Baudelaire, he happened to be born there—no longer native ground. It represents for him a theatrical display, an arena. [J66a,6]

Baudelaire never wrote a whore-poem from the point of view of the whore. (But compare Brecht, *Lesebuch für Städtebewohner,* no. 5.)[353] [J66a,7]

Preface to Dupont's poems in 1851; essay on Dupont in 1861. [J66a,8]

In the erotology of the damned—as that of Baudelaire might be called—infertility and impotence are the decisive factors. They *alone* are what give to the cruel and ill-famed moments of desire in sexual life a purely negative character—something that is lost, it goes without saying, in the act of procreation, as in relations designed to last an entire lifetime (that is, in marriage). These realities instituted for the long term—children, marriage—would lack all assurance of longevity, had not the most destructive energies of the human being entered into their creation, contributing to their stability not less but more than many another energy. But these relations are legitimated, through this contribution, only to the extent that this is really possible for decisive libidinal movements in present-day society. [J66a,9]

The social value of marriage rests decidedly on its longevity, insofar as this latter holds within it the idea of an ultimate and definitive—if continually deferred— "confrontation" of the spouses. From this confrontation the couple are preserved so long as the marriage itself lasts—which is to say, in principle, for the rest of their lives. [J67,1]

Relation between commodity and allegory: "value," as the natural burning-glass of semblance in history, outshines "meaning." Its luster ‹Schein› is more difficult to dispel. It is, moreover, the very newest. In the Baroque age, the fetish character of the commodity was still relatively undeveloped. And the commodity had not yet so deeply engraved its stigma—the proletarianization of the producers—on the process of production. Allegorical perception could thus constitute a style in the seventeenth century, in a way that it no longer could in the nineteenth. Baudelaire as allegorist was entirely isolated. He sought to recall the experience of the commodity to an allegorical experience. In this, he was doomed to founder, and it became clear that the relentlessness of his initiative was exceeded by the relentlessness of reality. Hence a strain in his work that feels pathological or sadistic only because it missed out on reality—though just by a hair. [J67,2]

It is one and the same historical night at the onset of which the owl of Minerva (with Hegel) begins its flight and Eros (with Baudelaire) lingers before the empty pallet, torch extinguished, dreaming of bygone embraces. [J67,3]

The experience of allegory, which holds fast to ruins, is properly the experience of eternal transience. [J67,4]

Prostitution can lay claim to being considered "work" the moment work becomes prostitution. In fact, the *lorette*[354] was the first to carry out a radical renunciation of the costume of lover. She already arranges to be paid for her time; from there, it is only a short distance to those who demand "wages." [J67,5]

Already at work in Jugendstil is the bourgeois tendency to set nature and technology in mutual opposition, as absolute antitheses. Thus, Futurism will later give to technology a destructive antinatural accent; in Jugendstil, the energies destined to operate in this direction are beginning to unfold. The idea of a world bewitched and, as it were, denatured by technological development informs a good many of its creations. [J67,6]

The prostitute does not sell her labor power; her job, however, entails the fiction that she sells her powers of pleasure. Insofar as this represents the utmost extension attainable by the sphere of the commodity, the prostitute may be considered, from early on, a precursor of commodity capitalism. But precisely because the commodity character was in other respects undeveloped, this aspect did not need to stand out so glaringly as would subsequently be the case. As a matter of fact, prostitution in the Middle Ages does not, for example, display the crudeness that in the nineteenth century would become the rule. [J67a,1]

The tension between emblem and commercial logo makes it possible to measure the changes that have taken place in the world of things since the seventeenth century. [J67a,2]

Strong fixations of the sense of smell, such as Baudelaire seems to have known, could make fetishism likely. [J67a,3]

The new ferment that enters into the *taedium vitae* and turns it to spleen is self-estrangement. [J67a,4]

Hollowing out of the inner life. Of the infinite regress of reflection that, in Romanticism, in a spirit of play, both expanded the space of life in ever-widening circles and reduced it within ever narrower frames, there remained to Baudelaire only the "somber and lucid exchange" with himself, as he represents it in the image of a conversation between the jack of hearts and the queen of spades in an old pack of cards. Later, Jules Renard will say: "His heart . . . more alone than an ace of hearts in the middle of a deck of cards."[355] [J67a,5]

There may well be the closest connection between the allegorical imagination and the imagination put in thrall to thinking during hashish intoxication. At work in the latter are different sorts of powers: a genius of melancholy gravity, another of Ariel-like spirituality. [J67a,6]

In view of its position immediately after "La Destruction," ‹in *Les Fleurs du mal*,› "Une Martyre" is rich in associations. The allegorical intention has done its work on this martyr: she is in pieces. [J67a,7]

In "La Mort des amants," correspondences weave away without any hint of allegorical intention. Sob and smile—as cloud formations of the human face—mingle in the tercets. Villiers de l'Isle-Adam saw in this poem, according to a letter he wrote to Baudelaire, the application of the latter's "musical theories." [J67a,8]

"La Destruction" on the demon: "he fills my burning lungs / with sinful cravings never satisfied."[356] The lung as the seat of desire is the boldest intimation of desire's unrealizability that can be imagined. Compare the invisible stream in "Bénédiction." [J68,1]

Of all the Baudelairean poems, "La Destruction" comprises the most relentless elaboration of the allegorical intention. The "bloody retinue," which the poet is forced by the demon to contemplate, is the court of allegory—the scattered apparatus by dint of which allegory has so disfigured and so unsettled the world of things that only the fragments of that world are left to it now, as object of its brooding. The poem breaks off abruptly; it itself gives the impression—doubly surprising in a sonnet—of something fragmentary. [J68,2]

Compare "Le Vin des chiffonniers" with "Dans ce Cabriolet," by Sainte-Beuve (‹*Les Consolations*,› vol. 2 [Paris, 1863], p. 193):

> Seated in this cabriolet, I examine the man
> Who drives me, the man who's little more than machine,
> Hideous with his thick beard, his long matted hair:
> Vice and wine and sleep weigh down his sottish eyes.
> How far then, I thought, can humanity sink?
> And I draw back to the other corner of the seat.

The poet goes on to ask himself whether his own soul is not just as unkempt as the soul of the coachman. Baudelaire mentions this poem in his letter of January 15, 1866, to Sainte-Beuve.[357] [J68,3]

The ragpicker is the most provocative figure of human misery. "Ragtag" ‹*Lumpenproletarier*› in a double sense: clothed in rags and occupied with rags. "Here we have a man whose job it is to pick up the day's rubbish in the capital. He collects and catalogues everything that the great city has cast off, everything it has lost, and discarded, and broken. He goes through the archives of debauchery, and the jumbled array of refuse. He makes a selection, an intelligent choice; like a miser hoarding treasure, he collects the garbage that will become objects of utility or pleasure when refurbished by Industrial magic" ("Du Vin et du haschisch," *Oeuvres,* vol. 1, pp. 249–250). As may be gathered from this prose description of 1851, Baudelaire recognizes himself in the figure of the ragman. The poem presents a further affinity with the poet, immediately noted as such: "a ragpicker stumbles past, wagging his head / and bumping into walls with a poet's grace, / pouring out his heartfelt schemes to one / and all, including spies of the police."[358]   [J68,4]

Much can be said on behalf of the supposition that "Le Vin des chiffonniers" was written around the time of Baudelaire's espousal of "beautiful utility." (The question cannot be settled with any certainty, because the poem first appeared in the book edition of *Les Fleurs du mal.*—"Le Vin de l'assassin" was published for the first time in 1848—in *L'Echo des marchands de vins!*) The ragpicker poem strenuously disavows the reactionary pronouncements of its author. The criticism on Baudelaire has overlooked this poem.   [J68a,1]

"Believe me, the wine of the *barrières* has effectively preserved the shocks to which governmental structures have been subject." Edouard Foucaud, *Paris inventeur: Physiologie de l'industrie française* (Paris, 1844), p. 10.   [J68a,2]

Apropos of "Le Vin des chiffonniers": "There's brass in our pockets, / Pierre, let's go on a binge; / On Mondays, you know, / I love to knock about. / I know of a wine for two sous / That's not half bad, / And so, let's go have some fun, / Let's walk up to the *barrière*." H. Gourdon de Genouillac, *Les Refrains de la rue, de 1830 à 1870* (Paris, 1879), p. 56.   [J68a,3]

Traviès often drew the type of the ragpicker.   [J68a,4]

The son of the proletarian figures in "L'Ame du vin" with the words, "this frail athlete of life"[359]—an infinitely sad correspondence of modernity and antiquity.
                                                                                                              [J68a,5]

With regard to the "sectioning of time": the hidden construction of "Le Vin des amants" is grounded in the fact that only rather far along does the now surprising light fall on the situation at hand: the ecstatic drunkenness which the lovers owe to the wine is a morning drunkenness. "Into the blue crystal of the morning"[360]—this is the seventh line of this fourteen-line poem.   [J68a,6]

In the situation of the lovers "cradled gently on the wing / of the conniving whirlwind,"[361] it is not far-fetched to hear a reminiscence of Fourier. "The whirlwinds of planetary spheres," we read in Silberling's *Dictionnaire de sociologie phalanstérienne* (Paris, 1911), p. 433, "so measured in their motion that at any one moment they pass over billions of places—are, in our eyes, the seal of divine justice on the fluctuations of matter" (Fourier, *Théorie en concret ou positive,* p. 320).   [J68a,7]

Baudelaire builds stanzas where it would seem almost impossible to construct them. Thus, in the sixth stanza of "Lesbos:" "ambitious hearts / that yearn, far from us, for a radiant smile / they dimly glimpse on the rim of other skies!"[362]

[J68a,8]

On the desecration of the clouds: "Wandering a wasteland at high noon / . . . I saw a dismal stormcloud bearing down / upon my head, bristling with vicious imps"[363]—this is a conception that could stem directly from a print by Meryon.

[J69,1]

It is rare in French poetry that the big city is evoked through nothing but the immediate presentation of its inhabitants. This occurs with unsurpassable power in Shelley's poem on London ‹cited in M18›. (Wasn't Shelley's London more populous than the Paris of Baudelaire?) In Baudelaire, one encounters merely traces of a similar perception—though a good many traces. In few of his poems, however, is the metropolis portrayed so exclusively in terms of what it makes of its inhabitants as in "Spleen I." This poem shows in a veiled way how the soulless masses of the big city and the hopelessly depleted existence of individuals come to complement one another. The first is represented by the cemetery and the suburbs—mass assemblages of citizens; the second, by the jack of hearts and the queen of spades. [J69,2]

The hopeless decrepitude of the big city is felt particularly keenly in the first stanza of "Spleen I." [J69,3]

In the opening poem of *Les Fleurs du mal,* Baudelaire accosts the public in a most unusual fashion. He cozies up to them, if not exactly in a cozy vein. You could say he gathers his readers about him like a camarilla. [J69,4]

The awareness of time's empty passage and the *taedium vitae* are the two weights that keep the wheels of melancholy going. In this regard, the last poem of the "Spleen et idéal" sequence corresponds exactly to the sequence "La Mort."

[J69,5]

The poem "L'Horloge" ‹The Clock› takes the allegorical treatment quite far. Grouped about the clock, which occupies a special position in the hierarchy of emblems, are Pleasure, the Now, Time, Chance, Virtue, and Repentance. (On the sylphid, compare the "wretched theater" in "L'Irréparable,"[364] and on the inn, the *auberge* in the same poem.) [J69,6]

The "grotesque and livid sky" of "Horreur sympathique"[365] is the sky of Meryon.

[J69,7]

On the "sectioning of time," and on "L'Horloge" in particular, Poe's "Colloquy of Monos and Una": "There seemed to have sprung up in the brain *that* of which no words could convey to the merely human intelligence even an indistinct conception. Let me term it a mental pendulous pulsation. It was the moral embodiment of man's abstract idea of *Time*. . . . By its aid I measured the irregularities of the clock upon the mantel, and of the watches of the attendants. Their tickings came sonorously to my ears. The slightest deviation from the true proportion . . . affected me just as violations of abstract truth are wont, on earth, to affect the moral sense" (Edgar Allan Poe, *Nouvelles Histoires extraordinaires* ⟨Paris, 1886⟩, pp. 336–337).[366] This description is nothing but one great euphemism for the utter void of time to which man is surrendered in spleen. [J69a,1]

". . . until night / voluptuously reaches for / the horizon, consoling all— / even hunger, concealing all— / even shame" ("La Fin de la journée")[367]—this is the summer lightning of social conflicts in the night sky of the metropolis. [J69a,2]

"**You seem, for setting off my darkness, more / mockingly to magnify the space / which bars me from those blue immensities**" (**"'Je t'adore à l'égal . . .'"**). **Juxtapose: "And the human face—which Ovid thought was made to mirror the stars— see it now, no longer expressing anything but a crazy ferocity, or rigid in a kind of death!"** (*Oeuvres*, **vol. 2, p. 628** [**"Fusées," no. 3**]).[368] [J69a,3]

In studying the allegorical in the work of Baudelaire, it would be a mistake to undervalue the medieval element in relation to the Baroque. It is something difficult to describe, but may be grasped most readily if we recall how very much certain passages, certain poems ("Vers pour le portrait de M. Honoré Daumier," "L'Avertisseur," "Le Squelette Laboureur"), in their pregnant simplicity, contrast with others that are overburdened with meanings. This bareness gives them the sort of expression one finds in portraits by Fouquet. [J69a,4]

A Blanquist look at the terrestrial globe: "I contemplate from on high the globe in its rondure, / and I no longer seek there the shelter of a hut" ("Le Goût du néant").[369] The poet has made his dwelling in space itself, one could say—or in the abyss. [J69a,5]

Representations pass before the melancholic slowly, as in a procession. This image, typical in this complex of symptoms, is rare in Baudelaire. It occurs in "Horreur sympathique": "your vast mourning clouds / are the hearses of my dreams."[370] [J70,1]

"Then all at once the raging bells break loose, / hurling to heaven their awful caterwaul" ("Spleen IV").[371] The sky that is assailed by the bells is the same in which Blanqui's speculations move. [J70,2]

"Behind the scenes, the frivolous decors / of all existence, deep in the abyss, / I see distinctly other, brighter worlds" ("La Voix"). These are the worlds of

L'Eternité par les astres. Compare "Le Gouffre" ‹The Abyss›: "my windows open on Infinity."[372]   [J70,3]

If we bring together "L'Irrémédiable" with the poem Mouquet attributed to Baudelaire, "Un Jour de pluie" ‹A Rainy Day›, then it becomes quite clear that what inspires Baudelaire is the state of surrender to the abyss, and we see also just where this abyss actually opens. The Seine localizes "Un Jour de pluie" in Paris. Of this locale we read: "In a fog heavy with poisonous vapors, / men are buried like sneaking reptiles; / though proud of their strength, they stumble blindly along / more painfully with each step" (vol. 1, p. 212). In "L'Irrémédiable," this image of the Parisian streets has become one of the allegorical visions of the abyss which the conclusion of the poem describes as "apt emblems": "A soul in torment descending / . . . into an echoing cavern / . . . of vigilant slimy monsters / whose luminous eyes enforce / the gloom" (vol. 1, pp. 92–93).[373]   [J70,4]

Apropos of the catalogue of emblems presented by the poem "L'Irrémédiable," Crépet cites a passage from de Maistre's *Soirées de Saint-Pétersbourg:* "That river which one crosses but once; that pitcher of the Danaides, *always* full and *always* empty; that liver of Tityus, *always* regenerated under the beak of the vulture that *always* devours it anew, . . .—these are so many speaking hieroglyphs, about which it is impossible to be mistaken."[374]   [J70,5]

The gesture of benediction, with outstretched arms, in Fidus (also in *Zarathustra?*)—the gesture of someone carrying something.   [J70,6]

From the draft of an epilogue to the second edition of *Les Fleurs du mal:* "your magic cobbles piled for barricades, / your cheap orators' baroque rhetoric, / ranting of love while your sewers run with blood, / swirling to hell like mighty rivers" (vol. 1, p. 229).[375]   [J70a,1]

"Bénédiction" presents the poet's path in life as Passion: "he sings the very stations of his cross." In places, the poem distantly recalls the fantasy in which Apollinaire, in *Le Poète assassiné* (ch. 16), has imagined the extermination of poets by unbridled philistines: "and blinding flashes of his intellect / keep him from noticing the angry mob."[376]   [J70a,2]

A Blanquist look at humanity (and, at the same time, one of the few verses by Baudelaire that unveils a cosmic aspect): "the Sky! black lid of that enormous pot / in which innumerable generations boil" ("Le Couvercle").[377]   [J70a,3]

It is, above all, the "recollections" to which the "familiar eye"[378] appertains. (This gaze, which is none other than the gaze of certain portraits, brings Poe to mind.)
                                                                                    [J70a,4]

"On solemn eves of Heavenly harvesting" ("L'Imprévu")[379]—an autumnal Ascension.   [J70a,5]

"Cybèle, qui les aime, augmente ses verdures"[380]—in Brecht's beautiful translation: "Cybele, die sie liebt, legt mehr Grün vor" ("Cybele, who loves them, shows more green"). A mutation of the organic is implicit here.   [J70a,6]

"Le Gouffre" is the Baudelairean equivalent of Blanqui's "vision."   [J70a,7]

"O worms, black cronies without eyes or ears"[381]—here is something like sympathy for parasites.   [J70a,8]

Comparison of eyes to illuminated shopwindows: "Your eyes, lit up like shops to lure their trade / or fireworks in the park on holidays, / insolently make use of borrowed power" ("Tu mettrais l'univers").[382]   [J70a,9]

Concerning "La Servante au grand coeur": the words, "of whom you were so *jealous,*"[383] in the first line, do not bear precisely *the* accent one would expect. The voice, as it were, draws back from *jalouse*. This ebbing of the voice is something extremely characteristic. (Remark of Pierre Leyris.)   [J70a,10]

The sadistic imagination tends toward mechanical constructions. It may be that, when he speaks of the "nameless elegance of the human armature," Baudelaire sees in the skeleton a kind of machinery. The point is made more clearly in "Le Vin de l'assassin": "That bunch! They feel about as much / as plowshares breaking ground— / plow or harrow! Which of them / has ever known True Love." And, unequivocally: "Blind and deaf machine, fertile in cruelties" ("Tu mettrais l'univers").[384]   [J71,1]

"Old-fashioned" and "immemorial" are still united in Baudelaire. The ‹things› that have gone out of fashion have become inexhaustible containers of memories. It is thus the old women appear in Baudelaire's poetry ("Les Petites Vieilles"); thus the departed years ("Recueillement"); it is thus the poet compares himself to a "stale boudoir where old-fashioned clothes / lie scattered among wilted fern and rose" ("Spleen II").[385]   [J71,2]

Sadism and fetishism intertwine in those imaginations that seek to annex all organic life to the sphere of the inorganic. "O living matter, henceforth you're no more / Than a cold stone encompassed by vague fear / And by the desert, and the mist and sun" ("Spleen II").[386] The assimilation of the living to dead matter was likewise a preoccupation of Flaubert's. The visions of his Saint Anthony are a triumph of fetishism, and worthy of those celebrated by Bosch on the Lisbon altar.   [J71,3]

If "Le Crépuscule du matin" opens with the sound of reveille in the barrack squares, one must remember that under Napoleon III, for reasons easy to understand, the interior of the city was filled with barracks. [J71,4]

Smile and sob, as cloud formation of the human face, are an unsurpassable manifestation of its spirituality. [J71,5]

In "Rêve parisien," the forces of production are seemingly brought to a standstill, put out of commission. The landscape of this dream is the dazzling mirage of the leaden and desolate terrain that in "De Profundis clamavi" becomes the universe. "A frozen sun hangs overhead six months; / the other six, the earth is in its shroud— / no trees, no water, not one creature here, / a wasteland naked as the polar north!"[387] [J71,6]

The phantasmagoria of "Rêve parisien" recalls that of the world exhibitions, where the bourgeoisie cried out to the order of property and production their "Abide, you are so fair!"[388] [J71,7]

Proust on "granting a kind of glory to the crowd": "It would seem impossible to better that."[389] [J71a,1]

"And which, on those golden evenings *when you feel yourself revive*"[390]—the second half of the line collapses on itself. Prosodically, it works to contradict what it affirms. This is, for Baudelaire, a characteristic procedure. [J71a,2]

"Whose name is known only to the buried prompter"[391]—this comes from the world of Poe (compare "Remords posthume," "Le Mort joyeux"). [J71a,3]

The only place in *Le Fleurs du mal* where the Baudelairean view of children is contravened is the fifth stanza of the first section of "Les Petites Vieilles": "the eyes of a child, a little girl who laughs / in sacred wonder at whatever shines!"[392] To arrive at this outlook on childhood, the poet takes the longest way—the way leading through old age. [J71a,4]

In Baudelaire's work, poems 99 and 100 of *Les Fleurs du mal* stand apart—as strange and solitary as the great stone gods of Easter Island. We know that they belong to the oldest parts of the text; Baudelaire himself pointed them out to his mother as poems referring to her, poems to which he had given no title because any advertisement of this secret connection was odious to him. What these poems mark out is a death-tranced idyll. Both, but especially the first, breathe an air of peace such as rarely obtains in Baudelaire. Both present the image of the fatherless family; the son, however, far from occupying the place of the father, leaves it empty. The distant sun that is setting in the first poem is the symbol of the father, of him whose gaze—"huge open eye in the curious sky"[393]—lingers without jealousy, sympathetic and remote, on the meal shared by mother and son. The second poem evokes the image of the fatherless family situated not around a table but around a grave. The sultriness of life pregnant with possibilities has entirely yielded to the cool night air of death.   [J71a,5]

The "Tableaux parisiens" begin with a transfiguration of the city. The first, second, and, if you like, third poem of the cycle work together in this. "Paysage" is the city's tête-à-tête with the sky. The only elements of the city to appear on the poet's horizon are the "workshop full of singing and gossip, and the chimney-pots and steeples."[394] Then "Le Soleil" adds the suburbs; nothing of the urban masses enters into the first three poems of "Tableaux parisiens." The fourth begins with an evocation of the Louvre, but it passes immediately, in the middle of the second stanza, into lamentation over the perishability of the great city.
[J72,1]

"Drawings to which the gravity / and learning of some forgotten artist / . . . / have communicated beauty"[395]—*la Beauté* appears here, thanks to the definite article, as sober and "impassive." It has become the allegory of itself.   [J72,2]

On "Brumes et pluies" ⟨Mists and Rains⟩: the city has become strange to the flâneur, and every bed "hazardous."[396] (Multitude of night lodgings for Baudelaire.)   [J72,3]

We may be surprised to find the poem "Brumes et pluies" among "Tableaux parisiens." It verges on imagery of the country. But already Sainte-Beuve had written: "Oh, how sad the plain around the boulevard!" ("La Plaine, octobre," mentioned by Baudelaire *contre* Sainte-Beuve on January 15, 1866).[397] The landscape of Baudelaire's poem is, in fact, that of the city plunged in fog. It is the preferred canvas for the embroideries of boredom.   [J72,4]

"Le Cygne" ⟨The Swan⟩ has the movement of a cradle rocking back and forth between modernity and antiquity. In his notes, Baudelaire writes: "Conceive a sketch for a lyrical or fairy *bouffonnerie,* a pantomime. . . . Steep the whole in an abnormal, dreamy atmosphere—the atmosphere of *great days.* Let there be something *lulling* about it" ("Fusées," no. 22).[398] These great days are the days of recurrence.   [J72,5]

On the "foul demons in the atmosphere":[399] they return as the "demons of the cities" in Georg Heym. They are grown more violent but, because they disclaim their resemblance to the "businessmen," they mean less.   [J72,6]

Closing stanza of "Die Dämonen der Städte" ⟨Demons of the Cities⟩, by Heym:

> But the demons are growing colossal.
> The horns on their heads draw blood from the sky.

Earthquakes rumble in the belly of the cities
Beneath their hooves, fire in their wake.

Georg Heym, *Dichtungen* (Munich, 1922), p. 19. [J72a,1]

"Je t'adore à l'égal de la voûte nocturne" ‹I adore you no less than the vault of Night›[400]—nowhere more clearly than in this poem is Sexus played off against Eros. One must turn from this poem to Goethe's "Selige Sehnsucht" ‹Blessed Longing›[401] to see, by comparison, what powers are conferred on the imagination when the sexual is joined with the erotic. [J72a,2]

"Sonnet d'automne" describes, in a reserved but scrupulous way, the state of being that conditions Baudelaire's erotic experiences: "My heart, on which everything jars, / . . . / is unwilling to disclose its hellish secret, / . . . / I hate all passion . . . / Let us love each other gently." This is like a distant reprise of the stanza in the *West-Östlicher Divan* where Goethe conjures out of the houris and their poet an image of the erotic as a sort of paradisal variant of sexuality: "Their friendship reward his endeavor, / Compliant with *sweet* devotions, / Let him live with them forever: / All the good have modest notions."[402] [J72a,3]

Marx on the Second Republic: "Passions without truth, truths without passion; heroes without heroic deeds, history without events; development, whose sole driving force seems to be the calendar, wearying with constant repetition of the same tensions and relaxations. . . . If any section of history has been painted gray on gray, it is this." Karl Marx, *Der achtzehnte Brumaire des Louis Bonaparte*, ed. Rjazanov (Vienna and Berlin ‹1927›), pp. 45–46.[403] [J72a,4]

The opposite poles of the Baudelairean sensibility find their symbols equally in the skies. The leaden, cloudless sky symbolizes sensuality in thrall to the fetish; cloud formations are the symbol of sensuality spiritualized. [J72a,5]

Engels to Marx on December 3, 1851: "For today, at any rate, the ass is as free . . . as the old man on the evening of the Eighteenth Brumaire, so completely unrestrained that he can't help exposing his asinine self in all directions. Appalling perspective of no resistance!"[404] (Karl Marx, *Der achtzehnte Brumaire des Louis Bonaparte*, ed. Rjazanov [Vienna and Berlin], p. 9). [J73,1]

Engels to Marx on December 11, 1851: "If, this time, the proletariat failed to fight *en masse*, it was because it was fully aware of its own . . . impotence and was prepared to submit with fatalistic resignation to a renewed cycle of Republic, Empire, restoration, and fresh revolution, until . . . it regained fresh strength"[405] (Marx, *Der achtzehnte Brumaire*, p. 10). [J73,2]

"As is known, May 15 [1848] had no other result save that of removing Blanqui and his comrades—that is, the real leaders of the proletarian party, the revolu-

tionary communists—from the public stage for the entire duration of the cycle."
Marx, *Der achtzehnte Brumaire*, ed. Rjazanov, p. 28.[406]   [J73,3]

America's spirit world enters into the description of the crowd in Poe. Marx
speaks of the republic which in Europe "signifies, in general, only the political
form of revolution of bourgeois society and not its conservative form of life—as,
for example, in the United States of North America, where . . . classes . . . have
not yet become fixed, . . . where the modern means of production . . . compensate for the relative deficiency of heads and hands, and where, finally, the feverish, youthful movement of material production . . . has left neither time nor
opportunity for abolishing the old spirit world." Marx, *Der achtzehnte Brumaire*,
p. 30.[407] It is remarkable that Marx invokes the world of spirits to help explain the
American republic.   [J73,4]

If the crowd is a veil, then the journalist draws it about him, exploiting his
numerous connections like so many seductive arrangements of the cloth.
                                                                              [J73,5]

The revolutionary by-elections of March 10, 1850, sent to the parliament in Paris
an exclusively social-democratic mandate. But these elections would find "a sentimental commentary in the April by-election, the election of Eugène Sue." Marx,
Der achtzehnte Brumaire, p. 68.[408]   [J73,6]

Apropos of "Le Crépuscule du matin." Marx sees in Napoleon III "a man who does
not decide by night in order to execute by day, but who decides by day and executes by night." Marx, *Der achtzehnte Brumaire*, ed. Rjazanov, p. 79.[409] [J73a,1]

Apropos of "Le Crépuscule du matin": "Paris is full of rumors of a coup d'état.
The capital is to be filled with troops during the night; the next morning is to bring
decrees." Quoted from the European daily press of September and October 1851.
Marx, *Der achtzehnte Brumaire*, p. 105.[410]   [J73a,2]

Marx calls the leaders of the Paris proletariat the "barricade commanders." *Der
achtzehnte Brumaire*, p. 113.[411]   [J73a,3]

Sainte-Beuve's remark about Lamartine, whose poems represented the sky over
André Chénier's landscapes (J51a,3), should be compared with the words of
Marx: "While, in its accord with society, in its dependence on natural forces and
its submission to the authority which protected it from above, the small holding
that had newly come into being was naturally religious, the small holding that is
ruined by debts, at odds with society and authority, and driven beyond its own
limitations naturally becomes irreligious. Heaven was quite a pleasing accession
to the narrow strip of land just won, more particularly as it makes the weather; it
becomes an insult as soon as it is thrust forward as substitute for the small
holding." Marx, *Der achtzehnte Brumaire*, p. 122.[412] Sainte-Beuve's analogy, com-

bined with this passage from Marx, provides the key to the character and duration of the political influence which Lamartine derived from his poetry. Compare, in this connection, his negotiations with the Russian ambassador, as
reported by Pokrovski ‹cited in d12,2›. [J73a,4]

Ambiguity of the heroic in the figure of the poet: the poet has about him something of the destitute soldier, something of the marauder. His fencing ‹*Fechten*›
often recalls the meaning of this word[413] in the argot of vagabonds. [J73a,5]

**Marx on the parasitic creatures of the Second Empire: "Lest they make a mistake
in the years, they count the minutes." Marx, *Der achtzehnte Brumaire*, p. 126.[414]**
[J73a,6]

Ambiguity of that conception of the heroic which is hidden in the Baudelairean
image of the poet. "The culminating point of the *idées napoléoniennes* is the preponderance of the army. The army was the *point d'honneur* of the small-holding
peasants; it was they themselves transformed into heroes. . . . But the enemies
against whom the French peasant has now to defend his property are . . . the tax
collectors. The small holding lies no longer in the so-called fatherland, but in the
register of mortgages. The army itself is no longer the flower of the peasant
youth; it is the swamp-flower of the peasant lumpenproletariat. It consists in large
measure of *remplaçants,* of substitutes, just as the second Bonaparte is himself
only a *remplaçant,* the substitute for Napoleon. . . . One see that ALL *idées
napoléoniennes* are ideas of the undeveloped small holding in the freshness of its
youth; for the small holding that has outlived its day, they are an absurdity."
Marx, *Der achtzehnte Brumaire,* ed. Rjazanov, pp. 122–123.[415] [J74,1]

**On Satanism: "When the puritans at the Council of Constance complained of the
dissolute lives of the popes . . ., Cardinal Pierre d'Ailly thundered at them: 'Only
the devil in person can still save the Catholic church, and you ask for angels.' In
like manner, after the coup d'état, the French bourgeoisie cried: Only the chief of
the Society of December 10 can still save bourgeois society! Only theft can still save
property! Only perjury can save religion! Only bastardy can save the family! Only
disorder can save order!" Marx, *Der achtzehnte Brumaire*, ed. Rjazanov,
p. 124.[416]** [J74,2]

**"One can visualize clearly this upper stratum of the Society of December 10, if one
reflects that Véron-Crevel is its preacher of morals and Granier de Cassagnac its
thinker." Marx, *Der achtzehnte Brumaire*, ed. Rjazanov, p. 127.[417]** [J74,3]

The "magic cobbles piled for barricades," in Baudelaire's draft of an epilogue,[418]
define the limit which his poetry encounters in its immediate confrontation with
social subjects. The poet says nothing of the hands which move these cobble-
stones. In "Le Vin des chiffonniers," he was able to pass beyond this limit. [J74,4]

Closing lines of "Le Vin des chiffonniers," in the version of 1852: "Already God had given them sweet sleep; / He added wine, divine son of the sun." The distinction between God and man ("Man added wine . . .") dates from 1857.   [J74a,1]

In the last section of "Salon de 1846" (section 18, "De l'Héroïsme de la vie moderne"), suicide appears, characteristically, as a "particular passion"—the only one, among those mentioned, of any real significance. It represents the great conquest of modernity in the realm of passion: "Except for Hercules on Mount Oeta, Cato of Utica, and Cleopatra, . . . what suicides do you see in the paintings of the old masters?" Ch. B., *Oeuvres,* vol. 2, pp. 133–134.[419] Suicide appears, then, as the quintessence of modernity.   [J74a,2]

In section 17 of "Salon de 1846," Baudelaire speaks of "the funereal and rumpled frock coat of today" (p. 136); and, before that, of this "uniform livery of mourning": "Do not these puckered creases, playing like serpents around the mortified flesh, have their own mysterious grace?" (p. 134). Ch. B., *Oeuvres,* vol. 2.[420]
       [J74a,3]

Nietzsche on the winter of 1882–1883, on the Bay of Rapallo: "Mornings, I would walk in a southerly direction on the splendid road to Zoagli, going up past pines with a magnificent view of the sea; in the afternoon, . . . I walked around the whole bay . . . all the way to Portofino. This place and this scenery came even closer to my heart because of the great love that Emperor Frederick III felt for them. . . . It was on these two walks that the whole of *Zarathustra I* occurred to me, and especially Zarathustra himself as a type. Rather, he *overtook* me." Friedrich Nietzsche, *Also Sprach Zarathustra,* ed. Kröner (Leipzig), pp. xx–xxi. Compare this with a description of the Fort du Taureau.[421]   [J74a,4]

Against the background of his "philosophy of the noontide"—the doctrine of eternal recurrence—Nietzsche defines the earlier stages of his thinking as philosophy of the dawn and philosophy of the morning. He, too, knows the "sectioning of time" and its great divisions. It is certainly legitimate to ask whether this apperception of time was not an element of Jugendstil. If in fact it was, then we would perhaps better understand how, in Ibsen, Jugendstil produced one of the greatest technicians of the drama.   [J74a,5]

The closer work comes to prostitution, the more tempting it is to conceive of prostitution as work—something that has been customary in the argot of whores for a long time now. This rapprochement has advanced by giant steps in the wake of unemployment; the "Keep smiling"[422] maintains, on the job market, the practice of the prostitute who, on the love market, flashes a smile at the customer.
       [J75,1]

The description of the labor process in its relation to nature will necessarily bear the imprint of its social structure as well. If the human being were not *authentically* exploited, we would be spared the *inauthentic* talk of an exploitation of nature. This talk reinforces the semblance of "value," which accrues to raw materials only by virtue of an order of production founded on the exploitation of human labor. Were *this* exploitation to come to a halt, work, in turn, could no longer be characterized as the exploitation of nature by man. It would henceforth be conducted on the model of children's play, which in Fourier forms the basis of the "impassioned work" of the Harmonians. To have instituted play as the canon of a labor no longer rooted in exploitation is one of the great merits of Fourier. Such work inspirited by play aims not at the propagation of values but at the amelioration of nature. For it, too, the Fourierist utopia furnishes a model, of a sort to be found realized in the games of children. It is the image of an earth on which every place has become an *inn*. The double meaning of the word ‹*Wirtschaft*› blossoms here: all places are worked by human hands, made useful and beautiful thereby; all, however, stand, like a roadside inn, open to all. An earth that was cultivated according to such an image would cease to be part of "a world where action is never the sister of dream."[423] On that earth, the act would be kin to the dream.

[J75,2]

Fashion determines, in each case, the acceptable limit of empathy. [J75,3]

The unfolding of work in *play* presupposes highly developed forces of production, such as only today stand at the disposal of humanity, and stand mobilized in a direction contrary to their possibilities—that is, they are poised for an emergency. Nevertheless, even in times of relatively undeveloped productivity, the murderous idea of the exploitation of nature, which has ruled over things since the nineteenth century, was in no sense determinative. Certainly this idea could have no place so long as the prevailing image of nature was that of the ministering mother, as reflected in Bachofen's conception of matriarchal societies. In the figure of the mother, this image has survived the inconstancies of history, though it obviously has grown more blurred during those periods in which mothers themselves become agents of the class that risks the life of their sons for its commercial interests. There is much to suggest that the second marriage of Baudelaire's mother was not made any more bearable for him by the fact that she elected to marry a general. This marriage evidently has a share in the evolution of the poet's libido; if the whore became the mastering image of the latter, this marriage plays its part. Of course, the whore is, fundamentally, the incarnation of a nature suffused with commodity appearance. She has even intensified its power of delusion insofar as, in commerce with her, an always fictive pleasure arises, one that is supposed to corresond to the pleasure of her partner. In other words, the capacity for pleasure itself now figures as a value in this commerce—as the object of an exploitation perpetrated no less by her than by her partner. On the other hand, one sees here the distorted, more than life-size image of an availability that holds for everyone and is discouraged by none. The unworldly ecstatic lasciviousness of the Baroque poet Lohenstein has stamped this image in a manner that is highly reminiscent of Baudelaire: "A beautiful woman, yes, arrayed in a thousand splendors, / Is a sumptuous table where the many sup and take their fill, / An inexhaustible wellspring of never failing waters, / Yes, of love's sweet milk; and from a hundred conduits / The luscious nectar runs" (Daniel Caspers von Lohenstein, *Agrippina* [Leipzig, 1724], p. 33). The "beyond" of the choice governing relations between mother and child, and the here and now of the choice governing relations between prostitute and client, make contact at a single point. This point defines the situation of Baudelaire's libido. (Compare X2,1: Marx on prostitution.) [J75a]

The lines from "Selige Sehnsucht"—"No distance can weigh you down, / You come flying, fascinated"[424]—describe the experience of the aura. The distance that is there in the eyes of the beloved and that draws the lover after it is the dream of a better nature. The decline of the aura and the waning of the dream of a better nature—this latter conditioned on its defensive position in the class struggle—are one and the same. It follows that the decline of the aura and the decline of sexual potency are also, at bottom, one. [J76,1]

The formula of *L'Eternité par les astres*—"The new is always old, and the old always new"[425]—corresponds most rigorously to the experience of spleen registered by Baudelaire. [J76,2]

A passage from *L'Eternité par les astres*—"The number of our doubles is infinite in time and space. . . . These doubles exist in flesh and bone—indeed, in trousers and jacket, in crinoline and chignon"—may be compared with "Les Sept Vieillards":

> Doubtless to you my dread seems ludicrous,
> unless a brotherly shudder lets you see:
> for all their imminent decrepitude,
> these seven monsters had eternal life!

> I doubt if I could have survived an eighth
> such apparition, father and son of himself,
> inexorable Phoenix, loathsome avatar!
> —I turned my back on the whole damned parade.

The "monstrous shoreless sea,"[426] which the poem evokes in the closing line, is the agitated universe of *L'Eternité par les astres*. [J76,3]

"The houses seemed to be stretched upward by the mist / and looked like the two quays of some swollen river."[427] An image reminiscent of Meryon. There is something similar in Brecht. [J76,4]

With gloomy irony, Blanqui demonstrates what a "better humanity" would be worth in a nature which can never be better. [J76,5]

Lamartine's industrial Christ reappears at the end of the century. Thus Verhaeren, in "Le Départ":

> And what would evils matter, and demented hours,
> And vats of vice in which the city ferments,
> If one day, from the depths of fogs and shadows,
> A new Christ rises, sculpted in light,
> Who lifts humanity toward him
> And baptizes it in the fire of newborn stars.[428]

Baudelaire was not possessed of any such optimism—and that was the great chance for his presentation of Paris. Cited in Jules Destrée, "Der Zug nach der Stadt," *Die neue Zeit*, 21, no. 2 (Stuttgart, 1903) ‹p. 571›. [J76,6]

In the historical action which the proletariat brings against the bourgeois class, Baudelaire is a witness; but Blanqui is an expert witness. [J76a,1]

If Baudelaire is summoned before the tribunal of history, he will have to put up with a great many interruptions; an interest that is in many respects foreign to him, and in many respects incomprehensible to him, conditions the line of questioning. Blanqui, on the other hand, has long since made the question on which he speaks entirely his own; hence, he appears as an expert where this question is tried. It is therefore not exactly in the same capacity that Baudelaire and Blanqui are cited to appear before the tribunal of history. (Compare N11,3.) [J76a,2]

Abandonment of the epic moment: a tribunal is no sewing circle. Or better: the proceedings are instituted, not reported. [J76a,3]

The interest which the materialist historian takes in the past is always, in part, a vital interest in its *being* past—in its having ceased to exist, its being essentially dead. To have certified this condition with respect to the whole is the indispensable prerequisite for any citation (any calling to life) of particular parts of this phenomenon of what-has-been. In a word: for the specific historical interest whose legitimacy it is up to the materialist historian to establish, it must be shown that one is dealing with an object which in its entirety, actually and irrevocably, "belongs to history." [J76a,4]

The comparison with Dante can serve both as an example of the perplexity of the early reception of Baudelaire and as an illustration of Joseph de Maistre's remark that the earliest judgments concerning an author are bequeathed to the subsequent criticism. ‹See J64a,4.› [J76a,5]

In addition to the Dante comparison, the concept of *décadence* figures as a keyword in the reception. It is there in Barbey d'Aurevilly, Pontmartin, Brunetière, Bourget. [J76a,6]

For the materialist dialectician, discontinuity is the regulative idea of the tradition of the ruling classes (and therefore, primarily, of the bourgeoisie); continuity, the regulative idea of the tradition of the oppressed (and therefore, primarily, of the proletariat). The proletariat lives more slowly than the bourgeois class. The examples of its champions, the perceptions of its leaders, do not grow old, or, at any rate, they grow old much more slowly than the epochs and great personages of the bourgeois class. The waves of fashion break against the compact mass of the downtrodden. The movements of the ruling class, by contrast, having once come into their ascendancy, maintain in themselves a reference to fashion. In particular, the ideologies of the rulers are by their nature more changeable than the ideas of the oppressed. For not only must they, like the ideas of the latter, adapt each time to the situation of social conflict, but they must glorify that situation as fundamentally harmonious. Such a business is managed only eccentrically and desultorily; it is modish in the fullest sense of the word. To undertake to "salvage" the great figures of the bourgeoisie means, not least, to conceive them in this most unstable dimension of their operation, and precisely from out of that to extract, to cite, what has remained inconspicuously buried beneath— being, as it was, of so little help to the powerful. To bring together Baudelaire and Blanqui means removing the bushel that is covering the light.[429]   [J77,1]

Baudelaire's reception by poets can be easily distinguished from his reception by theorists. The latter adhere to the comparison with Dante and the concept of decadence; the former, to the maxim of art for art's sake and the theory of correspondences.   [J77,2]

Faguet (where?) sees the secret of Baudelaire's influence in the extremely widespread chronic nervousness.   [J77,3]

The "jerky gait" of the ragpicker ‹see J79a,5› is not necessarily due to the effect of alcohol. Every few moments, he must stop to gather refuse, which he throws into his wicker basket.   [J77,4]

For Blanqui, history is the straw with which infinite time is stuffed.   [J77a,1]

"I come to a stop, for I am suddenly exhausted. Up ahead, it appears, the path descends without warning, precipitously: On all sides, abyss—I dare not look." Nietzsche, ‹Werke: Gross- und Kleinoktavausgabe,› vol. 12, p. 223 (cited in Karl Löwith, *Nietzsches Philosophie der ewigen Wiederkunft des Gleichen* [Berlin, 1935], p. 33).   [J77a,2]

The hero who asserts himself on the stage of modernity is, in fact, an actor first of all. He clearly appears as such in "Les Sept Vieillards," in a "scene to match the actor's plight," "steeling" his "nerves to play a hero's part."[430]   [J77a,3]

The figure of the poet in "Bénédiction" is a figure from Jugendstil. The poet appears, so to speak, in the nude. He displays the physiognomy of Joseph Delorme. [J77a,4]

The "natural benevolence" which Magnin (J50a,4) celebrates in Sainte-Beuve—his coziness, in short—is the complement of the hieratic bearing of Joseph Delorme. [J77a,5]

It can be seen from the portraits that Baudelaire's physiognomy very early showed the marks of old age. Among other things, this accounts for the oft-noted resemblance between his features and those of prelates. [J77a,6]

Vallès was perhaps the first to complain insistently (as Souday would do later) about Baudelaire's "backwardness" (J21,6). [J77a,7]

Allegory recognizes many enigmas, but it knows no mystery. An enigma is a fragment that, together with another, matching fragment, makes up a whole. Mystery, on the other hand, was invoked from time immemorial in the image of the veil, which is an old accomplice of distance. Distance appears veiled. Now, the painting of the Baroque—unlike that of the Renaissance, for example—has nothing at all to do with this veil. Indeed, it ostentatiously rends the veil and, as its ceiling frescoes in particular demonstrate, brings even the distance of the skies into a nearness, one that seeks to startle and confound. This suggests that the degree of auratic saturation of human perception has fluctuated widely in the course of history. (In the Baroque, one might say, the conflict between cult value and exhibition value was variously played out within the confines of sacred art itself.) While these fluctuations await further clarification, the supposition arises that epochs which tend toward allegorical expression will have experienced a crisis of the aura. [J77a,8]

Baudelaire mentions, among the "lyric subjects proposed by the Académie," "Algeria, or the conquering civilization." Ch. B., *Oeuvres,* vol. 2, p. 593 ("L'Esprit de M. Villemain"). Desecration of distance. [J78,1]

On the "abyss": "depths of space, allegorical of the depths of time." Ch. B., *Oeuvres*, vol. 1, p. 306 (*Les Paradis artificiels,* "L'Homme-dieu").[431] [J78,2]

Allegorical dismemberment. The music to which one listens under the influence of hashish appears, in Baudelaire, as "the entire poem entering your brain, like a dictionary that has come alive." Ch. B., *Oeuvres,* vol. 1, p. 307.[432] [J78,3]

During the Baroque, a formerly incidental component of allegory, the emblem, undergoes extravagant development. If, for the materialist historian, the medieval origin of allegory still needs elucidation, Marx himself furnishes a clue for understanding its Baroque form. He writes in *Das Kapital* (Hamburg, 1922), vol. 1, p. 344: "The collective machine . . . becomes more and more perfect, the more the process as a whole becomes a continuous one—that is, the less the raw material is interrupted in its passage from its first phase to its last; in other words, the more its passage from one phase to another is effected not only by the hand of man but by the machinery itself. In manufacture, the isolation of each detail process is a condition imposed by the nature of division of labor, but in the fully developed factory the continuity of those processes is, on the contrary, imperative." [433] Here may be found the key to the Baroque procedure whereby meanings are conferred on the set of fragments, on the pieces into which not so much the whole as the process of its production has disintegrated. Baroque emblems may be conceived as half-finished products which, from the phases of a production process, have been converted into monuments to the process of destruction. During the Thirty Years' War, which, now at one point and now at another, immobilized production, the "interruption" that, according to Marx, characterizes each particular stage of this labor process could be protracted almost indefinitely. But the real triumph of the Baroque emblematic, the chief exhibit of which becomes the death's head, is the integration of man himself into the operation. The death's head of Baroque allegory is a half-finished product of the history of salvation, that process interrupted—so far as this is given him to realize—by Satan. [J78,4]

The financial ruin of Baudelaire is the consequence of a quixotic struggle against the circumstances that, in his day, determined consumption. The individual consumer, who vis-à-vis the artisan commissions work, figures in the marketplace as customer. There he does his part in the clearance of a stock of commodities which his particular wishes have had no influence whatsoever in producing. Baudelaire wanted to have such particular wishes reflected not only in his choice of clothing—the tailor's was, of all the branches of business, the one that had to reckon longest with the consumer who commissions work—but also in his furniture and in other objects of his daily use. He thus became dependent on an antiquary who was less than honest, and who procured for him paintings and antique furniture that in some cases proved to be fakes. The debts which he incurred through these dealings weighed on him for the rest of his life. [J78a,1]

In the final analysis, the image of petrified unrest called up by allegory is a historical image. It shows the forces of antiquity and of Christianity suddenly arrested in their contest, turned to stone amid unallayed hostilities. In his poem on the sick muse, with its masterful verse that betrays nothing of the chimerical nature of the poet's wish, Baudelaire has devised, as ideal image of the muse's health, what is really a formula for her distress: "I'd wish . . . / Your Christian blood to flow in waves that scan / With varied sounds of ancient syllables." [434]

[J78a,2]

In the poetry of Baudelaire, notwithstanding the new and original signature which allegory inscribes there, a medieval substrate makes itself felt beneath the Baroque element. This involves what Bezold calls "the survival of the ancient gods in medieval humanism."[435] Allegory is the vehicle for this survival.   [J79,1]

At the moment when the production process closes itself off to people, the stock in trade becomes accessible to them—in the form of the department store.
[J79,2]

On the theory of dandyism. The tailor's is the last line of business in which the customer is still catered to on an individual basis. Story of the twelve frock coats.[436] More and more, the person commissioning work plays a heroic role.
[J79,3]

Insofar as the flâneur presents himself in the marketplace, his flânerie reflects the fluctuations of commodities. Grandville, in his drawings, has often depicted the adventures of the strolling commodity.   [J79,4]

On the phrase "racked by their labors":[437] with the Saint-Simonians, industrial labor is seen in the light of sexual intercourse; the idea of the joy of working is patterned after an image of the pleasure of procreation. Two decades later, the relation has been reversed: the sex act itself is marked by the joylessness which oppresses the industrial worker.   [J79,5]

It would be an error to think of the experience contained in the *correspondances* as a simple counterpart to certain experiments with synesthesia (with hearing colors or seeing sounds) that have been conducted in psychologists' laboratories. In Baudelaire's case, it is a matter less of the well-known reactions, about which effete or snobbish art criticism has made such a fuss, than of the medium in which such reactions occur. This medium is the memory, and with Baudelaire it was possessed of unusual density. The corresponding sensory data correspond in it; they are teeming with memories, which run so thick that they seem to have arisen not from this life at all but from some more spacious *vie antérieure*. It is this prior existence that is intimated by the "familiar eyes"[438] with which such experiences scrutinize the one who has them.   [J79,6]

What fundamentally distinguishes the brooder from the thinker is that the former not only meditates a thing but also meditates his meditation of the thing. The case of the brooder is that of the man who has arrived at the solution of a great problem but then has forgotten it. And now he broods—not so much over the matter itself as over his past reflections on it. The brooder's thinking, therefore, bears the imprint of memory. Brooder and allegorist are cut from the same cloth.   [J79a,1]

"While the *parliamentary party of Order* . . . destroy[ed] with its own hands, in the struggle against the other classes of society, all the conditions for its own regime, the parliamentary regime, the *extraparliamentary mass of the bourgeoisie,* on the other hand, . . . by its brutal maltreatment of its own press, invited Bonaparte to suppress and annihilate its speaking and writing section, its politicians and its *literati,* . . . in order that it might then be able to pursue its private affairs with full confidence in the protection of a strong and unrestricted government." Karl Marx, *Der achtzehnte Brumaire des Louis Bonaparte*, ed. Rjazanov (Vienna and Berlin ‹1927›), p. 100.[439] [J79a,2]

Baudelaire is quite as isolated in the literary world of his day as Blanqui is in the world of conspiracies. [J79a,3]

With the increase in displays of merchandise and with the rise, in particular, of *magasins de nouveautés,* the physiognomy of the commodity emerged more and more distinctly. Of course, even with his sensitive receptivity, Baudelaire never would have registered this development had it not passed like a magnet over the "precious metal of our will,"[440] over the iron ore of his imagination. In fact, the ruling figure of that imagination—allegory—corresponded perfectly to the commodity fetish. [J79a,4]

The bearing of the modern hero, as modeled on the ragpicker: his "jerky gait," the necessary isolation in which he goes about his business, the interest he takes in the refuse and detritus of the great city. (Compare Baudelaire, "De l'Héroïsme de la vie moderne," in vol. 2, p. 135: "The pageant of . . . life . . .")[441] [J79a,5]

The uncovering of the mechanical aspects of the organism is a persistent tendency of the sadist. One can say that the sadist is bent on replacing the human organism with the image of machinery. Sade is the offspring of an age that was enraptured by automatons. And La Mettrie's "man machine" alluded to the guillotine, which furnished rudimentary proof of its truths. In his bloody-minded fantasies, Joseph de Maistre—Baudelaire's authority on matters political—is cousin to the marquis de Sade. [J80,1]

The brooder's memory ranges over the indiscriminate mass of dead lore. Human knowledge, within this memory, is something piecemeal—in an especially pregnant sense: it is like the jumble of arbitrarily cut pieces from which a puzzle is assembled. An epoch fundamentally averse to brooding has nonetheless preserved its outward gesture in the puzzle. It is the gesture, in particular, of the allegorist. Through the disorderly fund which his knowledge places at his disposal, the allegorist rummages here and there for a particular piece, holds it next to some other piece, and tests to see if they fit together—that meaning with this image or this image with that meaning. The result can never be known beforehand, for there is no natural mediation between the two. But this is just how matters stand with commodity and price. The "metaphysical subtleties" in which the commodity delights, according to Marx,[442] are, above all, the subtleties of price formation. How the price of goods in each case is arrived at can never quite be foreseen, neither in the course of their production nor later when they enter the market. It is exactly the same with the object in its allegorical existence. At no point is it written in the stars that the allegorist's profundity will lead it to one meaning rather than another. And though it once may have acquired such a meaning, this can always be withdrawn in favor of a different meaning. The modes of meaning fluctuate almost as rapidly as the price of commodities. In fact, the meaning of the commodity *is* its price; it has, as commodity, no other meaning. Hence, the allegorist is in his element with commercial wares. As flâneur, he has empathized with the soul of the commodity; as allegorist, he recognizes in the "price tag," with which the merchandise comes on the market, the object of his broodings—the meaning. The world in which this newest meaning lets him settle has grown no friendlier. An inferno rages in the soul of the commodity, for all the seeming tranquillity lent it by the price. [J80,2; J80a,1]

On fetishism: "It may be that, in the emblem of the stone, only the most obvious features of the cold, dry earth are to be seen. But it is quite conceivable and . . . by no means improbable that the inert mass contains a reference to the genuinely theological conception of the melancholic which is found in one of the seven deadly sins. This is *acedia*." ‹Walter Benjamin,› *Ursprung des deutschen Trauerspiels* ‹Berlin, 1928›, p. 151.[443] [J80a,2]

On "the exploitation of nature" (J75,2): such exploitation was not always regarded as the basis of human labor. To Nietzsche, it quite rightly seemed worthy of remark that Descartes was the first philosophical physicist who "compared the discoveries of the scientist to a military campaign waged against nature." Cited in Karl Löwith, *Nietzsches Philosophie der ewigen Wiederkunft des Gleichen* (Berlin, 1935), p. 121 (‹Nietzsche, *Werke, Gross- und Kleinoktavausgabe*,› vol. 13, p. 55). [J80a,3]

Nietzsche calls Heraclitus "a star devoid of atmosphere."[444] Cited in Löwith, *Nietzsches Philosophie*, p. 110 (vol. 10, pp. 45ff.). [J80a,4]

The great physiognomic similarity between Guys and Nietzsche is worth emphasizing. Nietzsche ascribes to the pessimism of India "that tremendous, yearning rigidity of expression in which the Nothing is reflected" (cited in Löwith, *Nietzsches Philosophie,* p. 108 [vol. 15, p. 162]).[445] Compare this to the way Baudelaire describes the gaze of the oriental courtesan in Guys (J47,4): it is a gaze directed toward the horizon, one in which rigid attentiveness and profound distraction are united. [J80a,5]

On suicide as signature of modernity. "One cannot sufficiently condemn Christianity for having devalued the *value* of such a great *purifying* nihilistic movement, as was perhaps already being formed, . . . through continual deterrence from the *deed of nihilism*, which is suicide" (cited in Löwith, *Nietzsches Philosophie*, p. 108 ‹vol. 15, pp. 325, 186›).[446]   [J81,1]

On the abyss, and on the phrase "I balk at sleep as if it were a hole": "Do you know the terror which assails him who is falling asleep?—He is terrified down to his toes, because the ground seems to give way, and the dream begins" (‹Nietzsche,› *Zarathustra*, ed. Kröner [Leipzig], p. 215).[447]   [J81,2]

Comparison of the "sinuous fleece" with the "deep and spreading starless Night!" (final lines of "Les Promesses d'un visage").[448]   [J81,3]

The particulars of the boulevard press are, later, the sum and substance of the stock market reports. Through the role that it gives to the talk of the town, the *petite presse* paves the way for this stock market information.   [J81,4]

His confederates obstruct reality for the conspirator as the masses do for the flâneur.   [J81,5]

On the flight of images in allegory. It often cheated Baudelaire out of part of the returns on his allegorical imagery. One thing in particular is missing in Baudelaire's employment of allegory. This we can recognize if we call to mind Shelley's great allegory on the city of London: the third part of "Peter Bell the Third," in which London is presented to the reader as hell. ‹See M18.› The incisive effect of this poem depends, for the most part, on the fact that Shelley's *grasp* of allegory makes itself felt. It is this grasp that is missing in Baudelaire. This grasp, which makes palpable the distance of the modern poet from allegory, is precisely what enables allegory to incorporate into itself the most immediate realities. With what directness that can happen is best shown by Shelley's poem, in which bailiffs, parliamentarians, stock-jobbers, and many other types figure. The allegory, in its emphatically antique character, gives them all a sure footing, such as, for example, the businessmen in Baudelaire's "Crépuscule du soir" do not have.—Shelley rules over the allegory, whereas Baudelaire is ruled by it.   [J81,6]

Individuality, as such, takes on heroic outlines as the masses step more decisively into the picture. This is the origin of the conception of the hero in Baudelaire. In Hugo, it is a matter not of the isolated individual as such but of the democratic citizen. That implies a fundamental difference between the two poets. The resolution of this discord would have, as precondition, the dispelling of the illusion ‹*Schein*› which it reflects. This illusory appearance comes from the concept of the masses. Considered apart from the various classes which join in its formation, the mass as such has no primary social significance. Its secondary significance depends on the ensemble of relations through which it is constituted at any one time and place. A theater audience, an army, the population of a city comprise masses which in themselves belong to no particular class. The free market multiplies these masses, rapidly and on a colossal scale, insofar as each piece of merchandise now gathers around it the mass of its potential buyers. The totalitarian states have taken this mass as their model. The *Volksgemeinschaft* ‹People's Community› aims to root out from single individuals everything that stands in the way of their wholesale fusion into a mass of consumers. The one implacable adversary still confronting the state, which in this ravenous action becomes the agent of monopoly capital, is the revolutionary proletariat. This latter dispels the illusion of the mass through the reality of class. Neither Hugo nor Baudelaire could be directly at its side for that. [J81a,1]

On the inauguration of the heroine: Baudelaire's antiquity is Roman antiquity. At only one point—and it is, of course, irreplaceable—does Greek antiquity break into his world. Greece presents him with that image of the heroine which appeared to him worthy and capable of being carried over into modernity. Greek names stand at the head ‹?› of one of his greatest poems: "Femmes damnées: Delphine et Hippolyte." The heroine ‹is endowed› with the features of lesbian ‹love ›. [J81a,2]

"Thus, the poet's thought, after meandering capriciously, opens onto the vast perspectives of the past or future; but these skies are too vast to be everywhere pure, and the temperature of the climate too warm not to brew storms. The idle passerby, who contemplates these areas veiled in mourning, feels tears of hysteria come to his eyes." Ch. B., vol. 2, p. 536 ("Marceline Desbordes-Valmore").[449]
[J82,1]

On "Le Vin des chiffonniers": the reference to "police spies" suggests that the ragman dreams of returning to combat on the barricades. [J82,2]

"*City*. I am an ephemeral and not-too-discontented citizen of a metropolis obviously modern because every known taste has been avoided in the furnishings and in the outsides of the houses, as well as in the layout of the city. Here you would not discover the least sign of any monument of superstition. In short, morals and speech are reduced to their simplest expression. These millions of people, who have no need of knowing one another, conduct their education, their trade, and their old age with such similarity that the duration of their lives must be several times shorter than is the case, according to some insane statistics, with people on the continent." Arthur Rimbaud, *Oeuvres* (Paris, 1924), pp. 229–230 (*Illuminations*).[450] Disenchantment of "modernity"! [J82,3]

"Criminals disgust me as if they were castrates." Arthur Rimbaud, *Oeuvres* (Paris, 1924), p. 258 (*Une Saison en enfer*, "Mauvais Sang").[451] [J82,4]

One could try to show, using the example of Baudelaire, that Jugendstil arises out of weariness—a weariness that manifests itself, in his case, as that of the mime who has taken off his makeup. [J82,5]

Modernity, in this work, is what a trademark is on a piece of cutlery or an optical instrument. It may be as durable as one could wish; if the company which produced it at some point goes under, it will come to seem obsolete. But to impress a trademark on his work was Baudelaire's avowed intention. "To create a *poncif*."[452] And perhaps, for Baudelaire, there is no higher honor than to have imitated, to have reproduced, with his work this state of affairs, one of the most profane of all in the commodity economy. Perhaps this is Baudelaire's greatest achievement, and certainly it is one of which he is conscious: to have become so quickly obsolete while remaining so durable.   [J82,6; J82a,1]

The activity of the conspirator can be considered a sort of uprooting, comparable to that occasioned by the monotony and terror of the Second Empire.   [J82a,2]

The physiologies[453] were the first booty taken from the marketplace by the flâneur—who, so to speak, went botanizing on the asphalt.   [J82a,3]

Modernity has its antiquity, like a nightmare that has come to it in its sleep.[454]
[J82a,4]

England remained, until late in the previous century, the graduate school of social consciousness. From there, Barbier brought back his cycle of poems entitled *Lazare* ‹Lazarus› and Gavarni his sequence *Ce qu'on voit gratis à Londres* ‹What Can Be Seen for Free in London›, together with his character Thomas Vireloque, the figure of hopeless destitution.   [J82a,5]

> Between Augustus, calm of eye, and Trajan, pure of brow,
> Resplendent and unmoving in the great azure,
> On you, O pantheons, on you, O portals,
> Robert Macaire with his worn-out boots!

Victor Hugo, *Les Châtiments,* ed. Charpentier (Paris), p. 107 ("Apothéose").
[J82a,6]

"He has against him . . . the title of *Les Fleurs du mal*, which is a sham title, disagreeably anecdotal, and which particularizes to excess the universality of his impulse." Henry Bataille, "Baudelaire," *Comoedia* (January 7, 1921).   [J82a,7]

Apropos of "the nearly deafening street"[455] and other similar expressions, it should not be forgotten that the roads in those days were generally paved in cobblestone.   [J82a,8]

Nisard in the foreword to the first edition of *Le Poëtes latins de la décadence* (1834): "I endeavor to explain by what necessities . . . the human spirit arrives at this singular state of exhaustion, in which the most bountiful imaginations are no longer capable of true poetry and can manage only to debase their languages with scandal. . . . In conclusion, I touch on certain resemblances between the poetry of our time and that of the time of Lucan. . . . In a country where literature governs the minds of men, and even politics . . . lends its voice to everything progressive, . . . criticism . . . is . . . a task at once literary and moral." D. Nisard, *Etudes de moeurs et de critique sur les poëtes latins de la décadence* (Paris, 1849), vol. 1, pp. x, xiv.   [J83,1]

On the feminine ideal—"ghastly thin"—of Baudelaire: "But it is essentially the modern woman here, the French woman of the period preceding the invention of the bicycle." Pierre Caume, "Causeries sur Baudelaire, *La Nouvelle Revue* (Paris, 1899), vol. 119, p. 669.   [J83,2]

Nisard denounces, as a sign of decadence in Phaedrus, "a continual, affected employment of the abstract for the concrete. . . . Thus, instead of a long neck, he says: 'length of neck,' *colli longitudo*." D. Nisard, *Etudes de moeurs et de critique sur les poëtes latins de la décadence* (Paris, 1849), vol. 1, pp. 45.   [J83,3]

On the question of the declining birthrate and of barrenness: "There is no hopeful expectation of the future, nor any élan, without some guiding idea, some goal." Jules Romains, *Cela dépend de vous* (Paris ‹1939›), p. 104.   [J83,4]

"Into the depths of the Unknown"—with this, compare the great passage by Turgot on the known: "I cannot admire Columbus for having said, 'The earth is round, and therefore by traveling westward I shall meet the land again,' because the simplest things are often the most difficult to find.—But what distinguishes a hardy soul is the confidence with which it abandons itself to unknown waters on the faith of a deduction. What would genius and enthusiasm for truth be in a man to whom a *known truth* had given such courage!" Turgot, *Oeuvres* (Paris, 1844), vol. 2, p. 675 ("Pensées et fragments").[456]   [J83,5]

Being reduced to rags is a specific form of poverty—by no means the superlative form. "Poverty takes on the peculiar character of raggedness when it occurs amidst a society whose existence is founded on an intricate and richly articulated system for the satisfaction of needs. Insofar as poverty borrows bits and pieces from this system, fragments isolated from all context, it becomes subject to needs from which it can find no . . . lasting and decent deliverance." Hermann Lotze, *Mikrokosmos,* vol 3 (Leipzig, 1864), pp. 271–272.[457]   [J83a,1]

Lotze's reflections on the worker who no longer handles a tool but operates a machine aptly illuminate the attitude of the consumer toward the commodity produced under these conditions. "He could still recognize in every contour of the finished product the power and precision of his own formative touch. The participation of the individual in the work of the machine, by contrast, is limited to . . . manual operations which bring forth nothing directly but merely supply to an inscrutable mechanism the obscure occasion for invisible accomplishments." Hermann Lotze, *Mikrokosmos,* vol. 3 (Leipzig, 1864), pp. 272–273.   [J83a,2]

Allegory, as the sign that is pointedly set off against its meaning, has its place in art as the antithesis to the beautiful appearance ‹*Schein*› in which signifier and signified flow into each other. Dissolve this brittleness of allegory, and it forfeits all authority. That, in fact, is what happens with genre. It introduces "life" into allegories, which in turn suddenly wither like flowers. Sternberger has touched on this state of affairs (*Panorama* ‹Hamburg, 1938›, p. 66): "the allegory that has become a semblance of life, that has given up its lastingness and its rigorous validity for the red pottage" of life,[458] justly appears as a creation of the genre. In Jugendstil, a retrogressive process seems to set in. Allegory regains its brittleness.
[J83a,3]

On the foregoing remarks by Lotze: the idler, the flâneur, who no longer has any understanding of production, seeks to become an expert on the market (on prices).
[J83a,4]

"The chapters 'Persecution' and 'Murder' in Apollinaire's *Poète assassiné* contain the famous description of a pogrom against poets. Publishing houses are stormed, books of poems thrown on the fire, poets beaten to death. And the same scenes are taking place at the same time all over the world. In Aragon, 'Imagination,' in anticipation of such horrors, marshals its forces for a last crusade." Walter Benjamin, "Der Sürrealismus," *Die literarische Welt*, 5, no. 7 (February 15, 1929).[459]
[J84,1]

"It is hardly a coincidence that the century which has long been that of the strongest poetic language, the nineteenth century, has also been that of decisive progress in the sciences." Jean-Richard Bloch, "Langage d'utilité, langage poétique" (*Encyclopédie française,* vol. 16 [16–50], p. 13). Indicate how the forces of poetic inspiration, having been driven from their earlier positions by science, were compelled to make inroads into the commodity world.
[J84,2]

On the question raised by J.-R. Bloch, the question of the development of science and of poetic language, Chénier's "Invention":

> All the arts conjoin, and human science
> Could not extend the bounds of its alliance
> Without enlarging thus the scope for verse.
> What long travail to win the universe!
> . . . . .
> A new Cybele and a hundred different worlds befall
> Our Jasons first delivered from the ocean's thrall:
> What a wealth of worthy scenes, of images sublime,
> Born of those great subjects reserved for our time!
> [J84,3]

On "Les Sept Vieillards." The very fact that this poem stands isolated within Baudelaire's oeuvre fortifies the assumption that it occupies a key position there. If this position has remained unnoticed until now, this may have to do with the fact that a purely philological commentary has missed the mark with this poem. Yet the relevant datum is not so far afield. The piece corresponds with a particular passage from *Les Paradis artificiels*. It is this passage, however, that can shed light on the philosophical import of the poem.   [J84,4]

The following passage from *Les Paradis artificiels* is decisive for "Les Sept Vieillards." It makes it possible to trace the inspiration for this poem back to hashish: "The word 'rhapsodic,' which so well portrays a train of thought suggested and dictated by the outer world and the hazard of circumstance, has a great and more terrible truth in relation to hashish. Here, human reason becomes mere flotsam, at the mercy of all currents, and the train of thought is *infinitely more* accelerated and 'rhapsodic.'" Vol. 1, p. 303.[460]   [J84a,1]

Comparison between Blanqui and Baudelaire, in part deriving from Brecht's formulations: the defeat of Blanqui was the victory of Baudelaire—of the petty bourgeoisie. Blanqui succumbed; Baudelaire succeeded. Blanqui appears as a tragic figure; his betrayal has tragic greatness; he was brought down by the enemy within. Baudelaire appears as a comic figure—as the cock whose triumphal crowing announces the hour of betrayal.[461]   [J84a,2]

If Napoleon III was Caesar, then Baudelaire was the Catilinarian existence.
                                                                        [J84a,3]

Baudelaire unites the poverty of the ragpicker with the scorn of the cadger and the despair of the parasite.   [J84a,4]

The significance of the prose poem "Perte d'auréole" cannot be overestimated. First of all, there is the remarkable pertinence of the fact that it spotlights the threat to the aura posed by the experience of shock. (Perhaps this relation can be clarified by reference to metaphors of epilepsy.) Extraordinarily decisive, moreover, is the ending, which makes the exhibition of the aura from now on an affair of fifth-rate poets.—Finally, this piece is important because in it the inhabitant of the big city appears menaced more by the traffic of coaches than he is nowadays by automobiles.   [J84a,5]

Catiline figures in Baudelaire among the dandies.[462]   [J85,1]

Love for the prostitute is the apotheosis of empathy with the commodity.
                                                                        [J85,2]

"Recueillement" should be presented as Jugendstil poetry. The *défuntes années* ‹dead years›[463] as allegories in the style of Fritz Erler.   [J85,3]

The hatred for genre painting that can be discerned in Baudelaire's "Salons" is a sentiment typical of Jugendstil.   [J85,4]

Among the legends which circulated about Baudelaire is the following: he is supposed to have read Balzac while crossing the Ganges. In Henri Grappin, "Le Mysticisme poétique de Gustave Flaubert," *Revue de Paris* (December 1 and 15, 1912), p. 852.   [J85,5]

"Life has only one real charm—the charm of *gambling*. But what if we do not care whether we win or lose?" *Oeuvres complètes*, vol. 2, p. 630 ("Fusées").[464]   [J85,6]

"Commerce is essentially *satanic*. . . . Commerce is satanic because it is one of the forms of egoism—the lowest and vilest." *Oeuvres complètes*, vol. 2, p. 664 ("Mon Coeur mis à nu").[465]   [J85,7]

"What is love? The need to escape from oneself. . . . The more a man cultivates the arts, the less often he gets an erection. . . . To copulate is to aspire to enter into another—and the artist never emerges from himself." *Oeuvres complètes*, ⟨vol. 2,⟩ pp. 655, 663.[466]   [J85,8]

"It is partly a life of leisure that has enabled me to grow. To my great detriment— for leisure without fortune breeds debts. . . . But also to my great profit, as regards sensibility and meditation and the faculty of dandyism and dilletantism. Other men of letters are, for the most part, base ignorant drudges." *Oeuvres complètes*, vol. 2, p. 659 ("Mon Coeur . . .").[467]   [J85,9]

"As I have fully proved, to work is less wearisome than to amuse oneself." *Oeuvres complètes*, vol. 2, p. 647 ("Mon Coeur . . .").[468]   [J85,10]

On the dance of death (compare K7a,3, the passage from Huxley): "The woodcuts with which the Parisian printer Guyot Marchant ornamented the first edition of the *Danse Macabre* in 1485 were, very probably, imitated from the most celebrated of these painted death dances—namely, that which, since 1424, covered the walls of the cloister of the cemetery of the Innocents in Paris. . . . The dancing person whom we see coming back forty times to lead away the living originally represents not Death itself but a corpse: the living man such as he will presently be. In the stanzas, the dancer is called "the dead man" or "the dead woman." It is a dance of the dead and not of Death. . . . It is only toward the end of the century that the figure of the great dancer, of a corpse with hollow and fleshless body, becomes a skeleton, as Holbein depicts it." J. Huizinga, *Herbst des Mittelalters* (Munich, 1928), pp. 204–205.[469]   [J85a,1]

On allegory. "The characters in *Le Roman de la Rose*—Bel-Accueil, Doulce Mercy, Faux Semblant, Humble Requeste, Danger, Honte, Peur—are on a level with the authentic medieval representations of virtues and vices in human form: allegories or, something more than this, half-believed mythologems." J. Huizinga, *Herbst des Mittelalters* (Munich, 1928), p. 162.[470]   [J85a,2]

On "the metaphysics of the agent provocateur": "Without being too prejudiced in the matter, one may still feel a little uneasy in reading *Les Mystères galans* [*Les Mystères galans des théâtres de Paris*][471] to think that Baudelaire had a hand in this. If he himself has disowned this piece of youthful extravagance, there are nonetheless good reasons for believing, with M. Crépet, that he is in fact one of the authors. Here then is a Baudelaire on the brink of blackmail, spiteful toward all success? This would suggest that throughout his career, from these *Mystères* to the *Amoenitates Belgicae*, the great poet had need, from time to time, of voiding a sac of venom." Jean Prévost, review of the work mentioned, *La Nouvelle Revue française*, 27, no. 308 (May 1, 1939), p. 888.   [J85a,3]

Apropos of Baudelaire's "Au Lecteur." "The first six books of the *Confessions* have . . . a certain advantage built into their very subject: each reader, insofar as he is not the slave of literary or mundane prejudices, becomes an accomplice." André Monglond, *Le Préromantisme français*, vol. 2, *Le Maître des âmes sensibles* (Grenoble, 1930), p. 295.   [J86,1]

In an important passage by de Maistre, we not only encounter allegory in its satanic provenance, and in the very perspective that would later be that of Baudelaire; we also discover—here invested with the mysticism of Saint-Martin or Swedenborg—the *correspondances*. And these latter constitute, revealingly, the antidote to allegory. The passage is found in the eighth of *Les Soirées de Saint-Pétersbourg*, and reads: "One can form a perfectly adequate idea of the universe by considering it under the aspect of a vast museum of natural history exposed to the shock of an earthquake. The door to the collection rooms is open and broken; there are no more windows. Whole drawers have fallen out, while others hang by their hinges, ready to drop. Some shells have rolled out into the hall of minerals, and a hummingbird's nest is resting on the head of a crocodile. What madman, though, could have any doubt of the original intention, or believe that the edifice was built to look this way? . . . The order is as visible as the disorder; and the eye that ranges over this mighty temple of nature reestablishes without difficulty all that a fatal agency has shattered, warped, soiled, and displaced. And there is more: look closely and you can recognize already the effects of a restoring hand. Some beams have been shored up, some paths cut through the rubble; and, in the general confusion, a multitude of *analogues* have already taken their place once again and come into contact."[472]   [J86,2]

On Baudelaire's prosody. A phrase has been applied to it that originally referred to Racine: "graze the prose, but with wings."   [J86,3]

Concerning Baudelaire's "Voyage à Cythère":

> Cythera is there, depleted and lugubrious,
> Absurd death's head of the dream of love,
> And gleaming skull of pleasure . . .
> . . . . .

No more bees sipping dewdrop and thyme,
But always the blue sky above.

Victor Hugo, *Les Contemplations* ("Cérigo").   [J86a,1]

The theory of poetry as faculty of expression—"Where other men must suffer grief in silence, / A god gave me the power to speak my pain"[473]—is formulated with particular decisiveness by Lamartine in the "first" (it is actually the second) preface to his *Méditations* of 1849. The "striving for originality at all costs," to say nothing of an authentic reflection on original possibilities, preserves the poet—Baudelaire above all—from a poetics of mere expression. Lamartine writes: "I imitated no one; I expressed myself for myself. There was no art in this, but only an easing of my own heart. . . . I took no thought of anyone in putting down these lines here and there, unless it was of a ghost and of God." *Les Grands Ecrivains de la France,* vol. 2, "Lamartine" (Paris, 1915), p. 365.   [J86a,2]

Apropos of Laforgue's remark about the "crude comparisons" in Baudelaire ⟨J9,4⟩, Ruff observes: "The originality of these comparisons is not so much in their 'crudity' as in the artificial character—which is to say, *human* character—of the images: wall, lid, the wings of a stage. The 'correspondence' is understood in a sense opposite to that customarily proposed by the poets, who lead us back to nature. Baudelaire, by an invincible propensity, recalls us to the idea of the human. Even on the human plane, if he wishes to magnify his description by an image, he will often look for some other manifestation of humanity rather than having recourse to nature: 'the chimney-pots and steeples, the city's *masts.*'"[474] Marcel A. Ruff, "Sur l'Architecture des Fleurs du mal," *Revue d'histoire littéraire de la France,* 37, no. 3 (July–September 1930), p. 398. Compare the phrase "whose fingers point to heaven," in the paragraph on Meryon ⟨J2,1⟩.—The same motif, rendered innocuous and put into psychological terms, in Rattier's conversion of the flâneur to industrial activity.   [J86a,3]

In Barbier's poem "Les Mineurs de Newcastle," the eighth stanza concludes this way: "And many a one who dreams, within his secret soul, / Of domestic comforts, and his wife's blue eyes, / Discovers in the pit's embrace an everlasting tomb." Auguste Barbier, *Iambes et poèmes* (Paris, 1841), pp. 240–241; from the collection *Lazare,* which is dated 1837, and which records his impressions of England. Compare these lines to the last two lines of "Le Crépuscule du soir."   [J87,1]

Professional conspirator and dandy meet in the concept of the modern hero. This hero represents for himself, in his own person, a whole secret society.
                                                                         [J87,2]

On the generation of Vallès: "It is that generation which, under the starless sky of the Second Empire, grew up in the face of a . . . future without faith or greatness."

Hermann Wendel, "Jules Vallès," *Die neue Zeit*, 31, no. 1 (Stuttgart, 1912), p. 105. [J87,3]

"When is a courtier . . . not idle and contemplative?" La Bruyère. [J87,4]

Regarding "study": "The flesh is sad, alas! and all the books are read." Mallarmé, "Brise marine," *Poésies* (Paris, 1917), p. 43.[475] [J87,5]

On idleness: "Imagine a perpetual idleness, . . . with a profound hatred of that idleness." ‹Baudelaire,› letter to his mother of Saturday, December 4, 1847. *Lettres à sa mère* (Paris ‹1932›), p. 22.[476] [J87,6]

Baudelaire speaks [where?] of the "habit of putting off until the next day . . . so many important things for so many years."[477] [J87,7]

Early high capitalism, defined by Wiesengrund (letter of June 5, 1935) as "modernity in the strict sense." [J87,8]

On idleness: Baudelaire's satanism—of which so much has been made—is nothing more than his way of taking up the challenge which bourgeois society flings at the idle poet. This satanism is only a reasoned reprise of the cynical and destructive velleities—delusions, in the main—that emanate from the lower depths of society.[478] [J87,9]

On idleness. "Hercules . . . labored too, . . . but the goal of his career was really always a sublime leisure, and for that reason he became one of the Olympians. Not so this Prometheus, the inventor of education and enlightenment. . . . Because he seduced mankind into working, [he] now has to work himself, whether he wants to or not. He'll have plenty of opportunity to be bored, and will never be free of his chains." Friedrich Schlegel, *Lucinde* (Leipzig), pp. 34–35 ("Idylle über den Müssiggang" ‹An Idyll of Idleness›).[479] [J87a,1]

"And so this is what I said to myself . . . : 'O Idleness, Idleness! You are the life breath of innocence and inspiration. The blessed breathe you, and blessed is he who has you and cherishes you, you holy jewel, you sole fragment of godlikeness come down to us from Paradise!'" Schlegel, *Lucinde* p. 29 ("Idylle über den Müssiggang").[480] [J87a,2]

"Industry and utility are the angels of death who, with fiery swords, prevent man's return to Paradise. . . . And in all parts of the world, it is the right to idleness that distinguishes the superior from the inferior classes. It is the intrinsic principle of aristocracy." Schlegel, *Lucinde* (Leipzig), p. 32.[481] [J87a,3]

"Baudelaire's weighty phrasing, charged as though with fluid electricity." Jules Renard, *Journal* ‹inédit, 1887–1895›, ed. Gallimard (Paris ‹1925›), p. 7.

[J87a,4]

"Meanwhile darkness dawns, filled with demon familiars / Who rouse, reluctant as businessmen, to their affairs."[482]—It may not be out of place to find here a reminiscence of Poe's description of the crowd.   [J87a,5]

Just as in "A Une Passante" the crowd is neither named nor described, so the paraphernalia of gambling make no appearance in "Le Jeu."   [J87a,6]

In contrast to Cabet, to Fourier, and to the roving Saint-Simonian utopians, Blanqui can be imagined only in Paris. Moreover, he represents himself and his work as belonging only in Paris. At the opposite pole is Proudhon's conception of great cities (A11a,2)!   [J87a,7]

Extracts from the preface which Pyat wrote for the 1884 edition of *Le Chiffonnier de Paris* ‹The Ragpicker of Paris›. These statements are important as indirect evidence of the connections that exist between Baudelaire's oeuvre and radical socialism. "This painful but salubrious drama . . . has merely carried through the logical evolution of my thinking, in advance of . . . the same evolution in the people. . . . It is republican thinking in my first play, *Une Révolution d'autrefois* ‹A Revolution of Old›; republican-democratic in *Ango, le marin* ‹Ango, the Sailor›; democratic and social in *Les Deux Serruriers* ‹The Two Locksmiths›, *Diogènes,* and *Le Chiffonnier;* but it is always a progressivist thinking tending toward the ideal, toward . . . completion of the work of '89. . . . There is no doubt that national unity has been attained . . . and political unity as well . . . ! But social unity remains unachieved. There are still two classes having little in common but the air they breathe . . . ; nothing can unite them but mutual respect and love. How many wealthy French men marry poor French women? The crux lies there. . . . Let us come back to Jean. . . . I conceived this drama in prison, to which I had been condemned in 1844 for having avenged the republic on the monarchy. Yes, it is a product of imprisonment, like those other popular protestations *Don Quixote* and *Robinson Crusoe;* Jean has at least that in common with these immortal masterpieces. I conceived it the evening of the performance of its elder sibling *Diogènes,* which was produced while I was behind bars. By a very direct filiation of ideas, the Cynic suggested to me the Ragpicker; the lantern of philosophy suggested the candle of the pariah; the tub suggested the wicker basket; the disinterestedness of Athens suggested the zeal of Paris. Jean was the Diogenes of Paris, as Diogenes was the Jean of Athens. The natural inclination of my mind and spirit led me to the people; I am drawn to the cause of the masses. My poetic practice, ever in harmony with my politics, has not once separated the author from the citizen. Art, in my opinion, . . .—not art for art's sake, but art for the sake of humanity—should . . . gravitate toward the people. In fact, art follows what is sovereign, commencing with the gods, continuing with kings, nobles, and bourgeoisie, and ending with the people. And the initiative for that end, in *Les Serruriers,* had to reach its basic principle, its very center of gravity, in *Le Chiffonnier.* For while bourgeois art . . . displayed its radiance in Hernani, Ruy Blas, and other lovers of queens, . . . republican art . . . was announcing another dynasty, that of the ragpickers. . . . On February 24, 1848, at noon, after the victory over the monarchy of Louis Philippe, the drama of 'rags and tatters' was performed gratis before the armed and triumphant populace. It was during this memorable performance that the actor . . . recovered the crown in the basket. What a historic day! What an indescribable effect! Author, actors, director, and spectators, all standing together and clapping their hands to the singing of *La Marseillaise,* to the sound of cannon. . . . I have spoken of the birth and the life of Jean. As for his death: Jean was crushed, like the Republic, beneath the landslide of December.[483] The play had the honor of being condemned together with its author, who had seen it applauded in London, in Brussels, everywhere except Paris. Thus, in a society based on the family—and at a time when . . . the rights of incest, in *René,* the rights of adultery, in *Antony,* the rights of the brothel, in *Rolla,* all enjoyed an open field—*Jean,* representing the rights of the family, was proscribed by the saviors of family and society." Félix Pyat, *Le Chiffonnier de Paris,* drama in five acts (Paris, 1884), pp. iv–viii. [J88; J88a,1]

It would appear that Baudelaire has given no thought to the classical *corso* of flânerie—the arcade. But in the lyric design of "Le Crépuscule du matin," which concludes "Tableaux parisiens," the canon of the arcade can be recognized. The central portion of this poem is composed of nine couplets which, while chiming one with another, remain well sealed off from the preceding as well as the following pairs of lines. The reader moves through this poem as through a gallery lined with showcases. In each one, the immaculate image of naked misery is on display. The poem closes with two quatrains that, in their presentation of things earthly and celestial, match each other like pilasters. [J88a,2]

The infernal time of gaming is something Baudelaire got to know less through the actual practice of gambling than through those seasons when he was prey to spleen. [J88a,3]

"Paris, when seen in a ragpicker's hamper, is nothing much. . . . To think that I have all Paris here in this wicker basket . . . !" From Pyat, *Le Chiffonnier,* cited in ‹Jean› Cassou, *Quarante-huit* (Paris ‹1939›), p. 13. [J88a,4]

The Cité Dorée[484] was the ragpickers' metropolis. [J88a,5]

Portrait of Blanqui by Cassou: "Blanqui was formed to act—to act without ostentation or sentimentality; he could grasp whatever was strictly real and authentic in the situation at hand. But the poverty, obscurity, and feebleness of the situation restricted his action to a series of fruitless sorties and to an acceptance of long imprisonment. He knew himself condemned to a purely preparatory and symbolic existence, to an attitude of patience with the gloom and fetters. And his whole life was spent in this state of mind. He became, in time, a wan and emaciated old man. But he will never be conquered. He cannot be conquered." Jean Cassou, *Quarante-huit* (Paris), p. 24.   [J89,1]

Concerning Hugo, but also Baudelaire's "Les Petites Vieilles" (neither mentioned here by Cassou): "For such, indeed, is the novelty of the Romantic century: it is the scandalous presence of the satyr at the table of the gods, the public manifestation of beings without name, beings without any possibility of existence—slaves, Negroes, monsters, the spider, the nettle." Jean Cassou, *Quarante-huit* (Paris), p. 27. (One thinks here of Marx's description of child labor in England.)[485]   [J89,2]

It would perhaps not be impossible to find in Baudelaire's poem "Paysage" an echo of '48 and of the mysticism of work characteristic of that time. And it might not be inappropriate to think, in this connection, of the formula coined by Cassou with reference to Jean Reynaud's *Terre et ciel:* "The Workshop expands all the way to the stars and invades eternity." Jean Cassou, *Quarante-huit* (Paris), p. 47.   [J89,3]

Frégier, *Des Classes dangereuses de la population dans les grandes villes ‹et des moyens de les rendre meilleures›* (Paris, 1840), vol. 2, p. 347: "The wages of the ragpicker, like those of the worker, are inseparable from the prosperity of industry. The latter has, like nature itself, the sublime privilege of breeding with its own *débris.* This privilege is the more precious for humanity as it propagates life within the lower levels of society, while making the intermediate and highest levels the ornament of wealth." Cited in Cassou, *Quarante-huit,* p. 73.   [J89,4]

"For Dante is the constant model of these men of '48. They are imbued with his language and his tales, and, like him, are committed to proscription; they are bearers of a vagabond homeland, charged with prophetic tidings, accompanied by shadows and voices." Jean Cassou, *Quarante-huit* (Paris), p. 111.   [J89a,1]

Cassou, describing Daumier's models: "the hunched silhouettes of men in long shabby frock coats who are looking at engravings, and all those Baudelairean characters, descendants of Jean-Jacques' solitary walker." Jean Cassou, *Quarante-huit* (Paris), p. 149.   [J89a,2]

Regarding a connection that may be felt between Baudelaire's "generosity of heart" and his sadism, one should refer to Proust's portrait of Mlle. Vinteuil (which, by the way, was probably conceived as a self-portrait): "'Sadists' of Mlle. Vinteuil's sort are creatures so purely sentimental, so virtuous by nature, that even sensual pleasure appears to them as something bad, a privilege reserved for the wicked. And when they allow themselves for a moment to enjoy it, they endeavor to impersonate, to assume all the outward appearance of wicked people, for themselves and their partners in guilt, so as to gain the momentary illusion of having escaped beyond the control of their own gentle and scrupulous natures into the inhuman world of pleasure." Marcel Proust, *Du Côté de chez Swann,* vol. 1, p. 236.[486]—One might also think here of Anatole France's note on the Baudelairean erotic. Yet one is justified in asking whether every sadism is structured like this one, since the concept of evil to which Proust relates it seems to exclude awareness. Sexual intercourse between human partners (in contrast to that between animals) includes awareness, and would thus perhaps also include a more or less high degree of sadism. Baudelaire's reflections on the sexual act would therefore carry more weight than this Proustian apologetic.   [J89a,3]

On the subject of the ragpicker, compare the conditions in England described by Marx in the section "Die moderne Manufaktur," in *Das Kapital* (‹vol. 1,› ed. Korsch ‹Berlin, 1932›, p. 438).   [J89a,4]

Proust on the allegories by Giotto in Santa Maria dell'Arena: "In later years I understood that the arresting strangeness . . . of these frescoes lay in the great part played in each of them by its symbols, while the fact that these were depicted not as symbols (for the thought symbolized was nowhere expressed) but as real things, actually felt or materially handled, added something more precise and more literal to their meaning, something more concrete and more striking to the lesson they imparted. And even in the case of the poor kitchen-maid, was not our attention incessantly drawn to her belly by the load which filled it . . . ?" Marcel Proust, *Du Côté de chez Swann* (Paris), vol. 1, pp. 121–122.[487]   [J90,1]

In Baudelaire's theory of art, the motif of shock comes into play not only as prosodic principle. Rather, this same motif is operative wherever Baudelaire appropriates Poe's theory concerning the importance of surprise in the work of art.—From another perspective, the motif of shock emerges in the "scornful laughter of hell"[488] which rouses the startled allegorist from his brooding.   [J90,2]

On information, advertisements, and feuilletons: the idler[489] must be furnished with sensations, the merchant with customers, and the man in the street with a worldview.   [J90,3]

Apropos of "Rêve parisien," Crépet (‹in Baudelaire, *Les Fleurs du mal, Oeuvres complètes,*› Conard edition [Paris, 1930], p. 463) cites a passage from a letter to Alphonse de Calonne: "Movement generally implies noise, to the extent that Pythagoras attributed music to the *moving* spheres. But dream, which separates things and breaks them down, creates the *new*."[490] Crépet further cites an article which Ernest Hello published in *La Revue française* of November 1858, under the title "Du genre fantastique" ‹The Genre of the Fantastic›, and which Baudelaire would have seen. Hello writes: "In the symbolic order, beauty stands in inverse proportion to life. The naturalist thus classifies nature as follows: animal kingdom first, vegetable kingdom next, mineral kingdom last. He is guided by the order of life. The poet will say: mineral kingdom first, vegetable kingdom after that, and animal kingdom last. He will be guided by the order of beauty." [J90,4]

Apropos of "L'Horloge," Crépet (Conard, p. 450): "A correspondent for *L'Inter-médiaire des chercheurs et curieux* ‹The Organ of the Inquisitive and the Curi-ous›, M. Ch. Ad. C. (September 30, 1905), reported that Baudelaire had removed the hands from his clock and written on the face: 'It's later than you think!'" [J90a,1]

On novelty and the familiar: "One of my dreams was the synthesis . . . of a certain seagirt place and its medieval past. . . . This dream in which . . . the sea had turned gothic, this dream in which . . . I believed that I was attaining to the impos-sible—it seemed to me that I had often dreamed it before. But as it is the property of what we imagine in our sleep to multiply itself in the past, and to appear, even when novel, familiar, I supposed that I was mistaken." Marcel Proust, *La Côté de Guermantes* (Paris, 1920), vol. 1, p. 131.[491] [J90a,2]

A rigorously Baudelairean reminiscence in Proust, to which, above all, the com-ments on Meryon ‹in "Salon de 1859"› should be compared. Proust speaks of railroad stations as "those vast, glass-roofed sheds, like that of Saint-Lazare into which I must go to find the train for Balbec, and which extended over the rent bowels of the city one of those bleak and boundless skies, heavy with an accumu-lation of dramatic menaces, like certain skies painted with an almost Parisian modernity by Mantegna or Veronese, beneath which could be accomplished only some solemn and tremendous act, such as a departure by train or the Elevation of the Cross." Marcel Proust, *A l'Ombre des jeunes filles en fleurs* (Paris), vol. 2, p. 63.[492] [J90a,3]

The stanza beginning "If rape and arson," from "Au Lecteur," is cited by Proust (‹*La Prisonnière* (Paris, 1923), vol. 2› p. 241) with this characteristic addition: "But I can at least assume that Baudelaire is not sincere. Whereas Dosto-evsky . . ." At issue is the latter's "preoccupation with murder." This all in a conversation with Albertine.[493] [J90a,4]

Apropos of "A Une Passante": "When Albertine returned to my room, she was wearing a garment of black satin which had the effect of making her seem paler, of turning her into the pallid, ardent Parisian, etiolated by want of fresh air, by the atmosphere of crowds and perhaps by habitual vice, whose eyes seemed more restless because they were not brightened by any color in her cheeks." Marcel Proust, *La Prisonnière* (Paris, 1923), vol. 1, p. 138.[494] [J90a,5]

Meryon shows himself equal to the competition provided by photography. It was probably the last time this was possible for a graphic artist, as far as the image of the city is concerned. Writing about medieval Paris, Stahl says that on the site of the ancient *curia* "arose buildings that were much too large, against which the houses abutted with one yard after another, . . . and with blind alleys. Photography is useless here. Hence, we turn to the engravings of the great draftsman Meryon." Fritz Stahl, *Paris* (Berlin ‹1929›), p. 97.   [J91,1]

Insight into the physiognomy of "overpopulated Paris" is afforded by the background—empty of human beings—in Meryon's *Pont au change*. On this background we meet with one or two very narrow (window-wide) and, as it were, spindly houses. Their window openings strike the viewer like gazes; they bring to mind the gazes of those spindly, hollow-eyed children who appear—often gathered together in great numbers—in pictures of poor people from that era, and who stand there abashed and close-packed in a corner like the tenements in Meryon's engraving.   [J91,2]

Concerning Meryon's verses on the Pont Neuf ‹J2,3›, compare the old Parisian expression, "Il se porte comme le pont neuf" ("he is hale and hearty").   [J91,3]

Baudelaire, great despiser of the countryside, of greenery and fields, nevertheless has this peculiarity: No one could be less inclined to view the big city as something ordinary, natural, acceptable.[495]   [J91,4]

Baudelaire had the good fortune to be the contemporary of a bourgeoisie that could not yet employ, as accomplice of its domination, such an asocial type as he represented. The incorporation of a nihilism into its hegemonic apparatus was reserved for the bourgeoisie of the twentieth century.   [J91,5]

"I can understand how it is that city dwellers, who see only walls and streets and crimes, have so little religion." Jean-Jacques Rousseau, *Les Confessions*, ed. Hilsum (Paris ‹1931›), vol. 4, p. 175.[496]   [J91,6]

A criterion for deciding whether or not a city is modern: the absence of monuments. "New York is a city without monuments" (Döblin).—Meryon turned the tenements of Paris into monuments of modernity.   [J91a,1]

In the introduction to his published translation of one of Poe's tales in *L'Illustration* (April 17, 1852), Baudelaire characterizes the American author's field of interests, and mentions, among other things, Poe's "analysis of the eccentrics and pariahs of this world" (Ch‹arles› B‹audelaire›, *Oeuvres complètes,* ed. Crépet, *Traductions: Nouvelles Histoires extraordinaires* [Paris, 1933], p. 378).[497] The phrase corresponds, in the most striking manner, to the self-portrait which Blanqui introduced—as rebus image, so to speak—into *L'Eternité par les astres:* "Blanqui . . . recognized himself to be 'the pariah' of an epoch." Maurice Dommanget, *Auguste Blanqui à Belle-Ile* (Paris, 1935), pp. 140–141.   [J91a,2]

Re Meryon's *Pont au change*: "The block-tenements of Rome, such as the famous Insula Feliculae, rose, with a street breadth of only three to five meters, to heights that have never been seen in Western Europe and are seen in only a few cities in

America. Near the Capitol, the roofs already reached to the level of the hill-saddle. But always the splendid mass-cities harbor lamentable poverty and degraded habits, and the attics and mansards, the cellars and back courts are breeding a new type of raw man. . . . Diodorus tells of a deposed Egyptian king who was reduced to living in one of these wretched upper-floor tenements of Rome." Oswald Spengler, *Le Déclin de l'Occident* ‹trans. M. Tazerout›, vol. 2 (Paris, 1933), p. 143.[498]   [J91a,3]

On the decline in the birthrate: "When the ordinary thinking of a highly cultivated people begins to regard 'having children' as a question of pro's and con's, the great turning point has come. . . . At that point begins prudent limitation of the number of births. . . . In subsequent Roman times, it became appallingly general. At first explained by the economic misery of the times, very soon it ceased to explain itself at all." Oswald Spengler, *Le Déclin de l'Occident*, vol. 2 (Paris), p. 147. Compare p. 146: the peasant feels himself to be a link in the chain of forebears and descendants.[499]   [J91a,4]

Concerning the title, *Les Fleurs du mal:* "During naive epochs, and as late as 1824, the title of a volume of poetry simply indicated the genre taken up by the author. There were odes, epistles, light verse, heroic verse, satires. Today, the title is a symbol. Nothing is more refined. When the author harbors lyric intentions, he gives his collection a sonorous and musical label: *Melodies, Preludes* . . . Tender-hearted friends of nature prefer to take their titles from *The Good Gardener's Almanac*. Thus, we have *Dead Leaves, . . . Branches of Almond. . . .* We have *Palms* and *Cypresses. . . .* And then the flowers: *Flowers of Noon, Flowers of Provence, Flowers of the Alps, Flowers of the Fields*." Charles Louandre, "Statistique littéraire: La Poésie depuis 1830," *Revue des deux mondes*, 30 (Paris, June 15, 1842), p. 979.   [J92,1]

The original title of "Les Sept Vieillards": "Fantômes parisiens."[500]   [J92,2]

"From the beginning, the proclamation of Equality as a constitutional principle was not only an advance for thought, but a danger as well." (Max Horkheimer, "Materialismus und Moral," *Zeitschrift für Sozialforschung* [1933], no. 2, p. 188.)[501] Within the zone of this danger lie the absurd uniformities in Poe's description of the crowd. The hallucination of the seven identical old men is in the same mold.   [J92,3]

It is only as commodity that the thing has the effect of alienating human beings from one another. It produces this effect through its price. What is decisive is the empathy with the exchange value of the commodity, with its equalizing substrate. (The absolute qualitative invariance of the time in which labor that generates exchange value runs its course—such absolute equality is the grayish background against which the gaudy colors of sensation stand out.)   [J92,4]

Regarding spleen. Blanqui to Lacambre, September 16, 1853: "Even the news from the true Empire of the Dead must be more interesting than the news from this dismal hall in the Kingdom of the Shades where we are being quarantined. Nothing more wretched than this shut-away existence, this tossing and turning at the bottom of a jar, like spiders trying to find the way out." Maurice Dommanget, *Blanqui à Belle-Ile* ⟨Paris, 1935⟩, p. 250. [J92,5]

After a vain attempt at flight from Belle-Isle, Blanqui was thrown for a month into the dungeon known as "Château Fouquet." Dommanget refers to "the dreary and oppressive succession of hours and minutes that hammer the skull." Maurice Dommanget, *Blanqui à Belle-Ile*, p. 238. [J92a,1]

The following lines from Barbier should be compared with parts of Baudelaire's poem "Paysage." Cited in Sainte-Beuve, *Portraits contemporains*, vol. 2 (Paris, 1882), p. 234 ("Briseux et Auguste Barbier").

> What inexpressible happiness, what ecstasy,
> To be a living ray of divinity;
> To look down from the orbed canopy of heaven
> On the dust of worlds glistening below,
> To hear, at every instant of their bright awakening,
> A thousand suns at their song like the birds!
> Oh, what felicity to live among things of beauty,
> And to savor the sweetness without needing reasons!
> How lovely to be well without wishing to be better,
> And without ever having to tire of the skies! [J92a,2]

[Dream City and Dream House, Dreams of the Future, Anthropological Nihilism, Jung]

> My good father had been in Paris.
> —Karl Gutzkow, *Briefe aus Paris* (Leipzig, 1842), vol. 1, p. 58

> Library where the books have melted into one another and the titles have faded away.
> —Dr. Pierre Mabille, "Préface à l'*Eloge des préjugés populaires,*" *Minotaure,* 2, no. 6 (Winter 1935), p. 2

> The Pantheon raising its somber dome toward the somber dome of the sky.
> —Ponson du Terrail, *Les Drames de Paris,* vol. 1, p. 9[1]

Awakening as a graduated process that goes on in the life of the individual as in the life of generations. Sleep its initial stage. A generation's experience of youth has much in common with the experience of dreams. Its historical configuration is a dream configuration. Every epoch has such a side turned toward dreams, the child's side. For the previous century, this appears very clearly in the arcades. But whereas the education of earlier generations explained these dreams for them in terms of tradition, of religious doctrine, present-day education simply amounts to the distraction of children. Proust could emerge as an unprecedented phenomenon only in a generation that had lost all bodily and natural aids to remembrance[2] and that, poorer than before, was left to itself to take possession of the worlds of childhood in merely an isolated, scattered, and pathological way. What follows here is an experiment in the technique of awakening. An attempt to become aware of the dialectical—the Copernican—turn of remembrance.   [K1,1]

The Copernican revolution in historical perception is as follows. Formerly it was thought that a fixed point had been found in "what has been," and one saw the present engaged in tentatively concentrating the forces of knowledge on this ground. Now this relation is to be overturned, and what has been is to become the dialectical reversal—the flash of awakened consciousness. Politics attains primacy over history. The facts become something that just now first happened to us, first struck us; to establish them is the affair of memory. Indeed, awakening is the great exemplar of memory: the occasion on which it is given us to remember what is closest, tritest, most obvious. What Proust intends with the experimental rearrangement of furniture in matinal half-slumber, what Bloch recognizes as the darkness of the lived moment,[3] is nothing other than what here is to be secured on the level of the historical, and collectively. There is a not-yet-conscious knowledge of what has been: its advancement[4] has the structure of awakening.   [K1,2]

There is a wholly unique experience of dialectic. The compelling—the drastic—experience, which refutes everything "gradual" about becoming and shows all seeming "development" to be dialectical reversal, eminently and thoroughly composed, is the awakening from dream. For the dialectical schematism at the core of this process, the Chinese have often found, in their fairy tales and novellas, a highly pregnant expression. The new, dialectical method of doing history presents itself as the art of experiencing the present as waking world, a world to which that dream we name the past refers in truth. To pass through and carry out *what has been* in remembering the dream!—Therefore: remembering and awaking are most intimately related. Awakening is namely the dialectical, Copernican turn of remembrance.   [K1,3]

The nineteenth century a spacetime ‹*Zeitraum*› (a dreamtime ‹*Zeit-traum*›) in which the individual consciousness more and more secures itself in reflecting, while the collective consciousness sinks into ever deeper sleep. But just as the sleeper—in this respect like the madman—sets out on the macrocosmic journey through his own body, and the noises and feelings of his insides, such as blood pressure, intestinal churn, heartbeat, and muscle sensation (which for the waking and salubrious individual converge in a steady surge of health) generate, in the extravagantly heightened inner awareness of the sleeper, illusion or dream imagery which translates and accounts for them, so likewise for the dreaming collective, which, through the arcades, communes with its own insides. We must follow in its wake so as to expound the nineteenth century—in fashion and advertising, in buildings and politics—as the outcome of its dream visions.   [K1,4]

It is one of the tacit suppositions of psychoanalysis that the clear-cut antithesis of sleeping and waking has no value for determining the empirical form of consciousness of the human being, but instead yields before an unending variety of concrete states of consciousness conditioned by every conceivable level of wakefulness within all possible centers. The situation of consciousness as patterned and checkered by sleep and waking need only be transferred from the individual to the collective. Of course, much that is external to the former is internal to the latter: architecture, fashion—yes, even the weather—are, in the interior of the collective, what the sensoria of organs, the feeling of sickness or health, are inside the individual. And so long as they preserve this unconscious, amorphous dream configuration, they are as much natural processes as digestion, breathing, and the like. They stand in the cycle of the eternally selfsame, until the collective seizes upon them in politics and history emerges. [K1,5]

"Who will inhabit the paternal home? Who will pray in the church where he was baptized? Who will still know the room where he raised his first cry, where he witnessed a last breath? Who will be able to rest his brow above the sill of a window where, as a youth, he would have formed those waking dreams which are the grace of dawn within the long and somber servitude of life? O roots of joy torn from the human soul!" Louis Veuillot, *Les Odeurs de Paris* (Paris, 1914), p. 11. [K1a,1]

The fact that we were children during this time belongs together with its objective image. It had to be this way in order to produce this generation. That is to say: we seek a teleological moment in the context of dreams. Which is the moment of waiting. The dream waits secretly for the awakening; the sleeper surrenders himself to death only provisionally, waits for the second when he will cunningly wrest himself from its clutches. So, too, the dreaming collective, whose children provide the happy occasion for its own awakening. ☐ Method ☐
[K1a,2]

Task of childhood: to bring the new world into symbolic space. The child, in fact, can do what the grownup absolutely cannot: recognize the new once again. For us, locomotives already have symbolic character because we met with them in childhood. Our children, however, will find this in automobiles, of which we ourselves see only the new, elegant, modern, cheeky side. There is no more insipid and shabby antithesis than that which reactionary thinkers like Klages try to set up between the symbol-space of nature and that of technology. To each truly new configuration of nature—and, at bottom, technology is just such a configuration—there correspond new "images." Every childhood discovers these new images in order to incorporate them into the image stock of humanity. ☐ Method ☐ [K1a,3]

It is remarkable that constructions in which the expert recognizes anticipations of contemporary building fashions impress the alert but architecturally unschooled sense not at all as anticipatory but as distinctly old-fashioned and dreamlike. (Old railroad stations, gasworks, bridges.) [K1a,4]

"The nineteenth century: singular fusion of individualistic and collectivist tendencies. Unlike virtually every previous age, it labels all actions 'individualistic' (ego, nation, art) while subterraneanly, in despised everyday domains, it necessarily furnishes, as in a delirium, the elements for a collective formation. . . . With this raw material, we must occupy ourselves—with gray buildings, market halls, department stores, exhibitions." Sigfried Giedion, *Bauen in Frankreich* (Leipzig and Berlin), p. 15. [K1a,5]

It is not only that the forms of appearance taken by the dream collective in the nineteenth century cannot be thought away; and not only that these forms char-acterize this collective much more decisively than any other—they are also, rightly interpreted, of the highest practical import, for they allow us to recognize the sea on which we navigate and the shore from which we push off. It is here, therefore, that the "critique" of the nineteenth century—to say it in one word—ought to begin. The critique not of its mechanism and cult of machinery but of its narcotic historicism, its passion for masks, in which nevertheless lurks a signal of true historical existence, one which the Surrealists were the first to pick up. To decipher this signal is the concern of the present undertaking. And the revolu-tionary materialist basis of Surrealism is sufficient warrant for the fact that, in this signal of true historical existence, the nineteenth century gave supreme expres-sion to its economic basis. [K1a,6]

Attempt to develop Giedion's thesis. "In the nineteenth century," he writes, "construction plays the role of the subconscious."[5] Wouldn't it be better to say "the role of bodily processes"—around which "artistic" architectures gather, like dreams around the framework of physiological processes? [K1a,7]

Capitalism was a natural phenomenon with which a new dream-filled sleep came over Europe, and, through it, a reactivation of mythic forces. [K1a,8]

The first tremors of awakening serve to deepen sleep. [K1a,9]

"Strange, by the way, that when we survey this whole intellectual movement, Scribe appears as the only one to occupy himself directly and thoroughly with the present. Everyone else busies himself more with the past than with the powers and interests that set their own time in motion. . . . It was the past, moreover—it was the history of philosophy—that fueled eclectic doctrine; and, finally, it was the history of literature whose treasures were disclosed, in Villemain, by a criticism incapable of entering more deeply into the literary life of its own period." Julius Meyer, *Geschichte der modernen französischen Malerei* (Leipzig, 1867), pp. 415–416. [K2,1]

What the child (and, through faint reminiscence, the man) discovers in the pleats of the old material to which it clings while trailing at its mother's skirts—that's what these pages should contain. ☐ Fashion ☐ [K2,2]

It is said that the dialectical method consists in doing justice each time to the concrete historical situation of its object. But that is not enough. For it is just as much a matter of doing justice to the concrete historical situation of the *interest* taken in the object. And *this* situation is always so constituted that the interest is itself preformed in that object and, above all, feels this object concretized in itself and upraised from its former being into the higher concretion of now-being ‹*Jetztsein*› (waking being!). In what way this now-being (which is something other

than the now-being of "the present time" ‹*Jetztzeit*›, since it is a being punctuated and intermittent) already signifies, in itself, a higher concretion—this question, of course, can be entertained by the dialectical method only within the purview of a historical perception that at all points has overcome the ideology of progress. In regard to such a perception, one could speak of the increasing concentration (integration) of reality, such that everything past (in its time) can acquire a higher grade of actuality than it had in the moment of its existing. How it marks itself as higher actuality is determined by the image as which and in which it is comprehended. And this dialectical penetration and actualization of former contexts puts the truth of all present action to the test. Or rather, it serves to ignite the explosive materials that are latent in what has been (the authentic figure of which is *fashion*). To approach, in this way, "what has been" means to treat it not historiographically, as heretofore, but politically, in political categories. ▢ Fashion ▢
[K2,3]

The imminent awakening is poised, like the wooden horse of the Greeks, in the Troy of dreams.   [K2,4]

On the doctrine of the ideological superstructure. It seems, at first sight, that Marx wanted to establish here only a causal relation between superstructure and infrastructure. But already the observation that ideologies of the superstructure reflect conditions falsely and invidiously goes beyond this. The question, in effect, is the following: if the infrastructure in a certain way (in the materials of thought and experience) determines the superstructure, but if such determination is not reducible to simple reflection, how is it then—entirely apart from any question about the originating cause—to be characterized? As its expression. The superstructure is the expression of the infrastructure. The economic conditions under which society exists are expressed in the superstructure—precisely as, with the sleeper, an overfull stomach finds not its reflection but its expression in the contents of dreams, which, from a causal point of view, it may be said to "condition." The collective, from the first, expresses the conditions of its life. These find their expression in the dream and their interpretation in the awakening.   [K2,5]

Jugendstil—a first attempt to reckon with the open air. It finds a distinctive embodiment, for example, in the drawings of *Simplicissimus,* which clearly show how, in order to get a little air, one must become satirical. From another perspective, Jugendstil could blossom in the artificial light and isolation in which advertising presents its objects. This birth of *plein air* from the spirit of the interior is the sensuous expression of the situation of Jugendstil from the viewpoint of the philosophy of history: Jugendstil is the dream that one has come awake. ‹See S4a,1.› ▢ Advertising ▢   [K2,6]

Just as technology is always revealing nature from a new perspective, so also, as it impinges on human beings, it constantly makes for variations in their most primordial passions, fears, and images of longing. In this work I mean to wrest from primal history ‹Urgeschichte› a portion of the nineteenth century. The alluring and threatening face of primal history is clearly manifest to us in the beginnings of technology, in the living arrangements of the nineteenth century; it has not yet shown itself in what lies nearer to us in time. But it is also more intense in technology (on account of the latter's natural origin) than in other domains. That is the reason old photographs—but not old drawings—have a ghostly effect. [K2a,1]

On Wiertz's picture *Thoughts and Visions of a Severed Head,* and its explication. The first thing that strikes one about this magnetopathic experience is the grandiose sleight of hand which the consciousness executes in death. "What a singular thing! The head is here under the scaffold, and it believes that it still exists above, forming part of the body and continuing to wait for the blow that will separate it from the trunk." A. Wiertz, *Oeuvres littéraires* (Paris, 1870), p. 492. The same inspiration at work here in Wiertz animates Bierce in his extraordinary short story about the rebel who is hanged, and who experiences, at the moment of his death, the flight that frees him from the hangman.[6] [K2a,2]

Every current of fashion or of worldview derives its force from what is forgotten. This downstream flow is ordinarily so strong that only the group can give itself up to it; the individual—the precursor—is liable to collapse in the face of such violence, as happened with Proust. In other words: what Proust, as an individual, directly experienced in the phenomenon of remembrance, we have to experience indirectly (with regard to the nineteenth century) in studying "current," "fashion," "tendency"—as punishment, if you will, for the sluggishness which keeps us from taking it up ourselves.[7] [K2a,3]

Fashion, like architecture, inheres in the darkness of the lived moment, belongs to the dream consciousness of the collective. The latter awakes, for example, in advertising. [K2a,4]

"Very interesting . . . how the fascistization of science had to alter precisely those elements in Freud which still stem from the enlightened, materialistic period of the bourgeoisie. . . . In Jung, . . . the unconscious . . . is no longer individual—that is, not an acquired condition in the single . . . human being, but a stock of primal humanity renewing itself in the present; it is not repression but fruitful return." Ernst Bloch, *Erbschaft dieser Zeit* (Zurich, 1935), p. 254.[8] [K2a,5]

Historical index of childhood according to Marx. In his derivation of the normative character of Greek art (as an art springing from the childhood of the human race), Marx says: "Doesn't the child in every epoch represent the character of the period in its natural veracity?"[9] Cited in Max Raphael, *Proudhon, Marx, Picasso* (Paris, 1933), p. 175. [K2a,6]

More than a hundred years before it was fully manifest, the colossal acceleration of the tempo of living was heralded in the tempo of production. And, indeed, in the form of the machine. "The number of implements that he himself [that is, the human being] can use simultaneously is limited by the number of his own natural instruments of production, by the number of his bodily organs. . . . The jenny, on the other hand, even at its very birth, spun with twelve to eighteen spindles, and the stocking loom knits with many thousands of needles at once. The number of tools that a machine can bring into play simultaneously is, from the very first, emancipated from the organic limits that hedge in the tools of a handicraftsman." Karl Marx, *Das Kapital,* vol. 1 (Hamburg, 1922), p. 337.[10] The tempo of machine operation effects changes in the economic tempo. "In this country, the main thing is to reap a huge fortune with as little delay as possible. It used to be that the fortune resulting from a commercial house begun by the grandfather was scarcely run through by the time the grandson died. Things don't happen that way any more; people want to enjoy without waiting, without having to be patient." Louis Rainier Lanfranchi, *Voyage à Paris, ou Esquisses des hommes et des choses dans cette capitale* (Paris, 1830), p. 110.   [K3,1]

Simultaneity, the basis of the new style of living, likewise comes from mechanical production: "Each detail machine supplies raw material to the machine next in order; and since they are all working at the same time, the product is always going through the various stages of its fabrication, and is also constantly in a state of transition from one phase to another. . . . The collective machine, now an organized system of various kinds of single machines, and of groups of single machines, becomes more and more perfect, the more the process as a whole becomes a continuous one—that is, the less the raw material is interrupted in its passage from its first phase to its last; in other words, the more its passage from one phase to another is effected not by the hand of man but by the machinery itself. In manufacture the isolation of each detail process is a condition imposed by the nature of division of labor, but in the fully developed factory the continuity of those processes is, on the contrary, imperative." Karl Marx, *Das Kapital,* vol. 1 (Hamburg, 1922), p. 344.[11]   [K3,2]

Film: unfolding ‹result?›[12] of all the forms of perception, the tempos and rhythms, which lie preformed in today's machines, such that all problems of contemporary art find their definitive formulation only in the context of film. ☐ Precursors ☐
                                                                                        [K3,3]

A small piece of materialist analysis, more valuable than most of what exists in this field: "We love these hard, solid blocks of material which Flaubert raises and lets fall with the intermittent thud of a steam shovel. For if, as I found recounted in some book or other, sailors at sea used to catch the glow of Flaubert's lamp as he worked through the night, and take their bearings from it, as if from a lighthouse beam, so too it might be said that when he 'unloaded' a good round phrase, it had the regular rhythm of one of those machines used in excavating.

Happy are they who can feel the beat of this obsessive rhythm." Marcel Proust, *Chroniques* (Paris, 1927), p. 204 ("A Propos du 'style' de Flaubert").[13]   [K3,4]

In his chapter on the fetish character of the commodity, Marx has shown how ambiguous the economic world of capitalism seems. It is an ambiguity considerably heightened by the intensification of capital management—as we see exemplified quite clearly in the machines which aggravate exploitation rather than alleviate the human lot. Isn't there implicit here a general connection to the equivocalness of the phenomena we are dealing with in the nineteenth century? The significance of intoxication for perception, of fiction for thinking, such as was never before recognized? "One thing has disappeared in the general upheaval, and it was a great loss for art: the naive and therefore dependable accord of life and appearance"—so we read, characteristically, in Julius Meyer's *Geschichte der modernen französischen Malerei seit 1789* (Leipzig, 1867), p. 31.   [K3,5]

On the political significance of film. Socialism would never have entered the world if its proponents had sought only to excite the enthusiasm of the working classes for a better order of things. What made for the power and authority of the movement was that Marx understood how to interest the workers in a social order which would both benefit them and appear to them as just. It is exactly the same with art. At no point in time, no matter how utopian, will anyone win the masses over to a higher art; they can be won over only to one nearer to them. And the difficulty consists precisely in finding a form for art such that, with the best conscience in the world, one could hold that it *is* a higher art. This will never happen with most of what is propagated by the avant-garde of the bourgeoisie. Here, Berl's argument is perfectly correct: "The confusion over the word 'revolution'—a word which, for a Leninist, signifies the acquisition of power by the proletariat, and which elsewhere signifies the overturning of recognized spiritual values—is sufficiently attested by the Surrealists in their desire to establish Picasso as a revolutionary. . . . Picasso deceives them. . . . A painter is not more revolutionary for having 'revolutionized' painting than a tailor like Poiret is for having 'revolutionized' fashion, or than a doctor is for having 'revolutionized' medicine." Emmanuel Berl, "Premier pamphlet," *Europe,* 75 (1929), p. 401. The masses positively require from the work of art (which, for them, has its place in the circle of consumer items) something that is warming. Here the flame most readily kindled is that of hatred. Its heat, however, burns or sears without providing the "heart's ease" which qualifies art for consumption. Kitsch, on the other hand, is nothing more than art with a 100 percent, absolute and instantaneous availability for consumption. Precisely within the consecrated forms of expression, therefore, kitsch and art stand irreconcilably opposed. But for developing, living forms, what matters is that they have within them something stirring, useful, ultimately heartening—that they take "kitsch" dialectically up into themselves, and hence bring themselves near to the masses while yet surmounting the kitsch. Today, perhaps, film alone is equal to this task—or, at any rate, more ready for it than any other art form. And whoever has recognized this will be inclined to disallow the pretensions of abstract film, as important as its experiments may be. He will call for a closed season on—a natural preserve for—the sort of kitsch whose providential site is the cinema. Only film can detonate the explosive stuff which the nineteenth century has accumulated in that strange and perhaps formerly unknown material which is kitsch. But just as with the political structure of film, so also with other distinctively modern means of expression (such as lighting or plastic design): abstraction can be dangerous.   [K3a,1]

One can characterize the problem of the form of the new art straight on: When and how will the worlds of form which, without our assistance, have arisen, for example, in mechanics, in film, in machine construction, in the new physics, and which have subjugated us, make it clear for us what manner of nature they contain? When will we reach a state of society in which these forms, or those arising from them, reveal themselves to us as natural forms? Of course, this brings to light only one moment in the dialectical essence of technology. (*Which* moment, is hard to say: antithesis if not synthesis.) In any case, there lives in technology another impulse as well: to bring about objectives strange to nature, along with means that are alien and inimical to nature—measures that emancipate themselves from nature and master it.   [K3a,2]

On Grandville: "Between an uninformed vision of the streets and a knowledge of the occult derived from cartomancy or astrology, a knowledge openly tormented by flora and fauna and by a dream-humanity, he managed to lead a boundless imaginary life within a fabulous realm of primal poetry. . . . Grandville was perhaps the first draftsman ever to give the larval life of dreams a rational plastic form. Evident beneath this poised appearance, however, is that *flebile nescio quid*[14] which disconcerts and provokes disquietude—sometimes troubling enough." MacOrlan, "Grandville le précurseur," *Arts et métiers graphiques*, 44 (December 15, 1934), pp. 20–21. The essay presents ⟨Grandville⟩ as a forerunner of Surrealism, particularly of surrealist film (Méliès, Walt Disney).   [K4,1]

Confrontation between the "visceral unconscious" and the "unconscious of oblivion"—the first of which is predominantly individual, the second predominantly collective: "The other part of the unconscious is made up of the mass of things learned in the course of the centuries and in the course of a life, things which were conscious once and which, by diffusion, have entered oblivion. . . . Vast submarine fund, in which all cultures, all studies, all proceedings of mind and will, all social uprisings, all struggles are collected in a formless mire. . . . The passional elements of individuals have receded, dimmed. All that remain are the givens of the external world, more or less transformed and digested. It is of the external world that this unconscious is made. . . . Born of social life, this humus belongs to societies. The species and the individual count for little in it; only the races and the ages leave their mark. This enormous labor undertaken in the shadows comes to light in dreams, thoughts, decisions, and above all at moments of crisis or of social upheaval; it forms the great common ground, the reserve of peoples and individuals. Revolution and war, like a fever, are best suited to get it moving. . . . Seeing that the psychology of the individual is now outmoded, let us call upon a sort of natural history of volcanic rhythms and subterranean streams. There is nothing on the surface of the earth that was not once subterranean (water, earth, fire). Nothing in the intellect that has not been digested and circulated in the depths." Dr. Pierre Mabille, "Préface à l'*Eloge des préjugés populaires*," *Minotaure*, 2, no. 6 (Winter 1935), p. 2. [K4,2]

"The recent past always presents itself as though annihilated by catastrophes." Wiesengrund, in a letter ‹of June 5, 1935›.[15] [K4,3]

Apropos of Henry Bordeaux's recollections of his youth: "In sum, the nineteenth century ran its course without in the least appearing to announce the twentieth." André Thérive, "Les Livres," *Le Temps* (June 27, 1935). [K4,4]

> The embers blaze in your eyes,
> And you flash like a mirror.
> Have you hooves, have you wings,
> My black-flanked locomotive?
> See its mane ripple,
> Listen to that whinny;
> Its gallop is a rumble
> Of artillery and thunder.

Refrain:

> Feed your horse its oats!
> Saddled, bridled—whistle and we're off! Ride
> At a gallop across the bridge, under the arch,
> Plow your way through hill and dale—
> No mount can rival yours.

Pierre Dupont, "Le Chauffeur de locomotive" (Paris) ("Passage du Caire").
[K4a,1]

"Yesterday, looking down from the tower of Notre Dame, I was able to take in this gigantic city. Who built the first house, and when will the last one collapse? When will the ground of Paris look like that of Thebes or Babylon?" Friedrich von Raumer, *Briefe aus Paris und Frankreich im Jahre 1830* (Leipzig, 1831), vol. 2, p. 127. [K4a,2]

D'Eichthal's additions to Duveyrier's plan of the "new city." They have to do with the temple. Significant that Duveyrier himself says, "My temple is a woman!" Counters d'Eichthal: "I think that the temple will contain the palace of man and the palace of woman; the man will go to pass the night with the woman, and the woman will come to work during the day with the man. Between the two palaces will be the temple proper, the place of communion, where the man and the woman join with all women and all men; and there the couple will neither rest nor labor in isolation. . . . The temple ought to represent an androgyne, a man *and* a woman. . . . The same method of division should be employed throughout the city, throughout the realm, throughout the world: there will be the hemisphere of man and the hemisphere of woman." Henry-René d'Allemagne, *Les Saint-Simoniens, 1827–1837* (Paris, 1930), p. 310.   [K4a,3]

The Paris of the Saint-Simonians. From the draft plan sent by Charles Duveyrier to *L'Advocat*, with the expectation of having it incorporated into *Le Livre des cent-et-un* (which, evidently, it was not): "We wanted to give a human form to the first city inspired by our faith." "The Lord, in his goodness, has spoken through the mouth of man: he sends . . . Paris! It is on the banks of your river and within your walls that I shall impress the seal of my new bounty. . . . Your kings and your peoples have marched with the slowness of centuries, and they have finally arrived at a magnificent place. It is there that the head of my city will repose. . . . The palaces of your kings will be its brow, . . . and I shall tend to its beard of mighty chestnut trees. . . . From the top of that head I will sweep away the old Christian temple, . . . and in this clearing I will arrange a headdress of trees. . . . Above the breast of my city, in that sympathetic foyer where the passions all diverge and come together, where sorrows and joys vibrate, I will build my temple, . . . solar plexus of the giant. . . . The hills of Roule and Chaillot will form its flanks; there I will establish bank and university, marketplaces and publishing houses. . . . I will extend the left arm of the colossus along the bank of the Seine; it will run . . . opposite . . . Passy. The corps of engineers . . . will constitute the upper portion, which will stretch toward Vaugirard, and I will make the forearm from the union of all the specialized schools of physical science. . . . In between, . . . I will assemble all the grammar schools and high schools for my city to press to its breast, there on the left where the university is lodged. I will extend the right arm of the giant, as a show of force, all the way to the Gare de Saint-Ouen. . . . I will load this arm with workshops of small industry, arcades, galleries, bazaars. . . . I will form the right thigh and leg from all the large manufacturing establishments. The right foot will touch Neuilly. The left thigh will offer foreigners a long row of hotels. The left leg will reach to the Bois de Boulogne. . . . My city is in the posture of a man about to set off. His feet are bronze; they are resting on a double road of stone and iron. Here . . . vehicles of transport and instruments of communication are manufactured; here carriages race about. . . . Between its knees is an equestrian arena; between its legs, an immense hippodrome." Henry-René d'Allemagne, *Les Saint-Simoniens, 1827–1837* (Paris, 1930), pp. 309–310. The idea for this proposal goes back to Enfantin, who developed plans for the city of the future with the aid of anatomical charts.   [K5]

> But no, the Orient summons you
> To go irrigate its deserts;
> Raise high into the air
> The towers of the *ville nouvelle*.

F. Maynard, "L'Avenir est beau," in *Foi nouvelle: Chants et chansons de Bar-rault, Vinçard . . . , 1831 à 1834* (Paris, January 1, 1835), book 1, p. 81. Regarding the motif of the desert, compare Rouget de Lisle's "Chant des industriels" and "Le Désert" by Félicien David. [K5a,1]

Paris in the year 2855: "The city is 75 miles in circumference. Versailles and Fontainebleau—neighborhoods lost among so many others—send into less tranquil boroughs refreshing perfumes from trees that are twenty centuries old. Sèvres, which has become the regular market for the Chinese (French citizens since the war of 2850), displays . . . its pagodas with their echoing little bells; in its midst can still be found the factories of an earlier age, reconstructed in porcelain *à la reine*." Arsène Houssaye, "Le Paris futur," in *Paris et les Parisiens au XIXᵉ siècle* (Paris, 1856), p. 459. [K5a,2]

Chateaubriand on the Obelisk de la Concorde: "The hour will come when the obelisk of the desert will find once again, on Murderers' Square, the silence and solitude of Luxor."[16] Cited in Louis Bertrand, "Discours sur Chateaubriand," *Le Temps* (September 18, 1935). [K5a,3]

Saint-Simon once proposed "turning a mountain in Switzerland into a statue of Napoleon. In one hand, it would hold an occupied city; in the other, a lake." Count Gustav von Schlabrendorf, in Paris, on events and persons of his day [in Carl Gustav Jochmann, *Reliquien: Aus seinen nachgelassenen Papieren*, ed. Heinrich Zschokke, vol. 1 (Hechingen, 1836), p. 146]. [K5a,4]

Nocturnal Paris in *L'Homme qui rit*: "The little wanderer was suffering the indefinable depression made by a sleeping town. Its silence, as of a paralyzed ants' nest, makes the head swim. All its lethargies mingle their nightmares, its slumbers are a crowd."[17] Cited in R. Caillois, "Paris, mythe moderne," *Nouvelle Revue française*, 25, no. 284 (May 1, 1937), p. 691. [K5a,5]

"Because the collective unconscious is . . . a deposit of world-processes embedded in the structure of the brain and the sympathetic nervous system, it constitutes . . . a sort of timeless and eternal world-image which counterbalances our conscious, momentary picture of the world." C. G. Jung, *Seelenprobleme der Gegenwart* (Zürich, Leipzig, and Stuttgart, 1932), p. 326 ("Analytische Psychologie und Weltanschauung").[18] [K6,1]

Jung calls the consciousness—on occasion!—"our Promethean conquest." C. G. Jung, *Seelenprobleme der Gegenwart* (Zürich, Leipzig, and Stuttgart, 1932), p. 249 ("Die Lebenswende"). And in another context: "To be 'unhistorical' is the Promethean sin. In this sense, modern man lives in sin. *Higher consciousness is thus guilt.*" Ibid., p. 404 ("Das Seelenproblem des modernen Menschen").[19] [K6,2]

"There can be no doubt that from . . . the memorable years of the French Revolution onward, man has given a more and more prominent place to the psyche, his increasing attentiveness to it being the measure of its growing attraction for him. The enthronement of the Goddess of Reason in Notre Dame seems to have been a symbolic gesture of great significance to the Western world—rather like the hewing down of Wotan's oak by the Christian missionaries. For then, as at the Revolution, no avenging bolt from heaven struck the blasphemer down." C. G. Jung, *Seelenprobleme der Gegenwart* (Zürich, Leipzig, and Stuttgart, 1932), p. 419 ("Das Seelenproblem des modernen Menschen").[20] The "vengeance" for these two historical points of departure is being exacted today, it would seem, simultaneously. National Socialism takes the one affair in hand; Jung, the other.
[K6,3]

As long as there is still one beggar around, there will still be myth.   [K6,4]

"Moreover, an ingenious improvement had been introduced into the construction of squares. The administration bought them prefabricated, made to order. Trees of colored cardboard and taffeta flowers contributed greatly to these oases, and care had even been taken to conceal in the leaves some artificial birds that sang the whole day long. Thus, what is pleasant in nature had been preserved, while everything unfit and unworthy in nature had been eliminated." Victor Fournel, *Paris nouveau et Paris futur* (Paris, 1868), p. 252 ("Paris futur").   [K6,5]

"The works of M. Haussmann gave rise, at least in the beginning, to a host of rather strange or grandiose projects. . . . For example, the architect M. Hérard published, in 1855, a proposal for building footbridges at the intersection of the Boulevard Saint-Denis and the Boulevard de Sébastopol; these footbridges, incorporating galleries, would make for a continuous square, each side of which would be defined by the angle formed at the crossing of the two boulevards. M. J. Brame, in 1856, exhibited a series of lithographs detailing his plan for a metropolitan railway line—in Paris, specifically—with a system of arches supporting the rails, with walkways on the side for pedestrians, and with elevated crossovers to connect these sidewalks. . . . At around the same time, in a "Letter to the Minister of Commerce," a lawyer called for the establishment of a series of awnings running the length of the streets to shelter the pedestrian, . . . who would have no further need of a carriage or umbrella. Not long after this, an architect . . . proposed to reconstruct the entire historic city center in Gothic style, so as to bring it into harmony with Notre Dame." Victor Fournel, *Paris nouveau et Paris futur* (Paris, 1868), pp. 384–386.   [K6a,1]

From Fournel's chapter "Paris futur": "There were first-, second-, and third-class cafés, . . . and, for each category, the number of rooms, tables, billiard tables, mirrors, ornaments, and gildings was carefully regulated. . . . There were master streets and service streets, just as there are master stairways and service stairways in well-organized houses. . . . On the façade of the barracks, a bas-relief . . . depicted, in an ethereal nimbus, Public Order dressed as an infantryman: an aureole above his brow, he was busy laying low the hundred-headed Hydra of Decentralization. . . . Fifty sentinels, posted at the fifty windows of the barracks opposite the fifty boulevards, were able to see, through field glasses, at a distance of fifteen or twenty kilometers, the fifty sentinels at the fifty gates. . . . Crowning Montmartre was a dome decorated with a giant electric clock, which could be viewed from two sides and heard from four, and which served to regulate all the clocks in the city. The great goal so long sought had finally been achieved: that of making Paris an object of luxury and curiosity, rather than of use—a *ville d'exposition*, a display city placed under glass, . . . an object of admiration and envy to foreigners, unbearable for its inhabitants." V. Fournel, pp. 235–237, 240–241.

[K6a,2]

Critique by Fournel of Ch. Duveyrier's Saint-Simonian city: "We cannot continue with the exposition of this rash metaphor of M. Duveyrier's, which he develops . . . with a truly stupefying single-mindedness, and without any sense of the way in which his ingenious distribution would return the city of Paris, in the name of progress, to that period of the Middle Ages when each branch of industry or trade was confined to its own *quartier*." Victor Fournel, *Paris nouveau et Paris futur* (Paris, 1868), pp. 374–375 ("Les Précurseurs de M. Haussmann"). [K7,1]

"We shall speak of a monument especially dear to our heart, one which has come to seem, with a climate such as ours, a virtual necessity: . . . the *winter garden!* . . . Near the center of the city, a vast piece of ground capable of holding, like the Colosseum in Rome, a large part of the population, would be enclosed by a great lighted vault, a little like the Crystal Palace in London, or like our market halls of today; the columns would be of cast iron, with only a bit of stone to strengthen the foundations. . . . O, my winter garden, what use I would make of you for my Novutopians! In the great city of Paris, by contrast, they have built a heavy, clumsy, ugly monument of stone, which no one knows what to do with. Here, in recent months, the paintings of our artists have been displayed, facing away from the light, baking at only a slightly greater remove from the blazing sun." F. A. Couturier de Vienne, *Paris moderne: Plan d'une ville modèle que l'auteur a appelée Novutopie* (Paris, 1860), pp. 263–265. [K7,2]

On the dream house: "In all southern countries, where the popular conception of the street requires that the exteriors of houses appear more 'lived in' than their interiors, this exhibition of the private life of the residents confers on their dwellings the quality of a secret place, which piques the curiosity of foreigners. The impression made is the same in fairs: everything there is consigned to the street with such abandon that whatever is not there takes on the power of a mystery." Adrien Dupassage, "Peintures foraines," *Arts et métiers graphiques* (1939).

[K7,3]

Couldn't one compare the social differentiation present in architecture (see Fournel's description of cafés in K6a,2; or front stairs versus back stairs) with the social differentiation at work in fashion? [K7a,1]

On anthropological nihilism, compare N8a,1: Céline, Benn. [K7a,2]

"The fifteenth century . . . was a time when corpses, skulls and skeletons were extravagantly popular. Painted, sculpted, written about and dramatically represented, the Danse Macabre was everywhere. To the fifteenth-century artist, a good death-appeal was as sure a key to popularity as a good sex-appeal is at the present time." Aldous Huxley, *Croisière d'hiver: ‹Voyage› en Amérique centrale* (Paris ‹1935›), p. 58.[21] [K7a,3]

Concerning the interior of the body: "The motif and its elaboration go back to John Chrysostom's 'On Women and Beauty' (*Opera*, ed. B. de Montfaucon [Paris, 1735], vol. 12, p. 523)." "The beauty of the body is merely skin-deep. For if, like the legendary lynx of Boeotia, men were to see what lies beneath the skin, they would recoil in disgust at the sight of a woman. That well-known charm is nothing but mucus and blood, humors and bile. Just stop to consider what is hidden away in the nostrils, the throat, or the belly: everywhere filth. And if, in fact, we shrink from touching mucus or dung with even the tip of our finger, how could we ever wish to embrace the sack of excrements itself?" Odon of Cluny, *Collationum*, book 3 (Migne), vol. 133, p. 556; cited in J. Huizinga, *Herbst des Mittelalters* (Munich, 1928), p. 197.[22] [K7a,4]

Re the psychoanalytic theory of memory: "Freud's later researches made it clear that this view [the concept of repression] must be enlarged. . . . The machinery of repression . . . is . . . a special case of the . . . significant process which occurs when the ego is unequal to meeting certain demands made upon the mental mechanism. The more general process of defense does not cancel the strong impressions; it only lays them aside. . . . It will be in the interest of clarity for me to state the contrast between memory and reminiscence with deliberate bluntness: the function of memory [the author identifies the sphere of "forgetfulness" with "unconscious memory" (p. 130)] is to protect our impressions; reminiscence aims at their dissolution. *Essentially memory is conservative; reminiscence, destructive*." Theodor Reik, *Der überraschte Psychologe* (Leiden, 1935), pp. 130–132.[23] [K8,1]

"For instance, we experience the death of a near relative . . . and believe that we feel our grief in all its depth . . . , but our grief reveals its depths only long after we think that we have got the better of it." The "forgotten" grief persists and gains ground; compare the death of the grandmother in Proust. "To experience means to master an impression inwardly that was so strong we could not grasp it at once." This definition of experience in Freud's sense is something very different from what is meant by those who speak of having "had an experience." Theodor Reik, *Der überraschte Psychologe* (Leiden, 1935), p. 131.[24] [K8,2]

What is laid aside in the unconscious as content of memory. Proust speaks of the "thoroughly alive and creative sleep of the unconscious . . . in which the things that barely touch us succeed in carving an impression, in which our hands take hold of the key that turns the lock, the key for which we have sought in vain." Marcel Proust, *La Prisonnière* (Paris, 1923), vol. 2, p. 189.[25] [K8,3]

The classic passage on "involuntary memory" in Proust—prelude to the moment in which the effect of the madeleine on the narrator is described: "And so it was that, for a long time afterward, when I lay awake at night and revived old memories of Combray, I saw no more of it than this sort of luminous panel. . . . I must own that I could have assured any questioner that Combray did include other scenes. . . . But since the facts which I should then have recalled would have been prompted only by the voluntary memory, the intellectual memory, and since the information which that kind of memory gives us about the past preserves nothing of the past itself, I should never have had any wish to ponder over this residue of Combray. . . . And so it is with our own past. It is a labor in vain to attempt to recapture it: all the efforts of our intellect must prove futile. The past is hidden somewhere outside the realm, beyond the reach, of intellect, in some material object . . . which we do not suspect. And as for that object, it depends on chance whether we come upon it or not before we ourselves must die." Marcel Proust, *Du Côté de chez Swann,* vol. 1, pp. 67–69.[26] [K8a,1]

The classic passage on awakening at night in a dark room and the ensuing orientation: "When I awoke like this, and my mind struggled in an unsuccessful attempt to discover where I was, everything would be moving round me through the darkness: things, places, years. My body, still too heavy with sleep to move, would make an effort to construe the form which its tiredness took as an orientation of its various members, so as to deduce from that where the wall lay and the furniture stood, to piece together and to give a name to the house in which it must be living. Its memory, the composite memory of its ribs, knees, and shoulder-blades, offered it a whole series of rooms in which it had at one time or another slept, while the unseen walls kept changing, adapting themselves to the shape of each successive room that it remembered, whirling madly through the darkness. And even before my brain . . . had collected sufficient impressions . . . to identify the room, it, my body, would recall from each room in succession what the bed was like, where the doors were, how daylight came in at the windows, whether there was a passage outside, what I had in my mind when I went to sleep, and had found there when I awoke." Marcel Proust, *Du Côté de chez Swann,* vol. 1, p. 15.[27] [K8a,2]

Proust on nights of deep sleep after great exhaustion: "Good nights . . . turn so effectively the soil and break through the surface stone of our body that we discover there, where our muscles dive down and throw out their twisted roots and breathe the air of the new life, the garden in which as a child we used to play. There is no need to travel in order to see it again; we must dig down inwardly to discover it. What once covered the earth is no longer upon it but beneath; a mere excursion does not suffice for a visit to the dead city—excavation is necessary also." These words run counter to the injunction to revisit the sites of one's childhood. And they lose not a whit of their sense when taken as a critique of the *mémoire volontaire*. Marcel Proust, *Le Côté de Guermantes* (Paris, 1920), vol. 1, p. 82.[28] [K9,1]

Linking of Proust's oeuvre to the work of Baudelaire: "One of the masterpieces of French literature—*Sylvie*, by Gérard de Nerval—like the *Mémoires d'outre-tombe* ‹of Chateaubriand› . . . , contains a sensation of the same character as the savor of the madeleine. . . . And finally, in Baudelaire, these reminiscences are still more frequent and obviously less incidental and therefore, in my opinion, decisive. Here it is the poet himself who, with more variety and more indolence, purposely seeks in the odor of a woman's hair or her breast, for example, inspiring resemblances which shall evoke for him 'the canopy of overarching sky' and 'a harbor filled with masts and sails.' I was going to endeavor to recall the poems of Baudelaire which are based in similar manner on a transferred sensation, in order definitely to place myself again in line with such a noble literary heritage and reassure myself that the work I was now about to undertake without any further hesitation was worth the effort I was going to devote to it, when I reached the foot of the stairs . . . and suddenly found myself . . . in the midst of a fête." Marcel Proust, *Le Temps retrouvé* (Paris ‹1927›), vol. 2, pp. 82–83.[29] [K9,2]

"Man is himself, is man, only at the surface. Lift the skin, dissect: here begin the machines. It is then you lose yourself in an inexplicable substance, something alien to everything you know, and which is nonetheless the essential." Paul Valéry, *Cahier B, 1910* (Paris ‹1930›), pp. 39–40. [K9,3]

Dream city of Napoleon I: "Napoleon, who originally had wanted to erect the Arc de Triomphe somewhere inside the city, like the disappointing first effort made at the Place du Carousel, let himself be persuaded by Fontaine to start construction west of the city, where a large tract of land was at his disposal, on an imperial Paris that would surpass the royal city, Versailles included. Between the summit of the Avenue des Champs-Elysées and the Seine, . . . on the plateau where today the Trocadéro stands, was to be built, 'with palaces for twelve kings and their retinues,' . . . 'not only the most beautiful city that ever was, but the most beautiful city that ever could be.' The Arc de Triomphe was conceived as the first edifice of this city." Fritz Stahl, *Paris* (Berlin ‹1929›), pp. 27–28. [K9a,1]

L

[Dream House, Museum, Spa]

The genteel variant of the dream house. The entrance to the panorama of Gropius is described as follows: "One enters a room decorated in the style of Herculaneum; at its center the passerby is drawn for a moment to a basin inlaid with shells, in which a small fountain is plashing. Straight ahead, a little flight of stairs leads to a cheerful reading room where some volumes are displayed—notably, a collection of books designed to acquaint foreigners with the royal residence." Erich Stenger, *Daguerres Diorama in Berlin* (Berlin, 1925), pp. 24–25. Bulwer‹-Lytton›'s novel. When did the excavations begin? Foyers of casinos, and the like, belong to this elegant variant of the dream house. Why a fountain in a covered space is conducive to daydreaming has yet to be explained. But in order to gauge the shudder of dread and exaltation that might have come over the idle visitor who stepped across this threshold, it must be remembered that the discovery of Pompeii and Herculaneum had taken place a generation earlier, and that the memory of the lava-death of these two cities was covertly but all the more intimately conjoined with the memory of the great Revolution. For when the sudden upheaval had put an end to the style of the ancien régime, what was here being exhumed was hastily adopted as the style of a glorious republic; and palm fronds, acanthus leaves, and meanders came to replace the rococo paintings and *chinoiseries* of the previous century. ☐ Antiquity ☐ [L1,1]

"Suddenly, however, they want to transform the French, with one wave of a magic wand, into a people of classical antiquity; and on this whim of dreamers isolated in their private libraries (the goddess Minerva notwithstanding), numerous artistic endeavors have depended." Friedrich Johann Lorenz Meyer, *Fragmente aus Paris im IV‹ten› Jahr der französischen Republic* (Hamburg, 1797), vol. 1, p. 146. ☐ Antiquity ☐ [L1,2]

Dream houses of the collective: arcades, winter gardens, panoramas, factories, wax museums, casinos, railroad stations. [L1,3]

The Gare Saint-Lazare: a puffing, wheezing princess with the stare of a clock. "For our type of man," says Jacques de Lacretelle, "train stations are truly factories of dreams" ("Le Rêveur parisien," *Nouvelle Revue française*, 1927). To be sure:

today, in the age of the automobile and airplane, it is only faint, atavistic terrors which still lurk within the blackened sheds; and that stale comedy of farewell and reunion, carried on before a background of Pullman cars, turns the railway platform into a provincial stage. Once again we see performed the timeworn Greek melodrama: Orpheus, Eurydice, and Hermes at the station. Through the mountains of luggage surrounding the figure of the nymph, looms the steep and rocky path, the crypt into which she sinks when the Hermaic conductor with the signal disk, watching for the moist eye of Orpheus, gives the sign for departure. Scar of departure, which zigzags, like the crack on a Greek vase, across the painted bodies of the gods. [L1,4]

The domestic interior moves outside. It is as though the bourgeois were so sure of his prosperity that he is careless of façade, and can exclaim: My house, no matter where you choose to cut into it, is façade. Such façades, especially, on the Berlin houses dating back to the middle of the previous century: an alcove does not jut out, but—as niche—tucks in. The street becomes room and the room becomes street. The passerby who stops to look at the house stands, as it were, in the alcove. ⸆ Flâneur ⸆ [L1,5]

On the dream house. The arcade as temple: the habitué of those "obscure ba-zaars" of the bourgeois arcades "will find himself almost on foreign ground in the Passage de l'Opéra. He will be profoundly ill at ease there; he will be anxious to leave. Another moment and he will discover himself a master, as if he had pene-trated the temple of God." *Le Livre des cent-et-un,* vol. 10 (Paris, 1833), p. 71 (Amédée Kermel, "Les Passages de Paris"). [L1,6]

Apropos of the colored windowpanes which were beginning to be installed in stair-ways (and these stairs were often waxed!) Alphonse Karr writes: "The staircase has remained something that looks more like a machine of war for defending one's house against enemies than a means of communication and access offered to friends." Alphonse Karr, *300 pages,* new edition (Paris, 1861), pp. 198–199. [L1,7]

The house has always shown itself "barely receptive to new formulations." Sig-fried Giedion, *Bauen in Frankreich* ‹Berlin, 1928›, p. 78. [L1,8]

Arcades are houses or passages having no outside—like the dream. [L1a,1]

Museums unquestionably belong to the dream houses of the collective. In con-sidering them, one would want to emphasize the dialectic by which they come into contact, on the one hand, with scientific research and, on the other hand, with "the dreamy tide of bad taste." "Nearly every epoch would appear, by virtue of its inner disposition, to be chiefly engaged in unfolding a specific architectural problem: for the Gothic age, this is the cathedrals; for the Baroque, the palace; and for the early nineteenth century, with its regressive tendency to allow itself to be saturated with the past: the museum." Sigfried Giedion, *Bauen in Frankreich,* p. 36. This thirst for the past forms something like the principal object of my analysis—in light of which the inside of the museum appears as an interior magnified on a giant scale. In the years 1850–1890, exhibitions take the place of museums. Comparison between the ideological bases of the two.   [L1a,2]

"The nineteenth century provided all new creations, in every area of endeavor, with historicizing masks. This was no less true in the field of architecture than in the field of industry or society. New possibilities of construction were being introduced, but people felt almost fear at the advent of these new possibilities and heedlessly buried them in theatrical decoration. The enormous collective apparatus of industry was being put in place, but its significance was altered entirely by the fact that the benefits of the production process were allowed to accrue to only a small number. This historicizing mask is indissolubly bound to the image of the nineteenth century, and is not to be gainsaid." Sigfried Giedion, *Bauen in Frankreich*, pp. 1–2.   [L1a,3]

Le Corbusier's work seems to stand at the terminus of the mythological figuration "house." Compare the following: "Why should the house be made as light and airy as possible? Because only in that way can a fatal and hereditary monumentality be brought to an end. As long as the play of burden and support, whether actually or symbolically exaggerated (Baroque), got its meaning from the supporting walls, heaviness was justified. But today—with the unburdened exterior wall—the ornamentally accentuated counterpoint of pillar and load is a painful farce (American skyscrapers)." Giedion, *Bauen in Frankreich,* p. 85.   [L1a,4]

Le Corbusier's "contemporary city"[1] is yet another settlement along a highway. Only the fact that now its precincts are traveled over by autos, and that airplanes now land in its midst, changes everything. An effort must be made to secure a foothold here from which to cast a productive glance, a form-and-distance-creating glance, on the nineteenth century.   [L1a,5]

"The condominium is the last incarnation of the baronial manor. It owes its existence and its form to the brutal egoistic competition of individual landowners for the rights to territory that, in the struggle for existence, was being broken up and parceled out. We are therefore not surprised to see the *form* of the manor house reappearing as well—in the walled courtyard. One occupant secludes himself from another, and that in fact helps to explain why, in the end, a chance remnant of the whole survives." Adolf Behne, *Neues Wohnen—Neues Bauen* (Leipzig, 1927), pp. 93–94.   [L1a,6]

The museum as dream house. "We have seen how the Bourbons already thought it important that the ancestors of their house be glorified and that the earlier history of France, in all its splendor and significance, be recognized once again. Hence, they also arranged to have outstanding moments from French history and French cultural evolution depicted on the ceilings of the Louvre." Julius Meyer, *Geschichte der modernen französischen Malerei* (Leipzig, 1867), p. 424.   [L1a,7]

In June of 1837—"to the everlasting glory of France"—the historic museum of Versailles was opened. A suite of rooms that one needs almost two hours merely to traverse. Battles and scenes of parliament. Among the painters: Gosse, Larivière, Heim, Devéria, Gérard, Ary Scheffer, and others. Here, then, the collecting of pictures turns into: the painting of pictures for the museum.   [L2,1]

Interlacing of museum and domestic interior. M. Chabrillat (1882, director of the Ambigu theater) one day inherits a complete waxworks museum, "set up in the Passage de l'Opéra, right above the clock." (Perhaps it was the old Hartkoff Museum.) Chabrillat is friends with a certain *bohémien*, a gifted draftsman, who at the time is homeless. This man has an idea. Among the waxworks in this museum is one group representing the visit of Empress Eugénie to cholera patients in Amiens. At the right, the empress smiles on the patients; to the left is a Sister of Charity in white cornet; and lying on an iron cot, pale and emaciated beneath the fine clean bedclothes, is a dying man. The museum closes at midnight. The draftsman opines: Nothing simpler than to remove, with due care, the cholera patient, lay him on the floor, and take his place in the bed. Chabrillat gives his permission; the wax figures mean little to him. For the next six weeks, then, the artist, having just been thrown out of his hotel, spends the night in the bed of the cholera victim, and each morning he awakens under the gentle glance of the sicknurse and the smiling glance of the empress, who lets her blond hair fall on him. From Jules Claretie, *La Vie à Paris*, 1882 (Paris ‹1883›), pp. 301ff.   [L2,2]

"How much I admire those men who decide to be shut up at night in a museum in order to examine at their own discretion, at an illicit time, some portrait of a woman they illuminate by a dark lantern. Inevitably, afterward, they must know much more about such a woman than we do." André Breton, *Nadja* (Paris ‹1928›), p. 150.[2] But why? Because, in the medium of this image, the transformation of the museum into an interior has taken place.   [L2,3]

The dream house of the arcades is encountered again in the church. Encroachment of the architectural style of the arcades on sacred architecture. Concerning Notre Dame de Lorette: "The interior of this building is without doubt in excellent taste, only it is not the interior of a *church*. The splendid ceiling would suitably adorn the most brilliant ballroom in the world; the graceful lamps of bronze, with their frosted glass globes in different colors, look as though they came from the city's most elegant cafés." S. F. Lahrs ‹?›, *Briefe aus Paris,* in *Europa: Chronik der gebildeten Welt* (Leipzig and Stuttgart, 1837), vol. 2, p. 209.
    [L2,4]

"As for the new and not yet finished theaters, they appear to belong to no particular style. The intention, evidently, is to integrate private into public uses by con-

structing private residential dwellings all around the perimeter, so that these theaters can hardly become anything other than colossal containers, giant capsules for
all sorts of things." *Grenzboten,* 1861, 2nd semester, vol. 3, p. 143 ("Die Pariser
Kunstausstellung von 1861"). [L2,5]

Think of the arcade as watering place. What we would like is to stumble upon an
arcade myth, with a legendary source at its center—an asphalt wellspring arising
at the heart of Paris. The tavern advertising beer "on tap" still draws on this myth
of the waters. And the extent to which healing is a *rite de passage,* a transition
experience, becomes vividly clear in those classical corridors where the sick and
ailing turn into their recovery, as it were. Those halls, too, are arcades.[3] Compare
fountains in the vestibule. [L2,6]

The dread of doors that won't close is something everyone knows from dreams.
Stated more precisely: these are doors that appear closed without being so. It was
with heightened senses that I learned of this phenomenon in a dream in which,
while I was in the company of a friend, a ghost appeared to me in the window of
the ground floor of a house to our right. And as we walked on, the ghost
accompanied us from inside all the houses. It passed through all the walls and
always remained at the same height with us. I saw this, though I was blind. The
path we travel through arcades is fundamentally just such a ghost walk, on which
doors give way and walls yield. [L2,7]

The figure of wax is properly the setting wherein the appearance ‹*Schein*› of
humanity outdoes itself. In the wax figure, that is, the surface area, complexion,
and coloration of the human being are all rendered with such perfect and unsurpassable exactitude that this reproduction of human appearance itself is outdone,
and now the mannequin incarnates nothing but the hideous, cunning mediation
between costume and viscera. ☐ Fashion ☐ [L2a,1]

Description of a wax museum as dream house: "Once visitors reached the final
landing, they looked around the corner into a large, brightly lit room. There was,
so to say, no one within, though it was filled with princes, crinolines, uniforms, and
giants at the entrance. The woman went no further, and her escort paused beside
her, piqued by a baleful pleasure. They sat down on the steps, and he told her of
the terror he had experienced as a boy in reading about ill-famed castles where no
one lived any longer, but where on stormy nights there were lights burning at all
the windows. What was going on inside? What gathering was there? Where was
that light coming from? He had dreamed of catching a glimpse of this assembly
while hanging from the window ledge, his face pressed against the windowpanes of
the unspeakable room." Ernst Bloch, "Leib und Wachsfigur," *Frankfurter Zeitung* ‹December 19, 1929›. [L2a,2]

"Number 125: Castan's maze. At first, world travelers and artists suppose themselves transported into the forest of columns that is the magnificent mosque of
Cordova in Spain. As arch succeeds arch in that edifice, one column crowds upon

the next in perspective, offering fabulous vistas and unthinkably long avenues which no one could follow to the end. Then, suddenly, we behold an image that takes us into the very heart of the famous Alhambra of Granada. We see the tapestry pattern of the Alhambra, with its inscription 'Allah is Allah' (God is great), and already we are standing in a garden, in the orange grove of the Alhambra. But before the visitor arrives at this courtyard, he must pass through a series of labyrinthine divagations." Catalogue of Castan's panopticon[4] (from extracts in the *Frankfurter Zeitung*). [L2a,3]

"The success of the Romantic school gave rise, around 1825, to the market in modern paintings. Before that, art lovers went to the homes of artists. Sellers of artists' pigments—Giroux, Suisse, Binant, Berville—began to function as middlemen. The first retail house was opened by Goupil in 1829." ⟨Lucien⟩ Dubech and ⟨Pierre⟩ d'Espezel, *Histoire de Paris* (Paris, 1926), p. 359. [L2a,4]

"The Opéra is one of the characteristic creations of the Second Empire. It was designed by an unknown young architect, Charles Garnier, whose plan was selected from among 160 projects submitted. His theater, constructed in the years 1861–1875, was conceived as a place of pageantry. . . . It was the stage on which imperial Paris could gaze at itself with satisfaction. Classes newly risen to power and to fortune, blendings of cosmopolitan elements—this was a new world, and it called for a new name: people no longer spoke of the Court, but of *le Tout Paris* ⟨all fashionable Paris⟩. . . . A theater conceived as an urban center, a center of social life—this was a new idea, and a sign of the times." Dubech and d'Espezel, *Histoire de Paris*, pp. 411–412. [L2a,5]

To set up, within the actual city of Paris, Paris the dream city—as an aggregate of all the building plans, street layouts, park projects, and street-name systems that were never developed. [L2a,6]

The arcade as temple of Aesculapius, medicinal spring. The course of a cure. (Arcades as resort spas in ravines—at Schuls-Tarasp, at Ragaz.) The gorge as landscape ideal in the nineteenth century. [L3,1]

Jacques Fabien, *Paris en songe* (Paris, 1863), reports on the moving of the Porte Saint-Martin and the Porte Saint-Denis: "They are no less admired on the summits of the Faubourgs Saint-Martin and Saint-Denis" (p. 86). In this way, the areas around the gates, which had sunk quite noticeably, were able to regain their original level. [L3,2]

Proposal to cover the dead bodies in the morgue with an oilcloth from the neck down. "The public lines up at the door and is allowed to examine at its leisure the *nude* cadavers of the unknown dead . . . One day, morality will be given its due; and thereafter the worker who now goes at lunchtime to visit the morgue—hands in pockets, pipe in mouth, smile on lips—in order to crack jokes over the more or less putrefied naked bodies, of both sexes, will soon lose interest in the sparse *mise-en-scène*. I do not exaggerate. These smutty scenes are enacted every day at the morgue; people laugh there, smoke there, and chatter loudly." Edouard Foucaud, *Paris inventeur: Physiologie de l'industrie française* (Paris, 1844), pp. 212–213.   [L3,3]

An engraving from around 1830, perhaps a little earlier, shows copyists at work in various ecstatic postures. Caption: "Artistic Inspiration at the Museum." Cabinet des Estampes.   [L3,4]

On the beginnings of the museum at Versailles: "M. de Montalivet was in a hurry to acquire a quantity of paintings. He wanted them everywhere, and, since the Chambers had decried prodigality, he was determined to buy cheaply. The trend was toward thrift . . . M. de Montalivet willingly . . . let it be thought that it was he himself who, on the quays and in the dealers' shops, was buying up third-rate canvases. . . . No, . . . it was the reigning princes of art who were indulging in this hideous business . . . The copies and pastiches in the museum at Versailles are the most grievous confirmation of the rapacity of those master artists, who became entrepreneurs and barterers of art. . . . Business and industry decided to elevate themselves to the level of the artist. The latter, in order to satisfy his need for the luxuries which were beginning to tempt him, prostituted art to speculation and brought about the degeneration of the artistic tradition by his calculated reduction of art to the proportions of a trade." This last refers to the fact that [around 1837] painters were passing on to their students commissions they had accepted themselves. Gabriel Pélin, *Les Laideurs du beau Paris* (Paris, 1861), pp. 85, 87–90.
                                                                                          [L3,5]

On subterranean Paris—old sewers. "We shall form an image more closely resembling this strange geometric plan by supposing that we see spread upon a background of darkness some grotesque alphabet of the East jumbled as in a medley, the shapeless letters of which are joined to one another, apparently pell-mell and as if by chance, sometimes by their corners, sometimes by their extremities." Victor Hugo, *Oeuvres complètes*, novels, vol. 9 (Paris, 1881), pp. 158–159 *(Les Misérables)*.[5]   [L3a,1]

Sewers: "All manner of phantoms haunt these long solitary corridors, putridity and miasma everywhere; here and there a breathing-hole through which Villon within chats with Rabelais without." Victor Hugo, *Oeuvres complètes*, novels, vol. 9 (Paris, 1881), p. 160 *(Les Misérables)*.[6]   [L3a,2]

Victor Hugo on the obstacles which hindered Parisian digging and tunneling operations: "Paris is built upon a deposit singularly rebellious to the spade, to the hoe, to the drill, to human control. Nothing more difficult to pierce and to penetrate than that geological formation upon which is superposed the wonderful historical formation called Paris; as soon as . . . labor commences and ventures into that sheet of alluvium, subterranean resistance abounds. There are liquid clays, living springs, hard rocks, those soft deep mires which technical science calls *moutardes*. The pick advances laboriously into these calcareous strata alternating with seams of very fine clay and laminar schistose beds, encrusted with oyster shells contemporary with the pre-Adamite oceans." Victor Hugo, *Oeuvres complètes*, novels, vol. 9 (Paris, 1881), pp. 178–179 *(Les Misérables)*.[7]   [L3a,3]

Sewer: "Paris . . . called it the Stink-Hole. . . . The Stink-Hole was no less revolting to hygiene than to legend. The Goblin Monk had appeared under the fetid arch of the Mouffetard sewer; the corpses of the Marmousets had been thrown into the sewer of the Barillerie. . . . The mouth of the sewer of the Rue de la Mortellerie was famous for the pestilence which came from it. . . . Bruneseau had made a beginning, but it required the cholera epidemics to determine the vast reconstruction which has since taken place." Victor Hugo, *Oeuvres complètes*, novels, vol. 9 (Paris, 1881), pp. 166, 180 (*Les Misérables*, "L'Intestin de Léviathan").[8]   [L3a,4]

1805—Bruneseau's descent into the sewers: "Hardly had Bruneseau passed the first branchings of the subterranean network, when eight out of the twenty laborers refused to go further. . . . They advanced with difficulty. It was not uncommon for the stepladders to plunge into three feet of mire. The lanterns flickered in the miasmas. From time to time, a sewerman who had fainted was carried out. At certain places, a precipice. The soil had sunk, the pavement had crumbled, the sewer had changed into a blind well; they found no solid ground. One man suddenly disappeared; they had great difficulty in recovering him. On the advice of Fourcroy, they lighted from point to point, in the places sufficiently purified, great cages full of oakum saturated with resin. The wall, in places, was covered with shapeless fungi—one would have said with tumors. The stone itself seemed diseased in this unbreathable atmosphere. . . . They thought they recognized here and there, chiefly under the Palais de Justice, some cells of ancient dungeons built in the sewer itself. . . . An iron collar hung in one of these cells. They walled them all up. . . . The complete survey of the underground sewer system of Paris occupied seven years, from 1805 to 1812. . . . Nothing equaled the horror of this old voiding crypt, . . . cavern, grave, gulf pierced with streets, titanic molehill, in which the mind seems to see prowling through the shadow . . . that enormous blind mole, the past." Victor Hugo, *Oeuvres complètes*, novels, vol. 9 (Paris, 1881), pp. 169–171, 173–174 (*Les Misérables*, "L'Intestin de Léviathan").[9]   [L4,1]

In connection with the passage from Gerstäcker.[10] An undersea jeweler's shop: "We came into the underwater hall of the jeweler's. Never would one have believed it possible to be so far removed from terra firma. An immense dome . . . overspread the entire marketplace, which was filled with the brilliant glow of electricity and the happy bustle of crowds, and an assortment of shops with glittering display windows." Léo Claretie, *Paris depuis ses origines jusqu'en l'an 3000* (Paris, 1886), p. 337 ("En 1987"). It is significant that this image resurfaces just when the beginning of the end has arrived for the arcades.   [L4,2]

The sewers of Paris, 1861–1862. Photo by Nadar. Courtesy of the Bibliothèque Nationale de France. See L4,1.

Proudhon takes a keen interest in the paintings of Courbet and, with the help of vague definitions (of "ethics in action"), enlists them in his cause.   [L4,3]

Woefully inadequate references to mineral springs in Koch, who writes of the poems dedicated by Goethe to Maria Ludovica at Karlsbad: "The essential thing for him in these 'Karlsbad poems' is not the geology but . . . the thought and the sensation that healing energies emanate from the otherwise unapproachable person of the princess. The intimacy of life at the spa creates a fellow feeling . . . with the noble lady. Thus, . . . in the presence of the mystery of the springs, health comes . . . from the proximity of the princess." Richard Koch, *Der Zauber der Heilquellen* (Stuttgart, 1933), p. 21. [L4,4]

Whereas a journey ordinarily gives the bourgeois the illusion of slipping the ties that bind him to his social class, the watering place fortifies his consciousness of belonging to the upper class. It does this not only by bringing him into contact with feudal strata. Mornand draws attention to a more elementary circumstance: "In Paris there are no doubt larger crowds, but none so homogeneous as this one; for most of the sad human beings who make up those crowds will have eaten either badly or hardly at all. . . . But at Baden, nothing of the sort: everyone is happy, seeing that everyone's at Baden." Félix Mornand, *La Vie des eaux* (Paris, 1855), pp. 256–257. [L4a,1]

The meditative stroll through the pump room proves advantageous to business, chiefly through the agency of art. The contemplative attitude that schools itself on the work of art is slowly transformed into an attitude more covetous of the wares on display. "Having taken a turn before the *Trinkhalle*, . . . or beneath the frescoed peristyle of this Greco-German-Italianate colonnade, one will come indoors, . . . read the newspapers for a while, price the art objects, examine the watercolors, and drink a small glassful." Félix Mornand, *La Vie des eaux* (Paris, 1855), pp. 257–258. [L4a,2]

Dungeons of Châtelet ‹see also C5a,1›: "Those cells, the mere thought of which strikes terror into the hearts of the people, . . . have lent their stones to the one theater above all where people love to go for a good time, since there they hear of the undying glory of their sons on the fields of battle." Edouard Fournier, *Chroniques et légendes des rues de Paris* (Paris, 1864), pp. 155–156. The reference is to the Théâtre du Châtelet, originally a circus. [L4a,3]

The revised title page of Meryon's *Eaux-fortes sur Paris* ‹Etchings of Paris› depicts a weighty stone whose age is attested to by the encrusted shells and the cracks. The title of the cycle is engraved in this stone. "Burty remarks that the shells, and the imprint of moss preserved in the limestone, indicate clearly that this stone was chosen from among the specimens of ancient Parisian soil in the quarries of Montmartre." Gustave Geffroy, *Charles Meryon* (Paris, 1926), p. 47. [L4a,4]

In "Le Joueur généreux," Baudelaire meets with Satan in his infernal gambling den, "a dazzling subterranean dwelling of a fabulous luxury beyond anything the upper habitations of Paris could offer." Charles Baudelaire, *Le Spleen de Paris*, ed. R. Simon (Paris), p. 49.[11] [L4a,5]

The gate belongs in a context with the *rites de passage*. "However it may be indicated, one enters the way—whether it be between two sticks driven into the ground and sometimes set leaning toward each other, or through a tree trunk split in the middle and opened up, . . . or under a birch limb bent into an arch. . . . In these cases, it is always a matter of escaping a hostile . . . element, getting clear of some stain, separating off contagion or the spirits of the dead, who cannot follow through the narrow opening." Ferdinand Noack, *Triumph und Triumphbogen,* series entitled *Vorträge der Bibliothek Warburg,* vol. 5 (Leipzig, 1928), p. 153. Whoever enters an arcade passes through the gate-way in the opposite direction.[12] (Or rather, he ventures into the intrauterine world.)   [L5,1]

According to K. Meister, *Die Hausschwelle in Sprache und Religion der Römer,* Proceedings of the Heidelberg Academy of Sciences, Division of Philosophy and History, 1924–1925, Treatise 3 (Heidelberg, 1925), the threshold does not have for the Greeks, or indeed for any other people, the importance it has for the Romans. The treatise is concerned essentially with the genesis of the *sublimis* as the exalted (originally what is carried aloft).   [L5,2]

"Nevertheless, we see a continuous stream of new works in which the city is the main character, present throughout, and in which the name of Paris almost always figures in the title, indicating that the public likes things this way. Under these conditions, how could there not develop in each reader the deep-seated conviction (which is evident even today) that the Paris he knows is not the only Paris, not even the true one, that it is only a stage set, brilliantly illuminated but too *normal*—a piece of scenery which the stagehands will never do away with, and which conceals another Paris, the real Paris, a nocturnal, spectral, imperceptible Paris." Roger Caillois, "Paris, mythe moderne," *Nouvelle Revue française,* 25, no. 284 (May 1, 1937), p. 687.   [L5,3]

"Cities, like forests, have their dens in which all their vilest and most terrible monsters hide." Victor Hugo, *Les Misérables,* part 3 ⟨*Oeuvres complètes,* novels, vol. 7 (Paris, 1881), p. 306⟩.[13]   [L5,4]

There are relations between department store and museum, and here the bazaar provides a link. The amassing of artworks in the museum brings them into communication with commodities, which—where they offer themselves en masse to the passerby—awake in him the notion that some part of this should fall to him as well.   [L5,5]

"The city of the dead, Père Lachaise . . . The word 'cemetery' cannot properly be used for this particular layout, which is modeled on the necropolises of the ancient world. This veritable urban establishment—with its stone houses for the dead and its profusion of statues, which, in contrast to the custom of the Christian north, represent the dead as living—is conceived throughout as a continuation of the city of the living." (The name comes from the owner of the land, the father confessor of Louis XIV; the plan is by Napoleon I.) Fritz Stahl, *Paris* (Berlin ⟨1929⟩), pp. 161–162.   [L5a]

[The Flâneur]

A landscape haunts, intense as opium.
—Mallarmé ‹"Autrefois, en marge d'un Baudelaire," in *Divagations*›

To read what was never written.
—Hofmannsthal[1]

And I travel in order to get to know my geography.
—A madman, in Marcel Réja, *L'Art chez les fous* (Paris, 1907), p. 131

All that can be found anywhere can be found in Paris.
—Victor Hugo, *Les Misérables,* in Hugo, *Oeuvres complètes* (Paris, 1881), novels, vol. 7, p. 30, from the chapter "Ecce Paris, Ecce Homo"[2]

But the great reminiscences, the historical shudder—these are a trumpery which he (the flâneur) leaves to tourists, who think thereby to gain access to the genius loci with a military password. Our friend may well keep silent. At the approach of his footsteps, the place has roused; speechlessly, mindlessly, its mere intimate nearness gives him hints and instructions. He stands before Notre Dame de Lorette, and his soles remember: here is the spot where in former times the *cheval de renfort*—the spare horse—was harnessed to the omnibus that climbed the Rue des Martyrs toward Montmartre. Often, he would have given all he knows about the domicile of Balzac or of Gavarni, about the site of a surprise attack or even of a barricade, to be able to catch the scent of a threshold or to recognize a paving stone by touch, like any watchdog. [M1,1]

The street conducts the flâneur into a vanished time. For him, every street is precipitous. It leads downward—if not to the mythical Mothers, then into a past that can be all the more spellbinding because it is not his own, not private. Nevertheless, it always remains the time of a childhood. But why that of the life he has lived? In the asphalt over which he passes, his steps awaken a surprising resonance. The gaslight that streams down on the paving stones throws an equivocal light on this double ground. [M1,2]

An intoxication comes over the man who walks long and aimlessly through the streets. With each step, the walk takes on greater momentum; ever weaker grow the temptations of shops, of bistros, of smiling women, ever more irresistible the magnetism of the next streetcorner, of a distant mass of foliage, of a street name. Then comes hunger. Our man wants nothing to do with the myriad possibilities offered to sate his appetite. Like an ascetic animal, he flits through unknown districts—until, utterly exhausted, he stumbles into his room, which receives him coldly and wears a strange air. [M1,3]

Paris created the type of the flâneur. What is remarkable is that it wasn't Rome. And the reason? Does not dreaming itself take the high road in Rome? And isn't that city too full of temples, enclosed squares, national shrines, to be able to enter *tout entière*—with every cobblestone, every shop sign, every step, and every gateway—into the passerby's dream? The national character of the Italians may also have much to do with this. For it is not the foreigners but they themselves, the Parisians, who have made Paris the promised land of the flâneur—the "landscape built of sheer life," as Hofmannsthal once put it. Landscape—that, in fact, is what Paris becomes for the flâneur. Or, more precisely: the city splits for him into its dialectical poles. It opens up to him as a landscape, even as it closes around him as a room. [M1,4]

That anamnestic intoxication in which the flâneur goes about the city not only feeds on the sensory data taking shape before his eyes but often possesses itself of abstract knowledge—indeed, of dead facts—as something experienced and lived through. This felt knowledge travels from one person to another, especially by word of mouth. But in the course of the nineteenth century, it was also deposited in an immense literature. Even before Lefeuve, who described Paris "street by street, house by house," there were numerous works that depicted this storied landscape as backdrop for the dreaming idler. The study of these books constituted a second existence, already wholly predisposed toward dreaming; and what the flâneur learned from them took form and figure during an afternoon walk before the apéritif. Wouldn't he, then, have necessarily felt the steep slope behind the church of Notre Dame de Lorette rise all the more insistently under his soles if he realized: here, at one time, after Paris had gotten its first omnibuses, the *cheval de renfort* was harnessed to the coach to reinforce the two other horses. [M1,5]

One must make an effort to grasp the altogether fascinating moral constitution of the passionate flâneur. The police—who here, as on so many of the subjects we are treating, appear as experts—provide the following indication in the report of a Paris secret agent from October 1798(?): "It is almost impossible to summon and maintain good moral character in a thickly massed population where each individual, unbeknownst to all the others, hides in the crowd, so to speak, and blushes before the eyes of no one." Cited in Adolf Schmidt, *Pariser Zustände während der Revolution,* vol. 3 (Jena, 1876). The case in which the flâneur completely distances himself from the type of the philosophical promenader, and takes on the features of the werewolf restlessly roaming a social wilderness, was fixed for the first time and forever afterward by Poe in his story "The Man of the Crowd." [M1,6]

The appearances of superposition, of overlap, which come with hashish may be grasped through the concept of similitude. When we say that one face is similar to another, we mean that certain features of this second face appear to us in the first, without the latter's ceasing to be what it has been. Nevertheless, the possibilities of entering into appearance in this way are not subject to any criterion and are therefore boundless. The category of similarity, which for the waking consciousness has only minimal relevance, attains unlimited relevance in the world of hashish. There, we may say, everything is face: each thing has the degree of bodily presence that allows it to be searched—as one searches a face—for such traits as appear. Under these conditions even a sentence (to say nothing of the single word) puts on a face, and this face resembles that of the sentence standing opposed to it. In this way every truth points manifestly to its opposite, and this state of affairs explains the existence of doubt. Truth becomes something living; it lives solely in the rhythm by which statement and counterstatement displace each other in order to think each other.[3] [M1a,1]

Valery Larbaud on the "moral climate of the Parisian street." "Relations always begin with the fiction of equality, of Christian fraternity. In this crowd the inferior is disguised as the superior, and the superior as the inferior—disguised morally, in both cases. In other capitals of the world, the disguise barely goes beyond the appearance, and people visibly insist on their differences, making an effort to retain them in the face of pagans and barbarians. Here they efface them as much as they can. Hence the peculiar sweetness of the moral climate of Parisian streets, the charm which makes one pass over the vulgarity, the indolence, the monotony of the crowd. It is the grace of Paris, its virtue: charity. Virtuous crowd . . ." Valery Larbaud, "Rues et visages de Paris: Pour l'album de Chas-Laborde," *Commerce,* 8 (Summer 1926), pp. 36–37. Is it permissible to refer this phenomenon so confidently to Christian virtue, or is there not perhaps at work here an intoxicated assimilation, superposition, equalization that in the streets of this city proves to carry more weight than the will to social accreditation? One might adduce here the hashish experience "Dante und Petrarca,"[4] and measure the impact of intoxicated experience on the proclamation of the rights of man. This all unfolds at a considerable remove from Christianity. [M1a,2]

The "colportage phenomenon of space" is the flâneur's basic experience. Inasmuch as this phenomenon also—from another angle—shows itself in the mid-nineteenth-century interior, it may not be amiss to suppose that the heyday of flânerie occur in this same period. Thanks to this phenomenon, everything potentially taking place in this one single room is perceived simultaneously. The space winks at the flâneur: What do you think may have gone on here? Of course, it has yet to be explained how this phenomenon is associated with colportage.[5] ▯History▯   [M1a,3]

A true masquerade of space—that is what the British embassy's ball on May 17, 1839, must have been. "In addition to the glorious flowers from gardens and greenhouses, 1,000–1,200 rosebushes were ordered as part of the decoration for the festivities. It was said that only 800 of them could fit in the rooms of the embassy, but that will give you an idea of the utterly mythological magnificence. The garden, covered by a pavilion, was turned into a *salon de conversation*. But what a salon! The gay flower beds, full of blooms, were huge *jardinières* which everyone came over to admire; the gravel on the walks was covered with fresh linen, out of consideration for all the white satin shoes; large sofas of lampas and of damask replaced the wrought-iron benches; and on a round table there were books and albums. It was a pleasure to take the air in this immense boudoir, where one could hear, like a magic chant, the sounds of the orchestra, and where one could see passing, like happy shadows, in the three surrounding flower-lined galleries, both the fun-loving girls who came to dance and the more serious girls who came to sup." H. d'Almeras, *La Vie parisienne sous ‹le règne de› Louis-Philippe* ‹Paris, 1925›, pp. 446–447. The account derives from Madame de Girardin. ▯Interior▯ Today, the watchword is not entanglement but transparency. (Le Corbusier!)   [M1a,4]

The principle of colportage illustration encroaching on great painting. "The reports on the engagements and battles which, in the catalogue, were supposed to illuminate the moments chosen by the painter for battle scenes, but which failed to achieve this goal, were usually augmented with citations of the works from which these reports were drawn. Thus, one would find at the end, frequently in parentheses: *Campagnes d'Espagne,* by Marshal Suchet; *Bulletin de la Grande Armée et rapports officiels; Gazette de France,* number . . . ; and the like; *Histoire de la révolution française,* by M. Thiers, volume . . . , page . . . ; *Victoires et conquêtes,* volume . . . , page . . . ; and so forth and so on." Ferdinand von Gall, *Paris und seine Salons* (Oldenburg, 1844), vol. 1, pp. 198–199.   [M2,1]

Category of illustrative seeing—fundamental for the flâneur. Like Kubin when he wrote *Andere Seite,* he composes his reverie as text to accompany the images.
[M2,2]

Hashish. One imitates certain things one knows from paintings: prison, the Bridge of Sighs, stairs like the train of a dress.   [M2,3]

We know that, in the course of flânerie, far-off times and places interpenetrate the landscape and the present moment. When the authentically intoxicated phase of this condition announces itself, the blood is pounding in the veins of the happy flâneur, his heart ticks like a clock, and inwardly as well as outwardly things go on as we would imagine them to do in one of those "mechanical pictures" which in the nineteenth century (and of course earlier, too) enjoyed great popularity, and which depicts in the foreground a shepherd playing on a pipe, by his side two children swaying in time to the music, further back a pair of hunters in pursuit of a lion, and very much in the background a train crossing over a trestle bridge. Chapuis and Gélis, *Le Monde des automates* (Paris, 1928), vol. 1, p. 330.[6]   [M2,4]

The attitude of the flâneur—epitome of the political attitude of the middle classes during the Second Empire.   [M2,5]

With the steady increase in traffic on the streets, it was only the macadamization of the roadways that made it possible in the end to have a conversation on the terrace of a café without shouting in the other person's ear.   [M2,6]

The laissez-faire of the flâneur has its counterpart even in the revolutionary philosophemes of the period. "We smile at the chimerical pretension [of a Saint-Simon] to trace all physical and moral phenomena back to the law of universal attraction. But we forget too easily that this pretension was not in itself isolated; under the influence of the revolutionizing natural laws of mechanics, there could arise a current of natural philosophy which saw in the mechanism of nature the proof of just such a mechanism of social life and of events generally." ‹Willy› Spühler, *Der Saint-Simonismus* (Zürich, 1926), p. 29.   [M2,7]

Dialectic of flânerie: on one side, the man who feels himself viewed by all and sundry as a true suspect and, on the other side, the man who is utterly undiscoverable, the hidden man. Presumably, it is this dialectic that is developed in "The Man of the Crowd."   [M2,8]

"Theory of the transformation of the city into countryside: this was . . . the main theme of my unfinished work on Maupassant. . . . At issue was the city as hunting ground, and in general the concept of the hunter played a major role (as in the theory of the uniform: all hunters look alike)." Letter from Wiesengrund, June 5, 1935.   **[M2,9]**

The principle of flânerie in Proust: "Then, quite apart from all those literary preoccupations, and without definite attachment to anything, suddenly a roof, a gleam of sunlight reflected from a stone, the smell of a road would make me stop still, to enjoy the special pleasure that each of them gave me, and also because they appeared to be concealing, beneath what my eyes could see, something which they invited me to approach and take from them, but which, despite all my efforts, I never managed to discover." *Du Côté de chez Swann* ‹(Paris, 1939), vol. 1, p. 256.›[7]—This passage shows very clearly how the old Romantic sentiment for landscape dissolves and a new Romantic conception of landscape emerges—of landscape that seems, rather, to be a cityscape, if it is true that the city is the properly sacred ground of flânerie. In this passage, at any rate, it would be presented as such for the first time since Baudelaire (whose work does not yet portray the arcades, though they were so numerous in his day). [M2a,1]

So the flâneur goes for a walk in his room: "When Johannes sometimes asked for permission to go out, it was usually denied him. But on occasion his father proposed, as a substitute, that they walk up and down the room hand in hand. This seemed at first a poor substitute, but in fact . . . something quite novel awaited him. The proposal was accepted, and it was left entirely to Johannes to decide where they should go. Off they went, then, right out the front entrance, out to a neighboring estate or to the seashore, or simply through the streets, exactly as Johannes could have wished; for his father managed everything. While they strolled in this way up and down the floor of his room, his father told him of all they saw. They greeted other pedestrians; passing wagons made a din around them and drowned out his father's voice; the comfits in the pastry shop were more inviting than ever." An early work by Kierkegaard, cited in Eduard Geismar, *Sören Kierkegaard* (Göttingen, 1929), pp. 12–13. Here is the key to the schema of *Voyage autour de ma chambre*.[8] [M2a,2]

"The manufacturer passes over the asphalt conscious of its quality; the old man searches it carefully, follows it just as long as he can, happily taps his cane so the wood resonates, and recalls with pride that he personally witnessed the laying of the first sidewalks; the poet . . . walks on it pensive and unconcerned, muttering lines of verse; the stockbroker hurries past, calculating the advantages of the last rise in wheat; and the madcap slides across." Alexis Martin, "Physiologie de l'asphalte," *Le Bohême*, 1, no. 3, (April 15, 1855)—Charles Pradier, editor in chief. [M2a,3]

On the Parisians' technique of *inhabiting* their streets: "Returning by the Rue Saint-Honoré, we met with an eloquent example of that Parisian street industry which can make use of anything. Men were at work repairing the pavement and laying pipeline, and, as a result, in the middle of the street there was an area which was blocked off but which was embanked and covered with stones. On this spot street vendors had immediately installed themselves, and five or six were selling writing implements and notebooks, cutlery, lampshades, garters, embroidered collars, and all sorts of trinkets. Even a dealer in secondhand goods had opened a branch office here and was displaying on the stones his bric-à-brac of old cups, plates, glasses, and so forth, so that business was profiting, instead of suffering, from the brief disturbance. They are simply wizards at making a virtue of necessity." Adolf Stahr, *Nach fünf Jahren* (Oldenburg, 1857), vol. 1, p. 29.[9]

Seventy years later, I had the same experience at the corner of the Boulevard Saint-Germain and the Boulevard Raspail. Parisians make the street an interior. [M3,1]

"It is wonderful that in Paris itself one can actually wander through countryside." Karl Gutzkow, *Briefe aus Paris* (Leipzig, 1842), vol. 1, p. 61. The other side of the motif is thus touched on. For if flânerie can transform Paris into one great interior—a house whose rooms are the *quartiers,* no less clearly demarcated by thresholds than are real rooms—then, on the other hand, the city can appear to someone walking through it to be without thresholds: a landscape in the round.
[M3,2]

But in the final analysis, only the revolution creates an open space for the city. Fresh air doctrine of revolutions. Revolution disenchants the city. Commune in *L'Education sentimentale.* Image of the street in civil war. [M3,3]

Street as domestic interior. Concerning the Passage du Pont-Neuf (between the Rue Guénégaud and the Rue de Seine): "the shops resemble closets." *Nouveaux Tableaux de Paris, ou Observations sur les mœurs et usages des Parisiens au commencement du XIXᵉ siècle* (Paris, 1828), vol. 1, p. 34. [M3,4]

The courtyard of the Tuileries: "immense savannah planted with lampposts instead of banana trees." Paul-Ernest de Rattier, *Paris n'existe pas* (Paris, 1857). ☐ Gas ☐ [M3,5]

Passage Colbert: "The gas lamp illuminating it looks like a coconut palm in the middle of a savannah." ☐ Gas ☐ *Le Livre des cent-et-un* (Paris, 1833), vol. 10, p. 57 (Amédée Kermel, "Les Passages de Paris"). [M3,6]

Lighting in the Passage Colbert: "I admire the regular series of those crystal globes, which give off a light both vivid and gentle. Couldn't the same be said of comets in battle formation, awaiting the signal for departure to go vagabonding through space?" *Le Livre des cent-et-un,* vol. 10, p. 57. Compare this transformation of the city into an astral world with Grandville's *Un Autre Monde.* ☐ Gas ☐
[M3,7]

In 1839 it was considered elegant to take a tortoise out walking. This gives us an idea of the tempo of flânerie in the arcades. [M3,8]

Gustave Claudin is supposed to have said: "On the day when a filet ceases to be a filet and becomes a 'chateaubriand,' when a mutton stew is called an 'Irish stew,' or when the waiter cries out, '*Moniteur,* clock!' to indicate that this newspaper was requested by the customer sitting under the clock—on that day, Paris will have been truly dethroned!" Jules Claretie, *La Vie à Paris 1896* (Paris, 1897), p. 100.
[M3,9]

"There—on the Avenue des Champs-Elysées—it has stood since 1845: the Jardin d'Hiver, a colossal greenhouse with a great many rooms for social occasions, for balls and concerts, although, since its doors are open in summer too, it hardly deserves the name of winter garden." When the sphere of planning creates such entanglements of closed room and airy nature, then it serves in this way to meet the deep human need for daydreaming—a propensity that perhaps proves the true efficacy of idleness in human affairs. Woldemar Seyffarth, *Wahrnehmungen in Paris 1853 und 1854* (Gotha, 1855), p. 130. [M3,10]

The menu at Les Trois Frères Provençaux: "Thirty-six pages for food, four pages for drink—but very long pages, in small folio, with closely packed text and numerous annotations in fine print." The booklet is bound in velvet. Twenty hors d'oeuvres and thirty-three soups. "Forty-six beef dishes, among which are seven different beefsteaks and eight filets." "Thirty-four preparations of game, forty-seven dishes of vegetables, and seventy-one varieties of compote." Julius Rodenberg, *Paris bei Sonnenschein und Lampenlicht* (Leipzig, 1867), pp. 43–44. Flânerie through the bill of fare. [M3a,1]

The best way, while dreaming, to catch the afternoon in the net of evening is to make plans. The flâneur in planning. [M3a,2]

"Le Corbusier's houses depend on neither spatial nor plastic articulation: the air passes through them! Air becomes a constitutive factor! What matters, therefore, is neither spatiality per se nor plasticity per se but only relation and interfusion. There is but one indivisible space. The integuments separating inside from outside fall away." Sigfried Giedion, *Bauen in Frankreich* ‹Berlin, 1928›, p. 85. [M3a,3]

Streets are the dwelling place of the collective. The collective is an eternally unquiet, eternally agitated being that—in the space between the building fronts—experiences, learns, understands, and invents as much as individuals do within the privacy of their own four walls. For this collective, glossy enameled shop signs are a wall decoration as good as, if not better than, an oil painting in the drawing room of a bourgeois; walls with their "Post No Bills" are its writing desk, newspaper stands its libraries, mailboxes its bronze busts, benches its bedroom furniture, and the café terrace is the balcony from which it looks down on its household. The section of railing where road workers hang their jackets is the vestibule, and the gateway which leads from the row of courtyards out into the open is the long corridor that daunts the bourgeois, being for the courtyards the entry to the chambers of the city. Among these latter, the arcade was the drawing room. More than anywhere else, the street reveals itself in the arcade as the furnished and familiar interior of the masses. [M3a,4]

The intoxicated interpenetration of street and residence such as comes about in the Paris of the nineteenth century—and especially in the experience of the flâneur—has prophetic value. For the new architecture lets this interpenetration become sober reality. Giedion on occasion draws attention to this: "A detail of

anonymous engineering, a grade crossing, becomes an element in the architecture" (that is, of a villa). S. Giedion, *Bauen in Frankreich* ⟨Berlin, 1928⟩, p. 89.
[M3a,5]

"Hugo, in *Les Misérables*, has provided an amazing description of the Faubourg
Saint-Marceau: 'It was no longer a place of solitude, for there were people passing;
it was not the country, for there were houses and streets; it was not a city, for the
streets had ruts in them, like the highways, and grass grew along their borders; it
was not a village, for the houses were too lofty. What was it then? It was an
inhabited place where there was nobody, it was a desert place where there was
somebody; it was a boulevard of the great city, a street of Paris—wilder at night
than a forest, and gloomier by day than a graveyard.'"[10] ⟨Lucien⟩ Dubech and
⟨Pierre⟩ d'Espezel, *Histoire de Paris* (Paris, 1926), p. 366.   [M3a,6]

"The last horse-drawn omnibus made its final run on the Villette–Saint Sulpice
line in January 1913; the last horse-drawn tram, on the Pantin-Opéra line in April
of the same year." Dubech and d'Espezel, *Histoire de Paris*, p. 463.   [M3a,7]

"On January 30, 1828, the first omnibus began operation on the line running along
the boulevard from the Bastille to the Madeleine. The fare was twenty-five or
thirty centimes; the car stopped where one wished. It had eighteen to twenty seats,
and its route was divided into two stages, with the Saint-Martin gate as midpoint.
The vogue for this invention was extraordinary: in 1829, the company was running fifteen lines, and rival companies were offering stiff competition—Tricycles,
Ecossaises ⟨Scots Women⟩, Béarnaises ⟨Gascon Women⟩, Dames Blanches ⟨Ladies
in White⟩. Dubech and d'Espezel, *Histoire de Paris*, p. 358–359.   [M3a,8]

"After an hour the gathering broke up, and for the first time I found the streets of
Paris nearly deserted. On the boulevards I met only unaccompanied persons, and
on the Rue Vivienne at Stock Market Square, where by day you have to wind your
way through the crowd, there wasn't a soul. I could hear nothing but my own steps
and the murmur of fountains where by day you cannot escape the deafening buzz.
In the vicinity of the Palais Royal I encountered a patrol. The soldiers were advancing single file along both sides of the street, close to the houses, at a distance of
five or six paces from one another so as not to be attacked at the same time and so
as to be able to render mutual aid. This reminded me that, at the very beginning of
my stay here, I had been advised to proceed in this manner myself at night when
with several others, but, if I had to go home alone, always to take a cab." Eduard
Devrient, *Briefe aus Paris* (Berlin, 1840), p. 248.   [M4,1]

On the omnibuses. "The driver stops and you mount the few steps of the conven-
ient little staircase and look about for a place in the car, where benches extend
lengthwise on the right and the left, with room for up to sixteen people. You've
hardly set foot in the car when it starts rolling again. The conductor has once more
pulled the cord, and, with a quick movement that causes a bell to sound, he

advances the needle on a transparent dial to indicate that another person has entered; by this means they keep track of receipts. Now that the car is moving, you reach calmly into your wallet and pay the fare. If you happen to be sitting reasonably far from the conductor, the money travels from hand to hand among the passengers; the well-dressed lady takes it from the workingman in the blue jacket and passes it on. This is all accomplished easily, in routine fashion, and without any bother. When someone is to exit, the conductor again pulls the cord and brings the car to a halt. If it is going uphill—which in Paris it often is—and therefore is going more slowly, men will customarily climb on and off without the car's having to stop." Eduard Devrient, *Briefe aus Paris* (Berlin, 1840), p. 61–62.   [M4,2]

"It was after the Exhibition of 1867 that one began to see those velocipedes which, some years later, had a vogue as widespread as it was short-lived. We may recall that under the Directory certain Incroyables[11] could be seen riding velociferes, which were bulky, badly constructed velocipedes. On May 19, 1804, a play entitled *Vélocifères* was performed at the Vaudeville; it contained a song with this verse:

> You, partisans of the gentle gait,
> Coachmen who have lost the spur,
> Would you now accelerate
> Beyond the prompt velocifere?
> Learn then how to substitute
> Dexterity for speed.

By the beginning of 1868, however, velocipedes were in circulation, and soon the public walkways were everywhere furrowed. *Velocemen* replaced boatmen. There were gymnasia and arenas for velocipedists, and competitions were set up to challenge the skill of amateurs. . . . Today the velocipede is finished and forgotten." H. Gourdon de Genouillac, *Paris à travers les siècles* (Paris, 1882), vol. 5, p. 288.   [M4,3]

The peculiar irresolution of the flâneur. Just as waiting seems to be the proper state of the impassive thinker, doubt appears to be that of the flâneur. An elegy by Schiller contains the phrase: "the hesitant wing of the butterfly."[12] This points to that association of wingedness with the feeling of indecision which is so characteristic of hashish intoxication.   [M4a,1]

E. T. A. Hoffmann as type of the flâneur; "Des Vetters Eckfenster" ‹My Cousin's Corner Window› is a testament to this. And thus Hoffmann's great success in France, where there has been a special understanding for this type. In the biographical notes to the five-volume edition of his later writings (Brodhag?),[13] we read: "Hoffmann was never really a friend of the great outdoors. What mattered to him more than anything else was the human being—communication with, observations about, the simple sight of, human beings. Whenever he went for a walk in summer, which in good weather happened every day toward evening,

then . . . there was scarcely a tavern or pastry shop where he would not look in to
see whether anyone—and, if so, who—might be there." [M4a,2]

Ménilmontant. "In this immense *quartier* where meager salaries doom women and
children to eternal privation, the Rue de la Chine and those streets which join and
cut across it, such as the Rue des Partants and that amazing Rue Orfila, so fantastic with its roundabouts and its sudden turns, its fences of uneven wood slats, its
uninhabited summerhouses, its deserted gardens reclaimed by nature where wild
shrubs and weeds are growing, sound a note of appeasement and of rare calm. . . .
It is a country path under an open sky where most of the people who pass seem to
have eaten and drunk." J.-K. Huysmans, *Croquis Parisiens* (Paris, 1886), p. 95
("La Rue de la Chine"). [M4a,3]

Dickens. "In his letters . . . he complains repeatedly when traveling, even in the
mountains of Switzerland, . . . about the lack of street noise, which was indispensable to him for his writing. 'I can't express how much I want these [streets],' he
wrote in 1846 from Lausanne, where he was working on one of his greatest novels,
Dombey and Son. 'It seems as if they supplied something to my brain, which it
cannot bear, when busy, to lose. For a week or a fortnight I can write prodigiously
in a retired place . . . and a day in London sets me up again and starts me. But the
toil and labor of writing, day after day, without that magic lantern, is *immense.* . . . *My* figures seem disposed to stagnate without crowds about them. . . .
In Genoa . . . I had two miles of streets at least, lighted at night, to walk about in;
and a great theater to repair to, every night.'"[14] ⟨Franz Mehring,⟩ "Charles Dickens," *Die neue Zeit*, 30, no. 1 (Stuttgart, 1912), pp. 621–622. [M4a,4]

Brief description of misery; probably under the bridges of the Seine. "A bohemian
woman sleeps, her head tilted forward, her empty purse between her legs. Her
blouse is covered with pins that glitter in the sun, and the few appurtenances of her
household and toilette—two brushes, an open knife, a closed tin—are so well
arranged that this semblance of order creates almost an air of intimacy, the
shadow of an *intérieur*, around her." Marcel Jouhandeau, *Images de Paris* (Paris
⟨1934⟩), p. 62. [M5,1]

"⟨Baudelaire's⟩ 'Le Beau Navire' ⟨The Good Ship⟩ created quite a stir. . . . It was
the cue for a whole series of sailor songs, which seemed to have transformed the
Parisians into mariners and inspired them with dreams of boating. . . . In wealthy
Venice where luxury shines, / Where golden porticoes glimmer in the water, /
Where palaces of glorious marble reveal / Masterworks of art and treasures divine, / I have only my gondola, / Sprightly as a bird / That darts and flies at its
ease, / Skimming the surface of the waters." H. Gourdon de Genouillac, *Les Refrains de la rue, de 1830 à 1870* (Paris, 1879), pp. 21–22. [M5,2]

"'Tell me, what is that awful stew which smells so bad and is warming in that great
pot?' says a provincial sort to an old porter. 'That, my dear sir, is a batch of

paving stones that are being baked to pave our poor boulevard, which is looking so worn! . . . As if strolling wasn't nicer when you walked on the soil, the way you do in a garden!" *La Grande Ville: Nouveau Tableau de Paris* (Paris, 1844), vol. 1, p. 334 ("Le Bitume"). [M5,3]

On the first omnibuses: "Competition has already emerged in the form of 'Les Dames Blanches.' . . . These cars are painted entirely in white, and the drivers, dressed in . . . white, operate a bellows with their foot that plays the tune from *La Dame Blanche:* 'The lady in white is looking at you . . .'" Nadar, *Quand j'étais photographe* (Paris ‹1900›), pp. 301–302 ("1830 et environs"). [M5,4]

Musset once named the section of the boulevards that lies behind the Théâtre des Variétés, and that is not much frequented by flâneurs, the East Indies. ‹See M11a,3.› [M5,5]

The flâneur is the observer of the marketplace. His knowledge is akin to the occult science of industrial fluctuations. He is a spy for the capitalists, on assignment in the realm of consumers. [M5,6]

The flâneur and the masses: here Baudelaire's "Rêve parisien" might prove very instructive. [M5,7]

The idleness of the flâneur is a demonstration against the division of labor. [M5,8]

Asphalt was first used for sidewalks. [M5,9]

"A town, such as London, where a man may wander for hours together without reaching the beginning of the end, without meeting the slightest hint which could lead to the inference that there is open country within reach, is a strange thing. This colossal centralization, this heaping together of two and a half millions of human beings at one point, has multiplied the power of this two and a half millions a hundredfold; has raised London to the commercial capital of the world, created the giant docks and assembled the thousand vessels that continually cover the Thames. . . . But the sacrifices which all this has cost become apparent later. After roaming the streets of the capital a day or two, . . . one realizes for the first time that these Londoners have been forced to sacrifice the best qualities of their human nature to bring to pass all the marvels of civilization. . . . The very turmoil of the streets has something repulsive about it—something against which human nature rebels. The hundreds of thousands of all classes and ranks crowding past each other—aren't they all human beings with the same qualities and powers, and with the same interest in being happy? And aren't they obliged, in the end, to seek happiness in the same way, by the same means? And still they crowd by one another as though they had nothing in common, nothing to do with one another, and their only agreement is the tacit one—that each keep to his own side of the pavement, so as not to delay the opposing streams of the crowd—while no man thinks to honor another with so much as a glance. The brutal indifference, the unfeeling isolation of each in his private interest becomes the more repellent and offensive, the more these individuals are crowded together within a limited space. And however much one may be aware that this isolation of the individual, this narrow self-seeking, is the fundamental principle of our society everywhere, it is nowhere so shamelessly barefaced, so self-conscious, as just here in the crowding of the great city." Friedrich Engels, *Die Lage der arbeitenden Klasse in England*, 2nd ed. (Leipzig, 1848), pp. 36–37 ("Die grossen Städte").[15]   [M5a,1]

"By 'bohemians' I mean that class of individuals for whom existence is a problem, circumstances a myth, and fortune an enigma; who have no sort of fixed abode, no place of refuge; who belong nowhere and are met with everywhere; who have no particular calling in life but follow fifty professions; who, for the most part, arise in the morning without knowing where they are to dine in the evening; who are rich today, impoverished tomorrow; who are ready to live honestly if they can, and otherwise if they cannot." Adolphe d'Ennery and Grangé, *Les Bohémiens de Paris* ‹A play in five acts and eight tableaux› (Paris), pp. 8–9 (L'Ambigu-Comique, September 27, 1843; series entitled *Magasin théatral*).

[M5a,2]

"Then from out of Saint Martin's Gate / The romantic Omnibus flashed by." [Léon Gozlan,] *Le Triomphe des Omnibus: Poème héroï-comique* (Paris, 1828), p. 15.   [M6,1]

"When the first German railway line was about to be constructed in Bavaria, the medical faculty at Erlangen published an expert opinion . . . : the rapid movement would cause . . . cerebral disorders (the mere sight of a train rushing by could already do this), and it was therefore necessary, at the least, to build a wooden barrier five feet high on both sides of the track." Egon Friedell, *Kulturgeschichte der Neuzeit* (Munich, 1931), vol. 3, p. 91.   [M6,2]

"Beginning around 1845 . . . there were railroads and steamers in all parts of Europe, and the new means of transport were celebrated. . . . Pictures, letters, stories of travel were the preferred genre for authors and readers." Egon Friedell, *Kulturgeschichte der Neuzeit* (Munich, 1931), vol. 3, p. 92.   [M6,3]

The following observation typifies the concerns of the age: "When one is sailing on a river or lake, one's body is without active movement. . . . The skin experiences no contraction, and its pores remain wide open and capable of absorbing all the emanations and vapors of the surrounding environment. The blood . . . remains . . . concentrated in the cavities of the chest and abdomen, and reaches the extremities with difficulty." J.-F. Dancel, *De l'Influence des voyages sur l'homme et sur ses maladies: Ouvrage spécialement destiné aux gens du monde* (Paris, 1846), p. 92 ("Des Promenades en bateau sur les lacs et les rivières").   [M6,4]

Remarkable distinction between flâneur and rubberneck (*badaud*): "Let us not, however, confuse the flâneur with the rubberneck: there is a subtle difference. . . . The average flâneur . . . is always in full possession of his individuality, while that of the rubberneck disappears, absorbed by the external world, . . . which moves him to the point of intoxication and ecstasy. Under the influence of the spectacle, the rubberneck becomes an impersonal being. He is no longer a man—he is the public; he is the crowd. At a distance from nature, his naive soul aglow, ever inclined to reverie, . . . the true rubberneck deserves the admiration of all upright and sincere hearts." Victor Fournel, *Ce qu'on voit dans les rues de Paris* (Paris, 1858), p. 263 ("L'Odyssée d'un flâneur dans les rues de Paris"). [M6,5]

The phantasmagoria of the flâneur: to read from faces the profession, the ancestry, the character. [M6,6]

In 1851[16] there was still a regular stagecoach line between Paris and Venice. [M6,7]

On the colportage phenomenon of space: "'The sense of mystery,' wrote Odilon Redon, who had learned the secret from da Vinci, 'comes from remaining always in the equivocal, with double and triple perspectives, or inklings of perspective (images within images)—forms that take shape and come into being according to the state of mind of the spectator. All things more suggestive just because they do appear.'" Cited in Raymond Escholier, "Artiste," *Arts et métiers graphiques*, No. 47 (June 1, 1935), p. 7. [M6a,1]

The flâneur at night. "Tomorrow, perhaps, . . . noctambulism will have had its day. But at least it will be lived to the full during the thirty or forty years it will last. . . . The individual can rest from time to time; stopping places and waystations are permitted him. But he does not have the right to sleep." Alfred Delvau, *Les Heures parisiennes* (Paris, 1866), pp. 200, 206 ("Deux Heures de matin").—That nightlife was significantly extended is evident already from the fact that, as Delvau recounts (p. 163), the stores were closing at ten o'clock. [M6a,2]

In the musical revue by Barré, Radet, and Desfontaines, *M. Durelief, ou Petite Revue des embellissemens de Paris* (Paris, 1810), performed at the Théâtre de Vaudeville on June 9, 1810, Paris in the form of a model constructed by M. Durelief has migrated into the scenery. The chorus declares "how agreeable it is to have all of Paris in one's drawing room" (p. 20). The plot revolves around a wager between the architect Durelief and the painter Ferdinand; if the former, in his model of Paris, omits any sort of "embellishment," then his daughter Victorine straightaway belongs to Ferdinand, who otherwise has to wait two years for her. It turns out that Durelief has forgotten Her Majesty the Empress Marie Louise, "the most beautiful ornament" of Paris. [M6a,3]

The city is the realization of that ancient dream of humanity, the labyrinth. It is this reality to which the flâneur, without knowing it, devotes himself. Without knowing it; yet nothing is more foolish than the conventional thesis which rationalizes his behavior, and which forms the uncontested basis of that voluminous literature that traces the figure and demeanor of the flâneur—the thesis, namely, that the flâneur has made a study of the physiognomic appearance of people in order to discover their nationality and social station, character and destiny, from a perusal of their gait, build, and play of features. The interest in concealing the true motives of the flâneur must have been pressing indeed to have occasioned such a shabby thesis.　　　　　　　　　　　　　　　　　　　　　[M6a,4]

In Maxime Du Camp's poem "Le Voyageur," the flâneur wears the costume of the traveler:

> "I am afraid to stop—it's the engine of my life;
> . . . . .
> Love galls me so; I do not want to love."
> "Move on then, on with your bitter travels!
> The sad road awaits you: meet your fate."

Maxime Du Camp, *Les Chants modernes* (Paris, 1855), p. 104.　　　　[M7,1]

Lithograph. ***Cabmen Doing Battle with Omnibus Drivers***. Cabinet des Estampes.
　　　　　　　　　　　　　　　　　　　　　　　　　　　　　　　[M7,2]

As early as 1853, there are official statistics concerning vehicular traffic at certain Parisian nerve centers. "In 1853, thirty-one omnibus lines were serving Paris, and it is worth noting that, with a few exceptions, these lines were designated by the same letters used for the autobus lines operating at that time. Thus it was that the 'Madeleine–Bastille' line was already Line E." Paul d'Ariste, *La Vie et le monde du boulevard, 1830–1870* (Paris ‹1930›), p. 196.　　　　　　　[M7,3]

At connecting stations for the omnibus, passengers were called up in numerical order and had to answer when called if they wanted to preserve their right to a seat. (1855)　　　　　　　　　　　　　　　　　　　　　　　　　[M7,4]

"The absinthe hour . . . dates from the burgeoning . . . of the small press. In earlier times, when there was nothing but large serious newspapers, . . . there was no absinthe hour. This *heure de l'absinthe* is the logical consequence of the Parisian gossip columns and tabloids." Gabriel Guillemot, *Le Bohême* (Paris, 1869), p. 72 ("Physiognomies parisiennes").　　　　　　　　　　　　　[M7,5]

Louis Lurine, *Le Treizième Arrondissement de Paris* (Paris, 1850), is one of the most noteworthy testimonials to the distinctive physiognomy of the neighborhood. The book has certain stylistic peculiarities. It personifies the *quartier*. Formulas like "The thirteenth *arrondissement* devotes itself to a man's love only when it can furnish him with vices to love" (p. 216) are not unusual.[17]　　　　[M7,6]

Diderot's "How beautiful the street!" is a favorite phrase of the chroniclers of flânerie. [M7,7]

Regarding the legend of the flâneur: "With the aid of a word I overhear in passing, I reconstruct an entire conversation, an entire existence. The inflection of a voice suffices for me to attach the name of a deadly sin to the man whom I have just jostled and whose profile I glimpsed." Victor Fournel, *Ce qu'on voit dans les rues de Paris* (Paris, 1858), p. 270. [M7,8]

In 1857 there was still a coach departing from the Rue Pavée-Saint-André at 6 A.M. for Venice; the trip took six weeks. See Fournel, *Ce qu'on voit dans les rues de Paris* (Paris), p. 273. [M7,9]

In omnibuses, a dial that indicated the number of passengers. Why? As a control for the conductor who distributed the tickets. [M7,10]

"It is worth remarking . . . that the omnibus seems to subdue and to still all who approach it. Those who make their living from travelers . . . can be recognized ordinarily by their coarse rowdiness . . . , but omnibus employees, virtually alone among transit workers, display no trace of such behavior. It seems as though a calming, drowsy influence emanates from this heavy machine, like that which sends marmots and turtles to sleep at the onset of winter." Victor Fournel, *Ce qu'on voit dans les rues de Paris* (Paris, 1858), p. 283 ("Cochers de fiacres, cochers de remise et cochers d'omnibus"). [M7a,1]

"At the time Eugène Sue's *Mystères de Paris* was published, no one, in certain neighborhoods of the capital, doubted the existence of a Tortillard, a Chouette, a Prince Rodolphe." Charles Louandre, *Les Idées subversives de notre temps* (Paris, 1872), p. 44. [M7a,2]

The first proposal for an omnibus system came from Pascal and was realized under Louis XIV, with the characteristic restriction "that soldiers, pages, footmen, and other livery, including laborers and hired hands, were not permitted entry into said coaches." In 1828, introduction of the omnibuses, about which a poster tells us: "These vehicles . . . warn of their approach by sounding specially designed horns." Eugène d'Auriac, *Histoire anecdotique de l'industrie française* (Paris, 1861), pp. 250, 281. [M7a,3]

Among the phantoms of the city is "Lambert"—an invented figure, a flâneur perhaps. In any case, he is allotted the boulevard as the scene of his apparitions. There is a famous couplet with the refrain, "Eh, Lambert!" Delvau, in his *Lions du jour* ‹Paris, 1867›, devotes a paragraph to him (p. 228). [M7a,4]

A rustic figure in the urban scene is described by Delvau in his chapter "Le Pauvre à cheval" ‹Poor Man on Horseback›, in *Les Lions du jour.* "This horseman was a poor devil whose means forbade his going on foot, and who asked for alms as another man might ask for directions. . . . This mendicant . . . on his little nag, with its wild mane and its shaggy coat like that of a rural donkey, has long remained before my eyes and in my imagination. . . . He died—a rentier." Alfred Delvau, *Les Lions du jour* (Paris, 1867), pp. 116–117 ("Le Pauvre à cheval").

[M7a,5]

Looking to accentuate the Parisians' new feeling for nature, which rises above gastronomical temptations, Rattier writes: "A pheasant, displaying itself at the door of its leafy dwelling, would make its gold-and-ruby plumage sparkle in the sunlight . . . , so as to greet visitors . . . like a nabob of the forest." Paul-Ernest de Rattier, *Paris n'existe pas* (Paris, 1857), pp. 71–72. ☐ Grandville ☐ [M7a,6]

"It is emphatically not the counterfeit Paris that will have produced the rubber-neck. . . . As for the flâneur, who was always—on the sidewalks and before the display windows—a man of no account, a nonentity addicted to charlatans and ten-cent emotions, a stranger to all that was not cobblestone, cab, or gas lamp, . . . he has become a laborer, a wine grower, a manufacturer of wool, sugar, and iron. He is no longer dumbfounded at nature's ways. The germination of a plant no longer seems to him external to the factory methods used in the Faubourg Saint-Denis." Paul-Ernest de Rattier, *Paris n'existe pas* (Paris, 1857), pp. 74–75.

[M8,1]

In his pamphlet *Le Siècle maudit* (Paris, 1843), which takes a stand against the corruption of contemporary society, Alexis Dumesnil makes use of a fiction of Juvenal's: the crowd on the boulevard suddenly stops still, and a record of each individual's thoughts and objectives at that particular moment is compiled (pp. 103–104). [M8,2]

"The contradiction between town and country . . . is the crassest expression of the subjection of the individual to the division of labor, to a specific activity forced upon him—a subjection that makes one man into a narrow-minded city animal, another into a narrow-minded country animal." ‹Karl Marx and Friedrich Engels, *Die deutsche Ideologie*› in *Marx-Engels Archiv*, vol. 1, ed. D. Rjazanov (Frankfurt am Main ‹1928›), pp. 271–272.[18] [M8,3]

At the Arc de Triomphe: "Ceaselessly up and down these streets parade the cabriolets, omnibuses, swallows, velociferes, citadines, *dames blanches*, and all the other public conveyances, whatever they may be called—not to mention the innumerable whiskies, berlins, barouches, horsemen, and horsewomen." L. Rellstab, *Paris im Frühjahr 1843* (Leipzig, 1844), vol. 1, p. 212. The author also mentions an omnibus that carried its destination written on a flag. [M8,4]

Around 1857 (see H. de Pène, *Paris intime* [Paris, 1859], p. 224), the upper level of the omnibus was closed to women. [M8,5]

_ Quinze centimes un bain complet .....parole,c'est pas payé ! ...

A Paris omnibus. Lithograph by Honoré Daumier, 1856. The caption reads: "Fifteen centimes for a full bath! My word, what a bargain!" See M8,5.

"The genial Vautrin, disguised as the abbé Carlos Herrera, had foreseen the Parisians' infatuation with public transport when he invested all his funds in transit companies in order to settle a dowry on Lucien de Rubempré." Poëte, Beaurepaire, Clouzot, and Henriot, *Une Promenade à travers Paris au temps des romantiques: Exposition de la Bibliothèque et des Travaux historiques de la Ville de Paris* (1908), p. 28. [M8,6]

"Therefore the one who sees, without hearing, is much more . . . worried than the one who hears without seeing. This principle is of great importance in understanding the sociology of the modern city. Social life in the large city . . . shows a great preponderance of occasions to *see* rather than to hear people. One explanation . . . of special significance is the development of public means of transportation. Before the appearance of omnibuses, railroads, and streetcars in the nineteenth century, men were not in a situation where, for minutes or hours at a time, they could or must look at one another without talking to one another." G. Simmel, *Mélanges de philosophie rélativiste: Contribution à la culture philosophique* ‹trans. Alix Guillain› (Paris, 1912), pp. 26–27 ("Essai sur la sociologie des sens").[19] The state of affairs which Simmel relates to the condition of uneasiness and lability has, in other respects, a certain part to play in the vulgar physiognomy. The difference between this physiognomy and that of the eighteenth century deserves study.   [M8a,1]

"Paris . . . dresses up a ghost in old numbers of *Le Constitutionnel,* and produces Chodruc Duclos." Victor Hugo, *Oeuvres complètes,* novels, vol. 7 (Paris, 1881), p. 32 (*Les Misérables,* ch. 3).[20]   [M8a,2]

On Victor Hugo: "The morning, for him, was consecrated to sedentary labors, the afternoon to labors of wandering. He adored the upper levels of omnibuses—those 'traveling balconies,' as he called them—from which he could study at his leisure the various aspects of the gigantic city. He claimed that the deafening brouhaha of Paris produced in him the same effect as the sea." Edouard Drumont, *Figures de bronze ou statues de neige* (Paris ‹1900›), p. 25 ("Victor Hugo").   [M8a,3]

Separate existence of each *quartier:* around the middle of the century it was still being said of the Ile Saint-Louis that if a girl there lacked a good reputation, she had to seek her future husband outside the district.   [M8a,4]

"O night! O refreshing darkness! . . . in the stony labyrinths of the metropolis, scintillation of stars, bright bursts of city lights, you are the fireworks of the goddess Liberty!" Charles Baudelaire, *Le Spleen de Paris,* ed. Hilsum (Paris), p. 203 ("Le Crépuscule du soir").[21]   [M8a,5]

Names of omnibuses around 1840, in Gaëtan Niépovié, *Etudes physiologiques sur les grandes métropoles de l'Europe occidentale* (Paris, 1840), p. 113: Parisiennes, Hirondelles ‹Swallows›, Citadines, Vigilantes ‹Guardianesses›, Aglaias, Deltas.
                                                                                                           [M8a,6]

Paris as landscape spread out below the painters: "As you cross the Rue Notre-Dame-de-Lorette, lift up your head and direct your gaze at one of those platforms crowning the Italianate houses. You cannot fail to notice, etched against the sky seven stories above the level of the pavements, something resembling a scarecrow stuck out in a field. . . . At first you see a dressing gown upon which all the colors of the rainbow are blended without harmony, a pair of long trousers of outlandish shape, and slippers impossible to describe. Under this burlesque apparel hides a young painter." *Paris chez soi* (Paris ‹1854›), pp. 191–192 (Albéric Second, "Rue Notre-Dame-de-Lorette").   [M9,1]

Geffroy, under the impression made by the works of Meryon: "These are represented things which give to the viewer the possibility of dreaming them." Gustave Geffroy, *Charles Meryon* (Paris, 1926), p. 4.   [M9,2]

"The omnibus—that Leviathan of coachwork—crisscrosses with all the many carriages at the speed of lightning!" Théophile Gautier [in Edouard Fournier, *Paris démoli,* 2nd ed., with a preface by M. Théophile Gautier (Paris, 1855), p. iv].

(This preface appeared—presumably as a review of the first edition—in *Le Moniteur universel* of January 21, 1854. It would appear to be wholly or in part identical to Gautier's "Mosaïque de ruines," in *Paris et les Parisiens au XIXe siècle* [Paris, 1856].) [M9,3]

"The most heterogeneous temporal elements thus coexist in the city. If we step from an eighteenth-century house into one from the sixteenth century, we tumble down the slope of time. Right next door stands a Gothic church, and we sink to the depths. A few steps farther, we are in a street from out of the early years of Bismarck's rule . . . , and once again climbing the mountain of time. Whoever sets foot in a city feels caught up as in a web of dreams, where the most remote past is linked to the events of today. One house allies with another, no matter what period they come from, and a street is born. And then insofar as this street, which may go back to the age of Goethe, runs into another, which may date from the Wilhelmine years, the district emerges. . . . The climactic points of the city are its squares: here, from every direction, converge not only numerous streets but all the streams of their history. No sooner have they flowed in than they are contained; the edges of the square serve as quays, so that already the outward form of the square provides information about the history that was played upon it. . . . Things which find no expression in political events, or find only minimal expression, unfold in the cities: they are a superfine instrument, responsive as an Aeolian harp—despite their specific gravity—to the living historic vibrations of the air." Ferdinand Lion, *Geschichte biologisch gesehen* (Zürich and Leipzig ‹1935›), pp. 125–126, 128 ("Notiz über Städte"). [M9,4]

Delvau believes he can recognize the social strata of Parisian society in flânerie as easily as a geologist recognizes geological strata. [M9a,1]

The man of letters: "The most poignant realities for him are not spectacles but studies." Alfred Delvau, *Les Dessous de Paris* (Paris, 1860), p. 121. [M9a,2]

"A man who goes for a walk ought not to have to concern himself with any hazards he may run into or with the regulations of a city. If an amusing idea enters his head, if a curious shopfront comes into view, it is natural that he would want to cross the street without confronting dangers such as our grandparents could not have imagined. But he cannot do this today without taking a hundred precautions, without checking the horizon, without asking the advice of the police department, without mixing with a dazed and breathless herd, for whom the way is marked out in advance by bits of shining metal. If he tries to collect the whimsical thoughts that may have come to mind, very possibly occasioned by sights on the street, he is deafened by car horns, stupefied by loud talkers . . . , and demoralized by the scraps of conversation, of political meetings, of jazz, which escape slyly from the windows. In former times, moreover, his brothers, the rubbernecks, who ambled along so easily down the sidewalks and stopped a moment everywhere, lent to the stream of humanity a gentleness and a tranquillity which it has lost. Now it is a torrent where you are rolled, buffeted, cast up, and swept to one side and the other." Edmond Jaloux, "Le Dernier Flâneur," *Le Temps* (May 22, 1936).

[M9a,3]

"To leave without being forced in any way, and to follow your inspiration as if the mere fact of turning right or turning left already constituted an essentially poetic act." Edmond Jaloux, "Le Dernier Flâneur," *Le Temps* (May 22, 1936).   [M9a,4]

"Dickens . . . could not remain in Lausanne because, in order to write his novels, he needed the immense labyrinth of London streets where he could prowl about continuously. . . . Thomas De Quincey . . . , as Baudelaire tells us, was 'a sort of peripatetic, a street philosopher pondering his way endlessly through the vortex of the great city.'"[22] Edmond Jaloux, "Le Dernier Flâneur," *Le Temps* (May 22, 1936).   [M9a,5]

"Taylor's obsession, and that of his collaborators and successors, is the 'war on flânerie.'" Georges Friedmann, *La Crise du progrès* (Paris ‹1936›), p. 76.

[M10,1]

The urban in Balzac: "Nature appears to him in its magical aspect as the arcanum of matter. It appears to him in its symbolic aspect as the reverberation of human energies and aspirations: in the crashing of the ocean's waves, he experiences the 'exaltation of human forces'; and in the show of color and fragrance produced by flowers, he reads the cipher of love's longing. Always, for him, nature signifies something other, an intimation of spirit. The opposite movement he does not recognize: the immersion of the human back into nature, the saving accord with stars, clouds, winds. He was far too engrossed by the tensions of human existence." Ernst Robert Curtius, *Balzac* (Bonn, 1923), pp. 468–469.   [M10,2]

"Balzac lived a life . . . of furious haste and premature collapse, a life such as that imposed on the inhabitants of big cities by the struggle for existence in modern society. . . . In Balzac's case we see, for the first time, a genius who shares such a life and lives it as his own." Ernst Robert Curtius, *Balzac* (Bonn, 1923), pp. 464–465. On the question of tempo, compare the following: "Poetry and art . . . derive from a 'quick inspection of things.' . . . In *Séraphita*, velocity is introduced as an essential feature of artistic intuition: "that 'mind's eye' whose rapid perception can engender within the soul, as on a canvas, the most diverse landscapes of the world."[23] Ernst Robert Curtius, *Balzac* (Bonn, 1923), p. 445.   [M10,3]

"If God . . . has imprinted every man's destiny in his physiognomy, . . . why shouldn't the human hand sum up that physiognomy in itself, since the hand comprises human action in its entirety and is its sole means of manifestation? Hence palmistry. . . . To foretell the events of a man's life from the study of his hand is a feat . . . no more extraordinary than telling a soldier he is going to fight, a barrister that he is going to plead a cause, a cobbler that he is going to make boots or shoes, a farmer that he is going to fertilize and plough his land. Let us take a still more striking example: genius is a sort of immaterial sun whose rays give color to everything passing by. Cannot an idiot be immediately recognized by characteristics which are the opposite of those shown by a man of genius? . . . Most observant people, students of social nature in Paris, are able to tell the profession of a passerby as they see him approach." Honoré de Balzac, *Le Cousin Pons*, in *Oeuvres complètes*, vol. 18, *Scènes de la vie parisienne*, 6 (Paris, 1914), p. 130.[24]

[M10,4]

"What men call love is very small, very restricted, and very weak compared with this ineffable orgy, this holy prostitution of the soul which gives itself entirely, poetry and charity, to the unforeseen that reveals itself, to the unknown that happens along." Charles Baudelaire, *Le Spleen de Paris*, ed. R. Simon, p. 16 ("Les Foules").[25]

[M10a,1]

"Which of us, in his moments of ambition, has not dreamed of the miracle of a poetic prose, musical, without rhythm and without rhyme, supple enough and rugged enough to adapt itself to the lyrical impulses of the soul, the undulations of reverie, the jibes of conscience? / It was, above all, out of my exploration of huge cities, out of the medley of their innumerable interrelations, that this haunting ideal was born." Charles Baudelaire, *Le Spleen de Paris*, ed. R. Simon, pp. 1–2 ("A Arsène Houssaye").[26]

[M10a,2]

"There is nothing more profound, more mysterious, more pregnant, more insidious, more dazzling than a window lighted by a single candle." Charles Baudelaire, *Le Spleen de Paris*, ed. R. Simon (Paris), p. 62 ("Les Fenêtres").[27]

[M10a,3]

"The artist seeks eternal truth and knows nothing of the eternity in his midst. He admires the column of the Babylonian temple and scorns the smokestack on the factory. Yet what is the difference in their lines? When the era of coal-powered industry is over, people will admire the vestiges of the last smokestacks, as today we admire the remains of temple columns. . . . The steam vapor so detested by writers allows them to divert their admiration. . . . Instead of waiting to visit the Bay of Bengal to find objects to exclaim over, they might have a little curiosity about the objects they see in daily life. A porter at the Gare de l'Est is no less picturesque than a coolie in Colombo. . . . To walk out your front door as if you've just arrived from a foreign country; to discover the world in which you already live; to begin the day as if you've just gotten off the boat from Singapore and have never seen your own doormat or the people on the landing . . . —it is this that reveals the humanity before you, unknown until now." Pierre Hamp, "La Littérature, image de la société" (*Encyclopédie française*, vol. 16, *Arts et littératures dans la société contemporaine*, 1, p. 64).

[M10a,4]

Chesterton fastens on a specimen of English argot to characterize Dickens in his relation to the street: "He has the key to the street" is said of someone to whom the door is closed. "Dickens himself had, in the most sacred and serious sense of the term, the key to the street. . . . His earth was the stones of the street; his stars were the lamps of the street; his hero was the man in the street. He could open the inmost door of his house—the door that leads into that secret passage which is lined with houses and roofed with stars." G. K. Chesterton, *Dickens*, series entitled *Vies des hommes illustres*, vol. 9, translated from the English by Laurent and Martin-Dupont (Paris, 1927), p. 30.[28]   [M11,1]

Dickens as a child: "Whenever he had done drudging, he had no other resource but drifting, and he drifted over half London. He was a dreamy child, thinking mostly of his own dreary prospects. . . . He did not go in for 'observation,' a priggish habit; he did not look at Charing Cross to improve his mind or count the lamp-posts in Holborn to practice his arithmetic. But unconsciously he made all these places the scenes of the monstrous drama in his miserable little soul. He walked in darkness under the lamps of Holborn, and was crucified at Charing Cross. So for him ever afterwards these places had the beauty that only belongs to battlefields." G. K. Chesterton, *Dickens*, series entitled *Vie des hommes illustres*, vol. 9, translated from the English by Laurent and Martin-Dupont (Paris, 1927), pp. 30–31.[29]
                                                                                         [M11,2]

On the psychology of the flâneur: "The undying scenes we can all see if we shut our eyes are not the scenes that we have stared at under the direction of guide-books; the scenes we see are the scenes at which we did not look at all—the scenes in which we walked when we were thinking about something else—about a sin, or a love affair, or some childish sorrow. We can see the background now because we did not see it then. So Dickens did not stamp these places on his mind; he stamped his mind on these places." G. K. Chesterton, *Dickens*, series entitled *Vie des hommes illustres*, vol. 9, translated from the English by Laurent and Martin-Dupont (Paris, 1927), p. 31.[30]   [M11,3]

Dickens: "In May of 1846 he ran over to Switzerland and tried to write *Dombey and Son* at Lausanne. . . . He could not get on. He attributed this especially to his love of London and his loss of it, 'the absence of streets and numbers of figures. . . . My figures seem disposed to stagnate without crowds about them.'" G. K. Chesterton, *Dickens*, translated from the English by Laurent and Martin-Dupont (Paris, 1927), p. 125.[31]   [M11a,1]

"In . . . *Le Voyage de MM. Dunanan père et fils*, two provincials are deceived into thinking that Paris is not Paris but Venice, which they had set out to visit. . . . Paris as an intoxication of all the senses, as a place of delirium." S. Kracauer, *Jacques Offenbach und das Paris seiner Zeit* (Amsterdam, 1937), p. 283.[32]
                                                                                         [M11a,2]

According to a remark by Musset, the "East Indies" begin at a point beyond the boundary of the boulevards. (Shouldn't it be called instead the Far East?) (See Kracauer, *Offenbach*, p. 105.)[33]   [M11a,3]

Kracauer writes that "the *boulevardiers* . . . eschewed nature. . . . Nature was as Plutonic, as volcanic, as the people." S. Kracauer, *Jacques Offenbach* (Amsterdam, 1937), p. 107.[34]   [M11a,4]

On the detective novel: "We must take as an established fact that this metamorphosis of the city is due to a transposition of the setting—namely, from the *savannah* and *forest* of Fenimore Cooper, where every broken branch signifies a worry or a hope, where every tree trunk hides an enemy rifle or the bow of an invisible and silent avenger. Beginning with Balzac, all writers have clearly recorded this debt and faithfully rendered to Cooper what they owed him. Works like *Les Mohicans de Paris*, by Alexander Dumas—works where the title says all—are extremely common." Roger Caillois, "Paris, mythe moderne," *Nouvelle Revue française*, 25, no. 284 (May 1, 1937), pp. 685–686.   [M11a,5]

Owing to the influence of Cooper, it becomes possible for the novelist in an urban setting to give scope to the experiences of the hunter. This has a bearing on the rise of the detective story.   [M11a,6]

"It seems reasonable to say that there exists . . . a phantasmagorical representation of Paris (and, more generally, of the big city) with such power over the imagination that the question of its accuracy would never be posed in practice—a representation created entirely by the book, yet so widespread as to make up . . . part of the collective mental atmosphere." Roger Caillois, "Paris, mythe moderne," *Nouvelle Revue française*, 25, no. 284 (May 1, 1937), p. 684.   [M12,1]

"The Faubourg Saint-Jacques is one of the most primitive suburbs of Paris. Why is that? Is it because it is surrounded by four hospitals as a citadel is surrounded by four bastions, and these hospitals keep the tourists away from the neighborhood? Is it because, leading to no major artery and terminating in no center, . . . the place is rarely visited by coaches? Thus, as soon as one appears in the distance, the lucky urchin who spies it first cups his hands around his mouth and gives a signal to all the inhabitants of the faubourg, just as, on the seashore, the one who first spots a sail on the horizon gives a signal to the others." A. Dumas, *Les Mohicans de Paris*, vol. 1 (Paris, 1859), p. 102 (ch. 25: "Où il est question des sauvages du Faubourg Saint-Jacques"). The chapter describes nothing but the arrival of a piano before a house in the district. No one suspects that the object is a musical instrument, but all are enraptured by the sight of "a huge piece of mahogany" (p. 103). For mahogany furniture was as yet hardly known in this *quartier*.
                                                                     [M12,2]

The first words of an advertisement for *Les Mohicans de Paris:* "Paris—The Mohicans! . . . Two names as discordant as the qui vive of two gigantic unknowns, confronting each other at the brink of an abyss traversed by that electric light whose source is Alexandre Dumas."   [M12,3]

Frontispiece of the third volume of *Les Mohicans de Paris* (Paris, 1863): "The Virgin Forest" [of the Rue d'Enfer].   [M12,4]

"What wonderful precautions! What vigilance! What ingenious preparations and keen attention to detail! The North American savage who, even as he moves, obliterates his footprints in order to elude the enemy at his heels is not more skillful or more meticulous in his precautions." Alfred Nettement, *Etudes sur le feuilleton-roman*, vol. 1 ‹Paris, 1845›, p. 419.   [M12,5]

Vigny (according to Miss Corkran, *Celebrities and I* ‹London, 1902›, cited in L. Séché, *A. de Vigny*, vol. 2 ‹Paris, 1913›, p. 295), on viewing the chimneys of Paris: "I adore these chimneys. . . . Oh, yes, the smoke of Paris is more beautiful to me than the solitude of forests and mountains."   [M12,6]

One does well to consider the detective story in conjunction with the methodical genius of Poe, as Valéry does (in his introduction to *Les Fleurs du mal* [Paris, 1928], p. xx): "To reach a point which allows us to dominate a whole field of activity necessarily means that one perceives a quantity of possibilities. . . . It is therefore not surprising that Poe, possessing so . . . sure a method, became the inventor of several different literary forms—that he provided the first . . . examples of the scientific tale, the modern cosmogonic poem, the detective novel, the literature of morbid psychological states."[35]   [M12a,1]

Concerning Poe's "Man of the Crowd," this passage from an article in *La Semaine* of October 4, 1846, attributed to Balzac or to Hippolyte Castille (cited in Messac ‹*Le "Detective Novel" et l'influence de la pensée scientifique* [Paris, 1929]›, p. 424): "Our eye is fixed on the man in society who moves among laws, snares, the betrayals of his confederates, as a savage in the New World moves among reptiles, ferocious beasts, and enemy tribes."   [M12a,2]

Apropos of "The Man of the Crowd": Bulwer‹-Lytton› orchestrates his description of the big-city crowd in *Eugene Aram* (pt. 4, ch. 5) with a reference to Goethe's observation that every human being, from the humblest to the most distinguished, carries around with him a secret which would make him hateful to all others if it became known. In addition, there is already in Bulwer a confrontation between city and country that is weighted in favor of the city.   [M12a,3]

Apropos of detective fiction: "In the American hero-fantasy, the Indian's character plays a leading role. . . . Only the Indian rites of initiation can compare with the ruthlessness and savagery of rigorous American training. . . . In everything on which the American has really set his heart, we catch a glimpse of the Indian. His extraordinary concentration on a particular goal, his tenacity of purpose, his unflinching endurance of the greatest hardships—in all this the legendary virtues of the Indian find full expression." C. G. Jung, *Seelenprobleme der Gegenwart* (Zürich, Leipzig, Stuttgart, 1932), p. 207 ("Seele und Erde").[36]   [M12a,4]

Chapter 2, "Physiognomie de la rue," in the *Argument du livre sur la Belgique*: "Washing of the sidewalks and the façades of houses, even when it rains in torrents. A national mania, a universal mania. . . . No display windows in the shops. Flânerie, so dear to nations endowed with imagination, impossible in Brussels; nothing to see, and the roads impossible." Baudelaire, *Oeuvres*, vol. 2, ed. Y.-G. Le Dantec ⟨Paris, 1932⟩, pp. 709–710. [M12a,5]

Le Breton reproaches Balzac with having offered the reader "an excess of Mohicans in spencer jackets and of Iroquois in frock coats." Cited in Régis Messac, *Le "Detective Novel" et l'influence de la pensée scientifique* (Paris, 1929), p. 425. [M13,1]

From the opening pages of *Les Mystères de Paris:* "Everyone has read those admirable pages in which Fenimore Cooper, the American Walter Scott, has brought to life the fierce ways of the savages, their colorful and poetic speech, the thousand tricks they use when following or fleeing their enemies. . . . It is our intent to bring before the eyes of the reader some episodes in the lives of various other barbarians, no less removed from the civilized world than the tribes so well portrayed by Cooper." Cited in Régis Messac, *Le "Detective Novel"* (Paris, 1929), p. 425.[37] [M13,2]

Noteworthy connection between flânerie and the detective novel at the beginning of *Les Mohicans de Paris:* "At the outset Salvator says to the poet Jean Robert, 'You want to write a novel? Take Lesage, Walter Scott, and Cooper. . . .' Then, with characters like those of the *Thousand and One Nights,* they cast a piece of paper to the winds and follow it, convinced it will lead them to a subject for a novel, which is what in fact happens." Régis Messac, *Le "Detective Novel" et l'influence de la pensée scientifique* (Paris, 1929), p. 429. [M13,3]

On the epigones of Sue and Balzac, "who came swarming to the serial novels. The influence of Cooper makes itself felt here sometimes directly and sometimes through the mediation of Balzac or other imitators. Paul Féval, beginning in 1856 with *Les Couteaux d'or* ⟨The Golden Knives⟩, boldly transposes the habits and even the inhabitants of the prairie to a Parisian setting: we find there a wonderfully gifted dog named Mohican, an American-style duel between hunters in a Paris suburb, and a redskin called Towah who kills and scalps four of his enemies in a hackney cab in the middle of Paris, and performs this feat with such dexterity that the driver never notices. Later, in *Les Habits noirs* ⟨The Black Attire⟩ (1863), he multiplies those comparisons of which Balzac is so fond: 'Cooper's savages in the middle of Paris! Is not the big city as mysterious as the forests of the New World?'" An additional remark: "Compare also chapters 2 and 19, in which he brings two vagabonds on the scene, Echalot and Similor, 'Hurons of our lakes of mud, Iroquois of the gutter.'" Régis Messac, *Le "Detective Novel" et l'influence de la pensée scientifique,* series entitled *Bibliothèque de la revue de littérature comparée,* vol. 59, pp. 425–426. [M13,4]

"That poetry of terror which the stratagems of enemy tribes at war create in the heart of the forests of America, and of which Cooper has made such good use, was attached to the smallest details of Parisian life. The passersby, the shops, the hackney carriages, a person standing at a window—to the men who had been numbered off for the defense of Peyrade's life, everything presented the ominous interest which in Cooper's novels may be found in a tree trunk, a beaver's dam, a rock, a buffalo skin, a motionless canoe, a branch drooping over the water." Balzac, *A combien l'amour revient aux vieillards.*[38]   [M13a,1]

Preformed in the figure of the flâneur is that of the detective. The flâneur required a social legitimation of his habitus. It suited him very well to see his indolence presented as a plausible front, behind which, in reality, hides the riveted attention of an observer who will not let the unsuspecting malefactor out of his sight.   [M13a,2]

At the end of Baudelaire's essay on Marceline Desbordes-Valmore emerges the *promeneur,* who strolls through the garden landscape of her poetry; the perspectives of the past and future open before him. "But these skies are too vast to be everywhere pure, and the temperature of the climate too warm. . . . The idle passerby, who contemplates these areas veiled in mourning, feels tears of hysteria come to his eyes." Charles Baudelaire, *L'Art romantique* (Paris), p. 343 ("Marceline Desbordes-Valmore").[39] The *promeneur* is no longer capable of "meandering capriciously." He takes refuge in the shadow of cities: he becomes a flâneur.   [M13a,3]

Jules Claretie relates of the aged Victor Hugo, at the time when he was living on the Rue Pigalle, that he enjoyed riding through Paris on the upper level of omnibuses. He loved looking down, from this eminence, on the bustle of the streets. See Raymond Escholier, *Victor Hugo raconté par ceux qui l'ont vu* (Paris, 1931), p. 350—Jules Claretie, "Victor Hugo."   [M13a,4]

"Do you recall a tableau . . . , created by the most powerful pen of our day, which is entitled 'The Man of the Crowd'? From behind the window of a café, a convalescent, contemplating the crowd with delight, mingles in thought with all the thoughts pulsating around him. Having just escaped from the shadow of death, he joyfully breathes in all the germs and emanations of life; having been on the point of forgetting everything, he now remembers and ardently wishes to remember everything. Finally, he rushes into the crowd in search of an unknown person whose face, glimpsed momentarily, fascinated him. Curiosity has become a fatal, irresistible passion." Baudelaire, *L'Art romantique* (Paris), p. 61 ("Le Peintre de la vie moderne").[40]   [M14,1]

Already André Le Breton, *Balzac, l'homme et l'oeuvre* ⟨Paris, 1905⟩, compares Balzac's characters—"the usurers, the attorneys, the bankers"—to Mohicans, whom they resemble more than they do the Parisians. See also Remy de Gourmont, *Promenades littéraires*, second series (Paris, 1906), pp. 117–118: "Les Maîtres de Balzac.")   [M14,2]

From Baudelaire's *Fusées:* "Man . . . is always . . . in a state of savagery. What are the perils of jungle and prairie compared to the daily shocks and conflicts of civilization? Whether a man embraces his dupe on the boulevard, or spears his prey in unknown forests, is he not . . . the most highly perfected beast of prey?"[41]
                                                                          [M14,3]

There were representations (lithographs?) by Raffet of Ecossaises and Tricycles. ⟨See M3a,8.⟩   [M14,4]

"When Balzac lifts the roofs or penetrates the walls in order to clear a space for observation, . . . you listen at the doors. . . . In the interest of sparking your imagination, that is, . . . you are playing the role of what our neighbors the English, in their prudishness, call the 'police detective'!" Hippolyte Babou, *La Vérité sur le cas de M. Champfleury* (Paris, 1857), p. 30.   [M14,5]

It would be profitable to discover certain definite features leading toward the physiognomy of the city dweller. Example: the sidewalk, which is reserved for the pedestrian, runs along the roadway. Thus, the city dweller in the course of his most ordinary affairs, if he is on foot, has constantly before his eyes the image of the competitor who overtakes him in a vehicle.—Certainly the sidewalks were laid down in the interests of those who go by car or by horse. When?   [M14,6]

"For the perfect flâneur, . . . it is an immense joy to set up house in the heart of the multitude, amid the ebb and flow. . . . To be away from home, yet to feel oneself everywhere at home; to see the world, to be at the center of the world, yet to remain hidden from the world—such are a few of the slightest pleasures of those independent, passionate, impartial [!!] natures which the tongue can but clumsily define. The spectator is a *prince* who everywhere rejoices in his incognito. . . . The lover of universal life enters into the crowd as though it were an immense reservoir of electric energy. We might also liken him to a mirror as vast as the crowd itself; or to a kaleidoscope endowed with consciousness, which, with each one of its movements, represents the multiplicity of life and the flickering grace of all the elements of life." Baudelaire, *L'Art romantique* (Paris), pp. 64–65 ("Le Peintre de la vie moderne").[42]   [M14a,1]

The Paris of 1908. "A Parisian used to crowds, to traffic, and to choosing his streets could still go for long walks at a steady pace and even without taking much care. Generally speaking, the abundance of means of transportation had not yet given more than three million people the . . . idea that they could move about just as they liked and that distance was the last thing that counted." Jules Romains, *Les Hommes de bonne volonté*, book 1, *Le 6 octobre* (Paris ⟨1932⟩), p. 204.[43]
                                                                          [M14a,2]

In *Le 6 octobre,* in Chapter 17, "Le Grand Voyage du petit garçon" (pp. 176–184), Romains describes how Louis Bastide makes his journey through Montmartre, from the corner of the Rue Ordener to the Rue Custine: "He had a mission to accomplish. Somebody had commissioned him to follow a certain course, to carry something, or perhaps to bear news of something" (p. 179).[44] In this game of travel, Romains develops some perspectives—particularly the alpine land-scape of Montmartre with the mountain inn (p. 180)—which resemble those in which the flâneur's imagination can lose itself. [M14a,3]

Maxim of the flâneur: "In our standardized and uniform world, it is right here, deep below the surface, that we must go. Estrangement and surprise, the most thrilling exoticism, are all close by." Daniel Halévy, *Pays parisiens* (Paris ‹1932›), p. 153. [M14a,4]

In Jules Romains' *Crime de Quinette* (*Les Hommes de bonne volonté,* book 2), one finds something like the negative of the solitude which is generally companion to the flâneur. It is, perhaps, that friendship is strong enough to break through such solitude—this is what is convincing about Romains' thesis. "According to my idea, it's always rather in that way that you make friends with anybody. You are present together at a moment in the life of the world, perhaps in the presence of a fleeting secret of the world—an apparition which nobody has ever seen before and perhaps nobody will ever see again. It may even be something very little. Take two men going for a walk, for example, like us. Suddenly, thanks to a break in the clouds, a ray of light comes and strikes the top of a wall; and the top of the wall becomes, for the moment, something in some way quite extraordinary. One of the two men touches the other on the shoulder. The other raises his head and sees it too, understands it too. Then the thing up there vanishes. But they will know *in aeternum* that it once existed." Jules Romains, *Les Hommes de bonne volonté,* book 2, *Crime de Quinette* ‹Paris, 1932›, pp. 175–176.[45] [M15,1]

Mallarmé. "He had crossed the Place and the Pont de l'Europe almost every day (he confided to George Moore), gripped by the temptation to throw himself from the heights of the bridge onto the iron rails, under the trains, so as finally to escape this mediocrity of which he was prisoner." Daniel Halévy, *Pays parisiens* (Paris ‹1932›), p. 105. [M15,2]

Michelet writes: "I sprang up like a pale blade of grass between the paving stones" (cited in Halévy, *Pays parisiens*, p. 14). [M15,3]

The tangle of the forest as archetype of mass existence in Hugo: "An astonishing chapter of *Les Misérables* contains the following lines: 'What had just taken place in this street would not have surprised a forest. The trees, the copse, the heath, the branches roughly intertangled, the tall grass, have a darkly mysterious exist-ence. This wild multitude sees there sudden apparitions of the invisible; there, what is below man distinguishes through the dark what is above man.'"[46] Gabriel Bounoure: "Abîmes de Victor Hugo," *Mesures* (July 15, 1936), p. 49. ▯ Gerstäcker passage ▯   [M15,4]

"Research into that serious disease, hatred of the home. Pathology of the disease. Progressive growth of the disease." Charles Baudelaire, *Oeuvres*, ed. Le Dantec, vol. 2 (Paris, 1932), p. 653 ("Mon Coeur mis à nu").[47]   [M15,5]

Letter accompanying the two "Crépuscule" poems; to Fernand Desnoyers, who published them in his *Fontainebleau* (Paris, 1855): "I'm sending you two pieces of poetry that more or less sum up the reveries that assail me in the twilight hours. In the depths of the woods, shut in by those vaults that recall sacristies and cathedrals, I think of our amazing cities, and that prodigious music which rolls over the summits seems to me a translation of the lamentations of mankind." Cited in A. Séché, *La Vie des Fleurs du mal* (Paris, 1928), p. 110.[48] ▯ Baudelaire ▯
                    [M15a,1]

The classic early description of the crowd in Poe: "By far the greater number of those who went by had a satisfied, business-like demeanor, and seemed to be thinking only of making their way through the press. Their brows were knit, and their eyes rolled quickly; when pushed against by fellow-wayfarers they evinced no symptom of impatience, but adjusted their clothes and hurried on. Others, still a numerous class, were restless in their movements, had flushed faces, and talked and gesticulated to themselves, as if feeling in solitude on account of the very denseness of the company around. When impeded in their progress, these people suddenly ceased muttering, but redoubled their gesticulations, and awaited, with an absent and overdone smile upon the lips, the course of the persons impeding them. If jostled, they bowed profusely to the jostlers, and appeared overwhelmed with confusion." Poe, *Nouvelles Histoires extraordinaires*, trans. Ch. B. (Paris ‹1886›), p. 89.[49]   [M15a,2]

"What are the perils of jungle and prairie compared to the daily shocks and conflicts of civilization? Whether a man embraces his dupe on the boulevard, or spears his prey in unknown forests, is he not eternal man—that is to say, the most highly perfected beast of prey?" Charles Baudelaire, *Oeuvres*, ed. Le Dantec, vol. 2 ‹Paris, 1932›, p. 637 ("Fusées").[50]   [M15a,3]

The image of antiquity that so dazzled France is sometimes to be found in immediate proximity to the extremely modern image of America. Balzac on the commercial traveler: "See! What an athlete, what an arena, and what a weapon: he, the world, and his tongue! A daring seaman, he embarks with a stock of mere words to go and fish for money, five or six hundred thousand francs, say, in the frozen ocean, the land of savages, of Iroquois—in France!" H. de Balzac, *L'Illustre Gaudissart,* ed. Calmann-Lévy (Paris), p. 5.[51]   [M15a,4]

Description of the crowd in Baudelaire, to be compared with the description in Poe:

> The gutter, dismal bed, carries along its foulnesses,
> Carries, boiling, the secrets of the sewers;
> It slaps in corrosive waves against the houses,
> Rushes on to jaundice and corrupt the river Seine,
> Sloshing as high as the knees of pedestrians.
> On the slippery pavements everyone passes brutal and self-absorbed,
> Elbowing and spattering us with mud, or thrusting us aside
> In their hurry to arrive somewhere.
> Everywhere mire and deluge and opacity of sky:
> Dire tableau such as dark Ezekiel might have dreamt.

Ch. B., *Oeuvres*, vol. 1 ‹Paris, 1931›, p. 211 (*Poëmes divers*, "Un Jour de pluie").[52]   [M16,1]

On the detective novel:

> The man who hasn't signed anything, who left no picture,
> Who was not there, who said nothing:
> How can they catch him?
> Erase the traces.

Brecht, *Versuche* ‹4–7 (Berlin, 1930)›, p. 116 (*Lesebuch für Städtebewohner*, no. 1).[53]   [M16,2]

The masses in Baudelaire. They stretch before the flâneur as a veil: they are the newest drug for the solitary.—Second, they efface all traces of the individual: they are the newest asylum for the reprobate and the proscript.—Finally, within the labyrinth of the city, the masses are the newest and most inscrutable labyrinth. Through them, previously unknown chthonic traits are imprinted on the image of the city.   [M16,3]

The social base of flânerie is journalism. As flâneur, the literary man ventures into the marketplace to sell himself. Just so—but that by no means exhausts the social side of flânerie. "We know," says Marx, "that the value of each commodity is determined by the quantity of labor materialized in its use value, by the working-time socially necessary for its production" (Marx, *Das Kapital*, ed. Korsch ‹Berlin, 1932›, p. 188).[54] The journalist, as flâneur, behaves as if he too were aware of this. The number of work hours socially necessary for the production of his particular working energy is, in fact, relatively high; insofar as he makes it his business to let his hours of leisure on the boulevard appear as part of this work time, he multiplies the latter and thereby the value of his own labor. In his eyes, and often also in the eyes of his bosses, such value has something fantastic about it. Naturally, this would not be the case if he were not in the privileged position of making the work time necessary for the production of his

use value available to a general and public review by passing that time on the
boulevard and thus, as it were, exhibiting it. [M16,4]

The press brings into play an overabundance of information, which can be all the
more provocative the more it is exempt from any use. (Only the ubiquity of the
reader would make possible a utilization; and so the illusion of such ubiquity is
also generated.) The actual relation of this information to social existence is
determined by the dependence of the information industry on financial interests
and its alignment with these interests.—As the information industry comes into
its own, intellectual labor fastens parasitically on *every* material labor, just as
capital more and more brings *every* material labor into a relation of dependency.
[M16a,1]

Simmel's apt remark concerning the uneasiness aroused in the urbanite by other
people, people whom, in the overwhelming majority of cases, he sees without
hearing,[55] would indicate that, at least in their beginnings, the physiognomies
‹correction: physiologies› were motivated by, among other things, the wish to
dispel this uneasiness and render it harmless. Otherwise, the fantastic pretensions
of these little volumes could not have sat well with their audience. [M16a,2]

There is an effort to master the new experiences of the city within the framework
of the old traditional experiences of nature. Hence the schemata of the virgin
forest and the sea (Meryon and Ponson du Terrail). [M16a,3]

Trace and aura. The trace is appearance of a nearness, however far removed the
thing that left it behind may be. The aura is appearance of a distance, however
close the thing that calls it forth. In the trace, we gain possession of the thing; in
the aura, it takes possession of us. [M16a,4]

> Faithful to my old established way,
> I like to turn the street into a study;
> How often, then, as chance conducts my dreaming steps,
> I blunder, unawares, into a group of pavers!

Auguste-Marseille Barthélemy, *Paris: Revue satirique à M. G. Delessert, Préfet de
Police* (Paris, 1838), p. 8. [M16a,5]

"M. Le Breton says that it is the usurers, attorneys, and bankers in Balzac, rather
than the Parisians, who sometimes seem like ruthless Mohicans, and he believes
that the influence of Fenimore Cooper was not particularly advantageous for the
author of *Gobseck*. This is possible, but difficult to prove." Remy de Gourmont,
Promenades littéraires, 2nd series (Paris, 1906), pp. 117–118 ("Les Maîtres de
Balzac"). [M17,1]

"The jostling crowdedness and the motley disorder of metropolitan communication would . . . be unbearable without . . . psychological distance. Since contempo-

rary urban culture . . . forces us to be physically close to an enormous number of people, . . . people would sink completely into despair if the objectification of social relationships did not bring with it an inner boundary and reserve. The pecuniary character of relationships, either openly or concealed in a thousand forms, places [a] . . . functional distance between people that is an inner protection . . . against the overcrowded proximity." Georg Simmel, *Philosophie des Geldes* (Leipzig, 1900), p. 514.[56]   [M17,2]

Prologue to *Le Flâneur,* newspaper for the masses, published at the office of the town crier, 45 Rue de la Harpe (the first and, no doubt, only number, dated May 3, 1848): "To go out strolling, these days, while puffing one's tobacco, . . . while dreaming of evening pleasures, seems to us a century behind the times. We are not the sort to refuse all knowledge of the customs of another age; but, in our strolling, let us not forget our rights and our obligations as citizens. The times are necessitous; they demand all our attention, all day long. Let us be flâneurs, but patriotic flâneurs." (J. Montaigu). An early specimen of that dislocation of word and meaning which belongs among the devices of journalism.   [M17,3]

Balzac anecdote: "He was with a friend one day when he passed a beggar in rags on the boulevard. His companion was astonished to see Balzac touch his own sleeve with his hand; he had just felt there the conspicuous rip that gaped at the elbow of the mendicant." Anatole Cerfberr and Jules Christophe, *Répertoire de la Comédie humaine de H. de Balzac* (Paris, 1887), p. viii (Introduction by Paul Bourget).   [M17,4]

Apropos of Flaubert's remark that "observation is guided above all by imagination,"[57] the visionary faculty of Balzac: "It is important to note, first of all, that this visionary power could never be exercised directly. Balzac did not have time to live; . . . he did not have the leisure . . . to study men, after the fashion of Molière and Saint-Simon, through daily, familiar contact. He cut his existence in two, writing by night, sleeping by day" (p. x). Balzac speaks of a "retrospective penetration." "It would seem that he took hold of the givens of experience and then tossed them, as it were, into a crucible of dreams." A. Cerfberr and J. Christophe, *Répertoire de la Comédie humaine de H. de Balzac* (Paris, 1887), p. xi (Introduction by Paul Bourget).   [M17a,1]

Empathy with the commodity is fundamentally empathy with exchange value itself. The flâneur is the virtuoso of this empathy. He takes the concept of marketability itself for a stroll. Just as his final ambit is the department store, his last incarnation is the sandwich-man.   [M17a,2]

In a brasserie in the vicinity of the Gare Saint-Lazare, des Esseintes feels himself to be already in England.   [M17a,3]

Regarding the intoxication of empathy felt by the flâneur, a great passage from Flaubert may be adduced. It could well date from the period of the composition of *Madame Bovary:* "Today, for instance, as man and woman, both lover and mistress, I rode in a forest on an autumn afternoon under the yellow leaves, and I was also the horses, the leaves, the wind, the words my people uttered, even the red sun that made them almost close their love-drowned eyes."[58] Cited in Henri Grappin, "Le Mysticisme poétique ‹et l'imagination› de Gustave Flaubert," *Revue de Paris* (December 15, 1912), p. 856.   [M17a,4]

On the intoxication of empathy felt by the flâneur (and by Baudelaire as well), this passage from Flaubert: "I see myself at different moments of history, very clearly. . . . I was boatman on the Nile, *leno* [procurer] in Rome at the time of the Punic wars, then Greek rhetorician in Suburra, where I was devoured by bedbugs. I died, during the Crusades, from eating too many grapes on the beach in Syria. I was pirate and monk, mountebank and coachman—perhaps Emperor of the East, who knows?"[59] Grappin, "Le Mysticisme poétique ‹et l'imagination› de Gustave Flaubert," *Revue de Paris* (December 15, 1912), p. 624.   [M17a,5]

I

Hell is a city much like London—
  A populous and a smoky city;
There are all sorts of people undone,
And there is little or no fun done;
  Small justice shown, and still less pity.

II

There is a Castles, and a Canning,
  A Cobbett, and a Castlereagh;
All sorts of caitiff corpses planning
All sorts of cozening for trepanning
  Corpses less corrupt than they.

III

There is a * * *, who has lost
  His wits, or sold them, none knows which;
He walks about a double ghost,
And though as thin as Fraud almost—
  Ever grows more grim and rich.

IV

There is a Chancery Court; a king;
  A manufacturing mob; a set
Of thieves who by themselves are sent
Similar thieves to represent;
  An army; and a public debt.

V

Which last is a scheme of paper money,
    And means—being interpreted—
"Bees, keep your wax—give us the honey,
And we will plant, while skies are sunny,
    Flowers, which in winter serve instead."

VI

There is a great talk of revolution—
    And a great chance of despotism—
German soldiers—camps—confusion—
Tumults—lotteries—rage—delusion—
    Gin—suicide—and methodism;

VII

Taxes too, on wine and bread,
    And meat, and beer, and tea, and cheese,
From which those patriots pure are fed,
Who gorge before they reel to bed
    The tenfold essence of all these.

. . . . .

IX

Lawyers—judges—old hobnobbers
    Are there—bailiffs—chancellors—
Bishops—great and little robbers—
Rhymesters—pamphleteers—stock-jobbers—
    Men of glory in the wars,—

X

Things whose trade is, over ladies
    To lean, and flirt, and stare, and simper,
Till all that is divine in woman
Grows cruel, courteous, smooth, inhuman,
    Crucified 'twixt a smile and a whimper.

Shelley, "Peter Bell the Third" ("Part the Third: Hell").[60]   [M18]

Illuminating for the conception of the crowd: in "Des Vetters Eckfenster" ‹My Cousin's Corner Window›, the visitor still thinks that the cousin watches the activity in the marketplace only because he enjoys the play of colors. And in the long run, he thinks, this will surely become tiring. Similarly, and at around the same time, Gogol writes, in "The Lost Letter," of the annual fair in Konotop: "There were such crowds moving up and down the streets that it made one giddy to watch them." *Russische Gespenster-Geschichten* (Munich ‹1921›), p. 69.[61]

[M18a,1]

Tissot, in justifying his proposal to tax luxury horses: "The intolerable noise made day and night by twenty thousand private carriages in the streets of Paris, the continual shaking of the houses, the inconvenience and insomnia that result for so many inhabitants of the city—all this deserves some compensation." Amédée de Tissot, *Paris et Londres comparés* (Paris, 1830), pp. 172–173.   [M18a,2]

The flâneur and the shopfronts: "First of all, there are the flâneurs of the boulevard, whose entire existence unfolds between the Church of the Madeleine and the Théâtre du Gymnase. Each day sees them returning to this narrow space, which they never pass beyond, examining the displays of goods, surveying the shoppers seated before the doors of cafés. . . . They would be able to tell you if Goupil or Deforge have put out a new print or a new painting, and if Barbedienne has repositioned a vase or an arrangement; they know all the photographers' studios by heart and could recite the sequence of signs without omitting a single one." Pierre Larousse, *Grand Dictionnaire universel* (Paris ⟨1872⟩), vol. 8, p. 436.
[M18a,3]

On the provincial character of "Des Vetters Eckfenster." "Since that unfortunate period when an insolent and overbearing enemy inundated our country," the Berlin populace has acquired smoother manners. "You see, dear cousin, how nowadays, by contrast, the market offers a delightful picture of prosperity and peaceful manners." E. T. A. Hoffmann, *Ausgewählte Schriften,* vol. 14 (Stuttgart, 1839), pp. 238, 240.[62]   [M19,1]

The sandwich-man is the last incarnation of the flâneur.   [M19,2]

On the provincial character of "Des Vetters Eckfenster": the cousin wants to teach his visitor "the rudiments of the art of seeing."[63]   [M19,3]

On July 7, 1838, G. E. Guhrauer writes to Varnhagen about Heine: "He was having a bad time with his eyes in the spring. On our last meeting, I accompanied him part of the way along the boulevard. The splendor and vitality of that unique street moved me to boundless admiration, while, against this, Heine now laid weighty emphasis on the horrors attending this center of the world." Compare also Engels on the crowd ⟨M5a,1⟩. Heinrich Heine, *Gespräche*, ed. Hugo Bieber (Berlin, 1926), p. 163.   [M19,4]

"This city marked by a vitality, a circulation, an activity without equal is also, by a singular contrast, the place where one finds the most idlers, loungers, and rubbernecks." Pierre Larousse, *Grand Dictionnaire universel* (Paris ⟨1872⟩), vol. 8, p. 436 (article entitled "Flâneur").   [M19,5]

Hegel writing from Paris to his wife, September 3, 1827: "As I go through the streets, the people look just the same as in Berlin, everyone dressed the same, about the same faces, the same appearance, yet in a populous mass." *Briefe von und an Hegel,* ed. Karl Hegel (Leipzig, 1887), part 2, p. 257 (*Werke,* vol. 19, part 2).[64]   [M19,6]

Londres ‹London›

It is an immense place, and so spread out
That it takes a day to cross it by omnibus.
And, far and wide, there is nothing to see
But houses, public buildings, and high monuments,
Set down haphazardly by the hand of time.
Long black chimneys, the steeples of industry,
Open their mouths and exhale fumes
From their hot bellies to the open air;
Vast white domes and Gothic spires
Float in the vapor above the heaps of bricks.
An ever swelling, unapproachable river,
Rolling its muddy currents in sinuous onrush,
Like that frightful stream of the underworld,[65]
And arched over by gigantic bridges on piers
That mimic the old Colossus of Rhodes,
Allows thousands of ships to ply their way;
A great tide polluted and always unsettled
Recirculates the riches of the world.
Busy stockyards, open shops are ready
To receive a universe of goods.
Above, the sky tormented, cloud upon cloud,
The sun, like a corpse, wears a shroud on its face,
Or, sometimes, in the poisonous atmosphere,
Looks out like a miner coal-blackened.
There, amid the somber mass of things,
An obscure people lives and dies in silence—
Millions of beings in thrall to a fatal instinct,
Seeking gold by avenues devious and straight.

To be compared with Baudelaire's review of Barbier, his portrayal of Meryon, the poems of "Tableaux parisiens." In Barbier's poetry, two elements—the "description" of the great city and the social unrest—should be pretty much distinguished. Only traces of these elements still remain with Baudelaire, in whom they have been joined to an altogether heterogeneous third element. Auguste Barbier, *Iambes et poèmes* (Paris, 1841), pp. 193–194. The poem is from the sequence *Lazare* of 1837.   [M19a,1]

If one compares Baudelaire's discussion of Meryon with Barbier's "Londres," one asks oneself whether the gloomy image of the "most disquieting of capitals"[66]—the image, that is, of Paris—was not very materially determined by the texts of Barbier and of Poe. London was certainly ahead of Paris in industrial development.   [M19a,2]

Beginning of Rousseau's Second Promenade: "Having therefore decided to describe my habitual state of mind in this, the strangest situation which any mortal will ever know, I could think of no simpler or surer way of carrying out my plan than to keep a faithful record of my solitary walks and the reveries that occupy them, when I give free rein to my thoughts and let my ideas follow their natural course, unrestricted and unconfined. These hours of solitude and meditation are the only ones in the day when I am completely myself and my own master, with nothing to distract or hinder me, the only ones when I can truly say that I am what nature meant me to be." Jean-Jacques Rousseau, *Les Rêveries du promeneur solitaire;* preceded by *Dix Jours à Ermenonville,* by Jacques de Lacretelle (Paris, 1926), p. 15.[67]—The passage presents the integral link between contemplation and idleness. What is decisive is that Rousseau already—in his idleness—is enjoying himself, but has not yet accomplished the turning outward.　　[M20,1]

"London Bridge." "A little while ago I was walking across London Bridge and I paused to contemplate what is for me an endless pleasure—the sight of a rich, thick, complex waterway whose nacreous sheets and oily patches, clouded with white smoke-puffs, are loaded with a confusion of ships. . . . I leaned upon my elbows. . . . Delight of vision held me with a ravenous thirst, involved in the play of a light of inexhaustible richness. But endlessly pacing and flowing at my back I was aware of another river, a river of the blind eternally in pursuit of [its] immediate material object. This seemed to me no crowd of individual beings, each with his own history, his private god, his treasures and his scars, his interior monologue and his fate; rather I made of it—unconsciously, in the depths of my body, in the shaded places of my eyes—*a flux of identical particles*, equally sucked in by the same nameless void, their deaf headlong current pattering monotonously over the bridge. Never have I so felt solitude, mingled with pride and anguish." Paul Valéry, *Choses tues* ‹Paris, 1930›, pp. 122–124.[68]　　[M20,2]

Basic to flânerie, among other things, is the idea that the fruits of idleness are more precious than the fruits of labor. The flâneur, as is well known, makes "studies." On this subject, the nineteenth-century Larousse has the following to say: "His eyes open, his ear ready, searching for something entirely different from what the crowd gathers to see. A word dropped by chance will reveal to him one of those character traits that cannot be invented and that must be drawn directly from life; those physiognomies so naively attentive will furnish the painter with the expression he was dreaming of; a noise, insignificant to every other ear, will strike that of the musician and give him the cue for a harmonic combination; even for the thinker, the philosopher lost in his reverie, this external agitation is profitable: it stirs up his ideas as the storm stirs the waves of the sea. . . . Most men of genius were great flâneurs—but industrious, productive flâneurs. . . . Often it is when the artist and the poet seem least occupied with their work that they are most profoundly absorbed in it. In the first years of this century, a man was seen walking each and every day—regardless of the weather, be it sunshine or snow—around the ramparts of the city of Vienna. This man was Beethoven, who, in the midst of his wanderings, would work out his magnificent symphonies in his head before putting them down on paper. For him, the world no longer existed; in vain would people greet him respectfully as he passed. He saw nothing; his mind was elsewhere." Pierre Larousse, *Grand Dictionnaire universel* (Paris ⟨1872⟩), vol. 8, p. 436 (article entitled, "Flâneur"). [M20a,1]

Beneath the roofs of Paris: "These Parisian savannahs consisting of roofs leveled out to form a plain, but covering abysses teeming with population." Balzac, *La Peau de chagrin*, ed. Flammarion, p. 95.[69] The end of a long description of the roof-landscapes of Paris. [M20a,2]

Description of the crowd in Proust: "All these people who paced up and down the seawall promenade, tacking as violently as if it had been the deck of a ship (for they could not lift a leg without at the same time waving their arms, turning their heads and eyes, settling their shoulders, compensating by a balancing movement on one side for the movement they had just made on the other, and puffing out their faces), and who, pretending not to see so as to let it be thought that they were not interested, but covertly watching, for fear of running against the people who were walking beside or coming towards them, did, in fact, butt into them, became entangled with them, because each was mutually the object of the same secret attention veiled beneath the same apparent disdain; their love—and consequently their fear—of the crowd being one of the most powerful motives in all men, whether they seek to please other people or to astonish them, or to show them that they despise them." Marcel Proust, *A l'Ombre des jeunes filles en fleurs* (Paris), vol. 3, p. 36.[70] [M21,1]

The critique of the *Nouvelles Histoires extraordinaires* which Armand de Pontmartin publishes in *Le Spectateur* of September 19, 1857, contains a sentence that, although aimed at the overall character of the book, would nevertheless have its rightful place in an analysis of the "man of the crowd": "It was certainly there in a striking form, that implacable democratic and American severity, reckoning human beings as no more than numbers, only to end by attributing to numbers something of the life, animation, and spirit of the human being." But doesn't the sentence have a more immediate reference to the *Histoires extraordinaires,* which appeared earlier? (And where is "the man of the crowd"?) Baudelaire, *Oeuvres complètes,* Translations, *Nouvelles Histoires extraordinaires,* ed. Crépet (Paris, 1933), p. 315.—The critique is, at bottom, mean-spirited. [M21,2]

The "spirit of noctambulism" finds a place in Proust (under a different name): "The capricious spirit that sometimes leads a woman of high rank to say to herself 'What fun it will be!' and then to end her evening in a deadly tiresome manner, getting up enough energy to go and rouse someone, remain a while by the bedside in her evening wrap, and finally, finding nothing to say and noticing that it is very late, go home to bed." Marcel Proust, *Le Temps retrouvé* (Paris), vol. 2, p. 185.[71] [M21a,1]

The most characteristic building projects of the nineteenth century—railroad stations, exhibition halls, department stores (according to Giedion)—all have matters of collective importance as their object. The flâneur feels drawn to these "despised, everyday" structures, as Giedion calls them. In these constructions, the appearance of great masses on the stage of history was already foreseen. They form the eccentric frame within which the last privateers so readily displayed themselves. (See K1a,5.) [M21a,2]

[On the Theory of Knowledge, Theory of Progress]

> Times are more interesting than people.
>
> —Honoré de Balzac, *Critique littéraire,* Introduction by Louis Lumet
> (Paris, 1912), p. 103 [Guy de la Ponneraye, *Histoire de l'Amiral
> Coligny*]

> The reform of consciousness consists *solely* in . . . the awaken-
> ing of the world from its dream about itself.
>
> —Karl Marx, *Der historische Materialismus: Die Frühschriften* (Leipzig
> ‹1932›), vol. 1, p. 226 (letter from Marx to Ruge; Kreuzenach, Sep-
> tember 1843)[1]

In the fields with which we are concerned, knowledge comes only in lightning
flashes. The text is the long roll of thunder that follows.   [N1,1]

Comparison of other people's attempts to the undertaking of a sea voyage in
which the ships are drawn off course by the magnetic North Pole. Discover *this*
North Pole. What for others are deviations are, for me, the data which determine
my course.—On the differentials of time (which, for others, disturb the main
lines of the inquiry), I base my reckoning.   [N1,2]

Say something about the method of composition itself: how everything one is
thinking at a specific moment in time must at all costs be incorporated into the
project then at hand. Assume that the intensity of the project is thereby attested,
or that one's thoughts, from the very beginning, bear this project within them as
their telos. So it is with the present portion of the work, which aims to characterize and to preserve the intervals of reflection, the distances lying between the
most essential parts of this work, which are turned most intensively to the outside.   [N1,3]

To cultivate fields where, until now, only madness has reigned. Forge ahead with
the whetted axe of reason, looking neither right nor left so as not to succumb to
the horror that beckons from deep in the primeval forest. Every ground must at
some point have been made arable by reason, must have been cleared of the

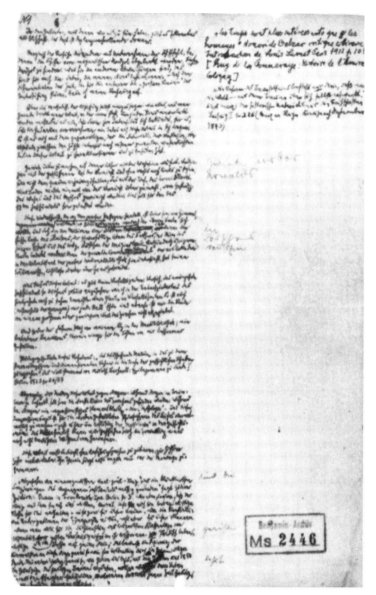

A page of Benjamin's manuscript, showing the beginning of
Convolute N.

undergrowth of delusion and myth. This is to be accomplished here for the
terrain of the nineteenth century.   [N1,4]

These notes devoted to the Paris arcades were begun under an open sky of
cloudless blue that arched above the foliage; and yet—owing to the millions of
leaves that were visited by the fresh breeze of diligence, the stertorous breath of
the researcher, the storm of youthful zeal, and the idle wind of curiosity—they've
been covered with the dust of centuries. For the painted sky of summer that looks

down from the arcades in the reading room of the Bibliothèque Nationale in Paris has spread out over them its dreamy, unlit ceiling. [N1,5]

The pathos of this work: there are no periods of decline. Attempt to see the nineteenth century just as positively as I tried to see the seventeenth, in the work on *Trauerspiel*. No belief in periods of decline. By the same token, every city is beautiful to me (from outside its borders), just as all talk of particular languages' having greater or lesser value is to me unacceptable. [N1,6]

And, later, the glassed-in spot facing my seat at the Staatsbibliothek. Charmed circle inviolate, virgin terrain for the soles of figures I conjured. [N1,7]

Pedagogic side of this undertaking: "To educate the image-making medium within us, raising it to a stereoscopic and dimensional seeing into the depths of historical shadows." The words are Rudolf Borchardt's in *Epilegomena zu Dante,* vol. 1 (Berlin, 1923), pp. 56–57. [N1,8]

Delimitation of the tendency of this project with respect to Aragon: whereas Aragon persists within the realm of dream, here the concern is to find the constellation of awakening. While in Aragon there remains an impressionistic element, namely the "mythology" (and this impressionism must be held responsible for the many vague philosophemes in his book),[2] here it is a question of the dissolution of "mythology" into the space of history. That, of course, can happen only through the awakening of a not-yet-conscious knowledge of what has been. [N1,9]

This work has to develop to the highest degree the art of citing without quotation marks. Its theory is intimately related to that of montage. [N1,10]

"Apart from a certain *haut-goût* charm," says Giedion, "the artistic draperies and wall-hangings of the previous century have come to seem musty." ⟨Sigfried⟩ Giedion, *Bauen in Frankreich* (Leipzig and Berlin ⟨1928⟩), p. 3. We, however, believe that the charm they exercise on us is proof that these things, too, contain material of vital importance for us—not indeed for our building practice, as is the case with the constructive possibilities inherent in iron frameworks, but rather for our understanding, for the radioscopy, if you will, of the situation of the bourgeois class at the moment it evinces the first signs of decline. In any case, material of vital importance politically; this is demonstrated by the attachment of the Surrealists to these things, as much as by their exploitation in contemporary fashion. In other words: just as Giedion teaches us to read off the basic features of today's architecture in the buildings erected around 1850, we, in turn, would recognize today's life, today's forms, in the life and in the apparently secondary, lost forms of that epoch. [N1,11]

"In the windswept stairways of the Eiffel Tower, or, better still, in the steel supports of a Pont Transbordeur, one meets with the fundamental aesthetic experience of present-day architecture: through the thin net of iron that hangs suspended in the air, things stream—ships, ocean, houses, masts, landscape, harbor. They lose their distinctive shape, swirl into one another as we climb downward, merge simultaneously." Sigfried Giedion, *Bauen in Frankreich* (Leipzig and Berlin), p. 7. In the same way, the historian today has only to erect a slender but sturdy scaffolding—a philosophic structure—in order to draw the most vital aspects of the past into his net. But just as the magnificent vistas of the city provided by the new construction in iron (again, see Giedion, illustrations on pp. 61–63) for a long time were reserved exclusively for the workers and engineers, so too the philosopher who wishes here to garner fresh perspectives must be someone immune to vertigo—an independent and, if need be, solitary worker.
[N1a,1]

The book on the Baroque exposed the seventeenth century to the light of the present day. Here, something analogous must be done for the nineteenth century, but with greater distinctness.
[N1a,2]

Modest methodological proposal for the cultural-historical dialectic. It is very easy to establish oppositions, according to determinate points of view, within the various "fields" of any epoch, such that on one side lies the "productive," "forward-looking," "lively," "positive" part of the epoch, and on the other side the abortive, retrograde, and obsolescent. The very contours of the positive element will appear distinctly only insofar as this element is set off against the negative. On the other hand, every negation has its value solely as background for the delineation of the lively, the positive. It is therefore of decisive importance that a new partition be applied to this initially excluded, negative component so that, by a displacement of the angle of vision (but not of the criteria!), a positive element emerges anew in it too—something different from that previously signified. And so on, ad infinitum, until the entire past is brought into the present in a historical apocatastasis.[3]
[N1a,3]

The foregoing, put differently: the indestructibility of the highest life in all things. Against the prognosticators of decline. Consider, though: Isn't it an affront to Goethe to make a film of *Faust,* and isn't there a world of difference between the poem *Faust* and the film *Faust?* Yes, certainly. But, again, isn't there a whole world of difference between a bad film of *Faust* and a good one? What matter are never the "great" but only the dialectical contrasts, which often seem indistinguishable from nuances. It is nonetheless from them that life is always born anew.
[N1a,4]

To encompass both Breton and Le Corbusier—that would mean drawing the spirit of contemporary France like a bow, with which knowledge shoots the moment in the heart.
[N1a,5]

Marx lays bare the causal connection between economy and culture. For us, what matters is the thread of expression. It is not the economic origins of culture that will be presented, but the expression of the economy in its culture. At issue, in other words, is the attempt to grasp an economic process as perceptible *Ur*-phenomenon, from out of which proceed all manifestations of life in the arcades (and, accordingly, in the nineteenth century).   [N1a,6]

This research—which deals fundamentally with the expressive character of the earliest industrial products, the earliest industrial architecture, the earliest machines, but also the earliest department stores, advertisements, and so on—thus becomes important for Marxism in two ways. First, it will demonstrate how the milieu in which Marx's doctrine arose affected that doctrine through its expressive character (which is to say, not only through causal connections); but, second, it will also show in what respects Marxism, too, shares the expressive character of the material products contemporary with it.   [N1a,7]

Method of this project: literary montage. I needn't *say* anything. Merely show. I shall purloin no valuables, appropriate no ingenious formulations. But the rags, the refuse—these I will not inventory but allow, in the only way possible, to come into their own: by making use of them.   [N1a,8]

Bear in mind that commentary on a reality (for it is a question here of commentary, of interpretation in detail) calls for a method completely different from that required by commentary on a text. In the one case, the scientific mainstay is theology; in the other case, philology.   [N2,1]

It may be considered one of the methodological objectives of this work to demonstrate a historical materialism which has annihilated within itself the idea of progress. Just here, historical materialism has every reason to distinguish itself sharply from bourgeois habits of thought. Its founding concept is not progress but actualization.   [N2,2]

Historical "understanding" is to be grasped, in principle, as an afterlife of that which is understood; and what has been recognized in the analysis of the "afterlife of works," in the analysis of "fame," is therefore to be considered the foundation of history in general.   [N2,3]

How this work was written: rung by rung, according as chance would offer a narrow foothold, and always like someone who scales dangerous heights and never allows himself a moment to look around, for fear of becoming dizzy (but also because he would save for the end the full force of the panorama opening out to him).   [N2,4]

Overcoming the concept of "progress" and overcoming the concept of "period of decline" are two sides of one and the same thing.   [N2,5]

A central problem of historical materialism that ought to be seen in the end: Must the Marxist understanding of history necessarily be acquired at the expense of the perceptibility of history? Or: in what way is it possible to conjoin a heightened graphicness ‹*Anschaulichkeit*› to the realization of the Marxist method? The first stage in this undertaking will be to carry over the principle of montage into history. That is, to assemble large-scale constructions out of the smallest and most precisely cut components. Indeed, to discover in the analysis of the small individual moment the crystal of the total event. And, therefore, to break with vulgar historical naturalism. To grasp the construction of history as such. In the structure of commentary. ☐ Refuse of History ☐ [N2,6]

A Kierkegaard citation in Wiesengrund, with commentary following: "'One may arrive at a similar consideration of the mythical by beginning with the imagistic. When, in an age of reflection, one sees the imagistic protrude ever so slightly and unobserved in a reflective representation and, like an antediluvian fossil, suggest another species of existence which washed away doubt, one will perhaps be amazed that the image could ever have played such an important role.' Kierkegaard wards off the 'amazement' with what follows. Yet this amazement heralds the deepest insight into the interrelation of dialectic, myth, and image. For it is not as the continuously living and present that nature prevails in the dialectic. Dialectic comes to a stop in the image, and, in the context of recent history, it cites the mythical as what is long gone: nature as primal history. For this reason, the images—which, like those of the *intérieur*, bring dialectic and myth to the point of indifferentiation—are truly 'antediluvian fossils.' They may be called dialectical images, to use Benjamin's expression, whose compelling definition of 'allegory' also holds true for Kierkegaard's allegorical intention taken as a figure of historical dialectic and mythical nature. According to this definition, 'in allegory the observer is confronted with the *facies hippocratica* of history, a petrified primordial landscape.'" Theodor Wiesengrund-Adorno, *Kierkegaard* (Tübingen, 1933), p. 60.[4] ☐ Refuse of History ☐ [N2,7]

Only a thoughtless observer can deny that correspondences come into play between the world of modern technology and the archaic symbol-world of mythology. Of course, initially the technologically new seems nothing more than that. But in the very next childhood memory, its traits are already altered. Every childhood achieves something great and irreplaceable for humanity. By the interest it takes in technological phenomena, by the curiosity it displays before any sort of invention or machinery, every childhood binds the accomplishments of technology to the old worlds of symbol. There is nothing in the realm of nature that from the outset would be exempt from such a bond. Only, it takes form not in the aura of novelty but in the aura of the habitual. In memory, childhood, and dream. ☐ Awakening ☐ [N2a,1]

The momentum of primal history in the past is no longer masked, as it used to be, by the tradition of church and family—this at once the consequence and condition of technology. The old prehistoric dread already envelops the world of our parents because we ourselves are no longer bound to this world by tradition. The perceptual worlds ‹*Merkwelten*› break up more rapidly; what they contain of the mythic comes more quickly and more brutally to the fore; and a wholly different perceptual world must be speedily set up to oppose it. This is how the accelerated tempo of technology appears in light of the primal history of the present. ☐ Awakening ☐ [N2a,2]

It's not that what is past casts its light on what is present, or what is present its light on what is past; rather, image is that wherein what has been comes together in a flash with the now to form a constellation. In other words, image is dialectics at a standstill. For while the relation of the present to the past is a purely temporal, continuous one, the relation of what-has-been to the now is dialectical: is not progression but image, suddenly emergent.—Only dialectical images are genuine images (that is, not archaic); and the place where one encounters them is language. ☐ Awakening ☐ [N2a,3]

In studying Simmel's presentation of Goethe's concept of truth,[5] I came to see very clearly that my concept of origin in the *Trauerspiel* book is a rigorous and decisive transposition of this basic Goethean concept from the domain of nature to that of history. Origin—it is, in effect, the concept of *Ur*-phenomenon extracted from the pagan context of nature and brought into the Jewish contexts of history. Now, in my work on the arcades I am equally concerned with fathoming an origin. To be specific, I pursue the origin of the forms and mutations of the Paris arcades from their beginning to their decline, and I locate this origin in the economic facts. Seen from the standpoint of causality, however (and that means considered as causes), these facts would not be primal phenomena; they become such only insofar as in their own individual development—"unfolding" might be a better term—they give rise to the whole series of the arcade's concrete historical forms, just as the leaf unfolds from itself all the riches of the empirical world of plants. [N2a,4]

"As I study this age which is so close to us and so remote, I compare myself to a surgeon operating with local anesthetic: I work in areas that are numb, dead—yet the patient is alive and can still talk." Paul Morand, *1900* (Paris, 1931), pp. 6–7. [N2a,5]

What distinguishes images from the "essences" of phenomenology is their historical index. (Heidegger seeks in vain to rescue history for phenomenology abstractly through "historicity.")[6] These images are to be thought of entirely apart from the categories of the "human sciences," from so-called habitus, from style, and the like. For the historical index of the images not only says that they belong to a particular time; it says, above all, that they attain to legibility only at a particular time. And, indeed, this acceding "to legibility" constitutes a specific critical point in the movement at their interior. Every present day is determined by the images that are synchronic with it: each "now" is the now of a particular recognizability. In it, truth is charged to the bursting point with time. (This point of explosion, and nothing else, is the death of the *intentio,* which thus coincides with the birth of authentic historical time, the time of truth.) It is not that what is past casts its light on what is present, or what is present its light on what is past; rather, image is that wherein what has been comes together in a flash with the now to form a constellation. In other words: image is dialectics at a standstill. For while the relation of the present to the past is purely temporal, the relation of what-has-been to the now is dialectical: not temporal in nature but figural ‹*bildlich*›. Only dialectical images are genuinely historical—that is, not archaic—images. The image that is read—which is to say, the image in the now of its recognizability—bears to the highest degree the imprint of the perilous critical moment on which all reading is founded. [N3,1]

Resolute refusal of the concept of "timeless truth" is in order. Nevertheless, truth is not—as Marxism would have it—a merely contingent function of knowing, but is bound to a nucleus of time lying hidden within the knower and the known alike. This is so true that the eternal, in any case, is far more the ruffle on a dress than some idea. [N3,2]

Outline the story of *The Arcades Project* in terms of its development. Its properly problematic component: the refusal to renounce anything that would demonstrate the materialist presentation of history as imagistic ‹*bildhaft*› in a higher sense than in the traditional presentation. [N3,3]

A remark by Ernst Bloch apropos of *The Arcades Project:* "History displays its Scotland Yard badge." It was in the context of a conversation in which I was describing how this work—comparable, in method, to the process of splitting the atom—liberates the enormous energies of history that are bound up in the "once upon a time" of classical historiography. The history that showed things "as they really were" was the strongest narcotic of the century. [N3,4]

"The truth will not escape us," reads one of Keller's epigrams.[7] He thus formulates the concept of truth with which these presentations take issue. [N3a,1]

"Primal history of the nineteenth century"—this would be of no interest if it were understood to mean that forms of primal history are to be recovered among the inventory of the nineteenth century. Only where the nineteenth century would be presented as originary form of primal history—in a form, that is to say, in which the whole of primal history groups itself anew in images appropriate to that century—only there does the concept of a primal history of the nineteenth century have meaning. [N3a,2]

Is awakening perhaps the synthesis of dream consciousness (as thesis) and waking consciousness (as antithesis)? Then the moment of awakening would be identical with the "now of recognizability," in which things put on their true—surrealist—face. Thus, in Proust, the importance of staking an entire life on life's supremely dialectical point of rupture: awakening. Proust begins with an evocation of the space of someone waking up. [N3a,3]

"If I insist on this mechanism of contradiction in the biography of a writer . . . , it is because his train of thought cannot bypass certain facts which have a logic different from that of his thought by itself. It is because there is no idea he adheres to that truly holds up . . . in the face of certain very simple, elemental facts: that workers are staring down the barrels of cannons aimed at them by police, that war is threatening, and that fascism is already enthroned. . . . It behooves a man, for the sake of his dignity, to submit his ideas to these facts, and not to bend these facts, by some conjuring trick, to his ideas, however ingenious." Aragon, "D'Alfred de Vigny à Avdeenko," *Commune,* 2 (April 20, 1935), pp. 808–809. But it is entirely possible that, in contradicting my past, I will establish a continuity with that of another, which he in turn, as communist, will contradict. In this case, with the past of Louis Aragon, who in this same essay disavows his *Paysan de Paris:* "And, like most of my friends, I was partial to the failures, to what is monstrous and cannot survive, cannot succeed. . . . I was like them: I preferred error to its opposite" (p. 807). [N3a,4]

In the dialectical image, what has been within a particular epoch is always, simultaneously, "what has been from time immemorial." As such, however, it is manifest, on each occasion, only to a quite specific epoch—namely, the one in which humanity, rubbing its eyes, recognizes just this particular dream image as such. It is at this moment that the historian takes up, with regard to that image, the task of dream interpretation. [N4,1]

The expression "the book of nature" indicates that one can read the real like a text. And that is how the reality of the nineteenth century will be treated here. We open the book of what happened. [N4,2]

Just as Proust begins the story of his life with an awakening, so must every presentation of history begin with awakening; in fact, it should treat of nothing else. This one, accordingly, deals with awakening from the nineteenth century. [N4,3]

The realization of dream elements in the course of waking up is the canon of dialectics. It is paradigmatic for the thinker and binding for the historian. [N4,4]

Raphael seeks to correct the Marxist conception of the normative character of Greek art: "If the normative character of Greek art is . . . an explicable fact of history, . . . we will have . . . to determine . . . what special conditions led to each renascence and, in consequence, what special factors of . . . Greek art these renascences adopted as models. For the totality of Greek art never possessed a normative character; the renascences . . . have their own proper history. . . . Only a historical analysis can indicate the era in which the abstract notion of a 'norm' . . . of antiquity was born. . . . This notion was created solely by the Renaissance—that is, by primitive capitalism—and subsequently taken up by classicism, which . . . commenced to assign it its place in a historical sequence. Marx has not advanced along this way in the full measure of the possibilities of historical materialism." Max Raphael, *Proudhon, Marx, Picasso* (Paris ‹1933›), pp. 178–179.

[N4,5]

It is the peculiarity of *technological* forms of production (as opposed to art forms) that their progress and their success are proportionate to the *transparency* of their social content. (Hence glass architecture.)

[N4,6]

An important passage in Marx: "It is recognized that where . . . the epic, for example, . . . is concerned, . . . certain significant creations within the compass of art are possible only at an early stage of artistic development. If this is the case with regard to different branches of art within the sphere of the arts, it is not so remarkable that this should also be the case with regard to the whole artistic realm and its relation to the general development of the society." Cited without references (perhaps *Theorien des Mehrwerts,* vol. 1?)[8] in Max Raphael, *Proudhon, Marx, Picasso* (Paris ‹1933›), p. 160.

[N4a,1]

The Marxian theory of art: one moment swaggering, and the next scholastic.

[N4a,2]

Proposal for a gradation of the superstructure, in A. Asturaro, *Il materialismo storico e la sociologia generale* (Genoa, 1904) (reviewed by Erwin Szabó in *Die neue Zeit,* 23, no. 1 [Stuttgart], p. 62): "Economy. Family and kinship. Law. War. Politics. Morality. Religion. Art. Science."

[N4a,3]

Strange remark by Engels concerning the "social forces": "But when once their nature is understood, they can, in the hands of the producers working together, be transformed from master demons into willing servants." (!) Engels, *Die Entwicklung des Sozialismus von der Utopie zur Wissenschaft* (1882).[9]

[N4a,4]

Marx, in the afterword to the second edition of *Das Kapital:* "Research has to appropriate the material in detail, to analyze its various forms of development, to trace out their inner connection. Only after this work is done can the actual movement be presented in corresponding fashion. If this is done successfully, if the life of the material is reflected back as ideal, then it may appear as if we had before us an a priori construction." Karl Marx, *Das Kapital,* vol 1, ed. Korsch (Berlin ‹1932›), p. 45.[10]

[N4a,5]

The particular difficulty of doing historical research on the period following the close of the eighteenth century will be displayed. With the rise of the mass-circulation press, the sources become innumerable.   [N4a,6]

Michelet is perfectly willing to let the people be known as "barbarians." "'Barbarians.' I like the word, and I accept the term." And he says of their writers: "Their love is boundless and sometimes too great, for they may devote themselves to details with the delightful awkwardness of Albrecht Dürer, or with the excessive polish of Jean-Jacques Rousseau, who does not conceal his art enough; and by this minute detail they compromise the whole. We must not blame them too much. It is . . . the luxuriance of their sap and vigor. . . . This sap wants to give everything at once—leaves, fruit, and flowers; it bends and twists the branches. These defects of many great workers are often found in my books, which lack their good qualities. No matter!" J. Michelet, *Le Peuple* (Paris, 1846), pp. xxxvi–xxxvii.[11]   [N5,1]

Letter from Wiesengrund of August 5, 1935: "The attempt to reconcile your 'dream' momentum—as the subjective element in the dialectical image—with the conception of the latter as model has led me to some formulations . . . : With the vitiation of their use value, the alienated things are hollowed out and, as ciphers, they draw in meanings. Subjectivity takes possession of them insofar as it invests them with intentions of desire and fear. And insofar as defunct things stand in as images of subjective intentions, these latter present themselves as immemorial and eternal. Dialectical images are constellated between alienated things and incoming and disappearing meaning, are instantiated in the moment of indifference between death and meaning. While things in appearance are awakened to what is newest, death transforms the meanings to what is most ancient." With regard to these reflections, it should be kept in mind that, in the nineteenth century, the number of "hollowed-out" things increases at a rate and on a scale that was previously unknown, for technical progress is continually withdrawing newly introduced objects from circulation.   [N5,2]

"The critic can start from any form of theoretical or practical consciousness, and develop out of the actual forms of existing reality the true reality as what it ought to be, that which is its aim." Karl Marx, *Der historische Materialismus: Die Frühschriften,* ed. Landshut and Mayer (Leipzig ‹1932›), vol. 1, p. 225 (letter from Marx to Ruge; Kreuzenach, September 1843).[12] The point of departure invoked here by Marx need not necessarily connect with the latest stage of development. It can be undertaken with regard to long-vanished epochs whose "ought to be" and whose aim is then to be presented—not in reference to the next stage of development, but in its own right and as preformation of the final goal of history.   [N5,3]

Engels says (*Marx und Engels über Feuerbach: Aus dem Nachlass,* Marx-Engels Archiv, ed. Rjazanov, vol. 1 [Frankfurt am Main ‹1928›], p. 300): "It must not be forgotten that law has just as little an independent history as religion."[13] What holds for law and religion holds for culture even more. It would be absurd for us to conceive of the classless society, its forms of existence, in the image of cultural humanity. [N5,4]

"Our election cry must be: Reform of consciousness not through dogmas, but through the analysis of mystical consciousness that is unclear to itself, whether it appears in a religious or a political form. Then people will see that the world has long possessed the dream of a thing—and that it only needs to possess the consciousness of this thing in order really to possess it." Karl Marx, *Der historische Materialismus: Die Frühschriften*, ed. Landshut and Mayer (Leipzig ‹1932›), vol. 1, pp. 226–227 (letter from Marx to Ruge; Kreuzenach, September 1843).[14]
[N5a,1]

A reconciled humanity will take leave of its past—and *one* form of reconciliation is gaiety. "The present German regime . . . , the nullity of the ancien régime exhibited for all the world to see, . . . is only the *comedian* of a world order whose *real heroes* are dead. History is thorough, and passes through many stages when she carries a worn-out form to burial. The last stage of a world-historical form is its *comedy*. The gods of Greece, who had already been mortally wounded in the *Prometheus Bound* of Aeschylus, had to die yet again—this time a comic death—in the dialogues of Lucian. Why does history follow this course? So that mankind may take leave of its past *gaily*." Karl Marx, *Der historische Materialismus: Die Frühschriften,* ed. Landshut and Mayer (Leipzig), vol. 1, pp. 268 ("Zur Kritik der Hegelschen *Rechtsphilosophie*").[15] Surrealism is the death of the nineteenth century in comedy. [N5a,2]

Marx (*Marx und Engels über Feuerbach: Aus dem Nachlass*, Marx-Engels Archiv, vol. 1 [Frankfurt am Main ‹1928›], p. 301): "There is no history of politics, law, science, etc., of art, religion, etc."[16] [N5a,3]

Die heilige Familie, on the subject of Bacon's materialism: "Matter, surrounded by a sensuous poetic glamor, seems to attract man's whole entity with winning smiles."[17] [N5a,4]

"I regret having treated in only a very incomplete manner those facts of daily existence—food, clothing, shelter, family routines, civil law, recreation, social relations—which have always been of prime concern in the life of the great majority of individuals." Charles Seignobos, *Histoire sincère de la nation française* (Paris, 1933), p. xi. [N5a,5]

Ad notam a formula of Valéry's: "What distinguishes a truly general phenomenon is its fertility."[18] [N5a,6]

Barbarism lurks in the very concept of culture—as the concept of a fund of values which is considered independent not, indeed, of the production process in which these values originated, but of the one in which they survive. In this way they serve the apotheosis of the latter ‹word uncertain›, barbaric as it may be.

[N5a,7]

To determine how the concept of culture arose, what meaning it has had in different periods, and what needs its institution corresponded to. It could, insofar as it signifies the sum of "cultural riches," turn out to be of recent origin; certainly it is not yet found, for example, in the cleric of the early Middle Ages who waged his war of annihilation against the teachings of antiquity.   [N6,1]

Michelet—an author who, wherever he is quoted, makes the reader forget the book in which the quotation appears.   [N6,2]

To be underlined: the painstaking delineation of the scene in the first writings on social problems and charity, like Naville, *De la Charité légale;* Frégier, *Des Classes dangereuses;* and various others.   [N6,3]

"I cannot insist too strongly on the fact that, for an enlightened materialist like Lafargue, economic determinism is not the 'absolutely perfect instrument' which 'can provide the key to all the problems of history.'" André Breton, *Position politique du surréalisme* (Paris ‹1935›), pp. 8–9.   [N6,4]

All historical knowledge can be represented in the image of balanced scales, one tray of which is weighted with what has been and the other with knowledge of what is present. Whereas on the first the facts assembled can never be too humble or too numerous, on the second there can be only a few heavy, massive weights.   [N6,5]

"The only attitude worthy of philosophy . . . in the industrial era is . . . restraint. The 'scientificity' of a Marx does not mean that philosophy renounces its task . . . ; rather, it indicates that philosophy holds itself in reserve until the predominance of an unworthy reality is broken." Hugo Fischer, *Karl Marx und sein Verhältnis zu Staat und Wirtschaft* (Jena, 1932), p. 59.   [N6,6]

It is not without significance that Engels, in the context of the materialist conception of history, lays emphasis on classicality. For the demonstration of the dialectic of development, he refers to laws "which the actual historical process itself provides, insofar as every momentum can be considered to be at the point of its full ripening, its classicality." Cited in Gustav Mayer, *Friedrich Engels,* vol. 2, *Engels und der Aufstieg der Arbeiterbewegung in Europa* (Berlin ‹1933›), pp. 434–435.   [N6,7]

Engels in a letter to Mehring, July 14, 1893: "It is above all this semblance of an independent history of state constitutions, of systems of law, of ideological conceptions in every separate domain, that dazzles most people. If Luther and Calvin 'overcome' the official Catholic religion, or Hegel 'overcomes' Fichte and Kant, or Rousseau with his republican *Contrat social* indirectly 'overcomes' the constitutional Montesquieu, this is a process which remains within theology, philosophy, or political science, represents a stage in the history of these particular spheres of thought and never passes beyond the sphere of thought. And since the bourgeois illusion of the eternity and finality of capitalist production has been added to this, even the overcoming of the mercantilists by the physiocrats and Adam Smith is regarded as a sheer victory of thought; not as the reflection in thought of changed economic facts, but as the finally achieved correct understanding of actual conditions subsisting always and everywhere."[19] Cited in Gustav Mayer, *Friedrich Engels*, vol. 2, *Engels und der Aufstieg der Arbeiterbewegung in Europa* (Berlin), pp. 450–451. [N6a,1]

"What Schlosser could say in response to these reproaches [of peevish moral rigor], and what he *would* say, is this: that history and life in general, unlike novels and stories, do not teach a lesson of superficial joie de vivre, even to the happily constituted spirit and senses; that the contemplation of history is more likely to inspire, if not contempt for humanity, then a somber vision of the world and strict principles for living; that, at least on the very greatest judges of the world and humankind, on men who knew how to measure outward affairs by their own inner life, on a Shakespeare, Dante, or Machiavelli, the way of the world always made the sort of impression that conduces to seriousness and severity." G. G. Gervinus, *Friedrich Christoph Schlosser* (Leipzig, 1861), in *Deutsche Denkreden*, ed. Rudolf Borchardt (Munich, 1925), p. 312. [N6a,2]

The relation of tradition to the technology of reproduction deserves to be studied. "Traditions . . . relate to written communications, in general, as reproduction of the latter by pen relates to reproduction by the press, as successive copies of a book relate to its simultaneous printings." Carl Gustav Jochmann, *Ueber die Sprache* (Heidelberg, 1828), pp. 259–260 ("Die Rückschritte der Poesie").[20]
[N6a,3]

Roger Caillois, "Paris, mythe moderne" (*Nouvelle Revue française,* 25, no. 284 [May 1, 1937], p. 699), gives a list of the investigations that one would have to undertake in order to illuminate the subject further. (1) Descriptions of Paris that antedate the nineteenth century (Marivaux, Restif de La Bretonne); (2) the struggle between Girondists and Jacobins over the relation of Paris to the provinces; the legend of the days of revolution in Paris; (3) secret police under the Empire and the Restoration; (4) *peinture morale* of Paris in Hugo, Balzac, Baudelaire; (5) objective descriptions of the city: Dulaure, Du Camp; (6) Vigny, Hugo (Paris aflame in *L'Année terrible*), Rimbaud. [N7,1]

Still to be established is the connection between presence of mind and the "method" of dialectical materialism. It's not just that one will always be able to detect a dialectical process in presence of mind, regarded as one of the highest forms of appropriate behavior. What is even more decisive is that the dialectician cannot look on history as anything other than a constellation of dangers which he is always, as he follows its development in his thought, on the point of averting. [N7,2]

"Revolution is a drama perhaps more than a history, and its pathos is a condition as imperious as its authenticity." Blanqui, cited in Geffroy, *L'Enfermé* (Paris, 1926), vol. 1, p. 232. [N7,3]

Necessity of paying heed over many years to every casual citation, every fleeting mention of a book. [N7,4]

To contrast the theory of history with the observation by Grillparzer which Edmond Jaloux translates in "Journaux intimes" (*Le Temps,* May 23, 1937): "To read into the future is difficult, but to see *purely* into the past is more difficult still. I say *purely,* that is, without involving in this retrospective glance anything that has taken place in the meantime." The "purity" of the gaze is not just difficult but impossible to attain. [N7,5]

It is important for the materialist historian, in the most rigorous way possible, to differentiate the construction of a historical state of affairs from what one customarily calls its "reconstruction." The "reconstruction" in empathy is one-dimensional. "Construction" presupposes "destruction." [N7,6]

In order for a part of the past to be touched by the present instant ‹*Aktualität*›, there must be no continuity between them. [N7,7]

The fore- and after-history of a historical phenomenon show up in the phenomenon itself on the strength of its dialectical presentation. What is more: every dialectically presented historical circumstance polarizes itself and becomes a force field in which the confrontation between its fore-history and after-history is played out. It becomes such a field insofar as the present instant interpenetrates it. ‹See N7a, 8.› And thus the historical evidence polarizes into fore- and after-history always anew, never in the same way. And it does so at a distance from its own existence, in the present instant itself—like a line which, divided according to the Apollonian section,[21] experiences its partition from outside itself. [N7a,1]

Historical materialism aspires to neither a homogeneous nor a continuous exposition of history. From the fact that the superstructure reacts upon the base, it follows that a homogeneous history, say, of economics exists as little as a homogeneous history of literature or of jurisprudence. On the other hand, since the different epochs of the past are not all touched in the same degree by the present day of the historian (and often the recent past is not touched at all; the present fails to "do it justice"), continuity in the presentation of history is unattainable.
  [N7a,2]

Telescoping of the past through the present. [N7a,3]

The reception of great, much admired works of art is an *ad plures ire*.[22] [N7a,4]

The materialist presentation of history leads the past to bring the present into a critical state. [N7a,5]

It is my intention to withstand what Valéry calls "a reading slowed by and bristling with the resistances of a refined and fastidious reader." Charles Baudelaire, *Les Fleurs du mal,* Introduction by Paul Valéry (Paris, 1928), p. xiii.[23]

[N7a,6]

My thinking is related to theology as blotting pad is related to ink. It is saturated with it. Were one to go by the blotter, however, nothing of what is written would remain. [N7a,7]

It is the present that polarizes the event into fore- and after-history. [N7a,8]

On the question of the incompleteness of history, Horkheimer's letter of March 16, 1937: "The determination of incompleteness is idealistic if completeness is not comprised within it. Past injustice has occurred and is completed. The slain are really slain. . . . If one takes the lack of closure entirely seriously, one must believe in the Last Judgment. . . . Perhaps, with regard to incompleteness, there is a difference between the positive and the negative, so that only the injustice, the horror, the sufferings of the past are irreparable. The justice practiced, the joys, the works, have a different relation to time, for their positive character is largely negated by the transience of things. This holds first and foremost for individual existence, in which it is not the happiness but the unhappiness that is sealed by death." The corrective to this line of thinking may be found in the consideration that history is not simply a science but also and not least a form of remembrance ‹*Eingedenken*›. What science has "determined," remembrance can modify. Such mindfulness can make the incomplete (happiness) into something complete, and the complete (suffering) into something incomplete. That is theology; but in remembrance we have an experience that forbids us to conceive of history as fundamentally atheological, little as it may be granted us to try to write it with immediately theological concepts. [N8,1]

The unequivocally regressive function which the doctrine of archaic images has for Jung comes to light in the following passage from the essay "Über die Beziehungen der analytischen Psychologie zum dichterischen Kunstwerk": "The creative process . . . consists in an unconscious activation of the archetype and in an . . . elaboration of this original image into the finished work. By giving it shape, the artist in some measure translates this image into the language of the present. . . . Therein lies the social significance of art: . . . it conjures up the forms in which the Zeitgeist, the spirit of the age, is most lacking. The unsatisfied yearning of the artist reaches back to the primordial image in the unconscious which is best fitted to compensate the . . . one-sidedness of the spirit of the age. This image his longing seizes on, and as he . . . brings it to consciousness, the image changes its form until it can be accepted by the minds of his contemporaries, according to their powers." C. G. Jung, *Seelenprobleme der Gegenwart* (Zürich, Leipzig, and Stuttgart, 1932), p. 71.[24] Thus, the esoteric theory of art comes down to making archetypes "accessible" to the "Zeitgeist." [N8,2]

In Jung's production there is a belated and particularly emphatic elaboration of one of the elements which, as we can recognize today, were first disclosed in explosive fashion by Expressionism. That element is a specifically clinical nihilism, such as one encounters also in the works of Benn, and which has found a camp follower in Céline. This nihilism is born of the shock imparted by the interior of the body to those who treat it. Jung himself traces the heightened interest in psychic life back to Expressionism. He writes: "Art has a way of anticipating future changes in man's fundamental outlook, and expressionist art has taken this subjective turn well in advance of the more general change." See *Seelenprobleme der Gegenwart* (Zürich, Leipzig, and Stuttgart, 1932), p. 415—"Das Seelenproblem des modernen Menschen").[25] In this regard, we should not lose sight of the relations which Lukács has established between Expressionism and Fascism. (See also K7a,4.) [N8a,1]

"Tradition, errant fable one collects, / Intermittent as the wind in the leaves." Victor Hugo, *La Fin de Satan* (Paris, 1886), p. 235. [N8a,2]

Julien Benda, in *Un Régulier dans le siècle,* cites a phrase from Fustel de Coulanges: "If you want to relive an epoch, forget that you know what has come after it." That is the secret Magna Charta for the presentation of history by the Historical School, and it carries little conviction when Benda adds: "Fustel never said that these measures were valid for understanding the role of an epoch in history." [N8a,3]

Pursue the question of whether a connection exists between the secularization of time in space and the allegorical mode of perception. The former, at any rate (as becomes clear in Blanqui's last writing), is hidden in the "worldview of the natural sciences" of the second half of the century. (Secularization of history in Heidegger.)[26] [N8a,4]

Goethe saw it coming: the crisis in bourgeois education. He confronts it in *Wilhelm Meister.* He characterizes it in his correspondence with Zelter. [N8a,5]

Wilhelm von Humboldt shifts the center of gravity to languages; Marx and Engels shift it to the natural sciences. But the study of languages has economic functions, too. It comes up against global economics, as the study of natural sciences comes up against the production process. [N9,1]

Scientific method is distinguished by the fact that, in leading to new objects, it develops new methods. Just as form in art is distinguished by the fact that, opening up new contents, it develops new forms. It is only from without that a work of art has one and *only* one form, that a treatise has one and *only* one method. [N9,2]

On the concept of "rescue": the wind of the absolute in the sails of the concept. (The principle of the wind is the cyclical.) The trim of the sails is the relative. [N9,3]

What are phenomena rescued from? Not only, and not in the main, from the discredit and neglect into which they have fallen, but from the catastrophe represented very often by a certain strain in their dissemination, their "enshrinement as heritage."—They are saved through the exhibition of the fissure within them.—There is a tradition that is catastrophe. [N9,4]

It is the inherent tendency of dialectical experience to dissipate the semblance of eternal sameness, and even of repetition, in history. Authentic political experience is absolutely free of this semblance. [N9,5]

What matters for the dialectician is to have the wind of world history in his sails. Thinking means for him: setting the sails. What is important is *how* they are set. Words are his sails. The way they are set makes them into concepts. [N9,6]

The dialectical image is an image that emerges suddenly, in a flash. What has been is to be held fast—as an image flashing up in the now of its recognizability. The rescue that is carried out by these means—and only by these—can operate solely for the sake of what in the next moment is already irretrievably lost. In this connection, see the metaphorical passage from my introduction to Jochmann, concerning the prophetic gaze that catches fire from the summits of the past.[27] [N9,7]

Being a dialectician means having the wind of history in one's sails. The sails are the concepts. It is not enough, however, to have sails at one's disposal. What is decisive is knowing the art of setting them. [N9,8]

The concept of progress must be grounded in the idea of catastrophe. That things are "status quo" *is* the catastrophe. It is not an ever-present possibility but what in each case is given. Thus Strindberg (in *To Damascus?*):[28] hell is not something that awaits us, but this life here and now. [N9a,1]

It is good to give materialist investigations a truncated ending. [N9a,2]

To the process of rescue belongs the firm, seemingly brutal grasp. [N9a,3]

The dialectical image is that form of the historical object which satisfies Goethe's requirements for the object of analysis: to exhibit a genuine synthesis. It is the primal phenomenon of history. [N9a,4]

The enshrinement or apologia is meant to cover up the revolutionary moments in the occurrence of history. At heart, it seeks the establishment of a continuity. It sets store only by those elements of a work that have already emerged and played a part in its reception. The places where tradition breaks off—hence its peaks and crags, which offer footing to one who would cross over them—it misses. [N9a,5]

Historical materialism must renounce the epic element in history. It blasts the epoch out of the reified "continuity of history." But it also explodes the homogeneity of the epoch, interspersing it with ruins—that is, with the present. [N9a,6]

In every true work of art there is a place where, for one who removes there, it blows cool like the wind of a coming dawn. From this it follows that art, which has often been considered refractory to every relation with progress, can provide its true definition. Progress has its seat not in the continuity of elapsing time but in its interferences—where the truly new makes itself felt for the first time, with the sobriety of dawn. [N9a,7]

For the materialist historian, every epoch with which he occupies himself is only prehistory for the epoch he himself must live in. And so, for him, there can be no appearance of repetition in history, since precisely those moments in the course of history which matter most to him, by virtue of their index as "fore-history," become moments of the present day and change their specific character according to the catastrophic or triumphant nature of that day. [N9a,8]

Scientific progress—like historical progress—is in each instance merely the first step, never the second, third, or $n + 1$—supposing that these latter ever belonged not just to the workshop of science but to its corpus. That, however, is not in fact the case; for every stage in the dialectical process (like every stage in the process of history itself), conditioned as it always is by every stage preceding, brings into play a fundamentally new tendency, which necessitates a fundamentally new treatment. The dialectical method is thus distinguished by the fact that, in leading to new objects, it develops new methods, just as form in art is distinguished by the fact that it develops new forms in delineating new contents. It is only from without that a work of art has one and *only* one form, that a dialectical treatise has one and *only* one method. [N10,1]

Definitions of basic historical concepts: Catastrophe—to have missed the opportunity. Critical moment—the status quo threatens to be preserved. Progress—the first revolutionary measure taken. [N10,2]

If the object of history is to be blasted out of the continuum of historical succession, that is because its monadological structure demands it. This structure first comes to light in the extracted object itself. And it does so in the form of the historical confrontation that makes up the interior (and, as it were, the bowels) of the historical object, and into which all the forces and interests of history enter on a reduced scale. It is owing to this monadological structure that the historical object finds represented in its interior its own fore-history and after-history. (Thus, for example, the fore-history of Baudelaire, as educed by current scholarship, resides in allegory; his after-history, in Jugendstil.) [N10,3]

Forming the basis of the confrontation with conventional historiography and "enshrinement" is the polemic against empathy (Grillparzer, Fustel de Coulanges). [N10,4]

The Saint-Simonian Barrault distinguishes between *époques organiques* and *époques critiques*. ‹See U15a,4.› The derogation of the critical spirit begins directly after the victory of the bourgeoisie in the July Revolution. [N10,5]

The destructive or critical momentum of materialist historiography is registered in that blasting of historical continuity with which the historical object first constitutes itself. In fact, an object of history cannot be targeted at all within the continuous elapse of history. And so, from time immemorial, historical narration has simply picked out an object from this continuous succession. But it has done so without foundation, as an expedient; and its first thought was then always to reinsert the object into the continuum, which it would create anew through empathy. Materialist historiography does not choose its objects arbitrarily. It does not fasten on them but rather springs them loose from the order of succession. Its provisions are more extensive, its occurrences more essential. [N10a,1]

[For] the destructive momentum in materialist historiography is to be conceived as the reaction to a constellation of dangers, which threatens both the burden of tradition and those who receive it. It is this constellation of dangers which the materialist presentation of history comes to engage. In this constellation is comprised its actuality; against its threat, it must prove its presence of mind. Such a presentation of history has as goal to pass, as Engels puts it, "beyond the sphere of thought."[29] [N10a,2]

To thinking belongs the movement as well as the arrest of thoughts. Where thinking comes to a standstill in a constellation saturated with tensions—there the dialectical image appears. It is the caesura in the movement of thought. Its position is naturally not an arbitrary one. It is to be found, in a word, where the tension between dialectical opposites is greatest. Hence, the object constructed in the materialist presentation of history is itself the dialectical image. The latter is identical with the historical object; it justifies its violent expulsion from the continuum of historical process. [N10a,3]

The archaic form of primal history, which has been summoned up in every epoch and now once more by Jung, is that form which makes semblance in history still more delusive by mandating nature as its homeland. [N11,1]

To write history means giving dates their physiognomy. [N11,2]

The events surrounding the historian, and in which he himself takes part, will underlie his presentation in the form of a text written in invisible ink. The history which he lays before the reader comprises, as it were, the citations occurring in this text, and it is only these citations that occur in a manner legible to all. To write history thus means to *cite* history. It belongs to the concept of citation, however, that the historical object in each case is torn from its context. [N11,3]

On the elementary doctrine of historical materialism. (1) An object of history is that through which knowledge is constituted as the object's rescue. (2) History decays into images, not into stories. (3) Wherever a dialectical process is realized, we are dealing with a monad. (4) The materialist presentation of history carries along with it an immanent critique of the concept of progress. (5) Historical materialism bases its procedures on long experience, common sense, presence of mind, and dialectics. (On the monad: N10a,3.) [N11,4]

The present determines where, in the object from the past, that object's fore-history and after-history diverge so as to circumscribe its nucleus. [N11,5]

To prove by example that only Marxism can practice great philology, where the literature of the previous century is concerned. [N11,6]

"The regions which were the first to become enlightened are not those where the sciences have made the greatest progress." Turgot, *Oeuvres,* vol. 2 (Paris, 1844), pp. 601–602 ("Second discours sur les progrès successifs de l'esprit humain").[30] The thought is taken up in the later literature, and also in Marx. [N11,7]

In the course of the nineteenth century, as the bourgeoisie consolidated its positions of power, the concept of progress would increasingly have forfeited the critical functions it originally possessed. (In this process, the doctrine of natural selection had a decisive role to play: it popularized the notion that progress was automatic. The extension of the concept of progress to the whole of human activity was furthered as a result.) With Turgot, the concept of progress still had its critical functions. In particular, the concept made it possible to direct people's attention to retrograde tendencies in history. Turgot saw progress, characteristically, as guaranteed above all in the realm of mathematical research. [N11a,1]

"But what a spectacle the succession of men's opinions presents! There I seek the progress of the human mind, and I find virtually nothing but the history of its errors. Why is its course—which is so sure, from the very first steps, in the field of

mathematical studies—so unsteady in everything else, and so apt to go astray? . . . In this slow progression of opinions and errors, . . . I fancy that I see those first leaves, those sheaths which nature has given to the newly growing stems of plants, issuing before them from the earth, and withering one by one as other sheaths come into existence, until at last the stem itself makes its appearance and is crowned with flowers and fruit—a symbol of late-emerging truth." Turgot, *Oeuvres,* vol. 2 (Paris, 1844), pp. 600–601 ("Second discours sur les progrès successifs de l'esprit humain").[31]   [N11a,2]

A *limes* to progress still exists in Turgot: "In later times, . . . it was necessary for them, through reflection, to take themselves back to where the first men had been led by blind instinct. And who is not aware that it is here that the supreme effort of reason lies?" Turgot, *Oeuvres,* vol. 2, p. 610.[32] This limit is still present in Marx; later it is lost.   [N11a,3]

Already with Turgot it is evident that the concept of progress is oriented toward science, but has its corrective in art. (At bottom, not even art can be ranged exclusively under the concept of regression; neither does Jochmann's essay develop this concept in an unqualified way.) Of course, Turgot's estimate of art is different from what ours would be today. "Knowledge of nature and of truth is as infinite as they are; the arts, whose aim is to please us, are as limited as we are. Time constantly brings to light new discoveries in the sciences; but poetry, painting, and music have a fixed limit which the genius of languages, the imitation of nature, and the limited sensibility of our organs determine. . . . The great men of the Augustan age reached it, and are still our models." Turgot, *Oeuvres,* vol. 2 (Paris, 1844), pp. 605–606 ("Second discours sur les progrès successifs de l'esprit humain").[33] Thus a programmatic renunciation of originality in art!   [N12,1]

"There are elements of the arts of taste which could be perfected with time—for example, perspective, which depends on optics. But local color, the imitation of nature, and the expression of the passions are of all times." Turgot, *Oeuvres*, vol. 2 (Paris, 1844), p. 658 ("Plan du second discours sur l'histoire universelle").[34]
                                              [N12,2]

Militant representation of progress: "It is not error that is opposed to the progress of truth; it is indolence, obstinacy, the spirit of routine, everything that contributes to inaction.—The progress of even the most peaceful of arts among the ancient peoples of Greece and their republics was punctuated by continual wars. It was like the Jews' building the walls of Jerusalem with one hand while defending them with the other. Their spirits were always in ferment, their hearts always high with adventure; and each day was a further enlightenment." Turgot, *Oeuvres,* vol. 2 (Paris, 1844), pp. 672 ("Pensées et fragments").   [N12,3]

Presence of mind as a political category comes magnificently to life in these words of Turgot: "Before we have learned to deal with things in a given position, they have already changed several times. Thus, we always perceive events too late, and politics always needs to foresee, so to speak, the present." Turgot, *Oeuvres,* vol. 2 (Paris, 1844), p. 673 ("Pensées et fragments").[35]   [N12a,1]

"The . . . radically altered landscape of the nineteenth century remains visible to this day, at least in traces. It was shaped by the railroads. . . . The focal points of this historical landscape are present wherever mountain and tunnel, canyon and viaduct, torrent and funicular, river and iron bridge . . . reveal their kinship. . . . In all their singularity, these things announce that nature has not withdrawn, amid the triumph of technological civilization, into the nameless and inchoate, that the pure construction of bridge or tunnel did not in itself . . . usurp the landscape, but that river and mountain at once took their side, and not as subjugated adversaries but as friendly powers. . . . The iron locomotive that disappears into the mountain tunnel . . . seems . . . to be returning to its native element, where the raw material out of which it was made lies slumbering." Dolf Sternberger, *Panorama, oder Ansichten vom 19. Jahrhundert* (Hamburg, 1938), pp. 34–35.   [N12a,2]

The concept of progress had to run counter to the critical theory of history from the moment it ceased to be applied as a criterion to specific historical developments and instead was required to measure the span between a legendary inception and a legendary end of history. In other words: as soon as it becomes the signature of historical process *as a whole,* the concept of progress bespeaks an uncritical hypostatization rather than a critical interrogation. This latter may be recognized, in the concrete exposition of history, from the fact that it outlines regression at least as sharply as it brings any progress into view. (Thus Turgot, Jochmann.)   [N13,1]

Lotze as critic of the concept of progress: "In opposition to the readily accepted doctrine that the progress of humanity is ever onward and upward, more cautious reflection has been forced to make the discovery that the course of history takes the form of spirals—some prefer to say epicycloids. In short, there has never been a dearth of thoughtful but veiled acknowledgments that the impression produced by history on the whole, far from being one of unalloyed exultation, is preponderantly melancholy. Unprejudiced consideration will always lament and wonder to see how many advantages of civilization and special charms of life are lost, never to reappear in their integrity." Hermann Lotze, *Mikrokosmos,* vol. 3 (Leipzig, 1864), p. 21.[36]   [N13,2]

Lotze as critic of the concept of progress: "It is not . . . clear how we are to imagine one course of education as applying to successive generations of men, allowing the later of these to partake of the fruits produced by the unrewarded efforts and often by the misery of those who went before. To hold that the claims of particular times and individual men may be scorned and all their misfortunes disregarded if only mankind would improve overall is, though suggested by noble feelings, merely enthusiastic thoughtlessness. . . . Nothing is progress which does not mean an increase of happiness and perfection for those very souls which had suffered in a previous imperfect state." Hermann Lotze, *Mikrokosmos,* vol. 3 (Leipzig, 1864), p. 23.[37] If the idea of progress extended over the totality of recorded history is something peculiar to the satiated bourgeoisie, then Lotze represents the reserves called up by those on the defensive. But contrast Hölderlin: "I love the race of men who are coming in the next centuries."[38]   [N13,3]

A thought-provoking observation: "It is one of the most noteworthy peculiarities of the human heart . . . that so much selfishness in individuals coexists with the general lack of envy which every present day feels toward its future." This lack of envy indicates that the idea we have of happiness is deeply colored by the time in which we live. Happiness for us is thinkable only in the air that we have breathed, among the people who have lived with us. In other words, there vibrates in the idea of happiness (this is what that noteworthy circumstance teaches us) the idea of salvation. This happiness is founded on the very despair and desolation which were ours. Our life, it can be said, is a muscle strong enough to contract the whole of historical time. Or, to put it differently, the genuine conception of historical time rests entirely upon the image of redemption. (The passage is from Lotze, *Mikrokosmos,* vol. 3 [Leipzig, 1864], p. 49.)[39]
                                                                                    [N13a,1]

Denial of the notion of progress in the religious view of history: "History, however it may move forward or fluctuate hither and thither, could not by any of its movements attain a goal lying out of its own plane. And we may spare ourselves the trouble of seeking to find, in mere onward movement upon this plane, a progress which history is destined to make not there but by an upward movement at each individual point of its course forward." Hermann Lotze, *Mikrokosmos,* vol. 3 (Leipzig, 1864), p. 49.[40]   [N13a,2]

Connection, in Lotze, between the idea of progress and the idea of redemption: "The reason of the world would be turned to unreason if we did not reject the thought that the work of vanishing generations should go on forever benefiting only those who come later, and being irreparably wasted for the workers themselves" (p. 50). This cannot be, "unless the world itself, and all the flourish about historical development, are to appear as mere vain and unintelligible noise. . . . That in some mysterious way the progress of history affects them, too—it is this conviction that first entitles us to speak as we do of humanity and its history" (p. 51). Lotze calls this the "thought of the preservation and restoration of all things" (p. 52).[41]   [N13a,3]

Cultural history, according to Bernheim, developed out of the positivism of Comte; Beloch's *Greek History* (‹vol. 1,› 2nd edition, 1912) is, according to him, a textbook example of Comtean influence. Positivist historiography "disregarded . . . the state and political processes, and saw in the collective intellectual development of society the sole content of history. . . . The elevation . . . of cultural history to the only subject worthy of historical research!" Ernst Bernheim, *Mit-*

telalterliche Zeitanschauungen in ihrem Einfluss auf Politik und Geschichtsschreibung (Tübingen, 1918), p. 8. [N14,1]

"'The logical category of time does not govern the verb as much as one might expect.' Strange as it may seem, the expression of the future does not appear to be situated on the same level of the human mind as the expression of the past and of the present. . . . 'The future often has no expression of its own; or if it has one, it is a complicated expression without parallel to that of the present or the past.' . . . 'There is no reason to believe that prehistoric Indo-European ever possessed a true future tense' (Meillet)." Jean-Richard Bloch, "Langage d'utilité, langage poétique" (*Encyclopédie française*, vol. 16 [16–50], 10). [N14,2]

Simmel touches on a very important matter with the distinction between the concept of culture and the spheres of autonomy in classical Idealism. The separation of the three autonomous domains from one another preserved classical Idealism from the concept of culture that has so favored the cause of barbarism. Simmel says of the cultural ideal: "It is essential that the independent values of aesthetic, scientific, ethical, . . . and even religious achievements be transcended, so that they can all be integrated as elements in the development of human nature beyond its natural state." Georg Simmel, *Philosophie des Geldes* (Leipzig, 1900), pp. 476–477.[42] [N14,3]

"There has never been a period of history in which the culture peculiar to it has leavened the whole of humanity, or even the whole of that one nation which was specially distinguished by it. All degrees and shades of moral barbarism, of mental obtuseness, and of physical wretchedness have always been found in juxtaposition with cultured refinement of life . . . and free participation in the benefits of civil order." Hermann Lotze, *Mikrokosmos*, vol. 3 (Leipzig, 1864), pp. 23–24.[43] [N14a,1]

To the view that "there is progress enough if, . . . while the mass of mankind remains mired in an uncivilized condition, the civilization of a small minority is constantly struggling upward to greater and greater heights," Lotze responds with the question: "How, upon such assumptions, can we be entitled to speak of one history of mankind?" Lotze, *Mikrokosmos*, vol. 3, p. 25.[44] [N14a,2]

"The way in which the culture of past times is for the most part handed down," Lotze says, "leads directly back to the very opposite of that at which historical development should aim; it leads, that is, to the formation of an *instinct* of culture, which continually takes up more and more of the elements of civilization, thus making them a lifeless possession, and withdrawing them from the sphere of that conscious activity by the efforts of which they were at first obtained" (p. 28). Accordingly: "The progress of science is not . . . , directly, human progress; it would be this if, in proportion to the increase in accumulated truths, there were also an increase in men's concern for them . . . and in the clearness of their insight concerning them." Lotze, *Mikrokosmos*, vol. 3, p. 29.[45]   [N14a,3]

Lotze on humanity: "It cannot be said that men grow to what they are with a consciousness of this growth, and with an accompanying remembrance of their previous condition." Lotze, *Mikrokosmos*, vol. 3, p. 31.[46]   [N14a,4]

Lotze's vision of history can be related to Stifter's: "that the unruly will of the individual is always restricted in its action by universal conditions not subject to arbitrary will—conditions which are to be found in the laws of spiritual life in general, in the established order of nature . . . " Lotze, *Mikrokosmos,* vol. 3, p. 34.[47]
                    [N14a,5]

To be compared with Stifter's preface to *Bunte Steine* ‹Colored Stones›: "Let us at the outset regard it as certain that a great effect is always due to a great cause, never to a small one." *Histoire de Jules César,* vol. 1 (Paris, 1865) (Napoléon III).
                    [N14a,6]

A phrase which Baudelaire coins for the consciousness of time peculiar to someone intoxicated by hashish can be applied in the definition of a revolutionary historical consciousness. He speaks of a night in which he was absorbed by the effects of hashish: "Long though it seemed to have been . . . , yet it also seemed to have lasted only a few seconds, or even to have had no place in all eternity." ‹Baudelaire, *Oeuvres,* ed. Le Dantec (Paris, 1931),› vol. 1, pp. 298–299.[48]
                    [N15,1]

At any given time, the living see themselves in the midday of history. They are obliged to prepare a banquet for the past. The historian is the herald who invites the dead to the table.   [N15,2]

On the dietetics of historical literature. The contemporary who learns from books of history to recognize how long his present misery has been in preparation (and this is what the historian must inwardly aim to show him) acquires thereby a high opinion of his own powers. A history that provides this kind of instruction does not cause him sorrow, but arms him. Nor does such a history arise from sorrow, unlike that which Flaubert had in mind when he penned the confession: "Few will suspect how depressed one had to be to undertake the resuscitation of Carthage."[49] It is pure *curiosité* that arises from and deepens sorrow.   [N15,3]

Example of a "cultural historical" perspective in the worse sense. Huizinga speaks of the consideration displayed for the life of the common people in the pastorals of the late Middle Ages. "Here, too, belongs that interest in rags and tatters which . . . is already beginning to make itself felt. Calendar miniatures note with pleasure the threadbare knees of reapers in the field, while paintings accentuate the rags of mendicants. . . . Here begins the line that leads through Rembrandt's etchings and Murillo's beggar boys to the street types of Steinlen." J. Huizinga, *Herbst des Mittelalters* (Munich, 1928), p. 448.[50] At issue, of course, is actually a very specific phenomenon.   [N15,4]

"The past has left images of itself in literary texts, images comparable to those which are imprinted by light on a photosensitive plate. The future alone possesses developers active enough to scan such surfaces perfectly. Many pages in Marivaux or Rousseau contain a mysterious meaning which the first readers of these texts could not fully have deciphered." André Monglond, *Le Préromantisme français,* vol. 1, *Le Héros préromantique* (Grenoble, 1930), p. xii.   [N15a,1]

A revealing vision of progress in Hugo, "Paris incendié" (*L'Année terrible*):

> What! Sacrifice everything! Even the granary!
> What! The library, arch where dawn arises,
> Unfathomable ABC of the ideal, where progress,
> Eternal reader, leans on its elbows and dreams . . .   [N15a,2]

On the style one should strive for: "It is through everyday words that style bites into and penetrates the reader. It is through them that great thoughts circulate and are accepted as genuine, like gold or silver imprinted with a recognized seal. They inspire confidence in the person who uses them to make his thoughts more understandable; for one recognizes by such usage of common language a man who knows life and the world, and who stays in touch with things. Moreover, these words make for a frank style. They show that the author has long ruminated the thought or the feeling expressed, that he has made them so much his own, so much a matter of habit, that for him the most common expressions suffice to express ideas that have become natural to him after long deliberation. In the end, what one says in this way will appear more truthful, for nothing is so clear, when it comes to words, than those we call familiar; and clarity is something so characteristic of the truth that it is often confused with it." Nothing more subtle than the suggestion: be clear so as to have at least the appearance of truth. Offered in this way, the advice to write simply—which usually harbors resentment—has the highest authority. J. Joubert, *Oeuvres* (Paris, 1883), vol. 2, p. 293 ("Du Style," no. 99).   [N15a,3]

The person who could develop the Joubertian dialectic of precepts would produce a stylistics worth mentioning. For example, Joubert recommends the use of "everyday words" but warns against "colloquial language," which "expresses things relevant to our present customs only" ("Du Style," no. 67 ‹ *Oeuvres,* vol. 2, p. 286›).   [N16,1]

"All beautiful expressions are susceptible of more than one meaning. When a beautiful expression presents a meaning more beautiful than the author's own, it should be adopted." J. Joubert, *Oeuvres* (Paris, 1883), vol. 2, p. 276 ("Du Style," no. 17).   [N16,2]

With regard to political economy, Marx characterizes as "its vulgar element" above all "that element in it which is mere reproduction—that is, representation of appearance." Cited in Korsch, *Karl Marx* ‹manuscript›, vol. 2, p. 22.[51] This vulgar element is to be denounced in other sciences as well.   [N16,3]

Concept of nature in Marx: "If in Hegel . . . 'physical nature likewise encroaches on world history,' then Marx conceives nature from the beginning in social categories. Physical nature does not enter directly into world history; rather, it enters indirectly, as a process of material production that goes on, from the earliest moment, not only between man and nature but also between man and man. Or, to use language that will be clear to philosophers as well: in Marx's rigorously social science, that pure *nature* presupposed by all human activity (the economic *natura naturans*) is replaced everywhere by nature as *material production* (the economic *natura naturata*)—that is, by a social 'matter' mediated and transformed through human social activity, and thus at the same time capable of further change and modification in the present and the future." Korsch, *Karl Marx*, vol. 3, p. 3.[52]
                                                                                [N16,4]

Korsch provides the following reformulation of the Hegelian triad in Marxian terms: "The Hegelian 'contradiction' was replaced by the struggle of the social classes; the dialectical 'negation,' by the proletariat; and the dialectical 'synthesis,' by the proletarian revolution." Korsch, *Karl Marx*, vol. 3, p. 45.[53]   [N16,5]

Restriction of the materialist conception of history in Korsch: "As the material mode of production changes, so does the system of mediations existing between the material base and its political and juridical superstructure, with its corresponding social forms of consciousness. Hence, the general propositions of materialist social theory concerning the relations between *economy* and *politics* or *economy* and *ideology*, or concerning such general concepts as *class* and *class struggle*, . . . have a different meaning for each specific epoch and, strictly speaking, are valid, in the particular form Marx gave them within the present bourgeois society, only for this society. . . . Only for contemporary bourgeois society, where the spheres of *economy* and *politics* are formally and entirely separated from each other, and where workers as citizens of the state are free and possessed of equal rights, does the scientific demonstration of their actual ongoing lack of freedom in the economic sphere have the character of a theoretical discovery." Korsch, vol. 3, pp. 21–22.
                                                                                [N16a,1]

Korsch makes "the seemingly paradoxical observation (which is nonetheless . . . suited to the final and most mature form of Marxian science) that in the materialist social theory of Marx the ensemble of social relations, which bourgeois sociologists treat as an independent domain . . . , already is investigated according to its objective . . . content by the historical and social science of economics. . . . *In this sense, Marx's materialist social science is not sociology but economics.*" Korsch, *Karl Marx*, vol. 3, p. 103.[54]   [N16a,2]

A citation from Marx on the mutability of nature (in Korsch, *Karl Marx*, vol. 3, p. 9): "Even the naturally grown variations of the human species, such as differences of race, . . . can and must be abolished in the historical process."[55]

[N16a,3]

Doctrine of the superstructure, according to Korsch: "Neither 'dialectical causality' in its philosophic definition, nor scientific 'causality' supplemented by 'interactions,' is sufficient to determine the particular kinds of connections and relations existing between the economic 'base' and the juridical and political 'superstructure . . . ,' together with the 'corresponding' forms of consciousness. . . . Twentieth-century natural science has learned that the 'causal' relations which the researcher in a given field has to establish for that field cannot be defined in terms of a general concept or law of causality, but must be determined specifically for each separate field.* [*See Philipp Frank, *Das Kausalgesetz und seine Grenzen* ⟨The Law of Causality and Its Limits⟩ (Vienna, 1932).] . . . The greater part of the results . . . obtained by Marx and Engels consist not in theoretical formulations of the new principle but in its specific application to a series of . . . questions, which are either of fundamental practical importance or of an extremely subtle nature theoretically. . . . * [*Here, for example, belong the questions raised by Marx at the end of the 1857 'Introduction' ⟨to the *Grundrisse*⟩ (pp. 779ff.), and which concern the 'unequal development' of different spheres of social life: unequal development of material production vis-à-vis artistic production (and of the various arts among themselves), the level of education in the United States as compared to that of Europe, unequal development of the relations of production as legal relations, and so forth.] The more precise scientific determination of the present contexts is still a task for the future . . . , a task whose center will lie, once again, not in theoretical formulation but in the further application and testing of the principles implicit in Marx's work. Nor should we adhere too strictly to the words of Marx, who often used his terms only figuratively—as, for instance, in describing the connections under consideration here as a relation between 'base' and 'superstructure,' as a 'correspondence,' and so on. . . . In all these cases, the Marxian concepts (as Sorel and Lenin, among the later Marxists, understood best) are not intended as new dogmatic fetters, as preestablished conditions which must be met in some particular order by any 'materialist' investigation. They are, rather, a wholly undogmatic guide to research and action." Korsch, *Karl Marx* (manuscript), vol. 3, pp. 93–96.[56]   [N17]

Materialist conception of history and materialist philosophy: "The formulas of materialist history that were applied by Marx and Engels . . . solely to the . . . investigation of bourgeois society, and transferred to other historical periods only with suitable elaboration, have been detached by the Marxist epigones from this specific application, and in general from every historical connection; and out of so-called historical materialism they have made a universal . . . sociological theory. From this . . . leveling . . . of materialist theory of society, it was only a step to the idea that once again today—or especially today—it was necessary to shore up the historical and economic science of Marx, not only with a general social philosophy but even with a . . . universal materialist worldview embracing the totality of nature and society. Thus, the . . . scientific forms into which the real kernel of eighteenth-century philosophical materialism had evolved . . . were ultimately carried back to what Marx himself had once unmistakably repudiated as 'the philosophical phrases of the Materialists about matter.' Materialist social science . . . does not need . . . any such philosophic support. This most important advance . . . carried out by Marx was later overlooked even by . . . 'orthodox' interpreters of Marx. . . . They have thus reintroduced their own backward attitudes into a theory which Marx had consciously transformed from a philosophy into a science. It is the almost grotesque historical fate of the Marx-orthodoxy that, in repulsing the attacks of revisionists, it ultimately arrives, on all important issues, at the very same standpoint as that taken by its adversaries. For example, the leading representative of this school, . . . Plekhanov, in his eager pursuit of that 'philosophy' which might be the true foundation of Marxism, finally hit upon the idea of presenting Marxism as 'a form of Spinoza's philosophy freed by Feuerbach of its theological addendum.'" Korsch, *Karl Marx* (manuscript), vol. 3, pp. 29–31.[57]

[N17a]

Korsch cites Bacon, from the *Novum Organum:* "'Recte enim veritas temporis filia dicitur non auctoritas.' On that authority of all authorities, *time,* he had based the superiority of the new bourgeois empirical science over the dogmatic science of the Middle Ages." Korsch, *Karl Marx* (manuscript), vol. 1, p. 72.[58]

[N18,1]

"For the *positive* use, Marx replaces the overweening postulate of Hegel that the truth must be concrete with the rational principle of *specification.* . . . The real interest lies . . . in the specific traits through which each particular historical society is *distinguished* from the common features of society in general and in which, therefore, its *development* is comprised. . . . In the same manner, an exact social science cannot form its general concepts by simply abstracting from some and retaining other more or less arbitrarily chosen characteristics of the given historical form of bourgeois society. It can secure the knowledge of the general contained in that particular form of society only by the minute investigation of all the historical conditions underlying its emergence from another state of society and from the actual modification of its present form under exactly established conditions. . . . Thus, the only genuine laws in social science are laws of development." Korsch, *Karl Marx* (manuscript), vol. 1, pp. 49–52.[59]   [N18,2]

The authentic concept of universal history is a messianic concept. Universal history, as it is understood today, is an affair of obscurantists.   [N18,3]

The now of recognizability is the moment of awakening. (Jung would like to distance awakening from the dream.)   [N18,4]

In his characterization of Leopardi, Sainte-Beuve declares himself "persuaded . . . that the full value and originality of literary criticism depends on its applying itself to subjects for which we have long possessed the background and all the immediate and more distant contexts." C.-A. Sainte-Beuve, *Portraits contemporains,* vol. 4 (Paris, 1882), p. 365. On the other hand, it must be admitted that the absence of certain of the conditions demanded here by Sainte-Beuve can have its value. A lack of feeling for the most delicate nuances of the text can itself cause the reader to inquire more attentively into the least of facts within the social relations underlying the work of art. Moreover, the insensitivity to fine shades of meaning can more readily procure for one (thanks to clearer apprehension of the contours of the work) a certain superiority to other critics, insofar as the feeling for nuances does not always go together with the gift for analysis.   [N18a,1]

Critical remarks on technical progress show up quite early. The author of the treatise *On Art* (Hippocrates?): "I believe that the inclination . . . of intelligence is to discover any one of those things that are still unknown, *if indeed it is better to have discovered them than not to have done so at all.*" Leonardo da Vinci: "How and why I do not write of my method of going underwater for as long as I can remain there without eating: if I neither publish nor divulge this information, it is because of the wickedness of men who would avail themselves of it to commit murder at the bottom of the sea—by staving in ships and sinking them with their crews." Bacon: "In . . . *The New Atlantis,* . . . he entrusts to a specially chosen commission the responsibility for deciding which new inventions will be brought before the public and which kept secret." Pierre-Maxime Schuhl, *Machinisme et philosophie* (Paris, 1938), pp. 7, 35.—"The bombers remind us of what Leonardo da Vinci expected of man in flight: that he was to ascend to the skies 'in order to seek snow on the mountaintops and bring it back to the city to spread on the sweltering streets in summer'" (Schuhl, *Machinisme et philosophie,* p. 95).
                                                                            [N18a,2]

It may be that the continuity of tradition is mere semblance. But then precisely the persistence of this semblance of persistence provides it with continuity.
                                                                            [N19,1]

Proust, apropos of a citation (from a letter by ‹Guez de› Balzac to M. de Forgues) which he evidently borrowed from Montesquiou, to whom his comments are addressed. (The passage may contain a nonsensical slip of the pen or a printer's error.) "It was fifteen days ago that I removed it [that is, the citation] from my proof sheets. . . . My book will no doubt be too little read for there to have been any risk of tarnishing your citation. Furthermore, I withdrew it less for your sake than for the sake of the sentence itself. In fact, I believe there exists for every beautiful sentence an imprescriptible right which renders it inalienable to all takers except the one for whom it waits, according to a destination which is its destiny." *Correspondance générale de Marcel Proust,* vol. 1, *Lettres à Robert de Montesquiou* (Paris, 1930), pp. 73–74.[60]   [N19,2]

The pathological element in the notion of "culture" comes vividly to light in the effect produced on Raphael, the hero of *The Wild Ass's Skin,* by the enormous stock of merchandise in the four-story antique shop into which he ventures. "To begin with, the stranger compared . . . three showrooms—crammed with the relics of civilizations and religions, deities, royalties, masterpieces of art, the products of debauchery, reason and unreason—to a mirror of many facets, each one representing a whole world. . . . The young man's senses ended by being numbed at the sight of so many national and individual existences, their authenticity guaranteed by the human pledges which had survived them. . . . For him this ocean of furnishings, inventions, fashions, works of art, and relics made up an endless poem. . . . He clutched at every joy, grasped at every grief, made all the formulas of existence his own, and . . . generously dispersed his life and feelings over the images of that empty, plastic nature. . . . He felt smothered under the debris of fifty vanished centuries, nauseated with this surfeit of human thought, crushed under the weight of luxury and art. . . . Alike in its caprices to our modern chemistry, which would reduce creation to one single gas, does not the soul distill fearful poisons in the rapid concentration of its pleasures . . . or its ideas? Do not many men perish through the lightning action of some moral acid or other, suddenly injected into their innermost being?" Balzac, *La Peau de chagrin,* ed. Flammarion (Paris), pp. 19, 21–22, 24.[61]   [N19,3]

Some theses by Focillon which have appearances on their side. Of course, the materialist theory of art is interested in dispelling such appearance. "We have no right to confuse the state of the life of forms with the state of social life. The time that gives support to a work of art does not give definition either to its principle or to its specific form" (p. 93). "The combined activity of the Capetian monarchy, the episcopacy, and the townspeople in the development of Gothic cathedrals shows what a decisive influence may be exercised by the alliance of social forces. Yet no matter how powerful this activity may be, it is still by no means qualified to solve problems in pure statics, to combine relationships of values. The various masons who bonded two ribs of stone crossing at right angles beneath the north tower of Bayeux . . . , the creator of the choir at Saint-Denis, were geometers working on solids, and not historians interpreting time. [!!] The most attentive study of the most homogeneous milieu, of the most closely woven concatenation of circumstances, will not serve to give us the design of the towers of Laon" (p. 89). It would be necessary to follow up on these reflections in order to show, first, the difference between the theory of milieu and the theory of the forces of production, and, second, the difference between a "reconstruction" and a historical interpretation of works. Henri Focillon, *Vie des formes* (Paris, 1934).[62]

                                                                                   [N19a,1]

Focillon on technique: "It has been like some observatory whence both sight and study might embrace within one and the same perspective the greatest possible number of objects and their greatest possible diversity. For technique may be interpreted in many various ways: as a vital force, as a theory of mechanics, or as a mere convenience. In my own case as a historian, I never regarded technique as the automatism of a 'craft,' nor as . . . the recipes of a 'cuisine'; instead I saw it as a whole poetry of action and . . . as the means for attaining metamorphoses. It has always seemed to me that . . . the observation of technical phenomena not only guarantees a certain controllable objectivity, but affords entrance into the very heart of the problem, *by presenting it to us in the same terms and from the same point of view as it is presented to the artist.* " The phrase italicized by the author marks the basic error. Henri Focillon, *Vie des formes* (Paris, 1934), pp. 53–54.[63]

[N19a,2]

The "activity on the part of a style in the process of self-definition . . . is generally known as an 'evolution,' this term being here understood in its broadest and most general sense. Biological science checked and modulated the concept of evolution with painstaking care; archaeology, on the other hand, took it simply as . . . a method of classification. I have elsewhere pointed out the dangers of 'evolution': its deceptive orderliness, its single-minded directness, its use, in those problematic cases . . . , of the expedient of 'transitions,' its inability to make room for the revolutionary energy of inventors." Henri Focillon, *Vie des formes* (Paris, 1934), pp. 11–12.[64]

[N20]

[Prostitution, Gambling]

> Love is a bird of *passage*.
>
> —*Nouveaux tableaux de Paris, ou Observations sur les moeurs et usages des Parisiens au commencement du XIXᵉ siècle* (Paris, 1828), vol. 1, p. 37

> . . . in an arcade,
> Women are as in their boudoir.
>
> —Brazier, Gabriel and Dumersan, *Les Passages et les rues, ou La Guerre déclarée* (Paris, 1827), p. 30

Hasn't his eternal vagabondage everywhere accustomed him to reinterpreting the image of the city? And doesn't he transform the arcade into a casino, into a gambling den, where now and again he stakes the red, blue, yellow *jetons* of feeling on women, on a face that suddenly surfaces (will it return his look?), on a mute mouth (will it speak?)? What, on the baize cloth, looks out at the gambler from every number—luck, that is—here, from the bodies of all the women, winks at him as the chimera of sexuality: as his type. This is nothing other than the number, the cipher, in which just at that moment luck will be called by name, in order to jump immediately to another number. His type—that's the number that pays off thirty-six-fold, the one on which, without even trying, the eye of the voluptuary falls, as the ivory ball falls into the red or black compartment. He leaves the Palais-Royal with bulging pockets, calls to a whore, and once more celebrates in her arms the communion with number, in which money and riches, absolved from every earthen weight, have come to him from the fates like a joyous embrace returned to the full. For in gambling hall and bordello, it is the same supremely sinful delight: to challenge fate in pleasure. Let unsuspecting idealists imagine that sensual pleasure, of whatever stripe, could ever determine the theological concept of sin. The origin of true lechery is nothing else but this stealing of pleasure from out of the course of life with God, whose covenant with such life resides in the name. The name itself is the cry of naked lust. This sober thing, fateless in itself—the name—knows no other adversary than the fate that takes its place in whoring and that forges its arsenal in superstition. Thus in gambler and prostitute that superstition which arranges the figures of fate and fills all wanton behavior with fateful forwardness, fateful concupiscence, bringing even pleasure to kneel before its throne. [O1,1]

"When I turn back in thought to the Salon des Etrangers, as it was in the second decade of our century, I see before me the finely etched features and gallant figure of the Hungarian Count Hunyady, the greatest gambler of his day, who back then took all society's breath away. . . . Hunyady's luck for a long time was extraordinary; no bank could withstand his assault, and his winnings must have amounted to nearly two million francs. His manner was surprisingly calm and extremely distinguished; he sat there, as it appeared, in complete equanimity, his right hand in the breast of his jacket, while thousands of francs hung upon the fall of a card or a roll of the dice. His valet, however, confided to an indiscreet friend that Monsieur's nerves were not so steely as he wanted people to believe, and that of a morning the count more often than not would bear the bloody traces of his nails, which in his excitement he had dug into the flesh of his chest as the game was taking a dangerous turn." Captain Gronow, *Aus der grossen Welt* ‹*Pariser und Londoner Sittenbilder, 1810–1860*, ed. Heinrich Conrad› (Stuttgart, 1908), p. 59.[1] [O1,2]

On the way Blücher gambled in Paris, see Gronow's book, *Aus der grossen Welt* ‹pp. 54–56›. When he had lost, he forced the Bank of France to advance him 100,000 francs so he could continue playing; after this scandal broke, he had to leave Paris. "Blücher never quit Salon 113 at the Palais-Royal, and spent six million during his stay; all his lands were in pledge at the time of his departure from Paris." Paris took in more during the occupation ‹of 1814› than it paid out in war reparations. [O1,3]

It is only by comparison with the ancien régime that one can say that in the nineteenth century the bourgeois takes to gambling. [O1,4]

The following account shows very conclusively how *public* immorality (in contrast to private) carries in itself, in its liberating cynicism, its own corrective. It is reported by Carl Benedict Hase, who was in France as an indigent tutor and who sent letters home from Paris and other stations of his wandering. "As I was walking in the vicinity of the Pont Neuf, a heavily made-up prostitute accosted me. She had on a light muslin dress that was tucked up to the knee and that clearly displayed the red silk drawers covering thigh and belly. '*Tiens, tiens, mon ami,*' she said, 'you are young, you're a foreigner, you will have need of it.' She then seized my hand, slipped a piece of paper into it, and disappeared in the crowd. Thinking I had been given an address, I looked at the missive; and what did I read?—An advertisement for a doctor who was claiming to cure all imaginable ailments in the shortest possible time. It is strange that the girls who are responsible for the malady should here put in hand the means to recover from it." Carl Benedict Hase, *Briefe von der Wanderung und aus Paris* (Leipzig, 1894), pp. 48–49. [O1,5]

A gallery of the Palais-Royal. From a watercolor entitled *La Sortie du numéro 113,* artist unknown, 1815. See O1,3.

"As for the virtue of women, I have but one response to make to those who would ask me about this: it strongly resembles the curtains in theaters, for their petticoats rise each evening three times rather than once." Comte Horace de Viel-Castel, *Mémoires sur le règne de Napoleon III* (Paris, 1883), vol. 2, p. 188.

[O1a,1]

"*Hirondelles*—women who work the window." Levic-Torca, *Paris-Noceur* (Paris, 1910), p. 142. The windows in the upper story of the arcades are choir lofts in which the angels that men call "swallows" are nesting. [O1a,2]

On what is "close" (Veuillot: "Paris is musty and close") in fashion: the "glaucous gleam" under the petticoats, of which Aragon speaks.[2] The corset as the torso's arcade. The absolute antithesis to this open-air world of today. What today is de rigueur among the lowest class of prostitutes—not to undress—may once have been the height of refinement. One liked the woman *retroussée,* tucked up. Hessel thinks he has found here the origin of Wedekind's erotics; in his view, Wedekind's fresh-air pathos was only a bluff. And in other respects? □ Fashion □ [O1a,3]

On the dialectical function of money in prostitution. It buys pleasure and, at the same time, becomes the expression of shame. "I knew," says Casanova of a procuress, "that I would not have the strength to go without giving her something." This striking admission reveals his knowledge of the most secret mechanism of prostitution. No girl would choose to become a prostitute if she counted solely on the stipulated payoff from her partner. Even his gratitude, which perhaps results in a small percentage more, would hardly seem to her a sufficient basis. How then, in her unconscious understanding of men, does she calculate? This we cannot comprehend, so long as money is thought of here as only a means of payment or a gift. Certainly the whore's love is for sale. But not her client's shame. The latter seeks some hiding place during this quarter-hour, and finds the most genial: in money. There are as many nuances of payment as there are nuances of lovemaking—lazy and swift, furtive or brutal. What does this signify? The shame-reddened wound on the body of society secretes money and closes up. It forms a metallic scab. We leave to the roué the cheap pleasure of believing himself devoid of shame. Casanova knew better: impudence throws the first coin onto the table, and shame pays out a hundred more to cover it. [O1a,4]

"The dance in which . . . vulgarity makes its appearance with unexampled impudence is the traditional French quadrille. When the dancers manage to offend against every tender feeling by their pantomime—without, however, going so far as to have to fear being ejected from the room by the on-duty police agents—then this type of dance is called *quincan.* But when all moral sentiment is trampled on by the manner of the dancing, when at last, after lengthy hesitation, the *sergeants de ville* feel compelled to recall the dancers to a sense of decorum with the customary words, "Dance more decently or you will be shown the door!"—then this intensification or, better, 'this degradation' is known as *chahue.* / . . . The bestial grossness . . . has led to the creation of a police ordinance. . . . Men, accordingly, are not allowed to appear at these balls either masked or in costume. This is in part to prevent their being tempted by their disguise to behave still more vilely but also, and chiefly, in the event a dancer should reach the Parisian ne plus ultra of depravity in dancing and subsequently be shown to the door by the *sergeants de ville,* to make sure he will be recognized thereafter and kept from reentering the room. . . . Women, on the other hand, are not allowed to appear unless they are masked." Ferdinand von Gall, *Paris und seine Salons* (Oldenburg, 1844), vol. 1, pp. 209, 213–214. [O1a,5]

Comparison of today's erotic fields of action with those of the middle of the previous century. The social play of eroticism turns today on the question: How far can a respectable woman go without losing herself? To represent the joys of adultery without its actual circumstances is a favorite device of dramatists. The terrain on which love's duel with society unfolds is thus, in a very broad sense, the realm of "free" love. For the Forties, Fifties, and Sixties of the previous century, however, things were entirely different. Nothing illustrates this more clearly than the account of the "pensions" which Ferdinand von Gall provides in his book *Paris und seine Salons* (Oldenburg, 1844–1845) ‹vol. 1, pp. 225–231›. There we learn that in many of these boardinghouses at the evening meal— which, with prior notification, strangers too could attend—it was the rule to bring in cocottes, whose job it was to play the part of girls from good families. In fact, they were not disposed to let down their masks too quickly, preferring instead to wrap themselves in endless layers of respectability and family connec- tion; to strip these away entailed an elaborate game of intrigues that ultimately served to raise the women's price. What is expressed in these relations, it goes without saying, is less the period's *pruderie* than its fanatical love of masquerade. [O2,1]

More on the mania for masks: "We know from the statistics on prostitution that the fallen woman takes a certain pride in being deemed by nature still worthy of motherhood—a feeling that in no way excludes her aversion to the hardship and disfigurement that goes along with this honor. She thus willingly chooses a middle way to exhibit her condition: she keeps it 'for two months, for three months,' naturally not longer." F. Th. Vischer, *Mode und Cynismus* (Stuttgart, 1879), p. 7. ▢ Fashion ▢ [O2,2]

In prostitution, one finds expressed the revolutionary side of technology (the symbolic side, which creates no less than discovers). "As if the laws of nature to which love submits were not more tyrannical and more odious than the laws of society! The metaphysical meaning of sadism is the hope that the revolt of man will take on such intensity as to summon nature to change its laws. For, with women no longer wanting to endure the ordeal of pregnancy, the risks and the sufferings of delivery and of miscarriage, nature will be constrained to invent some other means for perpetuating humanity on this earth." Emmanuel Berl, "Premier Pamphlet," *Europe,* 75 ‹1929›, pp. 405–406. And in fact: the sexual revolt against love not only springs from the fanatical, obsessional will to pleas- ure; it also aims to make nature adaptable and obedient to this will. The traits in question here appear more clearly still when prostitution (especially in the cynical form it took toward the end of the century, in the Paris arcades) is regarded less as the opposite than as the decline of love. It is then that the revolutionary aspect of this decline fuses, as though of its own accord, with the very same aspect in the decline of the arcades. [O2,3]

Feminine fauna of the arcades: prostitutes, grisettes, old-hag shopkeepers, female street vendors, glovers, *demoiselles.*—This last was the name, around 1830, for incendiaries disguised as women. [O2,4]

Around 1830: "The Palais-Royal is still enough in fashion that the renting of chairs brings in some 32,000 francs to Louis Philippe, and the tax on gaming some five and a half million to the treasury. . . . The gambling houses of the Palais-Royal rival those of the Cercle des Etrangers on the Rue Grange-Batelière and of Frascati on the Rue de Richelieu." ‹Lucien› Dubech and ‹Pierre› d'Espezel, *Histoire de Paris* (Paris, 1926), p. 365. [O2,5]

Rites de passage—this is the designation in folklore for the ceremonies that attach to death and birth, to marriage, puberty, and so forth. In modern life, these transitions are becoming ever more unrecognizable and impossible to experience. We have grown very poor in threshold experiences. Falling asleep is perhaps the only such experience that remains to us. (But together with this, there is also waking up.) And, finally, there is the ebb and flow of conversation and the sexual permutations of love—experience that surges over thresholds like the changing figures of the dream. "How mankind loves to remain transfixed," says Aragon, "at the very doors of the imagination!" *Paysan* ‹*de Paris* (Paris, 1926)›, p. 74.[3] It is not only from the thresholds of these gates of imagination that lovers and friends like to draw their energies; it is from thresholds in general. Prostitutes, however, love the thresholds of these gates of dream.—The threshold must be carefully distinguished from the boundary. A *Schwelle* ‹threshold› is a zone. Transformation, passage, wave action are in the word *schwellen,* swell, and etymology ought not to overlook these senses.[4] On the other hand, it is necessary to keep in mind the immediate tectonic and ceremonial context which has brought the word to its current meaning. ☐ Dream House ☐ [O2a,1]

Under the northeast peristyle of the Palais-Royal lay the Café des Aveugles. "There, a half-dozen blindmen from the Quinze-Vingts Hospital unceasingly performed more or less deafening music from six o'clock in the evening to one o'clock in the morning; for the underground establishments were open to the public only from dusk to dawn. They were the preferred rendezvous of those licensed Dryads and Nysiads, those impure Sirens who at least had the merit of conferring movement and life on this immense bazaar of pleasures—sad, somber and mute today as the brothels of Herculaneum." *Histoire des cafés de Paris extraite des mémoires d'un viveur* (Paris, 1857), p. 7. [O2a,2]

"On December 31, 1836, all the gambling houses were closed by authority of the police. At Frascati, there was a small riot. This was the mortal blow to the Palais-Royal, already dethroned since 1830 by the boulevard." Dubech and d'Espezel, *Histoire de Paris* (Paris, 1926), p. 389. [O2a,3]

"Talma, Talleyrand, Rossini, Balzac"—named as gamblers in Edouard Gourdon, *Les Faucheurs de nuit* (Paris, 1860), p. 14. [O2a,4]

"I submit that the passion for gambling is the noblest of all passions, because it comprehends all others. A series of lucky rolls gives me more pleasure than a man who does not gamble can have over a period of several years. I play by intuition, *par l'esprit*—that is to say, in the most keenly felt and delicate manner. Do you think I recognize gain only in terms of the gold that comes my way? You are mistaken. I see it in terms of the joys which gold procures, and I savor them to the full. These joys, vivid and scorching as lightning, are too rapid-fire to become distasteful, and too diverse to become boring. I live a hundred lives in one. If it is a voyage, it is like that of an electric spark. . . . If I keep my fist shut tight, and if I hold onto my banknotes, it is because I know the value of time too well to spend it like other men. To give myself to one pleasure alone would cause me to lose a thousand others. . . . I have spiritual pleasures, and I want no others." Edouard Gourdon, *Les Faucheurs de nuit* (Paris, 1860), pp. 14–15. The passage cited from La Bruyère!—Compare: " What? I no longer act as I might choose?" *Wallenstein.*[5]
[O2a,5]

"The gambling concessions included the Maison du Cercle des Etrangers, at 6 Rue Grange-Batelière; the Maison de Livry, known as Frascati, at 103 Rue Richelieu; the Maison Dunans, 40 Rue du Mont-Blanc; the Maison Marivaux, 13 Rue Marivaux; the Maison Paphos, 110 Rue du Temple; the Maison Dauphine, 36 Rue Dauphine; and at the Palais-Royal, no. 9 (through no. 24), no. 129 (through no. 137), no. 119 (extending from no. 102), no. 154 (extending from no. 145). These businesses, despite their great number, were not enough for the gamblers. Speculation brought about the opening of others which the police were not always able to monitor effectively. The patrons played écarté, bouillotte, and baccarat. The establishments were managed by . . . hideous-looking old women, disgraceful remnants of every vice. They gave themselves out to be widows of generals; they were protected by self-styled colonels, who received a share of the take. This state of things continued until 1837, when the gambling establishments were shut down." Edouard Gourdon, *Les Faucheurs de nuit* (Paris 1860), p. 34. [O3,1]

Gourdon notes that, in certain circles, the gamblers were almost exclusively women (*Les Faucheurs de nuit*, pp. 55ff.). [O3,2]

"The adventure of the municipal guardsman on horseback, placed like a fetish at the door of a gambler down on his luck, has remained in the annals of our circle. The worthy trooper, believing himself stationed there to pay honor to the guests at some reception, was greatly amazed at the silence of the street and the house, when suddenly, at around one o'clock in the morning, the sad victim of the green tables returned. As on other evenings, and despite the influence of the fetish, the gambler had lost heavily. He rings the bell; no one comes. He rings again; nothing stirs in the lodge of the sleeping Cerberus, and the door is unrelenting. Impatient, irritated, provoked above all by the losses he has just sustained, the tenant smashes a pane of glass with his walking-stick to rouse the porter. Here the municipal guardsman, until then a mere spectator of this nocturnal scene, believes it is his duty to intervene. He stoops down, seizes the troublemaker by the collar, hoists him onto his horse, and trots smartly off to his barracks, delighted to have a decent pretext for punishing a faction he dislikes. . . . Explanations notwithstanding, the gambler spent the night on a camp cot." Edouard Gourdon, *Les Faucheurs de nuit* (Paris, 1860), pp. 181–182. [O3,3]

On the Palais-Royal: "The former minister of police, Merlin, proposed turning this palace of luxury and intemperate pleasure into barracks, and so to shut out that vile breed of humanity from their habitual gathering place." F. J. L. Meyer, *Fragmente aus Paris im IV Jahr der französischen Republik* (Hamburg, 1797), vol. 1, p. 24. [O3,4]

Delvau on the lorettes of Montmartre: "They are not women—they are nights." Alfred Delvau, *Les Dessous de Paris* (Paris 1860), p. 142. [O3,5]

Isn't there a certain structure of money that can be recognized only in fate, and a certain structure of fate that can be recognized only in money? [O3,6]

Professors of argot:[6] "Possessed of nothing more than a perfect knowledge of martingales, series, and intermittences, they sat in the gambling dens from opening to closing time and ended their evening in those grottoes of bouillotte nicknamed Baural houses. Always on the lookout for novices and beginners . . . , these bizarre professors dispensed advice, talked over past throws of the dice, predicted the throws to come, and played for others. In the event of losses, they had only to curse the toss or put the blame on a drawn game, on chance, on the date of the month if it was the thirteenth, on the day of the week if it was Friday. In the event of a win, they would draw their dividend, over and above what they skimmed during their management of funds—a transaction which was known as 'feeding the magpie.' These operators divided into different classes: the aristocrats (all colonels or marquis of the ancien régime), the plebeians born of the Revolution, and finally those who offered their services for fifty centimes." Alfred Marquiset, *Jeux et joueurs d'autrefois, 1789–1837* (Paris, 1917), p. 209. The book contains valuable information on the role of the aristocracy and the military in the cultivation of gambling. [O3a,1]

Palais-Royal. "The second story is inhabited largely by the high-class *femmes perdues*. . . . On the third floor and *au paradis*, in the mansards, reside those of a lower grade. Their livelihood compels them to live in the center of the city, in the Palais-Royal, in the Rue Traversière, and surrounding areas. . . . Perhaps 600–800 live in the Palais-Royal, but a far greater number go walking there in the evenings, for that is where most of the idlers are to be found. On the Rue Saint-Honoré and some adjacent streets, at evening, they stand in a row just like the cabriolets for rent in the Palais during the day. But their numbers diminish as one moves further away, in the city, from the Palais-Royal." J. F. Benzenberg, *Briefe geschrieben auf einer Reise nach Paris* (Dortmund, 1805), vol. 1, pp. 261, 263. The author estimates the number of *femmes perdues* at "around 10,000"; "before the Revolution, according to a police report, they numbered 28,000" (p. 261).

[O3a,2]

"Vice had accomplished its customary task, for her as for the others. It had refined and rendered desirable the brazen ugliness of her face. Although the girl had lost none of the suburban quaintness of her origins, she had become—with her showy jewelry and her physical attractions ostentatiously worked up through creams—capable of stimulating and tempting the bored appetites and dulled sensibilities that are enlivened only by the provocations of makeup and the swirl of lavish gowns." J.-K. Huysmans, *Croquis parisiens* (Paris, 1886). p. 57 ("L'Ambulante").

[O3a,3]

"It is useless to expect that a bourgeois could ever succeed in comprehending the phenomena of the distribution of wealth. For, with the development of mechanical production, property is depersonalized and arrayed in the impersonal collective form of the joint stock company, whose shares are finally caught up in the whirlpool of the Stock Exchange. . . . They are . . . lost by one, won by another—indeed, in a manner so reminiscent of gambling that the buying and selling of stocks is actually known as 'playing' the market. Modern economic development as a whole tends more and more to transform capitalist society into a giant international gambling house, where the bourgeois wins and loses capital in consequence of events which remain unknown to him. . . . The 'inexplicable' is enthroned in bourgeois society as in a gambling hall. . . . Successes and failures, thus arising from causes that are unanticipated, generally unintelligible, and seemingly dependent on chance, predispose the bourgeois to the gambler's frame of mind. . . . The capitalist whose fortune is tied up in stocks and bonds, which are subject to variations in market value and yield for which he does not understand the causes, is a professional gambler. The gambler, however, . . . is a supremely superstitious being. The habitués of gambling casinos always possess magic formulas to conjure the Fates. One will mutter a prayer to Saint Anthony of Padua or some other spirit of the heavens; another will place his bet only if a certain color has won; while a third holds a rabbit's foot in his left hand; and so on. The inexplicable in society envelops the bourgeois, as the inexplicable in nature the savage." Paul Lafargue, "Die Ursachen des Gottesglaubens," *Die neue Zeit*, 24, no. 1 (Stuttgart, 1906), p. 512.

[O4,1]

Adolph Stahr mentions a certain Chicard as premier cancan dancer at the Bal Mabille, and maintains that he dances under the surveillance of two police sergeants whose sole responsibility is to keep an eye on the dancing of this one man. In connection with this: the statement—cited, without specific references, in Woldemar Seyffarth, *Wahrnehmungen in Paris, 1853 und 1854* (Gotha, 1855), p. 136—

"that only the superior strength of the police force can keep within certain barely adequate bounds the bestiality of the Paris crowds." [O4,2]

The "Original"—a sort of primitive man with enormous beard who can be seen in the Palais-Royal—is called Chodruc Duclos. [O4,3]

"Is it an insignificant delight to tempt fortune? Is it a pleasure devoid of intoxication to taste in one second months, years, a whole lifetime of fears and hopes? I was not ten years old when M. Grépinet, my master in the junior class, read us the fable *L'Homme et le génie* ⟨The Man and the Genie⟩. Yet I remember the tale better than if I had read it yesterday. A genie gives a boy a ball of thread, and tells him: 'This is the thread of your life. Take it. When you find time heavy on your hands, pull it out; your days will pass quick or slow, according as you unwind the ball rapidly or little by little. So long as you leave the thread alone, you will remain stationary at the same hour of your existence.' The boy took the thread; first he pulled at it to become a man, then to marry the girl he loved, then to see his children grow up, to win offices and profit and honor, to abridge anxieties, to escape griefs and the infirmities that come with the years, and finally, alas! to cut short a peevish old age. He had lived just four months and six days since the date of the genie's visit. Well, what is gambling, I should like to know, but the art of producing in a second the changes that Destiny ordinarily effects only in the course of many hours or even many years, the art of collecting into a single instant the emotions dispersed throughout the slow-moving existence of ordinary men, the secret of living a whole lifetime in a few minutes—in a word, the genie's ball of thread? Gambling is a hand-to-hand encounter with Fate. . . . The stake is money—in other words, immediate, infinite possibilities. . . . Perhaps the next card turned, the ball now rolling, will give the player parks and gardens, fields and forests, castles and manors lifting heavenward their pointed turrets and fretted roofs. Yes, that little bouncing ball holds within it acres of good land and roofs of slate with sculpted chimneys reflected in the broad bosom of the Loire; it contains treasures of art, marvels of taste, jewels of price, the most exquisite bodies in all the world, nay! even souls—souls no one ever dreamed were venal, all the decorations, all the distinctions, all the elegance, and all the puissance of the world. . . . And you would have me give up gambling? Nay; if gambling only availed to give endless hopes, if our only vision of it were the smile of its green eyes, it would be loved less fanatically. But it has nails of adamant; it is cruel and terrible. At its caprice it gives poverty and wretchedness and shame—that is why its votaries adore it. The fascination of danger is at the bottom of all great passions. There is no fullness of pleasure unless the precipice is near. It is the mingling of terror with delight that intoxicates. And what more terrifying than gambling? It gives and takes away; its logic is not our logic. It is dumb and blind and deaf. It is almighty. It is a God. . . . It has its votaries and its saints, who love it for itself, not for what it promises, and who fall down in adoration when its blow strikes them. It strips them ruthlessly, and they lay the blame on themselves, not on their duty. 'I played

a bad game,' they say. They find fault with themselves; they do not blaspheme
their God." Anatole France, *Le Jardin d'Epicure* (Paris), pp. 15–18.[7]   [O4a]

Béraud seeks to advocate, through extensive argumentation, the benefits of administrative—as opposed to judicial—proceedings against prostitutes: "Thus, the
sanctuary of justice will not have been publicly sullied by an unclean affair, and
the crime is punished, but in a discretionary manner, by virtue of a particular
ordinance of the Prefect of Police." F. F. A. Béraud, *Les Filles publiques de Paris
et la police qui les régit* (Paris and Leipzig, 1839), vol. 2, p. 50.   [O5,1]

"A *marlou* ⟨tomcat⟩ . . . is a handsome young man, strong and well built, who
knows how to defend himself, to dress well, to dance the *chahue* and the cancan
with elegance, to be obliging toward girls devoted to the cult of Venus, and to
provide for them in times of conspicuous danger; who knows also how to get them
respect and to force them to conduct themselves decently. . . . Here, then, we have
a class of individuals who, from time immemorial, have distinguished themselves
by their attractive appearance, by their exemplary conduct, and by the services
they have rendered society, and who now are reduced to dire circumstances."
*50,000 Voleurs de plus à Paris, ou Réclamation des anciens marlous de la capi-
tale, contre l'ordonnance de M. le Préfet de police, concernant les filles publiques;
Par le beau Théodore Cancan,* cited in F. F. A. Béraud, *Les Filles publiques de
Paris et la police qui les régit* (Paris and Leipzig, 1839), vol. 2, p. 109–110, 113–
114. [The pamphlet slightly antedates the work that cites it.]   [O5,2]

From the police edict of April 14, 1830, regulating prostitution: "Art. (1) . . . They
are forbidden to appear at any time, or on any pretext, in the arcades, in the
public gardens, or on the boulevards. Art. (2) *Filles publiques* are not permitted to
engage in prostitution except in licensed brothels (*maisons de tolérance*). Art. (3)
Filles isolées—that is to say, those who do not reside in licensed brothels—may not
enter these houses until after the lighting of the street lamps; they must proceed
directly there and be dressed simply and decently. . . . Art. (4) They may not, in a
single evening, leave one licensed brothel to go to another. Art. (5) Unattached
girls must leave the licensed brothels and return home by eleven o'clock in the
evening. . . . Art. (7) Licensed brothels shall be indicated by an entry light and, in
the early hours, by an older woman tending the door. . . . Signed: Mangin."
F. F. A. Béraud, *Les Filles publiques de Paris et la police qui les régit* (Paris and
Leipzig, 1839), vol. 2, p. 133–135.   [O5,3]

Bonuses earmarked for the *brigade d'ordre:* three francs for identification of a
prostitute under the age of twenty-one; fifteen francs for identification of an illicit
brothel; twenty-five francs for identification of a brothel of minors. Béraud, *Les
Filles publiques,* ⟨vol. 2,⟩ pp. 138–139.   [O5,4]

Explanations offered by Béraud concerning his proposals for new regulations. (1)
With respect to the old woman at the threshold: "The second paragraph prohibits

this woman from passing beyond the doorstep, because it often happens that she has the audacity to step out and intercept passersby. With my own eyes I have seen these panders take men by the arm or by the coat and, so to speak, force them to enter their houses." (2) With respect to the interdiction on commerce for prostitutes: "I would also forbid the opening of stores or shops in which *filles publiques* are installed as milliners, seamstresses, sellers of perfume, and the like. Women who work in these stores and shops will station themselves at open doors or windows in order to send signals to passersby. . . . There are others more ingenious who close their doors and windows but send signals through glass panes unprovided with curtains; or the curtains are left open just enough to permit easy communication between outside and interior. Some of these women rap against the front of the shop each time a man passes by, so that he returns to the spot where the noise was heard; and then such scandalous signs and beckonings ensue as could escape the attention of no one. All these shops are found in the arcades." F. F. A. Béraud, *Les Filles publiques de Paris et la police qui les régit* (Paris and Leipzig, 1839), vol. 2, pp. 149–150, 152–153. [O5a,1]

Béraud declares himself in favor of an unlimited number of brothels. "Art. (13) Every woman or girl of legal age who has suitable space in her living quarters (at least two rooms), and who is authorized by her husband if she is married, . . . will be able, as the proprietor or principal tenant of the house she inhabits, to become mistress of the house and to obtain a license for operating a brothel." Béraud, *Les Filles publiques de Paris*, vol. 2, p. 156. [O5a,2]

Béraud's proposal is that every girl, even a minor, should, if she so desires, be registered as a prostitute. From his argument: "Your feeling of duty demands a continual surveillance to protect these children. . . . To spurn them is to take on one's head all the consequences of cruel abandonment. . . . They must be registered, then, and surrounded with all the vigilance of authority. Instead of returning them to an atmosphere of corruption, let us submit these hardly nubile girls to a regular life in a house specially designed to receive them. . . . Notify their parents. As soon as they understand that the dissolute life of their daughters will remain undisclosed, that it is a secret religiously guarded by the administration, they will consent once again to acknowledge them." Béraud, *Les Filles publiques*, ‹vol. 2,› pp. 170–171. [O5a,3]

"Why don't . . . the police allow . . . some of the mistresses of the better-known houses of prostitution to give . . . evening parties, balls, and concerts, with the addition of tables for écarté? Then, at least, the sharpers could be carefully watched, whereas in other circles [gambling houses are meant] this is impossible, seeing that police action . . . there is . . . virtually nil." F. F. A. Béraud, *Les Filles publiques de Paris et la police qui les régit* (Paris and Leipzig, 1839), vol. 2, p. 202. [O6,1]

"There are . . . epochs, seasons of the year even, which are fatal to the virtue of a great many young *Parisiennes*. During these periods, in the licensed brothels and elsewhere, the investigations of the police turn up many more girls engaged in illicit prostitution than during all the rest of the year. I have often inquired into the causes of these periodic surges of debauchery, but there isn't anyone—even in the administration—who can answer this question. I have to rely on my own observations here, and, after much perseverance, I have finally succeeded in discovering the true principle of this increase in prostitution . . . at . . . certain times of the year. . . . With the approach of New Year's Day, of the Feast of Kings, and the festivals of the Virgin, . . . girls like to give and receive presents or to offer beautiful bouquets; they also want a new dress for themselves, or a hat in the newest fashion, and, lacking the necessary pecuniary means, . . . they turn for some days to prostitution to acquire such means. . . . Here, then, are the motives for the recrudescence in acts of debauchery at certain intervals and during certain holidays." F. F. A. Béraud, *Les Filles publiques de Paris et la police qui les régit* (Paris and Leipzig, 1839), vol. 1, pp. 252–254. [O6,2]

Against the medical examination at police headquarters: "Every woman seen walking along the Rue de Jérusalem, either to or from the police station there, is immediately stigmatized with the name *fille publique*. . . . It is a regular scandal. On the days set aside for visits, one always finds the approaches to the station overrun by a large number of men awaiting the appearance of these unhappy creatures, knowing, as they do, that those who leave by the dispensary have been deemed healthy." F. F. A. Béraud, *Les Filles publiques de Paris*, vol. 1, pp. 189–190. [O6,3]

The lorettes preferred the neighborhood around Notre Dame de Lorette because it was new, and because, as the first occupants of the recently constructed buildings, they paid lower rents. [O6,4]

"If it is a different sort of allure that you seek, go to the Tuileries, to the Palais-Royal, or to the Boulevard des Italiens. There you will see more than one urban siren seated on a chair, her feet resting on another chair, while beside her a third chair lies vacant. It is a magnet for the ladies' man. . . . The milliners' shops . . . likewise offer a multitude of resources for enthusiasts. There you dicker over hats—pink, green, yellow, lilac, or plaid. You agree on a price; you give your address; and next day, at the appointed hour, you see arrive at your place not only the hat but the girl who was positioned behind it, and who was crimping, with delicate fingers, the gauze, the ribbon, or some other frill so pleasing to the ladies." F. F. A. Béraud, *Les Filles publiques de Paris; Précédées d'une notice historique sur la prostitution chez les divers peuples de la terre*, by M.A.M., vol. 1, pp. cii–civ (Préface). [O6a,1]

"That the number of *filles publiques* at first seems very great is owing to a sort of phantasmagoria produced by the comings and goings of these women along a routine circuit, which has the effect of multiplying them to infinity. . . . Adding to this illusion is the fact that, on a single evening, the *fille publique* very often sports multiple disguises. With an eye just the least bit practiced, it is easy to convince oneself that the woman who at eight o'clock is dressed in a rich and elegant outfit is the same who appears as a cheap grisette at nine, and who will show herself at ten in a peasant dress. It is this way at all points in the capital to which prostitutes are habitually drawn. For example: follow one of these girls down the boulevard, between the Porte Saint-Martin and the Porte Saint-Denis. She is attired for the nonce in a hat with feathers and a silk gown covered by a shawl. She turns into the Rue Saint-Martin, keeping always to the right-hand side, comes to the narrow streets that border the Rue Saint-Denis, and enters one of the numerous houses of debauchery located there. A short time later, she comes out wearing her gray gown or rustic weeds." F. F. A. Béraud, *Les Filles publiques de Paris* (Paris and Leipzig, 1839), vol. 1, pp. 51–52. ☐ Fashion ☐   [O6a,2]

Les Filles de marbre ‹The Marble Maidens›, a play in five acts, with songs, by MM. Théodore Barrière and Lambert Thiboust; performed for the first time, in Paris, at the Théâtre du Vaudeville, May 17, 1853. The first act has the main characters appearing as ancient Greeks; the hero, Raphael, who later dies for love of the marble maiden, Marco, is here the sculptor Phidias, who creates the figures of marble. The act closes with a smile from the statues: they remained motionless when Phidias promised them fame, but turn smiling to Gorgias, who promises them money.   [O7,1]

"You see, . . . in Paris there are two kinds of women, just as there are two kinds of houses . . . : the bourgeois house, where one lives only after signing a lease, and the rooming house, where one lives by the month. . . . How are they to be distinguished? . . . By the sign. . . . Now, the outfit is the sign of the female . . . , and there are outfits of such eloquence that it is absolutely as if you could read on the second floor the advertisement, 'Furnished Apartment to Let'!" Dumanoir and Th. Barrière, *Les Toilettes tapageuses: Comédie en un acte* (Paris, 1856), p. 28.
                                                                         [O7,2]

Nicknames of the drum corps at the Ecole Polytechnique around 1830: Gavotte, Vaudeville, Mélodrame, Zéphir. Around 1860: Brin d'Amour ‹Blade of Love›, Cuisse de Nymphe ‹Nymph's Thigh›. ‹G.› Pinet, ‹*Histoire de l'Ecole polytechnique* (Paris, 1887),› p. 212.   [O7,3]

Bourlier proposes that the gambling houses reopen concessions and that the receipts be used to build an opera house—"one as magnificent as the Stock Exchange"—and a hospital. Louis Bourlier, *Epître aux détracteurs du jeu* (Paris, 1831), p. vii.   [O7,4]

Against the gambling firm of Benazet—which, among other things, engaged in illegal business practices by using, in its gambling houses, a higher exchange-rate on gold for its own transactions—the following tract appeared: Louis Bourlier, *Pétition à MM. les députés* (Paris [Galeries d'Orléans], June 30, 1839). Bourlier was a former employee of the firm.   [O7,5]

> On the floor of the Stock Exchange, as on our parquet,
> You come take your chances, wager what you may:
> Red and black at *trente et quarante*, rise and fall at the Bourse,
> Of every loss and every gain are equally the source,
> . . . . .
> For if playing the market is just like our roulette,
> Why proscribe the latter and the former abet?

Louis Bourlier, *Stances à l'occasion de la loi qui supprime la ferme des jeux; Addressées à la Chambre* (Paris, 1837), ⟨p. 5⟩. [O7,6]

A great print (lithograph) from 1852, *Maison de jeu* ⟨Gambling House⟩, shows at center the emblematic figure of a panther or tiger, on whose coat, as though on a rug, the better half of a roulette table is set. Cabinet des Estampes. [O7a,1]

"Lorettes were variously priced, according to the districts in which they lived." Going from the cheaper to the more expensive: Rue de Grammont, Rue du Helder, Rues Saint-Lazare and Chaussée-d'Antin, Faubourg du Roule. Paul d'Ariste, *La Vie et le monde du boulevard, 1830–1870* (Paris ⟨1930⟩), pp. 255–256. [O7a,2]

"Women are not allowed in the Stock Exchange when prices are being quoted, but they can be seen standing around in groups outside, impatiently awaiting the great oracle of the day." *Acht Tage in Paris* (Paris, July 1855), p. 20. [O7a,3]

"In the thirteenth *arrondissement* there are women who expire as they begin to make love; they whisper to love a last sweet nothing." Louis Lurine, *Le Treizième Arrondissement de Paris* (Paris, 1850), pp. 219–220. A nice expression for the Lady of Camellias, who appeared two years later. ⟨See O10a,7.⟩ [O7a,4]

At the time of the Restoration: "It was no disgrace to gamble. . . . Through the coming and going of soldiers, who were almost always adept at games of chance, the Napoleonic wars had spread abroad the pleasure of gambling." Egon Caesar Conte Corti, *Der Zauberer von Homburg und Monte Carlo* (Leipzig ⟨1932⟩), p. 30. [O7a,5]

January 1, 1838. "After the prohibition, the French bankers in the Palais-Royal, Benazet and Chabert, departed for Baden-Baden and Wiesbaden, and many employees went to Pyrmont, Aachen, Spa, and elsewhere." Egon Caesar Conte Corti, *Der Zauberer von Homburg und Monte Carlo* (Leipzig), pp. 30–31. [O7a,6]

From M. J. Ducos (de Gondrin), *Comment on se ruine à la Bourse* (Paris, 1858): "In no way desiring to attack legitimate rights, I have nothing to say against the serious operations of the Stock Market, operations for which stockbrokers were specifically created. My criticism concerns the commissions charged on fictitious markets, . . . as well as the usurious earnings" (p. 7). "No matter how favorable it might happen to be, there is no luck, in the playing of the Stock Exchange, that could withstand the exorbitant commissions of the stockbrokers. . . . On the Rhine, there are two gambling establishments (at Homburg and Wiesbaden) where they conduct a game of *trente et quarante* in which a slight commission of $62^1/_2$ centimes for every 100 francs is deducted in advance. . . . This is . . . one thirty-second of the stockbroker's commission and the earnings combined. *Trente et quarante* is played for red and black, just as on the Stock Market one plays for the rise and fall, with the difference that the odds are always exactly the same with the former and any kind of fraud is impossible—the weak, there, being not at all at the mercy of the strong" ⟨p. 16⟩.   [O7a,7]

In the provinces, speculation on the Stock Exchange was dependent on "getting news from Paris . . . about the fluctuations in the exchange of the most important stocks. . . . Special couriers and carrier pigeons had to serve this end, and one of the favorite methods in a France that, in those days, was dotted with windmills was to transmit signals from mill to mill. If the window of one of these mills was opened, that meant a rise in prices, and the signal was taken up by nearby mills and passed on; if the window remained closed, then a fall in prices was indicated. And the news traveled in this way, from mill to mill, out of the capital and into the provinces." The Blanc brothers, however, preferred to make use of the optical telegraph, which was legally reserved for the government. "One fine day in 1834, at the request of an agent for Blanc, a Parisian telegraphist in an official telegram sent an *H* to Bordeaux, which was supposed to indicate a rise in stocks. In order to mark this letter, and also to guard against discovery, he inserted after the *H* a symbol denoting error." Difficulties cropped up along this route, and so the Blancs combined this method with another. "If, for example, the French stocks at 3 percent showed an advance of at least 25 centimes, then the Paris agent for the Blancs, a certain Gosmand, sent a packet containing gloves to the telegraph official in Tours, whose name was Guibout, and who was prudently addressed on the parcel as a manufacturer of gloves and stockings. But if there was a decline of at least the same amount, then Gosmand sent stockings or neckties. The address written on this packet carried a letter or a number which Guibout then immediately dispatched, together with the error symbol, in an official telegram to Bordeaux." This system functioned for about two years. Reported in the *Gazette des Tribunaux* of 1837. Egon Caesar Conte Corti, *Der Zauberer von Homburg und Monte Carlo* (Leipzig ⟨1932⟩), pp. 17–19.   [O8,1]

Amorous Conversations of Two Girls of the Nineteenth Century at Fireside (Rome and Paris: Verlag Grangazzo, Vache & Cie). Some remarkable formulations: "Ah, ass and cunt, how simple these words, and yet so expressive. Look at me now—how do you like my ass, then, and my cunt, dear Lise?" (p. 12). "In the temple the sacrificer, in the anus the forefinger as sexton, on the clitoris two fingers as deacons; and thus I awaited the things that should come there. 'If my ass is in the right position, then please, my friend, begin!'"[8] The names of the two girls: Elise and Lindamine.   [O8,2]

Lecomte on the fashion correspondent Constance Aubert, who had an important position at *Le Temps*, and whose articles were paid for with deliveries of fashionable items from the houses about which she had written: "The pen becomes a true source of capital which, day by day, can fix the amount of revenue one wishes to obtain. All of Paris becomes a bazaar where nothing escapes the hand that reaches for it. It's already been quite a while since this hand was extended." Jules Lecomte, *Les Lettres de Van Engelgom*, ed. Henri d'Almeras (Paris, 1925), p. 190. Lecomte's letters first appeared in 1837 in the *Indépendant* of Brussels.

[O8a,1]

"It is by the tendency of the mind called reminiscence that the wishes of the man condemned to the glittering captivity of cities incline . . . toward a stay in the country, toward his original abode, or at least toward the possession of a simple, tranquil garden. His eyes aspire to rest on some greenery, sufficiently far away from the stresses of the shop counter or the intrusive rays of the living room lamp. His sense of smell, continually assaulted by pestilent emanations, longs for the scent of flowers. A border of modest and mild violets would altogether ravish his senses. . . . This happiness . . . denied him, he would push the illusion so far as to transform the ledge of his window into a hanging garden, and the mantelpiece of his unassuming parlor into an enamel bed of blossoms and leaves. Such is the man of the city, and such is the source of his passion for the flowers of the fields. . . . These reflections induced me to set up a number of looms on which I had weavers make designs imitating the flowers of nature. . . . The demand for these kinds of shawls was enormous. . . . They were sold before being made; the orders for their delivery streamed in. . . . This brilliant period of shawls, this golden age of manufacture . . . did not last long, yet in France it resulted in a virtual goldmine, from which flowed wealth that was all the more considerable in that its main source was foreign. Along with the fact of this remarkable demand, it may be of interest . . . to know in what manner it generally propagated itself. Just as I had expected, Paris bought up very few shawls with natural flowers represented on them. It was the provinces that demanded these shawls, in proportion to their distance from the capital; and foreign countries, in proportion to their distance from France. And their reign is not yet over. I still supply countries all across Europe, where there is hardly a chance for a shawl of cashmere bearing artificial designs. . . . On the basis of what Paris did *not* do in the case of shawls with natural-flower designs, . . . couldn't one conclude, recognizing Paris as the real center of taste, that the farther one gets from this city, the closer one comes to natural inclinations and feelings; or, in other words, that taste and naturalness have, in this case, nothing in common—and are even mutually exclusive?" J. Rey, Manufacturer of Cashmere Shawls, *Etudes pour servir à l'histoire des châles* (Paris, 1823), pp. 201–202, 204–206. The copy in the Bibliothèque Nationale contains, on the frontispiece, an inscription by an early reader: "This treatise on a seemingly trivial subject . . . is remarkable for the purity and elegance of its style, as well as for an erudition worthy of Anarcharsis."

[O8a,2]

Should the flower fashions of the Biedermeier period and the Restoration be linked to an unconscious discomfort with the growth of the big cities? [O8a,3]

"At the beginning of the reign of Louis Philippe, public opinion was also [like that of today concerning the Stock Market] opposed to games of chance. . . . The Chamber of Deputies . . . voted for their suppression, even though the state derived from them an annual revenue of twenty million francs. . . . At the present time, in Paris, play on the Stock Market does not provide anything like twenty million per year to the government; but, on the other hand, it does produce at least one hundred million for those stockbrokers, outside brokers,[9] and usurers . . . who reported earnings . . . , raising at times the interest rate to above 20 percent.—These hundred million are won from the four or five thousand undiscerning players who, by seeking naively to take advantage of one another, get completely taken themselves" (that is, by the stockbrokers). M. J. Ducos (de Gondrin), *Comment on se ruine à la Bourse* (Paris, 1858), pp. v–vi. [O9,1]

During the July Revolution, the Stock Exchange was used as a military hospital and munitions factory. Prisoners were employed in the manufacture of grapeshot. See Tricotel, *Esquisse de quelques scènes de l'intérieur de la Bourse* ‹Paris, 1830›. It was also used as a treasury. Silverware looted from the Tuileries was brought there. [O9,2]

There were shawls that took twenty-five to thirty days to weave. [O9,3]

Rey argues in favor of French cashmeres. Among other things, they have the advantage of being new. Which Indian shawls are not. "Need I mention all the revels it has witnessed, all the torrid scenes—to say no more—it has served to veil? Our modest and discreet Frenchwomen would be more than a little embarrassed if they came to know *the antecedents* of that shawl which makes them so happy!" Nevertheless, the author does not wish to endorse the opinion according to which all shawls have already been worn in India—a proposition just as false as that "which says that the tea coming out of China has already been steeped." J. Rey, *Etudes pour servir à l'histoire des châles* (Paris, 1823), pp. 226–227. [O9,4]

The first shawls appear in France in the wake of the Egyptian campaign.[10] [O9,5]

> Onward, my sisters, march on, night and day,
> At every hour, and at every price, to make love.
> Here below we are constrained by fate
> To save the home and all respectable women.

A. Barbier, *Satires et poèmes: Lazare* (Paris, 1837), p. 271; cited in Liefde, *Le Saint-Simonisme dans la poésie française* ‹entre 1825 et 1865 (Haarlem, 1927)›, p. 125. [O9,6]

In the sixteenth section of Baudelaire's *Spleen de Paris*, "L'Horloge" ‹The Clock›, we come upon a conception of time which can be compared to that of the gambler. [O9,7]

Regarding the influence of fashion on erotic life, a telling observation by Eduard Fuchs (*Die Karikatur der europäischen Völker*, vol. 2 ‹Munich, 1921›, p. 152): "Women of the Second Empire do not say, 'I love him,' but rather, 'I fancy him'—'*J'ai un caprice pour lui*.'" [O9,8]

J. Pellcoq depicts the high-kicking leg in the cancan with the inscription: "Present arms!" Eduard Fuchs, *Die Karikatur der europäischen Völker*, vol. 2, p. 171. [O9a,1]

"Many of the *galante* lithographs published in the 1830s featured simultaneous obscene variations for the lover of directly erotic images. . . . Toward the end of the Thirties, these novelties passed gradually out of fashion." Eduard Fuchs, *Illustrierte Sittengeschichte vom Mittelalter bis zur Gegenwart: Das bürgerliche Zeitalter*, supplement (Munich), p. 309. [O9a,2]

Eduard Fuchs mentions "the appearance of an illustrated catalogue of prostitutes, which could date from 1835–1840. The catalogue in question consists of twenty erotic lithographs in color, each one of which has printed at the bottom the address of a prostitute." Five different arcades figure among the first seven addresses in the catalogue. Eduard Fuchs, *Illustrierte Sittengeschichte vom Mittelalter bis zur Gegenwart: Das bürgerliche Zeitalter*, supplement (Munich), p. 157. [O9a,3]

As Engels was being trailed by police agents, in consequence of statements made by itinerant German artisans (among whom his agitation, up until the weakening of Grün's position, had met with little success), he writes to Marx: "If the suspicious-looking individuals who have been following me for the past fourteen days really are police spies, . . . then Headquarters will have handed out, of late, a good many admission tickets to the *bals* Montesquieu, Valentino, Prado, and the rest. I am indebted to M. Delessert for an acquaintance with some very lovely grisettes and for much *plaisir*."[11] Cited in Gustav Mayer, *Friedrich Engels*, vol. 1, *Friedrich Engels in seiner Frühzeit*, 2nd ed. (Berlin ‹1933›), p. 252. [O9a,4]

In 1848, on a trip through France's wine-producing regions, Engels discovers "that each of these wines produces a different intoxication, and that with a few bottles you can pass through . . . all intermediate stages, from the Musard quadrille to the Marseillaise, from the mad gaiety of the cancan to the wild ardor of revolutionary fever." Cited in Gustav Mayer, *Friedrich Engels*, vol. 1, *Friedrich Engels in seiner Frühzeit* (Berlin), p. 319.[12] [O9a,5]

"After the Café de Paris closed in 1856, the Café Anglais came to occupy a position during the Second Empire corresponding to that of the Café de Paris during the reign of Louis Philippe. It was a tall white building with a maze of corridors and innumerable public and private rooms." S. Kracauer, *Jacques Offenbach und das Paris seiner Zeit* (Amsterdam, 1937), p. 332.[13]   [O9a,6]

"The factory workers in France call the prostitution of their wives and daughters the Xth working hour, which is literally correct." Karl Marx, *Der historische Materialismus*, ed. Landshut and Mayer (Leipzig ‹1932›), p. 318.[14]   [O10,1]

"The print seller . . . will provide, on request, the address of the model who has posed for his obscene photographs." Gabriel Pélin, *Les Laideurs du beau Paris* (Paris, 1861), p. 153. In the shops of these *imagiers*, obscene pictures of individual models were hung in the window, while pictures of groups were found inside.
[O10,2]

Dance halls, according to *Le Caricaturiste* of August 26, 1849: Salon du Sauvage, Salon d'Apollon, Château des Brouillards. *Paris sous la République de 1848*, Exposition of the City of Paris (Paris, 1909), p. 40.   [O10,3]

"The regulation of the hours of work . . . was the first rational bridle on the murderous, meaningless caprices of fashion—caprices that consort so badly with the system of modern industry." Footnote here: "John Bellers remarked as far back as 1699: 'The uncertainty of fashions does increase necessitous poor' (*Essays about the Poor, Manufactures, Trade, Plantations, and Immorality*, p. 9)." Karl Marx, *Das Kapital*, ed. Korsch (Berlin ‹1932›), p. 454.[15]   [O10,4]

From the *Pétition des filles publiques de Paris à MM. le Préfet de police etc., rédigée par Mlle. Pauline et apostillée par MM. les épiciers, cabaretiers, limonadiers et marchands de comestibles de la capitale* . . . : "The business in itself is unfortunately quite ill-paid, but with the competition of other women and of elegant ladies, who pay no taxes, it has become wholly unprofitable. Or are we all the more blameworthy because we take cash while they take cashmere shawls? The city charter guarantees personal freedom to everyone; if our petition to Monsieur le Préfet proves unavailing, then we shall . . . apply to the Chambers. Otherwise, it would be better to live in the kingdom of Golconda, where girls of our sort formed one of the forty-four divisions of the populace and, as their sole responsibility, had only to dance before the king—which service we are prepared to render His Honor the prefect, should he ever wish it." Friedrich von Raumer, *Briefe aus Paris und Frankreich im Jahre 1830* (Leipzig, 1831), vol. 1, pp. 206–207.
[O10,5]

The author of the preface to Journet's *Poésies* speaks of "workshops involving different kinds of needlework, where, . . . for forty centimes per day, the women and young girls with no work would . . . squander . . . their . . . health. Nearly all of these unfortunate women . . . are forced to fall back on the fifth quarter of their day." Jean Journet, *Poésies et chants harmoniens* (Paris: A la Librairie Universelle de Joubert, 2 Passage du Saumon, et chez l'auteur, June 1857), p. lxxi (Editor's preface). [O10,6]

"Le Trottoir de la Rue des Martyrs" cites many of Gavarni's captions but makes no mention at all of Guys, who nevertheless could have furnished the immediate model for the following description: "It is a pleasure to see them walking down this asphalt pavement, one side of their dress hitched up jauntily to the knee, so as to flash in the sun a leg fine and nervous as that of an Arabian horse, full of exquisite quivers and tremors, and terminating in a half-boot of irreproachable elegance. Who cares about the morality of these legs! . . . What one wants is to go where they go." Alfred Delvau, *Les Dessous de Paris* (Paris, 1860), pp. 143–44 ("Les Trottoirs parisiens" ‹Parisian Sidewalks›). [O10a,1]

Proposal of Ganilh's: To use part of the proceeds from the state lottery as income for gamblers who have reached a certain age. [O10a,2]

Lottery agents: "Their shops always have two or three exits and several compartments, so as to facilitate the overlapping operations of gambling and usury and to show consideration for timid customers. It is not unusual for man and wife, without suspecting a thing, to be sitting right beside each other in these mysterious cubicles, which each thinks to utilize so cunningly alone." Carl Gustav Jochmann, *Reliquien*, ed. Heinrich Zschokke, vol. 2 (Hechingen, 1837), p. 44 ("Die Glücksspiele" ‹Games of Chance›). [O10a,3]

"If it is the belief in mystery that makes believers, then there are evidently more believing gamblers in the world than believing worshipers." Carl Gustav Jochmann, *Reliquien*, ed. Heinrich Zschokke, vol. 2 (Hechingen, 1837), p. 46 ("Die Glücksspiele"). [O10a,4]

According to Poisson, "Mémoire sur les chances que les jeux de hasard, admis dans les maisons de jeu de Paris, présentent à la banque" ‹Report on the Odds Presented to the Bank by the Games of Chance Operating in the Gambling Houses of Paris›, as read before the Academy of Sciences in 1820, the yearly turnover in *trente-et-un* was 230 million francs (bank's earnings, 2,760,000); in roulette, 100 million francs (with the bank earning 5,000,000). See Carl Gustav Jochmann, *Reliquien*, ed. Heinrich Zschokke, vol. 2 (Hechingen, 1837), p. 51 ("Die Glücksspiele"). [O10a,5]

Gambling is the infernal counterpart to the music of the heavenly hosts. [O10a,6]

On Halévy's *Froufrou:* "*Les Filles de marbre* had introduced the age of the courtesan, and *Froufrou* marked its end. . . . Froufrou breaks down under the . . .

strain of knowing that her life is ruined, and finally she returns to her family, a dying woman." S. Kracauer, *Jacques Offenbach und das Paris seiner Zeit* (Amsterdam, 1937), pp. 385–386. The comedy *Les Filles de marbre* was an answer to Dumas' *La Dame aux camélias* of the year before.[16]   [O10a,7]

"The gambler is driven by essentially narcissistic and aggressive desires for omnipotence. These, insofar as they are not immediately linked to directly erotic desires, are characterized by a greater temporal radius of extension. A direct desire for coitus may, through orgasm, be satisfied more rapidly than the narcissist-aggressive desire for omnipotence. The fact that genital sexuality, in even the most favorable cases, leaves a residue of dissatisfaction goes back, in turn, to three facts: not all pregenital desires, such as later are subsidiary to genitality, can be accommodated in coitus; and from the standpoint of the Oedipus complex, the object is always a surrogate. Together with these two . . . considerations goes . . . the fact that the impossibility of acting out large-scale unconscious aggression contributes to the lack of satisfaction. The aggression abreacted in coitus is very much domesticated. . . . Thus it happens that the narcissistic and aggressive fiction of omnipotence becomes above all a cause of suffering: whoever on that account has experienced the mechanism of pleasure as abreacted in games of chance, and possessing, as it were, eternal value, succumbs the more readily to it in proportion as he is committed to the 'neurotic pleasure in duration' (Pfeifer); and, as a consequence of pregenital fixations, he is less able to assimilate such pleasure to normal sexuality. . . . It should also be borne in mind that, according to Freud, the sexuality of human beings bears the stamp of a function that dwindles, whereas this cannot in any way be predicated of the aggressive and narcissistic tendencies." Edmund Bergler, "Zur Psychologie des Hasardspielers," *Imago*, 22, no. 4 (1936), pp. 438–440.   [O11,1]

"The game of chance represents the only occasion on which the pleasure principle, and the omnipotence of its thoughts and desires, need not be renounced, and on which the reality principle offers no advantages over it. In this retention of the infantile fiction of omnipotence lies posthumous aggression against the . . . authority which has 'inculcated' the reality principle in the child. This unconscious aggression, together with the operation of the omnipotence of ideas and the experience of the socially viable repressed exhibition, conspires to form a triad of pleasures in gambling. This triad stands opposed to a triad of punishments constituted from out of the unconscious desire of loss, the unconscious homosexual desire for domination, and the defamation of society. . . . At the deepest level, the game of chance is love's will to be extorted by an unconscious masochistic design. This is why the gambler always loses in the long run." Edmund Bergler, "Zur Psychologie des Hasardspielers," *Imago*, 22, no. 4 (1936), p. 440.   [O11,2]

Brief account of Ernst Simmel's ideas on the psychology of the gambler: "The insatiable greed that finds no rest within an unending vicious circle, where loss becomes gain and gain becomes loss, is said to arise from the narcissistic compulsion to fertilize and give birth to oneself in an anal birth fantasy, surpassing and replacing one's own father and mother in an endlessly escalating process. 'Thus, in the last analysis, the passion for gambling satisfies the claim of the bisexual ideal, which the narcissist discovers in himself; at stake is the formation of a compromise between masculine and feminine, active and passive, sadistic and masochistic; and in the end it is the unresolved decision between genital and anal libido that confronts the gambler in the well-known symbolic colors of red and black. The passion for gambling thus serves an autoerotic satisfaction, wherein betting is foreplay, winning is orgasm, and losing is ejaculation, defecation, and castration.'" Edmund Bergler, "Zur Psychologie des Hasardspielers," *Imago*, 22, no. 4 (1936), pp. 409–410; with reference to Ernst Simmel, "Zur Psychoanalyse des Spielers," *Internationale Zeitschrift für Psychoanalyse*, 6 (1920), p. 397.

[O11a,1]

With the discovery of Tahiti, declares Fourier, with the example of an order in which "large-scale industry" is compatible with erotic freedom, "conjugal slavery" has become unendurable.[17]   [O11a,2]

Apropos of Freud's conjecture that sexuality is a dwindling function "of" the human being, Brecht remarked on how the bourgeoisie in decline differs from the feudal class at the time of its downfall: it feels itself to be in all things the quintessence of humankind in general, and hence can equate its own decline with the death of humanity. (This equation, moreover, can play a part in the unmistakable crisis of sexuality within the bourgeoisie.) The feudal class, by virtue of privileges, felt itself to be a class apart, which corresponded to the reality. That enabled it, in its waning, to manifest some elegance and insouciance.   [O11a,3]

Love for the prostitute is the apotheosis of empathy with the commodity.

[O11a,4]

> Magistrate of Paris! March with the system,
> Pursue the good work of Mangin and Belleyme:
> Design, as châteaux for the filthy Phrynés,
> Pestilent, lonely, and dark *quartiers*.

‹Auguste-Marseille› Barthélemy, *Paris: Revue satirique à M. G. Delessert* (Paris, 1828), p. 22.   [O12,1]

A description of the lower class of prostitute that had settled in the vicinity of the city gate, the *barrière*. It comes from Du Camp, and would make an excellent caption for many of Guys's watercolors: "If one pushes open the barrier and the door that closes the entrance, one finds oneself in a bar furnished with marble or wooden tables and lighted by gas; through the clouds of smoke given off by the pipes, one distinguishes garbage men, diggers, carters—drinkers, for the most part—seated before a flask of absinthe and talking to creatures who are as grotesque as they are pitiable. All of these creatures are dressed, in almost the same way, in that red cotton fabric that is dear to African Negroes, and out of which the curtains in little provincial inns are made. What covers them cannot be called a dress; it is a beltless smock, puffed up with a crinoline. Exposing the shoulders with an outrageously low cut, and coming just to the level of the knees, this outfit gives them the look of large, inflated children, prematurely aged and glistening with fat, wrinkled, dazed, and with those pointed heads that are the sign of imbecility. When the inspectors, checking the registration book, call them and they get up to reply, they have all the charm of a circus dog." Maxime Du Camp, *Paris: Ses organes, ses fonctions et sa vie dans la seconde moitié du XIXe siècle,* vol. 3 (Paris, 1872), p. 447 ("La Prostitution"). (O12,2)

"The basic principle . . . of gambling . . . consists in this: . . . that each round is independent of the one preceding. . . . Gambling strenuously denies all acquired conditions, all antecedents . . . pointing to previous actions; and that is what distinguishes it from work. Gambling rejects . . . this weighty past which is the mainstay of work, and which makes for seriousness of purpose, for attention to the long term, for right, and for power. . . . The idea of beginning again, . . . and of doing better, . . . occurs often to one for whom work is a struggle; but the idea is . . . useless, . . . and one must stumble on with insufficient results." Alain ⟨Emile-Auguste Chartier⟩, *Les Idées et les ages* ⟨Paris, 1927⟩, vol. 1, pp. 183–184 ("Le Jeu"). [O12,3]

The lack of consequences that defines the character of the isolated experience ⟨*Erlebnis*⟩ found drastic expression in gambling. During the feudal age, the latter was essentially a privilege of the feudal class, which did not participate directly in the production process. What is new is that in the nineteenth century the bourgeois gambles. It was above all the Napoleonic armies that, on their campaigns, became the agents of gambling for the bourgeoisie. [O12a,1]

The significance of the temporal element in the intoxication of the gambler has been noticed before this by Gourdon, as well as by Anatole France. But these two writers see only the meaning time has for the gambler's pleasure in his winnings, which, quickly acquired and quickly surrendered, multiply themselves a hundredfold in his imagination through the numberless possibilities of expenditure remaining open and, above all, through the one real possibility of wager, of *mise en jeu*. What meaning the factor of time might have for the process of gambling itself is at issue in neither Gourdon nor France. And the pastime of gambling is, in fact, a singular matter. A game passes the time more quickly as chance comes to light more absolutely in it, as the number of combinations encountered in the course of play (of *coups*) is smaller and their sequence shorter. In other words, the greater the component of chance in a game, the more speedily it elapses. This state of affairs becomes decisive in the disposition of what comprises the authentic "intoxication" of the gambler. Such intoxication depends on the peculiar capacity of the game to provoke presence of mind through the fact that, in rapid succession, it brings to the fore constellations which work—each one wholly independent of the others—to summon up in every instance a thoroughly new, original reaction from the gambler. This fact is mirrored in the tendency of gamblers to place their bets, whenever possible, at the very last moment—the moment, moreover, when only enough room remains for a purely reflexive move. Such reflexive behavior on the part of the gambler rules out an "interpretation" of chance. The gambler's reaction to chance is more like that of the knee to the hammer in the patellar reflex. [O12a,2]

The superstitious man will be on the lookout for hints; the gambler will react to them even before they can be recognized. To have foreseen a winning play without having made the most of it will cause the uninitiated to think that he is "in luck" and has only to act more quickly and courageously the next time around. In reality, this occurrence signals the fact that the sort of motor reflex which chance releases in the lucky gambler failed to materialize. It is only when it does not take place that "what is about to happen," as such, comes clearly to consciousness. [O13,1]

Only the future that has not entered as such into his consciousness is parried by the gambler. [O13,2]

The proscription of gambling could have its deepest roots in the fact that a natural gift of humanity, one which, directed toward the highest objects, elevates the human being beyond himself, only drags him down when applied to one of the meanest objects: money. The gift in question is presence of mind. Its highest manifestation is the reading that in each case is divinatory. [O13,3]

The peculiar feeling of happiness in the one who wins is marked by the fact that money and riches, otherwise the most massive and burdensome things in the world, come to him from the fates like a joyous embrace returned to the full. They can be compared to words of love from a woman altogether satisfied by her man. Gamblers are types to whom it is not given to satisfy the woman. Isn't Don Juan a gambler? [O13,4]

"During the period of facile optimism, such as radiated from the pen of an Alfred Capus, it was customary on the boulevard to attribute everything to luck." Gaston Rageot, "Qu'est-ce qu'un événement?," _Le Temps,_ April 16, 1939.—The wager is a means of conferring shock value on events, of loosing them from the contexts of experience.[18] It is not by accident that people bet on the results of elections, on the outbreak of war, and so on. For the bourgeoisie, in particular, political affairs easily take the form of events on a gaming table. This is not so much the case for the proletarian. He is better positioned to recognize constants in the political process. [O13,5]

The Cemetery of the Innocents as promenade. "Such was the place which the Parisians of the fifteenth century frequented as a sort of lugubrious counterpart to the Palais-Royal of 1789. . . . In spite of the incessant burials and exhumations going on there, it was a public lounge and a rendezvous. Shops were established before the charnel houses, and prostitutes strolled under the cloisters." J. Huizinga, *Herbst des Mittelalters* (Munich, 1928), p. 210.[19]   [O13a,1]

Are fortunetelling cards more ancient than playing cards? Does the card game represent a pejoration of divinatory technique? Seeing the future is certainly crucial in card games, too.   [O13a,2]

Money is what gives life to number; money is what animates the marble maiden (see O7,1).   [O13a,3]

Gracian's maxim—"In all things, know how to win time to your side"—will be understood by no one better and more gratefully than the one to whom a long-cherished wish has been granted. With this, compare the magnificent definition which Joubert gives of such time. It defines, contrariwise, the gambler's time: "There is time even in eternity; but it is not a terrestrial or worldly time. . . . It destroys nothing; it completes." J. Joubert, *Pensées* (Paris, 1883), vol. 2, p. 162.   [O13a,4]

Concerning the heroic element in gambling—as it were, a corollary to Baudelaire's poem "Le Jeu": "A thought which regularly crosses my mind at the gambling table . . . : What if one were to store up all the energy and passion . . . which every year is squandered . . . at the gaming tables of Europe—would one have enough to make a Roman people out of it, and a Roman history? But that's just it. Because each man is born a Roman, bourgeois society aims to de-Romanize him, and thus there are games of chance and games of etiquette, novels, Italian operas and stylish gazettes, casinos, tea parties and lotteries, years of apprenticeship and travel, military reviews and changing of the guard, ceremonies and visits, and the fifteen or twenty close-fitting garments which daily, with a salutary loss of time, a person has to put on and take off again—all these have been introduced so that the overabundant energy evaporates unnoticed!" Ludwig Börne, *Gesammelte Schriften* (Hamburg and Frankfurt am Main, 1862), vol. 3, pp. 38–39 ("Das Gastmahl der Spieler" ‹Gamblers' Banquet›).   [O13a,5]

"But can you realize what delirium, what frenzy, possesses the mind of a man impatiently waiting for a gambling den to open? Between the evening gambler and the morning gambler the same difference exists as between the nonchalant husband and the ecstatic lover waiting under his mistress's window. It is only in the morning that quivering passion and stark need manifest themselves in all their horror. At that time of day, you can stare in wonderment at the true gambler—one who has not eaten or slept, lived or thought, so cruelly has he been scourged by the lash of his vice. . . . At that baleful hour, you will meet with eyes whose steady calm is frightening, with faces that hold you spellbound; you will intercept gazes which lift the cards and greedily peer beneath them. Gaming-houses then reach sublimity only at opening time." Balzac, *La Peau de chagrin*, Editions Flammarion (Paris), p. 7.[20]   [O14,1]

Prostitution opens a market in feminine types.   [O14,2]

On gambling: the less a man is imprisoned in the bonds of fate, the less he is determined by what lies nearest at hand.   [O14,3]

The ideal of the shock-engendered experience ‹*Erlebnis*› is the catastrophe. This becomes very clear in gambling: by constantly raising the stakes, in hopes of getting back what is lost, the gambler steers toward absolute ruin.   [O14,4]

[The Streets of Paris]

> In short, the streets of Paris
> Were set to rhyme. Hear how.
>
> —Beginning of *Dit des rues de Paris,* by Guillot (Paris, 1875), with
> preface, notes, and glossary by Edgar Marcuse (first word of the
> second line in the original: "Was")

We leave an imprint each time we enter into a history.[1]

They spoke of Paris as *la ville qui remue*—the city that never stops moving. But no less important than the life of this city's layout is here the unconquerable power in the names of streets, squares, and theaters, a power which persists in the face of all topographic displacement. Those little theaters which, in the days of Louis Philippe, still lined the Boulevard du Temple—how often has one of them been torn down, only to resurface, newly built, in some other *quartier.* (To speak of "city districts" is odious to me.) How many street names, even today, preserve the name of a landed proprietor who, centuries earlier, had his demesne on their ground. The name "Château d'Eau," referring to a long-vanished fountain, still haunts various *arrondissements* today. Even the better-known eating establishments are, in their way, assured of their small municipal immortality—to say nothing of the great literary immortality attaching to the Rocher de Cancall, the Véfour, the Trois Frères Provençaux. For hardly has a name made its way in the field of gastronomy, hardly has a Vatel or a Riche achieved its fame, than all of Paris, including the suburbs, is teeming with Petits Vatels and Petits Riches. Such is the movement of the streets, the movement of names, which often enough run at cross-purposes to one another.   [P1,1]

And then the timeless little squares that suddenly are there, and to which no name attaches. They have not been the object of careful planning, like the Place Vendôme or the Place des Grèves, and do not enjoy the patronage of world history, but owe their existence to houses that have slowly, sleepily, belatedly assembled in response to the summons of the century. In such squares, the trees hold sway; even the smallest afford thick shade. Later, however, in the gaslight, their leaves have the appearance of dark-green frosted glass near the street lamps, and their earliest green glow at dusk is the automatic signal for the start of spring in the big city. [P1,2]

The Quartier de l'Europe already existed as a project, incorporating the names of the European capitals, in 1820. [P1,3]

On February 4, 1805, houses were first numbered, by imperial decree. Previous attempts to do this—in January 1726—had met with violent resistance. Owners of houses declared themselves ready to number the side entrances, but not their carriage entrances. The Revolution had already introduced the numbering of houses according to districts; in some districts, there were 1,500–2,000 numbers. [P1,4]

After the assassination of Marat, Montmartre was renamed Mont-Marat. [P1,5]

The function of the saints in the naming of Parisian streets suddenly became clear during the Revolution. To be sure, the Rues Saint-Honoré, Saint-Roch, and Saint-Antoine were, for a while, known as Honoré, Roch, and Antoine, but it could not take hold; a hiatus had opened up that to the ear of the Frenchman was unendurable. [P1,6]

"An enthusiast of the Revolution once proposed transforming Paris into a map of the world: *all* streets and squares were to be rechristened and their new names drawn from noteworthy places and things across the world." Pursue this in imagination and, from the surprising impression made by such an optical-phonetic image of the city, you will recognize the great importance of street names. Pinkerton, Mercier, and C. F. Cramer, *Ansichten der Hauptstadt des französischen Kaiserreichs vom Jahre 1806 an,* vol. 1 (Amsterdam, 1807), p. 100 (ch. 8, "Neologie," by Pinkerton). [P1,7]

There is a peculiar voluptuousness in the naming of streets. [P1,8]

"The name La Roquette, given to two prisons, a street, and an entire district, comes from the plant of that name (*Eruca sativa*), which used to flourish in formerly uninhabited areas." La Grande Roquette was, for a long time, the prison in which those sentenced to death awaited the outcome of their appeal. Maxime Du Camp, *Paris*, vol. 3, p. 264. [P1,9]

The sensuality in street names—certainly the only sort which citizens of the town, if need be, can still perceive. For what do we know of streetcorners, curbstones, the architecture of the pavement—we who have never felt heat, filth, and the edges of the stones beneath our naked soles, and have never scrutinized the uneven placement of the paving stones with an eye toward bedding down on them. [P1,10]

"Pont d'Austerlitz! Its famous name evokes for me something quite other than the battle. Despite what people have maintained to me, and which I accept for form's sake, it was the battle that took its name from the bridge. An explanation for this took shape in my mind on the basis of my reveries, my recollection of distracted schooldays, and analogies in the savor and sound of certain words. As a child, I always kept this explanation under my hat; it was part of my secret language. And here it is: at the time of wars, crusades, and revolutions, on the eve of battle, the warriors would proceed with their ensigns to this bridge, old as the hills, and there, in all solemnity, would drink a cup of austerlitz. This austerlitz, formidable brew, was quite simply the hydromel of our ancestors, the Gauls, but more bitter and more filled with seltzer." Charles Vildrac ⟨Charles Messager⟩, ⟨*Les*⟩ *Ponts de Paris* ⟨Paris, ca. 1930⟩. [P1a,1]

Excursus on the Place du Maroc. Not only city and interior but city and open air can become entwined, and *this* intertwining can occur much more concretely. There is the Place du Maroc in Belleville: that desolate heap of stones with its rows of tenements became for me, when I happened on it one Sunday afternoon, not only a Moroccan desert but also, and at the same time, a monument of colonial imperialism; topographic vision was entwined with allegorical meaning in this square, yet not for an instant did it lose its place in the heart of Belleville. But to awaken such a view is something ordinarily reserved for intoxicants. And in such cases, in fact, street names are like intoxicating substances that make our perceptions more stratified and richer in spaces. One could call the energy by which they transport us into such a state their *vertu évocatrice,* their evocative power—but that is saying too little; for what is decisive here is not the association but the interpenetration of images. This state of affairs may be adduced, as well, in connection with certain pathological phenomena: the patient who wanders the city at night for hours on end and forgets the way home is perhaps in the grip of this power. [P1a,2]

Street names in Jean Brunet, *Le Messianisme—organisation générale de Paris: Sa constitution générale,* part 1 (Paris, 1858): Boulevard of Financiers, Boulevard of Jewelers, Boulevard of Merchants, Boulevard of Manufacturers, Boulevard of Metalworkers, Boulevard of Dyers, Boulevard of Printers, Boulevard of Students, Boulevard of Writers, Boulevard of Artists, Boulevard of Administrators.—Quartier Louis XIV (detailed argument for this name, p. 32, involving "embellishment" of the Saint-Martin and Saint-Denis gateways): Confection Street, Exportation Square, Ceramics Street, Bookbinding Street. [P1a,3]

"I read of a geographic scheme in which Paris would be the map, and hackney coaches the professors. Certainly, I would rather have Paris be a geographic map than a volume in the Roman calendar; and the names of saints, with which the streets are baptized, cannot compare, in either euphony or utility, with the names of the towns that have been proposed as substitutes for them. Thus, the Faubourg Saint-Denis, according to this plan, would be called the Faubourg de *Valenci-*

ennes; the Faubourg Saint-Marceau would become the Faubourg de Marseille; the Place de Grèves would be known as the Place de Tours or de Bourges; and so on." Mercier, *Le Nouveau Paris* ‹Paris, 1800›, vol. 5, p. 75. [P1a,4]

Rue des Immeubles Industriels—How old is this street? [P1a,5]

A surprising argument, a hundred years ago, in favor of an American system for demarcating streets: "You poor professors, who teach moral philosophy and belles lettres! Your names are posted in small black letters on a streetcorner, above a milestone. The name of this jeweler is as dazzling as a thousand fires—it shines like the sun. It is for sale, but it is expensive." Mercier, *Le Nouveau Paris,* vol. 4, pp. 74–75. [P1a,6]

Apropos of the theory of street names: "Proper names, too, have an effect that is conceptually unburdened and purely acoustic. . . . To borrow an expression from Curtius (p. 65), proper names are "bare formulas" which Proust can fill up with feelings because they have not yet been rationalized by language." Leo Spitzer, *Stilstudien* (Munich, 1928), vol. 2, p. 434. [P1a,7]

"Street," to be understood, must be profiled against the older term "way." With respect to their mythological natures, the two words are entirely distinct. The way brings with it the terrors of wandering, some reverberation of which must have struck the leaders of nomadic tribes. In the incalculable turnings and resolutions of the way, there is even today, for the solitary wanderer, a detectable trace of the power of ancient directives over wandering hordes. But the person who travels a street, it would seem, has no need of any waywise guiding hand. It is not in wandering that man takes to the street, but rather in submitting to the monotonous, fascinating, constantly unrolling band of asphalt. The synthesis of these twin terrors, however—monotonous wandering—is represented in the labyrinth. ☐ Antiquity ☐ [P2,1]

Whoever wishes to know how much at home we are in entrails must allow himself to be swept along in delirium through streets whose darkness greatly resembles the lap of a whore. ☐ Antiquity ☐ [P2,2]

How names in the city, though, first become potent when they issue within the labyrinthine halls of the Métro. Troglodytic kingdoms—thus they hover on the horizon: Solférino, Italie and Rome, Concorde and Nation. Difficult to believe that up above they all run out into one another, that under the open sky it all draws together. ☐ Antiquity ☐ [P2,3]

The true expressive character of street names can be recognized as soon as they are set beside reformist proposals for their normalization. For example, Pujoulx's proposal for naming the streets of Paris after the cities and localities of France, taking into consideration their geographic positions relative to one another, as well as their population, and having regard for rivers and mountains, whose names would go especially to long streets which cross several districts—all of this "in order to provide an ensemble such that a traveler could acquire geographic knowledge of France within Paris and, reciprocally, of Paris within France." J. B. Pujoulx, *Paris à la fin du dix-huitième siècle* (Paris, 1801), p. 81. ☐ Flânerie ☐

[P2,4]

"Seventeen of the gates correspond to imperial routes. . . . In these names, one would seek in vain for a general system. What are Antibes, Toulouse, and Bâle doing there beside La Villette and Saint-Ouen? . . . If one had wanted to establish some distinctions, one could have given to each gate the name of the French city most distant in that direction." E. de Labédollière, *Histoire du nouveau* (Paris), p. 5.

[P2,5]

"Some beneficial measures by the municipal magistracy date from the time of the Empire. On November 3, 1800, there was, by decree, a general revision of street names. Most of the grotesque vocables invented by the Revolution disappeared. The names of politicians were almost all replaced by the names of military men." Lucien Dubech and Pierre d'Espezel, *Histoire de Paris* (Paris, 1926), p. 336.

[P2,6]

"In 1802, in various neighborhoods—Rue du Mont-Blanc, Chaussée d'Antin— sidewalks were built, with an elevation of three or four inches. There was then an effort to get rid of the gutters in the center of the streets." Lucien Dubech and Pierre d'Espezel, *Histoire de Paris* (Paris, 1926), p. 336.   [P2,7]

"In 1805, the new system of sequential numbering of houses, begun on the initiative of Frochot and still in effect today: even numbers separated from odd, the even numbers on the right and the odd on the left, according as one moves away from the Seine or follows its course. The numbers were white and were placed on a red background in streets parallel to the river, on a black background in streets perpendicular to it." Lucien Dubech and Pierre d'Espezel, *Histoire de Paris* (Paris, 1926), p. 337.   [P2,8]

Around 1830: "The Chaussée d'Antin is the neighborhood of the nouveaux riches of the financial world. All these districts in the western part of town have been discredited: the city planners of the period believed that Paris was going to develop in the direction of the saltpeter works, an opinion that ought to instill prudence in today's developers. . . . A lot on the Chaussée d'Antin had trouble finding a buyer at 20,000 to 25,000 francs." Dubech and d'Espezel, *Histoire de Paris* (Paris, 1926), p. 364.   [P2a,1]

July Monarchy: "While most of the street names recalling political events were done away with, new ones appeared commemorating a date: the Rue du 29 Juillet." Dubech and d'Espezel, *Histoire de Paris*, p. 389.   [P2a,2]

"I know nothing more ridiculous and more inconsistent than the names of streets, squares, blind alleys, and culs-de-sac in Paris. Let us choose at random some of these names in one of the more beautiful neighborhoods, and we cannot but note this incoherence and caprice. I arrive by the Rue Croix-des-Petits-Champs; I cross the Place des Victoires; I turn into the Rue Vuide-Gousset, which takes me to the Passage des Petits-Pères, from which it is only a short distance to the Palais-Égalité. What a salmagundi! The first name calls to mind a cult object and a rustic landscape; the second offers military triumphs; the third, an ambush; the fourth, the memory of a nickname given to a monastic order; and the last, a word which ignorance, intrigue, and ambition have taken turns abusing." J. B. Pujoulx, *Paris à la fin du XVIIIᵉ siècle* (Paris, 1801), pp. 73–74.　　　　　　　　[P2a,3]

"Two steps from the Place de la Bastille in the Faubourg Saint-Antoine, people still say, 'I am going to Paris'. . . . This suburb has its own mores and customs, even its own language. The municipality has numbered the houses here, as in all other parts of Paris; but if you ask one of the inhabitants of this suburb for his address, he will always give you the name his house bears and not the cold, official number. . . . This house is known by the name 'To the King of Siam,' that by 'Star of Gold'; this house is called 'Court of the Two Sisters,' and that one is called 'Name of Jesus'; others carry the name 'Basket of Flowers,' or 'Saint Esprit,' or 'Bel Air,' or 'Hunting Box,' or 'The Good Seed.'" Sigmund Engländer, *Geschichte der französischen Arbeiterassociationen* (Hamburg, 1864), vol. 3, p. 126.　　　[P2a,4]

Excerpt from a proposal for naming streets which presumably stems from the Revolution: "Someone . . . proposed giving streets and alleys the names of virtues and generous sentiments, without reflecting that this moral nomenclature was too limited for the great number of streets to be found in Paris. . . . One senses that in this project there was a certain logic in the arrangement of names; for example, the Rue de la *Justice*, or that of *l'Humanité*, had necessarily to lead to the Rue du *Bonheur*, . . . while the Rue de la *Probité* . . . had to cross all of Paris in leading to the most beautiful neighborhoods." J. B. Pujoulx, *Paris à la fin du XVIIIᵉ siècle* (Paris, 1801), pp. 83–84.　　　　　　　　[P2a,5]

Concerning the magic of street names. Delvau on the Place Maubert: "It is not a square; it is a large blot, so full of filth and mire that even the lips sully themselves in pronouncing this name from the thirteenth century—not because it is old but because it exhales an odor of iniquity . . . which shocks the sense of smell." A. Delvau, *Les Dessous de Paris* (Paris, 1866), p. 73.　　　　　　　　[P2a,6]

"It is not superfluous to observe that a foreigner, who, on arriving in a city, starts out everywhere judging by appearances, could well suppose, in coming upon these unsystematic and insignificant street names, that the reasoning of those who live here was no less loosely connected; and, certainly, if several streets presented him with base or obscene names, he would have grounds for believing in the immorality of the inhabitants." J. B. Pujoulx, *Paris à la fin du XVIIIe siècle* (Paris, 1801), p. 77.   [P3,1]

Rationalism took particular offense at names like Rue des Mauvais-Garçons, Rue Tire-Boudin, Rue Mauvaises-Paroles, Rue Femme-sans-Tête, Rue du Chat qui Pêche, Rue Courtaud-Villain.[2] It is such places that are frequented, says Pujoulx, by those who won't listen to his proposals.   [P3,2]

"What a pleasure for the resident of the South of France to rediscover, in the names of the various districts of Paris, those of the place where he was born, of the town where his wife came into the world, of the village where he spent his early years." J. B. Pujoulx, *Paris à la fin du XVIIIe* siècle (Paris, 1801), p. 82.   [P3,3]

"The hawkers choose their newspapers according to which neighborhoods they want to work in, and even within these areas there are nuances that must be distinguished. One street reads *Le Peuple*, while another will have only *La Réforme*, but the street perpendicular to these, which connects them, takes *L'Assemblée nationale*, or perhaps *L'Union*. A good hawker ought to be able to tell you, with an eye to the promises made by all the aspiring legislators and written upon our walls, what percentage of the vote in a particular *arrondissement* each of these political mendicants can expect to have." A. Privat d'Anglemont, *Paris inconnu* (Paris, 1861), p. 154. ▯ Flâneur ▯   [P3,4]

What was otherwise reserved for only a very few words, a privileged class of words, the city has made possible for all words, or at least a great many: to be elevated to the noble status of name. This revolution in language was carried out by what is most general: the street.—Through its street names, the city is a linguistic cosmos.   [P3,5]

Apropos of Victor Hugo's "command of image. The few insights we have into his methods of composition confirm that the faculty of interior evocation was much stronger in him than in other people. This is why he was able—from memory, and without taking any notes—to describe the *quartier* of Paris through which Jean Valjean escapes in *Les Misérables*; and this description is strictly accurate, street by street, house by house." Paul Bourget, obituary notice for Victor Hugo in the *Journal des débats*: "Victor Hugo devant l'opinion" (Paris, 1885), p. 91.   [P3,6]

On an etching: "Rue Tirechape—in 1863 as it was in 1200." Cabinet des Estampes.   [P3,7]

In an engraving from 1830, one can see a man seated on a tree trunk in the Boulevard Saint-Denis.   [P3,8]

In 1865, on the Boulevard des Capucines, at the corner of the Rue de Sèze and the Rue Caumartin, the first *refuge*, or street-island, was installed.   [P3a,1]

"The way the cutups go to make faces at the entrance to the morgue; the way the showoffs come there to recite their grotesque jokes . . . in such a place; the way the crowd . . . gathers around to laugh their fill at the often indecent antics of a juggler, after gaping at five cadavers laid out side by side. . . . Now, that's what I call revolting . . . !" Victor Fournel, *Ce qu'on voit dans les rues de Paris* (Paris, 1858), p. 355 ("La Morgue"). [P3a,2]

Ghosts of the city: "Romanticism on the decline . . . delights in legends. While George Sand, dressed as a man, supposedly rides on horseback across Paris in the company of Lamartine, dressed as a woman, Dumas has his novels written in cellars and drinks champagne upstairs with various actresses. Or, better yet, Dumas does not exist; he is only a mythical being, a trade name invented by a syndicate of editors." J. Lucas-Dubreton, *La Vie d'Alexandre Dumas Père* (Paris ⟨1928⟩), p. 141. [P3a,3]

"Here, then, . . . is the . . . *Dictionnaire de la langue verte* ⟨Dictionary of Slang⟩, of which I would like people to say . . . what was said of Sébastien Mercier's *Tableau de Paris*—namely, that it was conceived in the street and written on a milestone." Alfred Delvau, *Dictionnaire de la langue verte* (Paris, 1866), p. iii. [P3a,4]

A nice description of elegant neighborhoods: "the nobility, silently bunkered in these cloistral streets as in an immense and splendid monastery of peace and refuge." Paul-Ernest Rattier, *Paris n'existe pas* (Paris, 1857), p. 17. [P3a,5]

Around 1860, the Paris bridges were still insufficient for the traffic between the two banks; there was frequent recourse to ferries. The fare for this service was two sous; proletarians, therefore, could only rarely make use of it. (From P.-E. Rattier, *Paris n'existe pas* (Paris, 1857), pp. 49–50. [P3a,6]

"In Hugo, the Vendôme Column, the Arc de Triomphe, and the Invalides go hand in hand, if I may put it this way. There is a historical and political, a real and literary connection among these three monuments. Today, . . . the position of these three terms, their relation, has changed. The Column has been effectively supplanted, in spite of Vuillaume. And it is the Pantheon that has come, as it were, to replace it—especially since Hugo's success in bringing it to yield, so to speak, to the great men. Today, the trilogy of monuments is the Arc de Triomphe, the Pantheon, and the Church of the Invalides." Charles Péguy, *Oeuvres complètes, 1873–1914: Oeuvres de prose* (Paris, 1916), p. 419 ("Victor-Marie, Comte Hugo"). ⟨See C6; C6a,1, section III.⟩ [P3a,7]

"The true Paris is by nature a dark, miry, malodorous city, confined within its narrow lanes, . . . swarming with blind alleys, culs-de-sac, and mysterious passages, with labyrinths that lead you to the devil; a city where the pointed roofs of the somber houses join together up there near the clouds and thus begrudge you

the bit of blue which the northern sky would give in alms to the great capital. . . .
The true Paris is full of freak shows, repositories at three centimes a night for
unheard-of beings and human phantasmagorias. . . . There, in a cloud of ammo-
niac vapor, . . . and on beds that have not been made since the Creation, reposing
side by side are hundreds, thousands, of charlatans, of match sellers, of accordion
players, of hunchbacks, of the blind and the lame; of dwarfs, legless cripples, and
men whose noses were bitten off in quarrels, of rubber-jointed men, clowns making a comeback, and sword swallowers; of jugglers who balance a greasy pole on
the tips of their teeth . . . ; children with four legs, Basque giants and other kinds,
Tom Thumb in his twentieth reincarnation, plant-people whose hand or arm is the
soil of a living tree, which sprouts each year its crown of branches and leaves;
walking skeletons, transparent humans made of light . . . and whose faint voice
can make itself heard to an attentive ear . . . ; orangutans with human intelligence;
monsters who speak French." Paul-Ernest de Rattier, *Paris n'existe pas* (Paris,
1857), pp. 12, 17–19. To be compared with this are Hugo's drawings, and also
Haussmann's vision of Paris. [P4,1]

Fate of the republican opposition under Guizot. "*L'Emancipation*, of Toulouse,
cites the words of a conservative to whom someone had expressed pity for the
plight of those political prisoners languishing behind bars: 'I will feel sorry for
them when mushrooms begin growing on their backs.'" Jean Skerlitch, *L'Opinion
publique en France d'après la poésie politique et sociale de 1830 à 1848*
⟨Lausanne, 1901⟩, pp. 162–163. [P4,2]

"With this magic title of *Paris*, a play or review or book is always assured of
success." Théophile Gautier, first sentence of the Introduction to *Paris et les
Parisiens au XIX*ᵉ *siècle* (Paris, 1856), p. i. [P4,3]

"The universe does nothing but gather the cigar butts of Paris." Théophile Gautier, Introduction, *Paris et les Parisiens au XIX*ᵉ *siècle* (Paris, 1856), p. iii. [P4,4]

"A long time ago, someone had the idea of peopling the Champs-Elysées with
statues. The moment for this has still not arrived." Th. Gautier, "Etudes philosophiques," *Paris et les Parisiens au XIX*ᵉ ⟨siècle,⟩ p. 27. [P4,5]

"Thirty years ago . . . it was still . . . virtually the sewer it had been in ancient
times. A very large number of streets, whose surface is now crowned, were then
hollow causeways. You very often saw, at the low point where the gutters of a street
or a square terminated, large rectangular gratings with great bars, the iron of
which shone, polished by the feet of the multitude, dangerous and slippery for
wagons, and making horses stumble. . . . In 1832, in many streets, . . . the old
Gothic cloaca still cynically showed its jaws. They were enormous, sluggish gaps of
stone, sometimes surrounded by stone blocks, displaying monumental effront-

ery." Victor Hugo, *Oeuvres complètes*, novels, vol. 9 (Paris, 1881), p. 181 *(Les Misérables).*[3]   [P4a,1]

On the wall of the Farmers-General, under Louis XVI: "The *mur* ‹wall› by which Paris is immured makes Paris murmur."   [P4a,2]

As a legend of the morgue, Maillard cites the following remarks from E. Texier, *Le Tableau de Paris* (1852): "In this building lives a clerk who . . . has a family. Who knows whether the clerk's daughter does not have a piano in her room and, on Sunday evenings, does not dance with her friends to the strains of the ritornellos of Pilodo or Musard." According to Maillard, however, the clerk did not live in the morgue in 1852. Cited in Firmin Maillard, *Recherches historiques et critiques sur la Morgue* (Paris, 1860), pp. 26–27. The account goes back, as Maillard himself explains, to a report of 1830 by Léon Gozlan, which for its part was somewhat feuilletonistic.   [P4a,3]

"The Place Maubert, accursed square which hides the name of Albertus Magnus." *Paris chez soi* ‹Paris, 1854›, p. 9 (Louis Lurine, "A travers les rues") .   [P4a,4]

In Mercier, *Nouveau Paris* (1800), vol. 6, p. 56, it is recounted that "the mysterious hornblowers . . . in fact made a pretty sinister noise. It was not to announce the sale of water that they made this noise; their lugubrious blare, dignified fanfare of terror, was most often a threat of arson: 'They were in the taverns, and they would communicate from one neighborhood to the next,' says Mercier. 'All their harmonized sounds were centrally coordinated, and when they played with redoubled force, one expected something to happen. You would listen for a long while, understanding nothing; but in all this uproar there was a language of sedition. These plots were no less deep for being hatched so blatantly. It has been remarked that, at the time of the fires, the signal was more prompt, more rapid, more shrill. When the blaze broke out at Les Célestins, . . . my brain had been dulled the day before by the noise of the horns. On another occasion, the ears were assailed by the cracking of whips; on some days, it was a banging on boxes. One trembles at these keen daily alarms.'" Edouard Fournier, *Enigmes des rues de Paris* (Paris, 1860), pp. 72–73 ("Sur quelques bruits de Paris").   [P4a,5]

C. Bouglé, *Chez les prophètes socialistes* (Paris, 1918), cites, in the essay "L'Alliance intellectuelle franco-allemande" (p. 123), Börne's phrase about the streets of Paris: those glorious streets "whose pavement one ought to tread with bare feet only."   [P5,1]

The Avenue Rachel leads to the cemetery of Montmartre. About this, Daniel Halévy writes (*Pays parisiens* [Paris ‹1932›], p. 276): "Rachel, the tragedienne, is here the herald and patroness."   [P5,2]

"The importance accorded the traffic of pilgrims—many people in those days went to venerate relics—is attested by the fact that the old Roman road, with its two sections, was named after the principal destinations of such pilgrimage: in the north, Saint-Martin, after the Cathedral of Tours; and in the south, Saint-Jacques, after the Spanish Jago di Compostella." Fritz Stahl, *Paris* (Berlin ‹1929›), p. 67. [P5,3]

The oft-formulated observation that the neighborhoods of Paris each have a life of their own is given support by Stahl (*Paris,* p. 28) in a reference to certain Parisian monuments. (He speaks of the Arc de Triomphe, and one could also mention Notre Dame or Notre Dame de Lorette.) Forming a background to important streets, these buildings give their districts a center of gravity and, at the same time, represent the city as such within them. Stahl says "that each monumental edifice . . . appears with an escort, like a prince with his train of followers, and by this retinue it is separated from the respectfully withdrawing masses. It becomes the ruling nucleus of a neighborhood that appears to have gathered around it" (p. 25). [P5,4]

[Panorama]

Does anyone still want to go with me into a panorama?

—Max Brod, *Über die Schönheit hässlicher Bilder*
(Leipzig, 1913), p. 59

There were panoramas,[1] dioramas, cosmoramas, diaphanoramas, navaloramas, pleoramas (*pleō*, "I sail," "I go by water"), fantoscope⟨s⟩, fantasma-parastases, phantasmagorical and fantasmaparastatic *expériences*, picturesque journeys in a room, georamas; optical picturesques, cinéoramas, phanoramas, stereoramas, cycloramas, *panorama dramatique*.

"In our time so rich in pano-, cosmo-, neo-, myrio-, kigo- and dio-ramas." M. G. Saphir, in the *Berliner Courier*, March 4, 1829; cited in Erich Stenger, *Daguerres Diorama in Berlin* (Berlin, 1925), p. 73.   [Q1,1]

The postrevolutionary Versailles as waxworks: "The leftover royal statues were remodeled. That of Louis XIV in the great Salle de l'Orangerie wears a liberty cap in place of the chiseled-away peruke, carries a pike instead of the official baton; and, so that no one mistakes the identity of the newly created god of war, there is written at the foot of the statue: 'French Mars, protector of the liberty of the world.' A similar prank was played with Coustou's colossal bas-relief, representing Louis XIV on horseback, in the large gallery of the château. The genius of fame, who descends from the clouds, holds a liberty cap over the bare head of the king, instead of the laurel wreath of former times." □ Colportage □ F. J. L. Meyer, *Fragmente aus Paris im IV. Jahr der französischen Republik* (Hamburg, 1797), vol. 2, p. 315.   [Q1,2]

On the exhibition of a group of thieves reproduced in wax, which (around 1785) was put together by Curtius or some other entrepreneur for the fair in Saint-Laurent: "Some were chained and clad in rags, while others were almost naked and lying on straw. It was a fairly graphic rendering. The only portraits that were likenesses were those of the two or three leaders; but since the gang was large, the owner had been obliged to find them some company. I took it for granted that he had fashioned these others more or less according to whim, and with this thought in mind I was rather casually strolling past the swarthy faces—often obscured by the coarse moustaches of these inferior brigands—when I thought I perceived beneath their repulsive appearance some characteristics that were not at all unfamiliar. As I looked more closely, I became convinced that the owner of the master thieves (who was also the owner of the other waxworks), wanting to make use of some wax figures that were no longer in fashion, or of some commissioned portraits that were subsequently rejected, had dressed them up in rags, loaded them with chains, and slightly disfigured them in order to place them here with the great thieves. . . . I could not help smiling when I considered that the wife of one of the subjects might well discover, among these gentlemen, the portrait of her husband that had once been so gloriously commissioned. And, really, I am not joking when I say that I saw among this group an excellent likeness of *Linguet,** who, several months earlier, had enjoyed a place of honor in the other room, and who undoubtedly had been transported here for economic reasons, and to fill out the prison." (*Simon-Nicolas-Henri Linguet, 1736–1794; polygraph and lawyer; executed on the guillotine.) J. B. Pujoulx, *Paris à la fin du XVIIIe siècle* (Paris, 1801), pp. 102–103. ⬜ Colportage ⬜ [Q1,3]

"Waiting" can be associated with the exhibition of imperial panoramas as much as with boredom. It is highly significant that Brod, in a gloss on "panorama," hits upon all the keywords of this investigation: "fashion," "boredom," "gaslight," and so on. [Q1,4]

"A mélange of Morgue and Musée de Luxembourg": this was how Jules Claretie characterized the battle panoramas. *La Vie à Paris, 1881* (Paris), p. 438. In these panoramas we perceive that wars, too, are subject to fashion. Max Brod, in his "Panorama," sees "inactive officers . . . searching about for suitable battlefields to wage their imaginary colonial wars." It is a wardrobe of battles: the impecunious come and look around to see if somewhere there is not a used battlefield they can make their own without going to great expense. [Q1,5]

Play on words with "-rama" (on the model of "diorama") in Balzac, at the beginning of *Père Goriot.*[2] [Q1,6]

Setup of the panoramas: View from a raised platform, surrounded by a balustrade, of surfaces lying round about and beneath. The painting runs along a cylindrical wall approximately a hundred meters long and twenty meters high. The principal panoramas of the great panorama painter Prévost: Paris, Toulon, Rome, Naples, Amsterdam, Tilsit, Wagram, Calais, Antwerp, London, Florence, Jerusalem, Athens. Among his pupils: Daguerre. [Q1a,1]

1838: the Rotonde des Panoramas constructed by Hittorff. ⬜ Iron ⬜ [Q1a,2]

Panorama at the Paris Exhibition of 1855. [Q1a,3]

A panorama under construction, in an image originally published in *L'Illustration*. Courtesy of the Syndicat Autoren- und Verlagsgesellschaft, Frankfurt am Main. See Q1a,1.

It remains to be discovered what is meant when, in the dioramas, the variations in lighting which the passing day brings to a landscape take place in fifteen or thirty minutes. Here is something like a sportive precursor of fast-motion cinematography—a witty, and somewhat malicious, "dancing" acceleration of time, which, by way of contrast, makes one think of the hopelessness of a mimesis, as Breton evokes it in *Nadja:* the painter who in late afternoon sets up his easel before the Vieux-Port in Marseilles and, in the waning light of day, constantly alters the light-relations in his picture, until it shows only darkness. For Breton, however, it was "unfinished."[3]   [Q1a,4]

To reflect rigorously on the particular pathos that lies hidden in the art of the panoramas. On the particular relation of this art to nature, but also, and above all, to history. How peculiar this relation was may be gathered from these sentences by Wiertz, whose painting, in fact, has a distinctly panoramic tendency. "There has been much talk of realism in painting. Generally speaking, paintings which are called 'realistic' are rarely in keeping with this rubric. Pure realism ought to manage things so that a represented object would seem within reach of your hand. . . . If, in general, what is properly termed trompe-l'oeil has been little appreciated, that is because up until now this genre of painting has been practiced only by mediocre painters, by sign painters, those restricted merely to the representation of certain still-life objects. . . . Will the example of M. Wiertz give birth to a new genre?" Commentary on *La Curieuse,* in the catalogue written by the painter himself and entitled *L'Atelier de M. Wiertz.* In *Oeuvres littéraires* ‹Paris, 1870›, pp. 501–502. [Q1a,5]

"Nocturnorama. A new sort of concert will entertain the fashionable society of Paris this winter. All that the music expresses, during these concerts, will be rendered visible through painted transparencies of superior quality. Haydn's *Creation* is in rehearsal and, accompanied by the appropriate phantasmagorias, will no doubt doubly captivate the senses of the audience. / To me, however, this arrangement seems more suited to gay and sentimental diversions than to this great work. / Thus, for example, a strikingly lifelike and moving portrait of Malibran is to appear, while, behind the scenes, a very fine singer delivers an Italian aria—as though one were hearing the shade of Malibran sing." August Lewald, *Album der Boudoirs* (Leipzig and Stuttgart, 1836), pp. 42–43. [Q1a,6]

From time to time in his diorama, Daguerre would have, among other things, the Church of Saint-Etienne du Mont. Midnight Mass. With organ. At the end: extinguishing of candles. [Q1a,7]

The fact that film today articulates all problems of modern form-giving—understood as questions of its own technical existence—and does so in the most stringent, most concrete, most critical fashion, is important for the following comparison of panoramas with this medium. "The vogue for panoramas, among which the panorama of Boulogne was especially remarkable, corresponds to the vogue for cinematographs today. The covered arcades, of the type of the Passage des Panoramas, were also beginning their Parisian fortunes then." Marcel Poëte, *Une Vie de cité Paris* (Paris, 1925), p. 326. [Q1a,8]

‹Jacques-Louis› David exhorted his students to make studies of nature in the panorama. [Q1a,9]

"Many people imagine that art can be perfected indefinitely. This is an error. There is a limit at which it stops. And here is why: it is because the conditions in which the imitation of nature is confined are immutable. One wants a picture—that is to say, a flat surface, surrounded or not surrounded by a frame—and on this surface a representation produced exclusively by means of various colored substances. . . . Within these conditions, which constitute the picture, everything has been attempted. The most difficult problem was perfect relief, deep perspectives carried to the most complete illusion. The stereoscope resolved it." A. J. Wiertz, *Oeuvres littéraires* (Paris, 1870), p. 364. This comment not only throws an interesting light on the points of view from which people looked at things like stereoramas in those days; it also shows very clearly that the theory of "progress" in the arts is bound up with the idea of the imitation of nature, and must be discussed in the context of this idea. [Q2,1]

The multiple deployment of figures in the wax museum opens a way to the colportage phenomenon of space and hence to the fundamental ambiguity of the arcades. The wax statues and busts—of which one is today an emperor, tomorrow a political subversive, and the next day a liveried attendant; of which another represents today Julia Montague, tomorrow Marie Lafargue, the day after tomorrow Madame Doumergue—all are in their proper place in these optical whispering-galleries. For Louis XI, it is the Louvre; for Richard II, the Tower; for Abdel Krim, the desert; and for Nero, Rome. ⬜ Flâneur ⬜   [Q2,2]

Dioramas take the place of the magic lantern, which knew nothing of perspective, but with which, of course, the magic of the light insinuated itself quite differently into residences that were still poorly lit. "Lanterne magique! Pièce curieuse!" With this cry, a peddler would travel through the streets in the evening and, at a wave of the hand, step up into dwellings where he operated his lantern. The *affiche* for the first exhibition of posters still characteristically displays a magic lantern.   [Q2,3]

There was a georama for a while in the Galerie Colbert.—The georama in the fourteenth *arrondissement* contained a small-scale natural reproduction of France.[4]   [Q2,4]

In the same year in which Daguerre invented photography, his diorama burned down. 1839. ⬜ Precursors ⬜   [Q2,5]

There is an abundant literature whose stylistic character forms an exact counterpart to the dioramas, panoramas, and so forth. I refer to the feuilletonist miscellanies and series of sketches from midcentury. Works like *La Grande Ville* ‹The Big City›, *Le Diable à Paris* ‹The Devil in Paris›, *Les Français peints par eux-mêmes* ‹The French as Painted by Themselves›. In a certain sense, they are moral dioramas—not only related to the others in their unscrupulous multiplicity, but technically constructed just like them. To the plastically worked, more or less detailed foreground of the diorama corresponds the sharply profiled feuilletonistic vesturing of the social study, which latter supplies an extended background analogous to the landscape in the diorama.   [Q2,6]

The sea—"never the same"[5] for Proust at Balbec, and the dioramas with their varied lighting, which sets the day marching past the viewer at exactly the speed with which it passes before the reader in Proust. Here, the highest and the lowest forms of mimesis shake hands.   [Q2,7]

The wax museum ‹*Panoptikum*› a manifestation of the total work of art. The universalism of the nineteenth century has its monument in the waxworks. Panopticon: not only does one see everything, but one sees it in all ways.   [Q2,8]

"Navalorama." Eduard Devrient, *Briefe aus Paris* (Berlin, 1840), p. 57.   [Q2,9]

Principal panoramic representations by Prévost for the panoramas of "passage." "Paris, Toulon, Rome, Naples, Amsterdam, Tilsit, Wagram, Calais, Antwerp, London, Florence, Jerusalem, and Athens. All were conceived in the same manner. His spectators, situated on a platform surrounded by a balustrade, as though on the summit of a central building, commanded a view of the entire horizon. Each canvas, affixed to the inner wall of a cylindrical room, had a circumference of 97 meters, 45 centimeters, 2 millimeters (300 feet) and a height of 19 meters, 42 centimeters (60 feet). Thus, the eighteen panoramas by Prévost represent a surface area of 86,667 meters, 6 centimeters (224,000 feet)." Labédollière, *Histoire du nouveau Paris* (Paris), p. 30.   [Q2a,1]

In *The Old Curiosity Shop*, Dickens speaks of the "unchanging air of coldness and gentility" about the waxwork.[6] ☐ Dream House ☐   [Q2a,2]

Daguerre and the Academy [Française?]: "Lemercier . . . gave me a ticket to a public session of the Institute. . . . At this session he is going to recite a poem about Daguerre's machine ‹See Q3a,1› in order to revive interest in the thing, for the inventor lost his whole apparatus in a fire in his room. And so, during my sojourn in Paris, there was nothing to see of the wondrous operation of this machine." Eduard Devrient, *Briefe aus Paris* (Berlin, 1840), p. 260 [letter of April 28, 1839].
                                                                                    [Q2a,3]

In the Palais-Royal, the "Café du Mont Saint-Bernard, a very odd sight, on the first floor opposite the staircase. (A coffeehouse where, roundabout on the walls, are painted Alpine pastures. At the height of the tables is a small gallery in which miniature models constitute the foreground of the painting: small cows, Swiss chalets, mills, sowers [should perhaps be cowherds], and the like—a very odd sight.)" J. F. Benzenberg, *Briefe geschrieben auf einer Reise nach Paris* (Dortmund, 1805), vol. 1, p. 260.   [Q2a,4]

A poster: "The French Language in Panorama." In J. F. Benzenberg, vol. 1, p. 265. In the same context, information concerning the regulation that applies to billstickers.   [Q2a,5]

An exceptionally detailed description of the program at the Pierre Theatre[7] in Benzenberg, vol. 1, pp. 287–292.   [Q2a,6]

The interest of the panorama is in seeing the true city—the city indoors. What stands within the windowless house is the true. Moreover, the arcade, too, is a windowless house. The windows that look down on it are like loges from which one gazes into its interior, but one cannot see out these windows to anything outside. (What is true has no windows; nowhere does the true look out to the universe.)   [Q2a,7]

"The illusion was complete. I recognized at first glance all the monuments and all the places, down to the little courtyard where I lived in a room at the Convent of the Holy Savior. Never did a traveler undergo such an arduous trial; I could not

have expected that Jerusalem and Athens would be transferred to Paris in order to convince me of truth or illusion." Chateaubriand, in the preface to his *Itinéraire de ‹Paris à› Jérusalem*, cited in Emile de Labédollière, *Le Nouveau* (Paris), p. 30.
[Q3,1]

The innermost glowing cells of the city of light, the old dioramas, nested in the arcades, one of which today still bears the name Passage des Panoramas. It was, in the first moment, as though you had entered an aquarium. Along the wall of the great darkened hall, broken at intervals by narrow joints, it stretched like a ribbon of illuminated water behind glass. The play of colors among deep-sea fauna cannot be more fiery. But what came to light here were open-air, atmospheric wonders. Seraglios were mirrored on moonlit waters; bright nights in deserted parks loomed large. In the moonlight you could recognize the château of Saint-Leu, where the last Condé was found hanged in a window. A light was still burning in a window of the château. A couple of times the sun splashed wide in between. In the clear light of a summer morning, one saw the rooms of the Vatican as they might have appeared to the Nazarenes; not far beyond rose Baden-Baden. But candlelight, too, was honored: wax tapers encircled the murdered Duc de Berry in the dusky cathedral that served as mortuary chapel, and hanging lamps in the silken skies of an isle of love practically put round Luna to shame. It was an ingenious experiment on the moonstruck magic night of Romanticism, and its noble substance emerged from the trial victorious.   [Q3,2]

The waxwork figure as mannequin of history.—In the wax museum the past enters into the same aggregate state that distance enters into in the interior.
[Q3,3]

On the world-travel panorama, which operated under the name "Le Tour du Monde" at the Paris world exhibition of 1900, and which animated a changing panoramic background with living figures in the foreground, each time costumed accordingly. "The 'World-Tour Panorama' is housed in a building that has already caused a general sensation because of its bizarre exterior. An Indian gallery crowns the walls of the edifice, while rising at the corners are the tower of a pagoda, a Chinese tower, and an old Portuguese tower." "Le Tour du Monde," in *Die Pariser Weltausstellung in Wort und Bild,* ed. Dr. Georg Malkowsky (Berlin, 1900), p. 59.—The similarity of this architecture to that in zoological gardens is worth noting.   [Q3,4]

Three stages in Lemercier's *Lampélie et Daguerre:* (1) presentation of stationary panoramas; (2) presentation of the technique of their animation, which Daguerre got from Lampélie; (3) description of the overcoming of Lampélie by the tireless Daguerre. In the following, the first stage (the third under ▢ Photography ▢).

Daguerre, in the tower where his erudite brush
Makes a radiant theater of optics,
Reveals in the dark of a giant enclosure
Bright horizons of awesome perspective.
His palette is magic; and his confluent lights,

Diorama on the Rue de Bondy, 1837. Courtesy of the Bibliothèque Nationale de France.
See Q3a,3.

> Once the scene is complete and in place all around,
> Transform a bare cloth covering circular walls
> To a mirror of nature itself.

Népomucène Lemercier, *Sur la Découverte de l'ingénieux peintre du diorama*
[afterward: *Lampélie et Daguerre*] (Institut Royal de France, Annual Public Session of the Five Academies, Thursday, May 2, 1839, chaired by M. Chevreul,
president [Paris, 1839], pp. 26–27).   [Q3a,1]

After the July Revolution, Daguerre's diorama included a view of "la Place de la
Bastille, July 28, 1830." Pinet, *Histoire de l'Ecole polytechnique* ⟨Paris, 1887⟩,
p. 208.   [Q3a,2]

Dioramas at the Château d'Eau (later the Place de la République) and on the Rue
de Bondy. Cabinet des Estampes.   [Q3a,3]

A print advertising the manufacture of precision instruments, J. Molteni and Co.,
62 Rue du Château d'Eau, refers (after 1856!) to, among other things, "apparatus
of phantasmagoria, polyoramas, dioramas, and such." Cabinet des Estampes.
                                                                         [Q3a,4]

Empire vignette: "The Panorama." An illustration plate, linen or paper, showing
tightrope walkers in the middle ground. Amor, with the pointed cap of a carnival
clown or of a town crier, points to a puppet theater in the foreground, where a

knight kneels before his lady while declaring his love. This all in a landscape. Cabinet des Estampes. [Q3a,5]

"I prepared myself to receive *the depositions* of the women she called his *panoramistes*—that is to say, those who walk up and down all the panoramas, particularly the one on the Boulevard Montmartre." P. Cuisin, *La Galanterie sous la sauvegarde des lois* (Paris, 1815), pp. 136–137. [Q3a,6]

"Carporama . . . specializing in the plants, flowers, and fruits of India." J.-L. Croze, "Quelques Spectacles de Paris pendant l'été de 1835" (*Le Temps*, August 22, 1935). [Q3a,7]

The panoramic principle in Balzac: "Our investigation has enabled us to take account of some three hundred real names in the Paris of the period 1800 to 1845, during which the characters of the *Comédie humaine* develop. If one added to this the political figures, the writers and playwrights, the celebrities of all kinds who . . . appear in Balzac's narratives . . . without any link to the action, the total would perhaps mount to five hundred." H. Clouzot and R.-H. Valensi, *Le Paris de la Comédie humaine: Balzac et ses fournisseurs* (Paris, 1926), p. 175. [Q4,1]

Passage des Panoramas. "You will have guessed that this arcade owes its name to a particular spectacle introduced in France in January 1799. The first Panorama in Paris was under the direction of a man from the United States . . . by the name of Robert Fulton. . . . Fulton, at the time of the plan to invade England, presented to the emperor a report on the immediate conversion of the imperial navy to steam. . . . Having been rejected in France, this engineer went on to succeed in America, and it is said that, when finally returning to Saint-Hélène to die, the emperor saw through his spyglass a steamboat which bore the name *The Fulton.*" Louis Lurine, "Les Boulevarts," in *Paris chez soi* (Paris ‹1854›), p. 60. [Q4,2]

Balzac: "When in 1822 he visits the diorama run by Daguerre, he enthusiastically calls it one of the miracles of the century—'a thousand problems are resolved.' And when the daguerreotype is developed twenty years later, he allows a photograph of himself to be made and writes altogether deliriously of this invention, which he claims to have prophesied already in *Louis Lambert* (1835)." [Note at this point: *Corr‹espondance* (1876)›, vol. 1, p. 68 (compare *Goriot*); *Lettres ‹à l'Etrangère›*, vol. 2 ‹1906›, p. 36.] Ernst Robert Curtius, *Balzac* (Bonn, 1923), p. 237. [Q4,3]

Dickens: "There floated before him a vision of a monstrous magazine, entirely written by himself. . . . One characteristic thing he wished to have in the periodical. He suggested an Arabian Nights of London, in which Gog and Magog, the giants of the city, should give forth chronicles as enormous as themselves." G. K. Chesterton, *Dickens,* trans. Laurent and Martin-Dupont (Paris, 1927), p. 81.[8] Dickens had numerous projects for serials. [Q4,4]

The world exhibition of 1889 had a "Panorama Historique," put together by Stevens and Gervex, at the conclusion of which a white-haired Victor Hugo was shown before an allegorical monument of France, which in turn was flanked by allegories of labor and of national defense. [Q4,5]

Balthasar's Feast, by the conductor and composer Jullien (circa 1836): "The chief role . . . devolved upon seven brilliantly colored transparents, which gleamed so fantastically in the darkness that Jullien's orchestra, instead of being the principal attraction, sank to being merely an accompaniment. This feast for the eyes, which was called a 'nocturnorama,' was produced by a mechanical device." S. Kracauer, *Jacques Offenbach und das Paris seiner Zeit* (Amsterdam, 1937), p. 64.[9] [Q4a,1]

"Panorama"[10]—the best known of the Greek-based coinages which emerged during the French Revolution. "On the seventh of Floréal, in the year VII, Robert Fretton ⟨Fulton?⟩ took out a patent 'for the purpose of exhibiting circular pictures called "panoramas."' This first attempt would lead to the idea of a 'peri-panorama,' then a 'cosmorama,' and later a 'panstereorama' (1813)." Ferdinand Brunot, *Histoire de la langue française des origines jusqu'à 1900*; vol. 9, *La Révolution et l'Empire*; section 2, *Les Evénements, les institutions et la langue* (Paris, 1937), p. 1212 ("Les Nomenclatures sous la Révolution"). [Q4a,2]

From Joseph Dufour (1752–1827) we have "hanging tableaux"—strips twelve to fifteen meters long, illustrated in the manner of panoramas. They show landscapes (Bosporus, Italy), genre scenes (savages of the South Seas), mythologies. [Q4a,3]

"I would rather return to the dioramas, whose brutal and enormous magic has the power to impose on me a useful illusion. I would rather go to the theater and feast my eyes on the scenery, in which I find my dearest dreams artistically expressed and tragically concentrated. These things, because they are false, are infinitely closer to the truth." Charles Baudelaire, *Oeuvres*, ed. Le Dantec, vol. 2 ⟨Paris, 1932⟩, p. 273 ("Salon de 1859," section 8, "Le Paysage").[11] [Q4a,4]

In Balzac's works, the number of supernumeraries runs to five hundred persons. Five hundred of his characters appear episodically without being integrated into the action. [Q4a,5]

R

[Mirrors]

The way mirrors bring the open expanse, the streets, into the café—this, too, belongs to the interweaving of spaces, to the spectacle by which the flâneur is ineluctably drawn. "During the day, often sober; in the evening, more buoyant, when the gas flames glow. The art of the dazzling illusion is here developed to perfection. The most commonplace tavern is dedicated to deceiving the eye. Through mirrors extending along walls, and reflecting rows of merchandise right and left, these establishments all obtain an artificial expansion, a fantastical magnitude, by lamplight." Karl Gutzkow, *Briefe aus Paris* (Leipzig, 1842), vol. 1, p. 225.

Thus, precisely with the approach of night, distant horizons bright as day open up throughout the city. [R1,1]

Here, in connection with the mirror motif, should be mentioned the story of the man who could not bear to have, in the interior of his shop or bistro, the legend on the outer windowpane incessantly before his eyes in mirror writing. To discover an anecdote that accords with this. [R1,2]

Brittle, too, are the mosaic thresholds that lead you, in the style of the old restaurants of the Palais-Royal, to a "Parisian dinner" for five francs; they mount boldly to a glass door, but you can hardly believe that behind this door is really a restaurant. The glass door adjacent promises a "Petit Casino" and allows a glimpse of a ticket booth and the prices of seats; but were you to open it—would it open into anything? Instead of entering the space of a theater, wouldn't you be stepping down to the street? Where doors and walls are made of mirrors, there is no telling outside from in, with all the equivocal illumination.[1] Paris is the city of mirrors. The asphalt of its roadways smooth as glass, and at the entrance to all bistros glass partitions. A profusion of windowpanes and mirrors in cafés, so as to make the inside brighter and to give all the tiny nooks and crannies, into which Parisian taverns separate, a pleasing amplitude. Women here look at themselves more than elsewhere, and from this comes the distinctive beauty of the Parisienne. Before any man catches sight of her, she already sees herself ten times reflected. But the man, too, sees his own physiognomy flash by. He gains his image more quickly here than elsewhere and also sees himself more quickly merged with this, his image. Even the eyes of passersby are veiled mirrors, and over that wide bed of the Seine, over Paris, the sky is spread out like the crystal mirror hanging over the drab beds in brothels. [R1,3]

Where were these mirrors manufactured? And when did the custom of furnishing bars with them arise? [R1,4]

Since when the custom of inserting mirrors, instead of canvases, into the expensive carved frames of old paintings? [R1,5]

Let two mirrors reflect each other; then Satan plays his favorite trick and opens here in his way (as his partner does in lovers' gazes) the perspective on infinity. Be it now divine, now satanic: Paris has a passion for mirror-like perspectives. The Arc de Triomphe, the Sacré Coeur, and even the Pantheon appear, from a distance, like images hovering above the ground and opening, architecturally, a fata morgana. ▢ Perspective ▢ [R1,6]

At the end of the 1860s, Alphonse Karr writes that no one knows how to make mirrors any more. [R1,7]

That the last but also the greatest work of this mirror magic is still around to be seen is owing, perhaps, more to its high production costs than to its drawing power and profitability, which today are already on the decline. This work is the "Cabinet des Mirages" at the Musée Grévin. Here were united, one final time, iron supporting beams and giant glass panes intersecting at countless angles. Various coverings make it possible to transform these beams into Greek columns one moment, Egyptian pilasters the next, then into street lamps; and, according as they come into view, the spectator is surrounded with unending forests of Greco-Roman temple columns, with suites, as it were, of innumerable railroad stations, market halls, or arcades, one succeeding another. A fluctuating light and gentle music accompany the performance, and coming before each transformation is the classic signal of the hand bell, and the jolt, which we recognize from our earliest trips around the world, when, in the Kaiserpanorama, before our eyes that were full of the pain of departure, an image would slowly disengage from the stereoscope, allowing the next one to appear. [R1,8]

Mallarmé as genius of mirrors. [R1a,1]

"The manufacture of mirrors in Paris and Saint-Gobain, 'mirrors known all over Europe and without serious rival,' continues unabated." Levasseur, *Histoire des classes ouvrières ‹et de l'industrie en France, de 1789 à 1870* (Paris, 1903)›, vol. 1, p. 446. [R1a,2]

"Our mirrors are growing larger by the day, which makes them more and more sought after throughout Europe. Today they are within range of the most middling

fortune, and whereas there is scarcely a household in France that does not possess at least one or two, nothing is rarer in England than to come upon one of our mirrors, even in castles." Adolphe Blanqui, *Histoire de l'exposition des produits de l'industrie française en 1827* (Paris, 1827), p. 130. [R1a,3]

Egoistic—"that is what one becomes in Paris, where you can hardly take a step without catching sight of your dearly beloved self. Mirror after mirror! In cafés and restaurants, in shops and stores, in haircutting salons and literary salons, in baths and everywhere, 'every inch a mirror'!" S. F. Lahrs⟨?⟩, *Briefe aus Paris*, in *Europa: Chronik der gebildeten Welt*, ed. August Lewald (Leipzig and Stuttgart, 1837), vol. 2, p. 206. [R1a,4]

Redon paints things as if they appeared in a somewhat clouded mirror. But his mirror world is flat, averse to perspective. [R1a,5]

"So long as the plate glass was produced solely through expansion of a glass cylinder blown with the mouth at the end of the pipe, its dimensions had a constant and relatively confined limit, one determined by the lung power expended in the blowing. Only recently was this replaced by compressed air. But with the introduction of the casting process . . . in 1688, these dimensions were immediately and significantly increased." A. G. Meyer, *Eisenbauten* (Esslingen, 1907), pp. 54–55. Note to this passage: "The first mirrors cast in Paris are said . . . to have measured 84 by 50 inches, as compared to a maximum of 50 by 45 inches before this." [R1a,6]

Actually, in the arcades it is not a matter of illuminating the interior space, as in other forms of iron construction, but of damping the exterior space. [R1a,7]

On the light that reigns in the arcades: "A glaucous gleam, seemingly filtered through deep water, with the special quality of pale brilliance of a leg suddenly revealed under a lifted skirt. The great American passion for city planning, imported into Paris by a prefect of police during the Second Empire and now being applied to the task of redrawing the map of our capital in straight lines, will soon spell the doom of these human aquariums. Although the life that originally quickened them has drained away, they deserve, nevertheless, to be regarded as the secret repositories of several modern myths." Louis Aragon, *Le Paysan de Paris* (Paris, 1926), p. 19.[2] ☐ Mythology ☐ [R2,1]

Outside surged "the green, transparent tide, filling the street to a level high above the houses; and there, up and down, swam the queerest fish, often nearly human in appearance. . . . The street itself could have come from some prehistoric book of images; gray gabled houses with high pointed roofs and narrow windows, the latter sometimes straight across, sometimes on a slant, the sides of the houses in some spots almost overgrown with shells and seaweed, though in other spots clean and well preserved, and adorned with tasteful paintings and shell figures. . . . Before every door stood a tall shady coral tree; and planted not infrequently along the walls, like the grapevines and roses we train on slender trellises at home, were polyps with spreading arms that reached in their luxuriance high above the windows, often to the very gables that protruded from the roofs." Friedrich Gerstäcker, *Die versunkene Stadt* (‹Berlin:› Neufeld and Henius, 1921), p. 30. If a work of literature, an imaginative composition, could arise from repressed economic contents in the consciousness of a collective, as Freud says it can from sexual contents in an individual consciousness, then in the above description we would have before our eyes the consummate sublimation of the arcades, with their bric-à-brac growing rankly out of their showcases. Even the vitreous radiance of the globes of the street lamps, the utter pomp and splendor of gas lighting, enters into this undersea world of Gerstäcker's. The hero sees, to his amazement, "that, with the gradual infusion of twilight, these undersea corridors just as gradually lit up by themselves. For everywhere in the bushes of coral and sponge, among the wreaths and thick curtains of seaweed and the tall waving seagrass towering up behind, were sitting broad-brimmed, glassy-looking medusas, which already at the outset had given off a weak, greenish phosphorescent light that quickly picked up strength at the approach of darkness and now was shining with great intensity." Gerstäcker, *Die versunkene Stadt,* p. 48. Here, the arcade in Gerstäcker in a different constellation: "Hardly had they left the house than they entered into a wide and airy, crystal-crowned passageway, onto which nearly all the neighboring houses seemed to issue; just beyond this, however, and divided from it only by a perfectly transparent partition that appeared to be formed of thin sheets of ice, lay the luminous waters." Gerstäcker*, Die versunkene Stadt,* p. 42. [R2,2]

As rocks of the Miocene or Eocene in places bear the imprint of monstrous creatures from those ages, so today arcades dot the metropolitan landscape like caves containing the fossil remains of a vanished monster: the consumer of the pre-imperial era of capitalism, the last dinosaur of Europe. On the walls of these caverns their immemorial flora, the commodity, luxuriates and enters, like cancerous tissue, into the most irregular combinations. A world of secret affinities opens up within: palm tree and feather duster, hairdryer and Venus de Milo, prostheses and letter-writing manuals. The odalisque lies in wait next to the inkwell, and priestesses raise high the vessels into which we drop cigarette butts as incense offerings. These items on display are a rebus: how one ought to read here the birdseed in the fixative-pan, the flower seeds beside the binoculars, the broken screw atop the musical score, and the revolver above the goldfish bowl— is right on the tip of one's tongue. After all, nothing of the lot appears to be new. The goldfish come perhaps from a pond that dried up long ago, the revolver was a corpus delicti, and these scores could hardly have preserved their previous owner from starvation when her last pupils stayed away. And since, to the dreaming collective itself, the decline of an economic era seems like the end of the world, the writer Karl Kraus has looked quite correctly on the arcades, which, from another angle, must have appealed to him as the casting of a dream: "In the

Berlin Arcade, there is no grass growing. It looks like the day after the end of the world, although people are still moving about. Organic life is withered, and in this condition is put on display. Castan's Panopticon. Ah, a summery day there, among the waxworks, at six o'clock. An orchestrion plays mechanical music to accompany Napoleon III's bladder-stone operation. Adults can see the syphilitic chancre of a Negro. Positively the very last Aztecs. Oleographs. Street youths, hustlers, with thick hands. Outside is life: a third-rate cabaret. The orchestrion plays 'You're a Fine Fellow, Emil.' Here God is made by machine." ⟨Karl Kraus,⟩ *Nachts* (Vienna and Leipzig, 1924), pp. 201–202. [R2,3]

On the Crystal Palace of 1851: "Of course, for sensuous perception, these glass surfaces are themselves practically dissolved in light. / In its basic principle, this is by no means something altogether new; rather, its prehistory goes back centuries at least, if not millennia. For it begins with the decision to cover the walls with shining metal plates. / . . . That is the first step on the way to the new valuation of space at work in the Crystal Palace. In the domed chamber of the Mycenaeans, this conception of space was already so decidedly in force that the entire space of the room could be dissolved in luster . . . In this way, however, one sacrificed that fundamental means of all spatial organization: contrast. The whole of the succeeding historical development was determined through this means—although, from the perspective of what concerns us at present, this development first begins only a thousand years later, and then no longer with the 'luster' of metal but with that of glass. / . . . The high point here is with the window of the Gothic cathedral. . . . The increasing transparency of glass in colorless glazing draws the outer world into the interior space, while covering the walls with mirrors projects the image of the interior space into the outer world. In either case the 'wall,' as a container of space, is deprived of its significance. The 'luster' increasingly forfeits the distinctive color that was part of its character and becomes ever more exclusively just a mirror of external light. / This process culminated in the profane interior space of the seventeenth century, where it was no longer only the embrasures of windows that were filled with plate glass clear as water, but also the remaining surfaces of the wall surrounding the room, particularly in places that lay opposite a window opening: in the 'mirror galleries of the rococo interiors.' / . . . But in this the principle of contrast still prevails. . . . In the Sainte-Chapelle, however, as in ⟨Versaille's⟩ Hall of Mirrors, this relation between surface and light was constituted in such a way that it is no longer the light that interrupts the surface area but the surface area that interrupts the light. / In terms of the unfolding valuation of space, therefore, we see a continuous progression. At its end stand the greenhouses, and the halls of the Crystal Palace in London." A. G. Meyer, *Eisenbauten* (Esslingen, 1907), pp. 65–66. [R2a,1]

One may compare the pure magic of those walls of mirrors which we know from feudal times with the oppressive magic worked by the alluring mirror-walls of the arcades, which invite us into seductive bazaars. ☐ *Magasins de Nouveautés* ☐ [R2a,2]

A look at the ambiguity of the arcades: their abundance of mirrors, which fabulously amplifies the spaces and makes orientation more difficult. For although this mirror world may have many aspects, indeed infinitely many, it remains ambiguous, double-edged. It blinks: it is always this one—and never nothing— out of which another immediately arises. The space that transforms itself does so in the bosom of nothingness. In its tarnished, dirty mirrors, things exchange a Kaspar-Hauser-look with the nothing. It is like an equivocal wink coming from nirvana. And here, again, we are brushed with icy breath by the dandyish name of Odilon Redon, who caught, like no one else, this look of things in the mirror of nothingness, and who understood, like no one else, how to join with things in their collusion with nonbeing. The whispering of gazes fills the arcades. There is no thing here that does not, where one least expects it, open a fugitive eye, blinking it shut again; but if you look more closely, it is gone. To the whispering of these gazes, the space lends its echo. "Now, what," it blinks, "can possibly have come over me?" We stop short in some surprise. "What, indeed, can possibly have come over you?" Thus we gently bounce the question back to it. ☐ Flânerie ☐[3]   [R2a,3]

"Images of interiors are at the center of the early Kierkegaard's philosophical constructions. These images are, in fact, produced by philosophy, . . . but they point beyond this stratum in virtue of the things they hold fast. . . . The great motif of reflection belongs to the *intérieur*. The 'seducer' begins a note: 'Why can't you be quiet and well behaved? You have done nothing the entire morning except to shake my awning, pull at my window mirror, play with the bell-rope from the third story, rattle the windowpanes—in short, do everything possible to get my attention!' . . . The window mirror is a characteristic furnishing of the spacious nineteenth-century apartment. . . . The function of the window mirror is to project the endless row of apartment buildings into the encapsulated bourgeois living room; by this means, the living room dominates the reflected row at the same time that it is delimited by it." Theodor Wiesengrund-Adorno, *Kierkegaard* (Tübingen, 1933), p. 45.[4] ☐ Flâneur ☐ Interior ☐   [R3,1]

To be cited in reference to the physiologies, even though coming later, is the passage from the "Lettre à Charles Asselineau," in which Babou gives free rein to his nonconformist and antimodernist sentiments. "I know that the public of today, being the most seemly of all publics, loves to admire itself *en famille* in those very large mirrors which adorn the cafés of the boulevard, or which the hand of an arty decorator has kindly installed in its bedroom." Hippolyte Babou, *Les Payens innocents* (Paris, 1858), p. xviii.   [R3,2]

S

[Painting, Jugendstil, Novelty]

> To create history with the very detritus of history.
> —Remy de Gourmont, *Le IIme Livre des masques* (Paris, 1924), p. 259

> Events profit from not being commented on.
> —Alfred Delvau, Preface to *Murailles révolutionnaires* (Paris), vol. 1, p. 4

> Pains eternal,
> And ever fresh,
> Hide from their hearts
> All your terrors.
> —Verse of the Devil, sung while he transforms a desolate and rocky
>   landscape into a boudoir; from Hippolyte Lucas and Eugène Barré,
>   *Le Ciel et l'enfer: Féerie* (Paris, 1853), p. 88

> While procreation used to be the fashion,
> We think of that, pardon, as tripe.
> —*Faust,* Part 2 (Wagner in the homunculus scene)[1]

"History is like Janus: it has two faces. Whether it looks to the past or to the present, it sees the same things." ‹Maxime› Du Camp, *Paris* ‹Paris, 1869–1875›, vol. 6, p. 315. ▯ Fashion ▯ [S1,1]

"It has often happened to me to note certain trivial events passing before my eyes as showing a quite original aspect, in which I fondly hoped to discern the spirit of the period. 'This,' I would tell myself, 'was bound to happen today and could not have been other than it is. It is a sign of the times.' Well, nine times out of ten, I have come across the very same event with analogous circumstances in old memoirs or old history books." Anatole France, *Le Jardin d'Epicure* (Paris), p. 113.[2] ▯ Fashion ▯ [S1,2]

The change in fashions, the eternally up-to-date ‹*das Ewig-Heutige*›, escapes "historical" consideration; it is truly overcome only through a consideration that is political (theological). Politics recognizes in every actual constellation the genu-

inely unique—what will never recur. Characteristic of a fashionable consideration, which proceeds from bad contemporariness, is the following item of information, which is found in Benda's *La Trahison des clercs* ‹The Betrayal of the
Intellectuals›: a German reports his amazement when, sitting at a *table d'hôte* in
Paris fourteen days after the storming of the Bastille, he heard no one speak of
politics. It is no different when Anatole France has the aged Pilate chatting in
Rome of the days of his governorship and saying, as he touches on the revolt of
the king of the Jews, "Now, what was he called?"[3]   [S1,3]

Definition of the "modern" as the new in the context of what has always already
been there. The always new, always identical "heathscape" in Kafka *(Der Prozeß)*
is not a bad expression of this state of affairs. "'Wouldn't you like to see a picture
or two that you might care to buy?' . . . Titorelli dragged a pile of unframed
canvases from under the bed; they were so thickly covered with dust that when
he blew some of it from the topmost, K. was almost blinded and choked by the
cloud that flew up. '*Wild Nature,* a heathscape,' said the painter, handing K. the
picture. It showed two stunted trees standing far apart from each other in darkish
grass. In the background was a many-hued sunset. 'Fine,' said K., 'I'll buy it.' K's
curtness had been unthinking and so he was glad when the painter, instead of
being offended, lifted another canvas from the floor. 'Here's the companion
picture,' he said. It might have been intended as a companion picture, but there
was not the slightest difference that one could see between it and the other; here
were the two trees, here the grass, and there the sunset. But K. did not bother
about that. 'They're fine prospects,' he said. 'I'll buy both of them and hang them
up in my office.' 'You seem to like the subject,' said the painter, fishing out a third
canvas. 'By a lucky chance I have another of these studies here.' But it was not
merely a similar study, it was simply the same wild heathscape again. The painter
was apparently exploiting to the full this opportunity to sell off his old pictures.
'I'll take that one as well,' said K. 'How much for the three pictures?' 'We'll settle
that next time,' said the painter. . . . 'I must say I'm very glad you like these
pictures, and I'll throw in all the others under the bed as well. They're
heathscapes every one of them—I've painted dozens of them in my time. Some
people won't have anything to do with these subjects because they're too somber,
but there are always people like yourself who prefer somber pictures.'" Franz
Kafka, *Der Prozeß* (Berlin, 1925), pp. 284–286.[4] ☐ Hashish ☐   [S1,4]

The "modern," the time of hell. The punishments of hell are always the newest
thing going in this domain. What is at issue is not that "the same thing happens
over and over," and even less would it be a question here of eternal return. It is
rather that precisely in that which is newest the face of the world never alters, that
this newest remains, in every respect, the same.—This constitutes the eternity of
hell. To determine the totality of traits by which the "modern" is defined would
be to represent hell.   [S1,5]

Of vital interest to recognize a particular point of development as a crossroads.
The new historical thinking that, in general and in particulars, is characterized by

higher concreteness, redemption of periods of decline, revision of periodization, presently stands at such a point, and its utilization in a reactionary or a revolutionary sense is now being decided. In this regard, the writings of the Surrealists and the new book by Heidegger[5] point to one and the same crisis in its two possible solutions. [S1,6]

Remy de Gourmont on the "Histoire de la société française pendant la Révolution et sous le Directoire": "It was the fundamental originality of the Goncourts to create history with the very detritus of history." Remy de Gourmont, *Le IIme Livre des masques* (Paris, 1924), p. 259. [S1a,1]

"If one takes from history only the most general facts, those which lend themselves to parallels and to theories, then it suffices, as Schopenhauer said, to read only the morning paper and Herodotus. All the rest intervening—the evident and fatal repetition of the most distant and the most recent facts—becomes tedious and useless." Remy de Gourmont, *Le IIme Livre des masques* (Paris, 1924), p. 259. The passage is not entirely clear. The wording would lead one to assume that repetition in the course of history concerns the great facts as much as the small. But the author himself probably has in mind only the former. Against this it should be shown that, precisely in the minutiae of the "intervening," the eternally selfsame is manifest. [S1a,2]

The constructions of history are comparable to military orders that discipline the true life and confine it to barracks. On the other hand: the street insurgence of the anecdote. The anecdote brings things near to us spatially, lets them enter our life. It represents the strict antithesis to the sort of history which demands "empathy," which makes everything abstract. The same technique of nearness may be practiced, calendrically, with respect to epochs. Let us imagine that a man dies on the very day he turns fifty, which is the day on which his son is born, to whom the same thing happens, and so on. If one were to have the chain commence at the time of the birth of Christ, the result would be that, in the time since we began our chronological reckoning, not forty men have lived. Thus, the image of a historical course of time is totally transformed as soon as one brings to bear on it a standard adequate and comprehensible to human life. This pathos of nearness, the hatred of the abstract configuration of history in its "epochs," was at work in the great skeptics like Anatole France. [S1a,3]

There has never been an epoch that did not feel itself to be "modern" in the sense of eccentric, and did not believe itself to be standing directly before an abyss. The desperately clear consciousness of being in the middle of a crisis is something chronic in humanity. Every age unavoidably seems to itself a new age. The "modern," however, is as varied in its meaning as the different aspects of one and the same kaleidoscope. ‹Compare N10,1.› [S1a,4]

Connection between the colportage intention and the deepest theological intention. It mirrors it back darkly, displaces into the space of contemplation what only holds good in the space of the just life. Namely: that the world is always the same (that all events could have taken place in the same space). On a theoretical plane, despite everything (despite the keen insight lurking within it), this is a tired and withered truth. Nevertheless, it finds supreme confirmation in the existence of the pious, to whom all things serve the greatest good, as here the space serves all that has happened. So deeply is the theological element sunk in the realm of colportage. One might even say that the deepest truths, far from having risen above the animal torpor of human being, possess the mighty power of being able to adapt to the dull and commonplace—indeed, of mirroring themselves, after their fashion, in irresponsible dreams. [S1a,5]

No decline of the arcades, but sudden transformation. At one blow, they became the hollow mold from which the image of "modernity" was cast. Here, the century mirrored with satisfaction its most recent past. [S1a,6]

Every date from the sixteenth century trails purple after it. Those of the nineteenth century are only now receiving their physiognomy. Especially from the data of architecture and socialism. [S1a,7]

Every epoch appears to itself inescapably modern—but each one also has a right to be taken thus. What is to be understood by "inescapably modern," however, emerges very clearly in the following sentence: "Perhaps our descendants will understand the second main period of history after Christ to have its inception in the French Revolution and in the turn from the eighteenth to the nineteenth century, while grasping the first main period in terms of the development of the whole Christian world, including the Reformation." At another place, it is a question of "a great period that cuts more deeply than any other into the history of the world—a period without religious founders, without reformers or lawgivers." Julius Meyer, *Geschichte der modernen Französischen Malerei* (Leipzig, 1867), pp. 22, 21. The author assumes that history is constantly expanding. But this is, in reality, a consequence of the fact that industry gives it its truly epochal character. The feeling that an epochal upheaval had begun with the nineteenth century was no special privilege of Hegel and Marx. [S1a,8]

The dreaming collective knows no history. Events pass before it as always identical and always new. The sensation of the newest and most modern is, in fact, just as much a dream formation of events as "the eternal return of the same." The perception of space that corresponds to this perception of time is the interpenetrating and superposed transparency of the world of the flâneur. This feeling of space, this feeling of time, presided at the birth of modern feuilletonism. ☐ Dream Collective ☐ [S2,1]

"What drives us into contemplation of the past is the similarity between what has been and our own life, which are somehow one being. Through grasping this identity, we can transport ourselves into even the purest of all regions—into death." Hugo von Hofmannsthal, *Buch der Freunde* (Leipzig, 1929), p. 111.[6]

[S2,2]

Very striking how Hofmannsthal calls this "somehow one being" a being in the sphere of death. Hence the immortality of his "religious novice," that fictional character of whom he spoke during his last meeting with me, and who was supposed to make his way through changing religions down the centuries, as through the suite of rooms of one grand apartment.[7] How it is that, within the narrowly confined space of a single life, this "being somehow one" with what has been leads into the sphere of death—this dawned on me for the first time in Paris, during a conversation about Proust, in 1930. To be sure, Proust never heightened but rather analyzed humanity. His moral greatness, though, lies in quite another direction. With a passion unknown to any writer before him, he took as his subject the fidelity to things that have crossed our path in life. Fidelity to an afternoon, to a tree, a spot of sun on the carpet; fidelity to garments, pieces of furniture, to perfumes or landscapes. (The discovery he ultimately makes on the road to Méséglise is the highest "moral teaching" Proust has to offer: a sort of spatial transposition of the *semper idem*.) I grant that Proust, in the deepest sense, "perhaps ranges himself on the side of death." His cosmos has its sun, perhaps, in death, around which orbit the lived moments, the gathered things. "Beyond the pleasure principle" is probably the best commentary there is on Proust's works. In order to understand Proust, generally speaking, it is perhaps necessary to begin with the fact that his subject is the obverse side, *le revers*, "not so much of the world but of life itself."

[S2,3]

The eternity of the operetta, says Wiesengrund in his essay on this form,[8] is the eternity of yesterday.

[S2,4]

"Perhaps no simulacrum has provided us with an ensemble of objects more precisely attuned to the concept of 'ideal' than that great simulacrum which constitutes the revolutionary ornamental architecture of Jugendstil. No collective effort has succeeded in creating a dream world as pure, and as disturbing, as these Jugendstil buildings. Situated, as they are, on the margins of architecture, they alone constitute the realization of desires in which an excessively violent and cruel automatism painfully betrays the sort of hatred for reality and need for refuge in an ideal world that we find in childhood neurosis." Salvador Dalí, "L'Ane pourri," *Le Surréalisme au service de la révolution*, 1, no. 1 (Paris, 1930), p. 12. ☐ Industry ☐ Advertising ☐

[S2,5]

"Here is what we can still love: the imposing block of those rapturous and frigid structures scattered across all of Europe, scorned and neglected by anthologies and studies." Salvador Dali, "L'Ane pourri," *Le Surréalisme au service de la révolution*, 1, no. 1 (Paris, 1930), p. 12. Perhaps no city contains more perfect examples of this Jugendstil than Barcelona, in the works of the architect who designed the Church of the Sagrada Familia.[9]   [S2a,1]

Wiesengrund cites and comments on a passage from Kierkegaard's *Repetition:* "One climbs the stairs to the first floor in a gas-illuminated building, opens a little door, and stands in the entry. To the left is a glass door leading to a room. One continues directly ahead into an anteroom. Beyond are two entirely identical rooms, identically furnished, as though one were the mirror reflection of the other." Apropos of this passage (Kierkegaard, ‹*Gesammelte*› *Werke*, vol. 3 ‹Jena, 1909›, p. 138), which he cites at greater length, Wiesengrund remarks: "The duplication of the room is unfathomable, seeming to be a reflection without being so. Like these rooms, perhaps all semblance in history resembles itself, so long as it itself, obedient to nature, persists as semblance." Wiesengrund-Adorno, *Kierkegaard* (Tübingen, 1933), p. 50.[10] ☐ Mirror ☐ Interior ☐   [S2a,2]

On the motif of the heathscapes in Kafka's *Der Prozeß:* in the time of hell, the new (the pendant) is always the eternally selfsame.   [S2a,3]

After the Commune: "England welcomed the exiles and did everything it could to keep them. At the exhibition of 1878, it became clear that she had risen above France and Paris to take the premier position in the applied arts. If the *modern style* returned to France in 1900, this is perhaps a distant consequence of the barbarous manner in which the Commune was repressed." Dubech and d'Espezel, *Histoire de Paris* (Paris, 1926), p. 437.   [S2a,4]

"The desire was to create a style out of thin air. Foreign influences favored the 'modern style,' which was almost entirely inspired by floral decor. The English Pre-Raphaelites and the Munich urbanists provided the model. Iron construction was succeeded by reinforced concrete. This was the nadir for architecture, one which coincided with the deepest political depression. It was at this moment that Paris acquired those buildings and monuments which were so very strange and so little in accord with the older city: the building in composite style designed by M. Bouwens at 27 Quai d'Orsay; the subway shelters; the Samaritaine department store, erected by Frantz Jourdain in the middle of the historic landscape of the Quartier Saint-Germain l'Auxerrois." Dubech and d'Espezel, *Histoire de Paris*, p. 465.   [S2a,5]

"What M. Arsène Alexandre, then, calls 'the profound charm of streamers blowing in the wind'—this serpentine effect is that of the octopus style, of green, poorly fired ceramics, of lines forced and stretched into tentacular ligaments, of matter tortured for no good reason. . . . Gourds, pumpkins, hibiscus roots, and volutes are the inspiration for an illogical furniture upon which appear hydrangeas, bats, polianthes, and peacock feathers—creations of artists in the grip of an unfortunate passion for symbols and 'poetry.' . . . In an era of light and electricity, what triumphs is the aquarium, the greenish, the submarine, the hybrid, the poisonous." Paul Morand, *1900* (Paris, 1931), pp. 101–103.   [S2a,6]

"This style of 1900, moreover, infects the whole of literature. Never was writing more pretentious. In novels, the *particule* is obligatory for names: there is Madame de Scrimeuse, Madame de Girionne, Madame de Charmaille, Monsieur de Phocas; impossible names: Yanis, Damosa, Lord Eginard. . . . The *Légendes du Moyen âge*, by Gaston Pâris, which has just come out, plays to the fervent cult of the neo-Gothic: it offers nothing but Grails, Isoldes, Ladies of the Unicorn. Pierre Louys writes "le throne," with the older Latinate spelling; everywhere are found abysses, ymages, gyres, and the like. . . . The triumph of the *y*." Paul Morand, *1900* (Paris, 1931), pp. 179–181.   [S3,1]

"It seemed to me worthwhile to bring together, in an issue of the journal [*Minotaure*, 3–4] containing several admirable specimens of Jugendstil art, a certain number of mediumistic designs. . . . In fact, one is immediately struck by similarities between these two modes of expression. What is Jugendstil, I am tempted to ask, but an attempt to generalize and to adapt mediumistic design, painting, and sculpture to dwellings and furniture? We find there the same discordance in the details; the same impossibility of repetition that guides the true, captivating stereotypy; the same delight in the never-ending curve (whether it be growing fern, or ammonite, or embryonic curl); the same profusion of minutiae, the contemplation of which seduces the eye away from pleasure in the whole. . . . It could be maintained that these two enterprises are actually conceived under the same sign, which might well be that of the octopus: "the octopus," as Lautréamont has said, "with the gaze of silk." From one part to another, in terms of plastic design, down to the very smallest feature, it is the triumph of the equivocal; in terms of interpretation, down to the most insignificant detail, it is the triumph of the complex. Even the borrowing, ad nauseam, of subjects, accessory or otherwise, from the plant world is common to these two modes of expression (which respond, in principle, to quite different needs for externalization). And both of them display, to an equal degree, a tendency to evoke superficially . . . certain ancient artforms of Asia and the Americas." André Breton, *Point du jour* (Paris ‹1934›), pp. 234–236.
                                                                                 [S3,2]

The painted foliage on the ceilings of the Bibliothèque Nationale. As one leafs through the pages down below, it rustles up above.   [S3,3]

"Just as pieces of furniture gravitate toward one another—davenport and coat rack are actually the fruit of such convergence—so it seems that walls, floors, and ceilings are possessed of a peculiar power of attraction. Increasingly, furniture is becoming untransportable, immovable; it clings to walls and corners, sticks fast to floors, and, as it were, takes root. . . . 'Detached' works of art, like paintings that need to be hung or sculpture that has to be placed, are wherever possible eschewed, and this tendency is very materially abetted by the revival of wall painting, frescoes, decorative tapestry, and glass-painting. . . . In this way, all permanent contents of the home are absorbed in exchange, while the occupant himself loses the power of moving about freely and becomes attached to ground and property." Dolf Sternberger, "Jugendstil," *Die neue Rundschau*, 45 (September 9, 1934), pp. 264–266. [S3a,1]

"It is by means of the rich and powerful contour that . . . the figure of the soul becomes ornament. . . . Maeterlinck . . . praises silence (in *Le Trésor des humbles* ⟨The Treasure of the Humble⟩), that silence which does not depend on the arbitrary will of two separate beings but rather wells up, so to speak, as a third being, sufficient to itself, thereafter growing to envelop the lovers and, in this way, first enabling their intimacy. This veil of silence reveals itself clearly enough as a form of contour or as a truly animated . . . form of ornament." Dolf Sternberger, "Jugendstil," *Die neue Rundschau*, 45 (September 9, 1934), p. 270. [S3a,2]

"Thus, every house appears . . . to be an organism which expresses its interior through its exterior, and van de Velde unmistakably betrays . . . the model for his vision of the city of characters . . .: 'To anyone who objects that this would be a carnival of confusion . . ., we would point to the harmonious and gladdening impression produced by a garden where terrestrial and aquatic plants are growing freely.' If the city is a garden full of freely growing house-organisms, it is not clear where, in such a vision, man would occupy a place, unless it be that he is caught within the interior of this plant life, himself rooted and attached to the soil—land or water—and, as if by enchantment (metamorphosis), rendered incapable of moving otherwise than as the plant that frames and encases him should move. . . . It is something like the astral body which Rudolf Steiner envisioned and experienced—Rudolf Steiner, . . . whose . . . school . . . endowed so many of its works . . . with an ornamental solemnity, the curved signature of which is nothing other than a vestige of Jugendstil ornament." See the essay's epigraph from Ovid, *Metamorphosis*, book 3, lines 509–510: "But when they sought his body, they found nothing, / Only a flower with a yellow center / Surrounded with white petals."[11] Sternberger, "Jugendstil," pp. 268–269, 254. [S3a,3]

The view of Jugendstil represented below is very problematic, for no historical phenomenon can be grasped exclusively under the category of flight; such flight is always registered concretely in terms of what is flown. "What . . . remains outside . . . is the din of cities, the unbridled fury not of the elements but of industry, the all-inclusive sovereignty of the modern economics of exchange, the world of ongoing activity, of technologized labor, and of the masses, the world that appeared to the exponents of Jugendstil as a general uproar, stifling and chaotic." Dolf Sternberger, "Jugendstil," *Die neue Rundschau,* 45 (September 9, 1934), p. 260. [S4,1]

"The most characteristic work of Jugendstil is the house. More precisely, the single-family dwelling." Sternberger, "Jugendstil," *Die neue Rundschau*, 45 (September 9, 1934), p. 264. [S4,2]

Delvau speaks, at one point, of the "future Benedictines who will write the history of Paris as it was in the nineteenth century." Alfred Delvau, *Les Dessous de Paris* (Paris, 1860), p. 32 ("Alexandre Privat d'Anglemont"). [S4,3]

Jugendstil and socialist housing policy: "The art of the future will be more personal than what has come before. At no other time has man's passion for self-knowledge been so strong as it is today, and the place where he can best fulfill and transform his individuality is the house, the house which each of us, according to his . . . heart's desire, will build. . . . In each of us slumbers a gift for ornamental invention . . . sufficiently compelling . . . to allow us to dispense with any middleman in order to build our house." After citing these lines from van de Velde's *Renaissance in modernen Kunstgewerbe* ‹Renaissance in the Modern Decorative Arts›, Karski continues: "For anyone who reads this, it must be absolutely clear that such an ideal is impossible in the present state of society, and that its realization is reserved for socialism." J. Karski, "Moderne Kunstströmungen und Sozialismus," *Die neue Zeit*, 20, no. 1 (Stuttgart ‹1901–1902›), pp. 146–147. [S4,4]

Among the stylistic elements that enter into Jugendstil from iron construction and technical design, one of the most important is the predominance of the *vide* over the *plein,* the empty over the full. [S4,5]

Just as Ibsen passes judgment on Jugendstil architecture in *The Master Builder,* so he passes judgment on its female type in *Hedda Gabler.* She is the theatrical sister of those *diseuses* and dancers who, in floral depravity or innocence, appear naked and without objective background on Jugendstil posters. [S4,6]

When we have to get up early on a day of departure, it can sometimes happen that, unwilling to tear ourselves away from sleep, we dream that we are out of bed and getting dressed. Such a dream was dreamed in Jugendstil by the bourgeoisie, fifteen years before history woke them with a bang. [S4a,1]

"That is the longing: to dwell midst the waves / and have no homeland in time." Rainer Maria Rilke, *Die frühen Gedichte* (Leipzig, 1922), p. 1 (epigraph). [S4a,2]

"The Paris Street," at the Paris world exhibition of 1900, realizes, in an extreme manner, the idea of the private dwelling that is characteristic of Jugendstil: "Here, in a long row, buildings of various kinds . . . have been erected . . . The satirical newspaper *Le Rire* has set up a Punch and Judy show. . . . The originator of the serpentine dance, Loie Fuller, has her theater in the row. Not far away . . . a house that appears to be standing on its head, with its roof planted in the earth and its doorsills pointing skyward, and which is known as 'The Tower of Wonders.' . . . The idea, at any rate, is original." Th. Heine, "Die Strasse von Paris," in *Die Pariser Weltausstellung in Wort und Bild,* ed. Dr. Georg Malkowsky (Berlin, 1900), p. 78. [S4a,3]

On the upside-down manor house: "This little house, constructed in Gothic style, stands . . . literally on its head; that is, its roof, with its chimneys and turrets, is stuck into the ground, while its foundation points to the heavens. Naturally, all the windows, doors, balconies, galleries, moldings, ornaments, and inscriptions are upside down too, and even the face of the grandfather clock obeys this tendency. . . . So far, this mad idea is amusing . . . , but once you are inside, it becomes tiresome. There, you are . . . yourself . . . upside down, together with . . . the objects on view. . . . One sees a table set for lunch, a rather richly furnished salon, as well as a bathroom. . . . The adjoining room . . . and some others, too, are actually lined with concave and convex mirrors. The contractors call them quite simply 'laughing chambers.'" "Le Manoir à l'envers," *Die Pariser Weltausstellung in Wort und Bild*, ed. Dr. Georg Malkowsky (Berlin, 1900), p. 474–475.   [S4a,4]

On the London world exhibition of 1851: "We still reside amid the aftereffects of what this exhibition achieved—not only in the realm of technology and machines, but in the realm of artistic development. . . . We ask ourselves today whether the movement that led to the production of monumental buildings in glass and iron . . . was not also heralded in the design of furniture and utensils. In 1851 this question could not have arisen, although there were many things that could be noted. In the first decades of the nineteenth century, mechanized industry in England had advanced to the point where furnishings and utensils were being stripped of superfluous ornamentation so as to be manufactured more easily through machines. In this way there emerged, for furniture especially, a series of very simple but thoroughly constructive and altogether sensible forms, in which we are again beginning to take an interest. The wholly modern furniture of 1900, which eschews all ornament and puts the accent on pure line, maintains a direct link to that delicately balanced and compact mahogany furniture of 1830–1850. But in 1850 no one appreciated what had already in fact been reached in the pursuit of new and fundamental forms." (People succumbed, instead, to the historicism that initially fostered a vogue for the Renaissance.) Julius Lessing, *Das halbe Jahrhundert der Weltausstellungen* (Berlin, 1900), p. 11–12.   [S5,1]

In connection with Kafka's Titorelli ‹S1,4›, compare the program of the naturalist painters around 1860: "According to them, the position of the artist toward nature ought to be . . . impersonal—so much so that he should be capable of painting the same picture ten times in succession, without hesitating and without having the later copies differ in any way from those that came before." Gisela Freund, *La Photographie au point de vue sociologique* (manuscript, p. 128).   [S5,2]

Perhaps an attempt should be made to extend the scope of this inquiry up to the threshold of the war, by tracing the influence of Jugendstil on the youth movement.[12]   [S5,3]

The façade of the "Information" Building on the Rue Réaumur is an example of Jugendstil in which the ornamental modification of supporting structures is seen particularly clearly.   [S5,4]

Influence of the processes of technological reproduction on the realists' theory of painting: "According to them, the position of the artist toward nature ought to be completely impersonal—so much so that he should be capable of painting the same picture ten times in succession, without hesitating and without having the later copies differ in any way from those that came before." Gisèle Freund, *La Photographie en France au XIXe siècle* (Paris, 1936), p. 106. [S5,5]

Careful attention should be given to the relation of Jugendstil to Symbolism, which brings out its esoteric side. Thérive writes, in his review of Edouard Dujardin, *Mallarmé par un des siens* (Paris, 1936): "In an astute preface to a book by Edouard Dujardin, Jean Cassou explains that *le symbolisme* was a mystical, magical enterprise, and that it posed the eternal problem of jargon—'argot essentialized, which signifies, on the part of the artistic caste, the will to absence and escape.' . . . What Symbolism liked best was the semiparodic play with dreams, with ambiguous forms; and this commentator goes so far as to say that the mélange of aestheticism and bad taste of the sort popularized by Le Chat Noir (*caf' conc'*, for *café concert;* leg-o'-mutton sleeves; orchids; and hairstyles inspired by wrought-iron designs) was a necessary and exquisite combination." André Thérive, "Les Livres" (*Le Temps,* June 25, 1936). [S5a,1]

Denner labored four years on a portrait that hangs in the Louvre, and along the way he did not scorn the use of a magnifying glass to obtain a reproduction perfectly faithful to nature. This at a time when photography had already been invented. ‹?› So difficult is it for man to relinquish his place and allow the apparatus to take over for him. (See Gisèle Freund, *La Photographie en France au XIXe siècle* [Paris, 1936], p. 112.) [S5a,2]

In a prefiguration of Jugendstil, Baudelaire sketches "a room that is like a dream, a truly *spiritual* room. . . . Every piece of furniture is of an elongated form, languid and prostrate, and seems to be dreaming—endowed, one would say, with a somnambular existence, like minerals and plants." In this text, he conjures an idol that might well call to mind the "unnatural mothers" of Segantini or Ibsen's Hedda Gabler: "the Idol . . . Yes, those are her eyes . . . those subtle and terrible eyes that I recognize by their dread mockery." Charles Baudelaire, *Le Spleen de Paris,* ed. R. Simon (Paris), p. 5 ("La Chambre double").[13] [S5a,3]

In the book *The Nightside of Paris,* by Edmund B. d'Auvergne (London, n.d., circa 1910), there is a mention, on page 56, of the old Chat Noir café (Rue Victor-Massé), where, over the door, there was an inscription that read: "Passerby, be modern!" (In a letter from Wiesengrund.)—Rollinat at Le Chat Noir. ‹See J55a,7.› [S5a,4]

"What could be further from us than the amazing ambition of a Leonardo, who, considering painting as a supreme end, a supreme display of knowledge, and deciding that it called for omniscience, did not hesitate to embark on a universal analysis whose depth and precision leave us overwhelmed? The passage from the ancient grandeur of painting to its present condition is quite perceptible in the artworks and writings of Eugène Delacroix. This modern, full of ideas, is tortured with restlessness and a sense of impotence; at each instant he encounters the limits of his resources in his efforts to equal the masters of the past. Nothing could better illustrate the diminution of that indefinable force and fullness of earlier days than the spectacle of that very noble artist, divided against himself, embarking nervously on a last struggle to attain the grand style in art." Paul Valéry, *Pièces sur l'art* (Paris), pp. 191–192 ("Autour de Corot").[14]   [S6,1]

"The victories of art seem bought by the loss of character." Karl Marx, "Die Revolutionen von 1848 und das Proletariat," speech to mark the fourth anniversary of the foundation of the ‹Chartist› *People's Paper*; published in *The People's Paper*, April 19, 1856. [In *Karl Marx als Denker, Mensch und Revolutionär*, ed. D. Rjazanov (Vienna, Berlin ‹1928›), p. 42.][15]   [S6,2]

Dolf Sternberger's essay "Hohe See und Schiffbruch" ‹High Seas and Shipwreck› is concerned with the "transformations of an allegory." "It is from allegory that genre is born. Shipwreck as allegory signifies . . . the ephemerality of the world in general; shipwreck as genre is a peephole looking out on a world beyond ours, on a dangerous life that is not our life but is nevertheless necessary. . . . This heroic genre remains the sign under which the reorganization and reconciliation of society . . . begins," as he writes in another passage with reference to Spielhagen's *Sturmflut* ‹The Breaking of the Storm› (1877). *Die neue Rundschau*, 46 (August 8, 1935), pp. 196, 199.   [S6,3]

"Private comfort was virtually unknown among the Greeks. These citizens of small towns, who raised in their midst so many admirable public monuments, resided in houses that were more than modest, houses in which vases (though masterpieces of elegance, to be sure) constituted the only furnishings. Ernest Renan, *Essais de morale et de critique* (Paris, 1859), p. 359 ("La Poésie à l'Exposition"). To be compared with this is the character of the rooms in the Goethe House.—Note the quite opposite love of comfort in Baudelaire's production.
                [S6,4]

"Far from saying that the progress of art is parallel to that made by a nation in the taste for 'comfort' (I am forced to use this barbarous word to express an idea quite un-French), we can unequivocally state, on the contrary, that the epochs and the countries in which comfort became the public's principal attraction have had the least talent for art. . . . Convenience excludes style; a pot from an English factory is better adapted to its end than all the vases of Vulci or Nola. These latter are works of art, whereas the English pot will never be anything but a household utensil. . . . The incontestable conclusion is that nowhere in history is the progress of industry in any way parallel to the progress of art." Ernest Renan, *Essais de moral et de critique* (Paris, 1859), pp. 359, 361, 363 ("La Poésie de l'Exposition").
                [S6a,1]

"The rapid overpopulation of the capital had the effect . . . of reducing the surface area in rooms. Already in his 'Salon de 1828,' Stendhal wrote: 'Eight days ago, I went to look for an apartment on the Rue Godot-de-Mauroy. I was struck by the smallness of the rooms. The century of painting is over, I said to myself with a sigh; only engraving can prosper.'" Amédée Ozenfant, "La Peinture murale," (in *Encyclopédie française*, vol. 16, *Arts et littératures dans la société contemporaine*, 1 〈Paris, 1935〉, p. 70). [S6a,2]

Baudelaire in his review of *Madame Bovary:* "*Realism*—a repulsive insult flung in the face of every analytic writer, a vague and elastic word which for the ordinary man signifies not a new means of creation, but a minute description of trivial details." Baudelaire, *L'Art romantique*, p. 413.[16] [S6a,3]

In Chapter 24, "Beaux-Arts," of the *Argument du livre sur la Belgique:* "Specialists.—One painter for sunshine, one for snow, one for moonlight, one for furniture, one for fabrics, one for flowers—and subdivision of specialties ad infinitum.—Collaboration a necessity, as in industry." Baudelaire, *Oeuvres*, vol. 2, ed. Y.-G. Le Dantec 〈Paris, 1932〉, p. 718. [S6a,4]

"The elevation of urban life to the level of myth signifies right away, for the more clearheaded, a keen predisposition of *modernity*. The position which this latter concept occupies in Baudelaire is well known. . . . For him, as he says, it is a 'principal and essential problem,' a question of knowing whether or not his age possesses 'a specific beauty inherent in our new passions.' We know his answer: it is the conclusion of that essay which, at least in its range, remains the most considerable of his theoretic writings: 'The marvelous envelops and permeates us, like the atmosphere itself; but we do not see it. . . . For the heroes of the *Iliad* cannot compare with you, O Vautrin, O Rastignac, O Birotteau—nor with you, O Fontanarès, who dared not publicly recount your sorrows wearing the funereal and rumpled frock coat of today; nor with you, O Honoré de Balzac, you the most heroic, the most amazing, the most romantic, and the most poetic of all the characters that you have drawn from your fertile bosom' (Baudelaire, 'Salon de 1846,' section 18)."[17] Roger Caillois, "Paris, mythe moderne, *Nouvelle Revue française*, 25, no. 284 (May 1, 1937), pp. 690–691. [S7,1]

In Chapter 24, "Beaux-Arts," of the *Argument du livre sur la Belgique:* "A few pages on that infamous poseur named Wiertz, a favorite of English cockneys." Baudelaire, *Oeuvres*, vol. 2, ed. Y.-G. Le Dantec 〈Paris, 1932〉, p. 718. And page 720: "Independent painting.—Wiertz. Charlatan. Idiot. Thief. . . . Wiertz, the philosopher-painter and littérateur. Modern moonshine. The Christ of humanitarians. . . . Inanity comparable to that of Victor Hugo at the end of *Les Contemplations*. Abolition of death's sting, infinite power of humanity. / Inscriptions on walls. Grave offenses against France and French critics. Wiertz's maxims, above all. . . . Brussels the capital of the world. Paris a province. Wiertz's books. Plagiarisms. He doesn't know how to draw, and his stupidity is as massive as his giants.

This phony, in sum, knows how to manage his affairs. But what will Brussels do with all this after his death? / Trompe-l'oeil. The bellows camera. Napoleon in hell. The book of Waterloo. Wiertz and Victor Hugo are out to save the world."

[S7,2]

Ingres, in his *Réponse au rapport sur l'Ecole des Beaux-Arts* (Paris, 1863), makes the bluntest possible defense of the institutions of the school before the Minister of Fine Arts, to whom the communication is directed. In this, he does not take sides against Romanticism. His response has to do, from the beginning (p. 4), with industry: "Now people want to marry industry to art. Industry! We want none of it! Let it keep to its place and not come plant itself on the steps of our school . . . !"—Ingres insists on making drawing the sole basis of instruction in painting. One can learn the use of colors in eight days.   [S7a,1]

Daniel Halévy remembers seeing Italian models in his childhood—women dressed in the costume of Sorrento with a tambourine in their hands, who used to stand chatting at the fountain in the Place Pigalle. See Halévy, *Pays parisiens* ‹Paris, 1932›, p. 60.   [S7a,2]

The life of flowers in Jugendstil: from the flowers of evil extends an arc, over the flower-souls of Odilon Redon, to the orchids which Proust weaves into the eroticism of his Swann.   [S7a,3]

Segantini's "unnatural mothers," as a motif of Jugendstil, closely related to *Les Lesbiennes* ‹see J19,4›. The depraved woman stays clear of fertility, as the priest stays clear of it. Jugendstil, in fact, describes two distinct lines. That of perversion leads from Baudelaire to Wilde and Beardsley; the hieratic line leads through Mallarmé to George. In the end, a third line stands out more vigorously, the only one that here and there emerges from the realm of art. This is the line of emancipation, which, taking its departure from *Les Fleurs du mal,* conjoins the underworld that produces the *Tagebuch einer Verlorenen*[18] with the heights of Zarathustra. (This, presumably, the point of the remark made by Capus.)   [S7a,4]

Motif of infertility: Ibsen's women characters don't sleep with their men; they go "hand in hand" with them to encounter something terrible.   [S7a,5]

The perverse flower-glance of Odilon Redon.   [S7a,6]

Formulas of emancipation in Ibsen: the ideal challenge; dying in beauty; homes for human beings ‹see I4,4›; one's own responsibility (*The Lady from the Sea*).

[S8,1]

Jugendstil is the stylizing style par excellence.   [S8,2]

The idea of eternal return in *Zarathustra* is, according to its true nature, a stylization of the worldview that in Blanqui still displays its infernal traits. It is a stylization of existence down to the tiniest fractions of its temporal process. Nevertheless: Zarathustra's style disavows itself in the doctrine that is expounded through it.   [S8,3]

The three defining "motifs" of Jugendstil: the hieratic motif, the motif of perversion, the motif of emancipation. They all have their place in *Les Fleurs du mal;* to each of them one can assign a representative poem from the collection. To the first, "Bénédiction"; to the second, "Delphine et Hippolyte"; to the third, "Les Litanies de Satan."   [S8,4]

Zarathustra has, first of all, appropriated to himself the tectonic elements of Jugendstil, in contrast to its organic motifs. The pauses especially, which are characteristic of his rhythmics, are an exact counterpart to the tectonic phenomenon so basic to this style—namely, the predominance of the hollow form over the filled form.   [S8,5]

Certain themes of Jugendstil are derived from technological forms. Thus the profiles of iron supports that appear as ornamental motifs on façades. See the essay [by Martin?] in the *Frankfurter Zeitung,* circa 1926–1929.   [S8,6]

"Bénédiction": "So thoroughly will I twist this miserable tree / that it will never put forth its evil-smelling buds!"[19] The plant motif of Jugendstil, and its line, appear here—and certainly not in a passage more ready to hand.   [S8,7]

Jugendstil forces the auratic. Never has the sun worn a more glorious aureole; never was the eye of man more radiant than with Fidus. Maeterlinck pushes the unfolding of the auratic to the point of absurdity. The silence of the characters in his plays is one of its manifestations. Baudelaire's "Perte d'auréole"[20] stands in the most decided opposition to this Jugendstil motif.   [S8,8]

Jugendstil is the second attempt on the part of art to come to terms with technology. The first attempt was realism. There the problem was more or less present in the consciousness of the artists, who were uneasy about the new processes of technological reproduction. (The theory of realism demonstrates this; see S5,5.) In Jugendstil, the problem as such was already prey to repression. Jugendstil no longer saw itself threatened by the competing technology. And so the confrontation with technology that lies hidden within it was all the more aggressive. Its recourse to technological motifs arises from the effort to sterilize them ornamentally. (It was this, we may say in passing, that gave Adolf Loos's struggle against ornament its salient political significance.)   [S8a,1]

The fundamental motif of Jugendstil is the transfiguration of infertility. The body is portrayed, preferably, in the forms that precede sexual maturity. [S8a,2]

Lesbian love carries spiritualization forward into the very womb of the woman. There it raises its lily-banner of "pure love," which knows no pregnancy and no family. [S8a,3]

The consciousness of someone prone to spleen furnishes a miniature model of the world spirit to which the idea of eternal recurrence would have to be ascribed. [S8a,4]

"There, man passes through forests of symbols / Which observe him with familiar eyes." "Correspondances."[21] It is the flower-gazes of Jugendstil that emerge here. Jugendstil wins back symbols. The word "symbol" is not often found in Baudelaire. [S8a,5]

The development that led Maeterlinck, in the course of a long life, to an extremely reactionary position is logical. [S8a,6]

The reactionary attempt to sever technologically constituted forms from their functional contexts and turn them into natural constants—that is, to stylize them—appears, in a mode similar to Jugendstil, somewhat later in Futurism. [S8a,7]

The sense of sorrow which autumn awakens in Baudelaire. It is the season of harvest, the time when the flowers are undone. Autumn is invoked in Baudelaire with particular solemnity. To it are consecrated the words that are perhaps the most mournful in all his poetry. Of the sun, it is said: "He bids the crops to grow and ripen / in the immortal heart that would always flower."[22] In the figure of the heart that would bear no fruit, Baudelaire has already passed judgment on Jugendstil, long before its appearance on the scene. [S9,1]

"This seeking for *my* home . . . was *my* affliction. . . . Where is—*my* home? I ask and seek and have sought for it; I have not found it. Oh, eternal Everywhere; oh, eternal Nowhere." Citation from *Zarathustra*, in Karl Löwith, *Nietzsches Philosophie der ewigen Wiederkunft* ⟨Berlin, 1935⟩, p. 35 [compare the Rilke epigraph, S4a,2], ed. Kröner, p. 398.[23] [S9,2]

It may be supposed that in the typical Jugendstil line—conjoined in fantastic montage—nerve and electrical wire not infrequently meet (and that the vegetal nervous system in particular operates, as a limiting form, to mediate between the world of organism and the world of technology). "The fin-de-siècle cult of the nerves . . . maintains this telegraphic image of exchange. It was said of Strindberg by his second wife, Frida, . . . that his nerves had become so sensitive to atmospheric electricity that an approaching thunderstorm would send its signal over them as if over electrical wires." Dolf Sternberger, *Panorama* (Hamburg, 1938), p. 33. [S9,3]

In Jugendstil, the bourgeoisie begins to come to terms with the conditions—not yet, to be sure, of its social dominion—but of its dominion over nature. Insight into these conditions engenders a strain at the threshold of its consciousness. Hence the mysticism (Maeterlinck) which seeks to deflect this pressure; but hence also the reception of technological forms in Jugendstil—for example, of hollow space. [S9,4]

The chapter in *Zarathustra* entitled "Unter Töchtern der Wüste" ‹Among the Daughters of the Desert› is instructive, not only for the fact that the flower maidens—an important Jugendstil motif—make an appearance here in Nietzsche, but also in view of Nietzsche's kinship with Guys. The phrase "deep but without thoughts"[24] perfectly captures the expression worn by the prostitutes in Guys. [S9a,1]

The extreme point in the technological organization of the world is the liquidation of fertility. The frigid woman embodies the ideal of beauty in Jugendstil. (Jugendstil sees in every woman not Helena but Olympia.) [S9a,2]

Individual, group, mass—the group is the principle of genre. For Jugendstil, the isolation of the individual is typical (see Ibsen). [S9a,3]

Jugendstil represents an advance, insofar as the bourgeoisie gains access to the technological bases of its control over nature; a regression, insofar as it loses the power of looking the everyday in the face. (That can still be done only within the security of the saving lie.)[25]—The bourgeoisie senses that its days are numbered; all the more it wishes to stay young. Thus, it deludes itself with the prospect of a longer life or, at the least, a death in beauty. [S9a,4]

Segantini and Munch; Margarete Böhme and Przybyszewski. [S9a,5]

Vaihinger's philosophy of the "as if" is Jugendstil's little death knell, sounding for those condemned. [S9a,6]

"With the early works of Hennebique and the Perret brothers, a new chapter opens in the history of architecture. The desire for escape and renewal, it should be added, had been seen in the efforts of the Jugendstil school, which failed miserably. These architects, it seemed, would torture stone to the point of exhaustion, and they thus prepared the way for a fierce reaction in favor of simplicity. Architectural art was to be reborn in serene forms through the utilization of new materials." Marcel Zahar, "Les Tendances actuelles de l'architecture," *Encyclopédie française*, vol. 17, p. 17). [S9a,7]

In his "Salons," Baudelaire has given himself out as an implacable foe of genre. Baudelaire stands at the beginning of that "modern style" which represents an attempt to liquidate genre. In *Les Fleurs du mal,* this Jugendstil emerges for the first time with its characteristic floral motif. [S10,1]

The following passage from Valéry (*Oeuvres complètes,* J, cited by Thérive, *Le Temps,* April 20, 1939) reads like a reply to Baudelaire: "Modern man is a slave to modernity. . . . We will soon have to build heavily insulated cloisters. . . . Speed, numbers, effects of surprise, contrast, repetition, size, novelty, and credulity will be despised there."[26] [S10,2]

Concerning sensation: this pattern—novelty and the depreciation that befalls it, with a shock—has found a peculiarly drastic expression since the middle of the nineteenth century. The worn coin loses nothing of its value; the postmarked stamp is devalued. It is probably the first sort of voucher whose validity is inseparable from its character of newness. (The registration of value goes together here with its cancellation.) [S10,3]

On the motif of sterility in Jugendstil: procreation was felt to be the least worthy manner of subscribing to the animal side of creation. [S10,4]

The "no" to be grasped as the antithesis of what goes "according to plan." On the subject of planning, compare Scheerbart's *Lesabéndio:* we are all so weary because we have no plan. [S10,5]

"Novelty. The cult of novelty. The new is one of those poisonous stimulants which end up becoming more necessary than any food; drugs which, once they get a hold on us, need to be taken in progressively larger doses until they are fatal, though we'd die without them. It is a curious habit—growing thus attached to that perishable part of things in which precisely their novelty consists." Paul Valéry, *Choses tues* ‹Paris, 1930›, pp. 14–15.[27] [S10,6]

Decisive passage in Proust concerning the aura. He speaks of his journey to Balbec and comments that it would probably be made today in an automobile, which, moreover, would have its advantages. "But, after all, the special attraction of the journey lies not in our being able to alight at places on the way . . . , but in its making the difference between departure and arrival not as imperceptible but as intense as possible, so that we are conscious of it . . . intact, as it existed in our mind when imagination bore us from the place in which we were living right to the very heart of a place we longed to see, in a single sweep which seemed miraculous to us not so much because it covered a certain distance as because it united two distinct individualities of the world, took us from one name to another name; and this difference is accentuated (more than in a form of locomotion in which, since one can stop and alight where one chooses, there can scarcely be said to be any point of arrival) by the mysterious operation that is performed in those peculiar places, railway stations, which do not constitute, so to speak, a part of the surrounding town but contain the essence of its personality, just as upon their signboards they bear its painted name. . . . Unhappily those marvelous places which are railway stations, from which one sets out for a remote destination, are tragic places also, for . . . we must lay aside all hope of going home to sleep in our own bed, once we have made up our mind to penetrate into the pestiferous cavern through which we may have access to the mystery, into one of those vast, glass-roofed sheds, like that of Saint-Lazare, into which I must go to find the train for Balbec, and which extended over the rent bowels of the city one of those bleak and boundless skies, heavy with an accumulation of dramatic menaces, like certain skies painted with an almost Parisian modernity by Mantegna or Veronese, beneath which could be accomplished only some solemn and tremendous act, such as a departure by train or the Elevation of the Cross." Marcel Proust, *A l'Ombre des jeunes filles en fleurs* (Paris), vol. 2, pp. 62–63.[28]   [S10a]

Proust on the museum: "But in this respect, as in every other, our age is infected with a mania for showing things only in the environment that properly belongs to them, thereby suppressing the essential thing: the act of mind which isolated them from that environment. A picture is nowadays 'presented' in the midst of furniture, ornaments, hangings of the same period, a secondhand scheme of decoration . . . ; and among these, the masterpiece at which we glance up from the table while we dine does not give us that exhilarating delight which we can expect from it only in a public gallery, which symbolizes far better by its bareness, by the absence of all irritating detail, those innermost spaces into which the artist withdrew to create it." Marcel Proust, *A l'Ombre des jeunes filles en fleurs* (Paris), vol. 2, pp. 62–63.[29]   [S11,1]

How does modernism become Jugendstil?   [S11,2]

Battlefield or bazaar? "In former times, we may recall, there was, in literature, a movement of generous and disinterested activity. There were schools and leaders of schools, parties and leaders of parties, systems combating other systems, intellectual currents and countercurrents . . . —a passionate, militant literary life. . . . Ah yes, around 1830, I should say, all the men of letters used to glory in being soldiers on an expedition, and what they required of publicity they got, in the shadow of some banner or other, from the proud summons to the field of battle. . . . What remains to us today of all this brave show? Our forefathers fought the good fight, and we—we manufacture and sell. Amid the confusion of the present, what is most clear to me is that in place of the battlefield have come myriad shops and workshops, where each day sees the production and vending of the newest fashions and what, in general, is known as the *Paris article*." "Yes, *modiste* is the word for our generation of thinkers and dreamers." Hippolyte Babou, *Les Payens innocents* (Paris, 1858), pp. vii–viii ("Lettre à Charles Asselineau").

                                                                                    [S11,3]

T

[Modes of Lighting]

Et nocturnis facibus illustrata.[1]

—Medal of 1667, commemorating the introduction
of street lighting

"Napoleon has coverings of wool, velvet, silk, embroidery, gold, and silver; a glass ball for his hat; wreaths of the immortals; and an eternal *gas* lamp." Karl Gutzkow, *Briefe aus Paris* (Leipzig, 1842), vol. 1, p. 270. ⟨See "The Ring of Saturn."⟩
[T1,1]

Note relating to 1824: "Paris was illuminated, this year, by means of 11,205 street lamps. . . . The entrepreneur has been hired to provide lighting for the entire city for at least forty minutes—that is to say, beginning twenty minutes before the hour prescribed daily, and finishing twenty minutes later; he can assign no more than twenty-five lamps to each lamplighter." J.-A. Dulaure, *Histoire* ⟨*physique, civile et morale*⟩ *de Paris depuis 1821 jusqu'à nos jours* (Paris ⟨1835⟩), vol. 2, pp. 118–119.
[T1,2]

"A dreamlike setting, where the yellowish flickering of the gas is wedded to the lunar frigidity of electric light." Georges Montorgueil, *Paris au hasard* (Paris, 1895), p. 65.
[T1,3]

1857, the first electric streetlights (at the Louvre).
[T1,4]

Originally gas was delivered to fashionable establishments in containers for daily consumption.
[T1,5]

"I boldly declare myself the friend of Argand lamps; these, to tell the truth, are content with shedding light and do not dazzle the eyes. Much less volatile than gas, their oil never causes explosions; with them we breathe more freely, and the odor is less offensive. Truly incomprehensible to me is the existence of all those shopkeepers who, entrenched in our arcades, remain—at all hours and in the warmest of weathers—within shops where, on account of the gas, it feels like the Tropics." ☐ Arcades ☐ *Nouveaux tableaux de Paris, ou Observations sur les moeurs et usages des Parisiens au commencement du XIXe siècle* (Paris, 1828), vol. 1, p. 39.
[T1,6]

"During this same period, the amount of street lighting more than doubled. Gas was now used instead of oil. New street lamps took the place of the older apparatus, and permanent lighting was substituted for intermittent lighting." M. Poëte, E. Clouzot, G. Henriot, *La Transformation de Paris sous le Second Empire*, ⟨Paris, 1910⟩, p. 65 (Exposition de la Bibliothèque et des Travaux historiques de la ville de Paris).   [T1,7]

On the ladies of the cash register: "All day long they go about in hair curlers and dressing gown; after sundown, however, when the gas is lit, they make their appearance, arrayed as for a ball. Seeing them, then, enthroned at the cashier's desk, surrounded by a sea of light, one may well think back to *The Blue Library*[2] and the fairy tale of the prince with golden hair and the enchanting princess, a comparison the more admissible inasmuch as Parisian women enchant more than they are enchanted." Eduard Kroloff, *Schilderungen aus Paris* (Hamburg, 1839), vol. 2, pp. 76–77.   [T1,8]

The tin racks with artificial flowers, which can be found at refreshment bars in railroad stations, and elsewhere, are vestiges of the floral arrangements that formerly encircled the cashier.   [T1,9]

Du Bartas called the sun "Grand Duke of Candles." Cited by M. Du Camp, *Paris* (Paris, 1875), vol. 5, p. 268.   [T1,10]

"The lantern carriers will have oil lanterns with 'six thick wicks'; they will be stationed at posts, each one separated from the next by a distance of eight hundred paces. . . . They will have a tinted lamp hung above their post that will serve as a beacon, and on their belts an hour glass of a quarter hour's duration, bearing the shield of the city. . . . Here, once again, it was a matter of empiricism; these wandering lamps provided no security at all to the city, and the carriers beat up the people they were accompanying on more than one occasion. Lacking anything better, however, the city used them; and they were used so long that they were still to be found at the beginning of the nineteenth century." Du Camp, *Paris*, vol. 5, p. 275.   [T1,11]

"They [the lantern carriers] would hail hackney cabs, would serve as crier-escorts for chauffeured carriages, and would accompany late-night passersby right to their homes, coming up to their apartments and lighting the candles. Some claim that these lantern carriers voluntarily gave accounts every morning to the lieutenant general of police on what they had noticed during the night." Du Camp, *Paris*, vol. 5, p. 281.   [T1a,1]

"The patent of importation taken out by Winsor for Paris is dated December 1, 1815; in January 1817, the Passage des Panoramas was illuminated. . . . The first attempts by businesses were not at all satisfactory; the public seemed resistant to this kind of lighting, which was suspected of being dangerous and of polluting breathable air." Du Camp, *Paris*, vol. 5, p. 290. [T1a,2]

"This place visited by commercial death, under this gas . . . which seems to tremble at the thought of not being paid for." Louis Veuillot, *Les Odeurs de Paris* (Paris, 1914), p. 182. [T1a,3]

"Glass is destined to play an important role in metal-architecture. In place of thick walls whose solidity and resistance is diminished by a large number of apertures, our houses will be so filled with openings that they will appear diaphanous. These wide openings, furnished with thick glass, single- or double-paned, frosted or transparent, will transmit—to the inside during the day and to the outside at night—a magical radiance." Gobard, "L'Architecture de l'avenir," *Revue générale d'architecture* (1849), p. 30 [S. Giedion, *Bauen in Frankreich* ‹Leipzig and Berlin, 1928›, p. 18]. [T1a,4]

Lamps in the form of vases. The rare flower "light," as done in oil. (The form on a fashionable copper engraving of 1866.) [T1a,5]

The old gas torches that burned in the open air often had a flame in the shape of a butterfly, and were known accordingly as *papillons*. [T1a,6]

In the Carcel lamp, a clockwork drives the oil up into the burner; whereas in the Argand lamp *(quinquet)*, the oil drips into the burner from a reservoir above it, thereby producing a shadow. [T1a,7]

Arcades—they radiated through the Paris of the Empire like fairy grottoes. For someone entering the Passage des Panoramas in 1817, the sirens of gaslight would be singing to him on one side, while oil-lamp odalisques offered enticements from the other. With the kindling of electric lights, the irreproachable glow was extinguished in these galleries, which suddenly became more difficult to find—which wrought a black magic at entranceways, and which looked within themselves out of blind windows. [T1a,8]

When, on February 12, 1790, the Marquis de Favras was executed for plotting against the Revolution, the Place de Grève and the scaffold were adorned with Chinese lanterns. [T1a,9]

"We said, in the first volume, that every historical period is bathed in a distinctive light, whether diurnal or nocturnal. Now, for the first time, this world has an artificial illumination in the form of gaslight, which burst onto the scene in London at a time when Napoleon's star was beginning to decline, which entered Paris more or less contemporaneously with the Bourbons, and which, by slow and tenacious advances, finally took possession of all streets and public localities. By 1840 it was flaring everywhere, even in Vienna. In this strident and gloomy, sharp and flickering, prosaic and ghostly illumination, large insects are busily moving about: shop-keepers." Egon Friedell, *Kulturgeschichte der Neuzeit*, vol. 3 (Munich, 1931), p. 86. [T1a,10]

On the Café Mille et Une Nuits: "Everything there was of an unprecedented magnificence. In order to give you a sense of it, it will suffice to say that the beautiful *limonadière* had, for her seat at the counter, . . . a throne, a veritable royal throne, on which one of the great potentates of Europe had sat in all his majesty. How did this throne get to be there? We could not say; we affirm the fact without undertaking to explain it." *Histoire des cafés de Paris, extraite des mémoires d'un viveur* (Paris, 1857), p. 31. [T1a,11]

"Gas has replaced oil, gold has dethroned woodwork, billiards has put a stop to dominoes and backgammon. Where one formerly heard only the buzzing of flies, one now listens to the melodies of Verdi or Aubert." *Histoire des cafés de Paris, extraite des mémoires d'un viveur* (Paris, 1857), p. 114. [T2,1]

Grand Café du XIXe Siècle—opens 1857 on the Boulevard de Strasbourg. "The green felt tops of numerous billiard tables can be seen there; a splendid counter is illuminated by gas jets. Directly opposite is a white marble fountain, on which the allegorical subject is crowned by a luminous aureole." *Histoire des cafés de Paris, extraite des mémoires d'un viveur* (Paris, 1857), p. 111. [T2,2]

"As early as 1801, Lebon had attempted to install gas lighting at the Hôtel Seignelay, 47 Rue Saint-Dominique. The system was improved at the beginning of January 1808: three hundred gas jets lit up the Hospital of Saint-Louis, with such success that three gas-jet factories were built." Lucien Dubech and Pierre d'Espezel, *Histoire de Paris* (Paris, 1926), p. 335. [T2,3]

"In matters of municipal administration, the two great works of the Restoration were gas lighting and the creation of omnibuses. Paris was illuminated in 1814 by 5,000 street lamps, serviced by 142 lamplighters. In 1822, the government decided that streets would be lit by gas in proportion as the old contracts came due. On June 3, 1825, the Compagnie du Gaz Portatif Français undertook, for the first time, to light up a square: the Place Vendôme received four multiple-jet street lamps at the corners of the column and two street lamps at the corners of the Rue de Castiglione. In 1826, there were 9,000 gas burners in Paris; in 1828, there were 10,000, with 1,500 subscribers, three gas companies, and four gas-jet factories, one of which was on the Left Bank." Dubech and d'Espezel, *Histoire de Paris*, p. 358. [T2,4]

From an eighteenth-century prospectus, "Lighting Project, Proposed by Subscription for Decorating the Famous Thoroughfare of the Boulevard Saint-Antoine": "The Boulevard will be illuminated by a garland of Lanterns that will extend on both sides between the trees. This illumination will take place twice weekly, on Thursdays and Sundays, and, when there is a Moon, on the days after the abovementioned weekdays. Lighting will begin at ten o'clock, and all will be illuminated by eleven. . . . Since this sort of evening Promenade is suited only to Lords and Men of Wealth who have carriages, it is only to them that we offer this subscription. Subscription for this year is at the rate of 18 pounds for each House; in subsequent years, however, it will cost only 12 pounds, the 6 additional pounds this year being for the initial expenses of installation" (p. 3). "The Cafés and Theaters that border this famous promenade are justly celebrated; Yes—I say this to their glory—it was the handsome Lanterns adorning their illustrious Booths that gave me the idea of universal Illumination. The celebrated Chevalier Servandoni has promised me designs for the Arcades, for the Garlands, and for the elegant Monograms, designs worthy of his fecund genius. Is there a single one of our wealthy style-setters who does not heartily support this brilliant Project? Adorned in this manner, the Boulevard will become a well-appointed Ballroom, one in which Carriages will serve as Box Seats."   [T2,5]

"After the theater I went to a café, which was all newly decorated in Renaissance style. The walls of the main room were entirely covered by mirrors set between gilded columns. The cashier sits at all times behind a large and sumptuous table placed upon a platform; before her is silverware, fruits, flowers, sugar, and the box for the *garçons*. It is customary for every paying customer to leave a small gratuity for the waiter; this is thrown by the latter into the box. Its contents are later equally divided." Eduard Devrient, *Briefe aus Paris* (Berlin, 1840), p. 20.
                    [T2a,1]

Between the February Revolution and the June Insurrection: "When the club meetings were over, workers took to the streets, and the sleeping bourgeois were either awakened by cries of 'Des lampions! Des lampions!' in consequence of which they would have to light their windows; or else wanton gunshots roused them from their beds in terror. . . . There were endless torchlight processions through the streets of Paris, and on one occasion it happened that a girl allowed herself to be undressed and shown naked to the crowd by torchlight; for the crowd, this was merely a reminiscence of the Goddess of Liberty of the first French Revolution. . . . At one point the prefect of police, Caussidière, issued a proclamation against these torchlight processions—but the edict terrified the citizenry of Paris still more, because it stated that the people were supposed to brandish torches only in the event of some threat to the republic." Sigmund Engländer, *Geschichte der französischen Arbeiter-Associationen* (Hamburg, 1864), vol. 2, p. 277–278.   [T2a,2]

"It was still the women who cleaned the oily street lamps by day, and lit them at night, climbing up and down with the aid of an extendable rope kept locked in a toolbox during the day—since gas, which for some years had been blazing in English towns, had yet to be supplied. The merchants who sold the oil and the Argand lamps wished to avoid all favorable mention of this other source of light, and they soon found two highly reputable writers, messieurs Charles Nodier and Amédée Pichot, . . . to denounce, . . . in octavo format, all the problems and perversities connected with gas, including the danger of our complete annihilation by explosion at the hands of malefactors." Nadar, *Quand j'étais photographe* (Paris ‹1900›), pp. 289–290. [T2a,3]

Fireworks and illuminations were already on the scene during the Restoration; they were set off whenever a measure proposed by the ultraroyalists was defeated in the Chamber. [T2a,4]

Apropos of an institute for the blind and the insane, this excursus on electric light: "I come now to the facts. The bright light of electricity served, at first, to illuminate the subterranean galleries of mines; after that, public squares and streets; then factories, workshops, stores, theaters, military barracks; finally, the domestic interior. The eyes, initially, put up rather well with this penetrating new enemy; but, by degrees, they were dazzled. Blindness began as something temporary, soon became periodic, and ended as a chronic problem. This, then, was the first result—sufficiently comprehensible, I believe; but what about the insanity lately visited on our leaders?—Our great heads of finance, industry, big business have seen fit . . . to send . . . their thoughts around the world, while they themselves remain at rest. . . . To this end, each of them has nailed up, in a corner of his office, electric wires connecting his executive desk with our colonies in Africa, Asia, and the Americas. Comfortably seated before his schedules and account books, he can communicate directly over tremendous distances; at a touch of the finger, he can receive reports from all his far-flung agents on a startling variety of matters. One branch-correspondent tells him, at ten in the morning, of a shipwrecked vessel worth over a million . . .; another, at five after ten, of the unexpected sale of the most prosperous house in the two Americas; a third, at ten after ten, of the glorious entrance, into the port of Marseilles, of a freighter carrying the fruits of a Northern California harvest. All this in rapid succession. The poor brains of these men, robust as they were, have simply given way, just as the shoulders of some Hercules of the marketplace would give way if he ventured to load them with ten sacks of wheat instead of one. And this was the second result." Jacques Fabien, *Paris en songe* (Paris, 1863), pp. 96–98. [T3,1]

Julien Lemer, *Paris au gaz* (Paris, 1861): "I close the curtains on the sun. It is well and duly put to rest; let us speak no more of it. Henceforth, I shall know no other light than that of gas" (p. 10). The volume contains three novellas in addition to the Parisian vignettes, of which the first gives it its title. [T3,2]

In the Place de l'Hôtel de Ville:[3]—around 1848—there was a Café du Gaz. [T3,3]

The misfortunes of Aimé Argand. The various improvements he made in the old oil lamp—the double current of air, the fuse woven in the shape of a hollow cylinder, the glass tubing, and so forth—were at first laid claim to by Lange in England (a man with whom Argand had been associated), before being stolen in Paris by Quinquet, who gave his name to the invention. And thus Argand ended in misery: "The misanthropy to which he succumbed after the withdrawal of his patent led him to seek a compensation of sorts in the occult sciences. . . . 'During the last years of his life, he was seen wandering through graveyards gathering bones and dust from tombs, which he would then submit to chemical processes in the hope of finding in death the secret of prolonging life.'" He himself died young. A‹ntoinette› Drohojowska, *Les Grandes Industries de la France: L'Eclairage* (Paris ‹1881›), p. 127.   [T3a,1]

Carcel, inventor of the lamp that operates by clockwork. Such a lamp has to be wound up. It contains a clockwork mechanism that pumps the oil from a reservoir at the bottom up into the wick. Carcel's advance over earlier oil lamps—which had the reservoir located above the wick, whence the oil dripped down—consisted in eliminating the shadow caused by this overlying reservoir. His invention dates from 1800. His *enseigne:* "B.-G. Carcel, inventor of the Lycnomènes, or mechanical lamps, manufactures said lamps."   [T3a,2]

"The chemical match is, without doubt, one of the vilest devices that civilization has yet produced. . . . It is thanks to this that each of us carries around fire in his pocket. . . . I . . . detest this permanent plague, always primed to trigger an explosion, always ready to roast humanity individually over a low flame. If you follow M. Alphonse Karr in his crusade against tobacco, you should likewise raise the banner in opposition to these matches. . . . If we did not have in our pockets the possibility of making smoke, we would smoke less." H‹enri› de Pène, *Paris intime* (Paris, 1859), pp. 119–120.   [T3a,3]

According to Lurine ("Les Boulevarts," in *Paris chez soi* ‹Paris, 1854›): the first gas lighting—1817, in the Passage des Panoramas.   [T3a,4]

Regarding the definitive installation of street lamps in the streets of Paris (in March 1667): "I know of no one but the abbé Terrasson, among the men of letters, who spoke ill of the lanterns. . . . According to him, decadence in the realm of letters began with the establishment of street lights. 'Before this period,' he once said, 'everyone returned home early, from fear of losing their lives, and this fact worked to the advantage of labor. Nowadays, people stay out at night, and work less.' Surely there is truth in this observation and the invention of gas is not likely to give it the lie." Edouard Fournier, *Les Lanternes: Histoire de l'ancien éclairage de Paris* (Paris, 1854), p. 25.   [T3a,5]

In the second half of the 1760s, a number of pamphlets were published that dealt with the new street lights in poetical form. The following verses come from the poem "Les Sultanes nocturnes et ambulantes contre Nosseigneurs les réverbères:

A la petite vertu" ‹The Strolling Sultanas of Night against Our Lords the Street Lamps: To Easy Virtue›, 1769:

> The poor woman finds, instead
> Of lovers, only lampposts
> In this dazzling town,
> Once a second Cythera,
> Where nymphs would walk.
> Tender mothers of delight,
> They are forced today
> To squeeze themselves into a box,
> In other words, an octogenarian fiacre,
> Which, by way of B., or F., takes them
> To where fiacres have nothing to do. . . .
> *Misericordia*, when once the night
> Will let you leave the hovel;
> For life is so needy.
> Not a single corner or carrefour
> The street light does not reach.
> It is a burning-glass that pierces through
> The plans we made by day. . . .

Edouard Fournier, *Les Lanternes: Histoire de l'ancien éclairage de Paris* (Paris, 1854), p. 5 (from the specially paginated printing of the poem).   [T4,1]

In 1799, an engineer installed gas lighting in his house, and thus put into practice what previously had been known only as an experiment in the physicist's laboratory.   [T4,2]

> It is possible, you know, to avoid these setbacks
> By choosing the shelter of covered arcades;
> Though, in these lanes the idler favors,
> Spirals of blue smoke rise from Havanas.
> . . . . .
> Make for us, by your efforts, a gentler life,
> Clear from our path all bumps and jolts,
> And ward off, for a time, the deadly volcanoes
> Of reading rooms and restaurants.
> At dusk, give orders to search
> Those spots defiled by the odorless gas,
> And to sound the alarm with cries of fear
> At the seeping in of flammable fumes.

Barthélemy, *Paris: Revue satirique à M. G. Delessert* (Paris, 1838), p. 16.   [T4,3]

"'What a splendid invention this gas lighting is!' Gottfried Semper exclaims. 'In how may different ways has it not enriched the festive occasions of life (not to mention its infinite importance for our practical needs)!' This striking preeminence of the festive over the daily, or rather the nightly, imperatives—for, thanks to this general illumination, urban nighttime itself becomes a sort of ongoing ani-mated festival—clearly betrays the oriental character of this form of lighting. . . . The fact that in Berlin, after what is now twenty years of operation, a gas company can boast of scarcely ten thousand private customers in the year 1846 can be . . . explained . . . in the following manner: 'For the most part, of course, one could point to general commercial and social factors to account for this phenomenon; there was still, in fact, no real need for increased activity during the evening and nighttime hours.'" Dolf Sternberger, *Panorama* (Hamburg, 1938), pp. 201, 202. Citations from Gottfried Semper, *Wissenschaft: Industrie und Kunst* (Brunswick, 1852), p. 12; and from *Handbuch für Steinkohlengasbeleuchtung*, ed. N. H. Schilling (Munich, 1879), p. 21. [T4a,1]

Apropos of the covering over of the sky in the big city as a consequence of artificial illumination, a sentence from Vladimir Odoievsky's "The Smile of the Dead": "Vainly he awaited the gaze that would open up to him." Similar is the motif of the blind men in Baudelaire, which goes back to "Des Vetters Eck-fenster." [4] [T4a,2]

Gaslight and electricity. "I reached the Champs-Elysées, where the *cafés concerts* seemed like blazing hearths among the leaves. The chestnut trees, brushed with yellow light, had the look of painted objects, the look of phosphorescent trees. And the electric globes—like shimmering, pale moons, like moon eggs fallen from the sky, like monstrous, living pearls—dimmed, with their nacreous glow, mysterious and regal, the flaring jets of gas, of ugly, dirty gas, and the garlands of colored glass." Guy de Maupassant, *Claire de lune* (Paris, 1909), p. 122 ("La Nuit cauche-mar" ‹The Nightmare›). [T4a,3]

Gaslight in Maupassant: "Everything was clear in the mild night air, from the planets down to the gas lamps. So much fire shone there above, just as in the town, that the shadows themselves seemed luminous. The glittering nights are merrier than the brightest of sunny days." Guy de Maupassant, *Claire de lune* (Paris, 1909), p. 121 ("La Nuit cauchemar"). In the last sentence, one finds the quintessence of the "Italian night." [T5,1]

The cashier, by gaslight, as living image—as allegory of the cash register. [T5,2]

Poe in the "Philosophy of Furniture": "*Glare* is a leading error in the philosophy of American household decoration. . . . We are violently enamored of gas and of glass. The former is totally inadmissible within doors. Its harsh and unsteady light offends. No one having both brains and eyes will use it." Charles Baudelaire, *Oeuvres complètes*, ed. Crépet (Paris, 1937), p. 207 (*Histoires grotesques et sérieuses par Edgar Poe*). [5] [T5,3]

U

[Saint-Simon, Railroads]

"Characteristic of the entire period up to 1830 is the slowness of the spread of machines. . . . The mentality of entrepreneurs, economically speaking, was still conservative; otherwise, the import duty on steam engines, which were not yet produced by more than a handful of factories in France, could not have been raised to 30 percent of the value. French industry at the time of the Restoration was thus still, in essence, thoroughly tied to the prerevolutionary regime." Willy Spühler, *Der Saint-Simonismus: Lehre und Leben von Saint-Amand Bazard* (Zurich, 1926), p. 12. [U1,1]

"Corresponding to the laborious development of large-scale industry is the slow formation of the modern proletariat. . . . The actual proletarianization . . . of the working masses is effected only at the end of the 1830s and 1840s." Spühler, *Der Saint-Simonismus*, p. 13. [U1,2]

"During the whole period of the Restoration . . . the Chamber of Deputies followed a commercial policy of the most extreme protectionism. . . . The old theory of a balance of trade was again in full swing, as in the days of mercantilism." Spühler, *Der Saint-Simonismus* (Zurich, 1926), pp. 10–11. [U1,3]

"It was only in 1841 that a modest little law concerning child labor was approved. Of interest is the objection of the famous physicist Gay-Lussac, who saw in the intervention "an onset of Saint-Simonianism or of phalansterianism." Spühler, *Der Saint-Simonismus*, p. 15. [U1,4]

"Aphrodite's birds travel the skies from Paris to Amsterdam, and under their wing is clipped a list of daily quotations from the Stock Exchange; a telegraph sends a message from Paris to Brussels concerning the rise in 3 percent annuities; couriers gallop over highways on panting horses; the ambassadors of real kings bargain with ideal kings, and Nathan Rothschild in London will show you, if you pay him a visit, a casket just arrived from Brazil with freshly mined diamonds intended to cover the interest on the current Brazilian debt. Isn't that interesting?" Karl Gutzkow, *Öffentliche Charaktere*, part 1 (Hamburg, 1835), p. 280 ("Rothschild"). [U1,5]

"The influence and development of Saint Simonianism, up until the end of the nineteenth century, had almost nothing to do with the working class. Saint-Simonianism provided an impetus and an ideal for the spirit of large-scale industry and for the realization of ambitious works. The Saint-Simonian Pereire brothers controlled the railroad, banking, and real estate operations of the July Monarchy and the Second Empire. The Suez Canal, for which Enfantin and Lambert-Bey would study the plans and work out the conception at a time when Ferdinand de Lesseps was consul in Cairo, has remained the prototype of the Saint-Simonian planetary enterprise. We may, without hesitation, contrast the *grand bourgeois* project of Saint-Simonianism, which is based on production and action, with the *petit bourgeois* project of the Fourierist phalanstery, which is based on consumption and pleasure." Albert Thibaudet, *Les Idées politiques de la France* (Paris, 1932), pp. 61–62. ☐ Secret Societies ☐   [U1,6]

"Girardin . . . founded *La Presse* in 1836; he invented the popular, low-priced newspaper and the *roman feuilleton,* or serial novel." Dubech and d'Espezel, *Histoire de Paris* (Paris, 1926), p. 391.   [U1,7]

"In the past several years, a complete revolution has occurred in the cafés of Paris. Cigars and pipes have invaded every corner. Formerly, there was smoking only in certain special establishments known as *estaminets* ‹public houses›, which were frequented solely by persons of low standing; today people smoke nearly everywhere. . . . There is one thing we cannot forgive the princes of the house of Orléans—namely, for having so prodigiously increased the vogue for tobacco, this malodorous and nauseating plant that poisons both mind and body. All the sons of Louis Philippe smoked like chimneys; no one encouraged the consumption of this nasty product more than they. Such consumption no doubt fattened the public treasury—but at the expense of public health and human intelligence." *Histoire des cafés de Paris, extraite des mémoirs d'un viveur* (Paris, 1857), pp. 91–92.
[U1a,1]

"Symbolism is so deeply rooted . . . that it is found not just in liturgical rites. In the previous century, didn't the disciples of Enfantin wear waistcoats that buttoned in the back, so as to draw attention to the fraternal assistance which one man renders another?" Robert Jacquin, *Notions sur le langage d'après les travaux du P‹ère› Marcel Jousse* (Paris, 1929), p. 22.   [U1a,2]

"In 1807, there were over 90,000 workers in Paris practicing 126 professions. They were subject to strict supervision: associations were prohibited, employment agencies were regulated, and work hours were fixed. Salaries went from 2 francs 50, to 4 francs 20, yielding an average of 3 francs 35. The worker ate a hearty breakfast, a light lunch, and an evening supper." Lucien Dubech and Pierre d'Espezel, *Histoire de Paris* (Paris, 1926), p. 335.   [U1a,3]

"On August 27, 1817, the steamship *Le Génie du commerce*, invented by the Marquis de Jouffroy, had sailed the Seine between the Pont-Royal and the Pont Louis XVI." Dubech and d'Espezel, *Histoire de Paris*, p. 359. [U1a,4]

The national workshops[1] "had been created according to the proposal of a moderate, ⟨Alexandre-Thomas⟩ Marie, because the Revolution had guaranteed the existence of the worker through his work, and because it was necessary to satisfy the demands of the extremists. . . . The workshops were organized, in a manner at once democratic and militaristic, into brigades, with elected chiefs." Dubech and d'Espezel, *Histoire de Paris*, pp. 398–399. [U1a,5]

The Saint-Simonians. "In the magnificent disorder of ideas that accompanied Romanticism, they had grown enough, by 1830, to abandon their loft on the Rue Taranne and to establish themselves on the Rue Taitbout. Here, they gave lectures before an audience of young men dressed in blue and women in white with violet scarves. They had acquired the newspaper *Le Globe*, and in its pages they advocated a program of reforms. . . . The government, . . . on the pretext of supporting the emancipation of women, decided to prosecute the Saint-Simonians. They came to the hearing in full regalia, and to the accompaniment of hunting horns. Enfantin wore written on his chest, in large letters, the two words *Le Père*, and he calmly declared to the presiding judge that he was in fact the father of humanity. He then tried to hypnotize the magistrates by staring into their eyes. He was sentenced to one year in prison, which effectively put an end to these follies." Dubech and d'Espezel, *Histoire de Paris*, pp. 392–393. ☐ Haussmann ☐ Secret Societies ☐ [U1a,6]

"Girardin published . . . a brochure with the title, "Why a Constitution?" It was his idea that the entire French constitution should be replaced by a simple declaration of ten lines, which . . . would be engraved on the five-franc piece." S. Engländer ⟨*Geschichte der französischen Arbeiter-Associationen* (Hamburg, 1864)⟩, vol. 4, pp. 133–134. [U1a,7]

"At the time of the Revolution, a new element began to appear in Paris: large-scale industry. This was a consequence of the disappearance of feudal guilds; of the reign of unfettered liberty that followed in their wake; and of the wars against England, which made necessary the production of items previously procured by import. By the end of the Empire, the evolution was complete. From the revolutionary period on, there were factories established for the production of saltpeter, firearms, woolen and cotton fabrics, preserved meat, and small utensils. Mechanical spinning mills for cotton and linen were developed, with the encouragement of Calonne, beginning in 1785; factories for the production of bronze were constructed under Louis XVI; and chemical and dying companies were founded by the Count d'Artois in Javel. Didot Saint-Léger ran a new machine for paper production on the Rue Sainte-Anne. In 1799, Philippe Lebon received a patent on a process for producing gas lighting. From September 22 to September 30, 1798, the first 'public exhibition of the products of French manufacturing and industry' was held on the Champ de Mars." Dubech and d'Espezel, *Histoire de Paris* (Paris, 1926), p. 324. ☐ Exhibitions ☐   [U2,1]

On the Saint-Simonians: "School constituted by a veritable corps of industrial engineers and entrepreneurs, representatives of big business underwritten by the power of the banks." A. Pinloche, *Fourier et le socialisme* (Paris, 1933), p. 47.
[U2,2]

"Although the worker associations were all run in exemplary fashion, ably and honestly, . . . members of the bourgeoisie were nevertheless unanimous in their disapproval. Most of the bourgeoisie would feel a certain apprehension in passing before one of the houses that bore the sign . . . and the emblem of a worker association. Though these shops were distinguished from other, similar businesses only by the inscription 'Association fraternelle d'ouvriers: Liberté, Egalité, Fraternité,' on the petit bourgeois they had the effect of snakes in the grass that might suddenly strike at any time. It sufficed for the bourgeois to think of the February Revolution, which had been the origin of these associations. . . . For their part, the associations of workers made every possible effort to conciliate the bourgeoisie, hoping to gain its support. It was for this reason that many of them furnished their shops in the most splendid manner, so as to draw their share of customers. The privations which the workers thus laid upon themselves, in an effort to withstand the competition, are beyond belief. While that part of the shop which was open to the public was fitted out in the costliest way, the worker himself would be sitting on the floor of a workroom that often was totally lacking in equipment." Sigmund Engländer, *Geschichte der französischen Arbeiter-Associationen* (Hamburg, 1864), vol. 3, pp. 106–108. ☐ Secret Societies ☐   [U2,3]

Influence of the feuilleton in its early days. "There are newspapers for one sou and newspapers for ten centimes. A dealer observes a solid bourgeois passing by, who, after carefully perusing his *Constitutionnel* . . . , negligently folds it and puts it in his pocket. The dealer accosts this plucky reader, presents him with either *Le Peuple* or *La Révolution*, which cost only a sou, and says to him: 'Monsieur, if you like, I will give you, in exchange for the paper you've just finished, *Le Peuple*, by citizen Proudhon, and its supplement containing a serial by the famous Ménars-Senneville.' The bourgeois allows himself to be persuaded. What good is a *Constitutionnel* you've already read? He gives up his newspaper and accepts the other, enticed, as he is, by the sovereign name of Ménars-Senneville. Often he forgets himself, in his delight at being rid of so tedious a burden, and adds another sou into the bargain." A. Privat d'Anglemont, *Paris inconnu* (Paris, 1861), pp. 155–156.   [U2a,1]

The well-known principle of Villemessant: "that an incident which is completely ordinary, but which occurs on the boulevards or their environs, has much more importance, from the point of view of journalism, than an event of great consequence in America or Asia." Jean Morienval, *Les Créateurs de la grande presse en France* (Paris ‹1934›), p. 132.   [U2a,2]

"*L'Autographe* was run by Bourdin,[2] because Villemessant, like Napoleon, loved to apportion kingdoms. That curious man, very independent of spirit, rarely acted alone. He would 'collaborate.'" Jean Morienval, *Les Créateurs de la grande presse en France* (Paris), p. 142.   [U2a,3]

Poetry of Saint-Simonianism: "In the preface to the first volume of *Le Producteur*, A. Cerclet launches an urgent appeal to artists. . . . And Buchez, who later succeeded to the leadership of the cooperative movement, appealed to the community of artists in similar terms. . . . It was Buchez who first observed . . . that classicism and romanticism share equally in the world with which they—the Saint-Simonians—are occupied, just as legitimacy and liberalism divide between themselves the political world. . . . In 1825, a monument was erected to the builder of the Languedoc Canal, Pierre Riquet. On this occasion, Soumet composed a stirring hymn. . . . The literary chronicler for *Le Producteur*, Léon Halévy, brother of the famous composer, hailed these verses, which he characterized as 'industrial poetry.' . . . Soumet, however, only partly fulfilled the hopes which the Saint-Simonians had placed in him. If later on, in his *Divine Epopée*, one can still hear the hammer's clang and the noisy grinding of the gears of industrial labor, it is precisely here, in the poet's greatest work, that the propensity for metaphysical abstractions is manifest. . . . Halévy, moreover, was himself a poet. . . . In 1828 Halévy published his *Poésies européennes*, . . . and in 1831 wrote an ode to Saint-Simon, who had died in 1825." H. Thurow, "Aus den Anfängen der sozialistischen Belletristik," *Die neue Zeit*, 21, no. 2 (Stuttgart, 1903), pp. 217–219.   ˙ [U2a,4]

On a review by Sainte-Beuve in the *Revue des deux mondes*, February 15, 1833: "The verses which Sainte-Beuve . . . reviewed were the literary remains of a poet by the name of Bruheille, who died very young. . . . In his account, furthermore, Sainte-Beuve draws attention to a novel which bore the characteristic title *La Saint-Simonienne*, and which . . . demonstrates the triumph of the Saint-Simonian idea. That the author, a certain Madame Le Bassu, brings about this triumph through a rather improbable course of events—namely, the transfusion of blood from the veins of a youth infected with Saint-Simonian doctrine into those of his ecclesiastically educated beloved—may be regarded in essence as an artistic expedient; at the same time, however, it brings out the mystical side of Saint-Simonianism. This mystical element had, shortly before, found stark expression during the sojourn by the 'family' in their last place of refuge, on the Rue Ménilmontant. This concluding episode in the life of the movement likewise engendered a corresponding literature—poems, songs, spiritual exercises in verse and prose—whose enigmatic symbolism could be understood only by the few initiates. . . . Thrown off course by the violence of political and economic developments, Saint-Simonianism had run aground on metaphysics." H. Thurow, "Aus den Anfängen der sozialistischen Belletristik," *Die neue Zeit*, 21, no. 2 (Stuttgart, 1903), pp. 219–220.   [U3,1]

Utopian socialism. "The class of capitalists . . . looked on its partisans as mere eccentrics and harmless enthusiasts. . . . These partisans themselves, furthermore, did all that was humanly possible . . . to warrant such an impression. They wore clothes of a very particular cut (Saint-Simonians, for example, buttoned their coats in the back so as to be reminded, while dressing, of their reliance on their fellow man and thereby of the need for union), or else they wore unusually large hats, very long beards, and so on." Paul Lafargue, "Der Klassenkampf in Frankreich," *Die neue Zeit*, 12, no. 2, p. 618.   [U3,2]

"After the July Revolution, the Saint-Simonians took over even the frontline organ of the Romantics, *Le Globe*. Pierre Leroux became the editor." Franz Diederich, "Victor Hugo," *Die neue Zeit*, 20, no. 1 (Stuttgart, 1901), p. 651.   [U3,3]

From a report on the November 1911 issue of the journal of Austrian social democracy, *Der Kampf:* "'On Saint-Simon's 150th birthday,' . . . Max Adler wrote: . . . He was known as a 'socialist' at a time when this word meant something entirely different from what it means today. . . . As far as the class struggle is concerned, he sees only the opposition of industrialism to the old regime; bourgeoisie and workers he considers together as a single industrial class, whose richer members he calls upon to take an interest in the lot of their impoverished fellow workers. Fourier had a clearer view of the need for a new form of society." Review of Periodicals, *Die neue Zeit*, 29, no. 1 (1911), pp. 383–384.   [U3,4]

Engels on Feuerbach's *Wesen des Christentums* ‹Essence of Christianity›. "Even the shortcomings of the book contributed to its immediate effect. Its literary, sometimes even high-flown, style secured for it a large public and was, at any rate, refreshing after long years of abstract and abstruse Hegelianizing. The same is true of its extravagant deification of love, which, coming after the now intolerable sovereign rule of 'pure reason,' had its excuse. . . . But what we must not forget is that it was precisely these two weaknesses of Feuerbach that 'true socialism,' which had been spreading like a plague in 'educated' Germany since 1844, took as its starting point, putting literary phrases in the place of scientific knowledge, the liberation of mankind by means of 'love' in place of the emancipation of the proletariat through the economic transformation of production—in short, losing itself in the nauseous fine writing and ecstasies of love typified by Herr Karl Grün." Friedrich Engels, "Ludwig Feuerbach und der Ausgang der klassischen deutschen Philosophie," *Die neue Zeit*, 4 (Stuttgart, 1886), p. 150 [review of C. N. Starcke, *Ludwig Feuerbach* (Stuttgart, 1885)].[3]   [U3a,1]

"Railroads . . . demanded, besides other impossibilities, a transformation in the mode of property. . . . Up until then, in fact, a bourgeois could run an industrial or a business concern with only his own money, or at most with that of one or two friends and acquaintances. . . . He managed the money himself, and was the actual proprietor of the factory or business establishment. But railroads had need of such massive amounts of capital that it could no longer be concentrated in the hands of only a few individuals. And so a great many bourgeois were forced to entrust their precious funds, which had never before been allowed out of their sight, to people whose names they hardly knew. . . . Once the money was given over, they would lose all control over its investment and could not expect to claim any proprietary rights over terminals, cars, locomotives, and the like. . . . They were entitled only to a share of the profits; in place of an object, . . . they were given . . . a mere piece of paper that represented the fiction of an infinitely small and ungraspable piece of the real property, whose name was printed at the bottom in large letters. . . . This procedure . . . stood in such violent contrast to what the bourgeoisie was used to . . . that its defense could be undertaken only by people who . . . were suspected of wanting to overthrow the order of society—socialists, in short. First Fourier and then Saint-Simon extolled this mobilization of property in the form of paper securities." Paul Lafargue, "Marx' historischer Materialismus," *Die neue Zeit*, 22, no. 1 (Stuttgart, 1904), p. 831.   [U3a,2]

"Every day, there is a riot. The students, all sons of the bourgeoisie, are fraterniz- ing here with the workers, and the workers believe the time has come. They are also seriously counting on the pupils from the Ecole Polytechnique." Nadar, *Quand j'étais photographe* (Paris ‹1900›), p. 287.   [U3a,3]

"It is not in proletarian circles, not even in democratic circles, that the initial impetus . . . for the establishment of labor exchanges is to be found. The idea was first advanced in 1842 by M. de Molinari, editor-in-chief of *Le Journal des écono- mistes*. It was Molinari himself who developed this idea in an article he . . . wrote entitled 'L'Avenir des chemins de fer' ‹The Future of the Railroads›. In order to indicate just how much times had changed, he referred to Adam Smith, who had said, in effect, that labor was the commodity most difficult to transport. Against this, he affirmed that labor power had now become mobile. Europe and the whole world now stands open to it as a market. . . . The main point of the conclusion which Molinari drew in 'L'Avenir des chemins de fer,' in favor of the institutions that were to serve as labor exchanges, was the following: the principal cause for the low rate of wages is the frequently recurring disproportion between the num- ber of workers and the demand for work; contributing further to the problem is the high concentration of workers population in certain centers of production. . . . Give to workers the means . . . by which they can change their place of residence at low cost; give them, too, the possibility of knowing where they will be able to find work in the most favorable circumstances. . . . If workers begin traveling quickly and, above all, cheaply, labor exchanges will soon arise." On the proposal to create a labor report: "This proposal, which was published in *Le Courrier français*, edited by Xavier Durrieu, turned matters directly to the workers . . . : 'We would like . . . to render a service to workers by publishing in our columns, next to the stock market quotations, a list of work available. . . . What is the purpose of stock market quotations? They report, as we know, the rate of exchange of government securities and shares of stock . . . on various markets around the world. . . . Without the aid of these market reports, the capitalists would often have no idea where to invest their money; without these lists, they would find themselves in the same situation as workers who . . . have no idea where to go to find work. . . . The worker is a vendor of work, and, as such, he has a very material interest in knowing what the market outlets are for his goods.'" Louis Héritier, "Die Arbeitsbörsen, *Die neue Zeit*, 14, no. 1 (Stuttgart, 1896), pp. 645–647.   [U4,1]

Notable difference between Saint-Simon and Marx. The former fixes the number of exploited as high as possible, reckoning among them even the entrepreneur because he pays interest to his creditors. Marx, on the other hand, includes all those who in any way exploit another—even though they themselves may be victims of exploitation—among the bourgeoisie.   [U4,2]

It is significant that the theoreticians of Saint-Simonianism are unfamiliar with the distinction between industrial and financial capital. All social antinomies dissolve in the fairyland which *le progrès* projects for the near future.   [U4a,1]

"Let us examine some of the large manufacturing cities of France. . . . Never, perhaps, has a defeated and retreating army presented a more lamentable spectacle than the triumphant industrial army. Gaze on the workers of Lille, Reims, Mulhouse, Manchester, and Liverpool, and tell me if they look like victors!" Eugène Buret, *De la Misère des classes laborieuses en Angleterre et en France* (Paris, 1840), vol. 1, p. 67.   [U4a,2]

On the political role of intellectuals. Important: the "Letter to M. Lamartine" by Emile Barrault, editor of *Le Tocsin des travailleurs*. ["Die socialistischen und communistischen Bewegungen seit der dritten französischen Revolution," appendix to ‹Lorenz von› Stein, *Socialismus und Communismus des heutigen Frankreichs* (Leipzig and Vienna, 1848), p. 240.]   [U4a,3]

To ascertain: whether or not, in the preimperial age, a relatively greater proportion of the profits of capital went into consumption and a relatively lesser proportion into new investments.   [U4a,4]

1860: "Napoleon entered into a trade agreement with the English government . . . ; according to the provisions of this treaty, customs duties were considerably lowered on French agricultural products imported by England, and on English manufactured goods imported by France. This treaty was very favorable to the mass public. . . . On the other hand, in order to hold their own against English competition, French industry was forced to lower the prices of its products. The immediate consequence was . . . a certain rapprochement with the opposition. Aiming to counter the resistance of . . . industrialists, Napoleon took steps to enlist the support of the liberals. This led, ultimately, to the transformation of the regime and the emergence of the Liberal Empire." A. Malet and P. Grillet, *XIXe Siècle* (Paris, 1919), p. 275. (Loosening of controls on the press, so as to enable coverage of debates in the Chamber.) [U4a,5]

Classification of the press under the Restoration. Ultras‹?›: *La Gazette de France, La Quotidienne, Le Drapeau blanc, Le Journal des débats* (until 1824). Independents: *Le Globe, Le Minerve,* and, from 1830, during the last year of the Restoration, *Le National, Le Temps.* Constitutionalists: *Le Constitutionnel, Le Courrier français,* and, after 1824, *Le Journal des débats.* [U4a,6]

Because of the rarity of newspapers, they were read by groups in the cafés. Otherwise, they were available only by subscription, which cost around eighty francs per year. In 1824, the twelve most widely circulating newspapers had, together, some 56,000 subscribers. For the rest, both the liberals and the royalists were concerned to keep the lower classes away from the newspaper. [U4a,7]

The "law of justice and of love," rejected by the Chamber of Peers: "One detail suffices to demonstrate the spirit of the project: every printed sheet, be it only a notification card, would have been subject to a tax of one franc per copy." A. Malet and P. Grillet, *XIXe Siècle* (Paris, 1919), p. 56. [U5,1]

"Saint-Simon lingers over the history of the fifteenth–eighteenth centuries, and gives to the social classes of this period a more concrete and specifically economic description. Hence, it is this part of Saint-Simon's system that is of greatest importance for the genesis of the theory of class struggle, and that exercises the strongest influence on its subsequent development. . . . Although, for later periods, Saint-Simon emphasizes the economic moment in his characterization of classes and the causes of their growth and decline . . . , in order to be consistent he would have had to see, in this economic activity, the true roots of the social classes as well. Had he taken this step, he would inevitably have attained to a materialist conception of history. But Saint-Simon never took this step, and his general conception remains idealist. . . . The second point that is so surprising in Saint-Simon's class theory, in view of its discrepancy with the actual relations among the classes of the period, is the representation of the class of industrialists as homogeneous. . . . The manifestly essential differences that exist between proletarians and entrepreneurs are for him external, and their antagonism is grounded in mutual misunderstanding: the interests of the directors of industrial enterprises, in reality, coincide with the interests of the masses. . . . This entirely unfounded assertion resolves for Saint-Simon the very real social contradiction, salvaging the unity of the industrial class and, with it, the perspective on a peaceful building-up of the new social system." V. Volgin, "Über die historische Stellung Saint-Simons," in *Marx-Engels Archiv,* ed. D. Rjazanov, vol. 1 (Frankfurt am Main ‹1928›), pp. 97–99. [U5,2]

Saint-Simon: "Least of all does the industrial system require the overseeing of individuals, for with a system in which the immediate goal is the well-being of the many, there ought not to be any energy wasted on maintaining power over these

people, who no longer threaten the existing order. . . . 'This function of maintaining order can then easily become . . . a task shared by all citizens, whether it be to contain troublemakers or to settle disputes.'⁴ Instead of an instrument for the domination of men, the state system becomes a system for the administration of things. . . . And the chief task of this administrative authority, whose agents will be the scholars, artists, and industrialists, . . . is to organize the cultivation of the terrestrial globe." V. Volgin, "Über die historische Stellung Saint-Simons," in *Marx-Engels Archiv*, ed. D. Rjazanov, vol. 1 (Frankfurt am Main), pp. 104–105.
[U5,3]

On the idea of the total work of art, according to Saint-Simon, *Oeuvres choisies*, vol. 3, pp. 358–360: "Saint-Simon indulges in fantasies about the development of a cult through the combined efforts of prophets, poets, musicians, sculptors, and architects. All the arts are to be united so as to make the cult useful to society, and so as, through the cult, to restructure humanity in the spirit of Christian morals." V. Volgin, "Über die historische Stellung Saint-Simons," in *Marx-Engels Archiv*, vol. 1 (Frankfurt am Main), p. 109.
[U5a,1]

Concerning the representation of Louis Philippe.—Saint-Simon teaches that "the industrial system is not in contradiction with royal power. The king will become the First Industrial, just as he has been the First Soldier in the kingdom."⁵ V. Volgin, "Über die historische Stellung Saint-Simons," in *Marx-Engels Archiv*, vol. 1 (Frankfurt am Main), p. 112.
[U5a,2]

Saint-Simon was a forerunner of the technocrats.
[U5a,3]

Two passages from *Le Globe* (October 31 and November 25, 1831), concerning the workers' uprising in Lyons: "we, defenders of ALL workers—from the leaders of industry to the humblest laborers"; and concerning the working class: "It is agonizing for us to see the workers degraded by brutality. Our heart bleeds at the sight of such moral privations, quite as hideous, in their way, as physical privations. . . . We would like . . . to inspire the workers with . . . our own sentiments of order, peace, and friendly accord." In the same publication, an expression of approval for the address of the Saint-Simonians from Lyons, who "have preserved Saint-Simonian calm." Cited in E. Tarlé, "Der Lyoner Arbeiteraufstand," in *Marx-Engels Archiv*, ed. Rjazanov, vol. 2 (Frankfurt am Main, 1928), pp. 108, 109, 111.
[U5a,4]

Important material relating to the history of the railroad, and particularly of the locomotive, in Karl Kautsky, *Die materialistische Geschichtsauffassung,* vol. 1 (Berlin, 1927), pp. 645ff. What emerges is the great importance of mining for the railroads, not only because locomotives were first used in mines but also because iron rails came from there. We are thus referred back to the use that was made of rails (originally, no doubt, of wood) in the operation of tipcarts.
[U5a,5]

On Saint-Simon's idea of progress (polytheism, monotheism, recognition of many laws of nature, recognition of a single law of nature): "Gravitation is supposed to play the role of the universal absolute idea and replace the idea of God." *Oeuvres choisies,* vol. 2, p. 219,[6] cited by V. Volgin, "Über die historische Stellung Saint-Simons," in *Marx-Engels Archiv,* vol. 1 (Frankfurt am Main), p. 106.   [U5a,6]

"In the system of the Saint-Simonians, banks not only play the part of forces that organize industry. They are the one antidote which the system now in place has developed to counter the anarchy that devours it; they are an element of the system of the future . . . , one that is free of the stimulant of personal enrichment; they are a social institution." V. Volgin, "Über die historische Stellung Saint-Simons," in *Marx-Engels Archiv,* ed. Rjazanov, vol. 1 (Frankfurt am Main), p. 94.
[U6,1]

"The chief task of an industrial system is said to be the establishment of a . . . plan of work that could be carried out by society. . . . But . . . his ideal is considerably closer to state capitalism than to socialism. With Saint-Simon, there is no talk of the abolition of private property, of expropriations. Only up to a certain point does the state submit the activity of industrialists to the general plan. . . . Throughout his career Saint-Simon . . . was drawn to large-scale projects . . . , beginning with the plans for the Panama and Madrid canals and ending with plans to transform the planet into a paradise." V. Volgin, "Über die historische Stellung Saint-Simons," in *Marx-Engels Archiv,* vol. 1 (Frankfurt am Main), pp. 101–102, 116.   [U6,2]

"Stocks have been 'democratized' so that all the world can share in the benefits of modern association. For it is under the banner of 'association' that people have glorified the accumulation of capital in joint-stock companies, over which grand financiers now exercise sovereignty at the expense of the shareholders." W. Lexis, *Gewerkvereine und Unternehmerverbände in Frankreich* (Leipzig, 1879), p. 143, cited in D. Rjazanov, "Zur Geschichte der ersten Internationale," in *Marx-Engels Archiv,* ed. D. Rjazanov, vol. 1 (Frankfurt am Main), p. 144.   [U6,3]

Emile Pereire, ex-Saint-Simonian, was the founder of Crédit Mobilier.—Chevalier presents him, in *La Religion Saint-Simonienne,* as "a former student at the Ecole Polytechnique."   [U6,4]

Re the history of newspapers. Differentiation according to social classes and mass circulation of literature, which, under Charles X, was mobilized against congregations. "Voltaire, more or less abridged, is adapted to the needs and circumstances of all levels of society! There is the rich man's Voltaire, the 'Voltaire for owners of medium-sized property,' and the cottager's Voltaire. There are also editions of *Tartuffe* at three sous. There are reprints of . . . Holbach, . . . Duprais<?>, . . . Volney. Things are set up in such a way that . . . more than

2,700,000 volumes were put into circulation in less than seven years." Pierre de la Gorce, *La Restauration,* vol. 2, *Charles X* (Paris), p. 58.   [U6,5]

Waiting for the *Révélateur,* who will bring on the end of the bourgeoisie and who "will render thanks to the father of the family for peacefully administering the Lord's estate." This, presumably, an allusion to Enfantin. At the beginning of the text, a sort of lament for the proletariat; the pamphlet also refers to this class in closing: "*Emancipateur pacifique!* He travels the world over, everywhere working for the liberation of the *proletarian* and of WOMAN." The lament: "If ever you have visited our workshops, you have seen those chunks of molten iron which we draw from the furnaces and cast into the teeth of cylinders that turn more rapidly than the wind. These furnaces emit a liquid fire that, in its boiling and heaving, throws off a shower of glowing drops into the air; and from the teeth of the cylinder, iron emerges drastically reduced. We too, in truth, are hard pressed like these masses of iron. If ever you have come to our workshops, you have seen those mining cables that are wound around a wheel, and that unwind in the search for blocks of stone or mountains of coal at a depth of twelve hundred feet. The wheel moans upon its axle; the cable stretches tight with the weight of its enormous charge. We, too, are drawn taut like the cable; but we do not moan like the wheel, for we are patient and strong. 'Great God! What have I done,' cries the voice of the people, consumed with a sorrow like that of King David. 'What have I done that my hardiest sons should become cannon fodder, and my loveliest daughters be sold into prostitution?' Michel Chevalier, "Religion Saint-Simonienne: Le Bourgeois, le révélateur" ‹pamphlet (Paris, 1830), pp. 3–4, i›.
                    [U6a,1]

Chevalier in 1848. He speaks of the forty-year sojourn of Israel in the wilderness, before it entered the Promised Land. "We, too, will have to pause for a time, before advancing into an era . . . of . . . prosperity for workers. Let us accept this season of waiting. . . . And if some persons endeavor to stir up the wrath of the populace . . . on the pretext of hastening the advent of better times, . . . then let us emblazon the words that Benjamin Franklin, *a worker* who became a great man, . . . once spoke to his fellow citizens: 'If anyone says to you that you can come into wealth by some means other than industry and frugality, then pay him no heed: He's a viper.'" Franklin, *Conseils pour faire fortune* (Paris, 1848), pp. i–ii (preface by Michel Chevalier).[7]   [U6a,2]

The press under Charles X: "One of the members of the court, M. Sosthène de la Rochefoucault, . . . conceived the grand project of absorbing the opposition newspapers by buying them up. But the only ones that would consent to the deal had no influence to sell." Pierre de la Gorce, *La Restauration,* vol. 2, *Charles X* (Paris), p. 89.   [U7,1]

The Fourierists looked forward to mass conversions among the public after they introduced a feuilleton in *La Phalange.* See Ferrari, "Des Idées et de l'école de Fourier," *Revue des deux mondes,* 14, no. 3 (1845), p. 432.   [U7,2]

"O Poets! You have eyes, but you do not see—and ears, but you do not hear! Great things are unfolding in your midst, and you give us war chants!" [There follows a characterization of the warlike inspiration for "La Marseillaise."] "This hymn to blood, these frightful imprecations bear witness not to any danger that might be threatening the country, but to the impotence of liberal poetry—poetry without inspiration beyond that of war, struggle, and endless complaint. . . . O people! Sing, nonetheless, sing "La Marseillaise," since your poets are silent or can only recite a pale imitation of the hymn of your fathers. Sing! The harmony of your voices will yet prolong the joy with which triumph had filled your soul; for you, the days of happiness are few and far between! Sing! . . . Your joy is sweet to those in sympathy with you! It has been so long since they heard anything but moans and groans from your lips!" "Religion Saint-Simonienne: La Marseillaise" (extract from *L'Organisateur,* September 11, 1830) [according to the catalogue of the Bibliothèque Nationale, the author is Michel Chevalier], pp. 3–4. The animating idea of this rhapsody is the confrontation of the peaceful July Revolution with the bloody Revolution of 1789. Hence, this observation: "Three days of combat sufficed to overturn the throne of legitimacy and divine right. . . . Victory went to the people, who live from their labors—the rabble that crowds the workshops, the populace that slaves in misery, proletarians who have no property but their hands: it was the race of men so utterly despised by salon dandies and proper folk. And why? Because they sweat blood and tears to get their bread, and never strut about in the balcony of the Comic Opera. After forcing their way into the heart of the palace, . . . they pardoned their prisoners . . . ; they bandaged the wounded. . . . Then they said to themselves: 'Oh, who will sing of our exploits? Who will tell of our glory and our hopes?'" ("La Marseillaise," as above, p. 1).   [U7,3]

From a reply to an unfriendly review (in *La Revue de Paris*) of Charles Pradier's literary labors: "For three years now, we have been appearing daily on the city's sidewalks, and you probably think we have grown accustomed to it all. . . . Well, you are mistaken. In fact, every time we step up on our soapbox, we hesitate and look around us for excuses; we find the weather unpropitious, the crowds inattentive, the street too loud. We dare not admit that we ourselves lack daring. . . . And now, perhaps, you understand . . . why sometimes we exult in the thought of our work; . . . and why, seeing us filled with enthusiasm, . . . you—and others with you—could take it for undue pride." Ch. Pradier, "Réponse à *La Revue de Paris,*" in *Le Bohême,* Charles Pradier, editor-in-chief, vol. 1, no. 8 (June 10, 1855). The passage is entirely characteristic of the bearing—at once honest and uncertain—of this newspaper, which did not make it past its initial year of publication. As early as the first issue, it marks itself off from the lax, morally emancipated *bohème* and makes mention of the pious Hussite sect, the Frères Bohèmes, founded by Michel Bradacz, which it would like to ensure a literary posterity.
                                                                        [U7a,1]

Sample of the style of the newspaper *Le Bohême:* "What suffers cruelly in the garrets is intelligence, art, poetry, the soul! . . . For the soul is a wallet containing only the banknotes of paradise, and the shopkeepers of this world would nail this money to their counter like a coin fallen from the hands of a counterfeiter." Alexandre Guérin, "Les Mansardes," *Le Bohême*, 1, no. 7 (May 13, 1855).   [U7a,2]

From a confrontation between the underclass intellectuals and the ruling-class intellectuals: "You princes of thought, jewels of the intellect . . . , since you have moved to disown us, we in turn have abjured your paternity; we have disdained your crowns and impugned your coats of arms. We have cast aside the grandiose titles you formerly sought for your labors: we are no longer "The Elan," "The Star," or "The Will-o'-the-Wisp," . . . but instead are "The Pretentious Fool," "The Penniless," "The Promised Land," "The Enfant Terrible," "The Tragic Pariah," or "The Bohemian," and thus we protest . . . your egotistical authority." Charles Pradier, "Pères et fils," *Le Bohême*, 1, no. 5 (April 29, 1855).   [U7a,3]

Le Bohême, in its first issue, bears the subtitle *Nonpolitical Newspaper.*   [U8,1]

"Do me the kindness of walking through the gambling dens, the little restaurants near the Pantheon or the Medical School. There you will find . . . poets who are moved only by envy and all the lowest passions, the self-proclaimed martyrs of the *sacred cause of progress*, who . . . smoke many a pipe . . . without doing anything . . . ; whereas Piconel, whose beautiful lines you have cited, Piconel the garment worker, who earns four and a half francs a day to feed eight people, is registered at the charity office!! . . . I have no . . . wish, paradoxical as it might seem, to commend the boasting of Dumas *père* or to excuse the indifference of some of his friends toward younger writers; but I declare to you that the greatest enemies of those who have been deprived of a literary legacy are not the writers of renown, the monopolizers of the daily feuilleton, but rather the falsely disinherited, those who do nothing but hurl insults, drink, and scandalize honest people, and all this from the vantage point of art." Eric Isoard, "Les Faux Bohêmes," *Le Bohême*, 1, no. 6 (May 6, 1855).   [U8,2]

It is significant that *Le Bohême,* which looks after the rights of the literary proletariat—who sympathize, to some extent, with the industrial proletariat—would see fit, in an article entitled "Du Roman en général et du romancier moderne en particulier" ‹On the Novel in General and the Modern Novelist in Particular›, by Paul Saulnier (vol. 1, no. 5), to condemn the practice of "slavers." Monsieur de Santis, as the novelist in vogue is named here, returns home after a day spent in idleness. "Directly upon his arrival home, Monsieur de Santis locks himself in . . . and goes to open a little door hidden behind his bookcase.—He finds himself, then, in a sort of little study, dirty and quite poorly lit. Here, with a long goose quill in his hand, with his hair standing on end, is a man with a face at once sinister and unctuous.—Oho! with this one, you can tell from a mile away he's a novelist—even if he is only a former employee of the ministry who learned the art of Balzac from the serials in *Le Constitutionnel*. It is the veritable author of *The Chamber of Skulls!* It is the novelist!"   [U8,3]

"In 1852 the brothers Pereire, two Portuguese Jews, founded the first great modern bank, Crédit Mobilier, of which one said that it was the biggest gambling hell in Europe. It undertook wild speculations in everything—railroads, hotels, colonies, canals, mines, theaters—and, after fifteen years, it declared total bankruptcy." Egon Friedell, *Kulturgeschichte der Neuzeit*, vol. 3 (Munich, 1931), p. 187.

[U8a,1]

"*Bohème* ⟨bohemian⟩ belongs to the vocabulary in use around 1840. In the language of that time, it is synonymous with 'artist' or 'student' or 'pleasure seeker'; it means someone who is light-hearted and unconcerned with the morrow, lazy and boisterous." Gabriel Guillemot, *Le Bohème* (Paris, 1868), pp. 7–8; cited in Gisela Freund, ⟨"La Photographie au point de vue sociologique," manuscript,⟩ p. 60.

[U8a,2]

"The *roman-feuilleton* ⟨serial novel⟩ was inaugurated in France by *Le Siècle* in 1836. The beneficent effects of the *roman-feuilleton* on the newspaper's receipts is revealed by the contract which *Le Constitutionnel* and *La Presse* together had with Alexandre Dumas in 1845. . . . Dumas received an annual salary of 63,000 francs for five years, in return for a minimum output of eighteen installments per year." Lavisse, *Histoire de la monarchie de juillet*, vol. 4 (Paris, 1892); cited, without page reference, in Gisela Freund.

[U8a,3]

A saying of Murger's (cited by Gisela Freund, p. 63): "The *bohème:* it is the training ground for the artistic life; it is the steppingstone to the Académie, to the Hôtel-Dieu ⟨hospital⟩, or to the Morgue."

[U8a,4]

Gisela Freund (p. 64) underlines the difference between the first generation of bohemians—Gautier, Nerval, Nanteuil—who were often of solid bourgeois origin, and the second: "Murger was the son of a concierge-tailor; Champfleury was the son of a secretary in the town hall of Laon; Barbara, the son of a sheet-music seller; Bouvin, the son of a village policeman; Delvau, the son of a tanner in the Faubourg Saint-Marcel; and Courbet was the son of a quasi-peasant." To this second generation belonged Nadar—the son of a poor printer. (He was later, for a long time, secretary to Lesseps.)

[U8a,5]

"M. de Martignac bequeathed . . . a troubled legacy to the newspapers, with his law of July 1828—a law that was more liberal, to be sure, but which, by making . . . dailies or periodicals more accessible to all, burdened them with certain financial obligations. . . . 'What will we do to cover the new expenses?' demanded the newspapers. 'Well, you will run advertisements,' came the response. . . . The consequences of advertising were quick to emerge and seemingly endless. It was all very well to want to separate, in the pages of the newspaper, that which remained conscientious and independent from that which became partisan and mercenary; but the boundary . . . was quickly crossed. The advertisement served as bridge. How could one condemn, five minutes before, . . . what five minutes afterward proclaimed itself the wonder of the age? The fascination of capital letters, which were growing ever larger, carried advertising away: it was the magnetic mountain that threw off the compass. . . . This wretched advertising had an influence no less fatal to the book trade. . . . Advertising represented . . . a doubling of expenses . . . : one thousand francs for promoting a new work. Because of this rise in costs, moreover, book dealers mercilessly demanded from authors two volumes instead of one—volumes in octavo rather than in smaller format, for that did not cost any more to advertise. . . . Advertising . . . would require a whole history unto itself: Swift, with his vitriolic pen, would be the one to write it." On the word *réclame* ⟨advertisement⟩, the following remark: "For those who may not know the facts, we merely observe that the *réclame* is the little notice slipped into the newspaper near the end, and ordinarily paid for by the bookseller; inserted on the same day as the advertisement, or on the day following, it gives in two words a brief and favorable judgment that helps prepare the way for that of the review." Saint-Beuve, "De la Littérature industrielle," *Revue des deux mondes*, 19, no. 4 (1839), pp. 682–683.   [U9,1]

"Writing and publishing will be less and less a sign of distinction. In keeping with our electoral and industrial customs, everyone, at least once in his life, will have his page, his treatise, his prospectus, his toast—will be an author. From there to penning a feuilleton is only a step. . . . In our own day, after all, who can say to himself that he does not, in part, write in order to live . . . ?" Sainte-Beuve, "De la Littérature industrielle," *Revue des deux mondes*, 19, no. 4 (1839), p. 681.
                                                                                                    [U9,2]

In 1860 and 1868, in Marseilles and Paris, appeared the two volumes of *Revues parisiennes: Les Journaux, les revues, les livres*, by Baron Gaston de Flotte, who took it upon himself to combat the thoughtlessness and unscrupulousness of the historical accounts in the press and, particularly, in the feuilletons. The rectifications concern the facts and the legends of cultural, literary, and political history.
                                                                                                    [U9,3]

Fees for feuilletons went as high as two francs per line. Authors would often write as much dialogue as possible so as to benefit from the blank spaces in the lines.
                                                                                                    [U9a,1]

In his essay, "De la Littérature industrielle" ⟨On Industrial Literature⟩, Sainte-Beuve discusses, among other things, the initial proceedings of the newly organized Société des Gens de Lettres (which originally campaigned, above all, against unauthorized Belgian reprints).   [U9a,2]

"In the beginning, Senefelder had thought only of facilitating the reproduction of manuscripts, and he publicized the new processes leading to this end in his *Vollständigen Lehrbuch der Steindruckerei* ⟨Complete Manual of Lithography⟩, which appeared in 1818. Others first exploited his ideas for the technique of lithography itself. These methods enabled a rapidity of drawing that was nearly equal to that of the word. . . . They opened the way to a journalism of the graver." Egon Friedell, *Kulturgeschichte der Neuzeit*, vol. 3 (Munich, 1931), p. 95.   [U9a,3]

Overview of the revolutionary press in Paris in 1848. *Curiosités revolutionnaires: Les Journaux rouges—Histoire critique de tous les journaux ultra-républicains,* by a Girondist (Paris, 1848).   [U9a,4]

"There is only one way of preventing cholera, and that is to work to elevate the morality of the masses. No person whose moral constitution is satisfactory has anything to fear from the plague. . . . There is clearly a place, today, for awakening moral salubrity among the masses. . . . What is needed are . . . extraordinary measures. . . . What is needed is a coup d'état, an industrial coup d'état. . . . This action would consist in changing, *by decree*, the law of expropriation, so that . . . the interminable delays occasioned by the current legislation would be reduced to a few days. . . . One could thus begin operations, for instance, on some thirty sites in Paris, from the Rue de Louvre to the Bastille, which would clean up and reform the worst neighborhood of the city. . . . One could . . . start up railways at the barrières. . . . The first stage of construction . . . would be accompanied by ceremonies and public festivals. All the official bodies of the state would be there with their insignia, to exhort the people. The king and his family, the ministers, the council of state, the court of cassation, the royal court, what is left of the two Chambers—all would drop by on a regular basis, wielding the shovel and pickaxe. . . . Military regiments would arrive on the scene to do service in full dress, with their military music to inspire them. . . . Theatrical performances would be put on there from time to time, and the best actors would consider it an honor to appear. The most radiant women would mix with the workers to provide encouragement. Exalted thus, and made to feel proud, the population would most certainly become invulnerable to cholera. Industry would be given an impetus; the government . . . would be . . . established on a firm foundation." Michel Chevalier, "Religion Saint-Simonienne: Fin du choléra par un coup d'état" ⟨pamphlet⟩ (Paris, 1832). The Saint-Simonians wanted to distribute medicine free of charge.   [U9a,5]

"What makes working on the omnibus train into truly painful drudgery: it departs Paris at 7:00 in the morning and arrives in Strasbourg at midnight. This makes for seventeen hours of continuous service, during which the conductor must get off at every station, without exception, to open the doors of the cars! . . . Surely, the employee who is required to climb down at each station, and to wade around in the snow for five or six minutes every half-hour, so as to open and close the car doors—and all this at twelve degrees below freezing, or worse—must suffer cruelly." A. Granveau, *L'Ouvrier devant la société* (Paris, 1868), pp. 27–28 ("Les Employés et le mouvement des chemins de fer").   [U10,1]

A remarkable apotheosis of the traveler—to some extent a counterpart, in the realm of sheer banality, to Baudelaire's "Le Voyage"—can be found in Benjamin Gastineau, *La Vie en chemin de fer* (Paris, 1861). The second chapter of the book is called "Le Voyageur du XIX⁰ siècle" ⟨The Nineteenth-Century Traveler⟩ (p. 65). This *voyageur* is an apotheosis of the traveler in which, in quite peculiar fashion, the traits of the Wandering Jew are mingled with those of a pioneer of progress. Samples: "Everywhere along his path, the traveler has sown the riches of his heart and his imagination: giving a good word to all and sundry, . . . encouraging the laborer, rescuing the ignorant from their gutter, . . . and raising up the humiliated" (p. 78). "The woman who seeks a love supreme: traveler!— The man who seeks a devoted woman: traveler!—. . . Artists avid for new horizons: travelers!—The mad who take their hallucinations for reality: travelers!—. . . Glory hunters, troubadours of thought: travelers!—Life is a journey, and every single being who departs the womb of woman to return to the womb of earth is a traveler" (pp. 79–81). "Humanity, 'tis thou who art the eternal voyager" (p. 84). [U10,2]

Passage from Benjamin Gastineau, *La Vie en chemin de fer* (Paris, 1861): "All of a sudden, the curtain is lowered abruptly on the sun, on beauty, on the thousand scenes of life and nature which your mind and heart have savored along the way. It is night and death and the cemetery; it is despotism—it is the tunnel! Nothing but beings that dwell in the shadows, never knowing the bright wing of freedom and truth! . . . Nonetheless, after hearing the cries of confusion and dismay from passengers on the train as it enters the gloomy archway, and their exclamations of joy on quitting the tunnel, . . . who would dare maintain that the human creature was not made for light and liberty?" (pp. 37–38). [U10,3]

Passages from Benjamin Gastineau, *La Vie en chemin de fer* (Paris, 1861): "Hail to you, noble races of the future, scions of the railway!" (p. 112). "All aboard! All aboard! The whistle pierces the sonorous vault of the station" (p. 18). "Before the creation of the railroads, nature did not yet pulsate; it was a Sleeping Beauty. . . . The heavens themselves appeared immutable. The railroad animated everything. . . . The sky has become an active infinity, and nature a dynamic beauty. Christ is descended from his Cross; he has walked the earth, and he is leaving, far behind him on the dusty road, the old Ahasuerus" (p. 50). [U10a,1]

"Michel Chevalier delighted the students [of the Ecole Polytechnique] when he retraced, in particular, the great historical epochs, recurring often to Alexander, Caesar, Charlemagne, and Napoleon, in order to emphasize the role of inventors and triumphant organizers." G. Pinet, *Histoire de l'Ecole polytechnique* (Paris, 1887), p. 205. [U10a,2]

"The disciples of Saint-Simon—recruited, for the most part, from the Ecole des Mines, which is to say, from among the best students of the Ecole Polytechnique— could not have failed to exert a considerable influence on their younger comrades. . . . Nevertheless, Saint-Simonianism did not have time to garner many converts at the Ecole Polytechnique. The schism of 1831[8] dealt it a fatal blow—the follies of Ménilmontant, the bizarre costumes, and the ridiculous names had killed it." G. Pinet, *Histoire de l'Ecole polytechnique*, pp. 204–205.   [U10a,3]

The idea for the Suez Canal goes back to Enfantin, who had sought a concession from the viceroy of Egypt, Muhammad Ali, and wanted to move there with forty pupils. England made sure that the concession was denied him.   [U10a,4]

"Saint-Simon attempted to found an association to take advantage of the easy terms mandated by the decree . . . of November 2, 1789, which made it possible to acquire national lands at a price that was payable in twelve annual installments by means of assignats. These terms allowed for the acquisition, with modest capital, of a considerable spread of rural properties. . . . 'Every financial speculation is based upon an investment of industry and an investment of funds. The returns on a financial speculation should be divided in such a way that industry and capital have shares proportionate to the influence they exercised. In the speculation I entered on with M. de Redern, capital played only a secondary role.'" The author cites a letter from Saint-Simon to Boissy-d'Anglas, dated November 2, 1807; it contains indications as to his theory of the relations between capital, labor, and talent. Maxime Leroy, *Les Spéculations foncières de Saint-Simon et ses querelles d'affaires avec son associé, le comte de Redern* (Paris ‹1925›), pp. 2, 23.   [U11,1]

"Saint-Simon believed in science. . . . But whereas, at the beginning of his studies, the mathematical and physical sciences . . . had almost exclusive claim on his attention, it was now from the realms of the natural sciences that he would seek the elusive key to those social problems that so vexed him. 'I distanced myself, in 1801, from the Ecole Polytechnique,' he writes, 'and I established myself in the vicinity of the Ecole de Médecine, where I was able to associate with the physiologists.'" Maxime Leroy, *La Vie véritable du comte Henri de Saint-Simon* (Paris, 1925), pp. 192–193.—The Ecole Polytechnique, at the time Saint-Simon lived near it, was housed in the Palais Bourbon.   [U11,2]

"The Nave of the Grand Café Parisien" reads the caption under an engraving from 1856. The view of the public offered here does, in fact, resemble the one seen in the nave of a church, or in an arcade. Visitors are mostly standing in place or wandering about—that is, among the billiard tables which are set up in the nave.   [U11,3]

Hubbard says—referring, with doubtful justification, to Saint-Simon's tears on parting from his wife at the time of their divorce:[9] "Perpetual sacrifice of the tender and compassionate being to the being that thinks and understands." Cited in Maxime Leroy, *La Vie véritable du comte Henri de Saint-Simon* (Paris, 1925), p. 211.   [U11,4]

"Let us put an end to honors for Alexander; and hail Archimedes!" Saint-Simon, cited in Leroy, *La Vie véritable du comte Henri de Saint-Simon*, p. 220.   [U11,5]

Comte worked for four years by the side of Saint-Simon.[10]   [U11,6]

Eugène Sue's *Juif errant* ‹Wandering Jew› in *Le Constitutionnel* as a replacement for Thiers's *Histoire du Consulat et de l'Empire*, which Véron had originally planned to publish there.   [U11,7]

Saint-Simon: "Considérations sur les mesures à prendre pour terminer la Révolution" ‹1820›.—Introduction to *Les Travaux scientifiques du XIXe siècle*.
[U11a,1]

Saint-Simon invented revolutionary playing cards: four geniuses (war, peace, art, commerce) as kings; four liberties (religion, marriage, the press, the professions) as queens; four equalities (duties, rights, dignities, colors) as jacks. Leroy, *La Vie véritable du comte Henri de Saint-Simon* (Paris, 1925), p. 174.   [U11a,2]

Saint-Simon dies in May 1825. His last words: "We are carrying on with our work." Leroy, p. 328.   [U11a,3]

On Saint-Simon: "As much as he astonishes us with his foresight in matters of labor and society, he nonetheless gives us the impression that he was lacking something: . . . a milieu, his milieu, the proper sphere in which to extend the optimistic tradition of the eighteenth century. Man of the future, he had to do his thinking almost entirely by himself, in a society that had been decapitated, bereft of its foremost minds by the Revolution. . . . Where was Lavoisier, founder of modern experimental science? Where was Condorcet, the leading philosopher of the age, and Chénier, the leading poet? They would have lived, in all likelihood, had Robespierre not had them guillotined. It was left to Saint-Simon to carry out, without their help, the difficult work of organization which they began. And faced with this immense and solitary mission, . . . he took upon himself too many tasks; he was obliged to be at once the poet, the experimental scientist, and the philosopher of the newborn age." Maxime Leroy, *La Vie véritable du comte Henri de Saint-Simon* (Paris, 1925), pp. 321–322.   [U11a,4]

A lithograph by Pattel represents "Engraving Doing Battle with Lithography." The latter seems to be getting the upper hand. Cabinet des Estampes.   [U11a,5]

A lithograph of 1842 depicts "The Divan of the Algerians in Paris" as "The Café Mauresque." In the background of a coffeehouse, in which exotic figures walk by the side of Europeans, three odalisques are sitting, pressed close together on a tiny divan beneath a mirror, and smoking water pipes. Cabinet des Estampes.
[U11a,6]

Graphics from 1830 display readily, and often allegorically, the conflict of the newspapers among one another. They love to show, in this same period, what happens when several people have to share in reading one newspaper. They picture the struggle that arises on this occasion, whether it be over possession of the paper or over the opinions it purveys. Cabinet des Estampes, a plate from 1817: "The Love of News, or Politicomania."   [U11a,7]

"At the Stock Exchange, one Saint-Simonian is worth two Jews." "Paris-Boursier," *Les Petits-Paris: Par les auteurs des mémoires de Bilboquet* [Taxile Delord] (Paris, 1854), p. 54.   [U12,1]

An uncommonly telling expression of the heyday of boulevard journalism. "What do you mean by the word 'wit'?—I mean something which, it is said, travels the streets but only very rarely enters the houses." Louis Lurine, *Le Treizième Arrondissement de Paris* (Paris, 1850), p. 192.   [U12,2]

The idea that newspaper advertisements could be made to serve the distribution not only of books but of industrial articles stems from Dr. Véron, who by this means had such successes with his Pâte de Regnauld, a cold remedy, that an investment of 17,000 francs yielded him a return of 100,000. "One can say, therefore, . . . that if it was a physician, Théophraste Renaudot, who invented journalism in France . . . , it was Dr. Véron who, nearly half a century ago, invented the fourth-page newspaper advertisement." Joseph d'Arçay, *La Salle à manger du docteur Véron* (Paris, 1868), p. 104.   [U12,3]

The "emancipation of the flesh," in Enfantin, should be compared to the theses of Feuerbach and the insights of Georg Büchner. The anthropological materialism is comprised within the dialectical.   [U12,4]

Villemessant: "Initially, he ran a business in ribbons. This concern . . . led the . . . young man to start up a fashion journal. . . . From there, Villemessant . . . soon moved into politics, rallied to the Legitimist party and, after the Revolution of 1848, turned himself into a political satirist. He organized three different newspapers in succession, among them the *Paris Chronicle*, which was suppressed by imperial decree in 1852. Two years after this, he founded *Le Figaro*." Egon Caesar Conte Corti, *Der Zauberer von Homburg und Monte Carlo* (Leipzig ‹1932›), pp. 238–239.   [U12,5]

François Blanc was one of the first great advertisers. Through contacts in the press, he had placed advertisements for the Homburg Casino in *Le Siècle* and *L'Assemblée nationale*. "He also personally arranged for entire series of eighteen—even fifty—advertisements to appear in newspapers . . . like *La Presse*, *Le National*, *La Patrie*, and *Le Galignani*." Egon Caesar Conte Corti, *Der Zauberer von Homburg und Monte Carlo* (Leipzig), p. 97.   [U12,6]

In Saint-Simon's day: "Independently of the New Jerusalem of Emanuel Swedenborg, advocated by Baron Portal, . . . there was the phalanstery of Charles Fourier. There was also the so-called Eglise Française of Abbé Châtel,

Primate of the Gauls; there was the restoration of the Order of the Templars, organized by M. Fabré-Palaprat; and there was the cult of Evadamism created by the Mapah."[11] Philibert Audebrand, *Michel Chevalier* ‹Paris, 1861›, p. 4.
[U12,7]

Saint-Simonian propaganda. "One of the followers of the doctrine, who was asked, one day, what his duties were, replied: 'I am a man about town, a respected speaker. I am elegantly dressed so that I can be presented everywhere; gold is put into my pocket so that I am ready to play whist. How can I fail?'" Philibert Audebrand, *Michel Chevalier*, p. 6.
[U12a,1]

The split in the ranks of the Saint-Simonians forced adherents of the doctrine to choose between Bazard and Enfantin.
[U12a,2]

At Ménilmontant, the members of the Saint-Simonian sect shared responsibility for the various *départements* of housekeeping: cooking (Simon and Rochette), tableware (Talebot), cleaning (d'Eichtel, Lambert), shoeshine (Barrault).
[U12a,3]

The Saint-Simonians at Ménilmontant: "A great musician of the future, M. Félicien David, composer of *The Desert*, of *The Pearl of Brazil* and of *Herculaneum*, was director of their orchestra. He composed the melodies they sang . . . , notably those which preceded and followed the meals." Philibert Audebrand, *Michel Chevalier* ‹Paris, 1861›, p. 11.
[U12a,4]

General celibacy, up until the marriage of Enfantin, was the rule at Ménilmontant.
[U12a,5]

After the dissolution of Ménilmontant, and after being sentenced to a year in prison, Chevalier was dispatched by Thiers to America. It is likewise Thiers who later sends him to England. After the February Revolution, which costs him his position, he becomes a reactionary. Under Napoleon, he is made senator.
[U12a,6]

By the end of the 1850s, *Le Siècle*, with 36,000 subscribers, had the largest circulation.—Milland founds *Le Petit Journal*, which he sells on the streets for one sou.
[U12a,7]

Balzac, commenting on *Aux Artistes: Du Passé et de l'avenir des beaux-arts—Doctrine de Saint-Simon* (Paris: Mesnier): "Apostleship is an artistic mission, but the author of this pamphlet has not shown himself worthy of that august title. The main idea of his work is truly important; what he has given us is inconsiderable. . . . Saint-Simon was a remarkable man, one who is yet to be understood. This fact has caused the leaders of his school to engage in the practice of proselytizing by speaking, like Christ, a language attuned to the times and to the men of those times, a language calculated to appeal less to the mind than to the heart." In this same text, with reference to Saint-Simon: "There, perhaps, lies the truth." Honoré de Balzac, *Critique littéraire*, ed. Louis Lumet (Paris, 1912), pp. 58, 60 ("Le Feuilleton des journaux politiques"). [U12a,8]

The immediate cause for the schism among the Saint-Simonians was Enfantin's doctrine of the emancipation of the flesh. To this was added the fact that others, like Pierre Leroux, had earlier already bridled at holding public confession. [U13,1]

The Saint-Simonians had little sympathy for democracy. [U13,2]

The press under Charles X: "The newspapers did not sell single copies to individuals. Newspapers were read only by subscribers, and subscription was expensive. It was a luxury, in fact, reserved for the nobility and the haute bourgeoisie. The total number of copies rose, in 1824, to only 56,000 (of which 41,000 were for the opposition newspapers)." Charles Seignobos, *Histoire sincère de la nation française* (Paris, 1933), pp. 411–412. Over and above that, the newspapers had to pay large deposits. [U13,3]

Girardin, as editor of *La Presse*, introduces advertisements, feuilletons, and sales of single copies. [U13,4]

"Newspaper salesmen have great difficulty procuring their stock. In order to get their supply, they have to stand in line—in the street, no less!—for part of the night." *Paris sous la République de 1848: Exposition de la Bibliothèque et des Travaux historiques de la Ville de Paris* (1909), p. 43. [U13,5]

Around 1848, the Café Chantant opens up: The founder is Morel. [U13,6]

Picture sheets: "Occupations of the Saint-Simonian Ladies According to Their Capacities" (*Imagerie populaire*, 1832). Colored prints, in which red, green, and yellow predominate: "Saint-Simonian Ladies Preaching the Doctrine," "This Bouquet Cannot Be Too Beautiful for Our Brother," "Saint Simonienne Dreaming of the Hunt," and so forth. Illustrations in Henry-René d'Allemagne, *Les Saint-Simoniens, 1827–1837* (Paris, 1930), opposite p. 228. A pendant to this: "Functions of the Apostles of Menil-Montant According to Their Capacity" (illustration, ibid., opposite p. 392). See in this context (ibid., opposite p. 296) the etiquette for launching a food item: "Liquor of the Saint-Simonians." A group of Enfantin's disciples; at center, Enfantin and the Republic waving a tricolored flag. Everyone raises a glass. [U13,7]

In 1831, Bazard, Chevalier, and a few others refuse, as members of the "clergy" of the Saint-Simonian church, to serve in the Garde Nationale. Twenty-four hours' imprisonment. [U13,8]

Le Globe (October 31, 1831), with regard to the uprising in Lyons, held that a raise in pay could place that city's industry in jeopardy: "Don't you see that, even if a direct intervention in the affairs of industry . . . is required of you, . . . you cannot, for some brief period, alleviate the suffering of one class of society without perhaps oppressing another? Let us now commend the benefits of competition, of that laissez-faire . . . which the liberal orators of late have once again been touting." H.-R. d'Allemagne, *Les Saint-Simoniens* (Paris, 1930), p. 140.   [U13,9]

The Saint-Simonians: a salvation army in the midst of the bourgeoisie.   [U13a,1]

Chevalier, writing to Hoart and Bruneau, on November 5, 1832: "Listen to that voice from Lyons! Lyons is calling you, is calling us, with a roar. Lyons is tottering. Lyons is trembling. What energy those proletarians have! They are descendants of Spartacus!" Henry-René d'Allemagne, *Les Saint-Simoniens, 1827–1837* ‹Paris, 1930›, p. 325.   [U13a,2]

Revealing:

> This people, whose head and hand you fear,
> Must march, must march—no halting!
> It's when you stop their steps
> They notice the holes in their shoes.

Léon Halévy, "La Chaussure," *Fables nouvelles* (Paris, 1855), p. 133; cited in de Liefde, *Le Saint-Simonisme dans la poésie française* ‹Haarlem, 1927›, p. 70.

        [U13a,3]

"Sappers of the army of peace"—a Saint-Simonian formula for the entire corps of workers.   [U13a,4]

A piece from Pierre Lachambeaudie's *Fables et poésies diverses* (Paris, 1851), "Fumée": smoke from the foundry meets with incense in the air, and they mingle at God's behest. This conception extends forward as far as Du Camp's poem on the locomotive, with its "sacred smoke."   [U13a,5]

Le Globe—at least for a time—was distributed gratis in Paris.   [U13a,6]

"The feminine and masculine element which they discover in God, and which they aim to revive in the priestly marriage, has not been celebrated in the poetry of the sect. We have found only one allusion to these doctrines . . . :

> God of male and female virtue. This world lacks all conviction;
> It yet doubts, and feels not the Father's iron affliction!
> The Mother—God above!—will be the saving grace
> That, in his joy, he'll hurry to embrace!"

Jules Mercier, "Dieu nous le rendra," in *La Foi nouvelle*, p. 15; cited in C. L. de Liefde, *Le Saint-Simonisme dans la poésie française* ⟨Haarlem, 1927⟩, pp. 146–147. [U13a,7]

George Sand, for whom love entails the unification of the classes, understands the matter in this way: "A young man of humble station, but genial and good looking, marries a beautiful and perfect young noblewoman, and voilà: the merger of the classes. . . . In *Le Meunier d'Angibault*, Lémor, the artisan hero, refuses the hand of a patrician widow because she is rich . . . , and then the widow rejoices at the fire which brings about her ruin, removing thus the last obstacle in the way of union with her lover." Charles Brun, *Le Roman social en France au XIXᵉ siècle* (Paris, 1910) pp. 96–97. [U13a,8]

Enfantin assumes that priests, artists, tradespeople, and so on will exhibit, in their different capacities, entirely different physical constitutions (and different ailments as well). [U13a,9]

Girardin's style: "Indentation with each new sentence, each sentence being but a line; the antithesis of ideas enveloped in the similitude of words; rhyme in prose . . . ; all nouns capitalized, enumerations that recall Rabelais, definitions that often recall nothing at all." Edouard Drumont, *Les Héros et les pitres* (Paris ⟨1900⟩), p. 131 ("Emile de Girardin"). [U14,1]

Drumont on Girardin: "To get this result—being forgotten eight days after his death—he rose all his life at five o'clock in the morning." Edouard Drumont, *Les Héros et les pitres* (Paris ⟨1900⟩), p. 134–135 ("Emile de Girardin"). [U14,2]

According to certain calculations, the Saint-Simonians distributed, between 1830 and 1832, some 18 million printed pages among the population. See Ch. Benoist, "L'Homme de 1848," *Revue des deux mondes* (July 1, 1913). [U14,3]

With their didactic contrast between worker bees and drones, the Saint-Simonians hark back to Mandeville's fable of the bees. [U14,4]

Regarding the movement within Saint-Simonianism: from the letters addressed to Lambert by Claire Démar and Perret Désessarts, before their joint suicide. Claire Démar: "But if his voice has not drawn me on, if it is not he who has come to invite me to this last festivity, at least I have not hastened his voyage: he has been ready for a long time." Désessarts: "The office and the officer are extinguishing themselves at the same time, as we have often said they must; for the one cannot depart without the other! Alas, I, who have always been a man of adversity and of solitude—I, who have always marched alone and apart, . . . protesting vigorously against order and unity—what could be surprising in my withdrawal, enacted at the very moment, it would seem, when the peoples are about to join in a religious federation, when their hands are now linked up to form that imposing chain. . . . Lambert, I do not doubt humanity, . . . nor do I doubt of Providence . . . ; but in the time in which we live, *everything is sacred*—even suicide! . . . Woe betide the man who does not bare his head before our cadavers, for he is truly impious! Adieu. August 3, 1833, at ten o'clock in the evening." Claire Démar, *Ma Loi d'avenir,*[12] work published posthumously by Suzanne (Paris: at the offices of *La Tribune des femmes,* and in association with all *marchands de nouveautés,* 1834), pp. 8, 10–11. [U14,5]

Statistics on the annual publication of newspapers, monthly periodicals, and fortnightly reviews. Included are new publications only:

1833: 251	*journaux*	1838: 184	*journaux*
1834: 180	"	1840: 146	"
1835: 165	"	1841: 166	"
1836: 151	"	1842: 214	"
1837: 158	"	1845: 185	"

Charles Louandre, "Statistique littéraire: De la Production intellectuelle en France depuis quinze ans," *Revue des deux mondes* (November 1, 1847), p. 442. [U14,6]

Toussenel remarks of Enfantin that, in order to make up for his conviction in court, and to console himself for the failure of his fascination on this occasion, he turned to speculation. Toussenel provides, moreover, the following portrait of him: "There was among them a man of godlike comportment who was named Enfantin. He was no less celebrated for the puissant maneuvers of his cue stick, in the noble game of billiards, than for the frequency and decisiveness with which he doubled the stakes at gaming. Relying on the faith of several charming women, . . . he passed himself off as someone ideally suited to a leading role, and had himself proclaimed the *Father*. . . . And since it was the aftermath of the July Revolution, . . . this man did not lack for followers." A. Toussenel, *Les Juifs rois de l'époque,* 3rd edition, ed. Gabriel de Gonet (Paris ‹1886›), vol. 1, p. 127. [U14a,1]

At the time of the cholera epidemics ‹in 1832?›, people laid the blame for the infection on liquor dealers. [U14a,2]

Le Journal des débats introduces the foreign correspondent: "Since M. Bertin sent Michel Chevalier on a diplomatic mission to the United States (which gained for his newspaper the publication of the famous *Lettres sur l'Amérique du Nord*), the latter has acquired a taste for these governmentally sponsored assignments. . . . Following the *Lettres sur l'Amérique du Nord* . . . came the *Lettres sur l'Espagne* . . . ; then there had to be *Lettres sur la Chine*." A. Toussenel, *Les Juifs roi de l'époque* (Paris), vol. 2, pp. 12–13. [U14a,3]

The Saint-Simonians looked for a female messiah (La Mère), who was to marry with their high priest, Le Père. [U14a,4]

"Le père Olinde ‹Rodrigues›: '. . . If you are a Saint-Simonian woman, be advised that it is not the republic that we want.'" Firmin Maillard, *La Légende de la femme émancipée* (Paris), p. 111. [U14a,5]

Heine dedicated *Deutschland* to Enfantin. Enfantin responded with a letter that was published in 1835, by Duguet, in a reprint, *Heine à Prosper Enfantin, en Egypt,* whose jacket bore the line *De l'Allemagne.*—8° M. Pièce 3319 ‹call number in the Bibliothèque Nationale›. The letter admonishes Heine to temper his sarcasm, above all in things religious. Heine should write books not about German thought but rather about the German reality, the heart of Germany—which, for Enfantin, was essentially an idyll. [U14a,6]

The conversion of Julie Fanfernot to Saint-Simonianism (she turned later to Fourierism) was made the subject of a theatrical work by the Saint-Simonians. Extracts from this publication, which appeared in the group's journal, are to be found in Firmin Maillard, *La Légende de la femme émancipée* (Paris), pp. 115ff. [U15,1]

Saint-Simon on the Rue Vivienne: "Dinners and evening parties followed one after another without interruption. . . . There were, in addition, some late-night scenes of amorous effusion, in which certain of the guests, it is reported, . . . let themselves be carried away in Anacreontic transports, while, from deep in his easy chair, a calm and impassive Saint-Simon looked on, taking no part at all in the conversation, but nonetheless taking it all in, and preparing himself withal to transform the human race." Firmin Maillard, *La Légende de la femme émancipée* (Paris), p. 27. [U15,2]

Many believed that the female messiah—who, according to Duveyrier, could issue as well from the ranks of the prostitutes as from any other stratum of society—would have to come from the Orient (Constantinople). Barrault and twelve comrades, therefore, set out for Constantinople to look for "the Mother." [U15,3]

Apropos of the schism among the Saint-Simonians: "Bazard . . . had been mortally wounded in consequence of the famous general confession, where he learned from his wife herself that, in spite of all the sympathy . . . which she had for him, she could never see him come up to her without feeling an instinctive repugnance. It was 'Hercules enchained,' as someone had said on seeing him struck by apoplexy." Firmin Maillard, *La Légende de la femme émancipée* (Paris), p. 35. [U15,4]

"Everyone knows about the retreat at Ménilmontant. . . . There they lived in celibacy so as to demonstrate that their ideas on marriage, and on the emancipation of women, were in no way the outcome of an epicurean design." Firmin Maillard, *La Légende de la femme émancipée* (Paris), p. 40. [U15,5]

Proudhon was a fierce opponent of Saint-Simonianism; he speaks of "Saint-Simonian rottenness." [U15,6]

"The arts can flourish only as conditioned within an organic age ‹*époque organique*›, and inspiration is strong and salutary only when it is social and religious." Thus E. Barrault speaks out, in *Aux artistes: Du Passé et de l'avenir des beaux-arts* (Paris, 1830), p. 73, against the barren "critical ages." [U15,7]

Last echo of the idea that inaugurated Saint-Simonianism: "One can compare the zeal and the ardor displayed by the civilized nations of today in their establishment of railroads with that which, several centuries ago, went into the building of cathedrals. . . . If it is true, as we hear, that the word 'religion' comes from *religare*, "to bind" . . . , then the railroads have more to do with the religious spirit than one might suppose. There has never existed a more powerful instrument for . . . rallying the scattered populations." Michel Chevalier, "Chemins de fer," in *Dictionnaire de l'économie politique* (Paris, 1852), p. 20. [U15a,1]

"The government wanted, on its own, to construct the railway system. There were various disadvantages to this course of action, . . . but, in the end, it would have given us railroads. The idea occasioned a terrific explosion; political rivalries dominated the scene. Science itself . . . came out in support of the spirit of systematic opposition. An illustrious savant was vain enough to lend the authority of his name to the plot against the railways. Construction by the state was thus rejected by an overwhelming majority. This occurred in 1838. Favorably disposed, as it was, toward the project, the government now turned to private industry. Take these marvelous thoroughfares, it said; I am offering you the concession for them. And no sooner were these words out than a new storm arose. What! The bankers, the capitalists are going to reap a fortune from this venture! . . . It is feudalism reborn from its own ashes!—The plans to offer concessions to companies were accordingly withdrawn, . . . or else spiked with clauses that made acceptance impossible for serious investors. We continued like this up until 1844." Michel Chevalier, "Chemins de fer," excerpt from *Dictionnaire de l'économie politique* (Paris, 1852), p. 100. [U15a,2]

Chevalier already sets up, for the transport of war materials in railroad cars, the equation: forty men equal six horses. See Michel Chevalier, "Chemins de fer," in *Dictionnaire de l'économie politique* (Paris, 1852), pp. 47–48. [U15a,3]

Theory of art in Saint-Simonianism. It rests on the division of history "into Organic or religious ages and Critical or irreligious ages. . . . The course of history treated in this work comprises two organic ages—the first constituted under the reign of Greek polytheism, the second under that of Christianity—and, in the wake of these organic ages, two critical ages, of which one extends from the era of Greek philosophy to the advent of Christianity, and the other from the end of the fifteenth century to the present." [E. Barrault,] *Aux artistes: Du Passé et de l'avenir des beaux-arts* (Paris, 1830), p. 6. ‹See N10,5.› [U15a,4]

Universal history appears, to the Saint-Simonian Barrault, as the new work of art: "Shall we venture to compare the last of the tragic or comic authors of Rome with the Christian orators intoning their eloquent sermons? No, Corneille, Racine, Voltaire, and Molière will not come back to life; dramatic genius has accomplished its mission. . . . In the end, the novel will fail no less in respect of what it has in common with these two genres as in its relations to the history of which it is the counterfeit. . . . History, in fact, will again take on a powerful charm . . . ; it will no longer be only a little tribe of the Orient that will make for sacred history; the history of the entire world will merit this title. Such history will become a veritable epic, in which the story of every nation will constitute a canto and the story of every great man an episode." [E. Barrault,] *Aux artistes: Du Passé et de l'avenir des beaux-arts* (Paris, 1830), pp. 81–82. The epic belongs to the organic age; the novel and drama, to the critical. [U16,1]

Barrault already has a vague idea of the importance, for art, of secularized cultic elements, although he puts the emphasis on periods that are consolidated through cult: "Although Greece never fostered a religious caste system like that of the Orient, its epic represented nothing less than an initial separation of poetry from cult. . . . Should orthodox movements survive into the critical periods, the course of these periods is imperceptibly drawn back into the bosom of orthodoxy." [E. Barrault,] *Aux artistes: Du Passé et de l'avenir des beaux-arts* (Paris, 1830), pp. 25–26. [U16,2]

Saint-Simon points with satisfaction to the fact that precisely those men who benefited humanity most decisively—Luther, Bacon, Descartes—were given to passions. Luther, the pleasures of eating; Bacon, money, Descartes, women and gambling. See E. R. Curtius, *Balzac* ‹Bonn, 1923›, p. 117. [U16,3]

With reference to Guizot, whose brochure, "Du Gouvernement de la France et du ministère actuel" (Paris, 1820) presents the accession of the bourgeoisie as the centuries-old struggle of a class (of course, his work *De la Démocratie* [Paris, 1849] sees in the class struggle, which has meanwhile arisen between bourgeoisie and proletariat, only a misfortune), Plekhanov portrays the visions of the socialist utopians as, "theoretically no less than practically," a great step backward. "The reason for this lay in the weak development of the proletariat at that time." Georgi Plekhanov, "Über die Anfänge der Lehre vom Klassenkampf," *Die neue Zeit,* 21, no. 1 (Stuttgart, 1903), p. 296. [U16,4]

Augustin Thierry, an "adopted son" of Saint-Simon. According to Marx, he describes very well how "from the first, or at least after the rise of the towns, the

French bourgeoisie gains too much influence by constituting itself the Parliament, the bureaucracy, and so on, and not, as in England, merely through commerce and industry." Karl Marx to Friedrich Engels, London, July 27, 1854 [Karl Marx and Friedrich Engels, *Ausgewählte Briefe*, ed. V. Adoratski (Moscow and Leningrad, 1934), p. 60].[13]   [U16a,1]

Aftereffects of Saint-Simonianism: "Pierre Leroux—who is represented, in engravings of the period, with hands clasped and eyes upraised in ecstasy—did his best to have an article on God published in *La Revue des deux mondes*. . . . We recall that Louis Blanc delighted Ruge with a lecture attacking the atheists. Quinet, along with Michelet, struggled furiously against the Jesuits, while privately harboring the wish to reconcile his compatriots with the Gospel." C. Bouglé, *Chez les prophètes socialistes* (Paris, 1918), pp. 161–162.   [U16a,2]

Heine's *Deutschland* is dedicated to Enfantin.   [U16a,3]

Schlabrendorf reports that Saint-Simon wanted to make physics, and nothing but physics, the true religion. "Teachers of religion were supposed to deliver lectures in church on the mysteries and wonders of nature. There, I imagine, they would have set up electrical apparatus on the altar and stimulated the faithful with galvanic batteries." *Graf Gustav von Schlabrendorf in Paris über Ereignisse und Personen seiner Zeit* [in Carl Gustav Jochmann, *Reliquien: Aus seinen nachgelassenen Papieren*, ed. Heinrich Zschokke, vol. 1 (Hechingen, 1836), p. 146].   [U16a,4]

Enfantin hailed the coup d'état of Louis Napoleon as the work of providence.   [U16a,5]

1846: enthusiastic reception, on its debut, of Félicien David's *Le Désert*. The project of the Suez Canal was then the order of the day. "Its theme was a poet's eulogy of the desert as the image of eternity, coupled with his pity for the townsman imprisoned between stone walls." S. Kracauer, *Jacques Offenbach und das Paris seiner Zeit* (Amsterdam, 1937), p. 133.[14] *Le Désert* was parodied by Offenbach.   [U16a,6]

"Among the dream architecture of the Revolution, Ledoux's projects occupy a special position. . . . The cubic form of his "House of Peace" seems legitimate to him because the cube is the symbol of justice and stability, and, similarly, all the elementary forms would have appeared to him as intelligible signs of intrinsic moment. The *ville naissante*, the city in which an exalted . . . life would find its abode, will be circumscribed by the pure contour of an ellipse. . . . Concerning the house of the new tribunal, the Pacifère, he says in his *Architecture:* 'The building drawn up in my imagination should be as simple as the law that will be dispensed there.'" Emil Kaufmann, *Von Ledoux bis Le Corbusier: Ursprung und Entwicklung der autonomen Architektur* (Vienna and Leipzig, 1933), p. 32.   [U17,1]

Ledoux, Temple de Mémoire (House of Women): "The narrative relief on the triumphal columns at four corners of a country house was intended to celebrate the glory of the bestowers of life, the mothers, in place of the customary monuments consecrated to the bloody victories of generals. With this unusual work, the artist wished to render thanks to the women he had come to know in his life." Emil Kaufmann, *Von Ledoux bis Le Corbusier* (Vienna and Leipzig, 1933), p. 38.

[U17,2]

On Ledoux: "Once the distinctions of rank within architecture fall by the wayside, then all architectural orders are of equal value. . . . The earlier thematic eclecticism, which was taken up almost exclusively with churches, palaces, the 'better' domiciles, and of course military fortifications, retreats before the new architectural universalism. . . . The revolutionary process of the suburbanizing of domestic housing parallels the disappearance of the baroque assemblage as art form. . . . A more extended complex, apparently conceived as a development at the entrance to the city, consists in a number of two- to four-room dwellings ranged around a square courtyard; each of these residences possesses the necessary closet space, while kitchen, pantries, and other utility rooms are located in a building at the center of the courtyard. We have here, probably, the earliest instance of the type of dwelling that is current today in the form of the apartment with shared kitchen." Emil Kaufmann, *Von Ledoux bis Le Corbusier* (Vienna and Leipzig, 1933), p. 38.

[U17,3]

"The Orient had been discovered, and some journeyed there to seek the Mother— La Mère—a representative figure of this century, covered with breasts like the Diana of Ephesus." Adrienne Monnier, "La Gazette des Amis des Livres," *La Gazette des Amis des Livres*, 1 (January 1, 1938) (Paris), p. 14.

[U17,4]

"*Man* remembers the *Past*; *Woman* divines the *Future*; the *Couple* sees the *Present*." Saint-Simonian formula, in Du Camp, *Souvenirs littéraires*, vol. 2 (Paris, 1906), p. 93.

[U17a,1]

"La Mère": "She was to be *la femme libre*. . . . This independent woman had to be a thinking woman, one who, . . . having fathomed the secrets of the feminine psyche, . . . would make confession for all her sex. . . . The quest for . . . the Mother was not an innovation of Enfantin's; well before him, Saint-Simon himself, during the period when Augustin Thierry was his secretary, had made an attempt to discover this . . . wonder . . . and evidently thought to have found her in Madame de Staël." The latter declined an invitation to beget a messiah for humanity with Saint-Simon (pp. 91–93).—"The mission to locate La Mère now formed, and was off. The pilgrims numbered twelve, including Barrault, the leader of the expedition. Their ultimate destination was Constantinople, . . . though they had no money. Dressed in white (as a sign of the vow of chastity they had taken on leaving Paris), staffs in hand, they begged their way from place to place, in the name of the Mother. In Burgundy, they hired themselves out to help with the harvest; in Lyons, they arrived on the day before an execution and, the following morning, demonstrated against the death penalty in front of the gallows. They embarked in Marseilles, and worked as sailors aboard a merchant vessel whose second mate was Garibaldi. . . . They slept in the Great Champ des Morts,[15] protected by cypresses from the morning dew; they wandered through the bazaars, occasionally stopping to preach the doctrines of Saint-Simon, speaking French to Turks who could not understand them" (pp. 94–95). They are arrested, then released. They set their sights on the island of Rotuma, in the South Pacific, as the place to seek the Mother, but they get only as far as Odessa, whence they are sent back to Turkey. According to Maxime Du Camp, *Souvenirs littéraires*, vol. 2 (Paris, 1906).

[U17a,2]

"Gaudissart demanded an indemnity of five hundred francs for the week he had to spend in boning up on the doctrine of Saint-Simon, pointing out what efforts of memory and brain would be necessary to enable him to become thoroughly conversant with this *article*." Gaudissart canvasses for *Le Globe* (and *Le Journal des enfants*). H. de Balzac, *L'Illustre Gaudissart*, ed. Calmann-Lévy (Paris), p. 11.[16]

[U18,1]

The Continental system[17] was, as it were, the first test for the example of Saint-Simonianism. Heine (*Sämtliche Werke* [Hamburg, 1876], vol. 1, p. 155—"Französische Zustände") calls Napoleon I a Saint-Simonian emperor. [U18,2]

In the Saint-Simonian jacket that buttoned in back, we may discern an allusion to the androgynous ideal of the school. But it has to be assumed that for Enfantin himself it remained unconscious. [U18,3]

Constantin Pecqueur, adversary of the Saint-Simonians, responds "to the question posed in 1838 by the Académie des Sciences Morales: 'How to assess . . . the influence of the . . . currently emerging means of transportation on . . . the state of a society . . . ?'" "The development of the railroads, at the same time that it induces travelers to fraternize in the cars, will overexcite . . . the productive activity of people." Pierre-Maxime Schuhl, *Machinisme et philosophie* (Paris, 1938), p. 67. [U18,4]

The historical signature of the railroad may be found in the fact that it represents the first means of transport—and, until the big ocean liners, no doubt also the last—to form masses. The stage coach, the automobile, the airplane carry passengers in small groups only. [U18,5]

"The anemic pallor of our civilization, as monotonous as a railway line," says Balzac. *La Peau de chagrin*, ed. Flammarion (Paris), p. 45.[18] [U18,6]

V

[Conspiracies, *Compagnonnage*]

"Those *agents provocateurs* who, during the Second Empire, often mingled with rioters were known as 'white smocks.'" Daniel Halévy, *Décadence de la liberté* (Paris ‹1931›), p. 152. [V1,1]

"In 1848, Louis Philippe had in Paris a security force of some 3,000 men, in place of the 950 gendarmes serving under Charles X, and some 1,500 police agents in place of 400. The Second Empire had great affection for the police, and it arranged magnificent installations for them. They owe to the Second Empire that vast edifice—at once barracks, fortress, and office building—which occupies the center of the Cité between the Palais de Justice and Notre Dame, and which, although larger and less beautiful, recalls those palaces in Tuscan cities where the podestas resided." Daniel Halévy, *Décadence de la liberté* (Paris), p. 150.
[V1,2]

"The secret files in police headquarters inspire a certain awe and a certain dread. When a new police commissioner first takes office, his personal file is brought up to him. He alone enjoys this privilege; neither the ministers nor even the president of the republic get to see their dossiers, which are shelved and maintained in archives that no one is permitted to examine." Daniel Halévy, *Décadence de la liberté* (Paris), pp. 171–172. [V1,3]

"Turning back toward the Quartier Latin, one ran into the virgin forest of the Rue d'Enfer, which extended between the Rue du Val-de-Grâce and the Rue de l'Abbé-de-l'Epée. There, one found the garden of an old hotel, abandoned and in ruins, where plane trees, sycamores, chestnut trees, and intertwined acacias grew haphazardly. In the center, a deep shaft gave access into the catacombs. It was said that the place was haunted. In reality, it served for the romantic gatherings of the Carbonari and of the secret society Aide-Toi, le Ciel t'Aidera ‹God Helps Him Who Helps Himself›." Dubech and d'Espezel, *Histoire de Paris* (Paris, 1926), p. 367. ▯ Gardens, The Seine ▯ [V1,4]

"The Garde Nationale was no laughing matter. Positioned between the royal troops and the popular insurgents, the armed bourgeoisie of Paris was the great mediating power, the good sense of the nation. . . . From 1830 to 1839, the bourgeois Garde Nationale lost 2,000 of their own in confrontation with the barricades, and it was due more to them than to the army that Louis Philippe was able to remain on his throne. . . . Whatever the reason—whether simple old age or a species of lassitude—it was always the bourgeoisie that wearied of this wasteful life which made it necessary, every six months, for hosiers and cabinetmakers to take up arms and shoot at each other. The hosiers, peaceful men, grew tired before the cabinetmakers. This remark would suffice to explain the February Revolution." Dubech and d'Espezel, *Histoire de Paris*, pp. 389–391.   [V1,5]

June Insurrection. "It was enough to have the appearance of poverty to be treated like a criminal. In those days there was something called 'a profile of the insurgent,' and anyone fitting the description was arrested. . . . The Garde Nationale itself had most certainly determined the outcome of the February Revolution,[1] but it never occurred even to them to give the name 'insurgents' to men struggling against a king. Only those who had risen up against property . . . were known as insurgents. Because the Garde Nationale . . . 'had saved society,' they could do at that time whatever they wanted, and no doctor would have dared refuse them entry into a hospital. . . . Indeed, the blind fury of the Guardsmen went so far that they would scream 'Silence!' to the fever patients speaking in delirium and would have murdered these people if the students had not stopped them." Engländer ‹*Geschichte der französischen Arbeiter-Associationen* (Hamburg, 1864),› vol. 2, pp. 320, 327–328, 327.   [V1,6]

"It goes without saying that the worker associations lost ground with the coup d'état of December 2, 1851. . . . All the associations of workers, those who had received subsidies from the government as well as the others, began by promptly removing their signs, on which symbols of equality and the words 'Liberty, Fraternity, Equality' were inscribed; it was as though they had been shocked by the blood of the coup. Hence, with the coup d'état, there were still unquestionably worker associations in Paris, but the workers no longer risked displaying this name. . . . It would be difficult to trace the remaining associations, for it is not only on the signboards but also in the city's directory of addresses that the name 'Workers Association' is missing. Worker associations survive, after the coup d'état, only in the guise of ordinary commercial concerns. Thus, the former fraternal association of masons is now going under the trade name 'Bouyer, Cohadon & Co.,' the association of gilders that likewise once existed as such now operates as the firm of 'Dreville, Thibout & Co.,' and, by the same token, in every surviving association of workers it is the managers who give their names to the business. . . . Since the coup d'état, not one of these associations has admitted a new member; any new member would be regarded with undisguised suspicion. If even the customers were each time received with distrust, this was because one everywhere sensed the presence of the police—and was the more justified in doing so as the police themselves would often show up officially on one pretext or another." Sigmund Engländer, *Geschichte der französischen Arbeiter-Associationen* (Hamburg, 1864), vol. 4, pp. 195, 197–198, 200. [V1a,1]

In regard to Cabet. "After the February Revolution, someone had discovered . . . , in the files of Toulouse's chief of police, a letter from Gouhenant, delegate or president of the first vanguard, who in 1843, during the trial in Toulouse,[2] had offered his services as police agent to the government of Louis Philippe. It was known that this poison of espionage in France had penetrated even into all the pores of family life; but that a police agent, this most disgusting excrescence of the old society, could have found his way to the leader of the vanguard of Icarians in order to cause his ruin, and at the risk of going under himself, aroused considerable surprise. Hadn't police spies been seen in Paris fighting and dying on the barricades, doing battle with the government in whose pay they stood!" Sigmund Engländer, *Geschichte der französischen Arbeiter-Associationen*, vol. 2, pp. 159–160. ☐ Utopians ☐ [V1a,2]

"With the development of proletarian conspiracies, the need arose for a division of labor. The members were divided into occasional conspirators, *conspirateurs d'occasion*—that is, workers who engaged in conspiracy alongside their other employment, merely attending meetings and holding themselves in readiness to appear at the place of assembly at the leaders' command—and professional conspirators, who devoted all their energy to the conspiracy and made their living from it. . . . The social situation of this class determines its entire character from the outset. Proletarian conspiracy naturally affords them only very limited and uncertain means of subsistence. They are therefore constantly obliged to dip into the cash boxes of the conspiracy. A number of them also come into direct conflict with civil society as such, and appear before the police courts with a greater or lesser degree of dignity. Their precarious livelihood, dependent in individual cases more on chance than on their activity, their irregular lives whose only fixed ports-of-call are the taverns of the *marchands de vin* (the conspirators' places of rendezvous), their inevitable acquaintance with all kinds of dubious people, place them in that social category which in Paris is known as the *bohème*. These democratic bohemians of proletarian origin are therefore either workers who have given up their work and have as a consequence become dissolute, or characters who have emerged from the lumpenproletariat and bring all the dissolute habits of that class with them into their new way of life. . . . The whole way of life of these professional conspirators has a most decidedly bohemian character. Recruiting sergeants for the conspiracy, they go from *marchand de vin* to *marchand de vin*, feeling the pulse of the workers, seeking out their men, cajoling them into the conspiracy and getting either the society's treasury or their new friends to foot the bill for the liters inevitably consumed in the process. Indeed, it is really the *marchand de vin* who provides a roof over their heads. It is with him that the conspirator spends most of his time; it is here he has his rendezvous with his colleagues, with the members of his section and with prospective recruits; it is here, finally, that the secret meetings of sections (groups) and section leaders take place. The conspirator, highly sanguine in character anyway like all Parisian proletarians, soon develops into an absolute *bambocheur* ‹boozer› in this continual tavern atmosphere. The sinister conspirator, who in secret session exhibits a Spartan self-discipline, suddenly thaws and is transformed into a tavern regular whom everybody knows and who really understands how to enjoy his wine and women. This conviviality is further intensified by the constant dangers the conspirator is exposed to; at any moment he may be called to the barricades, where he may be killed; at every turn the police set snares for him which may deliver him to prison or even to the galleys. . . . At the same time, familiarity with danger makes him utterly indifferent to life and liberty. He is as at home in prison as in the wine shop. He is ready for the call to action any day. The desperate recklessness which is exhibited in every insurrection in Paris is introduced precisely by these veteran professional conspirators, the *hommes de coups de main*. They are the ones who throw up and command the first barricades, who organize resistance, lead the looting of weapon-shops and the seizure of arms and ammunition from houses, and in the midst of the uprising carry out those daring raids which so often throw the government party into confusion. In a word, they are the officers of the insurrection. It need scarcely be added that these conspirators do not confine themselves to the general organizing of the revolutionary proletariat. It is precisely their business to anticipate the process of revolutionary development, to bring it artificially to the crisis point, to launch a revolution on the spur of the moment, without the conditions for a revolution. For them, the only condition for revolution is the adequate preparation of their conspiracy. They are the alchemists of the revolution, and are characterized by exactly the same chaotic thinking and blinkered obsessions as the alchemists of old. They leap at inventions which are supposed to work revolutionary miracles: incendiary bombs, destructive devices of magic effect, revolts which are expected to be all the more miraculous and astonishing in effect as their basis is less rational. Occupied with such scheming, they have no other purpose than the most immediate one of overthrowing the existing government, and they have the profoundest contempt for the more theoretical enlightenment of the proletariat about their class interests. Hence their plebeian rather than proletarian irritation at the *habits noirs* ("black frock coats")—people of a greater or lesser degree of education who represent that aspect of the movement, but from whom they can never make themselves quite independent, since they are the official representatives of the party. The *habits noirs* also serve, at times, as their source of money. It goes without saying that the conspirators are obliged to follow willy-nilly the development of the revolutionary party. . . . The chief characteristic of the conspirators' way of life is their battle with the police, to whom they have precisely the same relationship as thieves and prostitutes." At another point in this article, we read (in reference to Chenu's report on Lucien de La Hodde that follows): "As we see, this spy . . . turns out to be a political prostitute of the vilest kind who hangs about in the street in the rain for the payment of his 'tip' by the first officer of the peace who happens to come along." "'On one of my nocturnal excursions,' recounts Chenu, 'I noticed de La Hodde walking up and down the Quai Voltaire. . . . It was raining in torrents, a circumstance which set me thinking. Was this dear fellow de

La Hodde also helping himself from the cash box of the secret funds, by any chance? . . . "Good evening, de La Hodde, what on earth are you up to here at this hour and in this fearful weather?" "I am waiting for a rascal who owes me some money, and since he passes this way every evening at this time, he is going to pay me, or else"—and he struck the parapet of the embankment violently with his stick.' De La Hodde attempts to get rid of him and walks toward the Pont du Carrousel. Chenu departs in the opposite direction, but only to conceal himself under the arcades of the Institut ‹de France›. . . . 'A quarter of an hour later, I noticed the carriage with two little green lamps. . . . A man got out; de La Hodde went straight up to him. They talked for a moment, and I saw de La Hodde make a movement as though putting money into his pocket.'" Marx and Engels, review of Chenu, *Les Conspirateurs* (Paris, 1850) and de La Hodde, *La Naissance de la République* (Paris, 1850), published in the *Neuen rheinischen Zeitung* ‹1850›, rpt. in ‹*Die neue* Zeit,› 4 (Stuttgart, 1886), pp. 555–556, 552, 551.[3]   [V2;V2a]

The workers of 1848 and the great Revolution: "Although the workers suffered under the conditions created by the Revolution, they did not blame it for their misery; they imagined that the Revolution had failed to bring about the happiness of the masses because intriguers had perverted its founding principle. According to their thinking, the great Revolution was good in itself, and human misery could be eliminated only if people were to resolve on a new 1793. Hence, they turned away distrustfully from the socialists and felt drawn to the bourgeois republicans, who conspired with the aim of establishing a republic by revolutionary means. The secret societies in existence during the reign of Louis Philippe recruited a great many of their most active members from the working class." Paul Lafargue, "Der Klassenkampf in Frankreich," *Die neue Zeit*, 12, no. 2 (1894), p. 615.   [V3,1]

Marx on the "Communist League": "'As far as the secret doctrine of the League is concerned, it underwent all the transformations of French and English socialism and communism, as well as their German versions. . . . The secret form of the society goes back to its Paris origins. . . . During my first stay in Paris (from late October 1843 to February 1845), I established personal contact with the leaders of the League living there, as well as with the leaders of the majority of the secret French worker associations—without, however, becoming a member of any of them. In Brussels, . . . the London Central Authority entered into correspondence with us and . . . sent . . . a watchmaker called Joseph Moll . . . to invite us to join the League. Moll allayed our doubts . . . by revealing that the Central Authority intended to convoke a Congress of the League in London. . . . Accordingly, we joined it. The Congress . . . took place, and, after heated debate over several weeks, it adopted the *Manifesto of the Communist Party*, written by Engels and myself.' At the time Marx wrote these lines, he described their content as comprising 'histories long past and half forgotten.' . . . In 1860 the workers' movement, suppressed by the counterrevolution of the 1850s, was dormant throughout Europe. . . . One misunderstands the history of the *Communist Manifesto* if one sees the date of its publication as marking the commencement of the European workers' movement. In point of fact, the manifesto represented the close of this movement's first period, which stretched from the July Revolution to the February Revolution. . . . The most they could attain was theoretical clarification. . . . A secret league of workers that, over the years, could accompany and intellectually stimulate the English and French socialism of the day, as well as the reigning German philosophy, will have displayed an energy of thought that deserves the highest respect." "Ein Gedenktag des Kommunismus," *Die neue Zeit*, 16, no. 1 (Stuttgart, 1898), pp. 354–355. The passage from Marx is taken from the polemical pamphlet against Vogt.[4]   [V3,2]

"The practical programs of the communist conspirators of the period . . . set them apart advantageously from the socialist utopians, thanks to the firm conviction that the emancipation of the working class ('the people') is unthinkable without struggle against the upper classes ('the aristocracy'). Of course, the struggle of a handful of men who have hatched a conspiracy in the name of popular interests can in no case be considered a class struggle. If, nevertheless, the majority of these conspirators have come from the working class, then the conspiracy can be said to constitute the germ of the revolutionary struggle of that class. And the conception which the Society of Seasons[5] has of the 'aristocracy' shows how closely the ideas of the revolutionary communists in France, at that time, were connected to the ideas of the bourgeois revolutionaries of the eighteenth century and the liberal opposition during the Restoration. . . . Like Augustin Thierry, the French revolutionary communists began with the idea that the struggle against the aristocracy was necessarily in the interests of all the rest of society. But they rightly point out that the aristocracy of birth has been replaced by an aristocracy of money, and that, as a result, the struggle . . . must be waged against the bourgeoisie." Georgi Plekhanov, "Über die Anfänge der Lehre vom Klassenkampf" (from the introduction to a Russian edition of the *Communist Manifesto*), part 3, "Die Anschauungen des vormarxistischen Sozialismus vom Kassenkampf," *Die neue Zeit*, 21, no. 1 (1903), p. 297.   [V3a,1]

1851: "A decree of December 8 authorized the deportation, without hearing, . . . of any person presently or formerly belonging to a secret society. This was understood as referring to any society at all, whether a society for mutual aid or a literary society, that met—even in broad daylight—without the express permission of the prefect of police." A. Malet and P. Grillet, *XIXe Siècle* (Paris, 1919), p. 264.   [V3a,2]

"Following the assassination attempt by Orsini . . . , the imperial government immediately voted into law a general security measure giving it the power to arrest and deport, without hearing, . . . all persons previously punished on the occasion of the June Days of 1848 and the events of December 1851. . . . The prefect of each *département* was ordered to designate immediately a specific number of victims." A. Malet and P. Grillet, *XIXe Siècle* (Paris, 1919), p. 273.   [V3a,3]

"The Independents had their secret society, the Charbonnerie ‹Carbonari›, organized at the beginning of 1821 on the model of the Italian Carbonari. The organizers were a wine merchant, Dugied, who had spent time in Naples, and a medical student, Bazard. . . . Every member was required to contribute one franc a month, to possess a gun and fifty bullets, and to swear to carry out blindly the orders of his superiors. The Charbonnerie recruited among students and soldiers in particular; it ended up numbering 2,000 sections and 40,000 adherents. The Charbonniers wanted to overthrow the Bourbons, who had been 'brought back by foreigners,' and 'to restore to the nation the free exercise of its right to choose a suitable government.' They organized nine plots during the first six months of 1822; all failed." A. Malet and P. Grillet, *XIXᵉ Siècle* (Paris, 1919), p. 29. The uprisings of the Carbonari were military revolts; they had, perhaps, a certain analogy to those of the Decembrists. [V4,1]

April 29, 1827: dissolution of the Garde Nationale by order of Villèle, on account of a demonstration which it had organized against him. [V4,2]

About sixty students from the Ecole Polytechnique at the head of the July Revolution. [V4,3]

March 25, 1831: reinstatement of the Garde Nationale. "It named its own officers, except for the military chiefs. . . . The Garde Nationale constituted . . . a veritable army, numbering some 24,000 men . . . ; this army was a police force. . . . Also, care was taken to separate out the workers. . . . This was achieved by requiring the Garde Nationale to wear uniforms and to pay its own expenses. . . . This bourgeois guard, moreover, did its duty bravely in all circumstances. As soon as the drums had sounded the call, each man would leave his place of work, while the shopkeepers closed their stores, and, dressed in uniform, they would all go out to join their battalion, not needing to muster." A. Malet and P. Grillet, *XIXᵉ Siècle* (Paris, 1919), p. 77, 79. [V4,4]

"The republicans had belonged, for the most part, to the Charbonnerie; against Louis Philippe, they multiplied the number of secret societies. The most important . . . was that of the Droits de l'Homme ‹Rights of Man›. Founded in Paris (where it quickly grew to nearly 4,000 members), and modeled on the Charbonnerie, it had branches in most of the major cities. It was this secret society that organized the great insurrections in Paris and Lyons in June 1832 and April 1834. The principal republican newspapers were *La Tribune* and *Le National*, the first directed by Armand Marrast and the second by Armand Carrel." Malet and Grillet, *XIXᵉ Siècle* (Paris, 1919), p. 81. [V4,5]

Declaration of December 19, 1830, issued by students at the Ecole Polytechnique to the editorial office of *Le Constitutionnel:* "'If any man among the agitators,' they say, 'is found wearing the uniform of the Ecole, that man is an impostor. . . .' And so they had these men tracked down wherever they appeared in the faubourgs in the uniform of Polytechnicians, seeking to usurp the latter's influence. The best way to recognize them, according to Bosquet, was to ask them the *differential of sine x or of log x;* 'if they respond appropriately, they are former students; if not, we have them jailed.'" G. Pinet, *Histoire de l'Ecole polytechnique* (Paris, 1887), p. 187. Disturbances took place in connection with the trial against the ministers of Charles X.[6] Pinet adds: "In supporting the interests of the bourgeoisie, those with republican convictions seemed to fear they would be accused of deserting the cause of the people" (p. 187). In a further proclamation, the school came out decisively in favor of universal suffrage. [V4a,1]

"The students go to their student societies, whether publicly or secretly organized, to get the watchword of the day. . . . There, they learn what actions are being planned. . . . With all this going on, the Ecole Polytechnique has begun to view itself as a fourth estate within the nation. . . . It was the moment when the Republican party, which counted in its ranks the artillery of the Garde Nationale, the student, the proletariat, the worker, and the veteran of July, resumed . . . its activity; the moment when popular societies—like Les Amis du Peuple, Les Droits de l'Homme, and La Gauloise—were recruiting heavily; the moment when the Garde Nationale failed to maintain the peace; when the Saint-Simonians threatened to unsettle the order of society; . . . and when . . . *Le National* and *La Tribune* waged a daily struggle against those in power." G. Pinet, *Histoire de l'Ecole polytechnique* (Paris, 1887), pp. 192–193. [V4a,2]

During the cholera epidemic, the government was accused of having poisoned the fountains. For example, in the Faubourg Saint-Antoine. [V4a,3]

"Young people in the schools had adopted the red beret; and members of the secret societies looked forward to *the next time*, when the *national razor* would be well honed." Charles Louandre, *Les Idées subversives de notre temps* (Paris, 1872), p. 85. [V4a,4]

The secret societies of the democrats were chauvinistic. They wanted international propaganda for the republic by means of war. [V5,1]

"Response afterward made by a prisoner before the Court of Peers: / 'Who was your chief?' / *'I knew none, and I recognized none.'*" Victor Hugo, *Oeuvres complètes,* novels, vol. 8 (Paris, 1881), p. 47 (*Les Misérables,* "Faits d'où l'histoire sort et que l'histoire ignore").[7] [V5,2]

"From time to time, men 'disguised as bourgeois, and in fine coats' came, 'causing embarrassment,' and, having the air 'of command,' gave a grip of the hand *to the most important,* and went away. They never stayed more than ten minutes." Victor Hugo, *Oeuvres complètes,* novels, vol. 8 (Paris, 1881), pp. 42–43 (*Les Misérables,* "Faits d'où l'histoire sort et que l'histoire ignore").[8] [V5,3]

The Société des Droits de l'Homme ‹Society of the Rights of Man› employs, in its pamphlets, the calendar of the great Revolution. In the month of Pluviose,[9] year 42 of the Republican era, it counts 300 branch establishments throughout France, 163 in Paris alone, of which every one had its particular name. The wooing of the proletarians by the bourgeoisie had the benefit "that, instead of enlisting them through humiliation or material services, through the offer of money or other forms of assistance, it was by various attentions and tokens of respect, by joining together in balls and fêtes, that the leaders of the bourgeoisie worked to form attachments with the workers." Charles Benoist, "L'Homme de 1848," part 1, *Revue des deux mondes* (July 1, 1913), pp. 148–149.   [V5,4]

The Société de Propagande ‹Society of Propaganda›: "To this organization we owe, in part, the strike at the end of 1833, which extended to typographers, mechanics, stonecutters, rope makers, hackney drivers, camberers, glovers, sawyers, wallpaperers, hosiers, and locksmiths, and which involved no less than '8,000 tailors, 6,000 shoemakers, 5,000 carpenters, 4,000 jewelers, and 3,000 bakers.'" Ch. Benoist, "L'Homme de 1848," part 1, *Revue des deux mondes* (July 1, 1913), p. 151.   [V5,5]

The Comité Invisible ‹Invisible Committee›—name of a secret society in Lyons.   [V5,6]

Only after 1832, but above all around 1834 and 1835, did revolutionary propaganda gain a foothold in the proletariat.   [V5,7]

In the tightened organization of the secret societies after 1835, the mystagogic element was intensified. The names of the days of the week and of the months became codewords for assault detachments and commandos. An initiation ceremony influenced by freemasonry and reminiscent of the Vehme ‹medieval criminal tribunals› was introduced. According to de La Hodde, this ceremonial already includes, among other things, the question: "Must one make a political revolution, or a social revolution?"[10] See Ch. Benoist, "L'Homme de 1848," part 1, *Revue des Deux Mondes,* 7, no. 1 (1913), pp. 1959–1961.   [V5,8]

"It was all up with the Jacobins by 1840, just as with the Montagnards, the secret societies, the conspiracies, the journals, the ceremonial parades, and the raids. The 'communists' now held center stage. . . . The workers took part in the banquet in Belleville, at which the clockmaker Simard gave a speech. The great strike of 1840, during which, in Paris alone, 30,000 men stopped work, tightened their federation. . . . Heinrich Heine has given us, in ten passages of his *Lutèce,* a vivid picture of . . . the powerful hold which communism had on the workers from the Paris suburbs. Heine had the honor, in his letters to the *Augsburg Gazette,* of unveiling communism to the communists. . . . But . . . there are communists and communists. I transcribe, from *L'Almanach Icarien* of 1843, this notice . . . : 'Today, the communists can be divided into two main categories: communists pure

and simple, . . . who want to abolish marriage and the family, and Icarian communists, . . . who wish to preserve the family and marriage, but would do away with
secret societies, wanton violence, riots, and other such felonies." Charles Benoist,
"L'Homme de 1848," part 2, *Revue des deux mondes* (February 1, 1914),
pp. 638–641.   [V5a,1]

In the mid-Thirties, a crisis broke out in the traditions of the journeymen and
traveling artisans. The hierarchies handed down from the time of the guilds
began to lose their authority; many of the work songs had come to seem old-fashioned. An effort was made to elevate the intellectual and moral level of the
associations. Agricol Perdiguier put together a sort of journeyman's primer, with
songs and didactic or devotional readings. This document shows that the moribund customs of the trade guilds were a breeding ground for secret societies.
                                                                          [V5a,2]

Cenacles after 1839: La Goguette des Fils du Diable ‹Revels of the Sons of Satan›,
Les Communistes Matérialistes ‹The Materialist Communists›.   [V5a,3]

Network of wine merchants: "The current law gives them freedom, whereas the
Empire, in point of fact, had deprived them of freedom. Napoleon III looked on
the taverns as 'meeting places for the secret societies,' and the *Code annoté* [a
pamphlet by Julien Goujon, *Code annoté des limonadiers*] accuses him of having
wanted to 'strike with terror,' in order to 'transform three hundred thousand
inhabitants and their families into official watchmen.' Three hundred thousand
taverns—that is, political taverns (what Balzac calls 'the people's parliament')—
were thus consolidated . . . under the July Monarchy and the government of
1848." Maurice Talmeyr, "Le Marchand de vins," *Revue des deux mondes* (August
15, 1898), pp. 877–878.   [V5a,4]

Varia from Agricol Perdiguier, *Le Livre du compagnonnage* (Paris: by the author,
1840): "In 1830, the Aspirants Menuisiers ‹Apprentice Joiners› and the Aspirants
Serruriers ‹Apprentice Locksmiths› in Bordeaux revolted against their fellow
compagnons, or tradesmen, and formed among themselves the core of a new society. Since then, in Lyons, Marseilles, and Nantes, other apprentices have revolted
and formed societies. . . . These various societies corresponded with one another,
and the Société de l'Union ou des Indépendants was born. . . . It is distinguished
by no mystery, no initiation, no hierarchy. . . . All members of this society are
equal" (pp. 179–180). Customs: "When a *compagnon* goes to the house where the
society lodges, eats, and congregates, he says: 'I am going to the Mother's house'"
(pp. 180–181). Names: "The Rose of Carcassonne, the Resolved of Tournus, and
many others" (p. 185). Greeting—a prescribed form of introduction for trade-
guild members on first meeting: "They ask one another what side they are on or
what allegiance they hold to. If it is the same, there is a fête, and they drink from a
shared flask. . . . If not, there are insults to start with, and then blows" (p. 187).
Variously colored ribbons, worn in different ways, are insignia of the individual

trades. Common, as well, are earrings with distinctive little pendants on them (horseshoes, hammers, standard gauges, and the like), to which the different trades lay exclusive claim. "The T-square and compass are emblems of all the trade guilds, all *compagnonnage*, for it is thought . . . that the word *compagnon* derives from *compas* ‹compass›.[11] . . . The shoemakers and bakers have several times paid dearly for the honor of wearing the compass; all the *compagnons* with allegiance to other professions set upon them" (p. 189). "In the trade-guild societies, the word *monsieur* is never used. . . . The French, Spanish, Italians, and Swiss, whenever they happen to meet, address one another as countries—Country of Spain, Country of Italy, Country of Switzerland, and so on. . . . Since they all reside under the same starry vault, and tread the same ground, they are—and they call themselves—countries; the world for them, is one great country!" (p. 41).—Perdiguier was on the staff of *L'Atelier* (1840–1850), founded by Buchez. It went under in 1850 because it could not make a bail payment of 18,000 francs. [V6,1]

The July Days brought about an upsurge in secret societies, in consequence of a rapprochement between the republican bourgeoisie and the proletariat. [V6,2]

The Society of the Tenth of December. "On the pretext of establishing a charitable association, Louis Napoleon divided the Parisian lumpenproletariat, after his election to the presidency, into numerous secret sections, which were headed by Bonapartist agents." Eduard Fuchs, *Die Karikatur der europäischen Völker* (Munich ‹1921›), vol. 2, p. 102. [V6,3]

The tavern on the Place Belhomme. "Under Louis Philippe, it was run by an individual connected with the police. Its clientele was composed, in large part, of all the conspirators of the day, who assembled there twice a week, on Mondays and Thursdays. The names of confederates were proposed on Thursday, and they were admitted on Monday." A. Lepage, *Les Cafés politiques et littéraires de Paris* (Paris ‹1874›), p. 99. [V6a,1]

From a secret report, cited in Pokrowski, by the Russian informer Jakov Tolstoi, concerning his conversation with the director of the English colonial bank, Campbell, an agent of Prince Louis Napoleon: "The prince had apprised him of the difficulties of his situation, given that he has to battle against *Le National* {that is, against Cavaignac—M.N.P.}, no less than against the red republicans {that is, Ledru-Rollin—M.N.P.}, who have enormous sums at their disposal(!). . . . Afterward, . . . he asked me whether or not the Russian government was likely to entrust the prince with such a sum [which was needed for the electoral campaign and could not be raised in England]. . . . It became clear to me then that Mr. Campbell was a sort of emissary of Prince Louis and so, in order to divert his attention and to put an end to the conversation, I treated the whole affair as a joke. I asked him what Louis Napoleon could give to Russia in return for the million he requires.— 'Every possible concession,' answered Mr. Campbell, getting worked up. 'Then

Russia can buy the head of the Republic?' I asked. 'And for only a million francs? Distributed over the four years of his presidency, this comes to 250,000 a year. You will admit that it is not a great deal of money.'—'I guarantee you that, for this price, he will be entirely at your service.'—'Will he, at the very least, exert his full authority to rid France of Polish and Russian emigrants?'—'I say to you that he will make a formal commitment in this regard, for he presently finds himself in the most difficult situation that in general can befall a man!'" M. N. Pokrowski, *Historische Aufsätze* (Vienna and Berlin ⟨1928⟩), p. 120 ("Lamartine, Cavaignac, und Nikolaus I"). [V6a,2]

"The old journeymen's association of *compagnons*, the beginnings of which go back to the fourteenth, perhaps . . . the twelfth century . . . (a number of historians derive the Carbonari movement from it) . . . , must have especially interested Balzac. . . . The *compagnons* themselves . . . trace their origin to the construction of Solomon's temple. . . . In the preface to the *Histoire des Treize*, Balzac makes allusion to the *compagnons*, who even today would have their partisans among the French people." Ernst Robert Curtius, *Balzac* (Bonn, 1923), p. 34. [V7,1]

"In France, it was above all the secret society known as La Congrégation that furnished the public with materials for all sorts of thrilling and gruesome stories. The writers of the Restoration, in particular, ascribed to it the blackest machinations. The Comte d'Artois, the future Charles X, moved in its orbit. . . . With his *History of Secret Societies in the Army*, Charles Nodier enthralled his readers. He himself belonged to the Société des Philadelphes, founded in 1797. . . . Equally harmless was the Société du Cheval Rouge ⟨Society of the Red Horse⟩, which Balzac founded with Gautier and some others in the firm conviction that, by influencing the salons, its members . . . would garner power and glory for one another. . . . A secret alliance of prison convicts is the Société des Grands Fanandels, whose organization forms the background for . . . Vautrin." Ernst Robert Curtius, *Balzac* (Bonn, 1923), pp. 32–34. [V7,2]

The Faubourg Saint-Antoine and the Temple precinct owe their importance for handicraft to the fact that the laws which prohibited workers from establishing a residence before completing their term as journeymen were not in effect there. The journeyman's *tour de France* required three to four years. [V7,3]

Along with many other particulars concerning the *compagnons*, Chaptal reports of the enemy clans: "The tools of their trade were always their weapons of war." ⟨Jean-Antoine-Claude⟩ Chaptal, *De l'Industrie française* (Paris, 1819), vol. 2, p. 314. [V7,4]

"Apart from . . . meeting at night in small groups, the German craftsmen in Paris, in those years, liked to get together on Sundays with kith and kin in a restaurant on the outskirts of town. In January 1845, a former officer of the Garde Nationale, Adalbert von Bornstedt, who at that time was spying on radical writers and artisans in Paris for the Prussian government, described to the latter, in a report denouncing Marx and Hess, a gathering of this sort in the Avenue de Vincennes, where regicide, hatred of the rich, and the abolition of private property were openly advocated." Gustav Mayer, *Friedrich Engels*, vol. 1, *Friedrich Engels in seiner Frühzeit* (Berlin ‹1933›), p. 252.   [V7,5]

"Adalbert von Bornstedt . . . was . . . a spy . . . of the Prussian government. Engels and Marx made use of him, knowing well enough, however, whom they were dealing with." Gustav Mayer, *Friedrich Engels*, vol. 1, *Friedrich Engels in seiner Frühzeit*, second edition (Berlin), p. 386.   [V7a,1]

Flora Tristan attempted to free the workers from the terms of their journeyman's contract.   [V7a,2]

Schlabrendorf gives an account of the popular comedian Bobêche, who could be seen on the Boulevard du Temple. "His stage is so narrow, however, that he has no room to gesticulate when his brother-in-law, with whom he performs, is up there with him. So he has to stick his hands in his pockets. The other day he exclaimed, with reason: I must have a place, I absolutely *must* have a place!—But you surely know that a place must be filled, that you must do some work and *earn* your place?—Filled? You fill just one part of it and the rest is filled by others.—So what place do you want?—The Place Vendôme.—The Place Vendôme! It will surely be difficult for you to have that.—Nothing easier. I shall denounce the Column." *Graf Gustav von Schlabrendorf in Paris über Ereignisse und Personen seiner Zeit* [in Carl Gustav Jochmann, *Reliquien: Aus seinen Nachgelassenen Papieren*, ed. Heinrich Zschokke, vol. 1 (Hechingen, 1836), pp. 248–249].   [V7a,3]

The Carbonari looked on Christ as the first victim of the aristocracy.   [V7a,4]

"The police spies in Paris recognize one another by a badge bearing the so-called eye of providence." Carl Gustav Jochmann, *Reliquien*, ed. Heinrich Zschokke, vol. 3 (Hechingen, 1838), p. 220.   [V7a,5]

"For the work of Balzac . . . to appear authentically mythic, it suffices to recall that, even during the author's lifetime, there were groups of men and women in Venice and in Russia who would assume the parts of characters from his *Comédie humaine* and try to live like them." Roger Caillois, "Paris, mythe moderne," *Nouvelle Revue française*, 25, no. 284 (May 1, 1937), p. 698.   [V7a,6]

"As for Balzac, one need only . . . recall that he is the man whose earliest work (or nearly his earliest) happens to be his *Histoire impartiale des Jésuites,* which he considered an homage to 'the most beautiful society ever formed,' and that he is, at the same time, the creator of Vautrin and the author of the *Histoire des Treize*." Roger Caillois, "Paris, mythe moderne," *Nouvelle Revue française,* 25, no. 284

(May 1, 1937), pp. 695–696. The Jesuits, like the Assassins, play a role in the imaginative world of Balzac, as in that of Baudelaire. [V8,1]

"Ten French regiments, were they to descend into the catacombs, could not have laid a hand on a single Carbonaro, so many were the turns of those dark and dismal underground passages, leading to inaccessible retreats. It may be mentioned, furthermore, that the catacombs were admirably mined in five or six places, and a spark would have been enough . . . to blow up the entire Left Bank." A. Dumas, *Les Mohicans de Paris*, vol. 3 (Paris, 1863), p. 11. [V8,2]

The conspirators of 1830 were rigorously classical in orientation and bitter foes of Romanticism. Blanqui remained true to this type throughout his life. [V8,3]

Heine on a meeting of Les Amis du Peuple, at which over 1,500 in attendance listened to a speech by Blanqui. "The meeting had the odor of an old copy—much perused, greasy, and worn—of *Le Moniteur* of 1793." Cited in Geffroy, *L'Enfermé* ‹ed. 1926›, vol. 1, p. 59. [V8,4]

Secret societies after the July Revolution: Ordre et Progrès, Union des Condamnés Politiques, Réclamants de Juillet, Francs Régénérés, Société des Amis du Peuple, Société des Familles. [V8,5]

Organization of the Société des Saisons, successor to the Société des Familles: At the top, four seasons, of which the chief is spring. Each season has three months, the chief month being July. The month has four weeks, and their chief is Sunday.—The chiefs are not present at the meetings (or are not recognizable). See Geffroy, *L'Enfermé* ‹ed. 1926›, vol. 1, p. 79. [V8,6]

The sections of the Carbonari were known as *ventes*[12] (the name "Carbonari" goes back to a conspiracy organized in the house of a charcoal dealer during the struggle of the Ghibellines against the Guelphs). Supreme *vente*, district *ventes*, local *ventes*. Among the founders of the French section was Bazard. [V8,7]

J. J. Weiss on the Club des Halles: "The club met in a little room on the second floor above a café; it had few members, and these were serious and thoughtful. Think of the atmosphere of the Comédie Française on days when Racine or Corneille is performed; compare the audience on those days to the crowd that fills a circus where acrobats are executing perilous leaps, and you will understand the impression made on someone who ventured into this revolutionary club of Blanqui, compared with the impression made by the two clubs in vogue with the party of order, the club of the Folies-Bergère and that of the Salle Valentino. It was like a chapel consecrated to the orthodox creed of classical conspiracy, where the doors were open to all, but where you never felt like returning unless you believed. After the sullen parade of the oppressed who, every night, would present themselves at this tribunal in order always to denounce someone or something—the conspiracy of bankers, an office manager, an administrator of the railroad—the priest of the place would rise to his feet and, on the pretext of addressing the sorrows of his congregation, the people (represented by the half-dozen furious imbeciles who had just been heard), would clarify the situation. His appearance was distinguished, his bearing irreproachable; his countenance was delicate, fine, and composed, with a fierce and sinister flash that sometimes lit the small and piercing eyes, which, in their usual state, were more benevolent than harsh. His words were measured, colloquial, and precise; it was, along with that of M. Thiers, the least declamatory way of speaking I have ever heard. As to the content of his speech, almost everything in it was just. . . . 'Where, then, did Corneille learn the art of war?' cried the Grand Condé at the first performance of *Sertorius*. Blanqui, I would surmise, had no more studied war than had Corneille. But possessing, as he did, the political faculty to a superlative degree, he could manage, . . . even in military matters, all the signals that, when duly heeded, would have called forth a salute." Cited in Gustave Geffroy, *L'Enfermé* (Paris, 1897), pp. 346–348.

[V8a]

January 1870, after the murder of Victor Noir: Blanqui has the Blanquists, presented by Granger, file by before him, without letting the fact be known. "He went out, armed, bidding farewell to his sisters, and took up his post on the Champs-Elysées. It was there, as Granger had announced to him, that he would find, parading before him, the army of which he was the mysterious general. He recognized the squadron leaders, as they came into view, and, behind each of them, he saw the men grouped geometrically and marching in step, as though in regiments. It was all done according to plan. Blanqui held his review—strange spectacle—without arousing the slightest suspicion. Leaning against a tree, surrounded by the crowd of onlookers, the vigilant old man saw his comrades pass by, orderly amid the surging of the people, silent amid the steadily mounting uproar." Gustave Geffroy, *L'Enfermé* (Paris, 1897), pp. 276–277. [V9,1]

On the influence of Machiavelli, which Blanqui felt at Sainte-Pélagie: "In contrast to the French Blanqui—so lucid, so intelligent, so ironic—there appeared, from time to time, this old Italian Blanqui, denizen of Florence or of Venice, who put his faith in tenebrous schemes and in the possible success of an act of force." Gustave Geffroy, *L'Enfermé* (Paris, 1897), pp. 245–246. [V9,2]

A type of conspirator characteristic of the 1840s: Daniel Borme, a journeyman, half crazy, but above all ambiguous. He worked on assignment from Vidocq, who, for his part, took his orders from Caussidière as much as from Louis Napoleon. Borme put the regiment of the Vésuviennes on their feet; in 1848, he was granted an audience, in the company of several Vésuviennes, with Mme. de Lamartine. Lamartine himself refused to have any dealings with the Vésuviennes. There seems to have been a plan to set up workshops for them. Borme makes an appeal to the *citoyennes* on a poster dated February 28, 1848:

"To female citizens and patriots, my sisters in the Republic: . . . I have asked the Provisional Government to register you under the title of Vésuviennes. The engagement will be for one year; to enlist, you must be between fifteen and thirty, and unmarried. Apply at 14 Rue Sainte-Appoline, from noon to four o'clock." Cited in Roger Devigne, "Des 'Miliciennes' de 1937 aux 'Vésuviennes' de 1848," *Vendredi* (May 21, 1937).   [V9,3]

Baudelaire, in his review of *Les Martyrs ridicules*, by Léon Cladel: "The man of intelligence molds the people, and the visionary creates reality. I have known some poor wretches whose heads were turned by Ferragus XXIII and who seriously planned to form a secret coalition in order to share, like a rabble dividing up a conquered empire, all the functions and the wealth of modern society." Baudelaire, *L'Art romantique* (Paris), p. 434.[13]   [V9a,1]

Charles Prolès, in *Les Hommes de la révolution de 1871* ⟨Paris, 1898⟩, p. 9, on Raoul Rigault, Blanquist and prefect of police during the Commune: "In all things, . . . even in his fanaticism, he had a remarkable sang-froid, an indefinable air of the sinister and impassive *mystificateur*." Cited in Georges Laronze, *Histoire de la Commune de 1871* (Paris, 1928), p. 45. In the same text, p. 38, on Rigault's specialty, the unmasking of police spies: "Under the Empire, especially, he had thrived, . . . keeping his notebook up to date, denouncing, on their arrival, the disconcerted agents. 'So how are things with the boss?' And, with a sneer, he would announce their names. Blanqui saw in such perspicacity the mark of a serviceable talent. He let fall from his lips, one day, this unexpected word of praise: 'He is nothing but a gamin, but he makes a first-rate policeman.'"   [V9a,2]

Doctrine of the Blanquists during the Commune: "To issue decrees for the nation was to repudiate the utopia of federalism and . . . , from Paris as the abiding capital, to appear to govern France." Georges Laronze, *Histoire de la Commune de 1871* (Paris, 1928), p. 120.   [V9a,3]

The Blanquists venerated the memory of Hébert.   [V9a,4]

"Several editorial offices and boulevard cafés, in particular the Café de Suède, were the centers . . . of conspiracy. From there, the web spread out. It encompassed in its linkages the entire Commune, redoubtable less for the results obtained (these were effectively nullified by the profusion of plots) than for the atmosphere . . . of suspicion it produced. At the Hôtel de Ville, there were incessant leaks. No deliberation, no secret decision took place that was not immediately known by Thiers." Georges Laronze, *Histoire de la Commune de 1871* (Paris, 1928), p. 383.   [V9a,5]

Marx caps a detailed account of the Society of the Tenth of December, as an organization of the lumpenproletariat, with these words: "in short, the whole, indefinite, disintegrated mass, thrown hither and thither, which the French term *la bohème.*" Karl Marx, *Der achtzehnte Brumaire des Louis Bonaparte*, ed. Rjazanov (Vienna and Berlin ‹1927›), p. 73.[14]   [V10,1]

Re Balzac: "Sainte-Beuve . . . recounts an anecdote stranger . . . than all the others. At one point, a whole society meeting in Venice (one of the more aristocratic of the societies) decided to assign its members different roles drawn from the *Comédie humaine,* and some of these roles, adds the critic mysteriously, were taken to the very extreme. . . . This occurred around 1840." Anatole Cerfberr and Jules Christophe, *Répertoire de la Comédie humaine de H. de Balzac* (Paris, 1887), p. v (Introduction de Paul Bourget).   [V10,2]

In 1828 *The Conspiracy of Equals,* by Buonarroti, appears in Brussels. "Very quickly, his book becomes the breviary of conspirators." Title: ‹*History of Babeuf's*› *Conspiracy for Equality,* 60,000 copies sold in only a few days. In 1837, 15,000 people at Buonarroti's interment. Michelet's father had a relation to the beginnings of Babeuf; Michelet, to Buonarroti. See André Monglond, *Le Préromantisme français*, vol. 2, *Le Maître des âmes sensibles* (Grenoble, 1930), pp. 154–155.   [V10,3]

[Fourier]

Seas they fathom! Skies they reveal!
Each of these seekers after God
Takes an infinity upon his wing:
Fulton the green, Herschel the blue;
Magellan sails, Fourier soars.
The frivolous and ironical crowd
Sees nothing of their dreams.

> —Victor Hugo, *L'Année terrible: Les Précurseurs,* Epigraph
> to the brochure by Pellarin, *104ᵉ anniversaire natal de
> Fourier* (Paris, 1876), cited in A. Pinloche, *Fourier et
> le socialisme* (Paris, 1933), supplement

"The words of Jean Paul which I put at the head of this biography of Fourier—'Of the fibers that vibrate in the human soul he cut away none, but rather harmonized all'—these words apply admirably to this socialist, and in their fullest resonance apply only to him. One could not find a better way to characterize the phalansterian philosophy." Ch. Pellarin, *Notice bibliographique* (1839), p. 60, cited in A. Pinloche, *Fourier et le socialisme* (Paris, 1933), pp. 17–18.   [W1,1]

Fourier on his business career: "My best years were lost in the workshops of falsehood, where from all sides the sinister augury rang in my ears: 'A very honest boy! He will never be worth anything in business.' Indeed, I was duped and robbed in all that I undertook. But if I am worth nothing when it comes to practicing business, I am worth something when it comes to unmasking it." Charles Fourier, 1820, *Publication des manuscrits,* vol. 1, p. 17, cited in A. Pinloche, *Fourier et le socialisme* (Paris, 1933), p. 15.[1]   [W1,2]

Fourier wanted "every woman to have, first of all, a husband with whom she could conceive two children; second, a breeder *(géniteur)* with whom she could have only one child; then, a lover *(favorit)* who has lived with her and retained this title; fourth and last, mere possessors *(possesseurs),* who are nothing in the eyes of the law. . . . A man who expressly says that a girl of eighteen who has not yet found a man is entitled to prostitute herself; a man who directs that all girls be divided into two classes, the juveniles (under eighteen) and the emancipated (over eighteen), which last would have the right to take a lover and bear illegitimate children; a man who . . . maintains that unmarried young women who give themselves up to pleasure possess qualities superior to those of married women, . . . and describes in great detail how an entire army of women should enter into prostitution under the supervision of matrons—such a man does not understand the eternal bases of humanity." Sigmund Engländer, *Geschichte der französischen Arbeiter-Associationen* (Hamburg, 1864), vol. 1, pp. 245, 261–262.—In the same vein: "What are we to say of a system in which *filles publiques* are given the name *bacchantes* and in which it is argued that they are just as necessary as vestal virgins, and that they . . . exercise the virtue of fellowship? A system which describes in what manner innocent young people are supposed to lose their innocence?" (ibid., pp. 245–246).

[W1,3]

"Around 1803 or 1804, Fourier, who practiced the profession of commercial traveler—or 'shop-sergeant,' as he preferred to call it—found himself in Paris. Having before him a four-month wait for a position he had been promised, he looked around for some means of occupying his time and hit upon the idea of searching for a way to make all men happy. It was not with the expectation of obtaining any practical results that he entered on this project, but purely as a *jeu d'esprit*." Charles-M. Limousin, *Le Fouriérisme* (Paris, 1898), p. 3.   [W1,4]

"Fourier is so prodigal in his invention and his crazy descriptions that Lerminier justifiably compares him to Swedenborg. . . . Fourier, too, was at home in all skies and on all planets. After all, he calculated mathematically the transmigration of the soul, and went on to prove that the human soul must assume 810 different forms until it completes the circuit of the planets and returns to earth, and that, in the course of these existences, 720 years must be happy, 45 years favorable, and 45 years unfavorable or unhappy. And has he not described what will happen to the soul after the demise of our planet, and prophesied, in fact, that certain privileged souls will retire to the sun? He reckons further that our souls will come to inhabit all other planets and worlds, after spending 80,000 years on planet Earth. He calculates, in addition, that this termination of the human race will occur only after it has enjoyed the benefits of the boreal light for 70,000 years. He proves that by the influence, not of the boreal light, to be sure, but of the gravitational force of labor, . . . the climate of Senegal will become as moderate as summers in France are now. He describes how, once the sea has turned to lemonade, men will transport fish from the great ocean to the inland seas, the Caspian, Aral, and Black Seas, given that the boreal light reacts less potently with these salty seas; and so, in this way, saltwater fish will accustom themselves gradually to the lemonade, until finally they can be restored to the ocean. Fourier also says that, in its eighth ascending period, humanity will acquire the capacity to live like fish in the water and to fly like birds in the air, and that, by then, humans will have reached a height of seven feet and a life span of at least 144 years. Everyone, at that point, will be able to transform himself into an amphibian; for the individual will have the power of opening or closing at will the valve that connects the two chambers of the heart, so as to bring the blood directly to the heart without having it pass through the lungs. . . . Nature will evolve in such fashion, he maintains, that a time will come when oranges blossom in Siberia and the most dangerous animals have been replaced by their opposites. Anti-lions, anti-whales will be at man's service then, and the calm will drive his ships. In this way, according to Fourier, the lion will serve as the best of horses and the shark will be as useful in fishing as the dog is in hunting. New stars will emerge to take the place of the moon, which already, by then, will have begun to rot." Sigmund Engländer, *Geschichte der französischen Arbeiter-Associationen* (Hamburg, 1864), vol. 1, pp. 240–244.   [W1a]

"Fourier, . . . in his last years, . . . wanted to found a phalanstery that would be inhabited exclusively by children aged three to fourteen, of which he aimed to assemble 12,000; but his appeal went unheeded and the project was never realized. In his writings he left a detailed plan, which specifically describes how the children must be raised so as to further the idea of association. From the moment a child begins to walk, an attempt must be made to identify its tastes and passions, and, by this means, to discover its vocation. Children who show a liking for life in the street, who make a racket and refuse to learn neatness and cleanliness, are placed by Fourier in small bands which have charge of the more unpleasant tasks of the association. On the other side there are children in whom the taste for elegance and luxury is inborn; these again Fourier arranges in a group, so that by their presence on the scene the phalanx will not be lacking in luxury. . . . The children are to become . . . great artists of song. Every phalanx, Fourier says, will have 700 to 800 actors, musicians, and dancers, and the poorest canton in the Alps or the Pyrenees will have an opera company at least as good as the Grand Opera of Paris, if not much better. In order to foster the general sense for harmony, Fourier would have the children already singing duets and trios in the nursery." Sigmund Engländer, *Geschichte der französischen Arbeiter-Associationen* (Hamburg, 1864), vol. 1, pp. 242–243.   [W2,1]

"Among the disciples of Fourier, one of the most entertaining was this Alphonse Toussenel, who, in 1847 and 1852 respectively, published those works so popular in their day, *L'Esprit des bêtes* and *Le Monde des oiseaux*. . . . Like Fourier, . . . he sees in nature only animate beings: 'The planets,' he affirms, 'have great duties to fulfill, first as members of the solar system, then as mothers of families.' And he voluptuously describes the amours of the Earth and the Sun: 'As the lover dresses in his most beautiful robes, and glosses his hair, and perfumes his language for the visit of his love, thus every morning the Earth indues her richest attire to meet the rays of her star beloved. . . . Happy, thrice happy the Earth, that no council of the stars has yet thundered its anathema against the immorality of the kisses of the Sun!' . . . 'Professors of the officially sanctioned physical sciences dare not speak of the *two sexes* of electricity; they find it more moral to speak of its two *poles*. . . . Such absurdities are beyond me. . . . If the fire of love did not kindle all beings, metals and minerals as well as others, where, I ask, would be the reason for those ardent affinities of potassium for oxygen, of hydrochloric acid for water?'"

⟨Toussenel,⟩ *L'Esprit des bêtes* ⟨6th edition⟩ (Paris, 1862), pp. 9, 2–3, 102–106.[2] Cited in René de Planhol, *Les Utopistes de l'amour* (Paris, 1921), pp. 219–220.

[W2,2]

"Our planet goes into material decline once its inhabitants begin to backslide down the social scale. It is like a tree whose leaves the caterpillars have been allowed to devour over a period of years: the tree languishes and dies." From Fourier, *Théorie en abstrait ou négative*, p. 325. "Our vortex is young, and a column of 102 planets is presently on course for an entry into our universe, which is on the point of advancing from the third to the fourth power." From Fourier, *Théorie des quatre mouvements* (1808), pp. 75, 462, and *Théorie mixte ou spéculative et Synthèse routinière de l'association*, pp. 260, 263. Cited in E. Silberling, *Dictionnaire de sociologie phalanstérienne* (Paris, 1911), pp. 339, 338.   [W2a,1]

Gay's newspaper, *Le Communiste*: "What was noteworthy, in his case, was that he championed the view that communism could not possibly be achieved without a complete alteration in sexual relations. . . . 'In a communist society . . ., not only would all men and women enter into a great many intimate relationships with persons of the opposite sex, but even at their first encounter a genuine sympathy would spring up between them.'" Engländer, *Geschichte der französischen Arbeiter-Associationen*, vol. 2, pp. 93–94.   [W2a,2]

On Cabet: "The cry was not: Let us emigrate to America and there, with utmost exertion, found a colony in the wilderness. . . . Rather, Cabet was saying: 'Let us go to Icaria!' . . . Let us enter boldly into this novel, let us give life to Icaria, let us free ourselves from all privations . . . ! Every article in his newspaper would refer henceforth to Icaria; this went so far that he would describe, for example, how several workers were injured by the explosion of a steam engine in La Villette and conclude his account with the words, 'Let us go to Icaria!'" Engländer, vol. 2, pp. 120–121.   [W2a,3]

On Cabet: "Most of the correspondents write as though they have escaped the general destiny of humanity by journeying to America." [This pertains to the correspondents for *Le Populaire*.] Engländer, vol. 2, p. 128.   [W2a,4]

"Cabet, whom the radical republican party attacked because they considered him an opiate-monger," had to "remove to Saint-Quentin . . . so as to defend himself from accusations of revolutionary agitation. The accusation was to the effect that, even if the Icarians should embark with Cabet, they would disembark at another point on the coast of France, in order to begin the revolution." Engländer, vol. 2, p. 142. ☐ Secret Societies ☐   [W2a,5]

"Mercury taught us to read. He brought us the alphabet, the declensions, and finally the entire grammar of the unitary Harmonian language, as spoken on the sun and the harmonized planets." Citation from Fourier, in Maurice Harmel, "Charles Fourier," *Portraits d'hier*, vol. 2, no. 36 (Paris, 1910), p. 184.

[W2a,6]

"Among all the contemporaries of Hegel, Charles Fourier was the only one who saw through bourgeois relations as clearly as he himself did." G. Plekhanov, "Zu Hegels sechzigstem Todestag," *Die neue Zeit*, 10, no. 1 (Stuttgart, 1892), p. 243.

[W2a,7]

Fourier speaks "of the ascendancy of the principle of 'industrial passion' *(fougue industrielle)*, the universal enthusiasm that is ruled by the laws . . . of the 'composite' or the 'coincident.' On a cursory inspection, it might appear as though we had reached this stage today. Industrial passion is represented by the rage to speculate and the impulse to accumulate capital; the *passion coïncidente* (drive toward incorporation), by the consolidation of capital, its increasing concentration. But even though the elements discovered by Fourier are present in this relation, they are neither articulated nor regulated in the manner he envisioned and anticipated." Charles Bonnier, "Das Fourier'sche Prinzip der Anziehung," *Die neue Zeit*, 10, no. 2 (Stuttgart, 1892), p. 648. [W3,1]

"We can see from his works that Fourier expected his theory to be accomplished beginning in the year of their publication. In his *Prolégomènes*, he designates . . . 1822 as the year when the establishment of the experimental colony of the Harmonian association was to be prepared. This colony was supposed to be actually founded and put into practice the following year, whereupon 1824 would necessarily see its general imitation by the rest of the civilized world." Charles Bonnier, "Das Fourier'sche Prinzip der Anziehung," *Die neue Zeit*, 10, no. 2 (Stuttgart, 1892), p. 642. [W3,2]

Aftereffects: "In Zola's powerful novel *Le Travail* ‹Labor›, the great utopian was supposed to celebrate his resurrection. . . . Leconte de Lisle, later the famous leader of the Parnassian school, was, in his Sturm-und-Drang period, a singer of Fourierist socialism. A contributor to *La Revue socialiste* . . . [see the November 1901 issue] informs us that, at the invitation of the editors of *La Démocratie pacifique*, . . . the poet contributed first to this latter journal and then briefly to *La Phalange*." H. Thurow, "Aus den Anfängen der sozialistischen Belletristik," *Die neue Zeit*, 21, no. 2 (Stuttgart, 1903), p. 221. [W3,3]

"The political economists and politicians from whom the pre-1848 socialists had learned were, in every case, opposed to strikes. They explained to the workers that a strike, even though successful, would bring them no advantage, and that the workers should put their money into cooperatives for production and consumption rather than into plans for a strike." Proudhon "had . . . the ingenious idea of inciting the workers to strike in order not to increase their wages but to lower them. . . . In this way, the worker obtains two or three times more as a consumer than he earns as a producer." ‹Paul› Lafargue, "Der Klassenkampf in Frankreich," *Die neue Zeit*, 12, no. 2 (1894), pp. 644, 616.   [W3,4]

"Fourier, Saint-Simon, and other reformers recruited their followers almost exclusively from the ranks of the artisans . . . and from the intellectual elite of the bourgeoisie. With a few exceptions, it was educated people who gathered around them, people who thought they had not received from society consideration sufficient to their merits. . . . It was the *déclassés*, those who had transformed themselves into daring entrepreneurs, shrewd businessmen, or speculators. . . . M. Godin, for example, . . . founded in Guise (in the *département* of Aisne) a *familistère* according to Fourier's principles. In handsome buildings surrounding a spacious, glass-covered square courtyard, he provided accommodations for numerous workers from his plate-enameling factory; here they found, besides a home, all necessary articles for daily use . . . , entertainments in a theater, concerts, schools for their children, and so on. In short, M. Godin saw to all their physical and spiritual needs, and moreover realized . . . enormous profits. He earned the reputation of being a benefactor of mankind, and died a multimillionaire." Paul Lafargue, "Der Klassenkampf in Frankreich," *Die neue Zeit*, 12, no. 2 (Stuttgart, 1894), p. 617.   [W3a,1]

Fourier on stocks and bonds: "In his *Traité de l'unité universelle*, Fourier enumerates . . . the advantages which this form of property offers the capitalists: 'It does not run the danger of being stolen or damaged through fire or earthquake. . . . A minor never risks being taken advantage of in the administration of his money, since that administration is the same for him as for every other shareholder . . . ; a capitalist can realize his property at any moment, even though he owned a hundred million'; and so forth. . . . On the other hand, 'the poor man, though he have but one taler, can participate in the holding of public stock, which is divided up into quite small portions, . . . and hence . . . can speak of *our* palaces, *our* storehouses, *our* wealth.' Napoleon III and his cohorts in the coup d'état were very taken with these ideas; . . . they democratized state revenue, as one of them put it, by making it possible to purchase bonds for five francs or even one franc. By such methods, they thought to interest the masses in the solidity of public credit and preclude political revolutions." Paul Lafargue, "Marx' historischer Materialismus," *Die neue Zeit*, 22, no. 1 (Stuttgart, 1904), p. 831.   [W3a,2]

"Fourier is not only a critic; his imperturbably serene nature makes him a satirist, and assuredly one of the greatest satirists of all time." Engels,[3] cited in Rudolf Franz, review of E. Silberling's *Dictionnaire de sociologie phalanstérienne* (Paris, 1911), *Die neue Zeit*, 30, no. 1 (Stuttgart, 1912), p. 333.   [W3a,3]

The propagation of the phalanstery takes place through an "explosion." Fourier speaks of an "explosion du phalanstère."   [W3a,4]

In England, the influence of Fourier combined with that of Swedenborg.
                    [W3a,5]

"Heine was well acquainted with socialism. He could still see Fourier in person. In his articles entitled *Französische Zustände* ⟨French Affairs⟩, he writes at one point (June 15, 1843): 'Yes, Pierre Leroux is poor, just as Saint-Simon and Fourier were poor, and by the providential poverty of these great socialists the world was enriched. . . . Fourier likewise had recourse to the charity of friends. How often have I seen him scurrying past the columns of the Palais-Royal in his shabby gray coat, both pockets laden so that out of one was peeping the neck of a bottle and out of the other a long loaf of bread. The friend of mine who first pointed him out to me drew my attention to the indigence of the man, who had to fetch drink for himself at the wineshop and bread at the bakery.'"[4] Cited in "Heine an Marx," *Die neue Zeit*, 14, no. 1 (Stuttgart, 1896), p. 16; passage originally in ⟨Heine,⟩ *Sämtliche Werke*, ed. Bölsche (Leipzig), vol. 5, p. 34 ["Kommunismus, Philosophie, und Klerisei," part 1].   [W4,1]

"In his glosses to the memoirs of Annenkov, Marx writes: '. . . Fourier was the first to mock the idealization of the petty bourgeoisie.'" Reported by P. Anski, "Zur Charakteristik von Marx," *Russkaia Mysl* (August 1903), p. 63; in N. Rjasanoff, "Marx und seine russischen Bekannten in den vierziger Jahren," *Die neue Zeit*, 31, no. 1 (Stuttgart, 1913), p. 764.   [W4,2]

"Herr Grün finds it an easy matter to criticize Fourier's treatment of love; he measures Fourier's criticism of existing amorous relationships against the fantasies by which Fourier tried to get a mental image of free love. Herr Grün, the true German philistine, takes these fantasies seriously. Indeed, they are the only thing which he does take seriously. It is hard to see why, if he wanted to deal with this side of the system at all, Grün did not also enlarge upon Fourier's remarks concerning education; they are by far the best of their kind, and contain some masterly observations. . . . 'Fourier is the very worst expression of civilized egoism' (p. 208). He supplies immediate proof of this by relating that, in Fourier's world order, the poorest member eats from forty dishes every day, that five meals are eaten daily, that people live to the age of 144, and so on. With a naive sense of humor, Fourier opposes a Gargantuan view of man to the unassuming mediocrity of the men [in *Das Westphälische Dampfboot*, the following words . . . inserted after 'men': 'the infinitely small—Béranger'] of the Restoration period; but Herr Grün sees in this merely a chance of moralizing in his philistine way upon the most innocent side of Fourier's fancy, which he abstracts from the rest." Karl Marx writing about Karl Grün as historian of socialism (in an article originally published in *Das Westphälische Dampfboot*, August–September 1847), reprinted in *Die neue Zeit*, 18, no. 1 (Stuttgart, 1900), pp. 137–138.[5]   [W4,3]

The phalanstery can be characterized as human machinery. This is no reproach, nor is it meant to indicate anything mechanistic; rather, it refers to the great complexity of its structure ⟨*Aufbau*⟩. The phalanstery is a machine made of human beings.   [W4,4]

Fourier's point of departure: the reflection on small business. Compare, in this connection, the following: "When one considers the number of people in Paris whose lives depend on small business—the size of this formidable army exclusively occupied with measuring, weighing, packaging, and transporting from one end of town to the other—one is rightly alarmed. . . . It must be recalled that, in our industrial cities, a shop is generally run by three or four families. . . . 'Sordidi etiam qui mercantur a mercatoribus quod statim vendant; nihil enim proficiunt nisi admodum mentiantur. Nec vero quicquam est turpius vanitate' (*De Officiis*).[6] . . . The current president of the Chamber of Commerce last year formally requested once again, as a remedy for commercial anarchy, the reestablishment of guilds." Eugène Buret, *De la Misère des classes laborieuses en Angleterre et en France* (Paris, 1840), vol. 2, pp. 216–218. [W4a,1]

"The modern proletariat's lack of history, the detachment of the first generation of factory workers from every historical tradition of class and profession, and the diversity of its origin—in handicrafts, small landholdings, agrarian labor, and domestic concerns of every sort—made this category of economic man receptive to a vision of the world that would improvise ex novo a new state, a new economy, and a new morality. The novelty of what was to be achieved corresponded logically to the novelty of the situation in which the new men and women found themselves." Robert Michels, "Psychologie der antikapitalistischen Massenbewegungen," p. 313 [*Grundriss der Sozialökonomik*, vol. 9, no. 1, *Die gesellschaftliche Schichtung im Kapitalismus* (Tübingen, 1926)]. [W4a,2]

"Grandville's life is unremarkable enough: peaceful, remote from all excess, at the periphery of dangerous enthusiasms. . . . His youth was that of an honest clerk in a respectable shop, where, on rows of spotless shelves, were arrayed—not without malice—the various images that corresponded to the need for criticism which an 'average Frenchman' might feel in 1827." ⟨Pierre⟩ MacOrlan, "Grandville le précurseur," *Arts et métiers graphiques*, 44 (December 15, 1934) ⟨p. 20⟩.
[W4a,3]

Fourier and Saint-Simon: "Fourier is more interesting and more diversified in his economic analysis and in his critique of the existing social order. But, then, Saint-Simon has the advantage over Fourier in his representations of future economic development. Obviously, this development had to move . . . in the direction of a global economy . . . , and not in the direction of many self-sufficient little economies, such as Fourier imagined. Saint-Simon conceives the capitalist order . . . as a step . . . , while Fourier rejects it in the name of the petty bourgeoisie." V. Volgin, "Über die historische Stellung Saint-Simons," in (*Marx-Engels Archiv*, vol. 1 ⟨Frankfurt am Main, 1928⟩, p. 118. [W4a,4]

"In an exchange of views with the writer Camille Mauclair, . . . Zola . . . declared unequivocally that he bore no love for collectivism; he found it smallhearted and utopian. He was an anarchist rather than a socialist. . . . Utopian socialism, . . . as he saw it, took its rise from the individual workshop, proceeded to the idea of the association of producers, and aimed to achieve a communism of the general community. This was before 1848. . . . Zola, however, wanted to revive the method of this period; he . . . took up the . . . ideas of Fourier, which were conditioned by the embryonic relations of capitalist production, and attempted to ally them to the modern form of this production, which had grown to gigantic proportions." Franz Diederich, "Zola als Utopist" (on *Le Travail*), *Die neue Zeit*, 20, no. 1 (Stuttgart), pp. 326–327, 329. [W5,1]

Fourier (in *Le Nouveau Monde industriel et sociétaire*, 1829) disapproves of the contempt for gastronomy. "This gaucherie is yet another of those exploits of morality calculated to turn us into enemies of our own senses, and into friends of that commercial activity which serves merely to provoke the abuses of sensual pleasure." E. Poisson, *Fourier* [contains selected texts] (Paris, 1932), p. 131. Thus, Fourier here views immoral businesses as a complement to idealist morality. To both he opposes his hedonistic materialism. His position recalls, from afar, that of Georg Büchner. The words quoted above might have been spoken by Büchner's Danton. [W5,2]

"A phalanx does not sell a thousand quintals of flour of indifferent quality; it sells a thousand quintals classified according to a scale of five, six, or seven varieties of flavor, which it has tested in a bakery and distinguished in terms of the field where it was harvested and the method of cultivation. . . . Such an agricultural mechanism will contrast sharply with the practices of our backward world, our civilization so in need of perfecting. . . . We see among ourselves, furthermore, merchandise of inferior quality that is twenty times more abundant and more easily sold than better-quality goods. . . . As a result of this circumstance, we can no longer even recognize the inferior quality; morality accustoms the civilized to eating the good and the bad indiscriminately. From this coarseness of taste follow all the knaveries of mercantilism." *Théorie des quatre mouvements* (1828), cited in E. Poisson, *Fourier* (Paris, 1932), pp. 134–135.[7]—Already children are taught to "clean their plates." [W5,3]

"Knowing . . . that sometimes, in the region of the North Pole, there is generated an electrical discharge which lights up those lands plunged in darkness for six months of the year, Fourier announces that, when the earth shall have been rationally cultivated in all its parts, the aurora borealis will be continuous. Is this absurd?" The author endeavors, following this, to provide an explanation: the transformed earth will absorb less electricity from the sun, and whatever is not absorbed will encircle it as a ring of Northern Lights. Charles-M. Limousin, *Le Fouriérisme: Réponse à un article de Edmond Villey intitulé "Fourier et son oeuvre"* (Paris, 1898), p. 6. [W5a,1]

"There would be nothing very surprising in the fact that Fourier had been associated . . . with a Martinist lodge, or at the very least had felt the influence of a milieu in which such ideas flourished." Charles-M. Limousin, *Le Fouriérisme* (Paris, 1898), p. 9. [W5a,2]

Worthy of note is the fact—to which Limousin adverts—that, with Fourier, the desire for possession is not a "passion." This same commentator defines the concept of *passion mécanisante* as that passion which governs the play of the others. He remarks further (p. 15): "Fourier was surely wrong to make a joke of duty." Certainly apt is his observation (p. 17) that Fourier is more an inventor than a scientist. [W5a,3]

"In Fourier, occult science acquires a new form—that of industry." Ferrari, "Des Idées et de l'école de Fourier," *Revue des deux mondes*, 11, no. 3 (1845), p. 405. [W5a,4]

On Fourier's machinal mode of conception. The table entitled "Mesh of the Lodgments of Harmony" establishes, for apartments in street-galleries, twenty different categories of rentals, priced from 50 to 1,000 francs, and offers, among others, the following justification: "This meshing of the six series is a law of the twelfth passion. The simple progression, whether constantly increasing or decreasing, would have very serious drawbacks. In principle, it would be false and deleterious, insofar as it was simple. . . . In application, it would be injurious, insofar as . . . it gave to the body of dwellings in the wings . . . the appearance of an inferior class. Care must be taken to avoid this arrangement, which would be simple and therefore detrimental to the meshing of the different classes."[8] Thus, within a single section of the street-galleries, lodgers of different social standing will reside together. "I put off discussion of the stables . . . , about which I shall furnish . . . ample details in special chapters to follow. For now, our concern is with lodgments, of which one part alone—the street-gallery, the hall of universal linkage— conclusively proves that, after 3,000 years of research into architecture, civilized men have yet to learn anything about the bond of unity." Cited in E. Poisson, *Fourier* [anthology] (Paris, 1932), pp. 145–146. [W5a,5]

Aspects of Fourierist number mysticism, according to Ferrari, "Des Idées et de l'école de Fourier" (*Revue des deux mondes*, 14, no. 3 [Paris, 1845]): "Everything indicates that Fourierism bases itself on the Pythagorean harmony. . . . Its science was the science of the ancients" (p. 397). "Number reproduces its rhythm in the evaluation of earnings" (p. 398). The inhabitants of the phalanstery comprise $2 \times$ 810 men and women; for "the number 810 gives them a complete series of chords corresponding to the multitude of cabalist assonances" (p. 396). "If, with Fourier, the science of the occult takes on a new form, that of industry, it should not be forgotten that form per se counts for nothing in this airy poetry of the mystagogies" (p. 405). "Number groups all beings according to its symbolic laws; it develops all the groups through series; the series distributes the harmonies throughout the universe. . . . For the series . . . is perfect throughout all of nature. . . . Man alone is unhappy; hence, civilization inverts the number which should govern him. Let us rescue it from civilization. . . . The order that dominates physical movement—organic movement, animal movement—will thus radiate in . . . passional movement; nature itself will organize the association" (p. 395–396). [W6,1]

Foreshadowing of the bourgeois king in Fourier: "He speaks of kings who devote themselves to locksmithery, to woodworking, to selling fish, to the manufacture of sealing wax." Ferrari, "Des Idées et de l'école de Fourier," *Revue des deux mondes*, 14, no. 3 (1845) p. 393. [W6,2]

"All his life, Fourier was engaged in thinking; but he never once asked himself where his ideas came from. He portrays the human being as a *machine passionnelle*; his psychology begins with the senses and ends with the composite, without presupposing . . . the intervention of reason in the solution of the problem of happiness." Ferrari, "Des Idées et de l'école de Fourier," *Revue des deux mondes*, no. 3 (1845), p. 404. [W6,3]

Utopian elements: "The combined order comprises 'the glory of the arts and sciences, the spectacle of knight-errantry, gastronomy combined in a political sense, . . . and a *politique galante* for the levy of troops" (Ferrari, p. 399). "The world turns to its antitype, as dangerous and savage animals enter the service of mankind: lions are used for delivering the mail. The aurora borealis reheats the poles; the atmosphere, at the earth's surface, becomes clear as a mirror; the seas grow calm; and four moons light up the night. In short, the earth renews itself twenty-eight times, until the great soul of our planet (now enfeebled, exhausted) passes on, with all its human souls, to another planet" (Ferrari, p. 401). [W6,4]

"Fourier excels in the observation of animality, whether in beasts or in men. He has a genius for common matters." Ferrari, "Des Idées et de l'école de Fourier," *Revue des deux mondes*, 14, no. 3 (1845), p. 393. [W6a,1]

A Fourierist formula: "Nero will be more useful than Fénelon" (in Ferrari, p. 399). [W6a,2]

In the following scheme of twelve passions, the four in the second group represent the *passions groupantes*, the three in the third group the *passions sériantes*: "first the five senses; then love, friendship, family feeling, ambition; third, the passions for intrigue, for mutability, for union—in other words, the cabalist, the butterfly, the composite; a thirteenth passion, 'unityism,' absorbs all the others." Ferrari, "Des Idées et de l'école de Fourier," *Revue des deux mondes*, 14, no. 3 (1845), p. 394. [W6a,3]

From Fourier's last work, *La Fausse Industrie* ‹1835–1836›: "The celebrated American hoax associated with Herschel's discoveries about the world of the moon[9] had raised in Fourier, once the hoax was revealed as such, the hope of a direct vision of the phalanstery on other planets. . . . Here is Fourier's response:

'The American hoax,' he declares, 'proves, first, the anarchy of the press; second, the barrenness of storytellers concerned with the extraterrestrial; third, man's ignorance of the atmospheric shells; fourth, the need for a megatelescope.'" Ferrari, "Des Idées et de l'école de Fourier," *Revue des deux mondes*, 14, no. 3 (1845), p. 415.   [W6a,4]

Allegorical specimens from *La Fausse Industrie*. "On earth Venus creates the mulberry bush, symbol of morality, and the raspberry filled with verse, symbol of the countermorality preached in the theaters." Ferrari, "Des Idées et de l'école de Fourier," *Revue des deux mondes*, no. 3 (1845), p. 416.   [W6a,5]

"According to Fourier, the phalanstery should be able to earn, merely from spectators alone, 50 million francs in two years." Ferrari, "Des Idées et de l'école de Fourier," *Revue des deux mondes*, no. 3 (1845), p. 412.   [W6a,6]

"The phalanstery, for Fourier, was a veritable hallucination. He saw it everywhere, both in civilization and in nature. Never was he lacking for a military parade; the drilling of soldiers was for him a representation of the all-powerful play of the group and of the series inverted for a work of destruction." Ferrari, "Des Idées et de l'école de Fourier," *Revue des deux mondes*, no. 3 (1845), p. 409.   [W6a,7]

Fourier, in connection with a proposal for a miniature pedagogical colony: "Fulton was supposed to have constructed or merely drawn up plans for a delicate little launch that would have demonstrated, on a miniature scale, the power of steam. This skiff was to have transported from Paris to Saint-Cloud—without sails or oars or horses—a half-dozen nymphs, who, on their return from Saint-Cloud, would have publicized the prodigy and put all the Parisian *beau monde* in a flutter." Ferrari, "Des Idées et de l'école de Fourier," *Revue des deux mondes*, no. 3 (1845), p. 414.   [W7,1]

"The plan to encircle Paris with fortifications would squander hundreds of millions of francs for reasons of defense, whereas this magician, with only a million, would root out forever the cause of all wars and all revolutions." Ferrari, "Des Idées et de l'école de Fourier," *Revue des deux mondes*, 14, no. 3 (1845), p. 413.   [W7,2]

Michelet on Fourier: "Singular contrast between his boast of materialism and his self-sacrificing, disinterested, and spiritual life!" J. Michelet, *Le Peuple* (Paris, 1846), p. 294.[10]   [W7,3]

Fourier's conception of the propagation of the phalansteries through "explosions" may be compared to two articles of my "politics": the idea of revolution as an innervation of the technical organs of the collective (analogy with the child who learns to grasp by trying to get hold of the moon), and the idea of the "cracking open of natural teleology." ⟨See W8a,5 and X1a,2.⟩   [W7,4]

Fourier, *Oeuvres*, vol. ⟨3⟩, p. 260: "List of charges to be brought against God, on the hypothesis of a gap in the divine social code."   [W7,5]

A take on the ideas of Fourier: "King Clodomir, restored by harmony to his natural vocation, is no longer that ferocious Merovingian who has his confrere Sigismond thrown into a pit. 'He is a friend of flowers and of verse, an active partisan of musk roses, of golden plums and fresh pineapples, and many another growing thing. . . . He weds the vestal Antigone and follows her as troubadour to join the Hippocrene phalanx.' And Louis XVI, instead of filling so pitiably the job of king for which he was hardly cut out, makes magnificent door locks." Charles Louandre, *Les Idées subversives de notre temps* (Paris, 1872), p. 59 [citation given without indication of source].   [W7,6]

Delvau, in *Les Lions du jour* (Paris, 1867), p. 5, speaks of Fourier's "ingenious argot."   [W7,7]

"It is easy to understand that every 'interest' on the part of the masses . . . goes far beyond its real limits in the 'idea' or 'imagination' when it first comes on the scene, and is confused with human interest in general. This illusion constitutes what Fourier calls the 'tone' of each historical epoch." Marx and Engels, *Die heilige Familie*, in *Der historische Materialismus*, vol. 1 ⟨Leipzig, 1932⟩, p. 379.[11]
                                                    [W7,8]

Augustin-Louis Cauchy is mentioned by Toussenel (*L'Esprit des bêtes* [Paris, 1884], p. 111)[12] as a mathematician with Fourierist leanings.   [W7a,1]

In a passage concerned with Malthusianism, Toussenel explains that the solution to the problem resides in the double (= filled?) rose of Rhodes, whose stamen-filaments have been transformed into petals, "and which consequently becomes barren by exuberance of sap and of richness. In other words, . . . so long as misery shall continue increasing, the fecundity of the female sex will follow the same course; and there is but one method of curbing this continual prolification— namely, to surround all women with the delights of luxury. . . . Except through luxury . . . , except through general riches, no salvation!" A. Toussenel, *L'Esprit des bêtes: Zoologie passionnel* (Paris, 1884), p. 85.[13]   [W7a,2]

On the feminism of the Fourierist school: "On Herschel and Jupiter, botany courses are taught by young vestals of eighteen to twenty. . . . When I say 'eighteen to twenty,' I speak the language of Earth, since the years on Jupiter are twelve times longer than ours, and the vestalate begins only toward the hundredth year." A. Toussenel, *L'Esprit des bêtes* (Paris, 1884), p. 93.[14]   [W7a,3]

A model of Fourierist psychology in Toussenel's chapter on the wild boar. "Now, surrounding the dwellings of humanity are great quantities of broken glass bottles, rusty nails, and candle ends, which would be completely lost to society if some careful and intelligent hand did not charge itself with the collection of all these valueless relics, to reconstruct out of them a mass susceptible of being reworked and made fit for consumption again. This important task evidently belongs among the attributes of the miser. . . . Here the character and mission of the miser perceptibly rise: the pinch-penny becomes a ragpicker, a salvage operator. . . . The hog is the great salvager of nature; he fattens at nobody's expense." A. Toussenel, *L'Esprit des bêtes* (Paris, 1884), pp. 249–250.[15]   [W7a,4]

Marx characterizes the insufficiency of Fourier, who conceived "a particular form of labor—labor leveled down, parceled, and therefore unfree—. . . as the source of private property's perniciousness and of its existence in estrangement from men," instead of denouncing labor as such, as the essence of private property. Karl Marx, *Der historische Materialismus*, ed. Landshut and Mayer (Leipzig ‹1932›), vol. 1, p. 292 ("Nationalökonomie und Philosophie").[16]   [W7a,5]

Fourierist pedagogy, like the pedagogy of Jean Paul, should be studied in the context of anthropological materialism. In this, the role of anthropological materialism in France should be compared with its role in Germany. It might turn out that there, in France, it was the human collective that stood at the center of interests, while here, in Germany, it was the human individual. We must note, as well, that anthropological materialism attained sharper definition in Germany because its opposite, idealism, was more clearly delineated over there. The history of anthropological materialism stretches, in Germany, from Jean Paul to Keller (passing through Georg Büchner and Gutzkow); in France, the socialist utopias and the physiologies are its precipitate.   [W8,1]

Madame de Cardoville, a *grande dame* in *Le Juif errant* ‹The Wandering Jew›, is a Fourierist.   [W8,2]

In connection with Fourierist pedagogy, one should perhaps investigate the dialectic of the example: although the example as model (in the moralists' sense) is pedagogically worthless, if not disastrous, the gestic example can become the object of a controllable and progressively assimilable imitation, one that possesses the greatest significance.   [W8,3]

"*La Phalange, journal de la science sociale* (1836–1843), which appears three times a week, . . . will fade from the scene only when it can cede its place to a daily, *La Démocratie pacifique* (1843–1851). Here, the main idea . . . is 'the organization of labor' through the association." Charles Benoist, "L'Homme de 1848," part 2, *Revue des deux mondes* (February 1, 1914), p. 645.   [W8,4]

From Nettement's discussion of Fourier: "In creating the present world, God reserved the right to change its outward aspect through subsequent creations. These creations are eighteen in number. Every creation is brought about by a conjunction of austral fluid and boreal fluid." The later creations, following on the first, can eventuate only in Harmony. Alfred Nettement, *Histoire de la littérature française sous le gouvernement de juillet* (Paris, 1859), vol. 2, p. 58.   [W8,5]

"According to him ⟨Fourier⟩, souls transmigrate from body to body, and even from world to world. Each planet possesses a soul, which will go to animate some other, superior planet, carrying with it, as it does so, the souls of those people who have inhabited it. It is thus that, before the end of our planet earth (which is supposed to endure 81,000 years), the human souls upon it will have gone through 1,620 existences; they will have lived a total of 27,000 years on earth and 54,000 years on another planet. . . . In the exertions of its earliest infancy, the earth was struck by a putrid fever that eventually spread to the moon, which died as a result. But once organized in Harmony, the earth will resuscitate the moon." Nettement, *Histoire de la littérature française sous le gouvernement de juillet*, vol. 2, pp. 57, 59.   [W8,6]

The Fourierist on the subject of aviation: "The buoyant aerostat . . . is the chariot of fire, which . . . respects above all the works of God; it does not need to aggrade the valleys or tunnel through mountains in imitation of the murderous locomotive, which the speculator has dishonored." A. Toussenel, *Le Monde des oiseaux*, vol. 1 (Paris, 1853), p. 6.   [W8a,1]

"It is impossible . . . that zebras, quaggas, hemiones, and pygmy ponies, who know they are destined to serve as steeds for the children's cavalry of the future, are sympathetic with the policy of our statesmen, who treat as merely utopian the equestrian institutions where these animals are to hold a position of honor. . . . The lion likes nothing better . . . than having its nails trimmed, provided it is a pretty girl that wields the scissors." A. Toussenel, *Le Monde des oiseaux: Ornithologie passionnelle*, vol. 1 (Paris, 1853), pp. 19–20. The author sees in woman the intermediary between human and animal.   [W8a,2]

Memorable letter from Victor Cousin to Jean Journet, in response to writings sent him by the latter. It is dated October 23, 1843, and concludes: "When you are suffering, think not of social regeneration but of God, . . . who did not create man only for happiness but for an end quite otherwise sublime." The prefacer adds: "We would have consigned this little anecdote to oblivion, had not this poor letter . . . , a true masterpiece of perfect ignorance, summed up . . . the political science . . . of a coterie that, for the past twenty-one years, has overseen . . . the fortunes of our country." Jean Journet, *Poésies et chants harmoniens* (Paris, 1857), pp. xxvi–xxvii (editor's preface).   [W8a,3]

"The history of the . . . human races on Jupiter and Saturn teaches us that civilization . . . is on its way to guarantism . . . by virtue of the political equality between man and woman, and from guarantism to Harmony through the recognition of the superiority of woman." A. Toussenel, *Le Monde des oiseaux*, vol. 1 (Paris, 1853), p. 131.   [W8a,4]

Fourier's long-tailed men became the object of caricature, in 1849, with erotic drawings by Emy in *Le Rire*. For the purpose of elucidating the Fourierist extravagances, we may adduce the figure of Mickey Mouse, in which we find carried out, entirely in the spirit of Fourier's conceptions, the moral mobilization of nature. Humor, here, puts politics to the test. Mickey Mouse shows how right Marx was to see in Fourier, above all else, a great humorist. The cracking open of natural teleology proceeds in accordance with the plan of humor.   [W8a,5]

Affiliation of anti-Semitism with Fourierism. In 1845, *Les Juifs rois* ‹The Jewish Kings›, by Toussenel, appears. Toussenel is, moreover, the partisan of a "democratic royalty."   [W8a,6]

"The line . . . generally associated with the family group is the parabola. This postulate is demonstrated in the work of the Old Masters, and above all in Raphael. . . . From the approximation of this grouping to the parabolic type, there results, in the oeuvre of Raphael, a hymn to the family, . . . masterful and . . . divine. . . . The master thinker, who determined the analogies of the four conic sections, has recognized the correspondence of the parabola and of familyism. And here we find the confirmation of this proposition in the prince of painters, in Raphael." D. Laverdant, *De la Mission de l'art et du rôle des artistes: Salon de 1845* (Paris, 1845), p. 64.   [W9,1]

Delvau (*Les Dessous de Paris* ‹Paris, 1860›, p. 27) sees connections between Fourier and Restif de La Bretonne.   [W9,2]

Highly characteristic of the relation of the Fourierists to the Saint-Simonians is Considérant's polemic against the railroads. This polemic relies, for the most part, on Hoëné Wronski, *Sur la Barbarie des chemins de fer et sur la réforme scientifique de la locomotion*. Wronski's first objection is directed against the system of iron rails; Considérant indicts "the process operating under the name 'railway system,' that is to say, the construction of very long flat roads equipped with metallic rails and requiring enormous amounts of money and labor—a process 'not only opposed to the actual progress of civilization, but contrasting all the more strongly with this progress in that it presents something truly ridiculous: the barbarous contemporary reproduction of the massive and inert roadways of the Romans' (*Pétition aux Chambres,* p. 11)." Considérant opposes the "barbarous means," which is "simplistic," to the "scientific means," which is "composite" (pp. 40–41). At another point, he says explicitly: "For this *simplisme* has led, just as one would expect, to a result that is completely barbarian: that of the ever more ineluctable leveling of roads" (p. 44). By the same token: "Horizontality is a proper condition when it is a question of communications over water. The system of terrestrial locomotion, on the other hand, evidently ought to be capable of putting . . . different elevations in communication with one another" (p. 53). A second and related objection of Wronski's is directed against travel on wheels, which he describes as "a well-known and extremely vulgar process . . . , in use since the invention of the chariot." Here, too, he stresses the lack of any genuine scientific and complex character. Victor Considérant, *Déraison et dangers de l'engouement pour les chemins en fer* (Paris, 1838). The contents first appeared, in large part, in *La Phalange*. [W9,3]

Considérant argues that the work of engineers should be focused not on the improvement of the track but on the improvement of the means of transport. Wronski, to whom he refers, appears to be thinking primarily of an improved form of wheel or of its replacement by something else. Thus, Considérant writes: "Is it not clear . . . that the discovery of a machine that would facilitate locomotion over ordinary routes, and increase . . . the present speed of transportation on these routes, would devastate, from top to bottom, the entire enterprise of the railroads? . . . Hence, a discovery not only possible but indeed probable can annihilate, at one blow and forever, the extraordinary amounts of capital that some people have proposed be sunk into the railway system!" Victor Considérant, *Déraison et dangers de l'engouement pour les chemins en fer* (Paris, 1838), p. 63. [W9a,1]

"The operation of railroads . . . forced humanity into the position of combating nature's works everywhere on earth, of filling up valleys and breaching mountains, . . . of struggling finally, by means of a general system, against the natural conditions of the planet's terrain, . . . and replacing them *universally* by the opposite sort of conditions." Victor Considérant, *Déraison et dangers de l'engouement pour les chemins en fer* (Paris, 1838), pp. 52–53. [W9a,2]

Charles Gide on the "divinatory genius" of Fourier : "When he writes: 'A certain vessel from London arrives in China today; tomorrow the planet Mercury, having been advised of the arrivals and movements of ships by the astronomers of Asia, will transmit the list to the astronomers of London,' and if we transpose this prophecy into current vernacular so that it reads, 'When a ship arrives in China, the T. S. F. will transmit the news to the Eiffel Tower or to London,' then it is clear, I believe, that we have here an extraordinary anticipation. For what he means to say is precisely this: the planet Mercury is there to represent a force, as yet unknown, which would enable the transmission of messages—a force of which he has had a presentiment." Charles Gide, *Fourier précurseur de la coopération* (Paris ⟨1924⟩), p. 10–11.[17] [W9a,3]

Charles Gide on Fourier's nonsensical astrological speculations: "He tells us that the planets Juno, Ceres, and Pallas each produce a species of gooseberry, and that there ought to be a fourth and still more excellent kind, of which we are deprived because the planet Phoebe (the moon), which would have generated it, is unfortunately dead." Charles Gide, *Fourier précurseur de la coopération* (Paris), p. 10.[18] [W9a,4]

"When he speaks . . . of a celestial army which the Sidereal Council has resolved to send to the aid of Humanity, an army already dispatched some 1,700 years ago and having before it more than 300 years of travel until it arrives in the confines of our solar system, . . . we shudder a little at the hint of Apocalypse. In other places this lunacy is more amiable, bordering often on wisdom, abounding in fine and witty observations, a bit like the harangues on the topic of the Golden Age that Don Quixote in the Sierra Morena addressed to the astonished goatherds." Charles Gide, *Fourier précurseur de la coopération* (Paris), p. 11.[19]   [W10,1]

"One could say, and he says it himself, that his observatory—or his laboratory, if you prefer—is the kitchen. It is his point of departure for radiating into all the domains of social life." Charles Gide, *Fourier précurseur de la coopération* (Paris), p. 20.   [W10,2]

On the theory of attraction: "Bernardin de Saint-Pierre denied the force of gravity . . . because it signified an infringement on the free exercise of providence; and the astronomer Laplace struggled . . . no less violently . . . against the fanciful generalizations of this force. But that did not prevent the doctrines of an Azaïs and like-minded others . . . from finding their imitators. Henri de Saint-Simon . . . was occupied for years with the elaboration of a system of 'universal gravitation,' and in 1810 he came out with the following credo: 'I believe in God. I believe that God created the universe. I believe that God made the universe subject to the law of gravitation.' Fourier likewise founded . . . his . . . system on the 'force of universal attraction,' of which sympathy between one man and another is said to be but a special case." Ernst Robert Curtius, *Balzac* (Bonn, 1923), p. 45 (Azaïs, 1766–1845, *Des Compensations dans les destinées humaines*).   [W10,3]

Relation of the *Communist Manifesto* to the draft by Engels: "The organization of labor (a concession to Louis Blanc) and the construction, on state-owned lands, of large communal palaces designed to bridge the gap between city and country (a concession to the Fourierists of the *Démocratie Pacifique*) were items which derived from Engels' draft and which the final version of the manifesto left out." Gustav Mayer, *Friedrich Engels*, vol. 1, *Friedrich Engels in seiner Frühzeit*, 2nd ed. (Berlin ‹1933›), p. 288.   [W10,4]

Engels on Fourier: "'It is Morgan's work which throws into bold relief the whole brilliance of Fourier's critique of civilization,' he announced to Kautsky while working on his *Ursprung der Familie*. In this book itself, however, he wrote: 'The lowest interests . . . usher in the new, civilized society, the class-based society. The most outrageous means . . . topple the old, classless, gentile society.'" Cited in Gustav Mayer, *Friedrich Engels*, vol. 2, *Engels und der Aufstieg der Arbeiterbewegung in Europa* (Berlin ‹1933›), p. 439.[20]   [W10a,1]

Marx on Proudhon, in a letter to Kugelmann, October 9, 1866: "His sham criticism and sham opposition to the utopians (he himself is only a petty-bourgeois utopian, whereas in the utopias of a Fourier, an Owen, and others, there is the anticipation and imaginative expression of a new world) attracted and corrupted first the *jeunesse brilliante*, the students, and then the workmen, particularly those of Paris, who, as workers in luxury trades, are strongly attached, without knowing it, to the old rubbish." Karl Marx and Friedrich Engels, *Ausgewählte Brief*, ed. Adoratski (Moscow and Leningrad, 1934) ⟨p. 174⟩.[21]   [W10a,2]

"When property has been abolished throughout Germany, these ultra-clever Berliners will set up a *Démocratie Pacifique* on the Hasenheide. . . . Watch out! A new Messiah will presently arise in the Uckermark—a Messiah who will tailor Fourier to accord with Hegel, erect a phalanstery upon the eternal categories, and lay it down as an eternal law of the self-developing idea that capital, talent, and labor all have a definite share in the product. This will be the New Testament of Hegelianism; old Hegel will be the Old Testament; the 'state,' the law, will be a 'taskmaster over Christ'; and the phalanstery, in which the privies are located in accordance with logical necessity, will be the 'new Heaven' and the 'new Earth,' the new Jerusalem descending from heaven decked out like a bride." Engels to Marx, Barmen, November 19, 1844, in Karl Marx and Friedrich Engels, *Briefwechsel*, vol. 1, 1844–1853, ed. Marx-Engels-Lenin Institut (Moscow and Leningrad, 1935), p. 11.[22]   [W10a,3]

Only in the summery middle of the nineteenth century, only under its sun, can one conceive of Fourier's fantasy materialized.   [W10a,4]

"Cultivate in children the sharp ears of a rhinoceros or a cossack." Ch. Fourier, *Le Nouveau Monde industriel et sociétaire, ou Invention du procédé d'industrie attrayante et naturelle distribuée en séries passionnées* (Paris, 1829), p. 207.
                [W10a,5]

One readily grasps the importance of the culinary in Fourier; happiness has its recipes like any pudding. It is realized on the basis of a precise measuring out of different ingredients. It is an effect. Landscape, for example, signifies nothing to Fourier. He has no feeling for its romantic aspect; the miserable huts of the peasantry arouse his indignation. But let "composite agriculture" move into the area, let the little "hordes" and the little "bands"[23] spread out across it, let the noisy military marches of the industrial army play over its surface, and we have arrived at that proportion of elements needed for happiness to result.   [W11,1]

The kinship between Fourier and Sade resides in the constructive moment that is proper to all sadism. Fourier conjoins the play of colors of the imagination in a unique way with the play of numbers of his idiosyncrasy. It must be emphasized that Fourier's harmonies are not dependent on any of the traditional number-mysticisms, like that of Pythagoras or of Kepler. They are altogether his conception, and they give to the harmony something inaccessible and protected: they surround the *harmoniens* as though with barbed wire. The happiness of the phalanstery is a *bonheur barbelé*. On the other hand, Fourierist traits can be recognized in Sade. The experiences of the sadists, as presented in his *120 Jours de Sodome,* are, in their cruelty, exactly that extreme that is touched by the extreme idyllic of Fourier. *Les extremes se touchent.* The sadist, in his experiments, could chance on a partner who longs for just those punishments and humiliations which his tormentor inflicts. All at once, he could be standing in the midst of one of those harmonies sought after by the Fourierist utopia. [W11,2]

Simplism appears in Fourier as the mark of "civilization." [W11,3]

According to Fourier, the people in the vicinity of Paris, Blois, and Tours are especially suited to put their children into the trial phalanstery. The lower classes there are particularly well bred. See *Le Nouveau Monde*, p. 209. [W11a,1]

Fourier's system, as he himself explains, rests on two discoveries: that of attraction and that of the four movements (material, organic, animal, and social). [W11a,2]

Fourier speaks of a *transmission miragique* which will make it possible for London to have news from India within four hours. See Fourier, *La Fausse Industrie* (Paris, 1836), vol. 2, p. 711. [W11a,3]

"The social movement is the pattern for the three others. The animal, organic, and material movements are coordinated with the social movement, which is primary. This means that the properties of an animal, a vegetable, a mineral, or even a vortex of stars represent an effect of the human passions in the social order, and that everything, from atoms to stars, is an image of the properties of the human passions." Charles Fourier, *Théorie des quatre mouvements* (Paris, 1841), p. 47.[24] [W11a,4]

The contemplation of maps was one of Fourier's favorite occupations. [W11a,5]

Messianic timetable: 1822, preparation of the experimental canton; 1823, its opening and trial run; 1824, its imitation in all civilized nations; 1825, recruitment of the barbarians and savages; 1826, organization of the spherical hierarchy; 1826, dispatching of colonial squadrons.—The phrase *hiérarchie sphérique* should be taken to mean the "distribution of the scepters of sovereignty" (according to E. Silberling, *Dictionnaire de sociologie phalanstérienne* [Paris, 1911], p. 214). [W11a,6]

The model of the phalanstery comprises 1,620 persons—in other words, a male and a female exemplar of each of the 810 characters that, according to Fourier, exhaust all possibilities. [W11a,7]

In 1828, the poles were to become ice free. [W11a,8]

"The soul of man is an emanation of the great planetary soul, his body a portion of the planet's body. When a man dies, his body dissolves into the body of the planet and his soul fades into the planetary soul." F. Armand and R. Maublanc, *Fourier* (Paris, 1937), vol. 1, p. 111. [W11a,9]

"All children have the following dominant tastes: (1) *Ferreting*, or the penchant for handling things, exploring, running around, and constantly changing activities. (2) *Industrial din*, the taste for noisy jobs. (3) *Aping*, or the imitative mania. (4) *Working on a miniature scale*, the taste for little workshops. (5) *Progressive enticement* of the weak by the strong." Charles Fourier, *Le Nouveau Monde industriel et sociétaire* (Paris, 1829), p. 213.[25] [W12,1]

Two of the twenty-four "Sources for the blossoming of vocations": (3) The lure of hierarchical ornaments. A plume already suffices to bewitch one of our villagers to such an extent that he is ready to sign away his liberty. What, then, will be the effect of a hundred honorific adornments in the effort to enroll a child in the pleasurable association with his fellows? . . . (17) Harmony of matériel, or the unitary maneuver—something unknown in the workshops of civilization, but practiced in those of Harmony, where it is performed by the ensemble of soldiers and choreographers in a manner delightful to all children." Charles Fourier, *Le Nouveau Monde industriel et sociétaire* (Paris, 1829), pp. 215, 216. [W12,2]

Very characteristic that Fourier wants much more to keep the father away from the education of his children than the mother. "Disobedience toward the father and the teacher is . . . a perfectly natural impulse; and the child wants to command rather than obey the father." Charles Fourier, *Le Nouveau Monde industriel et sociétaire* (Paris, 1829), p. 219.[26] [W12,3]

Hierarchy of children: juveniles, gymnasians, lyceans, seraphim, cherubs, urchins, imps, weanlings, nurslings. The children are the only one of the "three sexes" that can enter "straightaway into the heart of harmony." [W12,4]

"Among the imps, we do not distinguish the two sexes by means of contrasting attire, like trousers and petticoat; that would be to risk stunting the growth of vocations and falsifying the proportion of the two sexes in each function." Fourier, *Le Nouveau Monde industriel et sociétaire* (Paris, 1829), pp. 223–224 (imps: ages one and a half to three; urchins: ages three to four and a half). [W12,5]

Tools in seven sizes. Industrial hierarchy of children: officers of various types, licentiates, bachelors, neophytes, aspirants. [W12,6]

Fourier conceives the departure for work in the fields as a sort of country outing, in large wagons and with music. [W12,7]

Qualifying examination for the choir of cherubim: (1) Musical and choreographic audition at the Opéra. (2) Washing of 120 plates in half an hour, without breaking one. (3) Peeling of half a quintal of apples in a given space of time, without allowing the weight of the fruit to drop below a certain level. (4) Perfect sifting of a quantity of rice or other grain in a fixed period of time. (5) Skill in kindling and screening a fire with intelligence and celerity." Charles Fourier, *Le Nouveau Monde industriel et sociétaire* (Paris, 1829), p. 231.   [W12a,1]

Fourier unveils "the prospect of attaining, at the age of twelve or thirteen, to a post of high dignity, such as commanding ten thousand men in a military or parade maneuver." Fourier, *Le Nouveau Monde industriel et sociétaire* (Paris, 1829), p. 234.   [W12a,2]

Names of children in Fourier: Nysas, Enryale. The educator: Hilarion.   [W12a,3]

"And so it is that, from his childhood on, a man is not compatible with simple nature; there is needed, for his education, a vast array of instruments, a multigrade and variegated apparatus, and this applies from the moment he first leaves the cradle. J.-J. Rousseau has denounced this prison in which the infant is pinioned, but he could not have known of the system of elastic mats, of the combined attentions and distractions, that would be enlisted in support of this method. Thus, the philosophers, in the face of evil, know only to oppose their sterile declamations, instead of building a road to the good—a system of roads that, far removed from simple nature, results only from composite methods." Fourier, *Le Nouveau Monde industriel et sociétaire* (Paris, 1829), p. 237. The "distractions" involve, among other things, letting neighboring children play with one another in hammocks.   [W12a,4]

Napoleon III belonged to a Fourierist group in 1848.   [W12a,5]

The Fourierist colony founded by Baudet-Dulary in 1833 still exists today in the form of a family-run pension. Fourier had disavowed it in his day.   [W12a,6]

Balzac knew and admired Fourier's work.   [W12a,7]

The flag of the phalanstery displayed the seven colors of the rainbow. Note by René Maublanc: "The colors are analogous to the passions. . . . By juxtaposing a series of tables wherein Fourier compares the passions to colors, to notes of the scale, to natural rights, to mathematical operations, to geometric curves, to metals, and to heavenly bodies, one finds, for example, that love corresponds to blue, to the note *mi*, to right of pasture, to division, to the ellipse, to tin, and to the planets." F. Armand and R. Maublanc, *Fourier* (Paris, 1937), vol. 1, pp. 227–228.
                                                                           [W12a,8]

Re Toussenel: "Fourier . . . claims to 'join together and enframe, within a single plan, the societary mechanics of the passions with the other known harmonies of the universe,' and for that, he adds, 'we need only have recourse to the amusing lessons to be drawn from the most fascinating objects among the animals and plants.'" Armand and Maublanc, *Fourier* (Paris, 1937), vol. 1, p. 227; citing Fourier, *Traité de l'association domestique-agricole* (Paris and London, 1822), vol. 1, pp. 24–25, and *Théorie de l'unité universelle* (1834), p. 31.   [W13,1]

Fourier reproaches Descartes with having, in his doubt, spared "that tree of lies one calls civilization." See *Le Nouveau Monde*, p. 367.   [W13,2]

Stylistic quirks reminiscent of Jean Paul. Fourier loves preambles, cisambles, transambles, postambles, introductions, extroductions, prologues, interludes, postludes, cismediants, mediants, transmediants, intermedes, notes, appendixes.   [W13,3]

Fourier appears very suggestive before the background of the Empire in this note: "The combined order will, from the outset, be as brilliant as it has been long deferred. Greece, in the age of Solon and Pericles, was already in a position to undertake it, having a degree of luxury sufficient to proceed to this form of organization." Armand and Maublanc, *Fourier* (Paris, 1937), vol. 1, pp. 261–262; citing *Traité de l'association domestique-agricole* (Paris and London, 1822), vol.1, pp. lxi–lxii; *Théorie de l'unité universelle* (1834), vol.1, p. 75.[27]   [W13,4]

Fourier recognizes many forms of collective procession and cavalcade: storm, vortex, swarm, serpentage.   [W13,5]

With 1,600 phalansteries, the association is already deployed in all its combinations.   [W13,6]

"Fourier put himself body and soul into his work because he could not put into it the needs of a revolutionary class, which did not yet exist." F. Armand and R. Maublanc, *Fourier* (Paris, 1937), vol. 1, p. 83. It should be added that Fourier appears, at many points, to prefigure a new type of human being, one conspicuous for its harmlessness.[28]   [W13,7]

"In his room, there was ordinarily but one free pathway, right in the middle, leading from door to window. The rest of the space was entirely taken up by his flowerpots, which offered in themselves the spectacle of a progressive series of sizes, shapes, and even qualities; there were pots of common clay, and there were pots of Chinese porcelain." Charles Pellarin, *Vie de Fourier* (Paris, 1871), pp. 32–33.   [W13,8]

Charles Pellarin, *Vie de Fourier* (Paris, 1871) reports (p. 144) that Fourier would sometimes go six or seven nights without sleeping. This happened because of excitement over his discoveries.   [W13a,1]

"The phalanstery will be an immense lodging house." (Fourier had no conception of family life.) F. Armand and R. Maublanc, *Fourier* (Paris, 1937), vol.1, p. 85.

[W13a,2]

The cabalist, the composite, and the butterfly form appear under the rubric "distributives," or ‹*passions*› *mécanisantes*. ‹See W15a,2.›   [W13a,3]

"The cabalist spirit always brings selfish motives into play with passion. All is calculation with the intriguer—the least gesture, a wink of the eye. Everything is done on reflection and with alacrity." *Théorie de l'unité universelle* (1834), vol. 1, p. 145.[29] This remark shows very clearly how Fourier takes account of egoism. (In the eighteenth century, workers who agitated were called *cabaleurs*.)

[W13a,4]

"The earth copulating with itself engenders the cherry; with Mercury, the strawberry; with Pallas, the black currant; with Juno, the raisin; and so on." Armand and Maublanc, *Fourier* (Paris, 1937), vol.1, p. 114.   [W13a,5]

"A series is a regular classification of a genus, species, or group of beings or of objects, arranged symmetrically with respect to one or several of their properties, and on both sides proceeding from a center or pivot, according to an ascending progression on one side, descending on the other, like two flanks of an army. . . . There are 'open' series, in which the world (!) of subdivisions is not determined, and 'measured' series, which comprehend, at various levels, 3, 12, 32, 134, 404 subdivisions." Armand and Maublanc, *Fourier* (Paris, 1937), vol. 1, p. 127.

[W13a,6]

According to Fourier, every passion corresponds to an organ of the human body.

[W13a,7]

"In Harmony . . . the relations arising from the series are so dynamic that one has little time for remaining in one's room." Cited in Armand and Maublanc, *Fourier* (Paris, 1937), vol. 2, p. 211.   [W13a,8]

The four "sources of virtue" in the Little Hordes: "These sources are the penchant for dirt, and the feelings of pride, impudence, and insubordination." Fourier, *Le Nouveau Monde industriel et sociétaire* (Paris, 1829), p. 246.[30]   [W14,1]

Work signal of the Little Hordes: "The charge of the Little Hordes is sounded in an uproar of bells, chimes, drums, and trumpets, a howling of dogs and a bellowing of bulls. Then the Hordes, led by their Khans and Druids, rush forward with a great shout, passing before the priests, who sprinkle them with holy water. . . . The Little Hordes should be associated with the priesthood as members of a religious brotherhood. When performing their work, they should wear a religious symbol

. . . on their clothing." "Although the Little Hordes perform the most difficult tasks . . . , they receive the least remuneration. They would accept nothing at all if that were permitted in association. . . . All authorities, even monarchs, owe the first salute to the Little Hordes. With their pygmy horses, the Little Hordes comprise the globe's foremost regiments of cavalry; no industrial army can begin a campaign without them. They also have the prerogative of initiating all work done in the name of unity." Charles Fourier, *Le Nouveau Monde industriel et sociétaire* (Paris, 1829), p. 247–248 and 244–246.[31]   [W14,2]

"*Manoeuvre tartare*—or curvilinear mode" of the Little Hordes, in contrast to the "*manoeuvre moderne*—or rectilinear mode" of the Little Bands. "The Horde resembles a square bed of variegated tulips: one hundred cavaliers will together display two hundred colors, artistically contrasted." Fourier, *Le Nouveau Monde*, p. 249.[32]   [W14,3]

"Whoever shall abuse quadrupeds, birds, fish or insects, either by hard usage or by unnecessary cruelty, will be liable to the tribunal of the Little Hordes. And whatever his age may be, he would be brought before this tribunal of children, and treated as inferior in moral sentiment to children themselves." Fourier, *Le Nouveau Monde* (Paris, 1829), p. 248.[33]   [W14,4]

The Little Hordes are obliged to look after the *concorde sociale*; the Little Bands, the *charme social*.   [W14,5]

"The Little Hordes will come to the beautiful by way of the good, by speculative defilement." Fourier, *Le Nouveau Monde*, p. 255.[34]   [W14,6]

"Just as the Little Hordes have their Druids and Druidesses, the Little Bands have their own adult associates, who are known as Corybants. They also have their own allies among the groups of voyagers who travel about Harmony. Whereas the Little Hordes are allied to the big hordes of Adventurers and Adventuresses, who belong to the industrial armies, the Little Bands are associated with the big bands of Knights and Ladies Errant, who are dedicated to the fine arts." Fourier, *Le Nouveau Monde* (Paris, 1829), p. 254.[35]   [W14a,1]

The Little Bands have jurisdiction over offenses against meadows and gardens, and over questions of language.   [W14a,2]

"If the vestalate is called upon to mislead the minds of the children concerning sexual relations, the tact manifest in the use of two sets of genital-urinary apparatus leaves the child in complete ignorance of sex." E. Silberling, *Dictionnaire de sociologie phalanstérienne* (Paris, 1911), p. 424 (s.v. "tact"). Likewise, the courtesy of the boys toward the girls in the Little Bands is designed to mask the meaning of gallant behavior among adults.   [W14a,3]

"Under the term 'opera' I comprehend all choreographic exercises, including those of the rifle and the censer." Fourier, *Le Nouveau Monde industriel et sociétaire* (Paris, 1829), p. 260. [W14a,4]

The phalanstery is organized like a land of milk and honey. Even amusements (hunting, fishing, making music, growing flowers, performing in theatricals) are remunerated. [W14a,5]

Fourier does not know the concept of exploitation. [W14a,6]

In reading Fourier, one is reminded of the sentence by Karl Kraus: "I preach wine and drink water." [W14a,7]

Bread plays only a small role in the diet of the *Harmoniens*. [W14a,8]

"The initiation of barbarians in the use of tactics is one of the signs of the degeneration . . . of civilization." E. Silberling, *Dictionnaire de sociologie phalanstérienne* (Paris, 1911), p. 424 (s.v. "tactics"). [W14a,9]

"The savage enjoys seven natural rights . . . : hunting, fishing, harvesting, pasture, external theft (that is, pillaging of what belongs to other tribes), the federal league (the intrigues and cabals internal to the tribe), and insouciance." Armand and Maublanc, *Fourier* (Paris, 1937), vol. 2, p. 78. [W14a,10]

The poor man speaks: "I ask to be advanced the necessary tools . . . and enough to live on, in exchange for the right to steal which simple nature has given me." Cited in Armand and Maublanc, *Fourier* (Paris, 1937), vol. 2, p. 82. [W15,1]

In the phalanstery, a caravansary is outfitted for the reception of foreigners. A structure characteristic of the phalanstery is the "tower of order." This building houses the optical telegraph, the control center for the signal lights, and the carrier pigeons. [W15,2]

The circulation of works useful to all the phalansteries amounts to 800,000 copies. Fourier thinks, above all, of publishing an *Encyclopaedie naturologique caluminée*. [W15,3]

Fourier loves to clothe the most reasonable sentiments in fanciful considerations. His discourse resembles a higher flower language.[36] [W15,4]

Fourier would like to see the people who serve no useful purpose in civilization—those who merely gad about in search of news to communicate—circulating among the tables of the Harmonians, so as to keep people there from losing time in reading newspapers: a divination of radio, born from the study of human character. [W15,5]

Fourier: "Every calling has its countermorality and its principles." Cited in Armand and Maublanc, *Fourier* (Paris, 1937), vol. 2, p. 97. Fourier mentions, as examples, *le monde galant* and the world of domestic servants. [W15,6]

"After three generations of Harmony, two-thirds of the women will be unfruitful, as is the case with all flowers which, by the refinements of cultivation, have been raised to a high degree of perfection." Fourier, *La Fausse Industrie* (Paris, 1835–1836), vol. 2, pp. 560–561.[37] [W15,7]

The voluntary submissiveness of the savage, with his seven natural rights, would be, according to Fourier, the touchstone of civilization. It is something first obtained in Harmony. [W15,8]

"The individual . . . is a being essentially false, for neither by himself alone nor with another can he bring about the development of the twelve passions, since these comprise a mechanism of 810 keys and their complements. It is therefore with the passional vortex alone that the scale begins, and not with the individual person." *Publication des manuscrits de Fourier,* 4 vols. (Paris, 1851–1858), *1857–1858,* p. 320. [W15,9]

After 70,000 years comes the end of Harmony, in the form of a new period of civilization, in descending tendency, which once more will give way to "obscure limbs." Thus, with Fourier, transience and happiness are closely linked. Engels observes: "Just as Kant introduced into natural science the idea of the ultimate destruction of the earth, Fourier introduced into historical science that of the ultimate destruction of the human race." Engels, *Anti-Dühring,* part 3, p. 12.[38]
[W15a,1]

The mechanics of the passions: "The tendency to harmonize the five sensual passions—(1) taste, (2) touch, (3) sight, (4) hearing, (5) smell—with the four affective passions—(6) friendship, (7) ambition, (8) love, (9) paternity. This harmony takes place through the medium of three little-known and abused passions, which I shall call: (10) the *cabalist,* (11) the *butterfly,* (12) the *composite.*" Cited from *Le Nouveau Monde,* in Armand and Maublanc, *Fourier* (Paris, 1937), vol. 1, p. 242.[39]
[W15a,2]

"A large number of universes (since one universe, along with man and planet, constitutes the third echelon, . . . Fourier calls it a "tri-verse") go to form a quatri-verse; and so on, up to the octi-verse, which represents . . . nature as a whole, the totality of the beings of Harmony. Fourier enters into some minute calculations and announces that the octi-verse is composed of 10^{96} universes." Armand and Maublanc, *Fourier* (Paris, 1937), vol. 1, p. 112. [W15a,3]

On "beautiful agriculture": "This plow that today is so despised will be taken up by the young prince, just as by the young plebeian; they will together compete in a

sort of industrial tournament, where each of the athletes will test his vigor and dexterity, and where each can show off to an audience of lovelies, who will bring the festivities to a close by serving lunch or a snack." Charles Fourier, *Traité de l'association domestique-agricole* (Paris and London, 1822), vol. 2, p. 584. To this *beau agricole* belong, further, the steles that are raised on flower-covered pedestals and the busts of deserving farm laborers or agriculturists placed on altars that are scattered through the fields. "These are the mythological demigods of the industrial sect or series." Cited in Armand and Maublanc, *Fourier* (Paris, 1937), vol. 2, p. 206. Offerings of incense are made to them through the Corybants.
[W15a,4]

Fourier recommends gearing the experiment, in the trial phalanx, toward precisely the most eccentric characters.
[W16,1]

Fourier was a chauvinist: he hated Englishmen and Jews. He saw the Jews not as civilized people but as barbarians who maintained patriarchal customs. [W16,2]

Fourier's apple—the pendant to that of Newton—which, in the Parisian restaurant Février, costs a hundred times more than in the province where it is grown. Proudhon, too, compares himself to Newton.
[W16,3]

To the Harmonians, Constantinople is the capital of the earth.
[W16,4]

Harmonians need very little sleep (like Fourier!). They live to the age of 150 at the very least.
[W16,5]

"The 'opera' stands at the forefront of educational directives. . . . The opera is a school of morality in outline: it is there that young people are imbued with a horror of anything prejudicial to truth, precision, and unity. At the opera, no favor can excuse the one whose note is false, whose timing, step, or gesture is off. The prince's child who has a part in the dance or the choir must endure the truth, must listen to the criticisms arising from the masses. It is at the opera that he learns, in every move he makes, to subordinate himself to unitary proprieties, to general accords." Cited in F. Armand and R. Maublanc, *Fourier* (Paris, 1937), vol. 2, pp. 232–233.
[W16,6]

"No one ever dreamed, in civilization, of perfecting that portion of our dress we call 'atmosphere.' . . . It does not suffice to change it merely in the rooms of certain idlers. . . . We must modify the atmosphere in general and systematically." Cited in F. Armand and R. Maublanc, *Fourier* (Paris, 1937), vol. 2, p. 145.   [W16,7]

Fourier's texts are rich in stereotypical locutions comparable to the *gradus ad parnassum*.[40] Almost every time he speaks of the arcades, it is to say that, under present circumstances, even the king of France gets wet when he steps into his carriage during a rainstorm.
[W16,8]

Ten million francs would be needed for the erection of the complete phalanstery; three million, for the trial phalanstery. [W16,9]

All flower beds of the Harmonians are "shielded" from too much sun and rain. [W16,10]

Of the beauties of agriculture among the Harmonians, Fourier gives an account that reads like a description of color illustrations in children's books: "The societary state will be able to establish, down to the most unsavory functions, a species-specific luxury. The gray overalls of a group of plowmen, the bluish overalls of a group of mowers, will be enhanced by the borders, belts, and plumes of their uniform, by glossy wagons and inexpensively adorned harnesses, all carefully arranged to protect the ornaments from the grime of work. If we should see, in a pretty vale of the medleyed English sort, all these groups in action, well sheltered by their colored tents, working in disseminated masses, circling about with flags and instruments, singing hymns in chorus while marching; and should the region be sprinkled with manor houses and belvederes enlivened by colonnades and spires, instead of with thatched cottages, we would verily believe that the landscape was enchanted, that it was a fairyland, an Olympian abode." Even the rape cutters, who lack high standing with Fourier, have a part in the splendor, and are found "at work in the hills, raising their pavilions above thirty belvederes crowned with golden rape." Cited in Armand and Maublanc, *Fourier* (Paris, 1937), vol. 2, pp. 203, 204. [W16a,1]

Forming a mesh—for example, between herding, plowing, and gardening: "It is not necessary that this interchange be total—say, that all of the twenty men engaged in tending flocks from 5:00 to 6:30 go off as a group to work in the fields from 6:30 to 8:00. All that is necessary is for each series to provide the others with several members taken from its different groups. The exchange of a few members will suffice to establish a linkage or meshing between the different series." Cited in Armand and Maublanc, *Fourier* (Paris, 1937), vol. 2, pp. 160–161 ("Essor de la 'papillonne'").[41] [W16a,2]

It is not just the despotism but also the moralism that Fourier hates in the great Revolution. He presents the subtle division of labor among Harmonians as the antithesis of *égalité,* and their keen competition as an alternative to *fraternité.* [W16a,3]

In *Le Nouveau Monde industriel* (pp. 281–282), Fourier's rancor against Pestalozzi is very evident. He says he took up Pestalozzi's "intuitive method" in his *Traité* ‹*de l'association domestique-agricole*› of 1822 because of the great success it had had with the public. Lacking such popular success, it would have created an unfavorable impression on its readers.—Of Yverdon he recounts, at best, tales of scandal calculated to prove that institutions of harmony cannot be introduced with impunity into civilization. [W17,1]

Under the heading "Le Garantisme d'ouïe" ⟨The Guaranteeism of Hearing⟩, and in conjunction with the amelioration of popular speech habits and of the musical education of the people (worker-choirs of the theater of Toulouse!), Fourier treats of measures to be taken against noise. He wants the workshops isolated and, for the most part, transferred to the suburbs. [W17,2]

Town-Planning: "A man who wishes to have a brilliant drawing room is keenly aware that the beauty of the principal room cannot do without that of the avenues. What is one to think of an elegant salon that requires the visitor, on his way there, first to pass through a courtyard littered with refuse, a stairwell full of rubbish, and an antechamber provided with old and uncouth furnishings? . . . Why is it, then, that the good taste evinced by each individual in the decoration of his private abode is not met with, as well, in our architects responsible for those collective abodes known as cities? And why hasn't one of the myriad princes and artists . . . ever had the idea of adorning, in appropriate degree, the three components: faubourgs, annexes, and avenues . . . ?" Charles Fourier, *Cités ouvrières: Modifications à introduire dans l'architecture des villes* (Paris, 1849), pp. 19–20. Among many other prescriptions for urban planning, Fourier imagines some that would allow one to recognize, from the increasing or decreasing decoration on the buildings, whether one was approaching or moving away from a city. [W17,3]

Barbarian, civilized, and harmonian town planning: "A barbarian town is formed of buildings haphazardly assembled . . . and confusedly grouped along streets that are tortuous, narrow, badly constructed, unsafe, and unhealthy. Such, in general, are the cities of France. . . . Civilized towns have a monotonous, imperfect order, a checkerboard pattern, as in . . . Philadelphia, Amsterdam, Nancy, Turin, the new parts of London and Marseilles, and other cities *which one knows by heart* as soon as one has looked at three or four streets. Further inspection would be pointless and dispiriting." In contrast to this: "neutral harmony," "which reconciles incoherent order with a combined order." Fourier, *Cités ouvrières*, pp. 17–18. [W17,4]

The Harmonians neither acknowledge nor desire any holidays. [W17a,1]

In *Die heilige Familie* (where?)[42] Marx refers to Fourier. [W17a,2]

Toussenel, in 1848, was among the founders of the Société Républicaine Centrale (Blanqui's club). [W17a,3]

Claude-Nicolas Ledoux: "Like all the communal dwellings envisioned for Chaux, the hospice (a low-rise structure ringed by arcades and enclosing a square courtyard) has the task of furthering the moral elevation of humankind, insofar as it carefully tests the people it shelters, allows the good their freedom, and detains the bad for compulsory labor. To what extent the artist was gripped by the reformist ideas of those days can be seen in the peculiar project of the 'oikema.' Already quite eccentric in its outward aspect, this elongated building with its Greco-Roman vestibule and windowless walls was to be the place where a new sexual ethic was pioneered. To reach the goal of higher sexual morality, the spectacle of human dissipation in the oikema, in the house of uninhibited passions, was supposed to lead to the path of virtue and to 'Hymen's altar.' Later, the architect decided that it would be better . . . to grant nature its rights. . . . A new, more liberated form of marriage was to be instituted in the oikema, which the architect wanted to situate in the most beautiful of landscapes." Emil Kaufmann, *Von Ledoux bis Le Corbusier: Ursprung und Entwicklung der autonomen Architektur* (Vienna and Leipzig, 1933), p. 36. [W17a,4]

"During a large part of his life, Grandville was much preoccupied with the general idea of Analogy." Ch. Baudelaire, *Oeuvres*, ed. Le Dantec, vol. 2 ‹Paris, 1932›, p. 197 ("Quelques caricaturistes français").[43] [W17a,5]

H. J. Hunt, *Le Socialisme et le Romantisme en France: Etude de la presse socialiste de 1830 à 1848* (Oxford, 1935), provides, on p. 122, a notably concise and felicitous statement of the main lines of Fourier's doctrine. The utopian element recedes into the background, and the proximity to Newton becomes clear. Passion is the force of attraction as experienced in the subject; it is what makes "work" into a process as natural as the fall of an apple. [W17a,6]

"In contrast to the Saint-Simonians, Fourier has no use for mysticism in aesthetic matters. In his general doctrine he is certainly mystical, utopian, messianic if you will, but in speaking of art he never once utters the word 'priesthood.' . . . 'Vanity takes over and impels artists and scientists to sacrifice their fortune [which they would have needed to preserve their independence] to the phantoms of pride.'" H. J. Hunt, *Le Socialisme et le Romantisme en France* (Oxford, 1935), pp. 123–124. [W18]

[Marx]

The man who buys and sells reveals something about himself more direct and less composed than the man who discourses and battles.

—Maxime Leroy, *Les Spéculations foncières de Saint-Simon et ses querelles d'affaires avec son associé, le comte de Redern* (Paris ‹1925›), p. 1

"We see how the history of industry and the established objective existence of industry are the open book of man's essential powers. . . . Hitherto this was conceived not in its inseparable connection with man's essential being, but only in an external relation of utility. . . . Industry is the actual historical relationship of nature—and therefore of natural science—to man." Karl Marx, "Nationalökonomie und Philosophie" (1844) [Karl Marx, *Der historische Materialismus*, ed. Landshut and Mayer (Leipzig ‹1932›), vol. 1, pp. 303–304].[1]   [X1,1]

"Not only wealth but, likewise, the poverty of man—under the assumption of socialism—receives, in equal measure, a human and therefore social significance. Poverty is the positive bond which causes the human being to experience the greatest wealth—the other human being—as need." Karl Marx, "Nationalökonomie und Philosophie" [Karl Marx, *Der historische Materialismus*, ed. Landshut and Mayer (Leipzig), vol. 1, p. 305].[2]   [X1,2]

"The conclusion Marx draws for the capitalist economy: with the purchasing power given him in the form of salary, the worker can purchase only a certain amount of goods, whose production required just a fraction of the labor he himself has provided. In other words, if the merchandise he produces is to be sold by his employer at a profit, he must always be expending surplus labor." Henryk Grossmann, "Fünfzig Jahre Kampf um den Marxismus," *Wörterbuch der Volkswirtschaft*, 4th ed., ed. Ludwig Elster, vol. 3 (Jena, 1933), p. 318.   [X1,3]

Origin of false consciousness: "Division of labor becomes truly such only from the moment when a division of material and mental labor appears. . . . From this moment onward, consciousness *can* really flatter itself that it is something other than consciousness of existing practice, that it *really* represents something without representing something real." "Marx und Engels über Feuerbach: Aus dem literarischen Nachlass von Marx und Engels," in *Marx-Engels Archiv*, ed. D. Rjazanov, vol. 1 (Frankfurt am Main ⟨1928⟩), p. 248.[3]   [X1,4]

A passage on the Revolution as a "Last Judgment" opposed to the one Bruno Bauer dreamt of—one that would usher in the victory of critical consciousness: "The holy father of the church will be greatly surprised when judgment day overtakes him, . . . a day when the reflection of burning cities in the sky will mark the dawn; when together with the 'celestial harmonies' the tunes of "La Marseillaise" and "Carmagnole" will echo in his ears accompanied by the requisite roar of cannon, with the guillotine beating time; when the infamous 'masses' will shout, "Ça ira, ça ira!" and suspend ⟨*aufhebt*⟩ 'self-consciousness' by the lamppost." "Marx und Engels über Feuerbach: Aus dem literarischen Nachlass von Marx und Engels," in *Marx-Engels Archiv*, ed. D. Rjazanov, vol. 1 (Frankfurt am Main), p. 258.[4]   [X1,5]

Self-alienation: "The worker produces capital; capital produces him—hence, he produces himself, and . . . his human qualities exist only insofar as they exist for capital *alien* to him. . . . The worker exists as a worker only when he exists *for himself* as capital; and he exists as capital only when some capital exists *for him*. The existence of capital is *his* existence, . . . since it determines the tenor of his life in a manner indifferent to him. . . . Production . . . produce[s] man as a . . . *dehumanized* being." Karl Marx, *Der historische Materialismus: Die Frühschriften*, ed. Landshut and Mayer (Leipzig), vol. 1, pp. 361–362 ("Nationalökonomie und Philosophie").[5]   [X1a,1]

On the doctrine of revolutions as innervations of the collective: "The transcendence of private property is . . . the complete emancipation of all human senses . . . , but it is this emancipation . . . because . . . the senses and minds of other men have become my *own* appropriation. Besides these direct organs, therefore, *social* organs develop . . . ; thus, for instance, activity in direct association with others . . . has become an organ for *expressing* my own *life*, and a mode of appropriating *human* life. It is obvious that the *human* eye enjoys things in a way different from that of the crude, nonhuman eye; the human *ear* different from the crude ear; and so on." Karl Marx, *Der historische Materialismus: Die Frühschriften* (Leipzig), vol. 1, pp. 300–301 ("Nationalökonomie und Philosophie").[6]   [X1a,2]

"The nature which develops in human history—the genesis of human society—is man's *real* nature; hence, nature as it develops through industry, even though in an *estranged* form, is true *anthropological* nature." Karl Marx, *Der historische Materialismus: Die Frühschriften*, ed. Landshut and Mayer (Leipzig), vol. 1, p. 304 ("Nationalökonomie und Philosophie").[7]   [X1a,3]

Point of departure for a critique of "culture": "The positive transcendence of private property, as the appropriation of human life, is . . . the positive transcendence of all estrangement; that is to say, the return of man from religion, family, state, and so on, to his human—that is, social—existence." Karl Marx, *Der historische Materialismus*, ed. Mayer and Landshut (Leipzig), vol. 1, p. 296 ("Nationalökonomie und Philosophie").[8]   [X1a,4]

A derivation of class hatred that draws on Hegel: "The annulling of objectivity in the form of estrangement (which has to advance from indifferent foreignness to real, antagonistic estrangement) means equally or even primarily, for Hegel, that it is objectivity which is to be annulled, because it is not the determinate character of the object but rather its objective character that is offensive and constitutes estrangement for self-consciousness." Karl Marx, *Der historische Materialismus* (Leipzig), vol. 1, p. 335 ("Nationalökonomie und Philosophie").[9]   [X1a,5]

Communism "in its first form." "Communism is . . ., in its first form, only a *generalization* and consummation of this relationship [that is, of private property]. . . . For it, the sole purpose of life and existence is *direct*, physical *possession*. The task of the *laborer* is not done away with, but extended to all men. It wants to do away *by force* with talent, and so forth. . . . It may be said that this idea of the *community of women* gives away the *secret* of this as yet completely crude and thoughtless communism. Just as woman passes from marriage to general prostitution, so the entire world of wealth . . . passes from the relationship of exclusive marriage with the owner of private property to a state of universal prostitution with the community. . . . How little this annulment of private property is really an appropriation is . . . proved by the abstract negation of the entire world of culture and civilization, the regression to the *unnatural* simplicity of the *poor* and undemanding man, who has not only failed to go beyond private property, but has not yet even reached it." Karl Marx, *Der historische Materialismus*, ed. Landshut and Mayer (Leipzig), vol. 1, pp. 292–293 ("Nationalökonomie und Philosophie").[10]   [X2,1]

It would be an error to deduce the psychology of the bourgeoisie from the attitude of the consumer. It is only the class of snobs that represents the standpoint of the consumer. The foundations for a psychology of the bourgeois class are much sooner to be found in the following sentence from Marx, which makes it possible, in particular, to describe the influence which this class exerts, as model and as customer, on art: "A certain stage of capitalist production dictates that the capitalist be able to devote the whole of the time during which he functions as a capitalist—that is, as personified capital—to the appropriation and therefore control of the labor of others, and to the selling of the products of this labor." Karl Marx, *Das Kapital,* ‹vol. 1,› ed. Korsch (Berlin ‹1932›), p. 298.[11]   [X2,2]

From Marx, *Kapital,* vol. 3, part 1 (Hamburg, 1921), p. 84: "The advice of the banker . . . more valuable than that of the priest." Cited in Hugo Fischer, *Karl Marx und sein Verhältnis zu Staat und Wirtschaft* (Jena, 1932), p. 56.[12]   [X2,3]

Time in technology: "As in a genuine political action, the choice . . . of the right moment is crucial. 'That a capitalist should command on the field of production is now as indispensable as that a general should command on the field of battle' (vol. 1, p. 278).[13] . . . 'Time' has here, in technology, a meaning different from the one it has in the historical events of the era, where . . . the 'actions all unfold on the same plane.' 'Time' in technology . . . also has a meaning different from the one it has in modern economics, which . . . measures labor-time in terms of the clock." Hugo Fischer, *Karl Marx und sein Verhältnis zu Staat und Wirtschaft* (Jena, 1932), p. 42; citation from *Kapital* ‹vol. 1› (Berlin, 1923). [X2,4]

"If you recall that Cournot died in 1877, and that his principal works were conceived during the Second Empire, you will recognize that, after Marx, he was one of the most lucid minds of his day. . . . Cournot goes well beyond Comte, who is misled by the dogma of his Religion of Humanity; beyond Taine, who is misled by the dogma of Science; and well beyond the nuanced skepticism of Renan. . . . He utters this admirable sentence: 'From being the king of creation, man has fallen—or risen (depending on how one understands it)—to the role of concessionaire for a planet.' The mechanized civilization of the future in no way represents for him 'the triumph of mind over matter' . . .; rather, it represents the triumph of the rational and general principles of things over the energy and qualities proper to the living organism." Georges Friedmann, *La Crise du progrès* (Paris ‹1936›), p. 246. [X2a,1]

"The dead matter was an advance over living labor power; second, it is consumed in the latter's blaze; and third, it once again takes its place on the throne. . . . For even before the entrance of the worker 'into the process of production, his own labor is estranged from him, appropriated by the capitalist, and incorporated into capital; and during the process, it is continually materialized as an alien product.' . . . The deadly thing that assails technology from all directions is economics. Economics has, for its object, the commodity. 'The process of production' that begins in a blaze, as labor engages its products, 'is extinguished in the commodity. The fact that labor power was expended in its fabrication now appears as a material property of the commodity, as the property of possessing value' (vol. 2, p. 361). . . . The action of a man, as the unique and 'entire connected act of production' (vol. 2, p. 201), is already more than the agent of this action. . . . The action already takes place in a higher sphere, which has the future for itself, the sphere of technics, while the agent of this action, as isolated individual, remains in the sphere of economics, and his product is likewise bound to this sphere. . . . Across the European continent, technology as a whole forms a single simultaneous action, insofar as it takes effect *as technology*; the physiognomy of the earth is from the outset transformed within the sphere of technics, and the gulf between city and country is ultimately spanned. But if the deadly force of economics should gain the upper hand, then the repetition of homologous magnitudes through absolutely interchangeable existences, the production of commodities through the agency of the worker, prevails over the singularity of the technological action."

Hugo Fischer, *Karl Marx und sein Verhältnis zu Staat und Wirtschaft* (Jena, 1932), pp. 43–45; the citations are from *Kapital* ‹vol. 2› (Hamburg, 1921).[14]

[X2a,2]

"'The same spirit that constructs philosophic systems in the brain of philosophers builds railroads with the hands of workers.' . . . In the desert of the nineteenth century, according to Marx, technology is the only sphere of life in which the human being moves at the center of a thing." Hugo Fischer, *Karl Marx und sein Verhältnis zu Staat und Wirtschaft* (Jena, 1932), pp. 39–40; the citation of Marx is apparently from Marx and Engels, *Gesammelte Schriften, 1841–1850* (Stuttgart, 1902), vol. 1, p. 259.[15]

[X3,1]

On the divine forebears of the charlatan: "The various divine ancestors had by now [at the end of the eighteenth century] revealed not only prescriptions for elixirs of life but also methods of dyeing, indications for spinning silk, and secrets of firing clay. The industry was mythologized." Grete de Francesco, *Die Macht des Charlatans* (Basel ‹1937›), p. 154.

[X3,2]

Marx emphasizes "the decisive importance of the transformation of value and price of labor power into the form of wages, or into the value and price of labor itself. This phenomenal form, which makes the actual relation invisible, and, indeed, shows the direct opposite of that relation, forms the basis of all the juridical notions of both laborer and capitalist, of all the mystifications of the capitalistic mode of production, of all its illusions as to liberty." Karl Marx, *Das Kapital* ‹vol. 1›, ed. Korsch (Berlin ‹1932›), p. 499.[16]

[X3,3]

"Had we gone further, and inquired under what circumstances all or even the majority of products take the form of commodities, we should have found that this can happen only with production of a very specific kind: capitalist production." Karl Marx, *Das Kapital* ‹vol. 1›, ed. Korsch, p. 171.[17]

[X3,4]

"This race of peculiar commodity-owners," as Marx at one point calls the proletariat (*Kapital* ‹vol. 1›, ed. Korsch, p. 173). Compare: "Natural instinct of the commodity-owners" (ibid., p. 97).[18]

[X3,5]

Marx opposes the idea that gold and silver are only imaginary values. "The fact that money can, in certain functions, be replaced by mere symbols of itself gave rise to that other mistaken notion: that it is itself a mere symbol. Nevertheless, under this error lurked a presentiment that the money-form of an object is not an inseparable part of that object but is simply the form under which certain social relations manifest themselves. In this sense, every commodity is a symbol, since, insofar as it is value, it is only the material envelope of the human labor spent upon it. But if it be declared that . . . the material forms assumed by the social qualities of labor under the regime of a definite mode of production are mere symbols, it is in the same breath also declared that these characteristics are arbitrary fictions sanctioned by the so-called universal consent of mankind." Note after "spent upon it": "'If we consider the concept of value, we must look on the thing itself as only a symbol; it counts not as itself but as what it is worth' (Hegel, *Rechtsphilosophie*, addition to paragraph 63)." Marx, *Das Kapital* ‹vol. 1›, ed. Korsch, pp. 101–102 ("Der Austauschprozeß").[19]   [X3,6]

Private property as origin of the alienation of human beings from one another: "Objects in themselves are external to man, and consequently alienable by him. In order that this alienation may be reciprocal, it is only necessary for men, by a tacit understanding, to treat one another as private owners of those alienable objects, and by implication as independent individuals. But such a state of reciprocal independence has no existence in a primitive society based on property in common. . . . The exchange of commodities, therefore, first begins on the boundaries of such communities." Karl Marx, *Das Kapital* ‹vol. 1›, ed. Korsch (Berlin, 1932), p. 99 ("Der Austauschprozeß").[20]   [X3a,1]

"In order that . . . objects may enter into relation with one another as commodities, their guardians must place themselves in relation to one another, as persons whose will resides in those objects." Marx, *Das Kapital* ‹vol. 1›, ed. Korsch (Berlin, 1932), p. 95 ("Der Austauschprozeß").[21]   [X3a,2]

Marx recognizes a climax in the development, and in the transparency, of the fetish character of the commodity: "The mode of production in which the product takes the form of a commodity, or is produced directly for exchange, is the most general and most embryonic form of bourgeois production. It therefore makes its appearance at an early date in history, though not in the same predominating and characteristic manner as nowadays. Hence, its fetish character is relatively easily seen through. But when we come to more concrete forms, even this appearance of simplicity vanishes." Marx, *Das Kapital* ‹vol. 1›, ed. Korsch (Berlin, 1932), p. 94 ("Fetischcharakter").[22]   [X3a,3]

The model according to which the polytechnical education demanded by Marxism must orient itself: "There are . . . states of society in which one and the same man does tailoring and weaving alternately, in which case these two forms of labor are mere modifications of the labor of the same individual, and not special and fixed functions of different persons" (Marx, *Kapital*, p. 57). These various modified acts of labor on the part of *one* individual are not compared with one another quantitatively, in terms of duration; to the abstraction "mere labor," which we can educe from them, corresponds nothing real; they stand within a unique concrete labor-context, the results of which bring no advantage to the owner of commodities. Compare the following: "For a society based upon the production of commodities, in which the producers in general enter into social relations with one another by treating their products as commodities . . . , whereby they reduce their individual private labor to the standard of homogeneous human labor—for such a society, Christianity with its *cultus* of abstract man

. . . is the most fitting form of religion." Marx, *Kapital,* p. 91 ("Fetischcharak-ter").[23]   [X3a,4]

"The body of the commodity, which serves as the equivalent, figures as the materialization of human labor in the abstract, and is at the same time the product of some specifically useful concrete labor. This concrete labor becomes, therefore, the medium for expressing abstract human labor." In this latter is contained, as Marx believes, all the misery of the commodity-producing society. (The passage is from *Kapital,* p. 70 ["Die Wertform oder der Tauschwert"].)[24] In addition, it is very important that Marx immediately after this (p. 71) refers to abstract human labor as the "opposite" of the concrete.—To formulate differ-ently the misery at issue here, one could also say: it is the misery of the commod-ity-producing society that, for it, "labor directly social in character" (p. 71) is always merely abstract labor. If Marx, in his treatment of the equivalent form, lays weight on the fact "that the labor of private individuals takes the form of its opposite, labor directly social in form" (p. 71), then this private labor is precisely the abstract labor of the abstract commodity-owning man.   [X4,1]

Marx has the idea that labor would be accomplished voluntarily (as *travail passionné*) if the commodity character of its production were abolished. The reason, according to Marx, that labor is not accomplished voluntarily would therefore be: its abstract character.   [X4,2]

"Value . . . converts every product into a social hieroglyphic. Later on, men try to decipher the hieroglyphic, to get behind the secret of their own social products; for the definition of the object of utility as value is just as much their social product as language." Marx, *Das Kapital* ‹vol. 1›, p. 86 ("Der Fetischcharakter der Ware und sein Geheimnis").[25]   [X4,3]

"The general value-form, which represents all products of labor as mere congela-tions of undifferentiated human labor, shows by its very structure that it is the social expression of the commodity world. Thus, it reveals that within this world the generally human [that is, the impoverished and abstract] character of the labor constitutes at the same time its distinguishing feature as social labor." Marx, *Das Kapital* ‹vol. 1›, p. 79 ("Die Wertform oder der Tauschwert").[26]—The ab-stract nature of the social labor and the abstract nature of the human being who relates to fellow humans as an owner correspond to each other.   [X4,4]

"How are we to express the fact that weaving creates the value of the linen not by virtue of being weaving, as such, but by reason of its general property of being human labor? Simply by opposing to weaving that other particular form of con-crete labor (in this instance tailoring), which produces the equivalent of the prod-uct of weaving. Just as the coat in its bodily form became a direct expression of value, so now does tailoring, a concrete form of labor, appear as the direct and palpable embodiment of human labor generally" (*Kapital* ‹vol. 1›, p. 71).[27] This is what Marx is referring to when he writes in the sentence preceding this passage: "In the value-expression of the commodity, the tables are turned." At this point a note: "This inversion, whereby the sensuous-concrete counts only as a phenomenal form of the abstract-general—rather than the abstract-general as a property of the concrete—is characteristic of the expression of value. . . . If I say: Roman law and German law are both systems of law, my statement is perfectly self-evident. But if I say: *the* law, that abstract concept, *realizes itself* in Roman law and in German law, those concrete legal systems, my context becomes mystical" (p. 71) ("Die Wertform oder der Tauschwert"). [X4a,1]

"When I state that coats or boots stand in a relation to linen because linen is the universal incarnation of abstract human labor, the absurdity of the proposition is manifest. Nevertheless, when the producers of coats and boots compare those articles with linen, or, what is the same thing, with gold or silver, as the universal equivalent, they express the relation between their own private labor and the collective labor of society in precisely this absurd form." Karl Marx, *Das Kapital*, ⟨vol. 1⟩, ed. Korsch (Berlin, 1932), p. 88 ("Fetischcharakter").[28] [X4a,2]

"Political economy has . . . never . . . asked the question why labor is represented by the value of its product, and labor-time by the magnitude of that value. These formulas, which bear it stamped upon them in unmistakable letters that they belong to a state of society in which the process of production has the mastery over man, instead of being controlled by him—such formulas appear to the bourgeois intellect to be as much a self-evident necessity imposed by nature as productive labor itself." Marx, *Das Kapital* ⟨vol. 1⟩, ed. Korsch, p. 92–93 ("Der Fetischcharakter der Ware und sein Geheimnis").[29] [X4a,3]

An extremely important passage relating to the concept of the "creative" is Marx's comment on the beginning of the first paragraph of the Gotha Program, "Labor is the source of all wealth and all culture": "The bourgeois have very good grounds for falsely ascribing *supernatural creative power* to labor, since precisely from the fact that labor depends on nature, it follows that the man who possesses no other property than his labor power must, in all conditions of society and culture, be the slave of other men who have made themselves owners of the material conditions of labor." Karl Marx, *Randglossen zum Programm der deutschen Arbeiterpartei*, ed. Korsch (Berlin and Leipzig, 1922), p. 22.[30] [X5,1]

"Within the cooperative society based on common ownership of the means of production, the producers do not exchange their products; just as little does the labor employed on the products appear here *at the value* of these products, as a material quality possessed by them, since now, in contrast to capitalist society, individual labor exists no longer in an indirect fashion, but directly as a component part of the total labor. The phrase 'proceeds of labor' . . . thus loses all meaning." The passage refers to the demand for "a fair distribution of the proceeds of labor." Marx, *Randglossen zum Programm der deutschen Arbeiterpartei* (Berlin and Leipzig, 1922), pp. 25, 24.[31]   [X5,2]

"In a higher phase of communist society, after the enslaving subordination of the individual to the division of labor, and therewith also the antithesis between mental and physical labor, has vanished; after labor has become not only a means of life but life's chief necessity; after the productive forces have also increased with the all-round development of the individual . . .—only then can the narrow horizon of bourgeois right be crossed in its entirety and society inscribe on its banners: 'From each according to his ability, to each according to his needs!'" Marx, *Randglossen zum Programm der deutschen Arbeiterpartei* (Berlin and Leipzig, 1922), p. 27.[32]   [X5,3]

Marx in his critique of the Gotha Program of 1875: "Lassalle knew the *Communist Manifesto* by heart. . . . If, therefore, he has falsified it so grossly, he has done so only to put a good face on his alliance with absolutist and feudal opponents against the bourgeoisie." Marx, *Randglossen zum Programm der deutschen Arbeiterpartei*, ‹ed. Korsch,› p. 28.[33]   [X5,4]

Korsch directs attention to a "scientific insight that is fundamental to the overall understanding of Marxist communism, though today it is often looked upon by the adversaries of Marxism, and even by many of its proponents, as 'meaningless'— the insight, namely, that the *wages of labor* are not, as bourgeois economists like to think, the value (or price) of the *labor*, but 'only a masked form of the value (or price) of the *labor power*, which is sold as a commodity on the labor market well before its productive utility (as labor) begins in the operation of the capitalist proprietor." Karl Korsch, Introduction to Marx, *Randglossen zum Programm der deutschen Arbeiterpartei*, ed. Korsch (Berlin and Leipzig, 1922), p. 17.
                                    [X5a,1]

Schiller: "Common natures pay with what they do; noble natures, with what they are."[34] The proletarian pays for what he is with what he does.   [X5a,2]

"In the course of the labor process, labor passes continually out of a state of unrest into a state of being, out of the form of motion into the form of objectivity. At the end of one hour's spinning, that act is represented by a definite quantity of yarn; in other words, a definite quantity of labor, namely that of one hour, has been objectified in the cotton. We say 'labor' because the work of spinning counts here only insofar as it is the expenditure of labor power in general, and not insofar as it is the specific work of the spinner. . . . Raw material and product appear here [in the production of surplus value] in quite a new light, very different from that in which we viewed them in the labor process pure and simple. The raw material serves now merely as an absorbent of a definite quantity of labor. . . . Definite quantities of product, these quantities being determined by experience, now represent nothing but definite quantities of labor, definite masses of crystallized labor time. They are nothing more than the materialization of so many hours or so many days of social labor." Karl Marx, *Das Kapital* ‹vol. 1›, ed. Korsch (Berlin ‹1932›), p. 191 ("Wertbildungsprozeß").[35] [X5a,3]

The petty-bourgeois-idealist theory of labor is given an unsurpassed formulation in Simmel, for whom it figures as the theory of labor per se. And with this, the moralistic element—here in antimaterialist form—is registered very clearly. "One may . . . assert in very general terms that . . . the distinction between mental and manual labor is not one between mental and material nature; that, rather, the reward is ultimately required in the latter case only for the internal aspect of work, for the aversion to exertion, for the conscription of will power. Of course, this intellectuality, which is, as it were, the thing-in-itself behind the appearance of work . . . , is not really intellectual but resides in emotion and the will. It follows from this that it is not coordinated with mental labor but rather is its basis. For at first the objective content . . . , the result . . . , the demand for reward is produced not in it but in . . . the expenditure of energy that it requires for the production of this intellectual content. In that an act of the *soul* is revealed to be the source of value . . . , physical and 'mental' labor contain a common (one might say, morally) value-grounding base, through which the reduction of labor value as such to physical labor loses its philistine and brutal materialistic appearance. This is roughly the case with theoretical materialism, which acquires a completely new and more seriously discussible basis if one emphasizes that matter itself is also a *conception,* not an essence which, . . . in the absolute sense, stands opposed to the soul but which in its cognizability is completely determined by the forms and presuppositions of our intellectual organization." Of course, with these reflections (‹*Philosophie des Geldes* (Leipzig, 1900),› pp. 449–450), Simmel is playing devil's advocate, for he does not want to admit the reduction of labor to physical labor. Indeed there is also, according to him, a valueless labor that still requires an expenditure of energy. "This means, however, that the value of labor is measured not by its amount but by the utility of its result!" Simmel goes on to reproach Marx, as it appears, for confusing a statement of fact with a demand. He writes: "socialism, in fact, strives for a . . . society in which the utility value of objects, in relation to the labor time applied to them, forms a constant" (‹ibid.,› p. 451). "In the third volume of *Capital,* Marx argues that the precondition of all value, of the labor theory too, is use value. Yet this means that so many parts of the total social labor time are used in each product as come in relation to its importance in use. . . . The approximation to this completely utopian state of affairs seems to be technically possible only if, as a whole, nothing but the . . . unquestionably basic life necessities are produced. For where this is exclusively the case, one work activity is of course precisely as necessary and useful as the next. In contrast, however, as long as one moves into the higher spheres in which, on the one hand, need and estimation of utility are inevitably more individual and, on the other, the intensity of labor is more difficult to prove, no regulation of the amounts of production could bring about a situation in which the relationship between need and labor applied was everywhere the same. On these points, all the threads of the deliberations on socialism intertwine. At this point, it is clear that the . . . difficulty . . . increases in relation to the cultural level of the product—a difficulty whose avoidance, of course, must limit production to that of the most primitive, most essential, and most average objects." Georg Simmel, *Philosophie des Geldes* (Leipzig, 1900), pp. 451–453.[36] With this critique, compare the counter-critique of this standpoint by Korsch, X9,1.   [X6;X6a]

"The individual significance of different objects of equal value is degraded through their exchangeability—however indirectly or imaginary this may be. . . . The disparagement of the interest in the individuality of a commodity leads to a disparagement of individuality itself. If the two sides to a commodity are its quality and its price, then it seems logically impossible for the interest to be focused on only one of these sides; for 'cheapness' is an empty word if it does not imply a low price for a relatively good quality. . . . Yet this conceptual impossibility is psychologically real and effective. The interest in the one side can be so great that its logically necessary counterpart completely disappears. The typical instance of one of these cases is the 'fifty-cent bazaar.' The principle of valuation in the modern money economy finds its clearest expression here. It is not the commodity that is the center of interest here but the price—a principle that in former times not only would have appeared shameless but would have been absolutely impossible. It has been rightly pointed out that the medieval town . . . lacked the extensive capital economy, and that this was the reason for seeking the ideal of the economy, not so much in the expansion (which is possible only through cheapness) as in the quality of the goods offered." Georg Simmel, *Philosophie des Geldes* (Leipzig, 1900), pp. 411–412.[37]   [X7,1]

"Political economy is now no longer a science of commodities. . . . It becomes a direct science of social labor": "in its present unambiguous, and definite, form of *labor producing a commodity for another person*—that is, of labor formally paid to its full value but actually exploited . . . , actually collective labor performed by proletarian wage laborers . . . to whom . . . the productive power of what would be under otherwise similar conditions the produce of an isolated worker, now increased a thousandfold by the social division of labor, stands opposed in the form of *capital*." ⟨Karl⟩ Korsch ⟨*Karl Marx*, manuscript⟩, vol. 2, p. 47.[38] Compare X11,1.   [X7,2]

On the bungled reception of technology. "The illusions in this sphere are reflected quite clearly in the terminology that is used in it, and in which a mode of thinking, proud of its . . . freedom from myth, discloses the direct opposite of these features. To think that we conquer or control nature is a very childish supposition, since . . . all notions of . . . conquest and subjugation have a proper meaning only if an opposing will has been broken. . . . Natural events, as such, are not subject to the alternatives of freedom and coercion. . . . Although . . . this seems to be just a matter of terminology, it does lead astray those who think superficially in the direction of anthropomorphic misinterpretations, and it does show that the mythological mode of thought is also at home within the natural-scientific worldview." Georg Simmel, *Philosophie des Geldes* (Leipzig, 1900), pp. 520–521.[39] It is the great distinction of Fourier that he wanted to open the way to a very different reception of technology. [X7a,1]

"The . . . *doctrine of 'surplus value,'* already largely anticipated . . . by the classic bourgeois economists and their earliest socialist adversaries, . . . and the reduction of the 'free labor contract' of the modern wage laborer to the sale of the 'commodity labor-power,' first acquire their real efficacy through the transfer of economic thought from the field of the exchange of commodities . . . to the field of material production . . .—that is, through the transition from . . . *surplus value,* existing in the form of goods and money, to . . . *surplus labor,* performed by real workers in the workshop under the social domination exerted upon them by the capitalist owner of the workshop." Korsch ‹*Karl Marx,* manuscript›, vol. 2, pp. 41–42.[40] [X7a,2]

Korsch, vol. 2, p. 47, cites a phrase from Marx ‹*Das Kapital,* vol. 1, 4th ed. (Hamburg, 1890), pp. 138–139›: "the hidden haunts of production, on whose threshold we are faced with the inscription: 'No admittance except on business.'"[41] Compare Dante's inscription on the Gate of Hell, and the "one-way street." [X7a,3]

Korsch defines surplus value as the "particularly 'deranged' form which the general fetishism attached to all commodities assumes in the commodity called 'labor-power.'" Karl Korsch, *Karl Marx,* manuscript, vol. 2, p. 53.[42] [X8,1]

"What Marx . . . terms the 'fetishism of the world of commodities' is only a scientific expression for the same thing that he had described earlier . . . as 'human self-alienation.' . . . The most important substantive difference between this philosophical critique of economic 'self-alienation' and the later scientific exposition of the same problem consists in the fact that, in *Das Kapital,* Marx . . . gave his economic critique a deeper and more general significance by tracing back the delusive character of all other economic categories to the fetish character of the *commodity*. Though even now that most obvious and direct form of the 'self-alienation of the human being,' which occurs in the relation between wage labor and capital, keeps its decisive importance for the practical attack on the existing order of society, the fetishism of *commodity labor power* is, at this stage, for theoretical purposes regarded as a mere derivative form of the more general fetishism which is contained in the *commodity* itself. . . . By revealing *all* economic categories to be mere fragments of one great fetish, Marx ultimately transcended all preceding forms and phases of bourgeois economic and social theory. . . . Even the most advanced classical economists remained caught in the . . . world of bourgeois appearance, or fell back into it, because they had never succeeded in extending their critical analysis either to the derived forms of economic fetishism [unmasking of the gold and silver fetishes, the physiocratic illusion that rent grows out of the earth, the interpretation of interest and rent as mere fractions of industrial profit] or to that general fundamental form which appears in the value-form of the labor products as commodity and in the value-relations of the commodities themselves." Korsch, *Karl Marx*, ‹vol. 2,› pp. 53–57.[43]   [X8,2]

"From the bourgeois point of view, the individual citizen thinks of 'economic' things and forces as of something entering into his private life from without. . . . According to the new conception, however, individuals in all they do are moving, from the outset, within definite social circumstances that arise from a given stage in the development of *material production*. . . . Such high ideals of bourgeois society as that of the free, self-determining individual, freedom and equality of all citizens in the exercise of their political rights, and equality of all in the eyes of the law are now seen to be nothing but *correlative concepts to the fetishism of the commodity*. . . . Only by keeping the people unconscious of the real contents of those basic relations of the existing social order . . ., only through the fetishistic transformation of the social relations between the class of capitalists and the class of wage laborers, resulting in the 'free and unhampered' sale of the 'commodity labor-power' to the owner of 'capital,' is it possible in this society to speak of freedom and equality." Korsch, *Karl Marx*, ‹vol. 2,› pp. 75–77.[44]   [X8a,1]

"The individual and collective bargaining over the conditions of sale of the commodity labor-power still belongs entirely to the world of fetishistic appearance ‹*Schein*›. Socially considered, and together with the material means of production, the propertyless wage laborers selling, through a 'free labor contract,' their individual labor-powers for a certain time to a capitalist entrepreneur are, as a class, from the outset and forever, a common property of the possessing class, which alone has the real means of labor at its disposal. It was therefore not the whole truth that was revealed by Marx in the *Communist Manifesto* when he said that the bourgeoisie had . . . replaced the veiled forms of exploitation practiced during the . . . Middle Ages by an altogether 'unveiled exploitation.' The bourgeoisie replaced an exploitation embroidered with religious and political illusions by a new and more refined system of *concealed exploitation*. Whereas in earlier epochs the openly proclaimed relations of domination and servitude appeared as the immediate springs of production, in the bourgeois period it is . . . , conversely, production that is . . . the pretext . . . for the . . . exploitation of laborers." ‹Korsch,› *Karl Marx*, ‹vol. 2,› pp. 64–65.[45]   [X8a,2]

On the doctrine of value: "The idea that there is an 'equality' inherent in all kinds of labor, by which economists are entitled to regard qualitatively different kinds of labor . . . as quantitatively different portions of a total quantity of 'general labor,' which forms the basis of the economic concept of value, is so little the discovery of a natural condition underlying the production and exchange of commodities that this 'equality' is, on the contrary, brought into existence by the social fact that, under the conditions prevailing in present-day capitalist 'commodity production,' all labor products are produced as commodities for such exchange. In fact, this 'equality' appears *nowhere else than in the 'value' of the commodities so produced.* The full development of the economic theory of 'labor value' coincided with a stage of the historical development when human labor, not just as a category but in reality, had long ceased to be, as it were, organically connected with either the individual or with small productive communities and, the barriers of the guilds having fallen under the new bourgeois banner of 'freedom of trade,' every particular kind of labor was treated henceforth as *equivalent* to every other particular kind of labor. It was precisely the advent of these historical and political conditions that was expressed (unconsciously, of course) by the classical economists when they traced back the 'value' appearing in the exchange of commodities to the quantities of labor incorporated therein, though most of them believed they had thus disclosed a natural law. . . . Those minor followers in the wake of the great scientific founders of political economy, no longer accustomed to such audacity of scientific thought, who have later pathetically bewailed the 'violent abstraction' by which the classical economists and Marxism, in tracing the value relations of commodities to the amounts of labor incorporated therein, have 'equaled the unequal,' must be reminded of the fact that this 'violent abstraction' results not from . . . economic science but from the real character of capitalist commodity production. *The commodity is a born leveler."* Korsch, *Karl Marx,* vol. 2, pp. 66–68. In "reality," of course, the "particular kinds of labor performed in the production of the various useful things are, according to Marx, effectively different also under the regime of the law of value" (ibid., p. 68).[46] This in opposition to Simmel; compare X6a.   [X9]

"Marx and Engels . . . pointed out that the equality-idea resulting from the epoch of bourgeois commodity-production and expressed in the economic 'law of value' is still bourgeois in its character. It is therefore only ideologically incompatible with the exploitation of the working class through capital, but not in actual practice. The socialist Ricardians, . . . on the basis of the economic principle that 'it is labor alone which bestows value,' . . . wanted to transform all men into actual workers exchanging equal quantities of labor. . . . Marx replied that 'this equalitarian relation . . . is itself nothing but the reflection of the actual world; and that therefore it is totally impossible to reconstitute society on the basis of what is merely an embellished shadow of it. In proportion as this shadow takes on substance again, we perceive that this substance, far from being the transfiguration dreamt of, is the actual body of existing society.'" The citation from *La Misère de la philosophie,* in Korsch, vol. 2, p. 4.[47]   [X9a,1]

Korsch: In the bourgeois epoch, "the production of the products of labor is pretext and cover for the . . . exploitation and oppression of the laborers. The scientific method of concealing this state of affairs is called political economy." Its function: to shift "responsibility for all the waste and hideousness which is already found at the present stage of development of the productive forces of society, and which emerges catastrophically during economic crises, from the realm of human action

to the sphere of so-called immutable, nature-ordained relations between things."
Korsch, *Karl Marx*, vol. 2, p. 65.[48]   [X9a,2]

"The distinction between use value and exchange value, in the abstract form in
which it had been made by the bourgeois economists, . . . did not provide any
useful starting point for an . . . investigation of bourgeois commodity production. . . . With Marx, . . . use value is not defined as a use value in general, but as
the *use value of a commodity*. This use value inherent in commodities . . . is,
however, not merely an extra-economic presupposition of their 'value.' It is an
element of the value. . . . The mere fact that a thing has utility for any human
being—say, for its producer—does not yet give us the economic definition of use
value. Not until the thing has . . . utility 'for other persons' . . . does the economic
definition of use value apply. Just as the use value of the commodity is economically defined as a social use value (use value 'for others'), so is the . . . labor which
goes into the production of this commodity defined economically as . . . labor 'for
others.' Thus, Marx's *commodity-producing labor* appears as social labor in a
twofold sense. It has . . . the *general social character* of being a 'specifically useful
labor,' which goes to the production of a definite kind of social use value. It has, on
the other hand, the *specific historical character* of being a 'generally social labor,'
which goes to the production of a definite quantity of exchange value. The capacity
of social labor to produce definite things useful to human beings . . . appears in the
use value of its product. Its capacity for the production of a value and a surplus
value for the capitalist (a particular characteristic of labor which derives from the
particular form of the social organization of the labor process . . . within the
present historical epoch) appears in the *exchange value* of its product. The fusion
of the two social characteristics of commodity-producing labor appears in the
'value-form' of the product of labor, or the *form of commodity*." Korsch, *Karl
Marx* ‹vol. 2›, pp. 42–44.[49]   [X10]

"The earlier bourgeois economists, when speaking of labor as a source of wealth,
had likewise thought of 'labor' in terms of the various forms of real work, though
they did so only for the reason that their economic categories were still in the
process of separation from their original material contents. . . . Thus, the Mercantilists, the Physiocrats, and so on successfully declared that the true source of
wealth lies in the labor expended in the export industries, in trade and shipping, in
agricultural labor, and the like. Even in Adam Smith—who, from the different
branches of labor, definitely advanced to the general form of commodity-producing labor—we find that concrete aspect retained, along with the new and more
formalistic definition which is also expressed in his system and was later to become
the exclusive definition of value in the work of Ricardo, and by which labor is
defined as an abstract and merely quantitative entity. This same abstract form of
labor, which he correctly defined as exchange-value-producing labor, he at the
same time . . . declared to be the only source . . . of the material wealth of the
community, or use value. This doctrine, which still obstinately persists in 'vulgar'
socialism . . . is, according to Marx, economically false." By its assumptions, "it

would be difficult to explain why, in present day . . . society, just those persons are poor who hitherto have had that unique source of all wealth at their exclusive disposal, and even more difficult to account for the fact that they remain unemployed and poor, instead of producing wealth by their labor. . . . But . . . in praising the creative power of 'labor,' Adam Smith was thinking not so much of the forced labor of the modern wage laborer, which appears in the value of commodities and produces capitalistic profit, as of the general natural necessity of human labor. . . . Likewise, his naive glorification of the 'division of labor' achieved in these 'great manufactures,' by which he understood the whole of modern capitalist production, refers not so much to the extremely imperfect form of contemporary capitalistic division of labor . . . as to the general form of human labor vaguely fused with it in his theoretical exposition." Korsch, *Karl Marx,* vol. 2, pp. 44–46.[50]   [X10a]

Decisive passage on surplus value, the final statement no doubt standing in need of further clarification: "Similarly, the *doctrine of surplus value,* which is usually regarded as the more particularly socialist section of Marx's economic theory, is neither a simple economic exercise in calculation which serves to check a fraudulent statement of value received and expended by capital in its dealing with the workers, nor a moral lesson drawn from economics for the purpose of reclaiming from capital the diverted portion of the 'full product of the worker's labor.' The Marxian doctrine, as an economic theory, starts rather from the opposite principle—that the industrial capitalist under 'normal' conditions acquires the labor-power of the wage laborers by means of a respectable and businesslike bargain, whereby the laborer receives the full equivalent of the 'commodity' sold by him, that is, of the 'labor-power' incorporated in himself. The advantage gained by the capitalist in this business derives not from economics but from his privileged social position as the monopolist owner of the material means of production, which permits him to exploit, for the production of commodities in his workshop, the specific *use value* of a labor-power which he has purchased at its economic '*value*' (exchange value). *Between the value of the new commodities produced by the use of the labor-power in the workshop, and the prices paid for this labor to its sellers, there is, according to Marx, no economic or other rationally determinable relation whatever.* The measure of value produced by the workers in the shape of their labor products over and above the equivalent of their wages (that is, the *mass of* '*surplus labor*' expended by them in producing this 'surplus value') and the quantitative relation between this surplus labor and the necessary labor (that is, the '*rate of surplus value*' or the '*rate of exploitation*' holding good for a particular time and a particular country) do not result from any exact economic calculation. They result from a battle between social classes." Korsch, *Karl Marx,* vol. 2, pp. 71–72.[51]   [X11]

"The ultimate meaning of this law of value, as shown in its workings by Marx, . . . does not consist . . . in supplying a theoretical basis for the practical calculations of the businessman seeking his private advantage, or for the economic-political measures taken by the bourgeois statesman concerned with the general maintenance and furtherance of the capitalist surplus-making machinery. The final scientific purpose of the Marxian theory is, rather, '*to reveal the economic law of motion of modern society*, and this means, at the same time, the law of its historical development.'" Korsch, *Karl Marx*, vol. 2, p. 70.[52]   [X11a,1]

"Complete determination of the actual social character of that fundamental process of modern capitalist production which is one-sidedly presented by the bourgeois economists, as by their adversaries from the camp of vulgar socialism, sometimes as production of consumer goods, and sometimes, by contrast, as production of value or as simple profitmaking": a "production of surplus value by means of the production of value by means of the production of consumer goods—in a society in which the material goods of production enter as capital into the process of production run by the capitalists, while the actual producers enter as the commodity labor-power." Korsch, *Karl Marx*, vol. 3, pp. 10–11.   [X11a,2]

The experience of our generation: that capitalism will not die a natural death.
                                                                           [X11a,3]

The confrontation of Lafargue with Jaurès is very characteristic for the *great* form of materialism.   [X11a,4]

Sources for Marx and Engels: "From the bourgeois historians of the French Restoration, they took the concept of social class and of class struggle; from Ricardo, the economic basis of the class antagonism; from Proudhon, the proclamation of the modern proletariat as the only real revolutionary class; from the feudal and Christian assailants of the new economic order . . ., the ruthless unmasking of the liberal ideas of the bourgeoisie, the piercing hate-filled invective. Their ingenious dissection of the unsolvable contradictions of the modern mode of production they took from the petty-bourgeois socialism of Sismondi; the humanism and the philosophy of action, from earlier companions among the left Hegelians, especially from Feuerbach; the meaning of political struggle for the working class, from the contemporary labor parties, French Social Democrats and English Chartists; the doctrine of revolutionary dictatorship, from the French Convention, and from Blanqui and his followers. Finally, they took from Saint-Simon, Fourier, and Owen the entire content of their socialist and communist agenda: the total upheaval of the foundations of existing capitalist society, the abolition of classes . . . , and the transformation of the state into a mere administration of production." Korsch, *Karl Marx*, vol. 3, p. 101.[53]   [X12,1]

"Through Hegel, the new materialism of proletarian theory linked itself to the sum of bourgeois social thought of the preceding historical period. It did so in the same antithetical form in which, on a practical level also, the social action of the proletariat continued the previous social movement of the bourgeois class." Korsch, *Karl Marx*, vol. 3, p. 99.[54]   [X12,2]

Korsch says very justly (and one might well think of de Maistre and Bonald in this connection): "To a certain extent, that . . . 'disenchantment' which, after the conclusion of the great French Revolution, was first proclaimed by the early French theorists of the counterrevolution and by the German Romantics . . . has in fact exerted a considerable influence upon Marx mainly through Hegel, and has thus directly entered into the . . . theory of the modern workers' movement." Korsch, *Karl Marx,* vol. 2, p. 36.[55]   [X12,3]

Concept of productive force: "'Productive force' is, in the first place, nothing else than the real earthly labor-power of living men: the force . . . by which . . . they produce . . . , under capitalistic conditions, 'commodities.' . . . Everything that increases the productive effect of human labor-power . . . is a new social 'productive force.' To the material forces of production belong nature, technology, and science; but to these forces belong, above all, the social organization itself and the . . . social forces created therein by cooperation and the industrial division of labor." Korsch, *Karl Marx,* vol. 3, pp. 54–55.[56]   [X12a,1]

Concept of productive force: "The Marxian concept of 'social' productive forces has nothing in common with the idealistic abstractions of the old and new 'technocrats,' who imagine they can define and measure the productive powers of society . . . in terms of natural science and technology. . . . 'Technocratic' prescriptions are not sufficient in themselves to remove the material obstacles which oppose any important change in present-day capitalistic society. . . . There is more power of resistance in the mute force of economic conditions . . . than well-meaning technocrats have ever dreamt of." Korsch, *Karl Marx,* vol. 3, pp. 59–60.[57]   [X12a,2]

In Marx—"Das philosophische Manifest der historischen Rechtsschule," *Rheinische Zeitung,* 221 (1842)—there appears, as a point of reference, "the correct idea . . . that the *primitive* conditions are naive 'Dutch pictures' of the *true* conditions." Cited in Korsch, vol. 1, p. 35.[58]   [X12a,3]

Against Proudhon, who looks on machine and division of labor as antithetical to each other, Marx emphasizes how much the division of labor has been refined since the introduction of machinery. Hegel, for his part, emphasized that the division of labor, in a certain sense, opened the way for the introduction of machinery. "This parceling out of their content . . . gives rise to the *division of labor. . . .* The labor which thus becomes more abstract tends, on one hand, by its uniformity, to make labor easier and to increase production; on another, to limit each person to a single kind of technical skill, and thus produce more unconditional dependence on the social system. The skill itself becomes in this way mechanical, and becomes capable of letting the machine take the place of human labor." Hegel, *Enzyklopädie der philosophischen Wissenschaften im Grundrisse* (Leipzig, 1920), p. 436 (paragraphs 525–526).[59]   [X12a,4]

The critique carried out by the young Marx on the "rights of man," as separated from the "rights of the citizen." "None of the so-called rights of man goes beyond egoistic man. . . . Far from the rights of man conceiving of man as a species-being, species-life itself, society, appears as a framework exterior to individuals. . . . The only bond that holds them together is natural necessity, need and private interest, the conservation of their property and egoistic person. It is . . . paradoxical . . . that citizenship, the political community, is degraded by the political emancipators to a mere means for the preservation of these so-called rights of man; that the citizen is declared to be the servant of egoistic man; that the sphere in which man behaves as a communal being is degraded below the sphere in which man behaves as a partial being; finally that it is not man as a citizen but man as a bourgeois who is called the real and true man. . . . The riddle has a simple solution. . . . What was the character of the old society? . . . Feudalism. The old civil society had a directly political character. . . . The political revolution . . . abolished the political character of civil society. It shattered civil society . . . on the one hand into individuals, on the other hand into the material and spiritual elements that make up the . . . civil position of these individuals. . . . The formation of the political state and the dissolution of civil society into independent individuals, who are related by law just as the estate and corporation men were related by privilege, is completed in one and the same act. Man as member of civil society, unpolitical man, appears necessarily as natural man. The rights of man appear as natural rights, because self-conscious activity is concentrated upon political action. Egoistic man is the passive, given result of the dissolved society, . . . a natural object. Political revolution's . . . attitude to civil society, to the world of need, to work, private interests, and private law, is that they are . . . its natural basis. Finally, man as a member of civil society counts for true man, for man as distinct from the citizen, because he is man in his sensuous . . . existence, while political man is only the abstract . . . man. . . . The abstraction of the political man is thus correctly described by Rousseau: 'He who dares to undertake the making of a people's institutions ought to feel himself capable . . . of changing human nature, of transforming each individual, who is by himself a complete and solitary whole, into part of a greater whole from which he . . . receives his life and being' (*Contrat social* [London, 1782], vol. 2, p. 67)." Marx, "Zur Judenfrage," in Marx and Engels, *Gesamtausgabe*, vol. 1, section 1, 1 (Frankfurt am Main, 1927), pp. 595–599.[60]   [X13]

The property appertaining to the commodity as its fetish character attaches as well to the commodity-producing society—not as it is in itself, to be sure, but more as it represents itself and thinks to understand itself whenever it abstracts from the fact that it produces precisely commodities. The image that it produces of itself in this way, and that it customarily labels as its culture, corresponds to the concept of phantasmagoria (compare "Eduard Fuchs, Collector and Historian," section 3).[61] The latter is defined by Wiesengrund "as a consumer item in which there is no longer anything that is supposed to remind us how it came into being. It becomes a magical object, insofar as the labor stored up in it comes to seem supernatural and sacred at the very moment when it can no longer be recognized as labor" (T. W. Adorno, "Fragmente über Wagner," *Zeitschrift für Sozialforschung*, 8, nos. 1–2 [1939], p. 17). In connection with this, from the manuscript on Wagner (pp. 46–47): "The art of Wagner's orchestration has banished . . . the role of the immediate production of sound from the aesthetic totality. . . . Anyone fully able to grasp why Haydn doubles the violins with a flute in *piano* might well get an intuitive glimpse into why, thousands of years ago, men gave up eating uncooked grain and began to bake bread, or why they started to smooth and polish their tools. All trace of its own production should ideally disappear from the object of consumption. It should look as though it had never been *made,* so as not to reveal that the one who sells it did not in fact make it, but rather appropriated to himself the labor that went into it. The autonomy of art has its origin in the concealment of labor."[62]   [X13a]

[Photography]

> Sun, look out for yourself!
>
> —A. J. Wiertz, *Oeuvres littéraires* (Paris, 1870), p. 374

> If one day the sun should sputter out,
> 'Twill be a mortal who rekindles it.
>
> —Laurencin and Clairville, *Le Roi Dagobert à l'exposition de 1844,*
>   Théâtre du Vaudeville, April 19, 1844 (Paris, 1844), p. 18 [lines
>   spoken by the Genius of Industry]

A prophecy from the year 1855: "Only a few years ago, there was born to us a machine that has since become the glory of our age, and that day after day amazes the mind and startles the eye. / This machine, a century hence, will be the brush, the palette, the colors, the craft, the practice, the patience, the glance, the touch, the paste, the glaze, the *trick*, the relief, the finish, the rendering. / A century hence, there will be no more bricklayers of painting; there will be only architects— painters in the full sense of the word. / And are we really to imagine that the daguerreotype has murdered art? No, it kills the work of patience, but it does homage to the work of thought. / When the daguerreotype, this titan child, will have attained the age of maturity, when all its power and potential will have been unfolded, then the genius of art will suddenly seize it by the collar and exclaim: 'Mine! You are mine now! We are going to work together.'" A. J. Wiertz, *Oeuvres littéraires* (Paris, 1870), p. 309. From an article, "La Photographie," that appeared for the first time in June 1855, in *La Nation,* and ended with a reference to the new invention of photographic enlargement, which makes it possible to produce life-size photos. Bricklayer-painters are, for Wiertz, those "who apply themselves to the material part only," who are good at "rendering." [Y1,1]

Industrialization in literature. On Scribe. "Although he made fun of the big industrialists and moneymen, he picked up the secret of their success. It did not escape his eagle eye that, in the last analysis, all wealth rests on the art of getting others to work for us. So then, groundbreaking genius that he was, he transferred the principle of the division of labor from the workshops of tailors, cabinetmakers, and manufacturers of pen nibs to the ateliers of dramatic artists, who, before this reform, working with only their *one* head and *one* pen, had earned merely the proletarian wages of the isolated worker. An entire generation of theatrical geniuses were in his debt for their training and development, their awards, and, not infrequently, even their riches and reputation. Scribe chose the subject, sketched out the main lines of the plot, indicated the places for special effects and brilliant exits, and his apprentices would compose the appropriate dialogue or verses. Once they had made some progress, their name would appear on the title page (next to that of the firm) as a just recompense, until the best would break away and begin turning out dramatical works of their own invention, perhaps also in their turn recruiting new assistants. By these means, and under the protection afforded by the French publishing laws, Scribe became a multimillionaire." Friedrich Kreyssig, *Studien zur französischen Cultur- und Literaturgeschichte* (Berlin, 1865) ⟨pp. 56–57⟩. [Y1,2]

Beginnings of the revue. "The French fairy plays[1] currently in vogue are practically all of recent origin; they derive, for the most part, from the revues which were customarily put on during the first fortnight of the new year, and which were a sort of fantastic retrospective of the year preceding. The character of these theatricals was initially quite juvenile; they were tailored specifically to schoolchildren, whose new year's festivities would be enlivened by productions of this kind." Rudolf Gottschall, "Das Theater und Drama des Second Empire," *Unsere Zeit: Deutsche Revue—Monatsschrift zum Konversationslexikon* (Leipzig, 1867), p. 931. [Y1,3]

From the start, to keep this thought in view and to weigh its constructive value: the refuse- and decay-phenomena as precursors, in some degree mirages, of the great syntheses that follow. These worlds ⟨?⟩ of static realities are to be looked for everywhere. Film, their center. ☐Historical Materialism☐ [Y1,4]

Fairy plays: "Thus, for example, in *Parisiens à Londres* (1866), the English industrial exhibition is brought to the stage and illustrated by a bevy of naked beauties, who naturally owe their appearance to allegory and poetic invention alone." Rudolf Gottschall, "Das Theater und Drama des Second Empire," *Unsere Zeit: Deutsche Revue—Monatsschrift zum Konversationslexikon* (Leipzig, 1867) p. 932. ☐Advertising☐ [Y1a,1]

"'Fermenters' are catalytic agents which provoke or accelerate the decomposition of relatively large quantities of other organic substances. . . . These 'other organic substances,' however, in reaction to which the fermenting agents manifest their destructive power, are the historically transmitted stylistic forms." "The fermenters . . . are the achievements of modern technology. They . . . can be grouped according to three great material divisions: (1) iron, (2) the art of machinery, (3) the art of light and fire." Alfred Gotthold Meyer, *Eisenbauten* (Esslingen, 1907), from the preface (unpaginated). [Y1a,2]

The photographic reproduction of artworks as a phase in the struggle between photography and painting.   [Y1a,3]

"In 1855, within the framework of the great exhibition of industry, special sections on photography were opened, making it possible for the first time to familiarize a wider public with the new invention. This exhibition was, in fact, the overture to the industrial development of photography. . . . The public at the exhibition thronged before the numerous portraits of famous and noted personalities, and we can only imagine what it must have meant to that epoch suddenly to see before it, in so lifelike a form, the celebrated figures of the stage, of the podium—in short, of public life—who, up until then, could be gazed at and admired only from afar." Gisela Freund, "Entwicklung der Photographie in Frankreich" [manuscript]. ▯ Exhibitions ▯   [Y1a,4]

Worthy of mention in the history of photography is the fact that the same Arago who made the famous expert report in favor of photography submitted, in that same year (?), 1838, an unfavorable report on the railroad construction planned by the government: "In 1838, when the government sent them the bill authorizing construction of railroad lines from Paris to Belgium, to le Havre, and to Bordeaux, the parliamentary reporter Arago recommended rejection, and his recommendation was approved by a vote of 160 to 90. Among other arguments, it was claimed that the difference in temperature at the entrance and exit of the tunnels would bring on mortal chills and fevers." Dubech and d'Espezel, *Histoire de Paris* (Paris, 1926), p. 386.   [Y1a,5]

Some successful stage plays from midcentury: Dennery, *La Naufrage* ‹Shipwreck› *de La Pérouse* (1859), *Le Tremblement de terre de Martinique* (1843), *Les Bohémiens de Paris* (1843); Louis François Clairville, *Les Sept Châteaux du diable* (1844), *Les Pommes de terre malades* (1845), *Rothomago* (1862), *Cendrillon* ‹Cinderella› (1866). Others by Duveyrier, Dartois. A *Kaspar Hauser* by Dennery?[2]   [Y1a,6]

"The most fantastic creations of fairyland are near to being realized before our very eyes. . . . Each day our factories turn out wonders as great as those produced by Doctor Faustus with his book of magic." Eugène Buret, *De la Misère des classes laborieuses en France et en Angleterre* (Paris, 1840), vol. 2, pp. 161–162.   [Y2,1]

From Nadar's splendid description of his photographic work in the Paris catacombs: "With each new camera setup, we had to test our exposure time empirically; certain of the plates were found to require up to eighteen minutes.—Remember, we were still, at that time, using collodion emulsion on glass negatives. . . . I had judged it advisable to animate some of these scenes by the use of a human figure—less from considerations of picturesqueness than in order to give a sense of scale, a precaution too often neglected by explorers in this medium and with sometimes disconcerting consequences. For these eighteen minutes of exposure time, I found it difficult to obtain from a human being the absolute, inorganic immobility I required. I tried to get round this difficulty by means of mannequins, which I dressed in workman's clothes and positioned in the scene with as little awkwardness as possible; this business did nothing to complicate our task. . . . This nasty ordeal of photographing in the sewers and catacombs, it must be said, lasted no less than three consecutive months. . . . Altogether, I brought back a hundred negatives. . . . I made haste to offer the first hundred prints to the collections of the City of Paris put together by the eminent engineer of our subterranean constructions, M. Belgrand." Nadar, *Quand j'étais photographe* (Paris ‹1900›), pp. 127–129.[3]   [Y2,2]

Photography by artificial light with the aid of Bunsen elements. "I then had an experienced electrician install, on a solid part of my balcony overlooking the Boulevard des Capucines, the fifty medium-sized elements I'd been hoping for and which proved sufficient. . . . The regular return, each evening, of this light (so little utilized at that time ‹1860–1861›) arrested the crowd on the boulevard and, drawn like moths to the flame, a good many of the curious—both the friendly and the indifferent—came to climb up the stairs to our studio to find out what was going on there. These visitors (some well known or even famous) represented every social class; they were the more welcome insofar as they furnished us with a free supply of models, variously disposed toward the novel experience. It was thus that I managed to photograph, during these evening affairs, Niépce de Saint-Victor, . . . Gustave Doré, . . . the financiers E. Pereire, Mirès, Halphen, and many others." Nadar, *Quand j'étais photographe* (Paris), pp. 113, 115–116.
[Y2,3]

At the end of the grand prospectus Nadar offers on the state of the sciences: "Here we are, well beyond even the admirable assessment of Fourcroy, at the hour supreme when the genius of the nation, in mortal danger, calls for discoveries." Nadar, *Quand j'étais photographe*, p. 3.   [Y2,4]

Nadar reproduces the Balzacian theory of the daguerreotype, which in turn derives from the Democritean theory of the *eidōla*. (Nadar seems to be unacquainted with the latter; he never mentions it.) Gautier and Nerval would have conformed to Balzac's opinion, "but even while speaking of specters, both of them . . . were among the very first to pass before our lens." Nadar, *Quand j'étais photographe,* p. 8. ‹Compare Y8a,1.›   [Y2a,1]

From whom does the conception of progress ultimately stem? From Condorcet? At any rate, by the end of the eighteenth century it does not yet appear to have taken very firm root. In the course of his eristic, among various suggestions for disposing of an adversary, Hérault de Séchelles includes the following: "Lead him astray through questions of moral freedom and progress to the infinite." Hérault de Séchelles, *Théorie de l'ambition* (‹Paris,› 1927), p. 132.   [Y2a,2]

1848: "The revolution . . . arose in the midst of a very severe economic crisis, provoked, on the one hand, by the speculations occasioned by railroad construction and, on the other hand, by two consecutive bad harvests, in 1846 and 1847. Once again the city of Paris, . . . as far out as the faubourg Saint-Antoine, was torn by hunger riots." A. Malet and P. Grillet, *XIXe Siècle* (Paris, 1919), p. 245.

[Y2a,3]

Declaration regarding Ludovic Halévy: "You may attack me on any grounds you like—but photography, no, that is sacred." Jean Loize, "Emile Zola photographe," *Arts et métiers graphiques*, 45 (February 15, 1935) ‹p. 35›. [Y2a,4]

"Whoever, at some point in his life, has had the chance to slip his head under the magic mantle of the photographer, and has peered into the camera so as to catch sight of that extraordinary miniature reproduction of the natural image—such a person will necessarily . . . have asked himself what is likely to come of our modern painting once photography has succeeded in fixing colors on its plates as well as forms." Walter Crane, "Nachahmung und Ausdruck in der Kunst," ‹trans. Otto Wittich,› *Die neue Zeit*, 14, no. 1 (Stuttgart ‹1895–1896›), p. 423. [Y2a,5]

The effort to launch a systematic confrontation between art and photography was destined to founder at the outset. It could only have been a moment in ‹the› confrontation between art and technology—a confrontation brought about by history. [Y2a,6]

The passage on photography from Lemercier's *Lampélie et Daguerre:*

> As, menaced by the birdcatcher's pitiless nets,
> The meadowlark, rousing the muses of morning,
> Flutters and foolishly comes to alight on a
> Lark-mirror, reef of its dalliances,
> So Lampélie's (= sunlight's) flight is cut short
> By the chemical snare of Daguerre.
> The face of a crystal, convex or concave,
> Will reduce or enlarge every object it marks.
> Its fine, lucid rays, through the depths of the trap,
> Catch the aspect of places in rapid inscription:
> The image imprisoned within the glass plate,
> Preserved from all threatening contact,
> Retains its bright life; and certain reflections
> Break through to the most distant spheres.

Népomucène Lemercier, *Sur la Découverte de l'ingénieux peintre du diorama* [Annual Public Session of the Five Academies, Thursday, May 2, 1839 (Paris, 1839), pp. 30–31]. ‹Compare Q3a,1.› [Y3,1]

"Photography . . . was first adopted within the dominant social class . . . : manufacturers, factory owners and bankers, statesmen, men of letters, and scientists." Gisela Freund, "La Photographie au point de vue sociologique" (manuscript, p. 32). Is this accurate? Shouldn't the sequence be reversed? [Y3,2]

Among the inventions that predate photography one should mention, in particular, the lithograph (invented in 1805 by Alois Senefelder and introduced into France some years later by Philippe de Lasteyrie) and the physionotrace, which, for its part, represents a mechanization of the process of cutting silhouettes. "Gilles Louis Chrétien, . . . in 1786, . . . successfully invented an apparatus which . . . combined two different modes of making portraits: that of the silhouette and that of the engraving. . . . The physionotrace was based on the well-known principle of the pantograph. A system of parallelograms was articulated in such a way as to be capable of transfer to a horizontal plane. With the aid of a dry stylus, the operator traces the contours of a drawing. An inked stylus traces the lines of the first stylus, and reproduces the drawing on a scale determined by the relative position of the two styluses." Gisela Freund, "La Photographie au point de vue sociologique" (manuscript, pp. 19–20). The apparatus was equipped with a viewfinder. Life-size reproductions could be obtained.   [Y3,3]

The reproduction time with the physionotrace was one minute for normal silhouettes, three minutes for colored ones. It is characteristic that the beginnings of the technologizing of the portrait, as instanced in this apparatus, set back the art of the portrait qualitatively as much as photography later advanced it. "One can see, on examining the quite enormous body of work produced with the physionotrace, that the portraits all have the same expression: stiff, schematic, and featureless. . . . Although the apparatus reproduced the contours of the face with mathematical exactitude, this resemblance remained expressionless because it had not been realized by an artist." Gisela Freund, "La Photographie au point de vue sociologique" (manuscript, p. 25). It would have to be shown here just why this primitive apparatus, in contrast to the camera, excluded "artistry."
                [Y3a,1]

"In Marseilles, around 1850, there were at most four or five painters of miniatures, of whom two, perhaps, had gained a certain reputation by executing fifty portraits in the course of a year. These artists earned just enough to make a living. . . . A few years later, there were forty to fifty photographers in Marseilles. . . . They each produced, on the average, between 1,000 and 1,200 plates per year, which they sold for 15 francs apiece; this made for yearly receipts of 18,000 francs, so that, together, they constituted an industry earning nearly a million. And this same development can be seen in all the major cities of France." Gisela Freund, "La Photographie au point de vue sociologique" (manuscript, pp. 15–16), citing Vidal, *Mémoire de la séance du 15 novembre 1868 de la Société Statistique de Marseille*. Reproduced in the *Bulletin de la Société française de Photographie* (1871), pp. 37, 38, 40.   [Y3a,2]

On the interlinking of technological inventions: "When he wanted to experiment with lithography, Niépce, who lived in the country, ran into the greatest difficulties in procuring the necessary stones. It was then that he got the idea of replacing the stones with a metal plate and the crayon with sunlight." Gisela Freund, "La Photographie au point de vue sociologique" (manuscript, p. 39), in reference to Victor Fouque, *Niépce: La Verité sur l'invention de la photographie* (Châlons sur Saône, 1867). [Y3a,3]

Following Arago's report to the Chamber: "A few hours later, opticians' shops were besieged; there were not enough lenses, not enough camera obscuras to satisfy the zeal of so many eager amateurs. They watched with regretful eye the setting sun on the horizon, as it carried away the raw material of the experiment. But on the morrow, during the first hours of the day, a great number of these experimenters could be seen at their windows, striving, with all sorts of anxious precautions, to capture on a prepared plate the image of a dormer-window opposite, or the view of a group of chimneys." Louis Figuier, *La Photographie: Exposition et histoire des principales découvertes scientifiques modernes* (Paris, 1851); cited, without page reference, by Gisela Freund (manuscript, p. 46). [Y4,1]

In 1840, Maurisset published a caricature of photography. [Y4,2]

"In the area of portraiture, a concern with 'situation' and the 'position' of a man, a concern that demands from the artist the representation of a 'social condition' and an 'attitude,' can be satisfied, in the end, only with a full-length portrait." Wilhelm Wätzold, *Die Kunst des Porträts* (Leipzig, 1908), p. 186; cited in Gisela Freund (manuscript, p. 105). [Y4,3]

Photography in the age of Disderi: "The characteristic accessories of a photographic studio in 1865 are the pillar, the curtain, and the pedestal table. Posed there, leaning, seated, or standing up, is the subject to be photographed: full-length, half-length, or bust. The background is filled, according to the social rank of the model, with other paraphernalia, symbolic and picturesque." Further on comes a very characteristic extract (without page reference) from *L'Art de la photographie* (Paris, 1862), by Disderi, who says, among other things: "In making a portrait, it is not a question only . . . of reproducing, with a mathematical accuracy, the forms and proportions of the individual; it is necessary also, and above all, to grasp and represent, while justifying and embellishing, . . . the intentions of nature toward this individual." Gisela Freund, "La Photographie au point de vue sociologique" (manuscript, pp. 106, 108).—The pillars: emblem of a "well-rounded education." ☐ Haussmannization ☐ [Y4,4]

Gisela Freund (manuscript, pp. 116–117) provides the following citation from Disderi's *L'Art de la photographie*: "Could not the photographer who was a master of all the effects of lighting, who had at his disposal a large and perfectly equipped studio with blinders and reflectors, who was provided with backdrops of all kinds, with settings, properties, costumes—could he not, given intelligent and skillfully dressed models, compose *tableaux de genre*, historical scenes? Could he not aspire to sentiment, like Scheffer, or to style, like Ingres? Could he not treat of history, like Paul Delaroche in his painting *The Death of the Duc de Guise?*" At the world exhibition of 1855, there were some photographs of this sort produced in England.　　　　　　　　　　　　　　　　　　　　　　　　　　　　　　　[Y4a,1]

The paintings of Delacroix escape the competition with photography, not only because of the impact of their colors, but also (in those days, there was no instant photography) because of the stormy agitation of their subject matter. And so a benevolent interest in photography was possible for him.　　　　　　　[Y4a,2]

What makes the first photographs so incomparable is perhaps this: that they present the earliest image of the encounter of machine and man.　　　　[Y4a,3]

One of the—often unspoken—objections to photography: that it is impossible for the human countenance to be apprehended by a machine. This the sentiment of Delacroix in particular.　　　　　　　　　　　　　　　　　　　　[Y4a,4]

"Yvon, . . . pupil of Delaroche, . . . decided, one day, to reproduce the Battle of Solférino. . . . Accompanied by the photographer Bisson, he goes to the Tuileries, gets the emperor to strike the right sort of pose, has him turn his head, and bathes everything in the light he wishes to reproduce. The painting that resulted in the end was acclaimed under the title *The Emperor in a Kepi.*" Following this, a courtroom battle between the painter and Bisson, who had put his photo on the market. He is convicted. Gisela Freund, "La Photographie au point de vue sociologique" (manuscript, p. 152).　　　　　　　　　　　　　　　　[Y4a,5]

Passing by the house of Disderi, Napoleon III halts a regiment he is leading down the boulevard, goes upstairs, and has himself photographed.　　　　[Y4a,6]

In his capacity as president of the Société des Gens de Lettres, Balzac proposed that all of the works of the twelve greatest living French authors should automatically be bought by the state. (Compare Daguerre.)　　　　　　[Y4a,7]

"At the Café Hamelin, . . . some photographers and night owls." Alfred Delvau, *Les Heures parisiennes* (Paris, 1866), p. 184 ("Une Heure du matin").　　[Y5,1]

On Népomucène Lemercier: "The man who spoke this pedantic, absurd, and bombastic idiom certainly never understood the age in which he lived. . . . Could anyone have done a better job of distorting contemporary events with the aid of outmoded images and expressions?" Alfred Michiels, *Histoire des idées littéraires en France au XIXᵉ siècle* (Paris, 1863), vol. 2, pp. 36–37.　　　　　[Y5,2]

On the rise of photography.—Communications technology reduces the informational merits of painting. At the same time, a new reality unfolds, in the face of which no one can take responsibility for personal decisions. One appeals to the lens. Painting, for its part, begins to emphasize color.　　　　　　　[Y5,3]

"Steam"—"Last word of him who died on the Cross!" Maxime Du Camp, *Les Chants modernes* (Paris, 1855), p. 260 ["La Vapeur"].   [Y5,4]

In "La Vapeur," part 3, Du Camp celebrates steam, chloroform, electricity, gas, photography. Maxime Du Camp, *Les Chants modernes* (Paris, 1855), pp. 265–272. "La Faulx" ‹The Scythe› celebrates the reaper.   [Y5,5]

The first two stanzas, and the fourth, from "La Bobine" ‹The Bobbin›:

> Near the cascading river—
> Each of its breakwaters
> A swirling relay station—
> In the midst of green meadows,
> And the flowering alfalfa,
> They have raised up my palace—
>
> My palace of a thousand windows,
> My palace of rustic vines
> Which climb to the rooftops,
> My palace where, without repose,
> The nimble wheel booms out its song,
> The wheel of rackety voice!
>
> Like those vigilant elves of Norway
> Who waltz across the snows
> To escape the sprite that stalks them,
> I turn, I turn, I turn!
> Through the hours of day, never resting,
> I turn, and I turn through the night!

Maxime Du Camp, *Les Chants modernes* (Paris, 1855), pp. 285–286.   [Y5,6]

"La Locomotive": "One day I shall be named a saint." Maxime Du Camp, *Les Chants modernes* (Paris, 1855), p. 301. This poem, like others, from the cycle "Chants de la matière."   [Y5,7]

"The press, that immense and sacred locomotive of progress." Victor Hugo, speech at the banquet of September 16, 1862, organized by the publishers of *Les Misérables* in Brussels. Cited in Georges Batault, *Le Pontife de la démagogie: Victor Hugo* (Paris, 1934), p. 131.   [Y5,8]

> It is a century that does us honor,
> The century of inventions;
> Unfortunately, it is also
> The century of revolutions.

‹Louis› Clairville and Jules Cordier, *Le Palais de Cristal, ou Les Parisiens à Londres*, Théâtre de la Porte Saint-Martin, May 26, 1851 (Paris, 1851), p. 31.
                    [Y5a,1]

Self-portrait by Nadar. Courtesy of the J. Paul Getty Museum, Los Angeles. See Y5a,5.

A locomotive pulling "several elegant coaches" appears on the stage. Clairville the elder and Delatour, *1837 aux enfers*, Théâtre du Luxembourg, December 30, 1837 (Paris, 1838) ‹p. 16›.   [Y5a,2]

To be demonstrated: the influence of lithography on the literary genre of panoramas. What, in the case of the lithograph, is perfunctory individual characterization often becomes, with the writer, equally perfunctory generalization.
                                                                                            [Y5a,3]

Fournel, in 1858 ("Ce qu'on voit dans les rues de Paris"), reproaches the daguerreotype for being unable to embellish. Disderi is waiting in the wings. On the other hand, Fournel condemns the conventional poses that relied on props such as Disderi had introduced. [Y5a,4]

Without indicating his source, Delvau cites this description of Nadar's appearance: "His hair has the reddish glow of a setting sun; its reflection spreads across his face, where bouquets of curly and contentious locks spill this way and that, unruly as fireworks. Extremely dilated, the eyeball rolls, testifying to a truly unappeasable curiosity and a perpetual astonishment. The voice is strident; the gestures are those of a Nuremberg doll with a fever." Alfred Delvau, *Les Lions du jour* (Paris, 1867), p. 219. [Y5a,5]

Nadar, speaking of himself: "A born rebel where all bondage is concerned, impatient of all proprieties, having never been able to answer a letter within two years, an outlaw in all houses where you cannot put your feet up before the fire, and finally—so that nothing should be lacking, not even a last physical defect, to complete the measure of all these amiable qualities and win him more good friends—nearsighted to the point of blindness and consequently liable to the most insulting amnesia in the presence of any face which he has not seen more than twenty-five times at a distance of fifteen centimeters from his nose." Cited in Alfred Delvau, *Les Lions du jour* (Paris, 1867), p. 222. [Y5a,6]

Inventions from around 1848: matches, stearin candles, steel pens. [Y5a,7]

Invention of the mechanical press in 1814. It was first utilized by the *Times*. [Y5a,8]

Nadar's self-characterization: "Formerly a maker of caricatures . . ., ultimately a refugee in the Botany Bay of photography." Cited in Alfred Delvau, *Les Lions du jour* (Paris, 1867), p. 220. [Y6,1]

On Nadar: "What will remain, one day, of the author of *Le Miroir aux alouettes* ⟨Lark-Mirror⟩, of *La Robe de Déjanire*, of *Quand j'étais étudiant?* I do not know. What I do know is that, on a cyclopean pile on the island of Gozo, a Polish poet, Czeslaw Karski, has engraved in Arabic, but with Latin letters, 'Nadar of the fiery locks passed in the air above this tower,' and that the inhabitants of the island very likely still have not left off worshiping him as an unknown God." Alfred Delvau, *Les Lions du jour* (Paris, 1867), pp. 223–224. [Y6,2]

Genre photography: the sculptor Callimachus, on viewing an acanthus plant, invents the Corinthian capital.—Leonardo paints the Mona Lisa.—*La Gloire et le pot au feu* ⟨Glory and Beef Stew⟩. Cabinet des Estampes, Kc 164a,1. [Y6,3]

An English etching of 1775, a genre scene, shows an artist making a silhouette of ⟨her⟩ model by following the shadow which the latter casts on the wall. It is entitled *The Origin of Painting*. Cabinet des Estampes, Kc 164a,1. [Y6,4]

NADAR élevant la Photographie à la hauteur de l'Art

Nadar in his balloon. Lithograph by Honoré Daumier, 1862. The caption reads: "Nadar raising photography to the level of art." See Y6,2.

There is a certain relation between the invention of photography and the invention of the mirror-stereoscope by Wheatstone in 1838. "It displays two different images of the same object: to the right eye, an image representing the object in perspective as it would be seen from the viewpoint of the right eye; to the left eye, an image of the object as it would appear to the left eye. This gives rise to the illusion that we have . . . before us a three-dimensional object" (Egon Friedell, *Kulturgeschichte der Neuzeit,* vol. 3 [Munich, 1931], p. 139). The exactness required of the images forming the material for this stereoscope would correspond more readily to photography than to painting. [Y6,5]

The apparent affinity between Wiertz and Edgar Quinet needs to be studied. [Y6,6]

"The lens is an instrument like the pencil or the brush, and photography is a process like drawing or engraving; for what the artist creates is the emotion and

The Origin of Painting. Etching by an English artist, 1775. Courtesy of the Bibliothèque Nationale de France. See Y6,4.

not the process. Whoever possesses the necessary skills and happy inspiration will be able to obtain the same effects from any one of these means of reproduction." Louis Figuier, *La Photographie au Salon de 1859* (Paris, 1860), pp. 4–5.   [Y6,7]

"M. Quinet . . . seemed to want to introduce into poetry the sort of genre that the English painter ⟨John⟩ Martin inaugurated in art. . . . The poet . . . did not shrink from having the cathedrals kneel before the sepulcher of Our Lord, and showing the towns absorbed in combing out upon their shoulders, with a comb of gold, their tresses of blond columns, while the towers danced a strange roundelay with the mountains." Alfred Nettement, *Histoire de la littérature française sous le gouvernement de Juillet* (Paris, 1859), vol. 1, p. 131.   [Y6a,1]

"At the world exhibition of 1855, photography, despite its lively claims, could gain no entry into the sanctuary of the hall on the Avenue Montaigne; it was condemned to seek asylum in the immense bazaar of assorted products that filled the Palais de l'Industrie. In 1859, under growing pressure, the museum committee . . . accorded a place in the Palais de l'Industrie for the exhibition of photography; the exhibition site was on a level with that made available to painting and engraving, but it had a separate entrance and was set, so to speak, in a different key." Louis Figuier, *La Photographie au Salon de 1859* (Paris, 1860), p. 2.   [Y6a,2]

"A skillful photographer always has a distinctive style, just like a draftsman or a painter; . . . and, what's more, . . . the distinctive character of the artistic spirit of each nation is clearly revealed . . . in the works produced in different countries. . . . A French photographer could never be confused . . . with one of his colleagues from across the Channel." Louis Figuier, *La Photographie au Salon de 1859* (Paris, 1860), p. 5.   [Y6a,3]

The beginnings of photomontage come out of the attempt to ensure that images of the landscape retain a painterly character. "M. Silvy has an excellent system for producing his pictures. . . . Instead of imposing, on all his landscapes indifferently, one and the same sky formed from a uniform negative, he takes the trouble, wherever possible, of separately enhancing, one after the other, the view of the landscape and that of the sky which crowns it. Here resides one of the secrets of M. Silvy." Louis Figuier, *La Photographie au Salon de 1859* (Paris, 1860), p. 9.   [Y6a,4]

It is significant that Figuier's booklet on the Salon of Photography of 1859 begins with a review of landscape photography.   [Y6a,5]

At the Salon de Photographie of 1859, numerous "voyages": to Egypt, to Jerusalem, to Greece, to Spain. In his account, Figuier observes: "Hardly had the practical processes of photography on paper come to be understood than a whole band of operators rushed forth . . . in all directions, to bring us back views of monuments, buildings, and ruins taken in all known lands of the world." Hence the new *voyages photographiques.* Louis Figuier, *La Photographie au Salon de 1859*, p. 35. [Y6a,6]

Among the works of reproduction to which Figuier gives special attention, in his *Photographie au Salon*, are the reproduction of the Raphael cartoon from Hampton Court—"the work . . . that dominates the entire photographic exhibition of 1859" (p. 51)—and that of a manuscript of Ptolemy's *Geography* dating from the fourteenth century and kept, at that time, in the monastery of Mount Athos. [Y7,1]

There were portraits specifically designed to be viewed through the stereoscope. This fashion was current in England, above all. [Y7,2]

Figuier (pp. 77–78) does not omit to mention the possibility that "microscopic photographs" could be used in time of war to transmit secret messages (in the form of miniature telegrams). [Y7,3]

"One thing . . . made clear by a careful inspection of the exhibition . . . is the present perfection . . . of the positive proof. Five or six years ago, photography was almost exclusively concerned with the negative, . . . and it was rare indeed that anyone gave thought to the utility of printing from a positive image." Louis Figuier, *La Photographie au Salon de 1859* (Paris, 1860), p. 83. [Y7,4]

Symptom, it would seem, of a profound displacement: painting must submit to being measured by the standard of photography: "We will be in agreement with the public in admiring . . . the fine artist who . . . has appeared this year with a painting capable of holding its own, in point of delicacy, with daguerrian prints." This assessment of Meissonnier is from Auguste Galimard, *Examen du Salon de 1849* (Paris ‹1850›), p. 95. [Y7,5]

"Photography in verse"—synonym for a description in verse. Edouard Fournier, *Chroniques et légendes des rues de Paris* (Paris, 1864), pp. 14–15. [Y7,6]

"The world's first movie theater opened on December 28, 1895, in the basement of the Grand Café, 14 Boulevard des Capucines, in Paris. And the first receipts for a brand of spectacle that would later net billions amounted to the considerable sum of thirty-five francs!" Roland Villiers, *Le Cinéma et ses merveilles* (Paris ‹1930›), pp. 18–19. [Y7,7]

"The year 1882 must be mentioned as a turning point in the history of photographic reportage. It was the year in which the photographer Ottomar Anschütz, from Leszno in Poland, invented the focal-plane shutter and thus made possible truly instantaneous photography." *Europäische Dokumente: Historische Photos aus den Jahren 1840–1900*, ed. Wolfgang Schade (Stuttgart, Berlin, Leipzig), p. [v]. [Y7,8]

The first photographic interview was conducted by Nadar with the ninety-seven-year-old French chemist Chevreul, in 1886. *Europäische Dokumente: Historische Photos aus den Jahren 1840–1900*, ed. Wolfgang Schade (Stuttgart, Berlin, Leipzig), p. 8–9.[4]   [Y7,9]

"The first experiment to launch research into scientifically produced motion . . . was that of Doctor Parès in 1825. The details are well known: on one side of a small square of cardboard, he had drawn a cage, and on the other side, a bird; by turning the piece of cardboard briskly on an axis, . . . he caused the two images to appear in succession, yet the bird seemed to be in the cage, just as though there had been only one drawing. This phenomenon, which in itself is the basis of all cinema, depends on the principle of the persistence of retinal impressions. . . . Once this principle is admitted, it is easy to understand that a movement decomposed, and presented in a rhythm of ten images or more per second, is perceived by the eye as a perfectly continuous movement. The first apparatus that actually wrought the miracle of artificial motion is the Phenakistiscope, constructed by the Belgian physician Plateau as early as 1833. Still known today as an optical toy, this apparatus . . . consisted of a disk on which were mounted drawings representing the successive phases of an action, which could be observed as the disk was rotated. . . . There . . . is an obvious relation here to the animated cartoons of today. . . . Researchers quickly saw . . . the interest in having . . . a succession of photographs substituted for the drawings. Unfortunately, . . . only images running at the minimum speed of a tenth of a second could work with such a design. For this, we had to await the gelatinobromide plates that permitted the first instantaneous exposures. It was astronomy that initially provided an occasion for testing chronophotography. On December 8, 1874, thanks to the passage of the planet Venus past the sun, the astronomer ‹Pierre› Janssen was able to try out his invention of a photographic revolver, which took a picture every seventy seconds. . . . But the process of chronophotography was soon to become much more rapid. . . . It was . . . when Professor Marey entered the lists with his photographic rifle . . . that the result of twelve images per second was obtained. . . . All these experiments were, up to then, purely scientific (!) in character. The researchers who conducted them . . . saw in chronophotography a simple 'means for analyzing the movements of humans and animals.' . . . At this point, in 1891, we meet with . . . Edison, who had constructed two devices. One, the Kinetograph, was for recording; the other, the Kinetoscope, was for projection. . . . Meanwhile, in 1891, Marey's collaborator, ‹Georges› Démeny, had built a machine that allowed for the recording of pictures and sound at the same time. His Phonoscope . . . was the first talkie." Roland Villiers, *Le Cinéma et ses merveilles* (Paris ‹1930›), pp. 9–16 ("Petite Histoire du cinéma").   [Y7a,1]

"Let us take as an example of technical progress, which actually is regress, the perfection of photographic devices. They are much more sensitive to light than the old boxes with which daguerreotypes were produced. One hardly need concern oneself about lighting when operating them now. They have a number of other advantages to boot, especially where photographing faces is concerned, although the portraits which one makes with them are doubtless much poorer than before. With the older, less light-sensitive apparatus, multiple expressions would appear on the plate, which was exposed for rather long periods of time; hence, on the final image there would be a livelier and more universal expression, and this had its function as well. Nevertheless, it would most certainly be false to regard the new devices as worse than the older ones. Perhaps something is missing from them which tomorrow will be found, and one can always do other things with them besides photographing faces. Yet what of the faces? The newer devices no longer work to compose the faces—but must faces be composed? Perhaps for these devices there is a photographic method which would decompose faces. But we can be quite sure of never finding this possibility realized . . . without first having a new function for such photography." Brecht, *Versuche* ‹8–10 (Berlin, 1931)›, p. 280 ("Der Dreigroschenprozeß" ‹The Threepenny Lawsuit›). [Y8,1]

The Bisson brothers, on the occasion of the visit by Napoleon III to their photographic studio on December 29, 1856—a visit which they say coincided with the eleventh anniversary of the opening of their business—published in pamphlet form a poem entitled, "Souvenir de la visite de Leurs Majestés l'Empereur et l'Impératrice aux magasins de Messieurs Bisson frères." The pamphlet comprises four pages. The first two pages contain another poem, "La Photographie." Both texts are unrelievedly fatuous. [Y8,2]

"It is worth noting that the better photographers of our day are not concerned to belabor the question . . . : 'Is photography an art?' . . . By their aptitude for creating the evocative shock, [these photographers] prove their power of expression, and that is their revenge for the skepticism of Daumier." George Besson, *La Photographie française* (Paris ‹1936›), pp. 5–6. [Y8,3]

The famous statement by Wiertz on photography can very likely be elucidated through the following statement by Wey (of course, it becomes clear by this that Wiertz's prognosis was mistaken): "In reducing to naught whatever is inferior to it, the heliograph predestines art to new forms of progress; in recalling the artist to nature, it links him with a source of inspiration whose fecundity is unlimited." Francis Wey, "Du Naturalisme dans l'art" [*La Lumière,* April 6, 1851]; cited in Gisèle Freund, *La Photographie en France au XIXe siècle* (Paris, 1936), p. 111. [Y8,4]

"If we consider only the practical side of divination, then to believe that previous events in a man's life . . . can be directly represented by the cards he shuffles and cuts, and which are then stacked by the fortuneteller in accordance with some mysterious laws, is to believe the absurd. But this criterion of absurdity once ruled out the harnessing of steam; it still rules out aerial navigation; it ruled out many inventions: gunpowder, printing, the telescope, engraving, and also the most recent great discovery of our time, the daguerreotype. If anyone had come and told Napoleon that a man or a building is incessantly, and at all hours, represented by an image in the atmosphere, that all existing objects have there a kind of specter which can be captured and perceived, he would have consigned him to Charenton as a lunatic. . . . Yet that is what Daguerre's discovery proved." Honoré de Balzac, *Le Cousin Pons*, in *Oeuvres complètes*, vol. 18, *La Comédie humaine: Scènes de la vie parisienne*, 6 (Paris, 1914), pp. 129–130. "Just as physical objects in fact project themselves onto the atmosphere, so that it retains this specter which the daguerreotype can fix and capture, in the same way ideas . . . imprint themselves on what we must call the atmosphere of the spiritual world, . . . and live on in it *spectrally* (one must coin words in order to express unnamed phenomena). If that be granted, certain creatures endowed with rare faculties are perfectly capable of discerning these forms or these traces of ideas" (ibid., p. 132).[5]　　　　　　[Y8a,1]

"Degas was the first to attempt, in his pictures, the representation of rapid movement such as we get in instantaneous photography." Wladimir Weidlé, *Les Abeilles d'Aristée* (Paris ⟨1936⟩), p. 185 ("L'Agonie de l'art").　　　　　　[Y8a,2]

What author is being cited by Montesquiou in the following passage, which is taken from a handwritten text forming part of a richly ornamented volume of memorabilia shown in a display case at the Guys exhibition, in Paris, in the spring of 1937? "And that, in a few hasty words, is how it was: the first exhibition of Constantin Guys—newest surprise to be served up to us from his treasure-box of malice by M. Nadar,[6] the famous aeronaut and (should I say?) illustrious photographer. Surely, this ingenious spirit, steeped in the past, has a right to that title, in its noblest acceptation, and according to the admirable definition provided by a powerful and subtle thinker, in the course of some sublime pages: 'Humanity has also invented, in its evening peregrinations—that is to say, in the nineteenth century— the symbol of memory; it has invented what had seemed impossible; it has invented a mirror that remembers. It has invented photography.'"　　　　　　[Y8a,3]

"At no time in the past has art responded to aesthetic exigencies alone. The Gothic sculptors served God in working for his faithful; the portraitists aimed at verisimilitude; the peaches and the hares of a Chardin had their place in the dining room, above the family dinner table. Individual artists in certain cases (and they were few and far between, to be sure) may have suffered from this state of affairs; art as a whole could only profit from it. This is the way it has been throughout all the great artistic epochs. In particular, the naive conviction that they were only 'copying nature' was as salutary for the painters of those fortunate epochs as it was theoretically unjustifiable. The old Dutch masters looked upon themselves less as artists than as photographers, so to speak; it is only today that the photographer is absolutely determined to pass for an artist. Formerly, an engraving was above all a document, less exact (on the average) and more artistic than a photograph, but having the same function, fulfilling by and large the same practical role." Together with this important insight we have, from this author, another no less important, according to which the photographer is distinguished from the graphic artist not through the fundamentally greater realism of his works, but through a more highly mechanized technique, which does not necessarily diminish his artistic activity. None of this prevents the author from going on to say: "What is *unfortunate* [my italics] is not that today's photographer believes himself an *artist;* what is unfortunate is that he actually has at his disposal certain resources proper to the art of the painter." Wladimir Weidlé, *Les Abeilles d'Aristée* (Paris), pp. 181–182, 184 ("L'Agonie de l'art"). Compare Jochmann on the epic poem: "The general interest which such a poem excites, the pride with which an entire people repeats it, its legislative authority over opinions and sentiments—all this is grounded in the fact that it is nowhere taken as a *mere* poem." [Carl Gustav Jochmann,] *Über die Sprache* (Heidelberg, 1828), p. 271 ("Die Rückschritte der Poesie"). [Y9,1]

In the period around 1845, illustrations are already appearing in advertisements. On July 6 of this year, the Société Générale des Annonces, which handled *publicité* for *Le Journal des débats, Le Constitutionnel*, and *La Presse*, publishes a prospectus that says: "We call . . . your attention to the illustrations which, for some years now, a great many businesses have been in the habit of joining to their announcements. The power of captivating the eye by the form and disposition of the letters is perhaps less decisive than the advantage to be gained by filling out an often arid exposition with drawings and designs." P. Datz, *Histoire de la publicité*, vol. 1 (Paris, 1894), pp. 216–217. [Y9,2]

In his "Morale du joujou" ‹Philosophy of Toys›, Baudelaire mentions, together with the stereoscope, the phenakistiscope. "The phenakistiscope, which is older, is less well known. Imagine some movement or other—for example, a dancer's or a juggler's performance—divided up and decomposed into a certain number of movements. Imagine that each one of these movements—as many as twenty, if you wish—is represented by a complete figure of the juggler or dancer, and that these are all printed round the edge of a circular piece of cardboard." Baudelaire then describes the mirror mechanism that enables the viewer to see, in the twenty openings of an outer circle, twenty little figures moving rhythmically in a continuous action. Baudelaire, *L'Art romantique* (Paris), p. 146.[7] Compare Y7a,1. [Y9a,1]

It was the pantograph, whose principle is equally at work in the physiognotrace, that undertook to transcribe automatically a linear scheme originally traced on paper to a plaster mass, as required by the process of photosculpture. Serving as model in this process were twenty-four simultaneous views taken from different sides. Gautier foresees no threat to sculpture from this process. What can prevent the sculptor from artistically enlivening the mechanically produced figure and its ground? "But there is more: for all its extravagance, the century remains economical. Pure art seems to it something expensive. With the cheekiness of a parvenu, it sometimes dares to haggle over masterworks. It is terrified of marble and bronze. . . . But photosculpture is not so daunting as statuary. . . . Photosculpture is used to modest proportions and is content with a set of shelves for pedestal, happy to have faithfully reproduced a beloved countenance. . . . It does not disdain an overcoat, and is not embarrassed by crinolines; it accepts nature and the world as they are. Its sincerity accommodates everything, and though its plaster casts of stearin can be transposed into marble, into terracotta, into alabaster, or into bronze, . . . it never asks, in return for its work, what its elder sister would demand in payment; it requests only the cost of materials." Théophile Gautier, "Photosculpture: 42 Boulevard de l'Etoile," ⟨*Le Moniteur universel*⟩ (Paris, ⟨January 4,⟩ 1864), pp. 10–11. The essay includes, at the end, a woodcut with photosculptures, one of which portrays Gautier.   [Y9a,2]

"He refined the illusionary art of the panorama and invented the diorama. He joined forces with another painter, and on July 11, 1822, on the Rue de Sanson in Paris . . . , he opened an exhibition whose fame quickly spread. . . . This inventor and entrepreneur . . . was dubbed a knight in the Legion of Honor. Midnight Mass, the Temple of Solomon, Edinburgh in the sinister glow of a conflagration, and Napoleon's Tomb transfigured naturally by the aureole of a rosy sunset: such are the wonders that were shown here. A translator of Daguerre's own account of his two inventions (1839) portrays very nicely the multiplicity of lights involved, great and small, splendid, secret, and terrifying: 'The spectator sits in a small amphitheater; the stage seems to him covered by a curtain which is still bathed in darkness. Gradually, however, this darkness yields to a twilight . . . : a landscape or prospect emerges more clearly; the dawn is beginning. . . . Trees stand out from the shadows; the contours of mountains, of houses, become visible . . . ; the day has broken. The sun climbs ever higher; through the open window of a house one sees a kitchen stove slowly flaming up, while in a corner of the landscape a group of campers is ranged round a cooking pot, under which the campfire is beginning to blaze; a forge becomes visible, its furnace giving off sparks as though . . . from continuous stoking. After a while, . . . the daylight begins to wane, and the reddish luster of the artificial flame grows stronger; once again there is advancing twilight, and finally nocturnal gloom. Soon, however, the moonlight asserts its rights, and the region is visible anew in the soft tints of the illuminated night: a mariner's lantern flares up on board a ship that is anchored in the foreground of a harbor; in the background of an admirable perspective of a church, the candles on the altar are lighted, and the previously invisible parishioners are now illuminated by the rays streaming down from the altar; or grief-stricken men are standing at the edge of a landslide, its devastations lit up by the moon at the very spot where, shortly before, the Ruffiberg had formed the background to the lovely Swiss landscape of Goldau.'" Cited as "Übersetzer von Daguerres Schrift über seine beiden Erfindungen (1839)," in Dolf Sternberger, "Das wunderbare Licht: Zum 150 Geburtstag Daguerres," *Frankfurter Zeitung* ⟨21⟩, November 1937.   [Y10,1]

The entrance of the temporal factor into the panoramas is brought about through the succession of times of day (with well-known lighting tricks). In this way, the panorama transcends painting and anticipates photography. Owing to its technological formation, the photograph, in contrast to the painting, can and must be correlated with a well-defined and continuous segment of time (exposure time). In this chronological specifiability, the political significance of the photograph is already contained *in nuce*.   [Y10,2]

"In these deplorable times, a new industry has developed, which has helped in no small way to confirm fools in their faith and to ruin what vestige of the divine might still have remained in the French mind. Of course, this idolatrous multitude was calling for an ideal worthy of itself and in keeping with its own nature. In the domain of painting and statuary, the present-day credo of the worldly-wise . . . is this: 'I believe . . . that art is, and can only be, the exact reproduction of nature. . . . Thus, if an industrial process could give us a result identical to nature, that would be absolute art.' An avenging God has heard the prayers of this multitude. Daguerre was his messiah. And then they said to themselves: 'Since photography provides us with every desirable guarantee of exactitude' (they believe that, poor madmen!), 'art is photography.' From that moment onward, our loathsome society rushed, like Narcissus, to contemplate its trivial image on the metallic plate. A form of lunacy, an extraordinary fanaticism, took hold of these new sun-worshippers. Strange abominations manifested themselves. By bringing together and posing a pack of rascals, male and female, dressed up like carnival-time butchers and washerwomen, and in persuading these 'heroes' to 'hold' their improvised grimaces for as long as the photographic process required, people really believed they could represent the tragic and charming scenes of ancient history. . . . It was not long before thousands of pairs of greedy eyes were glued to the peepholes of the stereoscope, as though they were the skylights of the infinite. The love of obscenity, which is as vigorous a growth in the heart of natural man as self-love, could not let slip such a glorious opportunity for its own satisfaction. . . . [p. 223] . . . I am convinced that the badly applied advances of photography—like all purely material progress, for that matter—have greatly contributed to the impoverishment of French artistic genius, already so rare. . . . Poetry and progress are two ambitious men who hate each other with an instinctive hatred, and when they meet along the same road one of them must give way." Charles Baudelaire, *Oeuvres* ⟨ed. Le Dantec⟩, vol. 2 ⟨Paris, 1932⟩, pp. 222–224 ("Salon de 1859: Le Public moderne et la photographie").[8]   [Y10a,1]

Baudelaire speaks, in "Quelques Caricaturistes français" (apropos of Monnier), of "the cruel and surprising charm of daguerreotypes." Charles Baudelaire, *Oeuvres*, ed. Le Dantec, vol. 2, p. 197.[9]   [Y10a,2]

"Poetry and progress are two ambitious men who hate each other with an instinctive hatred, and when they meet along the same road, one of them must give way. If photography is allowed to supplement art in some of its functions, it will soon have supplanted or corrupted it altogether, thanks to the stupidity of the multitude which is its natural ally. It is time, then, for it to return to its true duty, which is to be the servant of the sciences and arts—but the very humble servant, like printing or shorthand, which have neither created nor supplemented literature. Let it hasten to enrich the tourist's album and restore to his eye the precision which his memory may lack; let it adorn the naturalist's library, and enlarge microscopic animals; let it even provide information to corroborate the astronomer's hypotheses. In short, let it be the secretary and clerk of whoever needs absolute factual exactitude in his profession—up to that point nothing could be better. Let it rescue from oblivion those tumbling ruins, those books, prints, and manuscripts which time is devouring, precious things whose form is dissolving and which demand a place in the archives of our memory—it will be thanked and applauded. But if it be allowed to encroach upon the domain of the impalpable and the imaginary, upon anything whose value depends solely upon the addition of something of a man's soul, then it will be so much the worse for us!" Charles Baudelaire, *Oeuvres*, ed. Le Dantec, vol. 2, p. 224 ("Salon de 1859: Le Public moderne et la photographie").[10]   [Y11,1]

Cocteau's *Les Mariés de la tour Eiffel*[11] can perhaps be considered a "critique of the snapshot," insofar as in this piece the two aspects of shock—its technological function in the mechanism and its sterilizing function in the experience—both come into play.   [Y11,2]

Z

[The Doll, The Automaton]

> I was always, among human beings, the only doll[1] with a heart.
>
> —Amalie Winter, *Memoiren einer Berliner Puppe, für Kinder von 5 bis 10 Jahren und für deren Mütter* (Leipzig, 1852), p. 93

> Where, instead of the clock, the eyes indicate the hours.
>
> —Franz Dingelstedt, *Ein Roman;* cited in Adolf Strodtmann, *Dichterprofile,* vol. 1 (Stuttgart, 1879), p. 111

"The clever Parisiennes . . . , in order to disseminate their fashions more easily, made use of an especially conspicuous reproduction of their new creations—namely, tailors' dummies. . . . These dolls, which still enjoyed considerable importance in the seventeenth and eighteenth centuries, were given to little girls as playthings when their career as fashion figurines had ended." Karl Gröber, *Kinderspielzeug aus alter Zeit* (Berlin, 1927), pp. 31–32. ☐ Fashion ☐ Advertising ☐
[Z1,1]

They are the true fairies of these arcades (more salable and more worn than the life-sized ones): the formerly world-famous Parisian dolls, which revolved on their musical socle and bore in their arms a doll-sized basket out of which, at the salutation of the minor chord, a lambkin poked its curious muzzle. When Hackländer made use of this "newest invention of industrial luxury" for one of his fairy tales, he too placed the marvelous dolls in the dangerous arcade which sister Tinchen, at the behest of the fairy Concordia, has to wander in order finally to rescue her poor brothers. "Fearlessly, Tinchen stepped across the border into the enchanted land, all the while thinking only of her brothers. At first she noticed nothing unusual, but soon the way led through an enormous room entirely filled with toys. She saw small booths stocked with everything imaginable—carousels with miniature horses and carriages, swings and rocking horses, but above all the most splendid dollhouses. Around a small covered table, large dolls were sitting on easy chairs; and as Tinchen turned her gaze upon them, the largest and most beautiful of these dolls stood up, made her a gracious bow, and spoke to her in a little voice of exquisite refinement." The child may not want to hear of toys that are bewitched, but the evil spell of this slippery path readily takes the form, even today, of large animated dolls. □ Advertising □ [Z1,2]

"The fashion is supposed to have been invented by Longchamps. I've not seen anything new, but tomorrow in their bulletins all the "Friendly Sprites," all the "Petits Couriers des Dames," all the "Psyches" will report on new attire that was already designed and available before Longchamps ever came on the scene. I strongly suspect that in many of the coaches, instead of the lady who would seem to be seated inside, there was only a dummy which the owners of these fine vehicles had dressed according to their own taste in shawls and satins and silks." Karl Gutzkow, *Briefe aus Paris* (Leipzig, 1842), vol. 1, pp. 119–120. [Z1,3]

From the *Ombres Chinoises* ‹Chinese Shadows› of the Palais-Royal: "A . . . demoiselle gave birth on stage, and the children could immediately scamper about like moles. There were four of them, and they danced together a few moments after the birth in a pleasant quadrille. Another young woman started tossing her head vigorously, and in the twinkling of an eye a second demoiselle had stepped fully clothed from out of her head. This latter at once began dancing but, the next minute, was seized in turn with head-shaking; these were labor pains, and a third demoiselle stepped out of her head. She, too, immediately began dancing but soon took to tossing her head like the others, and out of her arose the fourth demoiselle. It continued in this manner until eight generations were there on the stage—all related to one another through spontaneous generation, like lice." J. F. Benzenberg, *Briefe geschrieben auf einer Reise nach Paris* (Dortmund, 1805), vol. 1, p. 294. [Z1,4]

At a certain point in time, the motif of the doll acquires a sociocritical significance. For example: "You have no idea how repulsive these automatons and dolls can become, and how one breathes at last on encountering a full-blooded being in this society." Paul Lindau, *Der Abend* (Berlin, 1896), p. 17. [Z1,5]

"In a shop on the Rue Legendre, in Batignolles, a whole series of female busts, without heads or legs, with curtain hooks in place of arms and a percaline skin of arbitrary hue—bean brown, glaring pink, hard black—are lined up like a row of onions, impaled on rods, or set out on tables. . . . The sight of this ebb tide of bosoms, this Musée Curtius of breasts, puts one vaguely in mind of those vaults in the Louvre where classical sculptures are housed, where one and the same torso, eternally repeated, beguiles the time for those who look it over, with a yawn, on rainy days. . . . How superior to the dreary statues of Venus they are—these dressmakers' mannequins, with their lifelike comportment; how much more provocative these padded busts, which, exposed there, bring on a train of reveries: libertine reveries, inspired by ephebic nipples and slightly bruised bubs; charitable reveries, recalling old breasts, shriveled with chlorosis or bloated with fat.— For one thinks of the sorrows of women who . . . experience the growing indifference of a husband, or the imminent desertion of a lover, or the final disarming of those charms which allowed them once to conquer, in the unavoidable battles they wage for the closed-up wallet of the man." J.-K. Huysmans, *Croquis parisiens* (Paris, 1886), pp. 129, 131–132 ("L'Etiage" ‹Ebb Tide›). [Z1a,1]

"Not long before the end of the Empire, a very special question arose: that of the Pupazzi. People wanted these wooden marionettes to perform *Le Roi Prudhomme* at the Théâtre des Variétés. The cast of characters for this playlet included the Emperor, Emile Olivier, . . . V. Hugo, . . . Gambetta, . . . and Rochefort. . . . The piece had been performed in drawing rooms and even in the Tuileries. But these private performances did not in the least prepare for the effects of any public performance, and the authorities refused to allow . . . the theater to embark on this path." Victor Hallays-Dabot, *La Censure dramatique et le théâtre (1850–1870)* (Paris, 1871), p. 86. [Z1a,2]

"In the competitions surrounding the material ornament . . . of attire, the popularity of dolls is put to use. . . . The Little Bands (in which girls make up the majority) are entrusted with the presentation of dolls and mannequins, among which a choice is to be made." Charles Fourier, *Le Nouveau Monde industriel et sociétaire* (Paris, 1829), p. 252. [Z1a,3]

While writing *Les Travailleurs de la mer* ‹The Toilers of the Sea›, Victor Hugo kept before him a doll dressed in the antique garb of a Guernsey woman. Someone had procured it for him; it served as a model for Déruchette. [Z1a,4]

Marx explains that "the two material bases on which the preparations for machine-operated industry proceeded within manufacture during the period from the sixteenth to the middle of the eighteenth century (the period in which manufacture was developing from handicraft into large-scale industry proper) were the clock and the mill (at first the corn mill, specifically, the water mill). Both were inherited from the ancients. . . . The clock was the first automatic device applied to practical purposes; the whole theory of the production of regular motion was developed through it. Its nature is such that it is based on a combination of semiartistic handicraft and direct theory. Cardanus, for instance, wrote about (and gave practical formulas for) the construction of clocks. German authors of the sixteenth century called clockmaking 'learned (nonguild) handicraft' and it would be possible to show from the development of the clock how entirely different the relation between science and practice was in the context of handicraft from what it is, for instance, in modern large-scale industry. There is also no doubt that in the eighteenth century the idea of applying automatic devices (moved by springs) to production was first suggested by the clock. It can be proved historically that Vaucanson's experiments along these lines had a tremendous influence on the imagination of English inventors. On the other hand, from the very beginning, as soon as the water mill was invented, the mill possessed the essential elements of the organism of a machine. The mechanical motive power. First, the motor, on which it depends; then the transmission mechanism; and finally the working machine, which deals with the material—each element existing independently of the others. The theory of friction, and with it the investigations into the mathematical forms of gear-wheels, cogs, and so forth, were all developed in connection with the mill; the same applies to the theory of measurement of the degree of motive power, of the best way of employing it, and so on. Almost all the great mathematicians since the middle of the seventeenth century, so far as they dealt with practical mechanics and worked out its theoretical side, started from the simple water-driven corn mill. And indeed this was why the name *Mühle*, 'mill,' which arose during the manufacturing period, came to be applied to all mechanical forms of motive power adapted to practical purposes. But in the case of the mill, as in that of the press, the forge, the plough, and other implements, the work proper—that of beating, crushing, grinding, pulverizing, and so on—has been performed from the very first without human labor, even though the moving force was human or animal. This kind of machinery is therefore very ancient. . . . Hence, it is practically the only machinery found in the manufacturing period. The industrial revolution begins as soon as mechanisms are employed where, from ancient times, the final result has required human labor; hence not where, as with the tools mentioned above, the material actually to be worked up has never been dealt with by the human hand." Marx to Engels, January 28, 1863, from London [in Karl Marx and Friedrich Engels, *Ausgewählte Briefe*, ed. V. Adoratski (Moscow and Leningrad, 1934), pp. 118–119].[2]   [Z2]

In his study "La Mante religieuse: Recherches sur la nature et la signification du mythe" ‹The Praying Mantis: Investigations into the Nature and Meaning of Myth›, Caillois refers to the striking automatism of reflexes in the praying mantis (there is hardly a vital function that it does not also perform decapitated). He links it, on account of its fateful significance, with the baneful automatons known to us from myths. Thus Pandora: "automaton fabricated by the blacksmith god for the ruin of humankind, for that 'which all shall / take to their hearts with delight, an evil to love and embrace' (Hesiod, *Works and Days*, line 58).[3] We encounter something similar in the Indian Krtya—those dolls, animated by sorcerers, which bring about the death of men who embrace them. Our literature as well, in the motif of femmes fatales, possesses the concept of a woman-machine, artificial, mechanical, at variance with all living creatures, and above all murderous. No doubt psycho-analysis would not hesitate to explain this representation in its own terms by envisaging the relations between death and sexuality and, more precisely, by finding each ambiguously intimated in the other." Roger Caillois, "La Mante religieuse: Recherches sur la nature et la signification du mythe," *Mesures*, 3, no. 2 (April 15, 1937), p. 110.   [Z2a,1]

Baudelaire, in the section, "Les Femmes et les filles" ‹Women and Prostitutes› in his essay on Guys, cites the words of La Bruyère: "Some women possess an artificial nobility which is associated with a movement of the eye, a tilt of the head, a manner of deportment, and which goes no further." Compare Baudelaire's "Le

Mensonge."—In the same section, Baudelaire cites the concept of "the *femina simplex* of the Roman satirist" (*L'Art romantique* [Paris], p. 109).[4]　　　[Z2a,2]

Beginnings of large-scale industry: "We find great numbers of peasants emigrating to the cities, where steam energy permits the concentration of factories that formerly were scattered along the banks of rivers." Pierre-Maxime Schuhl, *Machinisme et philosophie* (Paris, 1938), pp. 56–57.　　　[Z2a,3]

"Aristotle declares that slavery would cease to be necessary if only the shuttles and plectrums could set themselves going on their own. The idea accords admirably with his definition of the slave as animated instrument. . . . By the same token, the ancient poet Pherecydes of Syros had told how the Dactyls, after building a new house for Zeus, had fashioned for him male and female servants as well. We are in the realm of fable. . . . Yet before three centuries have passed, an Anthology poet, Antiphilos of Byzantium, offers a response to Aristotle by singing of the invention of the water mill, which liberates women from the arduous task of grinding: 'Spare the hand that grinds the corn, O miller girls, and softly sleep. Let Chanticleer announce the morn in vain! Demeter has commanded that the girls' work be done by Nymphs, and now they skip lightly over the wheels, so that the shaken axles revolve with their spokes and pull round the load of revolving stones. Let us live the life of our fathers, and let us rest from work and enjoy the gifts that Demeter sends us." (Note: "*Anthologie Palatine*, vol. 9, p. 418. This epigram . . . has already been related to the text of Aristotle, and for the first time, it would seem, by Marx"—presumably, in *Kapital*, vol. 3 ‹trans. Molitor [Paris, 1924]›, p. 61.) Pierre-Maxime Schuhl, *Machinisme et philosophie* (Paris, 1938), pp. 19–20.[5]

[Z3]

a

[Social Movement]

> Reveal to these depraved,
> O Republic, by foiling their plots,
> Your great Medusa face
> Ringed by red lightning.
>
> —French workers' song around 1850, cited in Adolf Stahr, *Zwei*
> *Monate in Paris* (Oldenburg, 1851), vol. 2, p. 199

> Rabble of the faithless, the soulless, the rootless,
> Who want to wipe out every art and industry,
> To crush underfoot the cult of the Cross,
> And drown in an ocean of blood and flames
> —Its waves have risen round the flanks of Paris—
> Temples, palaces, priests, peoples, and kings!
>
> —Edouard d'Anglemont, *L'Internationale* (Paris, 1871), p. 7

> Palermo has Etna; Paris, *la pensée*.
>
> —Victor Hugo, *Paris* [*Littérature et philosophie mêlée* (Paris, 1867),
> pp. 466–467], cited in Georges Batault, *Le Pontife de la démagogie:*
> *Victor Hugo* (Paris, 1934), p. 203

"Since the Surrealists constantly confuse moral nonconformism with proletarian revolution, they attempt, instead of following the course of the modern world, to relocate themselves to a historical moment when this confusion was still possible, a moment anterior to the Congress of Tours, anterior even to the development of Marxism: the period of the 1820s, '30s and '40s." Emmanuel Berl, "Premier Pamphlet," *Europe*, 75 (March 15, 1929), p. 402. And that is certainly no accident. For, on the one hand, we have here elements—anthropological materialism, hostility toward progress—which are refractory to Marxism, while, on the other hand, the will to apocatastasis speaks here, the resolve to gather again, in revolutionary action and in revolutionary thinking, precisely the elements of the "too early" and the "too late," of the first beginning and the final decay.   [a1,1]

It is really imperative that we understand, in precisely its polemical bearing, the apotheosis of organization and of rationalism which the Communist party has to promote unceasingly in the face of feudal and hierarchical powers, and that we be clear about the fact that the movement itself comprehends mystical elements as well, although of an entirely different sort. It is even more important, naturally, not to confuse these mystical elements, which pertain to corporality, with religious elements. [a1,2]

Episode of the February Revolution. On the twenty-third, at eleven o'clock in the evening, a fusillade on the Boulevard des Capucines: twenty-three dead. "The corpses are immediately paraded through the streets in a masterly, romantic *mise en scène*. 'Midnight is about to sound. The boulevards are still faintly lighted by the fading illumination [the celebratory illumination occasioned by the retreat of Guizot]. The doors and windows of the houses and shops are shut, everyone having returned home with heavy hearts. . . . All of a sudden, a muffled rumbling is heard on the paving stones, and some windows are cautiously opened. . . . In a cart drawn by a white horse, with a bare-armed worker holding the reins, five cadavers are arranged in horrible symmetry. Standing on the shaft is a child of the working class, sallow of complexion, a fixed and ardent look upon his face, his arm extended, nearly immobile, as though to represent the Genius of Vengeance; leaning backward, this boy lights up, with the beams of his torch, the body of a young woman whose livid neck and bosom are stained with a long trail of blood. From time to time another worker, positioned behind the cart, raises this lifeless body with a muscular arm and—his torch all the while emitting sparks and flakes of fire—casts his savage gaze over the crowd, shouting, "Vengeance! Vengeance! They are slaughtering the people!" "To Arms!" respond some voices; and the corpse falls back into the bottom of the cart, which continues on its way.'" (Daniel Stern). Dubech and d'Espezel, *Histoire de Paris* (Paris, 1926), p. 396. ▯ Lighting ▯ [a1,3]

The masses of workers mobilized by Haussmann were compared—unfavorably— to those incorporated in the national workshops of 1848. ▯ Haussmann ▯ [a1,4]

"The favorite readings of the working-class tailor are the histories of the Revolution of 1789. He likes it when these texts develop the idea that this revolution was a good thing, and that it improved the condition of the working class. He is inspired by the aura of drama lent to men and events by several famous authors. . . . Not perceiving that the principal cause of his social inferiority lies within himself, he likes to think that these men are the models for those who, in forging a new progress, will preserve him from all kinds of calamities." F. Le Play, *Les Ouvriers européens* ⟨Paris, 1855⟩, p. 277. [a1,5]

"Street warfare today has its own technique; it was perfected, after the armed takeover of Munich ⟨1848?⟩, in a curious little confidential work published with great secrecy by the government in Berlin. One no longer advances through the streets; they are left empty. A path is opened within the interiors of houses, by breaking through walls. As soon as one has taken a street, one organizes it; lines of communication are laid through the holes in the walls, while, to prevent the return of the adversary, one immediately mines the conquered ground. . . . Perhaps the clearest sign of progress, here, is that one need not concern oneself at all with sparing houses or lives. Compared with civil wars of the future, the episode of the Rue Transnonain ‹see a10a,5› will seem quite . . . innocent and archaic." Dubech and d'Espezel, *Histoire de Paris* (Paris, 1926), p. 479. ☐ Haussmann ☐   [a1a,1]

Family budget of a Parisian ragpicker, 1849–1851, according to F. Le Play, *Les Ouvriers européens* (Paris, 1855), pp. 274–275. An excerpt: "Section 4. Expenses for moral improvement, recreation, and health. . . . Instruction for the children: school fees paid by employer, 48 francs; books purchased, 1 franc 45 centimes; relief and alms (workers at this level ordinarily give no alms at all). Recreation and festivities: meal taken together by the entire family at one of the *barrières* of Paris (eight excursions per year), including wine, bread, and fried potatoes, 8 francs; meal of macaroni, with butter, cheese, and wine, taken on Christmas, Mardi Gras, Easter, and Pentecost: expenses included in the first section; chewing tobacco for the worker (cigar butts collected by the worker), 6.8 kilos worth 5–34 francs; snuff for the wife (purchased), 2.33 kilos worth 18 francs 66 centimes; toys and other gifts given to the child, 1 franc. . . . Correspondence with relatives: letters from the worker's brothers living in Italy, on average one per year. . . . Note: The main resource for the family, in case of accidents, is private charity. . . . Savings for the year (the worker—altogether incapable of prudent habits, and desirous, above all, of giving his wife and little girl all the comforts they deserve—never manages to save anything; he spends, day by day, all he earns)."   [a1a,2]

"The damage done to the morality of the improvident worker by the substitution of antagonism for solidarity consists precisely in the loss of all opportunity of exercising his natural virtues in the only way that would be practicable for him. The devotion displayed in the wish to do well, in the concern for the interests of the employer, or in the sacrifice of needs and desires irreconcilable with the regularity of work is, in fact, more feasible for the worker than the devotion which would lead to assisting his comrades with a sum of money. . . . The faculty of giving aid and protection of any consequence belongs to the upper classes; it can manifest itself among the workers as an immediate and short-lived enthusiasm, but the virtue most within their reach is clearly the performance of their task for the employer." M. F. Le Play, *Les Ouvriers européens* (Paris, 1855), "Printed by authority of the Emperor and the Imperial Press," p. 278.   [a1a,3]

The "small landowners of the suburbs." "They cultivate vines . . . that produce a wine of inferior quality, for which the consumption tax in effect inside the capital ensures a profitable market in the suburbs." F. Le Play, *Les Ouvriers européens* (Paris, 1855), p. 271.   [a1a,4]

"There is a tropical plant that for years remains unremarkable and brings forth no blossom, until finally, one day, an explosion resounds like a rifle shot and, some days later, from out of this thicket a wonderful giant of a flower arises, whose growth is so rapid that one can witness its unfolding with the naked eye. Just so paltry and stunted remained the French working class in a corner of society, until suddenly the explosion of the February Revolution was heard. But with that, a gigantic blossom shot up from the unremarkable bushes, and this bloom full of sap and vitality, full of beauty and significance, was called the association <a term derived from the Saint-Simonians>." Sigmund Engländer, *Geschichte der französischen Arbeiter-Associationen* (Hamburg, 1864), vol. 4, p. 217. [a2,1]

Organization of the state workshops *(ateliers nationaux)* by Thomas. "It suffices to mention that Emile Thomas divided the workers into brigades and companies, and that their chiefs were elected by universal suffrage of the workers. Every company had its flag, and Emile Thomas made use, for this organization, of other civil engineers and of students from the Ecole Polytechnique, who, through their youth, exerted a moral influence on the workers. . . . Nevertheless, although the minister of public works ordered the state engineers to come up with proposals for works . . . , the engineers in charge of bridges and roads decided not to comply with the minister's order, for in France there had long been a great rivalry between state engineers and civil engineers,[1] and it was the latter who directed the national workshops. Thomas was therefore left to his own resources, and he never could assign to such an army of workers, whose ranks were daily swelling, any sort of useful work. Thus, for example, he had trees from the outskirts of Paris brought into the city to be planted along the boulevards, because during the struggles of February the old trees on the boulevard had been cut down. The workers with the trees paraded slowly across Paris, singing as they went. . . . Other workers, who had the job, for example, of cleaning the railings of bridges, became an object of derision for passersby, and so the majority of these workers also wound up passing their time in mere cardplaying, singing, and the like. . . . The national workshops before long became . . . the gathering place for all sorts of vagabonds and idlers, whose labor consisted exclusively in marching through the streets with their standard bearers, here and there mending the pavement or turning up earth, but on the whole—singing and shouting, ragtag and unruly—doing whatever came into their heads. . . . One day, there suddenly appeared on the scene 600 actors, painters, artists, and agents, who together announced that, since the republic was guaranteeing work to all citizens, they too were putting forward their claim. Thomas made them inspectors." Sigmund Engländer, *Geschichte der französischen Arbeiter-Associationen* (Hamburg, 1864), vol. 2, pp. 268–271. ▢ Flâneur ▢
[a2,2]

"Neither the mayors nor the police commissioners, who had to sign the certificates attesting to the bearers' eligibility to work in Paris, could maintain the slightest control in view of the threats circulating against them. In their anxiety, they even gave certificates to ten-year-old children, who, with these in hand, presented themselves for admission to the national workshops." Sigmund Engländer, *Geschichte der französischen Arbeiter-Associationen* (Hamburg, 1864), vol. 2, p. 272. [a2a,1]

Episodes in the June Insurrection: "Women were seen pouring boiling oil or hot water on the soldiers while shrieking and bellowing. In many places, insurgents were given brandy mixed with various ingredients, so that they would be excited to madness. . . . Some women cut off the sexual organs of several imprisoned guardsmen, and we know that an insurgent dressed in woman's clothing beheaded a number of captured officers . . .; people saw the heads of soldiers on pikes that were planted atop barricades. Many things recounted were pure invention—for example, that the insurgents had pinioned captured guardsmen between two boards and sawed them, while alive, into pieces. On the other hand, things did in fact occur that were no less horrible. . . . Many insurgents used bullets of a type that could not be removed from wounds after shooting, because a wire had been inserted into these bullets which sprang out from the sides of them on impact. Behind numerous barricades were spray guns, which were used to spray sulphuric acid on attacking soldiers. It would be impossible to detail all the fiendish barbarities perpetrated by both sides in this action; we shall merely observe that world history can point to nothing comparable." Engländer, vol. 2, pp. 288–289.

[a2a,2]

June Insurrection. "On many closed shops, the insurgents would write: 'Respect Property! Death to Thieves!' Many flags on the barricades bore the words: 'Bread and Work.' On the Rue Saint-Martin, on the first day, a jeweler's shop stayed open without being threatened by any sort of harm, while, a few steps beyond, a store with a supply of scrap iron was plundered. . . . Many insurgents, during the battle, had assembled their wives and children on the barricades, and cried: 'Since we can no longer feed them, we want at least to die all together!' While the men fought, the women made gunpowder and their children cast bullets, using every piece of lead or tin that fell into their hands. Often the children molded the bullets with thimbles. At night, while the combatants were sleeping, girls would drag paving stones to the barricades." Engländer, vol. 2, pp. 291, 293.   [a2a,3]

Barricades of 1848: "More than 400 were counted. Many, fronted by trenches and battlements, reached a height of two stories." Malet and Grillet, *XIXe Siècle* (Paris, 1919), p. 249.   [a2a,4]

"In 1839, some workers in Paris founded a newspaper with the title *La Ruche populaire*.[2] . . . The editorial office of this publication was located in the poorest section of the city, on the Rue des Quatre Fils. It was one of the few worker-run newspapers to have an audience among the general population, which can be explained by the tendency it followed. That is, it took as its program the goal of bringing hidden misery to the notice of wealthy benefactors. . . . In the office of this journal a register of misery lay open, in which every starveling could inscribe his name. It was imposing, this register of misfortune, and since at this period *Les Mystères de Paris*, by Eugène Sue, had brought charity into fashion within high society, one often saw private carriages pull up before the dirty premises of the editorial office and blasé ladies step forth to secure addresses of the unfortunate;

they would then deliver alms personally to these people and, in this way, derive a novel stimulus for their jaded nerves. Each number of this workers' review began with a summary enumeration of the poor people who had registered with the editor; details of their plight could be found in the register itself. . . . Even after the February Revolution, at a time when all social classes looked on one another with distrust, . . . *La Ruche populaire* continued to facilitate personal contacts between rich and poor. . . . This is all the more remarkable in light of the fact that, even during this period, all articles in *La Ruche populaire* were written by actual workers engaged in some practical occupation." Sigmund Engländer, *Geschichte der französischen Arbeiter-Associationen* (Hamburg, 1864), vol. 2, pp. 78–80, 82–83. [a3,1]

"The expansion achieved by industry in Paris during the past thirty years has given a certain importance to the trade of ragpicker, which occupies the lowest level on the industrial scale. Men, women, and children can all easily devote themselves to the practice of this trade, which requires no apprenticeship and calls for tools that are as simple as its methods—a basket, a hook, and a lantern comprising the ragpicker's only equipment. The adult ragpicker, in order to earn 25–40 sous per day (depending on the season), is ordinarily obliged to make three rounds, two during the day and one at night; the first two take place from five o'clock in the morning until nine o'clock, and from eleven o'clock until [here, there are four pages missing from the copy in the Bibliothèque Nationale!]. Like salaried workers, they have a habit of frequenting taverns. . . . Like them, and more than them, they make a show of the expenditures which this habit entails. Among the older ragpickers and particularly among the older women, spirits hold an attraction like nothing else. . . . The ragpickers are not always content with ordinary wine in these taverns; they like to order mulled wine, and they take great offense if this drink does not contain, along with a strong dose of sugar, the aroma produced by the use of lemons." H.-A. Frégier, *Des Classes dangereuses de la population* ‹*dans les grandes villes et des moyens de les rendre meilleures*› (Paris, 1840), vol. 1, pp. 104, 109. [a3,2]

Frégier speaks at length about the public scriveners,[3] who must have stood in the worst repute, and from whose circles emerges one Lacenaire, esteemed for his beautiful handwriting.—"I heard tell of an old sailor endowed with a remarkable talent for fine handwriting, who, in the depths of the winter, had nary a shirt on his back, and would hide his nakedness by fastening his waistcoat with a pin. This individual, who was scarcely clothed, and who was not only ragged but nauseatingly filthy, would on occasion spend five to six francs on his dinner." H.-A. Frégier, *Des Classes dangereuses de la population* (Paris, 1840), vol. 1, pp. 117–118. [a3a,1]

"If it happens that an entrepreneur reproaches a worker in the presence of his comrades, and in a manner he feels to be unjust, . . . then the worker lays down his tools and heads for the tavern. . . . In many industrial establishments that are not rigorously monitored, the worker is not satisfied with going to the tavern before the hour when work begins and at his mealtimes, which are at nine o'clock and two o'clock; he goes there also at four o'clock and in the evening, on the way home. . . . There are women who have no compunctions about following their husbands to the *barrière*, in company with their children (who are already able to work), in order, as they say, to live it up. . . . There they spend a large portion of the income of the entire family, and return home Monday evening in a state bordering on drunkenness. Indeed, they often pretend—the children no less than their parents—to be more inebriated than they really are, so that everyone will know they've been drinking, and drinking well." H.-A. Frégier, *Des Classes dangereuses de la population* (Paris, 1840), vol. 1, pp. 79–80, 86.   [a3a,2]

On child labor among textile workers: "Unable to meet the costs of food and of caring for their children on their modest salary, which often does not exceed forty sous per day (not even when added to the salary of the wife, who earns barely half that amount), . . . workers find themselves obliged . . . to place their children, as soon as they are old enough to work (ordinarily, at age seven or eight), in the establishments of which we are speaking. . . . The workers keep their children working in the factory or mill until the age of twelve. At that point, they see that the children make their first Communion, and then they secure them an apprenticeship in a shop." H.-A. Frégier, vol. 1, pp. 98–100.   [a3a,3]

> There's brass in our pockets,
> Pierre, let's go live it up;
> On Mondays, don't you know,
> I love to knock about.
> I know of a sixpenny wine
> That's not half bad,
> So let's have some fun,
> Let's go up to the *barrière*.

H. Gourdon de Genouillac, *Les Refrains de la rue, de 1830 à 1870* (Paris, 1879), p. 56.   [a3a,4]

"And what wine! What variety—from bordeaux to burgundy, from burgundy to full-bodied Saint-Georges, to Lünel and the South's Frontignan, and from there to sparkling champagne! What a choice of whites and reds—from Petit Mâcon or chablis to Chambertin, to Château Larose, to sauterne, to Vin du Roussillon, and Aï Mousseux! Bear in mind that each of these wines produces a different sort of intoxication, and that with a few bottles one can pass through all the intervening stages from a Musard quadrille to "La Marseillaise," from the wanton pleasures of the cancan to the fiery ardor of revolutionary fever, thence to return, with a bottle of champagne, to the cheeriest carnival mood in the world! And only France has a Paris, a city in which European civilization attains its fullest flowering, in which all the nerve fibers of European history are intertwined, and from which arise, at regular intervals, those tremors which shake the terrestrial globe; a city whose population unites, like that of no other city on earth, the passion for enjoyment with the passion for historical action, whose inhabitants know how to live like the most refined of Athenian epicures and to die like the most unflinching Spartan— Alcibiades and Leonidas rolled up into one; a city which really is, as Louis Blanc says, the heart and brain of the world." Friedrich Engels, "Von Paris nach Bern: Ein Reisefragment," *Die neue Zeit*, 17, no. 1 (Stuttgart, 1899), p. 10.—In his foreword to this publication of the posthumous manuscript, Eduard Bernstein writes: "Although a fragment, this travel sketch gives us, perhaps, a better picture of its author than does any other of his works" (ibid., p. 8). [a4,1]

A song, "Jenny the Worker," whose refrain was inspiring to women:

> In a garden, 'neath a fragrant bower,
> You may hear a familiar bird:
> 'Tis the singing of Jenny the worker,
> At heart content, content with little.
> She could be rich, but prefers
> The things she has from God.

H. Gourdon de Genouillac, *Les Refrains de la rue, de 1830 à 1870* (Paris, 1879), pp. 67–68. [a4,2]

A reactionary song, after the June Insurrection:

> See, see this funeral procession!
> It's the archbishop—friends, remove your hats;
> Victim, alas, of sacrilegious combat,
> He is fallen for the *happiness* of all."[4]

H. Gourdon de Genouillac, *Les Refrains de la rue, de 1830 à 1870* (Paris, 1879), p. 78. [a4a,1]

"The proletarians have . . . composed a terrible, bitter "Marseillaise," which they sing in unison in the workshops, and which may be judged by the refrain: 'Sow the field, all you proles; / It's the idler who will reap.'" "Die socialistischen und communistischen Bewegungen seit der dritten französischen Revolution," opening of Stein's *Socialismus und Communismus des heutigen Frankreichs* (Leipzig and Vienna, 1848), p. 210 [from V. Considérant, *Théorie du droit de propriété et du droit de travail* ‹1848›]. [a4a,2]

Buret reports on a story in *La Revue britannique* of December 1839 (?), p. 29 (?): "The associated workers of Brighton consider machines to be absolutely beneficial. 'But,' they add, 'they are fatal as applied in the current regime. Instead of dutifully serving, as the elves served the shoemaker in the German fairy tale, the machines have behaved like Frankenstein's monster (German legend), who, after acquiring life, employed it only in persecuting the man who had given it to him.'" Eugène Buret, *La Misère des classes laborieuses en Angleterre et en France* (Paris, 1840), vol. 2, p. 219. [a4a,3]

"If the vices of the lower classes were limited, in their effects, to those who indulged in them, we may suppose that the upper classes would cease to concern themselves with all these dismal questions, and would happily leave the world at large to the sway of good and bad causes that rule over it. But . . . everything is linked together. If poverty is the mother of vices, then vice is the father of crime; and it is in this way that the interests of all the classes are conjoined." Eugène Buret, *La Misère des classes laborieuses en Angleterre et en France* (Paris, 1840), vol. 2, p. 262. [a4a,4]

"*Jenny the Worker* brings to life one of the most terrible afflictions of the social organism: the daughter of the working class . . . constrained to sacrifice her virtue for her family, and to sell herself . . . in order to provide bread for her loved ones. . . . As for the prologue to *Jenny the Worker,* it acknowledges neither the play's point of departure nor the details of poverty and hunger." Victor Hallays-Dabot, *La Censure dramatique et le théâtre, 1850–1870* (Paris, 1871), pp. 75–76. [a4a,5]

"In the mind of the factory boss, workers are not men but forces, and expensive ones at that—instruments more intractable and less economical than tools of iron and fire. . . . Without being cruel, he can be completely indifferent to the sufferings of a class of men with whom he has no moral commerce, no sentiments in common. Doubtless Madame de Sévigné was not an evil woman, . . . yet Madame de Sévigné, while detailing the atrocious punishments meted out to the people of Brittany who had rioted over a tax, Madame de Sévigné, the impassioned mother, speaks of hangings and of thrashings . . . in a light, cavalier tone that betrays not the slightest sympathy. . . . I doubt that, under the rule of the current laws of industry, there could be any more of a moral community between employers and their workers than there was, in the seventeenth century, between poor peasants and townsmen and a fine lady of the court." Eugène Buret, *De la Misère des classes laborieuses en Angleterre et en France* (Paris, 1840), vol. 2, pp. 269–271. [a5,1]

"Many girls . . . in the factories often leave the shop as early as six o'clock in the evening, instead of leaving at eight, and go roaming the streets in hopes of meeting some stranger whom they provoke with a sort of calculated bashfulness.—In the factories, they call this doing one's fifth quarter of the day." Villermé, *Tableau de l'état physique et moral des ouvriers*, vol. 1, p. 226, cited in E. Buret, *De la Misère des classes laborieuses* (Paris, 1840), vol. 1, p. 415. [a5,2]

The principles of philanthropy receive a classic formulation in Buret: "Humanity, and indeed decency, do not permit us to allow human beings to die like animals. One cannot refuse the charitable gift of a coffin." Eugène Buret, *De la Misère des classes laborieuses* (Paris, 1840), vol. 1, p. 266. [a5,3]

"The Convention, organ of the sovereign people, aims to make mendicancy and poverty disappear at a single stroke. . . . It guarantees work for all citizens who need it. . . . Unfortunately, the section of the law that was designed specifically to deal with mendicancy as a crime was more easily enforced than that which promised the benefits of national generosity to the poor. Repressive measures were taken, and they have remained within the letter as well as the spirit of the law, whereas the system of charity that motivated and justified these measures has never existed, except in the decrees of the Convention!" E. Buret, *De la Misère des classes laborieuses* (Paris, 1840), vol. 1, pp. 222–224. Napoleon adopted the position described here with his law of July 5, 1808; the law of the convention dates from October 15, 1793. Those convicted three times of begging could expect deportation for eight years to Madagascar. [a5,4]

Hippolyte Passy, ex-minister, in a letter addressed to the temperance society of Amiens (see *Le Temps*, February 20, 1836): "One is led to recognize that, however meager the share of the poor might be, it is the art of applying that share to his real needs, it is the capacity to encompass the future in his thoughts, that the poor man lacks. His plight is due more to this lack than to any other." Cited in E. Buret, *De la Misère des classes laborieuses* (Paris, 1840), vol. 1, p. 78. [a5a,1]

"There was a time, and it was not so long ago, when—all the while effusively singing the praises of work—one never let on to the worker that the means by which he derived his subsistence was not his freely willed labors but, in fact, a tax levied on him by certain persons who fattened themselves by the sweat of his brow. . . . It is what is called the exploitation of man by man. Something of this sinister and deceptive doctrine has remained in the songs of the street. . . . Work is still spoken of with respect, but this respect has something forced about it, something of a grimace. . . . It is nevertheless true that this way of viewing work is an exception. More often, it is praised like a law of nature, a pleasure, or a benefit . . .

> Against the lazy let us always do battle—
> Great enemies of our society.
> For if they complain of sleeping on straw,
> It is only what they deserve.
> In our stockyards, our factories, our mills,
> Let us answer the call at day's dawning;
> While we work our prodigious machines,
> Let us hymn a fraternal refrain . . ."
> —Antoine Rémy

Charles Nisard, *Des Chansons populaires* (Paris, 1867), vol. 2, pp. 265–267.
[a5a,2]

"The fifteen years of the Restoration had been years of great agricultural and industrial prosperity. . . . If we leave aside Paris and the large cities, we see that the institution of the press, along with the various electoral systems, engaged only part of the nation, and the least numerous part: the bourgeoisie. Many in this

bourgeoisie were already fearful of a revolution." A. Malet and P. Grillet, *XIXe*
Siècle (Paris, 1919), p. 72. [a5a,3]

"The crisis of 1857–1858 . . . marked a sudden end to all the illusions of imperial
socialism. All efforts to maintain wages at a level that would have corresponded in
some degree to the ever-rising prices of food and housing proved futile."
D. Rjazanov, *Zur Geschichte der ersten Internationale*, in *Marx-Engels Archiv*,
vol. 1 [Frankfurt am Main ‹1928›], p. 145. [a5a,4]

"In Lyons, the economic crisis had caused a reduction in the salary of the silk
weavers—the famous *canuts*—to eighteen sous for a workday of fifteen to sixteen
hours. The prefect had tried to induce the workers and bosses to agree to establish
a minimum salary level. The attempt having failed, an insurrection broke out on
November 12, 1831; it was nonpolitical in character, representing an uprising of
the poor. 'Live Working or Die Fighting' read the black banner which the *canuts*
carried before them. . . . After two days of fighting,[5] the troops of the line, which
the Garde Nationale had refused to support, were forced to evacuate Lyons. The
workers laid down their arms. Casimir Périer sent an army of 36,000 men to
reoccupy the city; furthermore, he removed the prefect from office, annulled the
tariff which the latter had succeeded in foisting upon the bosses, and disbanded
the Garde Nationale (December 3, 1831). . . . Two years later, . . . charges brought
against an association of Lyons workers, the Mutualists, were the occasion for an
uprising that lasted five days." A. Malet and P. Grillet, *XIXe Siècle* (Paris, 1919),
pp. 86–88. [a6,1]

"A study of working conditions in the textile industry in 1840 revealed that, for
one fifteen-and-a-half-hour day of active work, the average salary was less than
two francs for men and barely one franc for women. The suffering . . . got worse,
especially beginning in 1834, because, civil unrest being finally quelled, industrial
enterprises multiplied so rapidly that, within ten years, the population of the cities
increased by two million solely through the influx of peasants to the factories."
A. Malet and P. Grillet, *XIXe Siècle* (Paris, 1919), p. 103. [a6,2]

"In 1830, many believed that Catholicism in France was on its deathbed and that
the political role of the clergy was finished for good. . . . Yet . . . on February 24,
1848, the insurgents who commenced the sacking of the Tuileries removed their
hats in front of the Crucifix taken from the chapel and escorted it all the way to the
Eglise Saint-Roch. With the proclamation of the Republic, universal suffrage sent
to the National Assembly . . . three bishops and twelve priests. . . . This could
happen because, during the reign of Louis Philippe, the clergy had gotten closer to
the people." A. Malet and P. Grillet, *XIXe Siècle* (Paris, 1919), pp. 106, 107.
[a6,3]

On December 8, 1831, the procapitalist *Journal des débats* takes a stand on the
Lyons insurrection. "The article in *Le Journal des débats* produced a great sensa-

tion. The enemy of the workers had brought into clear relief the international significance of the Lyons symptom. Neither the republican nor the legitimist press, however, wished to present the question in such dangerous terms. . . . The legitimists . . . protested for purely demagogic reasons, since at that moment it was the intention of this party to play the working class off against the liberal bourgeoisie in the interests of reestablishing the elder line of Bourbons; the republicans, on the other hand, had an interest in playing down, as far as possible, the purely proletarian cast of the movement . . . in order . . . not to lose the working class as a future ally in the struggle against the July monarchy. Nevertheless, the immediate impression produced by the Lyons uprising was so wholly incommensurable, so painful for contemporaries, that for this reason alone it has already attained a special place in history. The generation which had witnessed the July Revolution . . . was thought, in effect, to have nerves of steel. Yet they saw in the Lyons insurrection something entirely new . . ., which alarmed them all the more insofar as the workers of Lyons themselves seemed manifestly not to see or understand this new dimension." E. Tarlé, "Der Lyoner Arbeiteraufstand," in *Marx-Engels Archiv*, ed. D. Rjazanov, vol. 2 (Frankfurt am Main, 1928), p. 102. [a6a,1]

Tarlé cites a passage from Börne on the Lyons insurrection, in which this writer vents his indignation over Casimir Périer because, as Tarlé writes, "Périer rejoices at the lack of political motive for the uprising in Lyons, satisfied that this is *only* a war of the poor against the rich." The passage—in Ludwig Börne, *Gesammelte Schriften* (Hamburg and Frankfurt am Main, 1862), vol. 10, p. 20—runs: "It is said to be nothing more than a war of the poor against the rich, of those who have nothing to lose against those who own something! And this terrible truth which, because it *is* a truth, ought to have been buried in the deepest of wells, the lunatic raises aloft and flaunts before all the world!" In E. Tarlé, "Der Lyoner Arbeiteraufstand," in *Marx-Engels Archiv*, vol. 2 (Frankfurt am Main, 1928), p. 112. [a6a,2]

Buret was a student of Sismondi. Charles Andler credits him with an influence on Marx (Andler, *Le Manifeste communiste* [Paris, 1901])—something which Mehring ("Ein methodologisches Problem," *Die neue Zeit* [Stuttgart], 20, no. 1, pp. 450–451) firmly denies. [a6a,3]

Influence of Romanticism on political phraseology, explaining an attack on the congregations. "We are at the beginning of Romanticism, and we clearly recognize it by the manner in which it dramatizes everything. A cross was set up atop Mount Valérien: this cross . . . is denounced as symbolizing the ascendancy of religious society over civil society. The Jesuit novitiate refers to itself only as 'the den of Montrouge.' A jubilee is announced for 1826, and already men of the cloth are thought to be looming on all sides." Pierre de la Gorce, *La Restauration* (Paris ‹1926–1928›), vol. 2, *Charles X*, p. 57. [a7,1]

> We are nothing but machines.
> Our Babels mount to the sky.
>
> Refrain: Let us love and, when we can,
> Let us meet to drink a round,
> Let the cannon fall silent or erupt—
> We drink, we drink, we drink
> To the independence of the world!

Pierre Dupont, *Le Chant des ouvriers* (Paris, 1848). [a7,2]

Last verse and refrain:

> If, in truth, a despicable mob,
> Having fire and iron in its store,
> Wants to shackle the body and soul
> Of the people, true child of God,
> Reveal to these depraved,
> O Republic, by foiling their plots,
> Your great Medusa face
> Ringed by red lightning!
>
> . . . . .
> O tutelary Republic,
> Do not ascend to the skies,
> Ideal incarnated here on earth
> By universal suffrage.

From the fourth verse:

> Ah! Let no nocturnal surprise
> Break in on the polls!
> Stand guard round the ballot box:
> 'Tis the arch of our destiny.

Pierre Dupont, *Le Chant du vote* (Paris, 1850). [a7,3]

In chapters like "Le Vrai Sublime," "Le Fils de Dieu," "Le Sublime des sublimes," "Le Marchand de vins," "Le Chansonnier des sublimes," Poulot treats of types intermediate between worker and apache. The book is reformist; first published in 1869. Denis Poulot, *Question sociale: "Le Sublime,"* new ed. (Paris). [a7,4]

A proposal from Louis Napoleon's *Extinction du paupérisme* (p. 123), cited in Henry Fougère, *Les Délégations ouvrières aux expositions universelles sous le Second Empire* (Montluçon, 1905), p. 23: "All managers of factories or farms, all entrepreneurs of any kind, would be obliged by law, as soon as they had employed more than ten workers, to have an arbitrator who would govern their affairs, and to whom they would pay a salary double that of the simple workers." [a7a,1]

"This people, victorious, who strode barefoot upon gold / Strewn across their path, and did not succumb" (Hégésippe Moreau). Motto of the newspaper *L'Aimable*

Faubourien: Journal de la canaille, cited in *Curiosités revolutionnaires: Les Journaux rouges,* by a Girondist (Paris, 1848), p. 26.   [a7a,2]

Theory of A. Granier de Cassagnac, *Histoire des classes ouvrières et des classes bourgeoises* (Paris, 1838): the proletarians were descended from thieves and prostitutes.   [a7a,3]

"Believe me, the wine of the *barrières* has preserved the governmental framework from many a shock." Edouard Foucaud, *Paris inventeur: Physiologie de l'industrie française* (Paris, 1844), p. 10.   [a7a,4]

Charras, from the Ecole Polytechnique, with reference to General Lobau, who had not wished to sign a proclamation: "'I will have him shot.'—'What are you thinking of?' demanded M. Mauguin, incensed. 'Have General Lobau shot! A member of the Provisional Government!'—'The very same,' responded the student, while leading the deputy to the window and showing him a hundred men outside, veterans of the fighting at the barracks in the Babylone district.[6] 'And were I to order these brave men to shoot the Lord God, they would do it!'" G. Pinet, *Histoire de l'Ecole polytechnique* (Paris, 1887), p. 158 [evidently a literal citation from Louis Blanc].   [a7a,5]

Léon Guillemin: "There are two sorts of providence, . . . God and the Ecole Polytechnique. If one should be found wanting, the other will be there." In G. Pinet, p. 161.   [a7a,6]

Lamennais and Proudhon wanted to be buried in a mass grave (Delvau, *Heures parisiennes* ‹Paris, 1866›, pp. 50–51).   [a7a,7]

Scene from the February Revolution. The Tuileries were plundered. "Nevertheless, the crowd had stopped, as a sign of respect, in front of the chapel. A student took advantage of this moment to steal the sacred vessels, and in the evening he had them taken to the Eglise Saint-Roch. He chose to carry, by himself, the magnificent sculpted Christ that found a place on the altar; a group of people followed quietly in his steps, their hats removed and heads bowed. This scene . . . was reproduced on a stamp that could be seen, for a long time afterward, in the windows of all the merchants who sell religious icons. The Polytechnician was represented holding the Christ in his arms, displaying it before a kneeling crowd, while he exclaimed: 'Here is the master of us all!' These words were not actually spoken, but they conform to the sentiments of the population at a time when . . . the clergy itself, persecuted by the Voltairean king, greeted the revolution with enthusiasm." G. Pinet, *Histoire de l'Ecole polytechnique* (Paris, 1887), pp. 245–246.   [a8,1]

The Polytechnicians "observed the proceedings of the Blanquist club that met in a hall on the ground floor, where demagogic orators, agitating for the most sinister of

incendiary deeds, spoke already of putting the Provisional Government on trial."
G. Pinet, *Histoire de l'Ecole polytechnique* (Paris, 1887), p. 250.   [a8,2]

During the February Revolution, students from the Ecole Polytechnique burned
papers in the Tuileries which appeared to them compromising for the signatories,
but which would have had great interest for the revolution: declarations of loyalty to Louis Philippe (Pinet, p. 254).   [a8,3]

Lissagaray, in an essay on *Les Misérables*, in *La Bataille*: "One need only be in
touch with the people to become revolutionary" [*Victor Hugo devant l'opinion*
(Paris, 1885), p. 129].   [a8,4]

"Around 1840, a certain number of workers formed the resolution to plead their
cause directly before the public. . . . From that moment, . . . communism, which
until then had been on the offensive, took prudently to the defense." A. Corbon,
Le Secret du peuple de Paris (Paris, 1863), p. 117. In question are the communist
organ *La Fraternité*, which began publishing already in 1845, the anticommunist
L'Atelier, L'Union, and *La Ruche populaire*, which was the earliest.   [a8,5]

On the worker: "He is, in general, incapable of understanding practical affairs.
The solutions that suit him best are therefore those which seem likely to exempt
him from incessant preoccupation with what he considers the humble sphere, the
drudgeries of life. . . . Let us take as a virtual certainty, then, that any system
which would tend to *rivet* . . . our worker . . . to the factory—though it promise far
more butter than bread—. . . would be repugnant to him." A. Corbon, pp. 186–
187.   [a8,6]

"The question of workers, like the question of the poor, was planted at the entryway to the Revolution. Since the children of the families of workers and artisans
could not cover the needs of a labor-starved industry, factories made use of orphans as well. . . . The industrial exploitation of children and women . . . is one of
the most glorious achievements of philanthropy. Cheap food for workers, with a
. . . view to lowering wages, was likewise one of the favorite philanthropic notions
of the factory owners and political economists of the eighteenth century. . . . When
the French finally study the Revolution with a cold eye and without class prejudice, they will realize that the ideas which made for its greatness came from Switzerland, where the bourgeoisie was already dominant: in fact, it was from Geneva
that A. P. Candolle imported the so-called 'economic soup' . . . which created such
a furor in the Paris of the Revolution. . . . Even the dry and unblinking Volney
could not help being moved 'at the sight of this alliance of men of respectable
position eagerly occupied in supervising a pot of boiling soup.'" Paul Lafargue,
"Die christliche Liebestätigkeit," *Die neue Zeit*, 23, no. 1 (Stuttgart), pp. 148–149.
         [a8a,1]

"Should three men happen to be in the street talking together about wages, or
should they happen to ask the entrepreneur who has grown rich on their labor for

a raise of one sou, then the bourgeois becomes terrified and cries out for strong measures. . . . Most of the time, our governments have exploited this sad progress of fear. . . . All I can say here is that . . . our grand Terrorists were by no means men of the people. They were bourgeois and nobles, men with cultivated, subtle, bizarre minds—sophists and scholastics." J. Michelet, *Le Peuple* (Paris, 1846), pp. 153–154.[7]   [a8a,2]

Frégier, the author of *Les Classes dangereuses*, was head clerk at the prefecture of police.   [a8a,3]

On the description of the February Revolution in Flaubert's *Education sentimentale*—which needs to be reread—one finds (with reference to Stendhal's description of the Battle of Waterloo):[8] "Nothing of the general movements, nothing of the great clashes, but rather a succession of details which can never form a whole. This is the model which M. Flaubert has imitated in his depiction of the events of February and June 1848; it is a model of description from the standpoint of the idler, and of politics from the standpoint of the nihilist." J.-J. Nescio, *La Littérature sous les deux Empires, 1804–1852* (Paris, 1874), ‹p. 114›.   [a8a,4]

Scene from the July Revolution. A woman donned men's clothing to fight alongside the others, and then afterward, as woman again, nursed the wounded who were lodged in the Stock Exchange. "Saturday evening, the cannoneers who were transferring the artillery pieces remaining at the Bourse to the Hôtel de Ville enthroned our young heroine on a cannon crowned with laurels and brought her with them. This evening, at around ten o'clock, they brought her back in triumph to the bourse by the light of torches; she was seated on an armchair decorated with garlands and laurels." C. F. Tricotel, *Esquisse de quelques scènes de l'intérieur de la Bourse pendant les journées des 28, 29, 30 et 31 juillet dernier: Au profit des blessés* (Paris, 1830), p. 9.   [a9,1]

Lacenaire composed an "Ode à la guillotine," in which the criminal is celebrated in the allegorical figure of a woman, of whom it is said: "This woman laughed with horrible glee, / As a crowd tearing down a throne will laugh." The ode was written shortly before Lacenaire's execution—that is, in January 1836. Alfred Delvau, *Les Lions du jour* (Paris, 1867), p. 87.   [a9,2]

A charity supper at the Hôtel de Ville, where unemployed workers—in winter, above all construction workers—gathered. "The hour for the public meal has just sounded. And now Little Bluecoat hands his ivory-tipped cane to one of his assistants, takes from his buttonhole a silver place-setting which is attached there, dips the spoon into one pot after another, tastes, pays the servers, presses the outstretched hands of the poor, takes up his cane, refastens his spoon, and goes tranquilly on his way. . . . He is gone. The serving of the food begins." Little Bluecoat was the nickname of the philanthropist Edmé Champion, who had risen out of very modest circumstances. ‹See a12a,1.› The passage from Ch.-L.

Chassin, *La Légende du Petit Manteau Bleu*, cited in Alfred Delvau, *Les Lions du jour* (Paris, 1867), p. 283.　　　　　　　　　　　　　　　　　　　　　　　　　[a9,3]

The author, in his pamphlet condemning the rural exodus, turns to the country girl: "Poor, lovely child! The journeyman's *tour de France*, which is of question-able utility to your brothers, is always an evil for you. Do not—if need be, until you are forty—let go of your mother's apron strings . . .; and should you be foolish enough to set out on your own, and should you find yourself sharing your unfur-nished room with intransigent unemployment and hunger, then call (like a virgin I knew once), call a last guest to your side: CHOLERA. At least in his fleshless arms, at least on his ghastly chest, you will no longer fear for your honor." And immedi-ately following this passage: "You men of conscience who will read this, I implore you once more, on my hands and knees, to make known, in every way possible, the substance of this penultimate chapter." Emile Crozat, *La Maladie du siècle, ou Les Suites funestes du déclassement social: Ouvrage écrit sous les tristes inspira-tions d'un avocat sans cause, d'un notaire et d'un avoué sans clientèle, d'un médecin sans pratiques, d'un négociant sans capitaux, d'un ouvrier sans travail* (Bordeaux, 1856), p. 28.　　　　　　　　　　　　　　　　　　　　　　　　　[a9,4]

Insurrectionist movements under Louis Philippe: "It was then, in 1832, that the red flag appeared for the first time." Charles Seignobos, *Histoire sincère de la nation française* (Paris, 1933), p. 418.　　　　　　　　　　　　　　　　　[a9a,1]

"In 1848, there were only four cities with a population above a hundred thousand souls—Lyons, Marseilles, Bordeaux, and Rouen; and only three with a population of seventy-five thousand to a hundred thousand—Nantes, Toulouse, and Lille. Paris alone was a great metropolis with more than a million inhabitants, not count-ing the faubourgs (annexed in 1860). France remained a country of small towns." Charles Seignobos, *Histoire sincère de la nation française* (Paris, 1933), pp. 396–397.　　　　　　　　　　　　　　　　　　　　　　　　　　　　　　　[a9a,2]

In 1840, the petty bourgeoisie makes a push toward the right to vote, by demand-ing it for the Garde Nationale.　　　　　　　　　　　　　　　　　　　　[a9a,3]

National Assembly of 1848. "Mlle.—— asks to borrow 600 francs from the Na-tional Assembly to pay her rent." Historical fact. *Paris sous la République de 1848: Exposition de la Bibliothèque et des Travaux historiques de la Ville de Paris* (1909), p. 41.　　　　　　　　　　　　　　　　　　　　　　　　　　　　　[a9a,4]

"As soon as they heard tell of a battalion of women, the designers set about to find them a uniform. . . . Eugénie Niboyet, editor of *La Voix des femmes*, . . . pro-nounced on the matter: 'The title "Vesuvian,"' she writes, 'means that every one of these conscripts is harboring, in the core of her heart, a volcano of revolution-ary fires.' . . . Eugénie Niboyet then summoned her 'sisters' to the downstairs galleries of the Bonne-Nouvelle bazaar and to the Salle Taranne." *Paris sous la*

République de 1848: Exposition de la Bibliothèque et des Travaux historiques de la Ville de Paris (1909), p. 28. [a9a,5]

Social subjects occupy a very large place in lyric poetry at midcentury. They take all possible forms, from the innocuous variety of a Charles Colmance ("La Chanson des locataires" ‹The Tenants' Song›, "La Chanson des imprimeurs" ‹"The Printers' Song›) to the revolutionary lyrics of a Pierre Dupont. Inventions are a favorite theme of such *chansons,* and their social significance is underscored. Thus was born a "poem in praise of the prudent entrepreneur who first renounced the manufacture of a noxious product [white lead] to adopt 'the white of innocent zinc.'" *Paris sous la République de 1848: Exposition de la Ville de Paris* (1909), p. 44. [a9a,6]

Apropos of Cabet: "It is toward the end of 1848 that the discovery of the deposits became known in Paris, and almost immediately companies were formed to facilitate the emigration of prospectors. By May 1849, fifteen such companies had begun to operate. The 'Compagnie Parisienne' had the honor of transporting the first group of travelers, and . . . these modern Argonauts entrusted themselves to a blind Jason who had never even seen California: one Jacques Arago, . . . whose account . . . of a voyage round the world was in part developed from another's notes. . . . Newspapers were founded: *La Californie,* a general-interest paper on the Pacific Ocean; the 'gold-bearing' *Aurifère,* monitor of the gold mines; *L'Echo du Sacramento.* Joint-stock companies offered shares of stock at exceptionally low prices, only five francs, on the floor of all the stock exchanges." Many cocottes make the trip overseas—the colonists are experiencing a shortage of women. *Paris sous la République de 1848: Exposition de la Ville de Paris* (1909), p. 32. ‹On Jacques Arago, see a12,5.› [a10,1]

There's a comparison to be drawn between Cabet and the following verse, which is, of course, directed against the Saint-Simonians. It comes from Alcide Genty, *A Monsieur de Chateaubriand: Poètes et prosateurs français—Satire* (Paris, 1838), cited in Carl Lodewijk de Liefde, *Le Saint-Simonisme dans la poésie française entre 1825 et 1865* ‹Haarlem, 1927›, p. 171: "The insinuating Rodrigues will peddle to the Iroquois / Barême and some unsmoked cigarettes." [a10,2]

Delphine Gay (Mme. E. de Girardin) shows herself, in her poem "Les Ouvriers de Lyons" (*Poésies complètes* [Paris, 1856], p. 210), to be a precursor of the philosophy of innkeeping: "The poor man is happy when the rich has his fun." [a10,3]

> With two arms of iron a magnificent track
> Will begird my republic: Peking to Paris.
> A hundred different peoples, mixing their tongues,
> Will make one colossal car a Babel.
> There, with wheel of fire, humanity's coach
> Will wear to the bone the muscles of the earth.
> From atop this gleaming vessel, men, all amazed,

>Will look out on an ocean of eatables.
>The world will become a fine china bowl
>Filled up for this human menagerie;
>And the clean-shaven globe, without beard or hair—
>A monumental pumpkin—will revolve through the skies.

Alfred de Musset, *Namouna* (Paris), p. 113 ("Dupont et Durand").　　　　[a10,4]

Saint-Simonian poetry—Savinien Lapointe, shoemaker, "L'Emeute" ‹The Riot›:

>No, the future will dispense with barricades!
>. . . . .
>You great ones, while your hands are building scaffolds,
>Mine are scattering flowers over the graves.
>To each his mission or his painful task:
>To the poet, the song; to power, the ax!

Olinde Rodrigues, *Poésies sociales des ouvriers* (Paris, 1841), pp. 237, 239.
　　　　[a10,5]

From Alfred de Vigny, "La Maison du berger" ‹The Shepherd's House›, treating of the railroad:

>May God guide the thundering steam to its end
>'Cross the mountains traversed by iron rails.
>Let an angel be perched on its loud-clanking boiler
>When it heads underground or rocks bridges.
>. . . . .
>Turn away from these tracks—they lack grace.
>Their iron lines will take you
>With the speed of an arrow through space,
>Shot whistling from bow to bull's-eye.
>Thus hurled like a bolt, human beings
>Lose their breath, lose their sight,
>In the smothering cloud rent by lightning.
>. . . . .
>Distance and time are now conquered by Science,
>Which encircles the world with its road sad and straight.
>The World is reduced by our experiment;
>The equator is now but a tight-fitting hoop.

Alfred de Vigny, *Poésies complètes*, new edition (Paris, 1866), pp. 218, 220–221.
　　　　[a10a,1]

To be compared with Cabet: the remarkable, beautiful poem "Le Havre," by Elise Fleury, embroiderer (Olinde Rodrigues, *Poésies sociales des ouvriers* [Paris, 1841], p. 9). It describes an ocean steamer, contrasting the luxury cabins with the lower deck.　　　　[a10a,2]

RUE TRANSNONAIN, LE 15 AVRIL 1834

Rue Transnonain, le 15 avril 1834 (Government Reprisal on the Rue Transnonain, April 15, 1834). Lithograph by Honoré Daumier. See a1a,1; a10a,5.

"An opuscule in verse (*Les Principes du Petit Manteau Bleu sur le système de la communauté* ‹see a9,3›, by Loreux, communist [Paris, 1847]) is a species of dialogue between a partisan and an adversary of communism. . . . In order to alleviate all . . . suffering, the communist Loreux appeals not to envy or to vengeance, but to kindness and generosity." Jean Skerlitch, *L'Opinion publique en France d'après la poésie politique et sociale de 1830 à 1848* (Lausanne, 1901), p. 194.   [a10a,3]

In 1847, a famine; many poems on the subject.   [a10a,4]

August 1834, uprising of Mutualists in Lyons, nearly contemporaneous with the uprising on the Rue Transnonain.[9] At Lyons: "The army reported 115 men killed and 360 wounded, and the workers reported 200 killed and 400 wounded. The government wanted to grant indemnities, and a commission was named, which proclaimed the following principle: 'The government does not want the triumph of the social order to cost any tears or regrets. It knows that time, which gradually effaces the anguish occasioned by the costliest personal losses, is powerless to redress the blows of fortune.' . . . The whole morality of the July Monarchy can be found in these words." Jean Skerlitch, *L'Opinion publique en France d'après la poésie politique et sociale* (Lausanne, 1901), p. 72.   [a10a,5]

"I will rouse the people with my unvarnished truths; / I will prophesy on every street corner." Hégésippe Moreau, cited in Jean Skerlitch, *L'Opinion publique en France d'après la poésie politique et sociale de 1830 à 1848*, p. 85.   [a11,1]

"In the days immediately following the Revolution of 1830, a song made the rounds in Paris: 'Requête d'un ouvrier à un Juste-Milieu.' Its refrain was particularly expressive:

> I am hungry!
> Well, then, eat your fist.
> Save the other for tomorrow.
> And that's my refrain.

. . . Barthélemy . . . says . . . that . . . the unemployed laborer has no choice but to work in 'the yard of upheaval.' . . . In Barthélemy's *Némésis* . . . the pontif Rothschild, with a multitude of the faithful, chants the 'Mass of stockjobbing,' sings the 'psalm of annuity.'" Jean Skerlitch, *L'Opinion publique en France d'après la poésie* (Lausanne, 1901), pp. 97–98, 159.   [a11,2]

"During the day of June 6, a search of the sewers had been ordered. It was feared that they would be used as a refuge by the vanquished. Prefect Gisquet was to ransack the hidden Paris, while General Bugeaud was sweeping the public Paris—a connected double operation which demanded a double strategy on the part of public power, represented above by the army and below by the police. Three platoons of officers and sewermen investigated the subterranean streets of Paris." Victor Hugo, *Oeuvres complètes*, novels, vol. 9 (Paris, 1881), p. 196 (*Les Misérables*).[10]   [a11,3]

> Unfolding its wings of gold,
> Million-armed industry, exultant,
> Traverses our domains
> And seeds the fields.
> The desert is peopled at the sound of its voice,
> The arid soil teems—
> And for the world's bounty
> It gives the world laws. ⟨p. 205⟩

Refrain: All honor to us, the offspring of industry!
           Honor, honor to our works!
           In all the arts we have conquered our rivals—
           And would be the hope, the pride, of our country. ⟨p. 204⟩

Cinquante Chants français, lyrics by various authors; set to music, with piano accompaniment, by Rouget de Lisle (Paris, 1825) [Bibliothèque Nationale, Vm7.4454], p. 202 (no. 49, "Chant des industriels," 1821, text by de Lisle). In the same volume, no. 23, "La Marseillaise."   [a11,4]

Revolutionary tactics and battles on the barricades, according to *Les Misérables*. The night before the barricade fighting: "The invisible police of the *émeute* watched everywhere, and maintained order—that is, night. . . . The eye which might have looked from above into that mass of shadow would have caught a glimpse in the distance here and there, perhaps, of indistinct lights, bringing out broken and fantastic lines, outlines of singular constructions, something like ghostly gleams coming and going among ruins; these were the barricades." *Oeuvres complètes*, novels, vol. 8 (Paris, 1881), pp. 522–523.—The following passage is from the chapter "Faits d'où l'histoire sort et que l'histoire ignore." "The meetings were sometimes periodic. At some, there were never more than eight or ten, and always the same persons. In others, anybody who chose to entered, and the room was so full that they were forced to stand. Some were there from enthusiasm and passion; others because 'it was on their way to work.' As in the time of the Revolution, there were in these wine shops some female patriots, who embraced the newcomers. Other expressive facts came to light. A man entered a shop, drank, and went out, saying: 'Wine merchant, whatever I owe, the revolution will pay.' . . . A worker, drinking with a comrade, made him put his hand on him to see how warm he was; the other felt a pistol under his vest. . . . All this fermentation was public, we might almost say tranquil. . . . No singularity was wanting in this crisis—still subterranean, but already perceptible. Bourgeois talked quietly with workers about the preparations. They would say, 'How is the uprising coming along?' in the same tone in which they would have said, 'How is your wife?'" Victor Hugo, *Oeuvres complètes*, novels, vol. 8 (Paris, 1881), pp. 43, 50–51 (*Les Misérables*).[11]   [a11a,1]

Barricade fighting in *Les Misérables*. From the chapter "Originalité de Paris." "Outside of the insurgent *quartiers*, nothing is usually more strangely calm than the physiognomy of Paris during an uprising. . . . There is firing at the streetcorners, in an arcade, in a cul-de-sac; . . . corpses litter the pavement. A few streets away, you can hear the clicking of billiard balls in the cafés. . . . The carriages jog along; people are going out to dine. Sometimes in the very *quartier* where there is fighting. In 1831 a fusillade was suspended to let a wedding party pass by. At the time of the insurrection of May 12, 1839, on the Rue Saint-Martin, a little infirm old man, drawing a handcart surmounted by a tricolored rag, in which there were decanters filled with some liquid, went back and forth from the barricade to the troops and from the troops to the barricade, impartially offering glasses of cocoa. . . . Nothing is more strange; and this is the peculiar characteristic of the uprisings of Paris, which is not found in any other capital. Two things are requisite for it: the greatness of Paris and its gaiety. It requires the city of Voltaire and of Napoleon." Victor Hugo, *Oeuvres complètes*, novels, vol. 8 ⟨Paris, 1881⟩, pp. 429–431.[12]   [a11a,2]

On the motif of exoticism, conjoined with that of emancipation:

> All the seraglios are opened,
> The imam finds his inspiration in wine,
> The Orient learns to read,
> Barrault crosses the seas.

Jules Mercier, "L'Arche de Dieu," in *Foi nouvelle: Chants et chansons de Barrault, Vinçard . . . 1831 à 1834* (Paris, January 1, 1835), book 1, p. 28.   [a12,1]

> Forge the liberty of the Orient:
> A cry of Woman, on the day of deliverance,
> Travels from the harem by repeated echo
> To break the horrid silence of the West.

Vinçard, "Le Premier Départ pour l'Orient," in *Foi nouvelle: Chants et chansons de Barrault, Vinçard . . . 1831 à 1834* (Paris, January 1, 1835), book 1, p. 48.
[a12,2]

A strange stanza from "Le Départ," by Vinçard:

> Cast off from a universe of serfdom,
> The old swaddling clothes[13] and the jargon;
> Learn the coarse and plain speech of the People,
> The light ditty and the oath.

Foi nouvelle, 1831 à 1834 (Paris, January 1, 1835), pp. 89–90.   [a12,3]

> Our flag has lost patience with the sky of France;
> Over the minarets of Egypt it now must wave.
> . . . . .
> Then will they see us, workers adept,
>   With our ribbons of iron
>   Subduing the desert sands;
> Cities, like palms, will spring up everywhere.

F. Maynard, "A l'Orient," in *Foi nouvelle* (Paris, January 1, 1835), pp. 85, 88.
[a12,4]

In Jacques Arago's pamphlet of 1848, "Aux Juges des insurgés," deportation appears as an instrument of colonial expansion. After the author, in picturesque language, has summoned up in turn each of France's overseas possessions without finding a single one suited to be the land of deportation, his eye lights on Patagonia. He gives a very poetical description of the land and its inhabitants. "These men, the tallest on earth; these women, of whom the youngest are so alluring after an hour's swim; these antelopes, these birds, these fish, these phosphorescent waters, this sky alive with clouds coursing to and fro like a flock of wandering hinds . . .—all this is Patagonia, all this a virgin land rich and independent. . . . Do you fear that England will come and tell you that you have no right to set foot on this part of the American continent? . . . Citizens, let England grumble, just let it, . . . and if it should arm, . . . then transport to Patagonia the men whom your laws have smitten. When the day of battle arrives, those you have exiled will have become staunch mobile barricades, standing implacable at the outposts." [a12,5]

Edmé Champion: self-made man,[14] philanthropist (1764–1852). "Whenever he had occasion to go across town, he would never forget to look into the morgue"—so reports Charles-Louis Chassin, *La Légende du Petit Manteau Bleu* (Paris, ca. 1860), p. 15. Champion had been a goldsmith and, during the Revolution, protected noble-born former customers—which endangered his own life.   [a12a,1]

Balzac, in *Eugénie Grandet,* with reference to the miser's dreams of the future: "That future which once awaited us beyond the requiem has been transported into the present."[15] This is still more true with reference to poor people's fears of the future.   [a12a,2]

From an analysis of the situation around 1830, by police prefect Gisquet. At issue are the workers: "Unlike the well-to-do classes of the bourgeoisie, they have no fear that, through a broader extension of liberal principles, they will be compromising an established fortune. . . . Just as the Third Estate profited from the suppression of the nobility's privileges . . . , the working class would profit today from all that the bourgeoisie would lose in its turn." Cited in Charles Benoist, "L'Homme de 1848," part 1, *Revue des deux mondes* (July 1, 1913), p. 138.
      [a12a,3]

"The great mob and the holy rabble / Made a rush at immortality." From a revolutionary song around 1830. Cited in Charles Benoist, "L'Homme de 1848," part 1, *Revue des deux mondes* (July 1, 1913), p. 143.   [a12a,4]

Rumford, in his economic essays, assembled recipes designed to lower the cost of soup-kitchen fare by using substitute ingredients. "His soups are not too expensive, seeing that for 11 francs 16 centimes, one has enough to feed 115 persons twice a day. The only question is whether they are being properly fed." Charles Benoist, "De l'Apologie du travail à l'apothéose de l'ouvrier," *Revue des deux mondes* (January 15, 1913), p. 384. Charity soups were variously introduced by French industries at the time of the great Revolution.   [a12a,5]

1837—the first banquets for universal suffrage and the petition with 240,000 signatures (equivalent to the number of registered voters at that time).   [a12a,6]

Around 1840, suicide is familiar in the mental world of the workers. "People are talking about copies of a lithograph representing the suicide of an English worker in despair at not being able to earn a living. At the house of Sue himself, a worker comes to commit suicide with this note in his hand: 'I am killing myself out of despair. It seemed to me that death would be easier for me if I died under the roof of one who loves us and defends us.' The working-class author of a little book much read by other workers, the typographer Adolphe Boyer, also takes his own life in despair." Charles Benoist, "L'Homme de 1848," part 2, *Revue des deux mondes* (February 1, 1914), p. 667.   [a12a,7]

From Robert (du Var), *Histoire de la classe ouvrière ‹depuis l'esclave jusqu'au proletaire de nos jours›* (1845–1848): "You have seen it witnessed in this history, O worker! When, as slave, you embraced the gospel, you became, unhesitatingly, a serf; when, as serf, you embraced the eighteenth-century *philosophes*, you became a proletarian. Well, today you have taken up socialism. . . . What is to prevent you from becoming a partner? You are king, pope, and emperor—your fate, in this regard, is in your own hands." Cited in Charles Benoist, "L'Homme de 1848," part 2, *Revue des deux mondes* (February 1, 1914), p. 668.
[a13,1]

A comment by Tocqueville on the spirit of the 1840s: "Wealthy proprietors liked to recall that they had always been enemies of the bourgeois class and always been friends of the people. The bourgeoisie themselves recalled with a certain pride that their fathers had been laborers, and if they could not trace their lineage . . . to a worker . . ., they would at least contrive to descend from some uncouth person who had made his fortune on his own." Cited in Charles Benoist, "L'Homme de 1848," part 2, *Revue des deux mondes* (February 1, 1914), p. 669.
[a13,2]

"The question of poverty . . . has, in a few years, passed through extremely varied phases. Toward the end of the Restoration, the debate turns entirely on the extinction of mendicancy, and society tries less to alleviate poverty than to . . . forget it by relegating it to the shadows. At the time of the July Revolution, the situation is reversed by means of politics. The republican party seizes on pauperism and transforms it into the proletariat. . . . The workers take up the pen. . . . Tailors, shoemakers, and typographers, who at that time constituted the revolutionary trades, march in the extreme avant-garde. . . . Around 1835, the debate is suspended in consequence of the numerous defeats dealt the republican party. Around 1840, it resumes, . . . and bifurcates . . . into two schools, culminating, on the one hand, in communism and, on the other, in the associations deriving from the mutual interests of workers and employers." Charles Louandre, "Statistique littéraire: De la Production intellectuelle en France depuis quinze ans," *Revue des deux mondes* (October 15, 1847), p. 279.
[a13,3]

The Blanquist Tridon: "O Might, queen of the barricades, . . . you who flash in the lightning and the riot, . . . it is toward you that prisoners stretch their manacled hands." Cited in Charles Benoist, "Le 'Mythe' de la classe ouvrière," *Revue des deux mondes* (March 1, 1914), p. 105.
[a13,4]

Against workhouses, and in favor of lowering the tax on the poor: F.-M.-L. Naville, *De la Charité légale et spécialement des maisons de travail et de la proscription de la mendicité*, 2 volumes (Paris, 1836).
[a13,5]

A coinage of 1848: "God is a worker."
[a13a,1]

Charles Benoist claims to find in Corbon, *Le Secret du peuple de Paris*, the proud consciousness of numerical superiority over the other classes. Benoist, "Le 'Mythe' de la classe ouvrière," *Revue des deux mondes* (March 1, 1914), p. 99.

[a13a,2]

Pamphlets from 1848 are dominated by the concept of organization.   [a13a,3]

"In 1867, it was possible to hold conferences in which 400 worker delegates, belonging to 117 professions, . . . discussed . . . the organization of Chambers of jointly unionized workers. . . . Up until then, however, workers' unions had been very rare—though on the other side, allied with the bosses, there had been forty-two Chambers of unionized workers. . . . Prior to 1867, in the margins and in defiance of the law, there had been associations only of typographers (1839), molders (1863), bookbinders (1864), and hatters (1865). After the meetings held in the Passage Raoul, . . . these syndicates multiplied." Charles Benoist, "Le 'Mythe' de la classe ouvrière," *Revue des deux mondes* (March 1, 1914), p. 111.   [a13a,4]

In 1848, Toussenel was a member of the Commission of Labor over which Louis Blanc presided in Luxembourg.   [a13a,5]

To present London in its significance for Barbier and Gavarni. Gavarni's series *Ce qu'on voit gratis à Londres* ⟨What Can Be Seen for Free in London⟩.   [a13a,6]

In *Der achtzehnte Brumaire*, Marx says of the cooperatives that in them the proletariat "renounces the revolutionizing of the old world by means of the latter's own great, combined resources, and seeks, rather, to achieve its salvation behind society's back, in private fashion, within its limited conditions of existence."[16] Cited in E. Fuchs, *Die Karikatur des europäischen Völker*, vol. 2 ⟨Munich, 1921⟩, p. 472.   [a13a,7]

On *Poésies sociales des ouvriers*, edited by Rodrigues, *La Revue des deux mondes* writes: "You pass from a reminiscence of M. de Béranger to a coarse imitation of the rhythms of Lamartine and Victor Hugo" (p. 966). And the class-bound character of this critique emerges unabashedly when its author writes of the worker: "If he aims to reconcile the exercise of his profession with literary studies, he will discover how uncongenial to intellectual development physical exhaustion can be" (p. 969). In support of his point, the author rehearses the fate of a worker poet who was driven mad. Lerminier, "De la Littérature des ouvriers," *Revue des deux mondes*, 28 (Paris, 1841).   [a13a,8]

Agricol Perdiguier's *Livre du compagnonnage* seeks to make use of the medieval guild-forms of alliance between workers for the new form of association. This undertaking is curtly dismissed by Lerminier in "De la Littérature des ouvriers," in *Revue des deux mondes*, 28 (Paris, 1841), pp. 955 ff.   [a14,1]

Adolphe Boyer, *De l'Etat des ouvriers et de son amélioration par l'organisation du travail* (Paris, 1841). The author of this book was a printer. It was unsuccessful. He commits suicide and (according to Lerminier) calls on the workers to follow his example. The book was published in German in Strasbourg, in 1844. It was very moderate and sought to make use of *compagnonnage* for worker associations. [a14,2]

"Anyone who considers the harsh and burdensome life which the laboring classes have to lead remains convinced that, among the workers, the most remarkable men . . . are not those who hurry to take up a pen . . ., not those who write, but those who act. . . . The division of labor that assigns to some men action and to others thought is thus always in the nature of things." Lerminier, "De la Littérature des ouvriers," *Revue des deux mondes,* 28 (Paris, 1841), p. 975. And by "action" the author means, first of all, the practice of working overtime! [a14,3]

Worker associations deposited their funds in savings banks or took out treasury bonds. Lerminier, in "De la Littérature des ouvriers" (*Revue des deux mondes* [Paris, 1841], p. 963), praises them for this. Their insurance institutions, he says further on, lighten the load of public assistance. [a14,4]

Proudhon receives an invitation to dinner from the financier Millaud. "Proudhon managed to extricate himself . . . by replying that he lived entirely in the bosom of his family and was always in bed by nine P.M." Firmin Maillard, *La Cité des intellectuels* (Paris ‹1905›), p. 383. [a14,5]

From a poem by Dauhéret on Ledru-Rollin:

> The red flag revered by the French everywhere
> Is the robe in which Christ was attired.
> Let us all render homage to brave Robespierre,
> And Marat who made him admired.

Cited in Auguste Lepage, *Les Cafés politiques et littéraires de Paris* (Paris ‹1874›, p. 11. [a14,6]

Georg Herwegh, "Die Epigonen von 1830," Paris, November 1841:

> Away, away with the Tricolor,
> Which witnessed the deeds of your fathers,
> And write on the gates as a warning:
> "Here is Freedom's Capua!"

Georg Herwegh, *Gedichte eines Lebendigen*, vol. 2 (Zürich and Winterthur, 1844), p. 15. [a14a,1]

Heine on the bourgeoisie during the February Revolution: "The severity with which the people dealt with . . . thieves who were caught in the act seemed to many

. . . rather excessive, and certain people became uneasy on learning that thieves were shot on the spot. Under such a regime, they said to themselves, who could be sure of his own life in the end?" Heinrich Heine, "Die Februarrevolution," *Sämtliche Werke*, ed. Wilhelm Bölsche (Leipzig), vol. 5, p. 363.[17]   [a14a,2]

America in the Hegelian philosophy: "Hegel . . . did not give direct expression to this consciousness of terminating an epoch of history; rather, he gave it indirect expression. He makes it known by the fact that, in thinking, he casts an eye over the past in 'its obsolescence of spirit,' even as he looks about for a possible discovery in the domain of spirit, all the while expressly reserving the awareness of such discovery. The rare indications concerning America—which at this period seemed the future land of liberty [note: A. Ruge, *Aus früherer Zeit*, vol. 4, pp. 72–84. Fichte had already thought of emigrating to America at the time of the collapse of old Europe (letter to his wife of May 28, 1807).]—and concerning the Slavic world, envision the possibility, for universal spirit, of emigration from Europe as a means of preparing new protagonists of the principle of spirit that was . . . completed with Hegel. 'America is therefore the land of the future, where, in the ages that lie before us, the burden of the World's History shall reveal itself—perhaps in a contest between North and South America.' . . . But 'what *has* taken place in the New World up to the present time is only an echo of the Old World—the expression of a foreign Life; and as a Land of the Future, it has no interest for us here. . . . In regard to *Philosophy* . . . we have to do with . . . that which *is*'" [Hegel, *Philosophie der Geschichte*, ed. Lasson, p. 200 (and 779?)].[18] Karl Löwith, "L'Achèvement de la philosophie classique par Hegel et sa dissolution chez Marx et Kierkegaard" [*Recherches philosophiques*, founded by A. Koyré, H.-Ch. Puech, A. Spaier, vol. 4 (Paris, 1934–1935), pp. 246–247].   [a14a,3]

Auguste Barbier represented the doleful pendant to Saint-Simonian poetry. He disavows this relationship as little in his works in general as in these closing lines of his prologue:

> If my verse is too raw, its tongue too uncouth,
> Look to the brazen century in which it sounds.
> Cynicism of manners must defile the word,
> And a hatred of evil begets hyperbole.
> Thus, I can defy the gaze of the prude:
> My ungentle verse is true blue at heart.

Auguste Barbier, *Poésies* (Paris, 1898), p. 4.   [a15,1]

Ganneau publishes "Waterloo" (Paris: Au Bureau des Publications Evadiennes, 1843) anonymously. The pamphlet is dedicated to the apotheosis of Napoleon— "Jesus the Christ-Abel, Napoleon the Christ-Cain" (p. 8)—and concludes with the invocation of "Evadian Unity" (p. 15) and the signature: "In the name of the Grand Evadah, in the name of God on High, Mother and Father, . . . the Mapah" (p. 16). ‹See U12,7.›   [a15,2]

Ganneau's "Page prophétique" was published for the first time in 1840, and again during the Revolution of 1848. The title page of the second edition bears the following announcement: "This 'Prophetic Page,' seized on July 14, 1840, was discovered by citizen Sobrier, former deputy in the Police Department, in the dossier of citizen Ganneau (The Mapah).—(The official report is labeled: 'Revolutionary page, one of 3,500 copies distributed under carriage entrances.')" [a15,3]

Ganneau's "Baptême, mariage" inaugurates the era of the Evadah, commencing on August 15, 1838. The pamphlet is published at 380 Rue Saint-Denis, Passage Lemoine. Signed: The Mapah. It proclaims: "Mary is no longer the Mother: she is the Bride; Jesus Christ is no longer the Son: he is the Bridegroom. The old world (of compression) is finished; the new world (of expansion) begins!" "Mary-Eve, female Genesiac unity" and "Christ-Adam, male Genesiac unity" appear "under the name Androgyne Evadam." [a15,4]

"The 'Devoir Mutuel' of Lyons, which played a crucial role in the insurrections of 1831 and 1834, marks the transition from the old Mutualité to the Resistance." Paul Louis, *Histoire de la classe ouvrière en France de la Révolution à nos jours* (Paris, 1927), p. 72. [a15,5]

On May 15, 1848, revolutionary demonstration of the Paris workers for the liberation of Poland. [a15,6]

"Jesus Christ . . . , who gave us no vestige of a political code, left his work incomplete." Honoré de Balzac, *Le Curé de village* (letter from Gérard to Grossetête), editions Siècle, vol. 17, p. 183.[19] [a15a,1]

The early inquests into workers' circumstances were conducted, for the most part, by entrepreneurs, their agents, factory inspectors, and administrative officials. "When the doctors and philanthropists who were conducting the inquest went to visit the families of workers, they were generally accompanied by the entrepreneur or his representative. Le Play, for example, advises one, when visiting the families of workers, 'to utilize the recommendation of a carefully chosen authority.' He counsels the adoption of utmost diplomacy in regard to individual members of the family, and even the payment of small indemnities or the distribution of gifts: one should 'praise with discretion the sagacity of the men, the grace of the women, the good behavior of the children, and, in suitable fashion, dispense little presents to all' (*Les Ouvriers européens* [Paris], vol. 1, p. 223). In the course of the detailed critique of inquest procedures which Audiganne promotes in the discussions of his workers' circle, Le Play is spoken of in the following terms: 'Never was a false path marked out, despite the best intentions. It is purely a question of the system. A mistaken point of view, an inadequate method of observation give rise to a wholly arbitrary train of thought having no relation at all to the reality of society and evincing, moreover, an incorrigible propensity for despotism and rigidity' (Audiganne, p. 61). A frequent error in the conduct of the inquests, according to

Audiganne, is the air of ceremony with which the investigators carry out their visits to the homes of the workers: 'If not a single special inquest undertaken during the Second Empire yielded concrete results of any kind, the blame for this rests, in large part, on the pomp with which the investigators paraded around' (p. 93). Engels and Marx describe further the methods by which the workers were induced to express themselves on the occasion of these *recherches sociales* and even to present petitions against the reduction of their work time." Hilde Weiss, "Die 'Enquête ouvrière' von Karl Marx" [*Zeitschrift für Sozialforschung*, ed. Max Horkheimer, 5, no. 1 (Paris, 1936), pp. 83–84]. The passages from Audiganne are taken from his book *Mémoires d'un ouvrier de Paris* ‹Paris, 1873›.
[a15a,2]

In 1854, the affair of the carpenters took place. When the carpenters of Paris decided to strike, proceedings were instituted against the leaders of the carpenters for violation of the ban on coalitions. They were defended, in the first instance and in the appeal, by Berryer. From his arguments before the court of appeals: "It cannot be this sacred resolve, this voluntary decision to abandon one's work rather than not derive a just income from it, that has been marked out for punishment by the law. No, it is the determination, instead, to restrain the freedom of others; it is the interdiction of work, the hindering of others from going to their place of work. . . . In order, then, for there to be a coalition, in the proper sense, there must be some sort of restraint on the liberty of persons, a violence done to the freedom of others. And, in fact, if this is not the true construction of articles 415 and 416, would there not be, in our law, a monstrous inequality between the condition of the workers and that of the entrepreneurs? The latter can take counsel together to decide that the cost of labor is too high. . . . The law . . . punishes the coalition of entrepreneurs only when their concerted action is unjust and abusive. . . . Without reproducing the same set of words, the law reproduces the same idea with respect to workers. It is by the sound interpretation of these articles that you will consecrate the equality of condition that ought to exist between these two classes of individuals." ‹Pierre-Antoine› Berryer, *Oeuvres: Plaidoyers*, vol. 2, *1836–1856* (Paris, 1876), pp. 245–246.
[a16,1]

Affair of the carpenters: "M. Berryer concludes his plea by rising to considerations . . . of the current situation, in France, of the lower classes—condemned, he says, to see two-fifths of their members dying in the hospital or laid out in the morgue." Berryer, *Oeuvres: Plaidoyers*, vol. 2, *1836–1856* (Paris, 1876), p. 250 (The principals accused in the trial were sentenced to three years in prison—a judgment that was upheld on appeal.)
[a16,2]

"Our worker-poets of late have been imitating the rhythms of Lamartine, . . . too often sacrificing whatever folk originality they might have. . . . When they write, they wear a suit and put on gloves, thus losing the superiority that strong hands and powerful arms give to the people when they know how to use them." J. Michelet, *Le Peuple*, 2nd ed. (Paris, 1846), p. 195. At another point (p. 107), the author accentuates the "peculiar character of meekness and melancholy" attaching to this poetry.[20] [a16,3]

"In Paris . . . Engels jotted down the 'creed' which the local branch of the Communist League had asked him to compose. He objected to the term 'creed,' by which Schapper and Moll had designated their draft, and he decided that the question-and-answer form which was usual in such programs, and to which Considérant and Cabet had ultimately had recourse as well, was no longer in place here." Gustav Mayer, *Friedrich Engels*, vol. 1 (Berlin ‹1933›), p. 283.[21] [a16,4]

Legislative repression of the working class goes back to the French Revolution. At issue are laws which punished any assembling and unionizing on the part of workers, any collective demands for higher wages, and any strikes. "The law of June 17, 1791, and that of January 12, 1794, contain measures that have proved sufficient, up through the present, to repress these offenses." Chaptal, *De l'Industrie françoise* (Paris, 1819), vol. 2, p. 351. [a16a,1]

"Since Marx was officially exiled from France, Engels decided, in August 1846, to shift his residence to the French capital so that he could meet with the German proletarians who were living there and recruit them for the cause of revolutionary communism. As it happened, however, the tailors and cabinetmakers and leather-workers whom Grün was trying to convert had nothing in common with the proletarian type on whom Engels was counting. . . . Paris was the headquarters of fashion and of the arts and crafts; most of the German workers who had come there to better their position in the trade, and then return home as master craftsmen, were still deeply imbued with the old spirit of the guild." Gustav Mayer, *Friedrich Engels*, vol. 1, *Friedrich Engels in seiner Frühzeit*, 2nd ed. (Berlin ‹1933›), pp. 249–250.[22] [a16a,2]

The Brussels "Communist Correspondence Committee" of Marx and Engels in 1846: "Marx and he . . . had tried in vain to convert Proudhon. Engels now undertook a fruitless mission to win over old Cabet, the leader of experimental utopian communism on the continent, . . . for participation in the Correspondence Committee. . . . It was some months . . . before he established closer relations with the *Réforme* group, with Louis Blanc and particularly with ‹Ferdinand› Flocon." Gustav Mayer, *Friedrich Engels*, vol. 1, *Friedrich Engels in seiner Frühzeit*, 2nd ed. (Berlin ‹1933›), p. 254.[23] [a16a,3]

Guizot writes, after the February Revolution: "I have long been subject to a double suspicion: one, that the disease is much more serious than we think and say; and, two, that our remedies are futile, scarcely more than skin deep. While I held the reins of my country and directed its affairs, this double awareness grew stronger by the day; and precisely in proportion as I succeeded and remained in power, I came to feel that neither my success nor my tenure in office was having much effect, that the defeated enemy was winning out over me, and that, in order truly to defeat him, one would have had to do things which it was impossible even to mention." Cited in Abel Bonnard, *Les Modérés*, in series entitled *Le Drame du présent*, vol. 1 (Paris ‹1936›), pp. 314–315. [a16a,4]

"If an agitator is to achieve lasting results, he must speak as the representative of a body of opinion. . . . Engels must have realized this during his first visit to Paris. On his second, he found that the doors at which he knocked opened more easily. French socialism still refused to have anything to do with political struggles. Therefore, he could look for allies in the coming battle only among those democrats connected with *La Réforme* who advocated state socialism in some degree. Under the leadership of a Louis Blanc and a Ferdinand Flocon, these men believed, as he did, that it was necessary to garner political power through democracy before attempting any social transformation. Engels was prepared to go hand in hand with the bourgeoisie whenever it took a confirmed democratic direction; he could not refuse to associate himself with this party whose program included the abolition of hired labor, although he must have known to what extent its parliamentary leader, Ledru-Rollin, was averse to communism. . . . He had learned from experience; he presented himself to Blanc as 'the official delegate of the German democrats in London, in Brussels, and on the Rhine' and 'the agent of the Chartist movement.'" Gustav Mayer, *Friedrich Engels*, vol. 1, *Friedrich Engels in seiner Frühzeit* (Berlin ‹1933›), pp. 280–281.[24] [a17,1]

"Under the Provisional Government it was customary, indeed it was a *necessity*, combining politics and enthusiasm at once, to preach to the generous workers who (as could be read on thousands of official placards) had '*placed three months of misery at the disposal of the republic*,' that the February Revolution had been waged *in their own interests*, and that the February Revolution was concerned above all with the *interests of the workers*. But, after the opening of the National Assembly, everyone came down to earth. What was important now was *to bring labor back to its old situation*, as Minister Trélat said." Karl Marx, "Dem Andenken der Juni-Kämpfer" [in *Karl Marx als Denker, Mensch und Revolutionär*, ed. D. Rjazanov (Vienna and Berlin ‹1928›), p. 38; first published in the *Neue rheinische Zeitung*, ca. June 28, 1848].[25] [a17,2]

Final sentence of the essay on the June combatants, coming directly after the description of the measures undertaken by the state to honor the memory of those victims who belonged to the bourgeoisie: "But the plebeians are tortured with hunger; reviled by the press; abandoned by doctors; abused by honest men as thieves, incendiaries, galley slaves; their women and children thrown into still-deeper misery; their best sons deported overseas; and it is the *privilege*, it is the *right of the democratic press* to entwine the laurels round their stern and threatening brows." Karl Marx, "Dem Andenken der Juni-Kämpfer" [in *Karl Marx als Denker, Mensch und Revolutionär*, ed. D. Rjazanov (Vienna and Berlin), p. 40; first published in the *Neue rheinische Zeitung*, ca. June 28, 1848].[26] [a17,3]

On Buret's *De la Misère des classes laborieuses en Angleterre et en France* and Engels' *Lage der arbeitenden Klasse in England:* "Charles Andler would like us to see in Engels' book only a 'recasting and sharpening' of the book by Buret. In our view, however, there is grounds for comparison here only in the fact that both books . . . partly draw from the same source material. . . . The evaluative criteria of the French writer remain anchored in the concept of natural right . . . , while the German author . . . adduces the tendencies of economic and social development . . . in his explanations. Whereas Engels looks to communism as the sole salvation from the worsening situation of the present, Buret places his hopes in the complete mobilization of landed property, in a social politics and a constitutional system of industry." Gustav Mayer, *Friedrich Engels*, vol. 1, *Friedrich Engels in seiner Frühzeit* (Berlin ‹1933›), p. 195.   [a17a,1]

Engels on the June Insurrection. "In a diary meant for publication on the literary page of the *Neue rheinische Zeitung*, he wrote: 'Between the old Paris and the new lay the fifteenth of May and the twenty-fifth of June. . . . Cavaignac's bombshells had effectively burst the invincible Parisian gaiety. "La Marseillaise" and "Le Chant du départ" ceased to be heard, and only the bourgeois still hummed to themselves their "Mourir pour la patrie," while the workers, unemployed and weaponless, gnashed their teeth in suppressed rage." Gustav Mayer, *Friedrich Engels*, vol. 1, *Freidrich Engels in seiner Frühzeit* (Berlin ‹1933›), p. 317.[27]
                    [a17a,2]

Engels, during the June Insurrection, referred to "Paris East and West as symbols for the two great enemy camps into which here, for the first time, the whole society splits." Gustav Mayer, *Friedrich Engels*, vol. 1, *Friedrich Engels in seiner Frühzeit* (Berlin ‹1933›), p. 312.   [a17a,3]

Marx calls the revolution "our brave friend, Robin Goodfellow, the old mole that can work in the earth so fast, that worthy pioneer—the Revolution." In the same speech, at the conclusion: "To avenge the misdeeds of the ruling class, there existed in the Middle Ages in Germany a secret tribunal called the Vehmgericht. If a red cross was seen marked on a house, people knew that its owner was doomed by the Vehm. All the houses of Europe are now marked with the mysterious red cross. History is the judge; its executioner, the proletarian." Karl Marx, "Die Revolutionen von 1848 und das Proletariat," speech delivered on the fourth anniversary of the foundation of *The People's Paper*. Published in *The People's Paper*, April 19, 1856[28] [in *Karl Marx als Denker, Mensch und Revolutionär*, ed. D. Rjazanov (Vienna and Berlin ‹1928›), pp. 42, 43].   [a17a,4]

Marx defends Cabet against Proudhon as "worthy of respect for his practical attitude toward the proletariat." Marx to ‹Johann› Schweitzer, London, January 24, 1865, in Karl Marx and Friedrich Engels, *Ausgewählte Briefe*, ed. V. Adoratski (Moscow and Leningrad, 1934), p. 143.[29]   [a18,1]

Marx on Proudhon: "The February Revolution certainly came at a very inconvenient moment for Proudhon, who had irrefutably proved only a few weeks before that the 'era of revolutions' was ended forever. His speech to the National Assembly, however little insight it showed into existing conditions, was worthy of every praise. Coming after the June Insurrection, it was an act of great courage. In addition, it had the fortunate consequence that Thiers—by his reply (which was then issued as a special booklet), in which he opposed Proudhon's proposals—proved to the whole of Europe what an infantile catechism formed the pedestal for this intellectual pillar of the French bourgeoisie. Compared with Thiers, Proudhon's stature indeed seemed that of an antediluvian colossus. . . . His attacks on religion, the church, and so on were of great merit locally at a time when the French socialists thought it desirable to show, by their religiosity, how superior they were to the bourgeois Voltaireanism of the eighteenth century and the German godlessness of the nineteenth. Just as Peter the Great defeated Russian barbarism by barbarity, Proudhon did his best to defeat French phrase-mongering by phrases." Marx to Schweitzer, London, January 24, 1865, in Karl Marx and Friedrich Engels, *Ausgewählte Briefe*, ed. V. Adoratski (Moscow and Leningrad, 1934), pp. 143–144.[30]   [a18,2]

"You'll be amused by the following: *Journal des économistes*, August of this year, contains, in an article on . . . communism, the following: 'M. Marx is a *cobbler*, as another German communist, Weitling, is a tailor. . . . Neither does M. Marx proceed beyond . . . abstract formulas, and he takes the greatest care to avoid broaching any truly practical question. According to him [note the nonsense], the emancipation of the German people will be the signal for the emancipation of the human race; philosophy would be the head of this emancipation, the proletariat its heart. When all has been prepared, the Gallic cock will herald the Teutonic resurrection. . . . Marx says that a universal proletariat *must be created* in Germany [!!] in order for the philosophical concept of communism to be realized.'" Engels to Marx, ca. September 16, 1846, in Karl Marx and Friedrich Engels, ⟨*Briefwechsel*,⟩ vol. 1, *1844–1853*, ed. Marx-Engels-Lenin Institute (Moscow, Leningrad, ⟨and Zürich,⟩ 1935), pp. 45–46.[31]   [a18,3]

"It is a necessary result of every victorious reaction that the causes of the revolution and especially of the counterrevolution should pass into utter oblivion." Engels to Marx, Manchester, December 18, 1868, apropos of Eugène Ténot's books on the coup d'état of 1851; in Karl Marx and Friedrich Engels, *Ausgewählte Briefe*, ed. V. Adoratski (Moscow and Leningrad, 1934), p. 209.[32]   [a18,4]

On national holidays, certain objects could be redeemed gratis from the pawn shops.   [a18a,1]

Laffitte calls himself "a citizen with possessions." Cited in Abel Bonnard, *Les Modérés*, in series entitled *Le Drame du présent*, vol. 1, (Paris ⟨1936⟩), p. 79.
                                                                                              [a18a,2]

"Poetry . . . has sanctioned the great error of separating the force of Labor from Art. Alfred de Vigny's denunciation of the railroads is succeeded by Verhaeren's invective against the 'tentacled cities.' Poetry has taken flight from the forms of modern civilization. . . . It has not understood that the elements of art can be found in any human activity whatsoever, and that its own powers are diminished by its refusal to entertain the possibility of inspiration in the things actually surrounding it." Pierre Hamp, "La Littérature, image de la société," *Encyclopédie française*, vol. 16, *Arts et littératures dans la société contemporaine*, 1 ‹Paris, 1935›, p. 64.   [a18a,3]

"From 1852 to 1865, France lent four and a half billion francs abroad. . . . The workers were even more directly affected than the bourgeois republicans by economic developments. The consequence of the trade treaty with England and the unemployment in the cotton industry caused by the American Civil War inevitably made them realize their own dependence upon the international economic situation." S. Kracauer, *Jacques Offenbach und das Paris seiner Zeit* (Amsterdam, 1937), pp. 328, 330.[33]   [a18a,4]

Pierre Dupont's hymn to peace was still sung in the streets during the world exhibition of 1878.   [a18a,5]

In 1852, establishment of Crédit Mobilier (Pereire) for financing the railroads. Establishment of Crédit Foncier ‹land bank› and of Au Bon Marché.   [a18a,6]

"In 1857, a year of crisis, a series of big financial trials started, under the influence of the opposition to the Saint-Simonian democratization of credit; they disclosed an enormous amount of corruption and shady practice, such as fraudulent bankruptcies, abuse of confidence, and artificial driving up of prices. An enormous sensation was caused by the trial of Mirès, which started in 1861 and dragged on for years." S. Kracauer, *Jacques Offenbach und das Paris seiner Zeit* (Amsterdam, 1937), p. 262.[34]   [a18a,7]

Louis Philippe to Guizot: "We shall never be able to effect anything in France, and a day will come when my children will have no bread." S. Kracauer, *Jacques Offenbach und das Paris seiner Zeit* (Amsterdam, 1937), p. 139.[35]   [a18a,8]

The manifesto of the Communist party was preceded by many others. (1843: Considérant's "Manifeste de la *Démocratie pacifique*.")   [a19,1]

Fourier speaks of cobblers as "men no less polite than others when they gather in association." Fourier, *Le Nouveau Monde industriel et sociétaire* (Paris, 1829), p. 221.   [a19,2]

In 1822, France had only 16,000 passive electors and 110,000 active electors. According to the law of 1817, a man was a passive elector ‹eligible for election to the Chamber of Deputies⟩ if he had reached the age of forty and paid 1,000 francs in direct taxation. He was an active elector ⟨eligible to vote for deputies⟩ if he had reached the age of thirty and paid 300 francs.[36] (Defaulting taxpayers had a man—a soldier?—quartered with them, whom they had to maintain until such time as they had settled their debt.)   [a19,3]

Proudhon on Hegel: "The antinomy is not resolved: here is the fundamental flaw of all Hegelian philosophy. The two terms of which the antinomy is composed balance out. . . . A balance is by no means a synthesis." "Let us not forget," adds Cuvillier, "that Proudhon was for a long time a bookkeeper." Elsewhere, Proudhon speaks of the ideas determining his own philosophy as "elementary ideas, common to bookkeeping and metaphysics alike." Armand Cuvillier, "Marx et Proudhon," *A la Lumière du marxisme*, vol. 2 (Paris, 1937), pp. 180–181.
                                                        [a19,4]

The following premise of Proudhon's, claims Marx in *Die heilige Familie* ⟨?⟩, had been previously advanced by the English economist Sadler in 1830. Proudhon says: "'This immense power that results from the union and harmony of laborers, from the convergence and simultaneity of their efforts, has not been recompensed by the capitalist.' Thus it is that 200 grenadiers succeeded, within several hours, in raising the obelisk of Luxor on the Place de la Concorde, whereas a single man working for 200 days would have obtained no result at all. 'Separate the laborers from one another, and the amount paid daily to each would perhaps exceed the value of each individual product, but this is not what is at issue here. A force of a thousand men working over a period of twenty days has been paid what a single man would earn in fifty-five years; but this force of a thousand has produced, in twenty days, what the power of a single man, multiplied across a million centuries, could not achieve. Is there equity in the marketplace?'" Cited in Armand Cuvillier, "Marx et Proudhon," *A la Lumière du marxisme*, vol. 2 (Paris, 1937), p. 196.
                                                        [a19,5]

Unlike Saint-Simon and Fourier, Proudhon was not interested in history. "The history of property among ancient peoples is, for us, nothing more than a matter of erudition and curiosity" (cited in Cuvillier, "Marx et Proudhon," p. 201). Conservatism bound up with a lack of historical sense is just as petty bourgeois as conservatism bound up with historical sense is feudal.   [a19a,1]

Proudhon's apology for the coup d'état: to be found in his letter to Louis Napoleon of April 21, 1858, where it is said of the dynastic principle "that this principle, which before '89 was simply the incarnation, in one chosen family, of divine right or religious thought, . . . is or can be defined today as . . . the incarnation, in one chosen family, of human right or the rational thought of the revolution." Cited in Armand Cuvillier, "Marx et Proudhon," *A la Lumière du marxisme*, vol. 2, part 1 (Paris, 1937), p. 219.   [a19a,2]

Cuvillier presents Proudhon as a precursor of "national socialism" in the fascist sense.   [a19a,3]

"Proudhon believed that one could abolish surplus value, along with unearned income, without transforming the organization of production. . . . Proudhon conceived this preposterous dream of socializing exchange within a context of nonsocialized production." A. Cuvillier, "Marx et Proudhon," *A la Lumière du marxisme*, vol. 2, part 1 (Paris, 1937), p. 210.   [a19a,4]

"Value measured by labor . . . is . . . , in Proudhon's eyes, the very goal of progress. For Marx, it is quite otherwise. The determination of value by labor is not an ideal; it is a fact. It exists in our current society." Armand Cuvillier, "Marx et Proudhon," *A la Lumière du marxisme*, vol. 2, part 1 (Paris, 1937), p. 208.
[a19a,5]

Proudhon spoke out extremely maliciously against Fourier, and he spoke no less derogatorily of Cabet. This last provoked a reprimand from Marx, who saw in Cabet, by reason of his political role in the working class, a highly respectable man.   [a19a,6]

Blanqui's exclamation, on entering the salon of Mlle. de Montgolfier on the evening of July 29, 1830: "The Romantics are done for!"[37]   [a19a,7]

Beginning of the June Insurrection: "On June 19, the dissolution of the national workshops was announced as imminent; a crowd gathered around the Hôtel de Ville. On June 21, *Le Moniteur* announced that, the following day, workers aged seventeen to twenty-five would be enlisted in the army or conducted to Sologne and other regions. It was this last expedient that most exasperated the Paris workers. All these men who were used to doing detailed manual work in front of a workbench and vise rejected the idea of going to till the earth and lay out roads in a marshland. One of the cries of the insurrection was: 'We won't go! We won't go!'" Gustave Geffroy, *L'Enfermé* (Paris, 1926), vol. 1, p. 193.   [a20,1]

Blanqui in *Le Libérateur*, March 1834: "He demolishes, by a comparison, the notorious commonplace, 'The rich put the poor to work.' 'Approximately,' he says, 'as plantation owners put Negroes to work, with the difference that the worker is not capital to be husbanded like the slave.'" Gustave Geffroy, *L'Enfermé* (Paris, 1926), vol. 1, p. 69.   [a20,2]

Garat's theme of April 2, 1848: "Establishment of a *cordon sanitaire* around the dwellings of the rich, who are destined to die of hunger." Gustave Geffroy, *L'Enfermé* (Paris, 1926), vol. 1, p. 152.   [a20,3]

Refrain of 1848: "Hat in hand when facing the cap, / Kneel down before the worker!"   [a20,4]

Fifty thousand workers in the June Insurrection in Paris.   [a20,5]

Proudhon defines himself as "a new man, a man of polemics and not of the barricades; a man who would know how to reach his goal by dining every day with the prefect of police and taking for his confidants all the De la Hoddes of the world." This in 1850. Cited in Geffroy, *L'Enfermé* (Paris, 1926), vol. 1, pp. 180–181.
                                                                             [a20,6]

"Under the Empire—to its very end, in fact—there was a renewal and development of the ideas of the eighteenth century. . . . People, in those days, readily called themselves atheists, materialists, positivists; and the vaguely religious or manifestly Catholic republican of 1848 became a . . . curiosity." Gustave Geffroy, *L'Enfermé* (Paris, 1897), p. 247.   [a20,7]

Blanqui, in the proceedings taken against the Société des Amis du Peuple, under questioning by the presiding judge: "'What is your profession?' Blanqui: 'Proletarian.' Judge: 'That is not a profession.' Blanqui: 'What! Not a profession? It is the profession of thirty million Frenchmen who live by their labor and who are deprived of political rights.' Judge: 'Well, so be it. Let the clerk record that the accused is a proletarian.'" *Défense du citoyen Louis Auguste Blanqui devant la cour d'assises, 1832* (Paris, 1832), p. 4.   [a20,8]

Baudelaire on Barbier's *Rimes héroïques:* "Here, to speak frankly, all the folly of the century appears, resplendent in its unconscious nakedness. Under the pretext of writing sonnets in honor of great men, the poet has celebrated the lightning rod and the automated loom. The prodigious absurdities to which this confusion of ideas and functions could lead us is obvious." Baudelaire, *L'Art romantique*, ed. Hachette, vol. 3 (Paris), p. 336.[38]   [a20a,1]

Blanqui, in his *Défense du citoyen Louis Auguste Blanqui devant la cour d'assises, 1832* (Paris, 1832), p. 14: "You have confiscated the rifles of July—yes. But the bullets have been fired. Every bullet of the workers of Paris is on its way round the world."   [a20a,2]

"The man of genius represents at once the greatest strength and the greatest weakness of humanity. . . . He tells the nations that the interests of the weak and the interests of genius coalesce, such that the one cannot be endangered without endangering the other, such that the ultimate limit of perfectibility will be reached only when the right of the weakest will have replaced, on the throne, the right of the strongest." Auguste Blanqui, *Critique sociale* (Paris, 1885), vol. 2, *Fragments et notes*, p. 46 ("Propriété intellectuelle," 1867—conclusion!).   [a20a,3]

On the compliments paid by Lamartine to Rothschild: "M. de Lamartine, this Captain Cook of oceangoing politics, this Sinbad the Sailor of the nineteenth century, . . . this voyager no less roving than Ulysses, though happier, who has taken

the Sirens to be crew of his ship and aired upon the shores of all the parties the
ever-varied music of his convictions, M. de Lamartine, in his never-ending odys-
sey, has just gently beached his aeolian bark under the porticoes of the Stock
Exchange." Auguste Blanqui, *Critique sociale* (Paris, 1885), vol. 2, p. 100 ("Lamartine et Rothschild," April 1850). [a20a,4]

Doctrine of Blanqui: "No! No one has access to the secret of the future. Scarcely
possible for even the most clairvoyant are certain presentiments, rapid glimpses, a
vague and fugitive coup d'oeil. The Revolution alone, as it clears the terrain, will
reveal the horizon, will gradually remove the veils and open up the roads, or
rather the multiple paths, that lead to the new order. Those who pretend to have in
their pocket a complete map of this unknown land—they truly are madmen."
Auguste Blanqui, *Critique sociale* (Paris, 1885), vol. 2, pp. 115–116 ("Les Sectes
et la Révolution," October 1866). [a20a,5]

Parliament of 1849: "In a speech delivered to the National Assembly on April 14,
M. Considérant, a disciple . . . of Fourier, had this to say: 'The time of obedience
is past: men feel that they are equal, and they want to be free. They do not believe any longer, and they wish to *enjoy themselves*. There you have the state
of souls.'—'You mean the state of brutes!' interrupted M. de La Rochejaque-
lein." L. B. Bonjean, *Socialisme et sens commun* (Paris, May 1849), pp. 28–29.
[a21,1]

"M. Dumas (of the Institut) exclaims: 'The blinding dust of foolish theories raised
by the whirlwind of February has dissipated in the air, and, in the wake of this
vanished cloud, the year 1844 reappears with its shining countenance and its
sublime doctrine of material interests.'" Auguste Blanqui, *Critique sociale* (Paris,
1885), vol. 2, p. 104 ("Discours de Lamartine," 1850). [a21,2]

In 1850, Blanqui pens a polemic: "Rapport gigantesque de Thiers sur l'assistance
publique." [a21,3]

"Will matter . . . assume the form of a single point in the sky? Or be content with a
thousand, ten thousand, a hundred thousand points that would barely enlarge its
meager domain? No—its vocation, its law, is infinity. It will not in the least allow
itself to be outflanked by the void. Space will not become its dungeon." A. Blanqui,
L'Eternité par les astres: Hypothèse astronomique (Paris, 1872), p. 54. [a21,4]

At the end of a meeting in the early days of the Third Republic: "Louise Michel
announced that an effort would be made to contact the wives and children of
imprisoned comrades. 'What we ask of you,' she said, 'is not an act of charity but
an act of solidarity; for those who bestow charity, when they do bestow it, are
proud and self-satisfied, but we—we are never satisfied.'" Daniel Halévy, *Pays
parisiens* (Paris ‹1932›), p. 165. [a21,5]

Nouvelle Némésis, by Barthélemy (Paris, 1844), contains, in chapter 16 ("The Workers"), a "satire" which very emphatically takes up the demands of the working class. Barthélemy is already acquainted with the concept of proletarian.
[a21,6]

Barricades: "At nine o'clock in the evening, on a beautiful summer night, Paris without streetlights, without shops, without gas, without moving vehicles, presented a unique tableau of desolation. At midnight, with its paving stones piled high, its barricades, its walls in ruins, its thousand carriages stranded in the mud, its boulevards devastated, its dark streets deserted, Paris was like nothing ever seen before. Thebes and Herculaneum are less sad. No noises, no shadows, no living beings—except the motionless worker who guarded the barricade with his rifle and pistols. To frame it all: the blood of the day preceding and the uncertainty of the morrow." Barthélemy and Méry, *L'Insurrection: Poème* (Paris, 1830), pp. 52–53 (note). ▯ Parisian Antiquity ▯
[a21a,1]

"Who would believe it! It is said that, incensed at the hour, / Latter-day Joshuas, at the foot of every clocktower, / Were firing on clock faces to make the day stand still." At this point a note: "This is a unique feature in the history of the insurrection: it is the only act of vandalism carried out by the people against public monuments. And what vandalism! How well it expresses the situation of hearts and minds on the evening of the twenty-eighth![39] With what rage one watched the shadows falling and the implacable advance of the needle toward night—just as on ordinary days! What was most singular about this episode was that it was observed, at the very same hour, in different parts of the city. This was the expression not of an aberrant notion, an isolated whim, but of a widespread, nearly general sentiment." Barthélemy and Méry, *L'Insurrection: Poème dédié aux Parisiens* (Paris, 1830), pp. 22, 52.
[a21a,2]

During the July Revolution, for a short time before the tricolor was raised, the flag of the insurgents was black. With it the female ‹body› was covered, presumably the same one carried by torchlight through Paris.[40] See Barthélemy and Méry, *L'Insurrection* (Paris, 1830), p. 51.
[a21a,3]

Railroad poetry:

> To a station 'neath the rails everybody is bound.
> Wherever the train crisscrosses the land,
> There's no more distinction twixt humble and grand;
> All classes are equal six feet underground.

Barthélemy, *Nouvelle Némésis*, no. 12, "La Vapeur" (Paris, 1845) ‹p. 46›.
[a22,1]

Opening of the preface to Tissot's *De la Manie du suicide et de l'esprit de révolte:* "It is impossible not to be struck by two moral phenomena which are like the symptoms of a disease that today, in its own particular way, is ravaging the body and limbs of society: we are speaking of *suicide* and *revolt*. Impatient with all law, discontented with all position, the individual rises up equally against human nature and against mankind, against himself and against society. . . . The man of our time, and the Frenchman perhaps more than any other, having violently broken with the past . . . and looked with fear toward a future whose horizon already seems to him so gloomy, kills himself if he is weak . . . , if he lacks faith in . . . the betterment of men and, above all, lacks faith in a providence capable of deriving good from evil." J. Tissot, *De la Manie du suicide et de l'esprit de révolte* (Paris, 1840) ⟨p. v⟩. The author claims not to have known the books by Frégier, Villermé, and Degéraude at the time he drafted his work.   [a22,2]

Concerning Flora Tristan's "Méphis": "This proletarian name, which now is so readily intelligible, . . . sounded extremely romantic and mysterious in those days. It marked the pariah, the galley slave, the *carbonaro*, the artist, the regenerator, the adversary of the Jesuits. From his encounter with a beautiful Spaniard was born the inspired woman who must redeem the world." Jean Cassou, *Quarante-huit* (Paris ⟨1939⟩), p. 12.   [a22,3]

With regard to the exotic enterprises of Considérant and Cabet, Blanqui speaks of experiments carried out "in a corner of the human species." Cited in Cassou, *Quarante-huit*, p. 41.   [a22,4]

The unemployment rate in England between 1850 and 1914 rose only once above 8 percent. (In 1930, it reached 16 percent.)   [a22,5]

"The typographer Burgy, in his book *Présent et avenir des ouvriers*, preaches . . . celibacy to his companions: the picture of the proletarian condition would not be complete if one left out the shadows of resignation and defeatism." Jean Cassou, *Quarante-huit* (Paris ⟨1939⟩), p. 77.   [a22a,1]

Guizot, in *Du Mouvement et du résistance en politique:* "Any man of above-average intelligence who has neither property nor business—that is to say, who is unwilling or unable to pay a tribute to the state—should be considered dangerous from a political standpoint." Cited in Cassou, *Quarante-huit*, p. 152.   [a22a,2]

Guizot in 1837, to the Chamber: "Today—apart from force of law—you have but one effective guarantee against this revolutionary disposition of the poorer classes: work, the constant necessity of work." Cited in Cassou, pp. 152–153.   [a22a,3]

Blanqui, in his letter to Maillard: "Thank heaven there are so many bourgeois in the camp of the proletariat. It is they who represent the chief strength of this camp, or at least its most lasting strength. They provide it with a contingent of luminaries such as the people themselves, unfortunately, cannot yet furnish. It was the bourgeois who first raised the flag of the proletariat, who formulated, propagated, and maintained the egalitarian doctrines, and who restored them after their downfall. Everywhere it is bourgeois who lead the people in their battles against the bourgeoisie." A passage immediately following deals with the bourgeoisie's exploitation of the proletariat as political shock troops. Maurice Dommanget, *Blanqui à Belle-Ile* (Paris, 1935>, pp. 176–177. [a22a,4]

"The terrible scourge of poverty, so relentless in its torments, requires a no less terrible remedy, and celibacy appears the most certain among those pointed out to us by social science." In connection with a reference to Malthus: "In our day the pitiless Marcus [evidently used for "Malthus"], unfolding the dismal consequences of a limitless increase in population . . . , has ventured to propose asphyxiating those babies born to indigent families that already have three children, and then compensating the mothers for suffering an act of such cruel necessity. . . . Here we have the last word of the economists of England!" [Jules Burgy,] *Présent et avenir des ouvriers* (Paris, 1847), pp. 30, 32–33.

[a22a,5]

> There exists on earth an infernal vat
> Named Paris; it is one large oven,
> A stony pit of wide circumference,
> Ringed by three bends of a muddy yellow river.
> It is a seething volcano that never stops erupting;
> Its shock waves travel through human matter.

Auguste Barbier, *Iambes et poèmes* (Paris, 1845), p. 65 ("La Cuve" ‹The Vat›).
[a23,1]

> The Paris purebred is this pale guttersnipe,
> Stunted growth, yellowed like an old penny,
> This boy hooting, out at all hours
> Strolling indolent down unfamiliar lanes,
> Routing the skinny mutts, or, all along the high walls,
> Chalking a thousand unchaste figures, whistling the while,
> This child, believing nothing, who turns up his nose at mother;
> The admonition to pray is for him a bad joke.

Auguste Barbier, *Iambes et poèmes,* p. 68 ("La Cuve"). Hugo had already retouched these traits in the figure of Gavroche. [a23,2]

b

[Daumier]

A paradoxical description of Daumier's art: "Caricature, for him, became a sort of philosophic operation which consisted in separating a man from that which society had made of him, in order to reveal what he was at bottom, what he could have been under different circumstances. He extracted, in a word, the latent self." Edouard Drumont, *Les Héros et les pitres* (Paris ‹1900›), p. 299 ("Daumier"). [b1,1]

On Daumier's bourgeois: "This ossified, inert, crystallized being who waits for the omnibus leans on an umbrella that expresses some unutterable idea of absolute petrifaction." Edouard Drumont, *Les Héros et les pitres* (Paris), p. 304 ("Daumier"). [b1,2]

"Many writers . . . acquired fame and fortune by mocking the faults and infirmities of others. Monnier, on the other hand, did not have to go very far to find his model: he planted himself before the mirror, listened to himself thinking and talking, and, finding himself highly ridiculous, he conceived this cruel incarnation, this prodigious satire of the French bourgeois, whom he named Joseph Prudhomme." Alphonse Daudet, *Trente ans de Paris*, p. 91. [b1,3]

"Not only does caricature greatly accentuate the techniques of drawing, . . . but it has always been the means of introducing new subject matter into art. It was through Monnier, Gavarni, and Daumier that the bourgeois society of this century was opened up to art." Eduard Fuchs, *Die Karikatur der europäischen Völker*, 4th ed. (Munich ‹1921›), vol. 1, p. 16. [b1,4]

"On August 7, 1830, Louis Philippe was . . . proclaimed . . . king. On November 4 of that same year, the first issue of *La Caricature* appeared, the journal created by Philipon." Eduard Fuchs, *Die Karikatur der europäischen Völker* (Munich), vol. 1, p. 326. [b1,5]

Michelet wanted to see one of his works illustrated by Daumier. [b1,6]

"Philipon invented a new character type, . . . which was said to have brought him nearly as much . . . popularity as his pears: 'Robert Macaire,' the type of the unscrupulous speculator and promoter."[1] Eduard Fuchs, *Die Karikatur der europäischen Völker* (Munich), vol. 1, p. 354. [b1,7]

"The last issue of *La Caricature*, dated August 27, 1835, was . . . devoted . . . to the promulgation of the . . . September Laws, . . . which . . . were represented in the form of pears." Eduard Fuchs, *Die Karikatur der europäischen Völker*, vol. 1, p. 352. [b1,8]

Traviès, the creator of Mayeux; Gavarni, the creator of Thomas Vireloque; Daumier, the creator of Ratapoil—the Bonapartist lumpenproletarian. [b1,9]

On January 1, 1856, Philipon rebaptizes *Le Journal pour rire* as *Le Journal amusant*. [b1,10]

"Whenever a priest . . . exhorted the girls of a village never to go to the dance, or the peasants never to frequent the tavern, Courier's epigrams would climb the bell tower and sound the alarm, proclaiming the advent of the Inquisition in France. His pamphlets, meanwhile, would make the whole country listen to the sermon." Alfred Nettement, *Histoire de la littérature française sous la Restauration* (Paris, 1858), vol. 1, p. 421. [b1a,1]

"Mayeux . . . is actually an imitation. Under Louis XIV, . . . a particular costume dance caused an uproar: children made up as old men, and sporting enormous hunchbacks, executed grotesque figures. It was known as the "Mayeux of Brittany" dance. The Mayeux who was made a member of the Garde Nationale in 1830 was merely a very ill-bred descendant of these old Mayeux." Edouard Fournier, *Enigmes des rues de Paris* (Paris, 1860), p. 351. [b1a,2]

On Daumier: "By no one more than Daumier has the bourgeois been known and loved (after the fashion of artists)—the bourgeois, this last vestige of the Middle Ages, this Gothic ruin that dies so hard, this type at once so commonplace and so eccentric." Charles Baudelaire, *Les Dessins de Daumier* (Paris ‹1924›), p. 14.[2]
[b1a,3]

On Daumier: "His caricature has formidable breadth, but it is quite without bile or rancor. In all his work there is a foundation of decency and bonhomie. We should note that he has often refused to handle certain very fine and violent satirical themes, because, he said, they exceeded the limits of the comic and could wound the feelings of his fellow men." Charles Baudelaire, *Les Dessins de Daumier* (Paris ‹1924›), p. 16.[3]
[b1a,4]

On Monnier: "But what a great source these merciless, imperturbable commentators remain! Balzac took the name . . . 'Cibot' from Monnier, as well as the names 'Desroches' and 'Descoings.' And Anatole France took from him the name 'Madame Bergeret,' just as Flaubert had taken, with a very slight alteration, the name

Honoré Daumier, ca. 1857. Photo by Nadar. Collection Société Française de Photographie.

'Monsieur Péguchet.'" Marie-Jeanne Durry, "De Monnier à Balzac," *Vendredi*, March 20, 1936, p. 5. [b1a,5]

When does Gavroche first appear? Who are his forebears? Is his first appearance in *Les Misérables?* Abel Bonnard on the *homme frelaté* ‹adulterated man›—"good only for provoking events he could not control." "This type of individual, originating in the nobility, has undergone a descent—and lost all his gilding in the process—through the whole spectrum of society, to the point where what was born in the foam at the surface has come to rest in the slime at the bottom. What began in persiflage has ended in a sneer. Gavroche is, very simply, the marquis of the gutter." Abel Bonnard, *Les Modérés,* in series entitled *Le Drame du présent,* vol. 1 (Paris ‹1936›), p. 294. [b1a,6]

"Everyone knew Daumier's mythological caricatures, which, in the words of Baudelaire, made Achilles, Odysseus, and the rest look like a lot of played-out tragic actors, inclined to take pinches of snuff at moments when no one was looking." S. Kracauer, *Jacques Offenbach und das Paris seiner Zeit* (Amsterdam, 1937), p. 237.[4] [b2,1]

Fourier. "Not content with extracting from his works the innumerable amusing inventions to be found there, the gazetteers add to them—for example, the business of the tail with an eye on its tip, supposedly an attribute of men of the future. He protests vehemently against this malicious fabrication." F. Armand and R. Maublanc, *Fourier* (Paris, 1937), vol. 1, p. 58. [b2,2]

The Pagan School is opposed not only to the spirit of Christianity but also to the spirit of modernity. Baudelaire illustrates this, in his essay "L'Ecole païenne," with the aid of Daumier: "Daumier did a remarkable series of lithographs, *L'Histoire ancienne,* which was, so to speak, the best paraphrase of the famous saying, 'Who will deliver us from the Greeks and Romans?' Daumier pounced brutally upon antiquity and mythology, and spit on them. The hotheaded Achilles, the prudent Ulysses, the wise Penelope, that great ninny Telemachus, the beautiful Helen who ruined Troy, the ardent Sappho, patroness of hysterical women—all were portrayed with a farcical homeliness that recalled those old carcasses of classical actors who take a pinch of snuff in the wings." Charles Baudelaire, *L'Art romantique,* ed. Hachette (Paris), vol. 3, p. 305.[5] [b2,3]

Types: Mayeux (Traviès), Robert Macaire (Daumier), Prudhomme (Monnier). [b2,4]

d

[Literary History, Hugo]

"Thiers argued that, since education was 'the beginning of ease, and since ease was not reserved for all,' then education should not be within reach of all. Moreover, he held lay instructors . . . responsible for the events of June . . . and declared himself 'ready to put the clergy in charge of all primary education.'" A. Malet and P. Grillet, *XIXᵉ Siècle* (Paris, 1919), p. 258. [d1,1]

February 25, 1848: "During the afternoon, armed mobs demanded that the red flag replace the tricolor flag. . . . After a violent debate, Lamartine managed to turn them back with an improvised address, whose concluding words have remained famous: 'I shall repudiate to the very death,' he cried, 'this flag of blood, and you ought to spurn it more than I. For this red flag that you wave before us has previously been unfurled only on the Champ de Mars, soaked with the blood of the people in '91 and '93, whereas the tricolor flag has been paraded the world over, with the name, the glory, and the liberty of the Fatherland." A. Malet and P. Grillet, *XIXᵉ Siècle* (Paris, 1919), p. 245. [d1,2]

"In an admirable article entitled 'Le Départ,' Balzac lamented the fall of the Bourbons, which for him meant the death knell of the arts and the triumph of the peddlers of political nostrums. Invoking the vessel on which the king was departing, he exclaimed: '*There* is law and logic; beyond this little boat are the storms.'" J. Lucas-Dubreton, *Le Comte d'Artois, Charles X* ‹Paris, 1927›, p. 233. [d1,3]

"Who knows the titles of all the books that bear the name of M. Dumas? Does he know them himself? If he does not keep a two-column record with debits and credits, he will no doubt have forgotten . . . more than one of those children of whom he is the legitimate father, or the natural father, or the godfather. His output in recent months has amounted to not less than thirty volumes." Paulin Limayrac, "Du Roman actuel et de nos romanciers," *Revue des deux mondes*, 11, no. 3 (Paris, 1845), pp. 953–954. [d1,4]

Ironical: "What a happy thought on the part of M. de Balzac—to predict a peasant revolt and demand the reestablishment of feudalism! What is so surprising in that? It is his idea of socialism. Mme. Sand has another, and M. Sue likewise. To each novelist his own." Paulin Limayrac, "Du Roman actuel et de nos romanciers," *Revue des deux mondes*, 11, no. 3 (Paris, 1845), pp. 955–956.   [d1,5]

"Citizen Hugo made his debut at the tribune of the National Assembly. He was what we expected: a phrasemaker and a gesticulator, full of empty, high-flown oratory. Continuing along the perfidious and slanderous path of his recent broadside, he spoke of the unemployed, of the indigent, of the idlers and do-nothings, the scoundrels who are the praetorians of the uprising, the *condottieri*. In a word, he ran the metaphor ragged to arrive at an attack on the national workshops." *Les Boulets rouges: Feuille du club pacifique des droits de l'homme*, ed. Pélin, 1st year, June 22–25 [1848] ("Faits divers").   [d1a,1]

"It is as though Lamartine had made it his mission to implement Plato's teaching on the necessity of banishing poets from the republic, and one cannot help smiling as one reads this author's account of the worker who was part of the large demonstration in front of the Hôtel de Ville, and who shouted at the speaker: 'You're nothing but a lyre! Go sing!'" Friedrich Szarvady, *Paris, 1848–1852*, vol. 1 (Berlin, 1852), p. 333.   [d1a,2]

Chateaubriand: "He brings into fashion that vague sadness, . . . 'le mal du siècle' ⟨the infirmity of the century⟩. A. Malet and P. Grillet, *XIXe Siècle* (Paris, 1919), p. 145.   [d1a,3]

"'If we could have our wish . . .' This desire, this regret—Baudelaire was the first to interpret it, twice giving voice, in *L'Art romantique*, to unexpected praise for a poet of his day, the author of a "Chant des ouvriers," that Pierre Dupont who, he tells us, 'after 1848 . . . attained great glory.' The specification of this revolutionary date is very important here. Without this indication, we might have trouble understanding the defense of popular poetry, and of an art 'inseparable from utility,'[1] on the part of a writer who could pass for the chief architect of the rupture of poetry and art with the masses. . . . 1848: that is the hour when the street beneath Baudelaire's window begins in very truth to tremble, when the theater of the interior must yield him up in all magnificence, to the theater of the exterior, as someone who incarnates, at the highest level, the concern for human emancipation in all its forms, as well as the consciousness, alas, of everything that is ridiculously ineffectual in this aspiration alone, whereby the gift of the artist and of the man becomes total—Baudelaire's anonymous collaboration on *Le Salut public* of February 27 and 28 effectively proving the point. . . . This communion of the poet, of the authentic artist, with a vast class of people impelled by their ardent hunger for freedom, even partial freedom, has every chance of emerging spontaneously at times of great social ferment, when reservations can be laid aside. Rimbaud, in whom the claims of the human tend, nonetheless, . . . to follow an infinite course, places, from the outset, all his confidence and *élan vital* in the Commune. Mayakovsky goes to great lengths to silence in himself—bottling it up to the point of explosion—everything born of individual feeling that might not conduce to the exclusive glory of the triumphant Bolshevik Revolution." André Breton, "La Grande Actualité poétique," *Minotaure*, 2, no. 6 (Winter 1935), p. 61.   [d2,1]

"Progress is the very footstep of God." Victor Hugo, "Anniversaire de la révolution de 1848," February 24, 1855 (on Jersey), p. 14.   [d2,2]

"Victor Hugo is the man of the nineteenth century, as Voltaire was the man of the eighteenth." "The nineteenth century thus comes to a close before its end. Its poet is dead." Obituary notices for Hugo in *Le National Républicain de l'Ardèche* and *Le Phare des Charentes* [*Victor Hugo devant l'opinion* (Paris, 1885), pp. 229, 224].   [d2,3]

> Students of the schools of France,
> Cheerful volunteers for progress,
> Let us follow the people in its wisdom;
> Let us turn our backs on Malthus and his decrees!
> Let us light up the new roadways
> Which labor shall open;
> For socialism soars on two wings,
> The student and the worker.

Pierre Dupont, *Le Chant des étudiants* (Paris, 1849).   [d2a,1]

A. Michiels, *Histoire des idées littéraires en France au XIXᵉ siècle* (Paris, 1863), vol. 2, provides, in his portrait of Sainte-Beuve, an outstanding description of the reactionary man of letters at midcentury.   [d2a,2]

> I caused a revolutionary wind to blow;
> I made the old lexicon don the insurgents' red cap.
> No more words, Senator! Commoner, no more!
> I raised a storm at the bottom of the inkwell.

Victor Hugo, cited in Paul Bourget, obituary for Victor Hugo in *Le Journal des débats* [*Victor Hugo devant l'opinion* (Paris, 1885), p. 93].   [d2a,3]

On Victor Hugo: "He was . . . the poet not of his own sufferings . . . but of the passions of those around him. The mournful voices of the victims of the Terror . . . made their way into the *Odes*. Then the trumpet blasts of the Napoleonic victories resounded in other odes. . . . Later on, he felt obliged to let the tragic cry of militant democracy pass through him. And what is *La Légende des siècles* . . . if not the echo of the great turmoil of human history? . . . It often seems as though he had collected the sighs of all families in his domestic verse, the breath of all lovers in his love poems. . . . It is for this reason that, . . . thanks to some mysterious quality in him that is always collective and general, Victor Hugo's poetry possesses an epic character." Paul Bourget, obituary notice for Victor Hugo in *Le Journal des débats* [*Victor Hugo devant l'opinion* (Paris, 1885), pp. 96–97].   [d2a,4]

Victor Hugo, ca. 1860. Photo by Etienne Carjat. Courtesy, Museum of Fine Arts, Boston. Reproduced with permission. © 1999 Museum of Fine Arts, Boston. All rights reserved.

It is worthy of note that the preface to *Mademoiselle de Maupin*[2] already seems to be pointing the way to *l'art pour l'art.* "A stage play is not a railroad train."

[d2a,5]

Gautier on the press: "Charles X alone has understood the question rightly. In ordering the suppression of the newspapers, he rendered a great service to the arts and to civilization. Newspapers are akin to courtiers and go-betweens, those who interpose themselves between artists and the public, between the king and the people. . . . These perpetual yelpings . . . create such an atmosphere of mistrust that . . . royalty and poetry, the two greatest things in the world, become impossible." Cited in A. Michiels, *Histoire des idées littéraires en France au XIXe siècle* (Paris, 1863), vol. 2, p. 445. This attitude earned Gautier the friendship of Balzac.

[d3,1]

"In the transports of his hatred [for the critics], M. Théophile Gautier denies all progress, especially in the area of literature and art, as does his master, Victor Hugo." Alfred Michiels, *Histoire des idées littéraires en France au XIXe siècle* (Paris, 1863), vol. 2, p. 444.

[d3,2]

"Steam will conquer cannon. In two hundred years—well before, perhaps—great armies from England, France, and America . . . will descend upon old Asia under the leadership of their generals. Their weapons will consist of pickaxes, and their horses will be locomotives. Singing, they will fall upon these uncultivated, unused lands. . . . It is thus, perhaps, that war will be waged, in the future, against all unproductive nations, by virtue of that axiom of mechanics which applies to all things: there must be no wasted energy!" Maxime Du Camp, *Les Chants modernes* (Paris, 1855), p. 20 ("Préface").

[d3,3]

In the preface to *La Comédie humaine*, Balzac declares himself on the side of Bossuet and Bonald, and affirms: "I write by the faint light of two eternal verities: Religion and Monarchy."

[d3,4]

Balzac on the press, in the preface to the first edition of *Un Grand Homme de province à Paris:* "The public is unaware of how many evils beset literature in its commercial transformation. . . . In the old days, newspapers . . . required a certain number of copies . . . This was over and above payment for articles attractive to . . . booksellers—payment often made without any guarantee that these articles would appear in print. . . . Today, this double tax has been driven up by the exorbitant price of advertising, which costs as much as the actual production of the book. . . . One can only conclude that newspapers are fatal for modern writers." Cited in Georges Batault, *Le Pontife de la démagogie: Victor Hugo* (Paris, 1934), p. 229.

[d3,5]

In the debate in the Chamber on November 25, 1848—June repression—Victor Hugo voted against Cavaignac.

[d3,6]

"The multiplication of readers is the multiplication of loaves. On the day Christ discovered this symbol, he foreshadowed the printing press." Victor Hugo, *William Shakespeare*, cited in Batault ⟨*Le Pontife de la démagogie* (Paris, 1934)⟩, p. 142. [d3,7]

Maxime Lisbonne comments, in *L'Ami du peuple*, on Victor Hugo's will. Beginning and conclusion of this statement: "Victor Hugo divides his fortune of 6 million francs as follows: 700,000 francs to the members of his family; 2.5 million francs to Jeanne and Georges, his grandchildren. . . . And for the revolutionaries who, since 1830, sacrificed with him for the republic, and who are still in this world, a lifetime annuity: twenty sous per day!" Cited in *Victor Hugo devant l'opinion* (Paris, 1885), pp. 167–168. [d3a,1]

In the debate in the Chamber on November 25, 1848, Victor Hugo voted against Cavaignac's repression of the June revolt. But on June 20 in the Chamber, during the discussion of the national workshops, he had coined the phrase: "The Monarchy had its idlers; the Republic will have its do-nothings." [d3a,2]

Seigneurial elements still obtain in nineteenth-century education. Saint-Simon's declaration is characteristic: "I used my money to acquire knowledge. Good food, fine wines, much alacrity vis-à-vis the professors, to whom my purse was opened—these things procured for me all the opportunities I could desire." Cited in Maxime Leroy, *La Vie véritable du comte Henri de Saint-Simon* (Paris, 1925), p. 210. [d3a,3]

As regards the physiognomy of Romanticism, attention might focus, first of all, on the colored lithograph in the Cabinet des Estampes, Sf. 39, vol. 2, which undertakes its allegorical representation. [d3a,4]

Engraving from the Restoration period, showing a crowd gathered before the shop of a publisher. A placard announces that the *Album pour 1816* has appeared. Caption: "Everything new is beautiful." Cabinet des Estampes. [d3a,5]

Lithograph. A poor devil looks on dolefully as a young gentleman signs the picture which the former has painted. Title: *L'Artiste et l'amateur du XIXᵉ siècle*. Caption: "It is by me, seeing that I sign it." Cabinet des Estampes. [d3a,6]

Lithograph, representing a painter walking along and carrying under his arm two long narrow planks, on each of which he has painted various garnishes and arrangements of meats. Title: *Les Arts et la misère* ⟨Poverty and the Arts⟩. "Dedicated to Messieurs the Pork Butchers." Caption: "The man of art in the toils of his trade." Cabinet des Estampes. [d3a,7]

Jacquot de Mirecourt publishes *Alexandre Dumas et Cie, fabrique de romans* ⟨Alexandre Dumas and Co., Manufactory of Novels⟩ (Paris, 1845). [d3a,8]

L'Artiste et l'amateur du dix-neuvième siècle (The Artist and the Amateur of the Nineteenth Century). Courtesy of the Bibliothèque Nationale de France. See d3a,6.

Dumas père. "In September 1846, Minister Salvandy proposed to him that he travel to Algeria and write a book about the colony. . . . Dumas, . . . who was read by five million Frenchmen at the very least, would give some fifty or sixty thousand of them a taste for colonialism. . . . Salvandy offered 10,000 francs to cover the cost of the voyage; Alexandre demanded, in addition to this, . . . a state vessel. . . . Why had the *Véloce*, which was charged with picking up freed prisoners in Melilla, gone to Cádiz . . . ? Members of Parliament seized on the incident. And M. de

Castellane pointedly questioned the logic of entrusting a scientific mission . . . to a journalistic entrepreneur: the French flag had debased itself in granting 'that fellow' its protection; 40,000 francs had been spent for no reason, and the ridicule was clearly audible on all sides." The affair ended in Dumas' favor after his challenge to a duel was declined by Castellane. J. Lucas-Dubreton, *La Vie d'Alexandre Dumas père* (Paris ⟨1928⟩), pp. 146, 148–149.   [d4,1]

Alexandre Dumas in 1848. "His proclamations . . . are . . . astonishing. In one of them, addressed to the working people of Paris, he enumerates his 'works for workers,' and proves, by citing figures, that in twenty years he has composed four hundred novels and thirty-five plays, which have enabled him to provide a living for 8,160 persons, including typesetters, foremen, machinists, usherettes, and

L'Homme de l'art dans l'embarras de son métier (The Man of Art in the Toils of His Trade). Courtesy of the Bibliothèque Nationale de France. See d3a,7.

Alexandre Dumas père, 1855. Photo by Nadar. Courtesy of the Bibliothèque Nationale de France.

professional applauders." J. Lucas-Dubreton, *La Vie d'Alexandre Dumas père* (Paris), p. 167. [d4,2]

"The bohemian of 1840 . . . is dead and gone.—Did he really exist? I have heard it said that he did not.—Whatever the case may be, you could comb through all of Paris at the present moment, and not come upon a single example. . . . There are certain neighborhoods, and a very great number of them, where the bohemian has never pitched his tent. . . . The bohemian flourishes along the boulevards, from the Rue Montmartre to the Rue de la Paix. . . . Less frequently in the Latin Quarter, formerly his main abode. . . . Where does the bohemian come from? Is he a product of the social or the natural order? . . . Who is to blame for the development of this species—nature or society? Without hesitation, I answer: nature! . . . As long as there are idlers and fops in the world, there will be bohemians." Gabriel Guillemot, *Le Bohême*, in the series entitled *Physionomies parisiennes* (Paris, 1869), pp. 11, 18–19, 111–112. Something similar on the grisettes in this series. [d4,3]

It would be useful to trace historically the "theses" of bohemia. The attitude of a Maxime Duchamps ⟨Du Camp?⟩, who holds success to be a proof of the lack of artistic quality, stems directly from that which is expressed in the statement, "There is nothing beautiful but what is forgotten," which occurs in Lurine's *Treizième arrondissement de Paris* ⟨Paris, 1850⟩, p. 190. [d4,4]

The Rafalers' Club (Cercle des Rafalés): "No famous names there. Should a member of the Rafalers' stoop so low as to make a name for himself—whether in politics, literature, or the arts—he would be mercilessly struck from the list." [Taxile Delord,] *Paris-Bohême* (Paris, 1854), pp. 12–13. [d4,5]

Victor Hugo's drawings, in his house at 6 Place des Vosges, where he lived from 1832 to 1848: *Dolmen Where the Voice of Shadow Spoke to Me; Ogive; My Destiny* (a giant wave); *The Sail Recedes, the Rock Remains* (gloomy rocky seashore; in the foreground a sailing ship); *Ego Hugo; VH* (allegorical monogram); *Lacework and Specter.* A sail with the inscription "Exile" and a tombstone with the inscription "France" (pendants, serving as homemade frontispieces, to two of his books); *The Borough of Angels; Village in Moonlight; Fracta Sed Invicta* (a wreck); a breakwater; a fountain in an old village, around which all the storms on earth seem to have gathered. [d4a,1]

"We have had novels about bandits purified by imprisonment—the tales of Vautrin and of Jean Valjean; and it was not to stigmatize them . . . that the writers evoked these melancholy figures. . . . And it is in a city where 120,000 girls live secretly from vice and 100,000 individuals live off girls, it is in a city infested with hardened criminals, cutthroats, housebreakers, carriage thieves, shop breakers, shoplifters, rabble rousers, con men, pickpockets, predators, shakedown artists, guardian angels,[3] swindlers, and lockpickers—in a city, I say, where all the wreckage of disorder and vice runs aground, and where the slightest spark can set fire to the sublimated populace, it is here that this corrupting literature— . . . *Les Mystères de Paris, Rocambole,* and *Les Misérables*—is produced." Charles Louandre, *Les Idées subversives de notre temps* (Paris, 1872), pp. 35–37.   [d4a,2]

"The incomplete copy in the Bibliothèque Nationale is sufficient for us to judge of the boldness and novelty of the project conceived by Balzac. . . . *Le Feuilleton des journaux politiques* aimed at nothing less than the elimination of booksellers. Direct sale from publisher to purchaser was the plan . . . by which everyone would benefit—the publisher and the author by making a profit, the purchaser by paying less for books. This arrangement . . . met with no success at all, doubtless because the booksellers were against it." Louis Lumet, introduction to Honoré de Balzac, *Critique littéraire* (Paris, 1912), p. 10.   [d4a,3]

The three short-lived periodicals founded by Balzac: *Le Feuilleton des journaux politiques* (1830), *La Chronique de Paris* (1836–1837), *La Revue parisienne* (1840).   [d4a,4]

"Recollection has value only as prediction. Thus, history should be classed as a science: practical application constantly proves its utility." Honoré de Balzac, *Critique littéraire,* introduction by Louis Lumet (Paris, 1912), p. 117 (review of *Les Deux Fous,* by P. L. Jacob, bibliophile).   [d4a,5]

"It is not by telling the poor to cease imitating the luxury of the rich that one will make the lower class happier. It is not by telling girls to stop permitting themselves to be seduced that one will suppress prostitution. We might as well tell them, '. . . When you have no bread, you will be so good as to cease being hungry.' But Christian charity, it will be said, is there to cure all these evils. To which we reply: Christian charity cures very little and prevents nothing at all." Honoré de Balzac, *Critique littéraire,* introduction by Louis Lumet (Paris, 1912), p. 131 (review of *Le Prêtre* [Paris, 1830]).   [d5,1]

"In 1750, no book—not even *L'Esprit des lois*[4]—reached more than three or four thousand people. . . . In our day, some thirty thousand copies of Lamartine's *Premières méditations* and some sixty thousand books by Béranger have been sold over the past ten years. Thirty thousand volumes of Voltaire, Montesquieu, and Molière have enlightened men's minds." Balzac, *Critique littéraire,* introduction by Louis Lumet (Paris, 1912), p. 29 ("De l'Etat actuel de la librairie" ‹On the Current State of the Bookstore›, sample from *Le Feuilleton des journaux politiques,* published in *L'Universel,* March 22–23, 1830).   [d5,2]

Victor Hugo hearkens to the inner voice of the crowd of his ancestors: "The crowd to which he listened admiringly in himself, and which he heard as the herald of his popularity, inclined him, in fact, toward the exterior crowd—toward the *Idola Fori,*[5] toward the inorganic body of the masses. . . . He searched in the tumult of the sea for the roar of applause." "He spent fifty years draping his love of confusion—of all confusion, provided it was rhythmic—in his love for the people." Léon Daudet, *Les Oeuvres dans les hommes* (Paris, 1922), pp. 47–48, 11.   [d5,3]

A saying of Vacquerie's about Victor Hugo: "The towers of Notre Dame were the *H* of his name." Cited in Léon Daudet, *Les Oeuvres dans les hommes* (Paris, 1922), p. 8.   [d5,4]

Renouvier wrote a book on Victor Hugo's philosophy.   [d5,5]

Victor Hugo in a letter to Baudelaire—with particular reference to "Les Sept Vieillards" and "Les Petites Vieilles" (both poems were dedicated to Hugo, and, as Baudelaire indicated to Poulet-Malassis, for the second of them Hugo's work served as the poet's model): "You have endowed the sky of art with an indescribable macabre gleam. You have created a new frisson."[6] Cited in Louis Barthou, *Autour de Baudelaire* (Paris, 1917), p. 42 ("Victor Hugo et Baudelaire").   [d5,6]

Maxime Leroy, *Les Premiers Amis français de Wagner,* suggests that a revolutionary impulse played a very large part in Baudelaire's enthusiasm for Wagner; indeed, Wagner's works inspired an antifeudal Fronde. The fact that his operas dispensed with ballet infuriated habitués of the Opéra.   [d5,7]

From Baudelaire's essay on Pierre Dupont: "We had been waiting so many years for some solid, real poetry! Whatever the party to which one belongs, whatever the prejudices one has inherited, it is impossible not to be moved by the sight of that sickly throng breathing the dust of the workshops, swallowing lint, becoming saturated with white lead, mercury, and all the poisons necessary to the creation of masterpieces, sleeping among vermin in the heart of districts where the humblest and greatest virtues live side by side with the most hardened vices and with the dregs from prisons. That sighing and languishing throng to which *the earth owes its marvels*, which feels *flowing in its veins an ardent red blood,* which looks long and sadly at the sunshine and shade of the great parks and, for its only comfort and consolation, bawls at the top of its voice its song of salvation: *Let us love one another* . . ."—"There will come a time when the accents of this workingman's Marseillaise will circulate like a Masonic password, and when the exiled, the abandoned, and the lost, whether under the devouring tropical sky or in the snowy wilderness, will be able to say, 'I have nothing more to fear—I am in France!' as he hears this virile melody perfume the air with its primordial fragrance: 'Nous dont la lampe le matin / Au clairon du coq se rallume, / Nous tous qu'un salaire incertain / Ramène avant l'aube à l'enclume . . .'"—On the "Chant des ouvriers": "When I heard that wonderful cry of melancholy and sorrow, I was awed and moved."[7] Cited in Maxime Leroy, *Les Premiers Amis français de Wagner* (Paris ‹1925›), pp. 51–53, 51.   [d5a,1]

On Victor Hugo: "He placed the ballot box on turning tables." Edmond Jaloux, "L'Homme du XIX⁰ siècle," *Le Temps*, August 9, 1935. [d5a,2]

"Eugène Sue . . . was in certain respects . . . similar to Schiller—not only in his preference for tales of crime, for colportage, for black-and-white depictions, but also in his predilection for ethical and social issues. . . . Balzac and Hugo viewed him as a competitor." Egon Friedell, *Kulturgeschichte der Neuzeit*, vol. 3 (Munich, 1931), p. 149. Foreigners, such as Rellstab, sought out the Rue aux Fèves, where *Les Mystères de Paris* was begun. [d5a,3]

On Victor Hugo: "This Ancient, this unique genius, this unique pagan, this man of unparalleled genius was ravaged by, at the very least, a double politician: a political politician that made him a democrat, and a literary politician that made him a Romantic. This genius was corrupted by talent(s)." Charles Péguy, *Oeuvres complètes, 1873–1914: Oeuvres de prose* (Paris, 1916), p. 383 ("Victor-Marie, comte Hugo"). [d6,1]

Apropos of Victor Hugo, Baudelaire "believed in the coexistence of genius and foolishness." Louis Barthou, *Autour de Baudelaire* (Paris, 1916), p. 44 ("Victor Hugo et Baudelaire"). Similarly, before the planned banquet for the tercentenary of Shakespeare's birthday (April 23, 1864), he speaks of the "book by Victor Hugo on Shakespeare, a book which—full of beauties and stupidities like all his books—is almost certain to vex even the most ardent of his admirers" (cited in Barthou, p. 50). And: "Hugo, priestlike, with his head always bent—too bent to see anything except his navel" (cited in Barthou, p. 57).[8] [d6,2]

The publishers of Balzac's *Feuilleton des journaux politiques* offered certain books at lower-than-official prices by bypassing book retailers. Balzac himself takes pride in this initiative, which he defends against criticisms from without, and which he expects will create the immediate bond between publisher and public that was his aim. In a sample issue of the newspaper, Balzac sketches the history of the book trade and of publishing since the Revolution of 1789, to conclude with the demand: "We must finally see to it that a volume is produced exactly like a loaf of bread, and is sold like a loaf of bread, so that there would be no intermediary between an author and a purchaser other than the bookseller. Then this business will be the most secure of all. . . . When a bookseller is required to lay out some twelve thousand francs for every project, he will no longer engage in any that are risky or ill-conceived. They will realize, then, that instruction is a necessity of their profession. A clerk who has learned in what year Gutenberg printed the Bible will no longer imagine that being a bookseller is only a matter of having one's name written over a shop." Honoré de Balzac, *Critique littéraire*, introduction by Louis Lumet (Paris, 1912), pp. 34–35. [d6,3]

Pélin publishes the letter of a publisher who declares himself ready to buy the manuscript of an author on the condition that he can publish it under the name of some other author of his choosing ("on the condition . . . that it be signed by someone whose name would be, according to my calculations, a spur to success"). Gabriel Pélin, *Les Laideurs du beau Paris* (Paris, 1861), pp. 98–99. [d6,4]

Fees. Victor Hugo receives 300,000 francs from Lacroix for *Les Misérables,* in exchange for rights to the novel for twelve years. "It was the first time Victor Hugo had received such a sum. 'In twenty-eight years of furious labor,' Paul Souday has said, 'with an oeuvre of thirty-one volumes . . . , he had made a total of about 553,000 francs. . . . He never earned as much as Lamartine, Scribe, or Dumas père. . . .' Lamartine, in the years 1838 to 1851, made close to five million francs, of which 600,000 were for the *Histoire des Girondins.*" Edmond Benoit-Lévy, *"Les Misérables" de Victor Hugo* (Paris, 1929), p. 108. Connection between income and political aspiration. [d6a,1]

"When Eugène Sue, following upon . . . *Les Mystères de Londres* ⟨by Paul Féval⟩, . . . conceived the project of writing *Les Mystères de Paris,* he did not at all propose to arouse the interest of the reader with a description of society's underworld. He began by characterizing his novel as an *histoire fantastique.* . . . It was a newspaper article that decided his future. *La Phalange* praised the beginning of the novel and opened the author's eyes: 'M. Sue has just set out on the most penetrating critique of society. . . . Let us congratulate him for having recounted . . . the frightful sufferings of the working class and the cruel indifference of society.' The author of this article . . . received a visit from Sue; they talked—and that is how the novel already underway was pointed in a new direction. . . . Eugène Sue convinced himself: he took part in the electoral battle and was elected . . . (1848). . . . The tendencies and the far-reaching effects of Sue's novels were such that M. Alfred Nettement could see in them one of the determining causes of the Revolution of 1848." Edmond Benoit-Lévy, *"Les Misérables" de Victor Hugo* (Paris, 1929), pp. 18–19. [d6a,2]

A Saint-Simonian poem dedicated to Sue as the author of *Les Mystères de Paris:* Savinien Lapointe, "De Mon Echoppe" ⟨My Workshop⟩,[9] in *Une Voix d'en bas* (Paris, 1844), pp. 283–296. [d6a,3]

"After 1852, the defenders of the educator's art are much less numerous. The most important is Maxime Du Camp." C. L. de Liefde, *Le Saint-Simonisme dans la poésie française* ⟨Haarlem, 1927⟩, p. 115. [d6a,4]

"*Les Jésuites,* by Michelet and Quinet, dates from 1843. (*Le Juif errant* ⟨The Wandering Jew⟩ appeared in 1844)." Charles Brun, *Le Roman social en France au XIXe siècle* (Paris, 1910), p. 102. [d6a,5]

"*Le Constitutionnel* going from 3,600 subscribers to more than 20,000 . . . 128,074 votes giving Eugène Sue an electoral mandate to become a deputy." Charles Brun, *Le Roman social en France au XIXe siècle* (Paris, 1910), p. 105. [d6a,6]

The novels of George Sand led to an increase in the number of divorces, nearly all of which were initiated by the wife. The author carried on a large correspondence in which she functioned as an adviser to women. [d6a,7]

Poor, but cleanly—is the philistine echo of a chapter title in *Les Misérables:* "La Boue, mais l'âme" ‹Mire, but Soul›.[10] [d7,1]

Balzac: "Mutual education produces 100-sous pieces made of human flesh. Individuals disappear in a population leveled by instruction." Cited in Charles Brun, *Le Roman social en France au XIXe siècle* (Paris, 1910), p. 120. [d7,2]

Mirbeau and Natanson, *Le Foyer* ‹The Hearth› (1, 4), Baron Courtin: "It is not desirable that education should be extended any further. . . . For education is the beginning of ease, and ease is not within everyone's reach." Cited in Charles Brun, *Le Roman social en France au XIXe siècle* (Paris, 1910), p. 125. Mirbeau merely repeats here, in satirical vein, a saying of Thiers ‹cited in d1,1›. [d7,3]

"Balzac—unbridled romantic by virtue of the lyrical tirades, the bold simplification of characters, and the complication of plot—is at the same time a realist by virtue of the evocation of place and social milieu, and a naturalist by virtue of his taste for vulgarity and his scientific pretensions." Charles Brun, *Le Roman social en France au XIXe siècle* (Paris, 1910), p. 129. [d7,4]

Napoleon's influence on Balzac, the Napoleonic in him. "The spirit and mettle of the Grande Armée in the form of greed, ambition, and debauchery: Grandet, Nucingen, Philippe Bridau, or Savarus."[11] Charles Brun, *Le Roman social en France au XIXe siècle* (Paris, 1910), p. 151. [d7,5]

"Balzac . . . quotes as authorities . . . Geoffroy Saint-Hilaire and Cuvier." Charles Brun, *Le Roman social* (Paris, 1910), p. 154. [d7,6]

Lamartine and Napoleon. "In *Les Destinées de la poésie*, in 1834, he speaks of . . . his contempt for this age . . . of calculation and power, of numbers and the sword. . . . It was the age in which Esménard sang the praises of navigation, Gudin of astronomy, Ricard of spheres, Aimé Martin of physics and chemistry. . . . Lamartine said it very well: 'Number alone is allowed, honored, protected, and recompensed. Since number does not think, since it is an . . . instrument . . . that never asks . . . whether it is made to serve the oppression of humankind or its deliverance, . . . the military leader of this era wanted no other emissary.'" Jean Skerlitch, *L'Opinion publique en France d'après la poésie* (Lausanne, 1901), p. 65. [d7,7]

"Romanticism proclaims the liberty of art, the equality of genres, and the fraternity of words (all under one entitlement as citizens of the French language)." Georges Renard, *La Méthode scientifique de l'histoire littéraire* (Paris, 1900), pp. 219–220, cited in Jean Skerlitch, *L'Opinion publique en France d'après la poésie* (Lausanne, 1901), pp. 19–20.   [d7,8]

The magnificent seventh book of the fourth part of *Les Misérables,* "L'Argot," winds up its penetrating and audacious analyses with a gloomy reflection: "Since '89, the entire people has been expanding in the sublimated individual; there is no poor man who, having his rights, has not his ray; the starving man feels within himself the honor of France; the dignity of the citizen is an interior armor; he who is free is scrupulous; he who votes reigns." Victor Hugo, *Oeuvres complètes,* novels, vol. 8 (Paris, 1881), p. 306 (*Les Misérables*).[12]   [d7a,1]

Nettement on the digressions in *Les Misérables:* "These bits of philosophy, of history, of social economy are like cold-water taps that douse the frozen and discouraged reader. It is hydrotherapy applied to literature." Alfred Nettement, *Le Roman contemporain* (Paris, 1864), p. 364.   [d7a,2]

"M. Sue, in *Le Juif errant*, hurls insults at religion . . . in order to serve the antipathies of *Le Constitutionnel.* . . . M. Dumas, in *La Dame de Monsoreau,* heaps scorn on royalty . . . to accommodate the passions of this same newspaper, . . . while in *La Reine Margot* he conforms to the taste of the gilded youth at *La Presse* for . . . risqué paintings, . . . and . . . in *Le Comte de Monte-Cristo* he deifies money and inveighs against the Restoration to please the world of civil servants who congregated around *Le Journal des débats.*" Alfred Nettement, *Etudes critiques sur le feuilleton-roman*, vol. 2 (Paris, 1846), p. 409.   [d7a,3]

Victor Hugo: owing to a law of his poetic nature, he has to stamp every thought with the form of an apotheosis.   [d7a,4]

A wide-ranging remark by Drumont: "Almost all the leaders of the movement of the school of 1830 had the same sort of constitution: high-strung, prolific, enamored of the grandiose. Whether it was a matter of reviving the epic on canvas, as with Delacroix, of portraying a whole society, as with Balzac, or of putting four thousand years of the life of Humanity into a novel, like Dumas, all . . . were possessed of shoulders that did not shrink from the burden." Edouard Drumont, *Les Héros et les pitres* (Paris ‹1900›), pp. 107–108 ("Alexandre Dumas père").
                                                                                   [d7a,5]

"'For the past fifty years,' said Doctor Demarquay to Dumas fils one day, 'all our moribund patients have died with one of your father's novels under their pillow.'" Edouard Drumont, *Les Héros et les pitres* (Paris ‹1900›), p. 106 ("Alexandre Dumas père").   [d7a,6]

In the preface to *Les Paysans,* Balzac speaks reproachfully of the year 1830, "which did not remember that Napoleon had preferred to risk failure rather than arm the masses." Cited in Ch. Calippe, *Balzac: Ses Idées sociales* (Reims and Paris ‹1906›), p. 94. [d7a,7]

"Bourget has remarked that Balzac's characters . . . appeared in real life even more frequently after the death of the novelist: 'Balzac,' he says, 'seems less to have observed the society of his age than to have contributed to the formation of an age. Certain of his characters were more true-to-life in 1860 than in 1835.' Nothing more just: Balzac deserves to be classed among anticipators of the first order. . . . Thirty years later, reality arrived on the terrain that his intuition had already crossed in a single bound." H. Clouzot and R.-H. Valensi, *Le Paris de la Comédie humaine* (Paris, 1926), p. 5 ("Balzac et ses fournisseurs"). [d8,1]

Drumont, too, inclines to the view that Balzac's gift was a prophetic one. Occasionally, however, he reverses the terms of the equation: "The people of the Second Empire wanted to be characters from Balzac." Edouard Drumont, *Figures de bronze ou statues de neige* (Paris ‹1900›), p. 48 ("Balzac"). [d8,2]

Balzac, speaking through his country doctor: "The proletarians seem to me to be the minors of the nation, and should always remain in a state of tutelage."[13] Cited in Abbé Charles Calippe, *Balzac: Ses Idées sociales* (Reims and Paris ‹1906›), p. 50. [d8,3]

Balzac (like Le Play) was opposed to the parceling out of large estates: "My God, how could anyone fail to realize that the wonders of art are impossible in a country without great fortunes!" (cited in Charles Calippe, p. 36). Balzac likewise draws attention to the disadvantages that result when peasants and petty bourgeois hoard their money, and calculates how many billions are in this way withdrawn from circulation. On the other hand, the only remedy he can recommend is for the individual, by hard work and wise economy, to become a landed proprietor himself. He thus moves within contradictions. [d8,4]

George Sand became acquainted with Agricol Perdiguier in 1840. She says: "I was struck by the moral importance of the topic, and I wrote the novel *Le Compagnon du tour de France* out of sincerely progressive ideas." Cited in Charles Benoist, "L'Homme de 1848," part 2, *Revue des deux mondes* (February 1, 1914), pp. 665–666. [d8,5]

Dumas père occupied almost simultaneously, with three of his novels, the feuilleton sections of *La Presse, Le Constitutionnel,* and *Le Journal des débats.* [d8,6]

Nettement on the style of Dumas père: "It is usually natural and relatively rapid, but it lacks force because the thought it expresses does not go very deep. It is to the style of great writers what lithography is to engraving." Alfred Nettement, *Histoire de la littérature française sous le Gouvernement de Juillet* (Paris, 1859), vol. 2, pp. 306–307. [d8,7]

Sue, compared with George Sand: "Once again we have a protest against the state of society, but, this time, a collective protest . . . undertaken in the name of the passions and interests of the largest classes of society." Alfred Nettement, *Histoire de la littérature française sous le Gouvernement de Juillet* (Paris, 1859), vol. 2, p. 322. [d8a,1]

Nettement points out that Sue's novels, which sought to undermine the July Monarchy, were published in newspapers, (*Le Journal des débats* and *Le Constitutionnel*) that were on its side. [d8a,2]

Regular customers at the brasserie on the Rue des Martyrs: Delvau, Murger, Dupont, Malassis, Baudelaire, Guys. [d8a,3]

Jules Bertaut sees Balzac's importance in terms of the action of significant figures in a milieu determined by the types of that day's society—which is to say, in terms of character study permeated by the study of manners. Apropos of the latter, he writes: "One need only peruse the innumerable *physiologies* . . . to see how far this literary vogue has come. From the Schoolboy to the Stockbroker, and taking account of the Dry Nurse, the Sergeant, and the Seller of Countermarks in between, it is an endless succession of *petits portraits*. . . . Balzac knows the genre well; he has cultivated it. Small wonder, then, that he seeks to give us, through these means, the picture of an entire society." Jules Bertaut, *"Le Père Goriot" de Balzac* (Amiens, 1928), pp. 117–118. [d8a,4]

"'Victor Hugo,' says Eugène Spuller, 'had gone along with the views of the reactionaries. . . . He had consistently voted on the right.' . . . As for the question of the national workshops, on June 20, 1848, he declares them a double error—from a political as well as a financial standpoint. . . . In the Legislative Assembly, on the other hand, he turns to the left, becoming one of its . . . most aggressive orators. Is this because of an evolution . . . , or is it due to wounded pride and personal bitterness against Louis Napoleon, under whom he supposedly wished—even expected—to become minister of public instruction?" E. Meyer, *Victor Hugo à la tribune* (Chambéry, 1927), pp. 2, 5, 7; cited in Eugène Spuller, *Histoire parlementaire de la Seconde République*, pp. 111, 266. [d8a,5]

"A discussion having opened between *Le Bon-Sens* and *La Presse* over the question of Girardin's forty-franc newspapers, *Le National* intervened. Because *La Presse* had taken this opportunity to mount a personal attack on M. Carrel, an encounter took place between the latter and the editor-in-chief of *La Presse*."—"It was the political press that fell, in the person of Carrel, before the industrial press." Alfred Nettement, *Histoire de la littérature française sous le Gouvernement de Juillet* (Paris, 1859), vol. 1, p. 254. [d8a,6]

"Communism, . . . that . . . logic of democracy, is already boldly attacking society in its moral assumptions, whence it is evident that the proletarian Samson, grown prudent, will henceforth sap the pillars of society in the cellar, instead of shaking them in the banquet hall." Balzac, *Les Paysans;*[14] (cited in Abbé Charles Calippe, *Balzac: Ses Idées sociales* (Reims and Paris ‹1906›), p. 108.   [d9,1]

Travel literature: "It is France that first . . . reinforced its armies with a brigade of geographers, naturalists, and archaeologists. The great achievements in Egypt . . . marked the advent of an order of works previously unknown. . . . The *Expédition scientifique de la Morée* and the *Exploration scientifique de l'Algérie* are worthy additions to this great line. . . . Whether scientific in spirit, serious or light, . . . accounts by travelers . . . have, in our time, found a considerable vogue. Along with novels, they form the staple fare in reading rooms, numbering, on average, some eighty works per year, or twelve hundred publications in fifteen years." This, on average, is not much more than in other fields of natural science. Charles Louandre, "Statistique littéraire: De la Production intellectuelle en France depuis quinze ans," *Revue des deux mondes* (November 1, 1847), pp. 425–426.   [d9,2]

From 1835 on, the average number of novels produced annually is 210—approximately the same as the number of vaudeville productions.   [d9,3]

Travel literature. It finds an unexpected application during the Chamber's debate on deportations (April 4, 1849). "Farconet, who was the first to oppose the project, brought up the question of the salubrity of the Marquesas Islands. . . . The member who had presented the report replied by reading some travel accounts which depicted the Marquesas as . . . a veritable paradise. . . . This, in turn, drew . . . the angry response: 'To offer idylls and bucolics on a subject so grave is ridiculous.'" E. Meyer, *Victor Hugo à la tribune* (Chambéry, 1927), p. 60.   [d9,4]

The idea for *La Comédie humaine* came to Balzac in 1833 (the year in which *Le Médecin de campagne* was published). The influence of Geoffroy Saint-Hilaire's theory of types was decisive. To this was added, on the literary side, the influence of Scott's and Cooper's cycles of novels.   [d9,5]

In its second year of publication, in 1851, the "*Almanach des réformateurs* . . . , in which the government is presented as a necessary evil, brings together the exposé of communist doctrine with verse translations of Martial and Horace, with sidelights on astronomy and medicine, and with all sorts of useful tips." Charles Benoist, "Le 'Mythe' de la classe ouvrière," *Revue des deux mondes* (March 1, 1914), p. 91.   [d9,6]

Derivation of the feuilleton novel, whose appearance in newspapers immediately entailed dangerous competition for periodicals and a marked decline in the production of literary criticism. The periodicals, in turn, had to decide whether to publish novels in installments. The first to do so were *La Revue de Paris* (edited by Véron?) and *La Revue des deux mondes*. "Under the old state of affairs, a journal with a subscription rate exceeding eighty francs was supported by those whose political convictions it expressed. . . . Under the new arrangements, a journal had to live by advertisements, . . . and in order to have lots of advertisements, the fourth page, which had become a publicity display, had to pass before the eyes of a great many subscribers. In order to have lots of subscribers, some bait had to be found that would speak to all opinions at the same time, and that would substitute, for political interest, an item of general interest. . . . This is how, by starting from the forty-franc newspaper and proceeding on to the advertisement, we arrive, almost inevitably, at the serial novel." Alfred Nettement, *Histoire de la littérature française sous le Gouvernement de Juillet* (Paris, 1859), vol. 1, pp. 301–302. [d9a,1]

Sometimes, in publishing a novel in serial form, one would leave out part of the work in order to get the newspaper-reading public to buy the book. [d9a,2]

In the editor's preface to Journet's *Poésies et chants harmoniens*, *Uncle Tom's Cabin*, by Harriet Beecher Stowe, is quite appropriately placed on an equal footing with *Les Mystères de Paris* and *Les Misérables*. [d9a,3]

"From time to time, one could read, in *Le Journal des débats*, articles by M. Michel Chevalier or M. Philarète Chasles, . . . articles of a socially progressive tendency. . . . The progressive articles in the *Débats* were customarily published during the fortnight preceding subscription renewals, which occurred every four months. On the eve of large renewals, *Le Journal des débats* could be found flirting with radicalism. This helps to explain how *Le Journal des débats* could undertake the bold publication of *Les Mystères de Paris* . . .—but this time, that imprudent newspaper had gone further than it realized. As a consequence, many wealthy bankers withdrew their support for the *Débats* . . . in order to found a new paper, . . . *Le Globe*. This worthy predecessor of *L'Epoque* . . . was aimed at doing justice to the incendiary theories of M. Eugène Sue and of *La Démocratie pacifique*." A. Toussenel, *Les Juifs, rois de l'époque*, ed. Gonet (Paris ‹1886›), vol. 2, pp. 23–24. [d9a,4]

The *bohème*. "With *Un Prince de la bohême* (1840), Balzac wanted to portray a . . . characteristic of this nascent *bohème*. The amorous preoccupations . . . of Rusticoli de la Palférine are only a Balzacian expansion upon the triumphs of Marcel and Rodolphe,[15] which would soon follow. . . . This novel contains a grandiloquent definition of bohemianism, . . . the first . . . : 'The *bohème*—what should be called the doctrine of the Boulevard des Italiens—consists of young people, . . . all men of genius in their way, men as yet little known, but soon to become known. . . . Here one meets writers, administrators, soldiers, journalists, artists! If the emperor of Russia purchased this bohemia for twenty million francs, . . . and if it were subsequently deported to Odessa, then in a year Odessa would be Paris.' . . . During this same period, George Sand . . . and Alphonse Karr . . . initiated bohemian circles. . . . But these were imaginary bohemias; and that of Balzac was entirely fantastic. The bohemianism of Théophile Gautier, on the other hand, and that of Murger, have been talked about so much . . . that today we can get an idea of what they were. To tell the truth, Gautier and his friends . . . did not realize right away, in 1833, that they were bohemians; they were content with calling themselves 'Jeune France' ‹Young France›. . . . Their poverty was merely relative. . . . This bohemianism . . . was the *bohème galante*; it could just as well be called gilded bohemianism, the *bohème dorée*. . . . Ten or fifteen years later, around 1843, there was a new bohemia . . . , the true *bohème*. Théophile Gautier, Gérard de Nerval, Arsène Houssaye were then approaching forty; Murger and his friends were not yet twenty-five. This time, it was a genuine intellectual proletariat. Murger was the son of a concierge tailor; Champfleury's father was a secretary at the town hall in Laon; . . . Delvau's father was a tanner in the Faubourg Saint-Marcel; Courbet's family were quasi-peasants. . . . Champfleury and Chintreuil wrapped packages in a bookstore; Bonvin was a working-class typographer." Pierre Martino, *Le Roman réaliste sous le Second Empire* (Paris, 1913), pp. 6–9. [d10,1]

In the early 1840s, there was a copying process known as the Rageneau press, evidently based on lithography. [d10,2]

Firmin Maillard, *La Cité des intellectuels* (Paris ‹1905›), pp. 92–99, offers an abundance of information about author's fees. [d10,3]

"Balzac . . . compared his critique of Parisian journalism to Molière's attacks on financiers, marquis, and doctors." Ernst Robert Curtius, *Balzac* (Bonn, 1923), pp. 354–355. [d10,4]

On Balzac: "What enables us to say that he was perhaps not very truthful after 1820 is the often expressed view that he wondrously painted in advance, and prophesied, the society of the Second Empire." Edmond Jaloux, "Les Romanciers et le temps," *Le Temps*, December 27, 1935. [d10,5]

From Lamartine's "Lettre en vers à M. Alphonse Karr":

> Every man can proudly sell the sweat of his brow;
> I sell my bunch of grapes as you do your flowers,
> Happy when its nectar, under the crush of my foot,
> Flows in amber streams through all my works,
> Producing for its master, drunk with its high price,
> Much gold with which to buy much freedom!
> Fate has reduced us to counting our wages;
> Day-wages you, night-wages me: two mercenaries.
> But bread well earned is bread well broken, too:
> O the glory of free men beholden to none for their salt!

Veuillot, who cites this text, has this to say: "Until now, it was felt that the freedom that can be purchased with money is not the sort that men of conscience are in the habit of pursuing. . . . What! . . . You don't know that the way to be free is to heap

scorn on gold? To secure this freedom acquired through gold, . . . you produce
your books in the same mercenary fashion as you produce vegetables and wine.
You will demand of your faculties a double or a triple harvest; you will start to
market your early produce; the muse will no longer visit voluntarily, but will toil
night and day like a drudge. . . . And in the morning, you will cast before the
public a page scribbled over in the course of your nocturnal lucubrations; you will
not even bother rereading the rubbish that covers it, though you will certainly
have counted the number of lines it contains." Louis Veuillot, *Pages choisies*, ed.
Antoine Albalat (Lyons and Paris, 1906), pp. 28, 31–32. (Karr sold flowers grown
on his estate near Nice.) [d10a,1]

"In vain Sainte-Beuve allows himself, out of a deep-rooted antipathy, to fly into a
rage against the author of *La Comédie humaine*. But he is right to observe that 'the
vogue for serial publication, which required, with each new chapter, that the
reader be struck a hearty blow, had driven the stylistic effects of the novel to an
extreme and desperate pitch.'" Cited in Fernand Baldensperger, "Le Raffermisse-
ment des techniques ⟨dans la littérature occidentale de⟩ 1840," *Revue de littérature comparée*, 15, no. 1 (January–March 1935), p. 82. [d10a,2]

In reaction to the serial novel, there arose—around 1840—novellas (Mérimée)
and regional novels (⟨Barbey⟩ d'Aurevilly). [d10a,3]

Eugène de Mirecourt, *Les Vrais Misérables* (Paris, 1862), recalls Lamartine's *Histoire des Girondins* and surmises that Hugo wanted to prepare his political career
with his novel as Lamartine had done with his popular history. [d10a,4]

Apropos of Lamartine and Hugo: "Instead of fostering the notion . . . that people
should follow devotedly in the steps of these sincere souls, we should investigate
the underside of all sincerity. But bourgeois culture and democracy are too greatly
in need of this value! The democrat is a man who wears his heart on his sleeve; his
heart is an excuse, a testimonial, a subterfuge. He is professionally heartwarming,
so he can dispense with being truthful." N. Guterman and H. Lefebvre, *La Conscience mystifiée* (Paris ⟨1936⟩), p. 151 ("Le Chantage et la sincerité" ⟨Blackmail
and Sincerity⟩). [d11,1]

On Lamartine: "The fatuity of the poet is indescribable. Lamartine deems himself
a statesman in the mold of Mirabeau, and he boasts (another Turgot!) of having
labored twenty years in the study of political economy. An eminent thinker, he's
convinced that he draws up from the depths of his soul ideas that he actually
catches on the wing and clothes in his own image." Emile Barrault, "Lamartine,"
extract from *Le National* of March 27, 1869 (Paris, 1869), p. 10. [d11,2]

Alfred Delvau (1825–1867): "He was a child of the *quartier* Mouffetard. . . . In
1848, he became private secretary to Ledru-Rollin, who was then minister of the

interior. Events having brusquely removed him from active politics, he devoted himself to letters, making his debut with several newspaper articles. . . . In *Le Journal amusant, Le Figaro*, and some other journals, he published articles dealing mainly with Parisian customs and practices. For some time, at *Le Siècle*, his special assignment was the Paris town council." During the second half of the 1850s, he was in exile in Belgium, where he had fled to escape a prison sentence incurred while he was editor of *Le Rabelais*. Later, he would endure prosecutions for plagiarism. Information in Pierre Larousse, *Grand Dictionnaire universel du XIXᵉ siècle*, vol. 6 (Paris, 1870), p. 385 (article: "Delvau").   [d11,3]

During the reign of Napoleon III, Benjamin Gastineau had already been twice deported to Algeria. "Under the Paris Commune, M. Gastineau was named inspector of communal libraries. The twentieth council of war, charged with trying his case, could find no evidence of any breach of common law. He was nevertheless condemned to deportation in a fortified cell." Pierre Larousse, *Grand Dictionnaire universel du XIXᵉ siècle*, vol. 8 (Paris, 1872), p. 1062.—Gastineau had begun his career as a typesetter.   [d11,4]

Pierre Dupont: "The poet, as he says in one of his little poems, 'listens, by turns, to the forests and the crowd.' And in fact it is the great rustic symphonies, the voices through which nature in its entirety speaks, as well as the clamor, the griefs, the aspirations and lamentations of the crowd, that make for his double inspiration. The song such as our fathers knew it . . . , the drinking song or even the simple ballad, is utterly foreign to him." Pierre Larousse, ‹Grand› *Dictionnaire universel du XIXᵉ siècle,* vol. 6 (Paris, 1870), p. 1413 (article: "Dupont"). Hence, with Baudelaire, hatred for Béranger is an element of his love for Dupont.
                [d11a,1]

Gustave Simon describes the scenes that took place in front of Paguerre's bookshop when the second and third parts of *Les Misérables* were delivered: "'On May 15, 1862,' he writes, 'a little before 6:00 in the morning, a dense crowd was gathering on the Rue de Seine before a shop that was still closed. The crowd kept growing larger and, impatient with waiting, became noisy, even riotous. . . . The pavement was obstructed by an impassable jumble of delivery carts, private carriages, cabs, carioles, and even wheelbarrows. People had empty baskets on their backs. . . . It was not yet 6:30 when the crowd, becoming more unruly by the minute, started pushing against the shopfront, while those in the vanguard knocked with redoubled force on the door. Suddenly, a window was opened on the second floor; a lady appeared and exhorted the assembled citizens to be more patient. . . . The shop to which they were preparing to lay siege was quite inoffensive; only books were sold there. It was Paguerre's bookshop. The people hurling themselves at the building were bookstore clerks, agents, buyers, and brokers. The lady who spoke from her second-floor window was Madame Paguerre.'" Albert de Besancourt, *Les Pamphlets contre Victor Hugo* (Paris), pp. 227–228; cited in Gustave Simon, "Les

Origines des *Misérables*," in *La Revue de Paris*, and in letters about the book which Simon published in *La Revue*). [d11a,2]

Perrot de Chezelles, in his pamphlet "Examen du livre des *Misérables* de M. Victor Hugo" (Paris, 1863), makes this more general contribution to the characterization of Victor Hugo: "In his dramas and novels he takes for his heroes a lackey like Ruy Blas, a courtesan like Marion Delorme, physically deformed beings like Triboulet and Quasimodo, a prostitute like Fantine, a convict like Jean Valjean."[16] Cited in Albert de Besancourt, *Les Pamphlets contre V.H.* (Paris), p. 243. [d11a,3]

Les Misérables depends, for its principal facts, on actual events. Underlying the condemnation of Jean Valjean is a case in which a man who had stolen a loaf of bread for his sister's children was condemned to five years' penal servitude. Hugo documented such things with great exactitude. [d12,1]

A detailed representation of Lamartine's behavior during the February Revolution is provided by Pokrowski in an article that bases itself, in part, on diplomatic reports by Kisseliov, the Russian ambassador to Paris at that time. These reports are cited in the course of the article. "'Lamartine . . . admitted,' Kisseliov writes, 'that, for the time being, France found itself in a situation that always tends to arise when one government has just fallen and the other is not yet firmly in place. He added, however, that the population had given proof of so much good sense, of such respect for family and property, that lawful order in Paris would be preserved through the momentum of things in themselves and through the good will of the masses. . . . In eight or ten days, continued Lamartine, a national guard of 200,000 men would be organized, in addition to which there were 15,000 mounted police, whose spirits were excellent, and 20,000 front-line troops, who already had encircled Paris and were to march on the city.' Here we must pause for a moment. It is well known that the pretext for recalling the troops, which since February had been stationed at a distance from Paris, was the workers' demonstration of April 16; the conversation between Lamartine and Kisseliov, however, took place on April 6. How brilliantly, therefore, Marx divined (in *Die Klassenkämpfe in Frankreich*) that the demonstration was provoked solely in order to be able to call back into the capital the most 'reliable' part of the 'forces of order.' . . . But let us go further. 'These masses, says Lamartine [that is, the bourgeois national guard, the mobile guard, and the line infantry—M.N.P.], will keep in check the club fanatics, who depend on a few thousand hooligans and criminal elements (!), and will nip every excess . . . in the bud.'" M. N. Pokrowski, *Historische Aufsätze* (Vienna and Berlin ⟨1928⟩), pp. 108–109 ("Lamartine, Cavaignac und Nikolaus I"). [d12,2]

On the sixth of April, a directive went out from Nesselrode in Petersburg to Kisseliov: "Nicholas and his chancellor did not conceal from their agent the fact that they needed the alliance with France against Germany—against the new red Germany that was beginning, with its revolutionary colors, to outshine the France which had already come rather far on the road to reason." M. N. Pokrowski, *Historische Aufsätze* (Vienna and Berlin), p. 112. [d12,3]

Michelet on Lamartine: "He glides on his great wing, rapid and oblivious." Cited in Jacques Boulenger, "Le Magie de Michelet," *Le Temps*, May 15, 1936. [d12a,1]

"A shrewd observer remarked, one day, that fascist Italy was being run like a large newspaper and, moreover, by a great journalist: one idea per day, with sidelights and sensations, and with an adroit and insistent orientation of the reader toward certain inordinately enlarged aspects of social life—a systematic deformation of the understanding of the reader for certain practical ends. The long and the short of it is that fascist regimes are publicity regimes." Jean de Lignières, "Le Centenaire de *La Presse*," *Vendredi*, June 1936. [d12a,2]

"Balzac was one of the collaborators on *La Presse* . . . , and Girardin was for him one of the best guides to the society in which the great man lived." Jean de Lignières, "Le Centenaire de *La Presse*," *Vendredi*, June 1936. [d12a,3]

"In general, the various currents of Realism between 1850 and 1860, that of Champfleury like that of Flaubert, are considered 'the school of Balzac.'" Ernst Robert Curtius, *Balzac* (Bonn, 1923), p. 487. [d12a,4]

"Modern mass production destroys the sense of art, and the sense of work, in labor: 'We have products; we no longer have works.'" Ernst Robert Curtius, *Balzac* (Bonn, 1923), p. 260; citation from *Béatrix* ⟨Balzac edition in *La Collection Michel-Lévy* (Paris, 1891–1899)⟩, p. 3. [d12a,5]

"The organization of intelligence is Balzac's goal. In this he sometimes, like the Saint-Simonians, entertains notions of corporation such as marked the Middle Ages. At these times, he returns to the idea . . . of an incorporation of intellectual labor into the modern system of credit. The idea of the state's remunerating intellectual production also surfaces here and there." Ernst Robert Curtius, *Balzac* (Bonn, 1923), p. 256. [d12a,6]

"Intelligential workers"—a coinage of Balzac's. See E. R. Curtius, *Balzac* (Bonn, 1923), p. 263. [d12a,7]

⟨J.-A.⟩ Chaptal, *De l'Industrie française*, vol. 2 (Paris, 1819), p. 198, estimates that the number of books published annually is 3,090. [d12a,8]

From the highly unfavorable "M. de Balzac," by Chaudes-Aigues: "Dungeons, brothels, and prisons would be asylums of virtue . . . compared to the civilized cities of M. de Balzac. . . . The banker is a man who has enriched himself through embezzlement and usury; the politician . . . owes his stature . . . to cumulative acts of treachery; the manufacturer is a prudent and skillful swindler; . . . the man of letters . . . is always hawking his opinions and his conscience. . . . The world as painted by M. de Balzac is . . . a cesspool." J‹acques› Chaudes-Aigues, *Les Ecrivains modernes de la France* (Paris, 1841), p. 227.　　　　　　　　　　[d13,1]

"Nowadays, so many attested and authenticated facts have emerged from the occult sciences that the time will come when these sciences will be taught at universities just as chemistry and astronomy are. Just now, when so many professorial chairs are being set up in Paris—chairs in Slavonic, in Manchurian studies, and in literatures so *unprofessable* as those of far northern lands; chairs which, instead of offering instruction, stand in need of it themselves . . .—is it not a matter of surprise that, under the name of anthropology, the teaching of occult philosophy, one of the glories of the old-time university, has not been restored? In this respect, Germany . . . is a step ahead of France." Honoré de Balzac, *Le Cousin Pons*,[17] in *Oeuvres complètes*, vol. 18, *La Comédie humaine: Scènes de la vie parisienne*, 6 (Paris, 1914), p. 131. ▢ Physiologies ▢　　　　　　　　　　　　　[d13,2]

On Lamartine: "He is the most feminine of men in a century which has seen a great many such men, several of whom seem to announce themselves by the very article preceding their names: Lafayette, Lamennais, Lacordaire, Lamartine. . . . There are very good reasons for thinking that he had prepared for the red flag the same speech he delivered for the tricolor flag." Abel Bonnard, *Les Modérés*, in the series entitled *Le Drame du présent*, vol. 1 (Paris ‹1936›), pp. 232–233.　　　[d13,3]

"The novel . . . is no longer only a way of telling a story but has become an investigation, a continual discovery. . . . Balzac stands at the limit of the literature of imagination *and* of the literature of exactitude. He has books in which the spirit of inquiry is rigorous, like *Eugénie Grandet* or *César Birotteau*; others in which the unreal is blended with the real, like *La Femme de trente ans*; and still others, like *Le Chef-d'oeuvre inconnu*, composed of elements drawn from a variety of jeux d'esprit." Pierre Hamp, "La Littérature, image de la société," *Encyclopédie française*, vol. 16, *Arts et littératures dans la société contemporaine*, 1, p. 64.
　　　　　　　　　　　　　　　　　　　　　　　　　　　　[d13,4]

"By 1862, the year in which Victor Hugo publishes *Les Misérables*, the number of illiterates has considerably diminished in France. . . . In proportion as an educated populace begins to patronize bookshops, authors begin choosing their heroes from the crowd, and the one in whom this phenomenon of socialization can best be studied is Hugo himself, the first great poet who gave to his literary works commonplace titles: *Les Misérables, Les Travailleurs de la mer*." Pierre Hamp, "La Littérature, image de la société," *Encyclopédie française*, vol. 16, *Arts et littératures dans la société contemporaine*, 1, p. 64).　　　　　[d13a,1]

These remarks on Scott might be applied to Victor Hugo: "He regarded rhetoric, the art of the orator, as the immediate weapon of the oppressed. . . . And it is odd to reflect that he was, as an author, giving free speech to fictitious rebels while he was, as a stupid politician, denying it to real ones." G. K. Chesterton, *Dickens,* trans. Laurent and Martin-Dupont (Paris, 1927), p. 175.[18]   [d13a,2]

The same holds for Victor Hugo as for Dickens: "Dickens stands first as a defiant monument of what happens when a great literary genius has a literary taste akin to that of the community. For this kinship was deep and spiritual. Dickens was not like our ordinary demagogues and journalists. Dickens did not write what the people wanted. Dickens wanted what the people wanted. . . . He died in 1870; and the whole nation mourned him as no public man has ever been mourned; for prime ministers and princes were private persons compared with Dickens. He had been a great popular king, like a king of some more primal age whom his people could come and see, giving judgment under an oak tree." G. K. Chesterton, *Dickens,* trans. Laurent and Martin-Dupont (Paris, 1927), pp. 72, 168.[19]   [d13a,3]

Le Nain jaune is founded by Aurélien Scholl; *La Vie Parisienne,* by Marcelin, a friend of Worth's. *L'Evénement* founded in 1865 by Villemessant, with the participation of Rochefort, Zola, and others in the opposition.   [d13a,4]

"Mirès and the Pereire brothers, following the example of the Rothschilds, would from time to time cause an unexpected shower, not of gold but of securities, to descend on well-known poets, journalists, and playwrights, without involving any direct obligation in return." S. Kracauer, *Jacques Offenbach und das Paris seiner Zeit* (Amsterdam, 1937), p. 252.[20]   [d14,1]

"A single one of the new sciences—that of analogy—ought to yield authors a profit of five million to six million francs for a sixteen-page installment." Charles Fourier, *Le Nouveau Monde industriel et sociétaire* (Paris, 1829), p. 35.   [d14,2]

Number of Paris newspaper subscribers: in 1824, ca. 47,000; in 1836, ca. 70,000; in 1846, ca. 200,000. (Details for 1824: 15,000 for the government papers *Journal de Paris, Etoile, Gazette, Moniteur, Drapeau blanc, Pilote;* 32,000 for the opposition papers *Journal des débats, Constitutionnel, Quotidienne, Courrier de Paris, Journal du Commerce, Aristarque.*)   [d14,3]

With the increase in public advertising, newspapers turned against the *annonces déguisées* ‹advertisements in disguise›, which no doubt had brought in more for journalists than for the administration.   [d14,4]

Around *Le Globe* gathered, as editors, the most important of the later Orleanists; this editorial staff included Cousin, Villemain, Guizot. In 1829, Blanqui entered the office as stenographer, particularly as parliamentary stenographer.   [d14,5]

The journalistic strain in the novels of Dumas: the first chapter of *Les Mohicans de Paris* already provides information about what impost must be paid, in the event one is arrested, for the privilege of an individual cell; where the Paris executioner lives; and what the best-known apache pubs of Paris are. [d14,6]

A young man from St. Petersburg called *Les Mystères de Paris* "the foremost book after the Bible." J. Eckardt, *Die baltischen Provinzen Russlands* (Leipzig, 1869), p. 406. [d14,7]

Valéry, in his introduction to *Les Fleurs du mal* (Paris, 1928), p. xv, on Hugo: "For more than sixty years, this extraordinary man was at his desk every day from five o'clock in the morning until noon! He unremittingly called up new combinations of language, willed them, waited for them, and had the satisfaction of hearing them respond to his call. He wrote one or two hundred thousand lines of poetry and acquired, by that uninterrupted exercise, a curious manner of thinking which superficial critics have judged as best they could."[21] [d14,8]

For nearly all the Romantics, the archetype of the hero is the bohemian; for Hugo, it is the beggar. In this regard, one should not lose sight of the fact that Hugo as writer made a fortune. [d14a,1]

Hugo in *Post-scriptum de ma vie: L'Esprit; Tas de pierre*, p. 1 (cited in Maria Ley-Deutsch, *Le Gueux chez Victor Hugo*, series entitled *Bibliothèque de la Fondation Victor Hugo*, vol. 4 [Paris, 1936], p. 435): "Do you want a measure of the civilizing power of art . . . ? Look in the prisons for a man who knows of Mozart, Virgil, and Raphael, who can quote Horace from memory, who is moved by *Orphée* and *Der Freischütz*. . . . Look for such a man . . . , and you will not find him." [d14a,2]

Régis Messac speaks of an "epic period" which the feuilleton under Louis Philippe enjoys, before it becomes a mass item in the Second Empire. The novels of Gabriel Ferry belong to the beginning of the latter era, as do those of Paul Féval. [d14a,3]

One can speak, in certain respects, of a contribution made by the physiologies to detective fiction. Only, it must be borne in mind that the combinative procedure of the detective stands opposed here to an empirical approach that is modeled on the methods of Vidocq, and that betrays its relation to the physiologies precisely through the Jackal in *Les Mohicans de Paris* (cited in Messac ‹*Le "Detective Novel" et l'influence de la pensée scientifique* [Paris, 1929]›, p. 434), of whom it is said: "One look at the ripped-open shutter, at the broken pane, at the knife slash was enough: 'Oh ho!' he said, 'I recognize this! It is the modus operandi of *one of them.*'" [d14a,4]

Véron pays 100,000 francs for *Le Juif errant* before a line has been penned. [d14a,5]

"Every time a serial novel threatened to carry off the prize, Balzac redoubled his efforts with Vautrin. It was in 1837–1838 that *Les Mémoires du diable* seemed to be dominating the serial format, and it was just at that point that the series entitled *Splendeurs et misères des courtisanes* began. In 1842–1843, *Les Mystères de Paris* appeared, and Balzac responded with *A Combien l'Amour revient aux vieillards*. In 1844 *Monte-Cristo*, and in 1846 *La Closerie des Genêts*; the latter year saw the publication of Balzac's *Où mènent les mauvais chemins*; the year after that, *La Dernière incarnation de Vautrin*.[22] If this dialogue . . . did not continue any further, it is because Balzac . . . died shortly afterward." Régis Messac, *Le "Detective Novel" et l'influence de la pensée scientifique* (Paris, 1929), pp. 403–404.

[d14a,6]

Under the Second Republic, an amendment to the law of July 16–19, 1850, designed "to strike out against an industry that dishonors the press and that is detrimental to the business of the bookstores." So declaims de Riancey, the author of the amendment. The law imposes on each feuilleton a tax of one centime per copy. The provision was annulled by the new and more severe press laws of February 1852, through which the feuilleton gained in importance.

[d15,1]

Nettement draws attention to the particular significance which the period for subscription renewal had for the newspapers. There was a tendency, at such times, to begin publishing a new novel in the feuilletons even before the old one had finished its run. In this same period of development, the reaction of readers to the novels started to make itself felt more immediately. Publishers took note of this tendency and gauged their speculations beforehand according to the title of the new novel.

[d15,2]

The novel published in installments can be seen as a precursor of the newspaper feuilleton. In 1836, a periodical of Karr's for the first time undertook to publish such installments—which later could be gathered under one cover—as a supplement for its readers.

[d15,3]

Political attitude of Romanticism, according to Baudelaire's conception in "Pétrus Borel": "If the Restoration had turned into a period of glory, Romanticism would not have parted company with royalty." "Later on, . . . a misanthropic republicanism joined the new school, and Pétrus Borel was the . . . most paradoxical expression of the spirit of the *Bousingots*. . . . This spirit, . . . contrary to the democratic and bourgeois passion which later so cruelly oppressed us, was excited both by an aristocratic hatred . . . for kings and the bourgeoisie, and by a general sympathy . . . for all that . . . was . . . pessimistic and Byronic." Charles Baudelaire, *L'Art romantique*, ed. Hachette, vol. 3 (Paris), pp. 354, 353–354.[23]   [d15,4]

"We in Paris have . . . seen the evolution of Romanticism favored by the monarchy, while liberals and republicans alike remained obstinately wedded to the routines of that literature called classical." Baudelaire, *L'Art romantique* (Paris), p. 220 ("Richard Wagner et *Tannhäuser*").[24]   [d15,5]

Three forms of bohemianism: "That of Théophile Gautier, Arsène Houssaye, Gérard de Nerval, Nestor Roqueplan, Camille Rogier, Lassailly, Edouard Our-liac—a voluntary *bohème* . . . where one played at poverty . . . , a bastard scion of the old Romanticism . . . ; that of 1848, of Murger, Champfleury, Barbara, Nadar, Jean Wallon, Schanne—truly needy, this *bohème*, but as quickly relieved, thanks to an intellectual camaraderie . . . ; and that finally of 1852, our *bohème*, not voluntary at all . . . but cruelly grounded in privation." Jules Levallois, *Milieu de siècle: Mémoires d'un critique* (Paris ‹1895›), pp. 90–91. [d15a,1]

Balzac sees human beings magnified through the mists of the future behind which they move. On the other hand, the Paris he describes is that of his own time; measured against the stature of its inhabitants, it is a provincial Paris. [d15a,2]

"What I have in mind here will become sufficiently clear if I say that I find in Balzac no interior life of any kind, but rather a devouring and wholly external curiosity, which takes the form of movement without passing through thought." Alain, *Avec Balzac* (Paris ‹1937›), p. 120. [d15a,3]

Laforgue on *La Fin de Satan:* "I remember a phrase by M. Mallarmé: Each morning, on rising from his bed, Hugo would go to the organ—like the great Bach, who piled up score upon score without concern for other consequences." Earlier, on the same page: "The organ continues as long as the score of the visible world lies open before his eager eyes, and as long as there is wind for the pipes." Jules Laforgue, *Mélanges posthumes* (Paris, 1903), pp. 130–131. [d15a,4]

"It has often been asked whether Victor Hugo had an easy time composing. It is clear that he was not endowed, or afflicted, with that strange facility in improvisation thanks to which Lamartine never crossed out a word. The iron pen of the latter sped rapidly along, barely touching the satiny paper it covered with light marks. . . . Victor Hugo makes the paper cry out under his pen, which itself cries out. He reflects on each word; he weighs every expression; he comes to rest on periods, as one might sit upon a milestone—to contemplate the finished sentence, along with the open space in which the next sentence will begin." Louis Ulbach, *Les Contemporains* (Paris, 1883); cited in Raymond Escholier, *Victor Hugo raconté par ceux qui l'ont vu* (Paris, 1931), p. 353. [d15a,5]

"Some of the letters which reached him were addressed simply: *Victor Hugo, Océan.*" Raymond Escholier, *Victor Hugo raconté par ceux qui l'ont vu* (Paris, 1931), p. 273 ("Automne"). [d15a,6]

An early, highly characteristic specimen of the feuilleton style in the *lettre parisienne* of January 12, 1839, from the pen of the vicomte de Launais (Madame de Girardin): "There is a great deal of excitement over M. Daguerre's invention, and nothing is more amusing than the explanations of this marvel that are offered in all seriousness by our salon savants. M. Daguerre can rest easy, however, for no one is going to steal his secret. . . . Truly, it is an admirable discovery, but we understand nothing at all about it: there has been too much explanation." Mme. de Girardin, *Oeuvres complètes,* vol. 4, pp. 289–290; cited in Gisèle Freund, *La Photographie en France au XIXe siècle* (Paris, 1936), p. 36.   [d16,1]

Baudelaire mentions "an immortal feuilleton" by Nestor Roqueplan, "Où vont les chiens?" ‹Where Do Dogs Go?›, in *Le Spleen de Paris,* ed. R. Simon (Paris), p. 83 ("Les Bons Chiens").[25]   [d16,2]

On Lamartine, Hugo, Michelet: "There is lacking to these men so rich in talent— as to their predecessors in the eighteenth century—that secret part of study whereby one forgets one's contemporaries in the search for truths, for that which afterward one can lay before them." Abel Bonnard, *Les Modérés,* in the series entitled *Le Drame du présent,* vol. 1 (Paris ‹1936›), p. 235.   [d16,3]

Dickens: "There was a great deal of the actual and unbroken tradition of the Revolution itself in his early radical indictments; in his denunciations of the Fleet Prison there was a great deal of the capture of the Bastille. There was, above all, a certain reasonable impatience which was the essence of the old Republican, and which is quite unknown to the Revolutionist in modern Europe. The old Radical did not feel exactly that he was 'in revolt'; he felt if anything that a number of idiotic institutions had revolted against reason and against him." G. K. Chesterton, *Dickens,* trans. Laurent and Martin-Dupont (Paris, 1927), pp. 164–165.[26]
                    [d16,4]

Gustave Geffroy (*L'Enfermé* ‹Paris, 1926›, vol. 1, pp. 155–156) points out that Balzac never described the unrest of the Parisian population in his days, the club life, the streetcorner prophets, and so on—with the possible exception of Z. Marcas, that slave of Louis Philippe's regime.   [d16,5]

During the July Revolution, Charles X had handwritten appeals distributed among the insurgents by his troops. See Gustave Geffroy, *L'Enfermé,* vol. 1, p. 50.
                    [d16,6]

"It is . . . important to conceive of the possibility of reorienting aesthetics . . . toward influences operating on man thanks to representations engendered by the morphology of society itself. . . . It is still more important to demonstrate that phenomena of this kind occur with the advent of universal literacy [that is to say, with the institution of compulsory primary school education, which was established at precisely the same time that the myth of Paris was formed (—*Note*)]." Roger Caillois, "Paris, mythe moderne," *Nouvelle Revue française,* 25, no. 284 (May 1, 1937), p. 699.   [d16a,1]

Gautier, in his "Victor Hugo," on the red waistcoats at the premiere of *Hernani:* "To avoid the infamous red of '93, we had added a slight amount of purple to our tint. We did not wish to have any political motive attributed to us." Cited in Raymond Escholier, *Victor Hugo raconté par ceux qui l'ont vu* (Paris, 1931), p. 162. [d16a,2]

1852: "The reputation of the author of *Hernani* had passed, by the peculiar conduits of *bohémerie* and utopianism, from the Latin Quarter to the faubourgs of Paris. Then, suddenly, the great metaphorist had had the revelation of the dogma of the sovereign people. . . . This revelation encompassed, at the same time, the projects of Michelet and Quinet and many another writer of lesser ability, such as Considérant." Léon Daudet, *La Tragique Existence de Victor Hugo* (Paris ⟨1937⟩), p. 98.—Around this time, Hugo made a speech to the troops. [d16a,3]

Hugo: "It was during one of those desolate excursions that the sight of a ship run aground on a nameless rock, its keel in the air, gave Hugo the idea for a new *Robinson Crusoe*, which he would call *Les Travailleurs de la mer* ⟨The Toilers of the Sea⟩, labor and the sea comprising the two poles of his exile. . . . Whereas in . . . *Les Contemplations* he had lulled his agonizing regret for the loss of his eldest daughter to the sea, he went on, in the prose of *Les Travailleurs*, to soothe the sadness he felt for the daughter who had sailed away. This marine element, then, was decidedly linked, by chains of black, to his destiny." Léon Daudet, *La Tragique Existence de Victor Hugo* (Paris), pp. 202–203. [d16a,4]

Juliette Drouet: "It is likely . . . that, beyond the question of former lovers and of debts, this propensity for ancillary amours, which attended the poet . . . from his thirtieth year until the end of his life, made him want to reduce his pretty actress to a subordinate position, to the position of beggar woman, . . . and the famous expiation might well have been only a metamorphosis of desire." Léon Daudet, *La Tragique Existence de Victor Hugo* (Paris), pp. 61–62. [d17,1]

Léon Daudet maintains that the failure of *Le Roi s'amuse* in 1832 turned Hugo against the monarchy. [d17,2]

Hugo's panegyrics to Louis Napoleon were published in *L'Evénement*. [d17,3]

From the record of the spiritualist sessions on Jersey (cited in Albert Béguin, *L'Ame romantique et le rêve* [Marseilles, 1937], vol. 2), to which Béguin appends the just remark (p. 397): "Hugo transports all that he takes up—and which could appear pure foolishness were reason alone to judge—into his mythology, a little like the primitive savage initiated into the beauties of free and compulsory public education. But his vengeance (and his destiny as well) will be to become, himself, the myth of an age devoid of all mythic meaning." Hence, Hugo transported spiritualism into his world. "Every great spirit carries on in his life two works: the work of the living person and the work of the phantom. . . . Whereas the living man performs the first work, the pensive phantom—at night, amid the universal silence—awakes within the man. O terror! 'What,' says the human being, 'that is not all?'—'No,' replies the specter. 'Get up! Up! There is a great wind abroad, the hounds and the foxes are yelping, darkness is everywhere, and nature shudders and trembles under the whipcord of God.' . . . The writer-specter sees the phantom ideas. Words take fright, sentences shiver, . . . the windowpane grows dim, the lamp is afraid. . . . Take care, living man, O man of a century, O proscript of a terrestrial idea! For this is madness, this is the tomb, this is the infinite—this is a phantom idea" (p. 390). The "great spirit," in the same context: "He encounters certitude sometimes as an obstacle on his path, and clarity sometimes as a fear" (p. 391).—From *Post-Scriptum de ma vie:* "There exists a hilarity of shadows. Nocturnal laughter floats in the air. There are merry specters" (p. 396).   [d17,4]

Hugo famously intoxicates himself—and not only in *William Shakespeare*—with long lists of the names of great geniuses. In this regard, one should recall the poet's passion for imagining his own name writ large; we know he read an *H* in the towers of Notre Dame. Another aspect of the matter is disclosed by his spiritualistic experiences. The great geniuses whose names he tirelessly rehearses, always in a different order, are his "avatars," incarnations of his own ego, and the more present for being ranged so before it.   [d17a,1]

Just as, during the writing of *Notre-Dame de Paris,* Hugo every evening would visit one of the towers of the cathedral, so on Guernsey (Jersey?) he sought out the *rocher des proscrits* ‹exiles' rock›, from which every afternoon he would contemplate the ocean.   [d17a,2]

This decisive passage, which explodes the status of consciousness within the century, from "Ce que dit la Bouche d'ombre":

> Weep for the unclean spider, for the worm,
> For the slug whose back is wet as winter,
> For the vile louse that hangs upon the leaf,
> For the hideous crab, and the appalling centipede,
> For the dreadful toad, poor monster with gentle eyes,
> Who is always gazing at the mysterious sky.

The last line should be compared with that of Baudelaire's "Les Aveugles."[27]   [d17a,3]

Sainte-Beuve on Lamartine's role in 1848: "What he did not foresee is that he would be the Orpheus who later, for a time, would direct and govern, with his golden lyre, this invasion of barbarians." C. A. Sainte-Beuve, *Les Consolations: Pensées d'août*, poems, part 2 (Paris, 1863), p. 118.   [d17a,4]

"One remembers that the china and the tables began to dance, while the rest of the world seemed to be standing still—in order to encourage the others." Karl Marx, *Das Kapital* ‹vol. 1›, ed. Korsch (Berlin ‹1932›) ‹p. 83›.[28]   [d17a,5]

In a note in *Das Kapital* (ed. Korsch, p. 541), Marx speaks of "Balzac, who so thoroughly studied every shade of avarice."[29]   [d17a,6]

Le Bohème—was, at first, the organ of the proletarianized intellectuals of Delvau's generation. [d18,1]

Bourget on Balzac: "Certain of his characters were more true-to-life in 1860 than in 1835." A. Cerfberr and J. Christophe, *Répertoire de la Comédie humaine* (Paris, 1887), p. v (introduction by Paul Bourget). ‹See d8,1.› [d18,2]

Taking a cue from Hofmannsthal (*Versuch über Victor Hugo* ‹Munich, 1925›, pp. 23–25), one could provide an account of the birth of the newspaper from the spirit of rhetoric,[30] and emphasize how the spirit of representative political discourse has conformed to that of empty chatter and civic gossip. [d18,3]

On the feuilleton: "Avid for gain, the editors of the big newspapers have not wanted to demand that their feuilletonists write criticism founded on conviction and on truth. Their convictions have too often changed." This the judgment of the Fourierist press. H. J. Hunt, *Le Socialisme et le romantisme en France: Etude de la presse socialiste de 1830 à 1848* (Oxford, 1935) ‹p. 142›. [d18,4]

Lamartine's politico-poetic program, model for fascist programs of today: "The ignorance and timidity of governments . . . has the effect, within all the parties, of disgusting one by one those men endowed with breadth of vision and generosity of heart. Each, in his turn, disenchanted with the mendacious symbols that no longer represent them, these men are going to congregate around ideas alone. . . . It is to help bring forth conviction, to add one voice more to this political group, that I temporarily renounce my solitude." Lamartine, "Des Destinées de la poésie" [second preface to *Les Méditations*], in *Les Grand Ecrivains de la France: Lamartine*, vol. 2 (Paris, 1915), pp. 422–423. [d18,5]

On the serial novel in Sue's day: "The need to which these fantasies respond is that of discovering some relation among events that appear to be utterly random. Obscurely, the imagination persuades itself that all these inequalities of social existence, these downfalls and ascents, constitute *one and the same great action*—in other words, that they proceed from a single cause and are connected one to another. The development of the serial novel parallels the creation of the social sciences." Cassou, *Quarante-huit* (Paris ‹1939›), p. 15. [d18,6]

Cassou on the "democratic lyricism of Lamartine": "We discover in this a secret thought: our possessions, along with all their train of spiritual delights, accompany us to the very threshold of immortality. Hardly broached in *Milly, ou la terre natale*, this theme bursts forth in *La Vigne et la maison*, expressing Lamartine's supreme desire—that of living on in a realm of physical immortality where every object preserves its perfect and savory reality. This eschatology, no doubt, differs a little from the pure spiritualism of *La Mort de Socrate*, with its Platonic inspiration. . . . But it reveals the profound nature of this aristocratic landowner." Jean Cassou, *Quarante-huit* (Paris), p. 173. [d18a,1]

The gargoyles of Notre Dame must be just about contemporary with Victor Hugo's novel. "Here Viollet-le-Duc, . . . whose work was so sharply criticized, has accomplished something remarkable. These devils and monsters are actually descendants of the grotesques created in the Middle Ages by the possessed imagination, everywhere seeing demons, really seeing them." Fritz Stahl, *Paris* (Berlin ‹1929›), p. 72. We meet with the analogous phenomenon, it seems, in Hugo. At stake here, perhaps, is a question, one that coincides with the question: Why is the nineteenth century the century of spiritualism? [d18a,2]

An important relation between information and feuilleton is indicated by Laverdant (this, at any rate, is how the signet "Lm" is read by Hunt, *Le Socialisme et le romantisme en France* [Oxford, 1935]): "The distressing disputes . . . between Germany and France, the war in Africa—do not such facts deserve as much attention as skillfully told stories of former times or of individual misfortunes? This being the case, if the public . . . reads these great national novels chapter by chapter, why do you wish to impose on it, all at one time, your tale or your doctrine? . . . *Division of labor* and *short sittings:* such are the requirements of the reader." Lm, "Revue critique du feuilleton," *La Phalange,* July 18, 1841; in *La Phalange,* 3rd series, vol. 3 (Paris, 1841), p. 540. [d18a,3]

"Victor Hugo, . . . according to a description by Théophile Gautier, would mix together on the same plate a cutlet, beans in oil, a ham omelette, and Brie cheese, and would drink café au lait seasoned with a dash of vinegar and a spot of mustard." R. B[runet], "La Cuisine régionale," *Le Temps,* April 4, 1940. [d19]

g

[The Stock Exchange, Economic History]

"Napoleon represented the last onslaught of revolutionary terror against the bourgeois society which had been proclaimed by this same Revolution, and against its policy. Napoleon, of course, already discerned the essence of the modern state; he understood that it is based on the unhampered development of bourgeois society, on the free movement of private interest, and so forth. . . . Yet, at the same time, he still regarded the state as an end in itself and civil life only as a purse-bearer. . . . He perfected the Terror by substituting permanent war for permanent revolution. . . . If he despotically suppressed the liberalism of bourgeois society—the political idealism of its daily practice—he showed no more consideration for its essential material interests, trade and industry, whenever they conflicted with his political interests. His scorn for industrial *hommes d'affaires* was the complement to his scorn for ideologues. . . . Just as the liberal bourgeoisie was opposed once more by revolutionary terror in the person of Napoleon, so it was opposed once more by counterrevolution during the Restoration, in the person of the Bourbons. Finally, in 1830, the bourgeoisie put into effect its wishes of the year 1789, the only difference being that its political enlightenment was now complete, that it no longer considered the constitutional representative state as a means for achieving the ideal of the state, the welfare of the world, and universal human aims but, on the contrary, had acknowledged it as the official expression of its own exclusive power and the political recognition of its own special interests." Karl Marx and Friedrich Engels, *Die heilige Familie*; cited in *Die neue Zeit*, 3 (Stuttgart, 1885), pp. 388–389.[1]   [g1,1]

A schema from Edgar Quinet's *De la Révolution et de la philosophie:* "The development of German philosophy . . . a sort of theory of the French political revolution. Kant is the Constituent Assembly, Fichte the Convention, Schelling the Empire (in light of his veneration of physical force), and Hegel appears as the Restoration and the Holy Alliance." ⟨Eduard⟩ Schmidt-Weissenfels, *Portraits aus Frankreich* (Berlin, 1881), p. 120 ("Edgar Quinet und der französische Nationalhaß" ⟨Edgar Quinet and French National Hatred⟩).   [g1,2]

Guizot ministry. "Corrupting the electoral colleges was a simple matter. These colleges generally comprised few electors; many contained less than 200, among

which were government bureaucrats. The latter obeyed the orders they were given; as to ordinary electors, one could buy them by giving their dependents and favorites things like tobacco shops or scholarships, or by giving the elector himself some important administrative post. In the Chamber, as in the electoral colleges, government bureaucrats were quite numerous: more than a third of the deputies (184 out of 459, in 1846) were prefects, magistrates, officials. The minister controlled them by fueling their hopes for advancement. . . . To reach a majority, thirty or forty deputies were needed. Guizot won them with concessions for large state projects (this was in the early days of railroad construction) or by giving them a share of the contract for supplies to the state. Corruption was thus built up into a system of government, and the numerous scandals at the end of the reign make glaringly clear that the underlings worked the system just as well as the prime minister." A. Malet and P. Grillet, *XIXe Siècle* (Paris, 1919), pp. 95, 97. Lamartine spoke, at this time, of the danger of an "electoral aristocracy" (1847).
[g1a,1]

"On July 28, 1831, a Parisian man displays his portrait together with that of Louis Philippe, providing them with the following caption: 'There is no distance separating Philippe from me. He is the citizen-king; I am the king-citizen.'" Gisela Freund, "La Photographie au point de vue sociologique" (manuscript, p. 31), citing Jean Jaurès, *Histoire socialiste: Le Règne de Louis-Philippe*, p. 49. [g1a,2]

"'Paris is as sad as possible,' wrote the author of *Colomba* at the height of the exhibition. 'Everyone is afraid without knowing why. It is a sensation akin to that produced by the music of Mozart when the Commendatore is about to enter.[2] . . . The least little incident is awaited like a catastrophe.'" Adolphe Démy, *Essai historique sur les expositions universelles de Paris* (Paris, 1907), pp. 173–174.
[g1a,3]

Some light on Napoleon's relation to the bourgeoisie around 1814. "The emperor had evinced the greatest reluctance at the prospect of arming the Paris population. Fearing the revolutionary spirit, he had refused the services of 50,000 workers, most of them former soldiers; he had wanted to organize companies . . . made up solely of citizens of the haute bourgeoisie—that is to say, those who were inclined to regard the allies as liberators. . . . People cursed Napoleon's name. Witness a letter to Colonel Greiner, second in command at the Ecole . . . : 'April 11, 1814.[3] Cowardly slave of an equally cowardly master! Give me back my son! Bloodthirstier even than the tyrant, you have outdone him in cruelty by delivering up to enemy fire the children we entrusted to your care—we who believe in the law that guaranteed their education. Where are they? You will answer for this with your head! All the mothers are marching against you, and I myself, I promise you, will wring your neck with my own two hands if my son does not reappear soon.'" G. Pinet, *Histoire de l'Ecole polytechnique* (Paris, 1887), pp. 73–74, 80–81. The letter is from the father of Enfantin.
[g2,1]

"Protestantism . . . did away with the saints in heaven so as to be able to abolish their feast days on earth. The Revolution of 1789 understood still better what it was about. The reformed religion had held on to Sunday; but for the revolutionary bourgeois, that one day of rest coming every seven days was too much, and they therefore substituted for the seven-day week the ten-day week ‹*la décade*›, so that the day of rest recurred but every ten days. And in order to bury all memory of the ecclesiastical holy days . . . , they replaced the names of saints, in the republican calendar, with the names of metals, plants, and animals." Paul Lafargue, "Die christliche Liebestätigkeit" [*Die neue Zeit*, 23, no. 1 (Stuttgart), pp. 145–146].   [g2,2]

"In the first days of the Revolution, the question of the poor assumed . . . a very distinct and urgent character. Bailly, who initially had been elected mayor of Paris for the express purpose of alleviating the misery of the . . . workers, packed them into masses and cooped them up—some 18,000 people—like wild animals, on the hill of Montmartre. Those who stormed the Bastille had workers with cannons emplaced there, lighted match in hand. . . . Had the war not drawn the unemployed and destitute laborers from town and countryside . . . into the army, and shuttled them off to the borders, . . . a popular uprising would have spread across the whole of France." Paul Lafargue, "Die christliche Liebestätigkeit" [*Die neue Zeit*, 23, no. 1 (Stuttgart), p. 147].   [g2,3]

"Our century, in which the sovereign is everywhere except on the throne." Balzac, Preface to *Un Grand Homme de province à Paris*; cited in Georges Batault, *Le Pontife de la démagogie: Victor Hugo* ‹Paris, 1934›, pp. 230–231.   [g2a,1]

On the writings of Napoleon III: "A set of commonplaces developed with sustained solemnity . . . , a perpetual clashing of antitheses, and then suddenly a striking formulation that captivates by its air of grandeur or seduces by its generosity . . . , along with ideas which are so confused that one can no longer distinguish them in the depths where they're apparently buried, but which, at the very moment one despairs of ever finding them, burst forth with the sound of trumpets." Pierre de la Gorce, *Napoléon III et sa politique* (Paris), pp. 4, 5; cited in Batault, *Le Pontife de la démagogie*, pp. 33–34.   [g2a,2]

Transition from the Napoleonic military regime to the peacetime regime of the Restoration. Engravings titled *The Soldier-Laborer, The Soldier-Reapers, Generosity of a French Soldier, The Tomb of the Brave*. Cabinet des Estampes.   [g2a,3]

"When, around 1829, M. de Saint-Cricq, director of Customs, announced the commercial shutdown, . . . we were incredulous. It was so serious that it caused the July Revolution. On the eve of February 1848, during the harsh winter that preceded it, the shutdown returned, and with it unemployment. Twenty years later, in 1869, here it is again. No one has any desire for enterprise. The current government, with its Crédit Mobilier and other companies, all so advantageous to the Stock Exchange, diverted for ten years the agricultural and industrial capital that earns comparatively little interest. Its free-trade treaty, opening France to English industry in 1860, . . . brought utter ruin from the outset. Normandy says it cannot recover. Much less the ironworks of the North." J. Michelet, *Nos fils* (Paris, 1879), pp. 300–301. [g2a,4]

A copper engraving of 1818: *Xenomania Impugned, or It's No Disgrace To Be French*. On the right, a column inscribed with the names of famous battles as well as famous works of art and literature. Under it, a young man with the honor roll of industry; his foot rests on a sheet bearing the inscription, "Products of Foreign Manufacture." Facing him, another Frenchman, who proudly points toward the column. In the background, an English civilian debates with a French soldier. All four persons provided with captions. Floating above in the sky and blowing into a trumpet, the figure—sharply reduced in scale—of an angel. From his horn hangs a tablet with the words: "To Immortality." Cabinet des Estampes. [g2a,5]

"If you pass in front of the Stock Exchange at noon, you will see a long line. . . . This line is composed of men from all walks of life—bourgeois, pensioners, shop-keepers, porters, errand boys, postmen, artists and actors—who come there to get a place in the first row, around the circular enclosure. . . . Positioned close to the floor, next to the public crier, they purchase shares of stock which they sell off during the same session. That old white-haired fellow who offers a pinch of snuff to the guard passing by is the dean of these speculators. . . . From the general look of the trading on the floor and off, and from the faces of the stockbrokers, he is able to divine, with a marvelous instinct, the rise or the fall of stocks." [Taxile Delord,] *Paris-Boursier* (Paris, 1854), pp. 44–46 ("Les Petits Paris"). [g3,1]

On the Stock Exchange: "The Bourse dates only from the time of M. de Villèle. There was more initiative and more Saint-Simonianism in the mind of this minister from Toulouse than is generally believed. . . . Under his administration, the position of stockbroker was sold for up to one million francs. The first words of speculation, though, were barely a lisp; the meager four billion in French debt, the several million in Spanish and . . . Neapolitan debt, were the alphabet by which it learned to read. . . . One put one's faith in the farm, in the house. . . . Of a rich man it was said: he has land in the sun and a house in town! . . . It was not until 1832, after the . . . sermons of Saint-Simonianism, . . . that the country found itself . . . suddenly ripe for its great financial destiny. In 1837, an irresistible force could be observed attracting attention to the Bourse; the creation of the railroad added new momentum to this force. . . . The *petite-coulisse* in the colonnade ‹see Convolute O, note 9› does the business of the petty bourgeoisie; just beyond, the *contre-petite-coulisse* handles the capital of the proletariat. The one operates for the porters, cooks, coachmen, grill-room proprietors, haberdashers, and waiters; the other descends a notch in the social hierarchy. One day we said to ourselves: 'The cobbler, the match seller, the boiler cleaner, and the fried-potato vendor know how to put their capital to use; let's make the great market of the Bourse

L'Etrangomanie blamée, ou D'Etre Français il n'y a pas d'affront
(Xenomania Impugned, or It's No Disgrace to Be French).
Courtesy of the Bibliothèque Nationale de France. See g2a,5.

available to them. . . . Thus, we opened up the *contre-petite-coulisse*, trading beyond the external market. We sold shares at a fixed rate of 3 francs, 50 centimes,
and made a profit of one centime. Business was booming in this market when the
debacle of last month occurred."[4] [Taxile Delord,] *Paris-Boursier* (Paris, 1854),
pp. 6–8, 56–57 ("Les Petits Paris"). [g3,2]

Commercial crisis of 1857 as cause of the Italian campaign. [g3,3]

"Enfantin exhorts his political comrades . . . to establish, in addition to the 'industrial credit' already in existence, an 'intellectual credit.'" This was in 1863! C. L.
de Liefde, *Le Saint-Simonisme dans la poésie française, 1825–1865* ⟨Haarlem,
1927⟩, p. 113. [g3a,1]

Balzac's portrait of the speculator Diard in *Les Marana:* "He demanded *thus-and-such percent* on the purchase of fifteen legislative votes, which passed, in the space of one night, from the benches of the Left to those of the Right. That sort of thing is no longer robbery, or any sort of crime; it is simply carrying on the government, becoming a silent partner in the national industry." Cited in Abbé Charles Calippe, *Balzac: Ses idées sociales* (Reims and Paris ‹1906›), p. 100.[5]

[g3a,2]

"It was in . . . 1838 that the government, in the person of M. Martin from Nord, had the good idea of bringing before the Chambers the project of a great network of national railways—a gigantic undertaking which the state alone would carry out. . . . Against this untoward governmental project *Le Journal des débats* launched a devastating attack, from which the project did not recover. Two years later, the concession for the two principal lines of the West and the South was granted by the state to two large companies. . . . Five years later, . . . Père Enfantin was secretary of the administrative council of the Lyons railroad, . . . and the pact between Saint-Simon and Judea . . . was sealed forever. . . . All this was the work of the Father ‹see U14a,1›. . . . Too many Jewish names appear on the membership rolls of the Saint-Simonian church for us to be surprised at the fact that the system of financial feudalism was established by the disciples of Saint-Simon." A. Toussenel, *Les Juifs, rois de l'époque* (Paris ‹1886›), ed. Gonet, pp. 130–133.

[g3a,3]

"It was not the French bourgeoisie as such that ruled under the bourgeois king, but merely . . . the financial aristocracy. The entire industrial corps, on the other hand, was in the opposition." Eduard Fuchs, *Die Karikatur der europäischen Völker* (Munich ‹1921›), vol. 1, p. 365.

[g3a,4]

"Before 1830, large-scale agriculture held sway over public policy; after 1830, the manufacturers took its place, but their reign had already developed under the regime which had been overthrown by the barricades. . . . Whereas 15 factories had been equipped with machines in 1814, there were 65 in 1820 and 625 in 1830." Paul Louis, *Histoire de la classe ouvrière en France, de la Révolution à nos jours* (Paris, 1927), pp. 48–49.

[g3a,5]

"The enslavement of governments is on the increase, and the influence of speculators has grown to such an extent that the gambling den of the Bourse has become the compass of public opinion." Cited in F. Armand and R. Maublanc, *Fourier* (Paris, 1937), vol. 2, p. 32.

[g4,1]

Fourier's Bourse: "There is much more animation and intrigue at the Stock Exchange of a Phalanx than there is at the stock exchanges of London and Amsterdam. For every individual must go to the Exchange to arrange his work and pleasure sessions for the following days. . . . Assuming that 1,200 individuals are present, and that each one has twenty sessions to arrange, this means that, in the meeting as a whole, there are 24,000 transactions to be concluded. Each of these transactions can involve twenty, forty, or a hundred individuals, who must be consulted and intrigued with or against. . . . Negotiations are carried on quietly, by means of signals. Each negotiator holds up the escutcheons of the groups or phalanxes which he represents, and by certain prearranged signs he indicates the approximate number of members he has recruited." *Publication des manuscrits de Fourier* (Paris, 1851–1858), 4 vols., Year 1851, pp. 191–192.[6]   [g4,2]

The term *Bourse de travail* ‹Labor Exchange› was coined by Fourier, or a Fourierist.   [g4,3]

In 1816 there were seven listings on the Stock Exchange; in 1847, more than two hundred.   [g4,4]

In 1825, according to Marx,[7] the first crisis of modern industry—that is, the first crisis of capitalism.   [g4,5]

[Reproduction Technology, Lithography]

"The social philosophy of the art of lithography at its beginnings . . . After the image makers of the Napoleonic legend, after the literary artists of Romanticism, came the chroniclers of the daily life of the French. The first group unwittingly paved the way for political upheavals, the second hastened the evolution of literature, and the third contributed to the profound demarcation between the aristocracy and the people." Henri Bouchot, *La Lithographie* (Paris ‹1895›), pp. 112, 114.   [i1,1]

Pigal portrays the people; Monnier, the petty bourgeoisie; Lami, the aristocracy.
                                                                                                                    [i1,2]

The important contribution of amateurs can be observed in the early days of lithography, exactly as it can later in photography.   [i1,3]

"The contest between lithography and stipple-engraving accelerates from day to day, but, since the end of 1817, the victory has belonged to lithography, thanks to the existence of caricature." Henri Bouchot, *La Lithographie* (Paris ‹1895›), p. 50.   [i1,4]

Bouchot looks on lithographs produced before 1817 as the incunabula of lithography. From 1818 to 1825, lithographic production in France steadily expands. Political circumstances made this upsurge much more visible there than in other countries. Its decline, too, is in part conditioned by politics: it coincides with the rise of Napoleon III. "The fact is . . . that, of the illustrious number present under the reign of Louis Philippe, there remained, in the early years of Napoleon III, barely four or five exhausted, disoriented survivors." Henri Bouchot, *La Lithographie* (Paris), p. 182.   [i1,5]

Lithography toward the end of the Second Empire: "So many things worked against it! The newly revived etching, the nascent heliographic processes, and to some extent the burin. Materially, it foundered under the difficulties associated with printing—the encumbrance of those very heavy stones, which the editors refused to warehouse as before." Henri Bouchot, *La Lithographie* (Paris), p. 193.
                                                                                                                    [i1,6]

Raffet undertook lithographic reportage in the Crimea.   [i1,7]

1835–1845: "It should . . . not be forgotten that the large-scale commercial operation which, at that time, was underway in wood engraving very quickly . . . led to
mass-production techniques. A woodcutter would make only the heads or figures
in a work, while another less skilled, or an apprentice, would make the accessories, the backgrounds, and so on. Out of such a division of labor nothing unified
could . . . emerge." Eduard Fuchs, *Honoré Daumier: Holzschnitte, 1833–1870*
(Munich ⟨1918⟩), p. 16.   [i1,8]

The first attempt at introducing lithography into France, undertaken by Senefelder's associate André d'Offenbach, was a complete failure. "He had . . . moved
to France solely with the intention of selling musical scores printed by means of
lithography. The patent had been taken out in his name in 1802, and he had
opened a shop, . . . little suspecting . . . what was in store for the discovery. . . . As
a matter of fact, it was not an auspicious moment for the minor arts of transcription. The master David expressed only the haughtiest disdain for engraving; at
most, he had a few kind words for the copper-plate technique. André's enterprise
was very soon in jeopardy." Henri Bouchot, *La Lithographie* (Paris ⟨1895⟩),
pp. 28–29.   [i1a,1]

On Doré's contributions to *Le Journal illustré* and *Le Journal pour tous*: "These
publications that sold for two sous—*Le Journal pour tous, Le Journal illustré, Le
Tour du monde*—where Doré gave of himself with stupefying prodigality and
verve, served him, above all, as a laboratory for his researches. Indeed, in the
grandes éditions sold in bookshops, produced at high cost (for those days) by
Hachette or Garnier, the imagination, the fantasy, the energy of Gustave Doré
were . . . , to a certain extent, disciplined and contained by the requirements of a
deluxe edition." Roger Dévigne, "Gustave Doré, illustrateur de journaux à deux
sous et reporter du crayon," *Arts et Métiers graphiques*, 50 (December 15, 1935),
p. 35.   [i1a,2]

"The Paris worker in revolt appears, in books and in illustrations, as a veteran of
the street wars, a seasoned revolutionary, going about half naked with a cartridge
belt and saber crisscrossed over his shirt, with a headdress like an African chief-
tain—a gold-braided kepi or a plumed hat—penniless, worn out, magnanimous,
blackened with powder and sweating from the sun, ostentatiously calling for water
when he is offered a glass of wine, installing himself comfortably on the upholstered throne in the manner of the *sans culottes* of '93, eyeing his companions at
the exit to the royal apartments, shooting any thieves. Take a look at drawings by
Charlet and by Raffet; read the accounts, in the form of glorifications that were
sold, a few days after a battle, for the benefit of widows, orphans, and the
wounded." Gustave Geffroy, *L'Enfermé* (Paris, 1926), vol. 1, p. 51.   [i1a,3]

Certain pamphlets by Marx were lithographed. (According to Cassou, *Quarante-
huit* ⟨Paris, 1939⟩, p. 148.)   [i2]

[The Commune]

"The history of the Paris Commune has become a touchstone of great importance for the question: How should the revolutionary working class organize its tactics and strategy in order to achieve ultimate victory? With the fall of the Commune, the last traditions of the old revolutionary legend have likewise fallen forever; no favorable turn of circumstances, no heroic spirit, no martyrdom can take the place of the proletariat's clear insight into . . . the indispensable conditions of its emancipation. What holds for the revolutions that were carried out by minorities, and in the interests of minorities, no longer holds for the proletarian revolution. . . . In the history of the Commune, the germs of this revolution were effectively stifled by the creeping plants that, growing out of the bourgeois revolution of the eighteenth century, overran the revolutionary workers' movement of the nineteenth century. Missing in the Commune were the firm organization of the proletariat as a class and the fundamental clarity as to its world-historical mission; on these grounds alone it had to succumb." [F. Mehring,] "Zum Gedächtnis der Pariser Kommune," *Die neue Zeit*, 14, no. 1 (Stuttgart, 1896), pp. 739–740.   [k1,1]

"We will say but two words about the lecture-presentations that have multiplied in recent years. . . . M. Ballande, who first thought of devoting Sunday afternoons to the inexpensive performance of masterpieces or the exhibition of certain monuments of art, preceded by a historical and literary explication of the work, had hit upon a happy and rewarding idea. . . . But success breeds imitation, and it is rare that the imitations do not bring out the troublesome aspects of the things they copy. This is indeed what happened. Daily presentations were organized at the Châtelet and the Ambigu. In these performances, questions of artistry were relegated to a position of secondary importance; politics predominated. Someone fetched up *Agnès de Méranie*; another exhumed *Calas* and *Charles IX, ou L'Ecole des rois*.[1] . . . From here, things could only go downhill; the most benign of works, by a strange inflection of the political madness, provided material . . . for the most heterogeneous declamations on the affairs of the day. Molière and Louis XIV would certainly have been surprised, at times, by the attacks . . . for which they served as pretexts. This type of 'theatrical' presentation completely defied all control."—"When revolutions break out, one often hears admissions that can be highly instructive. Here is what was said in *Le Mot d'ordre* of May 17, 1871, on the subject of the citizenship cards:[2] 'The overly assiduous reading of *Le Chevalier de Maison-Rouge* and other novels by Alexandre Dumas certainly inspired the members of the Commune to come up with this decree. We regret having to inform them that history is not made by reading novels.'" Victor Hallays-Dabot, *La Censure dramatique et le théâtre, 1850–1870* ⟨Paris, 1871⟩, pp. 68–69, 55. [*Le Mot d'ordre* is presumably an organ of Rochefort.]   [k1,2]

The Commune felt itself to be, in all respects, the heir of 1793.   [k1,3]

The passage in Hallays-Dabot, p. 55 ⟨cited in k1,2⟩, is very important for the connection between colportage and revolution.   [k1,4]

"At several intersections, our path opened out unexpectedly into vast arched domes. . . . Surely, each of these clandestine colosseums would provide a useful stronghold for the concentration of forces in certain eventualities, just as the infinity of subterranean networks, with its thousand galleries running under every corner of the capital, provides a ready-made sap from which to attack the city from below. . . . The lightning bolt that annihilated the Empire did not leave it time to act on this conception. It is harder to figure out why the leaders of the Commune, . . . so resolute in everything, did not make use of this formidable means of destruction when faced with the appearance of troops." Nadar, *Quand j'étais photographe* (Paris ⟨1900⟩), p. 121 ("Paris souterrain"). Refers to the "Letter from N— (Paris) to Louis Blanc (Versailles), May 1871," which voices just such an expectation.   [k1a,1]

"If Rimbaud is in fact admirable, it is not for having fallen silent but for having spoken. If he fell silent, it was doubtless for lack of a true audience. It was because the society in which he lived could not offer him this audience. One ought to keep in mind the very simple fact that Arthur Rimbaud came to Paris in 1871, quite naturally, to join the army of the Commune. . . . In the barracks of the Château-d'Eau, the young Rimbaud did not yet question the utility of writing and singing about the hands of the Wench, of the Jeanne-Marie of the faubourgs, who is not the plaster Marianne of the town halls:

> They are the hands not of a cousin
> But of working women with large foreheads
> Burned, in woods stinking of a factory,
> By a sun drunk on tar.
> . . . .
> They have paled, marvelous,
> Under the great sun full of love,
> On the bronze of machine guns,
> Throughout insurgent Paris![3]

Then, in the Assemblies of the Commune . . . , side by side with the workers of Paris . . . , with the warriors of socialism, one could see the poet of the International, Potier; the author of *L'Insurgé*, Jules Vallès; the painter of *L'Enterrement à Ornans*, Courbet; and the brilliant researcher into the physiology of the cerebellum, the great Flourens." ‹Louis› Aragon, "D'Alfred de Vigny à Avdeenko," *Commune*, 2 (April 20, 1935), pp. 810, 815. [k1a,2]

"The Commune, which accorded seats only to those elected from the workers' districts, was formed of a coalition of revolutionaries without a common program. Of the seventy-eight members, only a score were intent on projects of social reform; the majority were Jacobin democrats in the tradition of 1793 (Delescluze)." A. Malet, P. Grillet, *XIXe Siècle* (Paris, 1919), pp. 481–482. [k1a,3]

Within the Commune emerged the project of a Monument to the Accursed, which was supposed to be raised in the corner of a public square whose center would be occupied by a war memorial. All the official personalities of the Second Empire (according to the draft of the project) were to be listed on it. Even Haussmann's name is there. In this way, an "infernal history" of the regime was to be launched, although the intention was to go back to Napoleon I, "the villain of Brumaire—the chief of this accursed race of crowned bohemians vomited forth to us by Corsica, this fatal line of bastards so degenerated they would be lost in their own native land." The project, in the form of a printed placard, is dated April 15, 1871. (Exhibition entitled "La Commune de Paris," Municipal Offices of Saint-Denis.) [k2,1]

"There are your fruits, bloodthirsty Commune; / Yes, . . . you wanted to annihilate Paris." The last line is the refrain of a poem, "Les Ruines de Paris," printed as a pamphlet (Exhibition by the Municipality of Saint-Denis). [k2,2]

A lithograph by Marcier, *Le Départ de la Commune*, published by Deforet et César Editeurs, shows a woman (?) riding an animal that is half-nag and half-hyena, wrapped in a giant shroud, and brandishing the tattered, dirty red flag, while leaving behind her a murky alley filled with the smoke and flames of burning houses. (Exhibition, Municipality of Saint-Denis.) [k2,3]

After the taking of Paris, *L'Illustration* published a drawing entitled *Chasse à l'homme dans les catacombes* ‹Manhunt in the Catacombs›. In fact, the catacombs were searched one day for fugitives. Those found were shot. The troops entered at the Place Denfert-Rochereau, while the outlets of the catacombs toward the plain of Montsouris were guarded. (Exhibition.) [k2,4]

A Communard pamphlet publishes a drawing captioned *Les Cadavres découverts dans les souterrains de l'Eglise Saint-Laurent* ‹The Cadavers Discovered in the Vaults of the Church of Saint-Laurent›. It was claimed that female corpses had been discovered at this underground site—bodies which could not have been there longer than a couple of years, and whose thighs were forced open and hands bound. (Exhibition.)   [k2,5]

Leaflet; lithograph, *She*. The republic as a beautiful woman wrapped around by a snake, whose features are those of Thiers. The woman has a mirror high over her head. Beneath, a verse: "Many the ways you can take her— / She is for rent, but not for sale."   [k2,6]

The illusions that still underlay the Commune are given striking expression in Proudhon's formula, his appeal to the bourgeoisie: "Save the people and save yourselves—as your fathers did—by the Revolution." Max Raphael, *Proudhon, Marx, Picasso* (Paris ‹1933›), p. 118.   [k2a,1]

Remember the words of Chevalier: "Glory to us! We have entered into the treasury of kings, escorted by poverty and hunger; we have walked amid the purple, gold, and diamonds; when we came out, our companions were hunger and poverty." "Religion Saint-Simonienne: La Marseillaise" (Excerpt from *L'Organisateur* of September 11, 1830) [author Michel Chevalier, according to the Catalogue de la Bibliothèque Nationale], p. 2.   [k2a,2]

One of the Commune's last centers of resistance: the Place de la Bastille.   [k2a,3]

Charles Louandre, *Les Idées subversives de notre temps* (Paris, 1872), is a characteristic example of the reactionary pamphlets that followed in the wake of the Commune.   [k2a,4]

A caricature of Courbet: the painter standing on a broken column. Beneath, the caption: "Actuality." Cabinet des Estampes, kc 164 a I.[4]   [k2a,5]

"Louise Michel, recounting, in her memoirs, a conversation she had with Gustave Courbet, shows us the great Communard painter enraptured on the topic of the future, losing himself in visions which, though they are redolent of their own nineteenth century, are despite this—or perhaps because of it—marked by a wondrous and touching grandeur. 'Since everyone will be able to give himself over, unfettered, to his own special genius,' prophesied Courbet, 'Paris will double in importance. And Europe's international city will be able to offer to the arts, to industry, to commerce, to transactions of all kinds, and to visitors from all lands an imperishable order: the citizen-created order, which cannot be disrupted by the pretexts of monstrous pretenders.' It is a dream ingenuous as the world exhibitions, but one which nonetheless implies profound realities—above all, the certitude that a unanimous order will be founded, 'the citizen-created order.'" Jean Cassou, "La Semaine sanglante," *Vendredi*, May 22, 1936.   [k2a,6]

ACTUALITÉ

Actualité (Actuality), a caricature of the painter Gustave Courbet.
Courtesy of the Bibliothèque Nationale de France. See k2a,5.

In France's First Empire, and especially its Second, Engels sees states that could
appear as a court of mediation between an equally strong bourgeoisie and proletariat. See G. Mayer, *Friedrich Engels*, vol. 2 (Berlin ⟨1933⟩), p. 441.   [k2a,7]

The desperate struggle of the Commune: "Delescluze then issued his famous proclamation: 'Enough of this militarism! No more of these officers dripping gold braid
and embroidery! Make way for the people, for bare-armed fighters! The hour of
revolution has struck. . . . ' An impatient enthusiasm awakes in all hearts, and one
will go off to get oneself killed, as the Polish strategists intend.[5] Each man will
return to his neighborhood, his native turf, to the streetcorner where it is good to
live and bravely die—the traditional barricade! This proclamation is the last cry
of Blanquism, the supreme leap of the nineteenth century. One still wants to believe. To believe in the mystery, the miracle, the feuilleton, the magic power of the

epic. One has not yet understood that the other class has organized itself scientifically, has entrusted itself to implacable armies. Its leaders have long since acquired a clear vision of the situation. Not for nothing had Haussmann built broad, perfectly straight avenues to break up the swarming, tortuous neighborhoods, the breeding grounds for mystery and for the feuilleton, the secret gardens of popular conspiracy." Jean Cassou, "La Semaine sanglante," *Vendredi*, May 22, 1936.

[k3,1]

Engels and the Commune: "As long as the central committee of the Garde Nationale was directing the military operations, he remained hopeful. It was doubtless he who gave the advice which Marx transmitted to Paris: 'to fortify the northern slopes of Montmartre, the Prussian side.' He feared that, otherwise, the uprising 'would land in a mousetrap.' But the Commune failed to heed this warning and, as Engels regretfully confirmed, let the right moment for the offensive slip past. . . . Initially, Engels believed that the struggle would drag on. . . . In the General Council, he emphasized . . . that the Parisian workers were better organized militarily than in any earlier rebellion; that the street widening undertaken during the administration of Napoleon III would necessarily work to their advantage, should the assault on the city succeed; that for the first time, the barricades would be defended by cannons and regularly organized troops." Gustav Mayer, *Friedrich Engels*, vol. 2, *Engels und der Aufstieg der Arbeiterbewegung in Europa* (Berlin ⟨1933⟩), p. 227.[6]

[k3,2]

In 1884, Engels "admitted to Bernstein that Marx 'had upgraded the unconscious tendencies of the Commune into more or less conscious projects,' and he added that this improvement had been 'justified, even necessary, in the circumstances.' . . . The majority of the participants in the uprising had been Blanquists—that is to say, nationalistic revolutionaries who placed their hopes on immediate political action and the authoritarian dictatorship of a few resolute individuals. Only a minority had belonged to the ⟨First⟩ International, which at that time was still dominated by the spirit of Proudhon, and they could therefore not be described as social revolutionaries, let alone Marxists. That did not prevent the governments and the bourgeoisie throughout Europe from regarding this insurrection . . . as a conspiracy hatched by the General Council of the International." Gustav Mayer, *Friedrich Engels*, vol. 2, *Engels und der Aufstieg der Arbeiterbewegung in Europa* (Berlin), p. 228.[7]

[k3a,1]

The first *communio*: the city. "The German emperors—Frederick I and Frederick II, for instance—issued edicts against these *communiones* [communities], *conspirationes*, . . . quite in the spirit of the German Federal Diet. . . . It is quite amusing that the word *communio* was used as a term of abuse, just as 'communism' is today. The parson Guibert of Nogent writes, for instance: '*Communio* is a new and extremely bad word.' There is frequently something rather dramatic about the way in which the philistines of the twelfth century invite the peasants to flee to the cities, to the *communio jurata* ⟨sworn communes⟩." Marx to Engels, July 27,

A barricade of the Paris Commune, Rue Basfroi (11ᵉ *arrondissement*), March 18, 1871. Photographer unknown. See k4,5.

1854, from London [Karl Marx and Friedrich Engels, *Ausgewählte Briefe*, ed. V. Adoratski (Moscow and Leningrad, 1934), pp. 60–61].[8]   [k3a,2]

Ibsen saw further than many of the leaders of the Commune in France. On December 20, 1870, he writes to Brandes: "Up till now, we have been living on nothing but crumbs from the revolutionary table of last century, and I think we have been chewing on that stuff long enough. . . . Liberty, equality, and fraternity are no longer what they were in the days of the late-lamented guillotine. This is what the politicians will not understand; and that is why I hate them." Henrik Ibsen, *Sämtliche Werke,* vol. 10 ‹Berlin, 1905›, p. 156.[9]   [k3a,3]

It was the Proudhonist Beslay who, as delegate of the Commune, allowed himself to be persuaded on March 30, by de Ploeuc, deputy governor of the Banque de France, to leave untouched, in the interests of France, the two billion francs— "the true hostages." With the support of the Proudhonists on the council, his view prevailed.   [k4,1]

Blanqui, in *La Patrie en danger,* the newspaper he published during the siege:[10] "It is Berlin that supposedly will be the holy city of the future, the radiance that enlightens the world. Paris is the usurping and corrupted Babylon, the great prostitute which God's emissary, the exterminating angel, with Bible in hand, will wipe from the face of the earth. You mean you don't know that the Lord has marked the

German race with the seal of predestination? . . . Let us defend ourselves. It is the ferocity of Odin, magnified by the ferocity of Moloch, that advances against our cities; it is the barbarity of the Vandal and the barbarity of the Semite." Cited in Gustave Geffroy, *L'Enfermé* (Paris, 1897), p. 304.   [k4,2]

Georges Laronze in his *Histoire de la Commune de 1871* (Paris, 1928), p. 143, on the shooting of the hostages: "by the time the hostages fell, the Commune had lost power. But it remained accountable."[11]   [k4,3]

The Parisian administration during the Commune: "It preserved intact the entire organism, animated, as it was, by a keen desire to set its slightest cogwheels rolling again and to augment further—in good bourgeois fashion—the number of middle-class functionaries." Georges Laronze, *Histoire de la Commune de 1871* (Paris, 1928), p. 450.   [k4,4]

Military formations in the Commune: "A company little inclined to go beyond the city's ramparts, preferring, to combat in open country, the battle atmosphere of its own *quartier*, the fever of public meetings, the clubs, the police operations, and, if necessary, death behind the heaped-up paving stones of a Paris street." Georges Laronze, *Histoire de la Commune de 1871* (Paris, 1928), p. 532.   [k4,5]

Courbet took sides with several other Communards against Protot, to protect Thiers's collections from destruction.[12]   [k4,6]

The members of the International got themselves elected, on the advice of Varlin, to the Central Committee of the Garde Nationale.   [k4,7]

"This orgy of power, wine, women, and blood known as the Commune." Charles Louandre, *Les Idées subversives de notre temps* (Paris, 1872), p. 92.   [k4,8]

1

[The Seine, the Oldest Paris]

Around 1830: "The *quartier* was full of those gardens which Hugo has described in ⟨his poem of 1839⟩ 'Ce qui se passait aux Feuillantines.' The Luxembourg, rather more grand than it is today, was bordered directly by houses; the proprietors each had a key to the garden and could walk up and down there all night long." Dubech and d'Espezel, *Histoire de Paris* (Paris, 1926), p. 367.   [l1,1]

"Rambuteau had two rows of trees planted"—on the Boulevards Saint-Denis and Bonne-Nouvelle—"to replace those old and beautiful trees which had gone into the barricades of 1830." Dubech and d'Espezel, *Histoire de Paris*, p. 382.   [l1,2]

"Housewives go to draw their water from the Seine; the more distant neighborhoods are supplied by water carriers." Dubech and d'Espezel, *Histoire de Paris*, pp. 388–389 (section on the July Monarchy).   [l1,3]

Before Haussmann: "Prior to his day, the old aqueducts were capable of bringing water only as high as the second story." Dubech and d'Espezel, *Histoire de Paris*, p. 418.   [l1,4]

"Anglomania . . . has had an influence on ideas since the Revolution, on fashions since Waterloo. Just as the Constituents copied England's political institutions, the architects copied the parks and squares of London." Dubech and d'Espezel, p. 404.   [l1,5]

"The route of the Seine, as attested in Strabo, began to be used and appreciated. Lutetia became the center of an association of navigators or mariners, who, during the reign of Tiberius, raised to the emperor and to Jupiter the famous altar that was discovered under Notre Dame in 1711." Dubech and d'Espezel, p. 18.   [l1,6]

"The winter here is not severe. You can see vineyards and even fig trees, since care is taken to cover them with straw." Julian in the *Misopogon*; cited in Dubech and d'Espezel, p. 25.   [l1,7]

"The Seine seems to exhale the air of Paris all the way to its mouth." Friedrich Engels, "Von Paris nach Bern," *Die neue Zeit*, 17, no. 1 (Stuttgart, 1899), p. 11.
[11,8]

"If reading in the public gardens is now permitted, smoking there is not—liberty (as people are beginning to say) not being the same as license." Nadar, *Quand j'étais photographe* (Paris ‹1900›), p. 284 ("1830 et environs"). [11,9]

"Not long ago we witnessed the erection of the obelisk brought back from Luxor by the prince de Joinville.[1] We were made a bit nervous by noises that must not have been reassuring to the engineer Lebas, supervisor of the operation: the English, always so jealous, . . . were supposed to have paid a traitor to cut the insides of the cables. Oh, those English!" Nadar, *Quand j'étais photographe* (Paris), p. 291 ("1830 et environs"). [11,10]

Liberty trees—poplars [*peupliers*]—were planted in Paris in 1848. Thiers: "*People*, you will grow tall." They were cut down in 1850 by order of the prefect of police, Carlier. [11,11]

After the July Revolution: "The endless number of felled trees on the road to Neuilly, on the Champs-Elysées, on the boulevards. Not a single tree has been left standing on the Boulevard des Italiens." Friedrich von Raumer, *Briefe aus Paris und Frankreich im Jahre 1830* (Leipzig, 1831), vol. 2, pp. 146–147. [11,12]

"One sees gardens measuring only a few square feet, which offer nonetheless a bit of greenery in which to read a book; here and there, even a bird is chirping.—But the Place Saint-Georges is an altogether charming spot. Rustic and urban tastes are blended here. It is surrounded by buildings that look toward the city on one side and toward the country on the other." Add to this fountains, terraces, greenhouses, flower beds. L. Rellstab, *Paris im Frühjahr 1843: Briefe, Berichte und Schilderungen* (Leipzig, 1844), vol. 1, pp. 55–56. [11a,1]

"Paris is between two layers, a layer of water and a layer of air. The layer of water, lying at a considerable depth underground, . . . is furnished by the bed of green sandstone lying between the chalk and the Jurassic limestone. This bed can be represented by a disk with a radius of seventy miles. A multitude of rivers and brooks filter into it: we drink the Seine, the Marne, the Yonne, the Oise, the Aisne, the Cher, the Vienne, and the Loire in a single glass of water from the well of Grenelle. The layer of water is salubrious; it comes first from heaven, then from the earth. The layer of air is unwholesome, it comes from the sewers." Victor Hugo, *Oeuvres complètes*, novels, vol. 9 (Paris, 1881), p. 182 *(Les Misérables)*.[2]
[11a,2]

At the beginning of the nineteenth century, there were still *trains de bois* (timber rafts?) going down the Seine; and Ch. F. Viel finds fault, in his work *De l'Impuis-*

sance des mathématiques pour assurer la solidité des bâtiments, with the piers of the Pont du Louvre, on which such rafts are dashed to pieces. [11a,3]

On the "nets of Saint-Cloud" we have the testimony of Mercier (*Tableau de Paris* [Amsterdam, 1782], vol. 3, p. 197), among others: "The bodies of those unfortunates who have drowned are pulled up (except when the river is iced over) by the nets of Saint-Cloud." There are many, such as Dulaure, who speak of these nets; others, like Gozlan and Touchard-Lafosse, deny they ever existed. The archives of the Seine make no mention of them. Tradition maintains that they stopped being used in 1810. This according to Firmin Maillard, *Recherches historiques et critiques sur la Morgue* (Paris, 1860). The last chapter of this book (p. 137): "Les Filets de Saint-Cloud." [11a,4]

On "an underground river in Paris," which was, in large part, covered over at the beginning of the seventeenth century: "The stream thus . . . descended gradually along the slope, all the way to the house which, as early as the fifteenth century, had two salmon on its signboard, and which would be replaced by the Passage du Saumon. There, having swelled with the added flow of water coming from Les Halles, it plunged underground at the site where the Rue Mandar begins today, and where the entrance of the great sewer, which had long stood open, gave way . . . , after Thermidor . . . , to busts of Marat and Saint-Fargeau. . . . The stream disappeared . . . in the currents of the Seine, well below the city. . . . It was quite enough that this filthy stream created a stench in the districts it crossed, which happened to be among the most populous in Paris. . . . When the Plague broke out here, its first manifestations were in those streets which the stream, by its infectious contiguity, had already made a center of disease." Edouard Fournier, *Enigmes des rues de Paris* (Paris, 1860), pp. 18–19, 21–22 ("Une Rivière souterrain dans Paris"). [12,1]

"We recall the divine lamp with the silver burner, shining 'white like an electric light,' as it passes, in *Les Chants de Maldoror*, slowly down the Seine through Paris. Later, at the other extreme of the Cycle, in *Fantômas*, the Seine will also come to know, near the Quai de Javel, "inexplicable flashes of light in its depths." Roger Caillois, "Paris, mythe moderne," *Nouvelle Revue française*, 25, no. 284 (May 1, 1937), p. 687. [12,2]

"The quays of the Seine likewise owe their realization to Haussmann. It was only in his day that the walkways were constructed up above and the trees planted down below, along the banks; and these are what serve to articulate the form of that great thoroughfare, with its avenues and boulevards, that is the river." Fritz Stahl, *Paris* (Berlin ‹1929›), p. 177. [12,3]

"If Lutetia was not yet in direct communication with the great cities of northern lands, it was nevertheless on the commercial route that ran overland beside the river. . . . It was the great Roman way along the Right Bank which became the Rue

Saint-Martin. At the crossroads of Château-Landon, a second route branched off, that of Senlis. A third, the Melun road, a pathway cut through a thick marsh near the Bastille, came into existence perhaps, at the height of the empire . . . ; this would become the Rue Saint-Antoine." Dubech and d'Espezel, *Histoire de Paris* (Paris, 1926), p. 19.   [l2,4]

"Turning off from the boulevards, let us go down the Rue de Rougemont. You will notice that the Comptoir d'Escompte ‹Discount Bank› occupies the bottom of a marked depression: you are in the earliest bed of the Seine." Dubech and d'Espezel, *Histoire de Paris* (Paris, 1926), p. 14.   [l2a,1]

"The bourgeois center, Paris Ville, sharply distinguished from Paris Cité, grew up on the Right Bank and on the bridges which, at that time, were erected everywhere. The most influential segment of the population consisted of the merchants; here again, the hanse ‹merchants' guild› did its part to steer business to the water. The most important marketplace arose on a spot near the Church of Saint-Eustache, where the street by which ocean fish arrived crossed the street on which the marsh farmers of the region brought their vegetables to town. It is the same spot on which, today, the central market halls stand." Fritz Stahl, *Paris* (Berlin ‹1929›), p. 67.   [l2a,2]

m

[Idleness]

Noteworthy conjunction: in ancient Greece, practical labor is branded and pro-scribed. Although essentially left in the hands of slaves, it is condemned not least because it betrays a base aspiration for earthly goods (riches). This view after-ward plays a part in the denigration of the tradesman as the servant of Mammon: "Plato, in the *Laws* (VIII, 846), decrees that no citizen shall engage in a mechani-cal trade; the word *banausos,* signifying 'artisan,' becomes synonymous with 'con-temptible' . . . ; everything relating to tradespeople or to handwork carries a stigma, and deforms the soul together with the body. In general, those who practice these professions . . . are busy satisfying . . . this 'passion for wealth . . . which leaves none of us an hour's leisure.'[1] Aristotle, for his part, opposes the excess of the chrematistic to . . . the prudence of domestic economy. . . . In this way, the scorn felt for the artisan is extended to the merchant: in comparison to the liberal life, as absorbed in studious leisure *(scholē, otium),* the affairs of trade *(neg-otium, ascholia),* 'business affairs,' have mostly a negative value." Pierre-Maxime Schuhl, *Machinisme et philosophie* (Paris, 1938), pp. 11–12.　　　[m1,1]

Whoever enjoys leisure escapes Fortuna; whoever embraces idleness falls under her power. The Fortuna awaiting a person in idleness, however, is a lesser god-dess than the one that the person of leisure has fled. This Fortuna is no longer at home in the *vita activa;* her headquarters is the world at large.[2] "The artists of the Middle Ages depict those men who pursue an active life as bound to the wheel of fortune, ascending or descending according to the direction in which it turns, while the contemplative man remains immobile at the center." P.-M. Schuhl, *Machinisme et philosophie* (Paris, 1938), p. 30.　　　[m1,2]

Re the characterization of leisure. Sainte-Beuve, in his essay on Joubert: "'To converse and to seek to know—it was in this above all that, according to Plato, the happiness of private life consisted.' This class of connoisseurs and amateurs . . . has practically disappeared in France, now that everyone here has a trade." *Cor-respondance de Joubert* (Paris, 1924), p. xcix.　　　[m1,3]

In bourgeois society, indolence—to take up Marx's word—has ceased to be "heroic." (Marx speaks of the "victory . . . of industry over a heroic indolence."

Bilanz der preussischen Revolution, in *Gesammelte Schriften von Karl Marx und Friedrich Engels,* vol. 3 [Stuttgart, 1902], p. 211.)³   [m1a,1]

In the figure of the dandy, Baudelaire seeks to find some use for idleness, just as leisure once had a use. The *vita contemplativa* is replaced by something that could be called the *vita contemptiva.* (Compare part 3 of my manuscript ‹"Das Paris des Second Empire bei Baudelaire"›.)   [m1a,2]

Experience is the outcome of work; immediate experience is the phantasmagoria of the idler.⁴   [m1a,3]

In place of the force field that is lost to humanity with the devaluation of experience, a new field of force opens up in the form of planning. The mass of unknown uniformities is mobilized against the confirmed multiplicity of the traditional. To "plan" is henceforth possible only on a large scale. No longer on an individual scale—and this means neither *for* the individual nor *by* the individual. Valéry therefore says, with reason: "The long-hatched enterprises, the profound designs of a Machiavelli or a Richelieu, would today have the reliability and value of a *good tip on the Stock Exchange.*" Paul Valéry, *Oeuvres complètes,* J ‹(Paris, 1938), p. 30›.   [m1a,4]

The intentional correlate of "immediate experience" has not always remained the same. In the nineteenth century, it was "adventure." In our day, it appears as "fate," *Schicksal.* In fate is concealed the concept of the "total experience" that is fatal from the outset. War is its unsurpassed prefiguration. ("I am born German; it is for this I die"—the trauma of birth already contains the shock that is mortal. This coincidence ‹*Koinzidenz*› defines "fate.")   [m1a,5]

Would it be empathy with exchange value that first qualifies the human being for a "total experience"?   [m1a,6]

With the trace ‹*Spur*›, a new dimension accrues to "immediate experience." It is no longer tied to the expectation of "adventure"; the one who undergoes an experience can follow the trace that leads there. Whoever follows traces must not only pay attention; above all, he must have given heed already to a great many things. (The hunter must know about the hoof of the animal whose trail he is on; he must know the hour when that animal goes to drink; he must know the course of the river to which it turns, and the location of the ford by which he himself can get across.) In this way there comes into play the peculiar configuration by dint of which long experience appears translated into the language of immediate experience.⁵ Experiences can, in fact, prove invaluable to one who follows a trace—but experiences of a particular sort. The hunt is the one type of work in which they function intrinsically. And the hunt is, as work, very primitive. The experiences ‹*Erfahrungen*› of one who attends to a trace result only very remotely from any work activity, or are cut off from such a procedure altogether. (Not for nothing do we speak of "fortune hunting.") They have no sequence and no system. They are a product of chance, and have about them the essential interminability that distinguishes the preferred obligations of the idler. The fundamentally unfinishable collection of things worth knowing, whose utility depends on chance, has its prototype in study. [m2,1]

Idleness has little about it that is representative, though it is far more widely exhibited than leisure. The man of the middle class has begun to be ashamed of labor. He to whom leisure no longer means anything in itself is happy to put his idleness on display. [m2,2]

The intimate association between the concept of idleness and the concept of study was embodied in the notion of studio. Especially for the bachelor, the *studio* became a sort of pendant to the *boudoir*. [m2,3]

Student and hunter. The text is a forest in which the reader is hunter. Rustling in the underbrush—the idea, skittish prey, the citation—another piece "in the bag." (Not every reader encounters the idea.) [m2a,1]

There are two social institutions of which idleness forms an integral part: the news service and nightlife. They require a specific form of work-preparedness. This specific form is idleness. [m2a,2]

News service and idleness. Feuilletonist, reporter, photographer constitute a gradation in which waiting around, the "Get ready" succeeded by the "Shoot," becomes ever more important vis-à-vis other activities. [m2a,3]

What distinguishes long experience from immediate experience is that the former is inseparable from the representation of a continuity, a sequence. The accent that falls on immediate experience will be the more weighty in proportion as its substrate is remote from the work of the one having the experience—from the work distinguished by the fact that it draws on long experience precisely where, for an outsider, it is at most an immediate experience that arises. [m2a,4]

In feudal society, leisure—freedom from labor—was a recognized privilege. In bourgeois society, it is no longer so. What distinguishes leisure, as feudalism understands it, is that it communicates with two socially important types of behavior. Religious contemplation and court life represented, as it were, the matrices through which the leisure of the *grand seigneur,* of the prelate, of the warrior could be molded. These attitudes—that of piety no less than that of representation—were advantageous to the poet. His work in turn benefited them, at least indirectly, insofar as it maintained contact with both the religion and the life at court. (Voltaire was the first of the great literati to break with the church; so much the less did he disdain to secure a place at the court of Frederick the Great.) In feudal society, the leisure of the poet is a recognized privilege. It is only in bourgeois society that the poet becomes an idler. [m2a,5]

Idleness seeks to avoid any sort of tie to the idler's line of work, and ultimately to the labor process in general. That distinguishes it from leisure. [m3,1]

"All religious, metaphysical, historical ideas are, in the last analysis, merely preparations derived from the great experiences of the past—representations of the experience." Wilhelm Dilthey, *Das Erlebnis und die Dichtung* (Leipzig and Berlin, 1929), p. 198. [m3,2]

Closely connected with the shattering of long experience is the shattering of juridical certitudes. "In the liberalist period, economic predominance was generally associated with legal ownership of the means of production. . . . But after the development of technology in the last century had led to a rapidly increasing concentration . . . of capital, the legal owners were largely excluded from . . . management. . . . Once the legal owners are cut off from the real productive process . . . , their horizon narrows; . . . and finally the share which they still have in industry due to ownership . . . comes to seem socially useless. . . . The idea of a right with a fixed content, and independent of society at large, loses its importance." We finally arrive at "the loss of all rights with a determined content, a loss . . . given its fullest form in the authoritarian state." Max Horkheimer, "Traditionelle und Kritische Theorie," *Zeitschrift für Sozialforschung,* no. 2 (1937), pp. 285–287. Compare Horkheimer, "Bemerkungen zur philosophischen Anthropologie," *Zeitschrift für Sozialforschung,* no. 1 (1935), p. 12.[6] [m3,3]

"The authentic field of operations for the vivid chronicle of what is happening is the documentary account of immediate experience, reportage. It is directly aimed at the event, and it holds fast to the experience. This presupposes that the event also becomes an immediate experience for the journalist reporting on it. . . . The capacity for having an experience is therefore a precondition . . . of good . . . professional work." ⟨Emil⟩ Dovifat, "Formen und Wirkungsgesetze des Stils in der Zeitung," *Deutsche Presse*, July 22, 1939 (Berlin), p. 285. [m3,4]

Apropos of the idler: the archaic image of ships in Baudelaire. [m3,5]

The stringent work ethic and moral doctrine of Calvinism, it may be said, is most intimately related to the development of the *vita contemplativa*. It sought to build a dam to stem the melting of time into idleness, once such time was frozen in contemplation. [m3a,1]

On the feuilleton. It was a matter of injecting experience—as it were, intravenously—with the poison of sensation; that is to say, highlighting within ordinary experience the character of immediate experience.[7] To this end, the experience of the big-city dweller presented itself. The feuilletonist turns this to account. He renders the city strange to its inhabitants. He is thus one of the first technicians called up by the heightened need for immediate experiences. (The same need is evinced in the theory of "modern beauty" expounded by Poe, Baudelaire, and Berlioz. In this type of beauty, surprise is a ruling element.)   [m3a,2]

The process of the atrophy of experience is already underway within manufacturing. In other words, it coincides, in its beginnings, with the beginnings of commodity production. (Compare Marx, *Das Kapital* ‹vol. 1›, ed. Korsch ‹Berlin, 1932›, p. 336.)[8]   [m3a,3]

Phantasmagoria is the intentional correlate of immediate experience.   [m3a,4]

Just as the industrial labor process separates off from handicraft, so the form of communication corresponding to this labor process—information—separates off from the form of communication corresponding to the artisanal process of labor, which is storytelling. (See ‹Walter Benjamin,› "Der Erzähler," ‹*Orient und Occident,* new series, no. 3 (October 1936)› p. 21, par. 3 through p. 22, par. 1, line 3; p. 22, par. 3, line 1 through the end of the Valéry citation.)[9] This connection must be kept in mind if one is to form an idea of the explosive force contained within information. This force is liberated in sensation. With the sensation, whatever still resembles wisdom, oral tradition, or the epic side of truth is razed to the ground.   [m3a,5]

For the relations which the idler loves to enter into with the demimonde, "study" is an alibi. It may be asserted of the *bohème,* in particular, that throughout its existence it studies its own milieu.   [m3a,6]

Idleness can be considered an early form of distraction or amusement. It consists in the readiness to savor, on one's own, an arbitrary succession of sensations. But as soon as the production process began to draw large masses of people into the field, those who "had the time" came to feel a need to distinguish themselves en masse from laborers. It was to this need that the entertainment industry answered; and it immediately encountered specific problems of its own. Before very long, Saint-Marc Girardin was forced to conclude that "man is amusable only a small part of the time." (The idler does not tire as quickly as the man who amuses himself.)   [m4,1]

The true "salaried flâneur" (Henri Béraud's term) is the sandwich man.   [m4,2]

The idler's *imitatio dei:* as flâneur, he is omnipresent; as gambler, he is omnipotent; and as student, he is omniscient. This type of idler was first incarnated among the *jeunesse dorée.*[10]   [m4,3]

"Empathy" comes into being through a *déclic,* a kind of gearing action. With it, the inner life derives a pendant to the element of shock in sense perception. (Empathy is a synchronization,[11] in the intimate sense.)   [m4,4]

Habits are the armature of connected experiences. This armature is assailed by individual experiences.   [m4,5]

God has the Creation behind him; he rests from it. It is this God of the seventh day that the bourgeois has taken as the model for his idleness. In flânerie, he has the omnipresence of God; in gambling, the omnipotence; and in study, it is God's omniscience that is his.—This trinity is at the origin of the satanism in Baudelaire.—The idler's resemblance to God indicates that the old Protestant saying, "Work is the burgher's ornament," has begun to lose its validity.   [m4,6]

The world exhibitions were training schools in which the masses, barred from consuming, learned empathy with exchange value. "Look at everything; touch nothing."   [m4,7]

The classic description of idleness in Rousseau. This passage indicates, at one and the same time, that the existence of the idler has something godlike about it, and that solitude is a condition essential to the idler. In the last book of *Les Confessions,* we read that "the age for romantic plans was past. I had found the incense of vainglory stupefying rather than flattering. So the last hope I had left was to live . . . eternally at leisure. Such is the life of the blessed in the other world, and henceforth I thought of it as my supreme felicity in this. / Those who reproach me for my many inconsistencies will not fail to reproach me for this one, too. I have said that the idleness of society made it unbearable to me; and here I am, seeking for solitude solely in order to give myself up to idleness. . . . The idleness of society is deadly because it is obligatory; the idleness of solitude is delightful because it is free and voluntary." Jean-Jacques Rousseau, *Les Confessions,* ed. Hilsum (Paris ‹1931›), vol. 4, p. 173.[12]   [m4a,1]

Among the conditions of idleness, particular importance attaches to solitude. It is solitude, in fact, that first emancipates—virtually—individual experience from every event, however trivial or impoverished: it offers to the individual experience, on the high road of empathy, any passerby whatsoever as its substrate. Empathy is possible only to the solitary; solitude, therefore, is a precondition of authentic idleness.   [m4a,2]

When all lines are broken and no sail appears on the blank horizon, when no wave of immediate experience surges and crests, then there remains to the isolated subject in the grip of *taedium vitae* one last thing—and that is empathy.
                                                                     [m4a,3]

We may leave the question undecided as to whether, and in what sense, leisure is also determined by the order of production which makes it possible. We should, however, try to show how deeply idleness is marked by features of the capitalist economic order in which it flourishes.—On the other side, idleness, in the bourgeois society that knows no leisure, is a precondition of artistic production. And, often, idleness is the very thing which stamps that production with the traits that make its relation to the economic production process so drastic. [m4a,4]

The student "never stops learning"; the gambler "never has enough"; for the flâneur, "there is always something more to see." Idleness has in view an unlimited duration, which fundamentally distinguishes it from simple sensuous pleasure, of whatever variety. (Is it correct to say that the "bad infinity" that prevails in idleness appears in Hegel as the signature of bourgeois society?) [m5,1]

The spontaneity common to the student, to the gambler, to the flâneur is perhaps that of the hunter—which is to say, that of the oldest type of work, which may be intertwined closest of all with idleness. [m5,2]

Flaubert's "Few will suspect how depressed one had to be to undertake the revival of Carthage" makes the connection between study and *melencolia* ‹sic› transparent. (The latter no doubt threatens not only this form of leisure but all forms of idleness.) Compare "My soul is sad and I have read all the books" (Mallarmé); "Spleen II" and "La Voix" (Baudelaire); "Here stand I, alas, Philosophy / behind me" (Goethe).[13] [m5,3]

Again and again in Baudelaire, the specifically modern is there to be recognized as complement of the specifically archaic. In the person of the flâneur, whose idleness carries him through an imaginary city of arcades, the poet is confronted by the dandy (who weaves his way through the crowd without taking notice of the jolts to which he is exposed). Yet also in the flâneur a long-extinct creature opens a dreamy eye, casts a look that goes to the heart of the poet. It is the "son of the wilderness"—the man who, once upon a time, was betrothed, by a generous nature, to leisure. Dandyism is the last glimmer of the heroic in times of *décadence*. Baudelaire is delighted to find in Chateaubriand a reference to American Indian dandies—testimony to the former golden age of these tribes. [m5,4]

On the hunter type in the flâneur: "The mass of tenants and lodgers begins to stray from shelter to shelter in this sea of houses, like the hunters and shepherds of prehistory. The intellectual education of the nomad is now complete." Oswald Spengler, *Le Déclin de l'Occident* ‹trans. M. Tazerout›, vol. 2, part 1 (Paris, 1933), p. 140.[14] [m5,5]

"Man as civilized being, as *intellectual nomad,* is again wholly microcosmic, wholly homeless, as free intellectually as hunter and herdsman were free sensually." Spengler, vol. 2, p. 125.[15] [m5,6]

[Anthropological Materialism, History of Sects]

Gustav: "Your bottom is . . . divine!"
Berdoa: "And immortal as well, I hope."
Gustav: "What?"
Berdoa: "Nothing."

—Grabbe, *Herzog Theodor von Gothland*[1]

The grandiose and lachrymose *Mémoires de Chodruc-Duclos,* edited by J. Arago and Edouard Gouin (Paris, 1843), in two volumes, are occasionally interesting as the rudiments of a physiology of the beggar. The long preface is unsigned and says nothing about the manuscript. The memoirs could be apocryphal. We read at one point: "Let there be no mistake about it: it is not the refusal that humiliates so much as the almsgiving. . . . I never stretched out my hand in supplication. I would walk more quickly than the man who was going to accede to my request; passing him, I would open my right hand, and he would slip something into it" (vol. 2, pp. 11–12). At another point: "Water is sustaining! . . . I gorged myself with water, since I had no bread" (vol. 2, p. 19). [p1,1]

Scene in the dormitory of a prison at the beginning of the 1830s. The passage is cited in Benoist without indication of author: "In the evening, with the dormitory in an uproar, 'the republican workers, before going to bed, performed *La Révolution de 1830*, a theatrical charade they had composed. It reproduced all the scenes of the glorious week, from the decision of Charles X and his ministers to sign the July Ordinances, to the triumph of the people. The battle on the barricades was represented by a battle with bolsters carried on behind a lofty pile of beds and mattresses. At the end, victors and vanquished joined forces to sing "La Marseillaise."'" Charles Benoist, "L'Homme de 1848," part 1, *Revue des deux mondes* (July 1, 1913), p. 147. The passage cited presumably comes from Chateaubriand. [p1,2]

Ganneau. "The Mapah . . . appears to us under the aspect of the perfect dandy, who loves horses, adores women, and has a taste for the high life but is entirely impecunious. This lack of funds he makes up for through gambling; he is a habitué of all the gambling dens of the Palais-Royal. . . . He believes himself destined to be the redeemer of man's better half, and . . . takes the title of Mapah, a named formed from the first syllables of the two words 'mama' and 'papa.' He goes on to say that all proper names should be modified in this manner: you should no longer bear the name of your father, but rather should use the first syllable of your mother's maiden name combined with the first syllable of your father's name. And to mark the more clearly that he forever renounces his own former name . . . , he signs himself: 'He who was Ganneau.'" He distributes his pamphlets at the exits of theaters or sends them through the mail; he even tried to persuade Victor Hugo to patronize his doctrine. Jules Bertaut, "Le 'Mapah,'" *Le Temps*, September 21, 1935. [p1,3]

Charles Louandre on the physiologies, which he charges with corruption of morals: "This dreary genre . . . has very quickly run its course. The physiology, as produced in 32mo format suitable to be sold . . . to those out walking or driving, is represented in 1836, in the *Bibliographie de la France*, by two volumes; in 1838 there are eight volumes listed; in 1841 there are seventy-six; in 1842, forty-four; fifteen the year following; and hardly more than three or four in the two years since then. From the physiology of individuals, one moved to the physiology of cities. There was *Paris la nuit; Paris à table; Paris dans l'eau; Paris à cheval; Paris pittoresque; Paris bohémien; Paris littéraire; Paris marié*. Then came the physiology of peoples: *Les Français; Les Anglais peints par eux-mêmes*. These were followed by the physiology of animals: *Les Animaux peints par eux-mêmes et dessinés par d'autres*. Having finally run out of subjects, . . . the authors . . . turned in the end to portraying themselves, and gave us the *La Physiologie des physiologistes*." Charles Louandre, "Statistique littéraire: De la Production intellectuelle en France depuis quinze ans," *Revue des deux mondes* (November 15, 1847), pp. 686–687. [p1a,1]

Theses of Toussenel: "That the happiness of individuals is in direct proportion to female authority"; "that the rank of the species is in direct proportion to female authority." A. Toussenel, *Le Monde des oiseaux*, vol. 1 (Paris, 1853), p. 485. The first is the "formula of the gyrfalcon" (p. 39). [p1a,2]

Toussenel on his *Monde des oiseaux:* "The world of birds is only its incidental subject, whereas the world of men is its principal subject." Vol. 1, p. 2 (preface by the author). [p1a,3]

Toussenel in his preface to *Le Monde des oiseaux:* "He [the author] has sought to underline the importance of the culinary side of his subject by according the item "roast meat" a more prominent place than it usually occupies in scientific works." Vol. 1, p. 2. [p1a,4]

"We admire the bird . . . because with the bird, as in all well-organized politics, . . . it is gallantry that determines rank. . . . We feel instinctively that the woman, who came from the Creator's hand after the man, was made to command the latter, just as he was born to command the beasts who came before him" ‹*Le Monde des oiseaux*, vol. 1, p. 38›. [p1a,5]

According to Toussenel, the races that most look up to the woman stand highest: at times the Germans, but above all the French and the Greeks. "As the Athenian and the Frenchman are denoted by the falcon, so are the Roman and the Englishman by the eagle." (The eagle, however, "does not rally to the service of humanity.") A. Toussenel, *Le Monde des oiseaux*, vol. 1 (Paris, 1853), p. 125. [p1a,6]

Comic physiologies: *Musée pour rire*; *Musée Philipon*; *Musée* or *Magasin comique*; *Musée Parisien*; *Les Métamorphoses du jour*. [p2,1]

Series of drawings. *Les Vésuviennes*, by Beaumont: twenty prints. Daumier's series *Les Divorceuses* ‹Divorced Women›. A series (by whom?) titled *Les Bas-bleus* ‹The Bluestockings›.[2] [p2,2]

Rise of the physiologies: "The burning political struggle of the years 1830–1835 had formed an army of draftsmen, . . . and this army . . . was completely knocked out, politically speaking, by the September Laws. At a time, that is, when they had fathomed all the secrets of their art, they were suddenly restricted to a single theater of operations: the description of bourgeois life. . . . This is the circumstance that explains the colossal *revue* of bourgeois life inaugurated around the middle of the 1830s in France. . . . Everything came into the picture: . . . happy days and sad days, work and recreation, marriage customs and bachelor habits, family, house, child, school, society, theater, types, professions." Eduard Fuchs, *Die Karikatur der europäischen Völker*, 4th ed. (Munich ‹1921›), vol. 1, p. 362. [p2,3]

What sordidness once again, at the end of the century, in the representation of physiological affairs! Characteristic of this is a description of impotence in Maillard's book on the history of women's emancipation, which in its overall handling of the matter lays bare, in drastic fashion, the reaction of the established bourgeoisie to anthropological materialism. In connection with the presentation of Claire Démar's doctrine, one finds that "she . . . speaks of the deceptions that can result from that strange and enormous sacrifice, at the risk of which, under a torrid Italian sky, more than one young man tries his luck at becoming a famous *chanteur*." Firmin Maillard, *La Légende de la femme émancipée* (Paris), p. 98. [p2,4]

A key passage from the manifesto of Claire Démar: "The union of the sexes in the future will have to be the result of . . . deeply meditated sympathies . . . ; this will be the case even where the existence of an intimate, secret, and mysterious rapport between two souls has been recognized. . . . All such relations could very well come to nothing in the face of one last, indispensable, and decisive test: *the* TEST *of* MATTER *by* MATTER, the ASSAY of FLESH by FLESH!!! . . . Often enough, on the very threshold of the bedroom, a devouring flame has come to be *extinguished*; often enough, for more than one grand passion, the perfumed bedsheets have become a *death shroud*. More than one person . . . who will read these lines has entered, at night, into the bed of Hymen, *palpitating with desires and emotions*, only to awaken in the morning *cold and icy.*" Claire Démar, *Ma Loi d'avenir* (Paris, 1834), pp. 36–37. [p2,5]

Re anthropological materialism. Conclusion of Claire Démar's *Ma Loi d'avenir* ‹My Law of the Future›: "No more motherhood, no more law of blood. I say: no more motherhood. And, in fact, the woman emancipated . . . from the man, who then no longer pays her the price of her body, . . . will owe her existence . . . to her works alone. For this it is necessary that the woman *pursue* some work, fulfill a function. And how can she do this if she is always condemned to give up a more or less large part of her life to the care and education of one or more children? . . . You want to emancipate the *woman?* Well, then, take the newborn child from the breast of the *blood-mother* and give it into the arms of the *social mother,* a *nurse* employed by the state, and the child will be better raised. . . . Then, and then only, will man, woman, and child be freed from the law of blood, from the exploitation of humanity by humanity." Claire Démar, *Ma Loi d'avenir: Ouvrage posthume publié par Suzanne* (Paris, 1834), pp. 58–59. [p2a,1]

"What! Because a woman would rather not take the public into her confidence concerning her feelings as a woman; because, from among all the men who would lavish their attentions upon her, . . . only she could say which one she prefers— . . . is she then . . . to become . . . the slave of one man? . . . What! In such cases a woman is exploited. . . . For if she were not afraid of seeing them tear themselves to pieces, . . . she could give satisfaction to several men at once in their love. . . . I believe, with M. James de Laurence, in the need . . . for a freedom without . . . limits, . . . a freedom founded on mystery, which for me is the basis of the new morality." Claire Démar, *Ma Loi d'avenir* (Paris, 1834), pp. 31–32. [p2a,2]

The demand for "mystery"—as opposed to "publicity"—in sexual relations is closely connected, in Démar, with the demand for more or less extended trial periods. Of course, the traditional form of marriage would in general be supplanted by this more flexible form. It is logical, furthermore, that these conceptions should give rise to the demand for matriarchy. [p2a,3]

From the arguments directed against patriarchy: "Ah, it is with a huge pile of parricidal daggers at my side that, amid widespread groans of lamentation at the very mention of the words 'father' and 'mother,' I venture to raise my voice . . . against the law of blood, the law of generation!" Claire Démar, *Ma Loi d'avenir* (Paris, 1834), pp. 54–55. [p2a,4]

Caricature plays a considerable role in the development of the caption. It is characteristic that Henri Bouchot, *La Lithographie* (Paris ‹1895›) ‹p. 114›, reproaches Daumier with the length and indispensability of his captions. [p2a,5]

Henri Bouchot, *La Lithographie* (Paris), p. 138, compares the productivity of Devéria with that of Balzac and Dumas.   [p2a,6]

Several passages from Claire Démar's work *Ma Loi d'avenir* may be cited by way of characterizing her relation to James de Laurence. The first comes from the foreword written by Suzanne and has its point of departure in Claire Démar's refusal to contribute to *La Tribune des femmes:* "Up until the seventeenth issue, she had consistently refused, saying that the tone of this periodical was too moderate. . . . When this issue appeared, there was a passage in an article by me which, by its form and its moderation, exasperated *Claire.*—She wrote to me that she was going to respond to it.—But . . . her response became a pamphlet, which she then decided to publish on its own, outside the framework of the periodical. . . . Here, then, is the fragment of the article of which *Claire* has cited only a few lines. 'There is still in the world a man who interprets . . . Christianity . . . in a manner . . . favorable to our sex: I mean M. *James de Laurence,* the author of a pamphlet entitled *Les Enfants de dieu, ou La Religion de Jésus.* . . . The author is no Saint-Simonian; . . . he postulates . . . an inheritance through the mother. Certainly this system . . . is highly advantageous to us; I am convinced that some part of it will have a place . . . in the religion of the future, and that the principle of motherhood will become one of the fundamental laws of the state'" (Claire Démar, *Ma loi d'avenir: Ouvrage posthume publié par Suzanne* [Paris, 1834], pp. 14–16). In the text of her manifesto, Claire Démar makes common cause with Laurence against the reproaches leveled at him by *La Tribune des femmes,* which had claimed that he was advocating a form of "moral liberty . . . without rules or boundaries," something "which . . . would surely land us in a coarse and disgusting disorder." The blame for this is said to reside in the fact that in these things Laurence propounds mystery as a principle; on the strength of such mystery, we would have to render account in these things to a mystical God alone. *La Tribune des Femmes,* on the contrary, believes that "the Society of the Future will be founded not on mystery but on trust; for mystery merely prolongs the exploitation of our sex." Claire Démar replies: "Certainly, Mesdames, if, like you, I confused trust with publicity, and considered mystery as prolonging the exploitation of our sex, I would be bound to give my blessings to the times in which we live." She goes on to describe the brutality of the customs of these times: "Before the mayor and before the priest, . . . a man and a woman have assembled a long train of witnesses. . . . Voilà! . . . The union is called legitimate, and the woman may now without blushing affirm: 'On such and such a day, at such and such an hour, I shall receive a man into my *WOMAN'S BED!!!*' . . . Contracted in the presence of the crowd, the marriage drags along, across an orgy of wines and dances, toward the nuptial bed, which has become the bed of debauchery and prostitution, inviting the delirious imagination of the guests to follow . . . all the details . . . of the lubricious drama enacted in the name of the Wedding Day! If the practice which thus converts a young bride . . . into the object of impudent glances . . . , and which prostitutes her to unrestrained desires, . . . does not appear to you a horrible exploitation, . . . then I know not what to say" (*Ma Loi d'avenir,* pp. 29–30).   [p3,1]

Publication date of the first issue of *Le Charivari:* December 1, 1832.   [p3,2]

Lesbian confession of a Saint-Simonienne: "I began to love my fellow woman as much as my fellow man. . . . I left to the man his physical strength and his brand of intelligence in order to exalt at his side, and with equal right, the physical beauty of the woman and her distinctively spiritual gifts." Cited without indication of source or author in Firmin Maillard, *La Légende de la femme émancipée* (Paris), p. 65.   [p3a,1]

Empress Eugénie as successor to the Mother:

> Should you wish, O blessèd one,
> The whole of humankind with joy
> Will hail its EUGENIE—
> Archangel guiding us to port!!!

Jean Journet, *L'Ere de la femme, ou Le Règne de l'harmonie universelle* (January 1857), p. 8. ‹See U14a,4 and U17a,2.›   [p3a,2]

Maxims from James de Laurence, *Les Enfants de dieu, ou La Religion de Jésus réconciliée avec la philosophie* (Paris, June 1831): "It is more reasonable to claim that all children are made by *God* than to say that all married couples are joined together by *God*" (p. 14). The fact that Jesus does not condemn the woman taken in adultery leads Laurence to conclude that he did not approve of marriage: "He pardoned her because he considered adultery the natural consequence of marriage, and he would have accepted it were it to be found among his disciples. . . . As long as marriage exists, an adulterous woman will be found criminal because she burdens her husband with the children of others. *Jesus* could not tolerate such an injustice; his system is logical: he wanted children to belong to the mother. Whence those remarkable words: 'Call no man your father on earth, for you have one Father, who is in heaven'"[3] (p. 13). "The children of God, as descended from one woman, form a single family. . . . The religion of the Jews was that of *paternity,* under which the patriarchs exercised their domestic authority. The religion of Jesus is that of *maternity,* whose symbol is a mother holding a child in her arms; and this mother is called the Virgin because, while fulfilling the duties of a mother, she had not renounced the independence of a virgin" (pp. 13–14).   [p3a,3]

"Some sects . . . , during the first centuries of the church, seem to have divined the intentions of Jesus; the Simonians, the Nicolaitans, the Carpocratians, the Basilidians, the Marcionites, and others . . . not only had abolished marriage but had established the community of women." James de Laurence, *Les Enfants de dieu, ou La Religion de Jésus réconciliée avec la philosophie* (Paris, June 1831), p. 8.   [p3a,4]

The interpretation of the miracle at Cana[4] which James de Laurence offers, in an effort to prove his thesis that Jesus stood opposed to marriage, is wholly in the style of the early Middle Ages: "Seeing the wedded pair make a sacrifice of their

The Fourierist missionary Jean Journet, ca. 1858. Photo by Nadar. Courtesy of the Bibliothèque Nationale de France. See p3a,2.

liberty, he changed the water into wine so as to demonstrate that marriage was a foolhardy venture undertaken only by people whose brains are addled by wine." James de Laurence, *Les Enfants de dieu, ou La Religion de Jésus réconciliée avec la philosophie* (Paris, June 1831), p. 8. [p4,1]

"The Holy Spirit, or the soul of nature, descended upon the Virgin in the form of a dove; and since the dove is the symbol of love, this signifies that the mother of

Jesus had yielded to the natural inclination for love." James de Laurence, *Les Enfants de dieu* (Paris, June 1831), p. 5.   [p4,2]

Some of Laurence's theoretical motifs are already evident in his four-volume novel, *Le Panorama des boudoirs, ou L'Empire des Nairs* (Paris, 1817), which was published earlier in Germany and of which a fragment had appeared in 1793 in Wieland's *Deutsche Merkur*. Laurence (Lawrence) was English.   [p4,3]

"Balzac has described the physiognomy of the Parisian in unforgettable fashion: the faces drawn taut, tormented, livid, 'the almost infernal complexion of Parisian physiognomies';[5] not faces but masks." Ernst Robert Curtius, *Balzac* (Bonn, 1923), p. 243. (Citation from *La Fille aux yeux d'or*.)   [p4,4]

"Balzac's interest in longevity is one of the things he has in common with the eighteenth century. The naturalists, the philosophers, the charlatans of that age are agreed on this point. . . . Condorcet expected from the future era, which he painted in glowing colors, an infinite prolongation of the life span. Count Saint-Germain dispensed a 'tea of life,' Cagliostro an 'elixir of life'; others promoted 'sidereal salts,' 'tincture of gold,' 'magnetic beds.'" Ernst Robert Curtius, *Balzac* (Bonn, 1923), p. 101.   [p4,5]

In Fourier (*Nouveau Monde* ‹Paris, 1829–1830›, p. 275) there are outcries against wedding rites that recall the pronouncements of Claire Démar.   [p4,6]

Note of Blanqui's from the spring of 1846, when he was imprisoned in the Hospital of Tours: "On Communion days, the sisters of the hospice of Tours are unapproachable, ferocious. They have eaten God. They are churning with the pride of this divine digestion. These vessels of holiness become flasks of vitriol." ‹Cited in› Gustave Geffroy, *L'Enfermé* (Paris, 1926), vol. 1, p. 133.   [p4,7]

Apropos of the wedding at Cana. 1848: "A banquet for the poor was planned; it was to offer, for twenty-five centimes, bread, cheese, and wine, which would be eaten and drunk on the plain of Saint-Denis. It did not take place (initially scheduled for June 1, it was postponed to June 18, then to July 14); but the preparatory meetings that were held, the subscriptions that were collected, and the enrollments—which had mounted, by June 8, to 165,532—served to stir up public opinion." Gustave Geffroy, *L'Enfermé* (Paris, 1926), vol. 1, p. 192.   [p4a,1]

"In 1848, in the room of Jenny the worker, there were portraits of Béranger, Napoleon, and the Madonna pinned to the wall. People felt certain that the religion of *Humanity* was about to emerge. Jesus is a great man of '48. Among the masses, there were indications of a faith in omens. . . . The *Almanach prophétique* of 1849 announced the return of the comet of 1264—the warrior comet, produced by the influence of Mars." Gustave Geffroy, *L'Enfermé* (Paris, 1926), vol. 1, p. 156.   [p4a,2]

Babick, deputy of the tenth *arrondissement*, Pole, worker, then tailor, then perfumer. "He was . . . a member of the International and of the Central Committee, and at the same time an apostle of the fusionist cult—a religion of recent inspiration, intended for the use of brains like his. Formed by a certain M. de Toureil, it combined . . . several cults, to which Babick had conjoined spiritualism. As a perfumer, he had created for it a language which, for lack of other merits, was redolent of drugs and ointments. He would write at the top of his letters 'Paris-Jerusalem,' date them with a year of the fusionist era, and sign them 'Babick, child of the Kingdom of God, and perfumer.'" Georges Laronze, *Histoire de la Commune de 1871* (Paris, 1928), pp. 168–169.   [p4a,3]

"The whimsical idea conceived by the colonel of the twelfth legion was no more felicitous. It entailed forming a company of female citizen volunteers who were charged, for the greater shame of lawbreakers, with securing their arrest." Georges Laronze, *Histoire de la Commune de 1871* (Paris, 1928), p. 501.   [p4a,4]

Fusionisme begins its reckoning of time with December 30, 1845.   [p4a,5]

Maxime Du Camp, in his *Souvenirs littéraires*, makes a play on words with "Evadians" and "evaders." ‹See a15,2–4.›   [p4a,6]

From the constitution of the Vésuviennes: "Female citizens ought to do their part to serve the armies of land and sea. . . . The enlisted will form an army to be designated as reserve. It will be divided into three contingents: the corps of women workers, the corps of vivandières, and the corps of charity. . . . Since marriage is an association, each of the two spouses must share in all the work. Any husband refusing to perform his portion of domestic duties will be condemned . . . to assume responsibility for the service of his wife in the Garde Civique, in place of his own service in the Garde Nationale." Firmin Maillard, *La Légende de la femme émancipée* (Paris), pp. 179, 181.   [p5,1]

"The feelings Hegel stirred up among the members of Young Germany, and which fluctuated between strong attraction and even stronger repulsion, are reflected most vividly in Gustav Kühne's *Quarantäne im Irrenhause* ‹Quarantine in the Insane Asylum›. . . . Because the members of Young Germany placed the accent more on subjective volition than on objective freedom, the Young Hegelians heaped scorn upon the 'unprincipled meandering' of their 'belletristic egoism'. . . . Although the fear arose, within the ranks of Young Germany, that the inescapable dialectic of Hegelian doctrine might deprive Youth of the strength . . . to act, this concern proved unjustified." Quite the contrary: once these young Germans "were forced to recognize, after the ban on their writings was imposed, that they themselves had burned the hands by whose diligent labors they had hoped to live like good bourgeois, their enthusiasm quickly vanished." Gustav Mayer, *Friedrich Engels*, vol. 1, *Friedrich Engels in seiner Frühzeit* (Berlin ‹1933›), pp. 37–39.[6]   [p5,2]

Around the time that "physiologies" first appeared, historians like Thierry, Mignet, Guizot were laying emphasis on the analysis of "bourgeois life."   [p5,3]

Engels on the Wuppertal region: "Excellent soil for our principles is being prepared here; and once we are able to set in motion our wild, hot-tempered dyers and bleachers, you won't recognize Wuppertal. Even as it is, the workers during the past few years have reached the final stage of the old civilization; the rapid increase in crimes, robberies, and murders is their protest against the old social organization. At night the streets are unsafe, the bourgeois are beaten up, knifed, and robbed. If the local proletarians develop according to the same laws as the English proletarians, they will soon realize that it is useless to protest against the social system in this manner . . . and will protest in their general capacity, as human beings, by means of communism." Engels to Marx, October 1844, from Barmen [Karl Marx and Friedrich Engels, *Briefwechsel*, ed. Marx-Engels-Lenin Institut, vol. 1 (‹Zurich› 1935), pp. 4–5].[7]   [p5,4]

The heroic ideal in Baudelaire is androgynous. This does not prevent him from writing: "We have known the philanthropist woman author, the systematic priestess of love, the republican poetess, the poetess of the future, Fourierist or Saint-Simonian; and our eyes . . . have never succeeded in becoming accustomed to all this studied ugliness." Baudelaire, *L'Art romantique,* ed. Hachette, vol. 3 (Paris), p. 340 ("Marceline Desbordes-Valmore").[8]   [p5a,1]

One of the later sectarian developments of the nineteenth century is the fusionist religion. It was propagated by L. J. B. Toureil (born in Year VIII, died 1863 [or 1868?]). The Fourierist influence can be felt in his periodization of history; from Saint-Simon comes the idea of the Trinity as a unity of Mother-Father to which Sister-Brother or Androgyne is joined. The universal substance is determined in its working by three processes, in the definition of which the inferior basis of this doctrine comes to light. These processes are: "Emanation, . . . the property which the universal substance possesses of expanding infinitely beyond itself; . . . Absorption, . . . the property which the universal substance possesses of turning back infinitely upon itself; . . . Assimilation, . . . the property which the universal substance possesses of being intimately permeated with itself" (p. i).—A characteristic passage from the aphorism "Pauvres, riches" ‹Rich Men, Poor Men›, which addresses itself to the rich and speaks of the poor: "Moreover, if you refuse to elevate them to your level and scorn to involve yourselves with them, why then do you breathe the same air, inhabit the same atmosphere? In order not to breathe in and assimilate their emanation . . . , it will be necessary for you to leave this world, to breathe a different air and live in a different atmosphere" (p. 267).—The dead are "multiform" and exist in many places on the earth at the same time. For this reason, people must very seriously concern themselves, during their lifetime, with the betterment of the earth (p. 307). Ultimately, all unites in a series of suns, which in the end, after they have passed through the station of one light (*unilumière*), realize the "universal light" in the "universalizing region."

Religion fusionienne, ou Doctrine de l'universalisation réalisant le vrai catholicisme
(Paris, 1902).   [p5a,2]

"Me: Is there some particular facet of your religious cult that you could comment
on? M. de Toureil: We pray often, and our prayers ordinarily begin with the
words: 'O Map supreme and eternal.' Me: What is the meaning of this sound
'Map'? M. de Toureil: It is a sacred sound which combines the *m* signifying *mère*
(mother), the *p* signifying *père* (father), and the *a* signifying *amour* (love). . . .
These three letters designate the great eternal God." Alexandre Erdan [A. A.
Jacob], *La France mistique*, 2 vols. (Paris, 1855), vol. 2, p. 632 [continuous pagi-
nation].   [p6,1]

Fusionisme aims not at a syncretism but at the fusion of human beings with one
another and with God.   [p6,2]

"There will be no happiness for humanity until the day the republic sends the son
of God back to the carpenter's shop of Monsieur his father." This sentence is put
into the mouth of Courbet, in a pamphlet that presents the heroes of the February
Revolution to the public.   [p6,3]

[Ecole Polytechnique]

On commerce: "If competition between merchants, . . . or any other matter, prevents them from selling their wares in timely fashion, then the individual merchant is forced . . . to suspend business and cast the problem back onto the producers. . . . This is why we cannot distinguish between commercial and industrial crises, so dependent is industry on intermediaries. . . . A fearsome audit is conducted on all assets in circulation, and an enormous quantity of them are declared worthless. . . . The times when commercial assets are subjected to audit are called crises." Eugène Buret, *De la Misère des classes laborieuses en Angleterre et en France* (Paris, 1840), vol. 2, pp. 211, 213. [r1,1]

"In 1860, having long slumbered in the arms of protectionism, France abruptly awakened 'on the pillow of free trade.' Exercising the right conferred on him by the constitution of 1852, Napoleon III had bypassed parliament and negotiated to open our borders to products from other nations, at the same time opening several foreign markets to our entrepreneurs. . . . Long years of prosperity had made it possible for our industrial forces . . . to wage a global struggle." Henry Fougère, *Les Délégations ouvrières aux expositions universelles sous le Second Empire* (Montluçon, 1905), p. 28. [r1,2]

Founding of the Ecole Polytechnique:[1] "The Terror within, invaders at the borders . . . ; the country in ruins, disorganized, able neither to acquire the saltpeter needed for gunpowder nor to run the factories needed for manufacturing arms (since nearly all these factories were in the hands of insurgents)—such were the circumstances in which deliberations were held to found the new institution. . . . 'Everything that genius, labor, and concerted action were capable of,' as Biot had put it, 'was now called up, so that France alone could sustain itself against all of Europe . . . for the duration of the war, however long and terrible it might prove to be'. . . . Characteristic of the Ecole Polytechnique . . . was the coexistence of purely theoretic studies with a series of *vocational courses* geared to civil engineering, architecture, fortifications, mining, and even naval constructions. . . . Napoleon . . . made residence in the barracks obligatory for students. . . . Then came the events of . . . 1815, after which . . . one no longer concealed the hope of seeing the Ecole recruit more students from aristocratic families. . . . The institution thus ceased to have the character of a preparatory school for public service. . . . Pure science was to gain nothing by this; for . . . the graduating classes . . . of 1817 to 1830 contributed by far the lowest proportion of members to the Institut de France. . . . In 1848, the Ecole was in danger of being closed." A. de Lapparent, *Le Centenaire de l'Ecole polytechnique* (Paris, 1894), pp. 6–7, 12–15.   [r1,3]

Vote of March 18, 1871, at the Ecole Polytechnique, on the position to be adopted vis-à-vis the Commune: "Some . . . wonder what this committee is that claims to have been elected by the federation of 300,000 citizens. . . . Others . . . propose taking up the tradition of the past and putting themselves at the forefront of the movement. After a very lively but peaceful discussion, a vote is held: the partisans of the Central Committee are fourteen in number!" G. Pinet, *Histoire de l'Ecole polytechnique* (Paris, 1887), p. 293.   [r1a,1]

In 1871, the Ecole Polytechnique encountered justified mistrust. Voices were heard to say: "The Ecole is no longer what it was in 1830!" (Pinet, p. 297).
            [r1a,2]

Two characteristic passages from Edouard Foucaud, *Paris inventeur: Physiologie de l'industrie française* (Paris, 1844), on the conception of industry and of the worker before 1848: "Industrial intelligence is the daughter of heaven. It loves and surrenders itself only to those whom society . . . calls *manual laborers,* those whom intelligent persons know as *brothers* or *workers*" (p. 181). "Today, in the nineteenth century, the *chattel* of the Romans, . . . the *serf* of Charlemagne, the *peasant* of Francis I—this miserable trinity which slavery has brutalized but which the genius of emancipation has made radiant—is called *the people*" (pp. 220–221).
            [r1a,3]

"Without the advantages of wealth, . . . or a narrow mind, . . . the worker finds retirement on an annuity to be oppressive. The sky above may well be cloudless, and his home may well be verdant, perfumed with flowers, and enlivened by the song of birds; yet his inactive mind remains insensible to the charms of solitude. If, by chance, his ear should catch some sharp noise coming from a distant manufacturing plant, or even the monotonous churning of a factory mill, then his countenance immediately brightens; he no longer notices the birdsongs or the perfumes. The thick smoke escaping from the factory's high chimney, the ringing of the anvil, make him tremble with joy. These things remind him of the good old days of manual labor motivated by a mind inspired." Edouard Foucaud, *Paris inventeur: Physiologie de l'industrie française* (Paris, 1844), pp. 222–223.   [r1a,4]

"'Amid the reigning disorder,' writes Vaulabelle, 'their well-known uniform, beloved of all, gave them a sort of official character, which turned them into . . . the most active and most useful agents of the up and coming power'. . . . 'Whenever we had to give an order that required the backing of some kind of force,' says Mauguin, 'we would generally entrust its execution to a student of the Ecole

Polytechnique. The student would descend the flight of stairs leading out from the Hôtel de Ville. Before reaching the bottom step, he would address the crowd, which had become attentive; he would simply pronounce the words, "Two hundred men, able and willing!" Then he would complete his descent and turn alone into the street. At that very instant, one could see stepping forth from the walls and marching behind him—some with rifles, others just with swords—one man, two men, twenty men, and then one hundred, four hundred, five hundred men; more than twice the number needed.'" G. Pinet, *Histoire de l'Ecole polytechnique* (Paris, 1887), pp. 156–157. [The two passages cited are from ‹Achille› Vaulabelle, *Histoire des deux restaurations*, vol. 8, p. 291, and a letter of M. Mauguin to *La Presse*, Saumur, March 8, 1853.] [r2,1]

The students of the Ecole Polytechnique organize a relief fund to make it easier for *La Tribune* to pay a fine. (Pinet, p. 220.) [r2,2]

Lamartine in *Destinées de la poésie*, as cited in Michiels: "M. Lamartine, who has seen with his own eyes the intellectual servitude of the Empire, describes it. . . . 'It was a universal confederacy of the mathematical forms of study, in opposition to thinking and poetry. Number alone was permitted, was honored, protected, and paid. Since number does not think for itself, the military chief of that era had need of no other . . . henchman.'" Alfred Michiels, *Histoire des idées littéraires en France au XIXᵉ siècle* (Paris, 1863), vol. 2, p. 94. [r2,3]

Pinet ‹*Histoire de l'Ecole polytechnique* (Paris, 1887)› (p. viii) refers to the Encyclopédistes as "the true founders" of the Ecole Polytechnique. [r2,4]

"One tried by every means possible, but always without success, to win the Ecole over to the cause of the Bourbons." Pinet, *Histoire de l'Ecole polytechnique*, p. 86. [r2,5]

Customs and precepts of the student body at the Ecole Polytechnique, as assembled in the "Code X." "It rested entirely on this one principle, which had been upheld ever since the school was founded: 'Any resolution voted through is obligatory, no matter what the consequences might be.'" Pinet, pp. 109–110. [r2,6]

Michelet on the Ecole Polytechnique and the Ecole Normale: "After those great trials, there seemed to be a moment of silence for all human passions; one might have thought that there was no longer any pride, self-interest, or envy. The leading men in the state and in science accepted the most humble positions of public instruction. Lagrange and Laplace taught arithmetic. Fifteen hundred students—grown men who were in some cases already famous—came . . . to take their seats at the Ecole Normale and to learn to teach. They came as best they could, in the depth of winter, at that time of poverty and famine. . . . A great citizen, Carnot, . . . was the real founder of the Ecole Polytechnique. They learned with the zeal of soldiers. . . . Watching the uninterrupted inventions of their teachers, the students went on to invent as well. Imagine the spectacle of a Lagrange who suddenly stopped short in the middle of his lecture and was lost in thought. The room waited in silence. Finally he awoke and told them of his glowing new discovery, barely formed in his mind. . . . What a decline after those days! . . . After the reports made to the Convention, read those of Fourcroy and Fontanes; you sink . . . from manhood to old age." J. Michelet, *Le Peuple* (Paris, 1846), pp. 336–338.[2]   [r2a,1]

"Parnassus of the triangle and the hypotenuse"—this is what Paul-Ernest de Rattier, in *Paris n'existe pas* (Paris, 1857), calls the Ecole Polytechnique (p. 19).
    [r2a,2]

Ch. F. Viel, as an adversary of engineering construction, no less than as a royalist, was necessarily also an adversary of the Ecole Polytechnique. He laments the decline of architecture as art—a decline "that began with that terrible period when the throne of our king was toppled." Charles-François Viel, *De la Chute imminente de la science de la construction des bâtimens en France,* vol. 1 (Paris, 1818), p. 53. The study of architecture as art is, according to him, more difficult than the mathematical theory of construction; as proof, he cites the many prizes won in this field by students of the Ecole Polytechnique. The author speaks contemptuously of the new educational arrangements—"these new institutions professing everything with everything else"—and he writes on the same page: "Let us pay homage here to the government that has judged so well of the difference between mathematics and architecture, and which has preserved the special school in Paris for the teaching of this art, and recreated the private boarding school of Rome." Charles-François Viel, *De l'Impuissance des mathématiques pour assurer la solidité des bâtimens* (Paris, 1805), p. 63. Viel emphasizes (ibid., pp. 31–32) the irrational element in the genuine study of architecture: "The forms preexist the construction and constitute essentially the theory of the art of building," In 1819 (*De la Chute . . . ,* vol. 2, p. 120), he is still denouncing "the attitude of the century toward the fine arts in general, which it puts in a class with the *industrial* arts."   [r2a,3]

From the time of Napoleon I, the Ecole Polytechnique was subject to continual reproach for providing practical training with an overly broad theoretical foundation. These criticisms led, in 1855, to proposals for reform, against which Arago took a most determined stand. At the same time, he dismissed the charge that the school had become a breeding ground of revolutionary animus: "I have been told of a reproach directed against polytechnical instruction, and according to which the mathematical disciplines—the study of differential calculus and of integral calculus, for example—would have the effect of transforming their students into socialists of the worst stamp. . . . How has it escaped the author of such a reproach that its immediate consequence is nothing less than to range the likes of a Huygens, a Newton, a Leibniz, a Euler, a Lagrange, a Laplace among the most hot-headed of demagogues? It is truly shameful that someone was led to make comparisons of this kind." ‹François› Arago, *Sur l'ancienne Ecole polytechnique* (Paris, 1853), p. 42.   [r3,1]

In *Le Curé de village*, which Balzac wrote in the years 1837 to 1845, there are very violent attacks on the Ecole Polytechnique (coming in the letter of Grégoire Gérard to his patron, the banker Grossetête). Balzac fears that the forced study of the exact sciences would have devastating effects on the spiritual constitution and life span of the students. Still more characteristic are the following reflections: "I do not believe that any engineer who ever left the Ecole could build one of the miracles of architecture which Leonardo da Vinci erected—Leonardo who was at once engineer, architect, and painter, one of the inventors of hydraulic science, the indefatigable constructor of canals. They are so accustomed while not yet in their teens to the bald simplicity of geometry, that by the time they leave the Ecole they have quite lost all feeling for grace or ornament. A column, to their eyes, is a useless waste of material. They return to the point where art begins—on utility they take their stand, and stay there." H. de Balzac, *Le Curé de village*, ed. Siècle (Paris), p. 184.[3]   [r3,2]

Arago's speech on the question of fortifications[4] is directed against the report by Thiers and against Lamartine. The speech is dated January 29, 1841. One of its most important sections is headed: "The detached forts examined from the point of view of their political significance. Is it true that governments have never regarded citadels as a means of subduing and suppressing populations?" From this section: "M. Thiers does not like to admit that any government, in order to control the population, would ever resort to bombarding the towns . . . This illusion certainly does honor to his humanity and to his taste for fine arts; but . . . few others would share it. . . . And so . . . one may subscribe to the protestations of 1833 against the detached forts and the smaller fortresses without incurring the epithet of 'philistine,' or 'madman,' or other such compliments." Arago, *Sur les Fortifications de Paris* (Paris, 1841), pp. 87, 92–94.   [r3,3]

Arago fights for the "continuous *enceinte*" as opposed to the "detached forts": "The goal we should strive for, in fortifying Paris, is clearly to give this gigantic city the means of defending itself solely with the aid of its Garde Nationale, its workers, the population of surrounding areas, and some detachments of regular army troops. . . . This point granted, the best ramparts for Paris will be those the population finds to be best—the ramparts most intimately suited to the tastes, customs, ideas, and needs of an armed bourgeoisie. To pose the question in this manner is to reject out of hand the system of detached forts. Behind a continuous surrounding wall, the Garde Nationale would have news of their families at all times. The wounded would have access to care. In such a situation, the apprehensive guardsman would be as good as the seasoned veteran. On the other hand, we would be strangely deluded if we imagined that citizens under daily obligations as heads of families and as heads of businesses would go, without great reluctance, to shut themselves up within the four walls of a fort—that they would be prepared to sequester themselves at the very moment when circumstances of the most pressing kind would demand their presence at the domestic hearth or at the counter, store, or workshop. I can already hear the response to such imperious demands: the forts will be occupied by regular army troops! You admit then that, with a system of forts, the population could not defend itself alone. This is . . . an immense, a terrible admission." Arago, *Sur les Fortifications de Paris* (Paris, 1841), pp. 80– 81.　　　　　　　　　　　　　　　　　　　　　　　　　　　　　　　[r3a,1]

Marx on the June Insurrection: "In order to dispel the people's last illusion, in order to enable a complete break with the past, it was necessary for the customary poetic accompaniment of a French uprising, the enthusiastic youth of the bourgeoisie, the students of the Ecole Polytechnique, the three-cornered hats—all to take the side of the oppressors." Karl Marx, "Dem Andenken der Juni-Kämpfer" [*Karl Marx als Denker, Mensch und Revolutionär,* ed. D. Rjazanov (Vienna and Berlin ‹1928›, p. 36].[5]　　　　　　　　　　　　　　　　　　　　　[r3a,2]

Again, in 1871, in his strategy for the defense of Paris, Blanqui comes back to the uselessness of the forts which Louis Philippe erected against Paris.　　　[r3a,3]

The postrevolutionary tendencies of architecture, which gain currency with Ledoux, are characterized by distinct block-like structures to which staircases and pedestals are often appended in "standardized" fashion. One might discern in this style a reflection of Napoleonic military strategy. With this goes the effort to generate certain effects by means of structural massing. According to Kaufmann, "Revolutionary architecture aimed to produce an impression through giant masses, the sheer weight of the forms (hence the preference for Egyptian forms, which predates the Napoleonic campaign), and also through the handling of materials. The cyclopean embossment of the saltworks, the powerful ordonnance of the Palais de Justice at Aix, and the extreme severity of the prison designed for this city . . . speak clearly of that aim." Emil Kaufmann, *Von Ledoux bis Le Corbusier* (Vienna and Leipzig, 1933), p. 29.　　　　　　　　　[r4,1]

Ledoux's planned toll-belt for Paris: "From the beginning, he set his sights as high as possible. His tollgates were intended to proclaim from afar the glory of the capital. Of the more than forty guardhouses, not one resembled any of the others, and among his papers after his death were found a number of unfinished plans for expanding the system." Emil Kaufmann, *Von Ledoux bis Le Corbusier: Ursprung und Entwicklung der autonomen Architektur* (Vienna and Leipzig, 1933) , p. 27.　　　　　　　　　　　　　　　　　　　　　　　　　　　　　　[r4,2]

"Shortly after 1800, things were already so far along that the ideas which appear in Ledoux and Boullée—elemental outbursts of passionate natures—were being propounded as official doctrine. . . . Only three decades separate the late work of Blondel, which still . . . embodies the teachings of French classicism, from the *Précis des leçons d'architecture* of Durand, whose thinking had a decisive influence during the Empire and in the period following. They are the three decades of Ledoux's career. Durand, who announced the norm from his chair at the Ecole Royale Polytechnique in Paris, . . . diverges from Blondel on all essential points. His primer begins . . . with violent attacks on two famous works of classic Baroque art. St. Peter's in Rome, along with its square, and the Paris Pantheon are invoked as counterexamples. . . . Whereas Blondel warns of 'monotonous planimetry' and would not be unmindful of the function of perspective, Durand sees in the elementary schemata of the plan the only correct solutions." Emil Kaufmann, *Von Ledoux bis Le Corbusier* (Vienna and Leipzig, 1933), pp. 50–51.

[r4,3]

The institution of the Ponts et Chaussées ‹Civil Department of Bridges and Highways› had the unique privilege of coming through the great Revolution uncontested.

[r4a,1]

The students of the Ecole Polytechnique, according to Barthélemy:

> Glory to you, youths of banquets and darts!
> How we applauded in our poets' hearts
> When on the dusty street you took your stand,
> Elegantly dressed, with rifle in hand!

Barthélemy and Méry, *L'Insurrection* (Paris, 1830), p. 20.

[r4a,2]

FIRST SKETCHES

First Sketches

Paris Arcades ⟨I⟩

These early sketches for *The Arcades Project* (*Gesammelte Schriften,* vol. 5 [Frankfurt: Suhrkamp, 1982], pp. 991–1038) were written by Benjamin in a bound notebook that contains various other notes and drafts dating from mid-1927 to early 1930. Many of the sketches are crossed out in Benjamin's manuscript, presumably because in most cases they were revised and transferred to the manuscript of the convolutes; these canceled sketches are printed here in a smaller typesize, with cross-references to the corresponding entries in the convolutes and early drafts. (Some of the uncanceled sketches, in the larger typesize, were also transferred to the convolutes, and are accordingly cross-referenced.) Cross-references should not be considered exhaustive. The numbering here, as in "The Arcades of Paris," is that of the German editor and bears no relation to the numbering of the convolutes. The sign ⟨x⟩ indicates an illegible word.

The asphalt roadway in the middle: teams of harnessed humans, human carriages. Procession of human carriages.   ⟨A°,1⟩

The street that runs through houses. Track of a ghost through the walls of houses. ⟨See L2,7.⟩   ⟨A°,2⟩

People who inhabit these arcades: the signboards with the names have nothing in common with those that hang beside respectable entryways. Rather, they recall the plaques on the railings of cages at the zoo, put there to indicate not so much the dwelling place as the name and origin of the captive animals. ⟨See b°,2.⟩   ⟨A°,3⟩

World of particular secret affinities: palm tree and feather duster, hairdryer and Venus de Milo, champagne bottles, prostheses, and letter-writing manuals, ⟨broken off⟩ ⟨See a°,3 and R2,3.⟩   ⟨A°,4⟩

When, as children, we were made a present of those great encyclopedic works— *World and Mankind* or *The Earth* or the latest volume of the *New Universe*— wasn't it into the multicolored "Carboniferous Landscape" or "European Animal Kingdom of the Ice Age" that we plunged first of all, and weren't we, as though at first sight, drawn by an indeterminate affinity between the ichthyosaurs and bisons, the mammoths and the woodlands? Yet this same strange rapport and primordial relatedness is revealed in the landscape of an arcade. Organic world and inorganic world, abject poverty and insolent luxury enter into the most contradictory communication; the commodity intermingles and interbreeds as promiscuously as images in the most tangled of dreams. Primordial landscape of consumption. ⟨See a°,3.⟩   ⟨A°,5⟩

Trade and traffic are the two components of the street. Now, in the arcade the first of these ⟨error, corrected in A3a,7⟩ has all but died out: the traffic there is rudimentary. The arcade is a street of lascivious commerce only; it is wholly adapted to arousing desires. Thus, there is no mystery in the fact that whores feel spontaneously drawn there. Because in this street all the juices slow to a standstill, the commodity proliferates along the house fronts and enters into new and fantastic combinations, like the tissue in tumors. ⟨A°,6⟩

The will turns down the wide street into the teeth of pleasure and, as lust, drags with it into its gloomy bed whatever it finds in the way of fetish, talisman, and gage of fate across its path, drags with it the rotting debris of letters, kisses, and names. Love presses forward with the inquisitive fingers of desire down the winding street. Its way leads through the interior of the lover, which opens up to him in the image of the beloved who passes lightly before him. This image opens up his interior to him for the first time. For, as the voice of the truly beloved awakens in his heart an answering voice which he has never before heard in himself, the words which she speaks awaken in him thoughts of this new, much more hidden ego that reveals to him her image, while the touch of her hand awakens ⟨broken off⟩   ⟨A°,7]

Game in which children have to form a brief sentence out of given words. This game is seemingly played by the goods on display: binoculars and flower seeds, screws and musical scores, makeup and stuffed vipers, fur coats and revolvers.
                                                                                          ⟨A°,8⟩

Maurice Renard, in his book *Le Péril bleu,*[1] has told how inhabitants of a distant planet come to study the flora and fauna indigenous to the lower depths of the atmosphere—in other words, to the surface of the earth. These interplanetary travelers see in human beings the equivalent of tiny ⟨?⟩ deep-sea fish—that is to say, beings who live at the bottom of a sea. We no more feel the pressure of the atmosphere than fish feel that of the water; this in no way alters the fact that both sets of creatures reside on an ocean floor. With the study of the arcades, a closely related reorientation in space is opened up. The street itself is thereby manifest as ⟨x⟩ well-worn interior: as living space of the collective, for true collectives as such inhabit the street. The collective is an eternally awake, eternally agitated being that—in the space between the building fronts—lives, experiences, understands, invents as much as individuals do within the privacy of their own four walls. For it, for this collective, enameled shop signs are a wall decoration as good as, if not better than, the inexpensive oleograph above the hearth. Walls with their "Post No Bills" are its writing desk, newspaper stands its libraries, display windows its glazed inaccessible armoires, mailboxes its bronzes, benches its bedroom furniture, and the café terrace is the balcony from which it looks down on its household. As with a railing where pavers hang their coats before going to work, the vestibule is the hidden gateway which gives onto a row of courtyards—is, for it, the corridor that daunts the strangers and serves as the key to its dwelling. ⟨See d°,1 and M3a,4.⟩   ⟨A°,9⟩

A factory of 5,000 workers for weddings and banquets. Attire for bride and groom. Birdseed in the fixative pans of a photographer's darkroom.—Mme. de Consolis, Ballet Mistress. Lessons, Classes, Routines.—Mme. de Zahna, Fortuneteller. Possession by spirits, Illusions, Secret Embraces. ⟨See "Arcades" and a°,3.⟩   ⟨A°,10⟩

Everywhere stockings play a starring role. They are found in the photographer's studio, then in a doll hospital, and, one day, on the side table of a tavern, watched over by a girl. ‹See "Arcades" and b°,1.› ‹A°,11›

The arcade may be conceived as mineral spa ‹*Brunnenhalle*›. Arcade myth, with legendary source. ‹See L2,6.› ‹A°,12›

It is high time the beauties of the nineteenth century were discovered. ‹A°,13›

Arcade and railroad station: yes / Arcade and church: yes / Church and railroad station: Marseilles / ‹A°,14›

Poster and arcade: yes / Poster and building: no / Poster and ‹x›: open / ‹A°,15›

Conclusion: erotic magic / Time / Perspective / Dialetical reversal (commodity—type). ‹A°,16›

. . . .

There is, to speak once more of restaurants, a nearly infallible criterion for determining their rank. This is not, as one might readily assume, their price range. We find this unexpected criterion in the color of the sound that greets us when ‹broken off› ‹B°,1›

The solemn, reflective, tranquil character of the Parisian mealtime is measured less by the particular dishes served than by the stillness that surrounds you in the restaurant, whether it be before uncovered tables and plain white walls or in a carpeted and richly furnished dining room. Nowhere does one find the hubbub of a Berlin restaurant, where patrons like to give themselves airs and where food is only a pretext or necessity. I know a shabby, dark room in the very middle of which, a few minutes past noon, milliners from nearby shops gather around long marble tables. They are the only customers, keeping quite to themselves, and they have little to say to one another during their short lunch break. And yet—it is merely a whispering, from which the clinking of knives and forks (refined, dainty, as though punctuated) continuously rises. In a "Chauffeurs' Rendezvous," as the small bistros like to call themselves, a poet and thinker can have his breakfast and, in an international company of Russian, Italian, and French taxi drivers, advance his thoughts a good distance. If he wants, however, to enjoy the undivided sociable silence of a public repast, he will not turn his steps toward any of the venerable old Paris restaurants, and still less toward one of the newer chic establishments; rather, he goes to seek out, in a remote *quartier,* the new Parisian mosque. There he finds, along with the indoor garden and its fountains, along with the obligatory bazaar full of carpets, fabrics, and copperware, three or four medium-sized rooms furnished with stools and divans and lit by hanging lamps. He must of course bid adieu not only to French cooking, which he exchanges for a choice Middle Eastern cuisine, but above all to French wines. Nevertheless, within months of its opening, the best Parisian society had already discovered the "secrets of the mosque" and now takes its coffee in the little garden, or a late supper in one of the adjoining rooms. ‹B°,2›

If one wanted to characterize the inexhaustible charm of Paris in a few words, one could say that there is in this atmosphere a wisely apportioned mixture, such that ‹broken off›

⟨B°,3⟩

Carus on Paris, the atmosphere and its colors[2] / Paris as the city of painters / Chirico: the palette of gray ‹see D1a,7 and D1a,8›   ⟨B°,4⟩

Dreams vary according to where you are, what area and what street, but above all according to the time of year and the weather. Rainy weather in the city, in its thoroughly treacherous sweetness and its power to draw one back to the days of early childhood, can be appreciated only by someone who has grown up in the big city. It naturally evens out the day, and with rainy weather one can do the same thing day in, day out—play cards, read, or engage in argument—whereas sunshine, by contrast, shades the hours and is furthermore less friendly to the dreamer. In that case, one must get around the day from morning on; above all, one must get up early so as to have a good conscience for idleness. Ferdinand Hardekopf, the only honest decadent which German literature has produced, and whom I hold to be, of all the German poets now in Paris, the most unproductive and the most able, has in his "Ode vom seligen Morgen" ‹Ode to Blessed Morning›,"[3] which he dedicated to Emmy Hennings, laid out for the dreamer the best precautions to be taken for sunny days. In the history of the *poètes maudits,* the chapter describing their battle against the sun is yet to be written; the fogs of Paris, which is really what we are talking about here, were dear to Baudelaire ‹See D1a,9.›.   ⟨B°,5⟩

. . . .

Every year, one hears it said that the last Bastille Day did not measure up to previous ones. Unfortunately, and by way of exception, it was true this time. The reasons: First, the cool weather. Second, the city this year had refused to grant the usual funds to the holiday committee. Third, the franc has to some degree stabilized.[4] And everyone knows what a splendid basis for popular festivals a weakened currency is. Last year, when in July the franc was in the midst of a terrific slump, the currency communicated its impetuosity to the desperate public. People danced as they had seldom done before. At the streetcorners you could find the old image: long festoons of electric bulbs, platforms with musicians, crowds of the curious. But the dynamism of the tempos was undoubtedly weaker, and the three-day-long festivities did not extend so late into the night as in years past. On the other hand, its aftereffect was longer. A small assemblage of booths, strolling confectioners, target-shooting ‹stands› ‹broken off›   ⟨C°,1⟩

Death, the dialectical central station; fashion, measure of time.   ⟨C°,2⟩

In the first half of the previous century, theaters too, by preference, found a place in the arcades. In the Passage des Panoramas, the Théâtre des Variétés stands next to the Children's Theater of M. Comte;[5] another theater, the Gymnase des Enfants, was located in the Passage de l'Opéra, where later on, around 1896, the commentating ‹?› naturalist theater of Chirac housed the Théâtre de Vérité, in which one-act plays were performed by a nude couple. Today, one still finds in the Passage Choiseul the Bouffes Parisiennes, and if the other theaters have had to close their doors, the small bare booths of the ticket agents open ‹something› like a secret passage to all theaters. But this gives no idea of how strict the correlation between arcade and theater originally was. Under —, it was the custom to name fancy-goods shops after the most successful vaudevilles of the season. And since such shops, by and large, made up the most elegant part of the arcades, the gallery was, in places, like the mockup of a theater. These *magasins de nouveautés* played a particular role here. ‹C°,3›

Claretie speaks of the "stifled perspective" of certain pictures and compares it to the airlessness of the arcades. ‹See E1,5.› But the perspective of the arcades can itself be compared to this "suffocated" perspective, which is precisely that of the stereoscope. The nineteenth century ‹broken off› ‹C°,4›

Energies of repose (of tradition) which carry over from the nineteenth century. Transposed historical forces of tradition. What would the nineteenth century be to us if we were bound to it by tradition? How would it look as religion or mythology? We have no tactile ‹*taktisch*› relation to it. That is, we are trained to view things, in the historical sphere, from a romantic distance. To account for the directly transmitted inheritance is important. But it is still too early, for example, to form a collection. Concrete, materialistic deliberation on what is nearest is now required. "Mythology," as Aragon says, drives things back into the distance. Only the presentation of what relates to us, what conditions us, is important. The nineteenth century—to borrow the Surrealists' terms—is the set of noises that invades our dream, and which we interpret on awaking. ‹C°,5›

A walk through Paris will begin with an apéritif—that is, between five and six o'clock. I would not tie you down to this. You can take one of the great railroad stations as your point of departure: the Gare du Nord, with trains leaving for Berlin; the Gare de l'Est, with departures for Frankfurt; the Gare Saint-Lazare, where you can take off for London; and the Gare de Lyon, with its ‹xxxx› into the P.L.M. If you want my advice, I'd recommend the Gare Saint-Lazare. There you have half of France and half of Europe around you; names like Le Havre, Provence, Rome, Amsterdam, Constantinople are spread through the street like sweet filling through a torte. It is the so-called Quartier Europe, in which the greatest cities of Europe have all commissioned a street as emblem of their prestige. A rather precise and rigorous etiquette prevails in this diplomatic corps of European streets. Each one is clearly set off against the others, and if they have some business to transact with one another—at the corners—they come together very courteously, without the slightest ostentation. A foreigner who was unaware of the fact would perhaps never notice that he was in a royal household here. Atop this particular throne, however, is the Gare Saint-Lazare itself, a robust and dirty sovereign lady, a clanging puffing princess of iron and smoke. ‹See L1,4.› But we are by no means obliged to limit ourselves to railroad stations. Railroad stations make good starting points, but they also serve very well as destinations. Think now of the city's squares. Here, certain distinctions are called for: some are without history and without name. Thus, there is the Place de la Bastille and the Place de la République, the Place de la Concorde and the Place Blanche, but there are also others whose designers are unknown, and whose names are often not to be found on any wall. These squares are lucky accidents, as it were, in the urban landscape; they do not enjoy the patronage of history like the Place Vendôme or the Place de Grève, are not the result of long planning, but instead resemble architectural improvisations—those crowds of houses where the shabby buildings collide in a jumble. In these squares, the trees hold sway; here the smallest trees afford thick shade. At night, however, their leaves stand out against the gas-burning street lamps like transparent ‹x› fruits. These tiny hidden squares are the future ‹?› Gardens of the Hesperides. ‹See P1,2.› Let us suppose, then, that at five o'clock we sit down to an apéritif on the Place Sainte-Julie. Of one thing we may be sure: we will be the only foreigners and will have, perhaps, not even one Parisian near us. And should a neighbor present himself, he will most likely give the impression of being a provincial who has stopped in here at the end of the day to have a beer. Now, here we have a little secret password of freemasonry by which fanatical Paris-aficionados, French as well as foreign, recognize one another. This word is "province." With a shrug of the shoulders, the true Parisian, though he may never travel out of the city for years at a stretch, refuses to live in ‹Paris›. He lives in the *treizième* or the *deuxième* or the *dix-huitième;* not in Paris but in his *arrondissement*—in the third, seventh, or twentieth. And this is the provinces. Here, perhaps, is the secret of the gentle hegemony which the city maintains over France: in the heart of its neighborhoods, and ‹that is to say, its› provinces, it has welcomed the other into itself, and so possesses more provinces than the whole of France. For it would be foolish to depend on the bureaucratic division into *arrondissements* here: Paris has more than twenty of them and comprises a multitude of towns and villages. A young Parisian author, Jacques de Lacretelle, has recently taken as the theme of his dreamy ‹?› flânerie this quest for the secret Parisian districts, provinces, *arrondissements,* and has offered a description of a *rêveur parisien* ‹Parisian dreamer› that teaches us a great deal in twenty pages.[6] Paris has its South, with its Riviera and sandy beach where new construction plays; it has its foggy, rainy Breton coast on the banks of the Seine ‹?›, its Burgundian market corner not far from the Hôtel de Ville, and its harbor alleys of ill fame out of Toulon and Marseilles—naturally not on the knoll of Montmartre but just behind the respectable Place Saint-Michel. There are other spots that look as though, on the photo of a ‹broken off›   ‹C°,6›

And to have missed the onset of evening, with the question confided from the heart of the hour, is proof of a successful, abundant Parisian afternoon, which is much too beautiful to be merely a vestibule of the Moulin Rouge. On another occasion in nocturnal Paris, we will make sure to take our ‹x› only after dinner.

‹C°,7›

· · · · · · · · · · · · · ·

Surrealism—"wave of dreams"—new art of flânerie. New nineteenth-century past—Paris its classic locale. Here, fashion has opened the place of dialectical exchange between woman and ware. The clerk, death, tall and loutish, measures the century by the yard, serves as mannequin himself to save costs, and manages single-handedly the "liquidation" that in French is called "revolution." ‹See f°,1 and B1,4.› And all this we know only since yesterday. We look on the empty offices, and where ‹?› yesterday there was ‹?› . . . a room.　　　　　　‹D°,1›

Fashion was never anything other than: provocation of death through the woman. Here, with the victory of death, this provocation has ended. Death has erected the armature of the whores as a pallid battle memorial on the banks of the new Lethe, which as river of asphalt runs through the arcades. ‹See f°,1 and B1,4.›　　　　　　‹D°,2›

And nothing at all of what we are saying here actually existed. None of it has ever lived—as surely as a skeleton has never lived, but only a man. As surely, however, ‹broken off›　　　　　　‹D°,3›

Being past, being no more, is passionately at work in things. To this the historian trusts for his subject matter. He depends on this force, and knows things as they are at the moment of their ceasing to be. Arcades are such monuments of being-no-more. And the energy that works in them is dialectics. The dialectic takes its way through the arcades, ransacking them, revolutionizing them, turns them upside down and inside out, converting them, since they no longer remain what they are, from abodes of luxury to ‹x›. And nothing of them lasts except the name: *passages*. And: Passage du Panorama ‹sic›. In the inmost recesses of these names the upheaval is working, and therefore we hold a world in the names of old streets, and to read the name of a street at night is like undergoing a transformation ‹?›.　　　　　　‹D°,4›

Fashion as parody of the (motley) cadaver	Surrealism Primal landscape of consumption / Colors Inhabitants Inner spaces Dialectical reversal / Paris dolls
Fashion a dialogue with the body, even with putrefaction.	*Intérieur* / Salon Mirror / Perspective Theaters / Dioramas *Magasins de nouveautés* / Guides to Paris
Mold in which modernity is cast	Fashion / Time Lethe (modern)

Street as interior / the sitting room / *the dialectical reversal*
Last refuge of the commodity　　　　　　‹D°,5›

All this is the arcade in our eyes. And it was nothing of all this earlier. ⟨See a°,2 and C2a,9.⟩ So long as the gas lamps, even the oil lamps were burning in them, the arcades were fairy palaces. But if we want to think of them at the height of their magic, we must call to mind the Passage des Panoramas around 1870 ⟨?⟩: on one side, there was gaslight; on the other, oil lamps still flickered. The decline sets in with electric lighting. Fundamentally, however, it was no decline but, properly speaking, a reversal. As mutineers, after plotting for days on end, take possession of a fortified site, so the commodity by a lightning stroke seized power over the arcades. Only then came the epoch of commercial firms and figures. The inner radiance of the arcades faded with the blaze of electric lights and withdrew into their names. But their name was now like a filter which let through only the most intimate, the bitter essence of what had been. (This strange capacity for distilling the present, as inmost essence of what has been, is, for true travelers, what gives to the name its exciting and mysterious potency.)   ⟨D°,6⟩

Architecture as the most important testimony to latent "mythology." And the most important architecture of the nineteenth century is the arcade.—The effort to awaken from a dream as the best example of dialectical reversal. Difficulty of this dialectical technique.   ⟨D°,7⟩

. . . .

Lorgnette dealer.   ⟨E°,1⟩

In 1893 the arcades were closed to cocottes. ⟨See H1,4.⟩   ⟨E°,2⟩

Music in the arcades. "*Lanterne magique! Pièce curieuse!*" With this cry, a peddler would travel through the streets and, at a wave of the hand, step up into dwellings where he operated his lantern. The *affiche* for the first exhibition of posters characteristically displays a magic lantern. ⟨See Q2,3.⟩   ⟨E°,3⟩

Rage for tortoises in 1839. Tempo of flânerie in the arcades. ⟨See D2a,1.⟩   ⟨E°,4⟩

Names of *magasins de nouveautés* (most derived from successful vaudevilles): La Fille d'Honneur, La Vestale, Le Page Inconstant, Le Masque de Fer, Le Coin de la Rue, La Lampe Merveilleuse, Le Petit Chaperon Rouge ⟨Little Red Riding Hood⟩, Petite Nanette, Chaumière Allemande ⟨German Cottage⟩, Mamelouk. ⟨See A1,2.⟩   ⟨E°,5⟩

Sign above a confectioner's shop: "Aux Armes de Werther." A glover's: "Au Ci-Devant Jeune Homme" ⟨The Ci-Devant Young Man⟩. ⟨See A1,2.⟩   ⟨E°,6⟩

Olympia—continuation of the street.[7] Kinship with the arcade.   ⟨E°,7⟩

Musée Grévin: Cabinet des Mirages. Representation of a connection between temple, railroad station, arcades, and market halls where tainted (phosphorescent) meat is sold. Opera in the arcade. Catacombs in the arcade.   ⟨E°,8⟩

In 1857 the first electric streetlights in Paris (near the Louvre). ⟨See T1,4.⟩   ⟨E°,9⟩

Impasse Maubert, formerly d'Amboise. Around 1756, at Nos. 4–6, a poisoner resided with her two assistants. All three were found dead one morning—killed through inhalation of toxic fumes. ‹See A1a,8.›   ‹E°,10›

In the Passage de la Réunion there was once a courtyard; in the sixteenth century, it was a meeting place for thieves. At the beginning of the nineteenth or end of the eighteenth century, a dealer in muslins (wholesale) sets up shop in the arcade.   ‹E°,11›

Two pleasure districts in 1799: the Coblentz[8] (for returning émigrés) and the Temple.   ‹E°,12›

Le Charivari of 1836 has an illustration showing a poster that covers half a housefront. The windows are left uncovered, except for one, it seems, out of which a man is leaning while cutting away the obstructing piece of paper. ‹See G3,6.›   ‹E°,13›

Originally gas was delivered to fashionable establishments in containers for daily consumption. ‹See T1,5.›   ‹E°,14›

Thurn ‹?› as georama in the Galerie Colbert   ‹E°,15›

Félicien David, *Le Désert* (performed before ‹by?› Arabs), *Christophe Colomb* (panorama music). ‹See H1,5.›   ‹E°,16›

Passage du Pont-Neuf: described in Zola's *Thérèse Raquin,* right at the beginning (identical with the earlier Passage Henri IV ‹?›[9]).   ‹E°,17›

Elie Nachmeron ‹?› / Arcades: Bois-de-Boulogne (today:),[10] Caire, Commerce, Grosse-Tête, Réunion.   ‹E°,18›

"Winter, with the famed warmth of lamps . . . " Paul de Kock, *La Grande Ville,* vol. 4.   ‹E°,19›

Paul de Kock: "numerals of fire" on the fronts of gambling houses.   ‹E°,20›

Passage Vivienne—sculptures at the entrance representing allegories of commerce. In an inner courtyard, on a pedestal, a copy of a Greco-Roman Mercury.
                                                                                          ‹E°,21›

Years of industrial growth under Louis XVIII. ‹See A1a,9.›   ‹E°,22›

Louis Philippe drives out prostitution from the Palais-Royal, closes the gambling houses.   ‹E°,23›

Setup of the panoramas: view from a raised platform, surrounded by a balustrade, of surfaces lying round about and beneath. The painting runs along a cylindrical wall approximately a hundred meters long and twenty meters high. The principal panoramas of Prévost (the great painter of panoramas): Paris, Toulon, Rome, Naples, Amsterdam,

Tilsit, Wagram, Calais, Antwerp, London, Florence, Jerusalem, Athens. Among his pupils, Daguerre. ‹See Q1a,1.› ⟨E°,24⟩

Site of the Passage du Caire in the notorious "Cour des Miracles" (see Hugo, *Notre-Dame de Paris*). It was called the "court of miracles" because the beggars who made this place their guild hall shed their feigned infirmities there. ‹See A3a,6.› ⟨E°,25⟩

February 12, 1790: execution of the Marquis de Favras (accused of counterrevolutionary conspiracy). The Place de Grève and the scaffold decked with Chinese lanterns. ‹See T1a,9.› ⟨E°,26⟩

A Strasbourg piano manufacturer, Schmidt, made the first guillotine. ⟨E°,27⟩

Georama in the fourteenth *arrondissement*. Small nature-replica of France. ‹See Q2,4.› ⟨E°,28⟩

Passage Vivienne the "solid" arcade, in contrast to the Passage des Panoramas. No luxury shops in the former. Businesses in the Passage des Panoramas: Restaurant Véron, Marquis Chocolates, lending library, music shop, caricaturist, Théâtre des Variétés (tailors, bootmakers, haberdashers, wine merchants, hosiers). ‹See A2,1.› ⟨E°,29⟩

The perspective of the opera in the Musée Grévin (on the Passage de l'Opéra, compare *Le Fantôme de l'Opéra*).[11] ⟨E°,30⟩

The (caricaturist?) Aubert in the Passage Véro-Dodat. Marble pavement! ⟨E°,31⟩

Roi-Maçon ‹Mason King›—nickname of Louis Philippe. ‹See E1a,1.› ⟨E°,32⟩

In 1863 Jacques Fabien publishes *Paris en songe* ‹Paris in a Dream.› He explains there how electricity causes multiple blindings through excess of light, and induces madness because of the tempo of news services. ‹See B2,1.› ⟨E°,33⟩

Names of jewelers written in false gemstones above their shops. ‹See A1,2.› ⟨E°,34⟩

Transition from *boutique* to *magasin*. The shopkeeper buys provisions for a week and withdraws to the entresol. ‹See A1,3.› ⟨E°,35⟩

In great vogue around 1820: cashmere. ⟨E°,36⟩

Origin of the magic lantern. Inventor, Athanasius Kircher. ⟨E°,37⟩

In 1757, there were only three cafés in Paris. ‹See D3a,1.› ⟨E°,38⟩

Identify the frontispiece to volume 1 of *L'Hermite de la Chaussée d'Antin* (Paris, 1813).[12] ⟨E°,39⟩

"Praise God and all my shops"—saying attributed to Louis Philippe. ⟨E°,40⟩

Rachel resided in the Passage Véro-Dodat. ‹See A1a,4.› ⟨E°,41⟩

84 Rue Franciade, "Passage du Désir," which in the old days led to a *lieu galant*. ‹See A6a,4.› ⟨E°,42⟩

The panoramas in the Passage des Panoramas were closed in 1831. ⟨E°,43⟩

Gutzkow reports that the exhibition salons were full of oriental scenes calculated to arouse enthusiasm for Algiers. ‹See I2,2.› ⟨E°,44⟩

Query for the arcades project.
Does plush first appear under Louis Philippe? ⟨E°,45⟩

What is a "drawer play"? (Gutzkow, *Briefe aus Paris*, vol. 1, p. 84)—(*pièce à tiroirs?*)[13] ⟨E°,46⟩

At what tempo did changes in fashion take place in earlier times? ⟨E°,47⟩

Find out the meaning of *bec de gaz*[14] in argot and where it comes from. ⟨E°,48⟩

Read up on the manufacture of mirrors. ⟨E°,49⟩

When did it become customary to give streets names that had no intrinsic relation to them but were meant to commemorate a famous man, and so forth?
⟨E°,50⟩

Difference between *passage* and *cité?* ⟨E°,51⟩

Early writings on iron construction, technology of factory construction, and so on? ⟨E°,52⟩

What is an astral lamp? Invented in 1809 by Bordin-Marrell ‹?›.[15] ⟨E°,53⟩

What are the atmospherical railroads of Vallance?[16] ⟨E°,54⟩

Where does the citation of Apollinaire in Crevel come from?[17] ⟨E°,55⟩

Where is Picabia's proposal taken from—that of letting two mirrors face and look into each other? Likewise cited in Crevel. As epigraph to the section on mirrors.
⟨E°,56⟩

Information about the construction of the Carcel lamp, in which a clockwork mechanism drives the oil from below up into the wick, whereas in the Argand lamp (*quinquet*) the oil drips out of a reservoir into the wick from above, producing a shadow. ‹See T1a,7.›
⟨E°,57⟩

Where did Charles Nodier write against gas lighting?[18] ⟨E°,58⟩

What is *une psyché*?[19]   ⟨E°,59⟩.

· · · · · · · · · · · · · ·

The city made of markets. Thus Riga, when viewed from the other side of the river in the evening light, looks like a warehouse. When multicolored clouds gather over the ocean, Chinese legend says the gods are coming together to hold a market. They name this phenomenon *hai-thi,* or the sea-market.   ⟨F°,1⟩

Comparison of the arcades to the indoor arenas in which one learned to ride a bicycle. In these halls the figure of the woman assumed its most seductive aspect: as cyclist. That is how she appears on contemporary posters. Chéret as painter of this feminine pulchritude. ⟨See B1,2.⟩   ⟨F°,2⟩

Music in arcades. It seems to have settled into these spaces only with the decline of the arcades—that is to say, only with the advent of mechanical music. (Gramophone. The "theatrophone" in certain respects its forerunner.) Nevertheless, there was music that conformed to the spirit of the arcades—a panoramic music, such as can be heard today only in old-fashioned genteel concerts like those of the casino orchestra in Monte Carlo: the panoramic compositions of David (*Le Désert, Herculanum*). ⟨See H1,5.⟩   ⟨F°,3⟩

The nine ⟨sic⟩ muses of Surrealism: Luna, Cléo de Mérode, Kate Greenaway, Mors, Friederike Kempner, Baby Cadum, Hedda Gabler, Libido, Angelika Kauffmann, Countess Geschwitz.[20]   ⟨F°,4⟩

Amid the smoke of battle, on the printed picture sheets, is smoke in which spirits rise (from the *Thousand and One Nights*). ⟨See D2a,8.⟩   ⟨F°,5⟩

There is a wholly unique experience ⟨*Erfahrung*⟩ of dialectic. The compelling—the drastic—experience, which refutes everything "gradual" about becoming and shows all seeming "development" to be dialectical reversal, eminently and thoroughly composed, is the awakening from dream. For the dialectical schematism at the core of this magic process, the Chinese have found, in their fairy tales and novellas, the most radical expression. Accordingly, we present the new, the dialectical method of doing history: with the intensity of a dream, to pass through what has been, in order to experience the present as the waking world to which the dream refers! (And every dream refers to the waking world. Everything previous is to be penetrated historically.) ⟨See h°,4 and K1,3.⟩   ⟨F°,6⟩

Awakening as a graduated process that goes on in the life of the individual as in that of the generation. Sleep its initial stage. A generation's experience of youth has much in common with the experience ⟨*Erfahrung*⟩ of dreams. Its historical configuration is a dream-configuration. Every epoch has such a side turned toward dreams, the child's side. For the previous century, it is the arcades. But whereas the education of earlier generations explained these dreams for them in terms of tradition, of religious doctrine, present-day education simply amounts to the "distraction" of children. What follows here is an experiment in the technique of awakening. The dialectical—the Copernican—turn of remembrance ⟨*Wendung des Eingedenkens*⟩ (Bloch). ⟨See h°,4 and K1,1.⟩   ⟨F°,7⟩

Boredom and dust. Dream a garment one cannot turn. On the outside, the gray boredom (of sleep). Sleep state, hypnotic, of the dusty figures in the Musée Grévin. A sleeper is not

a good subject for wax. Boredom ‹*Langeweile*› is always the external surface of unconscious events. Therefore, it could appear to the great dandies as a mark of distinction. For
it is precisely ‹?› the dandy who despises new clothing: whatever he wears must appear
slightly frayed. As opposed to a theory of dreams that would reveal to us "psyches," the
world that comes to seem pointless. What about it? ‹See e°,2 and D2a,2.›   ‹F°,8›

Arcades: houses, passages, having no outside. Like the dream. ‹See L1a,1.›   ‹F°,9›

Catalogue of muses: Luna, Countess Geschwitz, Kate Greenaway, Mors, Cléo de
Mérode, Dulcinea ‹variant: Hedda Gabler›, Libido, Baby Cadum, and Friederike
Kempner. ‹See C1,3.›   ‹F°,10›

And boredom is the grating before which the courtesan teases death. ‹See B1,1.›
‹F°,11›

There are, at bottom, two sorts of philosophy and two ways of noting down
thoughts. One is to sow them in the snow—or, if you prefer, in the fire clay—of
pages; Saturn is the reader to contemplate their increase, and indeed to harvest
their flower (the meaning) or their fruit (the verbal expression). The other way is
to bury them with dignity and erect as sepulcher above their grave the image, the
metaphor—cold and barren marble.[21]   ‹F°,12›

Most hidden aspect of the big cities: this historical object, the new metropolis, with its
uniform streets and endless rows of houses, has given material existence to those architectures of which the ancients dreamed—the labyrinths. Man of the crowd. Impulse that
turns the big cities into a labyrinth. Fulfilled through the covered passageways of the
arcades. ‹See M6a,4.›   ‹F°,13›

Perspective: plush for silk ‹?›. Plush the material of the age of Louis Philippe. ‹See E1,7.›
‹F°,14›

Self-photography and the unrolling of the lived life before the dying. Two kinds of
memory (Proust). ‹See H5,1 and K8a,1.› Relationship of this kind of memory with the
dream.   ‹F°,15›

Hegel: in itself—for itself—in and for itself. In the *Phänomenologie,* these stages of
the dialectic become consciousness—self-consciousness—reason.   ‹F°,16›

Gamut in the word *passage*.   ‹F°,17›

"Rainshowers have given birth to many adventures."[22] Diminishing magical power of the
rain. Mackintosh. ‹See D1,7.›   ‹F°,18›

What the big city of modern times has made of the ancient conception of the
labyrinth. It has raised it, through the names of streets, into the sphere of language, raised it from out of the network of streets in which the city ‹x› designated
‹x› within language ‹x›.   ‹F°,19›

What was otherwise reserved for only a very few words—a privileged caste of words, the names—the city has made possible for all words, or at least a great many: to be elevated to the noble status of name. And this supreme revolution in language was carried out by what is most general: the street. And a vast order appears in the fact that all names in the cities run into one another without exercising any influence ‹?› on one another. Even those much-overused names of great men, already half-congealed into concepts, here once more pass through a filter and regain the absolute; through its street names, the city is image of a linguistic cosmos. ‹See P3,5.› ⟨F°,20⟩

Only the meeting of two different street *names* makes for the magic of the "corner." ⟨F°,21⟩

Names of streets written vertically (when? ‹x› book? at any rate German). On the invasion of the letters. ⟨F°,22⟩

The structure of books like *La Grande Ville, Le Diable à Paris, Les Français peints par eux-mêmes* is a literary phenomenon that corresponds to the stereoscopes, panoramas, and so forth. ‹See Q2,6.› ⟨F°,23⟩

The true has no windows. Nowhere does the true look out to the universe. And the interest of the panorama is in seeing the true city. "The city in the bottle"—the city indoors. What is found within the *windowless* house is the true. One such windowless house is the theater; hence the eternal pleasure it affords. Hence, also, the pleasure taken in those windowless rotundas, the panoramas. In the theater, after the beginning of the performance, the doors remain closed. Those passing through arcades are, in a certain sense, inhabitants of a panorama. The windows of this house open out on them. They can be seen out these windows but cannot themselves look in. ‹See Q2a,7.› ⟨F°,24⟩

Paintings of foliage in the Bibliothèque Nationale. This work was done in . . . ⟨F°,25⟩

With the dramatic signboards of the *magasins de nouveautés,* "art enters the service of the businessman." ‹See A1a,9.› ⟨F°,26⟩

Persian fashion makes its appearance in the mania for *magasins.* ⟨F°,27⟩

Fate of street names in the vaults of the Métro. ‹See P2,3.› ⟨F°,28⟩

On the peculiarly voluptuous pleasure in naming streets. ‹See P1,8.› Jean Brunet, *Le Messianisme, organisation générale Paris: Sa constitution générale,* part 1 (Paris, 1858). "Rue du Sénégal," "Place d'Afrique." ‹See P1a,3.› In this connection, something on the Place du Maroc. ‹See P1a,2.› Monuments are sketched out in this book, too. ⟨F°,29⟩

Red lights marking the entrance to the underworld of names. Link between name and labyrinth in the Métro. ‹See C1a,2.› ⟨F°,30⟩

Cashier as Danae. ‹See C1,4.› ⟨F°,31⟩

The true expressive character of street names can be recognized as soon as they are set beside reformist proposals for their normalization. ‹See P2,4.›   ‹F°,32›

Proust's remarks on the Rue de Parme and the Rue du Bac.[23]   ‹F°,33›

At the conclusion of *Matière et mémoire,* Bergson develops the idea that perception is a function of time. If, let us say, we were to live more calmly, according to a different rhythm, there would be nothing "subsistent" for us, but instead everything would happen right before our eyes; everything would strike us. But this is precisely what occurs in dreams. In order to understand the arcades from the ground up, we sink them into the deepest stratum of the dream; we speak of them as though they had struck us. A collector looks at things in much the same way. Things come to strike the great collector. How he himself pursues and encounters them, what changes in the ensemble of items are effected by a newly supervening item—all this shows him his affairs dissolved in constant flux, like realities in the dream. ‹See H1a,5.›   ‹F°,34›

Until ca. 1870 the carriage ruled. Flânerie, on foot, took place principally in the arcades. ‹See A1a,1.›   ‹F°,35›

Rhythm of perception in the dream: story of the three trolls.   ‹F°, 36›

. . . .

"He explains that the Rue Grange-Batelière is particularly dusty, that one gets terribly grubby in the Rue Réaumur." Aragon, *Paysan de Paris* (Paris, 1926), p. 88.[24] ‹See D1a,2.›
             ‹G°,1›

"The coarsest hangings plastering the walls of cheap hotels will deepen into splendid dioramas." Baudelaire, *Paradis artificiels,* p. 72.[25]   ‹G°,2›

Baudelaire on allegory (very important!), *Paradis artificiels,* p. 73.[26]   ‹G°,3›

"It has often happened to me to note certain trivial events passing before my eyes as showing a quite original aspect, in which I fondly hoped to discern the spirit of the period. 'This,' I would tell myself, 'was bound to happen today and could not have been other than it is. It is a sign of the times.' Well, nine times out of ten, I have come across the very same event with analogous circumstances in old memoirs or old history books." A. France, *Le Jardin d'Epicure,* p. 113.[27] ‹See S1,2.›   ‹G°,4›

The figure of the flâneur. He resembles the hashish eater, takes space up into himself like the latter. In hashish intoxication, the space starts winking at us: "What do you think may have gone on here?" And with the very same question, space accosts the flâneur. ‹See M1a,3.› In no other city can he answer it as precisely as he can here. For of no other city has more been written, and more is known here about certain stretches of the city's streets than elsewhere about the history of entire countries.   ‹G°,5›

Death and fashion. Rilke, the passage from the *Duineser Elegien*.[28]   ⟨G°,6⟩

Characteristic of Jugendstil are posters with full-length figures. So long as Jugendstil lasted, man refused to grant a place to things on the giant silver surface of the mirror, and claimed it for himself alone.   ⟨G°,7⟩

Definition of the "modern" as the new in the context of what has always already been there. ⟨See S1,4.⟩   ⟨G°,8⟩

"The clever Parisians . . . , in order to disseminate their fashions more easily, made use of an especially conspicuous reproduction of their new creations—namely tailors' dummies. . . . These dolls, which still enjoyed considerable importance in the seventeenth and eighteenth centuries, were given to little girls as playthings when their career as fashion figurines had ended." Karl Gröber, *Kinderspielzeug aus alter Zeit* (Berlin, 1927), pp. 31–32. ⟨See Z1,1.⟩   ⟨G°,9⟩

Perspective in the course of centuries. Baroque galleries. Scenography in the eighteenth century.   ⟨G°,10⟩

Play on words with "-rama" (on the model of "diorama") in Balzac at the beginning of *Père Goriot*. ⟨See Q1,6.⟩   ⟨G°,11⟩

Rückert: virgin forests in miniature.   ⟨G°,12⟩

To cultivate fields where, until now, only madness has reigned. Forge ahead with the whetted axe of reason, looking neither right nor left so as not to succumb to the horror that beckons from deep in the primeval forest. But every ground must at some point have been turned over by reason, must have been cleared of the undergrowth of delusion and myth. This is to be accomplished here for the terrain of the nineteenth century. ⟨See N1,4.⟩   ⟨G°,13⟩

Microcosmic journey which the dreamer makes through the regions of his own body. For he has this in common with the madman: the noises emanating from within the body, which for the salubrious individual converge in a steady surge of health and bring on sound sleep if they are not overlooked, dissociate for the one who dreams. Blood pressure, intestinal churn, heartbeat, muscle sensations become individually perceptible for him and demand the explanation which delusion or dream image holds ready. This sharpened receptivity is a feature of the dreaming collective, which settles into the arcades as into the insides of its own body. We must follow in its wake in order to expound the nineteenth century as its dream vision.[29] ⟨See K1,4.⟩   ⟨G°,14⟩

Rustling in the painted foliage under the vaulted ceilings of the Bibliothèque Nationale—produced by the many pages continually leafed through in the books here. ⟨See S3,3.⟩
          ⟨G°,15⟩

Heathscape, all remains ever new, ever the same (Kafka, *Der Prozeβ*). ⟨See S1,4.⟩
          ⟨G°,16⟩

Modernity, the time of hell. The punishments of hell are always the newest thing going in this domain. What is at issue is not that "the same thing happens over and over" (much less is it a question here of eternal return), but rather that the face of the world, the colossal head, precisely in what is newest never alters—that this "newest" remains, in every respect, the same. This constitutes the eternity of hell and the sadist's delight in innovation. To determine the totality of traits which define this "modernity" is to represent hell. ‹See S1,5.› ‹G°,17›

Re Jugendstil: Péladan. ‹See J18,6.› ‹G°,18›

Careful investigation into the relation between the optics of the myriorama and the time of the modern, of the newest. They are related, certainly, as the fundamental coordinates of this world. It is a world of strict discontinuity; what is always again new is not something old that remains, or something past that recurs, but one and the same crossed by countless intermittences. (Thus, the gambler lives in intermittence.) Intermittence means that every look in space meets with a new constellation. Intermittence the measure of time in film. And what follows from this: time of hell, and the chapter on origin in the book on Baroque.[30] ‹G°,19›

All true insight forms an eddy. To swim in time against the direction of the swirling stream. Just as in art, the decisive thing is: to brush nature against the grain. ‹G°,20›

Perspectival character of the crinoline, with its manifold flounces. In earlier times, at least six petticoats were worn underneath. ‹See E1,2.› ‹G°,21›

Wilde's Salome—Jugendstil—for the first time, the cigarette. Lethe flows in the ornaments of Jugendstil. ‹G°,22›

"The Gum-Resin Doll." Rilke's piece on dolls.[31] ‹G°,23›

Glass over oil paintings—only in the nineteenth century? ‹G°,24›

Physiology of beckoning. The nod of the gods (see introduction to Heinle's papers).[32] Waving from the mail coach, to the organic rhythm of the trotting horses. The senseless, desperate, cutting wave from the departing train. Waving has gone astray in the railroad station. On the other hand, the wave to strangers passing by on a moving train. This above all with children, who are waving to angels when they wave to the noiseless, unknown, never-returning people. (Of course, they are also saluting the passing train.) ‹G°,25›

Orpheus, Eurydice, Hermes at the train station. Orpheus the one who stays behind. Eurydice in the midst ‹?› of kisses. Hermes the stationmaster with his signal disk. ‹See L1,4.› This a neoclassical motif. With the neoclassicism of Cocteau, Stravinsky, Picasso, Chirico, and others, it has this in common: the transitional space of awakening in which we now are living is, wherever possible, traversed by gods. This traversal of space by gods is to be understood as lightning-like. And only certain of the gods may be thought of here. Above all,

Hermes, the masculine god. It is characteristic that, in neoclassicism, the muses who are so important for classical humanism mean nothing whatsoever. Moreover, there is much in Proust that belongs in the contexts of neoclassicism: names of gods. Also, the significance of homosexuality in Proust can be grasped from this perspective alone. More generally, the progressive leveling of the difference between masculine and feminine elements in love belongs in this space. But what is important above all in Proust is the stake which the entire work has in the supremely dialectical dividing point of life: waking up. Proust begins with a presentation of the space of someone awakening.—Where neoclassicism is basically lacking is in the fact that it builds an architecture for the gods passing by which denies the fundamental relations of their coming-to-appearance. (A bad, reactionary architecture.) ⟨G°,26⟩

It is one of the tacit suppositions of psychoanalysis that a clear-cut distinction between sleeping and waking has no value for the human being or for the empirical impressions of consciousness in general, but yields before an unending variety of conscious states determined, in each case, by the level of wakefulness of all psychic and corporeal centers. This thoroughly fluctuating situation of a consciousness each time manifoldly divided between waking and sleeping has to be transferred from the individual to the collective. Once this is done, it becomes clear that, for the nineteenth century, houses are the dream configurations of its deepest level of sleep. ⟨See K1,5.⟩ ⟨G°,27⟩

. . . .

All collective architecture of the nineteenth century constitutes the house of the dreaming collective. ⟨H°,1⟩

Railroad-station dreamworld of departure (sentimentality). ⟨H°,2⟩

Continuous assimilation of the various architectural capsules to forms of the dream house. ⟨H°,3⟩

Terrestrial atmosphere as undersea. ⟨H°,4⟩

Line of men around the woman to whom they are paying court. Train of suitors. ⟨H°,5⟩

Esprit de masque—when did this expression come into use? ⟨H°,6⟩

Collapse of the iron market-hall of Paris in 1842. ⟨H°,7⟩

Dennery, *Kaspar Hauser, Maréchal Ney, Le Naufrage de La Pérouse* (1859). *Le Tremblement de terre de la Martinique* (1843), *Bohémiens de Paris* (1843). ⟨See Y1a,6.⟩
⟨H°,8⟩

Louis-François Clairville, *Les Sept Châteaux du diable* (1844), *Les Pommes de terre malades* (1845), *Rothomago* (1862), *Cendrillon* (1866). ⟨See Y1a,6.⟩ ⟨H°,9⟩

Duveyrier. ‹See Y1a,6› ‹H°,10›

Dartois. ‹See Y1a,6.› ‹H°,11›

Specialty as a criterion for the fundamental ‹?› differentiation of items displayed according to the interests of buyers and collectors. Here is the historical-materialist key to genre painting. ‹See A2,6 and I2a,7.› ‹H°,12›

Wiertz the painter of the arcades: *The Premature Burial, The Suicide, The Burnt Child, Woman Reading a Novel, Hunger Madness and Crime, Thoughts and Visions of a Severed Head, The Lighthouse of Golgotha, One Second after Death, The Might of Man Knows No Bounds, The Last Cannon* (in this picture: airships and steam-powered dirigibles as the harbingers of achieved peace!). With Wiertz, "optical illusions." Under *The Triumph of Light:* "To be reproduced on an immense scale." A contemporary regrets that Wiertz was not given, say, "railway stations" to decorate. ‹H°,13›

To render the image of those salons where the gaze was enveloped in billowing drapery, where church doors opened within full-length mirrors and settees were gondolas in the eyes of those who sat there, on whom the gaslight from a vitreous globe shone down like the moon. ‹See I1,8.› ‹H°,14›

Important is the twofold character of the gates in Paris: border gates and triumphal arches. ‹See C2a,3.› ‹H°,15›

On the rhythm of today, which determines this work. Very characteristic is the opposition, in film, between the downright jerky rhythm of the image sequence, which satisfies the deep-seated need of this generation to see the "flow" of "development" disavowed, and the continuous musical accompaniment. To root out every trace of "development" from the image of history and to represent becoming—through the dialectical rupture between sensation and tradition—as a constellation in being: that is no less the tendency of this project. ‹H°,16›

Delimitation of the tendency of this project with respect to Aragon: whereas Aragon persists within the realm of dream, here the concern is to find the constellation of awakening. While in Aragon there remains an impressionistic element, namely, the "mythology" (and this impressionism must be held responsible for the many vacuous philosophemes in his book), here it is a question of the dissolution of "mythology" into the space of history. That, of course, can happen only through the awakening of a not-yet-conscious knowledge of what has been. ‹See N1,9.› ‹H°,17›

Interiors of our childhood days as laboratories for the demonstration of ghostly phenomena. Experimental relations. The forbidden book. Tempo of reading: two anxieties, on different levels, vie with one another. The bookcase with the oval panes from which it was taken. Vaccination with apparitions. The other prophylaxis: "optical illusions." ‹H°,18›

The writings of the Surrealists treat words like trade names and form texts that in reality act as prospectus for enterprises not yet off the ground. Nesting in the trade names are qualities that in earlier ages were looked for in the oldest words. ‹See G1a,2.›   ‹H°,19›

Daumier ‹?›, Grandville—Wiertz—   ‹H°,20›

. . . .

F. Th. Vischer, *Mode und Zynismus* (Stuttgart, 1879).   ‹I°,1›

Uprising of the anecdotes. The epochs, currents, cultures, movements always concern the bodily life in one and the same, identical fashion. There has never been an epoch that did not feel itself to be "modern" in the sense of most eccentric, and suppose itself to be standing directly before an abyss. A desperately clear consciousness of gathering crisis is something chronic in humanity. Every age unavoidably seems to itself a new age. But the "modernity" that concerns men with respect to the bodily is as varied in its meaning as the different aspects of one and the same kaleidoscope.—The constructions of history are comparable to instructions that commandeer the true life and confine it to barracks. On the other hand: the street insurgence of the anecdote. The anecdote brings things near to us spatially, lets them enter our life. It represents the strict antithesis to the sort of history which demands "empathy," which makes everything abstract. *"Empathy": this is what newspaper reading terminates in.* The true method of making things present is: to represent them in our space (not to represent ourselves in their space). Only anecdotes can do this for us. Thus represented, the things allow no mediating construction from out of "large contexts."—It is, in essence, the same with the aspect of great things from the past—the cathedral of Chartres, the temple of Paestum: to receive them into our space (not to feel empathy with their builders or their priests). We don't displace our being into theirs: they step into our life.—The same technique of nearness may be observed, calendrically, with regard to epochs. Let us imagine that a man dies on the very day he turns fifty, which is the day on which his son is born, to whom the same thing happens, and so on. The result would be: since the birth of Christ, not forty men have lived. Purpose of this fiction: to apply a standard to historical times that would be adequate and comprehensible to human life. This pathos of nearness, the hatred of the abstract configuration of human life in epochs, has animated the great skeptics. A good example is Anatole France. On the opposition between empathy and actualization: jubilees, Leopardi 13.[33] ‹See S1a,4; S1a,3; H2,3.›   ‹I°,2›

Benda reports on a German visitor's amazement when, sitting at a *table d'hôte* in Paris fourteen days after the storming of the Bastille, he heard no one speak of politics. Anatole France's anecdote about Pontius Pilate, who, in Rome, while washing his feet, no longer quite recalls the name of the crucified Jew.[34] ‹See S1,3.›   ‹I°,3›

Masks for orgies. Pompeian tiles. Gateway arches. Greaves. Gloves.   ‹I°,4›

Very important: bull's-eye windows in cabinet doors. But was there such a thing in France as well? ‹See I2a,4.›   ‹I°,5›

To make a truly palpable presentation of human beings—doesn't that mean bringing to light our memory of them?   ‹I°,6›

The flower as emblem of sin and its *via crucis* through the stations of the arcades, of fashion, of Redon's painting—which Marius and Ary Leblond have described by saying, "It is a cosmogony of flowers." ⟨I°,7⟩

More on fashion: what the child (and, through faint reminiscence, the man) discovers in the pleats of the old material to which it fastens while trailing at its mother's skirts. ⟨See K2,2.⟩ ⟨I°,8⟩

The arcades as milieu of Lautréamont. ⟨I°, 9⟩

. . . .

Various notes drawn from Brieger[35] and Vischer:
Around 1880, out-and-out conflict between the tendency to elongate the female figure and the rococo disposition to accentuate the lower body through multiplying underskirts. ⟨J°,1⟩

In 1876, the derrière disappears; but it comes back again. ⟨J°,2⟩

Floral forms in the drawings of cyclothymes, which for their part recall drawings made by mediums. ⟨J°,3⟩

Story of the child with its mother in a panorama. The panorama is presenting the Battle of Sedan. The child regrets that the sky is overcast. "That's what the weather is like in war," answers the mother. ⟨See D1,1.⟩ ⟨J°,4⟩

At the end of the 1860s, Alphonse Karr writes that no one knows how to make mirrors anymore. ⟨See R1,7.⟩ ⟨J°,5⟩

The rationalist theory of fashion appears very characteristically in Karr. It bears a resemblance to the religious theories of the Enlightenment. Karr thinks, for example, that long skirts come into fashion because certain women have an interest in concealing an unlovely foot. Or he denounces, as the origin of certain types of hats and certain hairstyles, the wish to compensate for thin hair. ⟨See B1,7.⟩ ⟨J°,6⟩

. . . .

Addendum to the remarks on Métro stations: it is owing to these stations that the names of places where Napoleon I gained a victory are transformed into gods of the underworld. ⟨K°,1⟩

The radical alterations to Paris under Louis Napoleon (Napoleon III), mainly along the axis running through the Place de la Concorde and the Hôtel de Ville, in ⟨Adolf⟩ Stahr, *Nach fünf Jahren* ⟨vol. 1 (Oldenburg, 1857)⟩, pp. 12–13.—Stahr, moreover, lived at that time on Leipziger Platz. ⟨See E1,6.⟩ ⟨K°,2⟩

The broad Boulevard de Strasbourg, which connects the Strasbourg *railway station* with the Boulevard Saint-Denis. ⟨K°,3⟩

Around the same time, the macadamization of the streets—which makes it possible, despite the heavy traffic, to carry on a conversation in front of a café without shouting in the other person's ear. ‹See M2,6.› ‹K°,4›

For the architectural image of Paris the war of 1870 was perhaps a blessing, seeing that Napoleon III had intended to alter whole sections of the city. Stahr thus writes, in 1857, that one had to make haste now to see the old Paris, "for the new ruler, it seems, has a mind to leave but little of it standing." ‹See E1,6.› ‹K°,5›

Ornament and boredom. ‹See D2a,2.› ‹K°,6›

Opposition of perspective and concrete, tactile nearness. ‹K°,7›

In the theory of collecting, the isolation, the segregation of every single object is very important. A totality—whose integral character always stands as far removed as possible from utility and, in preeminent cases, resides in a strictly defined, phenomenologically quite remarkable type of "completeness" (which is diametrically opposed to utility). ‹See H1a,2.› ‹K°,8›

Historical and dialectical relation between diorama and photography. ‹K°,9›

Important in regard to collecting: the fact that the object is detached from all original functions of its utility makes it the more decided in its meaning. It functions now as a true encyclopedia of all knowledge of the epoch, the landscape, the industry, and the owner from which it comes. ‹See H1a,2.› ‹K°,10›

There was pleorama (travels on water; *pleō,* "I go by ship"), navalorama, cosmorama, diaphanorama, picturesque views, pictorial voyages in a room, pictorial room-voyage, diaphanorama. ‹See Q1,1.› ‹K°,11›

Among the images: the sea of ice on the Grindelwald glacier in Switzerland, view of the harbor of Genoa from rooms of the Palazzo Doria, interior view of the cathedral of Brou in France, gallery of the Colosseum in Rome, Gothic cathedral in morning light. ‹K°,12›

The play on words with "-rama" (see Balzac, *Père Goriot*) in Germany as well. "Is ‹?› it ‹?› still in use?" ‹See Q1,6.› ‹K°,13›

Weather and boredom. The mere soporific, narcotizing effect which cosmic forces have on the ordinary man is attested in the relation of such a man to one of the highest manifestations of these forces: the weather. Comparison with the way Goethe (in his studies on meteorology)[36] managed to illuminate the weather.—On the weather which a fountain creates in its particular location. (Vestibule of Daguerre's diorama in Berlin.) Weather in the casinos. ‹See D1,3.› ‹K°,14›

A ballet whose principal scene takes place in the casino at Monte Carlo. Noise of rolling balls, of croupiers' rakes, of chips determining the character of the music. ‹K°,15›

Other names: optical belvedere. ⟨K°,16⟩

In the year in which Daguerre invented photography (1839) his diorama burned down. ⟨See Q2,5.⟩ ⟨K°,17⟩

It remains to be discovered what is meant when, in the dioramas, the variations in lighting which a day brings to a landscape take place in fifteen or thirty minutes. ⟨See Q1a,4.⟩ ⟨K°,18⟩

The Berlin diorama is closed on May 31, 1850; the pictures are sent, in part, to St. Petersburg. ⟨K°,19⟩

First London exhibition of 1851 brings together industries from around the world. Following this, the South Kensington museum is founded. Second world exhibition 1862 (in *London!*). With the Munich exhibition of 1875, the German Renaissance style came into fashion. ⟨See G2a,3.⟩ ⟨K°,20⟩

In 1903, in Paris, Emile Tardieu brought out a book entitled *L'Ennui,* in which all human activity is shown to be a vain attempt to escape from boredom, but in which, at the same time, what is, what was, and what will be appear as the inexhaustible nourishment of that feeling. In view of such a portrait, one might suppose the work to be some mighty classical monument of literature—a monument *aere perennius* erected by a Roman to the *taedium vitae.*[37] But it is only the self-satisfied, shabby scholarship of a new Homais, who aims to turn the most serious matters—asceticism and martyrdom included—into documents of his thoughtless, spiritually barren, petty-bourgeois discontent. ⟨See D1,5.⟩ ⟨K°,21⟩

To be mentioned in connection with the fashion in shawls: the characteristic and, properly speaking, sole decoration of the Biedermeier room "was afforded by the curtains, which—extremely refined and compounded preferably from several fabrics of different colors—were furnished by the upholsterer. For nearly a whole century afterward, interior decoration amounts, in theory, to providing instructions to upholsterers for the tasteful arrangement of draperies." Max von Boehn, *Die Mode im XIX Jahrhundert,* vol. 2 (Munich, 1907), p. 130. ⟨See E1,1.⟩ ⟨K°,22⟩

Mantlepiece clocks with genre scenes in bronze. Time looks out from the base. Double meaning of the term *temps* ⟨x⟩.[38] ⟨See D2a,3.⟩ ⟨K°,23⟩

Rue des Immeubles Industriels—how old is it? ⟨See P1a,5.⟩ ⟨K°,24⟩

"For our type of man, train stations are truly factories of dreams." Jacques de Lacretelle, "Le Rêveur parisien," *Nouvelle Revue française,* 1927. ⟨See L1,4.⟩ ⟨K°,25⟩

Within the frames of the pictures that hung on dining room walls, the advent of whiskey advertisements, of Van Houten Cocoa, of . . . is gradually heralded. Naturally, one can say that the bourgeois comfort of the dining room has survived longest in small cafés and other such places; but perhaps one can also say that the space of the café, within which every square meter and every hour is paid for much more precisely than in apartment houses, evolved out of the latter. Apartments laid out like cafés—in Frankfurt am Main, something very characteristic of that town. Attempt to formulate what there was inside. ⟨See G1,2.⟩ ⟨K°,26⟩

Empty, brightly lit streets as we enter cities at night. They surround us in fan-shaped formation, travel out and away from us like rays of a mandorla. And the glance into a room will always find a family at a meal or else occupied with some obscure niggling thing at a table under a hanging lamp, its white glass globe set into a metal frame. Such *eidōla* are the germ cells of Kafka's work. And this experience remains an inalienable possession of his generation, his only—and therefore ours, because only for it do the horror-furnishings of incipient high capitalism fill the scenes of its most luminous childhood experiences.—Unexpectedly, the street emerges here such as we never otherwise experience it, as way, as built-up thoroughfare. ⟨See I3,3.⟩ ⟨K°,27⟩

What, then, do we know of streetcorners, of curbstones, of the architecture of the pavement—we who have never felt the street, heat, filth, and the edges of the stones beneath our naked soles, and have never scrutinized the uneven placement of the wide paving stones with an eye toward bedding down on them.[39] ⟨See P1,10.⟩ ⟨K°,28⟩

. . . .

Mode und Zynismus[40]—from the copy in the ⟨Prussian⟩ National Library, one can see how often it was read in the past. ⟨L°,1⟩

Redon was on very friendly terms with the botanist Armand Clavaud. ⟨L°,2⟩

"I am not inspired by the supernatural. I do nothing but contemplate the external world; my works are true—whatever one may say." Odilon Redon. ⟨L°,3⟩

"A *cheval de renfort* ⟨spare horse⟩ which, at Notre Dame de Lorette, would make possible the hard climb up the Rue des Martyrs." ⟨See M1,1.⟩ ⟨L°,4⟩

André Mellerio, *Odilon Redon* (Paris, 1923). Refer to the plates on pp. 57 and 117. ⟨L°,5⟩

Say something about the method of composition itself: how everything one is thinking at a specific moment in time must at all costs be incorporated into the project then at hand. Assume that the intensity of the project is thereby attested, or that one's thoughts, from the very beginning, bear this project within them as their telos. So it is with the present portion of the work, which aims to characterize and to preserve the intervals of reflection, the distances lying between the most essential parts of this work, which are turned most intensively to the outside. ⟨See N1,3.⟩ ⟨L°,6⟩

The *Human Comedy* comprises a series of works which are not novels, in the ordinary sense of the term, but something like epic transcription of the tradition from the first decades of the Restoration. Entirely in the spirit of oral tradition is the interminability of this cycle, the antithesis to Flaubert's rigorous conception of form. No doubt about it—the nearer a work stands to the collective forms of expression of the epic, the more it tends, in varying and episodic development, to summon up the same recurrent circle of figures, according to the eternal paradigm of Greek legend. Balzac had secured this mythic constitution of his world through precise topographic contours. Paris is the breeding ground of his mythology, Paris with its two or three great bankers (like Nucingen), with its continually reappearing doctor, with its enterprising merchant (César Birotteau), with its four or five great courtesans, with its usurer (Gobseck), with its sundry soldiers and bankers. But above all—and we see this again and again—it is from the same streets and corners, the same little rooms and recesses, that the figures of this world step into the light. What else can this mean but that topography is the ground plan of every mythic space of tradition, ‹*Traditionsraum*›, and that it can become indeed its key—just as it became the key for Pausanias in Greece, and just as the history, layout, distribution of the Paris arcades are to become the key for the underworld of *this* century, into which Paris has sunk. ‹See C1,7.› ⟨L°,7⟩

Stahr reports that the premier cancan dancer at the Bal Mabille, a certain Chicard, dances under the surveillance of two police sergeants, whose sole responsibility is to keep an eye on the dancing of this one man. ‹See O4,2.› ⟨L°,8⟩

Portraits of famous cancan dancers on display in the arcades (Rigolette and Frichette). ‹See G1a,1.› ⟨L°,9⟩

On Redon: "Unconcerned with every quick and transitory effect, however se-ductive, he ultimately and above all wishes to give his flowers the very essence of life and, so to speak, a profound soul." André Mellerio, *Odilon Redon* (Paris, 1923), p. 163. ⟨L°,10⟩

Redon's plan to illustrate Pascal. ⟨L°,11⟩

Redon's nickname, after 1870, in the salon of Mme. de Rayssac: the prince of dream. ⟨L°,12⟩

Redon's flowers and the problem of ornamentation, especially in hashish. Flower world. ⟨L°,13⟩

"Rococo," at the time of the Restoration, has the meaning "antiquated." ⟨L°,14⟩

Chevet, at the Palais-Royal, "bestowed" dessert in exchange for a certain sum of money spent on the fruits and dainties consumed at dinner. ⟨L°,15⟩

Eugène Sue—a castle in Blogue ‹Bordes?›, a harem in which there were women of color. After his death, a legend that the Jesuits had poisoned him. ‹See I2,1.› ⟨L°,16⟩

The tin racks with artificial flowers which can be found at refreshment bars in railroad stations, and elsewhere, are vestiges of the floral arrangements that formerly encircled the ‹cashier›. ‹See T1,9.› ⟨L°,17⟩

The Palais-Royal is in its heyday under Louis XVIII and Charles X. ⟨L°,18⟩

Marquis de Sévry: director of the Salon des Etrangers. His Sunday dinners in Romainville. ⟨L°,19⟩

How Blücher gambled in Paris. (See Gronow, *Aus der grossen Welt* [Stuttgart, 1908], p. 56.) Blücher borrows 100,000 francs from the Bank of France. ‹See O1,3.›   ‹L°,20›

A bell sounds: departure for a journey ‹?› in the Kaiserpanorama. ‹See C3,5.›   ‹L°,21›

Concerning the mythological topography of Paris: the character given it by its gateways. Mystery of the boundary stone which, although located in the heart of the city, once marked the point at which it ended. Dialectic of the gate: from triumphal arch to traffic island. ‹See C2a,3.›   ‹L°,22›

When did industry take possession of the streetcorner? Architectural emblems of commerce: cigar shops have the corner, apothecaries the stairs . . . ‹See C2,4.›   ‹L°,23›

Panes of glass in which not the chandeliers but only the candles are reflected.
                                                                                            ‹L°,24›

Excursus on the Place du Maroc. Not only city and interior but city and open air can become entwined, and *this* intertwining can occur much more concretely. There is the Place du Maroc in Belleville: that desolate heap of stones with its rows of tenements became for me, when I happened on it one Sunday afternoon, not only a Moroccan desert but also, and at the same time, a monument of colonial imperialism; and topographic vision was entwined with allegorical meaning in this square, yet not for an instant did it lose its place in the heart of Belleville. But to awaken such a view is something ordinarily reserved for intoxicants. And in such cases, in fact, street names are like intoxicating substances that make our perception more stratified and richer in spaces than it is in everyday existence. The state into which these street names transport ‹us›, their *vertu évocatrice* (but this is saying too little, for what is decisive here is not the association but the interpenetration of images) ought also to be considered in connection with certain cycloid states. The patient who wanders the city at night for hours on end and forgets the way home is perhaps under the sway of this power. ‹See P1a,2.›   ‹L°,25›

Did the books of antiquity have prefaces?   ‹L°,26›

Bonhomie of revolutions *in the book on Baudelaire, E2.*[41]   ‹L°,27›

Arcades as temples of commodity capital. ‹See A2,2.›   ‹L°,28›

Passage des Panoramas, formerly Passage Mirès. ‹See A1a,2.›   ‹L°,29›

In the fields with which we are concerned here, knowledge comes only in lightning flashes. The text is the long roll of thunder that follows. ‹See N1,1.›   ‹L°,30›

The deepest enchantment of the collector: to put things under a spell, as though at a touch of the magic wand, so that all at once, while a last shudder runs over them, they are transfixed. All architecture becomes pedestal, socle, frame, antique memory room. It must not be assumed that the collector, the flâneur, would find anything strange in the *topos hyperouranios*—that place beyond the heavens where Plato locates the immutable archetypes of things. He loses himself, assuredly. But in return, he has the strength to raise himself up again to his full height—thanks to a project ‹?›. From out of the mists that envelop his sun, images arise like tables of the gods, islands in the Mediterranean. ‹See H1a,2.› ‹L°,31›

The need for sensation as king-size vice. To fasten on two of the seven deadly sins. Which ones? The prophecy that men would be blinded by the effects of too much electric light, and maddened by the rapidity of news reporting. ‹See B2,1.› ‹L°,32›

As introduction to the section on weather: Proust, the story of the little weather mannikin.[42] My joy whenever the morning sky is overcast. ‹L°,33›

Demoiselles: incendiaries disguised as women around 1830. ‹See O2,4.› ‹L°,34›

Around 1830 there was a newspaper in Paris with the name *Le Sylphe*. Find a ballet about newspapers. ‹See A2,9.› ‹L°,35›

‹xx› fasces, Phrygian caps, tripods. ‹L°,36›

‹xx› the "playing-card kings of stone" in Hackländer. ‹L°,37›

‹Carl› von Etzel—railroad constructions. ‹L°,38›.

. . . .

Various of the Berlin arcades should be mentioned: the colonnade in the vicinity of the Spittelmarkt (Leipziger Strasse), the colonnade in a quiet street of the clothiers' district, the arcade, the colonnade at the Halle Gate, the railing at the entry to private ways. Also to be kept in mind is the blue postcard of the Halle Gate, which showed all the windows lit up beneath the moon, illuminated by exactly the same light as came from the moon itself. Think further of the untouchable Sunday afternoon landscape that opens out somewhere at the end of a forlorn secluded street of "faded gentility"; in its nearness, the houses of this dubious neighborhood seem suddenly changed to palaces. ‹M°,1›

Magic of cast iron: "Hahblle was able then to convince himself that the ring around this planet was nothing other than a circular balcony on which the inhabitants of Saturn strolled in the evening to get a breath of fresh air." Grandville, *Un autre monde* ‹Paris, 1844›, p. 139. (Perhaps belongs also under the rubric "Hashish.") ‹See "The Ring of Saturn" and F1,7.› ‹M°,2›

Comparison of Hegel's *Phänomenologie* and the works of Grandville. Derivation of Grandville's work in terms of the philosophy of history. Important is the hypertrophy of the caption in this work. Also, the consideration of Lautréamont may be linked to Grandville. Grandville's works are a veritable cosmogony of fashion. Equally important, perhaps, a comparison between Hogarth and Grandville. A part of Grandville's work might be entitled "Fashion's Revenge on the Flowers." Grandville's works are the sibylline books of *publicité*. Everything that, with him, has its preliminary form as joke, or satire, attains its true unfolding as advertisement. ‹See B4,5 and G1,3.› ‹M°,3›

Superposition according to the rhythm of time. In relation to the cinema and to the "sensational" transmission of news. "Becoming" has for us—in regard to rhythm, according to our perception of time—no more claim as evidence. We decompose it dialectically into *sensation and tradition*.—Important to express these things analogously with respect to the biographical. ⟨M°,4⟩

Parallelism between this work and the *Trauerspiel* book. Common to both, the theme: theology of hell. Allegory⟨,⟩ advertisement, types: martyr, tyrant—whore, speculator. ⟨M°,5⟩

Hashish in the afternoon: shadows are a bridge over the river of light that is the street. ⟨M°,6⟩

Acquisition as decisive fact in collecting. ⟨M°,7⟩

Art of priming in reading and writing. Whoever can design at the most superficial level is the best author. ⟨M°,8⟩

Underground sightseeing in the sewers. Preferred route, Châtelet–Madeleine. ⟨See C2a,7.⟩ ⟨M°,9⟩

Passage du Caire erected in 1799 on the site of the garden of the Convent of the Daughters of God. ⟨See A3a,6.⟩ ⟨M°,10⟩

The best way, while dreaming, to catch the afternoon in the net of evening is to make plans. ⟨See M3a,2.⟩ ⟨M°,11⟩

Comparison of the human being with an instrument panel on which are thousands of electric bulbs. Some of them go out at one moment, some at another, ⟨and⟩ come back on again. ⟨M°,12⟩

The pathos of this work: there are no periods of decline. Attempt to see the nineteenth century just as positively as I tried to see the seventeenth, in the work on *Trauerspiel*. No belief in periods of decline. By the same token, every city is beautiful to me (from outside its borders), just as all talk of particular languages' having greater or lesser value is to me unacceptable. ⟨See N1,6.⟩ ⟨M°,13⟩

The dreaming collective knows no history. Events pass before it as always identical and always new. The sensation of the newest and most modern is, in fact, as much a dream formation of events as the "eternal return of the same." The perception of space that corresponds to this perception of time is superposition. Now, as these formations dissolve within the enlightened consciousness, political-theological categories arise to take their place. And it is only within the purview of these categories, which bring the flow of events to a standstill, that *history* forms, at the interior of this flow, as crystalline constellation.—The economic conditions under which a society exists not only determine that society in its material existence and ideological superstructure; they also come to expression. In the case of one who sleeps, an overfull stomach does not find its ideological superstructure in the contents of the dream—and it is exactly the same with the economic conditions of life for the collective. It interprets these conditions; it explains them. In the dream, they find their *expression;* in the awakening, their *interpretation.* ⟨See S2,1 and K2,5.⟩   ⟨M°,14⟩

The man who waits—a type opposed to the flâneur. The flâneur's apperception of historical time, set off against the time of one who waits. Not looking at his watch. Case of superposition while waiting: the image of the expected woman superimposes itself on that of some unknown woman. We are a dam holding back the time which, when the awaited woman appears, breaks upon us in a mighty torrent. "Tous les objets sont des maîtres" (Edouard Karyade).   ⟨M°,15⟩

The fact that we were children during this time belongs together with its objective image. It had to be this way in order to produce this generation. That is to say: we seek a teleological moment in the context of dreams. Which is the moment of waiting. The dream waits secretly for the awakening; the sleeper surrenders himself to death only provisionally, waits for the second when he will cunningly wrest himself from its clutches. So, too, the dreaming collective, whose children provide the happy occasion for its own awakening. ⟨See K1a,2.⟩   ⟨M°,16⟩

Look into the connection between colportage and pornography. Pornographic picture of Schiller—a litho: with one hand he gestures, picturesquely posed, into an ideal distance; with the other he masturbates. Pornographic parodies of Schiller. The ghostly and lascivious monk; the long train of specters and debauchery; in the *Mémoires des Saturnin,* by Mme. de Pompadour, the lewd procession of monks, with the abbot and his cousin at the head.   ⟨M°,17⟩

We are bored when we don't know what we are waiting for. And that we do know, or think we know, is nearly always the expression of our superficiality or inattention. Boredom is the threshold to great deeds. ⟨See D2,7.⟩   ⟨M°,18⟩

Clouded atmosphere, cloud-changeableness of things in the space of vision ⟨*Visionsraum*⟩.
⟨M°,19⟩

Task of childhood: to bring the new world into symbolic space ⟨*Symbolraum*⟩. The child, in fact, can do what the grownup absolutely cannot: remember the new once again. For us, locomotives already have symbolic character because we met with them in childhood. Our children, however, will find this in automobiles, of which we ourselves see only the new, elegant, modern, cheeky side. ⟨See K1a,3.⟩   ⟨M°,20⟩

⟨The⟩ glassed-in spot facing my seat at the Staatsbibliothek. Charmed circle inviolate, virgin terrain for the soles of figures I dreamed. ⟨See N1,7.⟩   ⟨M°,21⟩

"She was everybody's contemporary." ⟨Marcel Jouhandeau,⟩ *Prudence Hautechaume* ⟨Paris, 1927⟩, p. 129. ⟨See B2,5.⟩   ⟨M°,22⟩

⟨xxxxx⟩ world—and fashion.[43]   ⟨M°,23⟩

At the entrance to the skating rink, to the provincial pub, to the tennis court: *penates.* The hen that lays the golden praline-eggs, the machine that stamps our names on nameplates, slot machines, the mechanical fortuneteller—these guard the threshold. Oddly, such machines don't flourish in the city but rather are a component of excursion sites, of beer gardens in the suburbs. And when, in search of a little greenery, one heads for these places on a Sunday afternoon, one is turning as well to the mysterious thresholds. P.S.: Automatic scales—the modern *gnōthi seauton*.[44] Delphi. ‹See C3,4 and I1a,4.›

‹M°,24›

The gallery that leads to the Mothers is made of wood. Likewise, in the large-scale renovations of the urban scene, wood plays a constant though ever-shifting role: amid the modern traffic, it fashions, in the wooden palings and in the wooden planking over open substructions, the image of its rustic prehistory. ‹See C2a,4.› ‹M°,25›

Threshold and boundary must be very carefully distinguished. The *Schwelle* ‹threshold› is a *zone*. And indeed a zone of transition. Transformation, passage, flight ‹?› are in the word *schwellen* ‹swell›, and etymology ought not to overlook these senses. On the other hand, it is necessary to keep in mind the immediate tectonic framework that has brought the word to its current meaning. We have grown very poor in threshold experiences. "Falling asleep" is perhaps the only such experience that remains to us. But also the ebb and flow of conversation and the sexual permutations of love, like the world of figures in the dream, rise up over the threshold.—Out of the field of experience proper to the threshold evolved the gateway that transforms whoever passes under its arch. The Roman victory arch makes the returning general a conquering hero. Absurdity of the relief on the inner wall of the arch—a classicist misunderstanding. ‹See O2a,1 and C2a,3.›

‹M°,26›

. . . .

J. W. Samson, *Die Frauenmode der Gegenwart* (Berlin, 1927) (M1—marks and images‹?›).

‹N°,1›

Flower market: "There—without recurring to the efforts / Of the splendid architecture / To conceal from us its riches— / Flora in her *temple de verdure*." ‹N°,2›

Description ‹?› from Ferragus.[45] ‹N°,3›

Heinrich Mann, *Kaiserin Eugénie*.[46] ‹N°,4›

The Trojan horse—as snow ‹?›, as the imminent awakening steals into the dream. ‹See K2,4.›

‹N°,5›

Dusk: the hour when great works are inspired *(inspiration littéraire)*. According to Daudet, however, the hour when mistakes are made in reading ‹?›. ‹N°,6›.

. . . .

The indestructibility of the highest life in all things. Against the prognosticators of decline. One can make a film of Goethe's *Faust*. And yes, isn't it an outrage, and isn't there a world of difference between the poem *Faust* and the film *Faust?* Certainly, there is. But again, isn't there a whole world of difference between a bad film of *Faust* and a good one? What matter in culture are not the great contrasts but the nuances. ‹It is from them that› the world ‹is› always ‹born anew›. ‹See N1a,4.›   ‹O°,1›

Pedagogic side of this undertaking: "To educate the image-making medium within us, raising it to a stereoscopic and dimensional seeing into the depths of historical shadows." The words are ‹Rudolf› Borchardt's in *Epilegomena zu Dante,* vol. 1 (Berlin, 1923), pp. 56–57. ‹See N1,8.›   ‹O°,2›

From the start, to keep this thought in view and to weigh its constructive value: the refuse- and decay-phenomena as precursors, in some degree mirages, of the great syntheses that follow. These new synthetic realities are to be looked for everywhere: advertising, *film reality,* and so on. ‹See Y1,4.›   ‹O°,3›

Of vital interest to recognize, at a particular point of development, currents of thought at the crossroads—namely, the new view on the historical world at the point where a decision is forthcoming as to its reactionary or revolutionary application. In this sense, one and the same phenomenon is at work in the Surrealists and in Heidegger. ‹See S1,6.›
                    ‹O°,4›

It is said that the dialectical method consists in doing justice, at each moment, to the concrete historical situation of its object. But that is not enough. For it is just as much a matter of doing justice to the concrete historical situation of the *interest* taken in the object. And *this* situation is always so constituted as to be itself preformed in that object; above all, however, the object is felt to be concretized in this situation itself and upraised from its former being into the higher concretion of now-being ‹*Jetztsein*›. In what way *this* now-being (which is something other than the now-being of the present time ‹*Jetztzeit*›) already signifies, in itself, a higher concretion—this question, of course, can be entertained by the dialectical method only within the purview of a philosophy of history that at all points has overcome the ideology of progress. In regard to such a philosophy, one could speak of an increasing concentration (integration) of reality, such that everything past (in its time) can acquire a higher grade of actuality than it had in the moment of its existing. How it adapts to this, its own higher actuality, is something determined and brought to pass by the image as which and in which it is comprehended.—To treat the past (better: what has been) in accordance with a method that is no longer historical but political. To make political categories into theoretical categories, insofar as one dared to apply them only in the sense of praxis, because only to the present—that is the task. The dialectical penetration and actualization of former contexts puts the truth of all present action to the test. This means, however: the explosive materials latent in fashion (which *always* refers back to something past) have to be ignited. ‹See K2,3.›   ‹O°,5›

On the figure of the collector. One may start from the fact that the true collector detaches the object from its functional relations. But that is hardly an exhaustive description of this remarkable mode of behavior. For isn't this the foundation (to speak with Kant and Schopenhauer) of that "disinterested" contemplation by virtue of which the collector attains to an unequaled view of the object—a view which takes in more, and other, than that of the profane owner and which we would do best to compare to the gaze of the great physiognomist? But how his eye comes to rest on the object is a matter elucidated much more sharply through ‹another› consideration. ‹See H2,7; H2a,1.›   ‹O°,6›

It must be kept in mind that, for the collector, the world is present, and indeed ordered, in each of his objects. Ordered, however, according to a surprising and, for the profane understanding, incomprehensible connection. This connection stands to the customary ordering and schematization of things something as their arrangement in the dictionary stands to a natural arrangement. We need only recall what importance a particular collector attaches not only to his object but also to its entire past, whether this concerns the origin and objective characteristics of the thing or the details of its ostensibly external history: previous owners, price of purchase, current value, and so on. All of these—the "objective" data together with the other—come together, for the true collector, in every single one of his possessions, to form a whole magic encyclopedia, a world order, whose outline is the *fate* of his object. Here, therefore, within this circumscribed field, we can understand how great physiognomists (and collectors are physiognomists of the world of things) become interpreters of fate. It suffices to observe just one collector as he handles the items in his showcase. No sooner does he hold them in his hands than he appears inspired by them and seems to look through them into their distance, like an augur. (It would be interesting to situate the bibliophile as the only type of collector who has not unconditionally withdrawn his treasures from a functional context.) ⟨See H2,7; H2a,1.⟩

⟨O°,7⟩

Attempt to develop Giedion's thesis. "In the nineteenth century," he writes, "construction plays the role of the subconscious."[47] Wouldn't it be better to say "the role of bodily processes"—around which "artistic" architectures gather, like dreams around the framework of physiological processes? ⟨See K1a,7.⟩ ⟨O°,8⟩

Bear in mind that commentary on a reality (such as we are writing here) calls for a method completely different from that required by commentary on a text. In the one case, the scientific mainstay is theology; in the other case, philology. ⟨See N2,1.⟩ ⟨O°,9⟩

Interpenetration as principle in film, in new architecture, in colportage. ⟨O°,10⟩

Fashion inheres in the darkness of the lived moment, but in the collective darkness.— Fashion and architecture (in the nineteenth century) belong to the dream consciousness of the collective. We must look into how it awakes. For example, in advertising. Would awakening be the synthesis derived from the thesis of dream consciousness and the antithesis of waking consciousness? ⟨See K2a,4.⟩ ⟨O°,11⟩

The problem of space (hashish, myriorama) treated under the rubric "Flânerie." The problem of time (intermittences) treated under the rubric "Roulette."

⟨O°,12⟩

Interlacing of the history of the arcades with the whole presentation. ⟨O°,13⟩

Reasons for the decline of the arcades: widened sidewalks, electric light, ban on prostitution, culture of the open air. ⟨See C2a,12.⟩ ⟨O°,14⟩

To be developed: motif of boredom amid half-finished material. ⟨O°,15⟩

The "ultimate aims" of socialism hardly ever so clear as in the case of Wiertz. The basis here in vulgar materialism. ⟨O°,16⟩

The grandiose mechanical-materialistic divinations of Wiertz have to be seen in the context of the subjects of his painting—and, to be sure, not only the ideal utopian subjects but those allied to colportage and the ghastly. ⟨O°,17⟩

Advertisement by Wiertz: "Monsieur Wiertz requires a servant skilled in the painting of medieval accessories to do all his research work, etcetera, etcetera, such as ⟨x⟩, etcetera." A. J. Wiertz, *Oeuvres littéraires* (Paris, 1870), p. 235.
⟨O°,18⟩

Of particular importance, the great "legend" with which Wiertz has accompanied his *Pensées et visions d'une tête coupée* (Thoughts and Visions of a Severed Head). The first thing that strikes one about this magnetopathic *expérience* is the grandiose sleight of hand which the consciousness executes in death. "What a singular thing! The head is here under the scaffold, and it believes that it still exists above, forming part of the body, and continuing to wait for the blow that will separate it from the trunk." A. J. Wiertz, *Oeuvres littéraires* (Paris, 1870), p. 492. (At work here in Wiertz is the same inspiration that animates the unforgettable short story by Ambrose Bierce.[48] The rebel who is hanged from a bridge over the river.) ⟨See K2a,2.⟩ ⟨O°,19⟩

Does fashion die because it can no longer keep up the tempo—at least in certain fields? While, on the other hand, there are fields in which it can follow the tempo and even dictate it? ⟨See B4,4.⟩ ⟨O°,20⟩

Title of a painting by Wiertz: *Les Choses du présent devant les hommes de l'avenir* ⟨The Things of the Present on Display before the Men of the Future⟩. Noteworthy is the tendency of this painter toward allegory. For example, in the catalogue description of the picture *Une Second après la mort,* we read: "Consider the idea of a book that has fallen from one's hands, and on its cover these words: *Lofty Achievements of Humanity.*" *Oeuvres littéraires,* p. 496. Figure of "civilization" and many other allegories in *Le Dernier Canon.* ⟨O°,21⟩

Painting by Wiertz: *Le Soufflet d'une dame belge.* "This painting was executed with the intention of proving the necessity of having women trained in the use of firearms. It was Monsieur Wiertz, as we know, who had the idea of setting up a special rifle range for ladies and offering, as prize in the competition, a portrait of the victorious heroine." *Oeuvres littéraires,* p. 501 (catalogue of works, edited by the painter himself). ⟨O°,22⟩

Passage on the museum in Proust.[49] ⟨O°,23⟩

Boredom of the ceremonial scenes depicted in historical paintings, and boredom in general. Boredom and museum. Boredom and battle scenes. ⟨See D2a,8.⟩ ⟨O°,24⟩

Excursus on the battle scene! ⟨O°,25⟩

To the complex of boredom and waiting (a metaphysics of waiting is indispensable) one could no doubt assimilate, in a particular context, the metaphysics of doubt. In an allegory

of Schiller's we read of "the hesitant wing of the butterfly."[50] This points to that association of wingedness with the feeling of indecision which is so characteristic of hashish
intoxication. ‹See M4a,1.›   ‹O°,26›

Hofmannsthal's plan for *The Novice* and for *The Fortuneteller*.[51]   ‹O°,27›

Polemic against iron rails, in the 1830s. A. Gordon, *A Treatise in Elementary Locomotion*,
wanted to have the "steam carriage" run on lanes of granite. ‹See F3,4.›   ‹O°,28›

Great collectors. Pachinger, Wolfskehl's friend, who has put together a collection that, in
its array of proscribed and damaged objects, rivals the Figdor collection in Vienna. On the
Stachus, he suddenly stoops to pick up something he has been seeking for weeks: a
misprinted streetcar ticket that was in circulation for only one hour. Gratz in Wühlgarten.
The family in which everyone collects something, for example matchboxes. Pachinger
hardly knows any more how things stand in the world; explains to his visitors—alongside
the most antique implements—the use of pocket handkerchiefs, distorting mirrors, and
the like. "Beautiful foundation for a collection." Hoerschelmann. A German in Paris who
collects bad (only bad!) art. ‹See H2a,2.›   ‹O°,29›

Waxworks: mixture of the ephemeral and the fashionable. Woman fastening her garter.
Nadja ‹Paris, 1928›, p. ‹200›.[52] ‹See B3,4 and E2a,2.›   ‹O°,30›

Aporias of town planning (beauty of old districts), of museums, of street names, of
interiors. ‹See I2a,6.›   ‹O°,31›

One can characterize the problem of the form of the new art straight on: When and how
will the worlds of form which, without our having expected it, have arisen, for example,
in mechanics, or in machine construction, and subjugated us—when will they make
whatever nature they contain into primal history? When will we reach a state of society in
‹which these forms, or› those arising from them, ‹reveal› themselves to us as natural
forms? ‹See K3a,2.›   ‹O°,32›

On Veuillot's "Paris is musty and close." Fashions and the complete antithesis to the
open-air world of today. The "glaucous gleam" under the petticoats, of which Aragon
speaks. The corset as the torso's arcade. What today is de rigueur among the lowest class
of prostitutes—not to undress—may once have been the height of refinement. *Hallmark of
yesterday's fashions: to intimate a body that never knows full nakedness.* ‹See E2,2; O1a,3;
B3,1.›   ‹O°,33›

On the *renfermé*, much also in Proust. Above all, the retreat in the Bois.[53]
                                                                                    ‹O°,34›

Rue Laferriére formerly an arcade. See ‹Paul› Léautaud, *Le Petit ami*.   ‹O°,35›

Method of this project: literary montage. I needn't *say* anything. Merely show. I shall
appropriate no ingenious formulations, purloin no valuables. But the rags, the refuse—
these I will not describe but put on display. ‹See N1a,8.›   ‹O°,36›

Notes on montage in my journal. Perhaps, in this same context, there should be some indication of the intimate connection that ‹exists› between the intention making for nearest nearness and the intensive utilization of refuse—a connection in fact exhibited in montage.   ‹O°,37›

Fetish character of the commodity to be conveyed through the example of prostitution.   ‹O°,38›

On the interlacing of street and domestic interior: house numbers for the latter become cherished family photos.   ‹O°,39›

Utter ambiguity of the arcades: street and house.   ‹O°,40›

When and, above all, how did the name "Winter Garden" come to designate a variety theater? (Compare *Cirque d'hiver*.)   ‹O°,41›

Traffic at the stage of myth. Industry at the stage of myth. (Railroad stations and early factories.)   ‹O°,42›

Tedium of the railway journey. Stories of conductors. Here, Unold on Proust, *Frankfurter Zeitung,* 1926 or 1927.   ‹O°,43›

Relation of myth and topography. Aragon and Pausanias. (Bring in Balzac here as well.) ‹See C1,7.›   ‹O°,44›

Boredom and: the commodity's wait to be sold.   ‹O°,45›

Motif of dream time: atmosphere of aquariums. Water slackening resistance.
                              ‹O°,46›

Reasons for the decline of the arcades: widened sidewalks, electric light, ban on prostitution, cult of the open air. ‹See C2a,12.›   ‹O°,47›

On the doll motif: "You have no idea how repulsive these automatons and dolls can become, and how one breathes at last on encountering a full-blooded being in this society." Paul Lindau, *Der Abend* (Berlin, 1896), p. 17. ‹See Z1,5.›   ‹O°,48›

The modish green and red of recreation spots today, which corresponds obscurely—as a fashion phenomenon—to the knowledge we are trying to unfold here, has a capital interpretation in a passage by Bloch, where he speaks of "the green-papered chamber of memory with curtains red as sunset." *Geist der Utopie* (Munich and Leipzig, 1918), p. 351.   ‹O°,49›

The theory of not-yet-conscious knowing may be linked with the theory of forgetting (notes on *Der Blonde Eckbert*)[54] and applied to the collective in its various epochs. What Proust, as an individual, directly experienced ‹*erlebte*› in the phenomenon of remembrance, we have to experience ‹*erfahren*› indirectly (with regard to the nineteenth century) as "current," "fashion," "tendency"—in punishment, if you will, for the sluggishness which keeps us from taking it up ourselves. ‹See K2a,3.›   ‹O°,50›

These gateways are also thresholds. No stone step serves to mark them. But this marking is accomplished by the expectant posture of the handful of people. Tightly measured paces reflect the fact, altogether unknowingly, that a ‹decision lies› ahead. Citation ‹from Aragon› on people waiting in front of arcades.[55] ‹See C3,6.›   ‹O°,51›

This truly remarkable theory in Dacqué:[56] that man is a germ. (There are germinal forms in nature that present themselves as fully grown embryos, but without being trans-formed.) It is, accordingly, in the early stages of development that the human being—and the human-like animal species, anthropoid apes—would have their most proper, most genuinely "human" form: in the fully developed embryo of the human and the chimpan-zee (that is, in the fully developed human and chimpanzee), the properly animal re-emerges. But ‹broken off›   ‹O°,52›

Study of the theoreticians of Jugendstil is imperative. Following indication in A. G. Meyer, *Eisenbauten* (Esslingen, 1907): "Those endowed with an especially fine artistic conscience have hurled down, from the altar of art, curse after curse on the building engineers. It suffices to mention Ruskin" (p. 3). In the context of Jugenstil: Péladan. ‹See F5,1.›
                ‹O°,53›

"It is becoming more and more difficult to be revolutionary on both the spiritual plane and the social plane at once." Emmanuel Berl, "Premier pamphlet," *Europe*, 75 (1929), p. 40.   ‹O°,54›

Floral art and genre painting.   ‹O°,55›

We can speak of two directions in this work: one which goes from the past into the present and shows the arcades, and all the rest, as precursors, and one which goes from the present into the past so as to have the revolutionary potential of these "precursors" explode in the present. And this direction comprehends as well the spellbound elegiac consideration of the recent past, in the form of its revolutionary explosion.   ‹O°,56›

Shadow of myth which this agitated age casts onto the past, as myth-bearing Hellas (*mythotokos*) once did.   ‹O°,57›

Léon Daudet narrates his life topographically. *Paris vécu.*   ‹O°,58›

Passage and *procès*. Mirès.   ‹O°,59›

Movement of the life of fashion: change *a little*.   ‹O°,60›

In jazz, noise is emancipated. Jazz appears at a moment when, increasingly, noise is eliminated from the process of production, of traffic, and of commerce. Like-wise in radio.   ‹O°,61›

From *Der Bazar,* illustrated ladies' magazine published in Berlin (1857–): pearl embroidery for boxes of Communion wafers or gambling chips, men's shoes, glove box, small bolster, penwipers, needlecase, pincushion, slippers. *Christmas items:* lamp stands, game bags, bell pulls, firescreens, folder for musical scores, basket for knives, canister for wax tapers, pudding cloths, gambling chips.

⟨O°,62⟩

The type of the flâneur gains in distinctness when one thinks, for a moment, of the good conscience that must have belonged to the type of Saint-Simon's "industrial," who bore this title only as possessor of capital.　　⟨O°,63⟩

Notable difference between Saint-Simon and Marx. The former conceives the class of exploited (the producers) as broadly as possible, reckoning among them even the entrepreneur because he pays interest to his creditors. Marx, on the other hand, includes all those who in any way exploit another—even though they themselves may be victims of exploitation—among the bourgeoisie. ⟨See U4,2.⟩　　⟨O°,64⟩

Exacerbation of class divisions: the social order as a ladder along which the distance from rung to rung grows greater by the year. Infinite number of gradations between wealth and poverty in the France of the previous century.

⟨O°,65⟩

Byzantine mysticism at the Ecole Polytechnique. See Pinet, "L'Ecole polytechnique et les Saint-Simoniens," *Revue de Paris* (1894).　　⟨O°,66⟩

Didn't Marx teach that the bourgeoisie, as class, can never arrive at a perfectly clear awareness of itself? And if this is the case, isn't one justified in annexing to Marx's thesis the idea of the dream collective (that is, the bourgeois collective)? ⟨See S2,1.⟩　⟨O°,67⟩

Wouldn't it be possible, furthermore, to show how the whole set of issues with which this project is concerned is illuminated in the process of the proletariat's becoming conscious of itself?　　⟨O°,68⟩

The first tremors of awakening serve to deepen sleep—(tremors of awakening). ⟨See K1a,9.⟩　　⟨O°,69⟩

The *Comptes fantastiques d'Haussmann* ⟨by Jules Ferry (1868)⟩ first appeared as a series of articles in *Les Temps.*　　⟨O°,70⟩

Good formulation by Bloch apropos of *The Arcades Project:* history displays its Scotland Yard badge. That was in the context of a conversation in which I was describing how this work—comparable to the method of atomic fission, which liberates the enormous energies bound up within the atom—is supposed to liberate the enormous energies of history that are slumbering in the "once upon a time" of classic historical narrative. The history that was bent on showing things "as they really and truly were" was the strongest narcotic of the nineteenth century. ⟨See N3,4.⟩　　⟨O°,71⟩

Concretion extinguishes thought; abstraction kindles it. Every antithesis is abstract; every synthesis, concrete. (Synthesis extinguishes thought.) ⟨O°,72⟩

Formula: construction out of facts. Construction with the complete elimination of theory. What only Goethe in his morphological writings has attempted.
⟨O°,73⟩

On gambling. There is a certain structure of fate that can be recognized only in money, and a certain structure of money that can be recognized only in fate. ⟨See O3,6.⟩
⟨O°,74⟩

The arcade as temple of Aesculapius. Medicinal spring. The course of a cure. Arcades (as resort spas) in ravines. At Schuls-Tarasp, at Ragaz. The gorge as landscape ideal in our parents' day. ⟨See L3,1.⟩ As with the impact of very distant memories, the sense of smell is awakened. To me, as I stood before a shop window in Saint-Moritz and looked on mother-of-pearl pocketknives as "memories," it was as though at that moment I could smell them. ⟨O°,75⟩

The things sold in the arcades are souvenirs ⟨*Andenken*⟩. The "souvenir" is the form of the commodity in the arcades. One always buys only mementos of the commodity and of the arcade. Rise of the souvenir industry. As the manufacturer knows it. The custom-house officer of industry. ⟨See J53,1.⟩ ⟨O°,76⟩

How visual memories emerge transformed after long years. The pocketknife that came to me as I chanced upon one in a shop window in Saint-Moritz (with the name of the place inscribed between sprigs of mother-of-pearl edelweiss) had a taste and odor. ⟨O°,77⟩

Rather than pass the time, one must invite it in. To pass the time (to kill time, expel it): to be drained. Type: gambler, time spills from his every pore.—To store time like a battery: the type, flâneur. Finally, the synthetic type (takes in the energy "time" and passes it on in altered form): he who waits. ⟨See D3,4.⟩ ⟨O°,78⟩

"Primal history of the nineteenth century"—this would be of no interest if it were understood to mean that forms of primal history are to be recovered among the inventory of the nineteenth century. Only where the nineteenth century would be presented as originary form of primal history—as a form, that is to say, in which the *whole* of primal history so renews itself that certain of its older traits would be recognized only as precursors of these recent ones—only there does this concept of a primal history of the nineteenth century have meaning. ⟨See N3a,2.⟩ ⟨O°,79⟩

All categories of the philosophy of history must here be driven to the point of indifference. No historical category without its natural substance, no natural category without its historical filtration. ⟨O°,80⟩

Historical knowledge of the truth is possible only as overcoming the illusory appearance ⟨*Aufhebung des Scheins*⟩. Yet this overcoming should not signify sublimation, actualization of the object but rather assume, for its part, the configuration of a *rapid* image. The small quick figure in contrast to scientific complacency. This configuration of a rapid image goes together with the recognition of the "now" in things.[57] But not the future. Surrealist mien of things in the now; philistine mien in the future. The illusion overcome here is that an earlier time is in the now. In truth: the now ‹is› the inmost image of what has been. ‹O°,81›

. . . .

For the flower section. Fashion journals of the period contained instructions for preserving bouquets. ‹See I4,2.› ‹P°,1›

The mania for chamber and box. Everything came in cases, was covered and enclosed. Cases for watches, for slippers, for thermometers—all with embroidery on fine canvas. ‹See I4,4.› ‹P°,2›

Analysis of dwelling. The difficulty here is that on the one hand, in dwelling, the age-old—perhaps eternal—has to be recognized: image of that abode of the human being in the maternal womb. And then, on the other hand, this motif of primal history notwithstanding, we must understand dwelling in its most extreme form as a condition of nineteenth-century existence, one with which we have begun to break. The original form of all dwelling is existence not in the house but in the shell. The difference between the two: ‹the latter› bears quite visibly the impression of its occupant. In the most extreme instance, the dwelling becomes a shell. The nineteenth century, like no other century, was addicted to dwelling. It conceived the residence as the receptacle for the person, and it encased him, with all his appurtenances, so deeply in the dwelling's interior that one might be reminded of the inside of a compass case, where the instrument with all its accessories lies embedded in deep, usually violet folds of velvet. It is scarcely possible nowadays to think of all the things for which the nineteenth century invented étuis: pocket watches, slippers, egg cups, thermometers, playing cards. What didn't it provide with jackets, carpets, wrappers! The twentieth century, with its porosity and transparency, its tendency toward the well-lit and airy, has nullified dwelling in the old sense. Jumping-off point of things ‹?›, like the "homes for human beings" in Ibsen's *Master Builder*. Not by chance a drama rooted in Jugendstil, which itself unsettled the world of the shell in a radical way. Today this world is highly precarious. Dwelling is diminished: for the living, through hotel rooms; for the dead, through the crematorium. ‹See I4,4.› ‹P°,3›

Dialectics at a standstill—this is the quintessence of the method. ‹P°,4›

"To dwell" as a transitive verb. For example, "indwelt spaces"—this gives a sense of the hidden frenetic topicality of dwelling. This topicality consists in fashioning a shell. ‹See I4,5.› ‹P°,5›

Kitsch. Its economic analysis. In what way is manifest here: the overproduction of commodities; the bad conscience of producers. ‹P°,6›

Fashion. A sort of race for first place in the social creation. The running begins anew at every instant. Contrast between fashion and uniform. ‹P°,7›

Thomasius, *Vom Recht des Schlafs und der Träume* (Halle, 1723). ⟨P°,8⟩

Simmel, *Philosophische Kultur* ⟨Leipzig, 1911⟩ (fashion). ⟨P°, 9⟩

. . . .

Am I the one who is called W.B.? Or am I simply called W.B.? This, in fact, is the question which leads into the mystery of a person's name, and it is very aptly formulated in a posthumous fragment by Hermann Ungar: "Does the name attach to us, or are we attached to a name?" H. Ungar, "Fragment," in *Das Stichwort,* Newspaper of the Theater on Schiffbauer Damm (December 1929), p. 4. ⟨Q°,1⟩

Waxworks in Lisbon, in Joachim Nettelbeck's autobiography. ⟨Q°,2⟩

Anatole France, the series of novels with M. Bergeret. ⟨Q°,3⟩

Das Kapital, vol. 1, original edition, p. 40; vol. 3, pp. 1–200, especially 150ff.[58] Tendency of the profit rate and the average profit rate to fall. ⟨Q°,4⟩

Kafka, "Der Landarzt" ⟨A Country Doctor⟩ (a dream). ⟨Q°,5⟩

In *The Arcades Project,* contemplation must be put on trial. But it should defend itself brilliantly and justify itself. ⟨Q°,6⟩

Happiness of the collector, happiness of the solitary: tête-à-tête with things. Is not this the felicity that suffuses our memories—that in them we are alone with particular things, which range about us in their silence, and that even the people who haunt our thoughts then partake in this steadfast, confederate silence of things. The collector "stills" his fate. And that means he disappears in the world of memory. ⟨Q°,7⟩

E. T. A. Hoffmann, "Die Automate" ⟨Automata⟩ (*Serapionsbrüder* ⟨The Serapion Brethren, 1819–1821⟩, vol. 2). ⟨Q°,8⟩

Hoffmann as type of the flâneur. "Des Vetters Eckfenster" ⟨My Cousin's Corner Window⟩ the testament of the flâneur. Thus Hoffmann's great success in France. In the biographical notes to the five-volume collection of his later writings, we read: "Hoffmann was never really a friend of the great outdoors. What mattered to him more than anything else was the human being—communication with, observations about, the simple sight of, human beings. Whenever he went for a walk in summer, which in good weather happened every day toward evening, he always made for those public places where he would run into people. On the way, there was scarcely a tavern or pastry shop where he would not look in to see whether anyone—and if so, who—might be there." ⟨See M4a,2.⟩
⟨Q°,9⟩

Armature of physiognomic studies: the flâneur, the collector, the forger, the gambler.
⟨Q°,10⟩

Hans Kistemaecker, "Die Kleidung der Frau: Ein erotisches Problem" ‹Women's Clothing, A Problem in Erotics›, *Zürcher Diskuszionen,* vol. 8 (1898). The author probably Panizza. ‹Q°,11›

Louis Schneider, *Offenbach* (Paris, 1923).[59] ‹Q°,12›

Le Guide historique et anecdotique de Paris (Paris, Editions Argo).[60] ‹Q°,13›

We can be sure that the art of an earlier period—in its sociological sphere of influence, in the hierarchies that were founded on it, in the manner of its formation—was much more closely related to what today is fashion than to what today is known as art. Fashion: aristocratic-esoteric origin of the most widely distributed articles of use. ‹Q°,14›

Misunderstanding as constitutive element in the development of fashion. No sooner is the new fashion at a slight remove from its origin and point of departure than it is turned about and misunderstood. ‹Q°,15›

Metternich, *Denkwürdigkeiten* (Munich, 1921).[61] ‹Q°,16›

Hans von Veltheim, *Héliogabale, ou Biographie du XIXᵉ siècle de la France* (Braunschweig, 1843). ‹Q°,17›

Grässe and Jännicke, *Kunstgewerbliche Altertümer und Kuriositäten* (Berlin, 1909). ‹Q°,18›

On *La Muette de Portici.*[62] First performance 1828. An undulating musical extravaganza, an opera made of draperies, which rise and subside over the words. Very evident the success which this musical must have had at a time when *la draperie* was beginning its triumphal procession (at first, in fashion, as Turkish shawls). The *novarum rerum cupidus*[63] of the revolutionary is understood by this public to mean interest in fancy goods. With good reason it was shown a revolt whose premier task is to protect the king from its own effect. Revolution as drapery covering a slight reshuffle in the ruling circles, precisely what occurred in 1830. ‹See B4,3.› ‹Q°,19›

Henri Sée, *Französische Wirtschaftsgeschichte.*[64] ‹Q°,20›

On the dialectical image. In it lies time. Already with Hegel, time enters into dialectic. But the Hegelian dialectic knows time solely as the properly historical, if not psychological, time of thinking. The time differential ‹*Zeitdifferential*› in which alone the dialectical image is real is still unknown to him. Attempt to show this with regard to fashion. Real time enters the dialectical image not in natural magnitude—let alone psychologically—but in its smallest gestalt. ‹See N1,2.›— All in all, the temporal momentum ‹*das Zeitmoment*› in the dialectical image can be determined only through confrontation with another concept. This concept is the "now of recognizability" ‹*Jetzt der Erkennbarkeit*›. ‹Q°,21›

Fashion is intention that ignites; knowledge, intention that extinguishes.

⟨Q°,22⟩

What is "always the same thing" is not the event but the newness of the event, the shock with which it eventuates.   ⟨Q°,23⟩

Am I the one who is called W.B., or am I simply called W.B.? These are two sides of a medallion, but the second side is worn and effaced, while the first is freshly minted. This initial take on the question makes it evident that the name is object of a mimesis. Of course, it is in the nature of the latter to show itself not in what is about to happen, but always only in what has been—that is, in what has been lived. The habitus of a lived life: this is what the name preserves, but also marks out in advance. With the concept of mimesis, it is further asserted that the realm of the name is the realm of the similar. And since similarity is the organon of experience ⟨*Erfahrung*⟩, it may be said that the name can be recognized only in the contexts of experience. Only in them is its essence—that is, linguistic essence—recognizable.   ⟨Q°,24⟩

Point of departure for the foregoing considerations: a conversation with Wiesengrund on the operas *Electra* and *Carmen*. To what extent their names already contain within themselves their distinctive character, and thus make it possible for the child to have a presentiment of these works long before he comes to know them. (Carmen appears to him in the shawl which his mother has around her on evenings when she kisses him good night before going to the opera.) The knowledge contained in the name is developed most of all in the child, for the mimetic capability decreases with age in most people.   ⟨Q°,25⟩

EARLY DRAFTS

Arcades

This brief essay, dating from the summer or fall of 1927 (*Gesammelte Schriften,* vol. 5, [Frankfurt: Suhrkamp, 1982], pp. 1041–1043), is the only completed text we have from the earliest period of work on *The Arcades Project,* when Benjamin was planning to write a newspaper article on the Paris arcades in collaboration with Franz Hessel. The article may have been written by Benjamin and Hessel together. (See "Materials for 'Arcades.'")

On the Avenue Champs-Elysées, between modern hotels with Anglo-Saxon names, arcades were opened recently and the newest Parisian *passage* made its appearance. For its inaugural ceremony, a monster orchestra in uniform performed in front of flower beds and flowing fountains. The crowd broke, groaning, over sandstone thresholds and moved along before panes of plate glass, saw artificial rain fall on the copper entrails of late-model autos as a demonstration of the quality of the materials, saw wheels turning around in oil, read on small black plaques, in paste-jewel figures, the prices of leather goods and gramophone records and embroidered kimonos. In the diffuse light from above, one skimmed over flagstones. While here a new thoroughfare was being prepared for the most fashionable Paris, one of the oldest arcades in the city has disappeared—the Passage de l'Opéra, swallowed up by the opening of the Boulevard Haussmann. Just as that remarkable covered walkway had done for an earlier generation, so today a few arcades still preserve, in dazzling light and shadowy corners, a past become space. Antiquated trades survive within these inner spaces, and the merchandise on display is unintelligible, or else has several meanings. Already the inscriptions and signs on the entranceways (one could just as well say "exits," since, with these peculiar hybrid forms of house and street, every gate is simultaneously entrance and exit), already the inscriptions which multiply along the walls within, where here and there between overloaded coatstands a spiral staircase rises into darkness—already they have about them something enigmatic. "Albert at No. 83" will in all likelihood be a hairdresser, and "Theatrical Tights" will be silk tights; but these insistent letterings want to say more. And who would have the courage to take the dilapidated stairs up one flight to the beauty salon of Professor Alfred Bitterlin? Mosaic thresholds, in the style of the old restaurants of the Palais-Royal, lead to a *dîner de Paris;* they make a broad ascent to a glass door—but can there really be a restaurant behind it? And the glass door next to it, which announces a casino and permits a glimpse of something like a ticket booth with prices of seats posted—would it not, if one opened it, lead one into darkness rather than a theater, into a cellar or down to the street? And on the ticket booth hang stockings once again, stockings as in the doll hospital across the way and, somewhat earlier, on the side table of the tavern.—In the crowded arcades of the boulevards, as in the semi-deserted arcades of the old Rue Saint-Denis, umbrellas and canes are displayed in serried ranks: a phalanx of colorful crooks. Many are the institutes of hygiene, where gladiators are wearing orthopedic belts and bandages wind round the white bellies of mannequins. In the windows of the hairdressers, one sees the last women with long hair; they sport richly undulating masses, petrified coiffures. How brittle appears the stonework of the walls beside them and above: crumbling papier-mâché! "Souvenirs" and bibelots take on a hideous aspect; the odalisque lies in wait next to the inkwell; priestesses in knitted jackets raise aloft ashtrays like vessels of holy water. A bookshop makes a place for manuals of lovemaking beside devotional prints in color; next to the memoirs of a chambermaid, it has Napoleon riding through Marengo and, between cookbook and dreambook, old-English burghers treading the broad and the narrow way of the Gospel. In the arcades, one comes upon types of collar studs for which we no longer know the corresponding collars and shirts. If a shoemaker's shop should be neighbor to a confectioner's, then his festoons of bootlaces will resemble rolls of licorice. Over stamps and letterboxes roll balls of string and of silk. Naked puppet bodies with bald heads wait for hairpieces and attire. Combs swim about, frog-green and coral-red, as in an aquarium; trumpets turn to conches, ocarinas to umbrella handles; and lying in the fixative pans from a photographer's darkroom is birdseed. The concierge of the gallery has, in his loge, three plush-covered chairs with crocheted antimacassars, but next door is a vacant shop from whose inventory only a printed bill remains: "Will purchase sets of teeth in gold, in wax, and broken." Here, in the quietest part of the side-alley, individuals of both sexes can interview for a staff position within the confines of a sitting room set up behind glass. On the pale-colored wallpaper full of figures and bronze busts falls the light of a gas lamp. An old woman sits beside it, reading. For years, it would seem, she has been alone. And now the passage is becoming more empty. A small red tin parasol coyly points the way up a stair to an umbrella ferrule factory; a dusty bridal veil promises a repository of cockades for weddings and banquets. But no one believes it any longer. Fire escape, gutter: I am in the open. Opposite is something like an arcade again—an archway and, through it, a blind alley leading to a one-windowed Hôtel de Boulogne or Bourgogne. But I am no longer heading in that direction; I am going up the street to the triumphal gate that, gray and glorious, was built in honor of Louis the Great. Carved in relief on the pyramids that decorate its columns are lions at rest, weapons hanging, and dusky trophies.

⟨The Arcades of Paris⟩

⟨Paris Arcades II⟩

These originally untitled texts (*Gesammelte Schriften,* vol. 5, [Frankfurt: Suhrkamp, 1982], pp. 1044–1059), written on loose sheets of expensive handmade paper folded in half, date from 1928 or, at the latest, 1929, when Benjamin was planning to write an essay entitled "Pariser Passagen: Eine dialektische Feerie" (Paris Arcades: A Dialectical Fairyland). In the manuscript they are followed by citations which were largely transferred to the convolutes and which therefore are not reproduced in the German edition at this point. The ordering of the entries here is that of the German editor, who also gives their original order in the manuscript:

> Ms. 1154 recto: a°,1; a°,3; b°,1; b°,2.
> Ms. 1154 verso: c°,3; e°,1.
> Ms. 1155 recto: c°,1; c°,4; d°,1; d°,2; c°,2.
> Ms. 1155 verso: h°,5.
> Ms. 1160 verso: h°,1; a°,2; f°,1; h°,2; h°,3; h°,4; a°,5.
> Ms. 1161 verso: f°,2; e°,2; f°,3; a°,4; g°,1.

These texts were among those from which Benjamin read to Adorno and Horkheimer at Königstein and Frankfurt in 1929. Prominent correspondences to entries in the convolutes and to the essay "Arcades" are indicated in cross-references.

"In speaking of the inner boulevards," says the *Illustrated Guide to Paris,* a complete picture of the city on the Seine and its environs from the year 1852, "we have made mention again and again of the arcades which open onto them. These arcades, a recent invention of industrial luxury, are glass-roofed, marble-paneled corridors extending through whole blocks of buildings, whose owners have joined together for such enterprises. Lining both sides of these corridors, which get their light from above, are the most elegant shops, so that the arcade is a city, a world in miniature, in which customers will find everything they need. During sudden rainshowers, the arcades are a place of refuge for the unprepared, to whom they offer a secure, if restricted, promenade—one from which the merchants also benefit." The customers are gone, along with those taken by surprise. Rain brings in only the poorer clientele without waterproof or mackintosh. These were spaces for a generation of people who knew little of the weather and who, on Sundays, when it snowed, would rather warm themselves in the winter gardens than go out skiing. Glass before its time, premature iron: it was one single line of descent—arcades, winter gardens with their lordly palms, and railroad stations, which cultivated the false orchid "adieu" with its fluttering petals. They have long since given way to the hangar. And today, it is the same with the human material on the inside of the arcades as with the materials of their construction. Pimps are the iron bearings of this street, and its glass breakables are the whores. Here was the last refuge of those infant prodigies that saw the light of day at the time of the world exhibitions: the briefcase with interior lighting, the meter-long pocket knife, or the patented umbrella handle with built-in watch and revolver. And near the degenerate giant creatures, aborted and broken-down matter. We followed the narrow dark corridor to where—between a discount bookstore, in which colorful tied-up bundles tell of all sorts of failure, and a shop selling only buttons (mother-of-pearl and the kind that in Paris are called *de fantaisie*)—there stood a sort of salon. On a pale-colored wallpaper full of figures and busts shone a gas lamp. By its light, an old woman sat reading. They say she has been there alone for years, and collects sets of teeth "in gold, in wax, and broken." Since that day, moreover, we know where Doctor Miracle got the wax out of which he fashioned Olympia.[1] They are the true fairies of these arcades (more salable and more worn than the life-sized ones): the formerly world-famous Parisian dolls, which revolved on their musical socle and bore in their arms a doll-sized basket out of which, at the salutation of the minor chord, a lambkin poked its curious muzzle. ‹See A1,1; F3,2; H1,1; Z1,2.›   ‹a°,1›

All this is the arcade in our eyes. And it was nothing of all this. They ‹the arcades› radiated through the Paris of the Empire like grottoes. For someone entering the Passage des Panoramas in 1817, the sirens of gaslight would be singing to him on one side, while oil-lamp odalisques offered enticements from the other. With the kindling of electric lights, the irreproachable glow was extinguished in these galleries, which suddenly became more difficult to find—which wrought a black magic at entranceways, and peered from blind windows into their own interior. It was not decline but transformation. All at once, they were the hollow mold from which the image of "modernity" was cast. Here, the century mirrored with satisfaction its most recent past. Here was the retirement home for infant prodigies . . . ‹See C2a,9; T1a,8; S1a,6›   ‹a°,2›

When, as children, we were given those great encyclopedic works *World and Mankind, New Universe, The Earth,* wouldn't our gaze always fall, first of all, on the color illustration of a "Carboniferous Landscape" or on "Lakes and Glaciers of the First Ice Age"? Such an ideal panorama of a barely elapsed primeval age opens up when we look through the arcades that are found in all cities. Here resides the last dinosaur of Europe, the consumer. On the walls of these caverns, their immemorial flora, the commodity, luxuriates and enters, like cancerous tissue, into the most irregular combinations. A world of secret affinities: palm tree and feather duster, hair dryer and Venus de Milo, prosthesis and letter-writing manual come together here as after a long separation. The odalisque lies in wait next to the inkwell, priestesses raise aloft ashtrays like patens. These items on display are a rebus; and ‹how› one ought to read here the birdseed kept in the fixative-pan from a darkroom, the flower seeds beside the binoculars, the broken screws atop the musical score, and the revolver above the goldfish bowl—is right on the tip of one's tongue. After all, nothing of the lot appears to be new. The goldfish come perhaps from a pond that dried up long ago, the revolver will have been a corpus delicti, and these scores could hardly have preserved their previous owner from starvation when her last pupils stayed away. ⟨See R2,3.⟩

⟨a°,3⟩

Never trust what writers say about their own writings. When Zola undertook to defend his *Thérèse Raquin* against hostile critics, he explained that his book was a scientific study of the temperaments. His task had been to show, in an example, exactly how the sanguine and the nervous temperaments act on one another—to the detriment of each. But this explanation could satisfy no one. Nor does it explain the unprecedented admixture of colportage, the bloodthirstiness, the cinematic goriness of the action. Which—by no accident—takes place in an arcade. If this book really expounds something scientifically, then it's the death of the Paris arcades, the decay of a type of architecture. The book's atmosphere is saturated with the poisons of this process, and its people are destroyed by them. ⟨See H1,3.⟩

⟨a°,4⟩

One knew of places in ancient Greece where the way led down into the underworld. Our waking existence likewise is a land which, at certain hidden points, leads down into the underworld—a land full of inconspicuous places from which dreams arise. All day long, suspecting nothing, we pass them by, but no sooner has sleep come than we are eagerly groping our way back to lose ourselves in the dark corridors. By day, the labyrinth of urban dwellings resembles consciousness; the arcades (which are galleries leading into the city's past) issue unremarked onto the streets. At night, however, under the tenebrous mass of the houses, their denser darkness bursts forth like a threat, and the nocturnal pedestrian hurries past—unless, that is, we have emboldened him to turn into the narrow lane. ⟨See C1a,2.⟩

⟨a°,5⟩

Falser colors are possible in the arcades; that combs are red and green surprises no one. Snow White's stepmother had such things, and when the comb did not do its work, the beautiful apple was there to help out—half red, half poison-green, like cheap combs. Everywhere stockings play a starring role. Now they are lying under phonographs, across the way in a stamp shop; another time on the side table of a tavern, where they are watched over by a girl. And again in front of the stamp shop opposite, where, between the envelopes with various stamps in refined assortments, manuals of an antiquated art of life are lovelessly dispensed—*Secret Embraces* and *Maddening Illusions,* introductions to outmoded vices and discarded passions. The shop windows are covered with vividly colored Epinal-style posters, on which Harlequin betroths his daughter, Napoleon rides through Marengo, and, amid all types of standard artillery pieces, delicate English burghers travel the high road to hell and the forsaken path of the Gospel. No customer ought to enter this shop with preconceived ideas; on leaving, he will be the more content to take home a volume: Malebranche's *Recherche de la vérité,* or *Miss Daisy: The Journal of an English Equestrienne.* ‹See G1a,1 and "Arcades." ›   ‹b°,1›

To the inhabitants of these arcades we are pointed now and then by the signs and inscriptions which multiply along the walls within, where here and there, between the shops, a spiral staircase rises into darkness. The signs have little in common with the nameplates that hang beside respectable entryways but are reminiscent of plaques on the cages at zoos, put there to indicate not so much the dwelling place as the origin and species of the captive animals. Deposited in the letters of the metal or enameled signboards is a precipitate of all the forms of writing that have ever been in use in the West. "Albert at No. 83" will be a hairdresser, and "Theatrical Tights" will probably be silk tights, pink and light blue, for young chanteuses and ballerinas; but these insistent letterings want to say something more, something different. Collectors of curiosities in the field of cultural history have in their secret drawer broadsheets of a highly paid literature which seem, at first sight, to be commercial prospectuses or theatrical bills, and which squander dozens of different alphabets in disguising an open invitation. These dark enameled signs bring to mind the baroque lettering on the cover of obscene books.—Recall the origin of the modern poster. In 1861, the first lithographic poster suddenly appeared on walls here and there around London. It showed the back of a woman in white who was thickly wrapped in a shawl and who, in all haste, had just reached the top of a flight of stairs, where, her head half turned and a finger upon her lips, she is ever so slightly opening a heavy door to reveal the starry sky. In this way Wilkie Collins advertised his latest book, one of the greatest detective novels ever written, *The Woman in White.* Still color‹less›, the first drops of a shower of letters ran down the walls of houses (today it pours unremittingly, day and night, on the big cities) and was greeted like the plagues of Egypt.—Hence the anxiety we feel when, crowded out by those who actually make purchases, wedged between overloaded coatstands, we read at the bottom of the spiral staircase: "Institut de Beauté du Professeur Alfred Bitterlin." And the "Fabrique de Cravates au Deuxième"—Are there really neckties there or not? ("The Speckled Band" from Sherlock Holmes?) Of course, the needlework will have been quite inoffensive, and all the imagined horrors will be classified objectively in the statistics on tuberculosis. As a consolation, these places are seldom lacking institutes of hygiene. There gladiators wear orthopedic belts, and bandages are wrapped round the white bellies of mannequins. Something induces the owner of the shop to circulate among them on a frequent basis.—Many are the aristocrats who know nothing of the Almanach de Gotha: "Mme. de Consolis, Ballet Mistress—Lessons, Classes, Numbers." "Mme. de Zahna, Fortuneteller." And if, sometime in the mid-Nineties, ‹we had› asked for a prediction, surely it would have been: the decline of a culture. ‹See G1,6 and "Arcades."›

‹b°,2›

Often these inner spaces harbor antiquated trades, and even those that are thoroughly up to date will acquire in them something obsolete. They are the site of information bureaus and detective agencies, which there, in the gloomy light of the upper galleries, follow the trail of the past. In hairdressers' windows, you can see the last women with long hair. They have richly undulating masses of hair, which are "permanent waves," petrified coiffures. They ought to dedicate small votive plaques to those who made a special world of these buildings—to Baudelaire and Odilon Redon, whose very name sounds like an all too well-turned ringlet. Instead, they have been betrayed and sold, and the head of Salome itself made into an ornament—if that which sorrows there in the console is not the embalmed head of Anna Czyllak. And while these things are petrified, the masonry of the walls above has become brittle. Brittle, too, are the mosaic thresholds that lead you, in the style of the old restaurants of the Palais-Royal, to a "Parisian Dinner" for five francs; they mount boldly to a glass door, but you can hardly believe that behind this door is really a restaurant. The glass door adjacent promises a "Petit Casino" and allows a glimpse of a ticket booth and the prices of seats; but were you to open it—would it open into anything? Instead of entering the space of a theater, wouldn't you be stepping down to the street? Where doors and walls are made of mirrors, there is no telling outside from in, with all the equivocal illumination. Paris is a city of mirrors. The asphalt of its roadways smooth as glass, and at the entrance to all bistros glass partitions. A profusion of windowpanes and mirrors in cafés, so as to make the inside brighter and to give all the tiny nooks and crannies, into which Parisian taverns separate, a pleasing amplitude. Women here look at themselves more than elsewhere, and from this comes the distinctive beauty of the Parisienne. Before any man catches sight of her, she has already seen herself ten times reflected. But the man, too, sees his own physiognomy flash by. He gains his image more quickly here than elsewhere and also sees himself more quickly merged with this, his image. Even the eyes of passersby are veiled mirrors. And over that wide bed of the Seine, over Paris, the sky is spread out like the crystal mirror hanging over the drab beds in brothels. ‹See H1a,1; R1,3; "Arcades."›   ‹c°,1›

Let two mirrors reflect each other; then Satan plays his favorite trick and opens here in his way (as his partner does in lovers' gazes) the perspective on infinity. Be it now divine, now satanic: Paris has a passion for mirror-like perspectives. The Arc de Triomphe, the Sacré Coeur, and even the Pantheon appear, from a distance, like images hovering above the ground and opening, architecturally, a fata morgana. Baron von Haussmann, when he undertook to transform Paris during the period of the Third ‹correction: Second› Empire, was intoxicated with these perspectives and wanted to multiply them wherever possible. In the arcades, the perspective is lastingly preserved as in the nave of a church. And the windows in the upper story are choir lofts in which the angels that men call "swallows" are nesting.—"*Hirondelles* ‹—women› who work the window." ‹See R1,6 and O1a,2.›   ‹c°,2›

Ambiguity of the arcades as an ambiguity of *space*. Readiest access to this phenomenon would be afforded by the multiple deployment of figures in the wax museum. On the other hand, the resolute focus on the ambiguity of space, a focus obtained in the arcades, has to benefit the theory of Parisian streets. The outermost, merely quite peripheral aspect of the ambiguity of the arcades is provided by their abundance of mirrors, which fabulously amplifies the spaces and makes orientation more difficult. Perhaps that isn't saying much. Nevertheless: though it may have many aspects, indeed infinitely many, it remains—in the sense of mirror world—ambiguous, double-edged. It blinks, is always just this one—and never nothing—out of which another immediately arises. The space that transforms itself does so in the bosom of nothingness. In its tarnished, dirtied mirrors, things exchange a Kaspar-Hauser-look with the nothing: it is an utterly equivocal wink coming from nirvana. And here, again, we are brushed with icy breath by the dandyish name of Odilon Redon, who caught, like no one else, this look of things in the mirror of nothingness, and who understood, like no one else, how to join with things in their collusion with nonbeing. The whispering of gazes fills the arcades. There is no thing here that does not, where one least expects it, open a fugitive eye, blinking it shut again; and should you look more closely, it is gone. To the whispering of these gazes, the space lends its echo: "Now, what," it blinks, "can possibly have come over me?" We stop short in some surprise. "What, indeed, can possibly have come over you?" Thus we gently bounce the question back to it. Here, the coronation of Charlemagne could have taken place, as well as the assassination of Henri IV, the death of ‹Edward's› sons in the Tower, and the . . . That is why the wax museums are here. This optical gallery of princes is their acknowledged capital. For Louis XI, it is the throne room; for York, the Tower of London; for Abdel Krim, the desert; and for Nero, Rome. ‹See R2a,3 and Q2,2.›   ‹c°,3›

The innermost glowing cells of the *ville lumière,* the old dioramas, nested in these arcades, one of which today still bears the name Passage des Panoramas. It was, in the very first moment, as though you had entered an aquarium. Along the wall of the great darkened hall, broken at intervals by narrow joints, it stretched like a land of illuminated water behind glass. The play of colors among deep-sea fauna cannot be more fiery. But what came to light here were open-air, atmospheric wonders. Seraglios are mirrored on moolit waters; bright nights in deserted parks loom large. In the moonlight you can recognize the château of Saint-Leu, where a hundred years ago the last Condé was found hanged in a window. A light is still burning in a window of the château. A couple of times the sun splashes wide in between. In the clear light of a summer morning, one sees the rooms of the Vatican as they would have appeared to the Nazarenes; not far beyond rises Baden-Baden in its entirety, and were we not writing of 1860, one could perhaps make out among its figurines, on a scale of 1:10,000, Dostoevsky on the casino terrace. But candlelight, too, is honored. Wax tapers encircle the murdered duc de Berry in the dusky cathedral that serves as mortuary chapel, and hanging lamps in the skies beside[2] practically put round Luna to shame. It was an unparalleled experiment on the moonstruck magic night of Romanticism, and its noble substance emerged victorious from this ingenious trial. For anyone who was inclined to linger before the transparent image of the old thermal baths of Contrexéville, it was as though he had already wandered, in some previous life, along this sunny way between poplars, had brushed against the stone wall close by—modest, magical effects for domestic use, such as otherwise would be experienced only in rare cases, as before Chinese groups in soapstone or Russian lacquer-painting. ‹See Q3,2.› 〈c°,4〉

Streets are the dwelling place of the collective. The collective is an eternally wakeful, eternally agitated being that—in the space between the building fronts—lives, experiences, understands, and invents as much as individuals do within the privacy of their own four walls. For this collective, glossy enameled shop signs are a wall decoration as good as, if not better than, an oil painting in the drawing room of a bourgeois; walls with their "Post No Bills" are its writing desk, newspaper stands its libraries, mailboxes its bronze busts, benches its bedroom furniture, and the café terrace is the balcony from which it looks down on its household. The section of railing where road workers hang their jackets is the vestibule, and the gateway which leads from the row of courtyards out into the open is the long corridor that daunts the bourgeois, being for the courtyards the entry to the chambers of the city. Among these latter, the arcade was the drawing room. More than anywhere else, the street reveals itself in the arcade as the furnished and familiar interior of the masses. ‹See M3a,4.› 〈d°,1〉

The bourgeois who came into ascendancy with Louis Philippe sets store by the transformation of near and far into the interior. He knows but a single scene: the drawing room. In 1839, a ball is held at the British embassy. Two hundred rose bushes are ordered. "The garden," so runs an eyewitness account, "was covered by an awning and had the feel of a drawing room. But what a drawing room! The fragrant, well-stocked flower beds had turned into enormous *jardinières,* the graveled walks had disappeared under sumptuous carpets, and in place of the cast-iron benches we found sofas covered in damask and silk; a round table held books and albums. From a distance, the strains of an orchestra drifted into this colossal boudoir, and, along the triple gallery of flowers on the periphery, exuberant young people were passing to and fro. It was altogether delightful!" The dusty fata morgana of the winter garden, the dreary perspective of the train station, with the small altar of happiness at the intersection of the tracks—it all molders, even today, under spurious constructions, glass before its time, premature iron. ‹Toward the› middle of the previous century, no one as yet understood how to build with glass and iron. The problem, however, has long since been solved by the hangar. ‹Now› it is the same with the human material on the inside of the arcades as with the materials of their construction. Pimps are the iron bearings of this street, and its glass breakables are the whores. ‹See I4,1; F3,2; F1,2.› 〈d°,2〉

For the flâneur, a transformation takes place with respect to the street: it leads him through a vanished time. He strolls down the street; for him, every street is precipitous. It leads downward—if not to the mythical Mothers, then into a past that can be all the more profound because it is not his own, not private. Nevertheless, it always remains the past of a youth. But why that of the life he has lived? The ground over which he goes, the asphalt, is hollow. His steps awaken a surprising resonance; the gaslight that streams down on the paving stones throws an equivocal light on this double ground. The figure of the flâneur advances over the street of stone, with its double ground, as though driven by a clockwork mechanism. And within, where this mechanism is ensconced, a music box is palpitating <?> like some toy of long ago. It plays a tune: "From days of youth, / from days of youth, / a song is with me still." By this melody he recognizes what is around him; it is not a past coming from his own youth, from a recent youth, but a childhood lived before then that speaks to him, and it is all the same to him whether it is the childhood of an ancestor or his own.—An intoxication comes over the man who walks long and aimlessly through the streets. With each step, the walk takes on greater momentum; ever weaker grow the temptations of bistros, of shops, of smiling women, ever more irresistible the magnetism of the next streetcorner, of a distant square in the fog, of the back of a woman walking before him. Then comes hunger. He wants, however, nothing to do with the myriad possibilities offered to sate his appetite, but like an animal he prowls through unknown districts in search of food, in search of a woman, until, utterly exhausted, he stumbles into his room, which receives him coldly and wears a strange air. Paris created this type. What is remarkable is that it wasn't Rome. And the reason? Just this: does not dreaming itself take the high road in Rome? And isn't that city too full of themes, of monuments, enclosed squares, national shrines, to be able to enter *tout entière*—with every cobblestone, every shop sign, every step, and every gateway—into the passerby's dream? The national character of the Italians may also have much to do with this. For it is not the foreigners but they themselves, the Parisians, who have made Paris the holy city of the flâneur—the "landscape built of sheer life," as Hofmannsthal once put it. Landscape—that, in fact, is what Paris becomes for the flâneur. Or, more precisely, the city neatly splits for him into its dialectical poles: it opens up to him as a landscape, even as it closes around him as a room.—Another thing: that anamnestic intoxication in which the flâneur goes about the city not only feeds on the sensory data taking shape before his eyes but can very well possess itself of abstract knowledge—indeed, of dead facts—as something experienced and lived through. This felt knowledge, as is obvious, travels above all by word of mouth from one person to another. But in the course of the nineteenth century, it was also deposited in an immense literature. Even before Lefeuve (who quite aptly made the following formula the title of his five-volume work), "Paris street by street, house by house" was lovingly depicted as storied landscape forming a backdrop to the dreaming idler. The study of these books was, for the Parisian, like a second existence, one wholly predisposed toward dreaming; the knowledge these books gave him took form and figure during an afternoon walk before the apéritif. And wouldn't he necessarily have felt the gentle slope behind the church of Notre Dame de Lorette rise all the more insistently under his soles if he realized: here, at one time, after Paris had gotten its first omnibuses, the *cheval de renfort* was harnessed to the coach to reinforce the two other horses. ‹See M1,2–M1,5.›   ‹e°,1›

Boredom is a warm gray fabric lined on the inside with the most lustrous and colorful of silks. In this fabric we wrap ourselves when we dream. We are at home then in the arabesques of its lining. But the sleeper looks bored and gray within his sheath. And when he later wakes and wants to tell of what he dreamed, he communicates, by and large, only this boredom. For who would be able at one stroke to turn the lining of time to the outside? Yet to narrate dreams signifies nothing else. And in no other way can one deal with the arcades—structures in which we relive, as in a dream, the life of our parents and grandparents, as the embryo in the womb relives the life of animals. Existence in these spaces flows then without accent, like the events in dreams. Flânerie is the rhythmics of this slumber. In 1839, a rage for tortoises overcame Paris. One can well imagine the elegant set mimicking the pace of this creature more easily in the arcades than on the boulevards. Boredom is always the external surface of unconscious events. For that reason, it has appeared to the great dandies as a mark of distinction. ‹See D2a,1 and D2a, 2.›   ‹e°,2›

Here fashion has opened the business of dialectical exchange between woman and ware. The clerk, death, tall and loutish, measures the century by the yard, serves as mannequin himself to save costs, and manages single-handedly the liquidation that in French is called "revolution." For fashion was never anything other than the parody of the motley cadaver, the provocation of death through the woman, and bitter colloquy with decay whispered between loud outbursts of mechanical jubilation. This is why fashion changes so quickly: she titillates death and is already something different, something new, as he casts about to crush her. For a hundred years she holds her own against him. Now, finally, she is on the point of quitting the field. But he erects on the banks of a new Lethe, which rolls its asphalt stream through arcades, the armature of the whores as a battle memorial. ‹See B1,4.›   ‹f°,1›

When Hackländer made use of this "newest invention of industrial luxury" for one of his fairy tales, he too placed the marvelous dolls in the dangerous arcade which sister Tinchen, at the behest of the fairy Concordia, has to wander in order finally to rescue her poor brothers. "Fearlessly, Tinchen stepped across the border into the enchanted land, all the while thinking only of her brothers. At first she noticed nothing unusual, but soon the way led through an enormous room entirely filled with toys. She saw small booths stocked with everything imaginable—carousels with miniature horses and carriages, swings and rocking horses, but above all the most splendid dollhouses. Around a small covered table, large dolls were sitting on easy chairs; and as Tinchen turned her gaze upon them, the largest and most beautiful of these dolls stood up, made her a gracious bow, and spoke to her in a little voice of exquisite refinement." The child may not want to hear of toys that are bewitched, but the evil spell of this slippery path readily takes the form, even today, of large animated dolls. But who still remembers, nowadays, where it was that in the last decade of the previous century women would offer to men their most seductive aspect, the most intimate promise of their figure? In the asphalted indoor arenas where people learned to ride bicycles. The woman as cyclist competes with the cabaret singer for place of honor on Chéret's posters (the *affiches*) and gives to fashion its most daring line. ‹See Z1,2 and B1,8.› ‹f°,2›

Few things in the history of humanity are as well known to us as the history of Paris. Tens of thousands of volumes are dedicated solely to the investigation of this tiny spot on the earth's surface. For many streets, we know about the fate of every single house over a period of centuries. In a beautiful turn of phrase, Hugo von Hofmannsthal called this city "a landscape built of pure life." And at work in the attraction it exercises on people is the kind of beauty that is proper to great landscapes—more precisely, to volcanic landscapes. Paris is a counterpart in the social order to what Vesuvius is in the geographic order: a menacing, hazardous massif, an ever-active June of revolution. But just as the slopes of Vesuvius, thanks to the layers of lava that cover them, have been transformed into paradisal orchards, so the lava of revolution provides uniquely fertile ground for the blossoming of art, festivity, fashion. ‹See C1,6.› ‹f°,3›

Hasn't his eternal vagabondage everywhere accustomed him to reinterpreting the image of the city? And doesn't he transform the arcade into a casino, into a gambling den, where now and again he stakes the red, blue, yellow *jetons* of feeling on women, on a face that suddenly surfaces (will it return his look?), on a mute mouth (will it speak?)? What, on the baize cloth, looks out at the gambler from every number—luck, that is—here, from the bodies of all the women, winks at him as the chimera of sexuality: as his type. This is nothing other than the number, the cipher, in which just at that moment luck will be called by name, in order to jump immediately to another number. His type—that's the number that blesses thirty-six-fold, the one on which, without even trying, the eye of the voluptuary falls, as the ivory ball falls into the red or black compartment. He leaves the Palais-Royal with bulging pockets, calls to a whore, and once more finds in her arms the communion with number, in which money and riches, otherwise the most burdensome, most massive of things, come to him from the fates like a joyous embrace returned to the full. For in gambling hall and bordello, it is the same supremely sinful, supremely punishable delight: to challenge fate in pleasure. That sensual pleasure, of whatever stripe, could determine the theological concept of sin is something that only an unsuspecting idealism can believe. Determining the concept of debauchery in the theological sense is nothing else but this wresting of pleasure from out of the course of life with God, whose covenant with such life resides in the name. The name itself is the cry of naked lust. This holy thing, sober, fateless in itself—the name—knows no greater adversary than the fate that takes its place in whoring and that forges its arsenal in superstition. Thus in gambler and prostitute that superstition which arranges the figures of fate and fills all wanton behavior with fateful forwardness, fateful concupiscence, bringing even pleasure to kneel before its throne. ‹See O1,1.›

‹g°,1›

The father of Surrealism was Dada; its mother was an arcade. Dada, when the two first met, was already old. At the end of 1919, Aragon and Breton, out of antipathy to Montparnasse and Montmartre, transferred the site of their meetings with friends to a café in the Passage de l'Opéra. Construction of the Boulevard Haussmann brought about the demise of the Passage de l'Opéra. Louis Aragon devoted 135 pages to this arcade; in the sum of these three digits hides the number nine—the number of muses who presided as midwives at the birth of Surrealism. These stalwart muses are named Ballhorn, Lenin, Luna, Freud, Mors, Marlitt, and Citroen. A provident reader will make way for them all, as discreetly as possible, wherever they are encountered in the course of these lines. In *Paysan de Paris,* Aragon conducts as touching a requiem for this arcade as any man has ever conducted for the mother of his son. It is there to be read, but here one should expect no more than a physiology and, to be blunt, an autopsy of these parts of the capital city of Europe, parts that could not be more mysterious or more dead. ‹See C1,3.› ‹h°,1›

The Copernican revolution in historical perception is as follows. Formerly it was thought that a fixed point had been found in "what has been," and one saw the present engaged in tentatively concentrating the forces of knowledge on this ground. Now this relation is to be overturned, and what has been is to acquire its dialectical fixation through the synthesis which awakening achieves with the opposing dream images. Politics attains primacy over history. Indeed, historical "facts" become something that just now happened to us, just now struck us: to establish them is the affair of memory. And awakening is the great exemplar of memory—that occasion on which we succeed in remembering what is nearest, most obvious (in the "I"). What Proust intends with the experimental rearrangement of furniture, what Bloch recognizes as the darkness of the lived moment, is nothing other than what here is secured on the level of the historical, and collectively. There is a not-yet-conscious knowledge of *what has been:* its advancement has the structure of awakening. ‹See K1,2.› ‹h°,2›

In this historical and collective process of fixation, collecting plays a certain role. Collecting is a form of practical memory, and of all the profane manifestations of the penetration of "what has been" (of all the profane manifestations of "nearness") it is the most binding. Thus, in a certain sense, the smallest act of political reflection makes for an epoch in the antiques business. We construct here an alarm clock that rouses the kitsch of the previous century to "assembly." This genuine liberation from an epoch has the structure of awakening in the following respect as well: it is entirely ruled by cunning.[3] For awakening operates with cunning. Only with cunning, not without it, can we work free of the realm of dream. But there is also a false liberation, whose sign is violence. Here, too, that law prevails by which the exertion brings about its opposite. This fruitless exertion is represented, for the period in question here, by Jugendstil. ‹See H1a,2 and G1,7.›   ‹h°,3›

Dialectical structure of awakening: remembering and awaking are most intimately related. Awakening is namely the dialectical, Copernican turn of remembrance ‹Eingedenken›. It is an eminently composed reversal from the world of dreaming to the world of waking. For the dialectical schematism at the core of this physiological process, the Chinese have found, in their fairy tales and novellas, the most radical expression. The new, dialectical method of doing history teaches us to pass in spirit—with the rapidity and intensity of dreams—through what has been, in order to experience the present as waking world, a world to which every dream at last refers. ‹See K1,3.›   ‹h°,4›

These notes devoted to the Paris arcades were begun under an open sky of cloudless blue that arched above the foliage and yet was dimmed by the millions of leaves from which the fresh breeze of diligence, the stertorous breath of research, the storm of youthful zeal, and the idle wind of curiosity have raised the dust of centuries. The painted sky of summer that looks down from the arcades in the reading room of the Bibliothèque Nationale in Paris has stretched its dreamy, unlit ceiling over the birth of their insight. And when that sky opened to the eyes of this young insight, there in the foreground were standing not the divinities of Olympus—not Zeus, Hephaestus, Hermes, or Hera, Artemis, and Athena—but the Dioscuri.[4] ‹See N1,5.›   ‹h°,5›

The Ring of Saturn

or

Some Remarks on Iron Construction

According to Gretel Adorno, this text (*Gesammelte Schriften,* vol. 5 [Frankfurt: Suhrkamp, 1982], pp. 1060–1063) was "one of the first pieces Benjamin read to us in ‹1929 in› Königstein" (cited in *Gesammelte Schriften,* vol. 5, p. 1350). Benjamin himself filed the text at the beginning of Convolute G. Rolf Tiedemann suggests that it may have been intended as a radio broadcast for young people, but thinks it more likely to have been a newspaper or magazine article that was never published. The piece was written in 1928 or 1929.

The beginning of the nineteenth century witnessed those initial experiments in iron construction whose results, in conjunction with those obtained from experiments with the steam engine, would so thoroughly transform the face of Europe by the end of the century. Rather than attempt a historical account of this process, we would like to focus some scattered reflections on a small vignette which has been extracted from the middle of the century (as from the middle of the thick book that contains it), and which indicates, although in grotesque style, what limitless possibilities were seen revealed by construction in iron. The picture comes from a work of 1844—Grandville's *Another World*—and illustrates the adventures of a fantastic little hobgoblin who is trying to find his way around outer space: "A bridge—its two ends could not be embraced at a single glance and its piers were resting on planets—led from one world to another by a causeway of wonderfully smooth asphalt. The three-hundred-thirty-three-thousandth pier rested on Saturn. There our goblin noticed that the ring around this planet was nothing other than a circular balcony on which the inhabitants of Saturn strolled in the evening to get a breath of fresh air."

Gas candelabra appear in our picture as well. They could not be overlooked, in those days, when speaking of the achievements of technology. Whereas for us gas lighting often has about it something dismal and oppressive, in that age it represented the height of luxury and splendor. When Napoleon was interred in the church of Les Invalides, the scene lacked nothing: in addition to velvet, silk, gold and silver, and wreaths of the immortals, there was an eternal lamp of gas over the resting place. An engineer in Lancaster had invented a device that people regarded as a veritable miracle—a mechanism by which the church clock over the tomb was automatically illuminated by gaslight at dusk and by which the flames were automatically extinguished at daybreak.

For the rest, people were accustomed to seeing gas in conjunction with cast iron at those elegant establishments that were just then starting to appear: the arcades. The leading fancy-goods stores, the chic restaurants, the best confectioners, and so on found it necessary to secure a place in these galleries in order to preserve their reputations. Out of these galleries emerged, a little later on, the great department stores, of which the pioneering model, Au Bon Marché, was designed by the builder of the Eiffel Tower.

Iron construction began with winter gardens and arcades—that is, with genuine luxury establishments. Very quickly, however, it found its true range of technical and industrial application. What resulted were constructions that had no precedent and that were occasioned by wholly new needs: covered markets, railroad stations, exhibition halls. Engineers led the way. But poets, as well, displayed amazing foresight. Thus, the French Romantic Gautier declares: "A proper architecture will be created the moment we begin making use of the new materials furnished by the new industry. The advent of cast iron enables and calls for many new forms, as we can see in railroad terminals, suspension bridges, and the arches of winter gardens." Offenbach's *Parisian Life* was the first theatrical piece to be set in a railroad station. "Railway depots," they used to be called back then; and they inspired the strangest notions. A decidedly progressive Belgian painter, Antoine Wiertz, sought permission around midcentury to decorate the halls of railroad stations with frescoes.

Step by step, the technology of that era took possession of new fields; it did so in the face of difficulties and objections of which today we can scarcely form a conception. In the 1830s in England, for example, a bitter controversy arose over the issue of iron rails. Under no circumstances, it was argued, could enough iron ever be procured for the English railway system (at that time planned on only the smallest scale). The "steam carriages" would have to run on lanes of granite.

Alongside the theoretical battles were ongoing practical struggles with materials. The story of the bridge over the Firth of Tay is an especially memorable example. Six years were required for the construction of this bridge: 1872 to 1878. And shortly before its completion, on February 2, 1877, a hurricane (of the particularly violent sort that assail the inlet of the Tay and that also caused the catastrophe of 1879)[1] blew down two of the biggest supporting piers. And not only bridge construction made such demands on the patience of engineers; with tunnels, it was no different. When, in 1858, plans were afoot for the twelve-kilometer tunnel through Mont Cenis, the estimated length of time for the work was seven years.

Thus, while in great things heroic efforts were expended on precedent-setting, groundbreaking achievements, in little matters there was often—strange to say— something motley. It is as though people, and "artists" in particular, did not quite dare to acknowledge this new material, with all its possibilities. Whereas we allow our steel furnishings of today to be what they are, shiny and clean, a hundred years ago men took great pains, by means of subtle coating techniques, to make it appear that iron furniture—which was already being produced by then—was crafted from the finest wood. It was at this time that manufacturers began to stake their reputations on bringing out glasses that looked like porcelain, gold jewelry resembling leather straps, iron tables with the look of wickerwork, and other such things.

None of these efforts succeeded in covering over the chasm which the development of technology had opened up between the builder of the new school and the artist of the old type. Raging underneath was the battle between the academic architect, with his concern for stylistic forms, and the engineer, who dealt in formulas. As late as 1805, a leader of the old school published a work with the title: "On the Uselessness of Mathematics for Assuring the Stability of Buildings."[2] When this struggle finally, toward the end of the century, was decided in favor of the engineers, a reaction set in: an effort to renew art on the basis of technology's own rich store of forms. This was Jugendstil. At the same time, however, that heroic age of technology found its monument in the incomparable Eiffel Tower, of which the first historian of iron construction wrote: "Thus, the plastic shaping power recedes here before a colossal span of spiritual energy. . . . Every one of the twelve thousand metal fittings, each of the two and a half million rivets, is machined to the millimeter. . . . On this work site, one hears no chisel-blow liberating form from stone; here, thought reigns over muscle power, which it transmits via cranes and secure scaffolding."[3]

Walter Benjamin consulting the *Grand Dictionnaire universel du dix-neuvième siècle* at the Bibliothèque Nationale in Paris, 1937. Photo by Gisèle Freund.

Walter Benjamin at the card catalogue of the Bibliothèque Nationale in Paris, 1937.
Photo by Gisèle Freund.

ADDENDA

Exposé of 1935, Early Version

The earliest preserved draft of the exposé of 1935 (it is untitled in the manuscript) may constitute Benjamin's first draft. Some pages appear to be missing, and for some paragraphs there are two or even three separate versions. We have chosen to translate only passages presenting substantial differences from the definitive text of the exposé, which appears on pages 3–13 of this volume. Passages that Benjamin crossed out appear in curved brackets{ }. The complete draft is printed in *Das Passagen-Werk,* vol. 5 of Benjamin's *Gesammelte Schriften* (Frankfurt: Suhrkamp, 1982), pp. 1223–1237; it is followed by a version which Benjamin sent to Adorno and which, with respect to the translated texts, contains only minor variants.

I. Fourier, or the Arcades

. . . .

Chaque époque rêve la suivante.

—Michelet, "Avenir! Avenir!"

Corresponding to the form of the new means of production, which in the beginning is still ruled by the form of the old (Marx), are, in the social superstructure, wish images in which the new and the old interpenetrate in fantastic fashion. This interpenetration derives its fantastic character, above all, from the fact that what is old in the current of social development never clearly stands out from what is new, while the latter, in an effort to disengage from the antiquated, regenerates archaic, primordial elements. The utopian images which accompany the emergence of the new always, at the same time, reach back to the primal past. In the dream in which each epoch entertains images of its successor, the latter appears wedded to elements of primal history. The reflections of the base by the superstructure are therefore inadequate, not because they will have been consciously falsified by the ideologues of the ruling class, but because the new, in order to take the form of an image, constantly unites its elements with those of the classless society. The collective unconscious has a greater share in them than the consciousness of the collective. From the former come the images of utopia that have left their trace in a thousand configurations of life, from buildings to fashions.

These relations are discernible in the utopia conceived by Fourier . . .

. . . .

. . . In the dream in which each epoch entertains images of its successor, the latter appears wedded to elements of primal history—that is, to elements of a classless society. And the experiences of such a society—as stored in the unconscious of the collective—{never come to rest on the threshold of the most ancient cultures, but take up elements of natural history into their movement. This movement engenders,} engender, in combination with what is new, the utopia that has left its trace in a thousand configurations of life, from enduring edifices to passing fashions.

. . . .

III. Grandville, or the World Exhibition

. . . .

Fashion: "Madam Death! Madam Death!"

—Leopardi, "Dialogue between Fashion and Death"

World exhibitions propagate the universe of commodities. Grandville's late fantasies confer a commodity character on the universe. They modernize it. Thus, Saturn's ring becomes a cast-iron balcony on which the inhabitants of Saturn take the evening air. The literary counterpart to this graphic utopia is found in the books of the Fourierist Toussenel. Fashion prescribes the ritual according to which the commodity fetish demands to be worshipped. Grandville extends the scope of fashion to objects of everyday use, as well as to the cosmos. In taking it to an extreme, he reveals its nature. Fashion always stands in opposition to the organic. Not the body but the corpse is the most perfect object for its art. It defends the rights of the corpse before the living being, which it couples to the inorganic world. The fetishism that succumbs to the sex appeal of the commodity is its vital nerve. On the other hand, it is precisely fashion that triumphs over death. It brings the departed with it into the present. Fashion is contemporary with every past.

For the world exhibition of 1867, Victor Hugo issues a manifesto . . .

. . . .

V. Baudelaire, or the Streets of Paris

[1] Baudelaire's genius, in its affinity for spleen and melancholy, is an allegorical genius. "Tout pour moi devient allégorie." Paris as object of allegorical perception. The allegorical gaze as gaze of the alienated. Flâneur's lack of participation.

The flâneur as counterpart of the "crowd." The London crowd in Engels.
The man of the crowd in Poe. The consummate flâneur is a bohemian, a
déraciné. He is at home not in his class but only in the crowd—which is to
say, in the city. Excursus on the *bohémien*. His role in the secret societies.
Characterization of professional *conspirateurs*. The end of the old *bohème*.
Its dissociation into legal opposition and revolutionary opposition.

Baudelaire's ambivalent position. His flight into the asocial. He lives with a
prostitute. {The art theory of *l'art pour l'art*. It arises from the artist's pre-
monition that he will henceforth be obliged to create for the market.}

The motif of death in Baudelaire's poetry. It merges with his image of Paris.
Excursus on the chthonic side of the city of Paris. Topographic traces of
the prehistoric: the old bed of the Seine. The subterranean waterways.
The catacombs. Legends of subterranean Paris. Conspirators and communards in the catacombs. The undersea world of the arcades. Their importance for prostitution. Emphasis on the commodity character of the
woman in the market of love. The doll as wish symbol.

The phantasmagoria of the flâneur. The tempo of traffic in Paris. The city as
a landscape and a room. The department store as the last promenade for
the flâneur. There his fantasies were materialized. The flânerie that began
as art of the private individual ends today as necessity for the masses.

Art at war with its own commodity character. Its capitulation to the commodity with *l'art pour l'art*. The birth of the *Gesamtkunstwerk* from the spirit of
l'art pour l'art. Baudelaire's fascination with Wagner.

[2] Baudelaire's genius, which is nourished on melancholy, is an allegorical
genius. "Tout pour moi devient allégorie." For the first time, with Baudelaire, Paris becomes the subject of lyric poetry. Not as homeland; rather,
the gaze of the allegorist, as it falls on the city, is the gaze of the alienated
man.

The flâneur is a man uprooted. He is at home neither in his class nor in his
homeland, but only in the crowd. The crowd is his element. The London
crowd in Engels. The man of the crowd in Poe. The phantasmagoria of the
flâneur. The crowd as veil through which the familiar city appears transformed. The city as a landscape and a room. The department store is the
last promenade for the flâneur. There his fantasies were materialized.

The flâneur as *bohémien*. Excursus on the *bohémien*. He comes into being at
the same time as the art market. He works for the wide anonymous public
of the bourgeoisie, no longer for the feudal patron. He forms the reserve
army of the bourgeois intelligentsia. His initial efforts on behalf of conspirators in the army give way, later, to efforts on behalf of working-class
insurgents. He becomes a professional conspirator. He lacks political
schooling. Uncertainty of class consciousness. "Political" and "social" revolutions. The *Communist Manifesto* as their death certificate. The *bohème* dis-

solves into a legal opposition and an anarchist opposition. Baudelaire's ambivalent position between the two. His flight into the asocial.

The motif of death in Baudelaire's poetry penetrates the image of Paris. The "Tableaux parisiens," the *Spleen de Paris*. Excursus on the chthonic side of the city of Paris. The old bed of the Seine. The subterranean channels. Legends of subterranean Paris. Conspirators and communards in the catacombs. Twilight in the catacombs. Their ambiguity. They stand midway between house and street, between pavilion and hall. The undersea world of the arcades. Their importance for prostitution. Emphasis on the commodity character of the woman in the market of love. The doll as wish symbol.

Tout pour moi devient Allégorie.

—Baudelaire, "Le Cygne"

Baudelaire's genius, which is nourished on melancholy, is an allegorical genius. For the first time, with Baudelaire, Paris became the subject of lyric poetry . . .

. . . .

Facilis descensus Averni.

—Virgil

It is the unique disposition of Baudelaire's poetry that the image of the woman and the image of death intermingle in a third: that of Paris. The Paris of his poems is a sunken city, and more submarine than subterranean. It is the city of a death-fraught idyll. Yet the substrate of this idyll is nothing natural, and consists in neither the subterranean channels of Paris nor its catacombs and the legends that have grown up around them. It is, rather, a social, and that is to say, a modern substrate. But precisely the modern, *la modernité,* is always citing primal history. Here, this occurs through the ambiguity peculiar to the social relations and products of this epoch. The twilight of the arcades, which contemporaries compared to an undersea landscape, lies over the society that built them. Their construction itself is ambiguous. They stand midway between house and street, on the one hand; between pavilion and hall, on the other. At the same time, this ambiguity set the tone for the market of love. Prostitution, in which the woman represents merchant and merchandise in one, acquires a particular significance.

Je voyage pour connaître ma géographie.

The last poem of *Les Fleurs du mal:* "Le Voyage." The last journey of the flâneur: death. Its destination: the new. Newness is a quality independent of the use value of the thing. It is the last word of fashion. It is the semblance that forms the essence of the images which the dreaming subject of history engenders. The art that doubts its task must make novelty into its highest value . . .

. . . .

The press organizes the market in spiritual values, in which initially there is a boom. Eugène Sue becomes the first celebrity of the *feuilleton*. Nonconformists rebel against the commodity character of art. They rally round the banner of *l'art pour l'art*. From this watchword derives the conception of the total work of art, which would seal art off from the further development of technology. The *Gesamtkunstwerk* is a premature synthesis, which bears the seeds of death within it. The solemn rite with which it is celebrated is the pendant to the distractions which surround the apotheosis of the commodity. In their syntheses, both abstract from the social existence of human beings. Baudelaire succumbs to the rage for Wagner.

VI. Haussmann, or the Strategic Embellishment of Paris

. . . .

... increased the financial risks of Haussmannization.

The world exhibition of 1867 marked the high point of the regime and of Haussmann's power. Paris is confirmed as capital of luxury and of fashions. Excursus on the political significance of fashion. Fashion's innovations leave intact the framework of domination. For those who are ruled, it passes the time in which those who rule luxuriate. The insights of F.Th.Vischer.

Haussmann attempts to bolster his dictatorship . . .

. . . .

Fais voir, en déjouant la ruse,
O république, à ces pervers
Ta grande face de Méduse
Au milieu de rouges éclairs.

—Chanson d'ouvriers vers 1850

The barricade returns to life during the Commune. It is stronger and better secured than ever. It stretches across the great boulevards and shields the trenches behind it. If the *Communist Manifesto* ends the age of professional conspirators, then the Commune puts an end to the phantasmagoria according to which the proletariat and its republic are the fulfillment of 1789. This phantasmagoria conditions the forty years lying between the Lyons insurrection and the Paris Commune. The bourgeoisie did not share in this error . . .

. . . .

[1] {Balzac was the first to speak of the ruins of the bourgeoisie. But he still knew nothing about them. It was Surrealism which first got a glimpse of the field of debris left behind by the capitalist development of the forces of production.}

But it was Surrealism that first opened our eyes to them. These ruins became, for Surrealism, the object of a research no less impassioned than that which the humanists of the Renaissance conducted on the remnants of classical antiquity. Painters like Picasso and Chirico allude to this analogy. This unrelenting confrontation of the recent past with the present moment is something new, historically. Other contiguous links in the chain of generations have existed within the collective consciousness, but they were hardly distinguished from one another within the collective. The present, however, already stands to the recent past as the awakening stands to the dream. The development of the forces of production, in the course of the previous century, shattered that century's wish symbols even before the monuments representing them had collapsed, and before the paper on which they were rendered had yellowed. In the nineteenth century, this development of the forces of production worked to emancipate the forms of construction from art, just as in the sixteenth century the sciences freed themselves from philosophy. A start is made with architecture as engineered construction. Then comes the reproduction of nature as photography. The creation of fantasy prepares to become practical as commercial art. Literature submits to montage in the feuilleton. All these products are on the point of entering the market as commodities. But they linger on the threshold. They stop halfway. Value and commodity enter on a brief engagement before the market price makes their union legitimate. From this epoch derive the arcades and *intérieurs,* the exhibition halls and panoramas. They are residues of a dream world. But given that the realization of dream elements, in the course of waking up, is the paradigm of dialectical thinking, it follows that dialectical thinking is the organ of historical awakening. Only dialectical thinking is equal to the recent past, because it is, each time, its offspring. Every epoch, in fact, not only dreams the one to follow but, in thus dreaming, precipitates its awakening. It bears its end within itself and unfolds it—as Hegel already noticed—by cunning. The earliest monuments of the bourgeoisie began to crumble long ago, but we recognize, for the first time, how they were destined for this end from the beginning.

Materials for the Exposé of 1935

These materials consist of notations, schemes, and methodological reflections (*Gesammelte Schriften*, vol. 5 [Frankfurt: Suhrkamp, 1982], pp. 1206–1223, 1250–1251), which are connected to Benjamin's work on a "general plan" for *The Arcades Project*. Begun in March 1934, this work culminated in the exposé of 1935, "Paris, die Hauptstadt des XIX. Jahrhunderts." Certain of the notes, such as No. 3, may date from the late twenties. A relatively precise dating is possible only for No. 5, written February–May 1935, and for Nos. 20–25 (see Translators' Notes 9 and 10). The thematic ordering of the material is that of the German editor. Passages crossed out by Benjamin are in curved brackets { }. Editorial insertions are in angular brackets ‹ ›. Square brackets [ ] are Benjamin's. Words enclosed in double square brackets [[ ]] are later additions. The symbol ‹x› indicates illegible material.

No. 1

1848 December 10: election of Louis Bonaparte
    Bloc of Catholics, Legitimists, Orleanists; Napoleon promises freedom
      of instruction
    Ledru-Rollin gets 400,000 votes; Lamartine 8,000; Cavaignac
      1,500,000; Napoleon 5,500,000

1850 *Loi Falloux*
    Bail for the newspapers raised to 50,000 francs
    Electoral law, making the right to vote conditional on three years'
      residence in a municipality, as certified by tax lists

1851 Rejection of the Napoleonic amendments to the electoral law
    Victor Hugo tries in vain to mobilize the workers against the coup
      d'état
    December 20: plebiscite; 7,500,000 yes; 650,000 no

1852 November 20: plebiscite on reestablishment of the Empire. 7,839,000
      yes; 53,000 no; 20 percent abstaining

1863 Thiers and Berryer elected to the Chamber

1866 Formation of the Tiers Parti under Ollivier

1868 Restoration of freedom of the press and freedom of assembly

1869 Republicans 40 seats (Gambetta, Rochefort); Union Libérale 50; Tiers
      Parti 116. Bonapartists in the minority

1870   Plebiscite: 7,350,000 votes for the constitutional monarchy, against
        1,538,000 (Bonapartists and Republicans)

1864   Concession of the right to strike

1848   Abolition of the obligatory uniform for the Garde Nationale
        Increase of the number of electors through universal suffrage, from
            200,000 to over 9,000,000
        Emoluments for a member of parliament: 25 francs per day
        March 17 and April 16: violent demonstrations for the postponement
            of elections to the Constituent Assembly
        Cassation ‹?› of the Garde Mobile

1831ff. Parti du Mouvement: Laffitte, Lafayette, Barrot
        Parti de Résistance: Périer, Molé, Guizot, Thiers

No. 2

Fashion

1866   The head like a cloud, high above the valley of the dress
        Lamps in the form of vases: the rare flower "light" is put in oil

1868   The breast covered with a fringed border

—   Architectural forms on clothes

—   Visitation of the Virgin, as theme of fashion images

—   Fashionable clothing, as theme for confectioners

—   Motifs of hedges ‹?›, of gossamer ‹?› appear on clothes 1850–1860

—   Woman as equilateral triangle (crinoline)

—   Woman as X—End of the Empire—

        Jacket as double door

        Dress as fan

        Infinite possibility of permutation with the elements of fashion

No. 3

The Best Book on Paris

    Mirror city (the glass-plated armoire)

    Energies of the big city: gasoline tanks

    Illuminated advertising: new type of writing (no illuminated advertising in
        the arcades)

    Signboards: old type of writing

Gaslight in Baudelaire

Passage de l'Opéra

Aragon's technique compared with photographic technique

Fair in the basement ("Carnival of Paris")

| Teleology of Paris: Eiffel Tower and motorways

Parisian streets in French literature (statistically)

| The system of Parisian streets: a vascular network of imagination

{Bernouard: Parisian dialects during the war}

Sacré Coeur: ichthyosaur; Eiffel Tower: giraffe

Baby Cadum   [[Mme. Zahna]]

Fireproof walls

{Paris and the traveling <?> authors

Aragon   *Vague de rêves*

Nineteenth century: kitsch, new collections

Mirrors in the cafés: for the sake of the light, but also because the rooms are
so small}

No. 4

Themes of the Arcades Project

Entrance of the railroad into the world of dream and symbol

{Presentation of historical knowledge according to the image of awakening}

Fourier's "industrial fugue" as signature of an epoch that is crowned by the
world exhibitions

The Garde Nationale, military order of industry and commerce

{The domestic interior (furniture) in Poe and Baudelaire}

Sponsorship of the three kingdoms for the arcade: the mineral kingdom with
glass and iron; the vegetable kingdom with the palm: the animal kingdom
with aquatic fauna

The crisis that hits landscape painting with the advent of the diorama extends to the portrait with photography

{Wiertz as ennobler of the diorama}

From department store to world exhibition

{Haussmann's "strategic embellishment" of Paris}

{Fourier's archaic idyll: the child of nature as consumer; Pestalozzi's modern
utopia: the bourgeois as producer}

{Napoleon I as last representative of revolutionary terrorism, insofar as the
bourgeoisie is concerned}

The not-yet-conscious knowledge of what has been stems from the now

{History of the Paris Stock Exchange and the Salons des Etrangers}

The past unfolds in the wax museum like distance in the domestic interior.

No. 5

‹Themes of the Arcades Project II›

The camouflage of bourgeois elements in the *bohème*.

The *bohème* as form of existence of the proletarian intelligentsia.

The ideologues of the bourgeoisie: Victor Hugo, Lamartine. On the other hand, Rimbaud

The bourgeoisie's *maîtres de plaisir:* Scribe, Sue.

Industrialization of literature, the "negro"; industrialization of literature through the press

Industrial poetry of the Saint-Simonians

Beginnings of trade in modern artworks

{Panoramic literature}

{Beginnings of the *Gesamtkunstwerk* ‹total work of art› in the panoramas}

Literature and commerce (names of magazines derived from vaudevilles)

Specialty and originality

Inspiration for early photography: in ideas with Wiertz, in technology with Nadar.

{Arago's speech in the Chamber on photography} {/ Balzac's theory of photography}

{Photography at the industrial exhibition of 1855}

Meaning of the photographic reproduction of artworks; overcoming of art through ph‹otography›

Photography and electric light (Nadar)

{Attitude of the reactionary intelligentsia toward photography (Balzac)}

{The veristic art of photography founded on the fashionable illusionism of the panoramas}

Wiertz as precursor of montage (realism plus tendentiousness); stereorama and painting (Wiertz)

Three aspects of flânerie; Balzac, Poe, Engels; the illusionistic, psychological, economic

Flânerie as hothouse of illusion; Servandoni's project

The untranslatable literature of flânerie. "Paris street by street and house by house"

The flâneur and the collector; the archaic Paris of flânerie

{The flâneur skirts actuality}

{The city as a landscape and a room}

{*Egalité* as phantasmagoria}

{The tempo of flânerie and its cessation; exemplified by the restaurant and the means of transport}

Indecision of the flâneur; ambiguity of the arcades; opaqueness of class relations

{The doll in the annex to the cocotte's}

{Sexual-psychological interpretation of the cult of dolls; body and wax figure; disguise}

Interior and museum

{Jugendstil, or the end of the interior (Jugendstil and poster).}

Emancipation and prostitution

Girardin; the demoiselles of 1830; Fourier and Feuerbach

Emancipation and the Saint-Simonians; the cashier

Cult of love: attempt to deploy the technical force of production in opposition to the natural force of production

Rise of the proletariat; its awakening in the June Insurrection

{The labor exchanges}

The culture of the nineteenth century as a gigantic effort to stem the forces of production

{Premature syntheses. Insurance against the proletariat}

The Garde Nationale

Precursors of stocks and bonds

Change in the forms of property as a result of the railroad

Corruption in the awarding of contracts during construction on the railroad and during Haussmann's renovations

{Plekhanov on the world exhibition of 1889}

Museums and exhibitions

{The enthronement of the commodity (advertising and exhibitions)}

Influence of industry on language later than on the image (in the case of the Surrealists)

Allegory and advertisement (Baudelaire)

Police and conspirators; the *porte-lanternes* ‹lantern carriers›

{Construction has the role of the subconscious}

Physiognomic digressions
the flâneur / {the bohemian}
{the gambler} / the {dandy} /
  {the collector}
    Snob (the new)
    the new as antithesis to
      what conforms to a plan
    Fourier's serenity
    Godin and Ford
    The industrial Christ (Lamartine)
    Mercury in Fourier

Construction in city planning
The role of the big city in the
  nineteenth century
Flaubert's style

Image and destruction in history
Historical anamnesis
Not-yet-conscious knowledge
  of what has been
{Abolition of fashion}
Effect and expression

{The doubt about history}
Components of death / Excursus on
  Proust

{The Commune as test of the revolutionary legend}

{Fashion in Apollinaire} {Cabet and the end of fashion}[1]

{The city as object of fashion (Lefeuve)}

Relation between technology and art as key to fashion

{The phenomenon of the *quartiers* (Jules Janin)}

Participation of women ‹in› the nature of the commodity, by virtue of fashion

{Connection of fashion with death}

{Theories of fashion: Karr / Vischer}

Fashion and colportage: "everybody's contemporary"[2]

{Inclusion of sex in the world of matter}

{Razing of the Passage de l'Opéra during construction of the Boulevard Haussmann}

{Irruption of perspective into city planning: end of the arcades}

{Formation of workers' districts in the suburbs}

{The end of the *quartiers* with Haussmann}

{The language of the prefect of police}

{Decline of the arcades in *Thérèse Raquin*}

Tools and workers with Haussmann

{End of the arcade: the bicycle palaces}

Points of contact between Saint-Simonianism and fascism

{The knickknack ⟨?⟩}

{The collector}

{The curiosity shop as domestic interior}

{Early socialism, the police, conspirators (re Fourier)}

       Workers' associations   {After-effects of 1789}

       {Blurred class divisions}   {The Comm⟨unist⟩ Manifesto as

    {Conspirators and the *bohème*}   conclusion of the first period}
{Technical wonders in the service of insurrection}

Promiscuity and hostility among the classes; their communication in the omnibus

Huysmans describes Ménilmontant

The workers' associations

Toppling of illusionism in the cityscape: perspectives

{Their introduction into the interior through the mirror}

Why was there no French Idealism?

Sensual delights of the bourgeois

Hedonism and cynicism

Illusionism of the cocottes

The arcades as dream- and wish-image of the collective

Fermenters of intoxication in the collective consciousness

{Phantasmagoria of space (the flâneur); phantasmagoria of time (the gambler)}

{Lafargue on the gambler.}   {Phantasmagoria of society: (the bohemian)}

Atmosphere of the dream: climate

The dream of empire; the Muses / {Basing of the first factory buildings on residential homes}

{The Empire style as expression of revolutionary terrorism}

Empire form of the first locomotives; technology under control / Treasury of images of technology

Are there English influences on the Empire style? / Technology and the new

Attaching to the first appearance of the machine under the Empire was the sense of a restoration of antiquity

{Napoleon's attitude toward industrials and intellectuals}

{The world exhibition of 1867}

{Grandville and Toussenel; Cabet} / {Grandville and the advertisement}: dream and awakening

Bourgeois hedonism

{Rescue of the utopians; approaches to Fourier in Marx and Engels}

Fourier and Scheerbart; {Fourier's living on in Zola}

{Fourier and Jean Paul} / the true meaning of utopia: it is a precipitate of collective dreams

{The enthronement of the commodity on a cosmic scale / Commodity and fashion}

Advertisement and poster (business and politics)

{Dominance of finance capital under Napoleon III}

{Offenbach and the operetta}

The opera as center[3]

{Crinoline and Second Empire}

Polemic against Jung, who wants to distance awakening from dream.

No. 6

Provisional Schemata

Revolutionary praxis
    Technique of street fighting and barricade construction
    Revolutionary *mise en scène*
    Proletarians and professional conspirators

Fashion
    "everybody's contemporary"
    Attempt to lure sex into the world of matter

No. 7

Dialectical Schemata

Hell—golden age
    Keywords for hell: ennui, gambling, pauperism
    A canon of this dialectic: fashion
    The golden age as catastrophe

Dialectic of the commodity
  A canon for this dialectic to be drawn from Odradek[4]
  The positive in the fetish

Dialectic of the newest and oldest
  Fashion is a canon for this dialectic also
  The oldest as newest: the daily news
  The newest as oldest: the Empire

No. 8

First dialectical stage: the arcade changes from a place of splendor to a place of decay

Second dialectical stage: the arcade changes from an unconscious experience to something consciously penetrated

Not-yet-conscious knowledge of what has been. Structure of what-has-been at this stage. Knowledge of what has been as a becoming aware, one that has the structure of awakening.

Not-yet-conscious knowledge on the part of the collective

All insight to be grasped according to the schema of awakening. And shouldn't the "not-yet-conscious knowledge" have the structure of dream?

— {Dream kitsch
  Parisian chronicles}   {the terrifying knock on the door}
                            the ugliness of the object is the terrifying knock
                            on the door when we're asleep[5]

{We fashion an epoch in the history of the antiques trade and construct a clock by which to tell when objects are ripe for collecting.}

We construct an awakening theoretically—that is, we imitate, in the realm of language, the trick that is decisive physiologically in awakening, for awakening operates with cunning. Only with cunning, not without it, can we work free of the realm of dream.

Awakening is the exemplary case of remembering: the weighty and momentous case, in which we succeed in remembering the nearest (most obvious).

What Proust intends with the experimental rearrangement of furniture is no different from what Bloch tries to grasp as darkness of the lived moment.

Here the question arises: In what different canonical ways can man behave (the individual man, but also the collective) with regard to dreaming? And what sort of comportment, at bottom, is adequate to true waking being?

We conceive the dream (1) as historical phenomenon, (2) as collective phenomenon.

Efforts <?> to shed light on the dreams of the individual with the help of the doctrine of the historical dreams of the collective.

{We teach that, in the stratification of the dream, reality never simply is, but rather that it strikes the dreamer. And I treat of the arcades precisely as though, at bottom, they were something that has happened to me}

We have to wake up from the existence of our parents. In this awakening, we have to give an account of the nearness of that existence. Obedience as category of nearness in religious education. Collecting as profane category of nearness; the collector interprets dreams of the collective.

Freud's doctrine of the dream as a phenomenon of nature. Dream as historical phenomenon.

Opposition to Aragon: to work through all this by way of the dialectics of awakening, and not to be lulled, through exhaustion, into "dream" or "mythology." What are the sounds of the awakening morning we have drawn into our dreams? "Ugliness," the "old-fashioned" are merely distorted morning voices that talk of our childhood.

No. 9

Thesis and antithesis are to be drawn together into the dream-variation-image ‹*Traum-Wandel-Bild*›. The aspects of splendor and misery attaching to the arcades are dream vision. The dialectical reversal in synthesis is awakening. Its mechanism. How we free ourselves from the world of our parents through cunning. Antinomy of the sentimental. On the hallucinatory function of architecture. Dream images that rise up into the waking world.

Epitome of the false redemption: Jugendstil. It proves the law according to which effort brings about its opposite.

The motif of dialectic should be delineated specifically in reference to
perspective
luxury and fashion

Theory of awakening to be developed on the basis of the theory of boredom.

Theory of perspective in connection with Flaubert. Perspective and plush.

{Cite a remark of Aragon's that lies at the center of these questions: the arcades are what they are for us here through the fact that they no longer are (in themselves).} Removal of accents is characteristic of the dreamworld. An affinity with kitsch.

Economic rudiments
   the consumer
   luxury buildings
   fashion and boulevard

Reversal
   miscarried matter
   altered tempo
   date fatidique: 1893[6]

{New meaning of the arcades
   Aragon: new mythology
   relation to the nineteenth century
   awakening
   discovery of perspective}

{Chapters
   Street Names / Perspective / Collecting / Interior of the street / Fashion /}

Fashion always places its fig leaf on the spot where the revolutionary nakedness of society may be found. A slight adjustment and . . . But why is this adjustment fruitful only when it is carried out on the body of the recent past? (Noah ‹?› and his shame?)

No. 10

{Boredom}

{First treatment of decline: Aragon}		
Dialectic of the commodity	*Magasins de nouveautés* miscarried matter	{Theory of the collector Elevation of the commodity to the status of allegory}

Dialectic of sentimentality (sentences from "Dream Kitsch")[7]
                             {Archaeology of the ‹x›. Dream is the earth in which finds are made.}

Dialectic of flânerie	the interior as street (luxury)
	the street as interior (misery)

Dialectic of fashion   pleasure and cadaver

{Beginning: description of the present-
day arcades
Their dialectical development: commodity / perspective
Actuality of the arcades in their dream
structure}

{Attempt at a determination of the
essence of street names: they are
not pure allegories
Mythological T‹o›pography: Bal-
zac}

Thesis

Flowering of the arcades under
Louis Philippe

The panoramas
The magasins
Love

Antithesis

Decline of the arcades at the end
of the nineteenth century

Plush
Miscarried matter
The whore

Synthesis

Discovery of the arcades
The unconscious knowledge of what has
been becomes conscious

Theory of awakening

Dialectic of persp.
Dial. of fashion
Dial. of sentim.

{Dioramas
Plush-perspective
Rainy weather}

No. 11

Fundamental for Criticism

Systematic exterior architecture

Commodities—materials

Ur-history of the feuilleton

Golden age and hell

Theory of phantasmagoria: culture

More precise determination of the
commodity

Fetish and death's head

Erroneous

World exhibitions and working class

Fourier and arcades

Painting in the negative of the trace

Countinghouse and chamber of commerce

Saturn problem

Barcelona béton

No. 12

Methodological

Dialectical images are wish symbols. Actualized in them, together with the thing ‹*Sache*› itself, are its origin and its decline.

What sort of perceptibility should the presentation of history possess? Neither the cheap and easy visibility of bourgeois history books, nor the insufficient visibility of Marxist histories. What it has to fix perceptually are the images deriving from the collective unconscious.

The ‹development› of the productive forces of a society is determined not only by the raw materials and instruments at that society's disposal, but also by its milieu and the experiences it has there.

Waiting as form of existence of the parasitic elements.

No. 13

New Themes and Formulations

{With the expanded range of transportation, the informational merits of painting diminish. In reaction to photography it begins initially, over the course of half a century, to stress the elements of color in the picture. As Impressionism yields to Cubism, painting opens up a wider domain—one into which photography, for the moment, cannot follow.}

{For a subjective point of view on the presentation of the new, as it appears at midcentury in the society and its milieux, no one can take responsibility: hence the lens ‹*das Objektiv*›.}

Waiting and letting wait. Waiting as form of existence of the parasitic elements.

No. 14

Fundamental Questions

The historical significance of semblance ‹*Schein*›

{What are the ruins of the bourgeoisie?}

Where, within the new, runs the boundary between reality and semblance?

Ur-history of the nineteenth century

Relation between false consciousness and dream consciousness. Mirroring takes place in the dream consciousness. Collective dream consciousness and superstructure.

The dialectic, in standing still, makes an image. Essential to this image is a semblance.

The now of recognizability is the moment of awakening.

In the awakening, the dream stands still.

The historical movement is a dialectical movement. But the movement of false consciousness is not. This consciousness becomes dialectical also in the awakening.

No. 15

Methodological Reflections

Make use of studies on the "now of recognizability"

Make use of Proust's description of awakening

Awakening as the critical moment in the reading of dream images

Special claims of the recent past on the method of the historian

Demarcation from cultural history

Reread Hegel on dialectics at a standstill

The experience of our generation: that capitalism will not die a natural death.

Here, for the first time, the recent past becomes *distant* past. Primal history forms part of the recent past, just as mountains, seen from a great distance, appear to form part of the landscape lying before them.

No. 16

Wiesengrund

Dialectical image and dialectics at a standstill in Hegel

No. 17

The Fourierist utopia announces a transformation in the function of poetry

No. 18

Placed, thus, in the center of history, ‹broken off›

As man forms the center of the horizon that, in his eyes, stretches around him, so his existence forms for him the center of history. Looking about him at the midday hour, he invites the emaciated spirits of the past to dine at his table. {The historian presides} over a ghostly meal. The historian is the herald who summons the departed to this banquet of spirits.

The living generation ‹broken off›

{The merit of this little volume lies in the evocation of the different districts of a great city. It is not their picturesque aspect that concerns the author, nor anything exterior. It is, rather, the unique character conferred on each of these *quartiers* by the social strata informing them and the occupations of the residents.}

If the speculative phenomena attendant on "Haussmannization" remain for the most part in shadow, the tactical interests of the reform—interests which Napoleon III willingly concealed behind his imperial ambitions—emerge more clearly. A contemporary apology for Haussmann's project is comparatively frank on this subject. It commends the new streets for "not subserving the customary tactics of the local insurrections." Before this, Paris had already been paved in wood so as to deprive the revolution of its building material. As Karl Gutzkow writes in his *Pariser Briefen,* "no one builds barricades out of blocks of wood." To appreciate what is meant by this, recall that in 1830 some six thousand barricades were counted in the city.

Louis Philippe already had the nickname "Roi-Maçon" ‹Mason King›. With Napoleon III, the mercantile, hygienic, and military forces bent on transforming the city's image were allied with the aspiration to immortalize ‹oneself› in monuments of lasting peace. In Haussmann he ‹x› found the energy necessary for implementation of the plan. Putting the energy to work was, of course, not easy for him.

A careerist in the service of a usurper

Intran

Destructive-Pacific Imperialism
or
"The Haussmannization of Paris"

III. Haussmann and Napoleon III	The careerist serving the usurper
II. Strategic embellishment	
III. Fantastic accounts of Haussmann	

Strategic embellishment	Napoleon as pretender to the throne
The technique of barricade fighting	The coup d'état and Haussmann
The strategic lines	The police and Orsini's assassination
The theoretic base	attempt
Jurisprudence	Haussmann and the parliament
The spectacles; aesthetics	Haussmann's later career

Haussmann's means
Significance of substructions
The railroads
The world exhibitions
The new city planning

Plan of March 1934

[[Portrait of Haussmann;
destructive energies in him]]

Paris

Capital of the Nineteenth Century

+Haussmann, or Strategic
  Embellishment

Class warfare

Grandville, or the World Exhibition**)

Fetish character of the commodity

Baudelaire, or the Streets of Paris***)

Louis Philippe, or the
  Interior****)*****)++)

The *bohème*

+Daguerre, or the Panorama

The collective unconscious

Fourier, or the Arcades

[[Psychology of the newspaper:
the need for novelty]]

[[Cross-schemas

Paris   Metaphysics

Proletariat   Physiognomics (?)

Dialectics]]

****) Fashion
 ***) Flâneur
****) Boredom   *****)   Jugendstil (Jugendstil as end of the interior)

++   the collector   Zola: *Le Travail*

   I. Fourier, or the Arcades
      His figure set off against the Empire / Antiquity and Cockaigne / Historical
         hedonism***
      Fourier and Jean Paul / Why there was no French idealism
 {II. Daguerre, or the Panorama (Passage des Panoramas, 1800)
      Panoramas / Museums / Exhibitions / The premature syntheses / The
         breakthrough of the daguerreotype / Irruption of technology into the
         realm of art}
 III. Louis Philippe, or the Interior
      The dream house** / {The collector / The flâneur / The gambler}
 IV. Grandville, or the World Exhibition
      Happiness in machinery / The commodity in the cosmos /   Collector
         Fourier's dream   Gambler
      Plekhanov on 1889   Forger
   V. Haussmann, or the Embellishment of Paris   Flâneur

*** Origin of the arcades and
    primal history
** the chthonic Paris

| Fragments of the general layout |

VI. {Haussmann, or the "Strategic Embellishment" of Paris
    Excursus on the gambler
    The demolitions of Paris
    The end of the arcades
    Technique of street- and barricade-fighting
    The political function of fashion; critique of crinoline in F. Th. Vischer
    The Commune}

  I. Fourier, or the Arcades

> Transitory aims of constructions in iron.
> Moreover: iron, as the first artificial
> building material, is the first to
> undergo a development. This
> proceeded more and more rapidly in
> the course of the century. Arcades in
> Fourier are designed for dwelling.

    The Empire style
    Materialist tendencies in the bourgeoisie (Jean Paul, Pestalozzi; Fourier)
    Rise of the arcades   Marx and Engels on Fourier
    The arcades in Fourier   Theory of education as root of utopia
    Fourier's afterlife in Zola
    The beginnings of iron construction / The disguising of construction

 II. {Daguerre, or the Panorama
    Excursus on art ‹and› technology (Beaux-Arts and Ecole Polytechnique)
    The welcoming of photography (Balzac and Arago)
    The confrontation between art and technology in Wiertz
      Railroad stations and halls as new sites for art
    The panoramas as transitional phenomenon between art and the technique of reproducing nature
    Excursus on the later development: extension of the commodity world through the photo
    {Paris as panorama; the panoramic literature, 1830–1850
      (Life of the worker as subject of an idyll)}
    Photography at the industrial exhibition of 1855
    Rear-guard action by art against technology, in Talmeyr (1900)}

[margin: Passage des Panoramas]

III. Grandville, or the World Exhibitions
    Fashion as means of communicating commodity character to the cosmos
    Magic of cast iron in outer space and in the underworld
    Further development of the arcades in the exhibition halls; Paxton's
      Crystal Palace of 1851

The sex appeal of the commodity

Mobilization of the inorganic through fashion; its triumph in the doll

{The love market of Paris}

Paris as material of fashion; psychology of the *quartier* in Janin and
  Lefeuve

{The battle between utopia and cynicism in Grandville}

Grandville as precursor of advertising graphics

The world exhibition of 1867; triumph of cynicism; Offenbach as its
  demon

Grandville and the Fourierists (Toussenel's philosophy of nature)

The universal extension of commodity character to the world of things

Body and wax figure

Chthonic elements in Grandville / {Chthonic elements in the image of
  Paris}

The *spécialité*

No. 22

On V

{Critique of modernity (presumably a separate section). The new has the
  character of a semblance ‹*Scheincharakter*› and coincides with the semblance of the eternally recurrent. The dialectical semblance of the new and
  always identical is the basis of "cultural history."}

On V

Four digressions on boredom. The snob, who lives in the semblant world of
  the new and ever identical, has a constant companion: boredom. With
  Proust, snobbism becomes the key to the social analysis of the upper crust.

The total work of art represents an attempt to impose myth on society (myth
  being, as Raphael rightly says ‹in *Proudhon, Marx, Picasso* (Paris, 1933)›,
  p. 171, the precondition for *oeuvres d'art intégrales*).

No. 23[10]

[The eternal return as nightmare of historical consciousness]

{Jung wants to distance dream from awakening}

{Three aspects of flânerie: Balzac, Poe, Engels; the illusionistic, the psychological, the economic}

[Servandoni ‹?›]

{The new as antithesis to what conforms to a plan}

Allegory and advertising [the personification of commodities rather than of
  concepts; Jugendstil introduces the allegorical figure to advertising]

{The cashier as living image, as allegory of cash}

Cult of love: attempt to bring natural production into opposition with industrial production

[The concept of culture as the highest development of phantasmagoria]

[The concept of eternal return: the "last stand" against the idea of progress]

[Annihilation of the phantasmagoria of culture in the idea of eternal return]

[Odradek and the dialectic of the commodity]

[Attempt to banish ennui by dint of the new]

[Waiting for the new: in the last poem ‹of *Les Fleurs du mal*›—going to meet the new—but running into death]

No. 24

{Waiting as form of existence of parasitic elements}

Actualized in the dialectical image, together with the thing itself, are its origin and its decline. Should both be eternal? (eternal transience)

[Is the dialectical image free of semblance ‹*Schein*›?]

{The now of recognizability is the moment of awakening}

{[Proust: description of awakening]}

[Hegel on dialectics at a standstill]

{The experience of our generation: that capitalism will not die a natural death}

For the first time, here, the recent past becomes distant past

The *Gesamtkunstwerk* represents an attempt to impose myth on society (myth being, as Raphael rightly says, p. 171, the precondition for the *oeuvre d'art intégrale*).

"Everybody's contemporary" and eternal recurrence

No. 25

The question posed in I: What is the historical object?

The response of III: The dialectical image

The uncommon ephemerality of the genuine historical object (flame) compared with the fixity of the philological object. Where the text is itself the absolute historical object—as in theology—it holds fast to the moment of extreme ephemerality in the character of a "revelation."

The idea of a history of humanity as idea of the sacred text. In fact, the history of humanity—as prophecy—has, at all times, been read out of the sacred text.

The new and ever identical as the categories of historical semblance.—How stands the matter with regard to eternity?

The dissolution of historical semblance must follow the same trajectory as the construction of the dialectical image

Figures of historical semblance: I.
                                    II. Phantasmagoria
                                    III. Progress

Materials for "Arcades"

Among Benjamin's papers are the following materials, consisting of typewritten sheets with additions in his own and in Franz Hessel's hand. These notes and sketches (*Gesammelte Schriften,* vol. 5 [Frankfurt: Suhrkamp, 1982], pp. 1341–1347) evidently relate to the abortive collaboration with Hessel on the arcades. Typewritten text is printed here in italics; Benjamin's longhand notations, in underlined italics; and Hessel's longhand notations, in roman type. Passages that are crossed out in the manuscript are in curved brackets { } here.

Picture puzzles of the French Revolution or *Visible World History (Paris of the Romans, Middle Ages, ancien régime, revolution, and so on.) Balzac's streets and corners. (Sue, Hugo, and others.)*

May 1 on the Butte Rouge.

New and old catacombs, Métro, wine cellars, ancient sites.

Street vending.

Ghetto

The street where newspapers are printed

Lost animals (the pound)

The slaughterhouses

Social fortifications.

{*Stroll along vanished town walls (ancient)*

Philip Augustus, Louis XII, Farmers-General and the last fortification, now in the process of being demolished.}

Gasoline. (The perfect chauffeur in Paris)

Mirrors.

The fireside and the "Lanterne"

The last fiacres

Old signs.

Conveniences and inconveniences (tobacco, mailboxes, tickets, poster pillars, and so forth.)

Parisians on Paris.

Pickup, *môme,* streetwalker, tart, artiste, and so on.

Paris alpine.

Developmental and artistic history of the Eiffel Tower.

Afternoon in Montmartre.

Etiquette for mealtimes

Inoffensive monuments

Il faut amuser les enfants

Biography of a street (*Rue Saint-Honoré,* or Rivoli)

Annual fair.

Fashion houses

The bridges.

Doors and windows.

Architectures of chance. (Posters)

Arcades.

Hotel

Dance hall.

The smallest square in Paris.

Church windows

The parks from Monceau to Buttes-Chaumont.

Street of art dealers (1,000 meters of painted canvas)

The Sunday of the poorer classes

Tea in the Bois.

America and Asia in Paris

Reassuring advice for museum visits.

Lunch hour for dressmakers' assistants. (Fairy tale motif.)

(Physiology of the box)

Remarkable history of the development of small restaurants.

{*With Saint-Simon, Liselotte, and other revenants in Versailles.*}

All sorts of racing.

The Sunday of the poorer classes.

Staircases, windows, doors, and signboards of Paris.

Dance halls of different districts

Paris alpine.

The déjeuner of dressmakers' assistants.

How a first-class restaurant comes into being.

Apéritif, place, time, varieties

Fair.

How I drive my car in Paris

Theater with fewer than 500 seats.

(Purveyors of pleasure)

Fashionable teas.

Tavern with musical entertainment.

1,000 meters of modern art (Rue de la Boëtie)

Great and small labyrinth of Paris   Catacombs and Paris.

Paris translated ‹traduit›.

Underground newspapers

Parisian mirrors, from the bistro to Versailles.

Types of cocottes: streetwalkers, mômes, *call girls   (deluxe)   social relations
    tarts   lionesses   girlfriend   liaison   sweetheart   artiste*

Artiste sérieuse.

Toyshop   saddlers   harness makers   hardware store

Things of yesteryear and the like; Sacre Ferme 1.N.

A walk with the secret agent.

*Small side alley in the Passage des Panoramas: service passage with iron ladders on
    the walls.*

Visitors' cards are made immediately; boots immediately cleaned

*Mosaic thresholds, in the style of the old restaurants in the Palais-Royal, lead to a
    dîner de Paris at five francs—so broad and empty are they, that one cannot be-
    lieve there is really a restaurant up there. The same is true of the entrance to the
    Petit Casino. There you indeed see a ticket booth and prices of seats; but you have
    the feeling that, once through the glass door, you would wind up on the street
    again instead of in a theater.*

*Many institutes of hygiene   For the biceps, hip reducer, gladiators with orthopedic
    belts*   Bandages round the white bellies of mannequins

*In old hairdressing salons, the last women with long hair, undulating "permanent
    wave," petrified coiffures.*

*If these latter are petrified, the stonework of the arcades, by contrast, often has the
    effect of crumbling papier-mâché.*

Ridiculous "souvenirs" and bibelots—quite hideous

Odalisques stretched out next to inkwell; priestesses raise aloft ashtrays like
    patens.

"A la Capricieuse," lingerie de tout genre.

Doll mender.

Fan factory under the arch

Bookshop on the mezzanine: Etreintes secrètes, Art d'aimer, Affolantes Illusions, Les Insatiables, School of Love, Mémoires d'une bonne à tout faire. In their midst, Images d'Épinal. Harlequin betroths his daughter. Images of Napoleon. Artillery. Way to heaven and hell, with caption in French and German (in devotional shop on the Rue du Val de Grâce   English   the broad and the narrow way).

Typographies.

Visitors' cards while you wait

Everywhere, as addition to the program, as guest star: stockings. Now lying next to some photos, now in a tavern, watched over by a girl (we think of *the theater in Montrouge, where, during the day, they hang on the ticket booth that opens only at evening)*

Stairway to the Arabic restaurant, Kebab

Frequently, handbags (petits sacs) in open cardboard boxes, wrapped in tissue paper.

In the building next door, where there is a gateway, almost an arcade: *Mme. de Consolis, Maîtresse de Ballet—Leçons, Cours, Numéros. Mme. Zahna, Cartomancière.*

{Narrow alley} behind Hôtel de Boulogne, with one window above hairdresser. The girl waiting below and the one looking out of the window. The whole framed by the entryway.

‹Drawing by Hessel representing the gateway mentioned›

This in front of me (as seen from the café) and, to the right, the Gate of [Saint-Denis dedicated to] Louis the Great, with couchant lions, weapons, and vague trophies on pyramids.

In the arcades, bolder colors are possible. There are red and green combs.

Preserved in the arcades are types of collar studs for which we no longer know the corresponding collars or shirts.

Should a shoemaker's shop be neighbor to a confectioner's, his display of shoelaces will start to resemble licorice.

{There are many stamp shops (which, with their South American hummingbird stamps on paper stained by damp, remind the visitor from Berlin of childhood and cuckoos).}

One could imagine an ideal shop in an ideal arcade—a shop which brings together all métiers, which is doll clinic and orthopedic institute in one, which sells trumpets and shells, birdseed in fixative pans from a photographer's darkroom, ocarinas as umbrella handles.

A factory producing cockades for weddings and banquets, "finery for marrieds."

1. (*Not long ago, a piece of old Paris disappeared—the Passage de l'Opéra, which once led from the boulevards to the old opera theater. Construction of the Boulevard Haussmann swallowed it up. And so we turn our attention to the arcades that still exist, to the brighter, livelier, and in some cases renovated arcades of the opera district, to the narrow, often empty and dust-covered arcades of more obscure neighborhoods. They work, the arcades—sometimes in their totality, sometimes only in certain parts—as a past become space; they harbor antiquated trades, and even those that are thoroughly up to date acquire in these inner spaces something archaic.*) *Since the light comes only from above through glass roofs, and all stairways to the left or right, at entranceways between the shops, lead into darkness, our conception of life within the rooms to which these stairways ascend remains somewhat shadowy.*

1a. *The Illustrated Guide to Paris, a complete picture of the city on the Seine and its environs from the year 1852, writes of the arcades:* ‹there follows the citation found at the beginning of "The Arcades of Paris"›.

no responsibility toward the new age: it can come no more in the future

2. *At the entrance gates of the arcades (one could just as well say "exit gates," since, with these peculiar hybrid forms of house and street, every gate is simultaneously entrance and exit)—at the entrance gates one finds, on either side, remarkable and sometimes enigmatic inscriptions* and signs, *which oftentimes multiply along the walls within where, here and there, between the shops, a spiral staircase rises into darkness. We surmise that "Albert au 83" will be a hairdresser, and "Maillots de Théâtre" will most likely be silk tights, pink and light blue, for young singers and dancers; but these insistent letterings want to say more to us and something different. And should we find ourselves crowded out by those who actually buy and sell, and left standing between overloaded coatracks at the bottom of the spiral staircase, where we read "Institut de Beauté du Professeur Alfred Bitterlin," we cannot but feel anxious. And the "Fabrique de Cravates au 2ᵉ"—Does it make neckties for strangling? Oh, the needlework there will be quite inoffensive, of course, but these dark dilapidated stairs make us feel afraid.* But: "Union artistique de France au 3ᵉ"—What can that be? (*In all arcades—the wide and crowded ones of the boulevard, no less than the narrow deserted ones near the Rue Saint-Denis—there are displays of canes and umbrellas: serried ranks of colorful crooks.*)

3. {*Often, these inner spaces harbor antiquated trades, and even those that are thoroughly up to date will acquire in them something {archaic} obsolete*}
In the wide and crowded arcades of the boulevards, as in the narrow deserted arcades near the Rue Saint-Denis, there are always displays of umbrellas and canes: serried ranks of colorful crooks
{Many are the institutes of hygiene, where gladiators have on orthopedic belts, and there are bandages around the white bellies of mannequins.}
{In the shop windows of the hairdressers, one sees the last women with long hair; they have richly undulating masses of hair, which are "permanent waves," petrified coiffures.* And, while these are turned to stone, the masonry of the walls above is like crumbling papier-mâché.
Brittle, too, are the mosaic thresholds that lead you, in the style of the old restaurants of the Palais-Royal, to a "dîner de Paris" for five francs; they mount boldly to a glass door, but you can hardly believe that behind this door is really a restaurant. The glass door adjacent promises a "Petit Casino" and allows a glimpse of a ticket booth and prices of seats; but were you to open it and go in, wouldn't you rather come out on the street instead of into the space of a theater?** Or into a darkness such as that into which all stairs lead at the entranceways on either side?}

*{Baudelaire, "La chevelure." Redon, Baudelaire, who have made a special world out of hair. "Betrayed and sold"—that is a fate that first becomes intelligible within these spaces. Here, the head of Salome itself has become an ornament; or rather, a ghostly head that—now Salome's and now Anna Czyllak's—flits here and there undecided.}
**{The door, in fact, has a mirror in the middle and, since all walls are breached by mirrors, there is no telling outside from in, with all the equivocal illumination. Paris is the city of mirrors . . .}

4. {In the arcades {bolder} false colors are possible; that combs are red and green is not surprising, surprises no one. Snow White's stepmother had such things. And when the comb did not do its work, a red-green apple was needed.
Ticket agencies have large numbers of seats available for gapingly empty theaters. Shall we not, however, take advantage of this situation in order to have as neighbor some battered <?> creature who <broken off>
In such an agency the ticket was born
"Souvenirs" and bibelots can become particularly hideous; the odalisque lies in wait next to the inkwell; priestesses elevate ashtrays like patens.
Everywhere stockings play a starring role—now lying next to some photographs, now in a doll hospital, now on a side table in a tavern, watched over by a girl.

A bookstore places together on neighboring shelves {alluring manuals of the art of love,} introductions to outmoded vices, accounts of strange passions and vices, and memoirs of a maidservant, with vividly colored Epinal prints, on which Harlequin betroths his daughter, Napoleon rides through Marengo, and, close beside all types of artillery pieces, Old English burghers travel the broad path to hell and the narrow path of the Gospel.}

Preserved in the arcades are types of collar studs for which we no longer know the corresponding collars or shirts.

Should a shoemaker's shop   umbrella handles ‹broken off›

5. *At the entrance to one of the poorest arcades, we could read: "Bureau de Placement pour le Personnel des Deux Sexes,"* founded in 1859.*

   > **The personnel must live here—that can be inferred from the fact that a placement bureau for it exists* ‹marginal note›

   This stood above "Article de Paris, Spécialités pour Forains." We followed the narrow dark corridor to where—between a "librairie en solde," in which masses of books were stacked in dusty tied-up bundles, and a shop selling only buttons (mother-of-pearl, and the kind that in Paris is called "de fantaisie")— we discovered a sort of salon. On the pale-colored wallpaper full of figures and busts shone a gas lamp. By its light, an old woman sat reading. They say she has been there alone for years.

   {Having passed a stamp shop with South American hummingbird stamps on paper stained by damp, we come to an office shrouded in black: there, gold and silver is purchased.} There, the proprietor seeks sets of teeth in gold, in wax, or broken.*

   > **And not far from there must have stood the offices in which, toward the beginning of the Biedermeier period, Doctor Miracle created his Olympia. For they are the true fairies of these arcades (more salable and more worn than the life-size ones): the formerly world-famous Parisian dolls, which revolved on their musical socle and bore in their arms a doll-sized basket out of which, at the salutation of the minor chord, a lambkin poked its curious muzzle* ‹marginal note›

   But a small, red tin parasol, at the foot of a staircase close by, points the way coyly to a factory producing umbrella ferrules.

"Dialectics at a Standstill" / "The Story of Old Benjamin" Translators' Notes / Guide to Names and Terms / Index

The Passage Choiseul, 1908. Photographer unknown.

Dialectics at a Standstill

Approaches to the *Passagen-Werk*

By Rolf Tiedemann

There are books whose fate has been settled long before they even exist as books. Benjamin's unfinished *Passagen-Werk* is just such a case. Many legends have been woven around it since Adorno first mentioned it in an essay published in 1950.[1] Those legends became even more complexly embroidered after a two-volume selection of Benjamin's letters appeared, which abounded in statements about his intentions for the project. But these statements were neither complete nor coherent.[2] As a result, the most contradictory rumors spread about a book that competing Benjamin interpreters persistently referred to in the hope that it would solve the puzzles raised by his intellectual physiognomy. That hope has remained unrealized. The answer that the fragments of the *Passagen-Werk* give to its readers instead follows Mephisto's retort, "Many a riddle is made here," with Faust's "Many a riddle must be solved here."

In fact, for some years the texts that provide the most reliable information about the project Benjamin worked on for thirteen years, from 1927 until his death in 1940, and that he regarded as his masterpiece, have been available. Most of the more important texts he wrote during the last decade of his life are offshoots of the *Passagen-Werk*. If it had been completed, it would have become nothing less than a materialist philosophy of the history of the nineteenth century. The exposé entitled "Paris, the Capital of the Nineteenth Century" (1935) provides us with a summary of the themes and motifs Benjamin was concerned with in the larger work. The text introduces the concept of "historical schematism" (5:1150),[3] which was to serve as the basic plan for Benjamin's construction of the nineteenth century. On the other hand, "Das Kunstwerk im Zeitalter seiner technischen Reproduzierbarkeit" (The Work of Art in the Age of Technological Reproducibility; 1935–1936) has no thematic connection with the *Passagen-Werk* (dealing with phenomena belonging to the twentieth rather than to the nineteenth century), but is nevertheless relevant from the point of view of methodology. In that essay, Benjamin tries to "pinpoint the precise spot in the present my historical construction would take as its vanishing point' (Letters, 509). The great, fragmentary work on Baudelaire, which came into being in the years 1937–1939, offers a "miniature model" of *The Arcades Project*. The methodological problems raised by the "Work of Art" essay were, in their turn, addressed once more in the theses "Über den Begriff der Geschichte" (On the Concept of History). In Adorno's opinion, these theses "more or less summarize the epistemological considerations that developed concurrently with *The Arcades Project*."[4] What survives of this project—the countless notes and excerpts that constitute the fifth volume of Benjamin's

Gesammelte Schriften—rarely go theoretically beyond positions that have been formulated more radically in the texts mentioned above. Any study of the *Passagen-Werk* (Benjamin's intentions hardly lay themselves open to a simple perusal) must therefore deal with the "Work of Art" essay, the texts devoted to Baudelaire, and the theses "On the Concept of History." These must always be present to the student's mind, even though they are manifestly autonomous—writings either introductory to the *Passagen-Werk* or distinct from it.

The published volumes of the *Passagen-Werk* begin with two texts in which Benjamin presents the project in summary, first in 1935 and again in 1939. Together with the early essay "Der Saturnring, oder Etwas vom Eisenbau" (The Ring of Saturn, or Some Remarks on Iron Construction), these texts are the only ones belonging to the Arcades complex that may be said to be complete. They were not, however, intended for publication. The earlier, German one was written for the Institut für Sozialforschung, which, as a result, accepted the *Passagen-Werk* as one of its sponsored research projects. The other text, written in French, came into being at Max Horkheimer's instigation: Horkheimer hoped to make use of it to interest an American patron in Benjamin. The most important part, as well as the lengthiest section, of Volume 5 of the *Gesammelte Schriften* consists of the manuscript of the "Aufzeichnungen und Materialien" (Notes and Materials; here called the "Convolutes"), which is subdivided thematically. This is the manuscript that had been hidden in the Bibliothèque Nationale during World War II.

Benjamin probably worked on this manuscript from the fall or winter of 1928 until the end of 1929, and then again from the beginning of 1934. The last entries were made in the spring of 1940, immediately before Benjamin fled Paris. The present order of the notes does not correspond to the order in which they were originally entered. It seems that Benjamin would begin a new convolute, or sheaf of notes, whenever a new theme suggested itself and demanded to be treated. Within the different sheafs that were composed simultaneously, the notes may evince the chronological order in which they were written down. Yet even this chronology is not always identical with that of the notes' actual conception. At the beginnings of those rubrics that had guided his research in its earliest stage, we find notes Benjamin incorporated from older manuscripts. Here the notes have been rearranged, and therefore the first pages of the respective collections of material follow certain clear principles. By contrast, rubrics either added to or newly begun from 1934 onward generally owe their order to the coincidences of Benjamin's studies or, even more so, to his reading.[5]

The section "Erste Notizen" (5:991–1038), here called "First Sketches," consists of consecutive notes that were begun about the middle of 1927 and terminated in December 1929 or, at the latest, by the beginning of 1930. They are published in their entirety, even though their contents have for the most part been incorporated into the larger "Convolutes" section. It is only with their help that we can trace the "transformation process" that determined the transition from the first stage of the work to the second. The first of the "Frühe Entwürfe" (Early Drafts) entitled "Passagen" (Arcades), dates back to the very first phase of the work, mid-1927, when Benjamin intended to collaborate with Franz Hessel on a journal article. The draft may well have been written by Benjamin and Hessel together. "Pariser Passagen II" (here called "The Arcades of Paris") shows Benjamin's attempts in 1928 and 1929 to write the essay he thought the *Passagen-Werk* would become. Benjamin wrote these texts in a format totally unusual for him and on very expensive handmade paper, which he never used before or after. One can easily imagine that he approached their composition as he would a festive occasion. But he did not get very far. The discrete texts, whose sequence he did not establish, are soon interspersed with and finally overgrown by quotations and bibliographic notes, and in places with commentary. Both the "Convolutes" and the "First Sketches" are published in extenso as they are found in the manuscript, but "The Arcades of Paris" is treated in a different manner. The notes and quotations in this manuscript were never really worked out: they must have either been transferred to the "Convolutes" or been discarded. They have therefore not been included in this edition. Only fully formulated texts have been published; their order has been established by the editor. These texts, among the most important and, if I may say so, the most beautiful of Benjamin's texts, surface again at various places in the "Convolutes." Published as a whole, however, they convey an impression of the essay Benjamin mulled over but never actually wrote. The last text, "The Ring of Saturn, or Some Remarks on Iron Construction," also belongs to the first phase of his project. It may, in fact, be a journal or newspaper article, an offshoot of the *Passagen-Werk* which never made it into print.

The fragments of the *Passagen-Werk* can be compared to the materials used in building a house, the outline of which has just been marked in the ground or whose foundations are just being dug. In the two exposés that open the fifth volume of the *Gesammelte Schriften*, Benjamin sketches broad outlines of the plan as he had envisaged it in 1935 and in 1939. The five or six sections of each exposé should have corresponded to the same number of chapters in the book or, to continue the analogy, to the five or six floors of the projected house. Next to the foundations we find the neatly piled excerpts, which would have been used to construct the walls; Benjamin's own thoughts would have provided the mortar to hold the building together. The reader now possesses many of these theoretical and interpretive reflections, yet in the end they almost seem to vanish beneath the very weight of the excerpts. It is tempting to question the sense of publishing these oppressive chunks of quotations—whether it would not be best to publish only those texts written by Benjamin himself. These texts could have been easily arranged in a readable format, and they would have yielded a poignant collection of sparkling aphorisms and disturbing fragments. But this would have made it impossible to guess at the project attempted in the *Passagen-Werk*, such as the reader can discern it behind these quotations. Benjamin's intention was to bring together theory and materials, quotations and interpretation, in a new constellation compared to contemporary methods of representation. The quotations and the materials would bear the full weight of the project; theory and interpretation would have to withdraw in an ascetic manner. Benjamin isolated a "central problem of historical materialism," which he thought he could solve in the *Passagen-Werk*, namely:

> In what way is it possible to conjoin a heightened graphicness ‹*Anschaulichkeit*› to the realization of the Marxist method? The first stage in this undertaking will be to carry over the principle of montage into history. That is, to assemble large-scale constructions out of the smallest and most precisely cut components. Indeed, to discover in the analysis of the small individual moment the crystal of the total event. (N2,6)[6]

The components, the structural elements, are the countless quotations, and for this reason they cannot be omitted. Once familiar with the architecture of the whole, the reader will be able to read the excerpts without great difficulty and pinpoint in almost every one that element which must have fascinated Benjamin. The reader will also be able to specify which function an excerpt would have served in the global construction—how it might have been able to become a "crystal" whose sparkling light itself reflects the total event. The reader will, of course, have to draw on the ability to "interpolate into the infinitesimally small," as Benjamin defines the imagination in *Einbahnstrasse* (One-Way Street).[7]

For the reader endowed with such an imagination, the dead letters Benjamin collected from the holdings of the Bibliothèque Nationale will come to life. Perhaps even the building Benjamin did not manage to build will delineate itself before the imaginatively speculative eye in shadowy outlines.

These shadows, which prevent us from making a surveyable, consistent drawing of the architecture, are often traceable to problems of a philological nature. The fragments, which are mostly short and often seem to abbreviate a thought, only rarely allow us to glimpse how Benjamin planned to link them. He would often first write down ideas, pointed scribbles. It is impossible to determine whether he planned to retain them in the course of his work. Some theoretical notes contradict each other; others are hardly compatible. Moreover, many of Benjamin's texts are linked with quotations, and the mere interpretation of those citations cannot always be separated from Benjamin's own position. Therefore, to assist the reader in finding his bearings in the labyrinth this volume presents, I shall briefly sketch the essentials of Benjamin's intentions in his *Passagen-Werk,* point out the theoretical nodes of his project, and try to approach explication of some of its central categories.

The *Passagen-Werk* is a building with two completely different floor plans, each belonging to a particular phase of the work. During the first phase, from about mid-1927 to the fall of 1929, Benjamin planned to write an essay entitled "Pariser Passagen: Eine dialektische Feerie" (Paris Arcades: A Dialectical Fairyland).[8] His earliest references to it in letters characterize the project as a continuation of *One-Way Street* (Letters, 322), though Benjamin meant a continuation less in terms of its aphoristic form than in the specific kind of concretization he attempted there: "this extreme concreteness which made itself felt there in some instances—in a children's game, a building, and a situation in life"—should now be captured "for an epoch" (Letters, 348). Benjamin's original intention was a philosophical one and would remain so for all those years: "putting to the test" *(die Probe auf das Exempel)* "to what extent you can be 'concrete' in historical-philosophical contexts" (Letters, 333). He tried to represent the nineteenth century as "commentary on a reality" (O°,9), rather than construing it in the abstract. We can put together a kind of "catalogue of themes" from the "First Sketches" about the *Passagen-Werk.* The catalogue shows us what the work was supposed to treat at this level: streets and warehouses, panoramas, world exhibitions, types of lighting, fashion, advertising and prostitution, collectors, the flâneur and the gambler, boredom. Here the arcades themselves are only one theme among many. They belong to those urban phenomena that appeared in the early nineteenth century, with the emphatic claim of the new, but they have meanwhile lost their functionality. Benjamin discovered the signature of the early modern in the ever more rapid obsolescence of the inventions and innovations generated by a developing capitalism's productive forces. He wanted to recover that feature from the appearances of the unsightly, *intentione recta,* the physiognomic way: by showing rags, as a montage of trash (O°,36). In *One-Way Street* his thinking had similarly lost itself in the concrete and particular and had tried to wrest his secret directly, without any theoretical mediation. Such a surrender to singular Being is the distinctive feature of this thinking as such. It is not affected by the rattling mechanisms of undergraduate philosophy, with its transcendental tablets of commandments and prohibitions. Rather, it limits itself to the somewhat limitless pursuit of a kind of gentle empirical experience" *(Empirie).* Like Goethe's *Empirie,* it does not deduce the essence behind or above the thing—it knows it in the things themselves.

The Surrealists were the first to discover the material world characteristic of the nineteenth century, and in it a specific *mythologie moderne*. It is to that modern mythology that Aragon devotes the preface to his *Paysan de Paris,* while Breton's *Nadja* reaches up into its artificial sky. In his essay "Surrealism," which he called an "opaque folding screen placed before the *Passagen-Werk*" (Letters, 348), Benjamin praised the Surrealists as "the first to perceive the revolutionary energies that appear in the 'outmoded,' in the first iron constructions, the first factory buildings, the earliest photos, the objects that begin to be extinct, grand pianos in the salon, the dresses of five years ago, fashionable restaurants when the vogue has begun to ebb from them."[9] This stratum of material, the alluvium of the recent past, also pertains to the *Passagen-Werk*. Just as Aragon, sauntering through the Passage de l'Opéra, was pulled by a *vague de rêves* into strange, unglimpsed realms of the Real, so Benjamin wanted to submerge himself in hitherto ignored and scorned reaches of history and to salvage what no one had seen before him.

The nearly depopulated *aquarium humain,* as Aragon described the Passage de l'Opéra in 1927, two years after it had been sacrificed to the completion of the inner circle of boulevards—the ruins of yesterday, where today's riddles are solved—was unmatched in its influence on the *Passagen-Werk* (see Letters, 488). Benjamin kept quoting the *lueur glauque* of Aragon's arcades: the light that objects are immersed in by dreams, a light that makes them appear strange and vivid at the same time. If the concept of the concrete formed one pole of Benjamin's theoretical armature, then the Surrealist theory of dreams made up the other. The divagations of the first Arcades "sketch" take place in the field of tension between concretization and the dream.[10] Through the dream, the early Surrealists deprived empirical reality of all its power; they maltreated empirical reality and its purposive rational organization as the mere content of dreams whose language can be only indirectly decoded. By turning the optics of the dream toward the waking world, one could bring to birth the concealed, latent thoughts slumbering in that world's womb. Benjamin wanted to proceed similarly with the representation of history, by treating the nineteenth-century world of things as if it were a world of dreamed things. Under capitalist relationships of production, history could be likened to the unconscious actions of the dreaming individual, at least insofar as history is man-made, yet without consciousness or design, as if in a dream. "In order to understand the arcades from the ground up, we sink them into the deepest stratum of the dream" (F°,34). If the dream model is applied to the nineteenth century, then it will strip the era of its completeness, of that aspect that is gone forever, of what has literally become history. The means of production and way of life dominant in that period were not only what they had been in their time and place; Benjamin also saw the image-making imagination of a collective unconscious at work in them. That imagination went beyond its historical limits in the dream and actually touched the present, by transferring "the thoroughly fluctuating situation of a consciousness each time manifoldly divided between waking and sleeping," which he had discovered in psychoanalysis, "from the individual to the collective" (G°,27). Benjamin wanted to draw attention to the fact that architectonic constructions such as the arcades owed their existence to and served the industrial order of production, while at the same time containing in themselves something unfulfilled, never to be fulfilled within the confines of capitalism—in this case, the glass architecture of the future Benjamin often alludes to. "Each epoch" has a "side turned toward dreams, the child's side" (F°,7). The scrutiny this side of history was subjected to in Benjamin's observation was designed to "liberate the enormous energies of history . . . that are slumbering in the 'once upon a time' of classical historical narrative" (O°,71).

Almost concurrently with his first notes for the *Passagen-Werk,* Benjamin included in his writings many protocols of his own dreams; this was also when he began to experiment with drugs. Both represented attempts to break the fixations and the encrustations in which thinking and its object, subject and object, have been frozen under the pressure of industrial production.[11] In dreams as in narcotic intoxication, Benjamin watched "a world of particular secret affinities" reveal itself, a world in which things enter into "the most contradictory communication" and in which they could display "indefinite affinities" (A°,4–5). Intoxication and the dream seemed to unlock a realm of experiences in which the Id still communicated mimetically and corporeally with things. Ever since his earlier philosophical explorations, Benjamin sought a concept of experience that would explode the limitations set by Kant and regain "the fullness of the concept of experience held by earlier philosophers," which should restore the experiences of theology.[12] But the experiences of the Surrealists taught him that it was a matter not of restoring theological experience but of transporting it into the profane:

> These experiences are by no means limited to dreams, hours of hashish eating or opium smoking. It is a cardinal error to believe that, of "Surrealist experiences," we know only the religious ecstasies or the ecstasies of drugs. . . . But the true, creative overcoming of religious illumination certainly does not lie in narcotics. It resides in a *profane illumination,* a materialistic, anthropological inspiration to which hashish, opium, or whatever else can give a preliminary lesson. (*SW,* 2:208–209)

Benjamin wanted to carry such profane illuminations into history by acting as an interpreter of the dreams of the nineteenth-century world of things. The epistemic intention manifest here seems to fit in with the context of Benjamin's soon-to-be-formulated theory of mimetic ability, which is, at its core, a theory of experience.[13] The theory holds that experience rests on the ability to produce and perceive similarities—an ability that underwent significant change in the course of species history. In the beginning a sensuous, qualitative type of behavior of men toward things, it later transformed itself phylogenetically into a faculty for apperceiving nonsensuous similarities, which Benjamin identified as the achievements of language and writing. Vis-à-vis abstracting cognition, his concept of experience wanted to maintain immediate contact with mimetic behavior. He was concerned about "palpable knowledge" *(gefühltes Wissen),* which "not only feeds on the sensory data taking shape before his eyes, but can very well possess itself of abstract knowledge—indeed, of dead facts—as something experienced and lived through" (e°,1). Images take the place of concepts—the enigmatic and vexing dream images which hide all that falls through the coarse mesh of semiotics—and yet those images alone balance the exertions of cognition. The nineteenth-century language of images represents that century's "deepest level of sleep" (G°,27)—a sleep that should be awakened by the *Passagen-Werk.*

Benjamin knew that this motif of awakening separated him from the Surrealists. They had tried to abolish the line of demarcation between life and art, to shut off poetry in order to live writing or write life. For the early Surrealists, both dream and reality would unravel to a dreamed, unreal Reality, from which no way led back to contemporary praxis and its demands. Benjamin criticized Aragon for "persisting within the realm of dreams" and for allowing mythology to "remain" with him (H°,17). Aragon's mythology remains *mere* mythology, unpenetrated by reason. Surrealist imagery evens out the differences separating Now from Then; instead of bringing the past into the present, it drives "things back into the distance again" and remains bound, "in the historical sphere, [to] a romantic distance" (C°,5). Benjamin, on the other hand, wanted "to [bring] things near," to allow them to "step into our lives" (I°,2). What linked his methods to Surrealist ones, the immersion of what has been into layers of dreams, represented not an end in itself for the *Passagen-Werk,* but rather its methodological arrangement, a kind of experimental setup. The nineteenth century is the dream we must wake up from; it is a nightmare that will weigh on the present as long as its spell remains unbroken. According to Benjamin, the images of dreaming and awakening from the dream are related as expression is related to interpretation. He hoped that the images, once interpreted, would dissolve the spell. Benjamin's concept of awakening means the "genuine liberation from an epoch" (h°,3), in the double sense of Hegel's *Aufhebung:* the nineteenth century would be transcended *in* that it would be preserved, "rescued" for the present. Benjamin defines "the new, the dialectical method of doing history" in these words: "with the intensity of a dream, to pass through what has been [*das Gewesene*], in order to experience the present as the waking world to which the dream refers" (F°,6). This concept is based on a mystical conception of history that Benjamin was never to abandon, not even in his late theses "On the Concept of History." Every present ought to be synchronic with certain moments of history, just as every past becomes "legible" only in a certain epoch—"namely, the one in which human-ity, rubbing its eyes, recognizes just this particular dream image as such. It is at this moment that the historian takes up . . . the task of dream interpretation" (N4,1). Toward this end, we need not a dragging of the past into the mythological, but, on the contrary, a "dissolution of 'mythology' in the space of history" (H°,17). Benjamin demanded a "con-crete, materialist meditation on what is nearest" *(das Nächste);* he was interested "only in the presentation of what relates to us, what conditions us" (C°,5). In this way the historian should no longer try to enter the past; rather, he should allow the past to enter his life. A "pathos of nearness" should replace the vanishing "empathy" (I°,2). For the historian, past objects and events would not then be fixed data, an unchangeable given, because dialectical thinking "ransacks them, revolutionizes them, turns them upside down" (D°,4); this is what must be accomplished by awakening from the dream of the nineteenth century. That is why for Benjamin the "effort to awaken from a dream" represents "the best example of dialectical reversal" (D°,7).

The key to what may have been Benjamin's intention while working on the first phase of the *Passagen-Werk* may be found in the sentence, "Capitalism was a natural phenome-non with which a new dream-filled sleep came over Europe, and, through it, a reactivation of mythical forces" (K1a,8). Benjamin shares his project, the desire to investigate capital-ism, with historical materialism, from which he may well have appropriated the project in the first place. But the concepts he uses to define capitalism—nature, dream, and myth—originate from the terminology of his own metaphysically and theologically inspired thought. The key concepts of the young Benjamin's philosophy of history center around a critique of myth as the ordained heteronomous, which kept man banished in dumb dependence throughout prehistory and which has since survived in the most dissimilar forms, both as unmediated violence and in bourgeois jurisprudence.[14] The critique of capitalism in the first *Arcades* sketch remains a critique of myth, since in it the nineteenth century appears as a domain where "only madness has reigned until now." "But," Ben-jamin adds, "every ground must at some point have been turned over by reason, must have been cleared of the undergrowth of delusion and myth. This is to be accomplished here for the terrain of the nineteenth century" (G°,13). His interpretation recognizes forms still unhistorical, still imprisoned by myth, forms that are only preparing them-selves, in such an interpretation, to awaken from myth and to take away its power. Benjamin identifies them as the dominant forms of consciousness and the imagery of incipient high capitalism: the "sensation of the newest and most modern," as well as the image of the "eternal return of the same"—both are "dream formations of events," dreamed by a collective that "knows no history" (M°,14). He speaks in direct theological terms in his interpretation of the modern as "the time of hell":

> What matters here is that the face of the world, the colossal head, precisely in what is newest never itself changes—that this "newest" remains in all respects the same. This constitutes the eternity of hell and the sadist's delight in innovation. To determine the totality of traits which define this "modernity" is to represent hell. (G°,17)

Since it is a "commentary on a reality," which sinks into the historical and interprets it as it would a text, theology was called upon to provide the "scientific mainstay" of the *Passagen-Werk* (O°,9), though at the same time politics was to retain its "primacy over history" (h°,2). At the time of the first *Arcades* sketch, Benjamin was concerned less with a mediation of theological and political categories than with their identity. In this he was very much like Ernst Bloch in *Geist der Utopie* (Spirit of Utopia), which he explicitly took as his model. He repeatedly had recourse to Blochian concepts to characterize his own intentions, as in "fashion inheres in the darkness of the lived moment, but in the collective darkness" (O°,11). Just as for Bloch the experiencing individual has not yet achieved mastery over himself at the moment of experiencing, for Benjamin the historical phenomena remain opaque, unilluminated for the dreaming collective. In Bloch's opinion, individual experience is always experience of the immediate past; in the same way, Benjamin's interpretation of the present refers to the recent past: action in the present means awakening from the dream of history, an "explosion" of what has been, a revolutionary turn. He was convinced that "the whole set of issues with which this project is concerned" would be "illuminated in the process of the proletariat's becoming conscious of itself" (O°,68). He did not hesitate to interpret these facts as part of the preparation for the proletarian revolution. "The dialectical penetration and actualization of former contexts puts the truth of all present action to the test" (O°,5). It is not the action itself but its theory that is at stake here. This defines the task of the historian as "rescuing" the past or, as Benjamin formulated it with another concept taken from Bloch, "awakening a not-yet-conscious knowledge of what has been" (H°,17) by applying the "theory of not-yet-conscious knowing . . . to the collective in its various epochs" (O°,50). At this stage, Benjamin conceived of the *Passagen-Werk* as a mystical reconstitution: dialectical thinking had the task of separating the future-laden, "positive" element from the backward "negative" element, after which "a new partition had to be applied to this initially excluded, negative component so that, by a displacement of the angle of vision . . ., a positive element emerges anew in it too—something different from that previously signified. And so on, ad infinitum, until the entire past is brought into the present in a historical apocatastasis" (N1a,3). In this way, the nineteenth century should be brought into the present within the *Passagen-Werk*. Benjamin did not think revolutionary praxis should be allowed at any lesser price. For him revolution was, in its highest form, a liberation of the past, which had to demonstrate "the indestructibility of the highest life in all things" (O°,1). At the end of the 1920s, theology and communism converged in Benjamin's thought. The metaphysical, historical-philosophical, and theological sources that had nurtured both his esoteric early writings and his great aesthetic works until *Ursprung des deutschen Trauerspiels* (Origin of the German Trauerspiel) were still flowing and would also nurture the *Passagen-Werk*.

The *Passagen-Werk* was supposed to become all of that, and it became none of that—to echo a famous phrase of Benjamin's (D°,6). He interrupted work in the fall of 1929 for various reasons. Retrospectively, he placed responsibility on problems of representation: the "rhapsodic nature" of the work, which he had already announced in the first sketch's subtitle, "a dialectical fairyland" (Letters, 488). The "illicit 'poetic'" formulation he then thought he was obliged to use was irreconcilable with a book that was to have "our generation's decisive historical interests as its object" (Scholem Letters, 165). Benjamin believed that only historical materialism could safeguard those interests; the aporias he encountered while composing the *Passagen-Werk*, then, undoubtedly culminated in the project's position in relation to Marxist theory. Though Benjamin professed his commitment to Communist party politics to begin with, he still had to convince himself of the necessity to proceed from a political creed to the theoretical study of Marxism, which he thought could be appropriated for his purposes even prior to his actual study. His intention was to secure the *Passagen-Werk* "against all objections . . . provoked by metaphysics"; "the whole mass of thought, originally set into motion by metaphysics," had to be subjected to a "recasting process" which would allow the author to "face with equanimity the objects orthodox Marxism might mobilize against the method of the work" (Letters, 489). Benjamin traced the end of his "blithely archaic philosophizing, imprisoned by nature," which had been the basis of the "romantic form" and the "rhapsodic naiveté" of the first sketch, to conversations with Adorno and Horkheimer that he characterized as "historic" (Letters, 488–489). These took place in September or October 1929, in Frankfurt and Königstein. In all probability, both Horkheimer and Adorno insisted in discussions of the submitted texts—mainly the "Early Drafts" published with the *Passagen-Werk*—that it was impossible to speak sensibly about the nineteenth century without considering Marx's analysis of capital; it is entirely possible that Benjamin, who at that time had read hardly anything by Marx, was influenced by such a suggestion.[15] Be that as it may, Benjamin's letter to Scholem of January 20, 1930, contains the statement that he would have to study certain features of both Hegelian philosophy and *Capital* in order to complete his project (Letters, 359). Benjamin had by no means concluded such studies when he returned to the *Passagen-Werk* four years later. The "new face" (5:1103) the work unveiled, due not a little to Benjamin's political experiences in exile, revealed itself in an emphatic recourse to social history, which had not been wholly relinquished in the first sketch but which had been concealed by that sketch's surrealist intentions. None of the old motifs were abandoned, but the building was given stronger foundations. Among the themes added were Haussmann's influence, the struggles on the barricades, railways, conspiracies, *compagnonnage,* social movements, the Stock Exchange, economic history, the Commune, the history of sects, and the Ecole Polytechnique; moreover, Benjamin began assembling excerpts on Marx, Fourier, and Saint-Simon. This thematic expansion hardly meant that Benjamin was about to reserve a chapter for each theme (he now planned to write a book instead of an essay). The book's subject was now defined as "the fate of art in the nineteenth century" (Letters, 517) and thus seemed more narrowly conceived than it had been. That should not be taken too literally, however: the 1935 exposé, after all, in which Benjamin most clearly delineates his intentions in his work's second stage, still lists every theme the *Passagen-Werk* was to treat from the outset: arcades, panoramas, world exhibitions, interiors, and the streets of Paris. This exposé's title, "Paris, the Capital of the Nineteenth Century," remained the definitive title and was appropriated for another exposé—a French prospectus—in 1939. This prospectus contains a decisive reference to "the new and far-reaching sociological perspectives" of the second sketch. Benjamin wrote that these new perspectives would yield a "secure framework of interpretive interconnections" (Letters, 490). But his interpretation was now supposed to trace the book's subject matter—the cultural superstructure of nineteenth-century France—back to what Marx had called the fetish character of commodities. In 1935 the "unfolding of this concept" would "constitute the center" of the projected work (Scholem Letters, 159), and by 1938 the "basic categories" of the *Passagen-Werk* would "converge in the determination of the fetish character of commodities" (5:1166). This notion surfaces only once in the first sketch (O°,38); it was then by no means clear that commodity fetishism was destined to form the central schema for the whole project. When Benjamin wrote the first exposé in 1935, he was probably still unfamiliar with the relevant discussion in Marx's writings. He apparently only began to "look around . . . in the first volume of *Capital*" after completing the exposé (5:1122). He was familiar with the theory of commodity fetishism mainly in Lukác's version; like many other left-wing intellectuals of his generation, Benjamin largely owed his Marxist competency to the chapter on reification in Lukács's *History and Class Consciousness*.

Benjamin wished to treat culture in the era of high capitalism like Lukác's translation back into philosophy of the economic fact of commodity fetishism, as well as his application of the category of reification to the antinomies of bourgeois thought. Marx showed that capitalist production's abstraction of value begets an ideological consciousness, in which labor's social character is reflected as objective, thing-like characteristics of the products of that labor. Benjamin recognized the same ideological consciousness at work in the then-dominant "reified conception of culture," which obfuscated the fact that "the creations of the human mind . . . owe not just their origin, but also the ways in which they have been handed down, to a continuing social labor" (5:1255). The fate of nineteenth-century culture lay precisely in its commodity character, which Benjamin thereupon represented in "cultural values" as *phantasmagoria*. Phantasmagoria: a *Blendwerk,* a deceptive image designed to dazzle, is already the commodity itself, in which the exchange value or value-form hides the use value. Phantasmagoria is the whole capitalist production process, which constitutes itself as a natural force against the people who carry it out. For Benjamin, cultural phantasmagorias express "the ambiguity peculiar to the social relations and products of this epoch" (Exposé of 1935, section V). In Marx, the same ambiguity defines "the economic world of capitalism": an ambiguity "exemplified quite clearly in the machines which aggravate exploitation rather than alleviate the human lot" (K3,5). The concept of phantasmagoria that Benjamin repeatedly employs seems to be merely another term for what Marx called commodity fetishism. Benjamin's term can even be found in Marx's writings: in *Capital*'s first chapter (on fetishism), in the famous passage about the "definite social relation" which molds labor under capitalist conditions of production, that very relation is said to "assume . . . the phantasmagoric form of a relation between things" for the people concerned.[16] Marx had in mind the circumstances of the bourgeois economy's "necessarily false" consciousness, which is no less false for being necessary. Benjamin's interest in culture was less for its ideological content, however, whose depth is unearthed in ideology critique, than for its surface or exterior, which is both promising and deceptive. "The creations and life-styles that were mainly conditioned by commodity production and which we owe to the previous century" are "sensuously transfigured in their immediate presence" (5:1256). Benjamin was interested in that immediate presence; the secret he was tracking in the *Passagen-Werk* is a secret that comes to appear. The "luster with which the commodity-producing society surrounds itself" (5:1256) is phantasmagorical—a luster that hardly has less to do with the "beautiful appearance" of idealist aesthetics than with commodity fetishism. Phantasmagorias are the "century's magic images" (1:1153); they are the *Wunschbilder,* the wish symbols or ideals, by which that collective tried "both to overcome and to transfigure the immaturity of the social product and the inadequacies in the social organization of production"

(Exposé of 1935, section I). To begin with, the phantasmagoria seems to have a transfiguring function: world exhibitions, for example, transform the exchange value of commodities by fading, as in a film, from the abstractness of their valuation. Similarly, the collector transfigures things by divesting them of their commodity character. And in this same way, iron construction and glass architecture are transfigured in the arcades because "the century could not match the new technical possibilities with a new social order" (5:1257). As Benjamin in late 1937 came across Auguste Blanqui's *L'Eternité par les astres*—a cosmological phantasmagoria written by the revolutionary while in prison—he reencountered his own speculation about the nineteenth century as Hades. The semblance character *(Scheinhafte)* of all that is new and that the century liked to show off as modern par excellence was consummated in its highest concept, that of progress, which Blanqui denounced as a "phantasmagoria of history," as "something so old it predates thinking, which struts about in the clothes of the New," as the eternal recurrence of the same, in which mankind figures "as one of the damned" (5:1256). Benjamin learned from Blanqui that the phantasmagoria embraced "the most bitter criticism," the harshest indictment of society" (5:1256–1257). The transfiguring aspects of phantasmagoria change to enlightenment, into the insight "that mankind will remain under the power of mythical fear as long as phantasmagoria has a place in that fear (5:1256). The century always transcends the "old social order" in its cultural phantasmagoria. As "wish symbols," the arcades and interiors, the exhibition halls and panoramas are "residue of a dream world." They are part of Blochian dreaming ahead, anticipating the future: "Every epoch, in fact, not only dreams the one to follow, but, in dreaming, precipitates its awakening. It bears its end within itself." Insofar as dialectical thinking tries to define as well as to expedite this end of decaying bourgeois culture, it became for Benjamin the "organ of historical awakening" (Exposé of 1935, section VI, end).

"The property appertaining to the commodity as its fetish character attaches as well to the commodity-producing society—not as it is in itself, to be sure, but more as it represents itself and thinks to understand itself whenever it abstracts from the fact that it produces precisely commodities" (X13a). That was hardly Marx's opinion. He identifies the fetish character of the commodity through the fact that the features of man's labor *appear* to him as what they *are:* "as material relations between persons and social relations between things."[17] The analysis of capital establishes the quid pro quo of commodity fetishism as objective, not as a phantasmagoric. Marx would necessarily have rejected the notion that the commodity-producing society might be able to abstract from the fact that it produces commodities in any other way than by really ceasing to produce commodities in the transition to a higher social formation. It is not difficult—though also not very productive—to point out Benjamin's miscomprehensions of Marxist theory.

Benjamin showed little interest in a Marxist theory of art, which he considered "one moment swaggering, and the next scholastic" (N4a,2). He valued three short sentences by Proust more highly than most of what existed in the field of materialist analysis (K3,4). The majority of Marxist art theorists explain culture as the mere reflection of economic development; Benjamin refused to join them. He viewed the doctrine of aesthetic reflection as already undercut by Marx's remark that "the ideologies of the superstructure reflect relations in a false and distorted manner." Benjamin followed this remark with a question:

> If the infrastructure in a certain way (in the materials of thought and experience) determines the superstructure, but if such determination is not reducible to simple reflection, then how should it be characterized? As its expression. The superstruc-

ture is the expression of the infrastructure. The economic conditions under which society exists are expressed in the superstructure, precisely as, with the sleeper, an overfull stomach finds not its reflection but its expression in the contents of dreams, which, from a causal point of view, it may be said to "condition." (K2,5)

Benjamin did not set out according to ideology critique;[18] rather, he gave way to the notion of materialist physiognomics, which he probably understood as a complement, or an extension, of Marxist theory. Physiognomics infers the interior from the exterior; it decodes the whole from the detail; it represents the general in the particular. Nominalistically speaking, it proceeds from the tangible object; inductively it commences in the realm of the intuitive. The *Passagen-Werk* "deals fundamentally with the expressive character of the earliest industrial products, the earliest industrial architecture, the earliest machines, but also the earliest department stores, advertisements, and so on" (N1a,7). In that expressive character, Benjamin hoped to locate what eluded the immediate grasp: the *Signatur,* the mark, of the nineteenth century. He was interested in the "thread of expression": "the expression of the economy in its culture will be presented, not the economic origins of culture" (N1a,6). Benjamin's trajectory from the first to the second sketch of the *Passagen-Werk* documents his efforts to safeguard his work against the demands of historical materialism; in this way, motifs belonging to metaphysics and theology survived undamaged in the physiognomic concept of the epoch's closing stage. To describe the expression of economics in culture was an attempt "to grasp an economic process as perceptible *Ur*-phenomenon, from out of which proceed all manifestations of life in the arcades (and, accordingly, in the nineteenth century)" (N1a,6). Benjamin had already enlisted Goethe's primal phenomenon *(Urphänomen)* to explicate his concept of truth in *Origin of the German Trauerspiel:*[19] the concept of "origin" in the *Trauerspiel* book would have to be "a strict and compelling transfer of this Goethean first principle from the realm of nature to that of history." In the *Passagen-Werk,* then:

> I am equally concerned with fathoming an origin. To be specific, I pursue the origin of the forms and mutations of the Paris arcades from their beginning to their decline, and I locate this origin in the economic facts. Seen from the standpoint of causality, however (and that means considered as causes), these facts would not be primal phenomena; they become such only insofar as in their own individual development—"unfolding" might be a better term—they give rise to the whole series of the arcade's concrete historical forms, just as the leaf unfolds from itself all the riches of the empirical world of plants. (N2a,4)

Metaphysical subtleties and theological niceties reappear here in the theory of epistemology, even though they seemed vanquished after they learned of their ironic unmasking by economics. How could *Ur*-phenomena, which represent themselves as the expression of economic facts, distinguish themselves from those ideas in Benjamin's *Trauerspiel* book which represent themselves by empirical means? Benjamin resolves this problem with his early notion of a monadological truth, which presides at every phase of the *Passagen-Werk* and remains valid even in the theses "On the Concept of History." Whereas in the *Trauerspiel* book the idea as monad "contains the image of the world" in itself,[20] in the *Passagen-Werk* the expression as *Ur*-phenomenon contains the image of history in itself. The essence of capitalist production would be comprehended vis-à-vis the concrete historical forms in which the economy finds its cultural expression. The abstractions of mere conceptual thinking were insufficient to demystify this abhorrent state of affairs, such that a mimetic-intuitive corrective was imposed to decipher the code of the universal in the image. Physiognomic thought was assigned the task of "recognizing the monuments of the bourgeoisie as ruins even before they have crumbled" (Exposé of 1935, section VI, end).

The prolegomena to a materialist physiognomics that can be gleaned from the *Passagen-Werk* counts among Benjamin's most prodigious conceptions. It is the programmatic harbinger of that aesthetic theory which Marxism has not been able to develop to this day. Whether Benjamin's realization of his program was capable of fulfilling its promise, whether his physiognomics was equal to its materialist task, could have been proven only by the actual composition of the *Passagen-Werk* itself.

Modified concepts of history and of the writing of history are the link between both *Arcades* sketches. Their polemical barbs are aimed at the nineteenth-century notion of progress. With the exception of Schopenhauer (by no coincidence, his objective world bears the name "phantasmagoria"), idealist philosophers had turned progress into the "signature of historical process *as a whole*" (N13,1) and by doing so had deprived it of its critical and enlightenment functions. Even Marx's trust in the unfolding of the productive forces hypostatized the concept of progress, and it must have appeared untenable to Benjamin in light of the experience of the twentieth century. Similarly, the political praxis of the worker's movement had forgotten that progress in terms of proficiency and information does not necessarily mean progress for humanity itself—and that progress in the domination of nature corresponds to societal regress.[21] In the first *Arcades* sketch Benjamin already demanded "a philosophy of history that at all points has overcome the ideology of progress" (O°,5), one such as he later worked out in the historical-philosophical theses. There the image of history reminds the reader more of Ludwig Klages's lethal juggling with archetypal images *(Urbilder)* and phantoms than of the dialectic of the forces and the relations of production. It is that Angel of History who appears in one of the theses as an allegory of the historical materialist (in Benjamin's sense)[22] and who sees all history as a catastrophe "which keeps piling wreckage upon wreckage and hurls it in front of his feet" (*Illuminations*, p. 259). The Angel abolishes all categories which until then have been used for representing history: this materialist sees the "everything 'gradual' about becoming" as refuted, and "development" is shown to be only "seeming" (F°,6; K1,3). But more than anything else, he denounces the "establishment of a continuity" (N9a,5) in history, because the only evidence of that continuity is that of horror, and the Angel has to do with salvation and redemption. The *Passagen-Werk* was supposed to bring nothing less than a "Copernican revolution" of historical perception (F°,7; K1,1–3). Past history would be grounded in the present, analogous to Kant's epistemological grounding of objectivity in the depths of the subject. The first revolution occurred in the relationship in which subject and object, present and past meet in historical perception:

> Formerly it was thought that a fixed point had been found in "what has been," and one saw the present engaged in tentatively concentrating the forces of knowledge on this ground. Now this relation is to be overturned, and what has been is to become the dialectical reversal—the irruption of awakened consciousness. Politics attains primacy over history. The facts become something that just now first happened to us, first struck us; to establish them is the affair of memory. (K1,2)

The historical line of vision no longer falls from the present back onto history; instead it travels from history forward. Benjamin tried to "recognize today's life, today's forms in the life and in the apparently secondary, lost forms" of the nineteenth century (N1,11). Our contemporary interest in a historical object seems "itself preformed in that object, and, above all," it feels "this object concretized in itself and upraised from its former being into the higher concretion of now-being [*Jetztseins*] (waking being!)" (K2,3). The object of history goes on changing; it becomes "historical" (in this word's emphatic sense) only when it becomes topical in a later period. Continuous relationships in time, with which history deals, are superseded in Benjamin's thought by constellations in which the past coincides with the present to such an extent that the past achieves a "Now" of its "recognizability." Benjamin developed this "Now of Recognizability," which he sometimes referred to as his theory of knowledge (5:1148), from a double frontal position against both idealism and positivistic historicism. While the latter tried to move the historical narrator back into the past, so that he could comprehend "emphatically" (solely from within) the whole of the Then, which filled "homogeneous, empty time" as a mere "mass of data" (*Illuminations,* p. 264), idealist constructions of history, on the other hand, usurped the prospect of the future and posited in history the existence of the natural plan of a process, which runs on autonomously and can, in principle, never be completed. Both relegate "everything about history that, from the very beginning, has been untimely, sorrowful, unsuccessful" (*Trauerspiel,* p.166) to forgetting. The object of that materialist historical narrative Benjamin wanted to try out in the *Passagen-Werk* would be precisely what history started but did not carry out. That the lineaments of the past are first detectable after a certain period is not due to the historian's whim; it bespeaks an objective historical constellation:

> History is the object of a construct whose site is not homogeneous, empty time, but time filled by now-time [*Jetztzeit*]. Thus, to Robespierre ancient Rome was a past charged with now-time, which he blasted out of the continuum of history. The French Revolution viewed itself as Rome incarnate. It quoted ancient Rome. (*Illuminations,* p. 263)

Benjamin wished to continue along this line in the *Passagen-Werk*. The present would provide the text of the book; history, the quotations in that text. "To write history . . . means to *cite* history" (N11,3).

Benjamin's Copernican revolution of historical intuition also (and above all) meant that the traditional concept of truth was to be turned on its head:

> Resolute refusal of the concept of "timeless truth" is in order. Nevertheless, truth is not—as Marxism would have it—a merely contingent function of knowing, but is bound to a nucleus of time lying hidden within the knower and the known alike. This is so true that the eternal, in any case, is far more the ruffle on a dress than some idea. (N3,2)

The temporal core of history cannot be grasped as really happening, stretching forth in the real dimension of time; rather it is where evolution halts for a moment, where the *dynamis* of what is happening coagulates into *stasis,* where time itself is condensed into a differential, and where a Now identifies itself as the "Now of a particular recognizability." In such a Now, "truth is charged to the bursting point with time" (N3,1). The Now would have thus shown itself to be the "inmost image" (O°,81) of the arcades themselves, of fashion, of the bourgeois interior—appearing as the image of all that had been, and whose cognition is the pith of the *Passagen-Werk*. Benjamin invented the term "dialectical images" for such configurations of the Now and the Then; he defined their content as a "dialectic at a standstill." Dialectical image and dialectic at the standstill are, without a doubt, the central categories of the *Passagen-Werk*. Their meaning, however, remained iridescent; it never achieved any terminological consistency.[23] We can distinguish at least two meanings in Benjamin's texts; they remain somewhat undivulged, but even so cannot be brought totally in congruence. Once—in the 1935 exposé, which in this regard summarizes the motifs of the first draft—Benjamin localized dialectical images as dream and wish images in the collective subconscious, whose "image-making fantasy, which was stimulated by the new" should refer back to the "*Ur*-past": "In the dream, in which each epoch entertains images of its successor, the latter appears wedded to elements of *Ur*-history—that is, to elements of a classless society. And the experiences of such a society—as stored in the unconscious of the collective—engender, through interpenetration with what is new, the utopia" (Exposé of 1935, section I). The modern is said to quote *Ur*-history "by means of the ambiguity peculiar to the social relations and products of this epoch." In turn, "Ambiguity is the manifest imaging of dialectic, the law of dialectics at a standstill. This standstill is utopia, and the dialectical image, therefore, dream image. Such an image is afforded by the commodity per se: as fetish" (Exposé of 1935, section V). These statements drew the resolute criticism of Adorno, who could not concede that the dialectical image could be "the way in which fetishism is conceived in the collective consciousness," since commodity fetishism is not a "fact of consciousness" (Letters, 495). Under the influence of Adorno's objections, Benjamin abandoned such lines of thought; the corresponding passages in his 1939 exposé were dropped as no longer satisfactory to their author (see 5:1157). By 1940, in the theses "On the Concept of History," "dialectic at a standstill" seems to function almost like a heuristic principle, a procedure that enables the historical materialist to maneuver his objects:

> A historical materialist cannot do without the notion of a present which is not a transition, but in which time stands still and has come to a stop. For this notion defines the present in which he himself is writing history. . . . Materialist historiography . . . is based on a constructive principle. Thinking involves not only the flow of thoughts, but their arrest as well. Where thinking suddenly stops in a configuration pregnant with tensions, it gives that configuration a shock, by which it crystallizes into a monad. A historical materialist approaches a historical subject only where he encounters it as a monad. In this structure he recognizes the sign of a messianic cessation of happening, or, put differently, a revolutionary chance in the fight for the oppressed past. (*Illuminations,* pp. 264–265)

In fact, Benjamin's thinking was invariably in dialectical images. As opposed to the Marxist dialectic, which "regards every . . . developed social form as in fluid movement,"[24] Benjamin's dialectic tried to halt the flow of the movement, to grasp each becoming as being. In Adorno's words, Benjamin's philosophy "appropriates the fetishism of commodities for itself: everything must metamorphoze into a thing in order to break the catastrophic spell of things."[25] His philosophy progressed imagistically, in that it sought to "read" historical social phenomena as if they were natural historical ones. Images became dialectical for this philosophy because of the historical index of every single image. "In the dialectical image" of this philosophy, "what has been within a particular epoch is always simultaneously 'what has been from time immemorial'" (N4,1). By so being, it remained rooted in the mythical. Yet at the same time, the historical materialist who seized the image should possess the skill to "fan the spark of hope in the past," to wrest historical tradition "anew . . . from a conformism that is about to overpower it" (*Illuminations,* p. 255). Through the immobilizing of dialectic, the historical "victors" have their accounts with history canceled, and all pathos is shifted toward salvation of the oppressed.

For Benjamin, freezing the dialectical image was obviously not a method the historian could employ at any time. For him, as for Marx, historiography was inseparable from political practice: the rescuing of the past through the writer of history remained bound to the practical liberation of humanity. Contrasted with the Marxist conception, however, according to which "capitalist production begets, with the inexorability of a law of nature, its own negation,"[26] Benjamin's philosophy preserves anarchist and Blanquian elements:

> In reality, there is not one moment that does not carry *its own* revolutionary opportunity in itself. . . . The particular revolutionary opportunity of each historical moment is confirmed for the revolutionary thinker by the political situation. But it is no less confirmed for him by the power this moment has to open a very particular, heretofore closed chamber of the past. Entry into this chamber coincides exactly with political action. (1:1231)

Political action, "no matter how destructive," should always "reveal itself as messianic" (1:1231). Benjamin's historical materialism can hardly be severed from political messianism. In a late note, perhaps written under the shock of the Hitler-Stalin pact, Benjamin formulated as "the experience of our generation: that capitalism will not die a natural death" (X11a,3). In that case, the onset of revolution could no longer be awaited with the patience of Marx; rather, it had to be envisaged as the eschatological *end* of history: "the classless society is not the ultimate goal of progress in history but its rupture, so often attempted and finally brought about (1:1231). Myth is liquidated in the dialectical image to make room for the "dream of a thing" (1:1174); this dream is the dialectic at a standstill, the piecing together of what history has broken to bits (see *Illuminations,* p. 257), the *tikkun* of the Lurian Kabbalah.[27] Benjamin did quote the young Marx, who wanted to show "that the world has long possessed the dream of a thing that, made conscious, it would possess in reality" (N5a,1). But for the interpreter of dialectical images, true reality cannot be inferred from existing reality. He undertook to represent the imperative and the final goal of reality as "a preformation of the final goal of history" (N5,3). The awakening from myth would follow the messianic model of a history immobilized in redemption as the historian of the *Passagen-Werk* had imagined it. In his dialectical images, the bursting of time coincides with "the birth of authentic historical time, the time of truth" (N3,1). Since the dialectical images belong in such a way to messianic time, or since they should at least let that time reveal itself as a flash of lightning, messianism is introduced as a kind of methodology of historical research—an adventuresome undertaking if ever there was one. "The subject of historical knowledge is the struggling, oppressed class itself" (*Illuminations,* p. 260); one may imagine the historian of the dialectic at a standstill as the herald of that class. Benjamin himself did not hesitate to call him "a prophet turned backward," borrowing a phrase from Friedrich Schlegel (1:1237); he did not dismiss the Old Testament idea that prophecy precedes the Messiah, that the Messiah is dependent on prophecy. But Benjamin's historiographer is "endowed with a *weak* messianic power, a power to which the past has a claim." The historian honors that claim when he captures that "image of the past that is not recognized by the present as one of its own concerns" and thus "threatens to disappear irretrievably" (*Illuminations,* pp. 256–257). Benjamin was able to recognize only the mythical Ever-Same *(Immergleiche)* in historical evolutions and was unable to recognize progress, except as a *Sprung*—a "tiger's leap into the past" (*Illuminations,* p. 263), which was in reality a leap out of history and the entry of the messianic kingdom. He tried to match this mystical conception of history with a version of dialectics in which mediation would be totally eclipsed by reversal, in which atonement would have to yield to criticism and destruction. His "blasting" the dialectical image "out of the continuum of historical process" (N10a,3) was akin to that anarchistic impulse which tries to stop history during revolutions by instituting a new calendar, or by shooting at church clocks, as during the July revolution in Paris. The gaze, which exorcized images from objects blasted loose from time, is the Gorgon gaze at the *"facies hippocratica* of history," the "petrified primordial landscape" of myth (*Trauerspiel,* p. 166). But in that mystical moment when past and present enter "lightning-like" into a constellation—when the true image of the past "flashes" in the "now of its recognizability" (N9,7)—that image becomes a dialectically reversing image, as it presents itself from the messianic perspective, or (in materialistic terms) the perspective of the revolution.

From this perspective of "messianic time," Benjamin defined the present as catastrophe (1:1243), as the prolongation of that "one single catastrophe" which meets the Angelus Novus when he looks back on past history. It might appear as if Benjamin wished to reintroduce the "large hyphen between past and future,"[28] which was thought to be eradicated after Marx. Yet even Benjamin's late work does not fully forgo historical reference. Henri Focillon defined the classical in art as *"bonheur rapide,"* as the *chairou achme* of the Greeks, and Benjamin wanted to use that definition for his own concept of messianic standstill (see 1:1229). The dialectic at a standstill, the final coming to rest, the ending of the historical dynamic which Hegel, following Aristotle, wished to ascribe to the state, was, for Benjamin, prefigured only in art. A "real definition" of progress, therefore, could emerge only from the vantage point of art, as in the *Passagen-Werk:*

> In every true work of art there is a place where, for one who removes there, it blows cool like the wind of a coming dawn. From this it follows that art, which has often been considered refractory to every relation with progress, can provide its true definition. Progress has its seat not in the continuity of elapsing time but in its interferences. (N9a,7)

In this sense, it may even be possible to save that problematic definition from the first exposé, according to which in the dialectical image the mythical, *Ur*-historical experiences of the collective unconscious "engender, through interpenetration with what is new, the utopia"—and that utopia "has left its trace in a thousand configurations of life, from enduring edifices to passing fashions" (section I). Benjamin devised his dialectic at a standstill in order to make such traces visible, to collect the "trash of history," and to "redeem" them for its end. He undertook the equally paradoxical and astonishing task of presenting history in the spirit of an anti-evolutionary understanding of history. As a "messianic cessation of the event," it would have devolved upon the dialectic at a standstill to bring home in the *Passagen-Werk* the very insight Benjamin had long assimilated when he began that project: "the profane . . . although not itself a category of this [messianic] Kingdom, is at least a category, and one of the most applicable, of its quietest approach."[29] Benjamin's concept of profane illumination would remain "illuminated" in this way to the end; his materialist inspiration would be "inspired" in the same way, and his materialism would prove theological in the same way, despite all "recasting processes." Benjamin's historical materialism was historically true only as the puppet, "which enlists the services of theology." Nevertheless, it was supposed to "win" (*Illuminations,* p. 253). One can be excused for doubting whether this intricate claim could ever be honored. In that case, the reader, who has patiently followed the topography of the *Passagen-Werk,* including all the detours and cul-de-sacs this edition does not veil, may think he is, in the end, faced with ruins rather than with virginal building materials. What Benjamin wrote about German *Trauerspiel* however, holds true for the *Passagen-Werk:* namely, that "in the ruins of great buildings the idea of the plan speaks more impressively than in lesser buildings, however well preserved they are" (*Trauerspiel,* p. 235).

—Translated by Gary Smith and André Lefevere

The Story of Old Benjamin

By Lisa Fittko

This account was written in English, in November 1980, by Lisa Fittko, who accompanied Benjamin across the Pyrenees to the French-Spanish border at the end of September 1940 (and who later settled in the United States). It is printed in English in *Gesammelte Schriften,* vol. 5 (Frankfurt: Suhrkamp, 1982), pp. 1184–1194, with supplementary material (letters) relating mainly to the unsolved mystery of the "large black briefcase" which Benjamin was carrying. Included (p. 1203) is Benjamin's last letter, dated Port-Bou, September 25, 1940, and addressed both to Henny Gurland, who was with him at the end (see Gershom Scholem, *Walter Benjamin: The Story of a Friendship,* trans. Harry Zohn [New York: Schocken, 1981], pp. 224–226), and to Theodor Adorno; it is in French, in a form reconstructed from memory by Henny Gurland, who had felt it necessary to destroy the original: "In a situation presenting no way out, I have no other choice but to make an end of it. It is in a small village in the Pyrenees, where no one knows me, that my life will come to a close [*va s'achever*]. / I ask you to transmit my thoughts [*pensées*] to my friend Adorno and to explain to him the situation in which I find myself. There is not enough time remaining for me to write all the letters I would like to write."

This happened exactly forty years ago. I finally have to keep my promise to write down the story. People keep saying: Just write it the way it was . . .

I do remember everything that happened; I think I do. That is, I remember the facts. But can I re-live those days? Is it possible to step back and into those times when there was no time for remembering what normal life was like, those days when we adapted to chaos and struggled for survival . . . ?

The distance of the years—forty of them—has put events for us into perspective, many believe. It seems to me, though, that this perspective, under the pretense of insight, easily turns into simple hindsight, reshaping what was. . . . How will my recollections stand up against this trap?

And where do I start?

September 25, 1940
Port-Vendres (Pyrénées Orientales, France)

I remember waking up in that narrow room under the roof where I had gone to sleep a few hours earlier. Someone was knocking at the door. It had to be the little girl from downstairs; I got out of bed and opened the door. But it wasn't the child. I rubbed my half-closed eyes. It was one of our friends, Walter Benjamin—one of the many who had poured into Marseilles when the Germans overran France. Old Benjamin, as I usually referred to him, I am not sure why—he was about forty-eight. Now, how did he get here?

"*Gnädige Frau,*" he said, "please accept my apologies for this inconvenience." The world was coming apart, I thought, but not Benjamin's *politesse. "Ihr Herr Gemahl,*" he continued, "told me how to find you. He said you would take me across the border into Spain." He said *what?* Oh well, yes, *"mein Herr Gemahl"*—my husband—would say that. He would assume that I could do it, whatever "it" might be.

Benjamin was still standing in the open door because there was no room for a second person between the bed and the wall. Quickly I told him to wait for me in the bistro on the village square.

From the bistro, we went for a walk so that we could talk without being overheard. My husband had no way of knowing, I explained, but since my arrival here at the border region last week I had found a safe way to cross the frontier. I had started by going down to the port and chatting with some of the longshoremen. One of them led me to the union steward, who in turn directed me to Monsieur Azéma, the mayor of the next village, Banyuls-sur-Mer: the man, I had been told back in Marseilles, who would help me find a safe road for those of our family and friends who were ready to cross over. An old socialist, he was among those who had aided the Spanish republic by passing desperately needed doctors, nurses, and medicine across the border during the Spanish civil war.

What a great person, this Mayor Azéma, I went on to tell Benjamin. He had spent hours with me working out every detail. Unfortunately, the famous road along the cemetery walls of Cerbères was closed. It had been quite easy, and a good number of refugees had used it for a few months, but now it was heavily guarded by the Gardes Mobiles. On orders of the German Commission, no doubt. The only truly safe crossing that was left, according to the mayor, was *"la route Lister."** "That meant that we had to cross the Pyrenees farther west, at a greater altitude; it meant more climbing.

"That will be all right," Benjamin said, "as long as it is safe. I do have a heart condition," he continued, "and I will have to walk slowly. Also, there are two more persons who joined me on my trip from Marseilles and who also need to cross the border, a Mrs. Gurland and her teenage son. Would you take them along?"

Sure, sure. "But Mr. Benjamin, do you realize that I am not a competent guide in this region? I don't really know that road, I have never been up that way myself. I have a piece of paper on which the mayor penciled a map of the route from his memory, and then he described to me some details of turns to be taken, a hut on the left, a plateau with seven pine trees which has to remain to our right or we will end up too far north; the vineyard that leads to the ridge at the right point. You want to take the risk?"

"Yes," he said without hesitation. "The real risk would be not to go."

Glancing at him, I remembered that this was not Benjamin's first attempt to get out of the trap. Impossible for anyone who knew about his former try to forget it. The apocalyptic atmosphere in Marseilles in 1940 produced its daily absurd story of attempted escape: plans around fantasy boats and fable captains, visas for countries unknown to Atlas, and passports from countries that had ceased to exist. One had become accustomed to learning through the Daily Grapevine which foolproof plan had suffered today the fate of a House of Cards. We still were able to laugh—we had to laugh—at the comic side of some of these tragedies. The laughter was irresistible when Dr. Fritz Fraenkel, with frail body and gray mane, and his friend Walter Benjamin, with his sensitive scholar's head and pensive eyes behind thick glasses, were, through bribery, smuggled on a freighter, dressed up as French sailors. They didn't get very far.

Luckily, they did get away, though, due to the generalized state of confusion.

We agreed that we would try to see Mayor Azéma once more, this time together, so that we could both memorize every detail. I notified my sister-in-law—she, the baby, and I

* General Lister of the Spanish Republican Army had led his troops along that route.

were going to cross the border and go to Portugal the next week—and I went to Banyuls with Benjamin.

Here I have a lapse of memory. Did we dare to take the train in spite of the constant border checks? I doubt it. We must have walked the six or eight kilometers from Port-Vendres on the rocky path which by now was familiar to me. I do remember finding the mayor in his office, how he locked the door and then repeated his instructions and answered our questions.

Two days before, after he had drawn the sketch of the road for me, he and I had stepped to the window and he had pointed out the directions, the far-away plateau with the seven pine trees, and somewhere high up there the crest which we would have to cross. "On paper, it looked like an easy walk," I had said, "but it seems that we have to cross the high Pyrenees. . . ?" He had laughed: "That's where Spain is, on the other side of the mountains."

He now suggested that we take a walk this afternoon and do the first part of the route to test whether we would find our way. "You go up to this clearing here," he said pointing it out on his sketch. "Then you return and check it out with me. You spend the night at the inn and tomorrow morning around five o'clock, while it is still dark and our people go up to their vineyards, you start out again and go all the way to the Spanish border." Benjamin asked how far it was to the clearing. "Less than an hour . . . well, certainly not more than two hours. Just a nice walk." We shook hands. *"Je vous remercie infiniment, Monsieur le Maire,"* I heard Benjamin say. I can still hear his voice.

We got his companions who had been waiting at the inn and explained our plan. They seemed to be cooperative, not the complaining kind that I dreaded so much in ticklish situations. We walked slowly, like tourists enjoying the scenery. I noticed that Benjamin was carrying a large black briefcase which he must have picked up when we had stopped at the inn. It looked heavy and I offered to help him carry it. "This is my new manuscript," he explained. "But why did you take it for this walk?" "You must understand that this briefcase is the most important thing to me," he said. "I cannot risk losing it. It is the manuscript that *must* be saved. It is more important than I am."

This expedition won't be easy, I thought. Walter Benjamin and his puzzling ways. That's just what he is like. When trying to pass for a sailor in the port of Marseilles, had he toted the briefcase? But I better keep my mind on the road, I said to myself, and try to figure out Azéma's directions on the little map.

Here was the empty shed the mayor had mentioned, so we weren't lost . . . not yet. Then we found the path with a slight turn to the left. And the huge rock he had described. A clearing! That must be it. We had made it, after almost three hours.

This was about one third of the total route, according to Azéma. I don't remember it as being difficult. We sat down and rested for a while. Benjamin stretched out on the grass and closed his eyes, and I thought it must have been tiring for him.

We were ready to start the descent, but he didn't get up. "Are you all right?" I asked.

"I am fine," he answered, "you three go ahead."

"And you?"

"I am staying here. I am going to spend the night here, and you will join me in the morning."

This was worse than I had expected. What do I do now? All I can do is try and reason with him. This was wild mountain territory, there could be dangerous animals. As a matter of fact, I knew that there were wild bulls. It was late September and he had nothing with which to cover himself. There were smugglers around, and who knew what they might do to him. He would have nothing to eat or drink. Anyhow, this was insane.

He said that his decision to spend the night at the clearing was unshakable since it was based on simple reasoning. The goal was to cross the border so that he and his manuscript would not fall into the hands of the Gestapo. He had reached one third of this goal. If he had to return to the village and then do the entire way again tomorrow, his heart would probably give out. Ergo, he would stay.

I sat down again and said: "Then I too will stay."

He smiled. "Will you defend me against your wild bulls, *gnädige Frau?*"

My staying would not be reasonable, he explained quietly. It was essential that I check back with Azéma and that I get a good night's sleep. Only then would I be able to guide the Gurlands back before sunrise without possible error or delay, and continue to the border.

Of course, I knew all that. Above all, I had to get hold of some bread without ration stamps, and perhaps some tomatoes and black-market ersatz marmalade, to keep us going during the day. I think I had only tried to shock Benjamin into abandoning his plan, but of course it hadn't worked.

On the descent, I tried to concentrate on the road so that I would be able to find my way in the dark the next morning. But my mind kept nagging: he shouldn't be up there alone, this is all wrong. . . . Had he planned it this way all along? Or had the walk exhausted him so much that he had decided to stay only after we arrived? But there was this heavy briefcase that he had taken along. Were his survival instincts intact? If in danger, what would his peculiar way of reasoning tell him to do?

During the winter, before France's surrender, my husband and Benjamin had been together in one of the camps where the French government imprisoned the refugees from Nazi Germany—together with the Nazis. They were at the Camp de Vernuche, close to Nevers. In one of their conversations Benjamin, a heavy smoker, revealed that he had quit smoking a few days ago. It was painful, he added. "Wrong timing," Hans told him. Seeing Benjamin's inability to handle "the adversities of outer life which sometimes come . . . like wolves"[1]—at Vernuche all of life was adversity—Hans had become used to helping him cope.

He now tried to show Benjamin that in order to tolerate crises and keep one's sanity, the fundamental rule was to look for gratifications, not punishments. Benjamin answered, "I can bear the conditions in the camp only if I am forced to immerse my mind totally in an effort. To quit smoking requires this effort, and it will therefore save me."

The next morning everything seemed to be going well. The danger of being seen by the police or customs guards was greatest when leaving the village and starting up the foothills. Azéma had insisted: start out before sunrise, mingle with the vineyard workers on your way up, don't carry anything except a *musette,* don't talk. That way the patrols can't distinguish you from the villagers. Mrs. Gurland and her young son, to whom I had explained these rules, carefully followed them, and I had no trouble finding the way.

The closer we came to the clearing, the more tense I grew. Will Benjamin be there? Will he be alive? My imagination started turning like a kaleidoscope.

Finally. Here is the clearing. Here is old Benjamin. Alive. He sits up and gives us a friendly look. Then I stare at his face—what has happened? Those dark purple blotches under his eyes—could they be a symptom of a heart attack?

He guessed why I stared. Taking off his glasses and wiping his face with a handkerchief, he said: "Oh that. The morning dew, you know. The pads inside the frames, see? They stain when they get damp."

My heart stopped beating in my throat and slipped back down to where it belonged.

From here on, the ascent was steeper. Also, we began to be repeatedly in doubt about which direction to take. To my surprise Benjamin was quite able to understand our little map, and to help me keep our orientation and stick to the right road.

The word "road" became more and more symbolic. There were stretches of a path, but more often it became a hardly discernible trail among boulders—and then the steep vineyard which I will never forget.

But first I have to explain what made this route so safe.

Following the initial descent, the path ran parallel to the widely known "official" road along the crest of the mountain chain, which was quite passable. "Our" road—the *Route Lister* and an old, old smugglers' path—ran below and somewhat tucked inside the overhang of the crest, out of the sight of the French border guards patrolling above. At a few points the two roads approached each other closely, and there we had to keep silent.

Benjamin walked slowly and with an even measure. At regular intervals—I believe it was ten minutes—he stopped and rested for about one minute. Then he went on, at the same steady pace. He had calculated and worked this out during the night, he told me: "With this timing I will be able to make it to the end. I rest at regular intervals—I must rest *before* I become exhausted. Never spend yourself."

What a strange man. A crystal-clear mind; unbending inner strength; yet, a woolyheaded bungler.

The nature of his strength, Walter Benjamin once wrote, is "patience, conquerable by nothing." [2] Reading this years later, I saw him again walking slowly, evenly along the mountain path, and the contradictions within him lost some of their absurdity.

Mrs. Gurland's son, José—he was about fifteen years old—and I took turns carrying the black bag; it was awfully heavy. But, I recall, we all showed good spirits. There was some easy, casual conversation, turning mostly around the needs of the moment. But mainly, we were quiet, watching the road.

Today, when Walter Benjamin is considered one of the century's leading scholars and critics—today I am sometimes asked: What did he say about the manuscript? Did he discuss the contents? Did it develop a novel philosophical concept?

Good God, I had my hands full steering my little group uphill; philosophy would have to wait till the downward side of the mountain was reached. What mattered now was to save a few people from the Nazis; and here I was with this—this—*komischer Kauz, ce drôle de type*—this curious eccentric. Old Benjamin: under no circumstances would he part with his ballast, that black bag; we would have to drag the monster across the mountains.

Now back to the steep vineyard. There was no path. We climbed between the vinestalks, heavy with the almost ripe, dark and sweet Banyuls grapes. I remember it as an almost vertical incline; but such memories sometimes distort the geometry. Here, for the first and only time, Benjamin faltered. More precisely, he tried, failed, and then gave formal notice that this climb was beyond his capability. José and I took him between us; with his arms on our shoulders, we dragged him and the bag up the hill. He breathed heavily, yet he made no complaint, not even a sigh. He only kept squinting in the direction of the black bag.

After the vineyard, we rested on a narrow hillside—the same plateau where we met our Greek a few weeks later. But that is another story. The sun had climbed high enough to warm us, so it must have been about four to five hours since we had started out. We nibbled on the food I had brought in my *musette,* but nobody ate much. Our stomachs had shrunk during the last months—first the concentration camps, then the chaotic retreat—*la pagaille,* or The Total Chaos. A nation on the run, moving south; at our backs the empty villages and ghost towns—lifeless, soundless, till the rattling of the German tanks gulped up the stillness. But, again, that is another story, a very long one.

While we rested, I thought that this road across the mountains had turned out to be longer and more difficult than we could have guessed from the mayor's description. On the other hand, if one were familiar with the terrain and didn't carry anything, and were in good shape, it might really take considerably less time. Like all mountain people, Monsieur Azéma's ideas of distance and time were elastic. How many hours were "a few hours" to him?

During the following winter months, when we did this border crossing sometimes twice or even three times a week, I often thought of Benjamin's self-discipline. I thought of it when Mrs. R. started whining in the middle of the mountains: ". . . don't you have an apple for me . . . I want an apple . . .," and when Fräulein Mueller had a sudden fit of screaming ("acro-dementia," we called it); and when Dr. H. valued his fur coat more than his safety (and ours). But these again are different stories.

Right now I was sitting somewhere high up in the Pyrenees, eating a piece of bread obtained with sham ration tickets, and Benjamin was requesting the tomatoes: "With your kind permission, may I . . . ?" Good old Benjamin and his Castilian court ceremony.

Suddenly, I realized that what I had been gazing at drowsily was a skeleton, sun bleached. Perhaps a goat? Above us, in the southern blue sky, two large black birds circled. Must be vultures—I wonder what they expect from us. . . . How strange, I thought; the usual me would not be so phlegmatic about skeletons and vultures.

We gathered ourselves up and began trudging on. The road now became reasonably straight, ascending only slightly. Still, it was bumpy and, for Benjamin, it must have been strenuous. He had been on his feet since seven o'clock, after all. His pace slowed down some more and he paused a little longer, but always in regular intervals, checking his watch. He seemed to be quite absorbed by the job of timing himself.

Then we reached the peak. I had gone ahead and stopped to look around. The view came on so sudden, for a moment it struck me like a *fata morgana.* Down there below, from where we had come, the Mediterranean reappeared. On the other side, ahead, steep cliffs—another sea? But of course, the Spanish coast. Two worlds of blueness. In our back, to the north, Catalonia's *Roussillon* country. Deep down *La Côte Vermeille,* the autumn earth in a hundred shades of vermillion. I gasped: never had I seen anything so beautiful.

I knew that we were now in Spain, and that from here on the road would run straight until the descent into the town. I knew that now I had to turn back. The others had the necessary papers and visas, but I could not risk being caught on Spanish soil. But, no, I could not yet leave this group to themselves, not quite yet. Just another short stretch . . .

Putting down on paper the details which my memory brings back about this first time I crossed the border on the *Route Lister,* a nebulous picture surfaces from wherever it has been buried all these years. Three women—two of them I know vaguely—crossing our road; through a haze, I see us standing there and talking for a short while. They had come up a different road, and they then continued their way down to the Spanish side separately. The encounter did not particularly surprise or impress me, since so many people were trying to escape over the mountains.

We passed a puddle. The water was greenish slimy and stank. Benjamin knelt down to drink.

"You can't drink this water," I said, "it is filthy and surely contaminated." The water-bottle I had taken along was empty by now, but thus far he hadn't mentioned that he was thirsty.

"I do apologize," Benjamin said, "but I have no choice. If I do not drink, I might not be able to continue to the end." He bent his head down towards the puddle.

"Listen to me," I said. "Will you please hold it for a moment and listen to me? We have almost arrived; just a short while and you have made it. I know you can make it. But to drink this mud is unthinkable. You will get typhus . . ."

"True, I might. But don't you see, the worst that can happen is that I die of typhus . . . AFTER crossing the border. The Gestapo won't be able to get me, and the manuscript will be safe. I do apologize."

He drank.

The road was now running gently downhill. It must have been about two o'clock in the afternoon when the rocky wall gave way, and in the valley I saw the village, very close.

"That is Port-Bou down there! The town with the Spanish border control where you will present yourselves. This street leads straight down. A real road!"

Two o'clock. We had started out at five in the morning, Benjamin at seven. A total of almost nine hours.

"I have to go back now," I continued. "We are in Spain—we have been in Spain for almost an hour. The descent won't take long; it's so close that you can see every house from here. You will go directly to the border post and show your documents: the travel papers, the Spanish and Portuguese transit visas. When you have your entry stamp, you take the next train to Lisbon. But you know all that. . . . I must go now, *auf Wieder-sehen . . .*"

For a moment, my eyes followed them as they were walking down the road. It's time now for me to get out of here, I thought, and started to walk back. I walked on and felt: This isn't alien country any more, I am no stranger here, as I was only this morning. It also surprised me that I was not tired. Everything felt light, I was weightless and so was the rest of the world. Benjamin and his companions must have made it by now. How beautiful it was up here!

Within two hours I was back down in Banyuls. Nine hours uphill, two hours down.

During the following months, by the time we were able to find our way blindfolded, we once made it up to the border in two hours, and a few times in three to four hours. That was when our "freight" was young, strong, in good form and, above all, disciplined. I have never seen these people again, but from time to time a name comes up and suddenly something clicks. Henry Pachter, historian: Heinz and his friend, all-time record two hours. Or Prof. Albert Hirschman, economist at Princeton: young Hermant. I was critically ill when he came down to the border. He pressured a French hospital into admitting me, then crossed over, guided by my husband, in about three hours. I will write that story down another time.

For all that came later. Then, back in Banyuls, after my first trip on the Lister route, I thought: Good old Benjamin and his manuscript are safe, on the other side of the mountains.

In about a week the word came: Walter Benjamin is dead. He took his life in Port-Bou the night after his arrival.

The Spanish border authorities had informed the group that they would be returned to France. New orders, just received from Madrid: Nobody can enter Spain without the French exit visa. (Several different versions* exist of the reason Spain gave this time for closing the border: *apatrides*† may not travel through Spain; or Spanish transit visas issued in Marseilles were invalid.) Whatever the new directive was, it was lifted soon. Had there been time for the news to reach the French side of the frontier, crossings would have been halted while watching developments. We were living in the "Age of New Directives"; every governmental office in every country of Europe seemed to devote full time to decreeing, revoking, enacting, and then lifting orders and regulations. You just had to learn to slip through holes, to turn, to wind, and to wriggle your way out of this ever-changing maze, if you wanted to survive.

But Benjamin was not a wriggler . . .

". . . *faut se débrouiller*": one has to cut through the fog, work one's way out of the general collapse—that had become the only possible way of life in France. To most, it meant things like buying forged bread tickets or extra milk for the kids or obtaining some kind, any kind of permit; in other words, to get something that didn't officially exist. To some, it also meant to get such things by "collaborating." For us, the *apatrides,* it was primarily a matter of staying out of concentration camps and escaping from the Gestapo.

But Benjamin was no *débrouillard* . . .

In his remoteness, what counted was that his manuscript and he were out of the reach of the Gestapo. The crossing had exhausted him and he didn't believe that he could do it again—he had told me so during our climb. Here, too, he had calculated everything in advance: he had enough morphine on him to take his life several times over.

Impressed and shaken by his death, the Spanish authorities let his companions continue their travel.

July 1980

During a recent conversation with Professor Abramsky from London, we talked about Walter Benjamin and his work, and I mentioned his last walk.

Then I got a call from Professor Gershom Scholem, a trustee of Benjamin's literary estate and his closest friend. He had heard from Abramsky about our conversation and wanted to know more. I gave him a summarized description of the events on that day almost forty years ago.

He asked for every detail concerning the manuscript:

"There is no manuscript," he said. "Until now, nobody knew that such a manuscript ever existed."

I am hearing: there is no manuscript. Nobody knows about the heavy black briefcase carrying the papers that were more important to him than anything else.

---

* see F. V. Grunfeld, Hannah Arendt, G. Scholem et al.

† Stateless persons, literally "People without Fatherland"–official French term for refugees from Nazi Germany whose citizenship had been taken away by the Nazi government.

Hannah Arendt has written about the "little hunchback"* whose threat Benjamin felt throughout his life and against whom he took all precautions. Benjamin's "system of provisions against possible danger . . . invariably disregarded the real danger," she says.[3]

But it seems to me now that the "real danger" was not disregarded by Walter Benjamin during that night in Port-Bou; it was just that his real danger, his reality, differed from ours. He must have met again the little hunchback in Port-Bou . . . his very own, the Benjamin hunchback, and he had to come to terms with him.

Perhaps I will go to Port-Bou and try to pick up some tracks, to retrace what happened on that side of the mountains forty years ago, with the help of some of our old friends down there.

Perhaps there will be another ending to this story.

---

*A German fairy-tale figure who causes all of life's misfortunes; he trips you, he breaks your favorite toy, he spills your soup.

Translators' Notes

Abbreviations

GS   Walter Benjamin, *Gesammelte Schriften,* 7 vols. (Frankfurt: Suhrkamp, 1972–1989).

J.L.   Jean Lacoste, translator of the *Passagen-Werk* into French: *Paris, capitale du XIXe siècle* (Paris: Editions du Cerf, 1989).

R.T.   Rolf Tiedemann, editor of the *Passagen-Werk, GS,* vol. 5 (Frankfurt: Suhrkamp, 1982).

SW   Walter Benjamin, *Selected Writings.* Volume 1: *1913–1926* (Cambridge, Mass.: Harvard University Press, 1996). Volume 2: *1927–1934* (Cambridge, Mass.: Harvard University Press, 1999).

Previously published translations have been modified, where necessary, to accord with the passages cited by Benjamin.

Exposé of 1935

This synopsis of *The Arcades Project,* titled "Paris, die Hauptstadt des XIX. Jahrhunderts" (*GS,* vol. 5, pp. 45–59), was written by Benjamin in May 1935 at the request of Friedrich Pollock, codirector of the Institute of Social Research in New York. It was first published in Walter Benjamin, *Schriften,* 2 vols. (Frankfurt: Suhrkamp, 1955). The translators are indebted to the previous English translations by Quintin Hoare (1968) and Edmund Jephcott (1978).

1. The *magasin de nouveautés* offered a complete selection of goods in one or another specialized line of business; it had many rooms and several stories, with a large staff of employees. The first such store, Pygmalion, opened in Paris in 1793. The word *nouveauté* means "newness" or "novelty"; in the plural, it means "fancy goods."
2. Honoré de Balzac, "Histoire et physiolgie des boulevards de Paris," in George Sand, Honoré de Balzac, Eugène Sue, et al., *Le Diable à Paris,* vol. 2 (Paris, 1846), p. 91. [R.T.] See A1,4 in the Convolutes.
3. Karl Boetticher, "Das Prinzip der Hellenischen und Germanischen Bauweise hinsichtlich der Übertragung in die Bauweise unserer Tage" (address of March 13, 1846), in *Zum hundertjährigen Geburtstag Karl Böttichers* (Berlin, 1906), p. 46. [R.T.] See F1,1 in the Convolutes.
4. Sigfried Giedion, *Bauen in Frankreich* (Leipzig, 1928), p. 3. [R.T.]
5. Paul Scheerbart, *Glasarchitektur* (Berlin, 1914). [R.T.] In English, *Glass Architecture,* trans. James Palmes (New York: Praeger, 1972).

6. Jules Michelet, "Avenir! Avenir!" *Europe,* 19, no. 73 (January 15, 1929): 6. [R.T.]

7. See Karl Marx and Friedrich Engels, *Die deutsche Ideologie* (The German Ideology), part 2; in English in Marx and Engels, *Collected Works,* vol. 5, trans. C. P. Magill (New York: International Publishers, 1976). The passage in question is on pp. 513–514.

8. See Jean Paul, "Levana, oder Erziehungslehre" (1807); in English, "Levana, or Doctrine of Education," trans. Erika Casey, in *Jean Paul: A Reader* (Baltimore: Johns Hopkins University Press, 1992), pp. 269–274.

9. A. J. Wiertz, "La Photographie," in Wiertz, *Oeuvres littéraires* (Paris, 1870), pp. 309ff. [R.T.] See Y1,1 in the Convolutes.

10. Ferdinand Langlé and Emile Vanderburch, *Louis-Bronze et le Saint-Simonien: Parodie de Louis XI* (Théâtre du Palais-Royal, February 27, 1832), cited in Théodore Muret, *L'Histoire par le théâtre, 1789–1851* (Paris, 1865), vol. 3, p. 191.

11. Actually, it was Ernest Renan; see G4,5 and G13a,3 in the Convolutes.

12. Sigmund Engländer, *Geschichte der französischen Arbeiter-Associationen* (Hamburg, 1864), vol. 4, p. 52. [R.T.]

13. Marx, *Das Kapital,* vol. 1 (1867); in English, *Capital* trans. Samuel Moore and Edward Aveling (1887; rpt. New York: International Publishers, 1967), p. 76.

14. Giacomo Leopardi, "Dialogo della moda e della morte" (1827); in English in Leopardi, *Essays and Dialogues,* trans. Giovanni Cecchetti (Berkeley: University of California Press, 1982), p. 67.

15. Charles Baudelaire, "A Martyr," in Baudelaire, *Flowers of Evil,* trans. Wallace Fowlie (1964; rpt. New York: Dover, 1992), p. 85.

16. Baudelaire, "The Swan," ibid., p. 75.

17. Virgil, *The Aeneid,* trans. Allen Mandelbaum (New York: Bantam, 1971), p. 137 (book 6, line 126). Benjamin cites the Latin.

18. "The Voyage," in Baudelaire, *Les Fleurs du mal,* trans. Richard Howard (Boston: Godine, 1982), pp. 156–157.

19. Baudelaire, *Oeuvres complètes,* ed. Claude Pichois (Paris, 1976), vol. 2, p. 27. [R.T.] Idem, "Pierre Dupont," in *Baudelaire as a Literary Critic,* trans. Lois Boe Hyslop and Francis E. Hyslop, Jr. (University Park: Pennsylvania State University Press, 1964), p. 53.

20. *Confession d'un lion devenu vieux* [Confession of a Lion Grown Old] (Paris, 1888), 4 pp., was published anonymously, without year or place, by Baron Haussmann. [R.T.]

21. For Lafargue's comparison, see O4,1 in the Convolutes. [R.T.]

22. Maxime Du Camp, *Paris: Ses organes, ses fonctions et sa vie dans la seconde moitié du XIXᵉ siècle,* 6 vols. (Paris, 1869–1875). [R.T.] See Walter Benjamin, *Charles Baudelaire: Ein Lyriker im Zeitalter des Hochkapitalismus,* in *GS,* vol. 1, pp. 589–590; in English, *Charles Baudelaire: A Lyric Poet in the Era of High Capitalism,* trans. Harry Zohn (London: Verso, 1976), pp. 85–86.

23. Anonymous, *Paris désert: Lamentations d'un Jérémie haussmannisé* [Deserted Paris: Jeremiads of a Man Haussmannized] (Paris, 1868). [R.T.]

24. Engels' critique of barricade tactics is excerpted in E1a,5 in the Convolutes. [R.T.]

25. The verse derives from Pierre Dupont; see a7,3 in the Convolutes. [R.T.]

26. Frédéric Le Play, *Les Ouvriers européens: Etudes sur les travaux, la vie domestique et la condition morale des populations ouvrières de l'Europe, précédées d'un exposé de la méthode d'observation* (Paris, 1855). [R.T.]

27. See p. 24 and note 22 of the Exposé of 1939.

28. See C2a,8 in the Convolutes.

Exposé of 1939

The second exposé, "Paris, Capitale du XIXème siecle" (*Gesammelte Schriften,* vol. 5, pp. 60–77), was written by Benjamin in March 1939, in French, at the request of Max Horkheimer, who was attempting to enlist a New York banker named Frank Altschul as a backer for *The Arcades Project.* For this exposé, Benjamin added a theoretical Introduction and Conclusion. In reformulating his German exposé in French, he made a number of significant changes, particularly with regard to Fourier (A, II), Louis Philippe (C, II and III), and Baudelaire (D, II and III), while dropping much factual material. See his letter to Horkheimer of March 13, 1939, in *GS,* vol. 5, p. 1171. In our translation of the second exposé, we have tried to reproduce the often subtle divergences from the wording of the first, as well as the numerous verbal parallels (where it is a question of translating a translation).

1. See S1a,2 in the Convolutes. The formula does not appear in Schopenhauer. [R.T.]
2. Karl Marx and Friedrich Engels, *Die heilige Familie* (1845); in English, *The Holy Family,* trans. Richard Dixon and Clemens Dutt, in Marx and Engels, *Collected Works,* vol. 4 (New York: International Publishers, 1975), p. 81.
3. Charles Fourier, *Théorie des quatre mouvements et des destinées générales* (1808); in English in Fourier, *The Theory of the Four Movements,* trans. Ian Patterson (Cambridge: Cambridge University Press, 1996), p. 22.
4. Tony Moilin, *Paris en l'an 2000* [Paris in the Year 2000] (Paris, 1869). See C5a,3 in the Convolutes.
5. Marx and Engels, *Werke* (Berlin: Dietz, 1969–), vol. 3, p. 502: "die kolossalische Anschauung der Menschen."
6. Actually, it was Ernest Renan; see G4,5 and G13a,3 in the Convolutes.
7. Sigmund Engländer, *Geschichte der französischen Arbeiter-Associationen* (Hamburg, 1864), vol. 4, p. 52. [R.T.]
8. Marx, *Das Kapital,* vol. 1 (1867); in English, *Capital,* trans. Samuel Moore and Edward Aveling (1887; rpt. New York: International Publishers, 1967), p. 76.
9. Alphonse Toussenel, *Le Monde des oiseaux: Ornithologie passionnelle,* vol. 1 (Paris, 1853), p. 20. See W8a,2 in the Convolutes.
10. Giacomo Leopardi, "Dialogo della moda e della morte" (1827); in English in Leopardi, *Essays and Dialogues,* trans. Giovanni Cecchetti (Berkeley: University of California Press, 1982), p. 67.
11. Guillaume Apollinaire, *Le Poète assassiné* (1916); in English in Apollinaire, "*The Poet Assassinated" and Other Stories,* trans. Ron Padgett (San Francisco: North Point Press, 1984), p. 46.
12. Charles Baudelaire, "A Martyr," in Baudelaire, *Flowers of Evil,* trans. Wallace Fowlie (1964; rpt. New York: Dover, 1992), p. 85.
13. Friedrich Nietzsche, *Thus Spoke Zarathustra* (1891), trans. R. J. Hollingdale (Baltimore: Penguin, 1961), p. 286. "Affliction" translates *Heimsuchung.*
14. Marcel Proust, *Du Côté de chez Swann* (Swann's Way; 1913); in English in Proust, *Remembrance of Things Past,* vol. 1, trans. C. K. Scott Moncrieff (New York: Random House, 1925), p. 179. The expression *faire catleya* ("doing a cattleya") is Swann's euphemism for making love.
15. Reference is to the conclusion of Henrik Ibsen's play *The Master Builder* (1892). Throughout this section, in the original French, Benjamin uses the standard term *modern style* (in quotation marks) to refer to Jugendstil.
16. Baudelaire, "The Swan," in *The Complete Verse,* trans. Francis Scarfe (London: Anvil Press, 1986), p. 176.

17. "The Seven Old Men," in Baudelaire, *Flowers of Evil* (New York: Harper and Brothers, 1936), p. 185 (trans. Edna St. Vincent Millay).
18. "The Voyage," in Baudelaire, *Les Fleurs du mal,* trans. Richard Howard (Boston: Godine, 1982), pp. 156–157.
19. Ibid., p. 156.
20. *Spleen* came into French in 1745, from English; *idéal* in 1578, from Latin *(idealis)*.
21. *Confession d'un lion devenu vieux* [Confession of a Lion Grown Old] (Paris, 1888), 4 pp., was published anonymously, without year or place, by Baron Haussmann. [R.T.]
22. Apparently, a correction of the earlier exposé (see p. 13).
23. Louis-Auguste Blanqui, *Instructions pour une Prise d'Armes: L'Eternité par les astres—Hypothèse astronomique* (Paris: Société Encyclopédique Française, 1972), pp. 167–169. See D7; D7a. Benjamin first came upon this text by Blanqui at the end of 1937.

Convolutes

The central portion of the manuscript of *The Arcades Project* (*GS,* vol. 5, pp. 79–989) consists of 426 loose sheets of yellowish paper, each folded in half to form a 14 × 22 cm. folio, of which sides 1 and 3 are inscribed in Benjamin's tiny handwriting, with sides 2 and 4 left blank. These folios are gathered into thirty-six sheafs (the German word *Konvolut* means "sheaf" or "bundle") in accordance with a set of themes keyed to the letters of the alphabet. The titles of the convolutes, as well as the numbering of the individual entries, derive from Benjamin. In regard to the ordering, the use of lowercase *a* (as in "A1a,1") denotes the third page of a folio. The letters without corresponding titles in the Overview may indicate that Benjamin planned further convolutes.

In addition to Benjamin's cross-references (signaled with small squares) to rubrics of different convolutes, or to rubrics without convolutes, many of the citations and reflections in the manuscript are marked with a system of thirty-two assorted symbols (squares, triangles, circles, vertical and horizontal crosses—in various inks and colors), which do not appear in the published text. The symbols are linked to papers that Benjamin entrusted to Georges Bataille and that were discovered in the Bataille archive of the Bibliothèque Nationale in 1981. These papers contain a detailed plan for the Baudelaire book on which Benjamin was working in 1937–1938; the encoded items from the convolutes (more than 60 percent from Convolute J) are grouped there under a set of headings representing themes of the Baudelaire book as a whole. About half of the material was then further organized for the composition of the 1938 essay "Das Paris des Second Empire bei Baudelaire" (The Paris of the Second Empire in Baudelaire).

The convolutes were composed concurrently (rather than consecutively) in two stages: from the fall or winter of 1928 to the end of 1929, and from the beginning of 1934 until May 1940. The German editor of the *Passagen-Werk,* Rolf Tiedemann, provides a more specific dating of the entries on the basis of photocopies of manuscript pages made by Benjamin in June 1935 and December 1937 (*GS,* vol. 5, p. 1262). Within a particular convolute, the entries follow a roughly chronological order (some having been written earlier, then revised and transferred to the manuscript of the convolutes).

On the typographic differentiation between Benjamin's reflections and Benjamin's citations in the "Convolutes" section, see the Translators' Foreword.

A [Arcades, *Magasins de Nouveautés,* Sales Clerks]

1. Arthur Rimbaud, *Complete Works and Selected Letters,* trans. Wallace Fowlie (Chicago: University of Chicago Press, 1966), p. 254 (*Illuminations,* "Sale").

2. The Passage du Caire was the first glass-covered arcade in Paris outside the Palais-Royal. It opened in 1799, one year before the more luxurious Passage des Panoramas.
3. Space in a stock exchange set apart for unofficial business.
4. *The Utopian Vision of Charles Fourier,* ed. and trans. Jonathan Beecher and Richard Bienvenu (1971; rpt. Columbia: University of Missouri Press, 1983), pp. 242–244.
5. Friedrich Engels, *The Condition of the Working Class in England,* trans. Florence Wischnewetzky (1886; rpt. New York: Penguin, 1987), p. 71 ("The Great Towns")
6. *The Utopian Vision of Charles Fourier,* p. 245.
7. Ibid., pp. 242–245 (translation of sentences 2–4 added).
8. The Egyptian campaign of Napoleon Bonaparte took place in 1798–1799.
9. Heinrich Heine, *Jewish Stories and Hebrew Melodies* (New York: Markus Wiener, 1987), p. 122 (trans. Hal Draper). "Her" refers to the poet's wife.
10. Possibly a pun on *épicier,* "grocer." The final *e* in both *épée* and *sciée* has been sawed off; the sign is thus a typographical joke.
11. One of three main divisions of Balzac's writings.
12. From "Lutetia," Roman name for Paris. See C1,6.
13. G. K. Chesterton, *Charles Dickens* (1906; rpt. New York: Schocken, 1965), pp. 119–120. Corresponding to the sixth sentence quoted here, the translation used by Benjamin has: "Chaque boutique, en fait, éveillait en lui l'idée d'une nouvelle."
14. *De la justice dans la Révolution et dans l'église* (On Justice during the Revolution and in the Church) 3 volumes (1858).
15. Charles Baudelaire, *Baudelaire as a Literary Critic,* trans. Lois Boe Hyslop and Francis E. Hyslop, Jr. (University Park: Pennsylvania State University Press, 1964), p. 52. The reference is to Hugo's book of poems *Les Orientales* (1829).
16. Balzac, *Gaudissart the Great,* trans. James Waring, in *Balzac's Works* (Philadelphia: Gebbie Publishing, 1899), vol. 1, p. 343.
17. Baudelaire, *Paris Spleen,* trans. Louise Varèse (New York: New Directions, 1947), p. 60 ("The Generous Gambler").
18. Baudelaire, *"My Heart Laid Bare" and Other Prose Writings,* trans. Norman Cameron (1950; rpt. New York: Haskell House, 1975), p. 156 ("Fusées," no. 2).

B [Fashion]

1. Giacomo Leopardi, "Dialogo della moda et della morte" (1827); in English in Leopardi, *Essays and Dialogues,* trans. Giovanni Cecchetti (Berkeley: University of California Press, 1962), p. 67.
2. Rainer Maria Rilke, *Duino Elegies,* trans. J. B. Leishman and Stephen Spender (New York: Norton, 1939), p. 53 (fifth elegy).
3. Marginal annotation by Theodor W. Adorno: "I would think: counterrevolutions." [R.T.]
4. *Fan of Iris* and *The Moon (a Self-Portrait)* appear in Grandville's *Un Autre Monde* (1844); "the Milky Way . . . as an avenue illuminated by gas candelabra" is doubtless an allusion to the plate entitled *An Interplanetary Bridge.* [R.T.]
5. See Walter Benjamin, *Ursprung des deutschen Trauerspiels, GS,* vol. 1, p. 294. [R.T.] In English, *The Origin of German Tragic Drama,* trans. John Osborne (London: Verso, 1977), p. 115.
6. Guillaume Apollinaire, *"The Poet Assassinated" and Other Stories,* trans. Ron Padgett (San Francisco: North Point Press, 1984), pp. 45–47 (section 13).

7. André Breton, *Nadja,* trans. Richard Howard (New York: Grove Weidenfeld, 1960), p. 152.

8. See N3,2. [R.T.]

9. Apollinaire, *"The Poet Assassinated" and Other Stories,* p. 46.

10. *La Muette de Portici* (The Mute Girl of Portici), opera by D. F. E. Auber. A duet from this work, "Amour sacré de la patrie," is said to have been used as a signal for the Revolution of 1830 in Brussels.

11. A. E. Brehm (1829–1884), German zoologist, was the author of *Tierleben* (Life of Animals), 6 vols. (1864–1869). On Helen Grund, a friend of Franz Hessel, see the preface by J.-M. Palmier to the French translation of Hessel's *Spazieren in Berlin,* entitled *Promenades dans Berlin* (Grenoble: Presses Universitaires de Grenoble, 1989), pp. 17ff. [J.L.]

12. Paul Valéry, "On Italian Art," in *Degas, Manet, Morisot,* trans. David Paul (1960; rpt. Princeton: Princeton University Press, 1989), pp. 220, 224–225.

13. This passage does not appear in the English edition of von Jhering (also spelled "Ihering"), *Law as a Means to an End,* trans. Isaac Husik (New York: Macmillan, 1921).

14. Allusion to Louis Napoleon's coup d'état of December 2, 1851. Both the Second of December and the crinoline represent the triumph of reactionism.

15. Georg Simmel, "Fashion," trans. anonymous, *International Quarterly,* 10, no. 1 (October 1904), p. 136.

16. Ibid., p. 143.

17. This passage does not appear in the 1904 English translation of "Die Mode."

18. Simmel, "Fashion," p. 133.

19. Ibid., p. 151.

20. Valéry, "About Corot," in *Degas, Manet, Morisot,* p. 150.

21. Jules Michelet, *The People,* trans. John P. McKay (Urbana: University of Illinois Press, 1973), p. 44.

22. An echo of Mephistopheles' speech at lines 2038–2039, in Goethe's *Faust,* Part 1.

23. Henri Focillon, *The Life of Forms in Art,* trans. Charles Beecher Hogan and George Kubler (1948; rpt. New York: Zone Books, 1989), pp. 85, 87.

24. The essay, originally published in *Zeitschrift für Sozialforschung,* 6 (1937), is in *GS,* vol. 2; see p. 497, note 50. [R.T.] In English: "Eduard Fuchs: Collector and Historian," trans. Knut Tarnowski, *New German Critique,* 5 (Spring 1975); see p. 51, note 49.

25. Hermann Lotze, *Microcosmus,* trans. Elizabeth Hamilton and E. E. Constance Jones (New York: Scribner and Welford, 1888), vol. 1, pp. 486–487.

C [Ancient Paris, Catacombs, Demolitions, Decline of Paris]

1. Virgil, *The Aeneid,* trans. Allen Mandelbaum (New York: Bantam, 1971), p. 137 (Book 6, line 126). Benjamin cites the Latin.

2. Guillaume Apollinaire, *Oeuvres poétiques* (Paris: Gallimard, 1956), p. 39 (*Alcools,* "Zone"). [R.T.] In English: *Alcools: Poems, 1898–1913,* trans. William Meredith (Garden City, N.Y.: Doubleday, 1964), p. 3.

3. Certain of these muses of Surrealism can be identified more precisely: Luna, the moon; Kate Greenaway (1846–1901), English painter known for her illustrations of children's books; Mors, death; Cléo de Mérode (1875–1966), French dancer who epitomized the demimonde; Dulcinea, the beloved of Don Quixote and the image of idealized woman; Libido, an allusion to Freud; Baby Cadum, publicity and advertis-

ing; Friederike Kempner (1836–1904), German poet and socialite. A comparison with the two other "catalogues of muses" (see F°,4 and F°,10 in "First Sketches") reveals that Dulcinea is a variant of Ibsen's Hedda Gabler, and that Benjamin thought of adding the painter Angelika Kauffmann (1741–1807), a friend of Goethe's. Another list, presumably the earliest, is found in "The Arcades of Paris" (h°,1). [J.L.] Countess Geschwitz, a lesbian artist, is a character in Frank Wedekind's *Erdgeist* and *Die Büchse der Pandora,* plays which inspired Alban Berg's unfinished opera *Lulu.* The identity of Tipse remains a mystery. When Benjamin writes that the mother of Surrealism was *eine Passage,* he plays on the feminine gender of the noun in German.

4. The passage is cited in Benjamin's German translation. For the original French, see *GS,* vol. 5, p. 1326.
5. The reference is to Goethe's *Faust,* Part 2, Act 1 (lines 6264ff.), in which Faust visits "the Mothers"—vaguely defined mythological figures—in search of the secret that will enable him to discover Helen of Troy.
6. See H1a,3.
7. Louis Aragon, *Paris Peasant,* trans. Simon Watson Taylor (1971; rpt. Boston: Exact Change, 1994), p. 14.
8. "Know thyself."
9. Victor Hugo, *Les Misérables,* trans. Charles E. Wilbour (1862; rpt. New York: Modern Library, 1992), p. 103.
10. *Paris vécu* (Paris, 1930). See C9a,1.
11. Hugo, *Les Misérables,* p. 737.
12. Ibid., pp. 859–860.
13. Charles Baudelaire, *Selected Letters,* trans. Rosemary Lloyd (Chicago: University of Chicago Press, 1986), pp. 141–142.
14. Baudelaire, *Les Fleurs du mal,* trans. Richard Howard (Boston: Godine, 1882), p. 90 ("The Swan").
15. Marcel Raymond, *From Baudelaire to Surrealism,* trans. G. M. (1950; rpt. London: Methuen, 1970), p. 170.
16. Jules Romains, *Men of Good Will,* vol. 1, trans. Warre B. Wells (New York: Alfred A. Knopf, 1946), p. 146.
17. Oswald Spengler, *The Decline of the West,* vol. 2, trans. Charles Francis Atkinson (New York: Knopf, 1928), p. 107.

D [Boredom, Eternal Return]

1. Jakob van Hoddis (Hans Davidsohn), *Weltende* (1911), in *Gesammelte Dichtungen* (Zürich, 1958), p. 466 ("Klage"). [R.T.]
2. Johann Peter Hebel, *Werke* (Frankfurt am Main, 1968), vol. 1, p. 393. [R.T.]
3. In the collection *L'Autographe* (Paris, 1863). [J.L.]
4. *Aere perennius:* "more lasting than brass." *Taedium vitae:* tedium of life.
5. The Rue des Colonnes—formerly the Passage des Colonnes, transformed into a street in 1798—is located near the Stock Exchange. [J.L.]
6. Cited in French without references. Reading "bien des aventures" (F°,18 in "First Sketches") for "lieu des aventures."
7. Louis Aragon, *Paris Peasant,* trans. Simon Watson Taylor (1971; rpt. Boston: Exact Change, 1994), p. 71.
8. See note for B°,4 ("First Sketches").
9. See Ferdinand Hardekopf, *Gesammelte Dichtungen* (Zurich, 1963), pp. 50ff. [R.T.] See also B°,5 ("First Sketches").
10. "Time" and "weather."

11. Karl Marx, *Capital*, vol. 1, trans. Samuel Moore and Edward Aveling (1887; rpt. New York: International Publishers, 1967), p. 398.

12. André Gide, "Upon Rereading *Les Plaisirs et les jours* after the Death of Marcel Proust," trans. Blanche A. Price, in Gide, *Pretexts: Reflections on Literature and Morality,* ed. Justin O'Brien (New York: Meridian, 1959), p. 279.

13. *Dolce far niente:* Italian for "sweet idleness." *Images d'Epinal* were sentimental religious posters produced in the town of Epinal in southeastern France. Jean Lacoste suggests that Mogreby may be Maghrébin, the magician in "Aladdin and the Marvelous Lamp," in the Mardrus translation of *Les Mille et Une Nuits* (1925). Compare "Naples," in *SW,* vol. 1, p. 419.

14. This passage involves some wordplay in the German: *sich die Zeit vertreiben / austreiben,* as opposed to *die Zeit laden / zu sich einladen.*

15. Jules Michelet, *The People,* trans. John P. McKay (Urbana: University of Illinois Press, 1973), p. 46.

16. Siegfried Kracauer, *Orpheus in Paris: Offenbach and the Paris of His Time,* trans. Gwenda David and Eric Mosbacher (New York: Knopf, 1938), p. 268. Described is a scene from Offenbach's operetta *La Vie parisienne* (1866).

17. Charles Baudelaire, "The Painter of Modern Life," in *"The Painter of Modern Life" and Other Essays,* trans. Jonathan Mayne (1964; rpt. New York: Da Capo Press, 1986), p. 26.

18. Ibid., pp. 28–29.

19. Ibid., p. 29.

20. Ibid., p. 10.

21. Baudelaire, *The Complete Verse,* trans. Francis Scarfe (London: Anvil Press, 1986), p. 232.

22. An earlier version of this passage appears in *The Correspondence of Walter Benjamin,* trans. Manfred R. Jacobson and Evelyn M. Jacobson (Chicago: University of Chicago Press, 1994), p. 549 (where Benjamin announces his "rare find").

23. Friedrich Nietzsche, *The Will to Power,* trans. Walter Kaufmann and R. J. Hollingdale (New York: Vintage, 1968), pp. 35, 36.

24. Ibid., p. 38.

25. Ibid., pp. 546–547.

26. Ibid., p. 548.

27. Ibid., p. 550.

28. Ibid., p. 549.

29. *Gründerjahre:* years of reckless financial speculation, in this case following the Franco-Prussian War of 1870–1871.

30. Nietzsche, *Ecce Homo,* trans. Walter Kaufmann (New York: Vintage, 1969), p. 219: "Here no 'prophet' is speaking, none of those gruesome hybrids of sickness and will to power whom people call founders of religions."

31. Jean-Jacques Rousseau, *The Confessions,* trans. J. M. Cohen (Baltimore: Penguin, 1954), p. 415.

32. *The Portable Nietzsche,* trans. Walter Kaufmann (New York: Viking, 1954), pp. 101–102 *(The Gay Science).*

E [Haussmannization, Barricade Fighting]

1. Friedrich Engels, Introduction to Karl Marx, *The Class Struggles in France, 1848 to 1850,* trans. anonymous (New York: International Publishers, 1964), pp. 22–23.

2. Marx, *The Class Struggles in France,* p. 44.

3. Benjamin is quoting from an open letter by the economist Frédéric Bastiat to Lamartine, according to which the latter is actually citing Fourier. [R.T.]

4. Le Corbusier, *The City of Tomorrow and Its Planning,* trans. Frederick Etchells (1929; rpt. New York: Dover, 1987), p. 156.

5. Ibid., p. 155. See E5a,6.

6. Ibid., p. 261.

7. André Breton, *Nadja,* trans. Richard Howard (New York: Grove, 1960), p. 152.

8. Gisèle Freund, *Photographie und bürgerliche Gesellschaft: Eine kunstsoziologische Studie* (Munich, 1968), p. 67. [R.T.]

9. Le Corbusier, *The City of Tomorrow,* p. 156. Next sentence: "And in destroying chaos, he built up the emperor's finances!"

10. In chapter 14 of his popular utopian novel of 1888, *Looking Backward: 2000–1887,* Edward Bellamy describes a continuous waterproof covering let down in inclement weather to enclose sidewalks and streetcorners.

11. After the government, in July 1833, had bowed to public resistance and abandoned its plan to build fortifications around the city of Paris, it took its revenge by arresting a number of individuals (including four students from the Ecole Polytechnique) thought to be illegally manufacturing gunpowder and arms. The group was acquitted in December. G. Pinet, *Histoire de l'Ecole polytechnique* (Paris: Baudry, 1887), pp. 214–219.

12. This passage does not appear in the English-language edition: Gustav Mayer, *Friedrich Engels,* trans. Gilbert Highet and Helen Highet (1936; rpt. New York: Howard Fertig, 1969).

13. Siegfried Kracauer, *Orpheus in Paris: Offenbach and the Paris of His Time,* trans. Gwenda David and Eric Mosbacher (New York: Knopf, 1938) p. 190.

14. See below, E10a,3.

15. Honoré de Balzac, *Père Goriot,* trans. Henry Reed (New York: New American Library, 1962), p. 275.

16. *The Essential Rousseau,* trans. Lowell Bair (New York: New American Library, 1974), p. 17.

17. Friedrich Engels, *The Housing Question,* trans. anonymous in Marx and Engels, *Collected Works,* vol. 23 (New York: International Publishers, 1988), p. 365.

F [Iron Construction]

1. Emended to read "glass" in the German edition.

2. From *hâbleur,* "boastful chatterbox." A character in Grandville's book of illustrations *Un autre monde.* See *Fantastic Illustrations of Grandville* (New York: Dover, 1974), p. 49.

3. The term for "railroad" in German, *Eisenbahn,* means literally "iron track." The term came into use around 1820 and, unlike *Eisenbahnhof* (which became simply *Bahnhof*), continued to be used after steel rails had replaced the iron.

4. Karl Marx, *Capital,* vol. 1, trans. Samuel Moore and Edward Aveling (1887; rpt. New York: International Publishers, 1967), p. 362n. "Form of the tool," at the end, translates *Körperform des Werkzeugs* (literally, "bodily form"), and this is the term taken up by Benjamin in parenthesis.

5. "*Mehr Licht!*": Goethe's last words.

6. The German *Halle* and the English "hall" derive from a Germanic noun meaning "covered place," which in turn is traced back to an Indo-European root signifying "to cover, conceal." "Hall" is cognate with "hell." In earlier times, the hall—in contrast to

the room—was a spacious, half-open structure (with a roof supported by pillars or columns) designed to provide shelter from rain or sun.

7. Actually known as the Palais des Machines, it was built for the world exhibition of 1889 by the engineers Contamin, Pierron, and Chartron. [J.L.] The quotation, given without references, is in German.

8. On July 28, 1835, during a parade by the Garde Nationale down the Boulevard du Temple, the Corsican conspirator Giuseppe Fieschi made an unsuccessful attempt on the life of Louis Philippe. His "infernal machine"—a device made of several guns rigged to fire simultaneously—killed eighteen people.

9. Victor Hugo, *Notre-Dame of Paris,* trans. John Sturrock (New York: Penguin, 1978), p. 27.

10. Constructed by Viel and Barrault for the exhibition of 1855 on the Champs-Elysées. [J.L.]

11. Hugo, *Notre-Dame of Paris,* pp. 150–151.

12. The cast-iron bridge of Coalbrookdale, in Shropshire, was built by T. F. Pritchard. [J.L.]

13. Jules Michelet, *The People,* trans. John P. McKay (Urbana: University of Illinois Press, 1973), pp. 45, 43n.

G [Exhibitions, Advertising, Grandville]

1. Alexander von Humboldt's last and greatest work, *Kosmos* (5 vols., 1845–1862), was translated into nearly all European languages. The *schwindenden Doppelsterne* (disappearing twin stars) are discussed in volumes 1 and 3.

2. *Victoria! A New World! Joyous Proclamation of the Fact That on Our Planet, Especially in the Northern Hemisphere We Occupy, a Total Alteration in Temperature Has Begun, Thanks to the Increase in Atmospheric Warmth.*

3. 1867 was the year of Offenbach's biggest box-office success, *La Grande-Duchesse de Gerolstein,* with libretto by Henri Meilhac and Ludovic Halévy.

4. After Paxton's designs were initially rejected by the London Building Committee in 1850, he published them in the *London News,* and public response to his unusual concept was so overwhelmingly favorable that the committee capitulated.

5. The advertisement appears in Benjamin's German translation. Original French in *GS,* vol. 5, pp. 1327–1328.

6. Karl Marx, *Capital,* vol. 1, trans. Samuel Moore and Edward Aveling (1887; rpt. New York: International Publishers, 1967), pp. 76–77.

7. Ibid., p. 76.

8. The Crystal Palace was destroyed by a spectacular fire at Sydenham in south London in 1936.

9. At the end of the second Opium War (1856–1860), allied English and French forces captured Peking and burned the Chinese emperor's summer palace.

10. The royal ordinance of January 13, 1819, provided for the public exhibition of the products of French industry "in the rooms and galleries of the Louvre," at intervals not exceeding every four years; a jury was to decide which exhibitors deserved rewards from the government.

11. That is, 1801, according to the French revolutionary calendar.

12. *The Mysteries of Paris* (1842–1843), enormously popular novel by Eugène Sue.

13. Hugh Walpole, *The Fortress* (1932; rpt. Phoenix Mill, England: Alan Sutton Publishing, 1995), pp. 248, 247. The description of the "monster lodging-house" mentioned

in G10,1 is on p. 239. Benjamin cites the text in German (with an English title); translator unknown.

14. A. Toussenel, *Passional Zoology; Or, Spirit of the Beasts of France,* trans. M. Edgeworth Lazarus (New York: Fowlers and Wells, 1852), pp. 140, 142.

15. Ibid., p. 355.

16. Ibid., pp. 337–339.

17. Ibid., p. 340.

18. Ibid., pp. 135, 136.

19. Ibid., p. 346.

20. Ibid., pp. 91–92.

21. Ibid., pp. 346, 347.

22. Marx, *Capital,* vol. 1, pp. 293–294.

23. Victor Hugo, *Les Misérables,* trans. Charles E. Wilbour (1862; rpt. New York: Modern Library, 1992), p. 767.

24. The International Working Men's Association (the First International), the General Council of which had its seat in London, was founded in September 1864.

25. Marx, *Capital,* vol. 1, p. 76. "Material immaterial" translates *sinnlich übersinnlich.*

26. For another English version, translated from the Russian, see Nikolai Gogol, *Arabesques,* trans. Alexander Tulloch (Ann Arbor, Mich.: Ardis, 1982), p. 130.

27. J. W. Goethe, "Nachtgedanken," *Gedenkausgabe,* vol. 1, *Sämtliche Gedichte* (Zurich, 1961), p. 339. [R.T.] In English in *Selected Verse,* trans. David Luke (London: Penguin, 1964), p. 75. See J22a,1.

28. Charles Baudelaire, *The Mirror of Art,* trans. Jonathan Mayne (London: Phaidon, 1955), p. 84.

29. *Baudelaire as a Literary Critic,* trans. Lois Boe Hyslop and Francis E. Hyslop, Jr. (University Park: Pennsylvania State University Press, 1964), pp. 79–80.

30. See *SW,* vol. 2, pp. 85–90 ("Main Features of My Second Impression of Hashish"). Also below, I2,6, M1a,1, and M1a,3.

H [The Collector]

1. Letter of December 30, 1857, to his mother. In *Baudelaire: A Self-Portrait,* ed. and trans. Lois Boe Hyslop and Francis E. Hyslop, Jr. (London: Oxford University Press, 1957), p. 135.

2. Dr. Miracle and Olympia, the automated puppet, appear in *Les Contes d'Hoffmann* (1881), an opera by Jacques Offenbach. Dr. Miracle has been interpreted as genius of death; see Siegfried Kracauer, *Orpheus in Paris: Offenbach and the Paris of his Time,* trans. Gwenda David and Eric Mosbacher (New York: Knopf, 1938) p. 355.

3. The Passage du Pont-Neuf. See *Thérèse Raquin,* trans. Leonard Tancock (New York: Penguin, 1962), pp. 31–35. First published in 1867.

4. This reference remains obscure.

5. *Phaedrus,* 247c.

6. August Strindberg, "The Pilot's Trials," in Strindberg, *Tales,* trans. L. J. Potts (London: Chatto and Windus, 1930), pp. 45, 46, 50.

7. Baudelaire, *Artificial Paradise,* trans. Ellen Fox (New York: Herder and Herder, 1971), p. 68.

8. But see below, H2,7; H2a,1, on the singular "gaze" *(Blick)* of the collector.

9. Charles Dickens, *The Old Curiosity Shop* (London: Heron Books, 1970), p. 16 (ch. 1).

10. Theodor W. Adorno, "On Dickens' *The Old Curiosity Shop:* A Lecture," in *Notes to Literature,* vol. 2, trans. Shierry Weber Nicholsen (New York: Columbia University

Press, 1992), p. 177. Adorno's essay was first published in the *Frankfurter Zeitung* (April 18, 1931), pp. 1–2. The passages from Dickens are in chs. 12 and 44, respectively.

11. Karl Marx, "Economic and Philosophical Manuscripts [of 1844]," in *Karl Marx: Selected Writings,* ed. David McLellan (New York: Oxford University Press, 1977), p. 91.

12. *The Portable Karl Marx,* trans. Eugene Kamenka (New York: Viking Penguin, 1983), p. 151.

13. Marx, *Selected Writings,* p. 92.

14. Ibid., pp. 91–92.

15. This passage is not found in the English-language edition of Johan Huizinga's book *The Waning of the Middle Ages* (New York: Doubleday Anchor, 1954).

16. In this passage, "dispersion" translates *Zerstreuung,* "profundity" translates *Tiefsinn,* and "patchwork" translates *Stückwerk.*

17. Marcel Proust, *The Past Recaptured,* trans. Frederick A. Blossom, in *Remembrance of Things Past,* vol. 2 (New York: Random House, 1932), p. 1070. On the collector's relation to memory and the world of things, compare Q°,7 in "First Sketches."

I [The Interior, The Trace]

1. "Know thyself."

2. Le Corbusier, *The City of Tomorrow and Its Planning,* trans. Frederick Etchells (1929; rpt. New York: Dover, 1987), p. 259.

3. See I4a,2. In Sue's novel *The Mysteries of Paris,* the archvillain Ferrand, whose accomplice is a perfidious priest, is done in by the wiles of the Creole Cecily.

4. Jacques-Emile Blanche, *Mes modèles* (Paris, 1929), p. 117. Barrès' phrase, which Benjamin misquotes in French, is: "Un conteur arabe dans la loge de la portière!" [R.T.]

5. This whole passage is adapted from the protocol to Benjamin's second experience with hashish in January 1928. See *SW,* vol. 2, pp. 85–90.

6. See *GS,* vol. 6, p. 567 (where the passage is attributed to Ernst Bloch).

7. Marcel Proust, "About Baudelaire," in Proust, *A Selection from His Miscellaneous Writings,* trans. Gerard Hopkins (London: Allan Wingate, 1948), p. 199. Citing, respectively, from Baudelaire, *Pièces Condamnées,* "Une martyre," *Pièces condamnées.*

8. Sören Kierkegaard, *Stages on Life's Way,* trans. Walter Lowrie (1940; rpt. New York: Schocken, 1967), p. 30.

9. Theodor W. Adorno, *Kierkegaard: Construction of the Aesthetic,* trans. Robert Hullot-Kentor (Minneapolis: University of Minnesota Press, 1989), p. 60. "Primordial" translates *urgeschichtlich.* See pp. 48–49, on Kierkegaard as rentier.

10. Ibid., pp. 43–44 (the term *intérieur* has been translated after the first sentence). The passage from Kierkegaard is in *Either/Or,* vol. 1, trans. David F. Swenson and Lillian M. Swenson, with revisions by Howard A. Johnson (1944; rpt. New York: Anchor, 1959), pp. 384–386.

11. In Ibsen's *The Master Builder* (1892), Mrs. Solness had kept nine dolls hidden from her husband until a fire destroyed her family estate, catalyzing Solness's career of building homes for happy families. See *Four Major Plays,* trans. James McFarlane and Jens Arup (New York: Oxford University Press, 1981), pp. 314–315, 335.

12. "Wohnen als Transitivum—im Begriff des 'gewohnten Lebens' z.B."

13. The reign of Louis Philippe became known as the Middle-of-the-Road Regime (Juste Milieu). In a speech of 1831, he stated: "We must not only cherish peace; we must avoid everything that might provoke war. As regards domestic policy, we will en-

deavor to maintain a *juste milieu.*" Cited in *Daumier: 120 Great Lithographs,* ed. Charles F. Ramus (New York: Dover, 1978), p. xi.

14. Marx, *The Economic and Philosophic Manuscripts of 1844,* trans. Martin Milligan (New York: International Publishers, 1964), pp. 155–156.

15. Paul Valéry, "The Place of Baudelaire," in *Leonardo, Poe, Mallarmé,* trans. Malcolm Cowley and James R. Lawler (Princeton: Princeton University Press, 1972), p. 203.

16. A rather fantastic house near Versailles which Balzac built in 1838 and left in 1840.

17. Baudelaire, *Paris Spleen,* trans. Louise Varèse (New York: New Directions, 1947), p. 33.

18. Honoré de Balzac, *Modeste Mignon,* trans. anon. (New York: Fred de Fau, 1900), p. 68.

19. Georg Simmel, *The Philosophy of Money,* 2nd ed., trans. Tom Bottomore and David Frisby (London: Routledge, 1990), pp. 459–462.

20. Joseph Conrad, *"The Shadow-Line" and Two Other Tales* (New York: Anchor, 1959), pp. 189, 193.

21. Jean-Jacques Rousseau, *The Confessions,* trans. J. M. Cohen (Baltimore: Penguin, 1953), p. 280.

J [Baudelaire]

1. Pierre de Ronsard, *Oeuvres complètes,* vol. 2 (Paris: Pléiade, 1976), p. 282. [R.T.]

2. Paul Valéry, "The Place of Baudelaire," in *Leonardo, Poe, Mallarmé,* trans. Malcolm Cowley and James R. Lawler (Princeton: Princeton University Press, 1972), pp. 195, 197–198.

3. *Le poncif:* the banal, the trite; a conventional piece of writing, a cliché. Baudelaire writes in his notebook: "To create a new commonplace [*poncif*]—that's genius. I must create a commonplace." *"My Heart Laid Bare" and Other Prose Writings,* trans. Norman Cameron (1950; rpt. New York: Haskell House, 1975), p. 168 ("Fusées," no. 20). See also Baudelaire's "Salon of 1846," section 10.

4. Baudelaire's article "Richard Wagner and *Tannhäuser* in Paris" appeared on April 1, 1861.

5. Baudelaire, *"My Heart Laid Bare,"* p. 198: "Praise the cult of images (my great, my unique, my primitive passion)" ("My Heart Laid Bare"). *Primitive passion* can be translated as "earliest passion." Baudelaire's note could refer to the importance that pictures *(images)* had for him when he was a child; his father was an art lover and amateur painter. (He died when Baudelaire was six.)

6. *Baudelaire as a Literary Critic,* trans. Lois Boe Hyslop and Francis E. Hyslop, Jr. (University Park: Pennsylvania State University Press, 1964), pp. 53, 52. Pierre Dupont's *Chants et chansons* appeared in 1851. Baudelaire writes to his guardian Ancelle, on March 5, 1852, that Louis Napoleon's coup d'état of the previous December had "physically depoliticized" him (*Baudelaire as a Literary Critic,* p. 50).

7. Baudelaire had appeared on the barricades during the three-day revolution of February 1848.

8. In order to save Baudelaire from "the sewers of Paris," and to punish him for his monetary extravagance, his stepfather, General Aupick, sent him on a sea voyage to Calcutta. After departing in June 1841, and surviving a hurricane off the Cape of Good Hope, Baudelaire disembarked in Réunion and returned to France in February 1842.

9. *Selected Letters of Charles Baudelaire,* trans. Rosemary Lloyd (Chicago: University of Chicago Press, 1986), p. 142.

10. *The Mirror of Art: Critical Studies by Charles Baudelaire,* trans. Jonathan Mayne (London: Phaidon, 1955), pp. 282–283. The phrase "those spires 'whose fingers point to heaven'" *(montrant du doigt le ciel),* translates a line from Wordsworth's poem "The Excursion" (book 6, line 19), itself a citation from Coleridge. See *The Mirror of Art,* p. 282n2.

11. Baudelaire, *Paris Spleen,* trans. Louise Varèse (New York: New Directions, 1947), p. 8 ("To Every Man His Chimera").

12. Albert Thibaudet, *French Literature from 1795 to Our Era,* trans. Charles Lam Markmann (New York: Funk and Wagnalls, 1967), p. 289.

13. G. K. Chesterton, *Charles Dickens* (1906; rpt. New York: Schocken, 1965), p. 47. Reference is to the period of Dickens' youth when he worked in a factory pasting labels on blacking-bottles. In Benjamin's French edition, "That wild word" is translated as "Ce mot baroque."

14. Ibid., p. 60.

15. Valéry, *Leonardo, Poe, Mallarmé,* p. 207.

16. In August 1857, after the publication of *Les Fleurs du mal,* Baudelaire and his publishers were tried and found guilty of offending public morality; they were fined and six poems in the collection were suppressed. The verdict cites the "indecent realism" of the images.

17. Valéry, *Leonardo, Poe, Mallarmé,* p. 195.

18. *Baudelaire as a Literary Critic,* pp. 318–319 ("Advice to Young Men of Letters"). *L'Art romantique* was originally published in 1869 as volume 3 of the first collected edition of the poet's works; the title was evidently supplied by the editors.

19. *Baudelaire as a Literary Critic,* p. 69 ("The Respectable Drama and Novel").

20. Ibid., p. 73 ("The Pagan School").

21. Ibid., p. 77.

22. Ibid.

23. Ibid., p. 76. The passage conveys Baudelaire's disgust with certain classical notions of beauty, suggested by *la plastique,* "sculpted form" or "fine shaping."

24. Ibid., pp. 241–242.

25. Ibid., p. 251.

26. Ibid., p. 263.

27. Ibid., p. 262.

28. Ibid., pp. 265–266 ("Théodore de Banville").

29. Ibid., p. 278.

30. Ibid., pp. 285–286.

31. Ibid., p. 289.

32. Ibid., p. 147.

33. Ibid., pp. 144, 146.

34. Ibid., p. 146.

35. Ibid., p. 56.

36. Ibid., pp. 51–52, 52–53.

37. Ibid., p. 58 ("Pierre Dupont").

38. Ibid., p. 205.

39. Ibid., p. 222 ("Richard Wagner and *Tannhäuser* in Paris").

40. Baudelaire, *"The Painter of Modern Life" and Other Essays,* trans. Jonathan Mayne (1964; rpt. New York: Da Capo, 1986), p. 206. The reference that follows is to Jules Michelet's *Histoire de France au seizième siècle* (1855).

41. Baudelaire, "Painters and Etchers," in *Art in Paris, 1845–1862,* trans. Jonathan Mayne (London: Phaidon, 1965), pp. 220–221. Compare J2,1.

42. Baudelaire, *"The Painter of Modern Life,"* p. 21 ("The Painter of Modern Life").

43. Ibid., p. 24.

44. Ibid., p. 32.

45. Ibid., p. 40.

46. Baudelaire, *Selected Writings on Art and Literature,* trans. P. E. Charvet (1972; rpt. New York: Penguin, 1992), p. 435.

47. *Baudelaire as a Literary Critic,* pp. 296–297 ("The Painter of Modern Life," section 4, "Modernity"). Baudelaire here anticipates Nietzsche's critique of the antiquarian in the second of the *Unzeitgemässe Betrachtungen: Vom Nutzen und Nachteil der Historie für das Leben* ‹On the Advantage and Disadvantage of History for Life›. In the sentence that follows this quotation from Baudelaire, Benjamin delineates a dialectical process that is somewhat blurred in translation: the stamp of time that, literally, "impresses itself into" antiquity *(sich in sie eindrückt)* brings out of it *(treibt . . . aus ihr hervor)*— that is, brings into relief—the allegorical configuration.

48. *Baudelaire as a Literary Critic,* p. 296; and *"The Painter of Modern Life,"* pp. 14, 16. "Spleen et idéal" is the first book of *Les Fleurs du mal.*

49. Baudelaire, *"The Painter of Modern Life,"* pp. 29, 12.

50. Ibid., pp. 8, 66.

51. Ibid., pp. 10, 11.

52. Ibid., p. 48.

53. Ibid., p. 3.

54. Baudelaire, *Les Fleurs du mal,* trans. Richard Howard (Boston: Godine, 1982), p. 77.

55. Baudelaire, *"The Painter of Modern Life,"* p. 32.

56. Ibid., p. 14. See J6a,2.

57. *Selected Letters of Charles Baudelaire,* pp. 79–80. Baudelaire had received a copy of Alphonse Toussenel's book *L'Esprit des bêtes.*

58. Baudelaire's unsuccessful effort to gain membership in the Académie Française at the end of 1861 entailed mandatory visits to each of the forty Academicians. He was received by about half of them before he withdrew his application.

59. *Selected Letters of Charles Baudelaire,* p. 210 (November 13, 1864, to Ancelle).

60. Victor Hugo, *Poems,* trans. anonymous (Boston: Harcourt Bindery, 189?), pp. 190, 192. "Les Métamorphoses du vampire" (Metamorphoses of the Vampire) and "Les Petites Vieilles" (The Little Old Women) are poems in *Les Fleurs du mal.* For Athalie's dream of her dead mother, Jézabel, see scene 5 of Act 2 of Racine's *Athalie* (1691).

61. Jules Laforgue, *Selected Writings,* trans. William Jay Smith (New York: Grove Press, 1956), p. 212. References are to Baudelaire's poems "Le Balcon" and "Le Serpent qui danse," in *Les Fleurs du mal.*

62. Laforgue, *Selected Writings,* p. 213.

63. Ibid.

64. Ibid., pp. 215–217. Citations from *Les Fleurs du mal* (trans. Howard), p. 173 ("Meditation"), p. 14 ("Elevation"), p. 82 ("The Clock"), p. 87 ("Parisian Landscape").

65. *Baudelaire: A Self-Portrait,* ed. and trans. Lois Boe Hyslop and Francis E. Hyslop, Jr. (London: Oxford University Press, 1957), p. 51 ("Pauvre Belgique").

66. Baudelaire, *"My Heart Laid Bare,"* p. 177 ("My Heart Laid Bare").

67. Baudelaire, *The Complete Verse,* trans. Francis Scarfe (London: Anvil, 1986), pp. 326–327.

68. Laforgue, *Selected Writings,* p. 211.

69. Ibid., p. 213.

70. Baudelaire, *Intimate Journals,* trans. Christopher Isherwood (1930; rpt. Westport, Conn.: Hyperion, 1978), pp. 113–114.

71. See *The Mirror of Art,* p. 51. Baudelaire quotes from E. T. A. Hoffmann's *Höchst zerstreute Gedanken,* part of the "Kreisler papers" on music, named after the author's popular mouthpiece, Johannes Kreisler.

72. Baudelaire delivered the first of five public lectures in Brussels on May 2, 1864. It was well received, but the other four were dismal failures.

73. This is a play on the famous words of Henri of Navarre. When he assumed the French throne in 1593, as Henri IV, he converted to Catholicism with the words, "Paris vaut bien une messe."

74. *The Letters of Gustave Flaubert, 1830–1857,* trans. Francis Steegmuller (Cambridge, Mass.: Harvard University Press, 1980), pp. 232–233 (letter of July 13, 1857).

75. *Baudelaire as a Literary Critic,* p. 7 (letter of February 18, 1860, to Armand Fraisse).

76. "Elsewhere! Too far, too late, or never at all! / Of me you know nothing, I nothing of you—you / whom I might have loved and who knew that too!" "In Passing," *Les Fleurs du mal* (trans. Howard), p. 98.

77. *Selected Letters of Charles Baudelaire,* p. 175 (circa December 16, 1861, in reference to *Les Fleurs du mal*).

78. Gide, "Preface to *Les Fleurs du mal,*" in *Pretexts* (New York: Meridian, 1959), p. 257 (trans. Blanche A. Price).

79. Ibid., pp. 257–258. Gide quotes at the beginning from Baudelaire's first draft of a preface to *Les Fleurs du mal.* For the passages from Baudelaire's journals, see *"My Heart Laid Bare,"* p. 166 ("Fusées," no. 17).

80. Gide, *Pretexts,* p. 257.

81. Ibid., p. 256.

82. Ibid., p. 258.

83. Citations from *Les Fleurs du mal* (trans. Howard), pp. 170 ("Madrigal triste"), 37 ("Le Vampire"), 129 ("Femmes damnées").

84. Baudelaire, *"My Heart Laid Bare,"* p. 200 ("My Heart Laid Bare"). Lemaître's text has *dégoût* instead of *horreur.*

85. Baudelaire, *Flowers of Evil,* trans. Wallace Fowlie (1964; rpt. New York: Dover, 1992), p. 85.

86. Citations from *Les Fleurs du mal* (trans. Howard) pp. 20 ("L'Ennemi"), 22 ("Bohémiens en Voyage"), 62 ("Chant d'automne").

87. *Selected Letters of Charles Baudelaire,* p. 130. The passage continues: "This idea came to me when I was leafing through Hyacinthe Langlois' history of the 'Dance of Death' theme" (letter to Nadar, 1859). See J26,2.

88. Gide, *Pretexts,* p. 259. The reference is to a sentence in Baudelaire's private journals; see *"My Heart Laid Bare,"* p. 155 ("Fusées," no. 1).

89. Edgar Allan Poe, "The Imp of the Perverse," in Poe, *The Complete Tales and Poems* (New York: Modern Library, 1938), p. 281.

90. René Laforgue, *The Defeat of Baudelaire,* trans. Herbert Agar (London: Hogarth, 1932), pp. 163, 165.

91. Ibid., pp. 141, 143. Laforgue writes: ". . . the passive role, that of the woman, of the prisoner."

92. Ibid., p. 71.

93. *Baudelaire: A Self-Portrait,* p. 8. The editors date the letter August 13.

94. "New Notes on Edgar Poe," actually Baudelaire's third essay on Poe, served as a preface to his second volume of translations, published in 1857. The article on Gautier appeared in 1859. For the passages on passion, see *Baudelaire as a Literary Critic,* pp. 133, 162–166.

95. Ovid, *Metamorphoses,* book 1, lines 84–85. [J.L.] See Baudelaire, *"My Heart Laid Bare,"* p. 157 ("Fusées").

96. Baudelaire, *The Complete Verse,* p. 362.

97. Baudelaire, *Paris Spleen,* p. 69.

98. *Baudelaire: A Self-Portrait,* p. 135: "I haven't forgotten, near the city," and "The greathearted servant of whom you were jealous." After his father's death in 1827, Baudelaire lived for a time, along with his mother and nursemaid Mariette, in a house at Neuilly, just outside Paris.

99. Baudelaire, *The Mirror of Art,* p. 123 ("The Salon of 1846").

100. *Selected Letters of Charles Baudelaire,* p. 218.

101. "Je ne pouvais aimer . . . que si la mort mêlait son souffle à celui de la Beauté!" Cited in Seillière without references. Possibly an adaptation of a passage in "The Philosophy of Composition": "Of all melancholy topics, what . . . is the *most* melancholy? Death. . . . And when . . . is this most melancholy of topics most poetical? . . . When it most closely allies itself to Beauty: the death . . . of a beautiful woman is . . . the most poetical topic in the world—and . . . the lips best suited for such a topic are those of a bereaved lover." Poe, *"The Fall of the House of Usher" and Other Writings* (Harmondsworth: Penguin, 1986) p. 486. (Thanks to William Vance for this reference.)

102. Baudelaire, *Correspondance* (Paris: Gallimard, 1973), vol. 1, p. 410 (July 9, 1857, to Caroline Aupick). [R.T.] In English in *Selected Letters of Charles Baudelaire,* p. 97.

103. Baudelaire, *Oeuvres complètes* (Paris: Pléiade, 1976), vol. 1, p. 102 ("Rêve parisien"). [R.T.] In English in *Les Fleurs du mal* (trans. Howard), p. 107: "Architect of such conceits / I sent submissive seas / into the jewelled conduits / my will erected there."

104. *Baudelaire: A Self-Portrait,* pp. 26–27.

105. Jules Romains, *Men of Good Will,* vol. 1, trans. Warre B. Wells (New York: Knopf, 1946), p. 396. Citation from Baudelaire's "Elévation," *Les Fleurs du mal* (trans. Howard), p. 14.

106. Baudelaire, *Les Fleurs du mal* (trans. Howard), pp. 88, 45.

107. Baudelaire, *Oeuvres complètes,* vol. 1, p. 203 ("Je n'ai pas pour maîtresse"). [R.T.] Sarah was Baudelaire's first mistress.

108. See "The Bad Glazier," in *Paris Spleen,* pp. 12–14; and Gide's novel of 1914, *Les Caves du Vatican,* translated by Dorothy Bussy as *Lafcadio's Adventures* (Garden City, N.Y.: Doubleday, 1953), p. 183, where one finds the theory of the *acte gratuit* put into practice by Lafcadio's wanton murder of a pious old fool.

109. Baudelaire, *Les Fleurs du mal* (trans. Howard), p. 141.

110. *Flowers of Evil* (trans. Fowlie), p. 107.

111. Citations from *Les Fleurs du mal* (trans. Howard), pp. 77, 164, 107, 156. "Delphine et Hippolyte" is the subtitle of the longer of the two poems entitled "Femmes damnées."

112. Baudelaire, *Les Fleurs du mal* (trans. Howard), p. 73.

113. Ibid., p. 72 ("A l'heure où les chastes étoiles / Ferment leurs yeux appesantis").

114. Ibid., p. 97 ("crispé comme un extravagant").

115. Baudelaire, *The Complete Verse,* p. 159.

116. Baudelaire, *Les Fleurs du mal* (trans. Howard), p. 156.

117. Ibid., p. 41.

118. *The Works of Stefan George,* trans. Olga Marx and Ernst Morwitz (1949; rpt. New York: AMS Press, 1966), p. 6 (*Odes,* 1890).

119. Baudelaire, *Les Fleurs du mal* (trans. Howard), p. 116 ("The Solitary's Wine"). Compare the passage on Baudelaire and Berg in Theodor W. Adorno, *Alban Berg: Master of the Smallest Link,* trans. Juliane Brand and Christopher Hailey (Cambridge: Cambridge University Press, 1991), p. 120.

120. J. W. Goethe, *Selected Verse,* trans. David Luke (New York: Penguin, 1964), p. 75.

121. Baudelaire, *The Mirror of Art,* p. 120.

122. Baudelaire, *The Prose Poems and "La Fanfarlo,"* trans. Rosemary Lloyd (New York: Oxford University Press, 1991), p. 44 ("The Crowds").

123. "C'est un génie sans frontières." The last word is translated as "limits" in *Baudelaire as a Literary Critic,* p. 241 ("Reflections on Some of My Contemporaries").

124. Hugo, *Poems,* pp. 190, 192, 193 (in the sequence titled *Les Orientales*).

125. *The Poems of Victor Hugo* (New York: Little, Brown, 1909), pp. 175, 177 (trans. Henry Carrington).

126. *Baudelaire: A Self-Portrait,* p. 96.

127. Bourdin's article appeared in his father-in-law's paper on July 5, 1857, nine days before Thierry's favorable notice. It has been suggested that the conservative paper *Le Figaro* was at least partly responsible for the charges brought against Baudelaire. See J27a,3.

128. Probably a reference to the warning cut into stone above the Gate of Hell: "Lasciate ogne speranza voi ch'intrate" ("Abandon all hope, ye who enter here"). See Dante Alighieri, *The Inferno,* trans. John Ciardi (New York: New American Library, 1954), p. 42 (Canto 3).

129. "Rêve parisien" is dedicated to Guys.

130. See the end of Baudelaire's third draft for a preface to *Les Fleurs du mal,* in *The Complete Verse,* p. 389. Re: "the whole piece about Andromache."

131. Baudelaire, *Oeuvres complètes,* vol. 2, p. 68. [R.T.] From "Notes sur *Les Liaisons dangereuses*" (ca. 1864). "Sand est inférieure à Sade." Compare J49a,1.

132. Baudelaire, *Oeuvres complètes,* vol. 1, p. 5 ("Au Lecteur"). [R.T.] In English in *The Complete Verse,* p. 53.

133. Baudelaire, "The Exposition Universelle, 1855," in *The Mirror of Art,* pp. 213–214.

134. Baudelaire, *Oeuvres complètes,* vol. 2, p. 132. [R.T.] In English in *Baudelaire as a Literary Critic,* p. 238 ("Reflections on Some of My Contemporaries").

135. Baudelaire, *"My Heart Laid Bare,"* p. 178.

136. Sainte-Beuve's article "Sur les prochaines élections de l'Académie" (On the Forthcoming Academy Elections) contained a rather condescending section on Baudelaire as an "exemplary candidate, a nice young man."

137. *The Apocrypha,* Revised Standard Version (New York: Oxford University Press, 1977), p. 181 (40.8).

138. The dates are erroneous. *Questions de critique* (2nd ed.) appeared in 1889; *Essais sur la littérature contemporaine,* in 1892; *Nouveaux essais sur la littérature contemporaine,* in 1895; and *Evolution de la poésie lyrique en France,* in 1894. [R.T.]

139. Baudelaire, *"My Heart Laid Bare,"* p. 177 ("My Heart Laid Bare"). Benjamin's phrase at the end of this entry is "Das Historische ins Intime projiziert."

140. Baudelaire, *Oeuvres complètes,* vol. 1, p. 194. [R.T.] The notes in question were prepared by Baudelaire for the trial against *Les Fleurs du mal.*

141. Baudelaire, *"My Heart Laid Bare,"* p. 195 ("My Heart Laid Bare").

142. Baudelaire, *Flowers of Evil* (trans. Fowlie), p. 85 ("Destruction").

143. See Eugène Crépet, *Charles Baudelaire* (Paris: Léon Vanier, 1906), pp. 288–289. When Baudelaire, out walking with Asselineau on the boulevard, wants to have dinner at the early hour of 5 P.M., Asselineau, who has a head cold, assents on condition they go to his place first to get another handkerchief. Baudelaire, protesting that Asselineau must still have two or three places left on his present handkerchief sufficient to blow his nose during dinner, holds out his hand and cries, "Show me!"

144. Théophile Gautier, *A History of Romanticism,* trans. anonymous (1909; rpt. New York: Howard Fertig, 1988), pp. 301, 300.

145. Baudelaire, *Correspondance* (Paris: Gallimard, 1973), vol. 1, p. 30 (to his mother, probably written in Paris, 1845). [R.T.] In English in *Baudelaire: A Self-Portrait,* p. 32.

146. Baudelaire had written, on March 4, 1863, "So you really do want to compromise my dignity in a social set in which you've compromised your own?" *Selected Letters of Charles Baudelaire,* p. 193. For his letter of March 6, see pp. 193–194. The female admirer was Frédérique O'Connell, a painter whom Baudelaire mentions in the "Salons" of 1846 and 1859.

147. *Baudelaire: A Self-Portrait,* p. 133. The fine was reduced from 300 francs to 50 francs as a result of this letter.

148. Baudelaire, *"The Painter of Modern Life,"* p. 156 ("On the Essence of Laughter").

149. Ibid., p. 150.

150. Ibid., p. 157.

151. *Baudelaire as a Literary Critic,* p. 43.

152. Poe, *The Complete Tales and Poems,* p. 478 ("The Man of the Crowd").

153. *Baudelaire as a Literary Critic,* p. 127. Compare the classic distinction between imagination and fancy in Chapters 4 and 13 of Coleridge's *Biographia Literaria* (1817).

154. *Baudelaire as a Literary Critic,* p. 131. The sentence is a virtual quotation from Poe's "The Poetic Principle."

155. Baudelaire, *The Mirror of Art,* p. 251.

156. Ibid., p. 268. The journal in question was *Le Siècle.*

157. Ibid., p. 273. *Pro domo:* for his own cause.

158. Ibid., p. 274 ("Ce . . . je ne sais quoi de malicieux").

159. Alfred de Vigny, *Oeuvres complètes,* vol. 1 (Paris, 1883), pp. 251–252. [R.T.]

160. Baudelaire, *The Complete Verse,* p. 297 ("au plus noir de l'abîme, / Je vois distinctement des mondes singuliers").

161. Baudelaire, *The Mirror of Art,* p. 286. *Sursum, ad sidera:* upward, to the stars. *Vitai lampada:* torch of life.

162. Ibid., p. 283.

163. Ibid., p. 233.

164. Ibid., p. 224.

165. Baudelaire, *Intimate Journals,* pp. 29, 31. Baudelaire's word for both "ecstasy" and "intoxication" is *ivresse.*

166. Ibid., p. 33.

167. Ibid., p. 32.

168. Ibid., pp. 73–74.

169. Baudelaire, *"My Heart Laid Bare,"* pp. 155, 197.

170. *Baudelaire: A Self-Portrait,* p. 87.

171. *Selected Letters of Charles Baudelaire,* p. 159 (October 11, 1860).

172. *The Letters of Victor Hugo,* vol. 2, ed. Paul Meurice (Boston: Houghton, Mifflin, 1898), p. 152.

173. *Baudelaire as a Literary Critic,* p. 315.

174. Baudelaire, *Intimate Journals,* p. 39.

175. *Baudelaire as a Literary Critic,* p. 307. Baudelaire's article first appeared November 24, 1845, in *Le Corsaire-Satan* and was republished a year later in *L'Echo.*

176. Baudelaire, *The Mirror of Art,* p. 124. "Politics of art" translates *Kunstpolitik.*

177. Attributed to Poulet-Malassis by Marcel Ruff in his edition of Baudelaire, *Oeuvres complètes* (Paris: Seuil, 1968), p. 50 (where the entire sheet is reproduced).

178. Baudelaire, *Paris Spleen,* p. 8.

179. Baudelaire, *The Mirror of Art,* p. 118.

180. "A Strange Man's Dream"–poem in *Les Fleurs du mal.*

181. See *Selected Letters of Charles Baudelaire,* pp. 114–115.

182. Title of the volume of Baudelaire's criticism published posthumously in 1868 by Asselineau and Banville.

183. Baudelaire, *The Mirror of Art,* p. 191.

184. *Baudelaire as a Literary Critic,* p. 80.

185. Ibid., p. 81.

186. Ibid., pp. 83–84.

187. Ibid., p. 83.

188. Baudelaire, *The Mirror of Art,* pp. 195–196.

189. Ibid., p. 38.

190. *Baudelaire as a Literary Critic,* pp. 43–45.

191. Baudelaire, *The Mirror of Art,* p. 246.

192. Ibid., pp. 46, 68.

193. Ibid., p. 12.

194. Baudelaire, *Intimate Journals,* p. 97. *Gauloiserie:* licentious or improper remark, coarse jest.

195. Baudelaire, *"My Heart Laid Bare,"* p. 189. "In unison" here translates *en société.*

196. Ibid., p. 166.

197. Baudelaire, *Intimate Journals,* p. 45.

198. Baudelaire, *The Mirror of Art,* pp. 222–223 ("The Salon of 1859"); *Flowers of Evil* (trans. Fowlie), p. 97 ("The Voyage").

199. Baudelaire, *The Mirror of Art,* p. 99. On *gauloiserie,* see note 194 above. *Vaudevilles* were light theatrical entertainments with song and dance.

200. Ibid., p. 103 ("la loi fatale du travail attrayant").

201. Ibid., p. 68. Rolf Tiedemann points out that the emphasis on "fathomless" (*insondés*) is Benjamin's.

202. Ibid., p. 13.

203. Edmond and Jules de Goncourt, *The Goncourt Journals, 1851–1870,* trans. Lewis Galantière (Garden City, N.Y.: Doubleday, Doran, 1937), p. 35.

204. Baudelaire, *Oeuvres complètes,* vol. 1, p. 152 ("Femmes damnées: Delphine et Hippolyte"). [R.T.] In English in *The Flowers of Evil,* ed. Marthiel and Jackson Mathews (New York: New Directions, 1963), p. 152 (trans. Aldous Huxley).

205. Baudelaire, *Paris Spleen,* p. 3 ("Artist's Confiteor").

206. This article is not found in *Le Temps* of June 4, 1917. [R.T.]

207. Baudelaire, *"My Heart Laid Bare,"* p. 160 ("Fusées").

208. Baudelaire, *Les Fleurs du mal* (trans. Howard), p. 136 ("A Voyage to Cythera").

209. Baudelaire, *Intimate Journals,* p. 84 ("My Heart Laid Bare").

210. Gide, "Baudelaire and M. Faguet," *Pretexts,* p. 168.

211. Ibid., pp. 168, 170. Baudelaire's phrase is from "The Salon of 1859" (*The Mirror of Art,* p. 232). Gide emphasizes the importance of the critical faculty to Baudelaire's poetic production.

212. Gide, *Pretexts,* p. 167.

213. Ibid., p. 159.

214. Ibid., p. 163n. Baudelaire's phrase, "Je hais le mouvement," is from "La Beauté." In English in *Flowers of Evil* (trans. Fowlie), p. 37.

215. Proust, preface to Paul Morand, *Fancy Goods,* trans. Ezra Pound (New York: New Directions, 1984), pp. 5–6. For the line from Baudelaire's "Femmes damnées," see J41a,2.

216. See Proust, preface to Morand, *Fancy Goods,* pp. 6–8: "Sainte-Beuve, whose stupidity displays itself to the point where one asks whether it isn't a feint or a coward-

ice. . . . [He] thinks he has been very good to Baudelaire . . . in the complete dearth of encouragement."

217. Marcel Proust, "About Baudelaire," in *Marcel Proust: A Selection from His Miscellaneous Writings,* trans. Gerard Hopkins (London: Allan Wingate, 1948), p. 192. Proust cites the fourteenth stanza of "The Little Old Women," *Les Fleurs du mal* (trans. Howard), pp. 95–96.

218. *Marcel Proust: A Selection,* p. 204.

219. Ibid., p. 194.

220. Etienne Pivert de Senancour, *Obermann,* trans. anonymous (London: Philip Wellby, 1903), p. 231 (letter 52). Senancour actually wrote "naturelle à l'homme."

221. This passage does not appear in the English translation of Joseph de Maistre, "The Saint-Petersburg Dialogues," in *The Works of Joseph de Maistre,* trans. Jack Lively (New York: Macmillan, 1965).

222. *Selected Letters of Charles Baudelaire,* p. 123.

223. Ibid., p. 151 (ca. March 1860).

224. Baudelaire, *The Prose Poems and "La Fanfarlo,"* p. 115.

225. *Marcel Proust: A Selection,* pp. 191, 190.

226. Ibid., p. 199. Proust's phrase, several times cited in succeeding entries of Convolute J, is "un étrange sectionnement du temps."

227. Ibid., p. 199. Passages by Baudelaire are from *The Complete Verse,* pp. 236, 71.

228. *Marcel Proust: A Selection,* p. 202.

229. Ibid., pp. 203–204 (passages from Vigny translated into English).

230. Thomas à Kempis, *De imitatione Christi,* in Thomas à Kempis, *Opera Omnia,* vol. 7 (Freiburg, 1904), p. 38. [R.T.] In English in *The Imitation of Christ,* trans. anonymous (1504; rpt. London: J. M. Dent, 1910), pp. 38–39 ("On Love of Silence and Solitude"): "What canst thou see elsewhere that thou canst not see here? Lo here heaven earth and all elements and of these all things are made."

231. *Baudelaire: A Self-Portrait,* p. 43.

232. Ibid., p. 54.

233. Ibid., p. 65 ("hastily written in order to earn some money").

234. Ibid., p. 68.

235. Ibid., p. 95.

236. Ibid., p. 102.

237. *Selected Letters of Charles Baudelaire,* p. 97.

238. *Baudelaire: A Self-Portrait,* p. 172.

239. Ibid., p. 174.

240. *Selected Letters of Charles Baudelaire,* p. 190.

241. Ibid., p. 195.

242. The article, by Arthur Arnould, "Edgar Poe: L'homme, l'artiste et l'oeuvre," appearing in the April, June, and July issues, referred to Baudelaire's translations.

243. *Baudelaire: A Self-Portrait,* p. 234.

244. *Selected Letters of Charles Baudelaire,* p. 237.

245. *Baudelaire as a Literary Critic,* pp. 62, 63 (written in an album for Mme. Francine Ledoux in 1851, just before the appearance of "L'Ecole païenne").

246. Ibid., p. 74.

247. *"The Painter of Modern Life,"* p. 36.

248. See *GS,* vol. 1, p. 647n. [R.T.] In English in Benjamin, "On Some Motifs in Baudelaire," *Illuminations,* p. 200n17.

249. Baudelaire, *The Complete Verse,* p. 258.

250. Baudelaire, *"My Heart Laid Bare,"* pp. 171, 173–174.

251. Ibid., pp. 171, 172, 173. Nietzsche's doctrine of "the last man" is in section 5 of "Zarathustra's Prologue," in *Also sprach Zarathustra* (Thus Spoke Zarathustra).

252. Baudelaire, *"My Heart Laid Bare,"* p. 190.

253. Ibid., p. 179. The note continues: "Nevertheless, a most vivid liking for life and pleasure."

254. Baudelaire, *The Mirror of Art,* p. 42 ("La vérité, pour être multiple, n'est pas double").

255. Ibid., p. 18.

256. *Baudelaire as a Literary Critic,* p. 82.

257. Baudelaire, *Intimate Journals,* p. 114 (missing sentence supplied).

258. Ibid., p. 118.

259. *Baudelaire as a Literary Critic,* p. 75. "Gist" is intended to translate *Gehalt,* a term derived from Goethe. See Benjamin, *GS,* vol. 2, p. 105 (*Gehalt* as *innere Form*), and vol. 4, p. 107 (*Gehalt* as unity of *Form* and *Inhalt*). In English in Benjamin, *SW,* vol. 1, pp. 18, 459.

260. *Baudelaire as a Literary Critic,* pp. 75, 77.

261. See J44a,2. *Les Epaves* (Flotsam) was published in 1866; "Tableaux parisiens" is the second section of *Les Fleurs du mal.*

262. Baudelaire, *Les Fleurs du mal* (trans. Howard), p. 76.

263. See Baudelaire, *Paris Spleen,* pp. 50–51.

264. Ibid., p. 7. On being roused from an opium trance.

265. Baudelaire, *The Mirror of Art,* pp. 3–4.

266. He says this in his "Notes sur *Les Liaisons dangereuses*" (ca. 1864); see *Oeuvres complètes,* ed. Ruff, p. 644, and note to J27,3 (note 131 in Convolute J).

267. "A man of good will."

268. *Baudelaire as a Literary Critic,* p. 134.

269. Baudelaire, *Les Fleurs du mal* (trans. Howard), p. 136; *"My Heart Laid Bare,"* p. 177.

270. Baudelaire, *The Complete Verse,* p. 181.

271. See J44,5.

272. A play on words is lost here: "ding-fest gemacht . . . gegen die verdinglichte Welt."

273. *Selected Letters of Charles Baudelaire,* p. 244 (to Sainte-Beuve).

274. Ibid., p. 245. Followed by: "In truth, forgive me! I'M WANDERING. I've never dared say so much to you."

275. Ibid., p. 148.

276. Baudelaire, *"The Painter of Modern Life,"* p. 195. On *le poncif,* see note to J1,1 (note 3 in Convolute J).

277. Ibid., p. 188.

278. Ibid., p. 182.

279. Ibid., pp. 176–177.

280. Baudelaire, *Les Fleurs du mal* (trans. Howard), p. 75 ("Spleen II"). For the citation from Claudel, which appears in German here, see J33,8. On "souvenirs," see O°,76 in "First Sketches."

281. See Hermann Usener, *Götternamen: Versuch einer Lehre von der religiösen Begriffsbildung* (Bonn, 1896). [R.T.]

282. In *Les Fleurs du mal.*

283. Benjamin, *The Origin of German Tragic Drama,* trans. John Osborne (London: Verso, 1977), p. 226. "Experience," in this entry, translates *Erfahrung.*

284. Baudelaire, *"The Painter of Modern Life,"* pp. 152–153.

285. Benjamin, *The Origin of German Tragic Drama,* p. 227. "Experience," in this entry, translates *Erlebnis.*

286. Ibid., p. 183.

287. Ibid.
288. Ibid., p. 230. "Illusion" in this citation translates *Schein.*
289. Ibid., p. 232.
290. Baudelaire, *The Complete Verse,* p. 144.
291. Baudelaire, *Les Fleurs du mal* (trans. Howard), p. 170. "Experiences," in this entry, translates *Erlebnisse,* whereas, in J55,13 below, it translates *Erfahrungen.*
292. Baudelaire, *The Flowers of Evil,* pp. 197–198 (trans. Sir John Squire).
293. Ibid., p. 192 (trans. Doreen Bell).
294. Baudelaire, *Les Fleurs du mal* (trans. Howard), pp. 165; 164.
295. Ibid., p. 80.
296. Poem in *Les Fleurs du mal.*
297. Baudelaire, *Les Fleurs du mal* (trans. Howard), p. 33.
298. Ibid., p. 31.
299. Ibid., p. 155.
300. Baudelaire, *The Complete Verse,* pp. 231–232.
301. Baudelaire, *Les Fleurs du mal* (trans. Howard), p. 136.
302. Baudelaire, *The Flowers of Evil,* p. 111 (trans. Roy Campbell).
303. Baudelaire, *The Complete Verse,* p. 144.
304. Baudelaire, *Les Fleurs du mal* (trans. Howard), p. 164.
305. Ibid., p. 165.
306. See J15,1.
307. Baudelaire, *The Flowers of Evil,* p. xxx (trans. Jackson Mathews).
308. Ibid., p. xxix.
309. Baudelaire, *The Complete Verse,* p. 115 (versified).
310. Baudelaire, *Les Fleurs du mal* (trans. Howard), p. 45 ("Je te donne ces vers").
311. Ibid., p. 17 ("Les Phares").
312. Baudelaire, *Flowers of Evil* (trans. Fowlie), p. 31.
313. Baudelaire, *Les Fleurs du mal* (trans. Howard), pp. 18–19.
314. An allusion to the later philosophy of Edmund Husserl.
315. Baudelaire, *Intimate Journals,* p. 65.
316. Benjamin indicates in "Zentralpark" (no. 23) that these thoughts, as well as the words quoted in J57a,2, come from his friend Adrienne Monnier, publisher and bookseller, with whom he evidently had several conversations about Baudelaire. See Benjamin, *GS,* vol. 1, p. 673. In English in "Central Park," trans. Lloyd Spencer, *New German Critique,* no. 34 (Winter 1985), pp. 43–44.
317. For the source of the quotations, see note 316 above. *Le Rogne:* temper, choler, bad humor.
318. Baudelaire, *The Complete Verse,* p. 206. Benjamin indicates in "Zentralpark" (no. 25) that the remarks in this passage, and in the following one on *Gemütlichkeit* ("coziness"), stem from Bertolt Brecht.
319. See note to J1,1.
320. "Tendenz seiner Lyrik zur Scheinlosigkeit."
321. In the German text, the numbering of the entries goes directly from J58a,6 to J59,2; there is no J59,1.
322. See J1,6.
323. Title of prose poem 46 in *Spleen de Paris* (in English in *Paris Spleen,* p. 94). ("Perte d'auréole" can also be translated as "loss of aura.")
324. Baudelaire, *Intimate Journals,* p. 45. It is actually the sentence before this one in "Fusées" ("This book is not for my wives, my daughters, or my sisters") that Baudelaire used in the first and second drafts of a preface to *Les Fleurs du mal.*

325. Baudelaire, *Oeuvres complètes,* vol. 1, p. 89 ("Les Petites Vieilles"). [R.T.] In English in *The Complete Verse,* p. 180.

326. Baudelaire, *The Complete Verse,* p. 197.

327. Or, alternatively: The figure of impotence is the key to Baudelaire's solitude.

328. Mayeux and the ragpicker (*chiffonnier philosophe*) are characters created by the artist Charles Traviès de Villers (1804–1859), discussed by Baudelaire in "Quelques caricaturistes français" (Some French Caricaturists). Thomas Vireloque is a creation of Gavarni, and the Bonapartist Ratapoil is a creation of Daumier. See b1,9. The Parisian urchin Gavroche is a character in Hugo's *Les Misérables.*

329. Baudelaire, *Les Fleurs du mal* (trans. Howard), p. 62.

330. "Girls" is in English in the original. See J66,8.

331. Friedrich Nietzsche, *Die fröhliche Wissenschaft* (book 4, no. 295). [R.T.] In English in *Joyful Wisdom,* trans. Thomas Common (New York: Frederick Ungar, 1960), p. 229.

332. Sören Kierkegaard, *Either/Or,* vol. 1, trans. D. F. Swenson and L. M. Swenson, rev. H. A. Johnson (1944; rpt. New York: Anchor, 1959), p. 36. Baudelaire, *Les Fleurs du mal* (trans. Howard), p. 75.

333. Kierkegaard, *Either/Or,* vol. 1, p. 41.

334. Ibid., p. 281.

335. Ibid., p. 287.

336. Ibid.

337. Ibid., pp. 221–222.

338. Kierkegaard, *Either/Or,* vol. 2, trans. Walter Lowrie, rev. Howard A. Johnson (1944; rpt. New York: Anchor, 1959), p. 164.

339. Ibid., p. 234. On the "strange sectioning of time," see J44,5.

340. Baudelaire, *The Mirror of Art,* p. 267.

341. Gottfried Keller, "Tod und Dichter," *Werke,* vol. 1 (Zürich, 1971), p. 385. [R.T.]

342. Engels, "Socialism: Utopian and Scientific" (excerpt from *Anti-Dühring* first published in French in 1880), in Marx and Engels, *Basic Writings on Politics and Philosophy,* ed. Lewis Feuer (New York: Anchor, 1959), p. 77 (trans. E. Aveling). See W15a,1.

343. Immanuel Kant, *Critique of Practical Reason,* trans. Lewis White Beck (Chicago: University of Chicago Press, 1949), p. 258.

344. Baudelaire, *Oeuvres complètes,* ed. Pichois, vol. 1, p. 76 ("Le Goût du néant"). [R.T.] In English in *The Complete Verse,* p. 160.

345. "The Saint-Petersburg Dialogues," in *The Works of Joseph de Maistre,* trans. Jack Lively (New York: Macmillan, 1965), pp. 203–204.

346. Ibid., p. 253.

347. Ibid., pp. 268–269.

348. Ibid., p. 276.

349. "A dire mystery."

350. *The Works of Joseph de Maistre,* p. 254.

351. Baudelaire, *The Flowers of Evil,* p. 145 ("Destruction," trans. C. F. MacIntyre).

352. A term popularized by the National Socialists beginning in the early 1920s.

353. Bertolt Brecht, *Gesammelte Werke,* 8 vols. (Frankfurt am Main: 1967), vol. 4, pp. 271–273 ("Ich bin ein Dreck"). [R.T.] In English in Brecht, *Poems: 1913–1956,* ed. John Willett and Ralph Manheim (New York: Methuen, 1987), pp. 135–136 ("A Reader for Those Who Live in Cities").

354. *Lorettes* was a term originated by the journalist Nestor Roqueplan in 1840 for ladies of easy virtue, many of whom lived in the reconstructed quarter surrounding the church of Notre-Dame de Lorette.

355. Jules Renard, *Journal inédit, 1887–1895* (Paris, 1925), p. 11. [R.T.] Citation above from Baudelaire's "The Irremediable," in *The Complete Verse,* p. 166. The conversa-

tion between the jack of hearts and the queen of spades is at the end of "Spleen I."
Compare J69,2.

356. Baudelaire, *Les Fleurs du mal* (trans. Howard), p. 121.

357. Baudelaire, *Correspondance,* vol. 2, p. 584. [R.T.]

358. Baudelaire, *Artificial Paradise,* trans. Ellen Fox (New York: Herder and Herder, 1971), pp. 7–8. *Les Fleurs du mal* (trans. Howard), p. 114 ("Ragpickers' Wine").

359. Baudelaire, *The Complete Verse,* p. 205.

360. Ibid., p. 211. On the "sectioning of time," see J44,5.

361. Baudelaire, "Lovers' Wine," *Les Fleurs du mal* (trans. Howard), p. 117 ("tourbillon intelligent").

362. "Lesbos," *Les Fleurs du mal* (trans. Howard), p. 124.

363. Ibid., p. 132.

364. Ibid., p. 60.

365. Baudelaire, *The Complete Verse,* p. 162.

366. Poe, *The Complete Tales and Poems,* p. 449. The phrase "mental pendulous pulsation" appears in the Baudelaire translation used by Benjamin as "vibration du pendule mental" ("vibration of the mental pendulum").

367. Baudelaire, *Les Fleurs du mal* (trans. Howard), p. 150.

368. Ibid., p. 31; *"My Heart Laid Bare,"* p. 157.

369. Baudelaire, *The Complete Verse,* p. 160.

370. Ibid., p. 162.

371. Baudelaire, *Les Fleurs du mal* (trans. Howard), p. 77.

372. Ibid., pp. 166 ("other, brighter worlds" translates "mondes singuliers"); 174.

373. Baudelaire, *Vers retrouvés: Juvenilia, Sonnets,* introduction and notes by Jules Mouquet (Paris, 1929), pp. 57–59. [R.T.] In English in *The Complete Verse,* p. 378; *Les Fleurs du mal* (trans. Howard), p. 81.

374. Baudelaire, *Oeuvres complètes,* vol. 1: *Les Fleurs du mal. Les Epaves,* ed. Jacques Crépet, 2nd ed. (Paris, 1930), p. 449. [R.T.]

375. Baudelaire, *The Complete Verse,* p. 250.

376. Baudelaire, *Les Fleurs du mal* (trans. Howard), pp. 11, 12.

377. Ibid., p. 175.

378. Allusion to the "familiar eyes" of the poem "Correspondences," in Baudelaire, *The Flowers of Evil,* p. 12 (trans. Richard Wilbur).

379. Baudelaire, *Les Fleurs du mal* (trans. Howard), p. 168.

380. Baudelaire, "Bohémiens en voyage," *Oeuvres complètes,* vol. 1, p. 18. [R.T.]

381. Baudelaire, *The Complete Verse,* p. 152 ("Le Mort Joyeux").

382. Baudelaire, *Les Fleurs du mal* (trans. Howard), p. 32.

383. Baudelaire, *The Complete Verse,* p. 197.

384. Ibid., p. 193 ("The Dance of Death"); *Les Fleurs du mal* (trans. Howard), p. 116; *The Complete Verse,* p. 86.

385. *The Flowers of Evil,* p. 91 (trans. Anthony Hecht).

386. Ibid.

387. *Les Fleurs du mal* (trans. Howard), pp. 36–37 ("De Profundis Clamavi").

388. Goethe, *Faust,* trans. Walter Kaufmann (New York: Anchor, 1963), p. 469 (line 11,582).

389. See J43a,3 ("versent quelque héroïsme au coeur des citadins").

390. Baudelaire, *Oeuvres complètes,* vol. 1, p. 91 ("Et qui, dans ces soirs d'or *où l'on se sent revivre*"–Benjamin's emphasis. [R.T.] In English in *The Complete Verse,* p. 183 ("The Little Old Women," section 3).

391. Baudelaire, *Oeuvres complètes,* vol. 1, p. 90. [R.T.] In English in *The Complete Verse,* p. 182 ("The Little Old Women," section 2).

392. Baudelaire, *Les Fleurs du mal* (trans. Howard), p. 94.

393. Baudelaire, *The Complete Verse,* p. 196 ("I have not forgotten . . . ," and "The great-hearted servant . . . , " as numbered in the edition of 1861).

394. Ibid., p. 169 ("Parisian Landscape").

395. Baudelaire, *Oeuvres complètes,* vol. 1, p. 93 ("Le Squelette laboureur"). [R.T.] In English in *The Complete Verse,* p. 187.

396. Baudelaire, *The Flowers of Evil,* p. 128 (trans. Edna St. Vincent Millay).

397. Baudelaire, *Correspondance,* vol. 2, p. 585. [R.T.]

398. Baudelaire, *"My Heart Laid Bare,"* p. 170. Benjamin interprets Baudelaire's "grands jours" as "Tage der Wiederkehr."

399. Baudelaire, *Oeuvres complètes,* vol. 1, p. 94 ("Le Crépuscule du soir"). [R.T.] In English in *Les Fleurs du mal* (trans. Howard), p. 99.

400. Baudelaire, *The Complete Verse,* p. 85.

401. "Selige Sehnsucht," from Goethe's *West-Östlicher Divan;* in English in *Selected Verse,* trans. David Luke (New York: Penguin, 1964), p. 240.

402. Baudelaire, *The Complete Verse,* p. 144. Goethe, *West-Eastern Divan,* trans. J. Whaley (London: Oswald Wolff, 1974), p. 213 ("Resonances"). The emphasis, as Rolf Tiedemann points out, is Benjamin's.

403. Marx, *The Eighteenth Brumaire of Louis Bonaparte,* trans. anonymous (New York: International Publishers, 1963), pp. 43–44.

404. Karl Marx and Friedrich Engels, *Correspondence, 1846–1895,* trans. Dona Torr (London: Martin Lawrence, 1934), p. 50. The "ass" in question is Louis Bonaparte, who had just dissolved the National Assembly and the Council of State and, a year later, was to be proclaimed Emperor Napoleon III. The Eighteenth Brumaire (November 9, 1799) is the date of Napoleon I's coup d'état, in which he overthrew the Directory and dissolved the Council of Five Hundred.

405. Marx and Engels, *Collected Works,* vol. 38, trans. Peter and Betty Ross (New York: International Publishers, 1982), p. 511.

406. Marx, *The Eighteenth Brumaire of Louis Bonaparte,* p. 23.

407. Ibid., p. 25.

408. Ibid., pp. 69–70.

409. Ibid., p. 83.

410. Ibid., pp. 111–112.

411. Ibid., p. 120.

412. Ibid., p. 129.

413. *Fechten:* "to fence" and "to go begging."

414. Marx, *The Eighteenth Brumaire,* p. 134.

415. Ibid., p. 130.

416. Ibid., p. 131.

417. Ibid., p. 134. Marx's note at this point: "In his work *Cousine Bette,* Balzac delineates the thoroughly dissolute Parisian philistine in Crevel, a character which he draws after the model of Dr. Véron, the proprietor of *Le Constitutionnel.*"

418. Baudelaire, *Oeuvres complètes,* vol. 1, p. 192 ("Projets d'un épilogue pour l'édition de 1861"). [R.T.] In English in *The Complete Verse,* p. 250.

419. *Baudelaire as a Literary Critic,* p. 43.

420. Ibid., p. 44.

421. Friedrich Nietzsche, *Ecce Homo,* trans. Walter Kaufmann (New York: Vintage, 1969), pp. 297–298. On the Fort du Taureau, see the Conclusion to the Exposé of 1939.

422. In English in the original.

423. Baudelaire, *Oeuvres complètes,* vol. 1, p. 122 ("Le Reniement de Saint Pierre"). [R.T.]

In English in *The Complete Verse,* p. 228. Double meaning of the word *Wirtschaft:* "husbandry" and "lodging"; "farm" and "public inn." Baudelaire refers to life as an *auberge* ("inn") at the conclusion of *Les Paradis artificiels.*

424. Goethe, *Selected Verse,* p. 240.

425. Auguste Blanqui, *L'Eternité par les astres* (Paris, 1872), p. 74. [R.T.]

426. Blanqui, *L'Eternité par les astres,* p. 74. [R.T.] Baudelaire, *Les Fleurs du mal* (trans. Howard), p. 93; and *The Complete Verse,* p. 179.

427. Baudelaire, *Oeuvres complètes,* vol. 1, p. 87 ("Les Sept Vieillards"). [R.T.] In English in *The Complete Verse,* p. 177.

428. Emile Verhaeren, *Les Villes tentaculaires* (Paris, 1904), p. 119 ("L'Ame de la ville"). [R.T.]

429. Allusion to the Gospels. See Mark, 4:21.

430. Baudelaire, *The Flowers of Evil,* p. 111 (trans. Roy Campbell).

431. Baudelaire, *"My Heart Laid Bare,"* p. 110 ("The Poem of Hashish," section 4).

432. Ibid., p. 111.

433. Marx, *Capital,* vol. 1, trans. Samuel Moore and Edward Aveling (1887; rpt. New York: International Publishers, 1967), pp. 359–360.

434. Baudelaire, *The Flowers of Evil,* trans. James McGowan (New York: Oxford University Press, 1993), p. 25.

435. See Friedrich von Bezold, *Das Fortleben der antiken Götter im mittelalterlichen Humanismus* (Bonn and Leipzig, 1922). [R.T.]

436. Reference has not been traced.

437. Baudelaire, *Oeuvres complètes,* vol. 1, p. 104 ("Le Crépuscule du matin"). [R.T.] In English in *The Complete Verse,* p. 203: "The debauched made their way homeward, racked by their labors."

438. Baudelaire, *The Flowers of Evil,* p. 12, "Correspondences" (trans. Richard Wilbur).

439. Marx, *The Eighteenth Brumaire of Louis Bonaparte,* p. 106.

440. Baudelaire, *Les Fleurs du mal* (trans. Howard), p. 5 ("To the Reader").

441. "Jerky gait" (*pas saccadé*) is from Nadar's description of Baudelaire: see Benjamin, *GS,* vol. 1, p. 583 n.35. [R.T.] In English in *Charles Baudelaire: A Lyric Poet in the Era of High Capitalism,* trans. Harry Zohn (London: Verso, 1973), p. 80. The phrase of Baudelaire's is from "The Salon of 1846" (*The Mirror of Art,* p. 128).

442. Marx, *Capital,* vol. 1, p. 76.

443. Benjamin, *The Origin of German Tragic Drama,* p. 155. *Acedia:* sloth.

444. Nietzsche, *Philosophy in the Tragic Age of the Greeks,* trans. Marianne Cowan (Washington, D.C.: Regnery Gateway, 1962), p. 67.

445. Nietzsche, *The Will to Power,* trans. Walter Kaufmann and R. J. Hollingdale (New York: Vintage, 1968), p. 21 (no. 31).

446. Ibid., p. 143 (no. 247).

447. Baudelaire, *Les Fleurs du mal* (trans. Howard), p. 174 ("The Abyss"). Nietzsche, *Thus Spoke Zarathustra,* trans. R. J. Hollingdale (Baltimore: Penguin, 1961), p. 167 ("The Stillest Hour").

448. Baudelaire, *Les Fleurs du mal* (trans. Howard), p. 164.

449. *Baudelaire as a Literary Critic,* pp. 338–339.

450. Arthur Rimbaud, *Complete Works, Selected Letters,* trans. Wallace Fowlie (Chicago: University of Chicago Press, 1966), p. 239.

451. Ibid., p. 175.

452. Baudelaire, *"My Heart Laid Bare,"* p. 168 ("Fusées"). See note to J1,1.

453. A paperbound documentary literature popular in Paris during the 1840s. See Benjamin's *Charles Baudelaire: A Lyric Poet in the Era of High Capitalism,* pp. 35–36.

454. "Die Moderne hat die Antike wie einen Alb, der im Schlaf über sie gekommen ist." *Alb* can also mean "incubus."

455. Baudelaire, "To a Woman Passing By," *The Flowers of Evil* (trans. McGowan), p. 189.

456. Baudelaire, "The Voyage," *The Complete Verse,* p. 247. *The Life and Writings of Turgot,* ed. W. Walker Stephens (London: Longmans, Green 1895), p. 310.

457. Hermann Lotze, *Microcosmus,* trans. Elizabeth Hamilton and E. E. Constance Jones (New York: Scribner and Welford, 1888), vol. 2, p. 387. The excerpt quoted in J83a,2 is found on p. 388.

458. See the story of Jacob and Esau in Genesis 25, verses 29–34.

459. Benjamin, "Surrealism," trans. Edmund Jephcott, in *SW,* vol. 2, p. 213.

460. Baudelaire, *"My Heart Laid Bare,"* p. 107 ("The Poem of Hashish").

461. See Brecht, *Gesammelte Werke,* vol. 8. pp. 408–410 ("Die Schönheit in den Gedichten des Baudelaire") for the derivation of J84a,2, 3, and 4. [R.T.]

462. Baudelaire, *Oeuvres complètes,* vol. 2, p. 709. [R.T.] In English in *"The Painter of Modern Life,"* p. 26.

463. Baudelaire, *The Flowers of Evil,* p. 201 (trans. Robert Lowell).

464. Baudelaire, *"My Heart Laid Bare,"* p. 160.

465. Ibid., pp. 200–201.

466. Ibid., pp. 190, 199 ("My Heart Laid Bare"). "Qu'est-ce que l'amour? Le besoin de sortir de soi . . . et l'artiste ne sort jamais de lui-même."

467. Baudelaire, *Intimate Journals,* p. 85.

468. Ibid., p. 67.

469. Johan Huizinga, *The Waning of the Middle Ages,* trans. F. Hopman (New York: Anchor, 1954), pp. 145–146.

470. Ibid., p. 210.

471. Title of a book published in Paris in 1844 lampooning various actresses, such as Rachel, and playwrights, such as François Ponsard. Jacques Crépet republished the work in 1938, claiming Baudelaire as one of the authors.

472. Joseph de Maistre, *Oeuvres complètes* (Lyons, 1884), vol. 5, pp. 102ff. [R.T.] This passage is not found in the translation of de Maistre cited above (note 345).

473. Goethe, *Torquato Tasso,* Act V, scene 5 (lines 3432ff.). [R.T.] In English in *Torquato Tasso,* trans. Alan and Sandy Brownjohn (London: Angel Books, 1985), p. 136.

474. Baudelaire, *The Complete Verse,* p. 169 ("Townscape"). Ruff's emphasis. Compare the discussion in M. A. Ruff, *Baudelaire,* trans. Agnes Kertesz (New York: New York University Press, 1966), pp. 120–121, where *comparaisons crues* is rendered as "freshhewn comparisons."

475. Trans. Arthur Symons, *The Symbolist Movement in Literature* (1919; rpt. New York: Dutton, 1958), p. 67.

476. *Baudelaire: A Self-Portrait,* p. 41.

477. Ibid., p. 195 (letter to his mother of December 31, 1863).

478. Text written in French by Benjamin.

479. Friedrich Schlegel, *"Lucinde" and the Fragments,* trans. Peter Firchow (Minneapolis: University of Minnesota Press, 1971), pp. 67–68.

480. Ibid., pp. 63–64.

481. Ibid., pp. 65–66.

482. Baudelaire, *Oeuvres complètes,* vol. 1, p. 94 ("Le Crépuscule du soir"). [R.T.] In English in *The Flowers of Evil,* p. 120 (trans. David Paul).

483. The election of Louis Napoleon as president in 1848, with more than twice as many votes as all other candidates combined.

484. The *cité Dorée* ("gilded city" from the name of M. Doré, one-time owner of the land)

was a site in Paris occupied by workers from the national workshops in 1848, and gradually transformed into a sink of corruption. [J.L.]

485. See Marx, *Capital,* vol. 1, pp. 435–437 ("Modern Manufacture").

486. Marcel Proust, *Remembrance of Things Past,* vol. 1, trans. C. K. Scott Moncrieff (New York: Random House, 1925), p. 126. Proust goes on, in this paragraph, to define evil in terms of indifference to the suffering one causes. On the note by Anatole France mentioned by Benjamin at this juncture, see J17a,1.

487. Proust, *Remembrance of Things Past,* vol. 1, p. 62.

488. Benjamin, *The Origin of German Tragic Drama,* p. 227. See J53a,4.

489. Benjamin later wrote *Spekulant* (speculator) over *Müssiggänger* (idler) without striking the latter. [R.T.]

490. Baudelaire, *Selected Letters,* p. 151.

491. Proust, *Remembrance of Things Past,* vol. 1, p. 819.

492. Ibid., p. 490. For the passage on Meryon, see J2,1.

493. Baudelaire, *Les Fleurs du mal* (trans. Howard), p. 5. Proust, *Remembrance of Things Past,* vol. 2, *The Captive,* trans. C. K. Scott Moncrieff (New York: Random House, 1929), pp. 645–646.

494. Proust, *Remembrance of Things Past,* vol. 2, p. 449.

495. Written by Benjamin in French.

496. Jean-Jacques Rousseau, *The Confessions,* trans. J. M. Cohen (Baltimore: Penguin, 1954), p. 593.

497. *Baudelaire as a Literary Critic,* p. 116 (preface to "Berenice").

498. Oswald Spengler, *The Decline of the West,* vol. 2, trans. Charles Francis Atkinson (New York: Knopf, 1928), pp. 101–102.

499. Ibid., p. 104.

500. "Les Sept Vieillards" was written and published in 1859, as part of the series *Fantômes parisiens.*

501. Max Horkheimer, "Materialism and Morality," in *Between Philosophy and Social Science,* trans. G. Frederick Hunter, Matthew S. Kramer, and John Torpey (Cambridge, Mass.: MIT Press, 1993), p. 40.

K [Dream City and Dream House, . . . Jung]

1. Benjamin quotes here from Régis Messac, *Le "Detective Novel" et l'influence de la pensée scientifique* (Paris, 1929), p. 420. [R.T.]

2. *Eingedenken:* Benjamin's coinage from the preposition *eingedenk* ("mindful of") and the verb *gedenken* ("bear in mind," "remember"). This verbal noun has a more active sense than *Erinnerung* ("memory").

3. For the relevant passage from Proust, see K8a,2. On "the darkness of the lived moment," see Ernst Bloch, *The Principle of Hope,* trans. Neville Plaice, Stephen Plaice, and Paul Knight (Cambridge, Mass.: MIT Press, 1986), p. 290.

4. *Förderung,* which, in mining, has the sense of "drawing up," "hauling to the surface." Benjamin, like Heidegger, plays on the archaic verb *wesen* ("to be") embedded in the *Gewesenen* ("what has been"); he cites the being in what has been. Compare D°,6, on the power of "distilling" the present as inmost essence of what has been.

5. Sigfried Giedion, *Bauen in Frankreich* (Leipzig and Berlin, 1928), p. 3. [R.T.]

6. The reference is to Ambrose Bierce's short story "An Occurrence at Owl Creek Bridge," published in 1891 (part of Bierce's collection *In the Midst of Life*). Ben-

jamin's phrase, in the second sentence of this entry, is "magnetopathische Experience."

7. Benjamin contrasts Proust's *Erlebnis* with our *Erfahrung* ("was Proust . . . erlebte, das haben wir . . . zu erfahren"). The former is, for Benjamin, an experience of the moment; the latter is long experience over time, the fruit of work and tradition. *Erfahrung* is formed out of multiple *Erlebnissen* (*GS*, vol. 1, p. 1183). Compare m1a,3, and m2a,4.

8. Ernst Bloch, *Heritage of Our Times,* trans. Neville Plaice and Stephen Plaice (Berkeley: University of California Press, 1991), p. 313.

9. Karl Marx, *A Contribution to the Critique of Political Economy,* trans. S. W. Ryazanskaya (New York: International Publishers, 1970), p. 217.

10. Marx, *Capital,* vol. 1, trans. Samuel Moore and Edward Aveling (1887; rpt. New York: International Publishers, 1967), p. 354.

11. Ibid., pp. 359–60.

12. It is not certain whether Benjamin wrote *Auswicklung* here or *Auswirkung.*

13. *Marcel Proust: A Selection from His Miscellaneous Writings,* trans. Gerard Hopkins (London: Allan Wingate, 1948), p. 233.

14. That "doleful something."

15. This letter from Theodor Adorno to Benjamin has not been preserved. But see Adorno's *Minima Moralia,* section 29. [R.T.] In English in *Minima Moralia,* trans. E. F. N. Jephcott (London: Verso, 1974), p. 49.

16. The obelisk was originally erected in the Egyptian city of Luxor by Ramses II. In 1831, it was transplanted to the Place de le Concorde in Paris. Under the name of the Place de la Révolution, this square had served as the site of guillotining from 1793 to 1795.

17. Victor Hugo, *The Man Who Laughs,* trans. Joseph L. Blamire (1889; rpt. Milpitas, Calif.: Atlantean Press, 1991), p. 151. The sleeping town in question is actually Melcombe Regis, next to Weymouth, on the coast of England.

18. C. G. Jung, "Analytic Psychology and Weltanschauung," trans. R. F. C. Hull, *Collected Works,* vol. 8 (Princeton: Princeton University Press, 1960), p. 376.

19. Jung, *Modern Man in Search of a Soul,* trans. W. S. Dell and Cary F. Baynes (New York: Harcourt, Brace, 1934), pp. 110; 228.

20. Ibid., p. 241.

21. Aldous Huxley, *Beyond the Mexique Bay* (London: Chatto and Windus, 1934), pp. 56, 60.

22. This passage does not appear in the English-language edition of Huizinga, *The Waning of the Middle Ages* (1949; rpt. Garden City, N.Y.: Anchor, 1954).

23. Theodor Reik, *Surprise and the Psycho-Analyst: On the Conjecture and Comprehension of Unconscious Processes,* trans. Margaret M. Green (New York: Dutton, 1937), pp. 129–131. "Memory" here translates *Gedächtnis;* "reminiscence" translates *Erinnerung.*

24. Ibid., p. 130. "Experience" here translates *Erlebnis.*

25. Marcel Proust, *Remembrance of Things Past,* vol. 2 (New York: Random House, 1932), p. 619 (*The Captive,* trans. C. K. Scott Moncrieff).

26. Proust, *Remembrance of Things Past,* vol. 1, trans. C. K. Scott Moncrieff (New York: Random House, 1925), pp. 33–34 (*Swann's Way*). Moncrieff translates *la mémoire volontaire* here as "an exercise of the will."

27. Ibid., p. 5.

28. Ibid., p. 779 (*The Guermantes Way*).

29. Proust, *Remembrance of Things Past,* vol. 2, pp. 1030–1031 (*The Past Recaptured,* trans.

Frederick A. Blossom). The lines by Baudelaire are from *Les Fleurs du mal,* trans. Richard Howard (Boston: Godine, 1982), pp. 31 ("The Head of Hair"), 30 ("By Association").

L [Dream House, Museum, Spa]

1. See Le Corbusier, *The City of Tomorrow and Its Planning,* trans. Frederick Etchells (1929; rpt. New York: Dover, 1987), pp. 163–178. In this entry and elsewhere, "glance" translates *Blick,* which in earlier usage meant "a flashing," "a lighting up," "a shining."
2. André Breton, *Nadja,* trans. Richard Howard (New York: Grove, 1960), p. 112.
3. Possible allusion to the rite of incubation practiced in the temples of Aesculapius in ancient Greece. (See L3,1.) The incubant would sleep within the precincts of the temple for the purpose of receiving a dream vision of the healing god. Often these sanctuaries were equipped with theaters, gymnasia, and baths. On the other hand, Benjamin might be alluding here to the hospitals of Paris, such as the Hôtel-Dieu (near Notre Dame), a large classical-style building with an inner courtyard, ornamental gardens, frescoes, and long arcaded galleries around the courtyard and in the interior. "Corridors," in this entry, translates *Wandelhallen.* "Turn into their recovery" translates *ihrer Gesundung entgegenwandeln.* And "watering place," here, translates *Brunnenhalle* (literally, "hall of fountains"), elsewhere translated as "spa" and "medicinal spring."
4. Castan's panopticon was located inside the so-called Linden Arcade or Kaisergalerie in Berlin, before moving across the street in 1888.
5. Victor Hugo, *Les Misérables,* trans. Charles E. Wilbour (1862; rpt. New York: Modern Library, 1992), p. 1089.
6. Ibid., p. 1090.
7. Ibid., pp. 1098–1099.
8. Ibid., pp. 1093, 1099.
9. Ibid., pp. 1094, 1095, 1096.
10. See I4a,1, and R2,2. [R.T.]
11. Charles Baudelaire, *Paris Spleen,* trans. Louise Varèse (New York: New Directions, 1947), p. 60. ("The Generous Gambler").
12. That is, he travels back into the ghost world. (Compare L2,7.) "Gate-way," here, translates *Tor-Weg:* threshold as passage, or passage as threshold.
13. Hugo, *Les Misérables,* p. 644.

M [The Flâneur]

1. Hugo von Hofmannsthal, "Der Tor und der Tod" (1894), *Gesammelte Werke,* ed. Herbert Steiner (1952), p. 220. [R.T.]
2. Victor Hugo, *Les Misérables,* trans. Charles E. Wilbour (1862; rpt. New York: Modern Library, 1992), p. 513.
3. "Um sich zu denken" is what appears in the manuscript; *denken* is arguably a slip of the pen for *decken* ("in order to *coincide with* one another"), which would accord with *Überdeckung* ("covering," "overlap") in the first sentence. [R.T.]
4. See "Hashish in Marseilles," in *SW,* vol. 2, p. 677. "Intoxicated," in this entry and elsewhere in the *Arcades,* translates *rauschhaft.*
5. Last three sentences adapted from the protocol to Benjamin's second experience with

hashish (*GS,* vol. 6, p. 564; in English in *SW,* vol. 2, p. 88). See also I2,6; I2a,1; R2a,3; and G°,5.

6. "Far-off times and places" translates *Länder- und Zeitenfernen,* which could be rendered more literally as "geographic and temporal distances." At issue is a spatiotemporal "superposition" (M1a,1).

7. Marcel Proust, *Remembrance of Things Past,* vol. 1, trans. C. K. Scott Moncrieff (New York: Random House, 1925), p. 137.

8. *Voyage autour de ma chambre* (Voyage around My Room): title of a work published in 1794 by Xavier de Maistre, brother of Joseph. The work describes experiences undergone during a period of imprisonment when, as a soldier in the Piedmontese army, the author was being held in Turin and had to find compensation in mental traveling.

9. This citation could not be verified. [R.T.]

10. Hugo, *Les Misérables,* p. 374.

11. The Directory: executive body in charge of the French government from 1795 to 1799. Les Incroyables (the Incredibles): name given to a group of young men at this time who affected a studied elegance in their dress and speech.

12. "Des Schmetterlings zweifelnder Flügel." See J. C. F. Schiller, *Sämtliche Werke* (Munich, 1965), vol. 1, p. 229: "mit zweifelndem Flügel / Wiegt der Schmetterling sich über dem rötlichen Klee." See also Benjamin's notes on his first and second hashish experiences, in *GS,* vol. 6, pp. 560, 562. [R.T.]

13. Volumes 11–15 of Hoffmann's *Ausgewählten Schriften* appeared in 1839, published by Brodhag Verlag in Stuttgart. The following citation from Julius Eduard Hitzig appears in vol. 15, pp. 32–34. [R.T.]

14. *The Letters of Charles Dickens,* ed. Kathleen Tillotson, vol. 4 (Oxford: Oxford University Press, 1977), pp. 612–613 (August 30, 1846, to John Forster).

15. Friedrich Engels, *The Condition of the Working Class in England,* trans. Florence Wischnewetzky (1886; rpt., with revisions by V. G. Kierran, London: Penguin, 1987), pp. 68–69.

16. More exactly, 1857. See M7,9. [R.T.]

17. Prior to 1859, in the years when Paris comprised only twelve municipal wards, "the thirteenth *arrondissement*" was a name for illicit amours. [J.L.]

18. Karl Marx and Friedrich Engels, *The German Ideology,* in *Collected Works,* vol. 5 (New York: International Publishers, 1976), p. 64 (trans. Clemens Dutt).

19. Original title: "Exkurs über die Soziologie der Sinne." Translated by Robert E. Park and Ernest W. Burgess, in *Introduction to the Science of Sociology,* 2nd ed. (Chicago: University of Chicago Press, 1970); see p. 150.

20. Hugo, *Les Misérables,* p. 514. See also O4,3.

21. Baudelaire, *Paris Spleen,* trans. Louise Varèse (New York: New Directions, 1947), p. 45.

22. Baudelaire, *Artificial Paradise,* trans. Ellen Fox (New York: Herder and Herder, 1971), pp. 101–102.

23. Balzac, *Séraphita,* trans. Clara Bell (New York: Hippocrene, 1989), p. 6.

24. Balzac, *Cousin Pons,* trans. Herbert J. Hunt (London: Penguin, 1968), p. 132.

25. Baudelaire, *The Prose Poems and "La Fanfarlo,"* trans. Rosemary Lloyd (New York: Oxford University Press, 1991), p. 44 ("The Crowds").

26. Baudelaire, *Paris Spleen,* pp. ix–x.

27. Ibid., p. 77.

28. G. K. Chesterton, *Charles Dickens* (1906: rpt. New York: Schocken, 1965), pp. 44–45. We have taken the liberty of altering the phrase Chesterton cites from *Pickwick Papers,* "the key of the street," to accord with current usage.

29. Ibid., pp. 45–46. "Drifting" is translated in Benjamin's text as *flâner*.

30. Ibid., p. 46.

31. Ibid., pp. 178–179 (citing letter of August 30, 1846, to John Forster).

32. Siegfried Kracauer, *Orpheus in Paris: Offenbach and the Paris of His Time,* trans. Gwenda David and Eric Mosbacher (New York: Knopf, 1938), p. 213 (describing an operetta by Offenbach).

33. Ibid., pp. 75, 76–77. For the remark by Alfred de Musset, see "Le Boulevard de Gand," in Musset, *Oeuvres complètes* (Paris: Seuil, 1964), p. 896. [J.L.]

34. Kracauer, *Orpheus in* Paris, p. 79 (second sentence added).

35. Paul Valéry, "The Place of Baudelaire," in *Leonardo, Poe, Mallarmé,* trans. Malcolm Cowley and James R. Lawler (Princeton: Princeton University Press, 1972), p. 203.

36. C. G. Jung, *Collected Works,* vol. 10, trans. R. F. C. Hull (Princeton: Princeton University Press, 1978), p. 48.

37. This passage does not appear in the anonymous English translation: Eugène Sue, *The Mysteries of Paris* (Sawtry, Cambridgeshire: Dedalus, [1989?]).

38. In Balzac, *Splendeurs et misères des courtisanes,* part 2, in *Oeuvres complètes,* vol. 15 (Paris, 1913), pp. 310ff. [R.T.] In English, *A Harlot High and Low,* trans. Rayner Heppenstall (Harmondsworth: Penguin, 1970), p. 270.

39. *Baudelaire as a Literary Critic,* trans. Lois Boe Hyslop and Francis E. Hyslop, Jr. (University Park: Pennsylvania State University Press, 1964), pp. 338–339.

40. Ibid., p. 294.

41. Baudelaire, *"My Heart Laid Bare" and Other Prose Writings,* trans. Norman Cameron (1950; rpt. New York: Haskell House, 1975), p. 169 ("Fusées," no. 21). See M15a,3.

42. Baudelaire, *"The Painter of Modern Life" and Other Essays,* trans. Jonathan Mayne (1964; rpt. New York: DaCapo, 1986), p. 9.

43. Jules Romains, *Men of Good Will,* vol. 1, trans. Warre B. Wells (New York: Knopf, 1946), p. 157.

44. Ibid., p. 136 ("A Little Boy's Long Journey").

45. Ibid., pp. 399–400.

46. Hugo, *Les Misérables,* p. 884 ("Enchantments and Desolations," section 5). For the passage in Gerstäcker, see I,4a,1, and R2,2.

47. Baudelaire, *"My Heart Laid Bare,"* p. 188.

48. Baudelaire, *Selected Letters,* trans. Rosemary Lloyd (Chicago: University of Chicago Press, 1986), pp. 59–60.

49. Poe, *Complete Tales and Poems* (New York: Modern Library, 1938), p. 476 ("The Man of the Crowd").

50. Baudelaire, *"My Heart Laid Bare,"* p. 169.

51. Balzac, *Gaudissart the Great,* trans. James Waring (Philadelphia: Gebbie, 1899), p. 346.

52. Baudelaire, *The Complete Verse,* trans. Francis Scarfe (London: Anvil, 1986), p. 377.

53. Bertolt Brecht, *Poems, 1913–1956,* trans. Ralph Manheim et al. (New York: Methuen, 1987), p. 131 ("A Reader for Those Who Live in Cities").

54. Marx, *Capital,* vol. 1, trans. Samuel Moore and Edward Aveling (1887; rpt. New York: International Publishers, 1967), p. 181.

55. See M8a,1. On the "physiologies," a paperbound documentary literature popular in Paris during the 1840s, see Benjamin, *Charles Baudelaire: A Lyric Poet in the Era of High Capitalism,* trans. Harry Zohn (London: Verso, 1973), pp. 35–36. See also J82a,3.

56. Georg Simmel, *The Philosophy of Money,* 2nd ed., trans. Tom Bottomore and David

Frisby (London: Routledge, 1990), p. 477. The last phrase can be rendered more literally as "the all too pressing nearness."

57. "Voilà ce qui fait de l'observation artistique une chose bien différente de l'observation scientifique: elle doit surtout être instinctive et procéder par l'imagination, d'abord." Gustave Flaubert, *Correspondance* (Paris: Conard, 1926–1954) vol. 4, p. 230 (letter of June 6–7, 1853, to Louise Colet).

58. *The Letters of Gustave Flaubert, 1830–1857,* trans. Francis Steegmuller (Cambridge, Mass.: Harvard University Press, 1980), p. 203 (letter of December 23, 1853, to Louise Colet; see *Madame Bovary,* part 2, chap. 9).

59. *The Letters of Gustave Flaubert, 1857–1880,* trans. Francis Steegmuller (Cambridge, Mass.: Harvard University Press, 1982), p. 89 (September 29, 1866, to George Sand).

60. Shelley, *Poetical Works,* ed. Thomas Hutchinson and G. M. Matthews (1905; rpt. London: Oxford University Press, 1970), pp. 350–351. Benjamin cites a translation by Brecht, from the latter's manuscript.

61. *The Collected Tales and Plays of Nikolai Gogol,* trans. Constance Garnett, rev. Leonard J. Kent (New York: Pantheon, 1964), p. 78. See E. T. A. Hoffmann, "My Cousin's Corner Window," in *"The Golden Pot" and Other Tales,* trans. Ritchie Robertson (New York: Oxford University Press, 1992), pp. 379–380.

62. Hoffmann, *"The Golden Pot,"* pp. 399–400.

63. Ibid., p. 380.

64. *Hegel: The Letters,* trans. Clark Butler and Christiane Seiler (Bloomington: Indiana University Press, 1984), p. 650.

65. Allusion to Virgil's *Aeneid,* book 6, lines 296ff.: "Here starts the pathway to the waters of / Tartarean Acheron. A whirlpool thick / with sludge, its giant eddy seeth-ing, vomits / all of its swirling sand into Cocytus." Trans. Allen Mandelbaum (New York: Bantam, 1971), p. 142.

66. Baudelaire, *The Mirror of Art,* trans. Jonathan Mayne (London: Phaidon, 1955), p. 283 ("The Salon of 1859," section 8).

67. Jean-Jacques Rousseau, *Reveries of the Solitary Walker,* trans. Peter France (New York: Penguin, 1979), p. 35.

68. Valéry, *Poems in the Rough,* trans. Hilary Corke (Princeton: Princeton University Press, 1969), p. 155.

69. Balzac, *The Wild Ass's Skin,* trans. Herbert J. Hunt (London: Penguin, 1977), p. 108.

70. Proust, *Remembrance of Things Past,* vol. 1, trans. C. K. Scott Moncrieff (New York: Random House, 1925), p. 596 *(Within a Budding Grove).*

71. Proust, *Remembrance of Things Past,* vol. 2 (New York: Random House, 1932), p. 1084 *(The Past Recaptured,* trans. Frederick A. Blossom).

N [On the Theory of Knowledge, Theory of Progress]

In translating Convolute N, we have greatly benefited from the previous translation of this convolute, "Re the Theory of Knowledge, Theory of Progress," by Leigh Hafrey and Richard Sieburth, originally published in *Philosophical Forum* (Fall–Winter, 1983–1984), and reprinted in *Benjamin: Philosophy, History, Aesthetics,* ed. Gary Smith (Chicago: University of Chicago Press, 1989), pp. 38–83.

1. Karl Marx, *Selected Writings,* ed. David McLellan (New York: Oxford University Press, 1977), p. 38.

2. Reference is to Louis Aragon, *Le Paysan de Paris* (Paris, 1926). [R.T.] On the not-yet-conscious knowledge of what has been, see K1,2.

3. "Restoration of all things." Derived from Jewish apocalyptic, Stoic, and Neoplatonic-Gnostic traditions, the concept originally referred to the recurrence of a specific planetary constellation.

4. Adorno, *Kierkegaard: Construction of the Aesthetic,* trans. Robert Hullot-Kentor (Minneapolis: University of Minnesota Press, 1989), p. 54. The Kierkegaard passage is from *The Concept of Irony.* For the passage from Benjamin cited by Adorno, see Benjamin, *The Origin of German Tragic Drama,* trans. John Osborne (London: Verso, 1977), p. 166. The *facies hippocratica* is a death mask.

5. Georg Simmel, *Goethe* (Leipzig, 1913), esp. pp. 56–61; see also Benjamin, *GS,* vol. 1, pp. 953–954. [R.T.] "Origin" here translates *Ursprung.*

6. See Martin Heidegger, *Being and Time,* trans. John Macquarrie and Edward Robinson (New York: Harper and Row, 1962), Division 2, Chapter 5. On truth as "the death of the *intentio*" (parenthesis below), see Benjamin, *The Origin of German Tragic Drama,* p. 36. On time in the dialectical image, see Q°,21 in "First Sketches."

7. This sentence could not be found among Keller's epigrams. [R.T.]

8. The passage occurs in the Introduction to the *Kritik der Politischen Ökonomie,* in Karl Marx and Friedrich Engels, *Werke* (Berlin, 1964), vol. 13, pp. 640ff. [R.T.] In English, "Introduction to a Critique of Political Economy," in Marx and Engels, *The German Ideology,* trans. anonymous (New York: International Publishers, 1970), pp. 149–150.

9. Friedrich Engels, *Socialism, Utopian and Scientific,* trans. Edward Aveling (1935; rpt. Westport, Conn.: Greenwood, 1977), p. 68. Rolf Tiedemann informs us that Benjamin wrote in his manuscript, instead of "aus dämonischen Herrschern," the truly "strange" words "und dämonischen Herrscher." The sentence would then read: "they can, in the hands of associated producers and master demons, be transformed into willing servants."

10. Marx, *Capital,* vol. 1, trans. Samuel Moore and Edward Aveling (1887; rpt. New York: International Publishers, 1967), p. 28. Marx distinguishes between *Forschung* (research) and *Darstellung* (presentation, application).

11. Jules Michelet, *The People,* trans. John P. McKay (Urbana: University of Illinois Press, 1973), pp. 18–19.

12. Marx, *Selected Writings,* p. 37.

13. Marx and Engels, *The German Ideology,* vol. 1, trans. Clemens Dutt, in Marx and Engels, *Collected Works,* vol. 5 (New York: International Publishers, 1976), p. 91.

14. Marx, *Selected Writings,* p. 38.

15. Ibid., p. 66 (italics added).

16. Marx and Engels, *Collected Works,* vol. 5, p. 92 (*The German Ideology*).

17. Marx and Engels, *The Holy Family,* in *Collected Works,* vol. 4 (New York: International Publishers, 1975), p. 128 (trans. Richard Dixon and Clemens Dutt).

18. Paul Valéry, "The Place of Baudelaire," in *Leonardo, Poe, Mallarmé,* trans. Malcolm Cowley and James R. Lawler (Princeton: Princeton University Press, 1972), p. 203. See I5a,5.

19. Marx and Engels, *Selected Correspondence,* trans. I. Lasker (Moscow: Progress Publishers, 1975), pp. 434–435.

20. Benjamin's introduction to Jochmann's "Die Rückschritte der Poesie" (The Regressions of Poetry) appears in *GS,* vol. 2, pp. 572–585.

21. Benjamin's reference to the "apoll‹i›nischen Schnitt" remains obscure. The French translator of the *Passagen-Werk* renders this as "section d'or" ("golden section"), while the Italian translators offer the emendation "taglio di Apelle" ("Apelles' section"),

with reference to the fourth-century B.C. Greek painter who, in a contest, divided a narrow line by one yet narrower and of a different color.

22. This phrase (literally, "to go to the many") means "to die." It occurs, for example, in Petronius: "And now he's gone, joined the great majority" *(Tamen abiit ad plures). The Satyricon,* trans. William Arrowsmith (New York: New American Library, 1959), p. 50 (ch. 42). (Thanks to William Wyatt for this reference.)

23. Valéry, *Leonardo, Poe, Mallarmé,* p. 197.

24. C. G. Jung, "On the Relation of Analytical Psychology to Poetry," in Jung, *Complete Works* (Princeton: Princeton University Press, 1970–1992), vol. 15, pp. 82–83 (trans. R. F. C. Hull).

25. C. G. Jung, "The Spiritual Problem of Modern Man," in Jung, *Modern Man in Search of a Soul,* trans. W. S. Dell and Cary F. Baynes (New York: Harcourt, Brace, 1934), p. 237.

26. Blanqui's last work is *L'Eternité par les astres;* see D5a,1, and the entries following. Heidegger's outline of a *Problemgeschichte* ("history of problems") in *Being and Time,* paragraph 3, may stand behind Benjamin's reference to the philosopher here.

27. See Benjamin, *GS,* vol. 2, p. 578. [R.T.]

28. See August Strindberg, *To Damascus III,* in *Plays of Confession and Therapy,* trans. Walter Johnson (Seattle: University of Washington Press, 1979), p. 196.

29. Marx and Engels, *Selected Correspondence,* p. 434 (Engels to Mehring, July 14, 1893).

30. Turgot, "Second Discourse on the Successive Advances of the Human Mind," in *On Progress, Sociology and Economics,* trans. Ronald L. Meek (London: Cambridge University Press, 1973), p. 46.

31. Ibid., pp. 44, 46.

32. Ibid., p. 58. Benjamin has "perfection" for "reflection." *Limes* is Latin for "boundary," "limit."

33. Ibid., p. 52.

34. Ibid., p. 105.

35. *The Life and Writings of Turgot,* ed. W. Walker Stephens (London: Longmans, Green, 1895), p. 320.

36. Hermann Lotze, *Microcosmus,* trans. Elizabeth Hamilton and E. E. Constance Jones (New York: Scribner and Welford, 1888), vol. 2, p. 144.

37. Ibid., p. 146.

38. Friedrich Hölderlin, *Sämtliche Werke* (Stuttgart, 1954), vol. 6, p. 92 (letter of September 1793, to his brother). [R.T.]

39. Lotze, *Microcosmus,* vol. 2, p. 172.

40. Ibid., p. 171.

41. Ibid., pp. 173–174.

42. Simmel, *The Philosophy of Money,* 2nd ed., trans. Tom Bottomore and David Frisby (New York: Routledge, 1990), p. 447.

43. Lotze, *Microcosmus,* vol. 2, p. 147.

44. Ibid., p. 148.

45. Ibid., pp. 151–152.

46. Ibid., p. 154.

47. Ibid., p. 157.

48. Baudelaire, "The Poem of Hashish," in *"My Heart Laid Bare" and Other Prose Writings,* trans. Norman Cameron (1950; rpt. Haskell House, 1975), p. 102. Baudelaire claims here to be citing verbatim the letter of an unnamed woman.

49. *The Letters of Gustave Flaubert, 1857–1880,* trans. Francis Steegmuller (Cambridge, Mass.: Harvard University Press, 1982), p. 24.

50. This passage is not found in the English-language edition of *The Waning of the Middle Ages* (New York: Anchor, 1954).

51. Karl Korsch, *Karl Marx,* trans. anonymous (1938; rpt. New York: Russell and Russell, 1963), p. 106.

52. Ibid., pp. 190–191. Korsch cites Hegel's *Vorlesungen über die Philosophie der Geschichte* ‹Lectures on the Philosophy of History› (General Introduction, 2, i, a).

53. Korsch, *Karl Marx,* p 182.

54. Ibid., p. 234.

55. Ibid., p. 196. Korsch quotes from Marx and Engels, *Gesamtausgabe* (Berlin, 1927–1930), vol. 1, part v, p. 403. *(Die deutsche Ideologie).*

56. Korsch, *Karl Marx,* pp. 227–229. Korsch refers to the preface to Marx's *Zur Kritik der politischen Ökonomie* (1859).

57. Korsch, *Karl Marx,* pp. 168–169. Korsch cites phrases from *Die deutsche Ideologie* and from Georgi Plekhanov, *Fundamental Problems of Marxism* (1908).

58. Korsch, *Karl Marx,* p. 83. Quotation from Bacon is from the *Novum Organum,* book 1: "For it is rightly said that truth is the daughter of time and not of authority."

59. Korsch, *Karl Marx,* pp. 78–80.

60. The citation is from Guez de Balzac, letter of March 7, 1634: "And because I am not avaricious either in eye or in soul, I consider the emeralds of your peacocks as great a prize as those of the lapidary." In Proust, *Correspondance,* vol. 2: *1896–1901,* ed. Philip Kolb (Paris: Plon, 1976), pp. 52–53. Proust's letter is dated by the editor mid-April 1896. The book in question is *Les Plaisirs et les jours.*

61. Honoré de Balzac, *The Wild Ass's Skin,* trans. Herbert J. Hunt (London: Penguin, 1977), pp. 35, 37, 38, 40.

62. Henri Focillon, *The Life of Forms in Art,* trans. Charles Beecher Hogan and George Kubler (1948; rpt. New York: Zone, 1989), pp. 153–154, 148–149.

63. Ibid., pp. 102–103.

64. Ibid., p. 47.

O [Prostitution, Gambling]

1. This passage is drawn from *The Reminiscences and Recollections of Captain Gronow: Being Anecdotes of the Camp, Court, Clubs, and Society, 1810–1860,* vol. 1 (New York: Scribner and Welford, 1889), pp. 122–123 ("The Salon des Etrangers in Paris"), a text originally written in English. (Thanks to Susan Jackson for this reference.) We translate here the informative German translation used by Benjamin. On the Salon (Cercle) des Etrangers, see the Guide to Names and Terms, and "First Sketches," L°,19; Benjamin's "Marquis de Sévry" seems to be a mistake for the Marquis de Livry mentioned by Gronow (pp. 120–121).

2. Louis Aragon, *Paris Peasant,* trans. Simon Watson Taylor (1971; rpt. Boston: Exact Change, 1994), p. 14.

3. Ibid., p. 60.

4. *Schwelle,* cognate with the English word "sill," has the root sense of "board," "structural support," "foundation beam." According to current information, it is etymologically unrelated to *schwellen.*

5. Friedrich Schiller, *Wallenstein's Death* (act 1, scene 4), in *"The Robbers" and "Wallenstein,"* trans. F. J. Lamport (London: Penguin, 1979), p. 328. For the citation from La Bruyère, see J87,4 (?).

6. *Langue verte,* the Parisian slang catalogued by Alfred Delvau in his *Dictionnaire de la langue verte,* first published in Paris in 1865. See P3a,4.

7. Anatole France, *The Garden of Epicurus,* trans. Alfred Allinson (New York: Dodd, Mead, 1923), pp. 22–25.

8. The first passage uses the familiar form of the second-person dative, *Dir.* The other passage, within the single quotation marks, uses the formal form, *Sie.*

9. As distinct from the official stockbrokers *(agents de change),* these "outside brokers" *(courtiers de la coulisse)* were unauthorized. They took their name "from their habit of trading on the outskirts of the Bourse crowd—the wings of a theater, in French, being named *coulisse.*" See William Parker, *The Paris Bourse and French Finance* (New York: Columbia University Press, 1920), p. 26. Compare g3,2.

10. That is, of Napoleon, 1798–1799.

11. Marx and Engels, *Collected Works,* vol. 38, trans. Peter Ross and Betty Ross (New York: International Publishers, 1982), p. 91 (letter of November–December 1846).

12. Compare a4,1. Neither this nor the preceding passage appears in the English translation of Mayer's biography of Engels (see note to E9a,6).

13. Siegfried Kracauer, *Orpheus in Paris: Offenbach and the Paris of His Time,* trans. Gwenda David and Eric Mosbacher (New York: Knopf, 1938), p. 254.

14. Marx, *The Economic and Philosophic Manuscripts of 1844,* trans. Martin Milligan (New York: International Publishers, 1964), p. 151.

15. Marx, *Capital,* vol. 1, trans. Samuel Moore and Edward Aveling (1887; rpt. New York: International Publishers, 1967), pp. 450–451.

16. Kracauer, *Orpheus in Paris,* pp. 298, 133. *Les Filles de marbre* was produced in 1853; *Froufrou,* in 1869.

17. Charles Fourier, *The Theory of the Four Movements,* trans. Ian Patterson (New York: Cambridge University Press, 1996), p. 148.

18. "Events," in this entry, translates *Ereignisse;* "contexts of experience" translates *Erfahrungszusammenhängen* (which suggests "continuity of experience").

19. Johan Huizinga, *The Waning of the Middle Ages,* trans. F. Hopman (1949; rpt. New York: Anchor, 1954), p. 149.

20. Honoré de Balzac, *The Wild Ass's Skin,* trans. Herbert J. Hunt (London: Penguin, 1977), p. 23.

P [The Streets of Paris]

1. Cited by Benjamin in Latin without source.

2. Street of Bad Boys, Sausage-Maker Street, Street of Dirty Words, Street of the Headless Woman, Street of the Fishing Cat, Street of the Thickset Villain.

3. Victor Hugo, *Les Misérables,* trans. Charles E. Wilbour (1862; rpt. New York: Modern Library, 1992), p. 1100.

Q [Panorama]

1. Panoramas were introduced in France in 1799 by the American engineer Robert Fulton. But it was a certain James Thayer who, after acquiring the patent, developed the two rotundas on the Boulevard Montmartre which were separated by the arcade known as the Passage des Panoramas. These large circular tableaux, painted in trompe-l'oeil and designed to be viewed from the center of the rotunda, displayed scenes of battles and cities: "View of Paris," "Evacuation of Toulon by the English," "Encampment at Boulogne," "Rome," "Athens," "Jerusulem." As the number of panoramas increased and their popularity grew, new forms made their appearance: the cosmorama at the Palais-Royal, later transferred to Rue Vivienne; the neorama of M. Allaux, with its interior scenes; the georama, with its general and detailed views of

different parts of the world. But the decisive invention remains the diorama of Daguerre and Bouton, which was opened in 1822 on the Rue Sanson, near the Boulevard Saint-Martin, and then installed on the Boulevard de Bonne-Nouvelle. The pictures were painted on cloth transparencies, which by 1831 were being used with various lighting effects. The installation burned down in 1839, together with the laboratory where Daguerre and Niépce conducted their first experiments in photography. [J.L.]

2. See Honoré de Balzac, *Père Goriot,* trans. Henry Reed (New York: New American Library, 1962), pp. 53–56 (end of Part One).

3. André Breton, *Nadja,* trans. Richard Howard (New York: Grove Press, 1960), p. 148.

4. The georama was a large hollow globe or spherical chamber that was lined with a cloth depicting the geography of the earth's surface, to be viewed by a spectator from inside.

5. Marcel Proust, *Remembrance of Things Past,* vol. 1, trans. C. K. Scott Moncrieff (New York: Random House, 1925), p. 709 (*Within a Budding Grove*).

6. Charles Dickens, *The Old Curiosity Shop* (London: Heron Books, 1970), p. 267 (ch. 27).

7. Presumably, the picturesque and mechanized theater constructed by M. Pierre on the Carrefour Gaillon. [J.L.]

8. G. K. Chesterton, *Charles Dickens* (1906; rpt. New York: Schocken, 1965), pp. 117–118.

9. Siegfried Kracauer, *Orpheus in Paris: Offenbach and the Paris of His Time,* trans. Gwenda David and Eric Mosbacher (New York: Knopf, 1938), p. 42.

10. Word coined in 1789 by patentee Robert Barker (1739–1806), Scottish portrait painter and reputed inventor of panoramas. The patent mentioned in the passage following dates from 1800. (Floréal was the eighth month in the Revolutionary calendar established in 1793.)

11. Charles Baudelaire, *The Mirror of Art,* trans. Jonathan Mayne (London: Phaidon, 1955), p. 284.

R [Mirrors]

1. "So weiss man weder ein noch aus vor zweifelhafter Helle." The idiom *nicht aus noch ein wissen* ("not know which way to turn") is here taken literally ("know neither 'out' nor 'in'").

2. Louis Aragon, *Paris Peasant,* trans. Simon Watson Taylor (1971; rpt. Boston: Exact Change, 1994), p. 14.

3. See note to M1a,3. "Ambiguity," in the present passage, translates *Zweideutigkeit* (*zwei-deutig:* capable of two interpretations). "The whispering of gazes" is English for *Blickwispern.* Compare c°,3, in "The Arcades of Paris."

4. Theodor W. Adorno, *Kierkegaard: Construction of the Aesthetic,* trans. Robert Hullot-Kentor (Minneapolis: University of Minnesota Press, 1989), pp. 41–42. The Kierkegaard citation is from vol. 1 of *Either/Or,* trans. David F. Swenson and Lillian M. Swenson, rev. Howard A. Johnson (1944; rpt. New York: Anchor, 1959), pp. 349–350.

S [Painting, Jugendstil, Novelty]

1. Goethe, *Faust,* trans. Walter Kaufmann (New York: Anchor, 1963), p. 36 (lines 6838–6839).

2. Anatole France, *The Garden of Epicurus,* trans. Alfred Allinson (New York: Dodd, Mead, 1923), p. 129.

3. See Julien Benda, *The Betrayal of the Intellectuals,* trans. Richard Aldington (1928; rpt. Boston: Beacon, 1955), p. 166 (letter of August 13, 1789, from an Englishman, Arthur Young); and Anatole France, "The Procurator of Judaea," in *Mother of Pearl,* trans. Frederic Chapman (New York: Dodd, Mead, 1922), p. 26.

4. Franz Kafka, *The Trial,* trans. Willa and Edwin Muir, rev. E. M. Butler (1935; rpt. New York: Schocken, 1968), p. 163.

5. *Sein und Zeit* (Halle, 1927*).* [R.T.]

6. Hugo von Hofmannsthal, *Selected Prose,* trans. Mary Hottinger, Tania Stern, and James Stern (New York: Pantheon, 1952), p. 364. The *Buch der Freunde* (Book of Friends) was compiled from Hofmannsthal's notebooks of 1917–1922 and from quotations, and was first published in 1922.

7. Sketch for a play; now in Hofmannsthal, *Gesammelte Werke,* vol. 3, *Dramen* (Frankfurt am Main, 1957), pp. 491–493. [R.T.] Aside from the reference to Freud, the unidentified citations at the end of S2,3 are in French.

8. Theodor W. Adorno, "Arabesken zur Operette," in *Die Rampe: Blätter des Deutschen Schauspielhauses* (Hamburg, 1931–1932), p. 5. Adorno speaks of the "negative eternity of the operetta." [R.T.]

9. Benjamin refers to the great Catalan architect Antonio Gaudí (1852–1926).

10. Adorno, *Kierkegaard: Construction of the Aesthetic,* trans. Robert Hullot-Kentor (Minneapolis: University of Minnesota Press, 1989), pp. 45–46. The passage from *Repetition* describes the apartment Kierkegaard occupied during his residence in Berlin in 1843.

11. Ovid, *Metamorphoses,* trans. Rolfe Humphries (Bloomington: Indiana University Press, 1955), p. 73 (the reference is to Narcissus).

12. ". . . den Jugend*stil* bis in seine Auswirkung in die Jugend*bewegung* verfolgend."

13. Charles Baudelaire, *Paris Spleen,* trans. Louise Varèse (New York: New Directions, 1947), p. 5 ("The Double Room").

14. Paul Valéry, *Degas, Manet, Morisot,* trans. David Paul (Princeton: Princeton University Press, 1960), p. 152 ("About Corot").

15. Karl Marx, *Selected Writings,* ed. David McLellan (New York: Oxford University Press, 1977), p. 338.

16. *Baudelaire as a Literary Critic,* trans. Lois Boe Hyslop and Francis E. Hyslop, Jr. (University Park: Pennsylvania State University Press, 1964), p. 143.

17. Ibid., pp. 44, 45.

18. *Tagebuch einer Verlorenen* (Diary of a Lost Woman), anonymous memoir of a prostitute, ed. Margarete Böhme (Berlin, 1905). The reference to Alfred Capus that follows remains obscure. [R.T.]

19. Baudelaire, *The Complete Verse,* trans. Francis Scarfe (London: Anvil, 1986), p. 55.

20. "Loss of a Halo," section 46 of *Paris Spleen.*

21. Baudelaire, *"Flowers of Evil" and Other Works,* trans. Wallace Fowlie (1964; rpt. New York: Dover, 1992), p. 27.

22. Baudelaire, "The Sun" ("Le Soleil"), in *The Complete Verse,* p. 171.

23. Friedrich Nietzsche, *Thus Spoke Zarathustra,* trans. R. J. Hollingdale (1961; rpt. Baltimore: Penguin, 1968), p. 286 ("The Shadow").

24. Ibid., p. 315 ("Among the Daughters of the Desert").

25. See Henrik Ibsen, *The Wild Duck,* in *"Hedda Gabler" and Other Plays,* trans. Una Ellis-Fermor (1950; rpt. Harmondsworth: Penguin, 1982), pp. 243–244 ("the saving lie . . . is the stimulating principle of life, . . . to keep life going").

26. Paul Valéry, *History and Politics,* trans. Denise Follet and Jackson Mathews (Princeton: Princeton University Press, 1962), pp. 271–272.

27. Paul Valéry, *Analects,* trans. Stuart Gilbert (Princeton: Princeton University Press, 1970), p. 11.

28. Marcel Proust, *Remembrance of Things Past,* vol. 1, trans. C. K. Scott Moncrieff (New York: Random House, 1925), pp. 489–490.

29. Ibid., p. 490.

T [Modes of Lighting]

1. "Illuminated by nocturnal torches."

2. Apparent reference to a collection of fairy tales and humor, *Die blaue Bibliothek des Feenreichs, der Kobolde, Zwerge und Gnomen; oder Deutschlands Zaubermärchen, Herrengeschichten, und Schwanke zu ergötzlicher und bildender Unterhaltung für die Jugend und Erwachsene* (published in the 1840s).

3. The Hôtel de Ville (City Hall) was the meeting place of radical republican leaders in 1848; at the end of February, immediately after the abdication of Louis Philippe, members of the Chamber of Deputies proceeded there to join with these leaders and, under heavy pressure from the crowd outside, to proclaim a provisional republic.

4. See "Blind Men," in Baudelaire, *Les Fleurs du mal,* trans. Richard Howard (Boston: Godine, 1982), p. 97; and "My Cousin's Corner Window" in E. T. A. Hoffmann, *"The Golden Pot" and Other Tales,* trans. Ritchie Robertson (New York: Oxford University Press, 1992), p. 394.

5. Edgar Allan Poe, *The Complete Tales and Poems* (New York: Modern Library, 1938), p. 464. Poe goes on to recommend the Argand lamp.

U [Saint-Simon, Railroads]

1. *Ateliers nationaux:* an emergency relief agency, set up during the February Revolution of 1848, that attracted thousands of unemployed workers from all over France; it eventually satisfied neither radicals nor moderates and was abolished by the newly elected conservative majority in May, without any program of public works to replace it.

2. On Bourdin, see J27a,3.

3. Friedrich Engels, "Ludwig Feuerbach and the End of Classical German Philosophy," in Karl Marx and Friedrich Engels, *Basic Writings on Politics and Philosophy,* ed. Lewis S. Feuer (New York: Anchor, 1949), p. 205.

4. Henri Saint-Simon, *Selected Writings on Science, Industry and Social Organization,* trans. Keith Taylor (New York: Holmes and Meier, 1975), p. 210 (from *L'Organisateur,* 1820). On the replacement of "the government of persons . . . by the administration of things," see Friedrich Engels, "Socialism: Utopian and Scientific," in Marx and Engels, *Collected Works,* vol. 24 (New York: International Publishers, 1989), p. 321 (trans. Edward Aveling).

5. Henri Saint-Simon, *Selected Writings on Science, Industry and Social Organiziation,* p. 237 (from *Du Système industriel,* 1821).

6. Henri Saint-Simon, *Social Organization, the Science of Man, and Other Writings,* trans. Felix Markham (1952; rpt. New York: Harper, 1964), p. 18 ("Introduction to the Scientific Studies of the Nineteenth Century," 1808).

7. The passage quoted by Chevalier is evidently a free rendering of one of the maxims on industry from Benjamin Franklin's preface to the 1758 edition of his *Poor Richard*

Improved. The preface was extensively reprinted (and frequently revised) under such titles as *The Way to Wealth.*

8. Reference to the quarrel, at the end of 1831, between Enfantin (who soon withdrew to his estate at Ménilmontant, with forty disciples) and other leading Saint-Simonians, including Bazard, Rodrigues, and Leroux, over the question of relations between the sexes.

9. Saint-Simon married the young writer and musician Sophie de Champgrand in August 1801; having just assumed the role of patron of the sciences, he was in need of a hostess. The marriage was dissolved, by mutual consent, in June 1802. "I used marriage as a means of studying scientists" (*Selected Writings on Science, Industry and Social Organization,* p. 19).

10. Auguste Comte became Saint-Simon's assistant in 1817, following his expulsion from the Ecole Polytechnique for insubordination. It was in 1824—after *seven* years of collaboration—that a long-standing dispute between the two men finally led Comte to withdraw his support.

11. See a15,2–4, and p1,3. Evadamism: Eve + Adam + ism. Le Mapah (mater + pater) was the name taken by a sculptor named Ganneau, around 1835, in forming a cult that advocated the complete equality—and ultimate fusion—of men and women.

12. See p2,5, and entries following.

13. Karl Marx and Friedrich Engels, *Selected Correspondence,* 3rd ed., trans. I. Lasker (Moscow: Progress Publishers, 1975), p. 82.

14. Siefried Kracauer, *Orpheus in Paris: Offenbach and the Paris of His Time,* trans. Gwenda David and Eric Mosbacher (New York: Knopf, 1938), p. 95.

15. One of two cemeteries in the old Constantinople district of Pera (now called Beyoglu) in Istanbul, on the north side of the Golden Horn. There was a *grand* and a *petit* Champ des Morts, both destroyed by fire and renovations in the course of the nineteenth century.

16. Honoré de Balzac, *Gaudissart the Great,* trans. James Waring (Philadelphia: Gebbie, 1899), pp. 351–352.

17. Plan conceived by Napoleon I for blocking English merchandise from entering the Continent.

18. Honoré de Balzac, *The Wild Ass's Skin,* trans. Herbert J. Hunt (London: Penguin, 1977), p. 60.

V [Conspiracies, Compagnonnage]

Compagnonnage refers to trade guilds, solidarity associations among workers. The word comes from *compagnon:* "companion," "workman," "journeyman." A central feature of *compagnonnage,* up through the middle of the nineteenth century, was the *tour de France,* in which journeymen artisans traveled to various towns of France seeking employment in order to complete their professional training. The *tour* generally lasted three to four years and culminated in the production of a masterwork.

1. The army was persuaded to disarm by the passive conduct of the Garde Nationale.

2. The trial of Etienne Cabet for sedition.

3. Karl Marx and Friedrich Engels, *Collected Works,* vol. 10 (New York: International Publishers, 1978), pp. 316–319, 312–313, 312 (trans. Christopher Upward).

4. Marx and Engels, *Collected Works,* vol. 17, trans. Rodney Livingstone (New York: International Publishers, 1981), pp. 79–80 (*Herr Vogt* [1860]).

5. Société des Saisons: name of a secret society established by Blanqui, in 1837, with the

aid of two other young republicans. It utilized classical conspiratorial techniques to form a tightly disciplined and hierarchical organization. Three years earlier, Blanqui had founded its predecessor, the secret revolutionary Société des Familles, and in 1832 he had been a member of the republican Société des Amis du Peuple, which espoused a Saint-Simonian doctrine.

6. In the aftermath of the July Revolution, the ministers of Charles X were arrested and, in December, put on trial. Throughout the trial, troops of the Garde Nationale, led by the marquis de Lafayette, were required to control the crowds who gathered in the streets to demand the death sentence for the ministers. The latter were sentenced to life imprisonment on December 24, 1830, but they were all granted amnesty in 1836.

7. Victor Hugo, *Les Misérables,* trans. Charles E. Wilbour (1862; rpt. New York: Modern Library, 1992), p. 732 ("Facts from which History Springs, and which History Ignores").

8. Ibid., p. 730.

9. Fifth month (January 20–February 18) of the French revolutionary calendar, adopted in October 1793 by the First Republic.

10. This question from the catechism of neophyte revolutionaries of the Société des Familles—a question that was presented in evidence at the trial of Blanqui and other members of the organization in 1836—was answered: "One must make a *social* revolution." See Alan B. Spitzer, *The Revolutionary Theories of Louis Auguste Blanqui* (1957; rpt. New York: AMS Press, 1970), pp. 90, 92. Marx, too, calls for a social revolution.

11. *Compagnon* actually derives from the Old French word *compaignon,* which in turn comes from the Vulgar Latin *companio* (*com,* "with" + *panis,* "bread"). The word, meaning originally "one who eats bread with another," is unrelated to *compas,* "compass."

12. Related to the English word "vent," an obsolete term for "sale," "hostelry." The French word *vente* may have originally referred to a stand of timber.

13. *Baudelaire as a Literary Critic,* trans. Lois Boe Hyslop and Francis E. Hyslop, Jr. (University Park: Pennsylvania State University Press, 1964), p. 356.

14. Marx, *The Eighteenth Brumaire of Louis Bonaparte,* trans. anonymous (New York: International Publishers, 1963), p. 75. The Society of the Tenth of December was founded by Louis Napoleon in 1849 (as Marx writes in the sentence immediately preceding), on the pretext of establishing a charitable association (see V6,3). Napoleon was elected president of the republic on December 10, 1848.

W [Fourier]

1. Charles Fourier, *Harmonian Man: Selected Writings of Charles Fourier,* ed. Mark Poster (New York: Anchor, 1971), p. 151 (trans. Susan Hanson).

2. Alphonse Toussenel, *Passional Zoology; or, Spirit of the Beasts,* trans. M. Edgeworth Lazarus (New York: Fowlers and Wells, 1852), pp. 293, 289–290, 347–348.

3. Friedrich Engels, "Socialism: Utopian and Scientific," in Karl Marx and Friedrich Engels, *Basic Writings on Politics and Philosophy,* ed. Lewis S. Feuer (New York: Anchor, 1959), p. 76 (trans. Edward Aveling).

4. Heinrich Heine, *French Affairs: Letters from Paris,* trans. Charles Godfrey Leland (New York: Dutton, 1906), p. 460.

5. Karl Marx and Friedrich Engels, *Collected Works,* vol. 5 (New York: International Publishers, 1976), pp. 512–514 (*The German Ideology,* vol. 2, trans. C. P. Magill).

6. "Sullied also are those who buy from merchants in order immediately to sell; for they gain nothing unless they employ many deceptions. And, in truth, nothing is more

shameful than fraud." Cicero, *De Officiis* (Treatise on Duty), trans. Walter Miller (Cambridge, Mass.: Harvard University Press, 1921), p. 153.

7. This passage is not found in the English-language edition of Charles Fourier, *The Theory of the Four Movements,* trans. Ian Patterson (Cambridge, England: Cambridge University Press, 1996).

8. "Mesh" translates Fourier's *engrenage.* "Machinal" translates Benjamin's *maschinell,* which is distinguished from *mechanistisch,* "mechanistic" (W4,4).

9. In the summer of 1835, the *New York Sun* reported that Herschel, by means of a giant telescope, had observed paradisal woods and meadows, hills and valleys, even living organisms on the surface of the moon. News of these "discoveries" spread throughout Europe.

10. Jules Michelet, *The People,* trans. John P. McKay (Urbana: University of Illinois Press, 1973), p. 171n.

11. Marx and Engels, *Collected Works,* vol. 4 (New York: International Publishers, 1975), p. 81 (*The Holy Family,* trans. Richard Dixon and Clemens Dutt).

12. Toussenel, *Passional Zoology,* pp. 351–352.

13. Ibid., pp. 334–335.

14. Ibid., p. 341.

15. Ibid., pp. 231–232.

16. Karl Marx, *The Economic and Philosophic Manuscripts of 1844,* trans. Martin Milligan (New York: International Publishers, 1964), p. 132.

17. Charles Gide, Introduction to *Design for Utopia: Selected Writings of Charles Fourier,* trans. Julia Franklin (1901; rpt. New York: Schocken, 1971), p. 15.

18. Ibid., p. 16.

19. Ibid., p. 21.

20. Karl Marx and Friedrich Engels, *Selected Correspondence,* 3rd ed., trans. I. Lasker (Moscow: Progress Publishers, 1975), p. 351 (Engels to Karl Kautsky, April 26, 1884); Marx and Engels, *Collected Works,* vol. 26 (New York: International Publishers, 1990), p. 204 (Engels, *The Origin of the Family,* trans. anonymous).

21. Marx and Engels, *Selected Correspondence,* p. 172.

22. Marx and Engels, *Collected Works,* vol. 38, trans. Peter Ross and Betty Ross (New York: International Publishers, 1982), p. 13. Engels alludes to Galatians 3.24, and to Revelation 21.1–2, in the New Testament.

23. See below, W14,1 and entries following.

24. Fourier, *Theory of the Four Movements,* p. 38n.

25. Fourier, *The Utopian Vision of Charles Fourier,* trans. Jonathan Beecher and Richard Bienvenu (1971; rpt. Columbia: University of Missouri Press, 1983), pp. 308–309.

26. Ibid., p. 319 (first clause only).

27. Fourier, *Theory of the Four Movements,* p. 22.

28. *Harmlosigkeit,* meaning also "ingenuousness."

29. Fourier, *Harmonian Man,* p. 182.

30. Fourier, *Utopian Vision,* p. 319.

31. Ibid., pp. 320–321, 318–320.

32. The *petites hordes* are made up of two-thirds boys; the *petites bandes,* of two-thirds girls.

33. Fourier, *Harmonian Man,* p. 332.

34. Fourier, *Utopian Vision,* p. 316.

35. Ibid., p. 316n.

36. As a child, Fourier would fill his room with elaborately arranged flowers. See his *Utopian Vision,* p. 406, on the "language of flowers."

37. Fourier, *Design for Utopia,* p. 207n.

38. Marx and Engels, *Basic Writings on Politics and Philosophy,* p. 77. Compare J64,2.

39. Fourier, *Utopian Vision,* p. 217.

40. *A Step to Parnassus*—the title of a dictionary of prosody and poetic phrases once used in English schools as an aid in Latin versification. In general, the term refers to any dictionary of this type.

41. Fourier, *Utopian Vision,* p. 232.

42. There are references to Fourier scattered throughout *Die heilige Familie.* Compare W7,8.

43. Charles Baudelaire, *The Mirror of Art,* trans. Jonathan Mayne (London: Phaidon, 1955), pp. 170–171 ("Some French Caricaturists").

X [Marx]

1. Karl Marx, *The Economic and Philosophic Manuscripts of 1844,* trans. Martin Milligan (New York: International Publishers, 1964), pp. 142–143.

2. Ibid., p. 144.

3. Karl Marx and Friedrich Engels, *Collected Works,* vol. 5 (New York: International Publishers, 1976), pp. 44–45 (*The German Ideology,* vol. 1, trans. Clemens Dutt).

4. Ibid., p. 53n. The authors refer to three revolutionary songs of the period of the French Revolution; the refrain of the last was: "Ah! ça ira, ça ira, ça ira! Les aristocrates à la lanterne!" ("Ah, it will certainly happen! Hang the aristocrats from the lamppost!").

5. Marx, *Economic and Philosophic Manuscripts of 1844,* pp. 120–121.

6. Ibid., pp. 139–140.

7. Ibid., p. 143.

8. Ibid., p. 136.

9. Ibid., p. 183. "Annulling of objectivity" translates *Aufhebung der Gegenständlichkeit.*

10. Ibid., pp. 132–134.

11. Marx, *Capital,* vol. 1, trans. Samuel Moore and Edward Aveling (1887; rpt. New York: International Publishers, 1967), p. 292.

12. Karl Marx, *Capital,* vol. 3, trans. Ernest Untermann (1909; rpt. New York: International Publishers, 1967), p. 545. Marx cites G. M. Bell, *The Philosophy of Joint-Stock Banking* (London, 1840), p. 47.

13. Marx, *Capital,* vol. 1, p. 313.

14. Karl Marx, *Capital,* vol. 2, trans. anonymous (New York: International Publishers, 1967), pp. 390, 234. The first passage cited by Fischer is not found in this text.

15. See *Gesammelte Schriften von Karl Marx und Friedrich Engels: Von März 1841 bis März 1844* (Stuttgart, 1902), p. 259 (lead article in the *Kölnische Zeitung,* no. 179). [R.T.]

16. Marx, *Capital,* vol. 1, pp. 505–506.

17. Ibid., p. 166.

18. Ibid., pp. 168, 90.

19. Ibid., pp. 93–94 ("Exchange"). *Hegel's Philosophy of Right,* trans. T. M. Knox (London: Oxford University Press, 1952), p. 240. "Symbol," in these passages, translates *Zeichen.*

20. Marx, *Capital,* vol. 1, p. 91. "Primitive" translates *naturwüchsig.*

21. Ibid., p. 88.

22. Ibid., p. 86 ("Fetishism of Commodities").
23. Ibid., pp. 51, 83.
24. Ibid., p. 64 ("The Form of Value or Exchange Value").
25. Ibid., p. 79 ("The Fetishism of Commodities and the Secret Thereof").
26. Ibid., p. 72.
27. Ibid., p. 64. The note cited by Benjamin below does not appear in the English translation of the text.
28. Ibid., p. 80.
29. Ibid., p. 84–85.
30. Marx, "Critique of the Gotha Program," in Marx and Engels, *Basic Writings on Politics and Philosophy,* ed. Lewis S. Feuer (New York: Anchor, 1959), pp. 112–113.
31. Ibid., pp. 117, 115.
32. Ibid., p. 119.
33. Ibid., p. 121.
34. Benjamin quotes from memory. See Friedrich von Schiller, *Sämtliche Werke,* vol. 1 (Munich, 1965), p. 303. [R.T.] In English in *The Poems and Ballads of Schiller,* trans. Edward Bulwer-Lytton (New York: Clark and Maynard, 1864), p. 266: "By deeds their titles common men create— / The loftier order are by birthright great" ("Votive Tablets").
35. Marx, *Capital,* vol. 1, pp. 184–185 ("The Production of Surplus Value").
36. Georg Simmel, *The Philosophy of Money,* 2nd ed., trans. Tom Bottomore and David Frisby (London: Routledge, 1990), pp. 424–425, 425–426, 426, 426–427. "Cognizability" translates *Erkennbarkeit.*
37. Ibid., pp. 393–394.
38. Karl Korsch, *Karl Marx,* trans. anonymous. (1938; rpt. New York: Russell and Russell, 1963), p. 127.
39. Simmel, *Philosophy of Money,* pp. 482–483.
40. Korsch, *Karl Marx,* p. 122.
41. Ibid., p. 128. Marx wrote the inscription in English. With regard to Benjamin's comparison that follows, Rolf Tiedemann points to the concluding section of *One-Way Street,* "To the Planetarium," but it seems more likely that Benjamin is thinking here of the street sign. Dante's inscription is found at the beginning of Canto 3 of *The Inferno* (line 9): "Lasciate ogne speranza, voi ch'intrate" ("Abandon all hope, ye who enter here"). Trans. John Ciardi (New York: Signet, 1954), p. 42.
42. Korsch, *Karl Marx,* p. 132n.
43. Ibid., pp. 131–136.
44. Ibid., pp. 140–142.
45. Ibid., p. 134.
46. Ibid., pp. 151–153.
47. Ibid., pp. 90–91. Text written by Marx in French. In English in Marx, *Selected Writings,* ed. David McLellan (New York: Oxford University Press, 1977), p. 198 *(The Poverty of Philosophy).*
48. Korsch, *Karl Marx,* pp. 134, 137.
49. Ibid., pp. 123–124.
50. Ibid., pp. 124–126.
51. Ibid., pp. 154–155. It is Benjamin who underlines the third sentence from the end.
52. Ibid., p. 154.
53. Ibid., pp. 233–234. Compare U5,3.
54. Ibid., p. 232.
55. Ibid., p. 117.

56. Ibid., pp. 198–199.

57. Ibid., pp. 201–202.

58. Ibid., p. 50n. The passage from Marx is in Marx and Engels, *Collected Works,* vol. 1 (New York: International Publishers, 1975), p. 203 ("The Philosophical Manifesto of the Historical School of Law," trans. Clemens Dutt).

59. From G. W. F. Hegel, *Encyclopedia of the Philosophical Sciences,* trans. William Wallace, in *Hegel: Selections,* ed. Jacob Loewenberg (New York: Charles Scribner's Sons, 1929), pp. 237–238.

60. Marx, "On the Jewish Question," *Selected Writings,* pp. 54–56.

61. Now in *GS,* vol. 2, pp. 476–478. In English in Walter Benjamin, *"One-Way Street" and Other Writings* (London: Verso, 1979), pp. 359–361.

62. Theodor Adorno, *In Search of Wagner,* trans. Rodney Livingstone (London: Verso, 1981), pp. 82–83. It might be said that the method of citation in *The Arcades Project,* the polyphony of the text, works precisely to counter the phantasmagoria Adorno speaks of.

Y [Photography]

1. *Feenstücke* (a translation of the French *féeries*) are theatrical spectacles involving often pantomime, the appearance of supernatural characters like fairies and enchanters, and the use of stage machinery to create elaborate scenic effects.

2. Anicet Bourgeois and Adolphe Dennery, *Gaspard Hauser,* drama in four acts (Paris, 1838). [R.T.]

3. Nadar's account, "Paris souterrain," was first published in 1867, in connection with the Exposition Universelle. His photographs of the catacombs (former quarries refitted to house skeletons from overfull cemeteries) in 1861–1862, and of the Paris sewers in 1864–1865, in which he employed his patented new process of photography by electric light, followed on his experiments with aerial photography. See the catalogue of the exhibition *Nadar* (New York: Metropolitan Museum of Art, 1995), pp. 98–100, 248 (plate 93 shows one of Nadar's mannequins in the sewer).

4. Nadar actually interviewed the famous chemist on the latter's hundredth birthday. Eight of the series of twenty-seven instantaneous photos are reproduced in *Nadar,* pp. 102–103.

5. Honoré de Balzac, *Cousin Pons,* trans. Herbert J. Hunt (London: Penguin, 1968), pp. 131, 133.

6. Nadar helped organize an exhibition of the work of Constantin Guys in 1895.

7. Charles Baudelaire, *"The Painter of Modern Life" and Other Essays,* trans. Jonathan Mayne (1964; rpt. New York: Da Capo, 1986), p. 201.

8. Charles Baudelaire, *Selected Writings on Art and Literature,* trans. P. E. Charvet (1972; rpt. London: Penguin, 1992), pp. 295–296.

9. Ibid., p. 225.

10. Baudelaire, *The Mirror of Art,* trans. Jonathan Mayne (London: Phaidon, 1955), pp. 230–231; "factual exactitude" translates *exactitude matérielle.*

11. *Les Mariés de la tour Eiffel* (Marriage and the Eiffel Tower), ballet scenario of 1921. "Experience," in this entry, translates *Erlebnis.*

Z [The Doll, The Automaton]

1. *Puppe,* in German, can mean "puppet" as well as "doll."

2. Karl Marx and Friedrich Engels, *Selected Correspondence,* 3rd ed., trans. I. Lasker (Moscow: Progress Publishers, 1975), pp. 129–130.

3. *The Poems of Hesiod,* trans. R. M. Frazer (Norman: University of Oklahoma Press, 1983), p. 98.

4. Charles Baudelaire, *"The Painter of Modern Life" and Other Essays,* trans. Jonathan Mayne (1964; rpt. New York: Da Capo, 1986), pp. 36–37 (citing La Bruyère, *Les Caractères,* "Des Femmes," section 2, and Juvenal, Satire VI). Benjamin refers here to Baudelaire's poem "L'Amour du mensonge," in *Les Fleurs du mal.*

5. The epigram quoted here is actually by Antipatros of Sidon, a Greek poet who flourished around 120 B.C., and whose work is represented (together with that of Antiphilos) in the *Palatine Anthology,* the tenth-century Byzantine compilation of Greek poetic epigrams, of which the only manuscript was found in Count Palatine's library in Heidelberg. It is Antipatros whom Marx cites in volume *1* of *Das Kapital;* see *Capital,* trans. Samuel Moore and Edward Aveling (1887; rpt. New York: International Publishers, 1967), p. 385. Aristotle's discussion of the slave as "living instrument" is in book 1, chapter 3 of his *Politics,* trans. Benjamin Jowett, in *The Basic Works of Aristotle,* ed. Richard McKeon (New York: Random House, 1941), p. 1131.

a [Social Movement]

1. In France, in the nineteenth century, state engineers, in charge of public works, were distinguished from civil engineers, who were employed not by the state but by municipalities or private individuals. [J.L.]

2. That is, "The People's Hive."

3. *Ecrivains publics:* persons who, for a fee, would write out letters and documents for those who could not write.

4. On June 25, the archbishop of Paris, Monsignor Affre, was killed by a stray bullet in the Faubourg Saint-Antoine while trying to arrange a cease fire.

5. Fifteen thousand workers confronted the Garde Nationale in the streets of Lyons, and suffered some 600 casualties before capitulating.

6. In 1830, students of the Ecole Polytechnique led an attack on the Swiss Guards at the Babylone barracks and the Louvre; one student was killed.

7. Jules Michelet, *The People,* trans. John P. McKay (Urbana: University of Illinois Press, 1973), p. 86.

8. In *La Chartreuse de Parme* (chapter 3). For Flaubert's descriptions, see part 3, chapter 1, of *L'Education sentimentale.* Compare the passage by Nescio with Benjamin's idea of "interpretation in detail" *(Ausdeutung in den Einzelheiten)* in N2,1.

9. See "Mutualists," in the "Guide to Names and Terms." In response to a new law limiting free assembly, a republican insurrection broke out, on April 13, 1834, in the Marais district of Paris. During the quick suppression, all the occupants of a house on the Rue Transnonain were killed by General Bugeaud's troops, an incident depicted by Daumier in his lithograph of 1834, *Rue Transnonain.* See Baudelaire's essay "Quelques caricaturistes français," and Figure 29 in this volume.

10. Victor Hugo, *Les Misérables,* trans. Charles E. Wilbour (1862; rpt. New York: Modern Library, 1992), p. 1107 (re 1832).

11. Ibid., pp. 970–971 (re June 5, 1832); pp. 730–731 and 734–735 (re April 1832). *Emeute:* "riot," "disturbance."

12. Ibid., pp. 924–925.

13. *Langes,* perhaps a misprint for *langues,* "languages."

14. Benjamin writes in English: "selfmade-man."

15. Honoré de Balzac, *Eugénie Grandet,* trans. Marion Ayton Crawford (New York: Penguin, 1955), p. 126.

16. Karl Marx, *The Eighteenth Brumaire of Louis Bonaparte,* trans. anonymous (New York: International Publishers, 1963), p. 24. The sentence continues: "and hence necessarily suffers shipwreck."

17. Henrich Heine, *French Affairs,* in *The Works of Henrich Heine,* vol. 8, trans. Charles Godfrey Leland (New York: Dutton, 1906), p. 515.

18. G. W. F. Hegel, *The Philosophy of History,* trans. J. Sibree (1899; rpt. New York: Dover, 1956), pp. 86–87.

19. Honoré de Balzac, *The Country Parson,* trans. anonymous (New York: Fred De Fau, 1923), p. 182.

20. Michelet, *The People,* pp. 111–112, 60.

21. Gustav Mayer, *Friedrich Engels,* trans. Gilbert Highet and Helen Highet (1936; rpt. New York: Howard Fertig, 1969), p. 87. At issue is the drafting of the *Communist Manifesto.*

22. Ibid., p. 76.

23. Ibid., p. 78.

24. Ibid., p. 86. Engels' second visit to Paris took place in October and November 1847.

25. Karl Marx, *The Revolutions of 1848: Political Writings,* vol. 1, ed. David Fernbach (London: Penguin, 1973), pp. 131–132 (trans. anonymous). The essay actually appeared on June 29, 1848.

26. Ibid., p. 134.

27. Mayer, *Friedrich Engels,* p. 102. On May 15, 1848, after a demonstration in favor of Poland, a mob invaded the precincts of the newly elected, conservative Constituent Assembly; order was restored by the Garde Nationale. June 25 was the last full day of the insurrection; General Bréa, General Négrier, and Deputy Charbonnel were killed by rebels. General Cavaignac rejected the rebels' proposals in negotiations the next morning and launched an attack on the last rebel stronghold, in the Faubourg Saint-Antoine.

28. Karl Marx, *Selected Writings,* ed. David McLellan (New York: Oxford University Press, 1977), p. 339 (the original text is in English; the translation cited by Benjamin begins: "unseren guten Freund, unseren Robin Hood . . .").

29. Karl Marx and Friedrich Engels, *Selected Correspondence,* 3rd ed., trans. I. Lasker (Moscow: Progress Publishers, 1975), p. 146.

30. Ibid., pp. 146–147.

31. Karl Marx and Friedrich Engels, *Collected Works,* vol. 38, trans. Peter Ross and Betty Ross (New York: International Publishers, 1982), pp. 66–67 (Engels to the Communist Correspondence Committee).

32. Karl Marx and Friedrich Engels, *Selected Correspondence, 1846–1895,* trans. Dona Torr (New York: International Publishers, 1942), p. 256.

33. Siegfried Kracauer, *Orpheus in Paris: Offenbach and the Paris of His Time,* trans. Gwenda David and Eric Mosbacher (New York: Knopf, 1938), pp. 251–252.

34. Ibid., p. 196.

35. Ibid., p. 100.

36. This system had been established by the law of February 8, 1817, and was designed to put the new moneyed elite into power.

37. Blanqui appeared "at the height of the July Revolution in Mlle. de Montgolfier's salon. Blackened with gunpowder and blood, the young militant crashed his rifle butt against the floor and cried triumphantly: 'Enfoncés, les Romantiques!'" Alan B. Spitzer, *The Revolutionary Theories of Louis Auguste Blanqui* (1957; rpt. New York: AMS Press, 1970), p. 49, citing Geffroy, *L'Enfermé.*

38. *Baudelaire as a Literary Critic,* trans. Lois Boe Hyslop and Francis E. Hyslop, Jr. (University Park: Pennsylvania State University Press, 1964), pp. 252–253.

39. July 28, 1830, the second day of the three days of rioting in Paris known as *les trois glorieuses* ("the three glorious days"). See "July Revolution," in the "Guide to Names and Terms."

40. See a1,3, which concerns the February Revolution.

b [Daumier]

1. The pear (*poire* also means "fool") was Philipon's emblem for Louis Philippe; it became famous as an illustration in history books for generations afterward. The career of Robert Macaire was traced by Daumier in two series of lithographs, from 1836 to 1838 and from 1841 to 1843. The character was first created on the stage by the actor Fréderick Lemaître in a melodrama of 1823, and later in his own play *Robert Macaire,* suppressed in 1834. This archetype of the adroit swindler, who gave the name "Macairism" to all corruption and speculation, was based on Emile de Girardin.

2. Charles Baudelaire, *"The Painter of Modern Life" and Other Essays,* trans. Jonathan Mayne (1964; rpt. New York: Da Capo, 1986), p. 177 ("Some French Caricaturists").

3. Ibid., p. 179.

4. Siegfried Kracauer, *Orpheus in Paris: Offenbach and the Paris of His Time,* trans. Gwenda David and Eric Mosbacher (New York: Knopf, 1938), pp. 176–177.

5. *Baudelaire as a Literary Critic,* trans. Lois Boe Hyslop and Francis E. Hyslop, Jr. (University Park: Pennsylvania State University Press, 1964), p. 75.

d [Literary History, Hugo]

1. *Baudelaire as a Literary Critic,* trans. Lois Boe Hyslop and Francis E. Hyslop, Jr. (University Park: Pennsylvania State University Press, 1964), pp. 267 (1861) and 53 (1851).

2. Novel by Théophile Gautier, published 1835.

3. According to Alfred Delvau's *Dictionnaire de la langue verte,* 2nd ed. (Paris: Emil Dentu, 1867), an *ange gardien* ("guardian angel") is "a man whose trade . . . consists in leading drunks back to their domiciles, to spare them the disagreeable experience of being run over or robbed."

4. *L'Esprit des lois* (The Spirit of Laws; 1748) was a book by Montesquieu which profoundly influenced political thought in Europe and America.

5. "Idols of Fortune."

6. *Baudelaire as a Literary Critic,* p. 152 (letter of August 30, 1857, from Hugo to Baudelaire). The poems referred to are, in English, "The Seven Old Men" and "The Little Old Women." See Baudelaire's letter of September 23(?), 1859, to Hugo, in *Selected Letters of Charles Baudelaire,* trans. Rosemary Lloyd (Chicago: University of Chicago Press, 1986), p. 135: "['Les Petites Vieilles'] was written with the *aim of imitating you.*"

7. *Baudelaire as a Literary Critic,* pp. 56–57, 56. "We who light the lamp early while the cock crows, we whom an uncertain wage recalls, before dawn, to the anvil."

8. The last passage is translated in *Baudelaire as a Literary Critic,* p. 233. The other passage by Baudelaire is from the letter to the editor that was published in *Le Figaro* of April 14, 1864.

9. The title of this poem, which appears in a collection signed by "Savinien Lapointe, Workman Cobbler," and introduced by Sue, plays on the double meaning of *échoppe,*

"workshop" and "graver" or "burin" (the tool used by a cobbler to engrave on leather). In an engraving that accompanies the poem, Lapointe is shown working leather in his shop and, in a caption, lauding Sue as "an eminent surgeon wielding the scalpel" that will remove France's social ills—"scalpel" deriving from the same Latin root as *échoppe*. The work is thus a poem in praise of Sue's scalpel from the *échoppe* of Lapointe in both senses.

10. Part 5 ("Jean Valjean"), book 3.

11. Grandet the miser, Nucingen the German banker, and Bridau the amorous artist figure mainly in the novels *Eugénie Grandet, Splendeurs et misères des courtisanes,* and *Illusions perdues,* respectively. Balzac's *Albert Savarus* (1842) is about a man who labors for years to marry an Italian duchess.

12. Victor Hugo, *Les Misérables,* trans. Charles E. Wilbour (1862; rpt. New York: Modern Library, 1992), p. 864.

13. Honoré de Balzac, *The Country Doctor,* trans. G. Burnham Ives (Philadelphia: George Barrie, 1898), p. 202.

14. Honoré de Balzac, *The Peasantry,* trans. Ellen Marriage and Clara Bell (New York: A. L. Burt, 1899), p. 113.

15. Characters in Henri Murger's *Scènes de la vie bohème.* Marcel is a painter and Rodolphe a journalist, poet, and playwright.

16. Characters, respectively, in Hugo's plays *Ruy Blas* and *Marion de Lorme,* and in his novels *Le Roi s'amuse, Notre-Dame de Paris,* and *Les Misérables.*

17. Honoré de Balzac, *Cousin Pons,* trans. Herbert J. Hunt (London: Penguin, 1968), pp. 132–133.

18. G. K. Chesterton, *Charles Dickens* (1906; rpt. New York: Schocken, 1965), p 247.

19. Ibid., pp. 106, 237.

20. Siegfried Kracauer, *Orpheus in Paris: Offenbach and the Paris of His Time,* trans. Gwenda David and Eric Mosbacher (New York: Knopf, 1938), p. 188.

21. Paul Valéry, "The Place of Baudelaire," in Valéry, *Leonardo, Poe, Mallarmé,* trans. Malcolm Cowley and James R. Lawler (Princeton: Princeton University Press, 1972), p. 199.

22. *Les Mémoires du diable* and *La Closerie des Genêts* are serial novels by Frédéric Soulié. *Où mènent les mauvais chemins* and *La Dernière Incarnation de Vautrin* are titles of sections in Balzac's *Splendeurs et misères des courtisanes.*

23. *Baudelaire as a Literary Critic,* pp. 257, 256–257. Borel was "the leader of a group of stormy young Romantic writers called *bousingos,* presumably because of the wide-brimmed sailor-like hat which they affected" (Hyslops' introduction, p. 256).

24. Charles Baudelaire, *"The Painter of Modern Life" and Other Essays,* trans. Jonathan Mayne (1964; rpt. New York: Da Capo, 1986), p. 119.

25. Charles Baudelaire, *The Prose Poems and "La Fanfarlo,"* trans. Rosemary Lloyd (New York: Oxford University Press, 1991), p. 106.

26. Chesterton, *Charles Dickens,* p. 232.

27. "I ask myself—What are they seeking in the heavens, all those blind men?" In Baudelaire, *The Complete Verse,* trans. Francis Scarfe (London: Anvil, 1986), p. 185 ("Blind Men," 1860). The poem cited, "Ce que dit la Bouche d'ombre" (What the Mouth of Darkness Says), is from Hugo's volume *Les Contemplations* (1856). [R.T.]

28. This passage does not appear in Karl Marx, *Capital,* vol. 1, trans. Samuel Moore and Edward Aveling (1887; rpt. New York: International Publishers, 1967). It can be found in the second German edition of *Kapital* (1872), in a note at the end of the first paragraph of the famous section on commodity fetishism (part 1, chapter 1, section 4).

29. Marx, *Capital,* vol. 1, p. 552n.
30. "Der Ursprung der Zeitung aus dem Geiste der Rhetorik," playing on the title of Nietzsche's first book, *Die Geburt der Tragödie aus dem Geiste der Musik.*

g [The Stock Exchange, Economic History]

1. Karl Marx and Friedrich Engels, *The Holy Family,* trans. Richard Dixon and Clemens Dutt, in Marx and Engels, *Collected Works,* vol. 4 (New York: International Publishers, 1975), pp. 123–124.
2. *Colomba* (1840) is a novel by Prosper Mérimée. The Commendatore appears in the final scene of Mozart's opera *Don Giovanni.*
3. Date of Napoleon's abdication before the Allied armies at Fontainebleau. The letter that follows uses the *tu* form of address as a sign of the writer's contempt.
4. The author goes on (pp. 57–58) to describe the "debacle" in which he was "taken," by a speculator dealing in rabbit fur, to the tune of 12 francs, 15 centimes—a loss that proves ruinous for his finances.
5. Honoré de Balzac, *The Maranas,* trans. G. Burnham Ives (Philadelphia: George Barrie, 1899), p. 126.
6. *The Utopian Vision of Charles Fourier,* trans. Jonathan Beecher and Richard Bienvenu (1971; rpt. Columbia: University of Missouri Press, 1983) pp. 253–254.
7. Karl Marx, *Capital,* vol. 1, trans. Samuel Moore and Edward Aveling (1887; rpt. New York: International Publishers, 1967), p. 24.

k [The Commune]

1. *Agnès de Méranie* (1846), a drama by François Ponsard, is about a twelfth-century queen of France who was dethroned on orders from Pope Innocent III. *Calas* (1819), a play by Victor Ducange, concerns an eighteenth-century Huguenot executed on false charges by an intolerant Toulouse parliament. *Charles IX, ou L'Ecole des rois* (1788) is a verse tragedy by Marie-Joseph Chenier about a cowardly sixteenth-century king; it was a favorite with revolutionary audiences.
2. *Cartes de civisme* were identity cards which the Commune's Committee on Public Safety made compulsory for all citizens in May 1871, in response to heightened fears of spies.
3. *Rimbaud: Complete Works, Selected Letters,* trans. Wallace Fowlie (Chicago: University of Chicago Press, 1966), p. 89 ("The Hands of Jeanne-Marie").
4. It appears to have escaped Benjamin's notice that Courbet, in the caricature, is not standing on just any broken column but on the remains of the Place Vendôme column, which was torn down during the Commune—an act of destruction for which the painter was later convicted. [R.T.] See Figure 36 in this volume.
5. A reference to the dismemberment of Poland in 1815, after the Congress of Vienna.
6. Gustav Mayer, *Friedrich Engels,* trans. Gilbert Highet and Helen Highet (1936; rpt. New York: Howard Fertig, 1969), p. 220.
7. Ibid., pp. 220–221.
8. Karl Marx and Friedrich Engels, *Selected Correspondence,* 3rd ed., trans. I. Lasker (Moscow: Progress Publishers, 1975), pp. 82–83.
9. Henrik Ibsen, *Letters and Speeches,* ed. Evert Sprinchorn (New York: Hill and Wang, 1964), p. 106 (trans. Nilsen Laurvik and Mary Morison).
10. After the victory at Sedan and the capture of Napoleon III, on September 1, 1870, Prussian forces advanced on Paris and, by September 23, had surrounded the city.

The siege lasted until the end of January, when an armistice was signed, ending the Franco-Prussian War.

11. In the course of "Bloody Week" (May 21–28, 1871), the Communards resisted Thiers's forces street by street, retreating toward the heart of Paris. In their desperation, they executed a number of hostages, including the archbishop of Paris.
12. At issue is Thiers's art collection.

l [The Seine, The Oldest Paris]

1. Originally added to the temple at Luxor by Ramses II, the obelisk was installed on the Place de la Concorde in 1831. The prince de Joinville was François Ferdinand Philippe d'Orléans, son of Louis Philippe.
2. Victor Hugo, *Les Misérables,* trans. Charles E. Wilbour (1862; rpt. New York: Modern Library, 1992), pp. 1100–1101.

m [Idleness]

1. Plato, *The Collected Dialogues,* ed. Edith Hamilton and Huntington Cairns (New York: Pantheon, 1963), pp. 1397–1398 (*Laws,* 832a, trans. A.E. Taylor).
2. "Leisure" translates *Musse;* "idleness" translates *Müssiggang;* and "world at large" translates *Lebewelt.* On idleness, compare J87a,2–3.
3. Karl Marx, *The Revolutions of 1848: Political Writings,* vol. 1, ed. David Fernbach (London: Penguin, 1973), p. 192 (from the *Neue rheinische Zeitung,* Dec. 15, 1848). "Indolence" translates *Faulheit.*
4. "Experience" here translates *die Erfahrung;* "immediate experience," *das Erlebnis.* In the passages that follow in this convolute, the former is also translated by "long experience" and "connected experience," and the latter by "individual experience" and "experience" preceded by the definite or indefinite article. (Exceptions are indicated in angle brackets and notes.) *Erfahrung* (etymologically rooted in the notion of "going through") presupposes tradition and continuity; *Erlebnis,* something more spontaneous, entails shock and discontinuity. In notes connected with the composition of "Über einige Motive bei Baudelaire" ‹Some Motifs in Baudelaire›, Benjamin writes that experiences in the sense of *Erlebnisse* are "by nature unsuitable for literary composition," and "work is distinguished by the fact that it begets *Erfahrungen* out of *Erlebnissen*" (*GS,* vol. 1, p. 1183). See also, in the text below, "First Sketches," Q°,24, and *SW,* vol. 2, pp. 553 (on *Erfahrung*) and 582 (on *erlebte Erfahrung*).
5. Which is to say, tradition translated into the language of shock.
6. Max Horkheimer, "Traditional and Critical Theory," in Horkheimer, *Critical Theory,* trans. Matthew J. O'Connell (New York: Continuum, 1995), pp. 234–236; and idem, "Remarks on Philosophical Anthropology," in Horkheimer, *Between Philosophy and Social Science,* trans. G. Frederick Hunter, Matthew S. Kramer, and John Torpey (Cambridge, Mass.: MIT Press, 1993), p. 664.
7. ". . . der geläufigen Erfahrung den Erlebnischarakter abzumerken." In the sentence following, "the experience" translates *die Erfahrung.*
8. Marx, *Capital,* vol. 1, trans. Samuel Moore and Edward Aveling (1887; rpt. New York: International Publishers, 1967), pp. 333–334.
9. Reprinted in *GS,* vol. 2, p. 447, lines 13–20, and p. 448, lines 16–33. [R.T.] In English, "The Storyteller," in *Illuminations,* trans. Harry Zohn (New York: Schocken, 1969), pp. 91–92, 92–93 (section 9).
10. Literally, "gilded youth," fashionable and wealthy young people; specifically, in France, the fashionable set of the reactionary party in 1794.

11. *Gleichschaltung* ("alignment"—term used by the Nazis as a euphemism for the elimination of undesirable persons from public and professional life), chiming here with
Umschaltung ("gearing" or "switching") in the preceding sentence. "Empathy" translates *Einfühlung.*

12. Jean-Jacques Rousseau, *The Confessions,* trans. J. M. Cohen (Baltimore: Penguin,
1954), p. 591. The passage continues: "The idleness I love . . . is the idleness of a
child. . . . I love . . . to follow nothing but the whim of the moment."

13. *The Letters of Gustave Flaubert, 1857–1880,* trans. Francis Steegmuller (Cambridge,
Mass.: Harvard University Press, 1982), p. 24. "Mon âme est triste et j'ai lu tous les
livres" is Benjamin's exquisite misquotation of the opening of Mallarmé's poem
"Brise marine" (see J87,5). The line from Goethe is from *Faust,* trans. Louis Macneice
(New York: Oxford University Press, 1952), p. 19 (part 1, line 354).

14. Oswald Spengler, *The Decline of the West,* vol. 2, trans. Charles Francis Atkinson
(New York: Knopf, 1928), p. 100.

15. Ibid., p. 90.

p [Anthropological Materialism, History of Sects]

1. Christian Dietrich Grabbe, *Werke und Briefe,* vol. 1 (Darmstadt, 1960), pp. 142ff.
[R.T.]

2. Daumier's series of forty lithographs on career women was published under the title
Les Bas-bleus in *Le Charivari* in 1844. It was followed by series on socialist women and
divorced women.

3. *The New Oxford Annotated Bible* (New York: Oxford University Press, 1977), p. 1202
(Matthew 23.9). On the woman caught in adultery, see John 8.1–11.

4. John 2.1–11.

5. Honoré de Balzac, *The Girl with the Golden Eyes,* trans. G. B. Ives, with Walter
Robins and E. P. Robins (Philadelphia: George Barrie, 1896), p. 310. Curtius is
concerned here with the opening paragraph of Balzac's novel, in which Paris is
presented as a city of masks.

6. See Gustav Mayer, *Friedrich Engels,* trans. Gilbert Highet and Helen Highet (1936;
rpt. New York: Howard Fertig, 1969), pp. 14–16. The passages quoted by Benjamin
are not found in this English edition.

7. Karl Marx and Friedrich Engels, *Selected Correspondence,* 3rd ed., trans. I. Lasker
(Moscow: Progress Publishers, 1975), pp. 18–19.

8. *Baudelaire as a Literary Critic,* trans. Lois Boe Hyslop and Francis E. Hyslop, Jr.
(University Park: Pennsylvania State University Press, 1964), p. 336.

r [Ecole Polytechnique]

1. See "Ecole Polytechnique" in the "Guide to Names and Terms."

2. Jules Michelet, *The People,* trans. John P. McKay (Urbana: University of Illinois Press,
1973), pp. 195–196. Reference is to the extremely severe winter of 1794–1795 (Year
III, according to the Revolutionary calendar), after the guillotining of Robespierre,
on July 28, 1794, had ended the Reign of Terror.

3. Honoré de Balzac, *The Country Parson,* trans. anonymous (New York: Fred De Fau,
1923), p. 187.

4. In 1833, Thiers had presented to the Chamber of Deputies a project for erecting
detached forts outside the city. The proposal was abandoned; but in 1840, on account of new threats of war, a royal ordinance directed that Paris be encircled by
fortifications. This project was implemented in February 1841. The resulting *enceinte*

(destroyed in 1919) took in a number of neighboring townships, such as Montmartre and Belleville, which were not administratively attached to the capital until 1859. [J.L.]

5. Karl Marx, *The Revolutions of 1848: Political Writings,* vol. 1, ed. David Fernbach (London: Penguin, 1973), pp. 129–130.

First Sketches

1. *Le Péril bleu* (The Blue Peril) was published in Paris in 1911. [R.T.]
2. Benjamin knew Carl Gustav Carus' Paris journal through excerpts in Rudolf Borchardt's anthology *Der Deutsche in der Landschaft* (Munich, 1927), and through the texts selected by Eckart von Sydow (Leipzig, 1926); see his review of these two books in *GS,* vol. 3, pp. 91–94 and 56–57. [R.T.]
3. See note 9 in Convolute D.
4. Allusion to the stabilization of the franc by Raymond Poincaré in June 1928. [J.L.]
5. The Théâtre de Comte was located in the Passage des Panoramas before being moved to the Passage Choiseul in 1826. It combined demonstrations of physical agility, prestidigitation, and ventriloquy with playlets performed by child actors. [J.L.] On the shop names, see below, E°,5.
6. Jacques de Lacretelle, "Le Rêveur parisien," *Nouvelle Revue française,* 166 (July 1, 1927), pp. 23–39. [R.T.]
7. Benjamin this time may have in mind not the character in E. T. A. Hoffmann (see H1,1) but a large music hall built in 1893 on the Boulevard des Capucines. [J.L.]
8. The Petit-Coblentz is the name which, during the Directory (1795–1799), was given to a part of the Boulevard des Italiens that was frequented mainly by émigrés. [J.L.]
9. The Passage du Pont-Neuf was situated between the Rue Mazarine and the Rue de Seine, in the sixth *arrondissement.* The old Passage Henri IV was located near the Rue des Bons-Enfants, in the first *arrondissement.* [J.L.] On Zola's *Thérèse Raquin,* see H1,3.
10. The Passage du Bois-de-Boulogne became the Passage du Prado in 1929. [J.L.]
11. *Le Fantôme de l'Opéra,* a novel by Gaston Leroux, was published in Paris in 1910. After E°,30, a page was cut out of the manuscript. [R.T.]
12. *L'Hermite de la Chaussée d'Antin, ou Observations sur les moeurs et les usages parisiens au commencement du XIXᵉ siècle,* by Victor-Joseph Jouy (1764–1846), was first published as a newspaper serial and later collected in various book formats. The frontispiece of the 1813 edition is a drawing of the author sitting, quill in hand, at his writing desk in his library. Projected on the wall above him is an illuminated scene of Parisian street life; under this drawing is the following inscription in longhand: "My cell is like a CAMERA OBSCURA in which external objects are recalled."
13. A *pièce à tiroirs* is an episodic play in which the scenes unfold, one after another, like a row of drawers opening and closing in a chest. Gutzkow's term is *Schubladenstück.*
14. "Street lamp"; in argot, "policeman." [J.L.]
15. It was Bordier-Marcet who invented the ring-shaped, hanging *lampe astrale,* whose light filtered down from above. [J.L.]
16. The *Encyclopaedia Britannica* of 1875 (vol. 3, p. 36) indicates that a "Mr. Vallance of Brighton" first had the idea of utilizing the pneumatic principle—that is, a vacuum-tube system—to transport passengers. Experiments were run in the 1840s. [J.L.]
17. See René Crevel, "L'Esprit contre la raison," *Cahiers du Sud* (December 1927). [J.L.]
18. See T2a,3, and the entry on Nodier in the "Guide to Names and Terms."
19. A cheval glass, or swing-mirror.
20. Compare C1,3, including note 3, and F°,10.

21. Benjamin wrote this sketch in French.
22. Quoted in French without indication of source.
23. See Marcel Proust, *Remembrance of Things Past,* vol. 1, trans. C. K. Scott Moncrieff (New York: Random House, 1925), pp. 1023 and 995, respectively.
24. Louis Aragon, *Paris Peasant,* trans. Simon Watson Taylor (1971; rpt. Boston: Exact Change, 1994), p. 71.
25. Charles Baudelaire, *Artificial Paradise,* trans. Ellen Fox (New York: Herder and Herder, 1971), p. 68.
26. Ibid. See H2,1.
27. Anatole France, *The Garden of Epicurus,* trans. Alfred Allinson (New York: Dodd, Mead, 1923), p. 129.
28. See B1,5.
29. Or "dream face" *(Traumgesicht).*
30. See Walter Benjamin, *The Origin of German Tragic Drama,* trans. John Osborne (London: Verso, 1977), pp. 44–48, clearly a central passage for the logic of Benjamin's theory of reading. "Myriorama": a landscape picture made of a number of separate sections that can be put together in various ways to form distinct scenes.
31. Rainer Maria Rilke, "Puppen: Zu den Wachspuppen von Lotte Pritzel," in *Sämtliche Werke,* vol. 6 (Frankfurt am Main, 1966), pp. 1063–1074. [R.T.]
32. Benjamin's work on the poet Christoph Friedrich Heinle disappeared in 1933, together with Heinle's literary remains. [R.T.] The nod *(numen)* of the gods is intermittent.
33. Reference is to the thirteenth of Giacomo Leopardi's *Pensieri,* in the edition prized by Benjamin, *Gedanken* (Leipzig, 1922), pp. 16ff. [R.T.] In English: *Pensieri,* trans. W. S. Di Piero (Baton Rouge: Louisiana State University Press, 1981), pp. 46–47, on the subject of anniversaries. "Actualization" here, as in K2,3, translates *Vergegenwärtigung.* "Making things present," here as in H2,3, translates *sich gegenwärtig machen.* "The bodily life" translates *das leibliche Leben.*
34. See note 3 in Convolute S.
35. Presumably the writer Lothar Brieger-Wasservogel, who at one time was a friend of Benjamin's wife, Dora. [R.T.]
36. See, in particular, Goethe's *Versuch einer Witterungslehre* of 1825. [R.T.]
37. See note 4 in Convolute D.
38. That is, "time" and "weather."
39. Reading *betten* here (as in P1,10) for *leiten.*
40. *Mode und Zynismus* (Fashion and Cynicism), by Friedrich Theodor Vischer; see I°,1 and J°,1. [R.T.]
41. The object of this reference to the *Baudelaire-Buch* has not been identified. (Benjamin had been collecting materials on Baudelaire for *The Arcades Project* since the end of the 1920s, though his plan for making a book on Baudelaire out of these materials evidently did not take shape until 1938; see *GS,* vol. 1, p. 1160, 6.1.)
42. See Proust, *Remembrance of Things Past,* vol. 2 (New York: Random House, 1932), p. 385 (*The Captive,* trans. C. K. Scott Moncrieff). (Thanks to Julia Prewitt Brown for this reference.)
43. . . . *monde—und die Mode.*
44. "Know thyself."
45. Possibly refers to the description of the streets of Paris at the beginning of "Ferragus," the first episode of Balzac's *Histoire des treize.* [J.L.]
46. Heinrich Mann, *Eugénie, oder Die Bürgerzeit* (Berlin, Vienna, Leipzig, 1928). [R.T.]
47. Sigfried Giedion, *Bauen in Frankreich* (Leipzig and Berlin, 1928), p. 3. [R.T.]
48. See note 6 in Convolute K.

49. Proust, *A la Recherche du temps perdu,* vol. 1 (Paris, 1954), pp. 644ff. [R.T.] In English in *Remembrance of Things Past,* vol. 1, p. 490 (*Within a Budding Grove*). See S11,1.

50. See note 12 in Convolute M.

51. On the former plan, see note 7 in Convolute S; and on the latter, see the fragments in Hugo von Hofmannsthal, *Sämtliche Werke,* vol. 29 (Frankfurt, 1978), pp. 202–206. [R.T.]

52. André Breton, *Nadja,* trans. Richard Howard (New York: Grove Weidenfeld, 1960), p. 152.

53. Proust, *Remembrance of Things Past,* vol. 1, p. 323. (*Renfermé:* stuffy, close. *Ça sent le renfermé:* "It smells musty in here.")

54. Benjamin had planned to write on Ludwig Tieck's novella *Der Blonde Eckbert,* published in 1812. [R.T.]

55. Perhaps Aragon, *Paris Peasant,* pp. 81–84.

56. This passage appears also in Benjamin's review "Krisis des Darwinismus?" published in *Die literarische Welt,* April 12, 1929 (*GS,* vol. 4, p. 534). [R.T.]

57. "Agnoszierung des 'Jetzt' in den Dingen." The term *agnosziert,* "acknowledged," shows up in J51a,6.

58. Marx, *Capital,* vol. 1, trans. Samuel Moore and Edward Aveling (1887; rpt. New York: International Publishers, 1967), pp. 83–84; vol. 3, trans. Ernest Untermann (1909; rpt. New York: International Publishers, 1967), pp. 25–210, esp. 173ff. See, in this volume, Rolf Tiedemann, "Dialectics at a Standstill," note 15.

59. Louis Schneider, *Les Maîtres de l'opérette française: Offenbach* (Paris, 1923). [R.T.]

60. *Le Guide historique et anecdotique de Paris: L'Histoire de Paris, de ses monuments, de ses révolutions, de ses célébrités, de sa vie artistique, scientifique, mondaine,* published under the direction of E. Cuervo-Marquez (Paris, 1929). [R.T.]

61. The memoirs of Prince Metternich, published in two volumes. [R.T.]

62. *La Muette de Portici* (The Mute Girl of Portici), by Daniel Auber, was regarded as the archetype of grand opera. See note 10 in Convolute B.

63. "Eager for new things."

64. Henri Sée, *Französische Wirtschaftsgeschichte* (French Economic History), vol. 1 (Jena, 1930). [R.T.]

"The Arcades of Paris"

1. See note 2 in Convolute H.

2. *Seitenhimmeln,* possibly an error in transcription; in Q3,2, Benjamin has *Seidenhimmeln,* "silken skies." And in the third sentence of this passage, instead of *Land,* Q3,2 reads *Band,* "ribbon." See "Moonlit Nights on the Rue la Boétie," in *SW,* vol. 2, pp. 107–108.

3. In German, *List,* which originally meant "knowledge" and referred to techniques of hunting and war, to magical abilities and artistic skill.

4. Greek name for Castor and Pollux, twin sons of Leda who were transformed by Zeus into the constellation Gemini. They had a cult in Lacedaemon, where they were symbolized by the *dokana,* two upright pieces of wood connected by two crossbeams. Presumably an allusion to Benjamin's collaboration with Franz Hessel.

"The Ring of Saturn"

1. See *GS,* vol. 7, pp. 232–237. In English in *SW,* vol. 2, pp. 563–567.

2. Charles-François Viel, *De l'Impuissance des mathématiques pour assurer la solidité des bâtimens, et recherches sur la construction des ponts* (Paris, 1805). [R.T.]

3. Alfred Gotthold Meyer, *Eisenbauten: Ihre Geschichte und Ästhetik* (Esslingen, 1907), p. 93. [R.T.] Compare F4a,2.

Materials for the Exposé of 1935

1. In Etienne Cabet's novel *Voyage en Icarie* (1839), the narrator learns that in Icaria "fashion never changes; that there are only a certain number of different shapes for hats—toques, turbans, and bonnets; and that the model for each of these shapes had been . . . decided upon by a committee." *Oeuvres d'Etienne Cabet,* 3rd ed. (Paris: Bureau du Populaire, 1845), p. 137. See B4,2.
2. See B2,5. See also section 3 of the "Exposé of 1935, Early Version."
3. Presumably a reference to Fourier.
4. See Franz Kafka, "The Cares of a Family Man," in Kafka, *The Complete Stories* (New York: Schocken, 1971), pp. 427–429 (trans. Willa Muir and Edwin Muir). Odradek is a diminutive creature, resembling a flat star-shaped spool for thread, who can stand upright and roll around, but can never be laid hold of, and has no fixed abode. You might think he was a broken-down remnant, but in his own way he is perfectly finished. He can talk, but often remains mute.
5. Could also be construed as "the knocking that startles us out of sleep."
6. "Fateful date": possibly an allusion to the dramatic Socialist gains, that year, in the Chamber of Deputies.
7. "Traumkitsch" (first published in 1927) is in *GS,* vol. 2, pp. 620–622; in English in *SW,* vol. 2, pp. 3–5. Benjamin is concerned here with "distilling" the "sentimentality of our parents."
8. The second stage of work on *The Arcades Project* began in early 1934, when Benjamin was commissioned to write an article in French on Haussmann for *Le Monde,* a periodical edited at that time by Alfred Kurella. The article was never written, but Benjamin's preliminary studies remain, in the form of the drafts and outline printed here as No. 19. The first draft is in French; the second and third drafts are in German. The outline begins in French and switches to German after the second "embellissement stratégique."
9. The schemes printed as Nos. 20 and 21 were preparatory to the drafting of the exposé of 1935. The first is dated by Benjamin himself; the second most likely dates from the beginning of May 1935. The reflections contained in No. 22 appear to belong to a more extended scheme, which has not been preserved.
10. Nos. 23, 24, and 25 apparently date from after the drafting of the exposé of 1935. No. 25 was written by Benjamin on the back of a letter of December 22, 1938, addressed to him; while clearly connected to central concerns of the *Arcades* complex, it could relate as well to the project of a book on Baudelaire or to the theses "Über den Begriff der Geschichte" (On the Concept of History).

"Dialectics at a Standstill"

The following notes are by Rolf Tiedemann. Citations from the "Convolutes," the "First Sketches," and the "Early Drafts" are referenced by tags for the individual entries.

1. Translated as "A Portrait of Walter Benjamin," in T. W. Adorno, *Prisms,* trans. Samuel Weber and Shierry Weber (Cambridge, Mass.: MIT Press, 1981), pp. 221–241.
2. See Walter Benjamin, *Briefe,* ed. Gershom Scholem and Theodor W. Adorno (Frankfurt: Suhrkamp, 1966), passim. In English in *The Correspondence of Walter Benjamin,*

trans. Manfred R. Jacobson and Evelyn M. Jacobson (Chicago: University of Chicago Press, 1994). Subsequent references to the *Correspondence* will appear in the text as "Letters." For a complete compilation of Benjamin's statements in letters about the *Passagen-Werk* (within the limits of available correspondence), see Benjamin, *Gesammelte Schriften,* vol. 5 (Frankfurt: Suhrkamp, 1982), pp. 1081–1183 (annotations by Rolf Tiedemann). Subsequent references to the *Gesammelte Schriften* will appear in the text in parentheses, volume number followed by page number—e.g., "5:1063."

3. See *The Correspondence of Walter Benjamin and Gershom Scholem, 1932–1940,* trans. Gary Smith and André Lefevere (New York: Schocken, 1989), p. 121. Subsequent references to this work will appear in the text as "Scholem Letters."

4. Adorno, *Prisms,* p. 239.

5. See Rolf Tiedemann, *Dialektik im Stillstand* (Frankfurt: Suhrkamp, 1983), pp. 190–191, n. 18a, on the current legend of a "rearrangement" of the "Aufzeichnungen und Materialien" in the *Passagen-Werk.*

6. According to Adorno, Benjamin's intention was "to eliminate all overt commentary and to have the meanings emerge solely through a shock-like montage of the material. . . . His magnum opus, the crowning of his antisubjectivism, was to consist solely of citations" (Adorno, *Prisms,* 239). Though this thought may seem typical of Benjamin, I am convinced that Benjamin did not intend to work in that fashion. There is no remark in the letters attesting to this. Adorno supports his position with two entries from the *Passagen-Werk* itself (see N1,10 and N1a,8), which can hardly be interpreted in that way. One of these already turned up in the "First Sketches" of 1928 or 1929 (see O°,36), at a time when Benjamin stated that he was still considering an essay, which he had begun in the "Early Drafts"—by no means, however, in the form of a montage of quotations.

7. "One-Way Street," in Benjamin, *Selected Writings, Vol. 1: 1913–1926* (Cambridge, Mass.: Harvard University Press, 1996), p. 466. Subsequent references to the *Selected Writings* will appear in the text as *SW.*

8. This had been preceded by the plan—which probably did not last long—to collaborate with Franz Hessel on an article about arcades. See 5:1341.

9. "Surrealism," in Benjamin, *Selected Writings, Vol. 2: 1927–1934* (Cambridge, Mass.: Harvard University Press, 1999), p. 210.

10. Here and in what follows, references to the first and second sketch are in the same manner that Benjamin referred to them in his letter to Gretel Adorno of August 16, 1935: merely in quotation marks, so to speak. No single text is meant by "sketch"; the "second sketch," especially, does not denote the 1935 exposé. Benjamin had in mind the concept of the work, such as it can be inferred from an interpretation of the totality of the notes from both stages of his project.

11. See Hermann Schweppenhäuser, "Propaedeutics of Profane Illumination," in *On Walter Benjamin: Critical Essays and Recollections,* ed. Gary Smith (Cambridge, Mass.: MIT Press, 1988), pp. 33–50.

12. See mainly "On the Program of the Coming Philosophy," *Philosophical Forum* 15, 1–2 (Fall–Winter 1983–1984), pp. 41–51, now in *SW,* 1:100–110; this citation originates from an early fragment "Über die Wahrnehmung," 6:33–38 (*SW,* 1:93–96).

13. See "Doctrine of the Similar," in *SW,* 2:694–698; and "On the Mimetic Faculty," *SW,* 2:720–722. One of the latest texts in the "First Sketches" to the *Passagen-Werk* seems to be a germinating cell of Benjamin's theory of mimesis (see 5:1038; Q°,24).

14. See Rolf Tiedemann, *Studien zur Philosophie Walter Benjamins,* 2nd ed. (Frankfurt: Suhrkamp, 1973), pp. 76–77, 98–99.

15. In the "First Sketches," in which economic categories are used either metaphysically

or in a desultory fashion, we find uncommented references to two passages in the first and third volumes of *Capital,* and these references are to the "original edition" (see 5:1036; Q°,4). This could be especially instructive in the case of the first volume, whose first edition of 1867—the original edition referred to—is very rare and is almost never cited. We may surmise that Horkheimer or Adorno referred Benjamin to the pages in question during the "historical conversations" in the fall of 1929. The library of the Institut für Sozialforschung owned, at that time, a copy of the original edition, and at least Horkheimer was wont to quote from scarce editions. This conjecture is corroborated when one checks the relevant passage in the first edition of *Capital:* it deals with the definitive formulations of commodity fetishism—that is, the very concept whose "unfolding" would be "the central core" of the second *Passagen-Werk* sketch. Since the manuscript of the "First Sketches" was abandoned shortly after this entry, it is very possible that Benjamin's abandoning the manuscript may have been caused by the obstacles created by the suggestion that it was necessary for him to read *Capital.* Finally, a letter from Adorno to Horkheimer of June 8, 1935, which is absent from the fifth volume because it was made available only after the edition's publication, may well turn speculation into certainty. Adorno characterizes the first exposé as "an attempt to unlock the nineteenth century as 'style' by means of the category of 'commodity as dialectical image.'" He adds: "This concept owes as much to you as it is close to me (and as I have been beholden to it for many years). In that memorable conversation in the Hotel Carlton [in Frankfurt] which you, Benjamin, and I had about dialectical images, together with Asja Lacis and Gretel, it was you who claimed that feature of a historical image as central for the commodity; since that conversation, both Benjamin's and my thoughts on this matter have been reorganized in a decisive way. The Kierkegaard book [by Adorno] contains their rudiments, the 'Arcades' sketch embraces them quite explicitly."

16. Karl Marx, *Capital,* vol. 1, trans. Samuel Moore and Edward Aveling (1887; rpt. New York: International Publishers, 1967), p. 72.

17. Ibid., p. 73.

18. See Jürgen Habermas, "Walter Benjamin: Consciousness-Raising or Rescuing Critique," in Smith, ed., *On Walter Benjamin: Critical Essays and Recollections,* pp. 90–128.

19. See Tiedemann, *Studien,* pp. 79–89.

20. Walter Benjamin, *The Origin of German Tragic Drama,* trans. John Osborne (London: Verso, 1977), p. 48. Subsequent references to this work will appear in the text as *Trauerspiel.*

21. See Walter Benjamin, "Theses on the Philosophy of History," in Benjamin, *Illuminations,* trans. Harry Zohn (New York: Schocken, 1969), pp. 260–261. Subsequent references to this work will appear in the text as *Illuminations.*

22. See Tiedemann, "Historical Materialism or Political Messianism?" *Philosophical Forum* 15, nos. 1–2 (Fall–Winter 1983–1984), pp. 71–104.

23. Benjamin never brought himself to define these categories at length, yet they are the basis of all his thoughts on the *Passagen-Werk,* which he identified with the "world of dialectical images" and for which dialectic at a standstill was to be "the quintessence of the method" (P°,4). He apparently developed the theory of dialectical images mainly in conversations with Adorno. Although both concepts are absent from Benjamin's publications during his lifetime, the "dialectical image" appears—with reference to its Benjaminian origins—in Adorno's *Habilitationsschrift* on Kierkegaard, which was published in 1933 (Adorno, *Kierkegaard: Construction of the Aesthetic,* trans. Robert Hullot-Kentor [Minneapolis: University of Minnesota Press, 1988]). I shall here only allude to the fact that Adorno's interpretation of the concept differs from

Benjamin's in more than mere nuances. In his Kierkegaard book, Adorno equated the dialectical image with allegory, and later he also seems to liken it to phantasmagoria (see N5,2, and 5:1136). Benjamin characterized Adorno's definition of the "antinomy of appearance and meaning" as "fundamental" for both allegory and phantasmagoria, but he found it "confusing" in its application to the "dialectical image" (1:1174). The difference might be found in the connection Benjamin made between the dialectical image and elements of messianism—a connection to which Adorno, the more scrupulous Marxist, could not accede. One may try to put it this way: the phantasmagorias of the arcade or the collector as such are not dialectical images in Benjamin's sense; both the arcades and the collector become dialectical images only when the historical materialist *deciphers* them *as* phantasmagorias. But in Benjamin's opinion, the key that allows the historical materialist to unlock the code remains connected to the discovery of a messianic force in history (see 1:1232).

24. Marx, *Capital,* p. 20.
25. Adorno, *Prisms,* p. 233.
26. Marx, *Capital,* p. 763.
27. See Gershom Scholem, *Major Trends in Jewish Mysticism,* 3rd ed. (London: Thames and Hudson, 1955), pp. 283–287; and idem, *On the Kabbalah and Its Symbolism,* trans. Ralph Manheim (New York: Schocken, 1965), pp. 126ff. See also Tiedemann, *Dialektik im Stillstand,* pp. 102ff.
28. Karl Marx, *Briefe aus den "Deutsch-Französischen Jahrbüchern,"* in Karl Marx and Friedrich Engels, *Werke,* vol. 1, 2nd ed. (Berlin: Dietz, 1957), p. 346.
29. Walter Benjamin, "Theologico-Political Fragment," in Benjamin, *Reflections,* trans. Edmund Jephcott (New York: Schocken, 1978), p. 312.

"The Story of Old Benjamin"

1. Walter Benjamin, *Briefe,* vol. 1, ed. Gershom Scholem and Theodor W. Adorno (Frankfurt: Suhrkamp, 1966), p. 298. In English: *The Correspondence of Walter Benjamin, 1910–1940,* trans. Manfred R. Jacobson and Evelyn M. Jacobson (Chicago: University of Chicago Press, 1994), p. 206 (letter of February 24, 1923, to Florens Christian Rang).
2. In *Agesilaus Santander.* The translation here is by Lisa Fittko. See *GS,* vol. 6, p. 521 (August 12, 1933). In English in Walter Benjamin, *Selected Writings,* vol. 2 (Cambridge, Mass.: Harvard University Press, 1999), p. 713.
3. Hannah Arendt, *Men in Dark Times* (New York: Harcourt, Brace and World, 1968), p. 161.

Guide to Names and Terms

Abdel Krim (1885–1963). Leader of the Moors in the Rif region of Morocco. Ultimately defeated by French and Spanish forces in 1926, and exiled to Réunion.

About, Edmond (1828–1885). French novelist, playwright, and journalist.

Absalom. Son of King David in the Old Testament. He revolts against his father and is killed. See 2 Samuel 18.

Académie Française. Body founded in 1634 to promote the advancement of French literature.

Adler, Max (1873–1937). Austrian lawyer, student of Neo-Kantian and positivist philosophy. He was active in the Austrian Social Democratic Party, and cofounder of *Marx-Studien* (1904). Author of *Soziologie des Marxismus* (1930–1932).

Aimé Martin, Antoine-Louis (1786–1841). Man of letters, professor, and librarian at the Bibliothèque Sainte-Geneviève in Paris.

Alberti, Leon Battista (1404–1472). Italian architect, painter, writer; first to investigate the laws of perspective. Author of *De re aedificatoria* (1452).

Albertus Magnus. Pseudonym of Albert von Bollstädt (1193?–1280), German theologian, scientist, and philosopher. He was reputed to be a magician because of his scientific pursuits. Canonized in 1932.

Alhambra. Fortress and palace erected by the Moors near Granada, Spain, in the thirteenth and early fourteenth centuries.

Ambigu. Parisian theater built in 1827; a central venue for popular melodramas. It was demolished in 1966.

Amiel, Henri (1821–1881). Swiss poet and philosopher; author of the introspective *Journal intime* (1883–1884).

Anarcharsis. Scythian sage who, according to Herodotus, traveled widely to learn the customs of many nations.

Ancelle, Narcisse-Désiré (1801–1888). French lawyer. In 1844 Baudelaire's mother appointed him as her son's legal guardian.

Annenkov, Pavel (1812–1882). Russian man of letters, personally acquainted with Marx in the 1840s.

Anschütz, Ottomar (1846–1907). Polish-born German photographer who conducted experiments in high-speed photography; invented a tachyscope that was a forerunner of the motion-picture apparatus.

Antony. Play by Alexandre Dumas (1831). Its melancholy, star-crossed hero influenced a generation of young Frenchmen.

Arago, François (1786–1853). Scientist who investigated the theory of light and electromagnetism; director of the Paris observatory (1830). He took part in the July Revolution and was minister of war in the Provisional Government (1848). Opponent of Napoleon III.

Arago, Jacques (1790–1855). Brother of François Arago; traveler, novelist, and playwright.

Aragon, Louis (1897–1982). Novelist, poet, essayist; a leader of the Dadaists and later of the Surrealists. Author of *Feu de joie* (1920), *Une Vague de rêves* (1924), *Le Paysan de Paris* (1926), *Les Voyages de l'Impériale* (1940).

Argand, Aimé (1755–1803). Swiss physicist; inventor of a highly effective oil lamp.

Artois, comte d'. Title granted (1757) by Louis XV of France to his grandson, later Charles X.

Assassins. Islamic sect of the eleventh to thirteenth centuries that considered the murder of its enemies a religious duty.

Asselineau, Charles (1820–1874). French critic and bibliophile. Close friend and later editor and biographer of Baudelaire, who reviewed his collection of short stories, *La Double Vie,* in 1859.

Atala (1860). Fragmentary epic by Chateaubriand. Set in Louisiana in the eighteenth century and dealing with the lives of American Indians, it is said to mark the beginning of the Romantic movement in French literature.

L'Atelier. A monthly of French artisans and workers, influenced by Christian socialism, and committed to a moderate line. Published in Paris 1840 to 1850. It was subtitled *Organe spécial de la classe laborieuse rédigé par des ouvriers exclusivement.*

Auber, Daniel-François-Esprit (1782–1871). Regarded as the founder of French grand opera, he collaborated with Eugène Scribe on thirty-eight stage works between 1823 and 1864. Chapel master to Napoleon III.

Aubert, Gabriel (1787–1847). Former notary who, for many decades, operated a very successful print shop at 15 Galerie Véro-Dodat. Published the greater part of Daumier's works.

Aubert, Jacqueust (d. 1753). French violinist and composer of operas, sonatas, ballets.

Aupick, Jacques (1789–1857). Soldier, ambassador, senator; stamped out the insurrection organized by Blanqui in Paris in 1839. He was stepfather to Baudelaire, who turned against him.

Austerlitz. Town in southern Czechoslovakia where, on December 2, 1805, Napoleon decisively defeated the Russian and Austrian armies of Czar Alexander I and Emperor Francis II.

Azaïs, Pierre-Hyacinthe (1766–1845). French philosopher. In his *Système universel* (1800–1818), he developed a theory of forces and of "universal equilibrium."

Babeuf, François (1760–1797). Agitator and journalist during the French Revolution, advocating equal distribution of land and income. He organized a conspiracy to overthrow the Directory and return to the constitution of 1793; stabbed himself before being summoned to the guillotine. Author of a manifesto on social equality (1796).

Babou, Hippolyte (1824–1878). Critic and novelist, friend of Baudelaire.

Baby Cadum. Publicity. From the rosy-faced image of Bébé Cadum, symbol launched in France in 1912 for the popular Cadum soap.

Babylone. Neighborhood of Paris (today Sèvre-Babylone).

Bachofen, Johann (1815–1887). Swiss anthropologist and jurist. Author of works on Roman civil law and of *Das Mutterrecht* (1861), the first scientific history of the family as a social institution.

Bailly, Jean (1736–1793). French scholar and politician. As mayor of Paris (1789), he imposed martial law and called up the Garde Nationale to keep order (1791); lost popularity and was guillotined.

Bairam. Either of two Muslim religious festivals following the fast of Ramadan.

Ballhorn, Johann (1528–1603). Printer famous for his disastrous emendations (identity with figure named in h°,1 is speculative).

Baltard, Louis (1764–1846). French architect and engraver; professor at the Ecole des Beaux-Arts and the Ecole Polytechnique.

banquets. During the last months of Louis Philippe's reign, in 1847, the opposition organized a series of so-called Reform banquets, at which speakers called for electoral reforms.

Banville, Théodore de (1823–1891). Poet, playwright, critic. Close friend of Baudelaire and, with Charles Asselineau, editor of his works.

Barbara, Charles (1822–1886). Satirical writer active in the 1840s; associated with *Le Corsaire* and the group of bohemians around Henri Murger.

Barbès, Armand. Republican leader. Co-conspirator with, and later archenemy of, Louis-Auguste Blanqui, with whom he was imprisoned in the 1850s.

Barbey d'Aurevilly, Jules (1808–1889). French critic and novelist; long-time friend of Baudelaire.

Barbier, Auguste (1805–1882). Poet whom Baudelaire admired but criticized for moralistic tendencies. His *Iambes* (1831) satirized the monarchy of Louis Philippe.

Barnum, Phineas (1810–1891). American showman, connected with the circus business. Opened "The Greatest Show on Earth" in Brooklyn in 1871.

Barrault, Emile (1799–1869). Saint-Simonian writer and politician who published in *Le Globe* and wrote many works on Saint-Simonianism.

Barrès, Maurice (1862–1923). Writer and politician. Called for the restoration of "national energy" to France.

Barrot, Odilon (1791–1873). Leader of the liberal opposition in France prior to February 1848. From December 1848 to October 1849, he headed the ministry supported by monarchists.

Barthélemy, Auguste (1796–1867). French poet and satirist. He edited the weekly journal *Némésis,* which attacked the government of Louis Philippe in 1831–1832. Collaborated with Joseph Méry from 1824 to 1834.

Basilidians. Followers of Basilides, an Alexandrian Gnostic of the early second century, who preached a radical dualism and transcendence of the Creator-God of the Jews.

Batignolles. Village that became part of Paris in 1860; a meeting place of artists and politicians in the nineteenth century.

Bazard, Saint-Amand (1791–1832). Socialist, follower of Saint-Simon, and organizer of the French Carbonari (Charbonniers). He gave a long series of lectures in Paris (1828–1830), which won many adherents to Saint-Simonianism.

Beaumont, Charles (1821–1888). French graphic artist, contributor to *Le Charivari.* Illustrated works by Hugo and Sue.

Belgrand, Eugène (1810–1878). Engineer who modernized sewer service for the City of Paris. Arranged official support for Nadar's photography of the sewers. Author of *Les Travaux souterrains de Paris* (1875).

Bellamy, Edward (1850–1898). American author of *Looking Backward* (1888), a utopian romance based on socialist principles.

Bellangé. Pseudonym of François-Joseph Belanger (1744–1818), French architect famous for his innovative use of iron in the construction of the cupola of the old grain market in Paris.

Belle Isle. Island in the Bay of Biscay. From 1849 to 1857, it was a place of detention for French political prisoners; in particular, workers involved in the Paris uprising of June 1848 were imprisoned there.

Belleville. Working-class neighborhood in Paris.

Benda, Julien (1867–1956). French philosophical critic. Among his works are *La Bergsonisme, ou Une Philosophie sur la mobilité* (1912) and *La Fin de l'éternel* (1929).

Béraldi. Perhaps a mistake for Bérardi, Léon (1817–?), journalist and director of *L'Indépendance belge.*

Béranger, Pierre (1780–1857). Immensely popular lyric poet of liberal political sympathies.

Béraud, Henri (1885–1958). Novelist and essayist who promoted nationalism and anti-Semitism. Author of *Le Vitriol de la lune* (1921; Goncourt prize).

Bergeret, Madame. Character in Anatole France's series *L'Histoire contemporaine* (1896–1901).

Berl, Emmanuel (1892–1976). French writer and journalist, associated with the circle of Surrealists around Breton and Aragon.

Berlioz, Hector (1803–1869). French composer, a pioneer of modern orchestration.

Bernard, Claude (1813–1878). Noted physiologist. Investigated the sympathetic nervous system and the chemical phenomena of digestion.

Bernardin de Saint-Pierre, Jacques (1737–1814). Writer who anticipated French romanticism. Author of *Paul et Virginie* (1788).

Bernouard, François. French publisher. Friend of Benjamin during the 1920s and 1930s.

Bernstein, Eduard (1850–1932). German writer and politician. Co-editor of *Der Sozialdemokrat* (1881–1890). Associate of Engels.

Berry, Charles Ferdinand (1778–1820). Last duke of Berry, a nephew of Louis XVIII; in exile 1789–1814. His assassination in Paris by a fanatical Bonapartist led to a reactionary swing, countered by conspiracies.

Berryer, Pierre-Antoine (1790–1868). French lawyer and political figure; legitimist.

Bertin. Family famous for its association with *Le Journal des débats,* which Louis-François Bertin (1766–1841) purchased in 1799 and ran with his brother, Louis-François Bertin de Vaux (1771–1842). The sons of the former, Armand (1801–1854) and François-Edouard (1797–1871) took over as editors from their father.

Bibliographie de la France. Official weekly list of published books delivered by law to the Bibliothèque Nationale.

Biedermeier. Style of furniture in Germany (ca. 1815–1848), characterized by forms that are simpler and more sober than those of the Empire style, and by floral motifs. Also a style of landscape and genre painting.

Bierce, Ambrose (1842–?1914). American journalist and short-story writer. Served in the Civil War. He established his reputation with witty and caustic writings; his later work is often bitter and gruesome.

Biot, Jean Baptiste (1774–1862). French mathematician, physicist, and astronomer.

Bisson, Louis-Auguste. Pioneer photographer and early friend of Nadar, who owned a copy of Bisson's portrait of Balzac (1842).

Blanc, Louis (1811–1882). Socialist leader and journalist. Sponsored a guarantee of employment to workers during the Provisional Government of 1848. Author of *Histoire de la Révolution française* (1847–1862).

Blanqui, Jérôme (1798–1854). French economist; brother of Louis-Auguste Blanqui.

Blanqui, Louis-Auguste (1805–1881). Radical activist and writer committed to permanent revolution. After a classical lyceum education in Paris, he studied law and medicine, but devoted himself to conspiracy in the Carbonari and other secret societies, becoming a leading socialist agitator. He was often wounded in street fighting and spent a total of forty years in prison, yet maintained a fiery patriotism. Author of *L'Eternité par les astres* (1872) and *Critique social* (1885).

Blondel, Jacques François (1705–1774). Architect whose ideas greatly influenced his contemporaries. He opened in Paris the first art school to teach architecture (1743), and taught at the Académie Royale d'Architecture from 1756.

Blücher, Gebhard (1742–1819). Prussian field marshal. Defeated Napoleon at Laon (1814) and aided in the victory at Waterloo (1815), after which his army occupied Paris.

Boetticher, Karl Heinrich von (1833–1907). German architectural theorist; advisor to Bismarck. Author of *Tektonik der Hellenen* (1844–1852).

Böhme, Margarete. Editor of *Tagebuch einer Verlorenen* (Diary of a Lost Woman; 1905).

Boileau, Nicolas (1636–1711). Critic and poet in the classical tradition. Author of a highly influential didactic treatise in verse, *L'Art poétique* (1674).

Boissy-d'Anglas, comte François de (1756–1826). French statesman. Aided in the overthrow of Robespierre. He was a senator under Napoleon and a peer of France under Louis XVIII.

Bonald, Louis (1754–1840), Philosopher and publicist; minister of instruction under Napoleon (1808). He was an extreme conservative in his policies.

Bonaparte, Louis Napoleon. *See* Napoleon III.

Bonvin, François (1817–1887). Genre and still-life painter. The vitality of his portraits is noted by Baudelaire.

Bordeaux, Henry (1870–1963). Novelist and critic; known for his tales of French family life.

Borel d'Hauterive, Joseph Pétrus (1809–1859). French writer of extreme romantic tendencies. Published a collection of verse, *Rhapsodies* (1831), and two works of fiction.

Bornstedt, Adalbert von (1808–1851). Former officer of the Prussian Guard who edited *Die Deutsche-Brüsseler Zeitung*. Active in the Communist League until expelled by Marx.

Bossuet, Jacques (1627–1704). Catholic prelate and tutor to the dauphin. A theoretician of political absolutism and the divine right of kings.

Boucher, François (1703–1770). French painter. Designer of stage sets for the Opéra, and book illustrator noted for his ornate style.

Boullée, Etienne-Louis (1728–1799). Architect active in Paris in the restoration and construction of buildings during the eighteenth century.

Bourget, Paul (1852–1935). Novelist and critic. Molder of opinion among conservative intellectuals in the pre–World War I period.

Boyer, Philoxène (1827–1867). Poet and critic who, coming into a large inheritance in 1850, for two years held dinners at the best restaurants in Paris for a circle of writers that included Baudelaire.

Bracquemond, Félix (1833–1914). Painter and etcher. A friend of Baudelaire.

Brandes, Georg (1842–1927). Danish literary critic, with a reputation for radicalism. Professor of aesthetics at the University of Copenhagen, and author of studies on Shakespeare, Voltaire, Goethe, Kierkegaard.

Briseis. Concubine of Achilles, in the *Iliad*.

Brummell, George. Called Beau Brummell (1778–1840), he was an English dandy and gambler, a friend of the Prince of Wales. He died in an insane asylum in France.

Bruneseau. Character in Hugo's *Les Misérables* who supervises the cleaning and surveying of the Paris sewers under Napoleon I.

Brunet, Charles-Louis-Fortuné (1801–1862). French engineer and architect; student of Vandoyer.

Brunetière, Vincent (1849–1906). Critic and professor of literature at the Ecole Normale. Editor of *La Revue des deux mondes* (1893), and author of *Etudes critiques* (8 vols.; 1880–1907).

Buchez, Philippe (1796–1865). French Saint-Simonian; politician and historian. He was a founder of Christian socialism and president of the Constitutional Assembly (May 1848). Editor of *L'Atelier* (1840–1850).

Büchner, Georg (1813–1837). German poet. Author of the dramatic poem *Dantons Tod* (1835), the satire *Leonce und Lena* (1836), and the fragmentary tragedy *Woyzeck* (1836).

Bugeaud de la Piconnerie, Thomas (1784–1849). French soldier. Was made marshal of France in 1843.

Bulwer-Lytton, E. G. (1803–1873). English novelist and dramatist. Author of *The Last Days of Pompeii* (1834).

Buonarroti, Filippo (1761–1837). Italian-born elder statesman of French radicalism in the 1820s and 1830s. He was a member, with Louis-Auguste Blanqui, of the Society of Friends of the People in 1832, and leader of the Babeuvistes (after Babeuf), who advocated the revolutionary political role of education.

Buret, Antoine (1810–1842). French journalist who wrote on the poverty of the working classes.

Cabet, Etienne (1788–1856). French political radical, involved in the revolution of 1830. Exiled 1834–1839 for radical writings. Influenced by Robert Owen, he founded a utopian community called Icaria at Nauvoo, Illinois, in 1849, but withdrew in 1856 after dissension. Author of the socialist romance *Voyage en Icarie* (1839).

Cacus. Fire-breathing monster, a son of Vulcan. He lives in a cave on the Aventine hill, where he is killed by Hercules (*Aeneid*, book 8).

Cagliostro, Count Alessandro di. Real name Giuseppe Balsamo (1743–1795); Italian impostor. Born of poor parents, he traveled widely in Europe, posing as physician, alchemist, freemason.

Caillois, Roger (1913–1978). French writer who founded the Collège de Sociologie in 1937, together with Georges Bataille and Michel Leiris. Benjamin occasionally attended events there.

Calonne, Charles (1734–1802). Minister of finance under Louis XVI; in exile 1787–1802. He was a builder of roads and canals in the years before the Revolution.

Campanella, Tommaso (1568–1639). Italian philosopher. Author of *Civitas Solis* (City of the Sun; 1623), written during a long imprisonment and describing a utopian state similar to the one in Plato's *Republic*.

Candolle, Augustin (1778–1841). Swiss botanist; moved to Paris in 1796. Established a structural system of plant classification that replaced that of Linnaeus. Professor of natural science at Geneva (1816–1834).

Canning, George (1770–1827). British statesman. Pursued vigorous war policy (1807–1810).

Canova, Antonio (1757–1822). Italian neoclassical sculptor.

Capua. Strategically important ancient Roman city on the Appian Way, near Naples.

Capus, Alfred (1858–1922). French journalist and playwright; political editor of *Le Figaro* 1914–1922. His plays include *La Veine* (1901) and *Les Deux Hommes* (1908).

Carbonari. Italian revolutionary group organized around 1811 to establish a united republican Italy; named in honor of old conspirators who used to meet in huts of charcoal burners. French Carbonarism (Charbonnerie), directed against the Bourbon Restoration, was initiated in 1820 by several young republican militants, and spread with great secrecy through the schools of Paris into other towns.

Carcel, Bertrand (1750–1812). French clockmaker who, around 1800, invented the Carcel lamp, in which oil is pumped by clockwork into the wick tube.

Cardanus, Girolamo (1501–1576). Italian mathematician, physician, and astrologer.

Carjat, Etienne (1828–1906). One of the greatest of the early photographers. Photographed Baudelaire.

Carnot, Lazare (1753–1823). Statesman and military engineer. Member of the Committee of Public Safety (1793) and the Directory (1795–1797); afterward served Napoleon in various capacities. Author of works on mathematics and military strategy. *See* Ecole Polytechnique.

Carpocratians. Followers of the second-century Alexandrian Gnostic Carpocrates, who preached the transmigration of the soul and the superlative humanity of Christ.

Carrel, Nicolas Armand (1800–1836). Journalist and liberal political leader; co-founder, with Thiers and Mignet, and editor (1830–1836) of *Le National*. Killed by Emile de Girardin in a duel.

Carus, Carl Gustav (1789–1869). German physician and philosopher; follower of Schelling.

Casanova, Giovanni (1725–1798). Italian adventurer and writer; author *of Mémoires écrits par lui-même* (12 vols., 1826–1838).

Castellane, Victor Boniface (1788–1862). French politician who participated in military campaigns under Napoleon I. Was made a peer in 1837, and senator and maréchal in 1852.

Castlereagh, Robert Stewart (1769–1822). English statesman. Fought a duel with his rival George Canning in 1809.

Castles. An English government spy.

Catiline. Full name Lucius Sergius Catalina (108–62 B.C.), Roman aristocrat who conspired unsuccessfully to overthrow Cicero's government in 63–62 B.C. He was supported in Rome by debtors and discontented young patricians. Killed in battle.

Caussidière, Marc (1808–1861). Organizer of secret revolutionary societies under Louis Philippe. Prefect of Paris police after February Revolution (1848). He emigrated to England in June 1848.

Cavaignac, Louis (1802–1857). French army commander. As minister of war, he suppressed the Paris uprising in 1848. Unsuccessful candidate for president of France in December 1848.

Cazotte, Jacques (1719–1792). Author of *Le Diable amoureux* (1772) and of a continuation of the *Thousand and One Nights*. Guillotined as a Royalist in 1792.

Céline, Louis-Ferdinand. Pseudonym of Louis Destouches (1894–1961), French physician and novelist; fanatical anti-Semite. Author of the highly influential *Voyage au bout de la nuit* (1932) and *Mort à crédit* (1936).

Cham. Pseudonym of comte Amédée de Noé (1819–1879), French caricaturist.

Champfleury. Pseudonym of Jules Husson (1821–1889), novelist, critic; friend of Baudelaire. Author of *Le Réalisme* (1857).

Les Chants de Maldoror. Hallucinatory prose work by Lautréamont, written 1867–1870.

Chaptal, Jean-Antoine, comte de (1756–1832). French physicist and chemist. Minister of the interior (1800–1804). Founder of the first *école des arts et des métiers*.

Le Charivari. Daily journal founded by Charles Philipon (1831), to which Daumier was a constant contributor. The name signifies a jangling mock serenade meant to harass.

Charlet, Nicolas (1792–1845). French painter who glorified the soldiers of Napoleon's army, and whose works were extremely popular during the first decades of the nineteenth century.

Charras, Jean (1810–1865). French soldier and historian; undersecretary of state for war (1848). He opposed the policies of Napoleon III, and was banished after the coup d'état (1851).

Chasles, Philarète (1798–1873). Scholar and writer. On the editorial staff of *Le Journal des débats*. Author of *Etudes de littérature comparée* (11 vols).

Châtel, Ferdinand-François, abbé (1795–1857). Forbidden to preach because of his unorthodox views, he founded the Eglise Catholique Française in 1830, with services in French, no confessional, and married priests. In 1848, he was an advocate of women's rights and quick divorce.

Chaux. *See* Ledoux, Claude-Nicolas.

Chénier, André (1762–1794). French poet; guillotined in Paris, July 25, 1794. Considered by some to be the foremost practitioner of classical poetry in France after Racine and Boileau.

Chennevières, Philippe de (1820–1899). Writer, and director of the Ecole des Beaux-Arts. Friend of Baudelaire, who reviewed his collection of short stories, *Contes normands,* in 1845.

Chéret, Jules (1836–1932). French painter and lithographer, noted for his poster designs.

Chevalier, Michel (1806–1879). Economist, advocate of free trade, and follower of Saint-Simon. Co-editor of *Le Globe* (1830–1832), he was imprisoned with Enfantin in 1832–1833. Professor at the College de France and councillor of state under Napoleon III.

Chevet. Well-known *marchand de comestibles* in the Palais-Royal. Mentioned by Balzac.

Chevreul, Michel Eugène (1786–1889). Chemist; director of the natural history museum, Jardin des Plantes (1864–1879). Developed margarine and stearine.

Chintreuil, Antoine (1816–1873). Landscape painter whose technical excellence is noted by Baudelaire.

Chirico, Giorgio de (1888–1978). Italian painter. One of the founders of Surrealism.

Chodruc-Duclos (d. 1842). Called by Dumas a "modern Diogenes," he shows up as an associate of Socrates in a fragmentary drama by Baudelaire *(Idéolus).*

Chrysostom, Saint John (345?–407). A Father of the Greek church, born in Antioch. He was appointed bishop of Constantinople (398), later deposed and exiled to Armenia. Author of influential homilies, commentaries, letters.

Citroen, André (1878–1935). French automobile manufacturer; made munitions during World War I. After the war, he devoted his plant to the production of low-priced automobiles. Went bankrupt in 1934.

Cladel, Léon (1835–1892). French Symbolist writer, disciple of Baudelaire. Author of *Les Martyrs ridicules* (1862; collaboration with Baudelaire), *Les Va-nu-pieds* (1873), and other novels and tales.

Claës, Balthazar. Hero of Balzac's *La Recherche de l'absolu* (1834).

Clairville, Louis (1811–1879). Playwright. Wrote or co-authored more than 600 stage productions.

Claretie, Jules (1840–1913). Journalist and author of novels, plays, and literary studies. Director of the Comédie Française (1885).

Claudel, Paul (1868–1955). Poet, dramatist, and diplomat. Associated with the Symbolist movement.

Claudin, Gustave (1823–?). Writer for several Parisian newspapers, beginning in the 1840s.

La Closerie des Genêts. Play by Frédéric Soulié, first performed at the Théâtre Ambigu in 1846.

Cobbett, William (1763–1835). English political journalist. Shifted from attacking to defending political radicalism.

Cocteau, Jean (1889–1963). Author and filmmaker. Best known for his film *La Belle et la bête* (1946) and his play *La Machine infernale* (1934).

Collins, Wilkie (1824–1889). English novelist; friend of Dickens. Author of *The Woman in White* (1860), *The Moonstone* (1868), *The New Magdalen* (1873).

colportage. System of distributing books by traveling peddlers in the eighteenth and nineteenth centuries in France. From *col,* "neck," and *porter,* "to carry," reflecting the fact that colporteurs carried their wares on trays suspended from straps around their necks. They disseminated religious and devotional literature, manuals, almanacs, collections of folklore and popular tales, chivalric romances, political and philosophical works in inexpensive formats, and, after 1840, serial novels. In decline by the mid-nineteenth century, due to competition from the popular press.

Commune of Paris. Revolutionary government established in Paris on March 18, 1871, in the aftermath of the Franco-Prussian War. It was suppressed by Adolphe Thiers's government in bloody street-fighting that ended May 28, 1871, leaving 20,000 Communards dead.

Comte de Saint-Leu. Title assumed by Louis Bonaparte (1778–1846), brother of Napoleon Bonaparte and father of Napoleon III.

Condé, Le Grand (1621–1686). Louis II, prince de Condé, a member of the Bourbon family who was a military leader under Louis XIV.

Condé, Louis Henri Joseph (1756–1830). Last prince of the Condé family, a branch of the house of Bourbon. Wounded at Gibraltar (1782). It is thought that he committed suicide.

Condorcet, marquis de (1743–1794). Philosopher, mathematician, and revolutionary. Advocate of economic freedom, religious toleration, legal and educational reform. Outlawed as a Girondist by Robespierre, he died in prison. Author of *Esquisse d'un tableau historique des progrès de l'esprit humain* (1795).

Congress of Tours. Socialist party congress, at the end of 1920, marking a schism between partisans of the Second International and those of the Third International.

Considérant, Victor (1809–1893). Disciple of Fourier and a leader of the Fourierists after 1837. Author of *Destinée sociale* (1834). He tried to establish a phalansterian community near Dallas, Texas (1855–1857).

Constant, Benjamin (1767–1830). Franco-Swiss novelist and liberal politician; associate of the Schlegels and Madame de Staël. Author of *Adolphe* (1816).

Le Constitutionnel. Daily newspaper published in Paris 1815–1870. During the 1840s, it was the organ of moderate Orleanists.

Coppée, François (1842–1908). Poet, playwright, novelist. A leading member of the Parnassians.

Le Corsaire-Satan. Satirical newspaper issued in Paris 1844–1849. Its editor, Lepoitevin Saint-Alme, had been a friend of Balzac. It published the work of Baudelaire, Nadar, Banville, Murger, and others of their circle.

Courbet, Gustave (1819–1877). Leading French realist painter. Presided over the Committee of Fine Arts during the Commune (1871). He was imprisoned six months for destroying the column in the Place Vendôme, and was condemned (1875) to pay for restoration of the column.

Courier, Paul (1772–1825). French writer and political pamphleteer who was murdered. Opponent of the clergy and the Restoration.

Cournot, Antoine (1801–1877). Economist and mathematician, who sought to apply the calculus of probabilities to the solution of economic problems.

Court of Cassation. Established in 1790 as the highest court of appeals in the French legal system. During the Second Empire, it tended to serve the interests of the bourgeoisie, who had come to power under Louis Philippe, and thus represented a check on the power of Napoleon III and Baron Haussmann.

Cousin Pons. Main character in Balzac's novel *Le Cousin Pons* (1847).

Cousin, Victor (1792–1867). French philosopher and statesman; leader of the Eclectic school. Author of *Philosophie de Kant* (1842), and *Histoire générale de la philosophie* (1863).

Crépet, Eugène (1827–1892). French man of letters. Edited Baudelaire's *Oeuvres posthumes, précédées d'une notice biographique* (1887).

Crépet, Jacques (1874–1952). Son of Eugène Crépet, he continued the latter's work in editing Baudelaire and revising the *Etude biographique* (1906).

Crevel, René (1900–1935). Novelist, poet, essayist; among the first Surrealists. He committed suicide in Paris. Author of *Paul Klee* (1930) and *Dali, ou L'Anti-obscurantisme* (1935).

Curtius, Ernst Robert (1814–1896). German classical philologist and archaeologist. As director of antiquities in Berlin, he oversaw the German excavation of Olympia, Greece (1875–1881).

Cuvier, Georges (1769–1832). Naturalist and statesman; founder of comparative anatomy. He classified animals in terms of four distinct types.

d'Aurevilly. *See* Barbey d'Aurevilly, Jules.

d'Eichthals, Gustave (1804–1886). Saint-Simonian follower of Enfantin and collaborator on the newspaper *Le Globe*.

Dacqué, Edgar (1878–1945). French paleontologist.

Daguerre, Louis Jacques (1787–1851). French painter and inventor. Helped develop the diorama in Paris (1822), and collaborated with J. N. Niépce (1829–1833) on work leading to the discovery of the daguerreotype process, communicated to the Academy of Sciences in 1839.

Danae. In Greek mythology, the daughter of Eurydice and Acrisius, and mother of Perseus. She was imprisoned by her father in a chamber of bronze.

Dartois. Three brothers—François-Victor-Armand (1788–1867), Louis-Armand-Théodore (1786–1845), and Achille (1791–1868)—all active and occasionally working together in theater and vaudeville during the nineteenth century.

Daubrun, Marie (1827–1901). Noted French actress, beloved of Baudelaire. Inspired a number of poems in *Les Fleurs du mal*.

Daudet, Alphonse (1840–1897). Novelist who published a series of successful books from 1866 to 1898. Father of Léon Daudet.

Daudet, Léon (1867–1942). Son of Alphonse Daudet; journalist and writer. Founded, with Charles Maurras, the royalist journal *L'Action française* (1907). Author of novels, books on psychology and medicine, political works, literary criticism.

David, Félicien-César (1810–1876). French composer of popular and influential symphonic odes—e.g., *Le Désert* (1844), *Herculanum* (1859). Preached Saint-Simonian doctrine in the Middle East.

David, Jacques-Louis (1748–1825). French painter sympathetic to the Revolution of 1789; an admirer of Robespierre and, later, Napoleon. His neoclassical portraits of revolutionary heroes influenced the development of academic painting in France.

Deburau, Baptiste (1796–1846). Acrobat's son who transformed the character Gilles of commedia dell'arte into the wily chameleon Pierrot. His son Charles (1829–1873), a star during the Second Empire although without his father's genius, was photographed by Nadar.

Decembrists. Participants in the unsuccessful plot to overthrow Czar Nicholas I, in December 1825.

Delaroche, Paul (1797–1856). French portrait and historical painter. Founder of the Eclectic school, which united classical line with romantic color and subject matter.

Delatouche, Hyacinthe (1785–1851). Author of a novel about a hermaphrodite, *Fragoletta* (1829).

Delescluze, Louis Charles (1809–1871). Politician and journalist, active in the 1830 and 1848 revolutions. A leader of the Paris Commune, he was killed on the barricades in May 1871.

Delessert, Gabriel (1786–1858). Prefect of Paris police, 1836–1848.

Delord, Taxile (1815–1877). French journalist. Editor of *Le Charivari* 1848–1858, and author of *Physiologie de la Parisienne* (1841).

Delorme, Joseph. Main character in *Vie, poésies et pensées de Joseph Delorme,* by Sainte-Beuve (1829).

Delvau, Alfred (1825–1867). Journalist and friend of Baudelaire. Author of *Les Heures parisiennes* (1866).

de Maistre, Joseph (1753–1821). Diplomat and writer admired by Baudelaire. Author of *Les Soirées de Saint-Pétersbourg* (1821), which argued for the absolute rule of sovereign and pope.

Démar, Claire (1800–1833). Enthusiastic follower of Saint-Simonianism who committed suicide. Author of the manifesto *Ma Loi d'avenir* (1834).

La Démocratie pacifique. Fourierist daily edited by Victor Considérant; published in Paris 1843–1851.

Democritus. Greek atomist philosopher of the late fifth century B.C. He thought that images *(eidōla)* of a body are given off when this body is perceived, and that these images enter the pores of the viewer.

Denner, Balthasar (1685–1749). German portrait painter.

Dennery, Adolphe (1811–1899). French playwright and librettist.

des Esseintes. Hypersensitive hero of Huysmans' novel, *A Rebours* (1884).

Desnoyers, Fernand (1828–1869). Bohemian writer and friend of Baudelaire. Co-edited the *Festschrift* which published the two "Crépuscule" poems.

Deubel, Léon (1879–1913). French *poète maudit.*

Devéria, Eugène (1805–1865). French historical painter; brother of Achille Devéria (1800–1857). Both were praised by Baudelaire.

Diogenes (412?–323 B.C.). Greek cynic philosopher who, in pursuit of an ascetic ideal, lived in a tub. Supposed to have wandered the streets once holding up a lantern, "looking for an honest man."

Diorama. *See* panoramas.

Directory. In France, the period immediately following the Convention—that is, October 27, 1795, to November 9, 1799. It was a period of profligacy, of nouveaux riches, of the return of nobles from exile, and it ended with France on the verge of bankruptcy.

Disderi, Adolphe-Eugène (1818–1889). French entrepreneur. He introduced mass-manufacturing principles into portrait photography in 1859 and amassed a fortune before the collapse of the Second Empire. Inventor of the popular *carte de visite* (pocket portrait).

Döblin, Alfred (1878–1957). German physician and writer; in exile from 1934. Author of *Berlin Alexanderplatz* (1929).

Doré, Gustave (1833–1883). French artist best known for his illustrations of Balzac's *Contes drolatiques* (1856 edition) and Cervantes' *Don Quixote* (1863 edition).

Doumergue, Gaston (1863–1937). Left-wing statesman. Twelfth president of France (1924–1931).

Dozon, Auguste (1822–1891). French diplomat and scholar of the Balkans who translated poetry from Bulgarian and Albanian.

Drouet, Juliette (1806–1883). Actress with whom Hugo began a liaison in 1833. She renounced the stage to devote herself to him, discreetly, until her death.

Drumont, Edouard (1844–1917). Anti-Semitic and anti-Dreyfusard journalist who founded and edited *La Libre Parole.* Author of the influential *La France juive* (1886).

Du Bartas, Guillaume (1544–1590). French poet. Author of an epic of creation, *La Semaine* (1578).

Du Camp, Maxime (1822–1894). Writer; friend of Flaubert. Worked with Baudelaire on *La Revue de Paris*. Decorated by Cavaignac for service in the Garde Nationale during the June Days. Author of *Les Chants modernes* (1855) and a six-volume account of nineteenth-century Paris (1869–1875).

Ducange, Victor Henri (1783–1833). Author of novels and dramas during the Restoration. Imprisoned several times for his liberalism.

Ducasse, Isidor. *See* Lautréamont, comte de.

Dulamon, Frédéric (1825–1880). Literary bohemian, an associate of Baudelaire.

Dulaure, Jacques (1755–1835). Deputy during the Convention and active defender of the revolutionary cause during the Restoration. Author of an influential *Histoire de Paris* (1821–1827).

Dumas, Alexandre (père) (1802–1870). Enormously popular French novelist and dramatist who, thanks to his fine handwriting, became secretary to the future Louis Philippe and embarked on a successful literary career in the popular press.

Dumas, Jean (1800–1884). Chemist who founded the Ecole Centrale des Arts et Manufactures in Paris (1829). Studied vapor density and the composition of the atmosphere.

Dupont, Pierre (1821–1870). Popular lyric poet and songwriter. Author of *Les Deux Anges* (1842) and *Le Chant des ouvriers* (1846). Subject of two essays by Baudelaire.

Duquesnay, Jean (1800–1849). Architect for the original building of the Ecole des Mines and for the Gare de l'Est in Paris.

Duval, Jeanne. French mulatto, a prostitute and actress, who was Baudelaire's mistress for many years and the inspiration for several of his poems.

Duveyrier, Anne Honoré (1787–1865). Playwright who collaborated with Eugène Scribe and others, including his own brother Charles Duveyrier.

Duveyrier, Charles (1803–1866). French lawyer and writer; disciple of Saint-Simon. Founded the journal *Le Crédit*.

Ecole des Beaux-Arts. School of fine arts founded (as the Académie Royale d'Architecture) in 1671 in Paris, under Louis XIV. Merged with the Académie Royale de Peinture et de Sculpture (founded 1648) in 1793. Particularly influential in the field of architectural design during the Second Empire.

Ecole Normande. Group of young poets with a taste for technical virtuosity; flourished in the early 1840s at the Pension Bailly in the heart of bohemian Paris. It centered around Gustave Le Vavasseur, Ernest Prarond, and Philippe de Chennevières, and included Baudelaire. Most members were devout monarchists who, in 1848, became fierce opponents of the new republic.

Ecole Polytechnique. Engineering school established in 1794 by the National Convention as the Ecole Centrale des Travaux Publics, under the direction of Lazare Carnot and Gaspard Monge; took its present name in 1795. It was transformed into a military school by Napoleon in 1804.

Edison, Thomas Alva (1847–1931). American inventor. Invented the Kinetograph, the first true motion picture camera, in 1889, as an accompaniment to his vastly successful phonograph.

L'Education sentimentale. Novel by Flaubert of 1870, presenting a vast panorama of French daily life under the July Monarchy.

Eiffel, Alexandre-Gustave (1832–1923). French engineer, a founder of aerodynamics. Built several arched bridges of iron and, for the Paris Exhibition of 1867, the arched Galerie des Machines. He was known as "the magician of iron" after his construction of the Eiffel Tower (1887–1889).

Enfantin, Barthélemy-Prosper (1796–1864). Saint-Simonian leader, known as Père Enfantin. The model community he established at Ménilmontant in 1832 was characterized by fantastic sacerdotalism and freedom between the sexes. After serving on the Scientific Commission on Algeria, he became the first director of the Lyons Railroad Company (1845).

Engelmann, Godefroi (1788–1839). French lithographer responsible for the introduction of the Senefelder process in France.

Ennius, Quintus (239–169 B.C.). Roman poet, a founder of Latin literature. Author of tragedies, comedies, and the epic poem *Annales*. Only fragments of his work remain.

Epinal. Town in northeastern France famous for its production of sentimental religious paintings.

Erler, Fritz (1868–1940). German graphic artist prominent in Jugendstil; set designer for the Munich Artists' Theater. He was criticized by Kandinsky for his "willful originality."

Esménard, Joseph-Alphonse (1769–1811). French publicist and poet who wrote for *La Quotidienne* and other journals. Author of the long poem *La Navigation* (1805).

Etzel, Karl von (1812–1865). Engineer responsible for the construction of many central train stations and railroad networks in Germany and Switzerland.

Eugénie (1826–1920). Empress of France (1853–1871) as wife of Napoleon III.

Euler, Leonhard (1707–1783). Swiss mathematician and physicist.

Evadamism. *See* Ganeau.

Faguet, Emile (1847–1916). Literary critic and professor at the Sorbonne. Author of books on Corneille, La Fontaine, Voltaire, and Flaubert.

Falloux, comte Frédéric (1811–1886). French politician; minister of public instruction (1848–1849). He introduced the law known as the Loi Falloux, mandating freedom of instruction (passed 1850).

Fantômas. Cycle of popular twentieth-century thrillers by Marcel Allain (1885–1969).

Favras, marquis de (1744–1790). Army officer who planned the escape of the royal family at the outbreak of the Revolution (1789). Captured and hanged.

February Revolution. Refers to the overthrow of Louis Philippe's constitutional monarchy in February 1848.

Federal Diet *(Bundestag)*. Central organ of the German Confederation from 1815 to 1866. Consisting of representatives of the German states, it was used by German governments to carry through their policies.

Ferragus. Main character in Balzac's novel of the same name (1833).

Ferry, Gabriel. Pseudonym of Gabriel de Bellemare (1809–1852), French writer and contributor to *La Revue des deux mondes*.

Féval, Paul (1817–1887). Novelist and playwright. Author of *Les Mystères de Londres* (1844) and *Le Bossu* (1858).

Fidus. Pseudonym of Hugo Höppener (1868–1948), German architect and painter of Jugendstil.

Fieschi, Giuseppe (1790–1836). Corsican conspirator. Made an unsuccessful attempt on the life of Louis Philippe in 1835 with his "infernal machine," killing eighteen people.

Le Figaro. Conservative paper published in Paris from 1854; a daily from 1866. Connected with the government of the Second Empire.

Figuier, Guillaume Louis (1819–1894). Writer; popularizer of science.

La Fin de Satan. Unfinished and posthumously published epic poem by Victor Hugo (1886; written 1854–1860).

Flocon, Ferdinand (1800–1866). French politician and publicist; editor of the newspaper *La Réforme*. He was a member of the Provisional Government of 1848.

Flotte, Etienne-Gaston, baron de (1805–1882). Catholic royalist poet and writer from Marseilles who was the author of an essay on the literature of his city.

Flourens, Pierre (1794–1867). French physiologist; professor at the Collège de France. Author of *De l'Instinct et de l'intelligence des animaux* (1841).

Fontaine, Pierre (1762–1853). Chief architect for Napoleon. Retained the favor of Louis XVIII and Louis Philippe.

Fontanarès. Hero of Balzac's play *Les Ressources de Quinola* (1842), set in the sixteenth century.

Fontanes, Louis de (1757–1821). Writer and statesman. President of the Corps Législatif (1804); senator (1810); member of the privy council under Louis XVIII.

Ford, Henry (1863–1947). American automobile manufacturer. Introduced profit sharing in the Ford Motor Company (1914).

Formigé, Jean Camille (1845–1926). French architect.

Fouqué, Friedrich de La Motte (1777–1843). German romantic writer. Author of the popular fairy tale *Undine* (1811), which was set to music by E. T. A. Hoffmann.

Fouquet, Jean (1416?–1480). French painter at the court of Louis XI. Known especially for his illumination of *Livres d'heures*.

Fourcroy, Antoine (1755–1809). Chemist. Co-author, with Antoine Lavoisier, of *Méthode de nomenclature chimique* (1787).

Fourier, Charles (1772–1837). French social theorist and reformer who advocated a cooperative organization of society into communities of producers known as phalansteries. Author of *Théorie des quatre mouvements* (1808), *Traité de l'association agricole domestique* (1822), *Le Nouveau Monde industriel* (1829–1830), *La Fausse Industrie morcelée* (1835–1836).

Fournier, Marc (1818–1879). Swiss journalist and author; in Paris from 1838. Director of the Théâtre de la Porte de Saint-Martin (1851), for which he wrote many popular dramas in the 1850s.

Fraisse, Armand (1830–1877). Critic and journalist working out of Lyons. Admirer of Baudelaire's poems.

France, Anatole. Pseudonym of Jacques Thibault (1844–1924), satirical novelist, critic, poet, and playwright. Author of *Le Crime de Sylvestre Bonnard* (1881); and of an *Histoire contemporaine,* including the volumes *Le Mannequin d'Osier* (1897) and *Monsieur Bergeret à Paris* (1901).

François I (1494–1547). King of France (1515–1547). His reign was marked by a Renaissance of the arts.

Frederick III (1831–1888). Opponent of Bismarck; patron of literature and science. Succeeded his father, Wilhelm I, on March 9, 1888, but died of cancer after three months.

Frégier, Honoré-Antoine (1789–1860). Police officer. Author of *Des Classes dangereuses* (1840).

Der Freischütz. Opera by Carl Maria von Weber (1821).

Fuller, Loie (1862–1928). American dancer who achieved international acclaim through her innovations in theatrical lighting and her invention of the "serpentine" dance (1889), involving lengths of silk manipulated under colored lights.

Fustel de Coulanges, Numa Denis (1830–1889). French historian; specialist in ancient and medieval history.

Gambetta, Léon (1838–1882). Lawyer; leader of the opposition to Napoleon III. Escaped Paris by balloon during the Franco-Prussian war. Premier of France (1881–1882).

Ganeau (or Ganneau) (1805–1851). Sculptor and pamphleteer who, around 1835, founded the religion known as Evadamism (Eve + Adam), which called for the fusion of the sexes. Took the name *le Mapah* (mater + pater), and sent his androgynous sculptures to politicians.

Gautier, Judith (1850–1917). Poet and novelist; daughter of Théophile Gautier. Author of *Richard Wagner* (1882) and *Fleurs d'Orient* (1893).

Gautier, Théophile (1811–1872). French man of letters. A leader of the Parnassians.

Gavarni, Paul. Pseudonym of Sulpice Chevalier (1804–1866), French illustrator and caricaturist, best known for his sketches of Parisian life.

Gavroche. Character in *Les Misérables* (part IV, book 6).

Gay, Jules (1807–1876). French utopian communist.

Gay-Lussac, Joseph (1778–1850). French chemist and physicist.

Geffroy, Gustave (1855–1926). Parisian journalist and novelist; art critic for *La Justice*. Wrote biographies of Charles Meryon and Louis-Auguste Blanqui.

Geoffroy Saint-Hilaire, Etienne (1772–1844). French naturalist who propounded a single type of structure throughout the animal kingdom. Violently opposed by Georges Cuvier.

Gérard, François (1770–1837). French historical and portrait painter.

Gerstäcker, Friedrich (1816–1872). German traveler and author of adventure stories often set in North America.

Gervex, Henri (1852–1929). French painter, identified with the Impressionist school.

Gervinus, Georg (1805–1871). German historian.

Giedion, Sigfried (1888–1968). Swiss art historian. First secretary of the Congrès Internationale d'Architecture Moderne (1928). Professor at Harvard from 1938. Author of *Bauen in Frankreich* (1928).

Girardin, Emile de (1806–1881). Inaugurated low-priced journalism with his editorship of *La Presse* (1836–1856, 1862–1866), at an annual subscription rate of forty francs. Member of the Chamber of Deputies (1834–1851; 1877–1881).

Girardin, Mme. Delphine (1804–1855). Writing under the pseudonym Charles de Launay, she published novels, comedies, verse, and a series entitled *Lettres Parisiennes*.

Gisquet (1792–1866). Prefect of Paris police 1831–1836.

Le Globe. Important Parisian newspaper founded and edited by Pierre Leroux in 1824; became the organ of Saint-Simonianism in 1830.

Godin, Jean (1817–1888). French industrialist and social reformer, influenced by Fourier; established a familistère among his operatives. Author of *Solutions sociales* (1871).

Gorgias (485?–380 B.C.). Greek Sophist and rhetorician. Immortalized by Plato in his dialogue *Gorgias*.

Gosse, Nicolas-Louis-François (1787–1878). French painter who specialized in works for churches, museums, and public buildings.

Gotha. City of central Germany where, from 1763, the *Almanach de Gotha,* a record of Europe's aristocratic and royal houses, was published.

Gozlan, Léon (1803–1866). Journalist, novelist, and playwright. Author of *Le Triomphe des omnibus: Poëme héroï-comique* (1828), *Balzac en pantoufles* (1865).

Gozo. Island northwest of Malta.

Grabbe, Christian Dietrich (1801–1836). German dramatic poet. Among his plays are *Don Juan und Faust* (1829) and *Napoleon, oder Die Hundert Tage* (1831).

Gracian, Baltasar (1601–1658). Spanish writer and philosopher. Rector of Jesuit College at Tarragona. Author of *El Criticon* (1651–1657).

Grand-Carteret, John (1850–1927). French journalist. Author of *Le Décolleté et le retroussé: Un Siècle de gauloiserie* (1910) and other illustrated books on customs of the day.

Grand Châtelet. Ancient fortress in Paris that served as both courthouse and prison.

Grandville. Pseudonym of Jean-Ignace-Isidore Gérard (1803–1847), caricaturist and illustrator whose work appeared in the periodicals *Le Charivari* and *La Caricature. Un Autre Monde,* with illustrations by Grandville and text by Taxile Delord, editor of *Le Charivari,* appeared in 1844.

Granier de Cassagnac, Adolphe (1808–1880). Journalist and ardent Bonapartist after 1850. Editor of *Le Pays;* author of *Souvenirs du Second Empire* (1879).

Grillparzer, Franz (1791–1872). Austrian playwright and poet.

grisette. Refers to a type of proletarian young woman in Paris who was associated with such trades as seamstress, chambermaid, or milliner, and whose behavior was supposedly characterized by independence, loose morals, and a brash manner. The term derives from the gray color of the material used for working-class clothing.

Gronow, Captain Rees Howell (1794–1865). English military officer. Fought at Waterloo, and went on to become a London dandy and gambler. Resided in Paris from the late 1830s. Published four volumes of reminiscences (1861–1866).

Gropius, Karl Wilhelm (1783–1870). German architect who specialized in theater décor. Opened a diorama in Berlin in 1827, with views of Greece and Italy.

Gros, Baron Antoine (1771–1835). French historical painter; studied under David, whose classical theory he adopted.

Grün, Karl (1817–1887). German writer and publicist; follower of Feuerbach. Member of the Prussian National Diet. Representative of "true socialism" in the 1840s.

Gründerjahren. Refers to reckless financial speculation; specifically, four years of such speculation following the Franco-Prussian war of 1870–1871.

Guaita, Stanislas (1861–1897). Italian-born French poet and mystic, one-time associate of Maurice Barrès. Author of *Les Oiseaux de passage* (1881), *La Muse noire* (1883).

Gudin, Théodore (1802–1880). French painter of seascapes and landscapes.

Guilbert, Yvette (1868–1944). French singer.

Guillot, Adolphe (1836–1892). Member of the Académie des Sciences Morales. Published many works on sociology and on the city of Paris.

Guizot, François (1787–1874). Historian and statesman. Premier of France, 1840–1848; forced out of office by the Revolution of 1848.

Gutzkow, Karl (1811–1878). German journalist, novelist, playwright. A leader, from 1830 to 1850, of Young Germany's revolt against Romanticism. Author of *Die Ritter vom Geiste* (1850–1852), which initiated the modern German social novel.

Guys, Constantin (1802–1892). Dutch-born illustrator; won fame for sketches of Parisian life during the Second Empire. His ink drawings and watercolors are the subject of Baudelaire's essay "Le Peintre de la vie moderne."

Hackländer, Friedrich (1816–1877). German writer. Author of *Daguerreotypen* (1842), *Namenlose Geschichten* (1851), *Verbotene Früchte* (1876).

Halévy, Daniel (1872–1962). French writer. Author of *Essai sur le mouvement ouvrier en France* (1901), *La Vie de Frédéric Nietzsche* (1909), *Jules Michelet* (1928).

Halévy, Léon (1802–1883). French writer. Author of books on Jewish history, several volumes of verse, and a few plays.

Halévy, Ludovic (1834–1908). Playwright and novelist, son of Léon Halévy. Among his many works are *La Belle Hélène* (1864), *Froufrou* (1869), and *Mariage d'amour* (1881). He was Offenbach's most important collaborator.

Hardekopf, Ferdinand (1876–1954). German expressionist poet and translator of French writers. Influenced by Jugendstil. Friend of Emmy Hennings in prewar Munich.

Hauser, Kaspar (1812?–1833). German foundling. Popularly believed to be of noble birth, he died of stab wounds, which he said he received from a stranger promising information about his parentage. Subject of the novel *Caspar Hauser* (1909), by Jakob Wassermann, and other works of literature and film.

Haussmann, Baron Georges Eugène (1809–1891). Studied law and entered the French civil service in 1831. As prefect of the Seine (1853–1870), under Napoleon III, he inaugurated and carried through a large-scale renovation of Paris, which included the modernization of sanitation, public utilities, and transportation facilities, the construction of the Paris Opéra and the central marketplace Les Halles, the landscaping of the parks at Boulogne and Vincennes, and the creation of strategically organized *grands boulevards* that necessitated the demolition of many old Parisian neighborhoods and many arcades built in the first half of the century.

Haussoullier, William (1818–1891). French painter lauded by Baudelaire in "Le Salon de 1845."

Hébert, Jacques (1755–1794). Radical journalist and politician of the Revolution. Published the popular satiric newspaper *Le Père Duchesne* (whose title became his nickname). Executed in a struggle with the Jacobins' right wing under Danton.

Heim, François (1787–1865). French historical painter; praised by Baudelaire.

Heine, Heinrich (1797–1856). German poet and critic. Jewish-born Christian convert; resident in Paris (from 1831). Among his works are *Reisebilder* (1826–1831), *Buch der Lieder* (1827), *Romanzero* (1851).

Helena. Character in Goethe's *Faust,* Part 2.

Heliogabalus (204–222). Roman emperor, devoted to debauchery, who put to death many senators. Killed by praetorians.

Hello, Ernest (1828–1885). French philosopher and critic. Author of *Le Style* (1861), *Philosophie et athéisme* (1888).

Hennebique, François (1842–1921). French structural engineer who devised a kind of reinforced concrete using steel and iron (patented 1892).

Hennings, Emmy (1885–1948). German poet and cabaret artist in prewar Munich and later in Zurich, where, with her husband Hugo Ball, she launched Dada in 1916, founding Cabaret Voltaire. Friend of Benjamin.

Hérault de Séchelles, Jean (1759–1794). Lawyer and politician. Member of the National Convention (1792); helped to draft the new constitution (1793). Guillotined in Paris.

Herédia, José de (1842–1905). French poet of Spanish parentage; settled in Paris in 1859. A leader of the Parnassians and a disciple of Leconte de Lisle. Author of *Les Trophées* (1893).

Hernani. Play by Victor Hugo. Its first performance (February 25, 1830) resulted in the triumph of the Romantics over the literary classicists. The title character, a noble outlaw, wore a red waistcoat.

Herschell, Sir John (1792–1871). English astronomer and mathematician who followed in the path of his father William with the discovery and cataloguing of stellar phenomena.

Herwegh, Georg (1817–1875). German poet and revolutionary. Author of *Gedichte eines Lebendigen* (1841–1844).

Hess, Moses (1812–1875). Editor, with Friedrich Engels, of *Der Gesellschaftsspiegel* (1845–1846). Broke with Marx and Engels after 1848, and supported the socialist leader Ferdinand Lassalle in Paris.

Hessel, Franz (1880–1941). Writer and translator; an editor at Rowohlt Verlag in Berlin. Emigrated to Paris in 1938. He collaborated with Benjamin on translating Proust. His books *Heimliches Berlin* (1927) and *Spazieren in Berlin* (1929) were reviewed by Benjamin.

Heym, Georg (1887–1912). Leading German expressionist poet, influenced by Baudelaire and Rimbaud. Author of *Umbra vitae* (1912). Drowned while trying to save a friend.

Hittorff, Jacques (1792–1867). Government architect in Paris from 1830. Built the Gare du Nord and other public and private buildings.

Hoddis, Jakob van. Pseudonym of Hans Davidsohn (1887–1942), expressionist poet. Author of *Weltende* (1911).

Holbach, Baron Paul-Henri Thiry (1723–1789). German-born French materialist philosopher. Author of *Le Christianisme dévoilé* (1761), *Le Système de la nature* (1770), *Le Politique naturelle* (1773).

Homais. Freethinking provincial pharmacist in Flaubert's *Madame Bovary* (1857).

Honfleur. Port on the Normandy coast where Baudelaire's stepfather bought a house on a clifftop in 1855.

Hôtel de Ville. Paris city hall.

Hôtel-Dieu. Famous hospital in Paris, first established in the twelfth century near Notre-Dame. It burned down in 1772, was rebuilt, and then was torn down during the Second Empire. A new Hôtel-Dieu was built 1868–1878.

Houssaye, Arsène (1814–1896). Man of letters; manager of the Comédie Française 1849–1856. Author of novels, verse, literary criticism, histories.

Huygens, Christian (1629–1695). Dutch mathematician, physicist, and astronomer. Developed the wave theory of light. Worked in Paris 1666–1681, at the invitation of Louis XIV.

Huysmans, Joris-Karl (1848–1907). French novelist and art critic, descended from a family of Dutch artists. Worked in the Ministry of the Interior. His writings show the influence, successively, of Naturalism, aestheticism, occultism, and the Catholic revival. Author of *A Vau-l'eau* (1882), *A Rebours* (1884), *Là-bas* (1891), *En Route* (1895).

Icarians. *See* Cabet, Etienne.

Ile Saint-Louis. Small island in the Seine, next to the Ile de la Cité. Residence of Baudelaire in 1842.

Image d'Epinal. Sentimental religious poster, named after the town in northeastern France where this art was produced.

Institut de France. Name given in 1806 to the Institut National (established in 1795 by the Convention). After 1816, it was divided into *académies* devoted to literature, fine arts, and science.

Institute of Social Research *(Institut für Sozialforschung)*. Established 1923 in affiliation with the University of Frankfurt by a group of left-wing political scientists, including Felix Weil, Friedrich Pollock, and Max Horkheimer. Published the *Zeitschrift für Sozialforschung,* devoted mainly to cultural analysis, 1932–1941. The administrative center of the institute moved in 1933 to Geneva, with branch offices in Paris and London, and in 1934 to New York, where it was affiliated with Columbia University. Under the direction of Horkheimer and Theodor Adorno, the institute returned to Frankfurt in 1950.

Janin, Jules (1804–1874). Journalist, novelist, critic. Published an influential feuilleton in *Journal des débats.* Author of the six-volume *Histoire de la littérature dramatique en France.*

Janssen, Pierre (1824–1907). French astronomer. Established and directed the observatory on Mont Blanc (1893).

Jaurès, Jean (1859–1914). Author of *Histoire socialiste de la Révolution française* (1907), and leader of the democratic socialists in the Chamber of Deputies (1893–1914). Preached reconciliation with the state. His championing of Franco-German rapprochement led to his assassination at the outbreak of World War I.

Jehuda (Judah) ben Halevy (ca. 1085–ca. 1140). Jewish poet and philosopher, born in Toledo, Spain. Died on a pilgrimage to Jerusalem.

Joël, Charlotte. Wife of Ernst Joël, an old friend of Benjamin's from the youth movement days and later a physician in Berlin, who supervised Benjamin's experiments with hashish.

Joubert, Joseph (1754–1824). Thinker and moralist; associate of Diderot and Chateaubriand. He took part in the first period of the Revolution as a justice of the peace in his hometown, Montignac, but withdrew from politics in 1792. His *Pensées*, culled from his journals, were first published in 1838.

Jouffroy d'Abbans, marquis Claude (1751–1832). Engineer. A pioneer in steam navigation.

Journal des débats politiques et littéraires. Daily newspaper founded in Paris in 1789. Advocated views of the government during the July Monarchy.

Journet, Jean (1799–1861). Fourierist missionary and poet who gave up his pharmacy to wander for over twenty years, with knapsack and simple garb, preaching a doctrine of passional individualism. Photographed by Nadar.

Jugendstil. A style of architectural, figurative, and applied art that flourished in the last decade of the nineteenth century and the early years of the twentieth. Connected with Art Nouveau. In Germany, where it was known at first as the "modern style" and the "decorative movement," it was led by August Endell and Henry van de Velde. After 1896, it was associated with the periodical *Die Jugend* (Youth). It played an important part in exhibitions of applied art at Wassily Kandinsky's Phalanx society, beginning in 1901. It signified not only a crossing of the cultural barrier separating "higher" from "lower" arts, but an educational movement intent on restructuring the human environment.

Le Juif errant (The Wandering Jew). Novel by Eugène Sue, published 1844–1845.

Julian (Flavius Claudius Julianus, known as "Julian the Apostate"; 331–363). Roman emperor and author.

Jullien, Louis (1812–1860). French composer and musical director.

July Days. *See* July Revolution.

July Ordinances. Issued by Charles X and his ultra ministers on July 26, 1830, these ordinances dissolved the newly elected Chamber, restricted suffrage, and abolished liberty of the press. Annulled on July 30, one day before Louis Philippe and Lafayette, wrapped in a tricolor, embraced on the balcony of the Hôtel de Ville, as the crowd cheered.

July Revolution. Took place July 27–29, 1830, against Charles X. Led to the proclamation of Louis Philippe as "Citizen King" (July Monarchy).

June Insurrection. The so-called June Days (June 23–26, 1848), when workers in Paris, after the dissolution of the National Workshops, were joined by students and artisans in spontaneous demonstrations against the newly elected conservative majority. Suppressed in bloody battles on the barricades.

Karr, Alphonse (1808–1890). Journalist and novelist; editor of *Le Figaro* (1839), and founder of the satirical review *Les Guêpes*. Author of *Voyage autour de mon jardin* (1845).

Kautsky, Karl (1854–1938). German socialist writer; secretary to Engels in London (1881). Editor of *Die neue Zeit* (1883–1917). He opposed Bolshevism and the Russian Revolution.

Keller, Gottfried (1819–1890). Swiss German-language poet and novelist, who published his first poems in 1846. Author of *Der grüne Heinrich* (1854–1855), *Martin Salander* (1886), and other works. Subject of an important essay of 1927 by Benjamin.

Kircher, Athanasius (1601–1680). German Jesuit scholar who taught mathematics and

Hebrew at the College of Rome. In 1643 gave up teaching to study hieroglyphics. Credited with the invention of the magic lantern.

Klages, Ludwig (1872–1956). German philosopher, associated with the George circle. Author of *Vom Traumbewusstsein* (1919), *Vom kosmogonischen Eros* (1922), and *Der Geist als Widersacher der Seele* (1929–1932).

Kock, Paul de (1794–1871). French novelist and playwright, known for his depiction of bourgeois life. Author also of vaudevilles, pantomimes, light operas.

Korsch, Karl (1886–1961). German political philosopher. Author of *Marxismus und Philosophie* (1923). Excluded from the German Communist party in 1926; came to the U.S. in 1938. Met Benjamin through the medium of Brecht, with whom he stayed in 1934. His book on Marx was substantially drafted in Paris in 1936.

Kranzler Café. Berlin café established in the nineteenth century at the corner of Unter den Linden and Friedrichstrasse, near the Kaiser Galerie and Potsdam Place. It was frequented by stock jobbers toward the end of the century.

Kubin, Alfred (1877–1959). Austrian painter and writer. Illustrated books such as Paul Scheerbart's *Lesabéndio*.

Kugelmann, Ludwig (1830–1902). German physician, active in the revolution of 1848–1849 in Germany. Friend of Marx and Engels.

Kühne, Gustav (1806–1888). German novelist and critic; a leader of Young Germany. Editor of the weekly *Europa* 1846–1859.

Labrouste, Pierre François Henri (1801–1875). French architect.

Lacenaire, Pierre-François (1800–1836). French writer associated with the so-called "frenetic" literature. Composed his *Mémoires* in prison while awaiting execution for the murder of bank messengers.

La Chambaudie (1806–1872). Saint-Simonian writer of fables, poems, and essays. Associate of Louis-Auguste Blanqui.

Laclos, Pierre Choderlos de (1741–1803). Soldier and writer; a general under Napoleon. Author of *Les Liaisons dangereuses* (1782).

Lacordaire, Jean (1801–1870). Entomologist. Author of *Histoire naturelle des insectes* (1854–1868).

Lafargue, Marie (1816–1853). French woman convicted of poisoning her husband (1840). and condemned to life imprisonment at hard labor. She maintained her innocence, and was pardoned in 1852.

Lafargue, Paul (1842–1911). French radical socialist and writer; close associate of Marx and Engels. A founder of the French Workers' Party (1879), he edited, with Jules Guesde, *Le Citoyen* from 1881 to 1884. Rejected compromise with capitalistic government.

Lafayette, Marie Joseph (1757–1834). Statesman and officer; served in the American Revolution. Member of the French National Assembly (1789); aided in organizing the Garde Nationale, and was instrumental in securing the adoption of the tricolor flag. Opposed to the policies of Napoleon I. Leader of the opposition 1825–1830. Commander of the Garde Nationale in the July Revolution.

Laffitte, Jacques (1767–1844), Financier and statesman; partisan of Louis Philippe. Finance minister 1830–1831.

Laforgue, Jules (1860–1887). Poet and critic. One of the most distinguished of the Symbolists.

Lagrange, Joseph (1736–1813). Geometer and astronomer. Professor in Paris at the Ecole Normale (1795) and the Ecole Polytechnique (1797). Was made a senator under Napoleon.

La Hodde, Lucien de (1898–1865). Police spy and author of *Histoire des sociétés secrètes et du parti républicain* (1850).

Lamartine, Alphonse Prat de (1790–1869). Popular poet and orator who helped shape the Romantic movement in French literature. Foreign minister in the Provisional Government of 1848. Author of *Méditations poétiques* (1820), *La Chute d'un ange* (1838), *Histoire des Girondins* (1846).

Lamennais, Robert (1782–1854). French priest and philosopher. His advocacy of freedom in religious matters led to his censure and condemnation.

La Mettrie, Julien (1709–1751). Physician and materialist philosopher. Author of *Histoire naturelle de l'âme* (1745).

Lami, Louis Eugène (1800–1890). French historical painter and illustrator. Praised by Baudelaire.

Lampélie. Name given to a deity representing sunlight in Lemercier's homage to Daguerre (1839).

La Lanterne. Popular journal founded and edited by Henri Rochefort (1868).

Laplace, Pierre (1749–1827). Astronomer and mathematician. Author of *Théorie des attractions des sphéroïdes et de la figure des planètes* (1785), *Essai philosophique sur les probabilités* (1814).

Larchey, Etienne-Lorédon (1831–1902). Librarian at the Bibliothèque de l'Arsenal in Paris. Historian, linguist, publicist, and founder of the journal *La Mosaïque*.

Larivière, Philippe-Charles de (1798–1876). Painter who executed battle scenes for the museum established by Louis Philippe at Versailles.

La Rochejacquelein, Henri Auguste (1805–1867). Leader of the Legitimist party in the Chamber of Deputies (1842–1848). Later a senator under the Second Empire.

Lassailly, Charles (1806–1843). Bohemian poet and writer who was secretary, for a time, to Balzac. Died destitute.

Lautréamont, comte de. Pseudonym of Isidore Ducasse (1846–1870), writer who anticipated Surrealism. Born in Uruguay; settled in Paris in the 1860s. Author of *Les Chants de Maldoror* (1867–1870).

Laverdant, Gabriel-Desiré (1809–1884). Journalist and critic for the Fourierist newspaper *La Démocratie pacifique*.

Lavoisier, Antoine Laurent de (1743–1794). A founder of modern chemistry. Because his experiments were financed by the monarchy, he was condemned by the Revolution and executed.

Lawrence, James (1773–1840). Writer; son of an English colonist in Jamaica. Published in 1793 a study of marriage and inheritance customs among the Nair caste in Malabar. Became known as a feminist advocate in France. Friend of Schiller and Percy Shelley.

Leblond, Marius and Ary. Pseudonyms of French writers Georges Athenas (1877–1955) and Aimé Merlo (1880–1958). Authors of *Vies parallèles* (1902), *En France* (1909), *Le Paradis perdu* (1939).

Lebon, Philippe (1769–1804). Chemist and civil engineer. Pioneered the use of gas for illumination (1799).

Le Breton, André (1808–1879). French critic. Author of *Balzac: L'Homme et l'oeuvre* (1905).

Leconte de Lisle, Charles (1818–1894). Poet of disillusionment and skepticism; leader of the Parnassian school. Author of *Poèmes antiques* (1852), *Poèmes barbares* (1862), and other works.

Ledoux, Claude-Nicolas (1736–1806). French architect. Drew up plans for the "ideal city" of Chaux, conceived as an extension of the saltworks at Arc-et-Sénans.

Ledru-Rollin, Alexandre (1807–1874). Lawyer and politician, member of the Chamber of Deputies from 1841. A leader in the 1848 revolution, and minister of the interior in the Provisional Government. Instrumental in bringing universal suffrage to France.

Lefeuve, Charles (1818–1882). Writer and publicist, known for his archaeological and historical study *Les Anciennes Maisons des rues de Paris* (1857–1864).

Legitimists. Supporters of the Bourbon monarchy that was in power in France up to the Revolution of 1789 and during the Restoration (1815–1830). Also known as "ultras," they represented the interests of big landowners.

Lemaître, Jules (1853–1914). Writer and literary critic; enemy of critical dogmas. On the staff of *Le Journal des débats* and *La Revue des deux mondes*.

Lemercier, Louis Jean Népomucène (1771–1840). Playwright and poet. Upholder of classical tragedy against Romanticism, and originator of French historical comedy.

Lemonnier, Camille (1844–1913). Belgian novelist and art critic.

Lenin, Nikolai (1870–1924). Russian Communist leader. Became premier in 1918 and introduced far-reaching socialistic reforms, later modified by the New Economic Policy (1921).

Leopardi, Giacomo (1798–1837). Renowned Italian poet and scholar. Author of pessimistic and satirical lyrics and several works of philology.

Le Play, Frédéric (1806–1882). Engineer and economist. As senator (1867–1870), he represented a paternalistic "social Catholicism." Author of *Les Ouvriers européens* (1885).

Leroux, Gaston (1868–1927). French journalist and author of detective and mystery stories.

Leroux, Pierre (1797–1871). Saint-Simonian philosopher, economist, reformer; editor of *Le Globe* from 1824. In exile 1851–1859. Author of *De l'Humanité* (1840), *De l'Egalité* (1848).

Les Français peints par eux-mêmes. A celebrated and much imitated collection of essays and drawings that began publication in 1840. Grandville contributed several items.

Lesage, Alain (1668–1747). French novelist and playwright. Author of the picaresque masterpiece *L'Histoire de Gil Blas de Santillane* (1715–1735).

Lesseps, Ferdinand (1805–1894). French diplomat; minister of France in Madrid (1848–1849). Helped form the company that constructed the Suez Canal (1859–1869), and served as president of the company that began construction of the Panama Canal (1881–1888).

Le Vavasseur, Gustave (1819–1896). Writer, and good friend of Baudelaire.

Lévy, Michel (1821–1875). Founder of one of the largest publishing houses in nineteenth-century France. Published Baudelaire's translations of Poe and, after the poet's death, his *Oeuvres complètes*.

Le Libérateur. Newspaper founded by Louis-Auguste Blanqui in 1834 and dedicated to "exploited workers." Published one issue only.

Lion, Margo (1889–1989). Popular Berlin cabaret artist of the 1920s. Played the part of Pirate Jenny in the French production of Brecht's *Threepenny Opera* in 1931.

Liselotte. Nickname of Charlotte Elisabeth of Bavaria (1652–1722), duchess of Orléans, and sister-in-law of Louis XIV. Her *Letters* provide much intimate information about his court.

Lissagaray, Prosper (1838–1901). Journalist and historian. After participating in the Paris Commune, he emigrated to England.

Le Livre des cent-et-un. Periodical published in Paris 1831–1834. Contained essays and poems, many focused on life in Paris, by some of the most famous writers of the day.

Lobau, Georges (1770–1838). Highly decorated officer in Napoleon's army. Liberal deputy (1828–1830), and commander-in-chief of the Garde Nationale (1830).

Lohenstein, Daniel (1635–1683). German writer of tragedies, a book of lyrics, and a novel. Treated in Benjamin's *Ursprung des deutschen Trauerspiels.*

Loi Falloux. *See* Falloux, comte Frédéric.

Longchamps, Charles de (1768–1832). Popular dramatist and author of vaudevilles and operas, including *Le Séducteur amoureux* (1803).

Loos, Adolf (1870–1933). Moravian architect; opposed to Art Nouveau. He was a leader in establishing modernist architecture in Europe after World War I. Lived in Vienna and Paris. Author of *Ornament und Verbrechen* (1908).

Lotze, Hermann (1817–1881). German philosopher. Initiator of a teleological idealism that reinterpreted the Platonic ideas in terms of values. Helped found the science of physiological psychology.

Louis Napoleon. *See* Napoleon III.

Louis Philippe (1773–1850). Descendant of the Bourbon-Orléans royal line. Member of the Jacobin Club in 1790, and a colonel in the revolutionary army. Lived in Philadelphia (1796–1800), and later in England; was in France 1817–1830, administering his estates and great wealth. Proclaimed "Citizen King" by Thiers in the July Revolution, and elected by the Chamber of Deputies as a constitutional monarch on August 7, 1830. His reign, which sought to portray itself as middle-of-the-road and was therefore known as the "Juste Milieu," was marked by the rise of the bourgeoisie to power, especially through its domination of industry and finance. Overthrown by the February Revolution of 1848, on which he abdicated and escaped to England.

Louis the Great. Louis XIV (1638–1715), the longest-reigning king in European history (1643–1715), his court the most magnificent in Europe. French arts were in their golden age during his reign.

Louis XII (1462–1515). Known as Father of the People. Held the title duc d'Orléans 1465–1498. As king (1498–1515), he inaugurated widespread reforms.

Louis XVIII (1755–1824). After living as an émigré, he became king of France on Napoleon's downfall and the restoration of the Bourbons. Reigned 1814–1815, 1815–1824 (abdicating briefly during Napoleon's Hundred Days).

Louÿs, Pierre (1870–1925). French man of letters. Author of *Astarté* (verse, 1891), *Aphrodite* (novel, 1896), and other works.

Lucan. Full name Marcus Annaeus Lucanus (39–65 A.D.), Roman poet born in Cordova. Betrayed in a conspiracy against Nero. His sole extant work is the epic *Pharsalia,* about the war between Caesar and Pompey.

Lutèce. Ancient name for Paris. From Latin *Lutetia* ("city of mud").

Mabille, Pierre (1904–1952). Physician and writer, associated with the Symbolists. Editorial director of the famous art review *Minotaure.* His major works include *La Construction de l'homme* (1936), *Egrégores, ou La Vie des civilisations* (1938), and *Le Miroir du merveilleux* (1940).

MacOrlan, Pierre. Pseudonym of Pierre Dumarchais (1882–1970), writer associated with the group of Surrealists around Guillaume Apollinaire and Max Jacob. Among his novels, notable for their mixture of fantasy and realism, are *Le Quai des brumes* (1927) and *Le Nègre Léonard et Maître Jean Mullin* (1920).

Maeterlinck, Maurice (1862–1949). Belgian poet, dramatist, and essayist. Settled in Paris in 1896 and was influenced by the Symbolists. Author of *Pelléas et Mélisande* (1892), *Le Trésor des humbles* (1896), *L'Oiseau bleu* (1908).

Maillard, Firmin (1833–?). French journalist. Historian of the press and of Paris.

Maillard, L. Y. Young republican exile with whom Louis-Auguste Blanqui corresponded in 1852.

Makart, Hans (1840–1884). Austrian painter of historical scenes, with an opulent style imitative of sixteenth- and seventeenth-century Baroque.

Malassis. *See* Poulet-Malassis, Auguste.

Malebranche, Nicolas (1638–1715). Philosopher who sought to reconcile Cartesianism with the ideas of Augustine. His chief work, *De la Recherche de la verité* (1674–1678), argues that "we see all things in God," human nature being unknowable.

Malibran, Maria (1808–1836). French opera singer. Debuted in Rossini's *Il Barbiere di Siviglia* in 1825.

Mandeville, Bernard (1670?–1733). Dutch-born philosopher and satirist; settled in London. Author of the political satire *The Fable of the Bees, or Private Vices, Public Benefits* (1714).

Mapah. *See* Ganeau.

Marais. District of Paris; site of a republican insurrection in April 1834, during which, in a house on the Rue Transnonain, all occupants were butchered by government troops. This incident is the subject of Daumier's lithograph *La Rue Transnonain*.

Marat, Jean Paul (1743–1793). Swiss-born French Revolutionary politician; identified with the radical Jacobins. Assassinated by Charlotte Corday while in his bath.

Marcelin, Louis (1825–1887). Caricaturist on the staff of *Le Journal amusant;* associate of Nadar. In 1862 founded the journal *La Vie parisienne,* which published work by Baudelaire.

Marcionites. Believers in a Christian heresy of the second and third centuries that rejected the Old Testament. It likely included women in leadership roles.

Marengo. Village in northwest Italy where Napoleon gained a victory over the Austrians in 1800.

Marey, Etienne (1830–1904). Physiologist who studied electrical phenomena in animals. Invented the "chronophotographic gun" in 1882 to take series pictures of birds in flight.

Marie, Alexandre Thomas (b. 1795). French lawyer, associate of Ledru-Rollin; on the staff of *L'Atelier.* Member of the Provisional Government. Entrusted with the organization of the national workshops in 1848.

Marie-Louise (1791–1847). Daughter of Francis I of Austria; second wife (1810) of Napoleon I.

Marivaux, Pierre (1688–1763). French playwright and novelist.

Marlitt. Pseudonym of Eugénie John (1825–1887), popular German novelist, whose works appeared in the review *Die Gartenlaube.*

Martin du Nord, M. (1790–1847). Liberal opponent of the July Monarchy in the Chamber of Deputies. His proposal for government-financed railways in 1838 was voted down.

Martin, John (1789–1854). English painter known for works of wild imaginative power, like *Belshazzar's Feast* (1821), *The Fall of Ninevah* (1828), *The Eve of the Deluge* (1840).

Martinist. *See* Saint-Martin, Louis.

Maturin, Charles (1780–1824). Irish novelist and dramatist. Author of *Melmoth the Wanderer* (1820) and other Gothic romances.

Mauclair, Camille (1872–1945). Author of works on literature, music, and painting, including studies of Maeterlinck (1900), Baudelaire (1927), Heine (1930), Poe (1932), Mallarmé (1937).

Mayeux. Hunchbacked character of popular farce, appropriated by Traviès in some 160 lithographs published in *La Caricature* and elsewhere. Described as a "priapic puppet," he personified the patriotic petty bourgeois.

McAdam, John (1756–1836). British engineer who introduced the system of building roads of crushed stone, known as "macadamized" roads.

Mehring, Franz (1846–1919). German Socialist historian and pamphleteer. Helped organize the German Communist party.

Meilhac, Henri (1831–1897). French playwright. Collaborated with Ludovic Halévy on many light operas and comedies, including *Froufrou* (1869) and *Loulou* (1876).

Meissonier, Jean (1815–1891). Painter known for small genre paintings, often of military subjects, done with great delicacy.

Méliès, Georges (1861–1938). Professional magician and popular pioneer filmmaker. Director of *Le Voyage dans la lune* (1902) and other fantasies.

Mémoires du diable. Serial novel by Frédéric Soulié, published 1837–1838.

Mendès, Catulle (1841–1909). Founder of *La Revue fantaisiste* (1859) and editor of *La Parnasse contemporaine* (1866–1876). Friend of Baudelaire and Gautier.

Ménilmontant. *See* Enfantin, Barthélemy-Prosper.

Méphis. Novel by Flora Tristan, published 1838.

Merezhkovski, Dmitri (1865–1941). Russian writer, settled in Paris in 1917. Author of critical studies, historical novels, biographies, and plays.

Meryon, Charles (1821–1868). French etcher and engraver. Friend of Baudelaire.

Metternich, Prince Klemens von (1773–1859). Austrian statesman; created prince of the Austrian Empire in 1813. Largely responsible for the reactionary policy adopted by governments of Europe from 1815 to 1830.

Meyerbeer. Pseudonym of Jakob Beer (1791–1864), opera composer. Born in Berlin, he settled 1826 in Paris, where he composed in the French style.

Michel, Louise (1830–1905). French anarchist agitator. Participated in the Paris Commune (1871), and was deported to New Caledonia; returned after amnesty (1880) and resumed agitation. Sentenced to six years' imprisonment (1883); refused a pardon, out of solidarity with her comrades. Author of *La Commune* (1898). Photographed by Nadar.

Michelet, Jules (1798–1874). Historian and professor at the Collège de France 1838–1851. Democratic, anticlerical, anti-Semitic. Author of *Histoire de France* (1833–1867), *Histoire de la Révolution française* (1847–1853), *La Bible de l'humanité* (1864), and other works.

Mignet, François (1796–1884). Historian. Edited, with Adolphe Thiers, the anti-Bourbon journal *Le National* (1830). Author of *Histoire de la Révolution française* (1824).

Mirabeau, Victor Riqueti, marquis de (1715–1789). Soldier and economist, associated with the physiocrats. Author of *L'Ami des hommes, ou Traité sur la population* (1756).

Mirabeau, Honoré, comte de (1749–1791). Orator who became the most important figure of the first two years of the French Revolution. Son of Victor de Mirabeau.

Mirbeau, Octave (1850–1917). Radical journalist and novelist who attacked all forms of social organization. A founder of the satirical weekly *Grimaces* (1882).

Mirecourt, Eugène (Jacquot) de (1812–1880). French journalist. Author of a series of biographical sketches which led to his forced departure from Paris.

Mirès, Jules-Isaac (1809–1871). French financier; backer of railroads and newspapers. Photographed by Nadar. Convicted of fraud in 1861, he eventually won acquittal on appeal, but his reputation was ruined.

Misopogon. Fourth-century satire by Emperor Flavius Claudius Julianus.

Mistral, Frédéric (1830–1914). Leader of the Provençal cultural renaissance known as the Félibrige. Author of an epic poem, *Mirèio* (1859), written in Provençal and French and dealing with the lovelorn daughter of a wealthy farmer. Awarded the Nobel Prize for literature in 1904.

Moabit. District of Berlin, northwest of the Tiergarten. To the south of the park, Lützowstrasse gives onto Flottwellstrasse.

Modé, comte Louis (1781–1855). Premier of France 1836–1839. He was one of the deputies who opposed the coup d'état of 1851.

Mohammed Ali (1769–1849). Albanian-born soldier; viceroy of Egypt 1805–1848. Wrested control of Egypt from the Ottoman Empire and established a modern state.

Moilin, Tony (1832–1871). French utopian writer. Author of *Paris en l'an 2000* (1869).

Molènes, Paul de (1821–1862). French army officer and dandy. Friend of Baudelaire.

Molinari, Gustave de (1819–1912). Belgian political economist, in Paris 1843–1851, and from 1857 on. Became editor of *Le Journal des débats* (1867), and *Le Journal des économistes* (1881).

Moll, Joseph (1813–1849). German watchmaker. Member of the Central Committee of the Communist League. Killed in a revolt in Baden.

Le Moniteur universel. Daily newspaper published in Paris 1789–1901. From 1799 to 1869, an official government organ.

Monnier, Henri (1805–1877). Caricaturist and playwright. Creator (1830) of the popular character Joseph Prudhomme, the typical bourgeois. Discussed by Baudelaire in "Quelques Caricaturistes français."

Monselet, Charles (1825–1888). Critic and journalist. Founder of *La Semaine théatrale* (1851), in which Baudelaire published criticism and poetry.

Montesquieu, Charles (1689–1755). Lawyer, man of letters, and political philosopher whose liberal theories inspired the Declaration of the Rights of Man and the Constitution of the United States.

Montesquiou, Robert de (1855–1921). Aristocratic poet and essayist. Supposed model for Huysmans' des Esseintes and Proust's Charlus.

Moréas, Jean (1856–1910). Greek-born poet who settled in Paris in 1882. Associated with the Symbolists and later with the Ecole Romane. Author of *Les Syrtes* (1884), *Stances* (1899–1901).

Morgan, Lewis Henry (1818–1881). American ethnologist and archaeologist, student of American Indian culture. Author of *Ancient Society* (1877).

The Mother (*la Mère*). Female messiah of the Saint-Simonians. She was supposed by some to come from the East, possibly from the ranks of the prostitutes.

The Mothers. Mythologlogical figures in Goethe's *Faust,* Part 2 (Act 1). Faust visits the chthonic "Mothers" in search of the secret that will enable him to discover Helen of Troy.

Moulin Rouge. Well known spectacular Paris nightclub.

Munch, Edvard (1863–1944). Norwegian painter and designer; forerunner of Expressionism.

Munchausen (Münchhausen), Baron Karl (1720–1797). German huntsman and soldier. His name is proverbially associated with absurdly exaggerated adventure stories.

Murger, Henri (1822–1861). Writer who lived in poverty, supported by Nerval. Wrote pieces for the serial press that were collected in the 1848 book *Scènes de la vie de Bohème,* source for Puccini's opera *La Bohème.*

Murillo, Bartolomé (1617–1682). Spanish painter of the Andalusian school.

Musard, Philippe (1793–1859), Composer famous for his dance music; popular conductor at balls at the Opéra.

Musset, Alfred de (1810–1857). Distinguished poet and playwright of French Romanticism.

Mutualists. Secret society of weavers in Lyons who held that the factories should be taken over by associations of workers, operating through economic action rather than violent revolution. Name adapted by Proudhon for doctrines of credit banking and decentralized political organization.

Les Mystères de Londres. Novel by Paul Féval (11 vols.; 1844).

Les Mystères de Paris. Enormously popular novel by Eugène Sue (1842–1843).

The Mysteries of Udolpho. Novel by Ann Radcliffe (1794).

Nadar. Pseudonym of Félix Tournachon (1820–1910), French photographer, journalist, and caricaturist. Friend of Baudelaire, whom he photographed.

Nanteuil, Célestin (1813–1873). Romantic painter and graphic artist celebrated by Nadar.

Napoleon III. Full name Charles Louis Napoleon Bonaparte, known as Louis Napoleon (1808–1873). Nephew of Napoleon I, he lived in exile until assuming leadership of the Bonaparte family on the death of Napoleon II (1832). Elected to the National Assembly in 1848 and later to the presidency of the Republic (December 10, 1848). Made himself dictator by a coup d'état (December 2, 1851), and a year later proclaimed himself emperor as Napleon III. Having precipitated France's involvement in the Franco-Prussian War (1870–1871), he was himself captured at the Battle of Sedan (September 2, 1870) and held prisoner until the end of the war. Deposed by the National Assembly on March 1, 1871, he retired to England, where he died.

Nargeot, Clara (née Thénon; 1829–?). French painter. Did a portrait of Baudelaire.

Nash, Joseph (1809–1878). English watercolor painter and lithographer.

Le National. Daily newspaper published in Paris 1830–1851. During the 1840s, it was the organ of moderate republicans.

national workshops *(ateliers nationaux)*. An emergency relief agency, set up during the February Revolution of 1848, that attracted thousands of unemployed workers from all over France; it eventually satisfied neither radicals nor moderates and was abolished by the newly elected conservative majority in May, without any program of public works to replace it.

Naville, Pierre (1904–1993). Surrealist co-editor of the first numbers of *La Révolution surréaliste,* and writer on urban sociology.

Nazarenes. Group of young German painters active 1809–1830. Intent on restoring a religious spirit to art, they established themselves in Rome under the leadership of Johann Overbeck, Philipp Veit, and Franz Pforr.

Nerval, Gérard de. Pseudonym of Gérard Labrunie (1808–1855), celebrated French writer and eccentric, who committed suicide. Translated Goethe's *Faust.* Author of *Voyage en orient* (1848–1850), *Les Illuminés* (1852), *Les Filles de feu* (1854), *Aurélia* (1855).

Nesselrode, Karl (1780–1862). Russian statesman; chancellor 1845–1856. Concluded the Treaty of Paris after the Crimean War (1854–1856).

Nettelbeck, Joachim (1738–1824). Prussian officer whose memoirs, *Eine Lebensbeschreibung,* appeared in 1821.

Neufchâteau, François. Pseudonym of Nicolas François (1750–1828), French statesman and author. Minister of the interior 1797; member of the Directory 1797–1798; president of the Senate 1804–1806.

Niboyet, Eugénie (1804–?). Feminist who founded women's organizations in Lyons and Paris. Editor of the periodical *La Voix des femmes.*

Nicolaitans. Heretical sect in the early Christian church at Ephesus and Pergamum, possibly associated with the prophetess Jezebel, and condemned in Revelation (2.6,15) for immorality.

Niépce, Joseph (1765–1833). French physicist. In 1824 produced "heliotypes" by means of glass plates coated with bitumin. Associated with Daguerre (from 1829) in experiments leading to the invention of photography.

Nisard, Désiré (1806–1888). Journalist and literary critic. Director of the Ecole Normale Supérieure. Author of *Histoire de la littérature française* (1844–1861).

Nodier, Charles (1780–1844). Man of letters associated with the Romantic movement. Author of *Les Vampires* (1820). Collaborated with Amédée Pichot on *Essai critique sur le gaz hydrogène et les divers modes d'éclairage artificiel* (1823).

Noël, Jules (1815–1881). French landscape painter.

Noir, Victor (1848–1870). Journalist killed in an altercation with a cousin of Napoleon III. His funeral was the scene of a mob demonstration against the Empire.

Notre Dame de Lorette. Church in Paris. In its neighborhood, during Second Empire, many lorettes (ladies of easy virtue) lived in new housing.

Nouveauté. Newness, novelty, innovation; fancy article. The shops in Paris known as *magasins de nouveautés* offered a complete selection of goods in one or another specialized line of business. They had many rooms and several stories, with large staffs of employees. The first such store, Pygmalion, opened in Paris in 1793.

Obermann. Epistolary novel by Etienne Senancour (1804).

Odoievsky, Vladimir (1804–1869). Russian writer influenced by E. T. A. Hoffmann.

Offenbach, Jacques (1819–1880). Musician and composer. Born in Cologne, he became a nationalized Frenchman. Produced many successful operettas and opéras bouffes in Paris; managed the Gaîté-Lyrique there, 1872–1876. His famous *Contes d'Hoffmann* was produced after his death.

Ollivier, Emile (1825–1913). Politician. Headed the ministry (1870) that plunged France into the disasters of the Franco-Prussian war.

Olympia. Character in E. T. A. Hoffmann's story "Der Sandmann," a beautiful automaton.

Orleanists. Supporters of the Orléans branch of the French royal family, which was descended from a younger brother of Louis XIV and which included Louis Philippe.

Orléans, duc Ferdinand Philippe Louis (1810–1842). Son of Louis Philippe. Active in the Revolution of 1830; was made duc d'Orléans in 1830. In 1837, married Hélène Elisabeth, daughter of Grand Duke Frederick Louis of Mecklenburg-Schwerin.

Orphée et Eurydice (*Orfeo ed Euridice*). Opera by Christoph Gluck (1762).

Orsay, comte Alfred d' (1801–1852). French man of fashion, wit, painter in Paris and London.

Orsini, Felice (1819–1858). Italian revolutionary, active in the revolutions of 1848–1849. Attempted the assassination of Napoleon III (January 14, 1858). Executed in Paris.

Ourliac, Edouard (1813–1848). French writer; author of a physiology on the schoolboy. Early associate of Baudelaire.

Owen, Robert (1771–1858). Welsh socialist and philanthropist. Spent his fortune on social schemes. Founded communities of "Owenites" on the cooperative principle, in Great Britain and the U.S. (including one at New Harmony, Indiana, 1825–1828), all unsuccessful. Edited the influential journal *The New Moral World* (1836–1844). Author of *A New View of Society* (1813) and *Revolution in Mind and Practice* (1849).

Palais-Royal. Refers to the streets and shopping areas surrounding the palace of the dukes of Orléans in Paris. It was a center of prostitution and gambling, especially during the second quarter of the nineteenth century.

Panizza, Oskar (1853–1921). Controversial Bavarian playwright and poet. Argued in 1896 that the spirit of vaudeville was infusing modern culture.

panoramas. Large circular tableaux, usually displaying scenes of battles and cities, painted in trompe l'oeil and designed to be viewed from the center of a rotunda. Introduced in France in 1799 by the American engineer Robert Fulton. James Thayer acquired the patent, and developed two rotundas on the Boulevard Montmartre which were separated by the Passage des Panoramas. Subsequent forms included the Cosmorama at the Palais-Royal (later on the Rue Vivienne); the Neorama, showing interior scenes; the Georama, presenting views of different parts of the world. In 1822, on the Rue Sanson, Louis Daguerre and Charles Bouton opened their Diorama (later moved to the Boulevard de Bonne-Nouvelle). The pictures were painted on cloth transparencies, which by 1831 were being used with various lighting effects. Their installation burned down in 1839.

Parnassians. School of French poets, headed by Leconte de Lisle, stressing detachment, technical perfection, precise description. Anthologized in *Le Parnasse contemporain* (1866–1876).

Parusilippe. Hill near Naples, named after a Roman equestrian's care-dispelling villa.

Patin, Gui (1602–1672). Physician and dean of the Paris faculty of medicine. His witty letters, published posthumously, were widely read.

Pausanias. Greek traveler and geographer of the second century A.D. Author of *Periegesis of Greece,* documenting Greek topography, history, religion, architecture, and sculpture.

Paxton, Joseph (1801–1865). English architect and horticulturist. Designed the conservatory at Chatsworth (1836–1840), the model for his Crystal Palace, which was built of glass and iron for the London Exhibition of 1851, and reerected at Sydenham (1853–1854).

Pechméja, Ange. Rumanian poet influenced by Baudelaire. Published the first article on Baudelaire to appear beyond the Danube.

Péguchet, M. Caricature figure by Henri Monnier; adapted by Flaubert for his novel *Bouvard et Pécuchet* (1881).

Péladan, Joseph, called Joséphin (1858–1918). French writer and occultist who took the title "Sar." Published a series of novels under the general title *Décadence latine.*

Pelletan, Charles Camille (1846–1915). French journalist and politician. Son of Pierre Pelletan.

Pelletan, Pierrez (1813–1884). French journalist and politician. Author of *Les Droits de l'homme* (1858), *La Famille, la mère* (1865).

Perdiguier, Agricol (1805–1875). Worker-writer, political activist; model for characters in novels by George Sand and Eugène Sue. Trained as a joiner, he began writing for *La Ruche populaire,* and became an editor of *L'Atelier.* Elected to the Constituent Assembly (1848) and the Legislative Assembly (1849). Author of *Le Livre du compagnonnage* (1840), *Mémoires d'un compagnon* (1864).

Pereire. The brothers Jacob Emile (1800–1875) and Isaac (1806–1880) were financiers and brokers in Paris; associated with the Saint-Simonians. In 1852 founded Crédit Mobilier, which provided a model for new commercial banks across Europe.

Périer, Casimir (1777–1832). French banker and statesman, supporter of industry. A leader of the opposition to Charles X, who reigned 1824–1830. Prime minister under Louis Philippe 1831–1832.

Perret, Auguste (1874–1954). Architect who developed the structural possibilities of reinforced concrete. With his brothers Gustav and Claude, he built in Paris the first apartment block designed for reinforced concrete construction.

Pestalozzi, Johann Heinrich (1746–1827). Swiss educational reformer whose approach to instruction was influenced by Rousseau. Principal of a school at Yverdon 1805–1825.

Phaedrus. Roman fabulist of the early first century A.D. Author of a versified *Fabulae Aesopiae.*

La Phalange. Fourierist newspaper published in Paris 1832–1849. Subtitled *Revue de la science social.*

Phalanx. Fourierist term for an agriculturally based, self-supporting utopian community of 1,500–1,600 people. Its central edifice is known as the Phalanstery.

Pherecydes of Syros. Greek philosopher of the sixth century B.C. Author of a genealogy of the gods, of which only fragments remain.

Phidias. Fifth-century B.C. Athenian sculptor who executed the greatest of his city's monuments during the ascendancy of Pericles.

Philip Augustus, or Philip II (1165–1223). French king who engaged in various wars, consolidated new possessions, and built on a large scale.

Philipon, Charles (1800–1862). Oft-imprisoned French journalist and caricaturist. Founded and edited the weekly *La Caricature* and the daily *Le Charivari,* which attacked Louis Philippe. Became Daumier's editor in 1830.

Picabia, Francis (1879–1953). French painter, poet, and dandy. Associated with Cubism, Dadaism, and Surrealism. Constructor of imaginary "machines."

Pigal, Edme-Jean (1798–1872). Painter and illustrator. Discussed by Baudelaire in "Quelques Caricaturistes français."

Pinard, Ernest (1822–1909). Prosecuting counsel in the trials of *Madame Bovary* and *Les Fleurs du mal.* Became minister of the interior in 1867.

Pinelli, Bartolomeo (1781–1835). Italian painter and bohemian.

Piscator, Erwin (1893–1966). German expressionist theater director.

Plateau, Joseph (1801–1883). Belgian physicist. Originated a stroboscopic method for the study of vibratory motion. Invented the Phenakistiscope (Greek for "deceitful view") in 1832.

Plekhanov, Georgi (1857–1918). Russian political philosopher. After forty years in exile, he became the intellectual leader of the Russian Social Democratic movement, influencing the thought of Lenin.

Pokrovski, Mikhail (1868–1932). Russian Marxist historian and government official. Opposed Trotsky in the early 1920s. Author of *Russian History* (4 vols., 1924).

Pompadour, Madame de (1721–1764). Mistress of Louis XV of France; established at Versailles from 1745. She completely controlled the king and his policies.

Ponroy, Arthur. Writer whose father founded the conservative newspaper at Chateauroux, south of Paris, of which Baudelaire was briefly chief editor (1848).

Ponson du Terrail, Pierre-Alexis (1829–1871). Popular author of serial novels, such as *Exploits de Rocambole,* which were published in a twenty-two-volume collection in 1859.

Pontmartin, Armand de (1811–1890). Conservative critic whom Baudelaire called a "drawing-room preacher."

Posillipo. Promontory in the Bay of Naples.

Pottier (Potier), Eugène (1816–1887). Revolutionary poet and composer. Member of the Paris Commune and the Communist International. His poems are collected in *Chants révolutionnaires* (1887).

Poulet-Malassis, Auguste (1815–1878). French publisher and bibliophile. Close friend of Baudelaire in his later years. Published the first two editions of *Les Fleurs du mal.*

Pradier, James (1792–1852). French neoclassical sculptor.

Prarond, Ernest (1821–1909). French poet and historian of Picardy. Friend of Baudelaire.

La Presse. Daily newspaper published in Paris from 1836. Organ of the opposition in the 1840s. First paper to lower subscription rate to 40 francs, and to run advertisements and serial novels.

Prévost, Pierre (1764–1823). French painter.

Privat d'Anglemont, Alexandre (1815–1859). Bohemian man of letters who collaborated with Baudelaire on *Mystères galants de théâtre de Paris,* and wrote for *Le Siècle* and other journals. Author of *Paris inconnu* (1861).

Protot, Eugène (1839–1921). Lawyer and journalist. Blanquist, and member of the Paris Commune. Later attacked Engels and other Marxists.

Proudhon, Pierre-Joseph (1809–1865). Political thinker, regarded as the father of anarchism. Advocated a localized mutualist world federation to be achieved through economic action rather than violent revolution. Author of *Qu'est-ce que la propriété?* (1840) and other works.

Prudhomme, René. *See* Sully Prudhomme, René.

Przybyszewski, Stanislaw (1868–1927). Polish writer influenced by Nietzsche. Author of essays, novels, prose poems, and plays.

Pyat, Félix (1810–1889). French playwright and politician. A leader of the Paris Commune and a Revolutionary Socialist member of the Chamber of Deputies in 1888.

Quinet, Edgar (1803–1875). French writer and politician, associate of Jules Michelet. Hailed the 1848 revolution; in exile 1852–1870. Author of the epic poems *Napoléon* (1836) and *Prométhée* (1838), and of the prose poem *Ahasvérus* (1833), in which the figure of the Wandering Jew symbolizes the progress of humanity.

Rachel. Stage name of Elisa Félix (1820–1858), French actress famed for her roles as Phèdre, Lucrèce, Cleopatra. Died of tuberculosis.

Raffet, Denis (1804–1860). French illustrator. Classmate of Daumier. Best known for his lithographs of battle scenes.

Ragaz. Spa in the Rhine Valley near Chur, Switzerland.

Raphael, Max (1889–1952). French art historian; student of Georg Simmel and Heinrich Wölfflin. Lived in Paris 1932–1939.

Rastignac, Eugène. Character in *Père Goriot* (1834) and other novels by Balzac.

Ratapoil ("Hairy Rat"). Character created by Daumier in 1850 as a personification of militarism; he resembled Louis Napoleon.

Rattier, Paul Ernest de. Author of the utopian prose work *Paris n'existe pas* (1857).

Red Belt. Name for the suburbs immediately surrounding Paris proper in the later nineteenth century. Populated by many of the working class who were dislocated by Haussmann's urban renewal.

Redern, Sigismond, comte de (1755–1835). Prussian Ambassador to England who formed a business partnership in 1790 with Saint-Simon, with whom he shared an enthusiasm for science and social reform. The partnership was dissolved in 1797, but Redern later helped support Saint-Simon (1807–1811).

Redon, Odilon (1840–1916). French painter and engraver, identified with the post-Impressionist school. Famous for paintings of flowers.

La Réforme. Daily newspaper published in Paris (1843–1850) by republican democrats and socialists.

Reinach, Salomon (1858–1932). French archaeologist, director of the Musée de Saint-Germain. Author of *Orpheus: Histoire générale des religions* (1909) and other works.

Rellstab, Ludwig (1799–1860). Novelist, poet, and music critic for the Prussian *Vossische Zeitung.* Author of *Paris im Frühjahr 1843* (1844).

Renan, Ernest (1823–1892). French philologist and historian. Author of *De l'Origine du langage* (1858), *La Vie de Jésus* (1863).

René. Novel by Chateaubriand (1802).

Renouvier, Charles (1815–1903). Idealist philosopher. Author of *Le Personnalisme* (1902) and other works.

Restif de la Bretonne. Pseudonym of Nicolas Restif (1734–1806), novelist whose subject matter earned him the nickname "Rousseau of the Gutter."

Rethel, Alfred (1816–1859). German historical painter and graphic artist.

La Revue des deux mondes. Biweekly literary and political journal published in Paris since 1829.

Reynaud, Jean (1806–1863). Philosopher influenced by Saint-Simon. Author of *Terre et Ciel* (1854), which was condemned by a council of bishops at Périgueux.

Reynold de Cressier, Baron Frédéric Gonzague (1880–?). Swiss historian. Author of *La Démocratie et la Suisse* (1929), *L'Europe tragique* (1934), and other works.

Ricard, Louis-Gustave (1823–1873). Popular portrait painter praised by Gautier, Baudelaire, and Nadar.

Riquet, Pierre (1604–1680). Engineer who planned the Languedoc Canal, to connect the Mediterranean Sea with the Atlantic Ocean. He spent his personal fortune building the canal under Louis XIV; it was completed six months after his death.

Rivière, Jacques (1886–1925). Novelist and critic. Championed Proust, Stravinsky, Nijinsky. Editor of *Nouvelle Revue française* (1919–1925).

Robespierre, Maximilien François de (1758–1794). Radical Jacobin and Montagnard leader in the Revolution of 1789; responsible for much of the Reign of Terror. Attacked Jacques Hébert and Georges Danton. Executed by order of the Revolutionary Tribunal.

Rocambole. Popular multivolume serial novel by Pierre Ponson du Terrail (collected in 1859). Concerns a mysterious defender of the weak against the strong.

Rochefort, Henri (1830–1913). Journalist, playwright, and politician. In 1868 founded the satirical journal *La Lanterne,* opposed to Napoleon III. Involved in the Paris Commune (1871). Author of *La Grande Bohème* (1867), *Les Naufrageurs* (1876).

Rodenbach, Georges (1855–1898). Belgian poet. Associated with the Symbolists and with the nineteenth-century Belgian literary revival.

Rodrigues, Olinde (1794–1851). French intellectual and banker (of Jewish extraction) who became chief assistant to Saint-Simon in 1824, helped found *Le Producteur* (1825), and edited the first collected edition of Saint-Simon's writings (1832).

Roi Prudhomme. Play by Henri Monnier.

Rolla. Byronesque poem published by Musset in *La Revue des deux mondes* (1833).

Rollinat, Maurice (1846–1903). French poet known for his recitations at the Chat Noir café in Paris. His collection of poems, *Névroses* (1883), shows the influence of Baudelaire.

Romains, Jules (1885–1972). Novelist, poet, playwright. Author of *Les Hommes de bonne volonté* (27 vols.; 1932–1946), and other works. Moved to the U.S. in 1940.

Rops, Félicien (1833–1898). Belgian-French painter, engraver, and lithographer. Friend of Baudelaire.

Roqueplan, Nestor (1804–1870). Critic, and director of the Paris Opéra.

Rossini, Gioacchino (1792–1868). Celebrated Italian opera composer.

Rothschild, James (1792–1868). Founded the branch of his family's financial establishment at Paris. Gave support to the Restoration government and to the administration of Louis Philippe.

Rotrou, Jean de (1609–1650). French playwright. With Corneille, one of Cardinal Richelieu's "Five Poets." Author of *Saint Genest* (1646) and *Venceslas* (1647).

Rouget de Lisle, Claude (1760–1836). French army officer and songwriter; composer of "La Marseillaise" (1792).

Rückert, Friedrich (1788–1866). German poet, translator, professor of Oriental languages at Erlangen and Berlin. Author of *Deutsche Gedichte* (1814), *Die Weisheit des Brahmanen* (1836–1839).

Ruge, Arnold (1803–1880). German writer on philosophy and politics and editor of various leftist journals.

Rumford, Count. Title of Benjamin Thompson (1753–1814), American-born physicist and adventurer. From 1784 to 1795 he was in the service of the elector of Bavaria, who made him a count. Resident in Paris from 1802.

Ruy Blas. Play by Victor Hugo (1838).

Sabatier, Aglaé-Joséphine (1822–1890). French beauty; sponsor of Sunday dinners for the artistic world in the 1850s. Intimate friend of Baudelaire.

Sadler, Michael (1780–1835). English economist and politician. Leader of the philanthropic Tories.

Saint-Amant, Marc Antoine Girard (1594–1661). French burlesque poet and one of the first members of the Académie Française.

Sainte-Beuve, Charles Augustin (1804–1869). Leading man of letters in mid-nineteenth-century France. Author of *Vie, poésies, et pensées de Joseph Delorme* (1829), a novel, *Volupté* (1834), verse, and many volumes of literary criticism.

Sainte-Pélagie. Prison in Paris where Louis-Auguste Blanqui was held 1861–1865; demolished 1895.

Saint-Germain, comte de (d. ca. 1784). Adventurer in Paris from 1750. Claimed to possess the philosopher's stone and the elixir of life. Confidential diplomat of Louis XV.

Saint-Marc Girardin, François (1801–1873). Politician and man of letters. Member of the Chamber of Deputies (1835–1848). Professor of poetry at the Sorbonne. Author of *Cours de littérature dramatique* (1843–1863).

Saint-Martin, Louis (1743–1803). French mystic philosopher; one of the Illuminati, inspired by Jakob Böhme. Saint-Martin's followers were known as Martinists.

Saint-Simon, Henri (1760–1825). Philosopher and social reformer, considered the founder of French socialism. Fought in the American Revolution. Amassed a fortune by land speculation, but soon lost it and lived in relative poverty the last twenty years of his life. Author of *De la Réorganisation de la société européenne* (1814), *Du Système industriel* (1820–1823), *Le Nouveau Christianisme* (1825). His ideas were developed by disciples into the system known as Saint-Simonianism.

Salon. Annual public exhibitions of art in France, beginning in 1833, sponsored by the Academie Royale and held in the galleries of the Tuileries, adjoining the Louvre.

Salon des Etrangers. Luxurious Parisian gambling house frequented by the allies after Waterloo.

Salut public. Short-lived newspaper, founded by Baudelaire, Champfleury, and Charles Toubin. Two issues appeared, in February and March 1848. The name, recalling the infamous Committee of Public Safety formed under the Terror in 1793, came from Baudelaire. Its brief, unsigned articles were full of revolutionary enthusiasm for "the people," its republic, and a socialist Christ.

Salvandy, Narcisse, comte de (1795–1856). Colonial minister who invited Alexandre Dumas père to visit Tunis at the government's expense in order to publicize the colonies.

Sand, George. Pseudonym of Aurore Dudevant (1804–1876), Romantic novelist who stood for free association in all social relations, and whose protagonists are generally virtuous peasants or workmen. Famous for her love affairs with Prosper Mérimée, Alfred de Musset, and Frédéric Chopin.

Sandeau, Jules (1811–1883). Novelist and playwright. Curator of the Bibliothèque Mazarin in Paris.

Sarcey, Francisque (1827–1899). French journalist and drama critic.

Sauvageot, Charles (1781–1860). French archaeologist and violinist at the Opéra who assembled a vast collection, especially of Renaissance objects and art, during the 1830s. His collection was given to the Louvre in 1856.

Schapper, Karl (1812–1870). A leader in the German and international working-class movement, and a member of the Central Committee of the Communist League. Active in the 1848–1849 revolution in Germany.

Scheffer, Ary (1795–1858). Dutch-born French figure and portrait painter; criticized by Baudelaire.

Schinkel, Karl Friedrich (1781–1841). German architect and painter. Adapted classical Greek forms to modern architecture, as in the Royal Theater in Berlin.

Schlosser, Friedrich Christoph (1776–1861). German historian. Author of *Weltgeschichte für das Deutsche Volk* (19 vols.; 1843–1857).

Scholl, Aurélien (1833–1902). French journalist, friend of Offenbach, defender of Zola. Wrote for the *Le Figaro* before founding the satirical journal *Le Nain jaune* (1863). Author of *L'Esprit du boulevard.*

Schuls-Tarasp. Two neighboring towns in the Unter Engadin, in Switzerland.

Schweitzer, Johann Baptist (1834–1875). German politician and writer. Editor of *Der Sozial-Demokrat* (1864–1867). Succeeded Ferdinand Lasalle as president of the General Association of German Workers (1867–1871).

Scribe, Eugène (1791–1861). Popular playwright. Author or co-author of over 350 plays and librettos concerned with the predilections of the bourgeoisie.

Sedan, Battle of. Decisive victory of the Prussian army over the French on September 2, 1870, in which Napoleon III was taken prisoner. Led to the end of the Franco-Prussian War.

Segantini, Giovanni (1858–1899). Italian painter, influenced by French Impressionists. His *Punishment of the Unnatural Mothers, or The Infanticides* hangs in Vienna.

Senancour, Etienne (1770–1846). French writer of a pessimistic bent. Author of the epistolary novel *Obermann* (1804).

Senefelder, Aloys (1771–1834). Czech-born inventor of lithography (1796) and color lithography (1826). Inspector of maps at the royal Bavarian printing office in Munich.

September Laws. Passed in September 1835, they forbade any attack on the government or person of Louis Philippe, and required official authorization, as well as the deposit of a bond, for all publications and theatrical displays.

Serenus of Antissa. Greek geometer of Egypt who flourished circa the fourth century A.D.

Servandoni, Giovanni (1695–1766). Italian architect, painter, and stage designer. Called to Paris in 1724 to be architect to the king. Among his works are the neoclassical façade of the Church of Saint-Sulpice in Paris and the altar of the Church of the Chartreux in Lyons.

Sévigné, Madame de (1626–1696). French writer and lady of fashion, famed for her letters recording daily life in Paris and Brittany.

Le Siècle. Daily newspaper published in Paris 1836–1939. In the 1840s, it was oppositional; in the 1850s, moderate republican.

Silvy, Camille (1834–1910). Pioneer photographer, admired by Nadar.

Simonians. Syncretistic sect founded by a Samaritan magician of the first century A.D., Simon Magus, who converted to Christianity. He was accompanied in his ministry by a former prostitute named Helen.

Simplicissimus. Illustrated periodical founded in Munich in 1896 by Albert Langen and Frank Wedekind. It aimed to unsettle bourgeois complacency.

Sismondi, Jean Simonde de (1773–1842). Swiss historian and economist of Italian descent. Author of *Nouveaux Principes d'économie politique* (1819), *Histoire des Français* (1821–1844).

Solférino. Site of a major battle between Austrian and Franco-Piedmontese armies, June 24, 1859, in Lombardy. Heavy casualties led Napoleon III to seek a truce with Austria.

Sommerard, Alexandre du (1779–1842). French archaeologist who, during the 1830s, amassed a collection of French artifacts that was deposited in the Hôtel Cluny in 1832.

Soulié, Frédéric (1800–1847). Early practitioner of the serial novel. Author of popular sensational novels like *Mémoires du diable* (1837–1838).

Soumet, Alexandre (1788–1845). Poet and playwright, concerned with historical themes. Published *La Divine Epopée* in 1840.

Soupault, Philippe (1897–1990). Poet, novelist, and man of letters, associated with avant-garde movements of the early twentieth century. Published a biography of Baudelaire in 1931.

Spartacus (?–71). Leader of a slave revolt against Rome in the first century A.D.

Spielhagen, Friedrich (1829–1911). Popular German novelist and playwright, and partisan of democratic movements.

Spitzweg, Carl (1808–1885). German painter of landscape and genre scenes, associated with the Biedermeier style.

Stein, Lorenz von (1815–1890). German lawyer and historian, author of works on the socialist movement.

Steinlen, Théophile (1859–1923). French artist and illustrator, well-known for his posters and lithographs.

Stern, Daniel. Pseudonym of Marie Flavigny, comtesse d'Agoult (1805–1876), historian, novelist, and playwright who wrote extensively on the Revolution of 1848. Led a salon in Paris, and was the mistress of Franz Liszt, with whom she had a daughter, Cosima, later the wife of Richard Wagner.

Stevens, Alfred (1828–1906). Belgian painter, best known for his genre scenes of Parisian society.

Stifter, Adalbert (1805–1868). Austrian writer who believed that small everyday phenomena manifest the principles of nature more sublimely than prodigious phenomena. Author of *Die Mappe meines Urgrossvaters* (1842), *Bunte Steine* (1853). Subject of a short essay of 1918 by Benjamin.

Strabo (63 B.C.–A.D. 24). Greek geographer and historian working in Rome during the age of Augustus.

Suchet, Louis-Gabriel (1772–1826). Napoleonic general.

Sue, Eugène (1804–1857). Popular novelist of urban life and leading exponent of the newspaper serial. A Parisian dandy, he lived in exile after the coup d'état of 1851. Author of *Les Mystères de Paris* (1842–1843), *Le Juif errant* (1844–1845).

Sully Prudhomme, René (1839–1907). French poet, a leader of the Parnassians in their attempt to bring positivist philosophy to poetry.

Swedenborg, Emanuel (1688–1772). Swedish scientist, philosopher, and religious writer. Author of *Arcana Coelestia* (1749–1756). His followers organized the New Jerusalem church.

Taine, Hippolyte Adolphe (1828–1893). French philosopher and historian; leading exponent of positivism. Professor of aesthetics and the history of art at the Ecole des Beaux-Arts (1864–1883). Among his works are *Essais de critique et d'histoire* (1855), *Histoire de la littérature anglaise* (1865), *Origines de la France contemporaine* (1871–1894).

Talleyrand-Périgord, Charles (1754–1838). French clergyman and statesman. Grand chamberlain under Napoleon and later ambassador to Great Britain (1830–1834). Helped engineer the July Revolution. His *Mémoires* were published in 1891.

Talma, François (1763–1826). Outstanding French tragedian, a favorite with Napoleon.

Taylor, Frederick Winslow (1856–1915). American efficiency engineer. Author of *The Principles of Scientific Management* (1911).

Terrasson, Jean, abbé (1670–1750). Freemason and member of the Académie Française who championed the "moderns" in their debate with the "ancients." His novel *Séthos* (1731) combined political instruction with Masonic initiation.

Thierry, Augustin (1795–1856). French historian and assistant to Saint-Simon (1814–1817). Author of *Conquête de l'Angleterre par les Normands* (1825) and *Lettres sur l'histoire de France* (1827).

Thierry, Edouard (1813–1894). French poet and critic, known for his essays on drama. Friend of Baudelaire.

Thiers, Adolphe (1797–1877). Statesman and historian. Held cabinet posts under Louis Philippe, and was a leader of the Liberal opposition (1863–1870). In 1871, he helped crush the Paris Commune. Was elected first president of the Third Republic (1871–1873). Among his works are *Histoire de la Révolution française* (1823–1827) and *Histoire du Consulat et de l'Empire* (1845–1862).

Third Republic of France. 1875–1940.

Thomas, Emile (1822–1880). Civil engineer who, at age twenty-five, became director and chief architect of the National Workshops (February–May 1848).

Thomasius, Christian (1655–1728). German jurist and progressive philosopher. Taught at the University of Halle, where he departed from scholastic curriculum and lectured in vernacular German rather than Latin.

Three Glorious Days. *See* July Revolution.

Tiberius (42 B.C.–A.D. 37). Emperor of Rome (A.D. 14–37). Heir of Augustus.

Tieck, Ludwig (1773–1853). German author of lyric poetry, novels, dramas, and literary criticism.

Toubin, Charles (1820–1891). Professor who wrote for *La Revue des deux mondes*. Friend of Baudelaire and Courbet. Author of works on folklore and etymology.

Tournachon, Félix. *See* Nadar.

Toussenel, Alphonse (1803–1885). French naturalist; follower of Fourier. Editor of the journal *La Paix*. Author of *L'Esprit des bêtes* (1856), and other works in a droll mode.

Traviès de Villers, Charles (1804–1859). Painter and caricaturist; a founder of the periodicals *Le Charivari* (1831) and *La Caricature* (1838). Discussed by Baudelaire in "Quelques Caricaturistes français."

Trélat, Ulysse (1795–1879). Doctor and politician. On the editorial board of *Le National*, and minister of public works from May to June 1848.

Tridon, Gustav (1841–1871). French politician and publicist. Louis-Auguste Blanqui's favorite lieutenant. Active in the Paris Commune. Author of an anti-Semitic extravaganza, *Du Molochisme juif*.

Tristan, Flora (1803–1844). French radical writer who advocated a utopian socialism. Author of *Union ouvrière* (1843), *L'Emancipation de la femme* (1845).

Trophonius. Mythical builder of the Delphic oracle. According to legend, he gave prophetic answers after his death to those who slept in his cave in Boeotia.

Troyon, Constant (1813–1865). Landscape painter; a member of the Barbizon group. Renowned for paintings of animals.

Tuileries. A royal residence in Paris, begun in 1564 by Catherine de Médicis and burned in 1871. Now the site of the Tuileries Gardens, a park near the Louvre.

Turgot, Anne Robert (1727–1781). Statesman and economist; associated with the Physiocrats. His fiscal and political reforms met with opposition from high-ranking circles and led to his dismissal in 1776. Among his works are *Lettres sur la tolérance* (1753–1754) and *Réflexions sur la formation et la distribution du richesses* (1766).

Unold, Max (1885–1964). German writer and graphic artist. In France 1911–1913.

Usener, Hermann (1834–1905). German classical scholar and historian of religion. Teacher of Aby Warburg.

Vacquerie, Auguste (1819–1895). Journalist and playwright. Co-founded the radical journal *Le Rappel* (1869).

Vaihinger, Hans (1852–1933). German philosopher who developed Kantianism in the direction of pragmatism by espousing a theory of "fictions" for negotiating the maze of life. Author of *Die Philosophie des Als Ob* (1911).

Valjean, Jean. Leading character in Victor Hugo's *Les Misérables* (1862).

Vallès, Jules (1832–1885). French socialist journalist and novelist; founded *Le Cri du peuple* (1871). Member of the Paris Commune. Author of *Jacques Vingtras* (1879–1886).

van de Velde, Henry (1863–1957). Belgian architect and craftsman; leader of Jugendstil in architecture and arts. His most important work is *Vom neuen Stil* (1907).

Varlin, Louis-Eugène (1839–1871). Bookbinder and Proudhonist. He was a leader in the First International, as well as a member of the Central Committee of the Garde Nationale. Took part in the Paris Commune, and was killed by the forces of Thiers's government.

Varnhagen von Ense, Karl (1785–1858). German diplomat and writer. Author of *Biographische Denkmale* (1824–1830).

Vaucanson, Jacques de (1709–1782). Inventor. Constructed an automaton, "The Flute Player," in 1738, followed the next year by "The Duck," which imitated the motions of a live duck. Succeeded in automating the loom used for silk weaving.

Vautrin. Name assumed by the villainous character Jacques Collin in *Père Goriot, Illusions perdues,* and other of Balzac's novels.

Vehme, or Vehmgericht. System of secret tribunals that spread across Germany in the Middle Ages and allowed much scope for private revenge and judicial murder.

Vendée. A province in the west of France which gave its name to a royalist insurrection that took place there during the Revolution (1793).

Verhaeren, Emile (1855–1916). Belgian poet who fused techniques of Symbolism and Naturalism. An editor of *La Jeune Belgique*. Published *Les Villes tentaculaires* in 1895.

Verlaine, Paul (1844–1896). Leading Symbolist poet. Author of *Poèmes saturniens* (1866), *Sagesse* (1881), *Les Poètes maudits* (1884), *Elégies* (1893).

Véron, Louis (1798–1867). French journalist known as Docteur Véron. Founded *La Revue de Paris* (1829) and revived *Le Constitutionnel* (1835). Bonapartist after 1848.

Vésuviennes. Club de la Légion des Vésuviennes on the Rue Sainte-Apolline, one of many feminist clubs founded in France in 1848.

Veuillot, Louis (1813–1883). Journalist and editor of *L'Univers religieux* (1843). Author of *Le Pape et la diplomatie* (1861), *Les Odeurs de Paris* (1866).

Vicat, Louis (1786–1861). Engineer who specialized in building materials for bridges.

Vidocq, François (1775–1857). French adventurer and detective; served under Napoleon, Louis Philippe, and Lamartine. Published *Mémoires de Vidocq* (4 vols.; 1828–1829).

Vigny, Alfred de (1797–1863). Man of letters and army officer; leader of the Romantic school. His work is distinguished by an aristocratic pessimism.

Villèle, Jean Baptiste (1773–1854). Leader of the ultra-Royalists after the Restoration; premier 1822–1828. A critic of the financial policies of the July Monarchy.

Villemain, Abel (1790–1870). Writer and politician; secretary of the Académie Française. Author of *Eloge de Montesquieu* (1816), *Essai sur le génie de Pindare* (1859).

Villemessant, Jean (1812–1879). French journalist. Founder of *Le Figaro,* first (1854) as a weekly, and later (1866) as a daily newspaper.

Villiers de l'Isle-Adam, Auguste (1838–1889). Poet, dramatist, and short-story writer; reputed originator of the Symbolist school. Author of *Premières Poésies* (1856–1858), *Contes cruels* (1883), *Axel* (1890).

Viollet-le-Duc, Eugène (1814–1879). Architect; a leader of the Gothic revival in France. Designed the restoration of medieval buildings, including the cathedral of Notre-Dame in Paris.

Vireloque, Thomas. Character created by the illustrator Paul Gavarni.

Virginie. Character in Jacques Bernardin de Saint-Pierre's romance *Paul et Virginie* (1788).

Vischer, Friedrich Theodor (1807–1887). German poet and aesthetician of the Hegelian school. Author of *Kritische Gänge* (1844; 1860), *Ästhetik* (1846–1857), and a parody of Goethe, *Faust, Part III*.

Volney, Constantin-François (1757–1820). French scholar. Member of the States-General (1789). Author of *Voyage en Egypt et en Syrie* (1787), *Ruines, ou Méditation sur les révolutions des empires* (1791), *La Loi naturelle* (1793).

Wallon, Jean (1821–1882). Philosopher and friend of Baudelaire. Translated Hegel's *Logik*. Appears as Colline, a principal character in Henri Murger's *Scènes de la vie de Bohème*.

Walpole, Hugh (1884–1941). Prolific English novelist. Born in New Zealand, he served with the Russian Red Cross during World War I. His book *The Fortress* was published in 1932.

Watripon, Antonio (1822–1864). Journalist and critic. Friend of Baudelaire.

Werther. Sickly young German student, hero of Goethe's novel *Die Leiden des jungen Werthers* (1774).

Wheatstone, Charles (1802–1875). English physicist and inventor. Conducted experiments in electricity, light, and sound. The stereoscope, his invention for observing pictures in three dimensions, is still used in viewing X-rays and aerial photographs.

Wiertz, Antoine-Joseph (1806–1865). Belgian painter of colossal historical scenes. Lampooned by Baudelaire.

Wiesengrund. Theodor Wiesengrund Adorno.

Wolfskehl, Karl (1869–1948). German-Jewish philosopher and poet. A friend of Stefan George and Ludwig Klages, as well as of Benjamin, who wrote about him. Fled Germany in 1933.

Worth, Charles (1825–1895). Anglo-French couturier, patronized by Empress Eugénie. Arbiter of Paris fashions for thirty years.

Wronski, Józef (1778–1853). Polish mathematician and philosopher. Author of *Messianism: Final Union of Philosophy and Religion* (1831–1839).

Wühlgarten. An institute for epileptics in Berlin.

Young Germany. Literary movement arising after the death of Goethe (1832), and asserting the claims of the younger generation against the complacency of the elder.

Young Hegelians. Liberal movement arising after the death of Hegel (1831), and contesting dualism in church and state. Attacked by Marx and Engels in *Die deutsche Ideologie*.

Yverdon. *See* Pestalozzi, Johann Heinrich.

Yvon, Adolphe (1817–1893). French painter of historical scenes and portraits.

Z Marcas. Novel of 1840, forming part of Balzac's *Scènes de la vie politique*.

Zelter, Karl Friedrich (1758–1832). German composer; set poems by Goethe and Schiller to music. His correspondence with Goethe ran to six volumes.

Index

This book is set in the Adobe fonts Berthold Baskerville Book and Bodoni, contemporary adaptations of fonts created by John Baskerville in the mid-eighteenth century, and by Giambattista Bodoni in the early nineteenth century. The headings are set in Bodoni Poster, Bodoni Poster Compressed, and Bodoni Bold Condensed. The type was composed at Wellington Graphics in Boston, Massachusetts, in Corel Ventura Publisher on an IBM PC.

The book was printed web offset on 45-pound Glatfelter Offset Hi-Opaque paper at Hamilton Printing Company in Castleton, New York. The three-piece binding was done at Hamilton Printing with an Arrestox B spine and side papers printed in two colors at Henry N. Sawyer Company, Charlestown, Massachusetts, where the jacket was printed as well.

The book was designed by Gwen Nefsky Frankfeldt. The production was supervised by David Foss.